MCAT QBook

Over 2,000 Questions Covering Every MCAT Science Topic

NextStep

TEST PREP nextsteptestprep.com

Printed in the United States of America

Second Printing, 2018

ISBN 978-1-944935-24-5

Next Step Test Preparation, LLC
4256 N Ravenswood Ave
Suite 207
Chicago, IL 60613

www.nextsteptestprep.com

ABOUT THE AUTHORS

Clara Gillan is Next Step Test Prep's National Director for MCAT Content and an Elite MCAT Tutor. She has worked with hundreds of MCAT tutoring students over the past several years and helped develop many of Next Step's MCAT passages and discrete questions. She scored a 42 on her own MCAT, placing her in the top 0.1% nationally. With an extensive background in neuroscience and teaching, Clara enjoys helping students focus on learning methods and techniques that are proven effective by the latest in neuroscience research.

Bryan Schnedeker is Next Step Test Prep's Vice President for Tutoring and Content. He manages all of our MCAT and LSAT instructors nationally and counsels hundreds of students when they begin our tutoring process. He has over a decade of MCAT and LSAT teaching and tutoring experience (starting at one of the big prep course companies before joining our team). He has attended medical school and law school himself and scored a 44 on the old MCAT, a 525 on the new MCAT, and a 180 on the LSAT. Bryan has worked with thousands of MCAT students over the years and specializes in helping students looking to achieve elite scores.

Dr. Anthony Lafond is Next Step's MCAT Content Director and an Elite MCAT Tutor. He has been teaching and tutoring MCAT students for nearly 12 years. He earned his MD and PhD degrees from UMDNJ - New Jersey Medical School with a focus on rehabilitative medicine. Dr. Lafond believes that both rehabilitative medicine and MCAT education hinge on the same core principle: crafting an approach that puts the unique needs of the individual foremost.

To find out about MCAT tutoring directly with Clara, Anthony, or Bryan visit our website:

http://nextsteptestprep.com/mcat

Updates may be found here: http://nextsteptestprep.com/mcat-materials-change-log/

If you have any feedback for us about this book, please contact us at mcat@nextsteptestprep.com

Version: 1.2 (2018-04-01)

FREE ONLINE MCAT DIAGNOSTIC and

FULL-LENGTH EXAM

Want to see how you would do on the MCAT and understand where you need to focus your prep?

TAKE OUR FREE MCAT DIAGNOSTIC EXAM

Timed simulations of all 4 sections of the MCAT

Comprehensive reporting on your performance

Continue your practice with a free Full Length Exam

These two exams are provided free of charge to students who purchased our book

To access your free exam, visit:

http://nextsteptestprep.com/freemcat

TABLE OF CONTENTS

INTRODUCTION

Hello and welcome to Next Step's MCAT QBook. In this book you'll find over 2,000 questions dedicated to giving you the science review and MCAT practice that you need to succeed on Test Day.

To provide the broadest possible coverage, we have arranged this book as a series of independent discrete questions and we have provided coverage that is proportional to the MCAT itself. For example, on the real exam about 20% of all science questions will be based on biology, so about 20% of this book is biology questions.

The key to mastering this material involves taking a step-by-step approach, starting with content review, then untimed practice to master your question-solving technique, then short timed work, and finally 95-minute timed work to build endurance. To begin improving your MCAT performance, read "How to Use this Book" on the following page.

Everyone here at Next Step would like to wish you the best of luck with your studies!

Thank you,

Bryan Schnedeker
Vice President for MCAT Content
Next Step Test Preparation, LLC

STOP! READ THIS FIRST!

How to Use This Book

The book you're holding in your hands is one of the best supplements you can use to review and strengthen your MCAT science content. However, it is not complete prep. While the real MCAT does have about 45 discrete science questions (the kind of short independent question found in this book), it also has over 100 science questions that are based on descriptive passages. To best prepare for the exam, you will need to use this book in conjunction with several other resources.

All MCAT prep begins, first and foremost, with content review. There's a ton of stuff you just have to know when walking into the exam. While your science classes in college did a great job laying the foundations of your MCAT knowledge, most students find they need anywhere from one to three months to fully refresh themselves on MCAT science. The best way to do this review is through a combination of three things.

First, the AAMC has built a partnership with Khan Academy to provide a free series of video lectures covering nearly all MCAT topics (just Google "Khan MCAT" to find the site easily). These videos are good quality and totally free – a great place to start. From there, you will want to build on your understanding with a set of prep books. Many companies make excellent review books, but we're partial to the Next Step Content Review series (for obvious reasons!).

Finally and most importantly, you need to drill yourself on hundreds or thousands of practice questions to ensure that you've really mastered the content. That's where this book comes in. After you've finished your prep work in a given science, work your way through all of the questions in this book for that science. When you hit trouble with the questions, go back and re-watch the Khan videos or re-read the relevant chapters in your prep books.

After doing that content review work, you will need to move on to practicing full, timed sections and then full, timed MCAT practice tests. The Next Step Strategy and Practice books offer the former, and our online full lengths provide the latter. You can find both on our website at nextsteptestprep.com. Just click the "MCAT Books and Tests" link up at the top of front page.

Lastly, if you hit a big roadblock or think that you could use extra one-on-one MCAT help, contact Next Step to ask about our tutoring services at 888-530-NEXT.

Good luck with your practice and good luck on Test Day!

This page left intentionally blank.

Biology

1. Which of the following correctly describes the DNA double helix?

   I. It is held together by hydrogen bonding between the nitrogenous bases.
   II. Its backbone is composed of alternating ribose sugars and phosphate groups.
   III. It typically has a diameter of 20 angstroms.
   IV. It features pyrimidine-to-pyrimidine and purine-to-purine base pairings.

   A) II only
   B) I and III
   C) I, II, and IV
   D) I, III, and IV

2. The structure of a typical nucleoside includes:

   A) a six-carbon sugar.
   B) a nitrogenous base.
   C) phosphate groups.
   D) A and B only.

3. The gene encoding a protein involved in cell cycle regulation is analyzed, and researchers conclude that its sense strand contains the following sequence: 5'-AATTGCGCATTGC-3'. The sequence of the corresponding mRNA following transcription is:

   A) 5'-AAUUGCGCAUUGC-3'.
   B) 5'-GCAATGCGCAATT-3'.
   C) 5'-GCAAUGCGCAAUU-3'.
   D) 5'-AATTGCGCATTGC-3'.

4. Due to a point mutation during replication, one guanine base is now paired with adenine instead of cytosine. How might the cell's proofreading machinery be able to recognize this mistake?

   A) Because both adenine and guanine are pyrimidines, the DNA strand will be narrower at the site of the mutation.
   B) Because both adenine and guanine are purines, the DNA strand will be narrower at the site of the mutation.
   C) Because both adenine and guanine are pyrimidines, the DNA strand will be wider at the site of the mutation.
   D) Because both adenine and guanine are purines, the DNA strand will be wider at the site of the mutation.

5. A scientist is investigating the effect of single base pair mutations on the activity of a gene that is heavily expressed in neurons. He focuses on a sequence within the noncoding strand, 5'-CCTTGATCCATT-3'. Which of the following represents the sequence of a coding strand that could NOT be used to test these types of mutations?

A) 5'-AATGGATCCAGG-3'
B) 5'-AATTGATCCAGG-3'
C) 5'-AATGAATCAAGG-3'
D) 5'-AATGGATTAAGG-3'

Questions 6–7 rely on the figure to the right

The stability of three different samples of bacterial DNA is tested based on percent denaturation at various temperatures. The results are shown in the following graph.

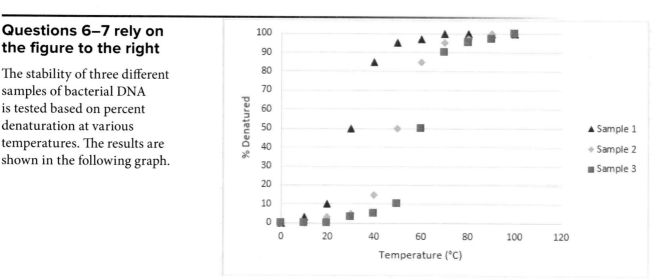

6. What is the approximate T_m of each of the samples?

A) Sample 1: 30°C; Sample 2: 50°C; Sample 3: 60°C
B) Sample 1: 70°C; Sample 2: 90°C; Sample 3: 100°C
C) Sample 1: 50°C; Sample 2: 30°C; Sample 3: 60°C
D) Sample 1: 20°C; Sample 2: 40°C; Sample 3: 50°C

7. Through sequencing, it was found that 20% of Sample 1 consists of cytosine, while Samples 2 and 3 contain 30% and 35% cytosine, respectively. Is this consistent with the experimental results?

A) Yes, because higher G-C content leads to a higher T_m due to the increased hydrophobic interactions within G-C pairings.
B) No, because higher G-C content leads to a lower T_m due to an increase in hydrogen bonding due to the G-C bases.
C) Yes, because higher G-C content leads to a higher T_m due to an increase in the hydrogen bonding due to the G-C bases.
D) No, because higher G-C content leads to a lower T_m due to the decreased hydrophobic interactions within G-C pairings.

Questions 8–9 rely on the figure below

Four different dsDNA samples taken from mammalian cells were analyzed to find their composition. The results were organized in the following table.

Sample	% Adenine	% Thymine	% Cytosine
A	15	15	35
B	29	29	21
C	27	27	23
D	35	unknown	unknown

8. A young lab assistant contaminated Sample D when testing for the percentages of thymine and cytosine. Based upon Chargaff's rules, predict the composition of this sample.

A) %T: 35; %G: 40; %C: 40
B) %T: 15; %G: 35; %C: 15
C) %T: 35; %G: 15; %C: 15
D) %T: 22; %G: 22; %C: 21

9. Thermal vents along the ocean floor emit water ranging from sixty to several hundred degrees Celsius. Which of the samples most likely came from bacteria that thrive in these vents?

   A) Sample A
   B) Sample B
   C) Sample C
   D) Sample D

10. A researcher is attempting to design a hypothetical new lifeform that does not rely on DNA for the storage of genetic information. He starts by identifying various molecules with properties that make them potential DNA alternatives. Which of the following characteristics should these alternative molecules possess?

    A) The ability to form a long, highly stable polymer
    B) The ability to be replicated with a high rate of accuracy and speed
    C) The ability to code for other macromolecules used throughout the cell
    D) All of the above are necessary characteristics.

11. Which of the following enzymes are involved in DNA replication in human cells?

    I. *Taq* polymerase
    II. Telomerase
    III. Ligase
    IV. Transcriptase

       A) I and III
       B) II and III
       C) II and IV
       D) I, II, and III

12. DNA replication is understood to be semiconservative. To ascertain this, a geneticist radiolabeled a fragment of dsDNA and allowed it to replicate. After four successive replication cycles, what fraction of the total DNA consists of the original parent material?

    A) 1/4
    B) 1/8
    C) 1/16
    D) 1/32

13. To perform a successful PCR reaction, all of the following reactants must be present EXCEPT:

    A) forward and reverse primers.
    B) *Taq* polymerase.
    C) a magnesium-containing buffer.
    D) dideoxynucleoside triphosphates (ddNTPs).

14. What purpose do primers serve in the initiation of DNA replication?

    A) They signal the location at which to form the replication fork.
    B) They provide sites to which a vital enzyme can bind.
    C) They indicate which of the two strands of parent DNA is to be replicated.
    D) They disrupt hydrogen bonding between base pairs, allowing the double helix to unwind more easily.

15. A certain X-linked disease inhibits the cell's ability to produce telomerase. With regard to chromosome structure, a male with one copy of the disease allele would differ from a healthy male in what way?

    A) His chromosomes would shorten over the course of several replication cycles.
    B) His newly synthesized DNA would be unable to rewind after replication.
    C) His total amount of supercoiled DNA would increase.
    D) The two individuals would not differ in their chromosome structure.

16. The figure below shows the nitrogenous bases involved in DNA base pairing.

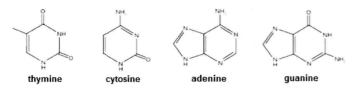

thymine   cytosine   adenine   guanine

What structural elements make AT-rich sequences especially appropriate targets for initiation proteins during replication?

A) The pairing of a purine and pyrimidine results in a low bond dissociation energy.

B) Thymine's ketone groups facilitate the binding of initiation proteins.

C) The interaction between adenine and thymine involves fewer hydrogen bonds than that between cytosine and guanine.

D) The AT pair exhibits resonance, making its binding especially stable and comparatively inert.

17. One of the fundamental qualities of DNA polymerase is its inability to initiate replication. In humans, for example, it can only begin to extend a strand when a short RNA primer is already present. A scientist thinks he has discovered a retrovirus that employs tRNA to initiate DNA synthesis rather than traditional primers. Is this possible?

A) Yes, tRNA has an innate ability to mimic the function of enzymes such as primase.

B) Yes, both the tRNA molecule and the RNA primers provide a free 3' –OH group as an attachment site for enzymes that elongate the chain.

C) No, retroviruses utilize reverse transcriptase instead of DNA polymerase.

D) No, tRNA only functions in the assembly of proteins at viral ribosomes.

18. Part of the replication fork on a eukaryotic dsDNA molecule is shown below.

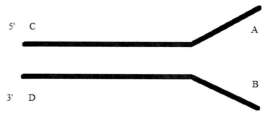

At which point does the lagging strand of the new DNA molecule begin to form?

A) A

B) B

C) C

D) D

19. One of the hallmarks of DNA polymerase is its quality of exclusively reading DNA from $3' \rightarrow 5'$ and synthesizing DNA from $5' \rightarrow 3'$. Imagine an organism whose DNA polymerase mutates and gains the ability to read DNA in both directions. How would the mutated polymerase differ from the original enzyme?

A) Due to changes in its proofreading ability, the mutated enzyme would produce strands with overlapping sequences.

B) The telomeres of the strand made by the mutated polymerase would be unusually short.

C) Replication mediated by the mutated polymerase would require increased ligase activity.

D) Okazaki fragments would not be observed in replication governed by the mutant polymerase.

20. How does the initiation step of transcription differ from that of DNA replication?

A) Replication involves a DNA-dependent DNA polymerase, while transcription utilizes an RNA-dependent RNA polymerase.

B) DNA replication is semiconservative and utilizes Okazaki fragments, while transcription forms a single-stranded product.

C) Transcription relies on sigma factors while DNA replication uses particular points in the DNA known as origins.

D) The processes do not differ notably; both transcription and replication require RNA primers due to the free -OH groups at their 3' ends.

21. An mRNA transcript begins with the sequence 5' CUUUACUGUAAG 3'. A point mutation into which of the following sequences will yield a truncated protein?

    I. 5'-CUUUAAUGUAAG-3'
    II. 5'-GUUUACUGUAAG-3'
    III. 5'-CUUUACUGAAAG-3'
    IV. 5'-CUUUACUGUAGG-3'

    A) I only
    B) I and III
    C) I, II, and IV
    D) I, III, and IV

22. Advantages of the triplet genetic code include all of these EXCEPT:

    A) each codon corresponds to one amino acid.
    B) the degeneracy of the system allows for silent single-base mutations.
    C) one mRNA sequence can code for multiple proteins.
    D) codon-anticodon binding allows for efficient translation of RNA to protein.

23. Which sequence of events correctly depicts the conversion of DNA into protein in a eukaryotic cell?

    A) DNA is translated into mRNA in the nucleus, then transcribed into an amino acid chain in the cytosol.
    B) DNA is transcribed into mRNA in the nucleus, then translated into an amino acid chain in the cytosol.
    C) DNA is transcribed into mRNA in the nucleus, then translated into an amino acid chain in the nucleus.
    D) DNA is transcribed into mRNA in the cytosol, then translated into an amino acid chain.

24. How does a codon recognize the correct anticodon?

    A) The anticodon binds to the codon via corresponding RNA sequences.
    B) The anticodon binds to the codon via a lock-and-key mechanism.
    C) The anticodon binds to the codon via corresponding DNA sequences.
    D) The anticodon binds to the codon via accessory proteins attached to the RNA.

25. A certain protease has a catalytic pocket that contains three consecutive glutamic acid residues. This region is coded for by the mRNA sequence 5'-GAAGAAGAA-3'. If mutated, which new sequence is most likely to yield the same protein product as the wild-type?

    A) 5'-GAAGGAGAA-3'
    B) 5'-GAGGAGGAA-3'
    C) 5'-GAAUAAGAA-3'
    D) 5'-GAACAAGAA-3'

Questions 26–27 rely on the figure below

Second letter

First letter	U	C	A	G	Third letter
U	UUU Phe	UCU Ser	UAU Tyr	UGU Cys	U
U	UUC Phe	UCC Ser	UAC Tyr	UGC Cys	C
U	UUA Leu	UCA Ser	UAA Stop	UGA Stop	A
U	UUG Leu	UCG Ser	UAG Stop	UGG Trp	G
C	CUU Leu	CCU Pro	CAU His	CGU Arg	U
C	CUC Leu	CCC Pro	CAC His	CGC Arg	C
C	CUA Leu	CCA Pro	CAA Gln	CGA Arg	A
C	CUG Leu	CCG Pro	CAG Gln	CGG Arg	G
A	AUU Ile	ACU Thr	AAU Asn	AGU Ser	U
A	AUC Ile	ACC Thr	AAC Asn	AGC Ser	C
A	AUA Ile	ACA Thr	AAA Lys	AGA Arg	A
A	AUG Met	ACG Thr	AAG Lys	AGG Arg	G
G	GUU Val	GCU Ala	GAU Asp	GGU Gly	U
G	GUC Val	GCC Ala	GAC Asp	GGC Gly	C
G	GUA Val	GCA Ala	GAA Glu	GGA Gly	A
G	GUG Val	GCG Ala	GAG Glu	GGG Gly	G

26. The sense strand of the DNA corresponding to a typical membrane-bound protein contains the segment 5'-TTTTTCGTG-3'. From the N to the C terminus, the associated protein sequence is:

    A) phenylalanine, leucine, valine.
    B) valine, phenylalanine, phenylalanine.
    C) histidine, glutamic acid, lysine.
    D) phenylalanine, phenylalanine, valine.

27. Part of an mRNA transcript created from the same gene reads 5'-CAUUCAGAA-3'. Where within the protein structure would this sequence most likely be found?

    A) The cytosolic domain
    B) The transmembrane domain
    C) The hydrophobic core
    D) B and C are equally likely.

28. Twenty standard amino acids are found in typical human proteins. How many unique mRNA codons exist?

    A) 16
    B) 20
    C) 32
    D) 64

29. The table below shows the relative binding energies of six distinct codon-anticodon pairings.

Codon	Amino acid bound to corresponding anticodon	Relative binding energy
AAA	lysine	1.00
AAG	lysine	0.66
CAC	histidine	1.23
CAU	histidine	0.71
GAA	glutamine	1.02
GAG	glutamine	0.57

    Which of the codons listed in the table likely attach to their anticodon via a wobble base pairing?

    A) AAA, CAC, GAA
    B) AAG, CAC, GAA
    C) AAG, CAU, GAG
    D) AAA, CAU, GAG

30. A wide variety of biological life forms carry their genetic information in the form of DNA. This genetic material is converted into RNA, which is then used to construct protein. One type of organism or agent that forms an exception to this rule is:

    A) archaebacteria.
    B) fungi.
    C) at least some dsDNA viruses.
    D) at least some positive-sense ssRNA viruses.

31. A researcher is comparing two proteins, a wild-type variant of albumin (A) and a mutant version of that same protein (B), by running them on an SDS-PAGE gel (samples loaded at the top), below.

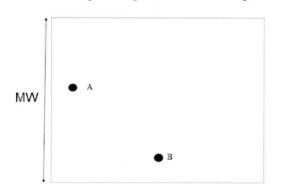

Which type of mutation likely occurred?

    A) Silent
    B) Missense
    C) Nonsense
    D) Frameshift

32. During replication, a single nucleotide was added to the coding portion of a gene, shown below in bold.

    5'-AUGGGACG**C**UAGAACGU-3'

    What type of mutation is exemplified by this change?

    I.   Insertion
    II. Nonsense
    III. Frameshift
    IV. Silent

       A) I only
       B) I and III
       C) I and IV
       D) I, II, and III

33. During the gene rearrangement involved in antibody production, important genes are enzymatically connected by random strings of nucleotides. However, for these genes to be "in frame," they must be read during translation using the same reading frame. Based on this information, what percentage of antibodies produced during this process will be out of frame, and therefore useless?

    A) 0%
    B) 33%
    C) 67%
    D) 100%

34. The concept of "wobble" is most closely related to:

    A) silent mutations.
    B) deletion mutations.
    C) translocation mutations.
    D) insertion mutations.

35. Suppose that the karyotype of a fetus shows an abnormally long chromosome 9 and an abnormally short chromosome 22. Which kind of error likely occurred during development?

    A) A nondisjunction
    B) A translocation
    C) A missense mutation
    D) A nonsense mutation

36. If a certain protein is known to be the product of a nonsense mutation, which of the following codons is most likely to appear prematurely in its mRNA transcript?

    A) AUG
    B) UUU
    C) CAG
    D) UAG

37. To confirm that a protein has a silent mutation, a scientist should use:

    A) one-dimensional gel electrophoresis.
    B) two-dimensional SDS-PAGE.
    C) a Western blot.
    D) Sanger sequencing.

38. The wild-type and mutated forms of an mRNA transcript are shown below.

    WT: 5'-CAUUAUGACCGGAGU-3'
    Mut: 5'-CAUUAGUGACCGGGAGU-3'

    What is the most specific way to classify this kind of mutation?

    A) Frameshift
    B) Substitution
    C) Silent
    D) Nonsense

39. The results of a protein activity assay are shown below.

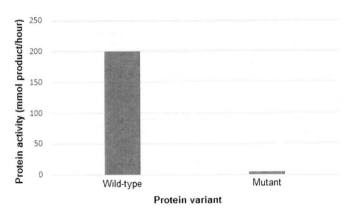

    Of the choices below, which is the most likely explanation for the reduced activity of the mutant variant?

    A) A single amino acid was replaced with another at a position far from the active site.
    B) A two-base insertion caused a change in the reading frame.
    C) A silent mutation occurred in the middle of a sequence involved in coding for the active site.
    D) A mutation coded for a less abundant tRNA instead of a common one, slowing translation significantly.

40. A missense mutation replaces an alanine residue located in the interior of a soluble protein with a serine residue. What will be the most likely effect of this change on the protein?

    A) Folding will be disrupted due to the mistaken inclusion of a polar amino acid.
    B) Folding will be disrupted due to the mistaken inclusion of an unusually bulky amino acid.
    C) The protein will completely lose its function.
    D) The protein will be completely unaffected.

41. Which of these statements concerning nucleic acids is / are accurate?

    I. DNA replication is more accurate than RNA transcription due to the existence of proofreading mechanisms.
    II. DNA and RNA are equally stable macromolecules.
    III. Due to the presence of different bases, DNA and RNA strands are unable to bind with one another.
    IV. The genome of an organism can be entirely composed of either DNA or RNA.

    A) I only
    B) I and IV
    C) II and IV
    D) I, II, and III

42. DNA is rarely found outside its double-helical form, while RNA is single-stranded and folds on itself to form various structures. RNA's wider structural variety results in:

    A) RNA having a wider range of functions than DNA.
    B) RNA being targeted less often for degradation.
    C) mRNA, tRNA, and rRNA being interchangeable and able to perform similar functions.
    D) RNA having less stability due to its single-stranded form.

43. Which of the following processes would be most affected if an organism lost its ability to synthesize snRNAs?

    A) Post-translational modification
    B) Post-transcriptional modification
    C) DNA synthesis
    D) RNA transcription

44. While DNA serves almost exclusively as the storage material for genetic information, RNA can perform a wide variety of functions. These functions include all of the following EXCEPT:

    A) catalyzing biochemical reactions.
    B) storing genetic information.
    C) forming organelles.
    D) establishing quaternary structures through disulfide bonding.

45. Which feature of RNA contributes most to its lack of stability in the cytosol?

    A) RNA is single-stranded.
    B) RNA is synthesized by RNA polymerase, an error-prone enzyme.
    C) RNA contains ribose rather than deoxyribose sugars.
    D) RNA contains uracil, in contrast with DNA's thymine.

Questions 46–47 rely on the figure below

The following diagram depicts a model of the structure of transfer RNA.

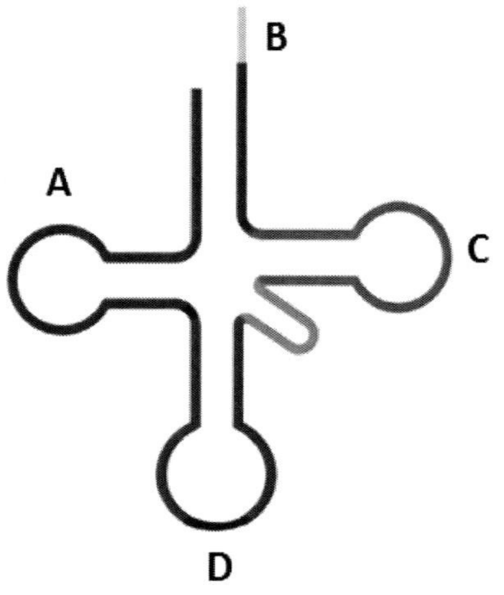

46. At which position do aminoacyl tRNA synthetases attach amino acid residues to the tRNA molecule?

    A) A
    B) B
    C) C
    D) D

47. The gene coding for a particular type of tRNA becomes mutated in a way that changes its anticodon sequence. What consequence will most likely result from this change?

    A) Due to wobble, this tRNA will serve the same function as non-mutated tRNA.
    B) Aminoacyl-tRNA synthetases will be unable to recognize this tRNA.
    C) This tRNA will no longer be able to take part in translation.
    D) This tRNA will recognize a different mRNA codon.

Questions 48–49 rely on the table below

The error rate for several cellular processes is shown in this table.

Process	Error rate (errors / base pair)
DNA replication	1×10^{-9}
RNA transcription	1×10^{-4}
Protein translation	4×10^{-4}

48. Which post-transcriptional process is responsible for the diversity of proteins that can be produced from a single gene?

    A) The addition of a 5' cap
    B) The removal of introns and joining of exons
    C) The addition of a poly (A) tail
    D) The use of uracil instead of thymine

49. The fidelity, or accuracy, of transcription is crucial to producing functional proteins. However, the error rate in transcription is significantly higher than that in DNA replication. All of the following statements are accurate regarding the error rate of transcription EXCEPT:

    A) RNA transcription lacks the proofreading mechanisms inherent to DNA replication.
    B) due to codon degeneracy, errors in transcription may still result in the desired polypeptide.
    C) errors in DNA replication are more lethal than errors in RNA transcription.
    D) the addition of the poly (A) tail and the 5' cap often change the sequence of the mRNA transcript.

50. snRNPs are comprised of which two types of molecules?

    A) RNA and protein
    B) DNA and RNA
    C) Introns and exons
    D) IgG and IgM antibodies

51. Post-transcriptional processing involves several modifications to pre-mRNA molecules. One such process, mRNA capping, occurs when the capping enzyme complex (CEC) attaches a modified guanine nucleotide to the 5' end of the newly transcribed pre-mRNA via an unusual 5' to 5' triphosphate linkage. Functions of the 5' cap include:

    I. protection of the transcript from exonuclease degradation.
    II. promotion of translation by serving as an attachment point for ribosomes.
    III. enabling of nuclear export.

    A) I and II
    B) I and III
    C) II and III
    D) I, II, and III

52. A spliceosome is a complex structure assembled from snRNAs and their associated proteins. If an organism was suddenly unable to produce spliceosomes, what would be the likely result?

    A) Transcription of mRNA from DNA would no longer occur.
    B) The dysfunctional machinery would severely limit DNA replication.
    C) The organism would produce mRNA identical to pre-mRNA.
    D) The recombination of different exons would not occur, limiting the diversity of gene products.

53. Which of these molecules is produced by the Dicer enzyme and is involved in RNA silencing?

    A) tRNA
    B) rRNA
    C) miRNA
    D) siRNA

54. A virus invades a cell and rapidly produces antisense RNA that is complementary to a gene's promoter sequence. What will happen to the transcription of the gene?

    A) Transcription will be unaffected.
    B) Transcription will be severely reduced.
    C) The sense strand of the gene will still be transcribed.
    D) Due to the presence of the virus, any mRNA transcribed will be rapidly degraded by miRNA.

55. RNA polymerase catalyzes the production of the mRNA transcript. How would this enzyme be adversely affected if it lacked its specific sigma factor?

    A) RNA polymerase would be unable to bind to gene promoters.
    B) The creation of the transcription bubble would be inhibited.
    C) A helicase enzyme would be required to unwind the DNA double helix.
    D) RNA polymerase would be unable to differentiate between nucleotides, leading to incorrect base pairing.

56. The figure below depicts a proposed example of alternative splicing.

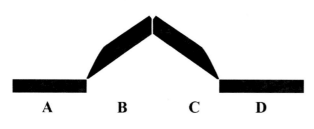

A, B, and D represent exons, while C represents an intron. Is this situation possible?

A) No, because alternative splicing involves the removal of introns only.

B) Yes, because alternative splicing can remove exons in addition to introns.

C) No, because alternative splicing does not relate to the removal of introns or exons.

D) Yes, because introns and exons are paired and can only be removed together.

57. The RNA-induced silencing complex (RISC) is a ribonucleoprotein that uses dsRNA fragments to target mRNA transcripts. This process is most accurately characterized as:

A) complementary base pairing.

B) RNA interference.

C) mRNA targeting.

D) intragenic RNA silencing.

58. The following image represents a mature eukaryotic mRNA that has undergone post-transcriptional modification.

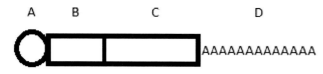

What best describes the function of D?

A) It contains the genetic information necessary for protein synthesis.

B) It promotes translation by serving as a docking point for ribosomes.

C) It forms part of the untranslated region that signals the termination of protein synthesis.

D) It prevents enzymatic degradation of the mRNA molecule.

59. Transcription differs from DNA replication in all of the following ways EXCEPT:

A) transcription produces a single-stranded product.

B) transcription requires a promoter, while DNA replication does not.

C) transcription only involves certain segments of the DNA sequence at a time.

D) transcription reads DNA from 3'-5'.

60. The most memorable difference between DNA and RNA relates to their composition. While thymine is a building block in DNA, it is replaced by uracil in RNA. Which of the following is another functional difference between DNA and RNA?

A) The genome of viruses is exclusively made up of DNA.

B) The inherent instability of RNA molecules renders them unable to store genetic information.

C) Certain RNA molecules possess the ability to catalyze biochemical reactions, while DNA molecules cannot.

D) RNA molecules, unlike DNA, are incapable of hydrogen bonding.

61. Which of the following statements about enzymes are true?

I. Enzymes are always composed of protein.

II. An enzyme reduces the activation energy of the forward reaction, while leaving the reverse reaction unchanged.

III. Enzymes are not consumed during the catalysis of a reaction.

IV. An enzyme's activity is heavily dependent on pH and temperature.

A) I and III

B) III and IV

C) I, II, and III

D) II, III and IV

62. The "lock and key" model was introduced in 1894 by Emil Fischer to explain enzyme specificity. This model was later revised to establish the modern "induced fit" model. All of the following are advantages of the "induced fit" model EXCEPT:

    A) it accounts for the flexibility of the active site.
    B) it describes the slight change in substrate conformation upon entering the active site of an enzyme.
    C) it more effectively explains molecular recognition in the presence of inhibitors and competitors.
    D) it states that substrates and enzymes possess complementary geometric shapes that facilitate specificity.

63. If there is a change in the amino acid sequence of a protein, which level of protein structure is guaranteed to be affected?

    A) Primary structure
    B) Secondary structure
    C) Tertiary structure
    D) Both A and B are correct.

64. A common phenomenon involving changes in protein structure can be observed when frying eggs. The transparent gel surrounding the yolk becomes opaque and hardens when exposed to high levels of heat. What specific mechanism is responsible for this change?

    A) Breaking of the hydrogen bonds that form the protein's secondary structure
    B) Disruption of the hydrophobic interactions that form the protein's tertiary structure
    C) Separation of the different polypeptide chains at the level of primary structure
    D) Formation of double and triple bonds between proteins to create quaternary structure

65. Cysteine is a semi-essential amino acid that is involved in numerous vital functions. In addition to the binding of metal ions, cysteine also participates in many post-translational modifications. What unique characteristic of cysteine allows it to play such a crucial role?

    A) Cysteine's versatility allows it to interact with both hydrophilic and hydrophobic amino acids.
    B) Cysteine is the only commonly found D-amino acid in the human body.
    C) Cysteine contains a thiol group that enables it to act in a tremendous variety of reactions.
    D) Cysteine is generally found bound to other cysteine residues via disulfide bonds.

66. This figure depicts proline, one of the twenty standard amino acids. Its uniqueness gives it a specific role in the formation of protein secondary structure.

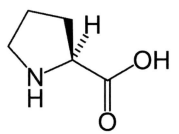

    The structural element of proline that enables this role is:

    A) the fact that proline, unlike most amino acids, is not chiral; this reduces its reactivity.
    B) its amino group, which can hydrogen bond in alpha helices and beta-pleated sheets.
    C) its terminal carboxyl group, which allows proline to bind to amino acids above and below it.
    D) the cyclic structure of its side chain bound to its own amino group, which gives it rigidity.

67. One important reactant in a polymerase chain reaction (PCR) is heat-resistant *Taq* polymerase, the enzyme responsible for elongating DNA strands. Why must this enzyme be heat-resistant?

    A) It prevents the polymerase from denaturing during the thermal cycling of PCR.
    B) *Taq* polymerase is responsible for maintaining the structure of the newly synthesized DNA.
    C) DNA replication is exothermic, and the heat released could denature normal polymerases.
    D) Heat resistance protects *Taq* polymerase from changes in pH.

68. The figure below depicts a model of enzyme regulation.

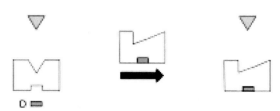

Which term accurately characterizes the function of the component marked "D"?

A) Substrate agonist
B) Allosteric regulator
C) Competitive inhibitor
D) Irreversible analog

69. The interaction between statins and grapefruit juice has long been an object of research, as certain components in grapefruit juice appear to inhibit cytochromes in the stomach. Why might this interaction be considered harmful?

A) Molecules in the juice bind irreversibly to the cytochromes, resulting in a toxic product.
B) Cytochromes are important in regulation of multiple systems, and inhibition of them halts digestion.
C) Stomach pH is regulated by cytochromes, and their inhibition results in significant fluctuations in acidity.
D) Inhibition of the cytochromes reduces breakdown of the statin, leading to potential overdose.

70. Feedback mechanisms are vital to maintaining the homeostasis of an organism. Due to a mutation in the gene encoding it, a certain enzyme suddenly displays an increased affinity for numerous other molecules present in the organism. How would this affect the catalysis of the enzyme's original substrate(s)?

A) Pathways involving this enzyme would terminate early.
B) Feedback mechanisms involved would take a longer period of time.
C) The enzyme's products would increase in concentration.
D) The metabolic pathway would shut down.

71. A scientist has created a drug that targets a pathogenic bacterium. After administering the drug, the bacterial cells exhibit normal levels of RNA and DNA, but low levels of protein. Which bacterial process is most likely interrupted by this drug?

A) DNA replication
B) Transcription
C) Translation
D) Binary fission, as bacteria do not undergo translation

72. Translation is the process by which protein is produced from mRNA. From beginning to end, the four phases of translation are:

A) translocation, initiation, elongation, and termination.
B) initiation, translocation, elongation, and termination.
C) translocation, elongation, initiation, and termination.
D) initiation, elongation, translocation, and termination.

73. Tetracycline is a broad-spectrum antibiotic used to treat conditions ranging from urinary tract infections to acne. It is known to specifically inhibit bacterial protein synthesis by binding to a ribosomal subunit. Based on this mechanism of action, tetracycline likely targets:

A) 30S, the smaller subunit.
B) 40S, the smaller subunit.
C) 70S, the smaller subunit.
D) 60S, the larger subunit.

Questions 74–76 rely on the figure below

In the following table, each trinucleotide mRNA codon corresponds to a charged amino acid present on a tRNA molecule.

First letter	Second letter: U	C	A	G	Third letter
U	UUU Phe	UCU Ser	UAU Tyr	UGU Cys	U
U	UUC Phe	UCC Ser	UAC Tyr	UGC Cys	C
U	UUA Leu	UCA Ser	UAA Stop	UGA Stop	A
U	UUG Leu	UCG Ser	UAG Stop	UGG Trp	G
C	CUU Leu	CCU Pro	CAU His	CGU Arg	U
C	CUC Leu	CCC Pro	CAC His	CGC Arg	C
C	CUA Leu	CCA Pro	CAA Gln	CGA Arg	A
C	CUG Leu	CCG Pro	CAG Gln	CGG Arg	G
A	AUU Ile	ACU Thr	AAU Asn	AGU Ser	U
A	AUC Ile	ACC Thr	AAC Asn	AGC Ser	C
A	AUA Ile	ACA Thr	AAA Lys	AGA Arg	A
A	AUG Met	ACG Thr	AAG Lys	AGG Arg	G
G	GUU Val	GCU Ala	GAU Asp	GGU Gly	U
G	GUC Val	GCC Ala	GAC Asp	GGC Gly	C
G	GUA Val	GCA Ala	GAA Glu	GGA Gly	A
G	GUG Val	GCG Ala	GAG Glu	GGG Gly	G

74. In theory, perfect one-to-one complementation between mRNA codons and tRNA anticodons would require 64 individual tRNAs. However, only 31 such molecules are actually required for translation. The phenomenon by which noncanonical Watson-Crick base pairs may form between tRNA and mRNA, thus reducing the minimum number of anticodons, is known as:

A) codon mutation; codons not exactly recognized by tRNA are deleted and replaced with a recognizable codon.
B) codon mutation; extra nucleotides are inserted before codons that are not perfectly recognized by tRNA.
C) wobble base pair; the first two nucleotides of a codon do not have to follow Watson-Crick base pairing rules.
D) wobble base pair; the last two nucleotides of a codon do not have to follow Watson-Crick base pairing rules.

75. A point mutation changes a UAU codon to UAA. What effect will this have on the polypeptide?

A) A stop codon will replace tyrosine, terminating translation.
B) A cysteine residue will replace tyrosine.
C) No effect; since both codons code for tyrosine, this will not affect the polypeptide product.
D) A stop codon will replace tyrosine, and translation will not occur.

76. A wild-type mRNA transcript is shown below.

5' AUG GAU GAA CAU UGU UCU GUU UUU ACU 3'

In a mutant polypeptide transcribed from this sequence, a point mutation results in a C5W amino acid mutation. The mRNA transcript coding for this mutant protein is most likely:

A) 5' AUG GAU GAA CAU UGU UCU GUU UUU ACU 3'.
B) 5' AUG GAU GAA CAU UGG UCU GUU UUU ACU 3'.
C) 5' AUG GAU GAA CAU GGC UCU GUU UUU ACU 3'.
D) 5' AUG GAU GAA CAU UGU UGG GUU UUU ACU 3'.

77. Although eukaryotes differ from prokaryotes in many significant ways, their replication, transcription, and translation mechanisms are fairly similar. Which of these are properties of translation that are shared by eukaryotes and prokaryotes?

I. The first amino acid of a polypeptide is some form of methionine.
II. The synthesized mRNA is monocistronic.
III. The ribosomes that are utilized are composed of two subunits.

A) I only
B) III only
C) I and III
D) I, II, and III

78. The eukaryotic translation termination factor 1 (eRF1) is a release factor (eRF) that recognizes and decodes all of the stop codons. How many such codons does eRF1 recognize?

A) 1
B) 2
C) 3
D) 4

79. The central dogma of molecular biology, shown below, attempts to explain the flow of biological information. However, since its introduction in 1956 by Dr. Francis Crick, many examples have been uncovered that do not follow this pathway.

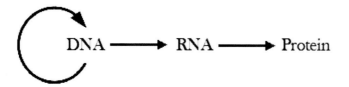

    All of the following fit with the traditional view of the central dogma EXCEPT:

    A) DNA in the human male zygote becoming demethylated to activate transcription.
    B) the Moloney murine leukemia virus using reverse transcriptase to synthesize DNA from an RNA template.
    C) pre-mRNAs from the *Drosophila melanogaster* gene *dsx* undergoing splicing prior to translation.
    D) *Bacillus acidocaldarius,* a thermoacidophilic eubacterium, possessing a DNA polymerase that can function at low pH.

80. Shown below is a prokaryotic ribosome along with an mRNA transcript, poised for translation.

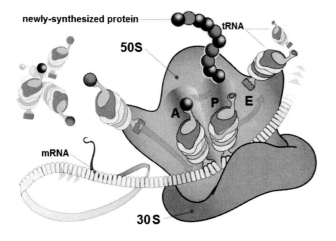

    Which choice gives the correct function of either the E, P, or A site?

A) At the A site, the growing polypeptide chain is released after translation.
B) At the E site, incoming charged aminoacyl-tRNAs bind to the complementary mRNA.
C) At the P site, the peptidyl tRNA is created through the covalent bonding of consecutive amino acids.
D) All of the above are correct.

81. What is a major difference between the human genome and that of *E. coli*?

A) The human genome contains 10^6 base pairs, while that of *E. coli* contains 10^9.
B) The genome of *E. coli* contains many more extraneous segments of DNA than the human genome.
C) The *E. coli* genome is contained within a few chromosomes, while the human genome is composed of 46.
D) The human genome includes multiple chromosomes, while that of *E. coli* is composed of a single circular chromosome.

82. The correct sequence of DNA packaging in chromosomes, from the smallest component to the most complete form, is:

A) double-stranded DNA → chromatin → histones → nucleosomes.
B) double-stranded DNA → histones → nucleosomes → chromatin.
C) chromatin → double-stranded DNA → histones → nucleosomes.
D) chromatin → double-stranded DNA → nucleosomes → histones.

83. What consequence is expected if a tumor cell is suddenly rendered unable to produce telomerase?

A) The cell would divide faster and more prolifically.
B) The cell would eventually stop dividing unless it found another way to produce telomeres.
C) The cell would be more resistant to apoptosis.
D) This change would have no effect, as tumor cells do not produce telomerase.

84. Two chromosomes are shown below.

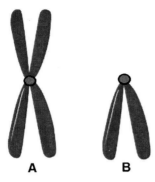

A   B

Given the positions of their centromeres, how would we label these two structures?

A) A: metacentric; B: telocentric
B) A: telocentric; B: metacentric
C) A: submetacentric; B: acrocentric
D) A: metacentric; B: antimetacentric

Questions 85–86 rely on the figure below

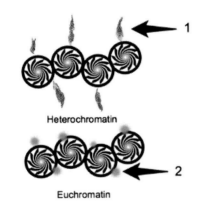

Heterochromatin

Euchromatin

85. What structure is denoted by the arrow marked "1," and what is its function?

A) It is an acetylated histone tail that increases the transcription of that segment of the chromosome.
B) It is an extra histone cluster that decreases the transcription of that segment of the chromosome.
C) It is an acetylated histone tail that decreases the transcription of that segment of the chromosome.
D) It represents methylation of guanine and cytosine nucleotides that decreases the transcription of that segment of the chromosome.

86. The arrow labeled "2" points to a particular feature of euchromatin. What is this feature, and what role does it play in the cell?

A) It is an extra histone cluster that decreases the transcription of that segment of the chromosome.
B) It represents methylation of guanine and cytosine nucleotides that increases the transcription of that segment of the chromosome.
C) It is an acetylated histone tail that increases the transcription of that segment of the chromosome.
D) It is an acetylated histone tail that decreases the transcription of that segment of the chromosome.

87. Which histone protein is associated with the "sealing off" of the DNA as it enters and exits the nucleosome?

A) H2A
B) H2B
C) H1
D) H3

88. When viewed under a light microscope, what visual difference exists between heterochromatin and euchromatin?

A) None; both heterochromatin and euchromatin are too small to be viewed under a light microscope. This action requires the use of an electron microscope.
B) Heterochromatin appears to be located outside of the nucleus, while euchromatin is intranuclear.
C) Heterochromatin appears extremely light, while euchromatin appears dark.
D) Heterochromatin appears extremely dark, while euchromatin appears light.

89. The human genome contains a large number of repetitive sequences that have no known function. What happens to these sequences during the life of a cell?

    A) These sequences are removed during meiosis to prevent their inheritance by the next generation.
    B) These sequences are translated, but the proteins that they code for are immediately destroyed.
    C) These sequences are spliced out before transcription takes place.
    D) The sequences are spliced out before translation takes place.

90. The function of DNA gyrase is to:

    A) unwind dsDNA to allow DNA polymerase to perform replication.
    B) help introduce supercoils in DNA by using ATP to twist the structure of the double helix.
    C) add nucleotides to the growing DNA molecule during replication.
    D) add RNA primers to each strand of DNA so that replication can occur.

91. Gene A, Gene B, and Gene C (shown below) are present in the same operon in a certain bacterial genome. They are transcribed to produce mRNA A, mRNA B, and mRNA C, respectively.

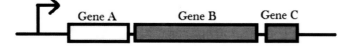

    The transcriptional mRNA products will be found in which relative amounts?

    A) mRNA A will be the most abundant.
    B) mRNA B will be the most abundant.
    C) mRNA C will be the least abundant.
    D) Equal mRNA levels will be observed.

92. An operon is a functional group of genes that can be organized together. All of the following are regulatory sequences within the operon EXCEPT:

    A) the operator.
    B) protein coding regions.
    C) the enhancer.
    D) the promoter.

93. In *E. coli*, the *lac* operon contains the genes that encode the transport and metabolism of lactose. The graph below shows the level of *lac* operon mRNA transcripts when lactose is first added to, then removed from, an *E. coli* culture.

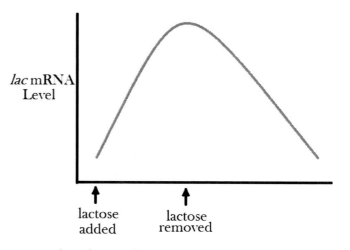

    Based on this graph, lactose is a(n):

    A) repressor.
    B) inducer.
    C) operator.
    D) operon.

94. In a positive repressible operon, an activator protein binds to the DNA and the genes are actively transcribed. In such a case, the addition of which of the following would stop transcription?

    A) An inducer
    B) RNA polymerase
    C) An inhibitor
    D) An activator

95. A scientist is attempting to characterize a novel bacterial operon. Genes on this operon generally are not transcribed due to a repressor protein that binds to the operator. However, the scientist discovers that the addition of an inducer activates transcription. Which of the following statements is accurate?

    A) This operon is regulated by negative induction.
    B) This operon is regulated by negative repression.
    C) This operon is regulated by positive induction.
    D) This operon is regulated by positive repression.

96. Which of the following are DNA-binding proteins that are NOT involved in eukaryotic transcription or transcriptional regulation?

    A) Transcription factors
    B) RNA polymerase
    C) Nucleases
    D) Histones

97. A scientist is developing a new class of antibiotics to target pathogenic prokaryotes without harming their eukaryotic hosts. Which of the following would be a logical target for these drugs?

    A) The Shine-Dalgarno sequence
    B) RNA polymerase II
    C) The TATA box
    D) Any of the above

98. Recent investigations have shown that mammalian cells use the gene amplification of specific DNA sequences to facilitate survival under stress. During a stressful period, the number of transcripts made from these genes:

    A) decreases.
    B) increases.
    C) remains constant.
    D) cannot be determined.

99. A species of fly has a set of genes (*yellow*) responsible for synthesizing black melanin. Production of this pigment results in dark, round colorations on the flies' white wings. Deletion of the *yellow* genes' enhancer sequence will result in which of the following phenotypes?

    A) Dark pigmented spots on the wings
    B) Asymmetrical wing size
    C) Smaller wing size
    D) A lack of pigmented spots on the wings

100. Which of the following are found in both prokaryotic and eukaryotic mechanisms of transcriptional regulation?

    I. Promoter sequences
    II. Operons
    III. Enhancers
    IV. Repressors

    A) I only
    B) I and IV
    C) I, II, and III
    D) I, III, and IV

101. Which of the following are true of eukaryotic mRNA before it leaves the nucleus?

    I. A 3' cap is added.
    II. A 5' cap is added.
    III. Exons are spliced out of the sequence.
    IV. Introns are spliced out of the sequence.

    A) I and III
    B) I and IV
    C) II and III
    D) II and IV

102. All of these modifications occur immediately after transcription in humans EXCEPT:

    A) a methyl and phosphate group are added to one end of the new transcript.
    B) one hundred or more adenine nucleotides are added to one end of the new transcript.
    C) introns are spliced out to yield a mature mRNA.
    D) the pre-mRNA leaves the nucleus for processing in the cytosol.

103. The *TP53* gene is found in many distinct cell types. Mutations of the wild-type *TP53* gene can be caused by environmental factors, diminishing the gene's expression and leading to uncontrolled cell division. Which of the following is most likely true of the *TP53* gene?

    A) It is an oncogene.
    B) It is a proto-oncogene.
    C) It is a tumor suppressor gene.
    D) It is found exclusively in unicellular organisms.

Questions 104–105 rely on the table below

Several geneticists aimed to assess the potential roles of three genes in human cancers. To do so, they constructed several experimental groups. Two consisted of lung cancer and leukemia patients, respectively, in their first month of treatment; the final group was a control. mRNA activity was measured using northern blotting and mapped below. Note that values are quantified relative to the cells of healthy patients. (Note: the mRNA activity level of healthy patients was normalized to 1.)

	Gene		
	RC18	AR12	JN87
Avg. reading for lung cancer patients	10	1	0.5
Avg. reading for leukemia patients	12	1.7	0.3

104. Which, if any, of these genes is implicated in a role as a tumor suppressor?

A) *RC18*
B) *AR12*
C) *JN87*
D) More than one of the above are correct.

105. Of the genes studied, the most likely candidate(s) for an oncogene is/are:

A) both *RC18* and *JN87*.
B) both *AR12* and *JN87*.
C) *RC18* only.
D) *JN87* only.

Questions 106–107 rely on the table below

Studies have shown that stress level plays a key role in the methylation and acetylation of certain genes in mice. Researchers constructed three experimental groups of mice of approximately the same age and weight. They subjected one of the experimental groups to periodic stress punctuated by periods of rest, while they made a second group subject to stress without rest. The scientists used northern blotting to measure the relative transcriptional activity of three genes and recorded their data as shown below.

	Gene 1	Gene 2	Gene 3
Healthy	1	1	1
Healthy and stressed in alternating fashion	5	0.6	6
Stressed	10	0.2	13

106. Considering the data above, which, if any, of the genes are likely acetylated in response to stress?

A) 1 and 2
B) 1 and 3
C) 2 and 3
D) None of the genes appear to be acetylated in response to stress.

107. It has been discovered that the methylation of certain genes in pregnant mice can be inherited by their offspring. Which of the three genes studied are most probably methylated in newborn mice whose mothers were exposed to severe long-term stress?

A) 1 only
B) 2 only
C) 3 only
D) 1 and 3

108. Unlike acetylation, DNA methylation:

A) inhibits transcription.
B) promotes transcription.
C) may either inhibit or promote transcription depending on the region of the chromosome.
D) none of the above; methylation and acetylation affect transcription in the same manner.

109. Post-transcriptional silencing is theorized to prevent some gene expression in response to stress. Which of these modifications could prevent functional mRNA from being translated?

A) Methylation
B) Acetylation
C) Binding to miRNA
D) Binding to tRNA

110. A sample of non-coding RNA is isolated from a cell's nucleus, where it was observed to exist in close proximity to pre-mRNA. This sample most likely contains:

A) snRNA.
B) rRNA.
C) tRNA.
D) snoRNA.

111. A certain bacterium has two different strains that are found in the human pharynx. These strains have a nearly identical complement of genetic material but exhibit very different virulence due to varying gene expression. These strains:

A) exhibit different behaviors due to major differences in their genotype.
B) must be from two different species.
C) exhibit different phenotypes.
D) will have different levels of antibiotic resistance.

112. A mother gives birth to dizygotic (fraternal) twin boys. Both boys appear healthy, behave similarly, and develop normally during the first few weeks of life. During a well-baby checkup, the physician administers a blood test revealing that only one of the boys has an elevated level of a certain plasma solute, indicating that the boy has inherited a recessive disease that runs in the father's family. These boys:

A) have the same genotype but different phenotypes.
B) have the same phenotype but different genotypes.
C) have the same genotype and phenotype.
D) have different genotypes and phenotypes.

113. A researcher has a fruit fly that demonstrates the dominant characteristics for eye color (E) and wing size (W) but does not know its genotype. To determine the fly's genotype, she could carry out which of the following procedures?

A) A test cross with an organism that has the genotype WWee
B) A test cross with an organism that has the genotype wwee
C) A northern blot to detect the DNA associated with the w and e genes
D) A western blot to detect the DNA associated with the W and E genes

114. The ABO blood antigen groups are an example of:

A) multiple possible alleles at a single locus.
B) multiple loci that can have a single allele.
C) a single allele and a single locus with variable expression.
D) degeneration in the genetic code due to inbreeding.

115. A geneticist wishing to carry out a hybridization experiment in pea plants in which every offspring is a hybrid should begin with which of the following crosses?

A) AABB x AABB
B) AABB x aabb
C) aabb x aabb
D) AaBb x AaBb

116. A flower displaying the dominant trait (long stem, L) is crossed with a flower displaying the recessive trait (short stem, l). Half of the offspring produced have long stems and half have short stems. The genotypes of the parent flowers must have been:

A) LL and ll
B) LL and LL
C) Ll and Ll
D) Ll and ll

117. In regions of the world where malaria is endemic, it has been observed that the frequency of the sickle cell allele is significantly higher than in other regions, despite the reduced survival rate for individuals born homozygous recessive (with the disease) in these regions. The persistence of the allele in these regions is likely due to:

A) hybrid vigor, or heterosis.
B) negative selection pressure on those with the disease.
C) enhanced survival rates among inbreeding populations with the allele.
D) better medical care leading to increased survival rates.

118. In a certain population of grasshoppers, black eyes (B) are dominant over yellow eyes (b) and approximately 3/4 of the population has black eyes. Over the course of several generations a number of events lead to a shift making yellow eyes the more common trait, with nearly 98% of the population demonstrating yellow eyes. In this population:

A) the trait for yellow eyes has become dominant.
B) having black eyes must have been strongly selected against.
C) yellow eyes are the wild type.
D) overall fitness has been reduced.

119. In Huntington's disease, the wild-type allele, h, is recessive to the disease allele, H. The persistence of an autosomal dominant allele that is fatal in 100% of cases is best explained by which of the following?

    A) The dominant allele only has moderate negative effects during adolescence and young adulthood.
    B) The wild-type h allele continues to spontaneously mutate into the dominant H allele.
    C) The persistence of any given allele in nature is determined almost wholly by chance.
    D) The disease has no effects until the individual has reached an age far past the normal age for reproduction.

120. In a certain individual, a genetic error led to a translocation in which a segment of the p arm on chromosome 14 was broken off and attached to the q arm of chromosome 16. The translocation created no observable changes in the individual's traits. For the genes located on the translocated segment:

    A) the loci have changed but the alleles have remained the same.
    B) the loci and the alleles have both changed.
    C) the loci have remained the same but at least some of the alleles must have been altered.
    D) the transcriptional machinery will be unable to read either strand of the DNA.

121. The carrier frequency for cystic fibrosis, an autosomal recessive disorder, in the Ashkenazi Jewish population is 1 out of every 24 individuals. A baby born to a couple from this demographic is tested for this mutation. A family history reveals that the mother's father was afflicted with cystic fibrosis. What is the approximate probability that the child will be a carrier of this disease?

    A) 1/1150
    B) 1/100
    C) 1/50
    D) 1/24

122. An orchid breeder crosses two types of orchid, one that is tall with a petite bloom and one that is short with a large bloom, with the goal of obtaining a tall orchid with a large bloom. The first cross yields all short flowers with petite blooms. What is the expected yield of tall orchids with large blooms if bred from the first generation?

    A) 6.25%
    B) 18.75%
    C) 25%
    D) 50%

123. A woman (but not her husband) suffers from Von Willebrand disease, an autosomal dominant condition that shows 50% penetrance. This condition is expected to be phenotypically expressed in what percent of her offspring?

    A) 25%
    B) 33%
    C) 50%
    D) 75%

124. A black, short-haired cat has a litter of kittens with an orange, long-haired cat. The litter is entirely long-haired with mottled black and orange fur. What must be the inheritance pattern for each trait?

    A) Short hair is dominant to long hair, and color shows incomplete dominance.
    B) Short hair is dominant to long hair, and color shows codominance.
    C) Long hair is dominant to short hair, and color shows incomplete dominance.
    D) Long hair is dominant to short hair, and color shows codominance.

Questions 125–126 rely on the figure below

A particular propensity for joint pain is inherited according to the following pedigree.

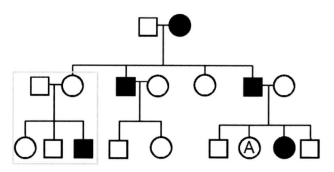

125. If only the individuals outlined by the gray box were considered, which type(s) of inheritance would this trait be thought to display?

    A) Autosomal dominant only
    B) Autosomal recessive only
    C) X-linked recessive only
    D) Autosomal recessive or X-linked recessive

126. What is the probability that the female labeled "A" is at least a carrier of this condition?

    A) 0%
    B) 25%
    C) 50%
    D) 100%

127. A trait is expressed in all individuals who carry a certain gene, but causes symptoms that vary in intensity depending on diet and exercise. What can be said about the penetrance and expressivity of this trait?

    A) The gene is 100% penetrant and lacks variable expressivity.
    B) The gene is 100% penetrant and variably expressive.
    C) The gene is less than 100% penetrant and lacks variable expressivity.
    D) The gene is less than 100% penetrant and variably expressive.

128. Which of the following is true about having a large gene pool?

    I.   It increases genetic diversity.
    II. It increases the chance of extinction of the species.
    III. It increases the chance that some individuals will be especially biologically fit.

    A) I only
    B) I and II
    C) I and III
    D) I, II, and III

129. A student performs a research study on a type of plant that expresses either waxy or smooth leaves, depending on the dryness of the season. The student obtains the following data on preferential expression and genetic analysis.

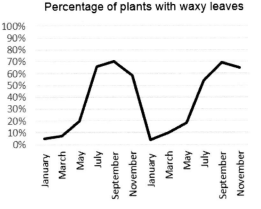

Percentage of plants with waxy leaves

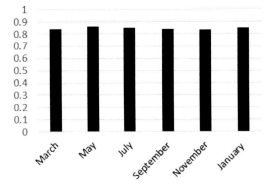

Plants carrying allele for waxy leaves

What can be concluded about the student's data?

    A) The trait for waxy leaves is completely penetrant with variable expressivity.
    B) The trait for waxy leaves is completely penetrant with invariable expressivity.
    C) The trait for waxy leaves displays incomplete penetrance with invariable expressivity.
    D) The trait for waxy leaves displays incomplete penetrance.

130. A man with blonde hair, blue eyes, and fair skin has a daughter with a woman with dark hair, brown eyes, and dark skin. (Assume that hair, eye, and skin color are each dependent on a single gene.) Based on their differences in these three traits, how many possible phenotypic combinations are possible for their child?

    A) 2
    B) 8
    C) 9
    D) 27

131. The instance of nondisjunction for the X chromosome in females over the age of 30 is about one out of every 130 live births. If a woman over 30 is pregnant, assuming that the risk of nondisjunction from the father is negligible, what is the approximate likelihood that the baby will be born with a trisomy in its sex chromosomes?

    A) 1/1000
    B) 1/300
    C) 1/200
    D) 1/125

132. Which of the following is true about an X-linked dominant trait?

    I. Fathers with the trait always pass the gene to their daughters.
    II. Mothers with the trait always pass the gene to their daughters.
    III. Mothers with the trait always pass the gene to their sons.
    IV. Females with one copy of the mutated allele will always express the trait.

    A) I and II
    B) I and IV
    C) I, II, and III
    D) II, III, and IV

133. A woman is experiencing symptoms of an X-linked recessive disease, but neither of her parents have this condition. Which of these explanations could NOT accurately describe this phenomenon?

    A) Her father and mother are carriers of the trait, and both passed mutated copies to their daughter.
    B) Her mother was a carrier of the trait and passed this chromosome to her daughter. The non-mutated chromosome was then randomly inactivated, leaving her with only the mutated chromosome.
    C) Her mother was a carrier of the trait and passed this chromosome to her daughter. Her father experienced nondisjunction and did not provide her with an additional X chromosome, leading to an X0 genotype with the only active X being a mutated one.
    D) Random mutation during development resulted in a new variant of this disease.

134. The Y chromosome contains very few genes of interest. Most important is the SRY gene, which activates male differentiation. During an error in replication, a father's X and Y chromosome underwent crossing over, causing the SRY gene to be left on the X chromosome. If this man passes his Y chromosome to his progeny, the child will be:

    A) genetically male and phenotypically female.
    B) genetically male and phenotypically male.
    C) genetically female and phenotypically female.
    D) genetically female and phenotypically male.

Questions 135–136 rely on the pedigree below

The following pedigree indicates the incidence of deafness in a large family.

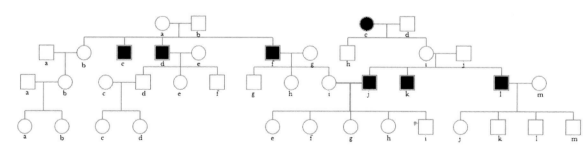

135. What type of inheritance is shown by the trait in the pedigree above?

    A) Autosomal dominant
    B) Autosomal recessive
    C) X-linked recessive
    D) There is not enough information to discern a concrete answer.

136. None of the children of Individuals "i" and "j" (from the third generation) suffer from this disease. What is the most likely reason for this occurrence?

    A) Individual "i" is not a carrier of the disease.
    B) Men cannot pass the disease to their children.
    C) Individual "i" had a germline nondisjunction event early in development that restored functionality.
    D) Deafness is multifactorial and arises from different genetic mutations for each family.

137. All of the following are true of mutations inherited on the Y chromosome EXCEPT that:

    A) only men are affected.
    B) mothers only pass the trait to their sons.
    C) they are rare, as the Y chromosome codes for relatively little genetic information.
    D) pedigrees will show that only the sons of afflicted fathers will possess the mutation.

138. The endosymbiont theory states that mitochondria and chloroplasts were initially prokaryotes that were engulfed by unicellular organisms. If true, which of these statements would support this hypothesis?

    A) Mitochondria and chloroplasts are surrounded by an additional plasma membrane.
    B) Mitochondria have long, straight chromosomes.
    C) Chloroplasts are incapable of dividing without other cellular machinery.
    D) Mitochondria and nuclear DNA contain some similar sequences.

139. MCAD is a mitochondrial disease that prevents the body from converting certain fats to energy, particularly during fasting. Which individual is at risk for MCAD and should be tested?

    A) The daughter of two healthy parents, whose grandfather had MCAD
    B) The son of a healthy father and an afflicted mother
    C) The daughter of an afflicted father and a healthy mother
    D) All of the above individuals are at risk and should be tested.

140. In some gastropods, the direction of spiral coiling is dependent on allelomorphic genes, with a sinistral coil (S) being recessive to dextral (S+) coiling. However, coiling only occurs due to proteins already expressed in the female gamete; therefore, for the first generation, coiling is maternally derived. If you cross a homozygous sinistral female (SS) with a homozygous dextral male (S+S+), what will be the spin of the majority of the offspring in the first and second generation?

    A) Sinistral, sinistral
    B) Sinistral, dextral
    C) Dextral, sinistral
    D) Dextral, dextral

141. Which of these sequences correctly lists all of the stages of meiosis?

    A) Prophase, anaphase, metaphase, telophase
    B) Prophase I, anaphase I, metaphase I, telophase I, prophase II, anaphase II, metaphase II, telophase II
    C) Prophase I, metaphase I, anaphase I, telophase I, prophase II, metaphase II, anaphase II, telophase II
    D) Prophase, metaphase, anaphase, telophase

142. How does the process of crossing over affect mitosis?

    A) It allows for a greater amount of genetic variation by creating recombinant chromosomes.
    B) It provides for the creating of two distinct diploid cells through recombination of parts of the chromosome.
    C) It allows the chromosomes to correctly split at the centromeres during anaphase.
    D) Crossing over does not occur during mitosis.

143. How does the behavior of the centromeres during meiosis differ from that during mitosis?

    A) During meiosis, the centromeres do not split during the first incarnation of anaphase.
    B) During meiosis, the centromeres do split during the first incarnation of anaphase, but this is followed by a second anaphase during meiosis II.
    C) The centromeres do not split at all during meiosis.
    D) The centromeres do not split at all during mitosis.

144. The figure below depicts the changes in chromosomal number that occur during mitosis and meiosis.

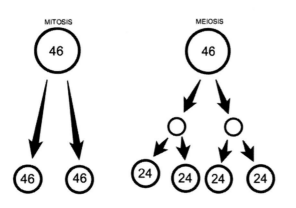

Are Figure 1 (the left-hand diagram) and Figure 2 (the right-hand diagram) labeled correctly?

A) Both Figures 1 and 2 have the process and number of chromosomes correctly labeled.

B) Both Figures 1 and 2 have the correct process labeled, but Figure 2 has the incorrect number of chromosomes in the finished product.

C) Neither Figure 1 nor Figure 2 have the process nor the number of chromosomes correctly labeled.

D) Figure 1 and 2 have the incorrect process labeled, but include the correct number of chromosomes.

145. How might failed synapsis affect the daughter cells produced by meiosis?

A) It would create two nonidentical daughter cells rather than two identical ones.

B) It would inevitably lead to the destruction and apoptosis of the daughter cells.

C) Synapsis occurs during mitosis, not meiosis; therefore, it would not affect the daughter cells at all.

D) It could create abnormalities through inversion, translocation, or nondisjunction, disrupting the genetic information of the gamete.

146. In the below figure, two different chromosomes are depicted with several genes labeled.

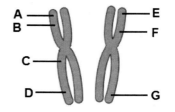

Which genes are most likely to be linked?

A) A and E

B) A and B

C) C and D

D) E and F

147. Which protein structure is intricately involved in chromosome pairing, synapsis, and recombination?

A) Spindle fibers

B) Telomeres

C) Synaptonemal complex

D) Golgi apparatus

148. What biological processes create the phenomenon of independent assortment?

A) Genes that help an organism survive are selected for while genes that hinder survival are selected against.

B) During sexual reproduction, the offspring receives genes from two parents.

C) During mitosis, chromosomes are pulled apart randomly and undergo recombination.

D) Homologous chromosomes undergo recombination and are randomly pulled apart during meiosis.

149. One way in which mitosis resembles meiosis is that:

A) both processes include the breakdown of the nuclear membrane.

B) in both processes, the number of chromosomes is reduced by half.

C) in both processes, crossing over increases the genetic variability of the daughter cells.

D) both processes can result in the production of somatic cells.

150. Two genes are found to have a recombination frequency of 50%. Are these genes likely on the same chromosome?

    A) Yes, they appear on the same chromosome and near the same location.
    B) Yes, they appear on the same chromosome far away from each other.
    C) No, they must be on different chromosomes.
    D) No, they probably are on different chromosomes, but they could be very far apart on the same chromosome.

151. Red hair is recessive to all other hair colors. If the incidence of red-headed individuals within a certain population is only 9%, what percent of that population are heterozygous for the "red hair" allele?

    A) 16%
    B) 21%
    C) 30%
    D) 42%

152. 845 of 1000 individuals lack a specific olfactory receptor for sulfur, even though the allele that codes for the receptor is dominant. Approximately what fraction of the population consists of people with two copies of this allele?

    A) 1%
    B) 16%
    C) 36%
    D) 84%

Questions 153–154 rely on the table below

The following data shows allele frequencies for albinism, a recessive trait, and pigmented scales in a population of salmon over time. Note that the values given represent the percent of the gene pool for each of the two alleles.

	1992	1993	1994	1995*	1996	1997	1998	1999	2000
Albino	4.01%	4.03%	3.99%	4.90%	6.89%	7.98%	11.34%	16.54%	25.73%
Pigmented	95.99%	95.97%	96.01%	95.10%	93.11%	91.94%	88.67%	83.46%	74.27%

*In early 1995, light-colored rocks were added to many riverbanks to prevent erosion.

153. The difference between the percentage of albino salmon in 1997 and that in 1993 is closest to:

    A) 0.001%.
    B) 0.5%.
    C) 4%.
    D) 50%.

154. Allele frequency did not stay consistent over time in this population study. Which of the following criteria for Hardy-Weinberg equilibrium was violated?

    A) Presence of a sufficiently large population
    B) Random mating
    C) No natural selection
    D) No migration

155. In a population where the allele frequency shifts by random chance, which mechanism of evolution is at work?

    A) Genetic drift
    B) Migration
    C) Mutation
    D) Natural selection

156. A biologist studying a gene finds that a change has occurred to the sequence, shown below (assume transcription begins at the second nucleotide).

    '5- CAGGUGAGAUAUUUA -3'

    ⬇

    '5 -CAGGUGAGAUUAAUA-3'

    What type of mutation does this exemplify?

    A) Silent
    B) Missense
    C) Nonsense
    D) Frameshift

157. An individual is experiencing symptoms related to the lack of a specific protein. However, genetic analysis using a cDNA library finds no mutation in the gene encoding this protein. If a mutation does indeed exist, it would most likely be found:

    A) in the promoter region of the gene of interest.
    B) in an intron within the gene of interest.
    C) downstream from the gene of interest.
    D) in a gene coding for RNA polymerase.

158. A researcher wants to know the carcinogenic risk of a particular polynuclear aromatic hydrocarbon (PAH). To find out, he plates *Salmonella*, which is unable to grow in the absence of histidine, on agar plates. Note that minimal media is a histidine-deficient carbon source. The researcher's results are shown below.

    Plate I: *Salmonella* alone on minimal media
    Plate II: *Salmonella* and PAH on minimal media
    Plate III: *Salmonella*, PAH, and human liver preparation (which contains histidine) on minimal media
    Plate IV: *Salmonella* and 2-aminoanthracene (a known carcinogen) on minimal media

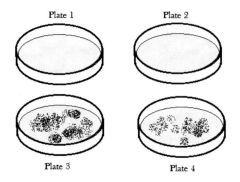

The scientist can conclude that the PAH is:

    A) a carcinogen, as evidenced by the growth on Plate 3.
    B) a carcinogen, as evidenced by the growth on Plate 4.
    C) not a carcinogen, as evidenced by the growth on Plate 3.
    D) not a carcinogen, as evidenced by the lack of growth on Plate 2.

159. Which of the following violate the principles of Hardy-Weinberg equilibrium?

    I. A very large population of foxes in a state where white foxes are often hunted for fur
    II. A group of crows that constantly loses members to a neighboring group
    III. A group of people subjected to so little pollution that only a small mutation rate is displayed
    IV. A small harem of rabbits with no natural predators

    A) I and II
    B) II and IV
    C) I, II, and IV
    D) I, II, III, and IV

160. Gene loci H, I, J, and K are in the same linkage group but do not necessarily appear in that order. Using several test crosses, the percent recombination was obtained for pairs of gene loci.

Pair of loci	H and I	H and J	I and K	J and K
Recombination rate	0.23	0.34	0.09	0.20

    Given this information, what is the order of the loci?

    A) HIJK
    B) HKIJ
    C) JKIH
    D) KIHJ

161. A rare type of orchid faces a unique challenge to find adequate sunlight. Plants that are too small are covered by undergrowth, while plants that reach too high are preyed upon by grazing herbivores. Over time, these orchids have, on average, grown to vary only slightly in height. This situation exemplifies which type of selection?

A) Speciation
B) Directional selection
C) Disruptive selection
D) Stabilizing selection

Questions 162–163 rely on the figure below

One species of hummingbird uses a specific food source, the trumpet climber, which changes the size of its blooms based on recent precipitation. The figure below shows this change in bloom size, along with its effect on the survival of birds with three different phenotypes. An upward arrow denotes a survival advantage, a downward arrow corresponds to a decrease in biological fitness, and a dash (---) means that no effect is observed.

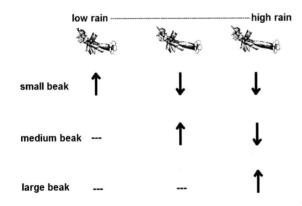

162. What form of natural selection is shown during periods of heavy rain?

A) Directional selection
B) Disruptive selection
C) Stabilizing selection
D) Genetic drift

163. Imagine that, over time, both trumpet climber blooms and hummingbird beaks gradually become longer. This relationship constitutes:

A) parallel evolution.
B) convergent evolution.
C) co-evolution.
D) divergent evolution.

164. A specific type of moth has been found in samples of wheat germ. This insect can vary in color from white to brown to black. In the past, brown moths have been most prevalent, as they are naturally camouflaged with the wheat germ, which allows them to avoid predators. After a fire, however, the earth becomes scorched black with white ash. Several generations later, hundreds of moths are counted and the new percentage of each phenotype in the population is determined.

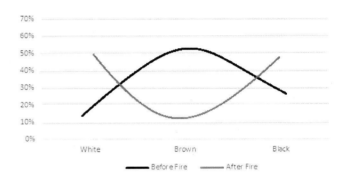

What type of selection has occurred?

A) Directional selection
B) Disruptive selection
C) Stabilizing selection
D) The bottleneck effect

165. The giant panda nearly became extinct several years ago, but recovery efforts have kept its population stable. However, nearly all giant pandas are now genetically very closely related. This is due to:

A) random mating.
B) stabilizing selection.
C) the bottleneck effect.
D) gene flow.

166. In a coral reef, genetic analysis shows that 18 different coral species originated from a common ancestor. This scenario best relates to:

    A) commensalism.
    B) adaptive radiation.
    C) an evolutionary bottleneck.
    D) stabilizing selection.

167. A population of beetles is taken from its mainland home to a neighboring island with very few shrubs. While mainland beetles create their nests in shrubbery, island beetles nest on the ground. After a long period of time, when the island beetles are reunited with their mainland relatives, it is observed that the two populations can no longer interbreed. Which form of speciation must have occurred?

    A) Sympatric speciation
    B) Allopatric speciation
    C) Parapatric speciation
    D) None of the above

168. The molecular clock hypothesis is based on which assumption?

    A) All mutations are neutral with regard to selection.
    B) All mutations are either advantageous or disadvantageous to the organism.
    C) Genetic mutations occur at a steady rate.
    D) Evolution of species has always occurred at a constant rate.

169. Natural selection is often referred to as "the survival of the fittest." In this sense, what is a "fit" individual?

    A) An organism with a very long lifespan
    B) An organism with many advantageous traits
    C) An organism who reproduces often
    D) An organism who has many fertile offspring

170. Hermit crabs often need to relocate to larger shells once they have outgrown their current ones. Sometimes, crabs scavenge empty shells from slightly different species that have been discarded on the ocean floor until an appropriate fit is found. This is an example of:

    A) commensalism.
    B) parasitism.
    C) mutualism.
    D) ectosymbiosis.

171. Which of these are found in a typical prokaryotic cellular membrane?

    I.   Phospholipids
    II. Cholesterol and other sterols
    III. Transmembrane proteins
    IV. Lipid-linked carbohydrates

    A) I only
    B) I and III
    C) I, II, and IV
    D) I, III, and IV

172. Of these pieces of scientific evidence, which provide support for the fluid mosaic model?

    A) Estrogen receptors are consistently found in the same location of the cell membrane of breast cancer cells.
    B) Phospholipids within a membrane separate based upon the length of their hydrophobic tails.
    C) The rate of protein diffusion in a cell membrane depends primarily on the viscosity of the membrane.
    D) Transport rate across the lipid bilayer depends on its relative viscosity.

173. Which of the following functions are performed by membrane-bound proteins?

    A) Transport of metabolites across the membrane
    B) Connection of the cell membrane to the cytoskeleton
    C) Initiation of signal transduction pathways
    D) All of the above are functions performed by membrane-bound proteins

174. In response to either bitter- or sweet-tasting substances, taste receptors cells release the molecule gustducin. This is accomplished through a signal transduction pathway initiated by a G protein-coupled receptor. Where within the cell would this receptor be found?

    A) In the cytoplasm
    B) Embedded in the nuclear membrane
    C) Embedded in the cellular membrane
    D) Not enough information is given to determine the location of this molecule.

175. Transmembrane proteins are able to freely diffuse throughout the cellular membrane, typically leading to a random distribution. However, in epithelial cells that line the small intestine, the

membrane possesses polarity. As a result, the transmembrane proteins found on one side of the cell have a different distribution from those on the other. How is this possible?

A) Epithelial cells are connected by tight junctions, which prevent movement of transmembrane proteins from one side of the cell to the other.

B) When transmembrane proteins are produced in epithelial cells, they are transported to a specific side based on their function(s).

C) Transmembrane proteins bind to the extracellular matrix, locking them in place in the epithelial cells.

D) Due to an increased amount of cholesterol in epithelial cell membranes, these proteins are unable to freely diffuse and become conformationally locked.

Questions 176–177 rely on the figure below

Two cells are shown below along with their relative concentrations of metabolites.

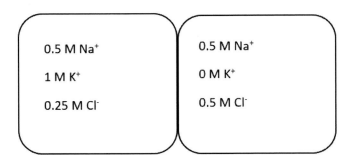

0.5 M Na⁺

1 M K⁺

0.25 M Cl⁻

0.5 M Na⁺

0 M K⁺

0.5 M Cl⁻

176. If solute is unable to travel between these cells, how can the voltage potential at the barrier between the two be described?

A) A voltage potential exists across the membrane, with the left more positive than the right.

B) A voltage potential exists across the membrane, with the right more positive than the left.

C) A voltage potential exists across the membrane, but to compensate, the cell on the left sequesters its K^+ ions in specialized proteins.

D) No voltage potential exists across the membrane.

177. If gap junctions are introduced to the membrane separating the two cells, which of the following would result from concentration gradients alone?

A) Nothing; no immediate ion flow would be observed.

B) Na^+ would have no net flow in either direction, while K^+ would flow to the right and Cl^- would flow to the left.

C) Na^+ would have no net flow in either direction, while K^+ would flow to the left and Cl^- would flow to the right.

D) Only K^+ would exhibit a net flow, and it would be to the right.

Questions 178–179 rely on the table below

The following table shows the results of FRAP experimentation on the cell membranes of five different mice, each of which was fed a different diet.

Sample	Time to Recovery (s)
1	5.6
2	4.5
3	9.9
4	3.0
5	4.5

178. During a FRAP experiment, cells are incubated with fluorescently-tagged lipids. The lipids are then bleached, and the time it takes for the fluorescence to recover is recorded. Based on the results in the table, which sample had the highest membrane fluidity?

A) Sample 1
B) Samples 2 and 5
C) Sample 3
D) Sample 4

179. Which sample was likely taken from a mouse who was fed a diet heavy in saturated fatty acids?

A) Sample 1
B) Samples 2 and 5
C) Sample 3
D) Sample 4

180. A recently-identified species of eukaryote is able to survive at extremely high temperatures. If a group of scientists were able to analyze the composition of the cell membrane of such a species, what would they expect to observe?

    A) High levels of cholesterol-like molecules and high levels of unsaturated fatty acids
    B) High levels of cholesterol-like molecules and low levels of unsaturated fatty acids
    C) Low levels of cholesterol-like molecules and high levels of unsaturated fatty acids
    D) Low levels of cholesterol-like molecules and low levels of unsaturated fatty acids

181. A scientist separates the two halves of a beaker with a membrane permeable only to water. On one side, the scientist adds an aqueous 3 M $Ca(OH)_2$ solution, and on the other a solution of 5 M glucose. The scientist leaves and returns after several hours. If the figure below shows the beaker immediately after addition of solute, which of the following diagrams depicts it upon the scientist's return? (Assume full dissociation of $Ca(OH)_2$.)

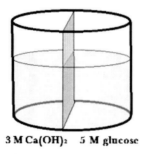

3 M Ca(OH)₂   5 M glucose

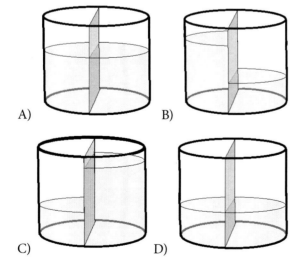

A)   B)

C)   D)

182. Which of the following directly impact(s) the rate of diffusion of a large polar substance across a plasma membrane?

    I. Concentration of the substance
    II. Fluidity of the membrane
    III. Volume of water
    IV. Number of transmembrane proteins

    A) I and II
    B) II and III
    C) I and IV
    D) I, II, and IV

183. During an action potential, voltage-gated channels open and result in a flow of sodium into the cell. This influx stabilizes at a membrane potential of +35 mV, even though the extracellular concentration of sodium is still higher than the Na^+ concentration inside the cell. How can this occurrence be explained?

    A) The total concentration of all solutes has equalized, stopping diffusion of sodium.
    B) Further depolarization of the cell would result in lysis.
    C) Sodium that enters the cell forms a chloride salt, making it inert.
    D) Electrochemical equilibrium has been reached due to the high intracellular concentration of K^+.

184. A scientist thinks that he has discovered a voltage-dependent pump that transports two Na^+ ions out of the cell for every K^+ ion it transmits inward. To study this, he places a neuron in an isotonic bath and connects it to a patch clamp, which immediately hyperpolarizes the cell. How would you expect this to affect the pump?

    A) The activity of the pump will increase.
    B) The activity of the pump will decrease.
    C) The activity of the pump will remain the same.
    D) The activity of the pump will cease entirely.

185. Which of the following substances is freely diffusible across the plasma membrane?

    A) Na^+
    B) Glucose
    C) ATP
    D) Estrogen

186. A vesicle contains 2.5 M of glucose and 3.5 M of sucrose. If it is placed in a solution of 5 M glucose and 1 M sucrose, in which direction will these solutes initially diffuse?

    A) Glucose will diffuse into the cell, while sucrose will diffuse outward.
    B) Both glucose and sucrose will diffuse into the cell.
    C) No diffusion will take place because equilibrium has already been reached.
    D) No diffusion will take place because neither glucose nor sucrose can cross the membrane.

187. In facilitated diffusion:

    A) energy, in the form of either ATP or GTP, is required.
    B) proteins are highly specific for the particular molecule involved.
    C) proteins are located only in the plasma membrane and not the nuclear or mitochondrial membranes.
    D) a molecule can be transported up its concentration gradient.

188. A scientist is studying the transport of zinc into epithelial cells. Two observations are made: first, that zinc can be moved inward even against its concentration gradient, and second, that as the metal ions enter the cell, the extracellular environment becomes more concentrated with solute. What can be concluded about this type of transport?

    A) Transport is passive and zinc diffuses through the plasma membrane.
    B) Transport is passive and zinc uses a protein channel to enter the cell.
    C) Transport is active and the cell uses an ATP-dependent mechanism to shuttle the zinc ion only.
    D) Transport is active and zinc movement is coupled with that of another ion.

189. Two different compounds are allowed to travel across a plasma membrane. The graph below shows the rates of transport for these substances versus their concentrations outside the cell. What are the most likely identities of the compounds?

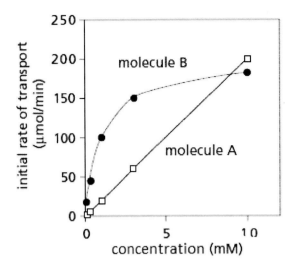

    A) Molecule A is CO_2, while molecule B is O_2.
    B) Molecule A is glycine, while molecule B is testosterone.
    C) Molecule A is O_2, while molecule B is glycine.
    D) Molecule A is testosterone, while molecule B is CO_2.

190. All of the following are true about the sodium-potassium pump EXCEPT:

    A) ATP is hydrolyzed when it is functioning.
    B) It is a transmembrane protein found on plasma membranes.
    C) For every two sodium ions pumped out of the cell, it transports three potassium ions inward.
    D) It plays a critical role in establishing the cell's resting potential.

191. Members of the genus *Ancistrus*, commonly known as the bristlenose pleco, are freshwater fish that are often kept in tanks. If one of these creatures were placed in a typical ocean, its cells would:

    A) shrink, as they would be hypotonic to their environment.
    B) swell, as they would be hypotonic to their environment.
    C) shrink, as they would be hypertonic to their environment.
    D) swell, as they would be hypertonic to their environment.

192. What is the definition of an isotonic solution?

    A) One that has the same concentration of charged solute as a reference compartment
    B) One that has the same concentration of overall solute as a reference compartment
    C) One that has the same concentration of overall solute as a typical human muscle cell
    D) One that has a higher concentration of solute than a solution to which it is compared

193. In normal human extracellular fluid, the concentration of Na^+ is approximately 140 mEq/L. A beaker of water is filled with a solution with exactly that sodium concentration. If a water-permeable synthetic cell is dropped in the beaker, what minimum NaBr concentration must it have to gain water from its environment?

    A) [NaBr] > 140 mEq/L
    B) [NaBr] < 140 mEq/L
    C) [NaBr] > 70 mEq/L
    D) [NaBr] < 70 mEq/L

194. Does the Na^+/K^+ ATPase exemplify a form of secondary active transport?

    A) No, because it requires the use of ATP for energy.
    B) No, because it involves movement of both ions against their concentration gradients.
    C) Yes, because it requires the use of ATP for energy.
    D) Yes, because it involves transport of two ions across a membrane in opposite directions.

195. SGLT1, a sodium/glucose cotransporter, utilizes the concentration gradient of sodium to actively force glucose molecules across the cell membrane of the nephron. Given this information, SGLT1 must:

    A) move sodium ions out of the cell.
    B) move glucose and sodium ions in opposite directions.
    C) move glucose molecules into the cell.
    D) move glucose molecules out of the cell.

196. Which of these statements is/are true?

    I.   All transmembrane proteins are integral proteins.
    II. All transmembrane proteins are eukaryotic.
    III. All integral proteins are transmembrane proteins.

    A) I only
    B) III only
    C) I and III
    D) I, II, and III

197. "Cell drinking" is also known as:

    A) endocytosis.
    B) minicytosis.
    C) phagocytosis.
    D) pinocytosis.

198. A protein is marked for degradation and enzymatically broken down in a lysosome. In which membrane-bound compartment did this protein likely reside immediately before this breakdown took place?

    A) A late endosome
    B) A secondary endosome
    C) A vesicle
    D) An early endosome

199. Phagocytosis, a technique often demonstrated by immune cells, involves the engulfment of pathogens for later destruction. Phagocytosis is a form of:

    I.   passive transport.
    II. active transport.
    III. pinocytosis.
    IV. endocytosis.

    A) I only
    B) I and III
    C) II and IV
    D) II, III, and IV

200. The image below depicts a form of cellular transport.

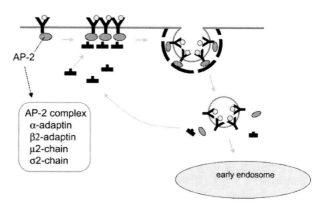

How can this process be accurately described?

A) As phagocytosis, a form of passive transport
B) As phagocytosis, a form of active transport
C) As receptor-mediated endocytosis, a form of passive transport
D) As receptor-mediated endocytosis, a form of active transport

201. Which of these correctly describe features in mitochondria but not other mammalian organelles?

I. Mitochondria have their own set of genetic material.
II. Mitochondria are able to self-replicate independently of the cell replication cycle.
III. Mitochondria are found only in eukaryotes
IV. Mitochondria are enclosed by a membrane bilayer.

A) I only
B) II only
C) I and II
D) I, II, III, and IV

202. Of the following, which is NOT a difference between prokaryotes and eukaryotes?

A) Prokaryotes have a circular genome, while eukaryotes have linear chromosomes.
B) Eukaryotes have mitochondria, while prokaryotes lack them entirely.
C) Eukaryotes divide via mitosis, while prokaryotes divide via binary fission.
D) Prokaryotes use alternative splicing to create multiple proteins from a single gene, while eukaryotes do not splice their gene transcripts.

203. Which of these processes occurs in the nucleolus?

A) Transcription of the genes that code for ribosomal components
B) Compaction of DNA that is not actively being transcribed
C) Translation of proteins that function in the nucleus
D) Transcription of genes that code for histone proteins

204. Of the four pairings below, which does NOT correctly match a cellular function with the location of its occurrence?

A) Splicing – nucleus
B) Transcription – nucleus
C) Electron transport chain – outer mitochondrial membrane
D) DNA replication – nucleus

205. Proteins enter and exit the nucleus through the nuclear pore complex. How do proteins specify which direction to travel through this pore?

A) Proteins or macromolecules bind to Ran, which enters the nucleus in its GDP state and exits in its GTP state.
B) Proteins have specific sequences that signal for nuclear import or export.
C) Proteins, as macromolecules composed of amino acids, change protonation states depending on their need for export or import from the nucleus.
D) Both A and B are correct.

206. Consider the evolutionary timeline below.

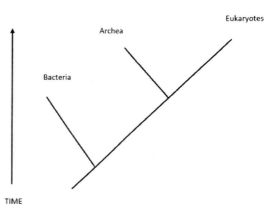

Based on the figure, around which point must the development of organelles have occurred?

A) Before eukaryotes and bacteria split
B) After bacteria split, but before Archaea did
C) After Archaea and eukaryotes split
D) It is impossible to know without more information.

207. The endosymbiotic hypothesis relates to:

A) mitochondria.
B) lysosomes.
C) the nucleolus.
D) the plasma membrane.

Questions 208–209 rely on the table below

A team of researchers observed the cellular locations of various proteins before and after the cell was exposed to EGF, or epithelial growth factor.

Protein	Location before Activation	Location after Activation
RAF	cytoplasm	cytoplasm
c-Jun	cytoplasm	nucleus
NF-κB	cytoplasm	nucleus
PTB1	nucleus	nucleus
S6-K	cytoplasm	cytoplasm

208. Which of the proteins listed in the table could be a transcription factor that is activated by EGF?

    A) S6-K
    B) c-Jun
    C) PTB1
    D) RAF

209. When activated, the S6-K protein directly affects intracellular protein synthesis. However, this macromolecule does not localize to the nucleus. Which of the following gives the best explanation for this observation?

    A) S6-K acts as a splicing factor to alter the proteins that are synthesized within the cell.
    B) S6-K activates another protein that can then enter the nucleus and act as a transcription factor.
    C) S6-K can act on mature mRNA and mitochondria to change protein synthesis.
    D) S6-K is able to act as a transcription factor even though it does not enter the nucleus.

210. A researcher sequences the genome of an unknown prokaryotic cell. When looking at the proteins coded for by this organism, she finds a protein that would not normally appear in a prokaryote. The molecule in question could be:

    A) a protein with sequential similarities to eukaryotic components of the spliceosome.
    B) a protein with a DNA-binding domain.
    C) a protein that is commonly seen in cell walls.
    D) a protein that is very similar in function to actin.

211. Which of the following correctly matches an organelle and its cellular function?

    I.   Lysosome - digestion of polysaccharides, proteins, and other cellular macromolecules
    II. Smooth ER - production of proteins
    III. Golgi apparatus - transport of vesicles to specific cellular locations
    IV. Mitochondria - cellular respiration

    A) I only
    B) I and III
    C) I, II, and IV
    D) I, III, and IV

212. The endoplasmic reticulum is directly attached to another cellular component. What is the identity of this structure?

    A) The Golgi apparatus
    B) The lysosome
    C) The nucleus
    D) The cell membrane

213. How does the lysosome form?

    A) The lysosome is formed by an invagination of the cellular membrane.
    B) The lysosome buds off from the Golgi apparatus as a vesicle.
    C) The lysosome forms in the endoplasmic reticulum during protein translation.
    D) The lysosome initially begins as part of the nucleus.

214. A student researcher accidentally injects the contents of a lysosome into his frog embryos. What will happen to one of these embryonic cells?

    A) The injected contents will be absorbed into the current lysosomes in the cell.
    B) The injected contents will be expelled by the frog embryo.
    C) The injected contents will begin to digest other proteins and macromolecules in the cell, possibly resulting in its death.
    D) The injected contents will be digested by the embryo.

215. What consequence is most likely if the Golgi apparatus were removed from a cell?

    A) The cell would no longer be able to target transmembrane proteins to the cell membrane as opposed to the nuclear membrane.
    B) The cell would no longer be able to properly excrete proteins.
    C) The cell would be incapable of forming lysosomes.
    D) All of the above would occur.

Questions 216–217 rely on the table below

An incredibly detail-oriented researcher analyzes the contents of a sample of human cells. He manages to document the number of each specific organelle, with the results that are displayed below.

Organelle	# of cells in which present	# of total organelles of this type
nucleus	500	475
mitochondria	500	50,005
lysosomes	500	10,130
peroxisomes	500	5,010
ribosomes	500	25,007

216. How many mitochondria, lysosomes, and peroxisomes are present per cell in the sample taken?

    A) Mitochondria: 100; lysosomes: 40; peroxisomes: 10
    B) Mitochondria: 100; lysosomes: 20; peroxisomes: 10
    C) Mitochondria: 500; lysosomes: 40; peroxisomes: 10
    D) Mitochondria: 500; lysosomes: 20; peroxisomes: 20

217. If the researcher drew up a second sample of the same cell type and found an increase in the number of ribosomes per cell, what would this indicate?

    A) The sample was contaminated with a small number of prokaryotic organisms.
    B) Many of the cells in the sample were preparing to undergo cell division.
    C) Some of the cells in the sample were beginning to experience apoptosis.
    D) A contaminant was added to the sample, which the cells were digesting.

Questions 218–219 rely on the table below

A sample of cells of an unknown tissue type is analyzed and compared to a known sample of human skin cells. Assume that the two samples included a roughly equal number of cells.

Sample	Rough ER	Smooth ER	Ribosomes
Human skin cells	.0067 g	.0035 g	0.05 g
Unknown cell sample	.0071g	.07 g	0.047 g

218. What is the cellular function of smooth ER?

    A) To produce intracellular proteins
    B) To produce enzymes used in the degradation of cellular materials
    C) To synthesize or function in the synthesis of lipids and fatty acids
    D) To package proteins and lipids into vesicles

219. What is the most likely identity of the unknown sample?

    A) Human liver cells
    B) Human muscle cells
    C) Human red blood cells
    D) Any of these are likely.

220. Which of the following correctly traces the location of a transmembrane protein from its location of translation to the cellular membrane?

   A) The protein is translated by a free ribosome, travels to the Golgi, is packaged in a vesicle and then merges with the plasma membrane.
   B) The protein is translated in the rough ER, packaged in a vesicle, enters the Golgi, and is placed in another vesicle, which then merges with the plasma membrane.
   C) The protein is translated in the rough ER, transported to the smooth ER, packaged in a vesicle that enters the Golgi, and moved to a second vesicle that then merges with the plasma membrane.
   D) The protein is translated by a ribosome that is directly attached to the plasma membrane.

221. A patient with persistent difficulties fighting off bacterial infections is found to have a genetic mutation that adversely impacts the speed of cytoskeletal reorganization in immune cells. This condition will most dramatically impact the function of:

   A) helper T cells.
   B) macrophages.
   C) plasma cells.
   D) killer T cells.

222. A scientist exposes yeast cells to a chemical that causes drastic, irreversible conformational changes in gamma-tubulin. Later, the scientist observes that these cells are unable to complete mitosis. At which stage of this process will these cells initially fail?

   A) Prophase
   B) Metaphase
   C) Anaphase
   D) None of the above; yeast cells normally do not undergo mitosis.

223. A neuron is observed to display impaired neurotransmitter (NT) secretion. Upon further study, this is found to be caused by a defect in the vesicular transport of newly synthesized NTs from the cell body down the axon. A problem with which class of cytoskeletal accessory proteins is most likely at fault?

   A) Kinesins, as they travel toward the + end of microtubules
   B) Kinesins, as they travel toward the − end of microtubules
   C) Dyneins, as they travel toward the + end of microtubules
   D) Dyneins, as they travel toward the − end of microtubules

224. The cytoskeleton does NOT play a direct role in which of the following functions?

   A) Cell movement
   B) Mitosis
   C) Ion transport
   D) Endocytosis

225. A young boy has a genetic defect that impairs the synthesis of keratin filaments. This condition is likely to most severely impact the structural integrity of:

   A) adipose tissue.
   B) epithelial tissue.
   C) muscular tissue.
   D) nervous tissue.

226. A newly proposed candidate for an antibiotic targets flagellin, the primary structural component of bacterial flagella. Does this medication pose a significant risk of attacking human cells as well?

   A) Yes; human flagellin would likely also be destroyed.
   B) No; human flagellin has a significantly different structure from bacterial flagellin.
   C) No; human flagellin is protected by the plasma membrane.
   D) No; human flagella are not composed of flagellin.

227. Progeria is a genetic disease characterized by symptoms resembling rapid aging; most sufferers do not live to be twenty. Its root cause is a point mutation in a single gene that results in abnormally-shaped, structurally-deficient nuclei, as visible below. (Note: the cell on the left results from untreated progeria, while that on the right has been treated with a medication.)

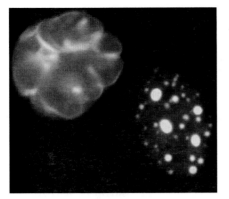

The mutation responsible for this disease is most likely found in a gene that codes for:

A) actin microfilaments.
B) intermediate filaments.
C) microtubules.
D) collagen.

228. Colchicine, a drug intended to treat gout, binds tightly to tubulin to prevent free dimers from polymerizing with microtubules. This medication will directly impair which process(es)?

I. Mitosis
II. Vesicular transport
III. Cytokinesis
IV. Extension of filipodia

    A) I only
    B) I and II
    C) I and IV
    D) II, III, and IV

229. The toxin phalloidin, produced by the "death cap" mushroom, acts by binding to actin microfilaments and thus preventing their depolymerization. A patient poisoned by this toxin will most likely experience disrupted:

A) vesicular transport.
B) organelle relocation.
C) cell movement.
D) intercellular signaling.

230. A scientist is taking an inventory of intracellular polymers in various cells. She determines that she can classify the compounds obtained into three types based on diameter, rigidity, and tensile strength.

Type	Diameter	Rigidity	Tensile strength
A	6 nm	low	intermediate
B	8-12 nm	intermediate	high
C	25 nm	high	low

Cells with a relatively high concentration of "type A" polymers were likely obtained from:

A) the myocardial layer of the heart.
B) the cerebral cortex.
C) the mucosa of the small intestine.
D) a deposit of adipose tissue.

231. According to Robert Hooke's cell theory, which of the following is true?

A) Living organisms are composed of more than one cell.
B) All living cells arise from pre-existing cells through division.
C) Protein is the fundamental unit of all living organisms.
D) No living organism is composed entirely of cells that are identical in nature.

232. A patient's blood is cultured and returns a positive test for peptidoglycan. This patient likely suffers from which type of infection?

A) A fungal infection
B) A bacterial infection
C) A viral infection
D) A parasitic infection

233. A pathologist observes the species below under a microscope.

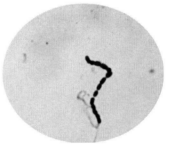

The bacteria in this image are of what type?

A) Spirochetes
B) Staphylococci
C) Streptobacilli
D) Diplobacilli

234. A patient comes to the clinic with a warm, raised rash. Upon culture and examination under a microscope, the cells pictured below are observed.

An appropriate diagnosis for the patient would be infection by:

A) *Streptococcus pneumoniae.*
B) *Streptobacillus epidermidis.*
C) *Staphylococcus aureus.*
D) *Borrelia burgdorferi* (a type of spirochete).

235. Which of these organisms possess membrane-bound organelles?

A) Protozoa
B) Archaea
C) Bacteriophage(s)
D) Bacteria

236. A scientist observes a bacterial culture (below) after exposure to Gram's iodine and crystal violet solution, washing, and exposure to a light pink counterstain.

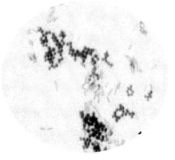

Which types of bacteria are depicted?

A) Gram-positive cocci and bacilli
B) Gram-negative cocci and bacilli
C) Gram-positive cocci and Gram-negative bacilli
D) Gram-positive bacilli and Gram-negative cocci

237. Which of these predictions accurately describes the relationship between the result of a Gram staining procedure and the qualities of a bacterial species' outer wall and membrane?

A) Cells with no outer membrane and a thick cell wall will stain positively in Gram's iodine.
B) Cells with an outer membrane and a thin cell wall will stain positively in Gram's iodine.
C) Cells with no outer membrane and a thin cell wall will stain negatively in Gram's iodine.
D) Cells with an outer membrane and a thick cell wall will stain negatively in Gram's iodine.

238. Some eukaryotic cells are covered with small ciliary projections used for absorption, while others contain larger flagella used for propulsion. These cellular structures are composed of:

A) intermediate filaments.
B) myosin.
C) microfilaments.
D) microtubules.

239. Flagella are used by prokaryotic cells for propulsion, allowing them to evade predation and find nutrients. Which eukaryotic cellular structures are composed of the same main cytoskeletal building blocks as the prokaryotic flagellum?

A) Kinetochores
B) Desmosomes
D) Microvilli
D) None of the above

240. Both eukaryotic and prokaryotic cells can utilize flagella for locomotion. Which of the following flagellar subunits acts as the motor and anchor for the structure in the plasma membrane?

A) The hook
B) The wheel
C) The basal body
D) The filament

241. Bacteria undergo binary fission, a process of self-division with no genetic exchange. Which of the following is NOT an advantage of this approach?

    A) It is rapid and results in exponential growth of the population.
    B) It increases genetic diversity.
    C) It does not involve a partner to share genetic material.
    D) It requires less cellular machinery to accomplish.

242. Which type of genetic exchange allows for the largest contribution to genetic diversity in a population of prokaryotes?

    A) Sexual transfer of genetic material
    B) Asexual reproduction
    C) Binary fission
    D) Conjugation

243. How can one account for the increased prokaryotic ability to adapt to changing environments and toxins, in contrast with their eukaryotic counterparts?

    A) Prokaryotes have a fast replication rate; therefore, advantageous mutations can be passed along more quickly than in eukaryotes.
    B) There is a vastly greater number of prokaryotic organisms in the ecosphere; therefore, they are better able to adapt.
    C) Prokaryotes are less likely to inherit deleterious mutations than eukaryotes.
    D) Prokaryotes have an earlier ancestral origin and can therefore adapt more quickly to the environment.

244. A strain of *Acetobactereae* has a doubling time of twelve minutes. A scientist observes a petri dish that is half covered with bacterial colonies. What is the minimum amount of time the scientist must allow for the dish to become entirely covered with these cells?

    A) 6 minutes
    B) 12 minutes
    C) 24 minutes
    D) 48 minutes

Questions 245–246 rely on the figure below

A dentist wishes to observe the oxygen consumption of several bacteria found in the oral cavity in order to develop a more comprehensive dental plan for his patients. The following represent the results of the study, where dots indicate bacterial growth in dense agar media.

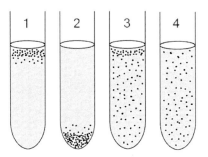

245. The bacteria in tube 3 could be described as a/an:

    A) obligate anaerobe.
    B) obligate aerobe.
    C) facultative anaerobe.
    D) aerotolerant anaerobe.

246. Two types of bacteria are common on tooth enamel: one that lives in areas open to the environment and another that uses the former bacteria as an air shield and lives between teeth under layers of secreted plaque for protection. In which test tube would you find each of these bacteria, respectively?

    A) 2, 4
    B) 1, 3
    C) 3, 1
    D) 4, 2

247. All of the following are true regarding a facultative anaerobe EXCEPT:

    I. it can live in the presence of oxygen.
    II. it cannot make ATP in the absence of oxygen
    III. it preferentially lives in the absence of oxygen.
    IV. it can switch between fermentation and aerobic respiration.

    A) I and II
    B) I and III
    C) II and IV
    D) III and IV

248. The table below indicates the growth of strains of *Streptomyces* and *Pseudomonas* on different media.

| | Exposed to light | | | | No light exposure | | | |
| | Minimal media | | Enriched media | | Minimal media | | Enriched media | |
	Sealed plate	Unsealed plate	Sealed plate	Unsealed plate	Sealed plate	Unsealed plate	Sealed plate	Unsealed plate
Streptomyces	- - -	- - -	+ + +	+ + +	- - -	- - -	+ + +	+ + +
Pseudomonas	- - -	+ + +	- - -	+ + +	- - -	+ + +	- - -	+ + +

Note: Minimal media includes no carbon source, while enriched media includes several organic carbon sources.

From this information, what must be the lifestyle of each respective prokaryote (*Streptomyces* and *Pseudomonas*)?

A) Photoheterotrophic, photoautotrophic
B) Photoautotrophic, photoautotrophic
C) Chemoheterotrophic, chemoautotrophic
D) Chemoautotrophic, chemoheterotrophic

249. A medical student is asked to plate a certain type of bacteria and leave the plates overnight to allow for growth. The student places the bacteria on enriched media (containing organic sugars), then moves them into an incubator at 37 °C overnight with a loose seal. Upon his return, the student notes no new growth on the bacterial plates. Which of the following could have resulted in this observation?

A) The bacteria are phototrophs and require sunlight.
B) The bacteria are heterotrophic and did not have an appropriate carbon source.
C) The bacteria are autotrophs and were not exposed to environmental CO_2 to obtain carbon.
D) The bacteria are still replicating and more time is needed to see visual growth.

250. Upon exposure to teratogens, *E. coli* moves to a location farther from these toxic compound. This is an example of:

A) positive chemotaxis.
B) neutral chemotaxis.
C) negative chemotaxis.
D) spontaneous mutation.

251. Which of the following is a difference between prokaryotic and eukaryotic transcription?

A) The site of transcription within the cell
B) The fact that transcription results in strands with uracil instead of thymine
C) The fact that initiation of transcription requires an RNA primer
D) The fact that AUG indicates a start codon

252. Translation can be inhibited by certain antibiotics that affect bacterial ribosomes. Why are these antibiotics not harmful to human cells?

A) These antibiotics target the 40S ribosomal subunit.
B) Eukaryotic ribosomes are protected by their own membranes.
C) These antibiotics target the 50S ribosomal subunit.
D) These antibiotics bind to tRNA when in the A site.

253. Consider the cell pictured below.

Which of the labeled structures is involved in post-translational processing in prokaryotes?

A) Structure A
B) Structure B
C) Structure C
D) None of the above

254. All of the following are true regarding plasmids EXCEPT:

A) that they are composed of single-stranded DNA.
B) that they can impart antibiotic resistance.
C) that they may contain a gene encoding for a sex pilus.
D) that they are small circular pieces of genetic material.

255. Which of the following is a characteristic of plasmid DNA that gives it research utility?

A) Plasmids can be incorporated into all types of cells through the process of transformation.
B) Plasmids have the ability to readily incorporate cloned DNA into certain organisms.
C) Plasmids are incapable of autonomous replication.
D) Plasmids are incapable of harming host genetic material upon insertion.

256. Which of the following correctly pairs the type of prokaryotic genetic exchange with its correct definition?

A) Transformation – a bacterium acquires genetic material from the external environment
B) Transformation – bacteriophage(s) transfer genetic material from one cell to another via infection
C) Transduction – one bacterium exchanges genetic material with another through the use of a pilus
D) Transduction – a bacterium acquires genetic material from the external environment

257. Transmission of the F factor, a plasmid that contains genes for a sex pilus, is facilitated by which process?

A) Transduction
B) Transposition
C) Conjugation
D) Transformation

258. A researcher wants to mix two distinct prokaryotic strains to observe conjugation between them. Which of these pairings could most likely result in the successful transfer of chromosomal genetic material?

A) A F$^+$ bacterium with another F$^+$ bacterium
B) A F$^+$ bacterium with a F$^-$ bacterium
C) A F$^+$ bacterium with an Hfr bacterium
D) An Hfr bacterium with a F$^-$ bacterium

259. Which of the following are true of Class I transposons?

I. They involve the action of reverse transcriptase, which transcribes RNA back to DNA.
II. They involve the normal transcription of DNA.
III. They act via a "copy-and-paste" mechanism.
IV. They act via a "cut-and-paste" mechanism.

A) I and III
B) II and IV
C) I, II, and III
D) I, II, and IV

260.

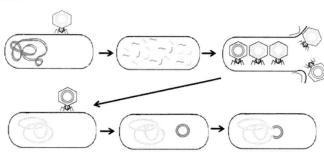

Which process does the above figure depict?

A) Transduction, which allows genetic material to be incorporated into the host genome using a bacteriophage in the lytic cycle

B) Transduction, which allows genetic material to be incorporated into the host genome using a bacteriophage in the lysogenic cycle

C) Transformation, which allows genetic material to be incorporated into the host genome using a bacteriophage in the lytic cycle

D) Transformation, which allows genetic material to be incorporated into the host genome using a bacteriophage in the lysogenic cycle

Questions 261–262 rely on the figure below

The structure shown below is a virus that infects humans in certain regions of Africa.

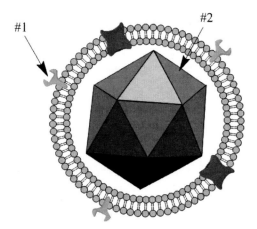

261. Structure #1:

A) will strongly bind to the variable domain of immunoglobulin.

B) is composed of hydrophilic and charged amino acids only.

C) is synthesized in the endoplasmic reticulum.

D) has an amino acid sequence that is encoded within the host cell genome.

262. A scientist uses a variety of techniques to assess the composition of structure #2. He will most likely find that it consists of:

A) primarily lipids.

B) many identical protein monomers.

C) a wide variety of structurally different protein monomers.

D) proteins encoded by host DNA.

263. All of the following statements are true of viruses EXCEPT:

A) they are composed of proteins and nucleic acids.

B) they often mutate at a high rate.

C) they contain a number of simple membranous organelles.

D) they are incapable of replicating without a host cell.

264. Human papillomavirus (HPV) is a non-enveloped DNA virus that has been implicated in the development of cervical cancer in humans. Vaccines containing a viral protein called L1 have proven effective in eliciting the formation of antibodies that block initial entry of HPV into the host cell. L1 is most likely a:

A) type of reverse transcriptase.

B) viral capsid protein.

C) tumor suppressor protein.

D) viral protease.

265. Lambda phage is a virus that infects *E. coli* cells. Which of these statements accurately characterizes this phage?

I.   It exclusively uses RNA as its genetic material.

II.   It is only capable of infecting prokaryotic organisms.

III. It synthesizes its own ribosomes to manufacture viral proteins.

IV.   It may be described as a parasitic species.

A) II only
B) I and II
C) II and IV
D) I, II, III, and IV

266. The following data maps the position of five essential genes within the HIV genome. The total length of this RNA genome is 9749 base pairs.

Gene	Position (bp)
gag	820-2435
pol	2201-5300
env	6230-8897
vif	5280-5700
nef	8890-9502

According to the information above, what must be true?

A) The viral RNA genome does not contain introns.
B) The virus utilizes multiple open reading frames to produce a variety of proteins.
C) The viral RNA does not contain a 5' cap or a poly(A) tail.
D) Only one copy of the genome is contained within a single viral particle.

267. Kaposi's sarcoma-associated herpesvirus (KSHV) leads to Kaposi's sarcoma, a type of cancer. The KSHV dsDNA genome contains a number of genes derived from host cell DNA, including a gene for a G protein-coupled receptor called cyclin-D. The KSHV virus:

A) injects viral DNA into the nucleus during KSHV infection.
B) uses G protein-coupled receptors to transduce signals across its cell membrane.
C) is a type of bacteriophage, making it vulnerable to antibiotics.
D) must also contain a gene for DNA polymerase within its genome.

268. A virologist obtains a purified sample of viral genetic material from a newly discovered virus. The virologist injects the genetic sample into the cytoplasm of healthy yeast cells in culture. Within hours, the cells die and free viral particles are detected in the growth medium. This new virus is most likely a:

A) (+) RNA virus.
B) (-) RNA virus.
C) dsDNA virus.
D) ssDNA virus.

269. Which of the following does NOT contribute to the relatively high mutation rate exhibited by most retroviruses?

A) RNA is chemically less stable than DNA.
B) Reverse transcriptase lacks the proofreading activity associated with DNA polymerase.
C) Unlike eukaryotic RNA, viral RNA does not contain uracil.
D) Different viral strains can exchange segments of their genomes, resulting in an antigenic shift.

270. Creutzfeldt-Jakob Disease (CJD) has been directly attributed to the consumption of misfolded, highly stable protein fragments called prions. However, alternative hypotheses have suggested a viral origin for this disease. Which of the following would most strongly support the prion hypothesis over the viral theory?

A) Patients with CJD do not improve after treatment with antibiotics.
B) In response to viral infection, human lymphocytes produce a prion-like protein with antiviral activity.
C) Crude brain lysates from CDJ mice cause classic CDJ pathology when fed to healthy mice.
D) Crude brain lysates subjected to toxic levels of ionizing radiation still reliably induce pathology when fed to healthy mice.

271. Down syndrome is a genetic condition that appears in about 0.1% of infants born each year. Also known as trisomy 21, it is caused by a genetic error in early development. What phenomenon and resulting genotype may be responsible for Down syndrome?

A) Chromosomal crossover results in an embryo with two copies of chromosome 21.
B) Chromosomal crossover results in an embryo with three copies of chromosome 21.
C) Nondisjunction results in an embryo with three copies of chromosome 21.
D) Nondisjunction results in an embryo with one copy of chromosome 21.

272. In order, the phases of mitosis are:

    A) metaphase, prometaphase, prophase, telophase, anaphase.
    B) prophase, prometaphase, metaphase, anaphase, telophase.
    C) prophase, prometaphase, metaphase, telophase, anaphase.
    D) metaphase, prometaphase, prophase, anaphase, telophase.

273. Paclitaxel is a drug often used during chemotherapy to treat various cancers. This compound binds to the beta-tubulin subunits of microtubules, stabilizing the tubulin polymer and preventing its disassembly. Which phase of mitosis does this most directly affect?

    A) Prophase; disrupting tubulin structures would inhibit the condensation of chromosomes.
    B) Prometaphase; stabilizing tubulin structures would prevent the nucleus from dissolving.
    C) Metaphase; stabilizing tubulin structures would prevent chromosomes from achieving the required configuration on the spindle apparatus.
    D) Telophase; stabilizing the tubulin polymer would prevent the nucleus from re-forming.

274. Chromosome instability is a phenomenon in which parts or even entire chromosomes are deleted or duplicated. This can result in an abnormal number of chromosomes in daughter cells, a condition known as aneuploidy. All of the following may cause chromosome instability EXCEPT:

    A) nondisjunction.
    B) merotelic attachment.
    C) multipolar spindles.
    D) homologous recombination.

275. A karyogram depicts the appearance of chromosomes in the nucleus of a eukaryotic cell. To prepare a karyogram, cells are arrested during mitosis, and the chromosomes are stained, imaged, and rearranged to give a chromosomal count for the organism. Shown here is a karyogram of a human male.

During which phase of mitosis were the cells arrested, and what is his chromosome count?

    A) The cells were arrested during prophase, and his chromosome count is 23.
    B) The cells were arrested during prophase, and his chromosome count is 46.
    C) The cells were arrested during metaphase, and his chromosome count is 44.
    D) The cells were arrested during metaphase, and his chromosome count is 46.

276. Mitosis and meiosis are two types of eukaryotic cell division. Although their mechanisms are similar, they have many differences as well. Which of the following characteristics are shared by both mitosis and meiosis I?

    I.   They are types of sexual reproduction.
    II. The daughter cells produced are genetically identical.
    III. The daughter cells produced are diploid.
    IV. They should be preceded by high-fidelity DNA replication.

        A) I only
        B) IV only
        C) II and III
        D) II, III, and IV

277. A geneticist stains a cell's chromosomes and views it under a microscope. He observes a line of chromosomes near the midline of the cell. The chromosomes are organized so that two sets of sister chromatids are side by side, forming a group of four chromatids. He also notices that this group contains two distinct centromeres. What

phase of the cell division is this cell currently in, and what is the scientist viewing?

A) Prophase I; the scientist is seeing the chromosomes condensing.

B) Metaphase I; the scientist is seeing the tetrad aligning at the metaphase plate.

C) Metaphase II; the scientist is seeing the chiasmata breaking at the metaphase plate.

D) Anaphase II; the scientist is seeing chromosomes dividing at the centromere.

278. Which of the following events does NOT occur prior to or during the transition from metaphase to anaphase of mitosis?

A) Every chromosome is bioriented.

B) Cohesin is severed.

C) Microtubules depolymerize.

D) The centromere decondenses.

Questions 279–280 rely on the figure below

Recently, it was discovered that a Chinese man had only 44 chromosomes. Part of his karyogram is depicted below. It can be assumed that in this case, chromosomes 1 – 12 are normal.

279. Although the man has fewer than the typical 46 chromosomes, he is asymptomatic and appears healthy, implying that he is missing very few important genes. What is the cause of his reduced number of chromosomes?

A) A Robertsonian translocation, resulting in a derivative chromosome containing genes from both chromosomes 14 and 15

B) A deletion, resulting in the loss of the quiescent chromosome 15

C) A translocation, resulting in the switching of chromosome 14's long q arm and short p arm

D) A nondisjunction event in early development, resulting in the loss of chromosome 15

280. This man's wife has a wild-type genotype, but the couple is struggling with infertility. What may be an underlying cause?

A) It cannot be determined without a karyogram of the wife.

B) The man's gametes do not contain any sex chromosomes.

C) The resulting zygote is aneuploid and unstable.

D) The man cannot produce gametes due to disruptions in meiosis.

281. Which of the following statements regarding interphase are correct?

I. DNA replication occurs during this time.

II. The cell increases in size by way of continued protein synthesis.

III. It encompasses more time in the cell cycle than other phases.

IV. The duration of each of its component phases is equal.

A) I and II

B) III and IV

C) I, II, and III

D) I, III, and IV

282. At which checkpoint does a cell commit to the cell cycle?

A) G_1-S

B) G_2-M

C) G_0

D) A cell never fully commits to the cell cycle.

283. Unrestricted cell division is a hallmark of cancer cells. What is a reasonable explanation for this characteristic?

A) Cancer cells can facilitate angiogenesis.

B) Cancer cells rely on anaerobic respiration for ATP.

C) Cancer cells can metastasize.

D) Cancer cells lack cell cycle checkpoints.

284. All of the following conditions are reasons for a cell to enter the G_0 phase EXCEPT:

A) a lack of growth factors.

B) a decreased presence of cyclin-dependent kinases.

C) a state of terminal differentiation.

D) the detection of incorrectly-replicated DNA.

285. The G_0 phase is generally conceptualized as a permanent quiescent state. However, some G_0 cells can return to the G_1 phase in the presence of certain growth factors. Which of these pairs includes two cell types that, once in it, never leave the G_0 phase?

    A) Liver cells and neurons
    B) Neurons and erythrocytes
    C) Muscle cells and epithelial cells
    D) Parenchymal and muscle cells

Questions 286–287 rely on the figure below

The following diagram shows a general schematic for the cell cycle.

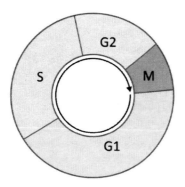

286. If a cell detects serious issues within replicated DNA, in which phase will it remain in to attempt to remedy it?

    A) G_1
    B) S
    C) G_2
    D) M

287. Generally, cells tend to spend around 90% of their time in interphase. What would be the most likely result if a mutation removed the G_1 checkpoint?

    A) The cell would not produce viable daughter cells.
    B) The resulting daughter cells would be smaller than those produced from the division of non-mutated cells.
    C) The daughter cells would possess numerous DNA errors.
    D) The cell would be unable to divide.

Questions 288–289 rely on the table below

The information below lists a number of regulators of the cell cycle, as well as their functions or notable characteristics.

Regulator	Function
Cyclin	Activates cyclin-dependent kinase enzymes (Cdk)
Cdk1/2	Active in G_1 phase, prepares cell for the S phase
Cyclin A	Present in G_1, S, and early G_2 phase
Cyclin B	Present in late G_2 phase
Cip/kip family	Arrests cell cycle in G_1

288. Which of the following statements is true?

    A) Cyclin and Cdk function together to halt the cell cycle.
    B) Cdk requires cyclin in order to exist in an active state.
    C) As inhibitors of the cell cycle, Cip and Kip can promote tumor growth.
    D) Removing Cdk 1 will prevent the cell from entering the S phase.

289. The level of cyclin and Cdks rise and fall during the cell cycle. What would be the consequence to a cell that, due to a missense mutation, displays perpetually high levels of both cyclin and Cdks?

    A) The cell cycle would cease entirely.
    B) The cell would be unable to divide.
    C) The cell would be arrested in the G_0 phase.
    D) The cell would rapidly move through the phases of the cell cycle.

290. At which point during the cell cycle is the cell the largest in size?

    A) The end of the G_1 phase
    B) The end of the G_2 phase
    C) The end of the S phase
    D) The end of the M phase

291. Human fingers are originally webbed when they first develop. How does the body create individual fingers from this webbed structure?

A) The fingers develop from totipotent stem cells that differentiate out of the webbing.

B) The fetus stretches its fingers, causing tears within the web that get repaired during development.

C) The cells of the web undergo apoptosis, resulting in the separation of fingers observed at birth.

D) The fetus develops an autoimmune response to its own epithelial cells.

292. Which of the following are labeled correctly?

I. Autocrine – cell communication whereby the signal acts on the same cell that secreted it

II. Paracrine – cell communication whereby the signal directly stimulates receptors of an adjacent cell

III. Juxtacrine – cell communication whereby the signal acts on cells in the local area

IV. Endocrine – cell communication whereby the signals involve secreted hormones that travel through the bloodstream

A) IV only
B) I and IV
C) II, III, and IV
D) I, II, III, and IV

293. In the context of cell specialization, what is the difference between determination and differentiation?

A) Determination refers to programmed cell death, while differentiation refers to the ability of an organism to regrow parts of its body.

B) Differentiation refers to programmed cell death, while determination refers to the ability of an organism to regrow parts of its body.

C) Differentiation refers to the cellular commitment to developing into a specific cell type, while determination refers to the changes that occur in the cell due to selective transcription of its appropriate cell lineage.

D) Determination refers to the cellular commitment to developing into a specific cell type, while differentiation refers to the changes that occur in the cell due to selective transcription of its appropriate cell lineage.

Questions 294–295 rely on the figure below

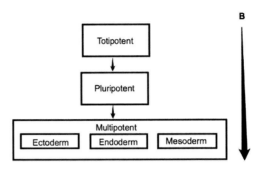

294. What qualities increase along the direction of the arrow marked "B"?

A) Lineage potential, expression of pluripotent genes

B) DNA methylation, expression of lineage-specific genes

C) "Open" chromatin, DNA methylation

D) Expression of pluripotent genes, "open" chromatin

295. Which cell types are derived from the ectoderm?

A) Epidermis, nervous system, eye lens, hair

B) Muscle, cardiac and skeletal systems, blood, heart, spleen

C) Linings of internal organs (stomach, lungs, intestines, etc.)

D) Epidermis, linings of internal organs, blood, spleen

296. What is meant by the term "senescence"?

A) It refers to a stem cell's ability to differentiate into many different types of cell.

B) It refers to an organism's ability to regrow body parts if they become damaged.

C) It refers to programmed cell death.

D) It refers to the biological process of aging and the degeneration that it includes.

Questions 297–298 rely on the figure below

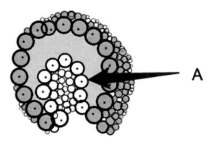

297. What embryonic structure is depicted above?

   A) The blastula
   B) The gastrula
   C) The zygote
   D) An egg cell

298. What type of cells differentiate from the layer of cells that is indicated by the arrow marked "A"?

   A) Epidermis, nervous system, eye lens, hair
   B) Muscle, cardiac and skeletal systems, blood, heart, spleen
   C) Linings of internal organs (stomach, lungs, intestines, etc.)
   D) Nothing develops from these cells, as they ultimately undergo apoptosis.

299. The human liver has high regenerative capacity. What does this mean?

   A) It has little, if any, ability to regrow itself, making whole-liver donation necessary during transplant.
   B) It can completely regrow itself; thus, if a liver is removed from the human body, a new one will systematically grow within a certain period of time.
   C) It can undergo extensive, but not complete, regrowth; thus, people can donate up to 50% of their livers and will eventually experience regeneration of the missing portion.
   D) The liver can be used to regenerate other organs because it contains a plethora of stem cells.

300. New research indicates that telomeres might play an integral part in the aging process. How may these structures contribute to aging?

   A) At a certain point during middle age, telomeres completely disappear, thus decreasing the ability of cells to undergo mitosis.
   B) Telomeres represent the portion of the chromosome to which the spindle fibers connect during mitosis. As they degenerate, the cell cannot appropriately separate the chromosomes, leading to higher prevalence of nondisjunction.
   C) During the process of aging, telomeres lengthen with each successive cell division, which makes mitosis more and more energetically costly to the cells of the body.
   D) Telomeres shorten with each round of DNA synthesis; as they degenerate, they may eventually become too short, and the cell cannot divide without losing useful DNA.

301. Which of the following correctly describes a feature of a particular meiotic stage?

   I. Metaphase I involves the lining up of homologous chromosomes along the center of the cell.
   II. Anaphase II involves the separation of sister chromatids from each other.
   III. Interphase II occurs after the first meiotic division, when the genetic material replicates a second time.
   IV. Prophase I involves the condensing of chromosomes.

   A) I only
   B) I and III
   C) I, II, and IV
   D) I, III, and IV

302. How does meiosis differ from mitosis?

  A) Meiosis involves two rounds of division that result in four diploid cells, while mitosis involves one round of division that results in two haploid cells.

  B) Meiosis involves two rounds of division that result in four haploid cells, while mitosis involves one round of division that results in two diploid cells.

  C) Meiosis involves one round of division that results in four diploid cells, while mitosis involves two rounds of division that result in two haploid cells.

  D) Meiosis involves one round of division that results in four haploid cells, while mitosis involves two rounds of division that result in two diploid cells.

303. Which of the following is a characteristic of both spermatogenesis and oogenesis?

  A) Both spermatogenesis and oogenesis result in four germ cells.

  B) Spermatogenesis produces four germ cells, while oogenesis produces one germ and three somatic cells.

  C) Spermatogenesis produces four germ cells, while oogenesis produces one germ cell and three dark polar bodies.

  D) Oogenesis produces four germ cells, while spermatogenesis produces one germ cell and three dark polar bodies.

304. A human cell has only 13 chromosomes. What type of cell is it?

  A) A muscle cell
  B) A germ cell
  C) A diploid cell
  D) A somatic cell

305. What is the most likely evolutionary advantage of the uneven cytoplasmic division that is seen during oogenesis?

  A) Only one egg is produced at a time, avoiding multiple births in animals that are not equipped to have a large number of offspring at one time.

  B) It slows the rate of reproduction, preventing overpopulation.

  C) It lessens the chance that genetic mutations will be passed on to the offspring.

  D) Oogenesis does not involve uneven division of the cytoplasm.

Questions 306–307 rely on the figure below

Below is a table that documents hormone levels throughout a typical menstrual cycle. Levels are reported as a percentage of the highest concentration observed for each hormone.

Day	LH	FSH	Estrogen	Progesterone
1	5	30	5	5
7	5	100	40	7
14	100	60	100	10
21	45	25	75	75
28	5	25	50	10

306. Which of the four hormones peaks latest in the cycle?

  A) LH
  B) FSH
  C) Estrogen
  D) Progesterone

307. How would the results change if fertilization and implantation had occurred?

  A) Estrogen levels would have remained high.
  B) Progesterone levels would have remained high.
  C) FSH levels would have remained high.
  D) Both A and B are correct.

Questions 308–309 rely on the table below

The total amount of DNA is measured in various cells, all of which are participating in distinct stages of oogenesis. Amounts are reported as a percentage of values measured for a somatic cell in the G_1 phase.

Cell	% of DNA
1	200
2	99
3	49
4	159
5	47

308. Which of the following statements is true?

    A) Cell 2 must be a primary oocyte.
    B) Cell 1 has yet to undergo any meiotic divisions.
    C) Cell 4 is a dark polar body.
    D) Cell 5 must be an ovum.

309. If the researchers had tested an ovum immediately following fertilization, what percentage of DNA would the cell be expected to have?

    A) 50%
    B) 75%
    C) 100%
    D) 200%

310. After numerous unsuccessful attempts to breed a male rabbit, a researcher decides to examine its sperm under a microscope. He finds that the sperm cells have normal tails and healthy motility. What is the most likely issue?

    A) The digestive enzymes in the acrosomes have been modified and are no longer functional.
    B) The sperm are no longer able to release toxins that kill the other sperm and allow for fertilization.
    C) The sperm do not have enough mitochondria to remain warm outside of the body.
    D) The sperm don't have enough energy stored in their fat cells to remain properly mobile.

311. The single diploid cell formed when an ovum is fertilized by a spermatozoon is known as a(n):

    A) embryo.
    B) zygote.
    C) morula.
    D) gastrula.

312. Order the stages of development from fertilization to organogenesis.

    A) Blastula, zygote, morula, gastrula
    B) Zygote, blastula, morula, gastrula
    C) Morula, blastula, gastrula, zygote
    D) Zygote, morula, blastula, gastrula

313. Spina bifida, or cleft spine, is a birth defect caused by incomplete neurulation and resulting in nerve damage. This condition is the product of the improper development of the:

    A) ectodermal germ layer.
    B) endodermal germ layer.
    C) mesodermal germ layer.
    D) diploblasmal germ layer.

314. A scientist uses a radioactive label to mark the cells on the outside of a gastrula. The labeled cells are shown below as those drawn with bolded black lines.

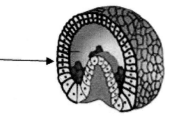

Following another 8 weeks of development and organogenesis, which of the following tissues would be labeled?

    A) Red blood cells, cardiac muscle, and gonads
    B) Lungs, thyroid, glands, mouth, and rectum
    C) Brain, skin, spine, hair, and nails
    D) Skin, brain, sweat glands, eyes, and red blood cells

315. All cells in a developing organism are initially identical. However, during embryogenesis, they are able to differentiate into various cell types and localize using positional information. This phenomenon, known as pattern formation, requires all of the following EXCEPT:

A) cell signaling pathways.
B) maternal growth factors.
C) a morphogen gradient.
D) cell-to-cell communication.

316. During human embryogenesis, limbs utilize pattern formation to develop from limb buds. A scientist has discovered that he can specify which limb (arm or leg) that a bud differentiates into by:

A) expressing different limb-specific transcription factors.
B) changing the anterior-posterior patterning.
C) changing the dorsal-ventral patterning.
D) dissecting and reattaching limb buds.

317. A developing zygote is exposed to a drug that inhibits cell differentiation. Which developmental process is this drug most likely to impede?

A) Intercalation
B) Pattern formation
C) Cell movement
D) Organogenesis

318. In vertebrates, neurulation results in the formation of the neural tube. Which of the following structures are then derived from this tube?

I. Spinal cord
II. Brain
III. Neural crest cells
IV. Vertebral column

A) I only
B) I and II
C) III and IV
D) I, II, and III

319. It is believed that a variety of factors, both genetic and environmental, interact to cause structural birth defects. These defects, such as spina bifida, oral clefts, and congenital heart defects, result from the complex influences that disrupt embryonic development. Which maternal factor(s) would increase the risk of developmental abnormalities in the embryo?

A) Exposure to teratogens
B) Genotype
C) Heart disease
D) All of the above

320. The figure below shows a developing chordate.

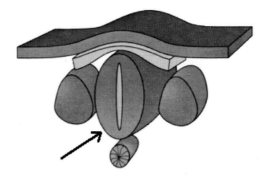

The name and function of the round structure indicated by the arrow is:

A) the neural tube; it develops into the central nervous system.
B) the neural tube; it develops into the peripheral nervous system.
C) the notochord; it develops into the central nervous system.
D) the notochord; it develops into the vertebral column.

321. Epithelial cells connect to underlying layers of connective tissue through cell adhesion proteins such as:

A) interleukins.
B) cadherins.
C) integrins.
D) connexins.

322. Tight junctions between cells are NOT likely to be found in which of the following areas?

A) The cerebral vascular epithelia
B) The mucosa of the small intestine
C) The glomerular capsules of the kidney
D) The capillaries of the lungs

323. The pancreas can be described as:

I. endocrine.
II. exocrine.
III. epithelial.

A) I only
B) I and III
C) II and III
D) I, II, and III

324. Scurvy, a form of malnutrition caused by an absence of vitamin C, is infamous as an ailment of sailors and other people who lack access to fresh food for long periods. Scurvy is characterized by a weakening of connective tissues in the gums and other mucous membranes, which will frequently display bleeding under slight stress. Vitamin C must therefore be key to the synthesis of which component of most connective tissues?

    A) Proteoglycans
    B) Collagen
    C) Keratin
    D) Connexins

325. In atherosclerosis, lipid deposits in the lining of arteries accumulate, inducing macrophages to attempt to absorb and "clean up" the deposits. If these cells are incapable of handling the volume, they die, inducing further immune cells to migrate to the deposit. Eventually, this cycle results in the formation of a plaque under the surface of the lining, which blocks the flow and reduces the flexibility of the artery. Under high mechanical stress, the plaque can rupture, creating a dangerous free-floating clot called a thrombus. A preventative treatment for the formation of thrombi would aim to strengthen which component of an artery?

    A) The lumen
    B) The endothelium
    C) The vascular smooth muscle
    D) The adventitia

326. A congenital dysfunction in the behavior of chondrocytes would LEAST likely make a patient prone to:

    A) knee pain.
    B) herniated discs.
    C) torn calf muscles.
    D) ankle sprains.

327. Ciliopathy refers to a group of conditions in which cilia fail to form or function properly. Ciliopathy of motile cilia is a possible cause of dysfunction in which of the following organ systems?

    A) Digestive
    B) Reproductive
    C) Lymphatic
    D) Auditory

328. The diagram below depicts a layer of epithelial cells with associated connective tissue and capillary.

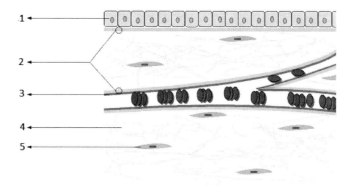

The basal lamina is a component of which of the labeled layers?

    A) 1
    B) 2
    C) 3
    D) 4

329. A physiology student views an unknown tissue sample (below) through a microscope.

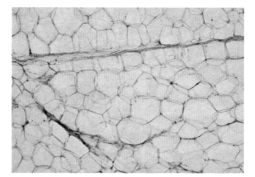

The most likely origin of this sample is:

    A) the cerebral cortex.
    B) the mucosa of the small intestine.
    C) the myocardial layer of the heart.
    D) a deposit of adipose tissue.

330. The cells comprising a cancerous tumor frequently suffer progressive genetic damage, caused by uncontrolled proliferation due to deactivation of genes that suppress errors in DNA replication. This genetic damage can cause the cancerous cells to engage in normal activity, such as the synthesis and secretion of various biomolecules, but in an uncontrolled fashion. A biopsy of a tumor reveals pockets of a fluid with heavy concentrations of proteoglycans

and glycoproteins. From which area do these cancerous cells most likely originate?

A) The cerebral cortex
B) The mucosa of the small intestine
C) A deposit of adipose tissue
D) The myocardial layer of the heart

331. A patient suffers from persistent indigestion and tachycardia, and various diagnostic tests reveal that his condition is neurological in origin. His symptoms are likely caused by diminished activation of:

A) the sympathetic nervous system.
B) the parasympathetic nervous system.
C) the limbic system.
D) the somatic nervous system.

332. Due to a rare genetic mutation, an individual's neurons synthesize very limited amounts of the neurotransmitter norepinephrine. This will likely lead to diminished efficacy of:

A) the sympathetic nervous system.
B) the enteric nervous system.
C) the parasympathetic nervous system.
D) the somatic nervous system.

333. A soldier suffers an injury to his spinal cord from a piece of shrapnel. Specifically, a shard of metal enters his spine from the rear between two thoracic vertebrae and severs many of the rearmost nerves, though it stops before severing any nerves in the front or middle of the cord. What symptoms will this injury likely cause for him?

A) The soldier will likely be paralyzed in parts of the body below the injury.
B) The soldier will likely lose feeling in parts of the body below the injury.
C) The soldier will likely lose both feeling and mobility in parts of the body below the injury.
D) The soldier will suffer paralysis of the digestive tract.

334. In Guillain-Barré syndrome, a viral infection triggers an autoimmune response, causing the immune system to demyelinate some of the body's own neurons. Symptoms include muscle weakness in the limbs along with tingling and numbness in the skin. Guillain-Barré syndrome triggers the death of which type of cell?

A) Microglial cells
B) Astrocytes
C) Oligodendrocytes
D) Schwann cells

335. Which of the following is true of reflex arcs?

A) Reflex arcs must contain an interneuron component.
B) Motor reflex arcs must be located at least partially within the brain's motor areas.
C) Reflex arcs can affect hormone balance.
D) Reflex arcs are always triggered by somatic sensory input from a skeletal muscle.

336. The following image depicts an important set of structures in the peripheral nervous system.

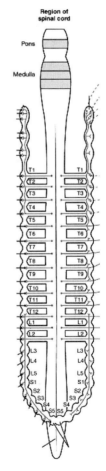

These structures can best be identified as:

A) dorsal root ganglia.
B) parasympathetic ganglia.
C) enteric ganglia.
D) sympathetic ganglia.

337. Locked-in syndrome is a condition in which the sufferer is otherwise healthy and aware of his surroundings, but cannot move or communicate due to paralysis of voluntary muscles. This results from a blockage of:

A) afferent autonomic pathways.
B) afferent somatic pathways.
C) efferent autonomic pathways.
D) efferent somatic pathways.

338. Several distinct neuron types are pictured in the figure below.

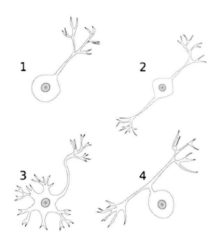

"Type 4" neurons are most likely to be found in:

A) the frontal lobe.
B) the dorsal root ganglia.
C) the cerebellum.
D) the retina.

339. An elderly male patient arrives at a clinic complaining of erectile dysfunction. Due to a family history of heart disease, he is hesitant to start taking Viagra. An alternate treatment regimen might prescribe supplements to increase the levels of which neurotransmitter?

A) Dopamine
B) Norepinephrine
C) Acetylcholine
D) Serotonin

340. The sympathetic nervous system promotes vasoconstriction in which of the following areas?

I. Large intestine
II. Skeletal muscles
III. Stomach
IV. Lungs

A) I and II
B) I and III
C) II and IV
D) I, III, and IV

Questions 341–342 rely on the figure below

A typical multipolar neuron is shown below.

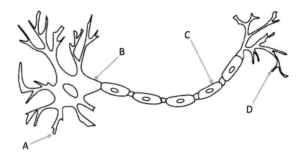

341. Suppose that this neuron receives a series of graded potentials that are sufficient in magnitude and timing to trigger an action potential. From which of the labeled points would this action potential originate?

A) Point A
B) Point B
C) Point C
D) Point D

342. With regard to structure and location, the neuron shown can be described as:

A) a myelinated cell located in the central nervous system.
B) an unmyelinated cell located in the peripheral nervous system.
C) a myelinated cell located in the peripheral nervous system.
D) an unmyelinated cell located in the central nervous system.

343. Which of the following hypothetical axons would likely propagate action potentials at the highest conducting velocity?

A) An unmyelinated axon with a diameter of 1.0 micron

B) A myelinated axon with a diameter of 1.0 micron

C) An unmyelinated axon with a diameter of 4.0 microns

D) A myelinated axon with a diameter of 4.0 microns

Questions 344–345 rely on the figure below

The following image shows the release of neurotransmitters between a glutamatergic presynaptic neuron and its target.

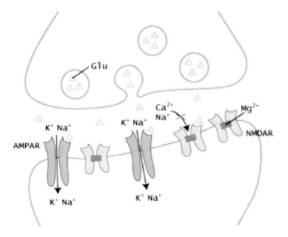

344. Assume the cells currently exist at the instant depicted in the figure. The postsynaptic neuron must subsequently:

A) use glutamate to excite a downstream neuron.

B) fire an action potential.

C) experience measurable membrane depolarization.

D) metabolize synaptic glutamate.

345. The molecule labeled "AMPAR" would best be classified as a:

A) voltage-gated ion channel.

B) "leaky" channel.

C) ligand-gated ion channel.

D) highly specific cation channel.

346. Synaptotagmin is a presynaptic protein that has been found to be essential in the fusion of intracellular neurotransmitter-laden vesicles with the presynaptic membrane. Synaptotagmin directly responds to the specific changes in local cytoplasmic conditions that occur when an action potential reaches the axon terminal, triggering the rapid and reliable fusion of docked vesicles with the plasma membrane. Structurally, synaptotagmin is most likely analogous to:

A) adenylate cyclase.

B) acetylcholinesterase.

C) calmodulin.

D) NMDAR.

347. Neuroplasticity has been a topic of considerable interest for several decades. Consistent stimulation at a particular synapse has been shown to induce a number of structural and metabolic changes in both pre- and postsynaptic neurons. These changes result in the "strengthening" of the synapse, making propagation of an action potential more efficient and sensitizing the synapse to further input. Considering that AMPA is a glutamate receptor, which of these actions would most likely contribute to the strengthening of a glutamatergic synapse?

I. CaMKII-mediated phosphorylation of AMPAR, which improves channel conduction

II. Calcium-mediated activation of intracellular scaffolding proteins with multiple AMPAR binding domains

III. Endocytosis of perisynaptic AMPA receptors without subsequent proteolysis

A) I only

B) III only

C) I and II

D) I, II, and III

348. Acetylcholinesterase, a membrane-bound, postsynaptic enzyme, is considered "catalytically perfect." This term is used because the rate-limiting step in the hydrolysis reaction catalyzed by this enzyme is actually the diffusion of acetylcholine into its extracellular active site. Acetylcholinesterase inhibitors, such as physostigmine, permit enhanced neuronal excitation in cholinergic circuits and are clinically effective in the management of symptoms associated with Alzheimer's disease. The presence of physostigmine in the synaptic cleft would most directly lead to:

A) an increased synaptic concentration of acetylcholine.

B) a decreased synaptic concentration of acetylcholine.

C) an increased cytoplasmic concentration of acetylcholine in the postsynaptic neuron.

D) a decreased cytoplasmic concentration of acetylcholine in the postsynaptic neuron.

349. Which of the following molecules is LEAST likely to be classified as a neurotransmitter?

A) Histamine, a small monoamine derived from the amino acid histidine

B) Carbon monoxide, a diatomic gas similar in structure to nitric oxide

C) Substance P, a soluble undecapeptide

D) Neuroglobin, a globular protein found in high concentrations in mammalian brain tissue

350. Succinylcholine, a charged, organic ester that is structurally analogous to acetylcholine, binds competitively to the nicotinic acetylcholine receptor without antagonistic activity. It is used in a hospital setting as a paralytic agent to facilitate procedures such as endotracheal intubation. When administered intravenously, succinylcholine most likely:

A) does not cause measurable postsynaptic depolarization and is degraded by acetylcholinesterase.

B) causes measurable postsynaptic depolarization and is degraded by acetylcholinesterase.

C) does not cause measurable postsynaptic depolarization and is not degraded by acetylcholinesterase.

D) causes measurable postsynaptic depolarization and is not degraded by acetylcholinesterase.

351. Which diagram accurately depicts the location and direction of ion movement during an action potential?

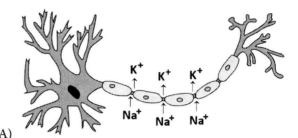

A)

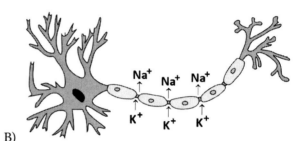

B)

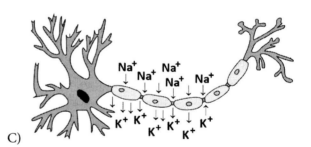

C)

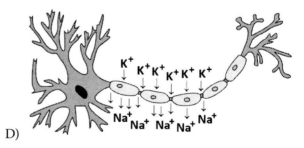

D)

Questions 352–353 rely on the figure below

The following diagram depicts changes in voltage during a typical action potential.

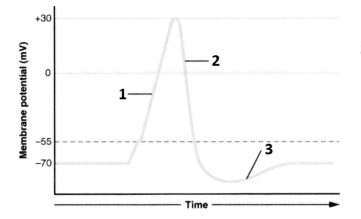

352. Between the points marked 2 and 3, the neuron:

    A) depolarizes, then hyperpolarizes.
    B) depolarizes, then repolarizes.
    C) repolarizes, then hyperpolarizes.
    D) hyperpolarizes, then repolarizes.

353. Prior to the point labeled 1, when the membrane potential is approximately -40 mV, what is the status of the majority of this neuron's voltage-gated sodium and potassium channels?

    A) Its sodium channels are closed, while its potassium channels are open.
    B) Its sodium channels are open, while its potassium channels are closed.
    C) Its sodium channels are open, while its potassium channels are inactivated.
    D) Both its sodium and potassium channels are closed.

354. Neurons in the human central nervous system generally possess many more leak channels for potassium than for sodium. In a hypothetical cell, the number of Na^+ leak channels is doubled while the number of K^+ leak channels is halved. The membrane potential of this neuron will:

    A) become more negative.
    B) become more positive.
    C) remain unchanged, because the opposing effects will cancel.
    D) remain unchanged, but it will be more difficult to reach the threshold level.

355. A hippocampal neuron with which of the following membrane potentials would most likely be considered to be hyperpolarized?

    A) +40 mV
    B) 0 mV
    C) -70 mV
    D) -85 mV

356. A neurobiology student notices that neurons of the basal ganglia hyperpolarize by approximately 3 mV when ambient temperature is reduced. He hypothesizes that this is due to the opening of additional voltage-gated, temperature-dependent potassium leak channels. Is the student's hypothesis sensible, and if not, why?

    A) Yes; this explanation makes sense.
    B) No; the opening of additional potassium channels would cause a depolarization, not a hyperpolarization.
    C) No; the opening of additional potassium channels would cause the neuron to become more negative, not more positive.
    D) No; leak channels cannot be voltage-gated.

357. Tetrodotoxin (TTX), a toxin found in pufferfish and other marine species, binds to and inhibits transmission through Na^+ voltage-gated channels in neurons. Neurons of an individual who has recently consumed raw pufferfish will:

    A) be more likely to fire, since sodium transmission out of a cell will hyperpolarize it.
    B) be more likely to fire, since sodium is integral for the initial depolarization phase of the action potential.
    C) be less likely to fire, since sodium transmission out of a cell will hyperpolarize it.
    D) be less likely to fire, since sodium is integral for the initial depolarization phase of the action potential.

358. What is the difference between an absolute and a relative refractory period, with regard to neurons?

A) During an absolute refractory period, the neuron cannot possibly fire again, but during a relative period, an especially strong stimulus is required to prompt firing. A neuron that experiences absolute periods will never experience relative ones.

B) During an absolute refractory period, the neuron cannot possibly fire again, but during a relative period, an especially strong stimulus is required to prompt firing. These two periods occur in the same neurons during different parts of the action potential.

C) During an absolute refractory period, no neurons are able to fire; during a relative refractory period, only some neurons are blocked from firing.

D) An absolute refractory period is one that exceeds a certain duration, while relative refractory periods are very short.

359. During observation of a particular chemical synapse, a student notices that a neurotransmitter is released, and that the membrane potential of the post-synaptic neuron quickly drops from -70 to -75 mV. This synaptic potential is:

A) an inhibitory potential, possibly provoked by the neurotransmitter GABA.

B) an inhibitory potential, possibly provoked by the neurotransmitter glutamate.

C) an excitatory potential, possibly provoked by the neurotransmitter GABA.

D) an excitatory potential, possibly provoked by the neurotransmitter glutamate.

360. A neurologist isolates a sensory neuron from the left foot and places it in an *in vitro* environment similar to that found within the body. He then exposes the neuron to various stimuli. In one case (Trial 1), he pokes it with a small probe and observes an immediate depolarization to -40 mV. In a separate trial (Trial 2), he uses mild electric stimulation to provoke a change to -54 mV over the same short interval. If this neuron has a threshold of -55 mV, during which trial will this neuron fire a stronger action potential?

A) During Trial 1, as it experienced a more drastic depolarization

B) During Trial 1, as Trial 2 does not even provide enough stimulation to reach the threshold value

C) During Trial 2, as the neuron then has a more negative membrane potential

D) The neuron will fire equally in both trials, as the nervous system operates under the "all-or-none" principle.

361. All of the following are true about endocrine glands EXCEPT:

A) they may secrete hormones that affect remote target cells.

B) their main function is to maintain homeostasis within the body.

C) they mainly serve to secrete enzymes that affect nearby target cells.

D) they may also serve an exocrine function.

362. Pilocaratine, a newly synthesized radioactive substance, can be metabolized in a similar manner to iodine. Pilocaratine (shown below) is given to mice both orally and intravenously.

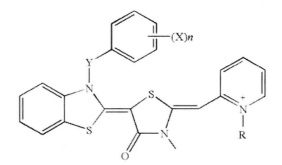

Over time, this substance would most likely accumulate in the:

A) thyroid gland.

B) stomach.

C) liver.

D) small intestine.

363. Which of these hormones is released by the adrenal cortex?

A) Growth hormone (GH)

B) Epinephrine

C) Glucagon

D) Cortisol

364. A student undergoes a blood test and finds that he is experiencing a dramatically increased secretion of corticosteroids. Which of the following events may have played a role in causing this condition?

A) Decreased release of CRH
B) Increased plasma cortisone levels
C) Decreased release of ACTH
D) Increased release of CRH

365. Hormones produced by the anterior pituitary include:

I. LH.
II. GHRH.
III. TSH.
IV. oxytocin.

    A) I and II
    B) I and III
    C) II and III
    D) II, III, and IV

366. Of the pairs below, which accurately matches the hormone with its organ of production?

A) FSH – hypothalamus
B) ADH – posterior pituitary
C) Melatonin – pineal gland
D) Insulin – thyroid gland

367. The table below contains lab results for a patient complaining of excess sweating, hunger, fatigue, racing heartbeat and high blood pressure. A hormone-secreting tumor is suspected.

	Normal range	Patient values
CRH	>0.01 (µg/dL)	>0.01 (µg/dL)
ACTH	9-52 (pg/mL)	2 (pg/mL)
Cortisone	2-28 (µg/dL)	250 (µg/dL)
Total T$_3$	75-200 (ng/dL)	127 (ng/dL)
Total T$_4$	4.5-11.5 ((µg/dL)	7.5 (µg/dL)

Based on this data, where is this tumor located?

A) The adrenal cortex
B) The hypothalamus
C) The anterior pituitary
D) The thyroid gland

368. A premedical student wants to take a supplement that will reduce urination in order to sit through a seven-hour exam. If the student plans to take this substance immediately before the test, which hormone should he aim to increase?

A) Aldosterone
B) Vasopressin
C) TSH
D) GH

369. Which of the following symptoms would be expected in someone with increased parathyroid gland activity?

A) Decreased bone density
B) Decreased blood calcium levels
C) Increased metabolic rate
D) Decreased metabolic rate

370. A patient presents with an aldosterone-secreting tumor in the adrenal medulla. Which of the following lab results would be expected from this patient?

A) Excess plasma calcium
B) Significantly lowered plasma sodium levels
C) Low blood pressure
D) Low plasma potassium levels

371. Cholesterol is a critical biological molecule for living organisms. Which of the following is NOT a role that cholesterol plays in the body?

A) A precursor to steroid hormones
B) A precursor to nucleic acids
C) A contributor to plasma membrane fluidity
D) A precursor to bile salts

372. What type of hormone exerts its effect upon the cell which released it?

A) Autocrine
B) Endocrine
C) Paracrine
D) Exocrine

373. A newly discovered factor is found to bind to extracellular receptors rather than enter the cell. Based on this observation, this factor is likely which type of hormone?

A) A peptide hormone
B) A tyrosine-based hormone
C) A gaseous hormone
D) A steroid hormone

374. The image below represents a newly discovered hormone.

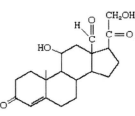

Based on its structure, what method of signaling is most probable?

A) Binding to extracellular hormone receptors that initiate a cAMP cascade

B) Binding to extracellular hormone receptors that initiate gene transcription changes

C) Binding to intracellular hormone receptors embedded in the plasma membrane that open extracellular Ca^{2+} channels

D) Binding to intracellular hormone receptors in the cytosol that initiate gene transcription and regulation

375. Steroid hormones are composed of cholesterol. In order for the cell to produce these hormones, they must be processed correctly with the help of the smooth endoplasmic reticulum and secreted through the Golgi apparatus. Based on this, which of the organs would be expected to have cells with the largest smooth ER and Golgi apparatus?

A) The anterior pituitary

B) The pancreas

C) The ovary

D) The adrenal medulla

376. Sonic hedgehog (SHH) is a developmental signaling hormone that is released from the notochord to create a concentration gradient that spans the dorsoventral axis. Higher concentrations of SHH are found ventrally, near the notochord, while lower concentrations are found dorsally. Based on this information, what type of signaling molecule is SHH?

A) Paracrine

B) Autocrine

C) Endocrine

D) Exocrine

377. Which of the following accurately describes a secondary messenger and its role in cell signaling?

A) cAMP is a secondary signaling molecule and attenuates the signal.

B) cAMP is a secondary signaling molecule and amplifies the signal.

C) GH is a secondary signaling molecule and attenuates the signal.

D) GH is a secondary signaling molecule and amplifies the signal.

378. Which of these statements must be true for Receptor A, a peptide hormone receptor?

A) It is exclusively hydrophilic in order to dissolve in the cytosol.

B) It contains both hydrophobic and hydrophilic regions, and the hormone binds the hydrophilic regions.

C) It contains both hydrophobic and hydrophilic regions, and the hormone binds the hydrophobic regions.

D) It is exclusively hydrophobic in order to be incorporated into the plasma membrane.

379. Describe the order in which a G protein-coupled receptor (GPCR) is activated.

A) Hormone binds to extracellular target → GDP is exchanged for GTP → GPCR undergoes conformational change → alpha subunit dissociates to adenylate cyclase → ATP is cyclized to cAMP

B) Hormone binds to extracellular target → GPCR undergoes conformational change → GDP is exchanged for GTP → alpha subunit dissociates to adenylate cyclase → ATP is cyclized to cAMP

C) Hormone binds to extracellular target → GPCR undergoes conformational change → ATP is cyclized to cAMP → GDP is exchanged for GTP → alpha subunit dissociates to adenylate cyclase

D) Hormone binds to extracellular target → GDP is exchanged for GTP → GPCR undergoes conformational change → ATP is cyclized to cAMP → alpha subunit dissociates to adenylate cyclase

380. Glucagon is a peptide hormone that binds to extracellular G protein-coupled receptors in order to exert its effect. If a competitive inhibitor to this receptor is injected intravenously, what symptoms will result in the patient?

    A) Glucagon secretion will decrease.
    B) Insulin secretion will increase.
    C) Blood glucose will increase.
    D) Blood glucose will decrease.

381. Albuterol is a sympathomimetic drug that acts on smooth muscle. This medication is frequently packaged in "rescue inhalers" used by asthmatic patients to relieve acute asthma and enable a return to normal breathing. Of the following cells, which are most likely to display receptors for albuterol?

    A) Smooth muscle cells surrounding alveolar sacs
    B) Smooth muscle cells surrounding the trachea
    C) Smooth muscle cells surrounding the terminal bronchioles
    D) Smooth muscle cells surrounding the glottis

382. PEEP, or positive end-expiratory pressure, refers to the pressure in the airway at the end of expiration. Patients with chronic respiratory conditions such as pulmonary edema or COPD often attempt to increase PEEP in order to prevent alveolar collapse and prolong gas exchange. Usually a subconscious effort, this is sometimes accomplished by forced exhalations through pursed lips. Which of the patients below is attempting to increase his or her PEEP?

    A) An asthmatic patient gasping sharply during inhalation
    B) A one-month premature infant grunting during exhalation
    C) An emphysema patient with reduced alveolar elasticity coughing up thick sputum
    D) A trauma patient with pneumothorax taking shallow, rapid breaths

383. Poultry farmers must carefully control the temperature of their coops to ensure production of healthy eggs. Interestingly, high blood pH and elevated temperature in chickens is associated with the abnormal formation of soft and delicate shells. With this in mind, a chicken raised in an excessively warm environment is most likely to:

    A) retain carbon dioxide and produce eggs with very hard shells.
    B) retain carbon dioxide and produce eggs with very soft shells.
    C) eliminate too much carbon dioxide and produce eggs with very hard shells.
    D) eliminate too much carbon dioxide and produce eggs with very soft shells.

384. Endotracheal (ET) intubation is considered the gold standard for airway control in the emergency medical setting. During this invasive procedure, the glottis is held open while an ET tube is inserted directly through the mouth and into the trachea. Unfortunately, this prevents the patient from using the nasal passages to breathe, leading to possible complications that include tracheobronchial mucosal necrosis and severe pneumonia. Functions of the nasal passages include:

    I. warming incoming air by exposing it to superficial blood vessels in the sinuses.
    II. using mucus and tiny hairs to trap airborne pathogens and debris before they can enter the lungs.
    III. humidifying incoming air to prevent damage to lower airway tissues.
    IV. containing a lining of simple squamous epithelial cells, allowing gas exchange to begin before incoming air reaches the lungs.

    A) I only
    B) I and III
    C) I, II, and IV
    D) I, II, and III

385. In the respiratory zone of the lungs, atmospheric air is separated from the interstitial fluid and capillaries by a single layer of squamous epithelial cells. What method is used by gases to move between the alveolar space and the pulmonary circulation?

    A) Active transport
    B) Binding to carrier proteins
    C) Simple diffusion
    D) Movement through hydrophobic protein channels

Questions 386–387 rely on the figure below

Several volumes have been defined based on their particular relevance to human breathing. The graph below shows the change in human lung volume as a function of time, with these volumes labeled.

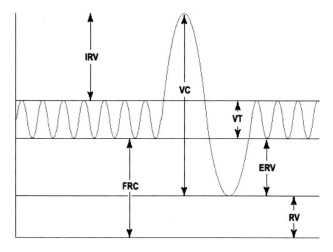

386. Asthma is characterized by a decrease in bronchiolar diameter, often secondary to irritation or inappropriate parasympathetic activity. Administration of bronchodilators such as albuterol and ipratropium can provide complete relief of symptoms in a matter of minutes. Which of the following lung volumes would most likely be abnormal in an asthmatic patient during an attack?

   A) VC
   B) VT
   C) IRV and ERV
   D) All values shown in the figure would essentially be normal.

387. Pregnancy causes marked changes in respiratory physiology. In part, these are due to the increased metabolic demand placed upon the mother by the developing fetus; they also result from increased physical pressure placed on internal organs by the gravid uterus. How can one best describe the respiratory parameters of a third-trimester pregnant female, compared to a female who is not pregnant?

   A) VT and VC decrease, while respiratory rate increases.
   B) VT, VC, and respiratory rate all decrease.
   C) VT and VC increase, while respiratory rate decreases.
   D) VT and VC decrease, while respiratory rate remains at the level of a person who is not pregnant.

388. Individuals who spend a significant portion of their early development at high altitudes tend to develop a barrel-chested appearance. Physical examination often reveals that these people move measurably more air during each breath than a comparably-sized individual living closer to sea level. This adaptation is beneficial because:

   A) a larger lung volume allows more air to be forced out of the alveolar space into circulation.
   B) the atmospheric partial pressure of oxygen is markedly lower at high altitude than at sea level.
   C) an increase in lung volume is usually accompanied by an increase in the rate of gas diffusion.
   D) surfactant is less effective at high altitude, so alveoli tend to spontaneously collapse.

389. Some debate exists regarding the administration of high-flow oxygen to patients with chronic obstructive pulmonary disease (COPD) out of concern for sudden respiratory arrest. Unlike healthy individuals, COPD patients are primarily driven to breathe by a decrease in circulating oxygen. Theoretically, then, providing them with 100% oxygen could eliminate their respiratory drive. In healthy individuals, central chemoreceptors are most directly stimulated to increase breathing rate by:

   A) decreased pH of the cerebrospinal fluid.
   B) increased pH of the cerebrospinal fluid.
   C) decreased plasma carbon dioxide.
   D) increased plasma carbon dioxide.

390. The complex process of breathing is controlled by a number of peripheral nerves and muscle groups. The diagram below provides a broad visual description of the gross anatomical regions of the brain.

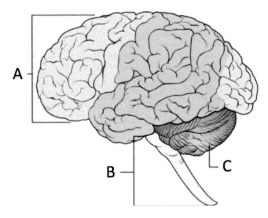

In a healthy human, which of the indicated regions may contribute to neural respiratory control?

A) A only
B) B only
C) A and B
D) B and C

391. In mammals, how does the circulatory system differ from the lymphatic system?

I. The circulatory system contains a single circuit, while the lymphatic system contains two.
II. Some vessels in the circulatory system contain valves, which are not present in any lymphatic vessels.
III. Only lymphatic vessels contain leukocytes.
IV. The circulatory system is closed, while the lymphatic system is open.

A) III only
B) IV only
C) II and IV
D) I, II, and IV

392. A cardiologist takes a biopsy of muscle tissue from the wall of the superior vena cava. Upon analysis of this tissue, what characteristics would he find?

A) Multinucleate, striated fibers with clearly defined sarcomeres
B) Uninucleate, non-striated cells with tapered ends
C) Highly branched, striated fibers that mainly appear to be uninucleate
D) As a vein, the vena cava does not contain muscle.

Questions 393–394 rely on the figure below

The following diagram shows a healthy human heart, with a number of vessels and valves labeled.

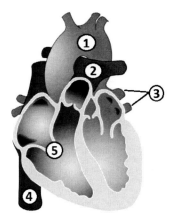

393. The partial pressure of CO_2 is highest in which of the numbered vessels?

A) 1
B) 2
C) 3
D) The partial pressure of CO_2 is roughly equal in all regions of the heart; it is the O_2 partial pressure that differs.

394. Which chambers are separated by the valve marked "5," and from which circuit do they receive blood?

A) The left atrium and the left ventricle; they receive blood from the pulmonary circuit.
B) The left atrium and the left ventricle; they receive blood from the systemic circuit.
C) The right atrium and the right ventricle; they receive blood from the pulmonary circuit.
D) The right atrium and the right ventricle; they receive blood from the systemic circuit.

395. In fluid dynamics, the continuity equation relates the cross-sectional area of a vessel to the speed of fluid moving through it. According to this equation:

   A) blood travels fastest in capillaries, since they have the smallest individual cross-sectional areas.

   B) blood travels slowest in capillaries, since they have the smallest individual cross-sectional areas.

   C) blood travels slowest in capillaries, since they have the largest combined cross-sectional area.

   D) blood travels fastest in capillaries, since they have the largest combined cross-sectional area.

396. The ductus arteriosus is a fetal circulatory adaptation that shunts blood directly from the pulmonary artery to the aorta. In a fetus, this is beneficial, as it bypasses underdeveloped lungs that are not yet required for gas exchange. However, many babies are born with a condition known as "patent ductus arteriosus," in which this shunt remains open after birth. When examining a 3-month-old male with this condition, one would expect to observe:

   A) a P_{CO2} in the aorta that is higher than expected.

   B) a P_{O2} in the pulmonary artery that is lower than expected.

   C) a P_{O2} in the tissues that is higher than expected.

   D) none of the above, as the pulmonary artery and aorta carry blood with roughly the same levels of C_{O2} and O_2.

397. The main role of serum albumin, a soluble 65 kDa protein, is to:

   A) bind to and carry oxygen via its many heme groups.

   B) bind to and carry carbon dioxide via its many heme groups.

   C) maintain plasma osmolarity, causing fluid to diffuse from the tissues into capillary beds.

   D) maintain plasma osmolarity, causing fluid to diffuse from the tissues into all blood vessels.

398. The graph below depicts blood pressure in various vessels throughout the human circulatory system.

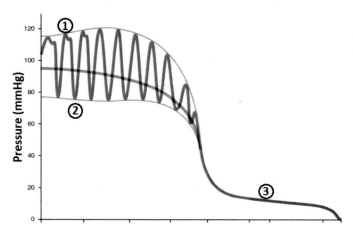

Labels 1, 2, and 3 most likely represent, respectively:

   A) the systolic pressure in the aorta, the diastolic pressure in the aorta, and the pressure in a vein of the lower chest.

   B) the diastolic pressure in the aorta, the systolic pressure in the aorta, and the pressure in a vein of the lower chest.

   C) the pressure in a coronary artery during systole, the pressure in a coronary artery during diastole, and the pressure in the vena cava during asystole.

   D) the pressure in a vein of the lower chest, the diastolic pressure in the aorta, and the systolic pressure in the aorta.

399. An inner lining of epithelial cells might be found in which type of blood vessel?

   A) Capillaries only, as this constitutes the one-cell-thick endothelium that comprises their entire wall

   B) Veins, arteries, and arterioles only, as these are the only types of vessel that contain smooth muscle

   C) All types, as gas diffusion must take place through vessel walls throughout the entire circulatory system

   D) All types, as well as lymphatic vessels

400. A physiology intern is testing the effects of nitric oxide (NO), a vasodilator, on thermoregulation. He hypothesizes that, in hot weather, NO can have a cooling effect on the body by promoting the vasodilation of smooth muscle in capillaries. What is this intern's mistake?

A) Blood vessels contain cardiac muscle, not smooth muscle.

B) Capillaries contain no muscle in their walls; it is arterioles that would undergo the majority of vasodilation.

C) Vasoconstriction, not vasodilation, cools the body when ambient temperatures are high.

D) Nothing; the intern is correct.

Questions 401–402 rely on the figure below

A biochemist is studying carbonic anhydrase and intends to isolate large amounts of this enzyme from whole blood. The researcher spins down a blood sample in a laboratory centrifuge; the tube after centrifugation is shown below. An assessment finds that samples of Layer 2 show immune activity.

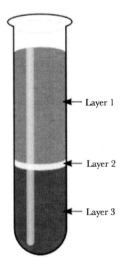

401. Following density gradient centrifugation, carbonic anhydrase will be found in which layer(s)?

A) Layer 1
B) Layer 2
C) Layer 3
D) Both Layers 1 and 3

402. As part of his experiments, the biochemist must determine the nucleotide sequence of the gene coding for carbonic anhydrase. Which layer should he isolate to obtain the most DNA for sequencing?

A) Layer 1
B) Layer 2
C) Layer 3
D) It is unlikely that DNA will be present in any of the layers.

403. A typical human red blood cell remains in circulation for approximately four months before being cleared by the spleen. Which characteristic of erythrocytes contributes to their short period of viability?

A) Erythrocytes have no mitochondria and have very low metabolic capabilities, reducing their capacity for cellular repair.

B) Since mature erythrocytes are anucleate and lack ribosomes, they do not contain any functioning enzymes.

C) Erythrocytes are exposed to high concentrations of oxygen free radicals, placing them at high risk for becoming cancerous.

D) Erythrocytes are frequent targets of viral infection due to their limited ability to produce antiviral peptides.

404. Albumin is an enzymatically inactive globular protein produced by the liver. It accounts for approximately 50% of human plasma protein. As a result of reduced albumin production, patients who develop liver failure are likely to exhibit:

A) swelling of the legs and feet.
B) increased susceptibility to viral infection.
C) reduced oxygen carrying capacity.
D) increased blood viscosity.

405. Which of the following is LEAST likely to reduce the oxygen-carrying capacity of human blood?

A) Complete removal of the stomach
B) Ablation of red bone marrow
C) Dietary iron deficiency
D) Intravenous erythropoietin supplementation

406. Epistaxis, also known as a nosebleed, is rarely a life-threatening condition in healthy individuals. However, in patients undergoing treatment with anticoagulant medications such as Coumadin, epistaxis can result in severe blood loss. Which of the following medications, if applied directly to a ruptured nasal blood vessel, would most likely improve patient outcome?

    A) Histamine, a potent endogenous vasodilator
    B) Lidocaine, an opioid analgesic related to morphine
    C) Tissue plasminogen activator, a drug often administered to patients suffering from ischemic stroke
    D) Ephedrine, a potent sympathomimetic drug related to amphetamine and epinephrine

407. Hemolytic disease of the newborn results when a pregnant female produces IgG antibodies specific for a particular erythrocyte antigen, known as "Rh." Although the placenta normally prevents mixing of fetal and maternal blood, the act of childbirth often involves bleeding that can permit sensitization of maternal immune cells to Rh. Which of the following scenarios carries the highest risk for development of hemolytic disease of the newborn?

    A) An Rh-negative mother on her first pregnancy, carrying an Rh-negative fetus
    B) An Rh-positive mother on her second pregnancy, carrying an Rh-positive fetus
    C) An Rh-negative mother on her first pregnancy, carrying an Rh-positive fetus
    D) An Rh-negative mother on her second pregnancy, carrying an Rh-positive fetus

408. Sickle-cell anemia is a genetic condition caused by the polymerization of abnormal hemoglobin within erythrocytes, which alters cellular structure. As oxygen dissociates from hemoglobin, the affinity of the abnormal hemoglobin molecules for each other increases. Which of the following could aggravate this?

    I.   Vigorous exercise
    II. Metabolic acidosis caused by diabetes mellitus
    III. Administration of 100% oxygen by an emergency physician

    A) I only
    B) II only
    C) I and II
    D) I and III

409. Neuroglobin is a monomeric, heme-containing protein found in mammalian cerebrospinal fluid. High levels of neuroglobin have been associated with improved outcomes in cases of ischemic stroke and traumatic brain injury.

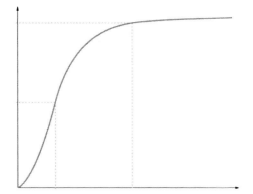

Compared to the sigmoidal oxygen dissociation curve for hemoglobin, shown above, the neuroglobin oxygen dissociation curve will most likely be:

    A) a sigmoidal curve, shifted left.
    B) a sigmoidal curve, shifted right.
    C) a rectangular hyperbolic curve, shifted left.
    D) a rectangular hyperbolic curve, shifted right.

410. Fetal hemoglobin (HbF) demonstrates a markedly greater affinity for oxygen compared to adult hemoglobin (Hgb). Which of the following, if true, provides a plausible explanation for this difference?

    A) HbF more avidly binds free radicals such as nitric oxide and carbon monoxide.
    B) The amino terminus of HbF subunits is more exposed to solution, facilitating conversion to carbaminohemoglobin.
    C) The iron center of HbF exists in the Fe(III) state, rather than the Fe(II) state found in Hgb.
    D) The 2,3-bisphosphoglycerate binding pocket of HbF contains a serine residue, which replaces the histidine found in Hgb.

411. The Bohr effect describes the relationship between hemoglobin-oxygen binding affinity and pH, which correlates to the concentration of carbon

dioxide. Which of the following conditions would decrease this binding affinity?

I.   High physiological pH
II.   High carbon dioxide concentrations
III. Low physiological pH
IV.   Low carbon dioxide concentrations

A) I and II
B) I and IV
C) II and III
D) III and IV

412. Of the below mechanisms, which best describes how gases, particularly oxygen and carbon dioxide, are exchanged between the alveoli and the blood?

A) Simple diffusion
B) Active transport
C) Osmosis
D) Facilitated diffusion

413. Hemoglobin has a quaternary structure composed of four subunits that primarily form alpha helices. However, it also contains a metal compound that is crucial for binding to oxygen. What is the metal in this compound?

A) Nickel
B) Magnesium
C) Zinc
D) Iron

414. Hemoglobin can bind a total of four oxygen molecules. Which of these molecules binds with most ease?

A) The first oxygen
B) The second oxygen
C) The third oxygen
D) The fourth oxygen

415. All of these listed molecules or compounds are substrates of hemoglobin EXCEPT:

A) oxygen.
B) carbon dioxide.
C) nitric oxide.
D) iron.

Questions 416–417 rely on the table below

Hemoglobin is the chief carrier of oxygen in the body. Below is the its dissociation curve.

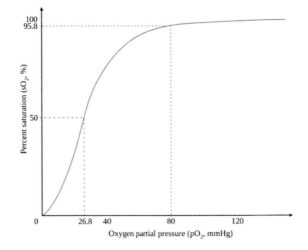

416. Which adjective best describes this curve, and how does it specifically relate to the dissociation of hemoglobin?

A) This graph is exponential, as hemoglobin has a low affinity for oxygen that increases as O_2 concentration increases.
B) This graph is logarithmic, as hemoglobin has a high affinity for oxygen; as the partial pressure of O_2 increases, the percent saturation is largely unaffected.
C) This graph is sigmoidal, as the binding of one oxygen molecule encourages the binding of additional oxygen molecules.
D) This graph is hyperbolic, as each oxygen molecule has an equal chance to bind to hemoglobin.

417. During pregnancy, the fetus acquires oxygen not through active breathing, but via gas exchange with its mother. In order for this to happen, what must the dissociation curve for fetal hemoglobin look like?

A) The curve is shifted to the right because fetal hemoglobin has a higher affinity for oxygen than adult hemoglobin.
B) The curve is shifted to the left to allow for the diffusion of oxygen through the placenta.
C) The curve is shifted to the right because maternal hemoglobin diffuses into the fetal bloodstream directly.
D) The curve is shifted to the left because fetal hemoglobin is composed of different subunits with increased oxygen affinity.

418. In general, how does breathing function to maintain the balance of carbon dioxide and oxygen in the lungs and bloodstream?

    A) Breathing keeps the concentration of oxygen high in the alveoli to facilitate diffusion into the bloodstream.
    B) Breathing rate decreases with physical activity to provide oxygen to the muscles.
    C) Breathing removes carbon dioxide from our system, thus reducing the pH of our blood.
    D) The rate of breathing is regulated depending on the body's demand for oxygen or carbon monoxide.

Questions 419–420 rely on the figure below

This equation represents a major contributor to acid-base balance in human beings.

$$H_2O + CO_2 \leftrightarrow H_2CO_3 \leftrightarrow H^+ + HCO_3^-$$

419. If one couldn't produce carbonic anhydrase, what condition would most directly result?

    A) Alkalosis
    B) Acidosis
    C) A reduced breathing rate
    D) An increased breathing rate

420. How does hyperventilation affect the pH of the blood?

    A) Increased breathing rate results in a lower pH.
    B) Decreased breathing rate results in a higher pH.
    C) Increased breathing rate results in a higher pH.
    D) Decreased breathing rate results in an unchanged pH.

421. Lymph is driven through the lymphatic vessels with the help of:

    A) one-way valves that prevent fluid backflow.
    B) the motion of beating cilia that push the fluid along.
    C) high systolic pressure in the parallel arterial circuit.
    D) the collective motion of highly motile leukocytes in the fluid.

422. The lymphatic system is involved in monitoring the immunological condition of the body. Lymph nodes are lymphatic organs that house high amounts of T and B cells. The lymphatic system ultimately drains back into venous circulation at the left subclavian vein. A severely infected laceration on the right foot would most likely lead to significant swelling of which lymph node?

    A) The axillary lymph node, located underneath the arm
    B) The inguinal lymph node, located in the groin
    C) The cervical lymph nodes, located in the oropharynx
    D) The popliteal lymph node, located behind the knee

423. A long-standing pharmaceutical challenge has been the effect of so-called "first pass metabolism" on oral medications. Blood from the small intestine travels directly to the liver via the hepatic portal system, and many drugs are extensively modified before they can reach their targets and exert desirable therapeutic effects. To circumvent this physiological roadblock, an intrepid pharmaceutical chemist might elect to cross-link an oral drug to:

    A) a large, acid-stable peptide.
    B) a long-chain fatty acid incorporated into a triglyceride.
    C) a simple sugar, such as glucose.
    D) a complex carbohydrate, such as starch.

424. Neutropenia is a condition characterized by abnormally low levels of circulating neutrophils in the body. Although a single neutrophil lives for only 2-3 hours, these cells are a critical part of the innate immune response. An individual with neutropenia would most likely:

    A) be more susceptible to reinfection with chicken pox, despite previous childhood infection.
    B) be advised by a physician to repeat all of his childhood vaccinations.
    C) suffer widespread tissue damage resulting from free reactive oxygen species.
    D) carry increased risk of opportunistic infection after stepping on a piece of broken glass.

425. Dendritic cells are often credited as being the link between the innate and adaptive immune systems. These cells are capable of sampling the membranes of somatic cells using a process called "nibbling." The dendritic cell then carries the cellular sample to the nearest lymph node and presents the antigen to another immune cell, in a process that involves direct membrane contact and utilizes MHC. Assuming the sampled cell was subject to a novel intracellular infection, the dendritic cell most likely interacts with:

A) a helper CD4+ T cell.
B) a macrophage.
C) a memory B cell.
D) a cytotoxic CD8+ T cell.

Questions 426–427 rely on the figure below

The following graph depicts serum immunoglobulin levels in three different patients as a function of time post infection. Note that all three patients are infected with the same pathogen.

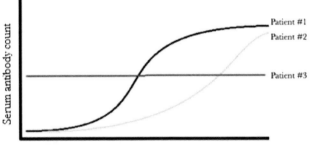

426. Given the data above, Patient #2 is most likely:

A) an adult with prior exposure to the pathogen and who has not been vaccinated.
B) an adult with no prior exposure to the pathogen.
C) an adult who has received an effective vaccine against the pathogen.
D) an adult who is unable to effectively combat his current infection.

427. Patient #3 is most likely:

A) a 50-year-old adult currently undergoing prophylactic broad-spectrum antibiotic therapy.
B) a 30-year-old adult in the late stages of AIDS.
C) a 16-day-old neonate who is being breast-fed by a vaccinated mother but has not been vaccinated herself.
D) a 28-day-old neonate who has been vaccinated against this pathogen but has not been breast-fed.

Questions 428–429 rely on the table below

Blood samples were collected from two different patients as part of a diagnostic procedure. Cell counts from these samples are shown below.

	Patient A	Patient B	Normal range
White blood cell count	$4.5 \times 10^9/L$	$4.9 \times 10^9/L$	$4.0 - 11.0 \times 10^9/L$
Absolute neutrophil count	$4.1 \times 10^9/L$	$6.8 \times 10^9/L$	$2.5 - 7.5 \times 10^9/L$
Red blood cell count	$2.5 \times 10^6/mL$	$5.1 \times 10^6/mL$	$4.2 - 6.1 \times 10^6/mL$
Platelet count	250,000/mcL	45,000/mcL	150,000 - 450,000/mcL
CD4 T cell count	$190/mm^3$	$780/mm^3$	$500 - 1500/mm^3$

428. Patient A is possibly suffering from which of the following clinical conditions?

   I.   Hemolytic anemia

   II. AIDS

   III. Pneumonia

      A) I and II

      B) I and III

      C) II and III

      D) I, II, and III

429. According to the data in the table above, Patient B is likely at risk of death from:

      A) a systemic septic infection.

      B) a hemorrhagic stroke.

      C) an anaphylactic reaction.

      D) a myocardial infarction.

430. The color of mucus produced by coughing or sneezing is usually dependent on cellular composition. Mucus may be green if it contains high levels of myeloperoxidase, an enzyme responsible for the synthesis of reactive oxygen species. A patient who has been coughing up green sputum likely has high numbers of which cell type in his lungs?

      A) Helper T lymphocytes

      B) Memory B lymphocytes

      C) Platelets

      D) Neutrophils

431. The number of unique human antibodies dramatically exceeds the number of human genes available to code for them. Which of the following mechanisms accounts for this fact?

      A) Alternative RNA splicing

      B) Post-translational modification

      C) Somatic (VDJ) recombination

      D) Clonal selection

432. Dithiothreitol (DTT) is a small organic molecule often used in a laboratory setting. It contains free thiol groups, making it capable of reducing disulfide bonds. The structure of DTT is shown below.

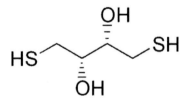

An immunologist isolates a pure sample of human IgG. After treating it with a solution of DTT, the immunologist loads the sample into an electrophoresis gel. How many bands will be visible after the gel has been run to completion?

      A) 1 band

      B) 2 bands

      C) 3 bands

      D) 4 bands

433. The structures of four common classes of immunoglobulin are show below.

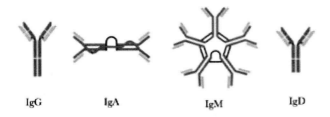

IgG   IgA   IgM   IgD

A laboratory technician wants to determine the antigenic profile of human red blood cells via a hemagglutination assay. Assuming that the technician has access to immunoglobulin molecules specific for human erythrocyte antigens A and B, which class of Ig would be the most useful laboratory reagent in this process?

A) IgG
B) IgA
C) IgM
D) IgD

434. Clonal selection occurs early in development to ensure proper education of immature lymphocytes. All T cells start their life expressing both CD4 and CD8, and are then termed "double positive" or "DP." Which of the following cells is most likely to survive clonal selection, assuming no pathologies are involved?

A) A DP T cell that fails to bind an MHC I complex loaded with a peptide fragment derived from a myelin sheath protein
B) A DP T cell that strongly binds an MHC I complex loaded with a peptide fragment derived from an androgen receptor
C) A DP T cell that weakly binds an MHC I complex loaded with a peptide fragment derived from an insulin receptor
D) A DP T cell that fails to bind an MHC II complex loaded with a peptide fragment derived from an insulin receptor

435. Hashimoto's disease is marked by decreased thyroid function, thyroid gland destruction, and symptomatic reduction in circulating thyroid hormone. Substantial evidence exists to suggest that this condition develops, at least in part, as a result of autoimmunity. Which of the following, if true, would provide the strongest evidence *against* this autoimmunity hypothesis?

A) Individuals with Hashimoto's disease often exhibit extremely high levels of circulating TSH and thyroglobulin.
B) Individuals with Hashimoto's disease often have a family history of type I diabetes mellitus.
C) CD8+ T cells isolated directly from the thyroid gland of a Hashimoto's patient display virtually no affinity for any thyrocyte surface antigens.
D) A monoclonal line of plasma B cells isolated from a Hashimoto's patient is capable of producing antibodies that are highly specific for TSH receptors, but cannot be induced to secrete antibodies for thyroid peroxidase or thyroglobulin.

436. Effective vaccines can provide lifelong immunity to certain pathogens without ever eliciting symptoms. Of the choices below, the molecule from which the most effective vaccine could be developed is:

A) a highly variable glycoprotein present on the surface of *Mycobacterium tuberculosis*.
B) a segment of viral DNA containing a gene that is conserved across all strains of the Epstein-Barr virus.
C) intact botulism toxin, produced by every strain of *Clostridium botulinum*.
D) whole poliovirus particles subjected to intense heat.

437. In addition to containing some form of antigen derived from the target pathogen, vaccines often include a substance known as an "adjuvant," which increases the immunologic insult of the foreign antigen. In many cases, the adjuvant does so by inducing immune cells to produce specific cytokines. These cytokines most likely exert their effects by all of the following mechanisms EXCEPT:

A) promoting local inflammation around the area of antigen introduction, which increases the presence of various immune cells.
B) inducing production of immunoglobulin by lymphocytes.
C) activating MHC production and loading by red blood cells proximal to the injection site.
D) promoting dendritic cell migration to lymph nodes for antigen presentation.

438. Organ transplant recipients are routinely screened against their potential donors to ensure that they share the same MHC subtypes. This dramatically reduces the chances of graft-versus-host disease and subsequent organ rejection. When a CD8+ T cell binds and kills an infected cell, the extracellular binding domain of the T cell receptor interacts specifically with:

    A) amino acid residues of the foreign antigen peptide fragment that are loaded into the MHC.
    B) amino acid residues of the MHC itself.
    C) amino acid residues of both the loaded foreign antigen peptide fragment and the MHC.
    D) amino acid residues of both the MHC and a peptide fragment derived from digested host cellular proteins.

439. A certain infected cell expresses MHC I. Binding of a CD8+ T cell to this complex results in:

    A) production of antibodies by the T cell.
    B) destruction of the infected cell by the T cell.
    C) destruction of the infected cell by macrophages following activation of the complement system.
    D) lysis of the T cell.

440. Superantigens are toxins produced by extracellular bacteria that bind to MHC II and trigger a rapid, systemic, non-specific T cell response. The resulting condition, known as toxic shock syndrome, is characterized by extremely high levels of inflammatory and proliferative cytokines shortly followed by widespread T cell anergy and apoptosis. Which of the following cell types is/are most likely involved in the development of this condition?

    I. CD4+ (helper) T cells
    II. CD8+ (cytotoxic) T cells
    III. Suppressor T cells

    A) I only
    B) I and III
    C) II and III
    D) I, II, and III

441. Which of these are functions of the large intestine?

    I. Water absorption
    II. Electrolyte absorption
    III. Fat absorption
    IV. Provision of an environment for *E. coli*

    A) III only
    B) IV only
    C) III and IV
    D) I, II, and IV

442. Starting from its location of synthesis, list the structures contacted by bile as it travels.

    A) Liver, gall bladder, cystic duct, common bile duct, duodenum
    B) Liver, common bile duct, gall bladder, cystic duct, duodenum
    C) Common bile duct, liver, cystic duct, gall bladder, stomach
    D) Gall bladder, common bile duct, liver, cystic duct, stomach

443. Starch in the digestive system is broken down by which enzyme?

    A) Lysozyme
    B) Amylase
    C) Pepsin
    D) Trypsin

444. Glucagon is released by the pancreas to regulate blood sugar levels. What is one function of this hormone?

    A) Lowering the level of fatty acids in the bloodstream
    B) Decreasing blood glucose levels
    C) Increasing glycogenolysis in the liver
    D) Increasing gluconeogenesis in the muscle

445. Which of the following does NOT occur in the stomach in the presence of a low pH?

    A) Autocleavage of pepsinogen
    B) Denaturation of ingested proteins
    C) Increased gastrin secretion by G cells
    D) Degradation of ingested bacteria

Questions 446–447 rely on the figure below

Doctors measured the glucose, blood pH, and insulin levels of a patient at intake and post-treatment and found the following results.

Time point	Glucose	Blood pH	Insulin
intake	low	low	high
post-treatment	normal	normal	low

446. What is the reason for the low blood pH of the patient at intake?

    A) Low glucose depletes bicarbonate buffers.
    B) Ketone body generation can promote acidosis.
    C) High insulin causes increased uptake of K⁺.
    D) High insulin causes increased lipolysis that releases large amounts of fatty acids into the blood.

447. At which point in the digestive cycle is the patient at the post-treatment test?

    A) During a meal
    B) Immediately after a meal
    C) A few hours after a meal
    D) Under a 24-hour fast

Questions 448–449 rely on the figure below

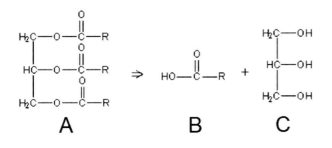

A   B   C

448. Where does this chemical reaction take place?

    A) In the mitochondria of skeletal muscle only
    B) In the mitochondria of all cells
    C) In the lacteals of the lymph system
    D) In the lumen of the small intestine

449. How is structure B transported in the bloodstream?

    A) It does not travel through the blood.
    B) It requires carrier proteins, like lipoproteins or albumin.
    C) It reacts with structure B to form structure A, which can travel through the circulatory system.
    D) It travels freely in the blood.

450. Which of the following is true?

    A) Trypsin cleaves sugars into monosaccharides and disaccharides.
    B) The duodenum is less acidic than the stomach due to bicarbonate ions released by the pancreas.
    C) Goblet cells in the digestive system epithelium secrete enzymes needed for digestion.
    D) Chief cells in the stomach directly release pepsin for the breakdown of protein.

451. The drawing below depicts a human kidney, with three major structures or regions labeled.

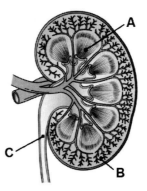

Respectively, labels A, B, and C refer to:

    A) the renal cortex, the renal medulla, and a ureter.
    B) the renal medulla, the renal cortex, and a ureter.
    C) the renal cortex, the renal medulla, and the urethra.
    D) the renal medulla, the renal cortex, and the urethra.

452. Which of these molecules represents a hormone secreted by the cortex of the endocrine gland positioned immediately above the kidney?

    A) Norepinephrine
    B) Renin
    C) Aldosterone
    D) Antidiuretic hormone

453. A physiology teacher is describing the nephron to her class. She mentions that, in healthy individuals, no glucose should be excreted in the urine. Instead, glucose monomers are reabsorbed from the lumen of the nephron into the interstitium surrounding the loop of Henle for later return to the bloodstream. What mistake, if any, did this teacher make?

    A) Glucose is removed from the filtrate in the proximal convoluted tubule, not the loop of Henle.
    B) Healthy humans tend to excrete a significant amount of glucose in the urine.
    C) The movement of solute out of the lumen of the nephron for retention in the body is termed secretion, not reabsorption.
    D) None of the above; the teacher's explanation is accurate.

454. How does secretion differ from filtration?

    A) Secretion refers to the transport of specific toxins and protons into the lumen of the nephron, while filtration relates to the original movement of fluid and solute into the Bowman's capsule.
    B) Secretion refers to the transport of specific toxins and protons into the lumen of the nephron, while filtration relates to the original movement of fluid and solute into the glomerulus.
    C) Secretion permits passage of all molecules except protein, while filtration is a specific process that only allows certain molecules to enter the nephron.
    D) Secretion takes advantage of passive diffusion, while filtration is accomplished mainly via secondary active transport.

455. A urologist is able to remove microscopic samples from particular regions of a mammalian nephron. One particular sample, Sample 1, contains simple cuboidal epithelial cells that lack any "brush border" or microvillus-based lining. The most likely origin of Sample A is the:

    A) collecting duct.
    B) glomerulus.
    C) proximal convoluted tubule.
    D) distal convoluted tubule.

456. Which part of the nephron functions to construct a solute gradient that facilitates the passive reabsorption of water in dehydrated individuals?

    A) The Bowman's capsule
    B) The collecting duct
    C) The loop of Henle
    D) The distal tubule

457. Hormones that are released from the posterior pituitary in either direct or indirect response to low blood pressure include:

    I. aldosterone.
    II. antidiuretic hormone.
    III. vasopressin.

    A) I only
    B) II only
    C) II and III
    D) I, II, and III

458. Which of the following molecules is most likely to be reabsorbed in the proximal convoluted tubule?

    A) Solute A, a large protein that serves multiple essential functions
    B) Solute B, a small, vital biomolecule
    C) Solute C, a medium-sized toxin
    D) Solute D, an ion with minor physiological uses

459. The enzyme ACE (angiotensin-converting enzyme) performs what specific function?

    A) It cleaves angiotensinogen into angiotensin I.
    B) It directly promotes the release of aldosterone when converted from its precursor, angiotensin I.
    C) It stimulates renin release from the juxtaglomerular cells of the kidney.
    D) It alters angiotensin I to form angiotensin II.

460. The urinary system is most closely tied to which of the other body systems?

    A) The integumentary system
    B) The endocrine system
    C) The digestive system
    D) The skeletal system

461. When the urine of an untreated diabetic patient is analyzed, which of the following are likely to be present?

I. Urea
II. Platelets
III. Potassium
IV. Glucose

    A) I and II
    B) II and III
    C) I, II, and IV
    D) I, III, and IV

462. Which three processes best describe urine formation by the nephron?

    A) Filtration, reabsorption, and secretion
    B) Formation, filtration, and secretion
    C) Formation, concentration, and dilution
    D) Filtration, concentration, and secretion

463. Frequent urination often occurs when an individual consumes alcohol. Often, the urine is clear, a common indicator of good hydration. However, hangover symptoms are consistent with those of dehydration. How can this apparent contradiction be explained?

    A) Alcohol reduces the blood pressure in the glomerulus, thus reducing water reabsorption.
    B) Alcohol causes the rapid excretion of water by disrupting the function of the distal convoluted tubule.
    C) Alcohol prevents water reabsorption in the proximal convoluted tubule.
    D) Alcohol disrupts water balance by preventing water reabsorption in the collecting duct.

464. Moderately high pressure in the Bowman's capsule most directly helps to:

    A) enable filtration.
    B) enable reabsorption.
    C) enable secretion.
    D) enable excretion.

465. The urea cycle is a cyclic process similar to the citric acid cycle. Ornithine is regenerated during one turn of the cycle and used for the next. Which pairing correctly matches the reactants and products of this cycle, respectively?

    A) Water and ammonium, urea
    B) Carbon dioxide and ammonia, urea
    C) Urea and water, uric acid
    D) Oxygen and ammonia, urea

Questions 466–467 rely on the figure below

A nephron is shown here, with labeled regions A, B, C, and D.

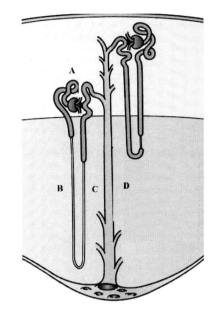

466. Which part of the nephron is permeable to water but not to salt?

    A) A
    B) B
    C) C
    D) D

467. Antidiuretic hormone serves to increase water reabsorption by inducing translocation of aquaporins into certain cells. A scientist is monitoring the change in number of aquaporins during this process. He would most likely focus his study on:

    A) region A, the collecting duct.
    B) region B, the descending limb of the loop of Henle.
    C) region C, the ascending limb of the loop of Henle.
    D) region D, the collecting duct.

468. A healthy human patient undergoes a variety of blood tests in an effort to become an organ donor. This individual's results for an electrolyte panel are shown below. If this patient were to drink abnormally large amounts of water, ion osmolarity in his plasma would:

Ion	Result	Normal concentration range (mmol*L^{-1})
sodium	140	135 – 145
potassium	4.0	3.6 – 5.1
chloride	98	95 – 105
calcium	2.2	2.1 – 2.8

A) increase, then slowly decrease.
B) decrease, then remain low until his next meal.
C) decrease, then remains low until urination.
D) decrease, then slowly increase.

469. The renin-angiotensin system is a regulatory system that helps control blood pressure. A critical catalyst within this system is angiotensin-converting enzyme (ACE), which transforms angiotensin I to angiotensin II. Drugs known as ACE inhibitors prevent the action of this enzyme. All of the following statements about the renin-angiotensin system are false EXCEPT:

A) even in an individual taking an ACE inhibitor, blood pressure can still change due to ADH.
B) inhibiting the renin-angiotensin system prevents any increases in blood pressure.
C) activation of the renin-angiotensin system results in vasodilation.
D) the renin-angiotensin system is directly activated when the salt content in the body exceeds a certain threshold.

470. In the presence of aldosterone, which of the following is most likely to be observed?

A) A decreased reabsorption of potassium
B) An increased reabsorption of sodium
C) An increase in urine pH
D) An inhibition of ADH secretion

471. Male patients who have sustained a traumatic lumbar spinal injury often present with a condition known as priapism, a prolonged and persistent erection. Most specifically, this condition results from damage to the:

A) parasympathetic nervous system.
B) sympathetic nervous system.
C) peripheral nervous system.
D) somatic nervous system.

472. Seminal vesicle dysfunction in males will most likely result in:

A) reduced fertility.
B) increased susceptibility to urinary tract infections.
C) decreased spermatogenesis.
D) malformation of spermatozoa.

473. Along with many other effects, surgical lesion of the anterior pituitary in an adult male would likely cause which of the following?

A) Increased serum testosterone
B) Increased GnRH production
C) Increased spermatogenesis
D) Increased osteogenesis

474. Activin is a small signaling protein with a number of biological roles. One of its functions involves the increase of FSH binding to the FSH receptor in the developing follicle. In males, an activin receptor agonist is most likely to cause:

A) increased spermatogenesis.
B) decreased spermatogenesis.
C) desensitization of Leydig cells.
D) desensitization of Sertoli cells.

475. The latter half of the menstrual cycle, shown below, is characterized by endometrial proliferation and vascularization. During the final days of the cycle, assuming implantation has not occurred, uterine contractions facilitate expulsion of the endometrium.

Which of the following hormones, if administered to a pregnant female, would be most effective in preventing pre-term birth?

A) Oxytocin
B) Prolactin
C) Estrogen
D) Progesterone

476. The structure of Bisphenol A (BPA) is shown below. Controversy still exists regarding the endocrine effects of this molecule. Many believe that it causes precocious puberty in females, which is defined as the development of secondary sexual characteristics before the age of 8.

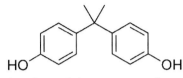

Assuming these claims are true, the structure and function of BPA most closely resemble:

A) luteinizing hormone.
B) follicle-stimulating hormone.
C) human chorionic gonadotropin.
D) estrogen.

477. Although *in utero* conditions can dramatically alter the course of fetal development, the rate of spontaneous DNA damage that occurs within the haploid oocyte is remarkably low. Which of the following, if true, constitutes a possible explanation for this finding?

I. The oocyte travels along the tube encased in a layer of metabolically-active maternal cells derived from the ovarian follicle.
II. The oocyte contains sufficient nutrients to nurture the embryo during the first zygotic divisions.
III. Oocyte chromatin displays a higher degree of supercoiling than that of most other known mammalian cell types.

A) I only
B) II only
C) I and III
D) I, II, and III

478. In a healthy intrauterine pregnancy, fertilization occurs in the:

A) uterine endometrium.
B) uterine myometrium.
C) Fallopian tube.
D) vaginal canal.

479. During the first weeks after fertilization, hCG levels can increase by a factor of over 10,000. However, excessively high hCG has been associated with multiple complications. Endometrial cells treated with high concentrations of the hormone display excessive apoptosis of CD8+ T cells. Pregnant females with abnormally high hCG are most likely at risk for the development of:

A) placenta percreta, a condition in which the placenta invades the uterine myometrium.
B) spontaneous abortion during the first trimester, caused by inadequate trophoblast implantation.
C) eclampsia, a seizure disorder that has been linked to exposure to novel paternal antigens.
D) endometriosis, the growth of normal uterine endometrial tissue in abnormal locations such as the Fallopian tubes.

480. Oxytocin, secreted by the posterior pituitary, increases the contractility and elasticity of the uterine wall. As a result, uterine contractions continue, eventually culminating in parturition (birth). Oxytocin production is most directly induced by:

A) progesterone secretion.
B) hCG secretion.
C) uterine contraction.
D) placental detachment.

481. Jon is a physiology student tasked with delineating the differences between cardiac muscle and skeletal muscle. He correctly explains how the two differ in:

A) the duration and "shape" of the action potential.
B) the presence of sarcomeres, including thick and thin filaments.
C) their dependence on ATP to provide energy for contraction.
D) their mechanism of contraction, including a cross-bridge cycle.

482. The autonomic nervous system is not involved in the control of which of the following muscles?

    A) Muscle lining the aorta
    B) Muscle of the left ventricle
    C) Arrector pili surrounding hair follicles
    D) The diaphragm

Questions 483–484 rely on the figure below

A physiology student is handed this schematic by his professor. Note that dark black lines represent neurons, while hexagonal structures denote muscle cells.

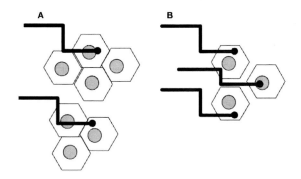

483. What is likely true of the relationship between A and B?

    I. Both A and B depict smooth muscle, but A indicates single-unit muscle and B indicates multiunit muscle.
    II. A is likely to have more gap junctions present than B.
    III. B is more likely to be found in the lining of the bowel.

    A) I only
    B) II only
    C) III only
    D) I, II, and III

484. Which structural elements are likely present in the depicted cells?

    I. Intermediate filaments, anchored to dense bodies
    II. Myosin filaments
    III. Actin filaments

    A) I only
    B) II only
    C) I and II only
    D) I, II, and III

485. In a routine neurological exam, a pediatrician taps a patient's knee, resulting in the child jerking his leg. The most likely physiological explanation of this reflex is that:

    A) an action potential is initiated in a sensory neuron, which excites a motor neuron innervating the quadriceps.
    B) an action potential is initiated in a motor neuron, which excites an interneuron that innervates the quadriceps.
    C) proteins in the tapped tissue react by contracting spontaneously.
    D) the child jerks his leg secondary to his appropriate sensation of pain.

486. Which of the following is the proper sequence of levels of organization, in order from smallest to largest, within skeletal muscle?

    A) Sarcomere; myofibril; muscle fiber; fasciculus
    B) Myofibril; sarcomere; muscle fiber; fasciculus
    C) Myofibril; muscle fiber; sarcomere; fasciculus
    D) Fasciculus; sarcomere; myofibril; muscle fiber

487. Slow-twitch or Type I skeletal muscle fibers are found in postural muscles. What is the most probable characteristic of such fibers?

    A) A high concentration of myoglobin
    B) A low concentration of myoglobin
    C) Rapid contraction velocity
    D) Low resistance to fatigue

488. Among the physiological functions of skeletal muscle are:

    A) temperature regulation.
    B) dilation and constriction of blood vessels.
    C) movement of fluids within the body.
    D) more than one of the above.

489. A biologist views the myosin head of a single thick filament, which is protruding in the form of a cross-bridge that is near, but not attached to, a thin filament. The cross-bridge is currently positioned at a 90° angle to the thin filament. This moment in time occurs immediately after:

    A) ATP is hydrolyzed to form ADP and inorganic phosphate.
    B) ADP is released from myosin.
    C) ATP binds to myosin.
    D) none of the above.

490. The giant muscle protein titin contains immunoglobulin domains that unfold in response to application of force, serving as shock absorbers in muscle tissue. In which region of the sarcomere is titin likely located?

A) I band
B) A band
C) H zone
D) None of the above

491. The sarcomere, the smallest functional unit in striated muscle, contains thick filaments that:

A) are composed of the muscle protein myosin and located in the A band of the sarcomere.
B) are composed of the muscle protein titin and located in the I band of the sarcomere.
C) contain a double helix of actin and myosin and are located in the H zone.
D) are composed of elastin and are located along the Z line.

492. A researcher is investigating Compound X. She hypothesizes that it is an acetylcholinesterase inhibitor (AChEI). What possible effects can she reasonably expect Compound X to promote, if administered to human patients in a future clinical trial?

I.   Decreased heart rate
II. Increased sympathetic nervous system activity at preganglionic nicotinic receptors
III. Hypotension

A) I only
B) II only
C) I and III
D) I, II, and III

493. A student in a physiology class isolates a muscle cell on a slide and notes that it has a single nucleus, as well as many gap junctions. He is uncertain as to whether the cell contains striations. He can reasonably conclude that his specimen is:

I.   skeletal muscle.
II. cardiac muscle.
III. smooth muscle.

A) I only
B) II only
C) II or III
D) I, II, or III

494. The diagram below shows a segment of skeletal muscle at two different times during the course of contraction.

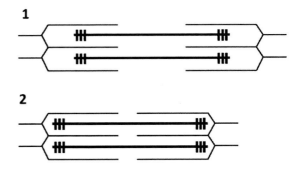

At Time 3, not pictured, the sarcomere has returned to the configuration that it is shown to have at Time 1. Which of the listed processes are likely to have occurred between Times 2 and 3?

A) The calcium concentration in the sarcoplasmic reticulum increased.
B) ATP was degraded into ADP and inorganic phosphate.
C) A conformational change in myosin took place.
D) Two or more of the listed choices are accurate.

495. To increase the force exerted by skeletal muscle, which of the following is required?

A) Increased frequency of action potentials within motor neurons
B) Sympathetic innervation of skeletal muscle tissue
C) Increased recruitment of motor units
D) Two or more of the above

496. After death, the limbs of the body stiffen in their current position in what is commonly known as rigor mortis. Physiologically, this is due to:

A) the decomposition of myosin and actin within the sarcomeres and the aggregation of thick and thin filaments.
B) the lack of ATP due to cessation of cellular respiration halting the cross-bridge formation cycle.
C) prolonged contraction of skeletal muscle due to decomposition of acetylcholinesterase.
D) none of the above.

497. Which of these conditions is promoted by high-frequency stimulation of an associated motor unit?

    A) Tetanus
    B) Rigor mortis
    C) Muscle adaptation
    D) Hypertrophy

498. Scientists studying excitation-contraction coupling modify various enzymes in skeletal muscle cells *in vitro*. As one result, they notice that, despite the initiation of depolarization of the sarcolemma, the muscle cell under observation does not contract effectively. A reasonable cause of this phenomenon might be:

    A) a mutated calcium channel within the sarcoplasmic reticulum.
    B) overactive nicotinic receptors on the sarcolemma.
    C) enhancement of myosin ATPase activity.
    D) none of the above.

499. A student observes a classmate squeezing a stress ball. She notes that, between every squeeze, the student's hand relaxes and the ball expands. The best physiological explanation one could offer for this relaxation is that:

    A) the motor neurons cease to depolarize the motor end plate, and acetylcholine is not released. The lack of signal, accompanied by the ATP-mediated detachment of thick and thin filaments, results in muscle relaxation.
    B) calcium is pumped back into the sarcoplasmic reticulum of the muscle cell, and accessory proteins cover myosin binding sites on thin filaments.
    C) the motor end plate receives a relaxation signal in the form of glutamine, which acts on postsynaptic receptors to increase the permeability of the sarcolemma to chlorine and temporarily hyperpolarizes the muscle cell.
    D) two or more of the above.

500. During skeletal muscle contraction, the dimensions of the various parts of the sarcomere change in what manner?

    I. The A band shortens.
    II. The I band shortens.
    III. The H zone lengthens.

    A) I only
    B) II only
    C) II and III
    D) I, II, and III

501. Which of these choices is an example of a flat bone?

    A) Femur
    B) Sternum
    C) Vertebra
    D) Metatarsal

502. All of the structures below represent long bones EXCEPT:

    A) the humerus.
    B) the femur.
    C) the mandible.
    D) the tibia.

503. Joints are defined as areas where bones connect. These structures allow for movement and provide mechanical support.

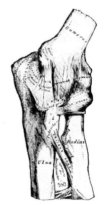

The joint between the humerus and ulna, as shown above, is characterized as which type of joint?

    A) A fibrous joint
    B) A synovial joint
    C) A cartilaginous joint
    D) More than one of the above

504. Which of the following correctly pairs a cell type with its function?

A) Osteoclasts are responsible for the creation of new and growing bone.

B) Osteoclasts are mature osteoblasts that will eventually become surrounded by their secreted matrix.

C) Osteoblasts are responsible for secretion of the bony matrix.

D) Osteoblasts are responsible for bone resorption.

505. Vitamin D is known to promote the absorption of calcium from the digestive tract. The resulting increase in blood Ca^{2+} levels will eventually stimulate the activity of which cells?

A) Osteoclasts

B) Osteoblasts

C) Hepatocytes

D) Leukocytes

506. How can the role of calcitonin, especially its control over serum $[Ca^{+2}]$, best be described?

A) Calcitonin stimulates osteoblasts, therefore decreasing serum $[Ca^{+2}]$.

B) Calcitonin stimulates osteoblasts, therefore increasing serum $[Ca^{+2}]$.

C) Calcitonin stimulates osteoclasts, therefore decreasing serum $[Ca^{+2}]$.

D) Calcitonin stimulates osteoclasts, therefore increasing serum $[Ca^{+2}]$.

507. A patient has contracted a very rare autoimmune disease that destroys the parathyroid gland. Which of the following symptoms could be expected in this individual?

A) Muscle cramping

B) Excessive urination

C) Osteoporosis

D) Constipation

508. Molecules that regulate blood calcium include:

I. dihydroxycholecalciferol.

II. calcitonin.

III. parathyroid hormone.

A) I

B) I and II

C) II and III

D) I, II, and III

509. All of the following describe differences between cartilage and bone EXCEPT:

A) cartilage is softer and more flexible.

B) cartilage is composed of collagen, while bone is made up of hydroxyapatite.

C) cartilage is avascular, while some bone is not.

D) cartilage may eventually turn to bone in development, but bone cannot be directly converted to cartilage.

510. Consider the anatomical drawing below.

The arrow indicates which type of connective tissue?

A) Cartilage B) Muscle

C) A ligament

D) A tendon

511. The epidermis, or most exterior layer of the skin, can best be described as:

A) a stratified columnar endothelium.

B) a stratified squamous epithelium.

C) a simple squamous epithelium.

D) a stratified cuboidal epithelium.

512. Sweat glands differ from sebaceous glands in that:

A) sweat glands secrete a fluid onto the exterior of the body, while sebaceous glands do not.

B) sweat glands are found near the surface of the body, while sebaceous glands secrete onto internal organs.

C) sweat glands are located solely in the epidermal layer, while sebaceous glands are buried in the hypodermis.

D) sweat glands play a major role in thermoregulation, while sebaceous glands serve to moisten the skin.

Questions 513–514 rely on the figure below

The following image shows a three-dimensional cross-section of human skin.

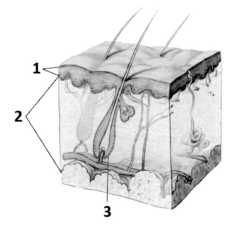

513. The layer marked "2" is known as:

    A) the epidermis.
    B) the hypodermis.
    C) the subepidermis.
    D) the dermis.

514. A dermatologist takes a biopsy of a patient's skin and finds that the sample is composed mainly of adipose cells. The dermatologist most likely biopsied which layer, as shown in the diagram?

    A) 1
    B) 2
    C) 3
    D) None of the above

515. Which of the biological actions below is NOT a thermoregulatory mechanism involving the skin?

    A) Angela exits her home into -10 °C conditions, but is kept warm by adipose deposits in her subcutaneous tissue.
    B) After running a marathon, Max cools down when capillaries in his skin undergo vasodilation.
    C) In cold weather, John notices that his skin turns pale and concludes that arterioles supplying his skin have constricted.
    D) Jake is embarrassed by his tendency to sweat, but notices that the evaporation of fluid from his skin keeps him cool.

516. A patient enters a doctor's clinic and is diagnosed with a melanin deficiency. Symptoms experienced by this individual likely include:

    A) weakened, breakable skin marked by blisters or redness.
    B) extra susceptibility to damage by sunlight with a wavelength of 700-1000 nm.
    C) unusually light-colored skin and eyes.
    D) extremely darkened skin and dark brown eyes.

517. The diagram below shows a type of epithelial layer.

This type of epithelium would most likely be found in which of the following locations?

    A) The epidermis, or external layer of the skin
    B) The lining of the small intestine
    C) The interior of the mouth
    D) The lining of the proximal convoluted tubule

518. As an extremely large external epithelium, the skin serves which of the following immune roles?

    A) It aids in providing innate immunity.
    B) It aids in providing adaptive immunity.
    C) It aids in providing cell-mediated immunity.
    D) The skin does not play an immune role.

519. The skin is technically classified as part of the:

    A) skeletal system.
    B) excretory system.
    C) integumentary system.
    D) muscular system.

520. Psoriasis is characterized by the appearance of red or white scaly plaques on an individual's skin. This disorder, which involves the rapid growth of keratinocytes, can have severe effects due to inflammatory and thermoregulatory disruption. A potential treatment for psoriasis might include:

A) a topical agent that lengthens the interphase portion of the cell cycle.

B) a growth factor that has been implicated in the appearance of various tumors, but is used to treat other conditions.

C) a lipoprotein thought to strengthen endothelial cells.

D) an orally administered form of cellulose that is quickly becoming a popular homeopathic remedy for a number of ailments.

This page intentionally left blank.

Biochemistry

521. In Anfisen's landmark experiment, the enzyme ribonuclease was denatured with 8 M urea and mercaptoethanol. The denaturing environment was subsequently removed via dialysis and the enzymatic activity of the protein was monitored after exposing the protein to the oxidizing environment of the atmosphere. What was the observed result?

A) The protein regained enzymatic activity.
B) The enzyme did not regain any of its enzymatic activity.
C) The enzyme aggregated to form large, white precipitated particles.
D) None of the above

522. A molecular biologist runs an SDS-PAGE on Protein A, using mercaptoethanol in the preparation of the protein sample. Protein A is known to possess quaternary structure. What will be the likely result after staining with Coomassie Blue?

A) Multiple bands that are further along the gel relative to Protein A's band in a native electrophoresis
B) Multiple bands that are closer to the start of the gel relative to Protein A's band in a native electrophoresis
C) A single band towards the start of the gel
D) A smear traversing the length of the gel

523. John runs a solution of Proteins A, B, and C through a size-exclusion chromatography column. The proteins elute out in the following order, from earliest to latest: C, A, B. What can John conclude?

I. Protein C will migrate a shorter distance in an SDS-PAGE gel than Protein B.
II. Protein B has quaternary structure.
III. Protein C is comprised of many hydrophobic residues.

A) I only
B) II only
C) III only
D) I, II, and III

524. A protein with a very high concentration of proline residues is likely deficient in which level of structure?

I. Primary
II. Secondary
III. Tertiary

A) I only
B) II only
C) I and II
D) I, II, and III

525. Leucine zipper motifs allow dimerization through the interaction of two alpha helices. The ensuing formation of heterodimers or homodimers is largely a result of which set of interactions?

A) Hydrophobic
B) London dispersion
C) Ionic
D) Dipole-dipole

526. A protein's sedimentation coefficient, measured in Svedbergs, depends upon:

A) only primary structure.
B) only tertiary and quaternary structure.
C) all the levels of protein structure.
D) none of the above.

527. Thomas, a biology undergrad, conducts an SDS-PAGE procedure on Proteins 1, 2, and 3. Note that mercaptoethanol was used to prepare the proteins involved.

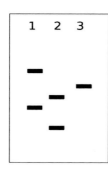

From the results above, Thomas may reasonably conclude all of the following EXCEPT:

A) Protein 2 contains the subunit with the smallest mass in kilodaltons.
B) Protein 1 contains the subunit with the greatest mass in kilodaltons.
C) Proteins 1 and 2 have quaternary structure in their native forms.
D) Protein 2 has a mass smaller than Protein 3.

528. Both myoglobin and hemoglobin are proteins that play crucial physiological roles. They are similar in that they:

A) both demonstrate the effect of cooperativity.
B) both contain the heme prosthetic group.
C) play the exact same physiological role.
D) more than one of the above.

529. The extinction coefficient for a particular protein is 0.685 Lmol⁻¹cm⁻¹. Which value is closest to the protein concentration if the absorbance is 7 and the path length is 1 cm?

A) 0.001 M
B) 0.1 M
C) 1 M
D) 10 M

530. A neurogenetic researcher is attempting to confirm the presence of a particular neurotrophic factor (called ABNF) in a cell extract. She runs a sample through an SDS-PAGE gel and observes a single dark band. Which of the below statements may be true?

I. Only ABNF is present in the sample.
II. Only a contaminant protein is present in the sample.
III. The sample could contain many distinct samples if all had equal or nearly equal masses.

A) I only
B) II only
C) I and II
D) I, II, and III

531. Which of these choices correctly identifies the function of a specific antibody?

I. IgA – present in mucosal areas to prevent colonization by pathogens
II. IgE – binds to allergens, causing the release of histamine
III. IgM – part of the early humoral response, secreted as a pentamer
IV. IgD – responsible for the majority of the humoral response

A) I only
B) I and III
C) I, II, and III
D) I, III, and IV

532. How is the human body able to produce enough unique antibodies to match up with a wide variety of pathogens?

A) The variable regions of the antibodies are altered by post-translational modifications.

B) Separate genes each code for the production of a unique variable region.

C) Random recombination and alternative splicing of gene segments produces the variable regions of the antibodies.

D) All antibodies are the same, but change structure in different ways when they come into contact with an antigen.

533. How does kinesin travel across a microtubule?

A) The hydrolysis of ATP triggers a conformational change in the protein, after which the replacement of ADP with ATP triggers another structural change and completes the cycle.

B) The kinesins bind to the microtubule and travel along with it as the microtubule grows and shrinks.

C) The kinesins only have affinity for alpha-tubulin and move down the microtubule as they switch between alpha-tubulin monomers.

D) The hydrolysis of water triggers a conformational change in the protein that allows it to travel down the microtubule.

534. How do the (+) and (-) ends of actin differ?

A) The monomers on the (+) end are bound to ATP, while those on the (-) end are bound to ADP.

B) The (+) end actin monomers have a greater binding affinity for each other than do those on the (-) end.

C) The (+) end is always closer to the outside of the cell.

D) Both A and B are correct.

535. Which of the following proteins travel down microtubules towards the outside of the cell?

A) Cadherins

B) Kinesins

C) Dyneins

D) Actin

Questions 536–537 rely on the figure below

The structure of an antibody is shown here.

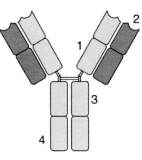

536. Which of the marked regions bind to antigens?

A) 1

B) 2

C) 3

D) 4

537. A scientist wants to create mass quantities of an antibody in a donor animal, then use them to treat human diseases. Which of the numbered parts of the figure would need to be modified after production?

A) 1 only

B) 2 only

C) 1, 3, and 4 only

D) 1 and 2 only

Questions 538–539 rely on the figure below

The graph shows the concentration of free actin monomers on the x-axis, along with whether the total polymer length is increasing or decreasing on the y-axis. The (+) and (-) ends of the actin polymer are each graphed.

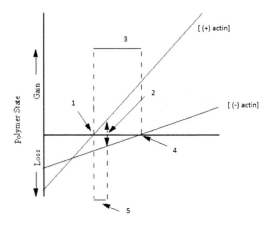

538. At which of the numbered regions will treadmilling occur?

A) 1

B) 4

C) 3

D) 5

539. What is happening at point 2?

A) The actin polymer is growing in size.

B) The rate of polymerization at the (+) end is equal to the rate of depolymerization at the (-) end.

C) The actin polymer is decreasing in size.

D) No polymerization or depolymerization is taking place.

540. A number of scientists are attempting to study the effects of mutating the genes coding for cadherin proteins in cancer cells. After assessing several random mutations, they find a cell culture that does not form desmosomes correctly. However, the gene coding for cadherins appear to be normal. What other cellular function must have been affected by the mutation?

A) The cell has lost the ability to form actin filaments.

B) The cell has lost the ability to produce proteins.

C) The cell has lost the ability to correct DNA mutations.

D) The cell has lost the ability to make intermediate filaments.

541. A biochemist is investigating a reaction featured in human metabolism. He notes that all necessary reactants are present in his test tube and that the process should proceed spontaneously given the conditions, but observes that no products are being made. The most likely explanation is that:

A) the rate of the uncatalyzed reaction is extremely slow.

B) a particular enzyme within live cells changes the mechanism of the reaction.

C) catalysts within human cells increase the amount of free energy released during the course of the reaction.

D) A and B only.

542. A researcher identifies an important metabolic catalyst, Enzyme G, as having a substrate of Protein Y. Enzyme G mediates the conversion of Protein Y into Protein Z via a transition state. The active site of Enzyme G best interacts with and stabilizes:

A) Protein Y.

B) Protein Z.

C) the transition state.

D) all of the above.

543. Catalase is an enzyme found in especially high concentrations in the liver. This molecule catalyzes the conversion of the reactive oxidative species hydrogen peroxide into water and oxygen. In the presence of this enzyme:

A) the conversion of hydrogen peroxide to water and oxygen gas is made spontaneous.

B) the rate of conversion of hydrogen peroxide to water and oxygen gas is increased.

C) the rate of conversion of water and oxygen gas to hydrogen peroxide is increased.

D) more than one of the above.

Questions 544–545 rely on the figure below

The diagram below outlines the first three steps of glycolysis. The letters refer to the enzymes mediating the respective reactions.

```
Glycolysis (Steps 1-3)

Glucose
A) ↓
Glucose-6-phosphate
B) ↓
Fructose-6-phosphate
C) ↓
Fructose-1,6-biphosphate
```

544. Enzyme A, which catalyzes the first step of glycolysis, most likely belongs to which of the following groups of enzymes?

    A) Kinases
    B) Phosphatases
    C) Oxidoreductases
    D) None of the above

545. Which enzyme is likely an example of an isomerase?

    A) A
    B) B
    C) C
    D) None of the above

546. Several distinct graphs are shown below, mapped on the same Cartesian coordinate system.

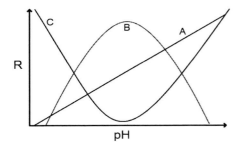

Which plot illustrates the correct relationship between the rate of an enzymatically catalyzed reaction (R) and pH occurring *in vivo*?

    A) A
    B) B
    C) C
    D) Both B and C are commonly exhibited, depending on the particular enzyme.

547. Which of the following enzymes are involved in protein digestion in the small intestine?

    A) Carboxypeptidase
    B) Salivary amylase
    C) Pepsin
    D) All of the above

548. In peripheral blood vessels, carbon dioxide from adjacent tissues diffuses into red blood cells. Here, it is converted into carbonic acid, which in turn dissociates into protons and bicarbonate; this process is catalyzed by the enzyme carbonic anhydrase. In the lungs, bicarbonate reenters the red blood cells, where it is turned back into carbon dioxide. What enzyme catalyzes the reverse reaction?

    A) Carbonic rehydrase
    B) Carboxylase
    C) Carbonic anhydrase
    D) None of the above

549. Priya is investigating the function of Enzyme D, which has a K_m value of 0.175 mM. She adds a large quantity of competitive inhibitor (Compound G) into her test tube. Which of the following is the apparent K_m value that she subsequently observes?

    A) 0.09 mM
    B) 0.10 mM
    C) 0.175 mM
    D) 0.500 mM

550. Which of the following changes may impact the V_{max}, or maximal reaction rate?

    A) Altering the amount of enzyme
    B) Altering the amount of noncompetitive inhibitor
    C) Altering the amount of mixed inhibitor
    D) All of the above

551. Which of these are classifications of water-soluble vitamins?

    I. Prosthetic groups
    II. Coenzymes
    III. Antioxidants
    IV. Carotenoids

    A) I and II
    B) II and IV
    C) III and IV
    D) I, II, and III

552. Which of the following characteristics regarding enzyme-substrate complexes can be explained by the "induced-fit," but not the "lock-and-key," model?

   A) Lowering of reaction activation energy
   B) Rigidity of enzyme tertiary structure
   C) Stabilization of transition state
   D) Enzyme specificity

553. Allosteric regulation is an important part of feedback regulation. All of the functions listed below can be performed by an allosteric molecule EXCEPT:

   A) catalysis of a reaction.
   B) activation of an enzyme.
   C) inhibition of an enzyme.
   D) conformational change of an enzyme.

554. Which statement accurately describes the difference between coenzymes and prosthetic groups?

   A) Coenzymes are covalently bound to their associated enzymes.
   B) Coenzymes are released from the enzyme's active site during a reaction.
   C) Prosthetic groups are metal ions that are located at the enzyme's core.
   D) Prosthetic groups can transport functional groups between enzymes.

555. Which of the following statements accurately describes active site-substrate interactions?

   A) Both the active site and the substrate can change shape to facilitate tight binding.
   B) The active site can change its shape to tightly bind to the substrate, but the substrate cannot change its own shape.
   C) The substrate can change its shape to tightly bind to the active site, but the active site cannot change its own shape.
   D) Neither the active site nor the substrate can change shape.

Questions 556–557 rely on the figure below

Consider this molecular diagram of hemoglobin.

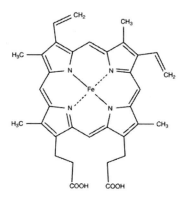

556. The iron atom at the center of the hemoglobin molecule is essential to its proper functioning. Which term most accurately describes this atom?

   A) Prosthetic group
   B) Cofactor
   C) Coenzyme
   D) Heme

557. If this iron atom acted like typical coenzymes, which are loosely bound to their associated enzymes and can dissociate immediately after the catalyzed reaction, how would hemoglobin's ability to transport oxygen be altered?

   A) Hemoglobin-oxygen binding affinity would dramatically decrease due to the prevention of cooperative binding.
   B) There would be no effect on hemoglobin's binding affinity to oxygen because the iron typically falls off after O_2 binds.
   C) Hemoglobin-oxygen binding affinity would be reduced due to increased competition from protons and carbon monoxide.
   D) Hemoglobin-oxygen binding affinity would increase due to reduced steric hindrance in the active site.

Questions 558–559 rely on the figure below

In this hypothetical metabolic pathway, the products of certain enzymatic reactions are used in subsequent reactions until product "P" is formed. Product "P" then binds to enzyme A, denaturing it.

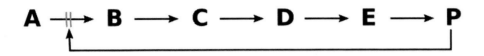

558. What kind of regulatory mechanism best describes this process?

    A) Allosteric inhibition
    B) Induced fit
    C) A feed-forward mechanism
    D) Feedback inhibition

559. If a researcher wanted to stop the production of product "P" *in vivo*, which point in the pathway would be the most reasonable to inhibit in order to minimize side effects?

    A) Enzyme A
    B) Enzyme E
    C) Any of the enzymes would be equally reasonable.
    D) None of the enzymes would be reasonable to inhibit.

560. The phosphorylation of proteins or DNA is an important regulatory mechanism. Which statement best explains the function of phosphorylation in regulation?

    A) Phosphorylation increases with age, allowing selective targeting of older DNA molecules for degradation.
    B) Kinase enzymes add phosphate groups to mitochondria during exercise to balance the charge distribution needed for ATP synthesis.
    C) Phosphorylation of enzymes changes their conformations, thereby allowing cells to determine when the enzyme is active.
    D) DNA is phosphorylated to increase the accuracy of replication during the cell cycle.

561. In the body, CO_2 is released by tissues and converted to bicarbonate and protons in a two-step reaction that is mediated by the catalyst carbonic anhydrase. The reaction scheme in the absence of this enzyme is shown below.

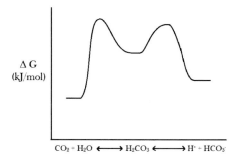

How will the reaction scheme appear when carbonic anhydrase is present?

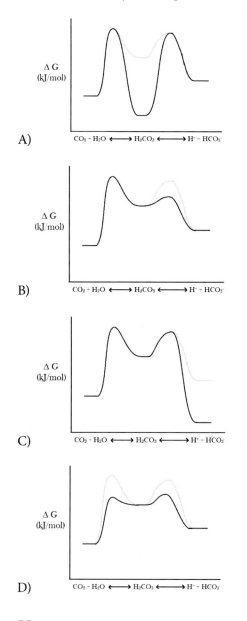

A)

B)

C)

D)

562. When hemoglobin binds to protons, its affinity for oxygen decreases. This is an example of:

A) positive cooperativity.
B) negative cooperativity.
C) competitive inhibition.
D) feedback inhibition.

563. The reaction below is a process in the citric acid cycle that is mediated by aconitase. Michaelis-Menten kinetics may be used to determine its initial velocity.

$$\text{Citrate} \underset{k_{-1}}{\overset{k_1}{\rightleftharpoons}} \text{Cis-Aconitase} \overset{k_2}{\longrightarrow} \text{Isocitrate}$$

Which of the following changes will result in an increased initial velocity for this reaction?

A) An increase in K_m
B) A decrease in the concentration of citrate
C) A decrease in k_{-1}
D) A decrease in V_{max}

564. The conversion of pyruvate to acetyl-CoA is mediated by the enzyme pyruvate dehydrogenase.

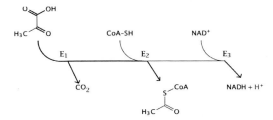

Which of the following equations relates to the rate in which the ES complex is formed? (Note: $[PD]_t$ = total concentration of pyruvate dehydrogenase, [PD-Y] = concentration of the pyruvate dehydrogenase complex bound to pyruvate, [Y] = concentration of pyruvate, [A] = concentration of acetyl-CoA, k_1 = rate constant for PD-Y formation from pyruvate and the pyruvate dehydrogenase complex, k_{-1} = rate constant of the reverse reaction)

A) $k_1[Y]$
B) $k_{-1}[Y]$
C) $k_1([PD]_t - [PD-Y])[Y]$

D) $k_{-1}([PD-Y] - [PD]_t)[Y]$

565. Consider the figure below.

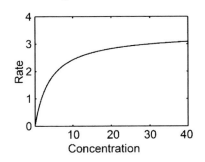

What value represents the K_m of this reaction?

A) 2
B) 10
C) 14
D) 22

566. What is the value for K_m if 50 M of substrate are present and the initial reaction velocity is ¼ of the V_{max}?

A) 25
B) 50
C) 100
D) 150

567. Consider the following Lineweaver-Burk plot.

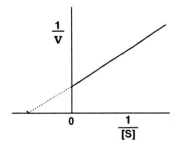

What can be said about the V_{max} of the corresponding process?

A) V_{max} = slope
B) V_{max} = slope(y-intercept)$^{-1}$
C) V_{max} = (y-intercept)$^{-1}$
D) V_{max} = -(x-intercept)

568. Consider the Lineweaver-Burk plot shown below.

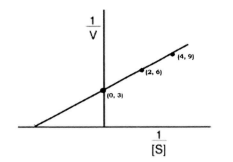

What is the value for K_m for this reaction?

A) -0.5
B) 0.5
C) 1.5
D) 3.0

569. If additional enzyme is added to a reaction flask, how the Lineweaver-Burk plot of the reaction be affected?

A)
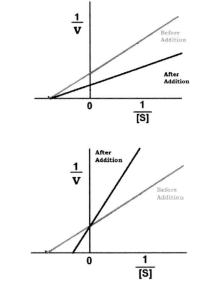

B)
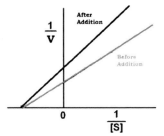

C)
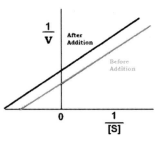

D)

570. The addition of an enzyme to a reaction will affect all of the following values EXCEPT:

A) the rate of the forward reaction.
B) the rate of the reverse reaction.
C) the energy released by the reaction.
D) the activation energy.

571. A digestive enzyme is present in a test tube along with Compound A, its substrate. When Compound B is included in the reaction mixture, the rate of decomposition of A is slowed considerably. If a large quantity of A is then added to the mixture, the decomposition can be restored to its maximal rate. Which of the following statements is most likely true about Compounds A and B?

A) Compound B structurally resembles Compound A and fits into the enzyme's active site.
B) Compound B binds with a position on the enzyme that is not the active site.
C) Compound B interacts with Compound A via noncovalent forces.
D) Compound A forms a heterodimer with Compound B.

572. The glycolytic enzyme phosphofructokinase mediates the phosphorylation of fructose-6-phosphate, resulting in fructose-1,6-biphosphate. Phosphofructokinase activity is allosterically inhibited by ATP, NADH, and citrate. This inhibition is probably an instance of:

A) competitive inhibition.
B) positive feedback.
C) negative feedback.
D) aerobic takeover.

Questions 573–574 rely on the graph below

An experiment is conducted to examine the kinetics of a metabolic enzyme under three different conditions. Curve A describes the kinetics of the enzyme in the absence of inhibition. Curves B and C describe the enzyme's kinetics after the addition of one of two different inhibitors, Compounds B and C, respectively.

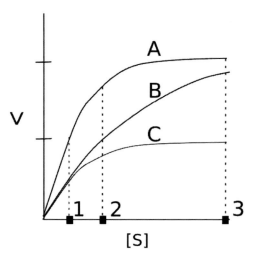

573. Substrate concentration at point 1 equals the enzyme's apparent K_m value under which of the following experimental conditions?

    I.   A
    II. B
    III. C

    A) I only
    B) II only
    C) I and III only
    D) I, II, and III

574. Upon further resolution with X-ray crystallography, the enzyme was shown to possess several potential binding positions in addition to the active site. One of these sites is likely the target of:

    A) Compound B.
    B) Compound C.
    C) both compounds.
    D) neither Compound B nor C.

575. The active site of Enzyme X features many aspartic and glutamic acid residues. Upregulated activity of this enzyme is implicated in a variety of diseases. A researcher at a pharmaceutical company isolates four different competitive inhibitors of Enzyme X for potential use as drugs. It is likely that these compounds all have:

    A) structures that complement the active site of Enzyme X.
    B) a concentration of lysine or arginine residues in certain parts of their structures.
    C) structures resembling that of Enzyme X.
    D) both A and B.

576. Luke is conducting an experiment with a particular enzyme in a reaction vessel. He knows that there may be a mystery inhibitor (Compound X) present in the vessel or no inhibitor at all. As he adds substrate to the tube, he observes an increase in the rate of reaction. Which of the following conclusions can Luke reasonably make?

    A) Compound X is present and is a competitive inhibitor.
    B) Compound X is present and is a noncompetitive inhibitor.
    C) No inhibitor is present.
    D) None of the above.

Questions 577–578 rely on the graph below

Catalase is an enzyme that facilitates the decomposition of hydrogen peroxide, a reactive species, into oxygen and water. The Lineweaver-Burk plot below describes experiments conducted with catalase. The dashed line corresponds to the control trial, in which the enzyme is uninhibited.

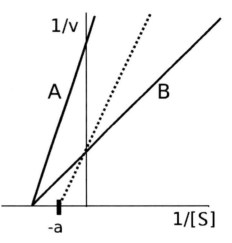

577. Catalase is noncompetitively inhibited, and the kinetics of the reaction as a function of substrate concentration are observed. Which of the plot lines describes the most likely result?

    A) A
    B) B
    C) No visible change is made to the Lineweaver-Burk plot, so the dashed line is observed again.
    D) None of the above.

578. The apparent K_m of the uninhibited enzyme is represented by the quantity:

    A) a.
    B) -a.
    C) 1/a.
    D) -1/a.

579. Molecule A is an inactive enzyme. Upon cleavage of some of its covalent bonds by an accessory enzyme, Molecule A is converted to Enzyme B, an enzymatically active, less massive protein. Which best describes the relationship between Molecule A and Enzyme B?

    A) Molecule A is the zymogen precursor to Enzyme B.
    B) Molecule A is a catalyst in the synthesis of Enzyme B.
    C) Molecule A and Enzyme B form an enzyme-substrate complex that is separated.
    D) None of the above.

580. In the presence of 2,3-biphosphoglyceric acid (2,3-BPG), the hemoglobin-O_2 saturation curve is shifted to the right. This is an instance of:

    A) competitive inhibition.
    B) covalent post-translational modification.
    C) zymogen activation.
    D) allosteric regulation.

581. Which of these zymogens could participate in autocatalytic cleavage at pH 3?

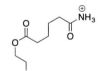

I.

II.

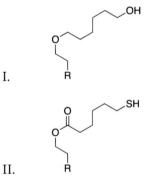

III.

IV.

    A) IV only
    B) I and II
    C) I and IV
    D) III and IV

582. Chymotrypsin is an intestinal enzyme that is used to digest proteins. In the absence of food, chymotrypsin does not digest any non-target proteins because chymotrypsin:

    A) is activated allosterically by leucine, an essential amino acid that can only be found in the diet.
    B) is synthesized as a zymogen, which is activated by other digestive enzymes in the presence of food.
    C) is localized to the duodenum, which is coated in an enzyme-resistant mucus.
    D) has an active site that can only bind to non-native proteins.

583.

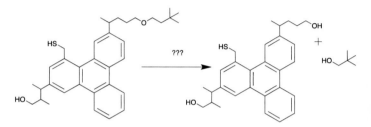

Which reagent is missing from the reaction above, which depicts the activation of a zymogen?

    A) EtOH
    B) H_2O_2
    C) H_2O
    D) NaOH

Questions 584–585 rely on the figure below

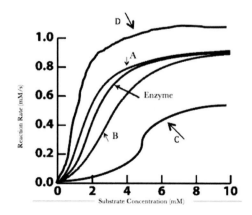

584. Which line in the above figure depicts the effect of an allosteric activator on the activity of an enzyme?

A) A
B) B
C) C
D) D

585. In the presence of an allosteric activator, doubling substrate concentration from 9 mM to 18 mM would:

A) increase the absolute value of V_{max}.
B) increase the rate of reaction to achieve V_{max}.
C) have no effect on the rate of reaction.
D) slow the rate of reaction.

586. There are many ways to covalently modify an enzyme. A kinase enzyme facilitates which covalent modification?

A) Phosphorylation
B) Acetylation
C) Hydration
D) Methylation

587. The figure below shows the reaction kinetics for Enzymes A and B, which correspond to Curves A and B, respectively.

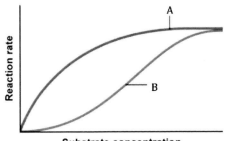

Given this figure, which of the following statements is true?

A) Enzyme A exhibits non-Michaelis-Menten kinetics.
B) Allosteric inhibition of enzyme B would slow the initial rate, but Curve B would eventually reach the same maximum.
C) If Enzyme A were competitively inhibited, Curve A would reach a lower maximum.
D) Allosteric activation of enzyme B would shift the curve up to reach a higher maximum value.

588. Hemoglobin consists of four subunits that bind O_2. The affinity for O_2 increases in each subunit as neighboring units bind the diatomic molecule. Hemoglobin exhibits which form of enzyme kinetics, and due to which effect(s) of its subunits?

A) Michaelis-Menten, allosteric
B) non-Michaelis-Menten, allosteric
C) non-Michaelis-Menten, amphiphilic
D) Michaelis-Menten, inhibiting

589. Consider the four simple plots below.

Which figure depicts the kinetics of hemoglobin?

A) A
B) B
C) C
D) D

590. The active site of an enzyme binds positively-charged molecules, but a researcher discovers that the enzyme is inhibited when it interacts with a certain large anion. This molecule likely:

A) dimerizes the enzyme.
B) competitively binds at the active site.
C) allosterically binds at the active site.
D) allosterically binds at a regulatory site.

591. A researcher isolates the human cDNA for β-globin, a protein present in high concentrations in certain stages of red blood cell development, and finds that it is 438 nucleotide pairs long. Using the cDNA clone as a probe, he isolates the DNA that encodes β-globin from a human genomic library. The genomic clone is sequenced and found to be 1328 nucleotide pairs long. What accounts for the difference in observed length between the two fragments?

A) All DNA clones in the human genomic library have highly repetitive telomere sequences that are absent in cDNA clones.
B) Post-transcriptionally modified mRNA is used as template to create cDNA.
C) Post-transcriptionally modified cDNA is used as template to create DNA clones in the human genomic library.
D) Exons had been excised from the cDNA clone.

592. Restriction enzymes recognize palindromic sequences in intact double-stranded DNA helices. Since the bases are located on the inside of the strand (surrounded by the sugar-phosphate backbone), how does the enzyme accomplish this?

    A) Restriction enzymes cleave only when helicase has unwound the DNA double helix during replication.
    B) Restriction enzymes bind to the minor groove in the double helix, allowing them to find the recognition sites by hydrogen bonding with the palindromic bases.
    C) Restriction enzymes bind to the major groove in the double helix, allowing them to find the recognition sites by hydrogen bonding with the palindromic bases.
    D) Restriction enzymes bind to the backbone of the double helix, allowing them to find the recognition sites by hydrogen bonding with phosphate groups corresponding to the palindromic bases.

Questions 593–595 rely on the figure below

An ampicillin-resistant, tetracycline-resistant plasmid, pBR413, is used to develop a *Drosophila* DNA library. The plasmid is cleaved with *Eco*RI, then ligated with *Eco*RI-digested *Drosophila* DNA. The mixture is used to transform *E. coli* cells.

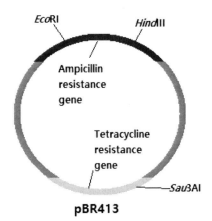

pBR413

593. Which antibiotic should be added to the medium to select *E. coli* cells that have incorporated the plasmid?

A) Ampicillin
B) Tetracycline
C) Both ampicillin and tetracycline
D) No antibiotic should be added.

594. What growth pattern should be selected to screen for plasmids that have successfully incorporated the *Drosophila* inserts?

A) Colonies that grow on both tetracycline and ampicillin media
B) Colonies that grow on an ampicillin medium but fail to show growth on a tetracycline medium
C) Colonies that fail to show growth on both tetracycline and ampicillin media
D) Colonies that grow on a tetracycline medium but fail to show growth on an ampicillin medium

595. A small number of colonies are able to grow in a medium containing both ampicillin and tetracycline. Which choice could NOT explain the presence of bacteria resistant to both antibiotics?

A) Cleavage with *Eco*RI was incomplete.
B) The cleaved ends of the plasmid were ligated together without incorporating the insert.
C) The bacteria failed to incorporate the plasmid.
D) The proper restriction enzyme was not used in developing the recombinant plasmid.

596. Which of the following DNA segments contains a restriction enzyme recognition sequence?

A) GTAAGGTTGAGT
B) GTAAGCTTCACG
C) GGATTCCTTGAG
D) GGATACCTTGAT

597. A researcher studying the efficacy of *Eco*RI decides to cleave a linear double-stranded DNA molecule with the restriction enzyme under non-optimal conditions. The dsDNA is 1000 base pairs long and contains two *Eco*RI recognition sites at base 12 and base 300. If the digested dsDNA is subjected to size-exclusion chromatography, what is the maximum possible number of elution peaks?

A) 3

B) 5

C) 6

D) Size-exclusion chromatography can only be used with protein.

598. You are attempting to isolate human pancreatic mRNAs to create a cDNA library. First, you successfully grow the pancreatic cells in a culture. You then apply a solution of labeled poly-thymine oligonucleotides that will hybridize to the complementary poly-adenine tails of the mRNAs. Unfortunately, you find that the labeled poly-T oligonucleotides do not bind to anything in the culture. What could explain this?

A) The pancreatic cell wall was not lysed before the labeled poly-T oligonucleotides were applied.

B) All mRNA that hybridized with the poly-T oligonucleotides was enzymatically degraded by mRNase enzymes.

C) In eukaryotic cells, poly-A tails are not attached to mRNA.

D) The pancreatic cell membrane was not rendered permeable to the poly-T oligonucleotides.

599. Which of the following are true statements regarding genomic and cDNA libraries?

I. A genomic library contains at least one copy of all of the sequences in an organism's genome.

II. A cDNA library contains only expressed sequences of a genome.

III. A cDNA library contains copies of DNA that was transcriptionally active in the cell at the time the library was made.

A) I only

B) II only

C) I and II only

D) I, II, and III

600. A DNA sequence implicated in certain cancers has been analyzed using the Sanger dideoxynucleotide sequencing technique. You have prepared the sequencing gel as shown in the figure above.

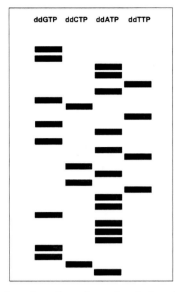

Assuming that the gel was loaded at the top, what is the sequence of the DNA?

A) 5'-CCTTATCGACTCTAGTG ATTCTTTCCGT-3'

B) 5'-GGAATAGCTGAGATCAC TAAGAAAGGCA-3'

C) 3'-CCTTATCGACTCTAGTGA TTCTTTCCGT-3'

D) 3'-GGAATAGCTGAGATCAC TAAGAAAGGCA-5'

601. A typical polymerase chain reaction is conducted using DNA polymerase derived from *T. aquaticus*, a bacterium. Which of these experimental conditions is LEAST likely to denature this species-specific polymerase?

A) Treatment with 12% trichloroacetic acid solution

B) Treatment with 6 M guanidinium chloride solution

C) Exposure to temperatures in excess of 90 °C

D) Exposure to sustained mechanical agitation

602. When selecting a buffer for PCR, it is most important to ensure that the solution contains:

A) magnesium cations.

B) free ribonucleotide triphosphates.

C) hydroxide anions.

D) pyrophosphate anions.

603. Circular dichroism (CD) spectroscopy is a versatile spectroscopic technique that is routinely employed to probe biomolecular secondary structure. If CD spectroscopy were used to follow the progress of a polymerase chain reaction, the resulting spectra would most likely:

    A) be identical for all phases of the thermal cycle, because the chirality of the individual nucleotides is constant.
    B) be identical regardless of reaction progress, because the DNA double helix is always right-handed in solution.
    C) vary depending on the particular phase of the thermal cycle, because heating disrupts the native double helix.
    D) vary depending on the particular phase of the thermal cycle, because *Taq* polymerase denatures during the heating phase.

604. Suppose that a biochemist wishes to monitor a polymerase chain reaction using simple calorimetric techniques. During the melting phase, how does the temperature of the reaction solution change?

    A) It rapidly increases.
    B) It rapidly decreases.
    C) It remains relatively constant.
    D) It slowly increases.

605. Which of the following must be completely disrupted for dissociation of the DNA double helix to occur?

    I.   Hydrophobic interactions between stacked bases
    II. Hydrogen bonding between complementary bases
    III. Charge-charge interactions between phosphate groups
    IV. Hydrogen bonding between DNA and solvating water molecules

    A) II only
    B) I and II
    C) III and IV
    D) I, II, and IV

606. Typically, the melting and annealing phases of PCR are run at approximately 96°C and 68°C, respectively. The polymerization phase, during which nucleotides are actively added to the growing 3' end, must proceed at 72°C for optimal activity. Which of these statements gives a plausible reason for the fact that optimal polymerization occurs at a temperature slightly higher than the annealing temperature?

    A) *Taq* polymerase is first synthesized as an inactive precursor that must be hydrolytically cleaved by high temperatures.
    B) The slightly elevated temperature prevents unproductive annealing of non-complementary strands.
    C) Since primers are very short and form few hydrogen bonds, their dissociation is inducible with only slight heating.
    D) Temperatures that are too low are likely to restrict changes in protein conformation.

607. Which of these procedural measures would contribute most to optimal PCR function and a high yield of the desired product?

    A) Selection of a primer sequence that does not complement itself
    B) Addition of metal chelating agents to the reaction solution
    C) Use of a dNTP solution with very high pyrimidine concentrations and relatively low purine concentrations
    D) Use of a DNA sample with an extremely high molecular weight

608. A simple denaturation curve for a sample of exon DNA is shown below.

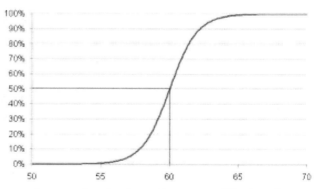

A researcher is attempting to amplify the telomere region of a eukaryotic chromosome using PCR. Compared to the curve depicted above, the segment of his curve at the labeled point, 50% denaturation ($T_m 50$), would most likely be:

A) shifted to the right, because telomeres contain abundant GC repeats.

B) shifted to the left, because telomeres contain abundant GC repeats.

C) higher in the vertical direction, because telomeres contain abundant GC repeats.

D) lower in the vertical direction, because telomeres contain abundant GC repeats.

609. Reverse transcription polymerase chain reaction (RT-PCR) is a variation on the classic PCR protocol. One essential difference is the presence of reverse transcriptase, the same enzyme produced by HIV virions during infection. Primers are generally six to nine bases in length and consist of random, non-repeating nucleotides that anneal to various points along the sample molecule. A rudimentary diagram of the RT-PCR process is depicted below.

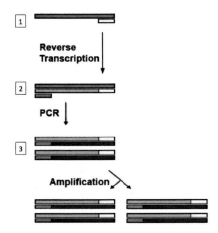

One researcher wants to assess for the presence of the original nucleic acid (labeled 1) in his final reaction solution following amplification. After separating the components of the solution by gel electrophoresis and transferring them to a nitrocellulose membrane, the most appropriate oligonucleotide probe to detect this leftover starting material would be composed of:

A) many repeating adenine nucleotides.

B) many repeating thymidine nucleotides.

C) alternating guanine and cytosine nucleotides.

D) alternating adenine and uracil nucleotides.

610. Far-western blotting is a variation on the more commonly used western blotting. In this technique, a tissue extract containing many proteins is transferred to a nitrocellulose membrane; proteins of interest are then detected using radiolabeled "bait" proteins. Generally, these bait molecules are recombinant products that are selected according to known protein-protein interactions with the "prey" species on the membrane. Considering that the far-western blotting protocol involves denaturation of the prey proteins before application of the bait molecules, it most likely detects the presence of "prey" using which type of interaction?

A) Covalent bonding between two amino acid residues

B) Hydrophobic interactions in specific binding pockets

C) A lock-and-key mechanism between two active sites

D) Hydrogen bonding between unique structural motifs

611. How can a western blot be used to analyze gene expression of a cell?

A) It can be used to amplify a gene to produce many copies for use in further analysis.

B) It can determine the specific nucleotide sequence of the gene.

C) It can determine the identity and size of a protein produced by the cell.

D) It can be used to identify mRNA products of the gene of interest.

612. One criticism of germ line gene therapy is it could ultimately lead to eugenics. What is eugenics?

A) The introduction of foreign DNA into the human genome

B) The practice of using stem cells from individuals without their consent

C) A set of belief and practices aimed at deliberately controlling and improving the genetic makeup of human populations

D) The resistance to pesticides and antibiotics through the manipulation of genomes

613. What type of human cells are the only known pluripotent cells?

A) Bone marrow stem cells

B) Embryonic stem cells

C) Adipose stem cells

D) Liver stem cells

Questions 614–615 rely on the figure below

A researcher theorizes that a particular gene is integral to metabolism of lactose in mice. She decides to run an experiment in which she knocks out two different genes. In Strain A, she knocks out Gene A, and in Strain B she knocks out Gene B. She then analyzes the mice for their ability to metabolize lactose. Her findings are shown in the figure below.

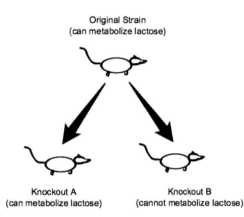

Original Strain
(can metabolize lactose)

Knockout A
(can metabolize lactose)

Knockout B
(cannot metabolize lactose)

614. What can we conclude from the experiment?

A) Gene A was integral to the metabolism of lactose.

B) Gene B was integral to the metabolism of lactose.

C) Neither Genes A nor B were integral to the metabolism of lactose.

D) Both Genes A and B were integral to the metabolism of lactose.

615. If the researcher created a new strain that knocked out a third gene, Gene C, and later found out that that strain could not metabolize lactose, what would this indicate?

A) Genes A and C are integral to the metabolism of lactose.

B) Gene C is the only gene integral to the metabolism of lactose.

C) Gene C is more important than Gene B in the metabolism of lactose.

D) Multiple genes must be responsible for the metabolism of lactose.

616. The surface protein of a harmful bacterium is cloned into a harmless virus. How could this be used therapeutically?

A) This type of virus could not be used therapeutically, as it would harm the patient.

B) The virus could be administered to a patient to promote viral attack of the harmful bacterium.

C) The virus could be used as a vector for the effective transfer of the gene coding for the surface protein into the genome of the participant.

D) The virus could be administered as a vaccine so the patient's immune system would recognize the surface protein in case of future contact.

Questions 617–618 rely on the figure below

A student performs a western blot, shown here. He uses samples from two separate bacterial colonies to determine whether each is producing a protein of interest. Lane A represents a marker, Lane B corresponds Colony B, and Lane C corresponds to Colony C. Figure 1 shows the primary blotting onto a nitrocellulose cellulose membrane, while Figure 2 depicts the blot after introduction of a fluorescently-marked antibody for the protein of interest.

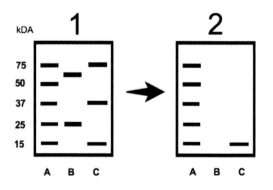

617. What can the student conclude about the expression of this protein in the two colonies?

A) Both Colonies B and C produce ample amounts of the protein of interest.

B) Only Colony C produces the protein, which is approximately 15 kDa in size.

C) Colony C produces approximately 33% more of the protein than Colony B.

D) Only Colony C produces the protein, which is approximately 25 kDa in size.

618. If the student mistakenly used an antibody for a different protein without realizing it, what can be concluded regarding the experiment?

    A) We cannot determine whether either colony produces the protein of interest.
    B) Neither Colony B nor C produces the protein of interest.
    C) Colony C produces the protein, but its size is likely represented incorrectly.
    D) Both Colonies B and C produce the protein of interest.

619. Severe combined immunodeficiency (SCID) was the first disease that was successfully treated using gene therapy. Unfortunately, a small number of patients later developed leukemia, representing one of the risks of gene therapy. How might these leukemias have developed?

    A) The virus used to transfer the cloned gene ended up attacking the patient and producing a cancer.
    B) As a result of viral infection, the immune function of these patients became impaired.
    C) The randomly integrated DNA may have activated an oncogene, causing leukemia.
    D) The virus could have triggered action of a tumor suppressor, causing leukemia.

620. Which technique could be used to determine protein expression in various cellular components in a sample of tissue?

    A) Immunohistochemistry
    B) Western blot
    C) Southern blot
    D) Enzyme-linked immunosorbent assay (ELISA)

621. Two proteins of interest are isolated from a cell lysate and run on a 2D SDS-PAGE, shown below.

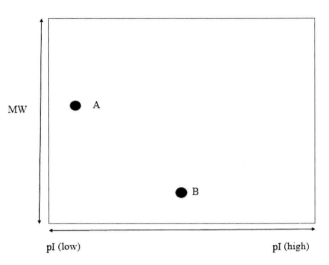

Which description of the locations of the two proteins is most consistent with the data in the figure?

    A) Both proteins A and B are soluble proteins.
    B) Both proteins A and B are contained within the plasma membrane.
    C) Protein A is contained within the plasma membrane, while protein B is soluble.
    D) Protein A is soluble, while protein B is contained within the plasma membrane.

622. What is the purpose of using SDS as a reagent when running an SDS-PAGE protocol?

    A) It ensures that the largest proteins are the first to reach the bottom of the gel.
    B) It reduces S-S bonds between cysteine residues.
    C) It denatures the primary structure of the protein.
    D) It linearizes the protein and provides a uniform charge-to-mass ratio for each sample.

623. Suppose a hereditary disease can be diagnosed using simple protein detection in fluid taken from a tissue biopsy. A family is tested to determine the pattern of inheritance, which is known to be based on a single gene and follow Mendelian laws.

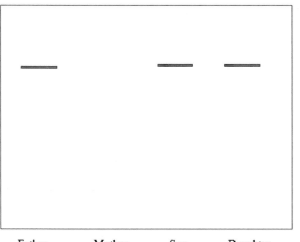

Father   Mother   Son   Daughter

Based on this nitrocellulose membrane after antibody incubation, what is the most likely inheritance pattern? Assume that presence of the protein indicates the diseased state and that those who do not display the disease phenotype are not carriers.

A) Autosomal dominant
B) Autosomal recessive
C) Sex-linked dominant
D) Sex-linked recessive

624. The mutant version of a murine protein weighs 50 kDa and contains more lysine residues than the 75-kDa wild-type protein. Which of the following pairs, based on the figure of the gel below, could represent these two proteins?

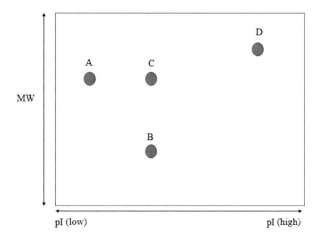

A) Protein A is the mutant protein and protein C is the wild-type protein.
B) Protein B is the mutant protein and protein D is the wild-type protein
C) Protein B is the mutant protein and protein A is the wild-type protein.
D) Protein D is the mutant protein and protein A is the wild-type protein.

625. A protein from a cell lysate was identified using separation in a gel followed by transfer to a nitrocellulose membrane and antibody detection. This method is called:

A) western blotting.
B) northern blotting.
C) ELISA.
D) 2D SDS-PAGE.

626. Which of the following assays would NOT help identify a protein found in the serum of a human patient during diagnostic testing?

A) ELISA
B) SDS-PAGE
C) FISH
D) Western blotting

627. An absorbance vs. time plot of the runoff from a protein separation column is shown below.

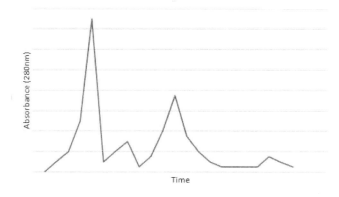

Time

Which conclusion can be drawn about the source of the proteins, assuming the column is designed by the researcher to elute small proteins first and larger ones later?

A) The source had few large proteins.
B) One of the smaller proteins was the most abundant.
C) The source had at most four different proteins.
D) The sample was heavily contaminated with DNA or RNA.

628. A researcher wants to use ELISA to measure the amount of a certain antigen in a blood sample. This procedure will require:

I.   SDS.
II. a reducing agent.
III. a capture antibody.
IV. an agarose gel.

   A) III only
   B) IV only
   C) I and II
   D) I, II, and III

629. When running an SDS-PAGE procedure, researchers often add a reducing agent such as beta-mercaptoethanol (BME). What purpose does this serve?

   A) BME denatures primary and secondary structure.
   B) BME adds a uniform charge to the protein.
   C) BME denatures the protein's tertiary structure.
   D) BME converts free thiol groups to disulfide bridges.

630. A protein is isolated from the blood of a patient undergoing a diagnostic test. After purification, the protein is run on an SDS-PAGE gel, where two distinct bands appear. What is a possible explanation for this result?

   A) The protein was handled poorly and degraded.
   B) SDS partially denatured the primary structure of the protein.
   C) The protein contained two subunits of different molecular weights.
   D) The sample actually contained two different proteins.

631. One of the many applications of high-performance liquid chromatography (HPLC) is the detection of performance-enhancing drugs in urine. What characteristic(s) of this technique make it advantageous over more traditional types of chromatography?

I.   Higher operational pressures
II. Smaller column dimensions
III. Smaller sorbent particles in the column
IV. A special solvent that gives superior resolving power

   A) I and II
   B) II and IV
   C) III and IV
   D) I, II, and III

632. Paper chromatography is conducted on chromatography paper made of cellulose, a polar substance. If a mixture of methane and vinegar is eluted with a nonpolar solvent such as chloroform, which compound would you expect to have the largest R_f value?

   A) Methane, because it migrated less than vinegar.
   B) Vinegar, because it traveled farther than methane.
   C) Methane, because it is nonpolar.
   D) Vinegar, because it is polar.

633. Three amino acids are subjected to reversed-phase chromatography: arginine, phenylalanine, and serine. From first to last, in what order will these compounds be eluted?

   A) Arginine, serine, phenylalanine
   B) Phenylalanine, serine, arginine
   C) Serine, arginine, phenylalanine
   D) All three amino acids will elute together.

634. If a biochemist wanted to purify a protein that was labeled with a His6 tag, which chromatographic technique would be the most appropriate?

   A) Ion-exchange chromatography
   B) Size-exclusion chromatography
   C) Thin-layer chromatography
   D) Affinity chromatography

635. Which of the following statements regarding size-exclusion chromatography is true?

   A) Smaller molecules take longer to elute because they are trapped by the stationary phase.
   B) Larger molecules take less time to elute because their movement is impeded by the stationary phase.
   C) Polar molecules take longer to elute because they interact with the polar stationary phase.
   D) Nonpolar molecules take longer to elute because they interact with the nonpolar stationary phase.

Questions 636–637 rely on the figure below

Two scientists created a chromatogram to describe the elution of a mixture of two unknown compounds.

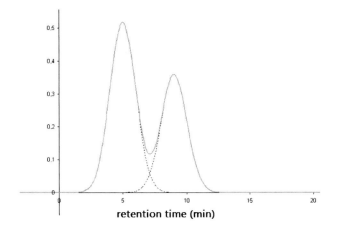

retention time (min)

636. If this were a size-exclusion chromatogram for a solution containing benzene and methane, which of the following would be accurate?

   A) The first peak must represent benzene because it is larger than the second peak.
   B) Benzene exhibits resonance, giving it a higher affinity for the beads within the column.
   C) Methane must have taken longer to elute because it is smaller and would be trapped by the stationary phase.
   D) Benzene must be represented by the second peak, since its movement is slowed by the beads within the column.

637. If the mixture consisted of alanine and glutamic acid and was run through a conventional ion-exchange column, in which peak would glutamic acid be found?

   A) The first peak, because glutamic acid is larger than alanine.
   B) The second peak, because glutamic acid interacts more with the functional groups on the ion-exchange resin.
   C) The first peak, because the charged side chain of the acid is repelled by the ion-exchange resin.
   D) Both peaks, because glutamic acid interacts with the resin and the nonpolar solvent equally.

Questions 638–639 rely on the figure below

A thin-layer chromatography experiment is conducted with an alumina stationary phase and a hexane solvent.

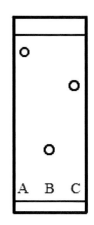

638. Rank the above samples in order of increasing polarity.

   A) A < B < C
   B) B < C < A
   C) A < C < B
   D) B < A < C

639. If the plate is 12 cm long, the solvent front traveled a total of 10 cm, and Sample C migrated exactly 4 cm, what would be its R_f value?

   A) 0.25
   B) 0.4
   C) 4
   D) 6

640. All of the following chromatographic methods are used to purify substances EXCEPT:

   A) size-exclusion chromatography.
   B) affinity chromatography.
   C) ion-exchange chromatography.
   D) thin-layer chromatography.

Questions 641–643 rely on the figure below

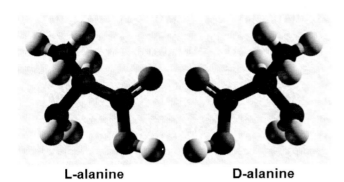

L-alanine   **D-alanine**

641. Most amino acids have two isomeric forms, known as L- and D-forms, that differ in arrangement around the chiral alpha carbon. What is the relationship between these two isomers?

A) They are enantiomers, but only L amino acids are used to build protein in cells.

B) They are enantiomers, but only D amino acids are used to build protein in cells.

C) They are diastereomers, but only L amino acids are used to build protein in cells.

D) They are diastereomers, but only D amino acids are used to build protein in cells.

642. A scientist finds a small bottle containing one or more amino acid(s). He attempts to further purify the solution into its separate enantiomers to assess optical activity. However, he discovers that none of the fractions rotate plane-polarized light. If the scientist has conducted his procedure properly, which is most likely to be true?

A) The scientist cannot possibly have any amino acids in solution.

B) The scientist has a bottle of leucine, because it is achiral.

C) The scientist has a bottle of isoleucine and leucine, because their net optical activities cancel.

D) The scientist has a bottle of glycine, because it is achiral.

643. Which type of chromatography would most effectively separate alanine from other amino acids with dissimilar properties in a sample at pH 1.0?

A) Cation-exchange chromatography

B) Anion-exchange chromatography

C) Size-exchange chromatography

D) Nickel affinity chromatography

644. Of the following amino acids, the one most likely to be a neutral zwitterion is:

A) alanine at pH 5.

B) tyrosine at pH 12.

C) lysine at pH 4.

D) glycine at pH 1.

645. Hair is composed of proteins known as keratins. In chemical hair-straightening treatments, curly hair is semi-permanently relaxed into straight hair. During these treatments, alkalis are used to reduce the disulfide bonds formed between residues in the keratin. Which amino acid is found in keratin, and how is it affected by the alkali treatment?

A) Threonine; the alkalis reduce, and thus form, new disulfide bonds between threonine residues.

B) Serine; the alkalis reduce, and thus form, new disulfide bonds between serine residues.

C) Cysteine; the alkalis reduce, and thus break, existing disulfide bonds between cysteine residues.

D) Methionine; the alkalis reduce, and thus break, existing disulfide bonds between methionine residues.

646. To study peptide bond formation, a scientist radiolabels an oxygen in the carboxyl group of an amino acid, as indicated by the arrow below.

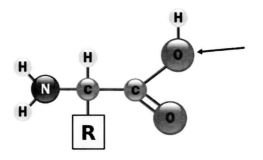

If the amino acid is then incorporated into a polypeptide, where would the scientist expect to find the labeled oxygen atom?

A) Included as part of a water molecule
B) Included as part of an oxygen molecule
C) On the N-terminus of the polypeptide
D) The answer to this question cannot be determined.

Questions 647–649 rely on the figure below

A 1 M solution of glycine is titrated with NaOH according to the following titration curve.

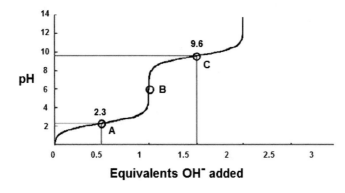

647. What is the approximate isoelectric point (pI) of glycine?

A) 2.3
B) 6.0
C) 8.0
D) 9.6

648. A student in the middle of performing this titration measures the current pH of the solution at 6.0. Suddenly, he accidentally drops a large vial of 1 M NaOH into the glycine solution. What

changes would we expect to see as a result of this mistake?

A) The solution's pH will stay roughly the same and glycine's net charge will become -1.
B) The solution's pH will stay roughly the same and glycine's net charge will become +1.
C) The solution's pH will increase and glycine's net charge will become +1.
D) The solution's pH will increase and glycine's net charge will become -1.

649. A professor attempts to purify glycine from a solution using anion-exchange chromatography. At which pH would he observe the largest amount of glycine adhering to the column?

A) 1.5
B) 6.5
C) 8.0
D) 10.0

650. Due to the planar properties of the peptide bond, proteins can easily assume various organized structures (for example, beta sheets). All of the following are characteristics of the peptide bond EXCEPT:

A) its rotation is restricted.
B) it has multiple resonance forms.
C) it frequently breaks and reforms to allow structural fluidity.
D) it exhibits partial double bond character.

651. Which of these statements describe(s) the amino acid K at physiological pH?

I. It has no net electrical charge.
II. It is not a zwitterion.
III. It is neither acidic nor basic.

A) I only
B) II only
C) I and II
D) I, II, and III

652. Ion-exchange chromatography with a positively-charged stationary phase is used to separate two polypeptides, A and B. Which of the below amino acids is LEAST likely to abound in the polypeptide that elutes first?

A) A
B) H
C) P
D) D

653. Which of the following amino acid sequences would incur the greatest entropic penalty if it were used to replace Tyr-Cys-Met in the surface region of a protein?

A) His-Gly-Gly
B) Ala-Gly-Ser
C) Leu-Val-Phe
D) Met-Thr-Glu

654. At pH = 1, what is the net electrical charge on Tyr?

A) -1
B) 0
C) +1
D) +2

655. All of the following L amino acids could be separated from their D enantiomers using chiral column chromatography EXCEPT:

A) G.
B) N.
C) R.
D) Q.

656. Which substitution, of those below, is most likely to cause a change in the tertiary structure of a protein?

A) Val to Met
B) Lys to Leu
C) Ser to Thr
D) Asp to Glu

657. Which of these amino acids is most likely to exist buried in the interior of a protein?

A) R
B) Q
C) T
D) F

Questions 658–659 rely on the table below

The information below gives the pK$_a$ values of an unknown amino acid, X.

Group	pK$_a$
1	2.10
2	4.07
3	9.47

658. Regarding amino acid "X," it must be true that:

A) Group 1 is negatively charged.
B) Group 2 is the R group.
C) the overall structure could resemble that of lysine.
D) at physiological pH, X is unlikely to have a net charge.

659. Where would residue X most likely predominate?

A) In the interior of mammalian hemoglobin
B) In prokaryotic DNA
C) In the extracellular domain of a G protein-coupled receptor
D) In the transmembrane domain of a cell surface receptor

660. A biochemistry student has an aqueous solution of the amino acid shown below.

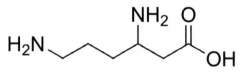

Upon performing a titration of this solution with NaOH, how many equivalence points would be observed?

A) 0
B) 1
C) 2
D) 3

661. Of the figures below, which depicts the amino acid that tends to introduce kinks in the secondary structures of proteins?

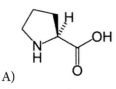

A)

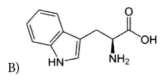

B)

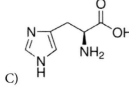

C)

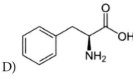

D)

662. If you were given a protein and a moderately concentrated solution of a reducing agent, what could you accomplish?

A) You could promote the formation of cysteine-cysteine disulfide linkages.
B) You could promote the breaking of cysteine-cysteine disulfide linkages.
C) You could promote the breaking of cystine-cystine disulfide linkages.
D) You could promote the dissociation of the protein's primary structure.

663. Aromatic amino acids include:

A) W, T, and F.
B) P, T, and W.
C) W, Y, and F.
D) Y, P, and W.

664. What structural characteristic marks the side chain of the amino acid N?

A) A four-carbon chain attached to an amine that makes the residue basic overall
B) A sulfur atom in the form of a thioether
C) A simple one-carbon group
D) An amide

665. Residue 127 is known to be an aromatic amino acid. To be classified in this manner, residue 127 must:

I. include at least one conjugated system, like threonine.
II. contain at least one ring that is marked by 4n + 4 pi electrons, like tyrosine.
III. contain at least one planar ring, like phenylalanine.

A) I only
B) III only
C) II and III
D) I, II, and III

666. A student is examining an essential amino acid with the chemical formula $C_5H_{11}NO_2S$. This structure:

A) is cysteine, and can form disulfide bonds due to its free thiol group.
B) is cystine, and can form disulfide bonds due to its free thiol group
C) is methionine, and can form disulfide bonds due to its free thiol group.
D) is methionine, and cannot form disulfide bonds because it lacks a free thiol group.

667. Consider the biomolecule shown below.

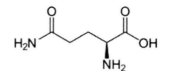

The three-letter and one-letter codes, respectively, for this amino acid are:

A) Gln and Q.
B) Glu and Q.
C) Glu and G.
D) Gln and E.

668. Which of the following amino acids exhibits the largest number of resonance structures?

A) Lysine
B) Isoleucine
C) Glutamate
D) Valine

669. The amino acid that is associated with the eukaryotic start codon is classified as:

A) aromatic.

B) acidic.

C) basic.

D) sulfur-containing.

670. The one-letter code for lysine is:

A) L.

B) Y.

C) K.

D) N.

671. Lactate dehydrogenase catalyzes the oxidation of lactate, which is depicted below.

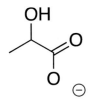

An amino acid in the active site of the enzyme initiates the reaction by deprotonating the hydroxyl group on carbon 2. Which amino acid(s) could serve this role in the active site?

I. Arginine

II. Aspartic acid

III. Histidine

IV. Proline

  A) I only

  B) II only

  C) I and III

  D) I, II, and III

672. Peptides are stable in water because:

A) peptide bonds cannot be cleaved by hydrolysis.

B) electron sharing between the carbonyl and amino group contributes resonance stabilization across the amide bond.

C) the breakdown of peptides into individual amino acids is entropically unfavorable.

D) peptides hydrogen bond with free-floating proline residues to promote stabilization.

673. The molecule below is cystine.

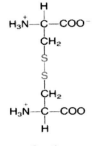

Cystine

Cystine is cleaved into two amino acids residues by:

A) hydrolysis.

B) acidic conditions.

C) oxidation.

D) reduction.

674. Aminotransferase is used to reversibly replace a ketone oxygen with an amino group. This enzyme is utilized during amino acid metabolism to convert certain amino acids into oxaloacetate, which is then incorporated into the TCA cycle.

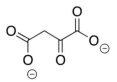

If an aminotransferase enzyme acts on oxaloacetate, picture above, which amino acid will be formed?

A) Arginine

B) Glutamate

C) Aspartic acid

D) Lysine

675. The following peptide sequence is phosphorylated.

TSGLVDSRTPEAGHAY

If all of the threonine R-groups have tert-butyl protecting groups attached, how many available phosphorylation sites are present?

A) 2

B) 5

C) 6

D) 7

676. Which statement is NOT true of disulfide bonds?

    A) They can stabilize secondary and tertiary structure.
    B) They are formed by cysteine-cysteine and methionine-methionine interactions.
    C) Disulfide bonds are formed and broken via oxidation/reduction reactions.
    D) A peptide's entropy is decreased by disulfide bond formation.

677. A researcher finishes synthesizing a peptide in a 3 mL reaction flask and wants to isolate it. The peptide is rich in threonine, glutamine, lysine, and glutamate resides. The researcher reduces the volume of the peptide solution to 0.5 mL, then plans to add 2.5 mL of a solvent that will cause the peptide to precipitate out, yielding a sample with higher purity. Which solvent should the researcher use?

    A) Water
    B) Ethanol
    C) Hexane
    D) THF

678. The cleavage of a Cys-Cys disulfide bond can be coupled with which reaction?

    A) $NADH \rightarrow NAD^+$
    B) $CH_3COO^- \rightarrow CH_3CHO$
    C) $FAD \rightarrow FADH_2$
    D) $2H_2O \rightarrow H_3O^+ + OH^-$

679. Trimethylsilyldiazomethane is a reagent used to methylate free carboxyl groups on amino acids *in vitro*. Which of the following peptide sequences will have 3 sites of methylation?

    A) TEPVL
    B) VEEEP
    C) DEPTS
    D) STIDL

680. Tertiary protein structure is determined by the protein's primary sequence. A protein with a sequence rich in isoleucine and alanine residues would likely fold in such a way to position this region:

    A) in the protein core.
    B) on the protein's exterior.
    C) within an alpha helix.
    D) in the active site.

681. Part of a certain amino acid sequence reads KRAKRRH. Where in a protein would this segment most likely be found?

    A) On the surface, because it is mainly hydrophobic
    B) On the surface, because it is mainly hydrophilic
    C) On the interior, because it is mainly hydrophobic
    D) On the interior, because it is mainly hydrophilic

682. During an electrophoresis procedure at pH = 7, which of the polypeptides below would migrate farthest towards the anode?

    A) Ala – Gly – Arg – Glu – Met
    B) Ala – Lys – Arg – Glu – Met
    C) Ala – Asp – Arg – Glu – Met
    D) Ala – Val – Arg – Asp – Met

Questions 683–684 rely on the table below

pK$_a$ values for lysine	
pK$_{a1}$	2.18
pK$_{a2}$	8.95
pK$_{a3}$	10.53

683. As a lysine molecule moves from a pH of 7 to a pH of 10, its charge changes from:

    A) 0 to -1.
    B) -1 to 0.
    C) 0 to +1.
    D) +1 to 0.

684. What is the approximate pI value for lysine?

    A) 5.6
    B) 7.2
    C) 8.9
    D) 9.7

Questions 685–686 rely on the figure below

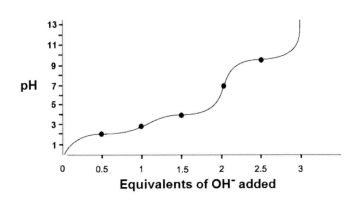

685. Which amino acid might exhibit the titration curve shown above?

A) Aspartic acid
B) Lysine
C) Glycine
D) Serine

686. Of the points marked with dots, which corresponds to a property of the molecule's side chain?

A) pK_{a1}
B) pK_{a2}
C) pK_{a3}
D) pI

687. Under certain conditions, the plasma pH (normally about 7.35) can drop, a phenomenon known as acidosis. How do amino acids play a role in buffering to mitigate this condition?

I. Due to increased hydrogen ion concentrations, the side chain of arginine can gain a proton.
II. Due to increased hydrogen ion concentrations, the side chain of glutamic acid can gain a proton.
III. Due to decreased hydrogen ion concentrations, the side chain of histidine can lose a proton.

A) I only
B) II only
C III only
D) I and II

688. Basic amino acid side chains may contain all of the following EXCEPT:

A) a guanidine group.
B) an azide group.
C) an amine group.
D) an imidazole ring.

689. Which of the lists below consists of three amino acids that do NOT contain a side chain with a gamma-carboxylic acid?

A) Aspartic acid, glutamine, asparagine
B) Aspartic acid, glutamic acid, asparagine
C) Lysine, glutamic acid, aspartic acid
D) Glutamic acid, glycine, aspartic acid

690. Basic amino acids are often found in the active sites of enzymes. Which of the following is NOT a possible explanation of this observation?

A) These amino acids can covalently bind to substrates.
B) These amino acids can hydrogen bond with the substrate to keep it in place.
C) These amino acids can alter the pH of the mini-environment.
D) These amino acids can take part in the enzymatic reaction.

691. According to Le Châtelier's principle, changes in which of these conditions will force the system to readjust to establish a new equilibrium?

I. Substrate concentration
II. Temperature
III. Catalyst concentration
IV. Pressure

A) I and II
B) II and IV
C) I, II, and III
D) I, II, and IV

692. The control of all of these qualities is considered a principal homeostatic process in mammals EXCEPT:

A) blood pH.
B) body height.
C) body temperature.
D) blood glucose concentration.

Questions 693–695 rely on the figure below

$$H_2O + CO_2 \leftrightarrow H_2CO_3 \leftrightarrow H^+ + HCO_3^-$$

693. This carbonic anhydrase-catalyzed reaction has negative ΔH and positive ΔS values, when experimentally determined at 25 °C and a pH of 7.2. What is the expected spontaneity and rate of this reaction?

   A) The reaction is spontaneous, and the rate depends on temperature, but not pH.
   B) The reaction is spontaneous, but the rate depends on both pH and temperature.
   C) The reaction is nonspontaneous, and the rate is independent of both temperature and pH.
   D) The reaction is nonspontaneous, but can become spontaneous depending on the temperature and pH.

694. In a human, what are the immediate effects of exercise and the concurrent production of higher levels of CO_2?

   A) The reaction quotient (Q) increases and the reactants are favored.
   B) The reaction quotient (Q) increases and the products are favored.
   C) The reaction quotient (Q) decreases and the reactants are favored.
   D) The reaction quotient (Q) decreases and the products are favored.

695. Acetazolamide is a potent carbonic anhydrase inhibitor. How would the administration of acetazolamide change the equilibrium (K_{eq}) of the carbonic anhydrase buffering system?

   A) The K_{eq} decreases because the products are favored.
   B) The K_{eq} decreases because more reactants are present.
   C) The K_{eq} increases because more products are present.
   D) The K_{eq} does not change.

Questions 696–698 rely on the figure below

Shown here is the reaction coordinate for a catalyzed form of alkene hydrogenation.

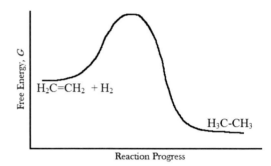

696. Would removing the enzyme catalyst from this reaction change its spontaneity?

   A) Yes, because $\Delta G > 0$, the reaction would become endergonic and nonspontaneous.
   B) Yes, because $\Delta G < 0$, the reaction would become exergonic and nonspontaneous.
   C) No, because $\Delta G > 0$, the reaction would remain endergonic and spontaneous.
   D) No, because $\Delta G < 0$, the reaction would remain exergonic and spontaneous.

697. Downstream metabolic needs remove $H_3C\text{-}CH_3$ from the system rapidly, resulting in low functional concentrations of this alkane. How does this affect ΔG and K_{eq}?

   A) ΔG increases and K_{eq} remains constant.
   B) ΔG decreases and K_{eq} remains constant.
   C) ΔG remains constant and K_{eq} increases.
   D) ΔG remains constant and K_{eq} decreases.

698. Changes in which of these quantities would affect the rate of a reaction?

   I.   Temperature
   II. Catalyst presence
   III. Enthalpy
   IV. Entropy

   A) I only
   B) III only
   C) I and II
   D) III and IV

699. How does the first law of thermodynamics apply to living systems?

 A) Energy is conserved during the transfer of energy from GTP to ATP.
 B) High-energy bonds cannot be spontaneously destroyed.
 C) ADP cannot spontaneously be phosphorylated into ATP.
 D) All of the above

700. Oftentimes, both anabolic and catabolic pathways are essential for an organism's survival, but contain steps that are nonspontaneous. Which is NOT a method used by cells to drive nonspontaneous reactions?

 A) Energy coupling of a nonspontaneous reaction to a spontaneous process
 B) Utilization of enzymes to increase steric probability
 C) Increasing of the environmental temperature around the reaction
 D) Temporary storage of energy in high-energy compounds to promote endergonic mechanisms

701. NADH is generated in the citric acid cycle. Which statement is NOT true regarding NADH?

 A) NAD$^+$ accepts a hydride ion to be reduced to NADH.
 B) NADH is irreversibly inhibited after acting as a coenzyme and must then be excreted.
 C) NADH generated in the mitochondria is converted to 2.5 ATP units by the electron transport chain.
 D) NADH cannot cross the mitochondrial membrane from the cytosol into the mitochondria.

702. The catabolism of which fuel yields the highest ATP output under aerobic conditions?

 A) Sugars
 B) Fatty acids
 C) Proteins
 D) Vitamins

Questions 703–704 rely on the figure below

This molecule is adenosine triphosphate, or ATP.

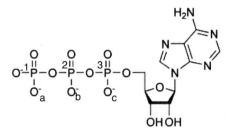

703. When ATP is converted to ADP, what is the site of nucleophilic attack?

 A) P$_1$
 B) P$_3$
 C) O$_a$
 D) O$_c$

704. When adenylate cyclase reacts with ATP, cyclic AMP is formed. What is/are the other product(s) of this reaction?

 A) 2 H$_2$O
 B) Pyrophosphate
 C) 2 P$_i$
 D) ADP

705. Which of the following is true of both NADH and FADH$_2$?

 A) They are flavoproteins that carry electrons and participate in the electron transport chain.
 B) They are used as coenzymes and store the energy that is released in oxidation reactions.
 C) They can be embedded in the mitochondrial membrane as ATP-producing complexes.
 D) As they can be used interchangeably, use of NADH vs. FADH$_2$ is determined by the location of the reaction within a cell.

706. Which reaction from the TCA cycle can be coupled with the conversion of NAD⁺ to NADH?

A)

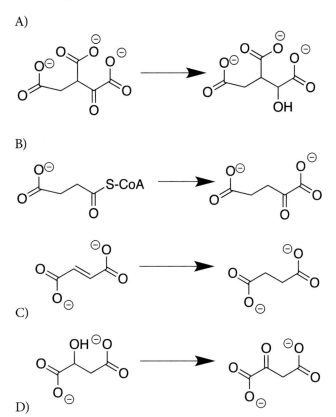

B)

C)

D)

707. If it actually costs two ATP molecules to add a single phosphate group, but the removal of a phosphate group still only generated one ATP molecule, what would be the net ATP production during one round of glycolysis?

   A) -2
   B) 0
   C) 2
   D) 4

708. The hydrolysis of ATP couples to other reactions that:

   I.   are exergonic.
   II. are thermodynamically unfavorable.
   III. are reversible.
   IV. can involve oxidization.

      A) II only
      B) I and II
      C) II and III
      D) I, II, and IV

709. Alcohol dehydrogenase catalyzes the reaction below.

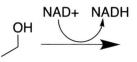

What would be the most likely product of this reaction?

   A) H_3C-CH_3

   B)

   C)

   D)

710. In glycolysis, aside from ATP hydrolysis, how else are phosphates incorporated into molecules?

   A) The addition of a phosphate is coupled with the oxidation of $FADH_2$ to FAD.
   B) The addition of a phosphate is coupled with the reduction of NAD⁺ to NADH.
   C) ADP donates a second phosphate, producing AMP.
   D) They are not; ATP is the lone phosphate source in glycolysis.

711. Which of the following process will not proceed without oxygen?

   A) The citric acid cycle
   B) Glycolysis
   C) Gluconeogenesis
   D) Oxidative phosphorylation

712. Consider the labeled eukaryotic cell below.

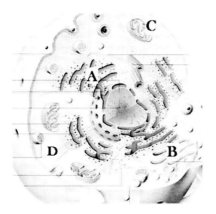

In which structure can NADH be produced?

A) C only
B) D only
C) C and D
D) A and B

713. Human cells are eukaryotic and can therefore utilize aerobic respiration to create ATP. However, one type of cell can only use glycolysis to obtain its energy. What is the identity of this cell?

A) A neuron
B) An epithelial cell
C) An erythrocyte
D) A T-cell

714. Which of the following processes occur in the presence or absence of oxygen?

I. Citric acid cycle
II. Gluconeogenesis
III. Glycolysis
IV. Fermentation

A) I and III
B) II and III
C) II, III, and IV
D) I, II, III, and IV

715. Which of the following is NOT a product of glycolysis?

A) Pyruvate
B) ATP
C) NADH
D) Acetyl-CoA

716. Which of the following enzymes is NOT found in the mitochondria?

A) Hexokinase
B) Pyruvate dehydrogenase
C) Citrate synthase
D) Succinate dehydrogenase

717. What is the net yield of ATP during glycolysis per molecule of glucose?

A) 2 ATP
B) 4 ATP
C) 13 ATP
D) 36 ATP

718. The following equation depicts the net reaction for the Krebs cycle.

$$\text{Acetyl-CoA} + NAD^+ + FAD^+ + GDP + P_i + H_2O \rightarrow CO_2 + NADH + FADH_2 + GTP + H^+ + CoA$$

What are the correct stoichiometric ratios?

A) 1 Acetyl-CoA, 1 NAD^+, 1 FAD^+, 1 CO_2, 1 NADH, 1 $FADH_2$, 1 CoA
B) 1 Acetyl-CoA, 3 NAD^+, 2 FAD^+, 1 CO_2, 3 NADH, 2 $FADH_2$, 1 CoA
C) 1 Acetyl-CoA, 2 NAD^+, 1 FAD^+, 2 CO_2, 2 NADH, 1 $FADH_2$, 2 CoA
D) 1 Acetyl-CoA, 3 NAD^+, 1 FAD^+, 2 CO_2, 3 NADH, 1 $FADH_2$, 1 CoA

719. DNP is a toxin that destroys the proton gradient created by the electron transport chain. Where in the cell does DNP act?

A) Plasma membrane
B) Mitochondrial matrix
C) Inner mitochondrial membrane
D) Nuclear membrane

720. Which of the following processes results in the largest amount of energy in the form of ATP?

A) Citric acid cycle
B) Glycolysis
C) Substrate-level phosphorylation
D) Oxidative phosphorylation

721. Consider the biological reaction below.

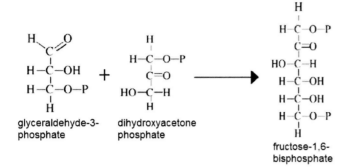

glyceraldehyde-3-phosphate   dihydroxyacetone phosphate   fructose-1,6-bisphosphate

This serves as an example of a(n):

A) isomerization.
B) decarboxylation.
C) hydrogenation.
D) aldol condensation.

722. The reaction between glyceraldehyde 3-phosphate and dihydroxyacetone phosphate is an:

A) isomerization.
B) decarboxylation.
C) hydrogenation.
D) aldol condensation.

723. Consider the biological reaction shown here.

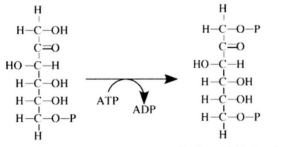

Fructose-6-phosphate   Fructose-1,6-bisphosphate

Which type of enzyme likely catalyzes such a process?

A) A dehydrogenase
B) A kinase
C) A phosphatase
D) A reductase

724. A deficiency in which of these listed reactants will result in a halt in glycolysis?

A) NAD^+
B) FAD
C) ATP
D) CO_2

725. All of the following are true about glycolysis EXCEPT that:

A) it occurs in the cytoplasm.
B) it is an anaerobic process.
C) it results in a net production of 4 ATP.
D) it requires ATP in order to be initiated.

726. During an early step of glycolysis, glucose is phosphorylated to form glucose 6-phosphate. This reaction is catalyzed by which enzyme?

A) Hexokinase in all cells
B) Glucokinase in all cells
C) Hexokinase in liver cells and glucokinase in all other cells
D) Glucokinase in liver cells and hexokinase in all other cells

727. Glycolysis is a process used to help regulate blood sugar. Eight hours after a meal, what is the expected level of glucose saturation for hexokinase and glucokinase?

A) Hexokinase will be saturated, while glucokinase will be unsaturated.
B) Hexokinase will be unsaturated, while glucokinase will be saturated.
C) Both enzymes will be saturated.
D) Both enzymes will be unsaturated.

728. Which of these enzymes catalyzes an irreversible step in glycolysis?

A) Pyruvate carboxylase
B) Aldolase
C) Phosphofructokinase
D) Citrate synthase

729. An aerobic organism placed in an oxygen-poor environment will begin to produce:

A) an excess of acetyl-CoA.
B) an excess of NADH.
C) an excess of ATP.
D) an excess of ADP.

730. In aerobic organisms, which glycolytic product contains the highest energy potential?

A) Pyruvate
B) ATP
C) NADH
D) $FADH_2$

731. Which statement is NOT true of phosphorylated intermediates in glycolysis?

A) Phosphate-ester bonds are formed to store the energy released in ATP hydrolysis.

B) Glycolytic intermediates must be phosphorylated to properly bind with the appropriate enzymes.

C) The attachment of a phosphate group allows the intermediate to freely pass through cellular membranes.

D) Phosphate groups form complexes with Mg^{2+} in the active site of enzymes.

732. If there is an excess of ATP present:

A) fructose 1,6-bisphosphatase will be downregulated, and will less actively convert fructose 6-phosphate to fructose 1,6-bisphosphate.

B) phosphofructokinase-1 will be downregulated and will less actively phosphorylate fructose 6-phosphate.

C) glycolytic pathways will be upregulated.

D) gluconeogenic pathways will be downregulated.

733. Pyruvate kinase, which converts PEP to pyruvate is regulated by:

I. ATP.
II. acetyl-CoA.
III. oxaloacetate.
IV. fructose 1,6-bisphosphate.

A) I only
B) I and II
C) I, II, and IV
D) I, II, III, and IV

734. Glucose monomers are stored in the form of glycogen. To free glucose from the glycogen chain, phosphate initiates nucleophilic attack that cleaves a single glucose from the chain. The freed glucose is phosphorylated as pictured below:

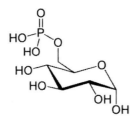

This glucose molecule can then enter directly into glycolysis. While glycolysis typically has a

net production of 2 ATP, in this circumstance glycolysis will instead have a net production of:

A) 1 ATP.
B) 3 ATP.
C) 4 ATP.
D) The net production of ATP will remain unchanged.

735. Which product of glycolysis can be produced both aerobically and anaerobically?

A) H_2O
B) Lactate
C) Acetyl-CoA
D) CO_2

736. Sucrose, pictured below, is a common disaccharide, and is digested by sucrase into two monosaccharides.

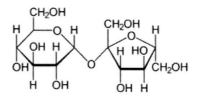

Which monosaccharides will be produced, and if hexokinase (a phosphorylating enzyme) acts on each of these monomers, will they be able to enter directly into glycolysis?

A) D-glucose and D-fructose; both will enter directly into glycolysis

B) L-glucose and D-mannose; both will enter directly into glycolysis

C) D-fructose and galactose; neither will enter directly into glycolysis

D) D-glucose and L-glucose; D-glucose will enter into glycolysis, but L-glucose will first need to be isomerized

737. 5 moles of glucose are added to a vial of yeast cells. All appropriate enzymes and coenzymes are present. How many moles of product will be generated?

A) 2 moles of ethanol, 2 moles of CO_2
B) 5 moles of ethanol, 10 moles of CO_2
C) 10 moles of ethanol, 5 moles of CO_2
D) 10 moles of ethanol, 10 moles of CO_2

738. What is the benefit to synthesizing lactate in the absence of oxygen, such as during strenuous exercise?

    A) Lactate builds up and triggers the body's emergency response, forcing the body to lose consciousness and take in oxygen.
    B) Lactate is energy-dense and can be metabolized by the citric acid cycle to yield 10+ ATP.
    C) Lactate will enter gluconeogenesis to produce new glucose to be metabolized into 2 ATP by glycolysis.
    D) Lactate is then converted into acetyl-CoA for fatty acid synthesis and metabolism.

739. A physician noticed anemia, splenomegaly, and jaundice in one of her patients. After a series of tests, she diagnosed the patient with a genetic disorder that is linked to glycolysis. Specifically, the patient was diagnosed with a deficiency in the enzyme that catalyzes this reaction:

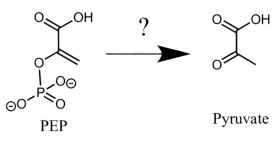

PEP   Pyruvate

What is the deficient enzyme?

A) Phosphoenolpyruvate kinase
B) Pyruvate kinase
C) Pyruvate hydrase
D) Phosphoenolpyruvate phosphatase

740. A new species of bacteria infects the mitochondria of eukaryotic cells and releases a toxin into the mitochondrial matrix to inhibit glyceraldehyde-3-dehydrogenase. What effect will this have on glycolysis?

    A) The formation of fructose 6-phosphate will be inhibited.
    B) Glycolytic reactions will be inhibited, but gluconeogenic reactions will proceed.
    C) This will have no effect on glycolysis.
    D) No ATP will be able to be produced through glycolysis.

741. During the Krebs cycle, isocitrate and NAD^+ come together to form alpha-ketoglutarate, NADH and H^+. Which of the following describe this type of chemical reaction?

    A) Dehydration
    B) Hydration
    C) Decarboxylation
    D) Oxidation

742. A new toxin has been found to overstimulate the citric acid cycle.

	Normal values	Result A	Result B	Result C	Result D
Blood pH	7.35-7.45	7.38	7.41	7.21	7.89
Bicarbonate (mmol/L)	22-28	25	27	15	32
[Na⁺] (mmol/L)	136-145	137	142	140	137
[K⁺] (mmol/L)	3.5-5.0	5.0	3.7	4.8	3.2
[Cl⁻] (mmol/L)	95-105	100	101	92	95

A patient who ingests this toxin will later show which of the following lab results?

A) Result A
B) Result B
C) Result C
D) Result D

743. In the Krebs cycle, NAD⁺ and FAD react with substrates to form NADH and FADH₂. Over the same period of time that nine molecules of FADH₂ are produced, how many units of NADH will be synthesized?

    A) 9 molecules
    B) 18 molecules
    C) 27 molecules
    D) 36 molecules

744. In what step of the citric acid cycle is GTP produced via substrate-level phosphorylation?

    A) During the conversion of succinyl-CoA to succinate
    B) During the conversion of succinate to fumarate
    C) During the conversion of malate to oxaloacetate
    D) During the conversion of pyruvate to acetyl-CoA

745. The mitochondrial membrane is not permeable to lard or polar ions. Therefore, carnitine, a shuttling protein, is required to transport molecules such as fatty acids across this membrane. A carnitine deficiency would directly impact which of the following metabolic reactions?

    A) Glycolysis
    B) The citric acid cycle
    C) Gluconeogenesis
    D) Oxidative phosphorylation

746. Fumarate, shown below, undergoes a hydration reaction that is catalyzed by the enzyme fumarase.

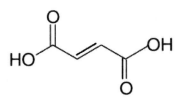

    What product is formed by this reaction?

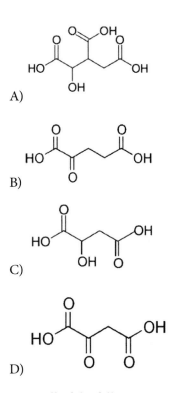

A)

B)

C)

D)

747. All of the following enzymes require NAD⁺ as a substrate EXCEPT:

    A) alpha-ketoglutarate dehydrogenase.
    B) isocitrate dehydrogenase.
    C) pyruvate dehydrogenase.
    D) succinate dehydrogenase.

748. High levels of acetyl-CoA stimulate which of the following enzymes?

    I.   Citrate synthase
    II. Pyruvate carboxylase
    III. Pyruvate dehydrogenase

    A) I only
    B) I and II
    C) II and III
    D) I, II, and III

749. Passage of one molecule of pyruvate through the Krebs cycle yields how many molecules of ATP when followed through oxidative phosphorylation?

    A) 13
    B) 15
    C) 30
    D) 36

750. High levels of which molecule will inhibit the TCA cycle?

    A) AMP
    B) ADP
    C) NADH
    D) NAD$^+$

751. Which of the following serve as electron donors or acceptors in the mitochondrial electron transport chain?

    I.   NADH dehydrogenase
    II. Ubiquinone
    III. Cytochrome c
    IV. Plastocyanin

    A) I only
    B) I and III
    C) I, II, and III
    D) I, III, and IV

752. The four major protein complexes along the inner mitochondrial membrane are crucial to the establishment of the proton gradient required for ATP synthesis. All of the following pump protons into the intermembrane space EXCEPT:

    A) Complex I.
    B) Complex II.
    C) Complex III.
    D) Complex IV.

753. If a mutation in the gene coding for NAD$^+$ resulted in a nonfunctional coenzyme, what change would occur to the rate of ATP synthesis?

    A) ATP production would no longer occur, since NADH is an electron donor that is required for proper functioning of the electron transport chain.
    B) ATP production would be unaffected, since a supply of electrons can be provided through other carriers.
    C) ATP production would increase, since free electrons would be picked up by existing electron carriers.
    D) ATP production would be reduced, since FADH$_2$ would still be capable of providing electrons through Complex II.

754. Oxidative phosphorylation is "coupled," meaning that it involves two processes, one of which facilitates the other. Which of the following steps most clearly highlights this phenomenon of coupling?

    A) The oxidation of electron carriers such as NADH and FADH$_2$ generate the electrochemical gradient.
    B) The rotating γ-subunit of ATP synthase generates free radical species.
    C) The proton gradient generated through electron transfer is used to regenerate ATP through ATP synthase.
    D) Oxygen serves as the final electron acceptor and is reduced to water.

755. Which of these statements regarding proton pumping is accurate?

    A) The intermembrane space becomes positive due to the protons being pumped into it.
    B) The mitochondrial matrix becomes positive due to the protons being pumped out of it.
    C) The intermembrane space becomes negative due to the protons being pumped out of it.
    D) The mitochondrial matrix becomes negative due to the protons being pumped into it.

Questions 756–757 rely on the figure below

Oligomycin, a potent inhibitor of oxidative phosphorylation, operates by preventing protons from flowing through the F$_0$ unit of ATP synthase. The following table shows the level of production of the proton gradient and the rate of ATP synthesis, in comparison to levels in normal cells, before and after applying an oligomycin solution.

	Proton gradient	ATP synthesis
Before	100%	100%
After	?	?

756. After applying oligomycin to an actively respiring cell, what change will occur to the rate of ATP synthesis within the mitochondria?

    A) It will increase to 150%.
    B) It will remain at 100%.
    C) It will decrease to a level below 100%, but not as low as 0%.
    D) It will decrease to 0%.

757. Oligomycin is administered to a pathogenic, aerobic species and immediately begins to take effect. Ten minutes later, the most likely level at which the proton gradient will exist, in comparison to its previous value, is:

    A) 200%.
    B) 100%.
    C) 50%.
    D) 0%.

Questions 758–759 rely on the figure below

The diagram below depicts ATP synthase.

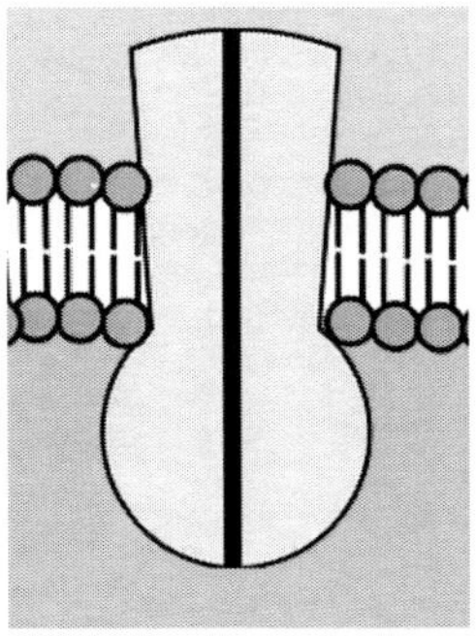

758. Where is the F_1 fraction of the enzyme located?

    A) Embedded in the mitochondrial membrane
    B) Inside the intermembrane space
    C) Inside the mitochondrial matrix
    D) The F_1 fraction is not depicted in the figure.

759. With respect to the figure above, during ATP synthesis, protons:

    A) flow downwards through the enzyme.
    B) flow upwards through the enzyme.
    C) translocate horizontally through the lipid bilayer.
    D) flow either direction through the enzyme, depending on the step of the process.

760. All of the following statements describe the net result of oxidative phosphorylation EXCEPT:

    A) NADH and $FADH_2$ are oxidized to generate a proton gradient.
    B) controlled proton flow through ATP synthase is used to regenerate ATP.
    C) oxygen is the final electron acceptor in the electron transport chain.
    D) the products of oxidative phosphorylation are retained for the next round of cyclic phosphorylation.

761. Which enzyme is exclusive to gluconeogenesis?

    A) Phosphohexose isomerase
    B) Fructose 1,6-bisphosphatase
    C) Phosphoglycerate kinase
    D) Pyruvate kinase

762. The process of gluconeogenesis can directly utilize all of the following molecules EXCEPT:

    A) glycerol.
    B) pyruvate.
    C) succinate.
    D) lactate.

Questions 763–764 rely on the figure below

The following figure depicts the ten steps of glycolysis.

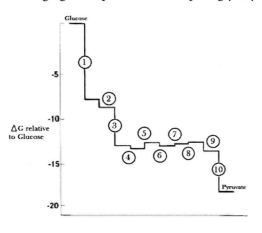

763. Which of these steps must be bypassed during gluconeogenesis?

    A) Step 2
    B) Step 3
    C) Step 5
    D) Step 7

764. Which gluconeogenesis enzyme bypasses step 1 in the figure above?

    A) Hexokinase
    B) Fructose 1,6-bisphosphatase
    C) Aldolase
    D) Glucose 6-phosphatase

765. With regard to human organs, gluconeogenesis occurs in the:

    A) liver.
    B) brain.
    C) muscle.
    D) pancreas.

766. Of the following, which accurately describes a difference between glycolysis and gluconeogenesis?

    A) Glycolysis can occur in all cells, while gluconeogenesis cannot.
    B) Glycolysis and gluconeogenesis occur in different parts of the cell.
    C) Only gluconeogenesis requires ATP to function.
    D) Glycolysis can occur in the absence of oxygen, while gluconeogenesis cannot.

767. The end goal of gluconeogenesis is the:

    A) formation of acetyl-CoA for use in the citric acid cycle.
    B) creation of ATP to facilitate the continuation of biological processes.
    C) regeneration of NAD^+ to allow glycolysis to continue.
    D) regulation of blood glucose levels.

768. Which of the following processes will be stimulated in conditions of elevated ATP and decreased ADP?

    I.   Glycolysis
    II. Gluconeogenesis
    III. The citric acid cycle

    A) I only
    B) II only
    C) I and II only
    D) I and III only

769. Elevated levels of which substrate will stimulate gluconeogenesis?

    A) ADP
    B) AMP
    C) Acetyl-CoA
    D) Glucose

770. A new toxin is found to inhibit pyruvate carboxylase.

	Reference values	Patient A	Patient B	Patient C	Patient D
Blood glucose (mg/dl)	70-100	150	20	80	75
Blood pH	7.35-7.45	7.38	7.41	7.28	7.89
Bicarbonate (mmol/L)	22-28	25	27	15	32
$[Na^+]$ (mmol/L)	136-145	137	142	140	137
$[K^+]$ (mmol/L)	3.5-5.0	5.0	3.7	4.8	3.2
$[Cl^-]$ (mmol/L)	95-105	100	101	92	95

Which of the patients in the table below has likely ingested this poison?

A) Patient A
B) Patient B
C) Patient C
D) Patient D

771. Which other metabolic processes are connected to the pentose phosphate pathway?

I. Gluconeogenesis
II. Glycolysis
III. Cellular respiration
IV. Nucleic acid synthesis

    A) I and II
    B) I, II, and III
    C) I, III, and VI
    D) I, II, III, and IV

772. All of the following are products of the pentose phosphate pathway EXCEPT:

A) ribulose 5-phosphate.
B) NADPH.
C) glyceraldehyde 3-phosphate.
D) xylulose 5-phosphate.

773. Under which conditions is the cell most likely to employ the pentose phosphate pathway?

A) Low NADPH, high glucose 6-phosphate
B) High NADPH, high glucose 6-phosphate
C) Low NADPH, low glucose 6-phosphate
D) High NADPH, low glucose 6-phosphate

774. The first step of the oxidative phase of the pentose phosphate pathway is the oxidation of glucose 6-phosphate by glucose 6-phosphate dehydrogenase and $NADP^+$. As expected, NADPH is a strong inhibitor of this reaction. What other substance would you expect to be an inhibitor of the first step of the oxidative phase?

A) Glyceraldehyde 3-phosphate
B) Acetyl-CoA
C) Pyruvic acid
D) Hydrogen ions

775. Of the three phases of the pentose phosphate pathway, which is most directly linked to the synthesis of fatty acids?

A) The isomerization phase
B) The rearrangement phase
C) The reduction phase
D) The oxidation phase

Questions 776–777 rely on the figure below

Below is the molecular structure of NADPH, an important biomolecule.

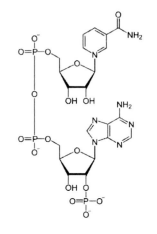

776. What would be the consequence to the identity and function of NADPH if a phosphatase were to remove the 2' phosphate group on the ribose-containing adenine?

   A) The molecule would have a different name and serve an entirely distinct function.
   B) The molecule would be assimilated into a new DNA double helix.
   C) The molecule could now be used in the creation of glycogen.
   D) This is a normal process that NADPH typically undergoes.

777. If a cell were infected and its NADPH degraded, all of the following cellular processes would be compromised EXCEPT:

   A) nucleic acid synthesis.
   B) protection against reactive oxygen species.
   C) fatty acid chain elongation.
   D) protein elongation.

778. The normal ratio of NADP⁺ to NADPH is:

   A) high, because NADPH is rapidly used in anabolic pathways.
   B) low, because NADPH functions as a reducing agent.
   C) high, because the generation of NADPH is unfavorable.
   D) low, because NADP⁺ is a highly reactive compound.

Questions 779–780 rely on the figure below

The protein structure for transketolase is shown below, along with the molecular structure of its cofactor, thiamine pyrophosphate.

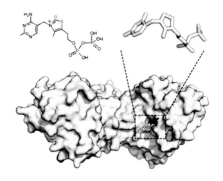

779. Which phase of the pentose phosphate pathway would be most affected if this enzyme were to become nonfunctional?

   A) Oxidative
   B) Initiation
   C) Non-oxidative
   D) Termination

780. Of the pathways fed into by the pentose phosphate pathway, which would be most affected if this enzyme were to lose functionality?

   A) Water retention pathways
   B) Glycolysis
   C) Nucleic acid synthesis
   D) Ketone body formation

781. The enzyme adenylate kinase catalyzes a particular reaction:

$$ADP + ADP \longleftrightarrow ATP + AMP$$

The forward reaction predominates when the cell is using ATP at a high rate. Which of these species likely upregulate(s) the activity of a glycolytic enzyme?

   I. AMP
   II. ADP
   III. ATP

   A) I only
   B) II only
   C) I and II
   D) I and III

782. Which of the ΔG° values below most likely corresponds to an irreversible step of glycolysis?

    A) 3.2 kJ/mol
    B) 20.9 kJ/mol
    C) -3.2 kJ/mol
    D) -20.9 kJ/mol

783. A well-fed person with type 1 diabetes receives an insulin injection in the hospital. As a result of this treatment, levels of all of the following will decrease EXCEPT:

    A) plasma glucose.
    B) intracellular pyruvate.
    C) intermediate gluconeogenesis species.
    D) intracellular AMP.

784. Which of these behaviors or physiological processes would NOT stimulate glycogenolysis?

    A) Stimulation of the sympathetic nervous system
    B) Release of glucagon
    C) Consumption of a carbohydrate-rich meal
    D) Participation in a marathon

785. Cardiac arrest, or the absence of cardiac activity, causes a cessation of blood flow and oxygen delivery to tissues. If untreated, this condition leads to death within minutes due to:

    A) the complete absence of ATP production in all cells.
    B) a severe drop in blood pH due to increased lactic acid production, leading to cell lysis.
    C) a reduction in ATP synthesis that prevents vital organs from performing their functions effectively.
    D) a severe increase in blood pH due to CO_2 buildup, leading to suffocation at the cellular level.

Questions 786–787 rely on the figure below

A group of scientists are studying enzyme X, a biological catalyst thought to play a metabolic role. The binding curves for this enzyme are shown here.

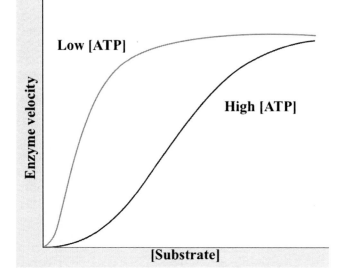

786. Based on this figure, in which metabolic process is this enzyme most likely involved?

    A) Glycogenesis, or the synthesis of glycogen
    B) Glycolysis
    C) Carbohydrate digestion
    D) Fatty acid digestion

787. What type of inhibition does ATP exert upon enzyme X, and how does it affect the K_m?

    A) High [ATP] increases the K_m of enzyme X and is a competitive inhibitor.
    B) High [ATP] decreases the K_m of enzyme X and is a competitive inhibitor.
    C) High [ATP] increases the K_m of enzyme X and is an allosteric inhibitor.
    D) High [ATP] decreases the K_m of enzyme X and is an allosteric inhibitor.

788. A woman trapped in the wilderness is forced to go several hours without eating. Expected changes in her metabolic regulation include:

    A) decreased fatty acid metabolism.
    B) decreased blood glucagon levels.
    C) increased glycogen synthesis.
    D) increased production of mRNA corresponding to proteins involved in gluconeogenesis.

789. A scientist radioactively labels the oxygen atoms in O_2 before tracing their journey through the citric acid cycle and mitochondrial respiration. At the end of the study, the radioactive atoms will be found in:

    A) glucose.
    B) CO_2.
    C) NADH.
    D) H_2O.

790. Intramuscular glucagon (IMG) can be administered via autoinjector pen in a similar fashion to the injection of epinephrine for allergic reactions. IMG is most likely used to treat:

    A) hyperglycemia.
    B) hypoglycemia.
    C) type 1 diabetes.
    D) type 2 diabetes.

791. A cholesterol deficiency would NOT be expected to have which effect on the body?

    A) Cell membranes would become too permeable.
    B) Cell membranes would become too rigid.
    C) Membrane lipids would become increasingly desaturated.
    D) Membrane proteins would be increasingly less secure in the lipid bilayer.

792. *V. cholerae* bacteria produce a toxin that binds to the α subunit of a certain G protein, G_s, causing it to lose the ability to hydrolyze GTP. As a result:

    A) the α subunit would be unable to separate from the β subunit.
    B) G_s would no longer be activated by receptor stimulation.
    C) the α subunit would be unable to activate its target protein(s).
    D) once stimulated, G_s would be stuck indefinitely in an activated state.

793. Some scientists have theorized that Saturn's moon Titan, despite having an average temperature of -179.2 ˚C, may be the best candidate for life elsewhere in the solar system. These researchers base their claim on its thick, high-pressure atmosphere composed almost entirely of nitrogen; they also cite its seas of liquid hydrocarbons such as ethane and methane, which might form a solvent for life and provide a source of complex carbon molecules. Which of the following most supports the idea that any life discovered on Titan must have biochemistry very different from that present on Earth?

    A) No known form of life can exist without oxygen.
    B) Cell membranes, at least as we know them, could not exist in Titan's seas.
    C) Complex carbon molecules become less stable at lower temperatures.
    D) Nitrogen is highly reactive and would interfere with the stability of complex hydrocarbons.

794. Suppose the electrical potential of a certain membrane were determined entirely by the relative concentrations of potassium ions on either side. If the value of $[K^+]$ both inside and outside the cell were squared, in comparison to before, the membrane potential:

    A) would be one hundred times larger.
    B) would be twice as large.
    C) would be unchanged.
    D) would be one-one hundredth as large.

795. Which of these species requires a channel or vesicle to cross the plasma membrane?

    A) Nitrous oxide
    B) Estrogen
    C) Dopamine
    D) Aldosterone

796. Palytoxin is a chemical isolated from certain species of coral; it effectively forces the Na^+/K^+ ATPase into an open conformation, allowing free diffusion of ions and rapid death. All of the listed effects would likely result from the administration of palytoxin EXCEPT:

A) cell membrane potentials would rapidly hyperpolarize.

B) glucose absorption in the gut would drastically decline.

C) Ca^{2+} ion levels in muscle cells would rise.

D) water absorption in the kidney would fall significantly.

797. A biologist exposes yeast cells to factors that stimulate the production of a certain lipid. After synthesis, this lipid typically inserts into the cytosolic leaflet of the endoplasmic reticulum's plasma membrane. The scientist simultaneously exposes the yeast cell to a chemical that disrupts vesicular transport. In which locations might this lipid be found shortly after these steps?

    I.   The inner leaflet of the endoplasmic reticulum

    II. The nuclear membrane

    III. The Golgi apparatus

    A) I only

    B) I and II

    C) II and III

    D) I, II, and III

Questions 798–799 rely on the figure below

A neurogeneticist is interested in the composition of a certain type of cell membrane. To study this concept, he saponifies various membrane lipids to remove their glycerol backbones. The resulting fatty acids are characterized below.

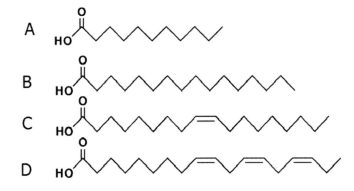

798. Which of the molecules above would most likely be found in lipids near membrane-embedded signaling proteins?

A) A
B) B
C) C
D) D

799. The geneticist then compares four different cell membranes that vary in their fatty acid composition and in their relative permeabilities. Which of the labeled fatty acids would likely dominate in the most permeable of the membranes?

A) A
B) B
C) C
D) D

800. The diagram below depicts the intracellular cascade associated with a certain insulin-linked transmembrane receptor.

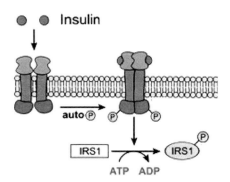

This receptor most likely auto-catalyzes the linkage of a phosphate group to which of the following amino acid residues within its structure?

A) Phenylalanine
B) Tryptophan
C) Tyrosine
D) Cysteine

801. During the beta-oxidation of fatty acids, which of these molecules are directly produced?

    I.   NADH

    II. FADH$_2$

    III. Acetyl-CoA

    IV. ATP

    A) I and II

    B) I, II, and III

    C) I, III, and IV

    D) I, II, III, and IV

802. Individuals that participate in the Atkins diet often report sweet-smelling breath and/or sweat, in addition to a metallic taste in the mouth. Based on this information, the Atkins diet most likely involves the metabolism of which molecule(s)?

    A) Glycogen
    B) Ketone bodies
    C) Amino acids
    D) Triacylglycerols

803. Which pathway does the metabolism of fatty acids most closely resemble?

    A) The pentose phosphate pathway
    B) Protein metabolism
    C) Glycolysis
    D) Production of acetyl-coA during cellular respiration

804. How many molecules of acetyl-CoA will be generated from the beta-oxidation of linoleic acid, which has the chemical formula $C_{18}H_{32}O_2$?

    A) 6 molecules
    B) 9 molecules
    C) 18 molecules
    D) Acetyl-CoA is not generated from the beta-oxidation of even-numbered fatty acid chains.

805. If a mutation in a eukaryotic cell eliminated all functioning protein kinase A, how would fatty acid metabolism be affected?

    A) Fatty acid metabolism would increase dramatically.
    B) Fatty acid metabolism would decrease dramatically.
    C) Fatty acid metabolism would be largely unaffected.
    D) The effect on fatty acid metabolism would be erratic and unpredictable.

Questions 806–807 rely on the figure below

Below is the molecular structure of a medium-chain fatty acid.

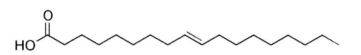

806. What is the identity of this organic molecule?

    A) *Trans*-oleic acid
    B) *Cis*-oleic acid
    C) *Trans*-linoleic acid
    D) *Cis*-linoleic acid

807. Compared to those who reside in warmer climates, would you expect the lipid bilayers of Arctic animals to include more saturated or unsaturated fats?

    A) Saturated fats, because the tighter packing reduces heat loss
    B) Unsaturated fats, because double bonds contain greater binding energy than single bonds
    C) Saturated fats, because they yield more energy per molecule
    D) Unsaturated fats, because the increased fluidity prevents freezing in subzero temperatures

808. Which sequence most accurately describes the ingestion and storage of fatty acids?

    A) They are ingested as triglycerides, absorbed as free fatty acids, transported by chylomicrons, and stored as triacylglycerols.
    B) They are ingested as fatty acids, absorbed as triglycerides, transported by lipoproteins, and stored as triacylglycerols.
    C) They are ingested as triglycerides, absorbed as triglycerides, transported by chylomicrons, and stored as fatty acids.
    D) They are ingested as fatty acids, absorbed as free fatty acids, transported by lipoproteins, and stored as fatty acids.

809. Below is a table that shows the typical contents of various classes of transport lipoproteins, in the form of percentages.

Class	Protein %	Cholesterol %	Phospholipid %	Triacylglycerol and cholesterol ester %
HDL	33	30	29	4
LDL	25	50	21	8
IDL	18	29	22	31
VLDL	10	22	18	50
Chylomicrons	<2	8	7	84

All of the following classes would serve as effective carriers of triacylglycerols EXCEPT:

A) chylomicrons.
B) IDL.
C) VLDL.
D) HDL.

810. If a human were suddenly rendered unable to synthesize chylomicrons, what would happen to the transport of free fatty acids from his digestive tract?

A) Transport would be unaltered.
B) Transport would decrease.
C) Transport would halt entirely.
D) Transport would increase.

811. The full breakdown of glucose involves glycolysis, the citric acid cycle, and the electron transport chain, with transitions between many intermediates along the way. One of these intermediates is used for fatty acid synthesis. How many glucose molecules are required to generate enough of this intermediate to synthesize an eight-carbon fatty acid chain?

A) 1
B) 2
C) 4
D) 8

Questions 812–813 rely on the figure below

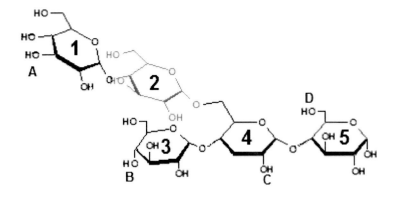

812. Glycogen synthase could be used to create a bond involving which hydroxyl group(s)?

A) An α-1,4 linkage on hydroxyl group A or B
B) An α-1,6 linkage on hydroxyl group C or D
C) An α-1,4 linkage on hydroxyl group D
D) An α-1,6 linkage on hydroxyl group B or D

813. A transferase enzyme might catalyze the cleavage of:

A) the bond between units 2 and 4, while reattaching units 1 and 2 to unit 3.
B) the bond between units 1 and 2, while reattaching unit 1 to unit 3.
C) the bond between units 3 and 4, while reattaching unit 3 to unit 1.
D) the bond between units 4 and 5, while reattaching unit 5 to unit 1 or 3, depending on the pH.

814. Acetyl-CoA, used in fatty acid synthesis, must travel between the cytosol and the mitochondrial matrix. By what means does this molecule cross the mitochondrial membrane?

A) Acetyl-CoA is hydrophobic and can thus diffuse across the membrane into the matrix.
B) Acetyl-CoA pairs with a Na^+/K^+ pump to be shuttled across the membrane via a transmembrane protein.
C) Coenzyme A is removed from acetyl-CoA, and the lone acetyl group is transferred with the aid of an enzyme.
D) Coenzyme A is removed from acetyl-CoA, and the lone acetyl group travels down a concentration gradient through a transmembrane protein.

815. Protein metabolism produces a toxic nitrogenous waste. Together, the liver and kidneys work to chemically alter this product into one that can be excreted by the body. Which toxic product is initially formed, and into which metabolite is it changed for excretion?

A) NH_3 is reduced to NH_2^-, which can be excreted.
B) NH_2^- is oxidized to NH_3, which can be excreted.
C) NO is converted to N_2 using ATP, which can be excreted.
D) NH_3 is converted to CH_4N_2O using ATP, which can be excreted.

816. Which of the following statements accurately characterize glycogen?

I. It represents a glucose polymer that is stored in order to increase intracellular osmotic pressure.
II. Entropy decreases when glucose is stored as glycogen, a process that is entropically unfavorable.
III. Glycogen is highly branched to maximize the number of exposed non-reducing sugars.
IV. The branching of glycogen increases its solubility in water.

A) II only
B) I and IV
C) II, III, and IV
D) I, III, and IV

817. Which metabolic pathway is NOT possible?

A) Proteins can be used to generate fatty acids.
B) Lactate can be used to generate glucose.
C) Glucose can be used to generate fatty acids.
D) Glucose can be used to generate proteins.

818. Typically, only 10-15% of an individual's energy comes from the metabolism of protein. A woman has a disorder that causes her body to preferentially degrade protein, leading her to obtain 85% of her energy from protein metabolism. What is a potential symptom of this disease?

A) Ketoacidosis
B) Organ failure
C) Low blood sugar
D) Decreased fat stores

Questions 819–820 rely on the figure below

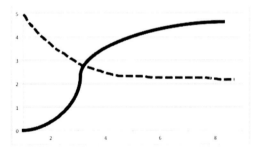

819. This graph plots the relative blood plasma concentration of a metabolite against days that an individual has spent fasting. Which combination below correctly assigns these lines?

A) The solid line is ketone bodies, while the dashed line is fatty acids.

B) The solid line is glycogen, while the dashed line is glucose.

C) The solid line is ketone bodies, while the dashed line is glucose.

D) The solid line is insulin, while the dashed line is fatty acids.

820. If the solid line soon plummeted, what would be the body's next fuel source?

A) Glycogen stores
B) Fatty tissue
C) Muscle
D) Acetyl-CoA from the Krebs cycle

821. An appropriate metabolic response to low blood glucose levels is:

I. decreasing the glycolytic rate.
II. increasing the rate of glycogenolysis.
III. increasing the rate of gluconeogenesis.
IV. decreasing ketone production.

A) I and II
B) I, II, and III
C) I, II, and IV
D) I, III, and IV

822. Which of these options correctly describes the function of glucagon in the human body?

A) Glucagon is released in response to low blood sugar and triggers an increase in glycogenolysis and gluconeogenesis.
B) Glucagon is released in response to low blood sugar and triggers an increase in glycolysis.
C) Glucagon is released in response to high blood sugar and triggers an increase in glycogenolysis and gluconeogenesis.
D) Glucagon is released in response to high blood sugar and triggers an increase in glycolysis.

823. In addition to the liver, where in the human body can gluconeogenesis occur?

A) The heart
B) The kidneys
C) The thyroid
D) Nowhere; gluconeogenesis only takes place in the liver.

824. Why must gluconeogenesis be localized to the kidney and liver and not other organs, such as the muscles or the heart?

   A) The liver and kidneys are the only organs that are directly attached to blood vessels. As such, only they are equipped to rapidly effect changes in blood sugar levels.
   B) Glycolysis occurs only in liver and kidney cells, so glucagon only affects these two organs.
   C) Muscle cells must be in a perfect homeostatic state to allow their consistent function.
   D) Muscle cells need a continually high supply of ATP; therefore, they require a high glycolytic, not gluconeogenic, rate.

825. A number of student researchers are investigating murine type II diabetes. They find that, despite consistently high insulin levels, the mice remain in a hyperglycemic state. How is this possible?

   A) The mice have a disease-induced need for added nutrients and continue to eat, which maintains the hyperglycemic state.
   B) The mice display high levels of glucagon and a high rate of gluconeogenesis, both of which promote hyperglycemia.
   C) The mice have developed a resistance to insulin, lessening its systematic effects.
   D) The mice are unable to metabolize sugar and therefore maintain a hyperglycemic state.

Questions 826–827 rely on the figure below

Blood glucose and insulin levels are tracked for three hours after a large meal in a diabetic and a non-diabetic patient.

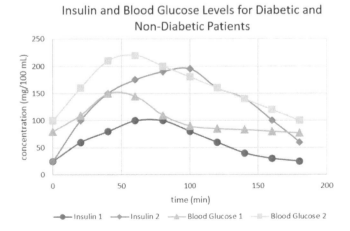

Insulin and Blood Glucose Levels for Diabetic and Non-Diabetic Patients

826. Which of these individuals is suffering from hyperglycemia and insulin resistance, and how can this be discerned?

   A) Patient 1, because he has lower blood sugar and insulin levels after eating.
   B) Patient 1, because he has higher blood sugar and insulin levels after eating.
   C) Patient 2, because he has lower blood sugar and insulin levels after eating.
   D) Patient 2, because he has higher blood sugar and insulin levels after eating.

827. If the researchers in the study had been measuring [glucagon] instead of [insulin], what results would be expected?

   A) In both patients 1 and 2, glucagon levels would be abnormally high.
   B) In patient 1, glucagon levels would fall near a baseline, while they would be increased in patient 2.
   C) In patient 1, glucagon levels would be increased, while they would fall near a baseline for patient 2.
   D) In both patients 1 and 2, glucagon levels would hover near a baseline.

Questions 828–829 rely on the table below

The following data shows the glucagon concentration and rate of gluconeogenesis in murine blood samples over a period of time.

Time (min)	[Glucagon] (mg / 100 mL)	Gluconeogenetic rate (mol / minute)
0	55.1	.005
25	53.8	.322
50	54.7	.005
75	55.1	.004
100	75.9	.222

828. What must have occurred to the mouse's plasma glucose levels between 75 and 100 minutes?

   A) The mouse's blood glucose levels must have risen.
   B) The mouse's blood glucose levels must have fallen.
   C) The mouse's blood glucose levels likely remained constant.
   D) We cannot be sure which changes are taking place during this time period.

829. At the 25-minute mark, the mouse showed a spike in its cellular rate of gluconeogenesis, but its glucagon concentration remained unchanged. What can explain this apparent contradiction?

   A) Gluconeogenic rate responded more rapidly to the low blood sugar levels than did glucagon secretion.
   B) The mouse may have consumed a meal, triggering an increase in gluconeogenesis.
   C) The mouse may have increased its epinephrine levels, possibly due to the stimulation of a fight-or-flight response.
   D) None of the above are sensible explanations.

830. Leptin is a hormone that is produced by adipose tissue and that regulates energy balance by triggering feelings of satiety (fullness). When tested, obese patients reported hunger at the end of a meal, despite displaying leptin levels much higher than their healthy-weight counterparts. Which of the following gives the best explanation for this observation?

   A) The obese patients have a mutated form of leptin.
   B) The obese patients have developed a tolerance to high levels of leptin.
   C) The brain chemistry of the obese patients has caused leptin to switch to trigger feelings of hunger instead of suppressing them.
   D) The obese patients have decreased insulin sensitivity, so they are unable to regulate their energy balance.

831. In which of the following cellular processes does a nucleotide directly participate?

   I. Storage and reproduction of genetic information
   II. Transfer of energy during metabolism
   III. Degradation of proteins
   IV. Intracellular signal transduction of hormonal signals

   A) I only
   B) I and III
   C) I, II, and IV
   D) I, III, and IV

832. How does the molecular structure of cAMP differ from that of AMP?

   A) cAMP has a cyclic phosphate group that is bound to carbons 5' and 3' of a ribose sugar.
   B) cAMP has a cyclic bond between the adenine and the 3' hydroxyl group.
   C) cAMP is a large protein that forms a cyclic structure around AMP.
   D) cAMP has a deoxyribose sugar, while AMP has a ribose sugar.

833. Which of these functional groups or bonds is NOT found in all nucleosides?

   A) An N-glycosidic linkage
   B) A pyrimidine ring
   C) A phosphodiester bond
   D) A pentose sugar

834. Which of the following is a cellular function of RNA in the human body?

   A) Post-transcriptional modification and splicing
   B) Storage and replication of genetic information
   C) Transport of molecules to the cell membrane
   D) All of the above are functions of RNA in the human body.

835. When asked to draw a nucleotide, a student draws a pyrimidine ring attached to an arabinose sugar, with a triphosphate group bound to the 2' carbon. Was the student correct?

   A) No, a nucleotide has phosphate groups attached to the 5' carbon only.
   B) No, he has drawn a nucleoside. Nucleotides do not have phosphate groups.
   C) No, a nucleotide must include either a ribose or a deoxyribose sugar.
   D) Yes, the student was correct.

Questions 836–837 rely on the figure below

The melting or denaturation curves for three distinct DNA samples are shown below.

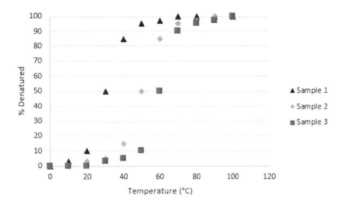

836. Which sample has the highest guanine content?
    A) Sample 1
    B) Sample 2
    C) Sample 3
    D) It cannot be determined from the graph.

837. If sample 3 were denatured, after which 1% of the bases on each strand were randomly mutated, what would happen to the resulting double-stranded DNA following reannealing?

    A) The two strands would no longer share enough sequence similarity to reanneal.
    B) The melting temperature of the final dsDNA would increase.
    C) The melting temperature of the resulting strand would remain the same.
    D) The melting temperature of the resulting strand would decrease.

Questions 838–839 rely on the table below

A sequencing analysis was conducted on the genomes of four different organisms.

Sample	% adenine	% cytosine	% thymine	% guanine	% uracil
1	26.6	23.4	0	23.6	26.4
2	13.0	37.2	10.9	36.8	2.1
3	21.3	28.9	20.7	29.1	0
4	23.5	26.5	18.3	26.5	5.2

838. Which of the samples represents a species with an RNA-based genome?

    A) Sample 1
    B) Sample 2
    C) Sample 3
    D) Sample 4

839. One of the nucleic acid samples was isolated from an organism that lives at extremely low temperatures. The most likely identity of this sample is:

    A) Sample 1.
    B) Sample 2.
    C) Sample 3.
    D) Sample 4.

840. Why is DNA found in a double-helical structure in eukaryotes, even though RNA is generally single-stranded?

A) Replacing thymine with uracil destabilizes the structure, as U is unable to hydrogen bond with other nucleotides.

B) The 2' OH group disrupts the double helical structure.

C) The DNA double helix is held together by accessory proteins that are not found in the environment of mRNA.

D) DNA only tends to form a double helix because it is compacted into the nucleus.

841. The nicotinic acetylcholine receptor, the principal ACh receptor expressed at the neuromuscular junction, responds to excitatory input from cholinergic motor neurons. Interestingly, no signal seems to exist to inhibit skeletal muscle contraction; instead, cholinergic input is rapidly suppressed by the action of synaptic acetylcholinesterase. In the absence of ACh release, contraction does not occur. Which of the following most accurately describes the relationship between the nicotinic receptor and its ligand?

A) The receptor binds its ligand with high affinity and high specificity.

B) The receptor binds its ligand with high affinity but low specificity.

C) The receptor binds its ligand with low affinity but high specificity.

D) The receptor binds its ligand with low affinity and low specificity.

842. The bacterial potassium channel operates in a similar manner to the eukaryotic K^+ channel that is involved in action potential propagation. Like neurons, bacteria are sensitive to subtle osmotic changes, and the potassium ions that pass through this channel are not hydrated. The most plausible explanation for the exclusion of sodium ions from this bacterial channel is that:

A) sodium ions have a larger atomic radius, excluding them from the channel due to steric constraints.

B) sodium ions have a smaller atomic radius, allowing them to maintain a more tightly-coordinated sphere of hydration.

C) sodium ions have a different charge distribution, and as a result interact unfavorably with residues lining the channel.

D) sodium ions have a slightly smaller positive charge, reducing their relative affinity for the channel.

Questions 843–844 rely on the figure below

The neuronal voltage-gated sodium channel has been extensively studied. A diagram of this transmembrane protein in its resting state is shown below. The channel has four separate transmembrane domains, each consisting of six membrane-spanning helices. Specific motifs are highly conserved and functionally relevant, namely the P-loops, S-loops, and I-loops.

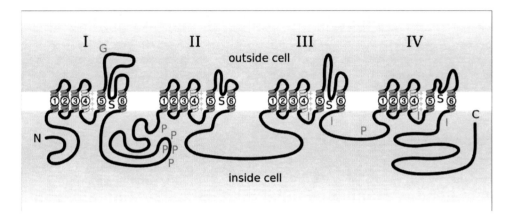

843. Elimination by hydrolytic cleavage of the S-loops permits free passage of sodium ions through the channel even in the absence of any change in membrane voltage. In contrast, substitution by mutagenesis of S-loop residues with alanine results in a channel that does not respond to voltage changes, but that also cannot be induced to conduct ions. Based on this information, the amino acid residues in the S-loop are most likely:

    A) positively charged, which results in a conformational change during depolarization that shifts the S-loop toward the extracellular side.
    B) positively charged, which results in a conformational change during depolarization that shifts the S-loop toward the intracellular side.
    C) negatively charged, which results in a conformational change during depolarization that shifts the S-loop toward the extracellular side.
    D) negatively charged, which results in a conformational change during depolarization that shifts the S-loop toward the intracellular side.

844. As the figure shows, the transmembrane domain of the sodium channel is primarily alpha-helical. With respect to amino acid composition, how can one best describe the alpha helices labeled 1-6?

    A) They are composed almost exclusively of hydrophobic residues.
    B) They are composed almost exclusively of hydrophilic resides.
    C) Roughly half of the residues are hydrophobic, while the other half are hydrophilic.
    D) The residues on the intracellular ends are primarily hydrophilic, while those on the extracellular ends are hydrophobic.

845. The Src Homology 2 (SH2) domain is highly specific for phosphorylated tyrosine residues and is expressed across nearly all species. Which of these proteins is most likely to contain an SH2 domain?

    A) PI3K, a cellular signaling enzyme activated when IGF-1 binds its receptor tyrosine kinase
    B) Adenylyl cyclase, an enzyme activated by G_s following stimulation of beta-adrenergic receptors
    C) CaMKII, a kinase stimulated by elevated intracellular calcium
    D) Phospholipase C (PLC), an enzyme that cleaves phosphate groups from a number of various phospholipids

Questions 846–847 rely on the figure below

Akt is a well-studied kinase with multiple effectors and extremely tight regulation. A highly simplified model of the Akt pathway is depicted here.

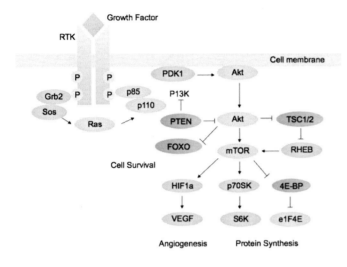

846. Which of the following would best be described as a tumor suppressor protein?

    A) mTOR
    B) VEGF
    C) PTEN
    D) PDK1

847. Decreased FOXO activity has been implicated in the development of a number of cancers. This protein has been found to exist in a number of different phosphorylation states. FOXO most likely functions as a:

    A) transcription factor that activates apoptosis and that is phosphorylated to prevent nuclear entry.
    B) transcription factor that inhibits apoptosis and that is phosphorylated to prevent nuclear entry.
    C) transcription factor that activates apoptosis and that is phosphorylated to permit nuclear entry.
    D) transcription factor that inhibits apoptosis and that is phosphorylated to permit nuclear entry.

848. G protein-coupled receptors can achieve signal amplification because:

    A) a single GPCR in its resting state is bound to multiple G proteins.
    B) multiple ligands are able to bind simultaneously to a single GPCR.
    C) a single G protein alpha subunit is able to interact with multiple target proteins.
    D) G proteins lack enzymatic activity.

849. Ras is a small protein with a structure similar to the alpha subunit of a typical heterotrimeric G protein. Ras, which is involved in cellular growth and cell cycle procession, is regulated in part by the actions of NF-1. NF-1 is a tumor suppressor and a member of a class of molecules known as GTPase-activating proteins (GAPs). Loss-of-function mutations in NF-1 are associated with the development of von Recklinghausen syndrome, a tumor disorder. In patients with von Recklinghausen syndrome, Ras activity is most likely:

    A) abnormally high, because NF-1 normally promotes Ras inactivation.
    B) abnormally high, because NF-1 normally promotes Ras activation.
    C) abnormally low, because NF-1 normally promotes Ras inactivation.
    D) abnormally low, because NF-1 normally promotes Ras activation.

850. Tyrosine kinase inhibitors (TKIs) were developed near the end of the twentieth century and proved highly effective in binding the receptor tyrosine kinase (RTK) and disrupting its interaction with its immediate partner, Grb2. Most forms of myelogenous leukemia involve a unique chromosomal abnormality, resulting in the formation of a constitutively-acting kinase variant called Bcr-Abl. The resulting uncontrolled growth signal leads to a rare form of cancer. Recently, even third-generation TKIs have become ineffective in the management of this previously treatable condition. Which of these genetic changes could account for this resistance?

   A) A mutation in the ligand-binding pocket of Bcr-Abl that confers higher affinity
   B) A mutation in Ras, a downstream effector of Bcr-Abl, that renders it constitutively active
   C) A mutation in Grb2 that reduces its affinity for the TKI
   D) A mutation in Grb2 that reduces its affinity for the RTK

851. Tumor necrosis factor alpha (TNFα) is a cytokine produced by activated macrophages, the receptor for which is normally expressed by nearly all somatic cells. Late-stage cancers frequently present with cachexia, a wasting disorder resulting from chronic elevation of TNFα. Which of the following mutations would one expect to find in metastatic cancer cells?

   I. Decreased expression of TNFα receptors
   II. A gain-of-function that enables production of NF-κB, a protein shown to inhibit neuronal TNFα-mediated apoptosis
   III. A gain-of-function that enables production of TNFα
   IV. Increased expression of VEGF, a transcription factor that is vital for angiogenesis

   A) I only
   B) II and IV only
   C) I, II, and IV
   D) I, II, III, and IV

852. Carboplatin, shown below, is a fairly new chemotherapeutic agent developed from a successful compound of similar structure, cisplatin.

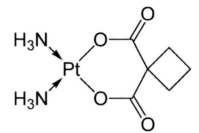

While the exact mechanism by which carboplatin exerts its cytotoxic effects is unclear, the coordinating ammonia molecules are believed to dissociate upon cellular uptake. Cells treated with carboplatin would most likely:

   A) undergo necrosis and release their cellular contents in membranous vesicles.
   B) undergo necrosis and release their cellular contents freely into the extracellular space following membrane collapse.
   C) undergo apoptosis and release their cellular contents in membranous vesicles.
   D) undergo apoptosis and release their cellular contents freely into the extracellular space following membrane collapse.

853. Caspases, also known as cysteine proteases, are instrumental in the progression of the apoptotic pathway. Prior to initiation of apoptosis, caspases exist as inactive pro-caspases in the cytosol. Caspase activation is tightly controlled and is actually mediated by the action of cytochrome c. Which of these targets is a likely substrate for cellular caspase?

   A) ATP synthase, causing the arrest of oxygen consumption and dissipation of the mitochondrial membrane potential
   B) The phosphate backbone of DNA, following caspase-mediated degradation of the nuclear structural lamina
   C) The small nuclear protein ICAD, resulting in its dissociation from its binding partner, a DNase
   D) The small cytosolic protein Bax, thus initiating pore formation in the outer mitochondrial membrane

854. Fas, which is expressed by most healthy somatic cells, is a membrane receptor that triggers apoptosis when bound by Fas ligand. Both Fas ligand and Fas itself are expressed on the surface of CD8+ T cells, the former of which enables, at least in part, their cytotoxic function. Cells that are LEAST likely to express Fas ligand include:

A) cells of the blood-testes barrier.
B) cells lining the placental capillaries.
C) CD4+ T cells.
D) cells of a metastatic carcinoma.

Questions 855–856 rely on the figure below

A portion of the phospholipase C (PLC) pathway is shown here.

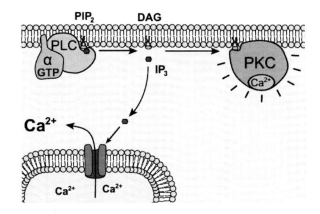

855. With regard to structure, DAG most closely resembles:

A) testosterone.
B) ATP.
C) histamine.
D) prostaglandin.

856. In addition to the role depicted in the figure, which of the following is likely performed by PLC?

A) Conversion of phosphatidylcholine to arachidonic acid
B) Conversion of arachidonic acid to thromboxanes
C) Conversion of inositol 1,4,5-trisphosphate to inositol
D) Conversion of cholesterol to vitamin D

857. The potential role of lipids in intracellular signaling has only recently become apparent; since most lipids are confined to a specific membrane, they were originally deemed unlikely signaling candidates. One lipid of considerable interest is ceramide, due in part to its proposed role in relaying apoptotic signals. Which statement, if true, would provide the strongest evidence AGAINST the hypothesis that ceramide acts as a proapoptotic signaling molecule?

A) Induced expression of Bax, a proapoptotic protein with a ceramide-binding domain, does not promote apoptosis in cells treated with a known ceramidase inhibitor.
B) Exposure to chemotherapeutic agents and ionizing radiation induces cellular accumulation of ceramide in the mitochondrial outer membrane, but not in the plasma membrane.
C) Cells treated with exogenous extracellular ceramide fail to show any bias toward an apoptotic fate.
D) Overexpression of Bcl-2, a known anti-apoptotic protein, can rescue cells from apoptosis but does not reduce ceramide levels in the mitochondrial or plasma membranes.

858. Cholesterol biosynthesis is tightly regulated by the action of SREBP; when cellular cholesterol levels are high, this species exists in complex with two other proteins, SCAP and INSIG-1. Upon dissociation from its binding partners, SREBP is able to enter the nucleus and act as a transcription factor. SREBP most likely activates transcription of the gene(s) for:

A) S1P and S2P, the Golgi-associated proteases responsible for the cleavage of SREBP from its partners.
B) the low-density lipoprotein (LDL) receptor, which has a high affinity for serum LDL.
C) HMG-CoA synthase, an enzyme responsible for producing HMG-CoA, which is then converted to mevalonate during the rate-limiting step of cholesterol biosynthesis.
D) Apolipoprotein B, which binds free cellular cholesterol to permit export and effective vascular transport.

859. Ganaxolone is an orally bioavailable, synthetic neurosteroid under investigation for the treatment of seizures and other neurological disorders. Ganaxolone binds the GABA receptor and rapidly alters the excitability of its target neuron, ultimately increasing the seizure threshold. Compared to most other steroids, ganaxolone is most accurately described as:

A) atypical, because it binds an extracellular receptor.

B) atypical, because it penetrates the blood-brain barrier.

C) typical, because it elicits a rapid cellular response.

D) typical, because it does not alter gene expression.

860. Aspirin is routinely prescribed to patients at risk of myocardial infarction. Aspirin irreversibly inhibits an enzyme necessary for the synthesis of thromboxane A2, a prostaglandin derivative produced by activated platelets. Likely actions of thromboxane A2 include:

A) deactivation of genes coding for tissue plasminogen.

B) stimulation of vascular smooth muscle.

C) formation of cross-links between multiple fibrin strands.

D) reduction of endothelial cell membrane fluidity.

Psychology

861. A waiter in a café measures the intensity of sound in the dining room to be 50 dB. As two customers leave, decreasing the sound intensity to 49 dB, he notices that the café becomes quieter. If the café is at 55 dB at peak hours and a large family enters, increasing the sound intensity to 60 dB, at what point would the waiter notice the increase in sound?

A) 49 dB
B) 59 dB
C) 56 dB
D) 60 dB

Questions 862–863 rely on the following scenario

At 0.5 dB, a sound does not even stir the hair cells in an animal's inner ear. However, the sound intensifies, reaching 2 dB, at which point the associated signal is sent to the animal's central nervous system. Finally, the sound further loudens to 130 dB, causing the animal discomfort before gradually returning to 0.5 dB.

862. At what point is the animal's absolute threshold reached?

A) 0.1 dB
B) 0.5 dB
C) 2 dB
D) 130 dB

863. The point at which the animal consciously perceives the sound is:

A) 0.5 dB.
B) 2.0 dB.
C) 130 dB.
D) It cannot be determined from the given information.

Questions 864–865 rely on the figure below

Some of a study's participants are deprived of sleep by being told to arrive at the lab extremely early in the morning. Upon arriving, these individuals are exposed to certain audible tones. Later, both sleep-deprived and healthy subjects are made to listen to "beeps" of gradually increasing intensity, while pushing a button as soon as they perceive a sound. The same individuals are also presented with noxious odors at random intervals and instructed to tell the researcher when they notice each smell. Average results for the two experimental groups are shown below. Note that the "sound" values represent the average lowest intensity at which participants noticed a beep, while "odor" values denote the average amount of time passed before subjects mentioned perceiving a smell.

	Stressed subjects	Healthy subjects
Sound	0 dB	0.5 dB
Odor	5 s	4 s

864. Which of the following statements regarding signal detection and this data, if assumed to be statistically significant, is most likely true?

   A) Because stressed subjects had been previously presented with more sound stimuli, the beeps became less noticeable.
   B) Because healthy subjects had no response bias, their threshold of conscious perception for sound was lower.
   C) Because stressed subjects had been previously presented with more sound stimuli, they began to perceive the sound at a lower intensity.
   D) Both A and B are sensible.

865. If both stressed and healthy subjects were also made to perform tasks while presented with sounds of increasing intensity, which of these statements describe adaptation? Assume that all experimental trends mentioned are true.

   I. The stressed subjects adapted more quickly because they noticed the sounds at lower decibel levels, making them more distracted.

   II. The healthy subjects adapted more quickly because they noticed the sounds at higher decibel levels, making them less distracted.
   III. The healthy subjects adapted more quickly because they had less of a response bias and were consequently less affected by the stimuli.
   IV. The stressed subjects adapted more quickly because they were more accustomed to the sounds and, as a result, tended to focus more than the healthy subjects.

   A) I only
   B) II only
   C) IV only
   D) I and III

866. Which sequence best describes the pathway taken by visual information in the human body?

   A) Optic tracts → occipital lobe → lateral geniculate nucleus → visual cortex
   B) Optic tracts → lateral geniculate nucleus → occipital lobe → visual cortex
   C) Lateral geniculate nucleus → optic tracts → occipital lobe → visual cortex
   D) Lateral geniculate nucleus → occipital lobe → optic tracts → visual cortex

867. A child riding a bicycle feels a bee lightly brush his face and then watches it as it flies blurrily by. All of the following sensory receptors were used when the child perceived the bee EXCEPT:

   A) magnocellular cells.
   B) cones.
   C) parvocellular cells.
   D) Meissner's corpuscles.

868. A group of patients have difficulty focusing on fixed objects when moving across the room or even rotating their heads. What structure is LEAST likely to be damaged in these individuals, based on their symptoms?

   A) Inferior colliculus
   B) Medial geniculate nucleus
   C) Lateral geniculate nucleus
   D) Auditory cortex

869. A case study describes a patient who has hair cells only in part of his cochlea. Which symptom is most likely to be caused by this deficiency?

    A) Unequalized pressure between the ear and the environment
    B) The perception of sounds of different frequencies as exactly the same
    C) The inability to hear sounds of certain frequencies
    D) The inability to hear any sounds at all

870. What is one example of adaptation in relation to signal detection?

    A) A child living near a bread factory begins to associate the smell of bread with home.
    B) A resident who spends long hours in fluorescent lighting more frequently looks downwards.
    C) A man who resides above a bakery stops noticing the smell wafting from below.
    D) A teacher learns to pause his lecture when he hears the intercom speaker begin to crackle.

871. The diagram below depicts the human eye.

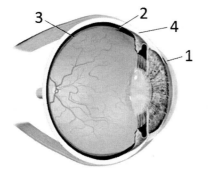

A middle-aged woman who must wear protective sunglasses in bright light most likely has a problem with which labeled structure?

    A) Structure 1, the cornea
    B) Structure 3, the sclera
    C) Structure 2, the choroid
    D) Structure 4, the retina

872. A patient is admitted to the emergency room with notably constricted pupils after taking recreational drugs. If a doctor wanted to dilate his pupils to a normal level, which division of the nervous system should he aim to stimulate?

    A) The sympathetic nervous system
    B) The parasympathetic nervous system
    C) Both A and B
    D) The answer to this question cannot be determined with the information given.

873. Individuals who have trouble seeing in the dark may have:

    A) low numbers of cones.
    B) low numbers of rods.
    C) an overexpression of rhodopsin.
    D) high numbers of both rods and cones.

874. James, a blind man, has a perfectly healthy occipital lobe. Additionally, visual information travels unhindered until it reaches his brain. Which part of James' visual pathway is probably damaged?

    A) The optic chiasm
    B) The visual cortex
    C) The lateral geniculate nucleus
    D) The optic tracts

Questions 875–876 rely on the figure below

A visuospatial study measured the visual capacities exhibited by several groups of individuals with distinct degenerative diseases. Members of each group were placed in a well-lit room and positioned seven meters from a screen. They were then told to identify a variety of fixed and moving objects. Results below show the percentage of properly identified objects for each case.

	Group 1	Group 2	Group 3
Fixed object	95%	97%	27%
Moving object	25%	98%	94%

875. Individuals in Group 1 most likely suffer from a deterioration of their:

    A) parvocellular cells.
    B) magnocellular cells.
    C) horizontal cells.
    D) none of the above.

876. Which of the statements below accurately summarize the data from this study?

   I. Members of Group 1 have healthy magnocellular cells.
   II. Members of Group 3 do not have damaged parvocellular cells.
   III. Members of Group 3 have healthy magnocellular cells.
   IV. Members of Groups 1 and 2 have healthy parvocellular cells.

   A) I and II
   B) II and IV
   C) III and IV
   D) I, II, and IV

877. When observing a certain blind patient, clinicians note that visual information reaches her healthy rods and cones; however, it never makes it to her ganglion cells. Which structure(s) may be damaged in this case?

   A) Horizontal cells
   B) Optic tracts
   C) Bipolar cells
   D) The optic nerve

878. A.K., an individual described in an advanced neurobiology textbook, can easily detect color and the shapes of objects, but not light and dark nor motion. Of the choices below, the most logical conclusion is that A.K. has an impairment of his:

   A) parvocellular cells and rods.
   B) magnocellular cells and cones.
   C) parvocellular cells and cones.
   D) magnocellular cells and rods.

879. In the complex process of "bionic eye" design, scientists are attempting to eliminate the natural blind spot exhibited by the human eye. Which solution, if possible, would best address this problem?

   A) Add more rods to the fovea
   B) Add more cones to the macula
   C) Add more cones and rods to the optic disc
   D) Change the shape of the eye from round to oval

880. All of the following statements regarding the visual pathway are true EXCEPT:

   A) the temporal fibers do not cross paths.
   B) the optic fibers closest to the nose do cross paths.
   C) at the optic chiasm, visual signals synapse from bipolar cells to ganglion cells.
   D) visual information travels through the temporal lobe.

881. A patient has suffered a head injury that is causing severe hearing loss. Sound appears to travel normally through his external auditory canal and tympanic membrane, but is not reaching the oval window of the organ of Corti. The damaged structure in this case is most likely the:

   A) pinna.
   B) stapes.
   C) basilar membrane.
   D) vestibule.

882. A number of individuals in a clinical trial have trouble balancing and remaining upright when running. These patients most likely have a deficiency in which part of or fluid within the ear?

   A) The endolymph
   B) The perilymph
   C) The vestibule
   D) The ampulla

883. A new species of desert iguana is discovered to possess structurally similar ears to those of humans. However, these reptiles do not have necks and never evolved to walk in curved or circular paths. As animals that only have the capacity to travel in straight lines, which structure do these iguanas most likely lack in comparison to humans?

   A) Scalae
   B) Eustachian tubes
   C) Vestibulocochlear nerves
   D) Semicircular canals

884. Researchers building a prosthetic hearing system want to create an auditory pathway as similar as possible to that of humans. The most appropriate order for this pathway would be:

A) organ of Corti → medial geniculate nucleus → auditory cortex.
B) superior olive → organ of Corti → medial geniculate nucleus → auditory cortex.
C) organ of Corti → medial geniculate nucleus → superior olive → auditory cortex.
D) organ of Corti → auditory cortex → medial geniculate nucleus.

Questions 885–886 rely on the figure below

Two groups of people with hearing problems, as well as one control group, were categorized according to the presence and type of structural damage in their ears. Each participant wore headphones, through which researchers played tones of increasing frequency and loudness. The individuals were told to press a button immediately after perceiving a tone. Finally, the researchers determined the lowest frequency and loudness at which each participant could hear a sound, then averaged those values for each group. The results of the study are summarized below.

	Group 1	Group 2	Group 3
Minimum frequency (Hz)	25	25	100
Minimum loudness (dB)	0	5	75

885. If the members of each experimental group were given cochlear implants, which group would benefit most?

A) Group 1
B) Group 2
C) Group 3
D) Both Group 2 and Group 3

886. One of the groups consists of individuals who have extreme difficulty perceiving their orientation in space. The most likely identity of this group is:

A) Group 1.
B) Group 2.
C) Group 3.
D) impossible to determine from the information given.

887. Five males between the ages of 15 and 35 are seated in a room equipped with a surround sound speaker system. A series of tones is then played from individual speakers; the participants must verbally identify which direction each tone comes from. Those who have trouble with this task may have suffered damage to their:

A) ampullae.
B) medial geniculate nuclei.
C) superior olives.
D) inferior colliculi.

888. The diagram below shows a section of the auditory canal.

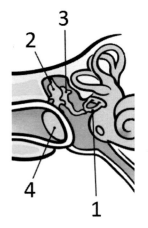

All of the following are present in the middle ear EXCEPT:

A) the vestibule, labeled here as structure 4.
B) the incus, labeled here as structure 3.
C) the malleus, labeled here as structure 2.
D) the stapes, labeled here as structure 1.

889. Jackie M., a patient in a case study, has significant trouble locating the sources of sounds. Additionally, she cannot focus her vision on a specific point in space while rotating her head. Which of these statements is likely true of Jackie M.?

 I. Her auditory cortex is damaged, since she cannot localize sounds.
 II. Her superior olive is damaged, since she cannot fixate on a point when rotating her head.
 III. Her inferior colliculus is damaged, leading to her inability to detect the locations of sounds.
 IV. Her semicircular canals are damaged, creating the issue with sound localization.

 A) I and II
 B) II and III
 C) II and IV
 D) None of these statements are true.

890. A certain astronaut has lived aboard the International Space Station for more than two years. If he begins to having trouble sensing rotational acceleration, which structure in his ear may be damaged?

 A) The utricle
 B) The saccule
 C) The superior olive
 D) The ampullae

891. Which of these statements are true regarding sensation and perception?

 I. The two-point threshold defines the minimum distance between two regions that allows them to be perceived as distinct touch stimuli when simultaneously stimulated.
 II. Physiological zero refers to the normal temperature of skin.
 III. Smell is intensely linked to emotion because it is processed directly by the limbic system.
 IV. Taste receptors are grouped together on the tongue so that certain areas of the tongue only detect specific flavors.

 A) I only
 B) I and III
 C) I, II, and III
 D) I, III, and IV

892. Which disease or trauma would most likely result in damage, whether permanent or temporary, to a patient's vestibular sense?

 A) An upper respiratory infection
 B) A fungal infection of the tongue
 C) An inner ear infection
 D) A spinal cord injury

893. Which of these pairings does NOT correctly link a sense to the part of the brain in which it is at least partially processed?

 A) Somatosensation – somatosensory cortex
 B) Taste – thalamus
 C) Smell – limbic system
 D) Hearing – medulla

894. After being diagnosed with a rare nerve disorder, a student is unable to recognize pain or distinguish temperature. However, he is able to perceive light touch, vibrations, and textures. Which nerve type is most likely affected by this student's condition?

 A) Olfactory chemoreceptors
 B) Meissner's corpuscles
 C) Merkel's disks
 D) Free nerve endings

895. A doctor runs a quick neurological assessment on a patient. First, the patient walks in a straight line with his eyes closed, then stands on one foot. Second, he is told to close his eyes and touch his nose and other parts of his body with his hand. Finally, he is asked to distinguish between two different objects based on touch. Which three senses, in order, has the doctor just tested?

 A) Vestibular sense, proprioception, somatosensation
 B) Proprioception, vestibular sense, somatosensation
 C) Somatosensation, vestibular sense, somatosensation
 D) Vestibular sense, proprioception, proprioception

Questions 896–897 rely on the figure below

Data is collected regarding five patients at a local clinic following the outbreak of an unknown bacterial disease. All responses are rated on a scale of 1 to 5, with 5 corresponding to a healthy human baseline and 1 corresponding to a complete loss of function.

Patient	Response light touch	Response to temperature	Response to vibration	Response to smell	Response to taste
1	3	5	4	5	5
2	3	5	4	5	5
3	5	5	5	5	5
4	2	4	3	5	5
5	1	3	2	5	5

896. Based on the given data, which type of receptors seem unaffected by the bacterium?

A) Light receptors
B) Chemoreceptors
C) Pain receptors
D) Mechanoreceptors

897. Considering the sensory impairments that are already evident, which additional symptom could be seen in these patients?

A) Loss of ability to detect vibrations
B) Loss of hearing
C) Loss of proprioception
D) Both A or B could be observed.

Questions 898–899 rely on the table below

The following table lists three female patients with various nerve disorders, as well as their rated responses to different stimuli. Responses are standardized to represent a percentage of average healthy human values.

Patient	Reported perception of taste	Reported perception of smell	Response to heat
1	99.5%	50%	99.5%
2	65%	150%	75%
3	175%	220%	160%

898. Which of the following statements is true?

A) Patient 1 is experiencing generalized decreased sensation to all stimuli.
B) Patient 2 is experiencing a decrease in sensation related to chemoreceptors.
C) Patient 3 is experiencing generalized increased sensation to stimuli.
D) Patient 3 is not experiencing any nerve issues.

899. It is found that Patient 2 has a fungal infection that is destroying his thalamus. Does this information match the results from the table?

A) No, the thalamus is involved all sensation; therefore, this patient should exhibit a reduced response to all stimuli.
B) Yes, smell bypasses the thalamus and goes directly to the limbic system, meaning that this patient's olfactory sense could be intact or even increased.
C) No, the response to heat would not be affected by the degeneration of the thalamus.
D) Yes, degeneration of the thalamus would directly cause an increase in smell perception.

900. Which of these listed conditions would most likely result in nausea, dizziness, and vertigo?

A) A puncture within the semicircular canal that has caused leakage of the fluid inside

B) A viral infection of the auditory nerve that does not affect the surrounding tissue

C) A large impaction of ear wax in the outer ear canal

D) An infection of the optic nerve

901. Which of the following is an example of bottom-up processing?

A) A series of broken lines is perceived as a triangle.

B) A man at the zoo can only see the legs of an animal, since a wall covers the rest of her body. He concludes that the animal is an elephant based on available information.

C) A banana is placed before a newborn. The baby's retina receives the light transmitted from the banana, causing a signal to ultimately be sent to the visual cortex of his brain. He perceives the characteristics of the banana without knowing what it is.

D) In a crowded and noisy cafeteria, a young woman clearly hears her name being called in the midst of many other sounds.

902. The figure below was shown to twenty participants in an experiment dealing with visuospatial perception.

Perceiving this picture as two parallel lines demonstrates which Gestalt principle?

A) Proximity

B) Closure

C) Feature detection

D) Parallel processing

903. All Gestalt principles are governed by the "law of Prägnanz." To what does this refer?

A) The underlying principle that, in organizing perceived objects, we will always seek to make things as precise, simple, symmetrical, and meaningful as we can

B) The law that we tend to recognize bright and colorful objects before drab or gray ones

C) The idea that bottom-up processing is preferential to top-down processing

D) The understanding that perception is a phenomenon unique to every individual and that different people will always perceive objects differently

904. A man is driving down an unfamiliar road and spots a sign for a restaurant. Although a few letters are missing, he can still read the name of the restaurant and stops for something to eat. Which perceptual technique did this man most directly utilize?

A) Bottom-up processing

B) Top-down processing

C) The law of similarity

D) The law of proximity

905. The difference between monocular and binocular cues is that:

A) monocular cues are perceived by one person, while binocular cues are perceived by two or more.

B) monocular cues depend on a single sensory system, while binocular cues require the orchestration of several.

C) monocular cues can be directly perceived, while binocular cues require conscious manipulation.

D) monocular cues can be perceived with one eye, while binocular cues require both eyes.

906. Which of these examples best demonstrates the Gestalt principle of closure?

    A) While in his bedroom, James hears the sound of the garage door closing and assumes that his mother has returned from work.
    B) Thomas closes one of his eyes and notices that part of his visual field disappears.
    C) The NBA symbol does not actually show a person, but rather an outline made by two separate shapes. Our brains then perceive this as a basketball player.
    D) Jessica visits France and, although she cannot read the signs on the door, she notices the symbol of a woman in a skirt and enters the woman's bathroom.

907. Monocular cues include:

    A) retinal disparities.
    B) convergence.
    C) somatosensation.
    D) relative size.

908. Which of the following situations describes the perceptual cue of motion parallax?

    A) While riding in a car, John looks out the window. His brain interprets that objects moving very fast are closer than those moving slowly.
    B) While running in the park, Jeff's brain filters out any bouncing that occurs to keep his field of vision relatively constant.
    C) Anna spins in a circle for two minutes; when she stops, the world still appears to spin.
    D) Objects must move at or above a minimum speed in order for us to perceive their motion.

909. A scientist conducts an experiment in which two groups of subjects view a series of photos. She notices that the first group can easily discern the relative sizes of the objects in the photos, but have a harder time determining depth. The second group can easily perceive both depth and relative size. According to these findings, what might we deduce about the difference between the two groups in the experimental design?

    A) The first group observed the photos from over ten feet away, while the second was allowed to stand much closer.
    B) The first group was composed of men, while the second was composed of women.
    C) The first group observed black-and-white photos, while the second looked at color photographs.
    D) The first group observed the photos with only one eye, while the second observed the photos with both eyes.

910. While at the local amusement park, two young women notice that as the sun sets, the blue color of the roller coaster changes slightly due to differences in lighting. One woman tells the other that the Gestalt principle of similarity explains why our brain still interprets this as the same object. What is incorrect about her statement?

    A) Gestalt principles relate to emotional, not visual, perception.
    B) She is not incorrect; the Gestalt principle of similarity does explain this phenomenon.
    C) The principle of similarity states that similar objects tend to be grouped together by the brain. The phenomenon described is actually explained by the concept of perceptual constancy.
    D) The principle of continuity, not that of similarity, explains this phenomenon.

911. A scientist uses electroencephalography to monitor the sleep cycles of several apparently healthy participants. What should be true of the EEG of someone who is fully awake?

    I.   It prominently features beta waves.
    II. It is marked by high-frequency, low-amplitude waveforms.
    III. It prominently features alpha waves.
    IV. It includes waves that are synchronous.

       A) I and II
       B) I and IV
       C) II and III
       D) II, III, and IV

912. All of the following are hallmarks of a state of alertness EXCEPT:

    A) raised cortisol levels.
    B) attentiveness to the self.
    C) possession of the capacity to think.
    D) diminished cortisol levels.

913. Exhibition of moderate activity on an EMG is typical of which of these listed sleep stages?

    A) Stage 1
    B) Stage 2
    C) Stage 3
    D) All of the above

914. In which sleep stage, when analyzed with electroencephalography, would a patient display beta waves?

    A) Stage 2
    B) Stage 3
    C) Stage 4
    D) REM sleep

915. The main observation that distinguishes REM sleep from a state of physiological awakeness is:

    A) different types of brainwaves.
    B) lowered heart rate.
    C) low EMG readings.
    D) increased respiration.

Questions 916–917 rely on the figure below

A pharmacologist intends to study the effect of proper sleep on cortisol concentration. To do so, he monitors the plasma of both healthy and sleep-deprived individuals immediately after meals throughout the day. The results are summarized in table form here.

Group	Plasma concentration (µg/dl)		
	Morning	Afternoon	Evening
Control	6	22	7
Sleep-deprived	9	27	8

916. Name the part of the brain that is likely overstimulated in sleep-deprived individuals.

    A) The posterior pituitary gland
    B) The anterior pituitary gland
    C) The temporal lobe
    D) The pineal gland

917. Which of these factors would be most helpful to know when evaluating the data yielded by the study?

    A) The brightness of the environment
    B) The age of individuals in the study
    C) The capacity of the participants to sense sound and taste stimuli
    D) The participants' professions

918. A scientist holds the personal belief that dreams are sequences of events randomly ordered by the brain while we sleep. This belief most closely coincides with which theory of dreams?

    A) Activation-synthesis theory
    B) Problem-solving dream theory
    C) Cognitive dream theory
    D) Activation-oriented theory

919. An individual who has somnambulism experiences which stages of sleep differently from a normal individual?

    A) Awakening and stage 1
    B) Stage 1 and 2
    C) Stage 2 and 3
    D) Stage 3 and 4

920. Which part of the brain acts abnormally in those who suffer short periods of anxiety and elevated heart rate and respiration during periods of slow-wave sleep?

    A) Occipital lobe
    B) Pons
    C) Cerebellum
    D) Pituitary gland

921. In the middle of her performance, a pianist notices with some annoyance that a cell phone is ringing in the audience. However, she still continues playing as usual. Which model of attention best explains this phenomenon?

    A) The Broadbent model of selective attention; she selectively pays attention to her performance.
    B) The Broadbent model of selective attention; the distraction is eliminated at the bottleneck, allowing her to focus on her music alone.
    C) Treisman's attenuation model; a filter lowers the intensity of, but does not fully eliminate, the distraction caused by the cell phone.
    D) Treisman's attenuation model; a selective filter prevents the cell phone from reaching this pianist's working memory.

922. All of these scenarios fit Treisman's attenuation model EXCEPT:

    A) a waiter hears diners at a table muttering about him, but focuses instead on speaking to the table he is currently serving.
    B) a student notices when the teacher calls her name, but continues to focus on finishing her exam as if she hadn't heard.
    C) a pizza delivery man makes sure he is biking safely to the next customer while ignoring phone calls from the previous one.
    D) a teacher devotes her efforts toward lecturing her class, not noticing the students in the back row who are talking.

923. A chef is attempting to listen to a football game while simultaneously cooking during peak dinner hours. The chef will succeed in dividing his attention if:

    A) watching the game and cooking require complementary, but not similar, types of attention.
    B) watching the game and cooking require similar modes of attention.
    C) this combination of tasks does not require more attentional resources than he has.
    D) he attenuates his attention to the game when he must focus on cooking.

Questions 924–925 rely on the figure below

A psychologist is researching participants' capacities to perform tasks when presented with distractions. First, he splits his test subjects into three groups. Group 1 is asked to cook an omelet while distracting sounds are played. In contrast, Group 2 must cook an omelet while answering math questions on paper. Finally, Group 3 is instructed to cook an omelet and answer the same math questions while hearing the distracting noises. The results of the study are summarized here.

	Group 1	Group 2	Group 3
Time of completion (min)	8	10	10

924. Which attentional model best explains why Groups 2 and 3 displayed such similar results?

    A) The Broadbent model of selective attention
    B) Treisman's attenuation model
    C) The resource model of attention
    D) Both A and B

925. If Group 3 instead completed their tasks in 15 minutes while Group 2, which consisted exclusively of professional chefs, remained at 10 minutes, what would best explain the discrepancy between these two groups?

    A) Group 2 utilized automatic processing.
    B) Group 3 utilized automatic processing.
    C) Group 2 utilized controlled processing.
    D) Group 1 utilized controlled processing.

926. An unknown compound is known to cause euphoria while simultaneously diminishing severe pain. This drug is most likely a:

    A) barbiturate.
    B) opioid.
    C) stimulant.
    D) hallucinogen.

927. As a class of psychoactive drug, stimulants:

    I.   can promote the release of neurotransmitters.
    II. can reduce the effects of neurotransmitters.
    III. can inhibit the reabsorption of neurotransmitters.
    IV. cause suppression of cerebellar activity.

    A) I and III
    B) II and III
    C) I, II, and III
    D) I, II, III, and IV

928. Which dopaminergic pathway is most closely associated with addictive responses to drugs?

    A) The nigrostriatal pathway
    B) The mesocortical pathway
    C) The mesolimbic pathway
    D) The tuberoinfundibular pathway

929. A heroin addict is experiencing painful withdrawal symptoms four days after quitting the drug. What is the main cause of these adverse effects?

    A) Her body is overproducing endorphins, resulting in sensitivity and pain.
    B) Her body is underproducing endorphins, resulting in sensitivity and pain.
    C) Her body has stopped producing GABA.
    D) One of her dopaminergic pathways has been seriously damaged.

930. It has recently been discovered that dogs have very similar attention patterns to humans. A dog may hear his name being called, but continue to focus on a hole he is digging. However, when he hears his name called more angrily, he might stop his task and decide to come inside. What model of attention best suits this scenario?

    A) The Broadbent model of selective attention, because the dog chooses to dig despite hearing his name
    B) The Broadbent model of selective attention, because the angry tone of his owner's voice changes the dog's mind
    C) Treisman's attenuation model, because the dog can initially focus on digging, but perceives the stimulus of the human voice to intensify as it grows angrier
    D) Treisman's attenuation model, because the dog first elects to continue digging, but later selectively filters out that desire when realizing the consequences of continuing

931. According to the cognitive developmental theory outlined by Jean Piaget, a child entering the preoperational stage would exhibit which of the following?

    A) She would begin to understand the perspectives of other people.
    B) She would start to be able to think logically using abstract ideas.
    C) She would begin to develop crystallized intelligence.
    D) She would gain an understanding of object permanence, or the idea that things do not cease to exist when they move out of view.

932. Which of these scenarios best demonstrates the use of fluid intelligence?

    A) A young adult who has never seen a Rubik's cube solves it after two hours of effort.
    B) An infant learns that crying and reaching for her bottle signals to her mother she wants to be fed.
    C) A college professor effortlessly solves a calculus problem in front of his students.
    D) A four-year-old child plays make-believe that he's a pirate in his backyard.

933. A psychologist conducts an experiment involving three different subjects. The participants watch behind a two-way mirror as a young man steals money from an elderly woman's purse. The researcher then asks the subjects to state whether what the man did was morally wrong, and if so, why. Their responses are summarized in the following figure.

Subject	Response
A	The man shouldn't steal from the woman because he might get caught and go to prison.
B	The man shouldn't steal from the woman because personal property is a universal right that needs to be respected.
C	The man shouldn't steal from the woman because stealing is wrong, and if everyone stole, society would not function.

According to Kohlberg's theory of moral reasoning, to which stages of morality does each individual belong?

A) Subjects A and B belong to the conventional stage, while subject C belongs to the postconventional stage.

B) Subject A belongs to the preconventional stage, subject B belongs to the postconventional stage, and subject C belongs to the conventional stage.

C) Subject A belongs to the preconventional stage, subject B belongs to the conventional stage, and subject C belongs to the postconventional stage.

D) Subject A belongs to the preconventional stage, while subjects B and C belong to the postconventional stage.

934. According to Piaget's stages of cognitive development, the emergence of symbolic thinking is a hallmark of:

A) the sensorimotor stage.
B) the concrete operational stage.
C) the formal operational stage.
D) the preoperational stage.

935. On his 80th birthday, an elderly man reflects on his life and accomplishments and emerges with a sense of wisdom, understanding, and peace regarding the idea of death. According to Erikson, which life conflict has this man successfully resolved?

A) Integrity vs. despair
B) Autonomy vs. shame and doubt
C) Intimacy vs. isolation
D) Initiative vs. guilt

936. The following data maps the risk of developing bipolar disorder for various populations.

Family history of bipolar disorder	Risk of developing the disease
One parent diagnosed	15-30%
Both parents diagnosed	50-75%
Brother or sister diagnosed	15-25%
Identical twin diagnosed	approximately 85%

Based on this information, we can conclude that:

A) bipolar disorder is inherited and genetic susceptibility is the only determining factor when analyzing risk.

B) genetics likely do not play a role in development of this disorder, as the study only measured diagnoses, which could depend on individual physicians.

C) both environment and genetics may be factors in development of bipolar disorder, with genetics likely playing a larger role.

D) both environment and genetics may be factors in development of bipolar disorder, with environment likely playing a larger role.

937. A young woman who is learning to play the piano is struggling to play a new piece by Bach. If learning this piece falls under Vygotsky's "zone of proximal development," what does this woman require to master the composition?

A) She needs to spend 10,000 hours playing the piano.

B) She needs to learn a different skill to take her mind off playing the piano.

C) She needs assistance from a more experienced piano player.

D) She needs to be around peers who are also learning to play the piano.

938. Erik Erikson developed a series of stages of development that involve resolving various conflicts between needs and social demands. According to Erikson, must an individual successfully resolve a stage before moving on to the next?

A) Yes, one cannot progress to the next stage of development without resolving the previous stage; its conflict must be played out until it is resolved.

B) No, one can progress to the next stage of development, as long the previous stage is resolved at some point in one's life.

C) No, one can progress to the next stage of development without resolving or obtaining mastery in the previous stage.

D) No, one can progress to the next stage of development if one has the help of a "more knowledgeable other."

939. According to Erikson, during which stage does an individual experience a "physiological revolution"?

    A) Industry vs. inferiority
    B) Identity vs. role confusion
    C) Intimacy vs. isolation
    D) Trust vs. mistrust

940. How might environment influence the genetic expression of a particular personality trait?

    A) A man could receive two alleles of a gene corresponding to a personality disorder and thus express the trait.
    B) A girl whose father has an anxiety disorder has a very tumultuous childhood; she later develops the same condition as a teenager.
    C) A young adult grows up in a very Catholic family and integrates Catholic traditions into his identity.
    D) A woman with an anxiety disorder takes a SSRI (selective serotonin reuptake inhibitor) to mitigate her symptoms.

941. Which of these are domains of intelligence as defined by Gardner's theory of multiple intelligences?

    I. Musical intelligence
    II. Interpersonal intelligence
    III. Logical-mathematical intelligence
    IV. Fluid intelligence

    A) I only
    B) I and III
    C) I, II, and III
    D) I, III, and IV

942. The Internet provides never-before-seen access to information and opposing viewpoints. However, psychologists find that, in spite of this, people have become even more steadfast in their beliefs. How can this apparent contradiction be explained?

    A) Internet users are suffering from skewed perception due to the affect heuristic.
    B) People are falling victim to the confirmation bias, causing them to overvalue information that agrees with their own viewpoints.
    C) The overload of information has rendered individuals incapable of forming strong opinions on key issues.
    D) The "hive mind" of the Internet has produced a constant state of groupthink.

943. After reading her psychology book, an MCAT student decides that she will only solve problems using algorithms from this point forward. What are the advantages and disadvantages of this strategy?

    A) The student will reach an answer quickly and efficiently when she is able to do so at all, but will often fail to obtain any definitive solution.
    B) The student will reach an answer quickly by relying on similar situations from her past, but will be unable to solve complex or unique questions.
    C) The student will be able to utilize her own emotions and biases, but this may lead to flawed solutions.
    D) The student will always reach a definitive answer, but algorithms are not very efficient and often require impractical amounts of time.

944. Which of the following exemplifies a sound and valid deductive argument?

    A) All athletes are able to run quickly; John is an athlete, so therefore John is able to run quickly.
    B) All cats have four paws; the animal I saw walking down the street had four paws, so therefore that animal was a cat.
    C) All atoms have mass; calcium is an atom, so therefore calcium has mass.
    D) All of the known atoms have mass, so if we discover a new atom, it must have mass as well.

945. Under which theory of intelligence would an autistic musical savant be considered a genius?

    A) A traditional IQ test
    B) The general intelligence factor
    C) The theory of multiple intelligences
    D) Sternberg's triarchic theory

Questions 946–947 rely on the figure below

A survey quizzed a large number of American adults on the prevalence of different adverse events, then compared the average participant answer to the correct one.

Question	Average response	Factual answer
What is the rate of violent crime?	25%	5%
What percentage of patients experience side effects from vaccines?	10%	<1%
What is the rate of plane crashes?	2%	<0.1%

946. Why might the survey participants have been so unable to answer these questions correctly?

  A) They used the availability heuristic.
  B) They used the representativeness heuristic.
  C) They relied overly on their own emotions.
  D) They fell victim to overconfidence.

947. If the participants in the survey were presented with the correct answer for each question immediately after their responses, how would this affect their beliefs going forward?

  A) Many participants would change their minds regarding the severity of these problems.
  B) Most participants would continue holding their initial beliefs, due to the effects of confirmation bias and belief perseverance.
  C) Participants would be less likely to trust their intuition in the future.
  D) None of the above would happen.

Questions 948–949 rely on the table below

The following data shows the results of twin studies conducted to compare the intelligence of identical and fraternal twins.

Group	Average difference in IQ between twins
Identical twins: raised in same household	3.77
Identical twins: raised in different households	7.56
Fraternal twins: raised in same household	5.65
Fraternal twins: raised in different households	9.97

948. Which of these conclusions is most likely to be drawn based on this data?

   A) Identical twins always have more similar IQ scores than fraternal twins.
   B) Identical twins tend to have more similar IQ scores than fraternal twins, assuming that all outside factors are controlled.
   C) Fraternal twins always have a larger variation in IQ scores than identical twins.
   D) Fraternal twins likely have greater IQ similarity than regular siblings.

949. Of these new findings, which would directly contradict the results shown in the table?

   A) When compared to unrelated individuals who grew up in the same household, identical twins displayed a greater variation in intelligence.
   B) When compared to unrelated individuals who grew up in the same household, identical twins displayed a smaller variation in intelligence.
   C) Genomic analysis reveals that random genetic mutations lead to significant variation in intelligence.
   D) Growing up in an environment that is non-conducive to learning greatly diminishes IQ scores later in life.

950. Mary's son was in an accident as a child and may have suffered brain damage. Years later, she notices that he struggles with planning and organizing. Which part of the brain was most likely damaged in the accident?

   A) The frontal lobe
   B) The amygdala
   C) The limbic system
   D) The hypothalamus

951. In the order that they occur, the three main stages of memory are:

   A) storage, encoding, retrieval.
   B) retrieval, encoding, storage.
   C) storage, retrieval, encoding.
   D) encoding, storage, retrieval.

952. Which of the following accurately depict(s) the order in which a fragment of information might progress through various types of memory during storage?

   I.   Echoic memory → short-term memory → long-term memory
   II. Iconic memory → short-term memory
   III. Sensory memory → iconic memory → short-term memory → long-term memory
   IV. Working memory → sensory memory → short-term memory

      A) I only
      B) I and II
      C) I and III
      D) II, III, and IV

953. If Bill wanted to use the self-reference effect to help him remember his coworkers' names, he could:

   A) visualize himself walking through the office, pairing each desk with the name of the person who sits there.
   B) use the rhyming sound of the words to remember that the financial directors' names are Derek and Eric.
   C) remind himself that his own middle name is Thomas, and Tom is the associate in the neighboring cubicle.
   D) repeat the list of names over and over in his own mind.

954. To choose the correct answer on a multiple-choice exam like the MCAT, students use:

A) recognition.
B) maintenance rehearsal.
C) recall.
D) procedural memory.

955. You need to memorize all of the amino acid structures by next week, but no matter how long you spend staring at the textbook, you can't remember any of them for longer than 45 seconds. Which study method would be LEAST effective?

A) Thinking about the appearance of the structure, sound of the word, and role of the functional groups to maximize the depth at which you process the information
B) Devising a mnemonic in which each one-letter abbreviation relates to the most memorable structural feature on the molecule
C) Separating the amino acids into five smaller groups instead of trying to remember each structure individually
D) Switching from using elaborative rehearsal six times per day to using maintenance rehearsal eight times per day

956. All of the following concepts are examples of retrieval cues EXCEPT:

A) the serial position effect.
B) context-dependent memory.
C) automatic processing.
D) priming.

957. A student must memorize the following list of numbers: 303, 197, 216, 42, 304, 76, 112. Which of the numbers will he probably retrieve the most easily?

A) 216 and 42, both due to the serial position effect
B) 303 (due to the primacy effect) and 112 (due to the recency effect)
C) 112 (due to the primacy effect) and 303 (due to the recency effect)
D) 42 and 76, both due to the spacing effect

958. When trying to retrieve the name "Abraham Lincoln" from memory, we might first think of "government," then "president," then "George Washington," etc. Within the concept of spreading activation, the word "government" in this example is a:

A) node.
B) network.
C) recency effect.
D) primacy effect.

Questions 959–960 rely on the graph below

A neuroscientist devises an experiment to test long-term potentiation and its relationship to memory in rats. In this procedure, one-third of the rats are wild-type, while an additional third (the HP4 strain) have been subjected to small lesions on their hippocampi. The remaining mice are treated with APV, an inhibitor of the NMDA receptor (a glutamate receptor found in the brain). The mice are each placed in a Morris water maze, a pool with a submerged platform as its only escape route. The average time it took each group to exit the maze during 13 identical trials is shown below.

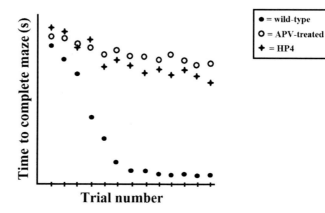

959. Which group likely experienced the greatest degree of long-term potentiation (LTP)?

A) The wild-type mice, because their effective storage and quick retrieval of the maze-related information was probably aided by strengthened synaptic connections

B) The wild-type mice, because they were the only group able to initially encode the memory of the platform's location

C) The APV-treated mice, because the inhibition of the NMDA receptor caused the memory impairments seen with high levels of LTP

D) The HP4 mice, because LTP is only known to occur in the hippocampus

960. APV is known to competitively inhibit a large number of NMDA receptors in various parts of the brain. Its effects would be most similar to that of:

A) an allosteric activator of a different glutamate receptor.

B) a new medication that selectively decreases the number of action potentials in hippocampal neurons.

C) a common glutamate agonist used for psychological research.

D) a GABA receptor agonist that acts on GABA receptors throughout almost the entire brain.

961. Recalling that lysine is a basic amino acid involves which division(s) of long-term memory?

I. Semantic memory
II. Declarative memory
III. Episodic memory
IV. Explicit memory

A) I only
B) I and IV
C) I, II, and IV
D) II, III, and IV

962. Spaced repetition would most likely be used to encode information into:

A) working memory, since the information can later be manipulated to solve problems.

B) semantic memory, since it involves the storage of facts and pieces of knowledge.

C) explicit memory, since it includes the unconscious memorization of details and concepts.

D) nondeclarative memory, since that area is where spaced repetition has the greatest advantage over massed practice.

963. Jack wants to eat pizza tonight, so he carefully leaves coupons for Italian food scattered around the house for his mother to see. He also changes her laptop background to a photo of him eating pizza. Miraculously, Jack's mother orders a pizza for dinner. However, when he tells her about his little "hints," she swears that she did not even notice. Jack used which type of memory to his advantage?

A) Procedural memory
B) Declarative memory
C) Implicit memory
D) Episodic memory

964. After damage to his prefrontal cortex, Philip's working memory started to show serious deficits. Which of these tasks would Philip have the LEAST trouble completing?

A) Playing a "concentration" game in which he must remember the identities of multiple playing cards at once

B) Multiplying seven and twelve in his head, then dividing the product by three

C) Closing his eyes and navigating through a room that he had only been present in for ten minutes

D) Reciting the names of the fifty states by singing them in tune with a song

965. Jade, a law student, successfully remembers all of the civil tax codes required for her morning exam. She then jumps on her motorcycle and rides home, where she relaxes by playing a video game in which she wins small tokens. Which choice correctly pairs each action with the type of memory or process involved?

   A) Remembering tax codes – semantic; riding her motorcycle – explicit; playing the video game – procedural
   B) Remembering tax codes – declarative; riding her motorcycle – procedural; playing the video game – operant conditioning
   C) Remembering tax codes – episodic; riding her motorcycle – procedural; playing the video game – explicit
   D) Remembering tax codes – semantic; riding her motorcycle – working; playing the video game – classical conditioning

966. All of the following statements about memory are incorrect EXCEPT:

   A) declarative memory can include learned responses to conditioned stimuli.
   B) nondeclarative and procedural memory are terms that have identical meanings.
   C) context effects can aid a person in recalling an episodic, but not a semantic, memory.
   D) nondeclarative memory can relate to the motor cortex.

967. According to Baddeley's model, working memory includes:

   A) a phonological loop and a visuospatial sketchpad.
   B) priming and the method of loci.
   C) implicit memory and explicit memory.
   D) echoic memory and iconic memory.

Questions 968–969 rely on the figure below

To win a card game, students must memorize all five of the playing cards shown below in a five-minute span. They must be able to correctly list the cards in order from left to right, and must accurately name the type of card (Jack, Ace, Queen, etc.), the color, and the symbol in the center.

968. John spends the entire five minutes repeating the details of the cards to himself over and over. He later finds that he can hardly remember a single detail. John could have encoded this information more efficiently by doing all of the following EXCEPT:

   A) increasing his depth of processing by thinking about the visual and phonetic connections between the letters J, A, etc.
   B) using a mnemonic to better solidify the cards' details into semantic memory.
   C) facilitating the conversion from short-term to declarative memory by using chunking.
   D) using elaborative rehearsal to commit the information to prospective memory.

969. During the second round of the game, students still must remember the five cards shown above, but two other cards – a black queen and a gray jack – are shown immediately after the five minutes ends. When quizzed later, several students wrongly recall that those two cards were present in the original set of five. What role do the black queen and gray jack play in this situation?

   A) They cause the students to experience retroactive interference.
   B) They cause the students to experience proactive interference.
   C) They prevent the students from making false alarm errors.
   D) They assist in priming for the recall that must be performed later.

970. A young child meets nearly every academic standard for her age, but cannot seem to learn how to hold a pencil. Though she practices every morning, her writing does not improve at all. This girl may be suffering from:

   A) genetic damage to part of her hippocampus.
   B) a viral infection that is impairing her declarative memory.
   C) a moderately underdeveloped cerebellum.
   D) a lesion on her auditory cortex.

971. Which of these pairings does NOT properly match a disease or condition with one of its manifestations?

   A) Parkinson's disease – destruction of dopaminergic neurons
   B) Alzheimer's disease – dementia
   C) Ataxia – loss of short-term memory
   D) Korsakoff's syndrome - confabulation

972. With regard to memory, the two main types of interference are:

   A) proactive and retrograde.
   B) retroactive and proactive.
   C) reactive and proactive.
   D) retrograde and anterograde.

973. A middle-aged woman is riding a bus when she sees a man steal another woman's purse. When visiting the police station to testify, she describes the man as tall and dark-haired, but is actually thinking of a main character from a recent movie. Which is true about this situation?

   A) The woman has made a source-monitoring error.
   B) The woman has been primed by the movie to aid proper retrieval of the suspect's face.
   C) The woman has made a serial positioning error.
   D) The woman has performed a correct rejection.

974. Which of the following diseases is/are able to cause retrograde memory impairments?

   I. Alzheimer's disease
   II. Korsakoff's syndrome
   III. Borderline personality disorder (BPD)
   IV. Ebbinghaus' disease

   A) I only
   B) I and II
   C) II and IV
   D) I, II, and III

975. William recently purchased a new cell phone with an unfamiliar ringtone. At first, he jumps up and reaches for his phone at the sound of any musical tones, but later begins to react only to his phone's unique melody. William is experiencing:

   A) retroactive interference, since recent memories of the phone's sound are blocking the retrieval of older information.
   B) Ebbinghaus' curve of forgetting, since his general memory of the sound fades over time.
   C) stimulus discrimination, since a learned association becomes more specific.
   D) anterograde amnesia, since he is struggling to remember past responses.

976. Jenny, a premed student, forgot several Spanish verbs when she visited Europe and became fluent in French. Additionally, she learned many French customs that led her to have trouble recalling American traditions. In this scenario, which type(s) of interference have influenced Jenny?

   A) Proactive when she forgot the Spanish verbs, and retroactive when she couldn't remember the American customs
   B) Retroactive when she forgot the Spanish verbs, and proactive when she couldn't remember the American customs
   C) Proactive both when she forgot the Spanish verbs and when she couldn't remember the American customs
   D) Retroactive both when she forgot the Spanish verbs and when she couldn't remember the American customs

977. A premed student has just memorized a list of commonly tested organic reagents. According to Ebbinghaus' forgetting curve, the student's retention of this material will decrease most sharply during:

A) the second week after memorization of the material.

B) the few days afterward, in which the material is stored and then encoded.

C) the few days immediately following the original memorization.

D) the weeks leading up to the exam, in which he utilizes the spacing effect.

Questions 978–979 rely on the table below

A psychologist is studying the processes involved in memorizing short lists of words. In his main experiment, he verbally presents a list of seven words to each participant over a 30-minute span. Instead of reading all of the terms in a consecutive list, he spreads them out so that each new word is presented five minutes after the previous one. The percent of participants who correctly recalled each word exactly one day later is given in the following table.

Time introduced (min)	Word	% correct recall by participants
1	flower	79
5	vacation	65
10	starstruck	48
15	pitiful	52
20	gardening	66
25	machine	50
30	literature	81

978. One participant has had a traumatic brain injury that prevents him from experiencing the recency effect. For which word would this man's results differ most from the majority of participants?

A) Flower

B) Literature

C) Gardening

D) The man's retrieval ability would be equally impaired for both "flower" and "literature."

979. The researcher alters the experiment to give an additional three words at the end: tulip, flowerpot, and soil. He finds that the percent of participants who properly recall the word "gardening"

drops to 39%. What most likely caused this phenomenon?

A) The subjects' poor results occurred due to context effects.

B) The subjects, like most people, had more difficulty with free recall than simple recognition.

C) The subjects experienced proactive interference due to the presentation of the new terms.

D) The subjects experienced retroactive interference due to the presentation of the new terms.

980. An elderly man has no trouble remembering how to play bridge and drive his car, but cannot remember his new nurse's name, no matter how many times she tells him. This man likely suffers from:

A) anterograde amnesia.

B) dissociative fugue.

C) a defect in his procedural memory.

D) retrograde amnesia.

981. A male patient arrives at a clinic, frustrated by his difficulties with verbal communication. On the basis of this information along, the man could be suffering from:

I. Broca's aphasia.

II. Wernicke's aphasia.

III. progressive damage to the frontal lobe.

IV. progressive damage to the temporal lobe.

A) I only

B) II only

C) I, II, and IV

D) I, II, III, and IV

982. How could one best describe the learning theory of language development?

A) An innate element exists within the human brain and allows humans to develop language.

B) Language is learned as a direct result of operant conditioning.

C) Language acquisition occurs passively, without conscious or unconscious rewards or punishments.

D) Language acquisition is driven by an innate desire to be social and coincides with neural development.

983. Which scenario provides the strongest evidence for the concept of a sensitive period with regard to language development?

   A) After studying a foreign language for several months, students typically experience a period of increased vocabulary growth and overall fluency.

   B) If a baby does not start speaking by the age of eighteen months, he or she will be unable to ever speak.

   C) When a young girl is isolated from human interaction throughout her childhood, she is unable to fully acquire the syntax of the language spoken in her community later in her life.

   D) There is little difference between the speaking styles of a six-year-old child and an average adult.

984. A series of scans revealed a correlation between the development of a specific region of the brain and a child's ability to understand syntax. This finding would best support the notion of a language acquisition device as described by the:

   A) the learning theory of language development.

   B) the biological theory of language development.

   C) the nativist theory of language development.

   D) the social interactionist theory of language development.

985. Following a car accident, a patient has retained the ability to speak and respond to sounds. However, she is unable to form coherent phrases and sentences. Which part of the brain has been damaged?

   A) Wernicke's area

   B) The limbic system

   C) Broca's area

   D) The auditory cortex

Questions 986–987 rely on the figure below

Local foster children were separated into three groups based on their living situations from age 2 onward. At age 11, a variety of tests were administered to assess their control of language and syntax, rated on a scale of 1 (worst) to 10 (best).

Living situation	Linguistic control
One stable, supportive home	8.75
One home with unsupportive absentee parents	5.0
Multiple distinct, supportive foster families	7.0

986. Assuming that the findings are statistically significant, which theory of language development best aligns with these results?

   A) The parental theory
   B) The learning theory
   C) The nativist theory
   D) The social interactionist theory

987. Suppose that further research finds that, when tested again between the ages of 20 and 30, children from all three groups display near-identical linguistic control scores. How would this affect the learning theory in particular?

   A) It would strengthen the theory, since the children from unsupportive homes were able to gain a grasp of language when in supportive environments.

   B) It would weaken the theory, since the children with the lowest original scores were able to develop linguistic control long after leaving the sensitive developmental period.

   C) It would weaken the theory, since growing up in an unsupportive environment had no lasting effect on that group's ability to develop language.

   D) It would neither weaken nor strengthen the theory, since the learning theory does not limit the development of language to a single age group.

Questions 988–989 rely on the figure below

A linguist isolated five distinct languages used by cultures from multiple continents. The following table shows these languages, numbered from 1 to 5, along with the number of words they have to describe several concepts: the color red, snow, and the physical perception of pain.

Language	"Red"	"Snow"	"Pain"
1	64	4	1
2	15	20	5
3	25	9	6
4	10	7	7
5	22	0	1

988. According to the Sapir-Whorf hypothesis, if memories of color are influenced by language, speakers of which language might be able to remember color in more detail?

    A) Language 1
    B) Language 3
    C) Language 4
    D) Regardless of the number of available words, individuals from all cultures should be able to remember and describe colors equally.

989. Language 5 most likely originated in:

    A) North America.
    B) the mountains of Nepal.
    C) the Amazon rainforest.
    D) eastern Europe.

990. A certain tribal language has a word for "one" and for "two" but any more than this is described as "many". An anthropologist attempts to teach members of the tribe to count, using Spanish words. According to the Sapir-Whorf hypothesis, which of the following would most likely be true?

    A) Young children will be totally incapable of developing numeracy.
    B) Adult members of the tribe will have an exceptionally difficult time developing numeracy.
    C) A baby taken from this tribe and brought to Spain will be unable to learn to count as it grows up.
    D) The tribe members will react with hostility to any attempt to modify their language.

991. Which of the following is NOT a universal emotion?

    A) Happiness
    B) Sadness
    C) Disgust
    D) Jealousy

992. Paul Ekman stated that the universal emotions have specific facial expressions. How can the expression corresponding to fear best be described?

    A) Upper lip raised, nose wrinkled, cheeks raised
    B) Penetrating stare, eyebrows lowered and drawn together, lips pressed together
    C) Eyebrows raised and drawn together, mouth open and lips pulled toward the ears, eyes widened
    D) Eyebrows arched, jaw open and dropped, eyes widened

993. Which of these statements explains the adaptive role of emotion in relation to Darwin's theory of evolution?

    A) At some point in human history, individuals who experienced emotion had an advantage over those who did not.
    B) A newborn baby quickly learns that screaming loudly will elicit attention from her parents.
    C) Sarah has been depressed for a few weeks, so every morning she starts her day with positive affirmations.
    D) Most human beings would prefer to feel love rather than hate or anger, and this leads to differences in the gene pool over time.

994. Which of the following statements accurately describes the James-Lange theory of emotion?

    A) An external stimulus triggers the simultaneous experience of physiological arousal and emotion.
    B) An external stimulus triggers physiological arousal, which is then interpreted as emotion.
    C) An external stimulus triggers physiological arousal; we then consciously identify the reason for this arousal, and an associated emotion is then experienced.
    D) An external stimulus triggers emotion, which we then interpret to produce physiological arousal.

Questions 995–996 rely on the figure below

A college student conducts an experiment on changes to skin temperature during emotional responses. He measures the temperature of the skin on his friend's forearm over the course of 15 seconds. At some point during this interval, he surprises his friend with a loud shout. The friend is told to push a button at the instant when he feels that he has experienced emotion. Results of this experiment are graphed below.

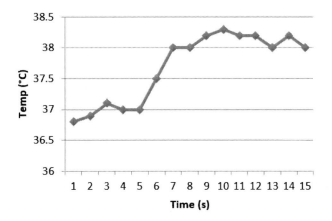

995. The experiment is found to strongly support the Cannon-Bard theory of emotion. Given the graph of skin temperature vs. time above, when did the experimenter's friend most likely press the button?

A) At the 3-second mark
B) At the 5.5-second mark
C) At the 8-second mark, since he felt no emotion until that time
D) At the 8-second mark, since he had to think about which emotion he should be experiencing

996. If the experimenter shouted at the 5-second mark, but the friend didn't push the button until two seconds later, which theory of emotion does the study validate?

A) The Cannon-Bard theory of emotion
B) The Schachter-Singer theory of emotion
C) The Garret-Luis theory of emotion
D) The Jesse-James theory of emotion

997. Which region of the human brain is most strongly associated with fear?

A) The cerebellum
B) The occipital lobe
C) The thalamus
D) The amygdala

998. The Yerkes-Dodson Law describes the relationship between arousal and performance. According to this law, people tend to perform the best:

A) when they have a very low level of arousal, because they are less nervous.
B) when they have a high level of arousal, because they are more attentive.
C) somewhere in the region between high and low arousal.
D) at entirely different levels of arousal, depending on the individual.

999. A patient arrives at a psychologist's office complaining of increased emotional thoughts, general anxiety, and trouble regulating inappropriate ideas. If the cause of this ailment is physiological, it most likely involves damage to which of these brain structures?

A) The prefrontal cortex
B) The amygdala
C) The hippocampus
D) The olfactory bulb

1000. The key difference between emotion and mood is that:

A) emotion is felt only by humans, while mood can be experienced by a variety of animal species.
B) emotion is relatively short-lived, while a mood can last for a long period of time.
C) emotion generally describes experiences in healthy people, while mood is more closely linked to conditions such as major depressive disorder.
D) emotions are caused external stimuli, while moods are internal states only.

1001. During finals week, John learns that his grandmother has recently died. He questions whether he will be able to handle dealing with this emotional situation while he studies for exams. Which type of stress appraisal is John performing?

A) Primary appraisal
B) Secondary appraisal
C) Virtual appraisal
D) Eustress appraisal

1002. Constant stress reappraisal is best exemplified by:

A) Isaac, who decides that the stress surrounding his upcoming soccer match will actually help him practice harder and play better.
B) Robert, who sees a bear while hiking one day; he stops walking for a moment, then decides to run the other way.
C) many people who developed anxiety, depression, and post-traumatic stress disorder after 9/11.
D) Elaine, who notices a man in a trench coat following her at night; as she walks home swiftly, she periodically looks behind her to see if the man is still there.

1003. A psychologist advises George to reframe the obstacles in his life so that they represent eustress. What is the psychologist telling George to do?

A) Identify which aspects of his life are producing the most stress and try to avoid them in the future
B) Reformulate his cognitive appraisal of these obstacles so that his reaction to them is positive and they affect him in a healthy way
C) Admit that stress is inevitable, but attempt to feel as little of it as possible
D) Isolate the stressors that cause him the most discomfort, are most difficult to deal with, and are most significantly damaging his health

1004. PTSD involves three clusters of symptoms: avoidance, hyperarousal, and re-experiencing. Symptoms falling within the "hyperarousal" cluster might include:

A) having frightening thoughts, nightmares, and flashbacks.
B) feeling emotionally numb, strong guilt, depression, and a loss of interest in life.
C) talking very fast, having racing thoughts, and experiencing delusions of grandeur.
D) being tense and on edge, having difficulty sleeping, having angry outbursts, and being easily startled.

1005. Give the correct sequence of the mechanism by which cortisol is released.

A) The hypothalamus sends a signal via nerve fibers and stimulates the adrenal gland to release cortisol.
B) The hypothalamus releases adrenocorticotropic hormone, causing the anterior pituitary to release corticotropin-releasing hormone; the adrenal gland then releases cortisol.
C) The hypothalamus releases corticotropin-releasing hormone, causing the anterior pituitary to release adrenocorticotropic hormone; the adrenal gland then releases cortisol.
D) The hypothalamus releases adrenocorticotropic hormone, causing the thyroid to release T_3 and T_4; the adrenal gland then releases cortisol.

Questions 1006–1007 rely on the graph on the right

Jennifer is conducting a study on stress reduction techniques with her fellow PhD students and faculty. To do so, she establishes three groups of participants. Members of one group then undergo two months of cognitive behavioral therapy (CBT), while those of another experience daily meditation; participants in the third group use both techniques. After the interval is over, Jennifer uses a questionnaire designed to measure perceived stress reduction as a percentage. Her results are detailed below.

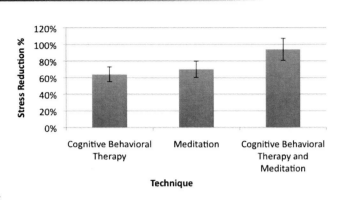

1006. From the data above, we can conclude that:

A) meditation works better than cognitive behavioral therapy, but a combination of the two works the best.

B) no significant difference can be detected between meditation and cognitive behavioral therapy, but a combination of the two reduces stress significantly more than CBT alone.

C) cognitive behavioral therapy reduces stress by the largest percentage, followed by meditation, then a combination of the two.

D) Due to statistical error, we cannot conclude anything from this study.

1007. Specifically, how might cognitive behavioral therapy be used to reduce stress?

A) It could assist in identifying and resolving the conflict between the ego and the superego.

B) It could help a person move toward self-actualization by removing obstacles that hinder personality development.

C) It could allow a person to gain better access to childhood memories, thus helping him or her to overcome the past and relieve present anxiety.

D) It could facilitate the identification of potential triggers of stress, then assist the individual to adjust his or her perception of those stressors to a healthier one.

1008. The physiological effects of long-term stress include:

A) decreased blood pressure, increased immune response, and additional blood supply to the skin.

B) smoking of cigarettes, consumption of alcohol, and excessive eating.

C) increased blood pressure, susceptibility to infection, and skin problems.

D) increased feelings of anger, depression, and irritability.

1009. Which of the following is an example of acute stress?

A) Andrew can't find his car keys and frantically searches the house before leaving for work.

B) Gerald experiences flashbacks and anxiety from traumatic experiences during the Vietnam War.

C) Sarah lives in a dysfunctional family that fights constantly, causing her associated stress.

D) Katrina, a PhD student, feels extreme pressure during the last two years of her education due to heavy responsibility.

1010. While stress generally carries negative connotations, not all stressors produce adverse physiological and emotional reactions. Positive responses of the human body to stress include:

A) increased susceptibility to depression and increased risk of heart disease.

B) impaired memory, elevated blood pressure, a higher risk of infertility, and a deteriorated immune response.

C) increased alertness, increased blood flow to muscles, temporary suppression of reproductive organs, and a lowered perception of pain.

D) a higher IQ, increased cardiovascular fitness, and a sense of tranquility.

1011. The treatment of patients with multiple neurological or psychiatric disorders is made more difficult by the fact that some disorders have opposing effects on the underlying brain chemistry. The treatment of a patient with both schizophrenia and Parkinson's disease would be complicated by the fact that these disorders are related to imbalances in production and sensitivity, but in opposite ways, of which neurotransmitter?

A) Norepinephrine
B) Acetylcholine
C) Dopamine
D) Serotonin

1012. Monoamine oxidase inhibitors (MAOIs) are a type of drug that act to inhibit monoamine oxidase, the enzyme that breaks down monoamine neurotransmitters (NTs) to clear them from synapses. Due to the risk of a potentially lethal buildup of NTs, MAOIs should not be prescribed at the same time as other drugs that increase the levels of monoamines. Which of the following substances would be contraindicated to use along with MAOIs?

A) Benzodiazepines
B) SSRIs
C) Melatonin
D) Nitrous oxide

1013. In Huntington's disease, cells produce a defective form of protein known as huntingtin (Htt) that contains a long chain of glutamine amino acids. This chain interferes with the normal folding of the protein and results in the formation of Htt plaques in many neurons, causing cell death; however, certain neuron types are more vulnerable than others. One of the first areas affected is the striatum, which is part of the darker central structure pictured below.

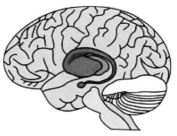

Early signs of Huntington's disease include jerky, random motions known as chorea, which later progress to more severe writhing motions and difficulties with eating, chewing, and speaking. From this information, the striatum is most likely part of the:

A) cerebellum.
B) hippocampus.
C) thalamus.
D) basal ganglia.

1014. Reflex arcs, particularly those involving the hypothalamus and brain stem, are crucial to the maintenance of homeostasis. However, not all homeostatic processes involve input from these arcs. Which of the following processes does NOT directly involve a neural reflex arc?

A) A person's blood pressure increases, resulting in the dilation of blood vessels to compensate.

B) A person's body temperature falls, triggering goosebumps.

C) The body experiences low temperatures over several days, triggering an increase in the body's basal metabolic rate.

D) Lung blood vessels with a low partial pressure of O_2 constrict to divert blood to better-ventilated vessels with a high partial pressure of O_2.

1015. Among other symptoms, withdrawal from opiates such as morphine and heroin is associated with physical hallmarks including cramps, aches and pains. This occurs because the brain has become habituated to opiate stimulation and, in response, has reduced its sensitivity to which naturally-occurring neurotransmitters?

A) Cholinergics
B) Epinephrines
C) Endorphins
D) Oxytocins

1016. One of the developmentally toxic effects of childhood lead exposure is the downregulation of neuronal NMDA receptors, which respond to the neurotransmitter glutamate. Glutamate is used in many neural pathways, particularly those involving learning, and this blocking effect on its action may account for aspects of lead toxicity like lowered IQ and impulsivity. Which of the following statements most accurately describes the described pathophysiology for lead toxicity?

A) Lead blocks the release of glutamate, preventing the NMDA receptor from being activated.
B) The lead atoms adhere to glutamate molecules, blocking them from binding to the NMDA receptor and activating it.
C) The lead atoms adhere to the binding site of the NMDA receptor, blocking glutamate from binding and activating it.
D) Lead exposure lowers the number of NMDA receptors present in the postsynaptic neuron's cell membrane, giving glutamate fewer sites to bind.

1017. In Parkinson's disease, aggregates of misfolded alpha-synuclein protein known as Lewy bodies begin to accumulate in many neurons. The disease takes a particular toll on dopaminergic neurons in the substantia nigra, a structure near the basal ganglia, where the Lewy bodies are thought to lower the rate of synthesis and vesicular release of dopamine. Parkinson's is characterized by a paradoxical set of symptoms displaying both hyper- and hypomobility: sufferers have dramatic, involuntary resting tremors, especially in the hands, but also have difficulty initiating smooth and rapid voluntary movements. Which of the following must NOT be true of the neurons in the substantia nigra?

A) They must be involved in inhibitory effects on movement.
B) They must be involved in excitatory effects on movement.
C) Their function in a Parkinson's sufferer could be improved by treatment with a dopamine receptor antagonist.
D) Their function in a Parkinson's sufferer could be improved by treatment with a biosynthetic precursor to dopamine.

1018. After a stroke, a formerly confident and decisive woman has difficulty making even the simplest choices, such as deciding which pair of socks to wear in the morning, though she otherwise seems to have no other psychological deficits. This stroke most likely affected:

A) the frontal lobe of her brain.
B) the temporal lobe of her brain.
C) her cerebellum.
D) the occipital lobe of her brain.

1019. Which of the following neurotransmitters is found in large amounts in both the central and peripheral nervous systems?

A) Dopamine
B) GABA
C) Acetylcholine
D) Serotonin

1020. GABA is an inhibitory neurotransmitter that affects Cl⁻ ion channels. When stimulated by GABA, what will most likely happen to a neuron's cell potential?

A) It will be depolarized to -60 mV.
B) It will be hyperpolarized to -60 mV.
C) It will be depolarized to -80 mV.
D) It will be hyperpolarized to -80 mV.

1021. The results of blood work show that a patient has high levels of cortisol in her system. What could be the cause of this elevation?

   A) The patient has a tumor in her thyroid gland.
   B) The patient is experiencing high levels of stress, which activate the parasympathetic nervous system and promote cortisol release.
   C) The patient is experiencing high levels of stress, which activate the sympathetic nervous system and promote cortisol release.
   D) The patient likely suffers from major depressive disorder.

1022. During part of his day, Doug's parasympathetic nervous system becomes especially active. Doug could be:

   A) taking an organic chemistry final for which he did not study, except for cramming the night before.
   B) just finishing a meal and sitting down to watch his favorite television show.
   C) doing high-intensity interval training at the gym with sprints and heavy weights.
   D) watching a horror film that he finds very scary.

1023. Which part of the endocrine system is associated with high levels of arousal, aggression, and sexual behavior?

   A) Thalamus
   B) Hypothalamus
   C) Thyroid gland
   D) Parathyroid gland

1024. How do environmental and genetic factors interact to impact the behavior of an organism?

   A) Genetics entirely determine behavior, which is why it remains constant regardless of environment.
   B) Environment can actually change the genetic composition of an individual in a way that is always transmitted to the next generation.
   C) Environment can influence behavior, but not temperament, of an individual.
   D) Environment can influence the expression of genetic components, thus altering behavior.

1025. During prenatal development, what is observed in the stage of neurulation?

   A) The ectoderm furrows beneath the notochord, forming the neural groove.
   B) The neural tube differentiates into the spinal cord.
   C) The neural tube forms the three main parts of the brain: the rhombencephalon, mesencephalon, and prosencephalon.
   D) The prefrontal cortex is formed and fully develops.

1026. Of the following designations for the organization of the developing brain, which are labeled appropriately?

   I. Prosencephalon – limbic system, cerebral cortex, hypothalamus, thalamus
   II. Mesencephalon – inferior and superior colliculus
   III. Rhombencephalon – medulla oblongata, reticular formation, cerebellum

   A) I only
   B) III only
   C) II and III
   D) I, II, and III

1027. Epigenetic modification is one method by which environment can influence the behavior of an organism. A way in which such a modification could influence behavior is:

   A) over time, the adrenal cortex releases extra glucocorticoids in response to a very stressful environment.
   B) during crossing over, genes related to depression are transferred to a chromosome that later is found in the gamete.
   C) in response to stress, certain genes are methylated and "turned off."
   D) during pregnancy, a fetus is exposed to SSRIs (selective serotonin reuptake inhibitors) and goes through withdrawal symptoms after birth.

1028. A group of researchers studied concordance rates of schizophrenia between monozygotic and dizygotic twins. Their findings are presented below.

	Monozygotic twins	Dizygotic twins
Concordance rate	11.0% – 13.8%	1.8% – 4.1%

What possible conclusion could be drawn from this data, assuming that the results display a p-value that is less than 0.05?

A) Genetics play a major role in the development of schizophrenia, as identical twins display a greater concordance rate than fraternal ones.

B) Genetics play a major role in the development of schizophrenia, as fraternal twins display a greater concordance rate than identical ones.

C) Genetics do not play a major role in the development of schizophrenia, as identical twins display a greater concordance rate than fraternal ones.

D) Genetics do not play a major role in the development of schizophrenia, as fraternal twins display a greater concordance rate than identical ones.

1029. Adolescents frequently engage in behavior that appears to be more emotional than rationally-driven. What could explain this phenomenon?

A) The prefrontal cortex is fully formed by adolescence, while the cerebellum is still developing.

B) The limbic system develops more rapidly than the prefrontal cortex during adolescence.

C) The limbic system largely overrides the rest of the brain during adolescence.

D) The hippocampus is still rapidly developing during adolescence, while the limbic system is fully formed.

1030. Compared to the number of neurons at birth, the number in an adult human being is:

A) considerably greater, due to rapid neurogeneration during childhood.

B) considerably less, due to pruning of these nervous cells during one's lifetime.

C) different from person to person, depending on genetic and environmental factors.

D) approximately the same, as the brain does not create new neurons, but rather reforms connections.

1031. Which of the following disorders are characterized by eccentric or disjointed patterns of thoughts or beliefs and abnormal perceptions of the significance of ordinary events?

I. Schizophrenia
II. Schizoid personality disorder
III. Schizotypal personality disorder

A) I only
B) I and II
C) I and III
D) I, II, and III

1032. Borderline personality disorder may have the least informative name of all major personality disorders; in fact, the APA has considered changing its official name in future editions of the DSM. Based on the symptoms of BPD, what might be a more fitting name for the disorder?

A) Emotionally unavailable personality disorder

B) Emotionally unstable personality disorder

C) Emotional devaluation personality disorder

D) Emotional miscomprehension personality disorder

1033. Narcissistic personality disorder is characterized by a tendency toward self-aggrandizing behavior designed to feed the sufferer's need for admiration. Individuals with this disorder have trouble seeing the impact of their behavior on others. Relationships are mainly viewed in terms of their effect on the narcissist's self-image, as opposed to genuine interest in the needs or wants of the other person. In other words, those with NPD tend to deal with others in way that lacks:

A) emotions.
B) self-esteem.
C) empathy.
D) self-regard.

1034. Which of the following personality disorders is most overrepresented in the prison population compared to the population at large?

A) Avoidant personality disorder
B) Antisocial personality disorder
C) Schizoid personality disorder
D) Paranoid personality disorder

1035. Obsessive-compulsive disorder (OCD) should not be confused with obsessive-compulsive personality disorder (OCPD). While both are marked by obsessive patterns of thought and behavior, rigidity, and a preoccupation with orderliness, they differ in that symptoms of OCD cause distress for its sufferers, while those with OCPD experience their symptoms as rational and desirable. Another way of saying this is that OCPD symptoms are:

A) trait-compatible.
B) ego-syntonic.
C) personality-aligned.
D) amorbid.

1036. A man walking down the street sees a brand-new, unattended, unlocked bicycle. While he is tempted to steal it and go on a joyride, and while he knows that his friends would be very impressed by the bike, he recalls that stealing is morally wrong. As a result, he locks up the bicycle and goes on his way. According to Freud, which component of the personality dominated in this interaction?

A) The id
B) The ego
C) The superego
D) The libido

1037. The situational approach to personality argues that behavior is predominately influenced by external factors (rather than internal ones) and that the idea of a consistent personality is illusory. Which famous psychological experiment would NOT be cited in support of this view?

A) Zimbardo's Stanford prison experiment
B) Milgram's obedience test
C) Bandura's "Bobo doll" social learning experiments
D) Piaget's cognitive development experiments

1038. According to Kohlberg's theory of the stages of moral development, someone who follows moral rules in order to avoid being punished would fit into:

A) the conventional stage.
B) the unconventional stage.
C) the post-conventional stage.
D) the pre-conventional stage.

1039. All of the following are listed among Goldberg's five factors of personality EXCEPT:

A) neuroticism.
B) extraversion.
C) agreeableness.
D) rigidity.

1040. Twin studies are frequently used to control for the effects of "nature," or genetic inheritance, and examine the effects of "nurture," or the environment in which an individual grows up. A psychologist studying the effects of family influence on political views gave questionnaires regarding various political issues to two 20-pair groups of twins adopted into different families. One group of twins was identical, while the other consisted of fraternal pairs. The questionnaires were then converted into "liberalism scales" denoting the level of agreement of the respondent with the positions of the political left on economic or social policy. The degree of correlation between each participant and his or her twin was then calculated for each scale, as was the margin of error based on the sample size. The overall results are presented below.

	Identical twins	Fraternal twins
Average correlation of economic liberalism	0.51 ± 0.06	0.45 ± 0.10
Average correlation of social liberalism	0.79 ± 0.07	0.52 ± 0.12

The results for the correlation of social liberalism would offer the most support to which set of theories about personality?

A) Psychoanalytic
B) Humanistic
C) Biological
D) Situationist

1041. Of the individuals described below, who is / are intrinsically motivated?

A) Dave, a young boy who mows the lawn because he truly loves money
B) Pauline, a teenage girl who completes her homework to get an A in the class
C) Joseph, a toddler who sings the alphabet song because he likes the way it sounds
D) Both A and C are correct.

1042. A seven-year-old child loves playing with her older brother's science kit, which she found on her own and experiments with for hours each day. If her parents want to reinforce this behavior, they should:

A) offer occasional praise, but mainly leave her alone with the kit.
B) reward her with a favorite snack each time she opens the kit.
C) tell her that each time she plays with the kit for one hour, she will be given one dollar.
D) tell her that each time she plays with the kit for one hour, she will be allowed to avoid one of her chores for the day.

1043. A drive can best be defined as:

A) an automatic behavior that always results from a certain stimulus, like the knee-jerk reflex.
B) a pleasant sensation that motivates individuals to perform actions that increase the drive.
C) a tense feeling or conscious urge to fulfill a need, like hunger.
D) a natural tendency to complete a certain behavior, like the movement of baby sea turtles toward the ocean.

1044. The Yerkes-Dodson law hypothesizes a relationship between performance on a task and level of arousal. Which of the following graphs accurately depicts this relationship?

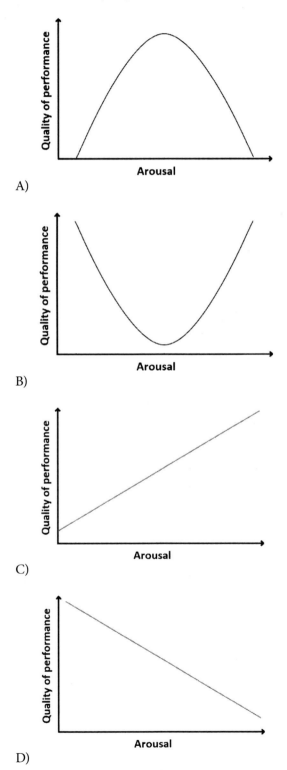

A)

B)

C)

D)

1045. According to the expectancy-value theory, which college course will a student be most motivated to attend?

A) A class that is famous for being extremely easy, but is not required and will have no benefit on her chosen career path
B) A course that she thinks she will perform fairly well in and is also strongly recommended for her major
C) A course that she is sure she will fail, but is mandatory for every student at her university
D) A course that she thinks she will perform fairly well in, that is not a required subject

1046. Which of the following are NOT examples of primary drives?

I. The desire to earn money to buy necessities for one's family
II. The pressure to eat some of every dish one's grandma cooked, even without being hungry
III. The desire to find a warm shelter in -10° weather
IV. The need to prove oneself in a football game

A) III only
B) I and IV
C) I, II, and IV
D) I, II, III, and IV

1047. You are extremely dehydrated, so you feel a strong urge to drink some water. This scenario best relates to which theory of motivation?

A) Drive augmentation theory
B) Drive reduction theory
C) Arousal theory
D) Incentive theory

1048. A heroin addict who decides to quit the drug immediately begins to experience leg tremors, trouble sleeping, and violent illness. Which theory of motivation is most commonly cited to explain this situation?

A) The expectancy-value theory, which attributes motivation to the need to reduce unpleasant tensions such as thirst

B) Arousal theory, which states that people act to maintain a specific level of arousal (excitement)

C) The opponent-process theory, which describes two contrasting emotional or physical components to many behaviors

D) Drive reduction theory, which states that people act to maximize the number of pleasant drives they perceive

Questions 1049–1050 rely on the figure below

In 1943, a psychologist named Abraham Maslow developed his now-famous "hierarchy of needs" to explain human motivation. This hierarchy is displayed in the diagram below.

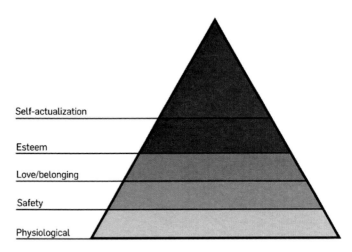

Self-actualization
Esteem
Love/belonging
Safety
Physiological

1049. If a certain individual's strongest motivation is currently to meet new friends, which must be true?

A) He has already achieved self-actualization and esteem-related goals.

B) He will not experience safety-related or physiological motivation until his current goal has been met.

C) He currently does not have a pressing need related to hunger, thirst, or lack of safety.

D) He may have strong physiological needs at the same time.

1050. If an individual has met all of her esteem-related goals and has no other immediate concerns, she will next be motivated to achieve:

A) love / belonging goals, since they appear next on Maslow's pyramid.

B) self-actualization, or the devotion of oneself to others.

C) physiological needs, since they are always experienced after other needs have been met.

D) self-actualization, since it appears next on Maslow's pyramid.

1051. A driver always avoids freeways after being involved in a multi-car accident on a large highway during his childhood. He often remembers this trauma when he drives near freeways and is faced with a choice between taking one and finding an alternate route. Which component of his attitude toward freeways is represented by his memory of the childhood accident?

A) The affective component

B) The cognitive component

C) The behavioral component

D) The associative component

1052. Which of these statements is most likely accurate?

A) A person who does not believe in consuming alcohol will not go to many parties.

B) A person who wants to be fit will avoid eating at fast-food restaurants.

C) A person who wants to gains muscle mass will decide to lift weights.

D) A person who feels lonely will opt to try out an online dating site.

1053. Of these individuals, who would be most influenced by his or her own behavior to believe that recycling is a moral imperative?

    A) A researcher who studies global warming
    B) An environmentalist who speaks to others about the importance of recycling
    C) A man who works at a recycling plant
    D) A student who has been taught for her entire life about the importance of sustainable living

1054. The concept of role-playing affecting a personal attitude is best exemplified by:

    A) a newly-elected politician who starts to lose sleep as the realities of her job sink in.
    B) a Nazi conscript who had several Jewish friends during childhood but begins to believe and make anti-Semitic remarks.
    C) a child in an affluent family who befriends a less wealthy boy at school.
    D) a second-year teacher who begins to dread the end of the summer.

Questions 1055–1056 rely on the figure below

Two speakers give opposing perspectives on gun control at a rural town hall meeting that is attended mainly by military veterans, hunters, and their spouses. After leaving the meeting, attendees that were initially identified as either pro- or anti-control were asked to list three points that each speaker made, along with whether their personal attitude was changed as a result of the meeting. The following table gives the survey results for both groups of attendees with regard to the speaker who was supportive of gun control.

Original attendee stance	Percent who could accurately list three points	Percent who experienced an attitude change
Pro-control	85%	0%
Anti-control	35%	5%

1055. According to the elaboration likelihood model, if 65% of the anti-control listeners processed the pro-control speaker's message peripherally, then they:

    A) had the motivation, but not the ability, to evaluate specific points of the argument.
    B) had the ability, but not the motivation, to evaluate specific points of the argument.
    C) had the ability, but not the motivation, to form general impressions of the speaker's presentation.
    D) had neither the ability nor the motivation to form general impressions of the speaker's presentation.

1056. In additional notes, the poll-takers mentioned that the 5% attitude shift amongst anti-control attendees was not specified as either a short- or a long-term change. However, it was noted that these individuals were persuaded peripherally. With the elaboration likelihood model in mind, we would expect this attitude change to be:

    A) long-term, because the shift required these listeners to overcome significant bias.
    B) long-term, because the shift resulted from meaningful impressions.
    C) short-term, because the shift resulted from superficial impressions.
    D) short-term, because the shift required these listeners to overcome significant bias.

1057. Social cognitive theory explains which of the following patterns of behavior:

    A) a child who watches many violent horror movies with his parents and, as a teenager, begins to exhibit aggressive tendencies.
    B) a boy whose parents regularly cook aromatic meals and who, as a result, is positively biased towards others who cook regularly.
    C) the father of two successful professional athletes who gains weight as he feels less of a need to prove his athleticism.
    D) the sibling of a successful artist who intentionally leaves the walls of his apartment bare.

1058. The idea of cognitive dissonance holds that a married mother who is torn between continuing an unhappy marriage and getting a divorce would:

A) make the decision based on her values.

B) make the decision based on advice from a role model.

C) internalize the values she uses to justify her decision.

D) internalize a hybrid of the two conflicting perspectives, making the decision difficult.

1059. A couple that has been married for forty years has spent the last decade deciding against divorce because they believe their marriage to be the admirable result of considerable effort. Which of these factors that may affect attitude change is most relevant to this example?

A) Role-playing

B) Public declaration

C) Justification of effort

D) The continuity paradox

1060. Which of the following statements does NOT correctly describe a factor that may impact attitude or attitude change?

A) A motivational speaker always expresses confidence in himself and his decisions as a result of public declaration.

B) After loudly reprimanding a coworker, a chef stops cooking without gloves on as a result of public declaration.

C) A soldier with a criminal history engages in roleplaying and acts aggressively towards his commanding officer.

D) Role-playing influences an uneducated caretaker to begin making real medical decisions for his patient.

1061. Of the choices below, which accurately lists two types of nonassociative learning?

A) Stimulus discrimination and stimulus generalization

B) Classical conditioning and habituation

C) Classical conditioning and operant conditioning

D) Habituation and sensitization

1062. An individual hears a loud tapping noise due to construction outside his building. At first, he jumps each time he hears the noise, and his heart rate and breathing increase. After two days, he barely responds to the noise at all. This process is:

A) not a form of learning.

B) not a form of associative learning.

C) not a form of nonassociative learning.

D) a form of associative learning.

1063. Which of the following statements about learning are true?

I. Stimulus generalization is the opposite of stimulus discrimination.

II. Dishabituation and sensitization are synonyms.

III. Escape and avoidance learning are both types of positive punishment.

A) I only

B) II only

C) I and III

D) I, II, and III

1064. Donnie, a theoretical patient discussed in a college psychology class, is incapable of experiencing habituation or sensitization. If Donnie is otherwise normal, he would likely have the most trouble:

A) lifting a large weight after two hours of hard exercise.

B) experiencing sensory neuron adaptation leading to feeling less cold after being outside for a long period of time.

C) copying a complex series of dance steps shown to him by an instructor.

D) gradually ceasing to notice the sound of a coworker's typing after hearing it all day.

1065. A student is researching mirror neurons and the processes in which they are involved. He would benefit most from studying which of the following famous experiments?

A) Bandura's "Bobo doll" experiment, in which children began to abuse an inflatable doll after watching adults do the same

B) Simons' "invisible gorilla" experiment, in which participants did not notice an obvious gorilla due to inattentional blindness

C) Harlow's "wire mother" experiment, in which young rhesus monkeys were more comforted by fake toys that resembled themselves

D) Schachter and Singer's "adrenaline" experiment, which dealt with the potential misattribution of emotion

1066. Biological factors related to learning and memory include all of the following EXCEPT:

A) long-term potentiation, or the strengthening of synaptic connections due to high-frequency stimulation.

B) synaptic pruning, or the removal of synapses that are not heavily used during development.

C) ataxia, or an impairment in an individual's ability to learn language.

D) neuroplasticity, or the ability of the brain's pathways to change over time.

Questions 1067–1068 rely on the figure below

In a developmental psychology study, participants are divided into groups of three, with each group either containing children ages 4-6 or adults ages 30-55. A group of children is placed in a room with a large stuffed bear. At the same time, a group of adults enters an adjacent room, separated only by a clear glass window and also containing a similar bear. At first, the children respond to the bear affectionately, while the adults are told to punch and yell at it. The number of abusive actions toward the bear, for both the "child" and the "adult" groups, are shown graphically below.

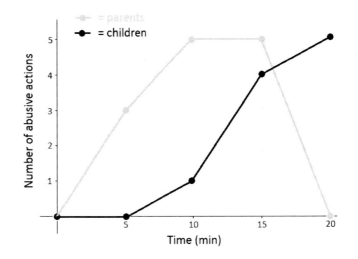

1067. If researchers monitored the children's brains using a functional MRI machine, where would they find additional activity relevant to the interaction with the adult group?

A) In the cerebellum

B) In the occipital lobe

C) In specific neurons in the auditory cortex

D) In specific neurons in the parietal and frontal lobes

1068. The experiment is repeated with an identical procedure, except the "child" group is replaced with teenagers ages 14-17. During one trial, one of the teenagers noticed that one adult's shirt is inside out, and immediately feels embarrassed. That participant:

A) is mirroring the adult's behavior.

B) is perceiving the vicarious emotion of embarrassment.

C) likely is not using mirror neurons, since she is not performing an actual action.

D) is currently in Piaget's preoperational stage of development.

1069. A member of the species *Aplysia californica* is being observed by a team of scientists. They poke the animal in its siphon, causing it to pull both its gill and siphon away. After twenty such stimuli, the animal no longer responds. The researchers could restore the gill- and siphon-withdrawal responses by:

   A) presenting the animal with a mild shock, causing habituation.
   B) introducing a secondary reinforcer to reward the desired responses.
   C) waiting for a period of time before poking the animal again, causing habituation.
   D) presenting the animal with a mild shock, causing dishabituation.

1070. A higher-order cognitive process that may include the trial-and-error approach is known as:

   A) observational learning.
   B) problem solving.
   C) shaping.
   D) classical conditioning.

1071. An unconditioned stimulus can accurately be described in all of the following ways EXCEPT:

   A) as an event or object that automatically produces a response in the subject.
   B) as a stimulus that elicits the same response as the conditioned stimulus later does.
   C) as an event or object that later becomes conditioned.
   D) as something either naturally desirable or undesirable.

1072. In classical conditioning, the process of acquisition involves:

   A) a neutral stimulus becoming a conditioned stimulus.
   B) an unconditioned stimulus becoming a conditioned stimulus.
   C) a conditioned stimulus becoming an unconditioned stimulus.
   D) a specific stimulus becoming generalized.

1073. A local elementary school uses a bell to signal that students should move to a different classroom. Over time, Johnny, a third-grader, begins to automatically stand up when he hears similar sounds, like his mother's ringtone. This situation exemplifies:

   A) operant conditioning.
   B) observational learning.
   C) stimulus discrimination.
   D) stimulus generalization.

1074. A daycare teacher keeps all of her fun toys and colorful blocks in a closet near the back of the room. When playtime is about to start, she turns around abruptly to go open the closet door. After two months, the toddlers in the class look up and become more active whenever the teacher turns around for any reason. During at least part of this scenario:

   A) the toys and blocks are neutral stimuli.
   B) the sight of the teacher turning around is a conditioned stimulus.
   C) the teacher's action of opening the closet door is a conditioned response.
   D) the children becoming especially active when the teacher turns around is an unconditioned response.

1075. An animal trainer needs to teach a chimpanzee to swing through a series of hoops. To reward this behavior, she can use:

   I. a primary reinforcer: a favorite food.
   II. a primary reinforcer: a token the chimp can trade back to her for a banana.
   III. a secondary reinforcer: a clicking sound that is associated with a food reward.
   IV. a secondary reinforcer: water for the thirsty chimp.

   A) I only
   B) I and III
   C) I, II, and III
   D) I, III, and IV

1076. Which of the following situations relates best to stimulus discrimination?

A) A child often receives candy packaged in a bright wrapper. Over time, he starts jumping up and down whenever he sees brightly colored pieces of paper.

B) A monkey is conditioned to avoid one corner of its cage, but after the experiment ends, he gradually begins going in that corner again.

C) A rat is first rewarded whenever any light is flashed, causing him to run to a food dispenser. The experimenter starts reinforcing only the brightest flashes, and weeks later, the rat does not even respond to dim flashes.

D) A circus tiger needs to be trained to complete a long series of tricks. His handler begins by rewarding the animal for attempting the simplest steps of the procedure.

Questions 1077–1078 rely on the table below

A student hears about Pavlov's dogs and decides to try an experiment of his own with his cat. He moves the cat's favorite treats to a drawer that creaks loudly when opened. The student's actions and his pet's responses over one month are shown in the following table.

Days	Student's action	Animal's response
1-3	Opens drawer, gives no food	Ignores drawer opening
4-13	Opens drawer, gives food	Cat ignores drawer, but comes running at sight of food
14-20	Opens drawer, gives no food	Cat comes running at sound of drawer
21-24	Opens drawer, gives no food	Cat ignores drawer
25-26	Opens drawer, gives no food	Cat comes running at sound of drawer
27-31	Opens drawer, gives no food	Cat ignores drawer

1077. On day 2, the sound of the drawer opening is a(n):

A) unconditioned stimulus.
B) neutral stimulus.
C) conditioned stimulus.
D) generalized stimulus.

1078. During which phase of the experiment does spontaneous recovery take place?

    A) Days 14-20
    B) Days 21-24
    C) Days 25-26
    D) Days 27-31

1079. In a particular psychology lab, rabbits have recently learned to associate small gold coins with food. The sight of one coin makes them hop repeatedly and salivate, just as if food itself was presented. One scientist wants to teach the rabbits to hop and salivate when he plays a loud tone, so he decides to present a coin whenever the tone is played. What single change to this experimental procedure would maximize his chance of success?

    A) Playing the tone more often during the first few days of the experiment, but only occasionally pairing it with a coin
    B) Waiting until the response to the coin undergoes spontaneous recovery, then beginning to pair it with the tone
    C) Pairing the coins with the tone for a drastically increased time period
    D) Removing the coins from the experiment entirely, and instead pairing food with the tone

1080. Which of the following concepts is NOT a type of associative learning?

    A) Habituation
    B) Operant conditioning
    C) Instrumental conditioning
    D) Classical conditioning

1081. A football coach plans to condition his players to follow his instructions from the sidelines. If he wants them to learn as quickly as possible but only needs this conditioning to last until the championship game next month, he should use:

    A) a variable-interval schedule.
    B) a fixed-interval schedule.
    C) an intermittent reinforcement schedule.
    D) a continuous reinforcement schedule.

1082. Which of the following scenarios best exemplifies shaping?

    A) A baby is praised for saying the word "da-da" when he sees his father. Over time, the child spontaneously learns to use more words and speak in complex sentences.
    B) A young boy trying to learn to brush his teeth is first rewarded for picking up his toothbrush, later for putting toothpaste on the brush, and finally for combining those behaviors and placing the brush in his mouth.
    C) A teenager prefers to ride his motorcycle after school, but realizes that he gets more approval from his parents when he focuses on schoolwork. He adjusts his behavior to increase his frequency of studying.
    D) A dolphin is trained to perform a complex series of tricks. One month later, his trainer teaches him an entirely different, but equally complex, sequence as well.

1083. An MCAT instructor checks in on his students every one to three days, giving them praise if they've completed their assigned work. Which reinforcement schedule is involved in this situation?

    A) Fixed-interval
    B) Variable-interval
    C) Fixed-ratio
    D) Variable-ratio

1084. All of the following statements about reinforcement are false EXCEPT:

    A) fixed-ratio reinforcement schedules are less resistant to extinction than variable-interval schedules.
    B) positive reinforcement includes both escape learning and avoidance learning.
    C) positive punishment is used to increase the frequency of a certain behavior.
    D) fixed reinforcement schedules are always more effective than variable schedules.

1085. A researcher trains rats to exhibit a variety of behaviors. In one experiment, the researcher plays a high-pitched sound, then presses a button to make the floor of the cage uncomfortably cold. If the rat pulls a lever within three seconds of hearing the sound, the researcher does not press the button and the cage remains room temperature. After just a few trials, all of the rats learn to pull the lever. Which of the following concepts are involved here?

I. Negative reinforcement
II. Positive punishment
III. Avoidance learning
IV. Escape learning

    A) I and III
    B) I and IV
    C) II and III
    D) II and IV

1086. If you keep a book past its due date, the library revokes your book-borrowing privileges for one week. The library is using:

A) negative reinforcement.
B) positive punishment.
C) negative punishment.
D) positive reinforcement.

1087. In which situation would a variable-ratio schedule be most advantageous over a variable-interval one?

A) A parent wants to incentivize her third-grade child to practice reading after school, but hopes that he will eventually read on his own for the fun of it.
B) A dealership owner needs to motivate his salesmen to sell as many cars as possible, as quickly as they can.
C) A manager wants to encourage his employees to come to work early, but has very little available money to use as a reward.
D) A yoga teacher needs to motivate her students to show up to class, and wants them to do so even after she has stopped rewarding them.

1088. Operant and classical conditioning differ in that classical conditioning:

A) can convert a neutral stimulus into a conditioned one.
B) involves rewarding unconditioned responses to increase the frequency that they are performed.
C) is a type of associative learning.
D) was pioneered by B. F. Skinner.

Questions 1089–1090 rely on the data below

A college professor is annoyed that so few of his students seem to ask questions, or even raise their hands at all, during his lecture. He implements a procedure in which every third student who raises his hand is given a point of extra credit. The scatter plot below shows instances of proper hand-raising behavior over time.

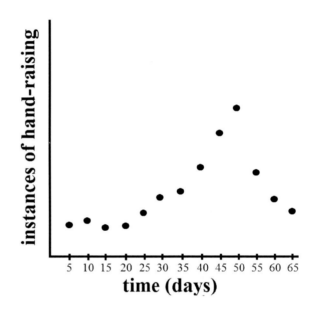

1089. Though the professor implemented his new reward procedure on day 1, he sees very little increase in the number of desired behaviors for the first three weeks. On day 23, he changes his method to:

A) a variable-ratio schedule in which every other student is rewarded.
B) a fixed-ratio schedule in which every tenth student is rewarded.
C) a positive punishment method in which every student who does not raise his hand is not allowed to watch the end-of-semester class movie.
D) a continuous reinforcement schedule.

1090. On day 47, the professor leaves for his sabbatical, and the replacement teacher does not reward any students for hand-raising. This change results in:

    A) spontaneous recovery.
    B) a switch from positive reinforcement to negative punishment.
    C) extinction.
    D) shaping.

1091. Self-concept and identity are very similar psychological concepts that are often thought to be synonymous. However, they do differ in a subtle way. How can this distinction best be summarized?

    A) Self-concept relates to the groups and categories that we belong to, while identity is the entirety of our ideas about ourselves.
    B) Identity relates to the groups and categories that we belong to, while self-concept is the entirety of our ideas about ourselves.
    C) Identity refers to how we actually perceive ourselves, while self-concept refers to how we desire to perceive ourselves.
    D) Self-concept refers to how we actually perceive ourselves, while identity refers to how we desire to perceive ourselves.

1092. Which of the following statements regarding self-efficacy is accurate?

    A) An individual with high self-efficacy must also have high self-esteem.
    B) An individual with high self-esteem must also have high self-efficacy.
    C) An individual with high self-efficacy must have low self-esteem.
    D) An individual with high self-efficacy could have either high or low self-esteem.

1093. A single, healthy individual may possess:

    A) multiple self-concepts.
    B) multiple identities.
    C) both multiple self-concepts and multiple identities.
    D) neither multiple self-concepts nor multiple identities.

1094. The three major components of the self-discrepancy theory are:

    A) the id, the ego, and the superego.
    B) identity, self-esteem, and self-efficacy.
    C) the actual self, the ideal self, and the ought self.
    D) the conscious self, the unconscious self, and the subconscious self.

1095. When Jeffrey places second in an important golf tournament, he loudly states, "I only lost because I'm not strong enough." This statement most clearly exemplifies:

    A) an external self-concept.
    B) an external locus of control.
    C) an external locus of command.
    D) none of the above.

1096. Which of the choices below accurately define(s) a type of identity?

    I. Gender identity: a person's perception of being male, female, or other
    II. Class identity: the socioeconomic group to which a person belongs
    III. Ethnic identity: the collection of a person's genetic physical features, such as skin tone and hair color
    IV. Racial identity: the non-physical aspects of a person's culture, such as traditions and language

    A) I and II only
    B) III and IV only
    C) I, III, and IV
    D) I, II, III, and IV

1097. A psychiatrist wishes to determine whether his new patient has an internal or external locus of control as soon as possible. Which question would be most productive for the psychiatrist to ask?

    A) Do you generally feel like you are a valuable person?
    B) Do you usually begin an exam or sporting event with the belief that you will perform well?
    C) When did you most recently face a major obstacle in your life?
    D) When you last did poorly on a test or other challenge, what reason did you give for that occurrence?

Questions 1098–1099 rely on the table below

An eighth-grade math teacher decides to implement a new method of administering exams. At the beginning of the year, he asks each student what range they expect to score within on their first test. One week later, they are given their first exam (Test #1), which is scored between 0 and 100. The two subsequent exams, Test #2 and Test #3, are given three and six months later, respectively. The predicted and actual scores of four students are shown in the following table.

Student name	Predicted score range	Score on Test #1	Score on Test #2	Score on Test #3
Shirley	88-92	89	91	94
Kaleb	80-84	80	78	83
Max	62-66	63	59	68
Denise	91-95	71	71	35

1098. A student's self-esteem could be directly measured using which values from the table?

A) The predicted score range only, with high predictions correlating with high self-esteem

B) The predicted score range and the score on Test #1, with a more accurate prediction correlating with high self-esteem

C) The scores on all three exams, with higher scores correlating with high self-esteem

D) No values in the table can be used to accurately measure self-esteem.

1099. Of the four individuals, which one most likely developed learned helplessness during the course of the year?

A) Max, since he performed the worst on two of the three exams

B) Max, since his predicted score was already very low before any of the tests were administered

C) Denise, since her high predicted score indicates an internal locus of control

D) Denise, since an external locus of control may have caused her to give up and perform poorly on Test #3

1100. A woman considering a career change thinks that she should become a firefighter because others will see her as a hero. This perception is an example of the woman's:

A) actual self.

B) ideal self.

C) ought self.

D) identity.

1101. Social interactionism, a sociological perspective related to the work of George Herbert Mead, holds that:

A) we only improve and further ourselves as people when we interact with others.

B) certain objects and ideas have universal meaning, but this can only be discovered through interactions with society.

C) as children, we pass through a number of libidinal stages that must be resolved to avoid neurosis.

D) we assign meaning to concepts and objects based on our interactions with society, and act based on these systems of meaning.

1102. Anthony, a member of a college fraternity, tends to be impulsive and often earns poor grades. However, he believes that all of his friends see him as a successful, outgoing role model. According to Cooley's concept of the looking-glass self, Anthony will:

A) shape a more confident and positive sense of self, as he believes that others view him positively.
B) shape a more insecure and negative sense of self, as his friends actually see his personality in a negative way.
C) shape a more confident and positive sense of self, as he clearly displays a remarkable ability to be optimistic.
D) shape a more insecure and negative sense of self, due to the poor decisions that he actually makes.

1103. A first-grade child struggles to write her name, but succeeds in doing so when a teacher guides her pencil. This situation best exemplifies which developmental theory?

A) Kohlberg's stages of moral development
B) Vygotsky's zone of proximal development
C) Erikson's stages of psychosocial development
D) Freud's concept of the id and the ego

1104. All of the following are Freudian concepts EXCEPT:

I. the latency stage.
II. the death drive.
III. fixation.
IV. the ought self.

A) II only
B) IV only
C) II and IV
D) I, II, and III

1105. James, a 45-year-old male, works at a high-level position in an accounting firm. When faced with an ethical dilemma, he usually focuses on what others might want him to choose. Due to his busy schedule, he often makes decisions quickly without regard for the greater good of society. James most likely falls into:

A) Erikson's initiative vs. guilt phase.
B) Erikson's integrity vs. despair phase.
C) Kohlberg's conventional morality phase.
D) Kohlberg's postconventional morality phase.

1106. Identity formation is often affected when a young individual chooses to join a group. However, groups often fall victim to a variety of psychological phenomena, including groupthink and peer pressure. All of the following are part of Irving Janis' eight symptoms of groupthink EXCEPT:

A) an illusion of morality, or the idea that the group is doing the right thing.
B) unusually low stereotyping, or the tendency to accept members of the group regardless of race, ethnicity, gender, etc.
C) mindguards, or individuals within the group who voluntarily control the information accessed by group members.
D) an illusion of invulnerability, leading to often-unhealthy risk-taking.

Questions 1107–1108 rely on the figure below

The psychologist George Herbert Mead described three stages of the development of the self, all typically occurring at a fairly young age. These stages are described in table form below.

Stage	Description
Imitation	An infant is only able to comprehend his own perspective, but can learn through copying his parents and others.
Play	A child can use language and behavior to take on the roles of others, but only sees one perspective at a time. In this stage, children often play "house" and similar games.
Game	A child can now understand multiple roles at once and how they interact, leading to a more complex understanding of society.

1107. An eleven-year-old boy is playing the role of Bottom in the play A Midsummer Night's Dream. When onstage, he must predict the lines of his co-stars, while also gauging the reactions of his audience and teacher. This boy most likely falls under which of Mead's stages?

   A) Imitation
   B) Play
   C) Game
   D) None of the above

1108. After the game stage, a child is typically able to use his understanding to perceive others' expectations of him. According to Mead, when an individual acts according to these perceived expectations, he is viewing himself from the perspective of the:

   A) discriminated other.
   B) generalized other.
   C) more knowledgeable other.
   D) looking-glass other.

1109. According to George Herbert Mead, the me is best characterized as:

   A) one's instinctive, often aggressive set of natural drives.
   B) the part of oneself that consciously, morally represses one's innate urges with the intent of reaching perfection.
   C) the free will that one uses to uniquely respond to a situation, generally within the constraints of societal norms.
   D) an internalized collection of others' attitudes regarding one and how one should be, resulting in the socialized identity.

1110. Erika, a twelve-year-old girl, has recently begun to spend time with members of her brother's clique, or gang. While she does not participate in any violence or consume any drugs, she spends every weekend walking around town with these individuals. Erika is most significantly at risk of:

   A) social loafing.
   B) social facilitation.
   C) deindividuation.
   D) individuation.

1111. After failing his organic chemistry final, Dave experiences a wide variety of emotions. First, he blames his professor for speaking so quietly he could barely hear; later, he feels personal regret for not working hard enough, and finally, he decides to write off the failure as plain old bad luck. In chronological order, Dave made which types of attribution?

   A) Dispositional, situational, and dispositional again
   B) Dispositional, situational, and situational again
   C) Situational, dispositional, and dispositional again
   D) Situational, dispositional, and situational again

1112. Attribution theory can best be defined as:

    A) the study of our tendency to assign causes to events, most notably to the behavior of others and ourselves.

    B) the study of our tendency to predict the consequences of events, most notably of our own and others' behavior.

    C) the human tendency to relegate our own successes to dispositional factors and our failures to situational ones.

    D) the human tendency to cite dispositional factors when analyzing the behaviors of others.

1113. One Monday morning, both you and your cousin happen to be late to school. You decide that this isn't your fault because you were stuck in traffic, but that your cousin is just lazy and unmotivated. In making these judgments, you are falling victim to:

    A) neither the fundamental attribution error nor the self-serving bias.

    B) the self-serving bias alone.

    C) the fundamental attribution error alone.

    D) both the fundamental attribution error and the self-serving bias.

1114. Kelley's covariation model outlined three types of cues that are used to assist in making attributions. Which of the following terms is NOT one of these three categories?

    A) Familiarity cues

    B) Distinctiveness cues

    C) Consensus cues

    D) Consistency cues

1115. Mike, an American service member, prevents a mugging on a train one day and is lauded as a hero. Which type of cue likely aided the public in making this dispositional attribution?

    A) Distinctiveness – Mike's behavior was unusual, so he likely acted due to his heroic nature.

    B) Consensus – Mike performed an action that most individuals did not have the foresight or quick thinking to do, so his actions can be attributed to his personality.

    C) Consensus – Mike did what most people would want to do, so he can be categorized as a selfless and true hero.

    D) Familiarity – Mike's face was seen on television for weeks after the event, so Americans grew accustomed to him and began to believe that he was a good person.

1116. Amanda and Kyle have just begun dating. Though she observes Kyle being mean to younger members of his fraternity, she concludes that he is not a bad person because he acts kindly and thoughtfully in all other types of situation. Amanda is using:

    A) a distinctiveness cue.

    B) a consensus cue.

    C) a consistency cue.

    D) none of the above.

1117. Dr. Ozzy, a psychologist, firmly agrees with the correspondent inference theory. Dr. Ozzy would most likely expect us to attribute which of these behaviors to dispositional factors?

    A) The person walking next to you accidentally trips on a wet floor and knocks you over.

    B) A woman in front of you in a drive-thru chooses to pay for both her bill and yours.

    C) A young college student at a party, like nearly everyone else there, drinks a beer.

    D) The human resources director at a large company fires a number of low-level employees because the company would inevitably fail otherwise.

1118. In which of the nations described below would citizens be LEAST likely to be affected by the fundamental attribution error?

    A) Country A, where the group is seen as all-important and individuals often put personal goals on hold to assist family members
    B) Country B, where individual achievement is prized and rewarded highly
    C) Country C, a nation that is settled in a "middle ground" between an individualist and a collectivist mindset
    D) People from all three of these nations are equally likely to fall victim to the error.

1119. A twenty-year-old college student tragically dies in a car crash. According to the defensive attribution hypothesis, how might Alice (another young person in college) respond to this news?

    A) "That exact fate could have happened to me, so I need to drive more carefully."
    B) "It wasn't my fault that he died, so I don't need to feel guilty about it."
    C) "He was probably drunk and driving too fast, which I would never do."
    D) "He had his entire life ahead of him; this is so terribly sad."

1120. The table below lists four ninth-grade athletes, along with their accounts of events that occurred during their most recent game or match.

Name	Sport	Personal account of event
Joshua	Lacrosse	"I missed an obvious shot on the goal – I'm so embarrassed that I let the team down."
Margaret	Softball	"She caught that fly ball that was heading right for me – I can't believe she would try to make me look bad like that."
Alex	Football	"The referee made some poor calls all night, but I heard that his wife just got diagnosed with cancer."
Zane	Soccer	"I can't believe I missed warm-ups; it's because my brother was getting in my way."

From this information alone, which student most likely committed the fundamental attribution error?

    A) Joshua
    B) Margaret
    C) Alex
    D) Zane

1121. A heuristic is:

    A) a shortcut or rule of thumb that nearly always leads to biased decision-making.
    B) a shortcut or rule of thumb that is usually helpful, but can lead to biased decision-making.
    C) a mental outline describing the steps involved in a certain task or activity.
    D) our tendency to see people as either all good or all bad, depending on the information we know about them.

1122. When another driver cuts you off on the freeway, you think, "Hmm, he must be late for work." What kind of attribution is this?

    A) Situational
    B) Dispositional
    C) Positional
    D) Relational

1123. A student best exemplifies the self-serving bias when he:

A) modestly states that his high MCAT score was "just luck," but blames his low chemistry grade on a bad professor.

B) maintains that the Green Bay Packers are the best football team in the NFL, while ignoring statistics about their recent poor performance.

C) attributes his winning bowling game to his own talent, but constantly repeats "I'm so stupid" when he performs poorly on math homework.

D) proudly speaks about his athletic ability when he wins tennis matches, but blames weather conditions when he loses.

1124. Mental organization patterns that help us make decisions or perform complex actions include:

I. scripts.
II. schemas.
III. working memory.
IV. heuristics.

A) III only
B) I and III
C) I, II, and IV
D) I, II, III, and IV

1125. A mother sees three news stories in a row about patients who died from a new variant of swine flu. She begins to believe that this flu must be especially deadly. When told that 98% of people who contract the flu fully recover, she continues to tell her friends that the flu kills most people that it infects. The mother is using:

A) confirmation bias first, and the representativeness heuristic later.

B) the availability heuristic first, and belief perseverance later.

C) the availability heuristic first, and object permanence later.

D) belief perseverance first, and the availability heuristic later.

1126. A novelist is attempting to create a character who believes in the just-world hypothesis. Which of these traits or behaviors should this character exhibit?

A) He firmly believes in karma and often says "what goes around comes around."

B) He approves of the way a neighbor dresses for work and concludes that she must be a good employee.

C) He strongly prefers food from his own culture over cuisine from others.

D) Both A and B are correct.

Questions 1127–1128 rely on the table below

A local family, the Robertsons, have six children (one boy and five girls). A psychologist decides to use them as an example to study cognition and problem-solving in his research participants.

Child's name	Age	Gender
Maura	15	female
Jeremy	14	male
Samantha	12	female
Jennifer	8	female
Carly	5	female
Sarah	2	female

1127. The gambler's fallacy is the incorrect assumption that the results of previous events affect future outcomes. For example, one might wrongly conclude that since the Robertsons' last four children were female, they are now more likely to have a male child. This fallacy is most closely related to:

A) the affect heuristic.
B) the fundamental attribution error.
C) the representativeness heuristic.
D) confirmation bias.

1128. Participants are given the ages and genders of only some of the Robertson children and asked to make predictions. Which of the following responses is LEAST biased?

A) Stating that, since four of the Robertsons' first five children were female, their sixth child is unusually likely to be female as well

B) Stating that, since four of the Robertsons' first five children were female, their sixth child is unusually likely to be male to "balance things out"

C) Stating that, since the Robertsons first had one female and one male child, their third child has an equal chance of being male or female

D) Stating that, since the probability of having a male child is generally 50%, the Robertsons' seventh child has an equal chance of being male or female

1129. Robert and George are both comedians. When George sees Robert tell an offensive joke, he assumes that Robert is a crass and thoughtless person. However, when George later tells a similar joke, he attributes it to the general attitude within the audience. From the perspective of the actor-observer bias:

A) George is the actor, while Robert is the observer.

B) George is the actor when he tells the joke, and the observer when he sees Robert do the same.

C) George is the actor when Robert tells the joke, and the observer at all other times.

D) George is neither actor nor observer because he does not fall victim to the bias.

1130. A conspiracy theorist is certain that aliens repeatedly land in his backyard. While he has never seen or heard of this happening to anyone else, he constantly asserts that he is "the only one who knows the truth." He ignores the comments of anyone except his sympathetic Aunt Mildred, who nicely tries to agree with him. Which of the following mental patterns is NOT used by this individual?

A) Overconfidence
B) Belief perseverance
C) Confirmation bias
D) The availability heuristic

1131. Which of these chemical imbalances can lead to or promote depression?

I. Low levels of serotonin
II. Low levels of glucocorticoids
III. Low levels of norepinephrine
IV. High levels of dopamine

A) I only
B) I and III
C) I, II, and IV
D) I, III, and IV

1132. A patient is experiencing hypomanic periods that do not cause serious psychosis or delusions, but cycle back and forth with major depressive episodes. This patient most likely has which psychological condition?

A) Major depressive disorder
B) Seasonal affective disorder
C) Bipolar II disorder
D) Bipolar I disorder

1133. How can one correctly describe the biopsychosocial approach to defining mental illness?

A) Each mental illness is caused by a specific chemical imbalance in the brain.

B) Mental illnesses are caused by a combination of chemical imbalances, psychological influences, and sociocultural factors.

C) Mental illnesses are entirely psychological in basis and should not be treated with medication.

D) Mental illnesses differ from physical diseases because they are significantly harder to treat.

1134. If a patient is diagnosed with reactive attachment disorder, which of the following must be true?

A) The patient must lack healthy bonds with its parents or caregivers.

B) The patient cannot have autism spectrum disorder.

C) The patient must also have major depressive disorder.

D) Both A and B are true.

1135. A patient comes in for a severe unexplainable tremor of the left hand. A thorough medical examination, including neurological testing, finds no underlying neurological cause for the patient's symptoms. Additionally, when the patient is distracted the tremor is reduced. Which of the following disorders does the patient have?

A) Acute stress disorder
B) Generalized anxiety disorder
C) Conversion disorder
D) There is no disorder that matches this patient's symptoms.

Questions 1136–1137 rely on the figure below

Researchers tracked the rate at which members of a set of identical twins developed the same psychological disorder as their twin, then compared it to similar measurements between siblings.

Group	Rate of same mental illness seen in both relations
Twins (male)	10%
Twins (female)	9.5%
Brothers	6.7%
Sisters	6.5%

1136. Based on the data in the figure, does a genetic basis for mental illness exist?

A) Yes, because the rate of overall mental illness was higher in males than in females.
B) No, because the twins showed a higher rate of shared mental illness than the siblings.
C) No, because the rate of overall mental illness was higher in males than females.
D) Impossible to determine, as we have no data regarding statistical significance and did not look at a control group of unrelated individuals.

1137. With the data in mind, which of these new findings would weaken the conclusion that at least some psychological disorders are caused by genetic factors?

A) Mental illnesses co-occur in more than 7% of mothers and their children.
B) The rate of the same mental illness seen in two random people is 12%.
C) The rate of mental illness in general is higher in identical than fraternal twins.
D) None of the above

Questions 1138–1139 rely on the table below

Just for fun, a doctor gives a short survey measuring "Happiness Rating" to each patient who waits to see him. Happiness is ranked on a scale of 1 to 10 and was measured throughout the course of a year. In addition, the doctor made an effort to disqualify any outliers, or participants who were very happy or sad for specific reasons.

Season	Average "happiness rating"
summer	8
fall	7
winter	4
spring	7

1138. The doctor notes that this trend repeats over the course of multiple years. What underlying condition are his patients most specifically experiencing?

A) Major depressive disorder
B) Seasonal affective disorder
C) Cyclothymic disorder
D) Bipolar disorder

1139. Which of these actions would NOT serve as an appropriate treatment for the patients in question?

A) Sitting in a warm, dark room
B) Using antidepressants
C) Participating in bright light therapy
D) Attending one-on-one therapy to address any underlying issues

1140. How do somatic disorders differ from other mental illnesses?

A) They can only be treated pharmacologically.

B) They relate strongly to biological symptoms but often lack a biological explanation.

C) They can only be treated non-pharmocologically.

D) They are long-lasting and often resistant to initial treatment.

1141. Which of the individuals described below, if given access to a mental health professional, is most likely to be diagnosed with schizophrenia?

A) Patient A, a man who has had extremely vivid hallucinations for sixteen months with no other symptoms

B) Patient B, a woman who spent the past year believing that the government is watching her, occasionally speaks in a monotone, and has lost motivation to go to work

C) Patient C, a man who has gradually lost his ability to remember fairly recent events, often misplaces items, and sometimes becomes angered

D) Patient D, a teenager who suddenly started telling others that he was blind despite no damage to his brain, optic nerves, or retinas

1142. With regard to schizophrenia, a negative symptom is defined as:

A) a symptom that adversely affects the patient's life, such as paranoid delusions.

B) a symptom that occurs in addition to normal experience, such as lack of motivation.

C) a symptom that represents a lack of normal experience, such as flat affect.

D) a symptom that is unresponsive to medication, such as hallucinations.

1143. A psychologist is attempting to study the stress-diathesis model in relation to schizophrenia. Of the individuals below, he would most likely be interested in:

A) Robert, a healthy thirty-year-old man with no family history of schizophrenia.

B) Amelie, a healthy six-year-old girl with no family history of schizophrenia.

C) Jackson, a twenty-four-year-old schizophrenic man with loving parents and no history of trauma.

D) Oscar, a twenty-one-year-old, recently abused man thought to be in the prodromal phase of schizophrenia.

1144. All of the following are positive symptoms of schizophrenia EXCEPT:

I. disorganized speech.
II. anterograde amnesia.
III. anhedonia.
IV. delusions.

A) II only
B) III only
C) I and IV
D) II and III

Questions 1145–1146 rely on the table below

A team of scientists is mapping the prevalence of borderline personality disorder (BPD) among individuals in various populations within a mid-size city in Ohio. Their data is shown in the following table.

Population	Prevalence of BPD
Healthy, white females with no history of sexual abuse	2.8%
Healthy, white males with no history of sexual abuse	1.3%
White female substance abusers with no history of sexual abuse	6.0%
White females who were sexually abused between the ages of 5 and 12	6.5%

1145. What conclusion can be logically drawn based on the data in the table?

　　A) It would be sensible to expect slightly under 3% of the healthy, white female population in the United States to be newly diagnosed with BPD next year.

　　B) Substance abuse directly causes an increased rate of BPD.

　　C) BPD may have a higher rate of occurrence in females than in males.

　　D) Both A and C are logical conclusions.

1146. Which of the following personality disorders would you expect to be categorized most similarly to BPD in the DSM-V?

　　A) Narcissistic personality disorder

　　B) Dependent personality disorder

　　C) Schizoid personality disorder

　　D) Seasonal affective disorder (SAD)

1147. Though Anna has been diagnosed with a psychological disorder, she feels completely normal and even perceives some of her symptoms as "just how she is." Anna most likely has:

　　A) a personality disorder, since many tend to be ego-syntonic.

　　B) an anxiety disorder, since many tend to be ego-dystonic.

　　C) a somatic disorder, since many tend to be ego-dystonic.

　　D) an anxiety disorder, since many tend to be ego-dystonic.

1148. Which of the following pairings properly matches the symptom of a psychological disorder with its description?

　　A) Echopraxia – repeating the speech of others word-for-word

　　B) Anhedonia – depression or long-term sadness that does not yet fulfill the diagnostic criteria for major depressive disorder

　　C) Mania – a period of depressed mood, decreased appetite, and drastically increased sleep

　　D) Catalepsy – rigid, immovable muscles and lowered sensitivity to stimuli

1149. Both Roxanne and Marisol were recently diagnosed with psychological disorders. Though Roxanne has a psychotic disorder and Marisol has a personality disorder, they display similar symptoms, including beliefs in aliens and other superstitions. Which conditions are these two women most likely to have?

A) Roxanne has schizoid personality disorder and Marisol has narcissistic personality disorder.

B) Roxanne has schizoid personality disorder and Marisol has schizophrenia.

C) Roxanne has schizophrenia and Marisol has schizotypal personality disorder.

D) Roxanne has bipolar I disorder and Marisol has schizoid personality disorder.

1150. The DSM-IV, published in 1994, renamed multiple personality disorder due to perceived inaccuracies in the name. One major issue is that sufferers of this disorder do not actually have many distinct "personalities"; they possess multiple "personality states" that cause them to lack a cohesive identity. The current name for this condition is:

A) depersonalization / derealization disorder.

B) dissociative fugue.

C) dissociative identity disorder.

D) hypochondriasis.

1151. Who is most likely to be part of a visiting football player's in-group when he is playing in another team's stadium?

I. His teammates
II. The crowd in the stadium
III. The fans watching from home
IV. His parents watching in the bleachers

A) I and III
B) I and IV
C) I, II, and III
D) I, III, and IV

1152. An American pilot is deployed in Iraq and flies missions above both Iraq and Syria. All of the following are likely to be in this pilot's out-group EXCEPT:

A) combatants that are housed in the targets that he bombs.

B) civilians living near the targets that he bombs.

C) enemy pilots flying near him and targeting allied positions.

D) American politicians that oppose military involvement.

1153. American soldiers that were entrenched in the same positions for weeks at a time during World War I most likely viewed their French allies that fought in separate trenches as part of a:

A) reference group.
B) outlier group.
C) out-group.
D) primary group.

1154. An infant who is abandoned by her parents goes on to live with multiple foster families, but eventually breaks off relations with all of them. During the course of her life, this individual has:

A) had no primary group but multiple secondary groups.

B) had temporary primary groups that evolved into secondary groups.

C) had one long-lasting primary group in her original parents and multiple secondary groups in her foster families.

D) had neither primary nor secondary groups.

1155. With regard to athletic performance, social facilitation is exemplified by:

A) virtually all soccer players performing best when extremely excited.

B) swimmers performing very poorly when moderately alert.

C) experienced NFL players performing worse than usual in a public environment.

D) amateur golfers who are new at the sport making many extra mistakes in front of a large group of their friends.

1156. Ellen and Patricia were best friends and members of the same dance team for ten years. Recently, Ellen transferred to another team, causing their friendship to suffer as they were forced to compete against instead of with each other. In fact, Ellen actually beat Patricia in the individual round. According to the stereotype content model, Patricia likely views Ellen:

A) with an admiration stereotype.
B) with an envious stereotype.
C) with a paternalistic stereotype.
D) with a contemptuous stereotype.

1157. An orchestra performs a piano concerto for a live audience. Who is most likely to be considered in the reference group of the first-chair violinist?

A) Members of the violin section
B) A stranger who stopped to watch the performance
C) The conductor
D) The violinist's parents and siblings in the audience

1158. Social loafing explains why:

A) a beginning chess player does better when playing against a computer than in public.
B) a government auditor is less thorough when assigned to the same project as other auditors.
C) a politician delays the legislative process because she has a majority.
D) a chef cooks meals slowly to encourage diners to order more drinks while they wait.

1159. Which of the following explains why an experienced spelling bee contestant does better when practicing with her parents than when onstage?

A) Social facilitation
B) Social loafing
C) The Yerkes-Dodson law
D) None of the above

1160. A biker who is grazed by a bus and falls off his bike has visible scrapes that cover his legs, as well as minor head trauma. Although he stands bloodied and dazed by the side of the road, nobody in the crowd of people walking by stops to assist. The bystander effect addresses this phenomenon by explaining that:

A) people in the crowd are less likely to assist someone in need because other individuals are present.
B) people in the crowd diffuse the effort of exertion onto others.
C) people in the crowd diffuse apathy for the victim onto others.
D) the plight of the victim is averaged with the well-being of the crowd.

1161. A researcher is conducting a social experiment with a group of test subjects on a blocked-off street. The participants are escorted out of an apartment building and told to cross the street. After they exit the building, an elderly woman walks by on the sidewalk and pretends to drop her purse, spilling the contents everywhere. The researcher records whether the subject offers to help pick up the woman's belongings. The experiment is then repeated with different subjects while progressively adding confederates, also walking on the sidewalk near the elderly woman. The percentage of subjects that help the woman is recorded in the graph below.

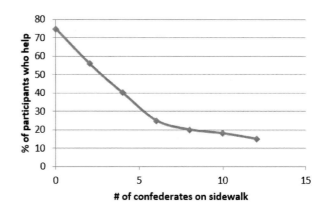

What social phenomenon is demonstrated by this experiment?

A) Deindividuation
B) The bystander effect
C) Social facilitation
D) Groupthink

1162. Deindividuation is best exemplified by:

A) a tenth-grade teenager who has his mother buy him Nike gear because all his friends wear Nike.
B) a group of Republican leaders who make very extreme, right-wing decisions when they come together as a group.
C) an inner-city protest in which all of the members wear masks, and which becomes violent even though its participants are typically peaceful people.
D) a group of ten soldiers at boot camp who carry a log across a field, with two of the soldiers bearing very little of the load.

1163. Peer pressure has been explained by the concept of identity shift. To what does this term refer?

A) Compared to adults, young people have somewhat less established senses of self, so they tend to adopt the identities of their peers more frequently.

B) Peer pressure can be avoided if one shifts one's mindset to be less reliant on approval from others.

C) A person's sense of internal harmony is disrupted when exposed to external conflict or the threat of rejection. The person resolves this disruption by conforming to the expectations of the group.

D) Younger individuals tend to adjust their identities to resemble those they respect, such as celebrities and sports figures.

1164. A small town in Africa experiences several violent attacks by members of a different village. Town leaders meet to resolve the issue, and because none of them wish to disagree with their fellow villagers, they decide to instigate an attack on the other village – even though most of them know this is not the best decision. This situation best illustrates:

A) peer pressure.
B) deindividuation.
C) social loafing.
D) groupthink.

1165. How does group polarization differ from groupthink?

A) Group polarization describes the tendency of competing groups to become increasingly extreme over time, while groupthink refers to the idea that people tend to arrive at better and more intelligent decisions as a group.

B) Groupthink refers to the social phenomenon in which groups make poor decisions based on a desire for harmony, while group polarization describes the tendency of groups to hold viewpoints that are more extreme than those of the individual members.

C) Groupthink describes the tendency of groups to hold viewpoints that are more extreme than those of the individual members, while group polarization refers to the social phenomenon in which groups make poor decisions based on a desire for harmony.

D) Groupthink describes the general process of group decision-making, while group polarization refers to the process of resolving conflicting ideas within the group.

1166. A social scientist is analyzing an instance of group polarization. She concludes that the most common ideas to emerge out of this group discussion were those that were most in line with the dominant, or majority, viewpoint. What type of influence is this?

A) Normative influence
B) Informational influence
C) Viewpoint influence
D) Congratulatory influence

1167. Informal social control relates is best exemplified by:

A) a law that prohibits young people staying out after 10 PM.
B) a sanction that restricts the number of people who can fly to a particular country.
C) the shame that a man feels after having an extramarital affair.
D) volunteers at a local fun run who direct people along the appropriate route.

1168. Eric was just hired at a new company. All of the employees go out to eat every Friday for lunch, and although the company doesn't have an explicit rule mandating this activity, Eric feels that he must also go out to eat even though he would prefer to eat lunch alone. This example illustrates which of the following?

    A) Deindividuation
    B) Peer pressure
    C) Groupthink
    D) Social facilitation

1169. Members of a group of Tea Party advocates are surveyed before and after attending a Tea Party discussion forum. Their overall acceptance and support of party ideals is displayed below as either weak, moderate, or strong agreement.

	Weakly agree	Moderately agree	Strongly agree
Before attending forum	47%	40%	13%
After attending forum	11%	27%	62%

    The above data demonstrates the psychological phenomenon of:

    A) peer pressure.
    B) social loafing.
    C) group polarization.
    D) bystander effect.

1170. Is peer pressure always negative or positive?

    A) Negative; peer pressure causes people to exhibit deviant or immoral behavior.
    B) Negative; peer pressure causes individuals to lose a sense of self and engage in behavior contrasting with their natural identities.
    C) Positive; peer pressure helps individuals conform and thereby aids in maintaining necessary social norms.
    D) Neither; peer pressure can be positive or negative depending on the circumstance.

1171. According to impression management theory, the three selves that operate during self-presentation are:

    A) the id, ego, and superego.
    B) front stage, back stage, and middle stage.
    C) the authentic self, ideal self, and tactical self.
    D) verbal, non-verbal, and intuitive.

1172. What might be a biological advantage of aggression?

    A) Aggression serves no biological advantage, since it does not directly alter the genes of the individual.
    B) Aggression can cause the organism that uses it to become ostracized and potentially lose access to resources.
    C) Aggression is closely tied to epigenetic modifications, especially methylation.
    D) Aggression protects against threats and can assist in the gaining of access to resources and potential mates.

1173. When Paul first attends college, he finds that he is more attracted to the women who sit near him in class than those on the opposite side of the room. What principle of attraction does this demonstrate?

    A) Reciprocal liking
    B) The primacy effect
    C) The proximity effect
    D) The serial position effect

1174. Which of the following demonstrates an ambivalent attachment style?

    A) Neither a father nor his child cares significantly about the other.
    B) A caregiver shows little or no response to her child in distress.
    C) A mother displays unpredictable and inconsistent responses to her child, sometimes with appropriate attention, sometimes neglectfully.
    D) A guardian gives a moderate amount of attention to his child, allowing her to feel safe to explore and grow.

1175. The golden ratio refers in part to:

    A) the body proportions that human beings find most attractive.
    B) the appropriate balance between verbal and non-verbal communication.
    C) the healthy medium between front-stage and back-stage selves.
    D) the precise amount of care and attention that a caregiver should give a child.

1176. A group of college students conducted an experiment in which they showed a photograph of a person's face to other students on campus, then asked whether they found the person attractive. In the first group, they told each subject that the person in the photo also found them (the subject) to be good-looking. In contrast, subjects in the second group were told nothing. The results of the experiment are shown here.

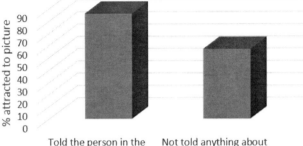

Which phenomenon is demonstrated here?

A) Selfish attraction
B) Reciprocal liking
C) The mere exposure effect
D) The familiarity effect

1177. A high school counselor decides to create an initiative to provide added network support to troubled students. To establish this form of support, she could:

A) create a series of fliers to remind them of their special skills and talents.
B) found a scholarship fund to help them with money to buy school supplies and clothes.
C) invite them to individual sessions, where she would listen attentively and empathize with their situations.
D) create a group meeting after school and invite the students to participate.

1178. Generally, women and men experience the feeling of empathy differently. Describe this difference.

A) Men rarely feel empathy, while women feel it very often.
B) Men feel empathy towards people whom they feel are socially beneath them, while women feel it toward people across social strata.
C) Both men and women feel empathy, but women are more likely to express it through overt communication.
D) Men feel empathy regarding feelings of anger, while women feel empathy relating to happiness or sadness.

1179. A psychologist tells her patient that he often employs the defensive impression management strategy of self-handicapping. The psychologist means that:

A) the patient is physically and emotionally hurting himself in order to avoid taking responsibility.
B) the patient creates excuses and obstacles in order to anticipate and mitigate poor performance.
C) the patient believes that he does not possess any intrinsic talent or skill.
D) the patient feigns weakness in order to gain sympathy from others.

1180. A middle-aged man's home behavior differs greatly from his actions when he is at the office, running his company. According to the dramaturgical approach, what is this man doing?

A) He is employing manifest functions at the office and latent functions in his home.
B) He is taking drama from the office into his home, thus relieving stress but impacting his behavior.
C) He is expressing his tactical self at the office and his genuine self at home.
D) He is expressing his back-stage self at home and his front-stage self at the office.

1181. An environmental biologist observes a group of Alaskan eagles and concludes that they are performing a foraging behavior. The eagles could be:

    A) building a nest for their offspring.
    B) copulating after engaging in an elaborate ritual.
    C) flying over a pond and searching for fish near the water.
    D) fighting for territory over a lake in midair.

1182. Can most animal species learn foraging behavior?

    A) No, foraging happens as a direct result of gene expression and cannot be consciously altered.
    B) Yes, but only if humans teach the behavior to the animal using Pavlovian conditioning techniques.
    C) No, this type of advanced learning is only demonstrated in humans and some primates.
    D) Yes, they can learn from experience or via observational learning from elder members of the group.

Questions 1183–1185 rely on the figure below

The Hawk-Dove game represents a classic hypothetical application of game theory to animal behavior. The game assumes that the hawk and the dove compete for a non-sharable resource. The two bird species have very different strategies. The hawk displays aggression and will escalate this behavior until he is victorious or injured. The dove also initially displays aggression, but will flee in the face of a major escalation. The following matrix describes potential payoffs of a number of scenarios in this game. Note that W = the value of the resource, while C = the cost of losing a fight.

	Meets hawk	Meets dove
If hawk	W/2 – C/2	W
If dove	0	W/2

1183. If a dove meets another dove when competing for the resource, how can his payoff most accurately be described?

    A) He will lose the entire resource because he will run away.
    B) He will win the entire resource half of the time because he will win, on average, half of the fights.
    C) He will win half of the resource because the two doves will share it.
    D) He will win the entire resource because he will fight while the other dove will run.

1184. A large male hawk, Bird A, encounters another similarly-sized hawk, Bird B. If the two are both aiming to earn the same resource, the payoff for Bird A will most likely be:

    A) W/2 – C/2, because the hawks will fight and the winner will take half of the resource.
    B) W/2 – C/2, because Bird A will win the fight (on average) half of the time, then take the resource minus any damage from the fight.
    C) W, because Bird A will win the entire resource in the ensuing fight.
    D) W/2 – C/2, because half of the time Bird B will run and Bird A will win the entire resource.

1185. In theory, this game states that the hawk population will be governed by the quantity W/C. Assuming that the population of hawks temporarily rises, what might cause it to return to an equilibrium between the two species?

    A) No equilibrium is possible, as the hawks always beat the doves in the matrix.
    B) As the population of hawks rises, the remaining doves will be forced to fight, thus winning resources and bringing the populations back to an equilibrium level.
    C) If the population of hawks rises, fewer doves will be playing the game; for a particular hawk, the V value will thus increase while C decreases.
    D) If the population of hawks rises, fewer doves will be playing the game; for a particular hawk, the V value will thus decrease while C increases.

1186. Altruism is often explained by the concept of the selfish gene. To what does this term refer?

A) A particular gene has been isolated that confers altruistic behavior to some species; animals lacking this gene are termed selfish.

B) Some organisms within a population are intrinsically self-serving, while others are intrinsically altruistic; these attributes manifest on a genetic level.

C) Organisms display altruistic behavior toward other individuals that share the same genes; thus, altruism ultimately helps genes survive within a population.

D) Contrary to popular expectation, an altruistic organism will always outcompete a selfish organism on the species level.

1187. Males of some species, like peacocks, display elaborate ornamentation that seems too metabolically costly to be evolutionarily beneficial. Which theory helps explain this apparent contradiction?

A) Fisherian selection
B) Inclusive fitness
C) The selfish gene
D) Nash equilibrium

1188. Of the statements below, which best exemplifies the evolutionary concept of sensory bias?

A) Organisms need distinct sensory faculties to best survive and exploit resources; thus, different species develop their senses to different degrees.

B) When a certain feature is already preferred in a non-mating context, animals that share that trait may obtain more mating opportunities.

C) Organisms with more highly-developed senses will always have greater biological fitness than organisms with less advanced sensory mechanisms.

D) More extreme-looking or ornamental organisms, even if otherwise unfit, can be selected for because they are preferred in a mating context.

1189. Facial expressions appear to be more highly conserved between species than body language. One behavior that exemplifies this trend is:

A) bees dancing in order to communicate the location of food.

B) all humans laughing and smiling when they find something humorous.

C) some species rising up on their hind legs to communicate aggression.

D) the baring of teeth conveying aggression and imminent attack in a number of species.

1190. During a lecture, a behavioral evolutionist explains that foraging behavior can be subject to natural selection. Which of these foraging behaviors will be most obviously selected for?

A) A bear journeys multiple miles in order to feast on a few berries.

B) A bird competes for access to fish in a lake, but often loses fights against a competing bird of a different species.

C) A species of monkey starts eating a new plant that is readily available and that other monkey species do not touch.

D) Females in a tiger population habitually eat all of their young soon after birth.

This page intentionally left blank.

CHAPTER 4

General Chemistry

1191. A sample of earth from a recently discovered cave is found to contain a significant amount of ^{238}U. How many protons does one atom of this element have?

A) 92
B) 119
C) 238
D) Not enough information is available.

1192. The ratio of protons to neutrons in radon-222 is:

A) 1:1.
B) 1:2.
C) 43:68.
D) 86:222.

1193. In a theoretical procedure, one-half of the uncharged nucleons in a chlorine-35 atom are isolated and weighed. Noting that the mass of a proton is 1.672×10^{-27} kg while that of a neutron is 1.675×10^{-27} kg, the total mass of this collected sample will be closest to:

A) 2.5×10^{-25} kg.
B) 6.0×10^{-25} kg.
C) 1.5×10^{-26} kg.
D) 3.0×10^{-26} kg.

1194. A new element, Z, is discovered and is found to contain 120 protons and 125 neutrons. What is the correct atomic notation for this element?

A) $^{120}_{245}Z$
B) $^{245}_{120}Z$
C) $^{245}_{125}Z$
D) $^{125}_{245}Z$

1195. A 1-L beaker is filled with 2 moles of liquid methanol and 0.25 moles of NaCl. The ratio of ions to atoms in this solution is:

A) 0.5:2.
B) 1:6.
C) 1:25.
D) 3:1.

Questions 1196–1197 rely on the table below

A sample of Martian water is collected by a Mars rover and analyzed. Distillation results in the separation of three distinct molecules. After further testing, the results of the analysis were summarized in a table.

	Molecule 1	Molecule 2	Molecule 3
Number of molecules	2.4×10^{46}	6.0×10^{26}	1.2×10^{92}
Mass (kg)	0.5	0.2	0.1

1196. How many moles of Molecule 3 are present in the sample?

    A) 2.0×10^2

    B) 2.0×10^4

    C) 2.0×10^{68}

    D) 2.0×10^{368}

1197. The molar mass of Molecule 2 is:

    A) 0.2 g/mol.

    B) 0.5 g/mol.

    C) 5 g/mol.

    D) 20 g/mol.

Questions 1198–1199 rely on the table below

Three samples of different pure substances are weighed, then mixed with water. The original number of moles of each compound is summarized in the following table.

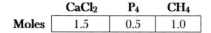

	$CaCl_2$	P_4	CH_4
Moles	1.5	0.5	1.0

1198. How many moles of ions are present in solution after the sample of calcium chloride is dissolved in water?

    A) 1.5

    B) 4.5

    C) 9.0×10^{23}

    D) 1.2×10^{24}

1199. How many moles phosphorus atoms are present in the sample of P_4?

    A) 0.13 moles

    B) 0.5 moles

    C) 2.0 moles

    D) 4.0 moles

1200. All of the following statements are false regarding CH_4 EXCEPT:

    I. it is a molecule.

    II. it is a compound.

    III. two moles of it contain eight moles of hydrogen.

    IV. when mixed with water, one mole yields 5 ions in solution.

    A) I and III

    B) I and IV

    C) I, II, and III

    D) I, II, III, and IV

1201. All of the following are true regarding the relationship between carbon and nitrogen EXCEPT:

    A) nitrogen has a greater electron affinity than carbon.

    B) nitrogen has a greater ionization energy than carbon.

    C) nitrogen is more electronegative than carbon.

    D) nitrogen has a smaller atomic radius than carbon.

Questions 1202–1203 rely on the figure below

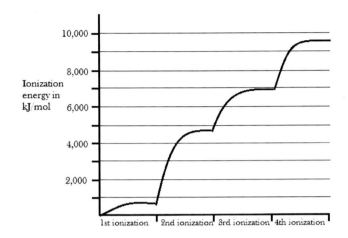

1202. An element from which of the following groups could have given these results?

A) Alkaline earth metals
B) Alkali metals
C) Noble gases
D) Halogens

1203. Which of the following represents the electron configuration of this element after the third ionization?

A) $1s^2 2s^2$
B) $1s^2 2s^2 2p^2$
C) $1s^2 2s^2 2p^6 3s^2 3p^3$
D) $1s^2 2s^2 2p^6 3s^2 3p^4$

1204. Place the following elements in order of decreasing atomic radius: F, O, Rb, Sr.

A) Rb > Sr > O > F
B) Sr > Rb > O > F
C) F < O < Sr < Rb
D) F > O < Sr < Rb

1205. Which choice is an accurate statement about electron affinity?

A) It reflects an endothermic process for both bromine and potassium.
B) It reflects an exothermic process for both bromine and potassium.
C) The process that it reflects is endothermic for bromine but exothermic for potassium.
D) The process that it reflects is exothermic for bromine but endothermic for potassium.

1206. Of the ions listed below, the largest atomic radius will be held by:

A) K.
B) K^+.
C) Mg.
D) Mg^{2+}.

1207. Which of the following bonds would exhibit the most ionic character?

A) A single bond between F and O
B) A single bond between B and S
C) A single bond between H and F
D) A single bond between Li and N

1208. Of the elements listed below, which would have an electron affinity of zero?

A) Ar, because it is a noble gas
B) Be, because it has a stable, fully-filled s subshell
C) Na, because it prefers to lose, not gain, an electron
D) C, because it easily forms four single bonds

1209. The carbon of a carbonyl group is a strong electrophile due to what property?

A) Due to the difference in electron affinity, polarization occurs between the oxygen and carbon atoms.
B) The carbon has an sp^2 hybridization.
C) Due to the difference in electronegativity, polarization occurs between the oxygen and carbon atoms.
D) Carbon is saturated with electron density gained from its double bond to oxygen, making it more electrophilic.

1210. Alkali metals, when placed in water, are highly reactive and sometimes capable of causing large explosions. Which of the following properties of these metals serves as a cause of this reactivity?

A) Alkali metals have very low electronegativities.
B) Alkali metals have very high electron affinities.
C) Alkali metals are catalysts in combustion reactions.
D) Alkali metals have very low ionization energies.

1211. Alkali metals are characterized by their:

    I.   reactivity with water.
    II.   ability to act as strong reducing agents.
    III. ability to form strong acids when bound to hydrogen.
    IV.   ground-state valence shell configuration of ns^1.

    A) I only
    B) I and III
    C) I, II, and IV
    D) I, III, and IV

1212. Why are noble gases unreactive in nature?

    A) They form stable diatomic molecules.
    B) They possess complete valence shells.
    C) The have highly stable half-full valence shells.
    D) They tend to exist in an inert crystalline form.

1213. Is a halogen more likely to be reduced or oxidized, and why?

    A) Reduced, because a halogen will gain one electron to fill its valence shell.
    B) Reduced, because a halogen will lose one electron to fill its valence shell.
    C) Oxidized, because a halogen will gain one electron to fill its valence shell.
    D) Oxidized, because a halogen will lose one electron to fill its valence shell.

1214. An unknown molecule, which has the ability to form multiple stable oxidation states, tends to exist in brightly-colored compounds. This species is most likely a:

    A) noble gas.
    B) halogen.
    C) alkaline earth metal.
    D) transition metal.

1215. Which of the following correctly orders these elements from the least to the most reactive with water?

    A) K, Na, Li, Be
    B) Be, K, Na, Li
    C) Be, Li, Na, K
    D) Li, Na, K, Be

Questions 1216–1217 rely on the figure below

The table below shows the properties of three atoms.

Atom	Oxidation state	Oxide formed	Forms diatomic molecule?
1	+1	XOH (amphipathic)	Yes
2	+2	$X(OH)_2$ (basic)	No
3	-2	XO_2 (acidic)	No

1216. To which group does atom 2 most likely belong?

    A) The alkaline earth metals
    B) The transition metals
    C) The halogens
    D) The alkali metals

1217. Which of the following identities for atoms 1 and 3 would best fit the data?

    A) Atom 1: Na; Atom 3: O
    B) Atom 1: K; Atom 3: S
    C) Atom 1: H; Atom 3: S
    D) Atom 1: H; Atom 3: O

Questions 1218–1219 rely on the figure below

The table below shows the properties of three atoms.

Atom	Oxidation State	Reactivity with water	Reducing potential	Magnetism of pure element	Identity of atom
1	-1	low	low	diamagnetic	-
2	-2, +1, +2, +3, +4	low	high	diamagnetic	
3	-	-	-	-	Ca

1218. To which groups do atoms 1 and 2 belong, respectively?

   A) Atom 1: halogens; atom 2: transition metals
   B) Atom 1: halogens; atom 2: alkali metals
   C) Atom 1: transition metals; atom 2: transition metals
   D) Atom 1: oxygen group; atom 2: alkaline earth metals

1219. How might you correctly complete row 3 of the above table, assuming that you are dealing with a lone Ca atom in a vacuum?

   A) +1, high, low, paramagnetic
   B) +2, high, high, paramagnetic
   C) +2, high, high, diamagnetic
   D) +1, high, low, diamagnetic

1220. A student is trying to identify the group of an unknown substance. Given that it forms a positive charge in water, which of the following tests would NOT be helpful to run?

   A) Ion-exchange chromatography, followed by titration for identification of charge
   B) Analysis of its relative reactivity with H_2O compared to that of a known molecule
   C) Analysis of the solubility of the nitrate salt of the molecule
   D) All of these tests would help identify the group of the mystery species.

1221. Which of these atoms or ions are forms of hydrogen?

   I.   Protium
   II. Deuterium
   III. Tritium
   IV. He^{2+}

   A) I only
   B) II and III only
   C) I and IV only
   D) I, II, and III only

1222. Of the following statements, which gives the best description of the Bohr model of the atom?

   A) An atom is an extremely small, indivisible particle that makes up larger molecules. The atoms that constitute one element are fundamentally different from the atoms that constitute another.
   B) The atom is a body of positive charge that has negative particles interspersed throughout its structure.
   C) The atom contains a positively-charged nucleus surrounded by electrons that orbit the nucleus in defined paths, similar to planetary bodies that circle the sun.
   D) The atom contains a positively-charged nucleus surrounded by an electron cloud. The precise position and momentum of an electron in that cloud cannot be determined.

1223. How does the Bohr model account for the emittance of electromagnetic radiation at specific wavelengths and frequencies?

   A) Bohr proposed that electrons could only stably orbit the nucleus at specific distances, and that jumping between these distances was responsible for the emittance of electromagnetic waves.

   B) The Bohr model includes the specific energy levels of each orbit and the associated electromagnetic wave that would be emitted based on each electronic transition.

   C) The Bohr model suggested that the atom would attenuate any incoming or outgoing electromagnetic radiation, and that only radiation of specific wavelengths would remain.

   D) At the time of the inception of the Bohr model, electromagnetic radiation had not yet been discovered.

1224. A set of four quantum numbers can describe all of the following EXCEPT:

   A) the electron shell and subshell of an atom.

   B) the specific orbital of a subshell.

   C) the angular momentum of an electron.

   D) the charge density of an atom.

1225. What is the electron configuration for Ni^{2+}?

   A) $[Ar]4s^2 3d^8$

   B) $[Ar]3d^8$

   C) $[Ar]4s^1 3d^7$

   D) $[Ar]4s^2 3d^6$

Questions 1226–1227 rely on the figure below

The diagram below depicts the electron configuration of a particular element, according to a college student.

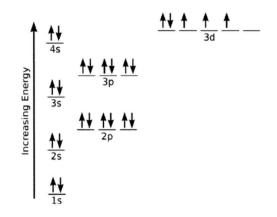

1226. Which rule, if any, is most clearly violated in this diagram?

   A) The Pauli exclusion principle

   B) Hund's rule

   C) The Heisenberg uncertainty principle

   D) Schrödinger's equation

1227. Is it possible to stimulate a lower-energy electron to enter a higher-energy orbit, such as from 3p to 3d?

   A) Yes, electrons can be physically removed from their orbits and placed into higher ones.

   B) No, electrons can only stably exist in their ground-state orbits.

   C) Yes, electrons can be excited into higher energy states from photons or particulate collisions.

   D) No, because the 3p orbit possesses higher energy than the 3d orbit.

1228. The Heisenberg uncertainty principle states that it is impossible to measure which two characteristics of a particle with absolute precision?

   A) Velocity and momentum

   B) Mass and acceleration

   C) Kinetic energy and acceleration

   D) Position and momentum

Questions 1229–1230 rely on the table below

The following table shows possible quantum numbers that an electron may possess, up to the principal quantum number of n = 4.

n	1	2	3	4
l	0	0, 1	0, 1, 2	0, 1, 2, 3
m	0	-1, 0, 1	-2, -1, 0, 1, 2	-3, -2, -1, 0, 1, 2, 3
m_s	+1/2, -1/2	+1/2, -1/2	+1/2, -1/2	+1/2, -1/2

1229. Which set of quantum numbers is possible for a valence electron of nitrogen from the p-block?

A) 2, 0, -1, +1/2
B) 3, 2, 1, -1/2
C) 2, 0, 0, +1/2
D) 2, 1, 1, -1/2

1230. In the ground state of cobalt, how many d orbitals contain an electron?

A) Two orbitals
B) Three orbitals
C) Five orbitals
D) Seven orbitals

1231. Which of these statements accurately describe(s) the behavior of photoelectrons?

I. A photoelectron's energy cannot exceed that of the incident photon.
II. A photoelectron's energy may equal the energy of the incident photon.
III. The threshold frequency is proportional to the likelihood that an electron will be ejected.
IV. The intensity of incident light is proportional to the energy of the ejected photoelectrons.

A) I only
B) II only
C) I and II
D) I and III

1232. Of the following, the only diamagnetic element is:

A) oxygen.
B) sodium.
C) iron.
D) cadmium.

1233. What is the effective nuclear charge of an electron in the n = 4 shell of iodine?

A) 15
B) 25
C) 53
D) Insufficient information is available.

1234. When an electron transitions to or from an excited state, all of the following are true EXCEPT:

A) the electron moves to an excited state after absorbing a discrete amount of energy.
B) the difference between the energies of the initial and final orbits is equal to the energy absorbed or released by the electron.
C) light is released when an electron transitions to a higher-energy state.
D) each subshell is associated with a defined radius and a definite energy.

1235. What is the frequency of a photon emitted by an electron with an initial energy of 5.0×10^{-34} J and a final energy of 2.5×10^{-34} J? Note that Planck's constant = 6.63×10^{-34} Js.

A) 4.0×10^{-2} Hz
B) 6.0×10^{-2} Hz
C) 0.4 Hz
D) 0.6 Hz

Questions 1236–1237 rely on the figure below

A physicist is researching the properties of light rays emitted by unidentified metals found in a salvaged shipwreck. The following table shows the type of ray emitted by each sample.

	Sample 1	**Sample 2**	**Sample 3**
Mode of light	infrared	ultraviolet	visible

1236. Electrons in Sample 1 may have made which of the following jumps, as indicated by their principal quantum numbers?

   A) 6 to 2
   B) 6 to 3
   C) 3 to 1
   D) 3 to 2

1237. Which of the samples may have contained atoms with excited electrons that had a principal quantum number of 6?

   A) Sample 1
   B) Sample 2
   C) Sample 3
   D) All of the above

Questions 1238 –1239 rely on the figure below

The diagram below represents the electronic configuration of a selenium atom. It is implied that all shells other than the outermost shell, which contains 4 electrons, are full.

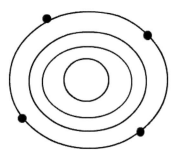

1238. With regard to this atom, what is the effective nuclear charge when n = 4?

   A) 4
   B) 6
   C) 18
   D) 22

1239. If the above atom is oxidized twice, what is the new effective nuclear charge when n = 4?

   A) 4
   B) 6
   C) 18
   D) 22

1240. A scientist observes an emitted photon in the form of an infrared ray. He knows only that in its excited state, the principal quantum number of the associated electron was 6. What is the frequency of this ray of light? R = 2.18×10^{-18} J; h = 6.64×10^{-34} Js.

   A) 1.0×10^{14} Hz
   B) 1.5×10^{14} Hz
   C) 2.75×10^{14} Hz
   D) 5.5×10^{14} Hz

1241. Which equation correctly represents the combustion of calcium?

   A) $Ca_2(s) + O_2(g) \rightarrow 2CaO(s)$
   B) $Ca(s) + O(g) \rightarrow CaO(s)$
   C) $2Ca(s) + O_2(g) \rightarrow 2CaO(s)$
   D) None of the above

1242. At high temperatures, magnesium carbonate can be decomposed to produce a metal oxide used in various industrial applications. The decomposition of magnesium carbonate is given by which equation?

   A) $MgCO_3(s) \rightarrow MgO(s) + CO_2(g)$
   B) $MgCO_3(s) \rightarrow Mg(s) + CO_3(g)$
   C) $Mg_2CO_3(s) \rightarrow 2Mg(s) + CO_3(g)$
   D) $Mg_2CO_3(s) \rightarrow 2MgO(s) + CO_2(g)$

Questions 1243–1244 rely on the chemical equation below

A student mixes 10 mL of 0.2 M potassium bromide with 30 mL of 0.15 M lead nitrate. The equation involved in this process is as follows:

$$KBr\,(aq) + Pb(NO_3)_2\,(aq) \rightarrow PbBr_2\,(s) + KNO_3\,(aq)$$

1243. As shown above, this equation exemplifies:

A) a single-displacement reaction.
B) a double-displacement reaction.
C) a precipitation reaction.
D) both a double-displacement and a precipitation reaction.

1244. Which statements describing the process are true?

I.   For every molecule of potassium bromide consumed, two molecules of potassium nitrate are formed.
II. For every molecule of lead nitrate consumed, two molecules of potassium nitrate are formed.
III. For every two molecules of potassium bromide consumed, one molecule of lead bromide is formed.
IV. For every atom of bromine that reacts, three oxygen atoms must be consumed as well.

A) I and II
B) I and III
C) II and III
D) II, III, and IV

1245. Write the balanced equation for the oxidation of zinc by hydrochloric acid.

A) $Zn_2\,(s) + 4HCl\,(aq) \rightarrow 2ZnCl_4\,(aq) + 4H^+\,(aq)$
B) $Zn\,(s) + 2HCl\,(aq) \rightarrow ZnCl_2\,(aq) + 2H^+\,(aq)$
C) $Zn\,(s) + 2HCl\,(aq) \rightarrow ZnCl_2\,(aq) + H_2\,(g)$
D) $2Zn\,(s) + 2HCl\,(aq) \rightarrow Zn_2Cl_2\,(aq) + H_2\,(aq)$

1246. The combustion of sodium in oxygen, a redox reaction, can be written as:

A) $2Na + O + 2e^- \rightarrow 2NaO + 2e^-$
B) $4Na + 2O_2 + 2e^- \rightarrow 2Na_2O_2 + 2e^-$
C) $4Na + O_2 + 4e^- \rightarrow 2Na_2O + 4e^-$
D) $2Na + O_2 + 4e^- \rightarrow Na_2O_2 + 4e^-$

1247. Write a balanced chemical equation for the single-displacement reaction of iron(II) nitrate and aluminum, which forms aluminum nitrate and solid iron.

A) $4FeNO_3\,(aq) + Al_2\,(s) \rightarrow 2Al(NO_3)_2\,(aq) + 4Fe\,(s)$
B) $FeNO_3\,(aq) + Al\,(s) \rightarrow Al(NO_3)\,(aq) + Fe\,(s)$
C) $Fe(NO_3)_2\,(aq) + Al\,(s) \rightarrow Al(NO_3)_2\,(aq) + Fe\,(s)$
D) $3Fe(NO_3)_2\,(aq) + 2Al\,(s) \rightarrow 2Al(NO_3)_3\,(aq) + 3Fe\,(s)$

1248. The reaction of magnesium sulfide with hydrogen peroxide produces both magnesium sulfate and water. What is the balanced equation for this process, and which element is reduced?

A) $MgS\,(s) + 4H_2O_2\,(aq) \rightarrow MgSO_4\,(aq) + 4H_2O\,(l)$; oxygen
B) $MgS\,(s) + 2H_4O_4\,(aq) \rightarrow MgSO_4\,(aq) + 4H_2O\,(l)$; oxygen
C) $MgS\,(s) + 4H_2O_2\,(aq) \rightarrow MgSO_4\,(aq) + 4H_2O\,(l)$; magnesium
D) $MgS\,(s) + 4H_2O_2\,(aq) \rightarrow MgSO_4\,(aq) + 2H_2O\,(l)$; magnesium

Questions 1249–1250 rely on the chemical equation below

$$Ba(NO_3)_2\,(aq) + H_2SO_4\,(aq) \rightarrow BaSO_4\,(s) + HNO_3\,(aq)$$

1249. All of the following are true of this reaction EXCEPT:

A) that it is a precipitation reaction.
B) that it is a redox reaction.
C) that it is a double-displacement reaction.
D) All of the above are true.

1250. How many molecules of product form when 5 molecules of barium nitrate completely react with 5 molecules of sulfuric acid?

A) 5 molecules
B) 10 molecules
C) 15 molecules
D) Not enough information is given.

1251. What is the molecular formula of an amino acid that contains 36.1% carbon, 5.3% hydrogen, 10.5% nitrogen, and 48.08% oxygen by mass, if it has a molar mass of 133.1 g / mol?

   A) $C_5H_{14}NO_3$
   B) $C_8H_{14}N_2O_8$
   C) $C_4H_7NO_4$
   D) $C_4H_7N_2O_3$

1252. An unknown organic compound weighing 1980 mg is fully combusted at high pressure, yielding 900 mg of carbon dioxide and 360 mg of water. What is its empirical formula?

   A) $C_2H_4O_{10}$
   B) CH_2O_5
   C) CHO_3
   D) CH_6O_{10}

1253. Which of the following is an appropriate method for determining the number of particles in a certain mass of a compound?

   A) # of particles = mass × MM × Avogadro's number
   B) # of particles = mass × 1 / MM × Avogadro's number
   C) # of particles = mass × MM × 1 / Avogadro's number
   D) # of particles = mass × 1 / MM × 1 / Avogadro's number

1254. A fluid is estimated to contain 3.0×10^{24} molecules of resveratrol ($C_{14}H_{12}O_3$), a phenol found in grapeskins and wine. The approximate mass of the resveratrol present is:

   A) 45.6 g.
   B) 1.1 kg.
   C) 5 kg.
   D) 1100 kg.

1255. A 0.1 cm³ sample of nitroglycerin has a mass of 160 mg. What is the density of nitroglycerin?

   A) 1.6×10^{-3} kg / m³
   B) 1.6×10^2 kg / m³
   C) 1.6×10^3 kg / m³
   D) 1.6×10^6 kg / m³

Questions 1256–1257 rely on the chemical equation below

The combustion of sucrose is represented as follows:

$C_{12}H_{22}O_{11}$ (s) + 12 O_2 (g) $\rightarrow$ 12 CO_2 (g) + 11 H_2O (l)

1256. The molar ratio of oxygen to water is:

   A) 24:23.
   B) 12:11.
   C) 12:23.
   D) 24:11.

1257. If 684 grams of sucrose are reacted with excess oxygen, how many total moles of gas are produced?

   A) 46 moles
   B) 23 moles
   C) 11 moles
   D) 12 moles

Questions 1258–1259 rely on the chemical structure shown below

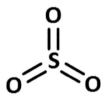

1258. The formal charges on the sulfur atom and on each of the three oxygens atoms are, respectively:

   A) +3 and -1.
   B) +1 and -3.
   C) +6 and -2.
   D) 0 and 0.

1259. Sulfur trioxide acts as an electrophile in sulfonation reactions. When the sulfur atom is attacked by a benzene ring, a single bond forms and one oxygen atom loses its double bond character. At that time, the formal charges on the sulfur atom and the single-bonded oxygen are, respectively:

A) -3 and -1.
B) -1 and -3.
C) 0 and +1.
D) 0 and -1.

1260. A sample of an unknown gas produced by gut bacteria is analyzed in a laboratory. If the gas has a mass of 50 mg and occupies a volume of 2.5×10^4 cm³, what is its density?

A) 30 mg / m³
B) 300 mg / m³
C) 3 mg / m³
D) 20 mg / m³

Questions 1261–1262 rely on the chemical equation below

Sulfates react with methane through the following reaction:

$$CH_4 (g) + SO_4^{2-} (aq) \rightarrow H_2O (l) + HS^- (aq) + HCO_3^- (aq)$$

1261. In a college biology experiment, 50 mg of methane and 60 mg of sulfate are mixed in a closed container. What is the limiting reagent, and how much excess reagent remains when that species has been exhausted?

A) CH_4; 55 mg SO_4
B) CH_4; 50 mg SO_4
C) SO_4; 40 mg CH_4
D) SO_4; 10 mg CH_4

1262. The above experiment is repeated, and again, 50 mg of methane and 60 mg of sulfate are mixed in a closed vessel. What is the theoretical yield of hydrosulfide ion?

A) 0.6 mg HS⁻
B) 10 mg HS⁻
C) 20 mg HS⁻
D) 60 mg HS⁻

1263. A balloon is filled with 100 mg of various gases to mimic those present in the Martian atmosphere. The balloon contains equimolar amounts of nitrogen and oxygen, argon with a mole fraction of 0.10, and carbon dioxide with a mole fraction of 0.26. In this system, the percent composition by mass of carbon is:

A) 9%.
B) 12%.
C) 26%.
D) 33%.

1264. What is the percent composition by mass of nitrogen in glutamine ($C_5H_{10}N_2O_3$)?

A) 9%
B) 17%
C) 21%
D) 25%

Questions 1265–1266 rely on the chemical equation below

Ammonium dichromate decomposes in a violent reaction that is often used in science demonstrations due to its "volcano-like" appearance. The equation for this process is as follows:

$$(NH_4)_2Cr_2O_7 (s) \rightarrow Cr_2O_3 (aq) + H_2O (l) + N_2 (g)$$

1265. Theoretically, how many grams of nitrogen gas should be obtained from the decomposition of 750 grams of ammonium dichromate?

A) 21 g of N_2
B) 42 g of N_2
C) 84 g of N_2
D) 168 g of N_2

1266. A student attempts to decompose 500 grams of ammonium dichromate but only measures 12 grams of N_2 gas produced. The absolute value of the percent error for this student's experiment is:

A) 21%.
B) 35%.
C) 66%.
D) 79%.

1267. Copper(II) sulfide and nitric acid are reacted, yielding copper(II) nitrate, sulfur, water, and nitrogen monoxide. When two moles of copper(II) sulfide and twelve moles of nitric acid are mixed in a reaction vessel, which is the limiting reagent?

A) Copper(II) sulfide
B) Nitric acid
C) Neither reagent is limiting.
D) Not enough information is given to determine the limiting reagent.

1268. What is the percent composition by mass of copper in a covered beaker containing equimolar amounts of copper(II) nitrate (molar mass 187.6 g/mol), sulfur (molar mass 32.06 g/mol), water, and nitrogen monoxide? Assume none of the species react in the beaker.

A) 10%
B) 24%
C) 31%
D) 48%

Questions 1269–1270 rely on the chemical equation below

$$H_3PO_4 + Mg(OH)_2 \rightarrow H_2O + Mg_3(PO_4)_2$$

1269. When 2 moles of phosphoric acid react with 6 moles of magnesium hydroxide, what is the theoretical yield of magnesium phosphate?

A) 1 mol $Mg_3(PO_4)_2$
B) 2 mol $Mg_3(PO_4)_2$
C) 3 mol $Mg_3(PO_4)_2$
D) 6 mol $Mg_3(PO_4)_2$

1270. Again, a student reacts exactly 2 moles of phosphoric acid with 6 moles of magnesium hydroxide. This time, he measures 13.15 grams of magnesium phosphate (molar mass 263 g/mol) produced. What is the percent yield?

A) 5%
B) 10%
C) 45%
D) 95%

1271. 150 mL of 0.75 M ethylene glycol, one of the primary reagents used in the manufacture of polyester clothing, is diluted with 1.85 L of water. What is the final molarity of the solution?

A) 6.0×10^{-3} M
B) 6.0×10^{-2} M
C) 0.56 M
D) 56 M

1272. 174 g of acetone (C_3H_6O) is mixed with 350 mL of an unknown solvent (density 2 g/mL). Assuming that the addition of acetone does not change the total volume substantially, the molarity of acetone in the solution is:

A) 4.2×10^{-3} M.
B) 8.6×10^{-3} M.
C) 4.2 M.
D) 8.6 M.

1273. To enhance the flavor of a homemade soda, 49 g of phosphoric acid (H_3PO_4) is mixed with 2 L of carbonated water. If the density of the water is 1.5 g/mL, what is the solution's molality?

A) 0.02 m
B) 0.17 m
C) 0.25 m
D) 2.00 m

1274. As the volume of solvent increases while the mass of solute remains constant, what must be true of the overall solution?

A) Both the molarity and the molality decrease.
B) The molarity decreases while the molality remains the same.
C) The molarity increases while the molality decreases.
D) Both the molarity and the molality increase.

1275. Succinic acid ($C_4H_6O_4$) is a dicarboxylic acid with a variety of uses. When 472 g of succinic acid is mixed with water to fill a 2 L container, what is the normality of the [H^+] in solution? (Assume full deprotonation.)

A) 0.5 N
B) 2 N
C) 4 N
D) 8 N

Questions 1276–1277 rely on the chemical equation below

Sodium bicarbonate, a commonly used antacid, produces carbon dioxide and salt water when mixed with hydrochloric acid in the gut. The reaction for this process is as follows:

$$HCl\ (aq) + NaHCO_3\ (aq) \rightarrow H_2O\ (l) + CO_2\ (g) + NaCl\ (aq)$$

1276. 250 mL of 2 M HCl is mixed with excess sodium bicarbonate in a closed container and allowed to react. If the carbon dioxide produced is then transferred to a glass vessel with 0.5 mol water vapor and 0.5 mol gaseous ammonia, what will be the mole fraction of CO_2 in the vessel?

A) 0.05
B) 0.33
C) 0.50
D) 0.75

1277. The reaction is run to completion in an open container, after which all excess sodium bicarbonate is filtered and removed. What is the percent by mass of salt in the remaining solution?

A) 0.25% NaCl
B) 25% NaCl
C) 50% NaCl
D) 75% NaCl

Questions 1278–1279 rely on the figure below

The following is the structure of phosphoric acid, an inorganic acid with multiple biological and industrial uses.

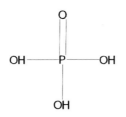

1278. When 100 mL of 5 M phosphoric acid is completely deprotonated by water at high temperature, what is the mole fraction of the phosphate anion in solution? Note that the solution contains 18 mol of water.

A) 0.025
B) 0.25
C) 0.33
D) 0.95

1279. The phosphate anion (molecular weight = 95 g) commonly forms complex ions with metals. 140 grams of an unidentified metal complexes with 2 moles of phosphate anions. What is the percent by mass of phosphate anion in one mole of this complex?

A) 23%
B) 40%
C) 58%
D) 68%

1280. A well-sealed flask found in a laboratory is said to contain a 3 M solution of an unidentified compound. The solution is measured to be 2.5 L and to have a density of 2 g/mL. The molar mass of this compound is closest to:

A) 15 g/mol.
B) 67 g/mol.
C) 150 g/mol.
D) 667 g/mol.

1281. Which of the following statements regarding chemical kinetics is/are always true?

I. According to collision theory, reaction rate increases with increasing concentration.
II. Raising the temperature will always increase the total amount of products formed.
III. The activation energy for a forward reaction is equal to that of the reverse reaction.
IV. Catalysts decrease the ΔG of a reaction.

A) I only
B) I and III
C) I, II, and IV
D) I, II, III, and IV

1282. The reaction below depicts a theoretical chemical process that is being studied by a university aeronautics lab.

    $5X + 2Y \rightarrow 3Z$

    What is the rate law for this reaction?

    A) Rate $= \dfrac{Z^3}{X^5Y^2}$
    B) Rate $= k[5X][2Y]$
    C) Rate $= k[X]^5[Y]^2$
    D) This answer cannot be determined with the information given.

Questions 1283–1284 rely on the table below

Initial rate (mM/s)	[A] (mM)	[B] (mM)	[C] (mM)
0.004	0.5	1.0	1.0
0.016	2.0	1.0	1.0
0.036	0.5	3.0	1.0
0.004	0.5	1.0	2.0

1283. Based on the experimental data in the table above, determine the rate law for this reaction.

    A) Rate $= k[A]^2[B][C]$
    B) Rate $= k[A][B]^3$
    C) Rate $= k[A][B]^2[C]$
    D) Rate $= k[A][B]^2$

1284. In a fifth trial, the initial concentrations of reagents A, B, and C are 2 mM, 4 mM, and 0.5 mM, respectively. The initial rate of the reaction will be:

    A) 0.064 mM/s.
    B) 0.256 mM/s.
    C) 0.512 mM/s.
    D) 32 mM/s.

Questions 1285–1286 rely on the figure below

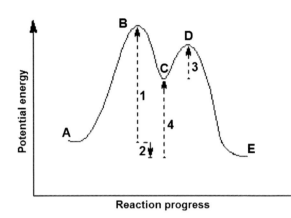

1285. Which point(s) correspond(s) to the reaction intermediate(s)?

    A) B and D
    B) C only
    C) C and E
    D) B, C, and D

1286. The dashed line or arrow that corresponds to the ΔG of the forward reaction's second step is:

    A) 1.
    B) 2.
    C) 3.
    D) 4.

1287. A one-step reaction between two alkenes can produce a cyclic structure like that shown below.

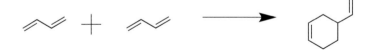

    Given the information above, determine the overall reaction order and the units of the rate constant.

    A) 1st order; Ms^{-1}
    B) 1st order; s^{-1}
    C) 2nd order; $Lmol^{-1} s^{-2}$
    D) 2nd order; $M^{-1}s^{-1}$

1288. The following zeroth-order reaction is carried out under UV light.

$$H_2 (g) + Cl_2 (g) \rightarrow 2 \, HCl$$

What will be the effect of tripling the concentration of H_2 (g)?

A) The rate will increase by a factor of 3.
B) The rate will increase by a factor of 9.
C) The rate will remain constant.
D) The reaction given cannot be zeroth order.

1289. A mixture of reagents K, L, and M react in one bimolecular step to yield product P. The rate law for this reaction CANNOT be:

A) rate = k[K][L].
B) rate = k[M]^2.
C) rate = k[L][K][M].
D) rate = [L][M].

1290. Consider the following multistep reaction:

$$2 \, A \rightarrow D$$

Step 1: $A + A \rightarrow B$ k_1
Step 2: $B \rightarrow C$ k_2
Step 3: $C \rightarrow D$ k_3

If the unimolecular steps are extremely fast, what is the rate law for the overall reaction?

A) Rate = k[A][B]
B) Rate = k_1[A]^2
C) Rate = $k_1 k_2 k_3$[A][B]^2[C]
D) Rate = $k_1 k_3$[A][C]

1291. A concentration profile of the reaction H_2 (g) + I_2 (g) $\longleftrightarrow$ 2HI (g) is shown below.

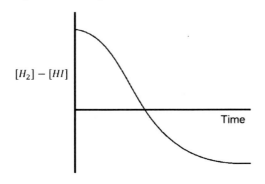

If the initial partial pressures of H_2 and I_2 are equal, which species will be present in the highest concentration at equilibrium?

A) H_2
B) I_2
C) HI
D) All species reach identical concentrations at equilibrium.

1292. Suppose that the equilibrium position of a reaction, $N_2 + 3 \, H_2$ (g) $\longleftrightarrow$ 2 NH_3 (g), is described by these concentrations.

[N_2] = 0.23 M   [H_2] = 0.33 M   [NH_3] = 2.99 M

What would happen if 1.00 mole of gaseous H_2 is injected into the system?

A) [N_2] would decrease and [NH_3] would decrease.
B) [N_2] would decrease and [NH_3] would increase.
C) [N_2] would increase and [NH_3] would decrease.
D) [N_2] would increase and [NH_3] would increase.

Questions 1293–1294 rely on the reaction below

$$C_5H_6O_3 \text{ (g)} \longleftrightarrow C_2H_6 \text{ (g)} + 3 \, CO \text{ (g)}$$

1293. Equilibrium amounts of each compound are added to a flask. If C_2H_6 placed in the flask is labeled with radioactive ^{14}C, where will ^{14}C be found after a substantial amount of time has passed?

A) ^{14}C will be found only in C_2H_6 indefinitely.
B) ^{14}C will be found only in $C_5H_6O_3$ and C_2H_6.
C) ^{14}C will be found only in C_2H_6 and CO.
D) ^{14}C will be found in all species.

1294. If the pressure of the system is increased, which of these observations are likely?

I. The concentration of CO will increase.
II. The partial pressure of $C_5H_6O_3$ will increase.
III. The number of molecules of $C_5H_6O_3$ will increase.
IV. When equilibrium is re-established, the partial pressure of each species will be equal to its prior value.

A) I only
B) IV only
C) I and II
D) II and III

1295. What is the correct equilibrium expression for the reaction $2\ NOCl\ (g) \longleftrightarrow 2\ NO\ (g) + Cl_2\ (g)$?

A) $K_{eq} = \dfrac{[NOCl]^2}{[NO]^2[Cl_2]}$

B) $K_{eq} = [NO]^2[Cl]^2$

C) $K_{eq} = \dfrac{[NO]^2[Cl_2]}{[NOCl]^2}$

D) $K_{eq} = \dfrac{[NO]^2[Cl]^2}{[NOCl]^2}$

1296. A researcher is attempting to study the equilibrium of an unknown reaction when he determines that the initial product-to-reactant concentration is too small. In this concentration profile:

A) Q is equal to K.
B) Q is greater than K.
C) Q is less than K.
D) none of the above.

Questions 1297–1298 rely on the information below

Reaction 1: $C \longleftrightarrow D$

$K_1 = 1 \qquad \Delta G_1° = 90.2$ kJ/mol

Reaction 2: $A + F \longleftrightarrow 2\ D + E$

$K_2 = 2 \qquad \Delta G_1° = -132.4$ kJ/mol

Reaction 3: $B + C \longleftrightarrow A + F$

$K_3 = 4 \qquad \Delta G_1° = 12.7$ kJ/mol

1297. Calculate the equilibrium constant for the reaction $B \longleftrightarrow D + E$.

A) $K_{eq} = K_2 + K_3 - K_1$

B) $K_{eq} = \dfrac{K_1}{K_2 K_3}$

C) $K_{eq} = K_1 - K_2 - K_3$

D) $K_{eq} = \dfrac{K_2 K_3}{K_1}$

1298. Which of these statements correctly characterizes the thermodynamics of the reaction $B \longleftrightarrow D + E$?

A) It is nonspontaneous because both K_{eq} and $\Delta G_{rxn}°$ are negative.
B) It is spontaneous because both K_{eq} and $\Delta G_{rxn}°$ are positive.
C) It is nonspontaneous because K_{eq} is positive.
D) It is spontaneous because $\Delta G_{rxn}°$ is negative.

1299. Which of the following is FALSE?

A) K_{eq} will be affected by a change in temperature.
B) K_{eq} will be unaffected by a change in product concentration.
C) K_{eq} will be unaffected by a change in reactant concentration.
D) K_{eq} will be affected by change in pressure.

1300. Consider the following reaction.

$2A_3\ (g) \longleftrightarrow A_6\ (g)$

If $K_p = 10$ and the partial pressure of A_6 is 0.1 atm at equilibrium, what is the mole fraction of A_3 at equilibrium?

A) 0.2
B) 0.5
C) 20
D) 50

1301. A laboratory assistant, in a hurry before class, pours dilute HCl into what she believed was a clean glass vessel. However, a thick white precipitate quickly forms along the bottom of the container. The vessel was most likely contaminated with:

A) ammonium nitrate.
B) a small amount of potassium chloride.
C) silver ion.
D) sodium hydroxide.

1302. The solubility product of calcium hydroxide is equal to:

A) $[Ca^{2+}][OH^-]$.
B) $([Ca^{2+}][OH^-]^2) / [CaOH_2]$.
C) $[Ca^{2+}]^2[OH^-]$.
D) $[Ca^{2+}][OH^-]^2$.

1303. The K_{sp} of zinc phosphate is 9.0×10^{-33}. Jack, an organic chemistry student, adds 0.010 mol of Na_3PO_4 to a solution of 0.0002 mol $Zn(NO_3)_2$ in 2 L of water. Should Jack expect to see a solid precipitate?

A) Yes, because the ion product is less than the K_{sp} of zinc phosphate.
B) Yes, because the ion product exceeds the K_{sp} of zinc phosphate.
C) No, because the ion product is less than the K_{sp} of zinc phosphate.
D) No, because zinc phosphate is a soluble salt.

1304. The table below gives the K_{sp} values for a number of salts in water.

Compound	K_{sp}
Copper (II) sulfide	2.2×10^{-20}
Magnesium hydroxide	1.8×10^{-11}
Manganese (II) hydroxide	1.9×10^{-13}

Given this information, which of the following statements are true?

I. CuS is the most soluble of the three salts.
II. $Mn(OH)_2$ is less soluble than $Mg(OH)_2$.
III. $Mg(OH)_2$ has a higher molar solubility than $Mn(OH)_2$.

A) I only
B) II only
C) I and III
D) II and III

1305. A researcher observes that, under certain conditions, the K_{sp} value for iron(II) carbonate is 3.2×10^{-11}. To increase this value, she could:

A) increase the number of moles of $FeCO_3$ present in the solvent.
B) add $Fe(NO_3)_2$, a soluble salt, to her solution.
C) change the ambient temperature.
D) All of the above could accomplish the researcher's goal.

1306. The molar solubility of chromium(II) hydroxide is 7×10^{-9}. What is the K_{sp} of this compound?

A) 2×10^{-20}
B) 4.9×10^{-17}
C) 1×10^{-16}
D) 1.4×10^{-24}

1307. Which of these choices most accurately characterizes the common ion effect?

A) When additional calcium carbonate is added to an already-saturated solution of that salt, a precipitate forms.
B) A student has a beaker containing an unsaturated solution of barium fluoride. When he adds a small amount of sodium fluoride, a precipitate forms.
C) An Erlenmeyer flask holds a solution of aluminum phosphate with a solid substance at the bottom. When ammonium phosphate is added, the solid disappears.
D) A glass jug contains both sodium bromide and calcium fluoride in water.

1308. Calcium oxalate, a salt found in large amounts in kidney stones, dissociates according to the equilibrium below.

$$CaC_2O_{4\,(s)} \longleftrightarrow Ca^{2+} + C_2O_4^{2-} \quad K_{sp} = 2.7 \times 10^{-9}$$

If 5 moles of calcium oxalate are added to 1 L of distilled water, what concentration of oxalate ion will exist in solution?

A) 2.7×10^{-9} M
B) 5.2×10^{-5} M
C) 2.6×10^{-4} M
D) 1.7×10^{-3} M

1309. Molar solubility is defined as:

A) the equilibrium constant associated with the dissolution of a particular solid in aqueous solution.
B) the amount of solvent required to dissociate one mole of a particular solid.
C) the number of moles of a particular solid that dissociate in one liter of solution.
D) the number of moles present in an unsaturated aqueous solution of a particular solid.

1310. The diagram below depicts the structure of the tetraaminodiaquacopper(II) ion, a complex ion.

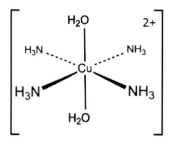

With this in mind, how would the solubility of $CuCO_3$ in a water / ammonia solution differ from its solubility in water alone? Assume that copper ions do not form complexes in pure water.

A) It would be more soluble in the water / ammonia solution.
B) It would be less soluble in the water / ammonia solution.
C) It would be completely insoluble in both solutions.
D) It would be completely soluble in both solutions.

1311. Which of the following compounds is a strong acid?

    A) Nitrous acid
    B) Hypochlorous acid
    C) Perchloric acid
    D) Sulfurous acid

1312. All of the following statements about K_a are false EXCEPT:

    A) the product of the K_a of HSO_4^- and the K_b of HSO_4^- is always equal to 10^{-14}.
    B) the product of the K_a of HSO_4^- and the K_b of HSO_4^- is equal to the value of K_w at that temperature.
    C) the product of the K_a of H_2SO_4 and the K_b of HSO_4^- is always equal to 10^{-14}.
    D) the product of the K_a of HSO_4 and the K_b of SO_4^{2-} is equal to the value of K_w at that temperature.

1313. Acetic acid is titrated with NaOH according to the reaction below:

$$HC_2H_3O_2 + NaOH \rightarrow NaC_2H_3O_2 + H_2O$$

Which choice accurately expresses the role of acetate in this reaction?

    A) It is a Lewis acid.
    B) It is the conjugate base of a Brønsted-Lowry acid.
    C) It is a weak Brønsted-Lowry acid.
    D) It is a strong Brønsted-Lowry base.

1314. The conjugate base of $HClO_2$ is:

    A) ClO_2^-, a weak base.
    B) ClO_2^-, a strong base.
    C) ClO_2^-, a neutral ion.
    D) $HClO$, a weak acid.

1315. Which of the following equations correctly designates the relationship between pH, pOH, K_a, and K_b?

    I. $pH + pOH = pK_w$
    II. $K_a + K_b = K_w$
    III. $K_a = \dfrac{Kw}{Kb}$

    A) I only
    B) I and II
    C) I and III
    D) II and III

1316. A student combines 50 mL of 0.80 M HF with 40 mL of 0.75 M KOH. He predicts that, since he is mixing a weak acid with a strong base, the final pH of the solution will be greater than 7. However, a piece of blue litmus paper dipped into the beaker immediately turns red. Which choice accurately describes the student's mistake?

    A) HF is actually a strong acid, making the pH of this solution lower than expected.
    B) Since KOH is strong, it is the pOH of the solution that will be greater than 7, not the pH.
    C) pH depends on the concentrations of H^+ and OH^-, regardless of acid and base strength, and the final solution contains more moles of H^+ than OH^-.
    D) The student did not make a mistake; blue litmus paper becomes red in basic solution.

1317. Acid A has a $pK_a < 4.7$, while Acid B has a $pK_a > 5.8$. In aqueous solution at 25 °C, Acid B:

    A) will have a percent dissociation that is over ten times greater than that of Acid A.
    B) has a conjugate base with a larger K_b than the conjugate of Acid A.
    C) has a conjugate base with a larger pK_b than the conjugate of Acid A.
    D) has a K_a that is between 10^{-4} and 10^{-5}.

1318. The following figure shows two carboxylic acids.

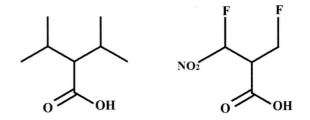

The acid with the lower pK_a is:

    A) the acid on the left, due to the presence of additional alkyl groups.
    B) the acid on the left, due to the additional stabilizing effects of resonance.
    C) the acid on the right, due to the electron-donating substituents.
    D) the acid on the right, due to the added inductive effect.

Questions 1319–1320 rely on the table below

The following table shows four polyprotic acids and their K_a values at 25 °C:

Acid	K_{a1}	K_{a2}	K_{a3}
H_2CO_3	4.3×10^{-7}	4.8×10^{-11}	N/A
H_2SO_3	1.5×10^{-2}	1.0×10^{-7}	N/A
H_3PO_4	7.5×10^{-3}	6.2×10^{-8}	4.8×10^{-13}
$H_2C_2O_4$	5.9×10^{-2}	6.4×10^{-5}	N/A

1319. Which of the following ions is the most basic?

    A) HSO_3^-

    B) HPO_4^{2-}

    C) $C_2O_4^{2-}$

    D) CO_3^{2-}

1320. What is the approximate pK_b for $H_2PO_4^-$ at 25°C?

    A) 2.2

    B) 6.6

    C) 11.8

    D) 13.0

1321. 10 ml of a 1.0 M hydrochloric acid solution is added to a 100 mL flask. Next, 90 mL of distilled water is added to the flask, bringing the total volume to 100 mL. What is the pH of the final solution?

    A) 0

    B) 1

    C) 2

    D) 10

1322. A student makes a solution by mixing equimolar amounts of hydrofluoric acid and sodium hydroxide. Which of these choices constitutes a true statement regarding the pH of the solution produced?

    A) Its pH is 7, because both HF and NaOH are strong.

    B) Its pH is 7, because both F^- and H_2O are negligibly weak.

    C) Its pH is greater than 7, because F^- is a moderately strong base.

    D) Its pH is greater than 7, because NaOH will remain after all of the HF is neutralized.

Questions 1323–1324 rely on the chemical equations below

HCN (aq) + H_2O (l) $\longleftrightarrow$ H_3O^+ (aq) + CN^- (aq) $pK_a = 9.2$

$2 H_2O$ (l) $\longleftrightarrow$ H_3O^+ (aq) + OH^- (aq) $pK_w = 14$

1323. In a 0.5 M aqueous solution of HCN, what major species are present?

    A) H_3O^+ (aq) and H_2O (l)

    B) H_2O (l) and CN^- (aq)

    C) H_3O^+ (aq) and OH^- (aq)

    D) H_2O (l) and HCN (aq)

1324. What is the pH of a 1 M aqueous HCN solution?

    A) 0

    B) 4.6

    C) 9.4

    D) 11.44

1325. All of the following are true EXCEPT:

    A) a weak acid in aqueous solution has a pH that is less than 7.

    B) under standard conditions, the pH scale ranges from 0 to 14.

    C) weak acids produce relatively strong conjugate bases.

    D) 10 mL of 2 M KOH is fully neutralized by 20 mL of 1 M HF.

Questions 1326–1327 rely on the table below

The following table shows some pH and pOH values for pure water at various temperatures.

Temperature (°C)	pH	pOH
0		7.48
25	7	
50	6.63	
75		6.35
100	6.13	

1326. At which tabulated temperature is $[OH^-] > [H^+]$?

    A) 0 °C and 25°C

    B) 50°C

    C) 75°C and 100°C

    D) None

1327. Which choices accurately describe the auto-ionization of water?

    I.   It exemplifies an exothermic process.
    II. K_w is temperature-dependent.
    III. pH + pOH = 14 at all temperatures.
    IV. Pure water becomes acidic at some temperatures greater than 25°C.

    A) II
    B) I and II
    C) II and III
    D) I, II, and IV

1328. The correct expression for K_w is:

    A) $\dfrac{[H^+][OH^-]}{[H_2O]}$.

    B) $\dfrac{[H^+][OH^-]}{[H_2O]^2}$.

    C) $[H+][OH-]$.

    D) $\dfrac{[H_2O]^2}{[H^+][OH^-]}$.

1329. A student needs to increase the calcium ion concentration in a particular solution. He adds a large chunk of solid calcium hydroxide, but is dismayed to note that it hardly dissolves at all. To best remedy this situation, the student should:

    A) add 1 M KOH.
    B) add 0.05 M $HC_2H_3O_2$.
    C) add 2 M HI.
    D) none of the above; none of these changes would alter K_{sp}.

1330. Jasmine is titrating a 250 mL solution of 8 M acetic acid. To reach the half-equivalence point, she would need to add:

    A) less than 1 mole of LiOH, since lithium hydroxide is a strong acid.
    B) exactly 1 mole of LiOH, since that is enough to neutralize half of the acid that is initially present.
    C) less than 2 moles of LiOH, since lithium hydroxide is a strong acid.
    D) exactly 2 moles of LiOH, since that is enough to neutralize all of the acid that is initially present.

1331. Which of these combinations of solutions could be used to create an effective buffer?

    I. 500 mL of 1 M HCN and 500 mL of 1 M KCN

    II. 250 mL of 1.5 M $HC_2H_3O_2$ and 250 mL of 1.5 M NH_3
    III. 500 mL of 1 M HCN and 350 mL of 1 M KCN
    IV. 500 mL of 1.5 M $HC_2H_3O_2$ and 500 mL of 0.75 M NaOH

    A) I only
    B) I and III
    C) I, II, and IV
    D) I, III, and IV

1332. A scientist wishes to set up a buffer at a pH of 4.80. Of the following acids, the scientist should use:

    A) hydrofluoric acid ($K_a = 7.2 \times 10^{-4}$).
    B) benzoic acid ($K_a = 6.3 \times 10^{-5}$).
    C) acetic acid ($K_a = 1.8 \times 10^{-5}$).
    D) hydrocyanic acid ($K_a = 6.2 \times 10^{-10}$).

1333. Which of the following is an accurate representation of the Henderson-Hasselbalch equation?

    A) $pH = pK_a - \log \dfrac{[\text{conjugate base}]}{[\text{acid}]}$

    B) $-\log[H^+] = K_a - \log \dfrac{[\text{conjugate base}]}{[\text{acid}]}$

    C) $-\log[OH^-] = pK_b + \log \dfrac{[\text{base}]}{[\text{conjugate acid}]}$

    D) $pOH = pK_b + \log \dfrac{[\text{conjugate acid}]}{[\text{base}]}$

1334. For carbonic acid, $K_{a1} = 4.3 \times 10^{-7}$ and $K_{a2} = 5.6 \times 10^{-11}$. What is the pH of a solution made with equimolar amounts of sodium bicarbonate and potassium carbonate?

    A) 5.6
    B) 6.37
    C) 10.25
    D) 11.44

1335. Exactly 1 L of a 0.5 M solution of HF is titrated with 1 M NaOH. Which of the following statements is NOT accurate?

    A) After 0.5 L of NaOH has been added, the pH of the solution is greater than 7.
    B) When the neutralization is complete, a weak base is present in solution.
    C) At the equivalence point, the solution contains equal concentrations of HF and F^-.
    D) Exactly 0.25 L of NaOH is required to reach the half-equivalence point of the titration.

Questions 1336–1337 rely on the figure below

0.75 M H_2CO_3 is titrated with 2.25 M NaOH to generate the following titration curve:

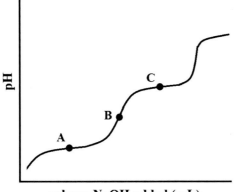

volume NaOH added (mL)

1336. At which labeled point(s) on the curve is $[HCO_3^-]$ > $[H_2CO_3]$?

A) A only
B) C only
C) B and C
D) A, B, and C

1337. If the initial volume of H_2CO_3 was 500 mL, what volume of NaOH is required to reach point A on the curve?

A) 83 mL
B) 166.5 mL
C) 333 mL
D) 1000 mL

Questions 1338–1339 rely on the table below

The following table shows pK_w values for pure water with respect to temperature.

Temperature (°C)	pK_w
0	14.95
25	13.99
50	13.26
75	12.70
100	12.25

1338. Which of the following statements is true?

A) The pH of a neutral solution is always 7.0.
B) Since pK_w is not always equal to 14, in a solution of pure water, pH is not necessarily equal to pOH.
C) As temperature increases, the pOH of a container of water must decrease.
D) A single H_2O molecule is least likely to dissociate at a temperature of 100°C.

1339. What is the pH of pure water at 75°C?

A) 6.35
B) 6.70
C) 7.00
D) 7.65

1340. In its fully protonated form, gamma-aminobutyric acid (GABA) has the structure shown below:

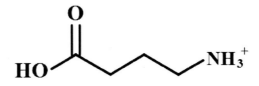

A biochemistry student decides to try titrating GABA with 1 M NaOH. At which regions on the titration curve would the solution serve as an acceptable buffer?

A) At the first half-equivalence point only
B) At both the first and second half-equivalence points
C) At both the first equivalence point and the second half-equivalence point
D) This solution would never function as a buffer.

1341. What is the oxidation state of carbon in H_2CO_3, HCO_3^-, and CO_3^{2-}, respectively?

A) -4, -5, and -6
B) +4, +3, and +2
C) +4, +4, and +4
D) 0, -1, and -2

1342. A researcher is attempting to create a fuel from trans-2-octene, an eight-carbon hydrocarbon. The combustion of this molecule is shown in the following reaction.

$$C_8H_{16} + 12\ O_2 \rightarrow 8\ CO_2 + 8\ H_2O$$

In this reaction, what changes in oxidation state occur?

A) Carbon is oxidized and oxygen is reduced.
B) Hydrogen is oxidized and oxygen is reduced.
C) Carbon is reduced and oxygen is oxidized.
D) Carbon is oxidized and hydrogen is reduced.

1343. Na^+ has a reduction potential of -2.71, while Mg^{2+} has a reduction potential of -2.38. Which metal serves as the better reducing agent?

A) Na^+, because it is more prone to gaining electrons.
B) Mg^{2+}, because it is more prone to gaining electrons.
C) $Na(s)$, because it more readily gives up electrons.
D) $Mg(s)$, because it more readily gives up electrons.

Questions 1344–1345 rely on the table below

The following table gives standard reduction potentials for eight half-reactions.

Half-reaction	E° (volts)
$Na^+ + e^- \rightarrow Na\ (s)$	-2.71
$Al^{3+} + 3e^- \rightarrow Al\ (s)$	-1.66
$Zn^{2+} + 2e^- \rightarrow Zn\ (s)$	-0.76
$Cd^{2+} + 2e^- \rightarrow Cd\ (s)$	-0.40
$2H^+ + 2e- \rightarrow H_2\ (g)$	0.00
$Cu^{2+} + 2e^- \rightarrow Cu\ (s)$	0.34
$Fe^{3+} + e^- \rightarrow Fe^{2+}$	0.77
$Cl_2\ (g) + 2e^- \rightarrow 2Cl^-$	1.36

1344. From the data above, the best oxidizing and reducing agents, respectively, are:

A) $Na\ (s)$ and $Cl_2\ (g)$.
B) $Cl_2\ (g)$ and $Na\ (s)$.
C) Na^+ and Cl^-.
D) Cl^- and Na^+.

1345. In a galvanic cell at standard conditions:

A) Zn^{2+} will reduce at the cathode and $Cu(s)$ will oxidize at the anode.
B) $Zn(s)$ will oxidize at the cathode and Cu^{2+} will reduce at the anode.
C) $Zn(s)$ will oxidize at the anode and Cu^{2+} will reduce at the cathode.
D) Zn^{2+} will reduce at the anode and $Cu(s)$ will oxidize at the cathode.

1346. Thermite is a compound with a variety of uses in metalworking and construction. Thermite can be made from aluminum and iron oxide according to this reaction:

$$2\ Al + Fe_2O_3 \rightarrow 2\ Fe + Al_2O_3$$

Al^{3+} has a standard reduction potential of -1.66, while Fe^{3+} has a standard reduction potential of -0.04. What change could be made to increase the total yield of aluminum oxide from aluminum and Fe_2O_3?

A) Decreasing the total E_{cell} of the reaction by increasing the number of moles of solid iron present
B) Decreasing the total E_{cell} of the reaction by increasing the number of moles of Fe_2O_3 present
C) Increasing the total E_{cell} of the reaction by increasing the number of moles of Fe_2O_3 present
D) None of the above; E_{cell} is a set value and cannot be changed by changing concentrations.

1347. Which choice properly identifies the location of oxidation in the two major types of electrochemical cells?

A) Electrolytic cells – cathode; galvanic cells – anode
B) Electrolytic cells – anode; galvanic cells – cathode
C) Electrolytic cells – anode; galvanic cells – anode
D) Electrolytic cells – cathode; galvanic cells – cathode

Questions 1348–1349 rely on the table below

Half-reaction	E°
Pb (s) → Pb²⁺ + 2e⁻	0.13
Ni (s) → Ni²⁺ + 2e⁻	0.23

A student is devising an electrochemical cell using lead and nickel electrodes. Oxidation potentials of those metals are shown below.

1348. Which of the following standard state potentials is possible for the overall cell?

I.   -0.36 V
II. -0.10 V
III. +0.10 V
IV. +0.36 V

   A) I and IV
   B) II and III
   C) III and IV
   D) I, II, III, and IV

1349. The student decides to create a galvanic cell with a lead electrode as the cathode. What would be the ΔG and K values for the reaction that takes place?

   A) ΔG < 0, K > 1
   B) ΔG > 0, K < 1
   C) ΔG < 0, K < 1
   D) It is impossible to create a galvanic cell with a lead cathode.

1350. Perchloric acid is a strong acid with a pK_a of -1.58. Two moles of perchloric acid is reacted with 4 L of a 0.5 M solution of NaOH, resulting in water and Species A. The oxidation state of oxygen in Species A is:

   A) -2
   B) -1
   C) 0
   D) +2

1351. The oxidation potentials of Na (s), Cd (s), and Ni (s) are 2.71, 0.40, and 0.28, respectively. A student sets up a galvanic cell with a cadmium anode and a nickel cathode under standard conditions. If he wished to make the cell potential of this apparatus more positive, which change should he implement?

   A) He could replace the cadmium anode with solid sodium metal in aqueous solution.
   B) He could increase the concentration of Ni²⁺.
   C) He could increase the concentration of Cd²⁺.
   D) None of the above; given the information above, a galvanic cell could never have a cadmium anode and a nickel cathode.

1352. The table below gives the reduction potentials of two metals.

Half-reaction	E°
Pb²⁺ + 2 e⁻ → Pb (s)	-0.13 V
Cu²⁺ + 2 e⁻ → Cu (s)	0.34 V

If a student were to construct an electrochemical cell using lead and copper electrodes, and if the species above were the only ones that react in the solution, the cell potential (E_{cell}) for this system could be:

   A) -0.47 V.
   B) 0.21 V.
   C) 0.47 V.
   D) All of the above are possible values.

1353. Which of these choices best exemplifies a concentration cell?

   A) A galvanic cell with two half-cells that contain 2 M Sn(NO₃)₂ and 0.05 M MgCl₂, respectively
   B) A galvanic cell with two half-cells that contain 2 M Sn(NO₃)₂ and 0.10 M SnCl₂, respectively
   C) An electrolytic cell with two half-cells that contain 2 M Sn(NO₃)₂ and 0.05 M MgCl₂, respectively
   D) An electrolytic cell with two half-cells that contain 2 M Sn(NO₃)₂ and 0.10 M SnCl₂, respectively

Questions 1354–1356 rely on the figure below

A laboratory intern set up the galvanic cell shown below and conducted a number of measurements. Unfortunately, he left his notebook at the lab and cannot remember anything about the cell. He does know that Ag^+ is more likely to reduce than Zn^{2+} and that he did not make any obvious mistakes when constructing the apparatus.

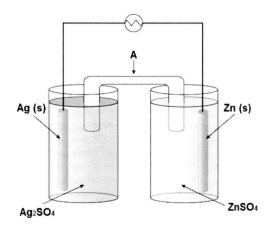

1354. In the diagram above, the anode is:

    A) the silver electrode, because Ag can be oxidized to Ag^+.
    B) the silver electrode, because electrons flow away from it.
    C) the zinc electrode, because current flows toward it.
    D) the zinc electrode, because Zn^{2+} is reduced to solid zinc at that position.

1355. What is the function of the structure marked "A"?

    A) It allows the transmission of electrons from right to left.
    B) It allows the transmission of electrons from left to right.
    C) It prevents the buildup of charge by allowing sulfate anions to travel from left to right.
    D) It prevents the buildup of charge by allowing sulfate anions to travel from right to left.

1356. The student finds his notebook and realizes that his memory had deceived him. While the electrodes had been composed of silver and zinc, it was sodium cation, not sulfate anion, that served as the other species in both half-cells. How does this revelation change what we know about this apparatus?

    A) Nothing changes, since sulfate was only a spectator ion.
    B) We now know that ions traveled through the salt bridge from right to left, not left to right.
    C) We now know that ions traveled through the salt bridge from left to right, not right to left.
    D) Due to the extremely positive reduction potential of Na^+, it will now participate in the redox reaction as well.

1357. A certain electrochemical cell contains a positive (+) anode. What type of cell must it be?

    A) An electrolytic cell
    B) A galvanic cell
    C) Either an electrolytic or a galvanic cell
    D) Neither an electrolytic nor a galvanic cell

1358. The Nernst equation allows for the relatively easy calculation of a cell potential under non-standard conditions. This equation can be written as follows:

$$E = E° + \frac{RT}{nF} \ln(Q)$$

With this in mind, which statement is true?

    A) When Q = 0, E = E°.
    B) When Q = 1, E = E°, but only if the temperature is 0 °C.
    C) If Q > 3 and conditions are otherwise standard, E < E°.
    D) If Q > 3 and conditions are otherwise standard, E > E°.

1359. Nickel-metal hydride (NiMH) batteries are rechargeable cells used in many hybrid and all-electric vehicles. An NiMH battery in the process of recharging is similar to:

    A) an electrolytic cell.
    B) a galvanic cell.
    C) a concentration cell.
    D) a half-cell.

1360. While the Nernst equation can be written in a variety of ways, one particularly biologically relevant iteration is shown below:

$$V_m = \frac{61}{z} \log \frac{[ion_{outside}]}{[ion_{inside}]}$$

Here, V_m represents the equilibrium membrane potential (in mV) for a particular ion, while z represents the valence of that ion. Under what conditions will the membrane potential for ion X equal -61 mV?

A) $[X_{outside}]$ = 320 mM; $[X_{inside}]$ = 32 mM; z = +1
B) $[X_{outside}]$ = 3 × 10^{-2} mM; $[X_{inside}]$ = 3 × 10^{-3} mM; z = +1
C) $[X_{outside}]$ = 13 mM; $[X_{inside}]$ = 130 mM; z = +1
D) $[X_{outside}]$ = 4.2 × 10^{-4} mM; $[X_{inside}]$ = 4.2 × 10^{-3} mM; z = -1

1361. Which of the following are found in sodium dodecyl sulfate, $NaC_{12}H_{25}SO_4$ (s)?

I. A sigma bond
II. A pi bond
III. An ionic bond
IV. A covalent bond

A) I only
B) I and III
C) I, II, and IV
D) I, II, III, and IV

1362. Which type of bond is formed in a molecule of sodium hydride (NaH)?

A) A covalent bond
B) An ionic bond
C) A coordinate covalent bond
D) A hydrogen bond

1363. A methane molecule includes:

A) polar covalent bonds.
B) coordinate covalent bonds.
C) nonpolar covalent bonds.
D) hydrogen bonds.

1364. Describe the potential energy curve for two hydrogen atoms as they are brought increasingly close together.

A) The potential energy begins at a baseline, then drops as the atoms move closer together. It reaches a trough and, as they are brought even closer, rises back above the baseline.
B) The potential energy begins at a baseline, then drops continuously until the bond is formed.
C) The potential energy begins at a baseline, then rises continuously until the bond is formed.
D) The potential energy begins at a baseline, then rises as the atoms move closer together. It reaches a peak and, as they are brought even closer, falls back below the baseline.

1365. How can one order the simple two-carbon hydrocarbons in terms of increasing bond length?

A) Ethyne, ethene, ethane
B) Ethyne, ethane, ethene
C) Ethene, ethane, ethyne
D) Ethane, ethene, ethyne

Questions 1366–1367 rely on the figure below

Consider the structure of epinephrine.

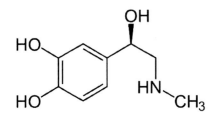

1366. How many π bonds are present in this molecule as pictured above?

A) 2
B) 3
C) 4
D) 13

1367. The structure of epinephrine contains how many sp^3-hybridized carbons?

A) 3
B) 4
C) 6
D) 9

Questions 1368–1369 rely on the table below

The following table gives the bond lengths for various nitrogen- and oxygen-containing bonds. Note that all lengths are given in angstroms.

Bond type	Bond length
N-N	1.47
N=N	1.24
Unknown #1	1.10
N-O	1.36
Unknown #2	1.22

1368. What are the expected bond orders of unknown 1 and unknown 2, respectively?

A) 3 and 2
B) 2 and 2
C) 2 and 2
D) 2 and 1

1369. A researcher wants to create a double bond with a length of 1.6 angstroms and that contains at least one nitrogen atom. Based on the table, which of the following bonds should the researcher try?

A) N=N
B) N=S
C) N=P
D) Both B and C

1370. A researcher places a large number of ammonia molecules into a magnetic field and notices that they align with the field. He then attempts the same process with carbon dioxide. Despite the fact that both of these compounds contain polar covalent bonds, CO_2 does not align with the magnetic field. How can this observation be explained?

A) Carbon dioxide is a linear molecule, so although its bonds are polar covalent, it has no net dipole.
B) Carbon dioxide molecules interact with each other and block the magnetic field from having an effect.
C) The carbon-to-oxygen bond is not sufficiently polar enough to be affected by the magnet.
D) The researcher has made a mistake; CO_2 should align with the magnetic field.

1371. Which of the figures below best represents the Lewis structure of PO_4^{3-}?

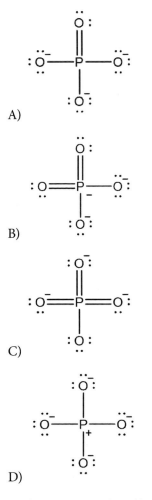

A)

B)

C)

D)

1372. Carbonate anion (CO_3^{2-}) is able to exhibit:

A) 2 resonance structures.
B) 3 resonance structures.
C) 4 resonance structures.
D) 5 resonance structures.

1373. What is the molecular geometry of SO_4^{2-}?

A) Octahedral
B) Square pyramidal
C) Tetrahedral
D) Square planar

Questions 1374–1375 rely on the figure below

Acetophenone, an aromatic ketone, is commonly used as a precursor to a number of scents and fragrances. Its structure is shown here.

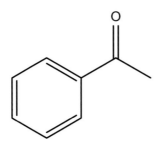

1374. The molecular geometry of the tertiary carbon on the benzene ring is:

A) tetrahedral.
B) trigonal planar.
C) square planar.
D) trigonal pyramidal.

1375. Of the resonance structures for acetophenone, how many contain a carbocation?

A) 0
B) 2
C) 3
D) 4

1376. The Lewis dot structure of phosphorus pentabromide is best represented as:

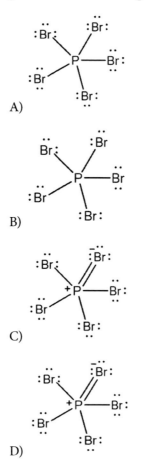

Questions 1377–1378 rely on the figure below

Nitrogen triiodide, shown below without lone pairs drawn, is an extremely explosive compound that releases a thick purple gas when contacted.

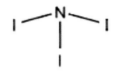

1377. The molecular geometry of nitrogen triiodide is:

A) trigonal planar.
B) tetrahedral.
C) trigonal bipyramidal.
D) trigonal pyramidal.

1378. If nitrogen triiodide were to lose one iodine atom without gaining bonds to any other substituents, what would be its new molecular geometry?

A) Trigonal planar
B) Linear
C) Bent
D) Square planar

1379. Which of the following statements is / are true?

I. Given its molecular formula, the molecular geometry of a compound can be determined.
II. The overall molecular geometry is affected by valence electrons on peripheral atoms as well as the central atom.
III. Lone pairs repel other bonding groups.
IV. Lone pairs attract other bonding groups.

A) I only
B) I and II
C) I and III
D) I, II, and IV

1380. Sulfur trioxide exhibits all of the features below EXCEPT:

A) it has three contributing resonance structures.
B) it has a trigonal planar molecular geometry.
C) it has no formal charge.
D) all of the above are true.

1381. Imagine that the carboxylate ion depicted below is placed in a solution of pH 1.2.

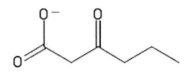

What is the strongest intermolecular force that the resulting molecule will be able to exert?

A) Dipole-dipole
B) Hydrogen bonding
C) London dispersion
D) Covalent bonding

1382. Which of these hydrocarbons is expected to have the highest boiling point?

A) 2-methyl-2-butene
B) Trans-2 pentene
C) 1-octene
D) Cis-2-pentene

1383. Of the molecules below, which should produce the lowest vapor pressure? Assume that all are present at the same temperature.

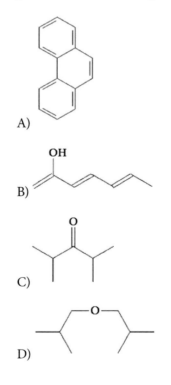

1384. A student generates the ketone below from a reaction with benzene.

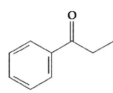

The strongest form of intermolecular force that can be exerted by this species results from:

A) its ability to donate hydrogen bonds.
B) its conjugated structure.
C) its carbonyl functionality.
D) its six-membered ring.

1385. The strongest attractive force or linkage, of those below, is:

A) a nonpolar covalent bond.
B) a hydrogen bond.
C) a dipole-dipole force.
D) a London dispersion force.

1386. Gaseous hydrogen is a diatomic gas. Which intermolecular forces can H_2 exert?

A) Ionic bonding
B) Dipole-dipole forces
C) Hydrogen bonding
D) London forces

1387. G-C bonding in DNA is more stable than A-T bonding due to increased:

A) interactions between hydrogen atoms.
B) interactions between oxygen atoms.
C) interactions between hydrogen and oxygen atoms of the same nucleotide.
D) interactions between hydrogen and oxygen atoms of complementary nucleotides.

1388. Which of these compounds should have the lowest boiling point?

A) 3-nonanone
B) 2-octanone
C) 3-butanone
D) 2-propanone

1389. A student is considering the four molecules below. Which of them is expected to most readily enter the gas phase?

A) H_2O
B) $CaCl_2$
C) Ne
D) Al

1390. Which of the below strands of dsDNA will have the highest melting or denaturation point?

A) One that is 10% thymine
B) One that is 29% guanine
C) One that is 38% adenine
D) One that is 39% cytosine

1391. According to Boyle's law, which of these statements is accurate?

A) Doubling the temperature of a gas will cause it to double in volume, as long as it is held in a flexible container.
B) Tripling the volume of a gas will cause it to triple in temperature when pressure is held constant.
C) Halving the volume of a gas will cause its pressure to be reduced by half as well.
D) Quadrupling the volume of a gas will cause its pressure to drop to a quarter of its previous value.

1392. 2 moles of oxygen gas is sequestered in a 3 L container at 1 atm and 15°C. For the temperature of this gas to increase to 83°C, what increase in pressure is necessary? Assume that the volume of the container cannot change.

A) The pressure must be changed to 1.25 atm.
B) The pressure must be changed to 2 atm.
C) The pressure must be changed to 2.5 atm.
D) The pressure should be increased to 5.5 atm.

1393. Since no real gas behaves truly ideally, the ideal gas law involves a variety of approximations. Two of these assumptions are that ideal gases:

A) have particles of negligible volume and have no attractive forces between particles.
B) occupy a negligible volume and have no attractive forces between particles.
C) have particles of negligible volume and exert no force on the walls of the container.
D) occupy a negligible volume and exert no force on the walls of the container.

1394. 20 moles of gaseous ammonia are held in a flexible balloon. Under which conditions should this gas behave LEAST ideally?

A) When $P = 1 \times 10^5$ Pa and T = 298 K
B) When $P = 1 \times 10^2$ GPa and T = 25 K
C) When P = 25 kPa and T = 800 K
D) When $P = 1 \times 10^7$ Pa and T = 400 K

1395. A biologist is making a variety of measurements for a sample of CO_2 generated by a colony of aerobic bacteria. The sample contains exactly 1 mole of gas and is being held in a 0.05 L container. When the biologist calculates the PV/RT ratio of the gas, he finds that it is 1.05. How could this finding be explained?

A) The sample may be held at a high temperature, causing deviation from the ideal gas law.
B) The sample may be held at a low temperature, causing a lower PV/RT ratio than expected.
C) The relatively low pressure within the flask is causing intermolecular forces to exert a substantial effect.
D) The relatively high pressure within the flask is causing particle volume to exert a substantial effect.

1396. According to the kinetic molecular theory of gases, which gas particle should have the smallest amount of kinetic energy?

A) An O_2 particle (molecular weight = 32 amu) at 400 K and a pressure of 670 torr
B) An Ar particle (molecular weight = 40 amu) at 560 °C and a pressure of 760 torr
C) A Cl_2 particle (molecular weight = 70.9 amu) at 95 K and a pressure of 200 torr
D) A He particle (molecular weight = 4 amu) at 135 °C and a pressure of 540 torr

1397. At STP, a number of moles of argon gas has a volume of 67.2 L. If the approximate molar masses of argon and krypton are 39.95 g/mol and 84.8 g/mol, respectively, what volume will the same number of moles of Kr gas occupy at STP?

A) 22.4 L
B) 33.1 L
C) 67.2 L
D) 135 L

1398. A sealed flask is filled with three gases: 0.5 mol ammonia, 0.25 mol oxygen, and 0.75 mol helium. If the partial pressure of NH_3 is 415 torr, what is the total pressure in the flask?

A) 630 torr
B) 830 torr
C) 1245 torr
D) 2490 torr

1399. Gas A, a compound used in industrial cleaning, is observed to diffuse through a room at approximately 0.1 m/s. If helium gas diffuses through the same room at 0.8 m/s, the molar mass of Gas A is:

A) 16 g/mol.
B) 32 g/mol.
C) 256 g/mol.
D) 512 g/mol.

1400. Which of the following statements is/are accurate regarding the diffusion of gases?

I. A heavier gas will diffuse and effuse more slowly than a lighter one.
II. Diffusion rate is directly proportional to the reciprocal of the molar mass of a gas.
III. Diffusion rate is directly proportional to the reciprocal of the square root of the density of a gas.

A) I only
B) I and II
C) I and III
D) I, II, and III

1401. Solid carbon dioxide, commonly known as "dry ice," has a variety of uses in the cooling and packaging industries. A reaction involving this compound is shown below.

$CO_2(g) \rightarrow CO_2(s)$

This type of reaction is known as:

A) sublimation.
B) condensation.
C) deposition.
D) decomposition.

1402. Of the following processes, which require(s) the input of energy in the form of heat?

    I.   A block of ice at -10°C and 1 atm transitioning into a pool of water at 15°C and 1 atm

    II. A beaker of water at 100°C and 1 atm fully transitioning into steam at 100°C and 1 atm

    III. A block of ice at 230 K and 10 Pa transitioning into water vapor at 50 Pa

    IV. A balloon filled with steam at 395 K transitioning into water at 350 K

    A) I only
    B) IV only
    C) I and II
    D) I, II, and III

1403. A student wants to transform 100 g of ice at -5 °C into water at 15 °C. If he does so under standard conditions, how much heat will the entire process require? Note that c_{ice} = 2.03 J / (g°C), c_{water} = 4.18 J / (g°C), and $H_{fusion (water)}$ = 334 J/g.

    A) 7285 J
    B) 7619 J
    C) 38535 J
    D) 40685 J

1404. The heat of vaporization of water is 2256 kJ/kg, while the heat of fusion is 334 kJ/kg. What amount of heat is required to completely transform 80 mL of distilled water at 100 °C into steam, also at 100 °C?

    A) 0 J, since ΔT for this transition is 0
    B) 180 J
    C) 2.7×10^4 J
    D) 1.8×10^5 J

Questions 1405–1406 rely on the graph below

A team of researchers has synthesized what appears to be a novel compound. They conduct a simple test to determine the thermodynamic properties of this substance. The diagram below depicts the phase changes of 50 g of this unknown solid as heat is added at a constant rate.

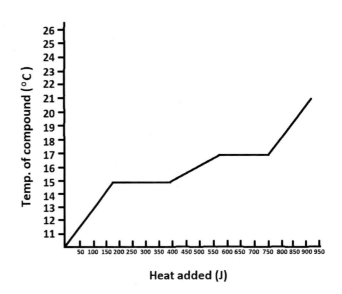

1405. What is the approximate specific heat capacity of the unknown compound in the liquid phase?

    A) 0.75 J / (g°C)
    B) 1 J / (g°C)
    C) 1.75 J / (g°C)
    D) 5 J / (g°C)

1406. The scientists finally decide on a name for the new compound: joulium, abbreviated Jo. Of the choices below, the substance with the largest specific heat is:

    A) Jo (s).
    B) Jo (l).
    C) Jo (g).
    D) All three phases of joulium have the same specific heat capacity.

1407. A student has a sample of carbon dioxide. While it begins as vapor, he finds that a 90-Pa decrease in pressure converts it to solid, while a 15-K decrease in temperature converts it to liquid. The original conditions of the sample were likely closest to:

    A) the critical point of CO_2, since all three phases meet under those conditions.
    B) the critical point of CO_2, since liquid and vapor become indistinguishable above this temperature and pressure.
    C) the triple point of CO_2, since all three phases meet under those conditions.
    D) none of these choices, since these findings are impossible.

1408. Fusion is best represented by which of the following?

A) A sample of gaseous acetic acid that is cooled into liquid
B) A beaker of ethanol that is subjected to extremely low temperatures until frozen
C) A CO_2-containing vessel that is rapidly compressed into solid "dry ice"
D) A cube of ice that is heated until thoroughly melted

Questions 1409–1410 rely on the figure below

The figure below shows the phase diagram for water.

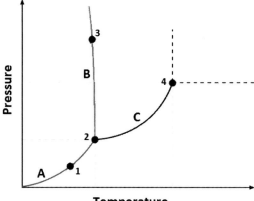

1409. If a student were instead to map the phase diagram of ethanol, which line would differ most radically from the figure above?

A) Line A
B) Line B
C) Line C
D) None of the above; all phase diagrams resemble the one shown.

1410. All of the following statements about a 100-g sample of H_2O are true EXCEPT:

A) if initially held at the conditions present at point 3, an increase in temperature promotes melting.
B) if initially held at conditions anywhere along line C, the sample is in equilibrium between liquid and vapor.
C) if initially held at conditions immediately below point 1, freezing can be induced by increasing the pressure.
D) as its temperature and pressure increase, the liquid and vapor phases gradually begin to resemble one another.

1411. A college chemistry student is examining a variety of solutes. If he wishes to produce a solution with the highest possible freezing point, he should add which of the following to one liter of water?

A) 2 moles of solid calcium phosphate
B) 1.5 moles of solid sodium chloride
C) 1 liter of a 2.5 M aqueous solution of potassium hydroxide
D) 1 liter of a 4 M aqueous solution of glucose

1412. Exactly 0.05 kg of diethyl ether, a common organic solvent, is weighed and poured into a beaker. When 0.35 mol of glucose is added, the boiling point of the solution is measured at 49.7°C. If diethyl ether has a K_b value of 2.16 °C*kg / mol, what would its boiling point be with no solute present?

A) 15.1°C
B) 19.5°C
C) 34.6°C
D) 47.5°C

1413. If the atmospheric pressure on the side of a mountain is measured at 660 torr, a container of pure methanol would boil at a vapor pressure of:

A) slightly less than 660 torr.
B) exactly 660 torr.
C) slightly greater than 660 torr.
D) Insufficient information is available to answer this question; the relationship between vapor pressure and boiling point is only consistent for water.

1414. 17.1 grams of sucrose (table sugar) is added to 10 mL of water (K_f = 1.86 °C/m). The freezing point of the water is then measured at -9.3°C. The molecular weight of sucrose is closest to:

A) 34.2 g/mol.
B) 85.5 g/mol.
C) 171 g/mol.
D) 342 g/mol.

1415. Which of these pairs of properties would most likely be observed in the same solution?

A) Boiling point elevation and vapor pressure depression
B) Freezing point elevation and boiling point elevation
C) Freezing point depression and vapor pressure elevation
D) Boiling point elevation and vapor pressure elevation

Questions 1416–1417 rely on the figure below

A college physiology class is asked to devise an apparatus to model diffusion across capillary walls. To construct the device, students use glass beakers, a variety of mesh membranes, and distilled water. On one side of the membrane, they then add sodium chloride, glucose, and a 65-kD protein similar to albumin. One student's apparatus is shown here.

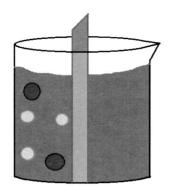

1416. At the very beginning of the experiment, the student measures the osmotic pressure across the membrane. All of the following changes would result in a higher calculated value EXCEPT:

I. doubling the amount of NaCl added to the solution.
II. quadrupling the amount of albumin added to the solution.
III. doubling the amount of water used, while leaving all solute concentrations the same.
IV. increasing the temperature by 45 K.

A) III only
B) I and IV
C) III and IV
D) I, II, and IV

1417. After two hours, the student returns and finds that the water level in his solution has not changed, but ions, glucose, and protein appear on both sides of the membrane. What mistake did he most likely make?

A) He used a membrane permeable to water, but impermeable to solute.
B) He used a membrane with pores large enough to allow movement of molecules up to 100 Da.
C) He used a membrane with pores large enough to allow movement of molecules up to 100 kDa.
D) His initial concentrations of all solutes were too low.

1418. If equimolar amounts of the molecules below are added to two identical containers of pure water, which solution will display the lower boiling point?

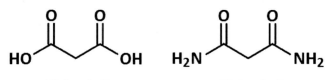

Molecule Z   Molecule X

A) the solution containing Molecule Z, due to its higher molecular weight
B) the solution containing Molecule X, due to its lower molecular weight
C) the solution containing Molecule Z, due to its higher Van't Hoff factor
D) the solution containing Molecule X, because it dissociates into fewer total particles

1419. All of the following statements about vapor pressure are accurate EXCEPT:

    A) ethanol in an open flask will evaporate even when vapor pressure is less than atmospheric pressure.

    B) at 25°C, pure water will have a lower vapor pressure than an identical container of pure acetone.

    C) addition of a volatile solute, such as NaCl, can affect vapor pressure.

    D) if the vapor pressure above a flask of pure water is 380 torr and the atmospheric pressure is 0.5 atm, an equilibrium has been established.

1420. Osmotic pressure can be calculated using the formula $\pi = iMRT$. If π is given units of atmospheres (atm), what are the units for R?

    A) (kg * atm) / (mol * K)

    B) (L * atm) / (mol * K)

    C) (mol * K) / (L * atm)

    D) R is the gas constant and thus is always unitless.

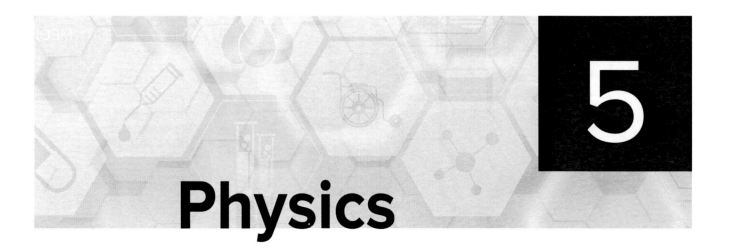

Physics

1421. If an ant is crawling at 56 mm/min, how long will it take to travel 1 m?

A) 18 seconds
B) 56 seconds
C) 1080 seconds
D) 1800 seconds

1422. Which of the following are vector quantities?

I.   Displacement
II. Speed
III. Work
IV. Velocity

A) IV only
B) I and II
C) I and IV
D) I, III, and IV

1423. A security guard is patrolling his sector by traveling in large circles around a house. The guard's displacement is:

A) always equal to the distance he has traveled.
B) sometimes equal to the distance he has traveled.
C) sometimes equal to zero.
D) never a negative value.

1424. Several environmental scientists are monitoring the movement of a cheetah on an Ethiopian plain. They find that at t = 5 min, the cheetah is traveling at 5 m/s due west. At t = 15 min, it is moving at 12 m/s toward the west, while at t = 30 min it is moving at 2 m/s toward the east. If we call western movement positive, when is the cheetah's speed negative?

A) During the entire interval from t = 15 to t = 30 min
B) Only during part of the interval from t = 15 to t = 30 min
C) During at least part of the interval from t = 15 to t = 30 min, and possibly at other times
D) Never, since speed is not a vector quantity

1425. Acceleration and velocity, respectively, can be defined as:

A) the change in velocity over time and the change in position over time.
B) the change in position over time and the change in velocity over time.
C) the change in speed over time and the change in displacement over time.
D) the change in distance over time and the change in position over time.

1426. Which of the following velocities is the largest?

A) 800 μm/ms
B) 34 m/s
C) 0.100 km/min
D) 320 cm/hr

Questions 1427–1428 rely on the figure below

A scientist uses the following graph to map the velocity of a projectile over the course of approximately ten seconds.

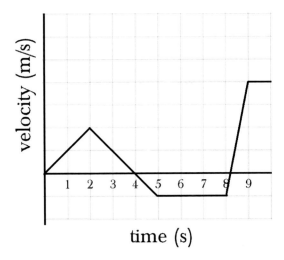

1427. At time = 6 s, the projectile's motion could be described as:

    A) standing still, behind its starting position.
    B) standing still, in front of its starting position.
    C) moving backwards with a constant velocity.
    D) moving forwards, but slowing down.

1428. Which of the pairings below give two times at which the magnitude of the projectile's acceleration is equal?

    A) t = 1 s and t = 3 s
    B) t = 3 s and t = 7 s
    C) t = 6 s and t = 9.5 s
    D) Both A and C are correct.

1429. A planet is orbiting a distant sun with a velocity of 200 m/s. If the orbit has a radius of 160 km, after how many minutes will the planet be in the same position in which it started?

    A) 42
    B) 83
    C) 166
    D) 5000

1430. A student wants to perform a series of calculations, but first must convert all given values to SI units. He should use:

    A) centimeters for length, hours for time, and kilograms for mass.
    B) meters for length, seconds for time, and grams for mass.
    C) meters for length, seconds for time, and kilograms for mass.
    D) meters for length, hours for time, and kilograms for mass.

1431. A 7.5 kg box starts at rest and is pushed along the ground with a constant force of 150 N. Assuming that no friction is present, how far has it traveled when its velocity reaches 40 m/s?

    A) 1 m
    B) 40 m
    C) 50 m
    D) 80 m

1432. A lemming runs directly off a 20 m cliff at 10 m/s. How far from the base of the cliff will he land?

    A) 12 m
    B) 16 m
    C) 20 m
    D) 40 m

1433. An angry wife is throwing her husband's possessions out his bedroom window (20 ft above the ground). If she were able to drop a 5 kg bowling ball at the exact same time that she threw a 2 kg briefcase horizontally outward, which would hit the ground first? Air resistance can be neglected.

    A) The bowling ball
    B) The briefcase
    C) It depends on the shapes of the two objects.
    D) Both objects will reach the ground at the same time.

1434. Timothy, the kicker on a local football team, wants the ball to stay in the air for a longer time after he kicks it. Right now, he tends to kick at a 30° angle from the ground and an 8 m/s total velocity. What change(s) can Timothy make to increase the time of flight of his kicks?

I. Increasing the total velocity to 10 m/s while keeping all other factors constant
II. Increasing the horizontal velocity of the ball while keeping all other factors constant
III. Changing the angle to 45° with respect to the ground
IV. Changing the angle to 89° with respect to the ground and lowering the velocity to 6 m/s

A) I only
B) I and III only
C) I, III, and IV only
D) I, II, III, and IV

1435. An 80 kg kangaroo jumps forward at an angle of 60° with respect to the ground. If he is in the air for a total of 1.7 s and possesses 1000 J of kinetic energy at the highest point of his arc, how far away will he land from his starting position?

A) 1.25 m
B) 3.5 m
C) 8.5 m
D) This scenario is impossible; at the top of the projectile arc, the kangaroo should only have potential energy.

1436. Jake throws a baseball horizontally at 10 m/s off of a 30-m platform. Phil simultaneously drops a different baseball from a 60-m platform on the other side of a field. How far will Phil's ball have fallen at the instant when Jake's ball hits the ground?

A) 13.6 m
B) 19 m
C) 30 m
D) 40 m

1437. A stuntman is launched at a 65° angle with an initial total velocity of 20 m/s. The man is in the air for a total of 3.6 seconds. The horizontal range of the performer can be found by using:

A) $\Delta x = v_i t + \frac{1}{2}at^2$, with $v_i = 20 \cos(65°)$, $a = 9.8$ m/s^2, and $t = 3.6$ s
B) $\Delta x = v_i t + \frac{1}{2}at^2$, with $v_i = 20 \sin(65°)$, $a = 9.8$ m/s^2, and $t = 3.6$ s
C) $\Delta x = v_i t$, with $v_i = 20$ m/s and $t = 3.6$ s
D) $\Delta x = v_i t$, with $v_i = 20 \cos(65°)$ m/s and $t = 3.6$ s

Questions 1438–1439 rely on the figure below

Students in a physics class map the velocity of a remote-control car as they pilot it through an obstacle course. Assume that every vertical line represents a one-second interval, and each horizontal line is a 1 m/s interval. For example, at the point labeled A, the car has been traveling for three seconds and is moving at 3 m/s.

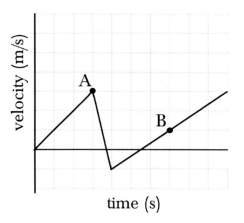

1438. If the car continues accelerating at the same rate as at point B, how fast will it be traveling 15 seconds after passing that point?

A) 10 m/s
B) 11 m/s
C) 16 m/s
D) 18 m/s

1439. All of the following statements are true EXCEPT:

A) the car is slowing down between t = 3.8 s and t = 5.5 s.
B) the car is moving backwards between t = 3.8 s and t = 5.5 s.
C) if the car were to fly off a cliff at point A and take 4 s to land, it would hit the ground 12 m horizontally from the cliff.
D) the magnitude of the car's acceleration is greater at t = 3.9 s than at t = 6 s.

1440. A crane does exactly 1800 J of work to lift a steel beam from the ground. The beam is accidentally dropped and falls back to its starting position in 0.9 s. What is the mass of the beam?

A) 18 kg
B) 22.5 kg
C) 45 kg
D) 450 kg

1441. An object is in a uniform gravitational field. Which of the following is conserved as the object falls? (Ignore friction and air resistance.)

   I. Kinetic energy
   II. Total energy
   III. Momentum
   IV. Potential energy

   A) I only
   B) II only
   C) I, II, and IV
   D) I, III, and IV

1442. A small metal ball is in free fall, during which it is acted upon by air resistance. If air resistance is directly proportional to velocity squared, and if k is a constant related to the ball's size and shape, the equation describing its acceleration is:

   A) $a = (g - kv^2) / m$.
   B) $a = (g + kv^2) / m$.
   C) $a = g$.
   D) $a = g + kv^2$.

1443. Urbanium, a planet with twice the circumference and twice the mass of Earth, has an acceleration due to gravity at its surface that is closest to:

   A) 5 m/s^2.
   B) 10 m/s^2.
   C) 14 m/s^2.
   D) 20 m/s^2.

1444. A box with mass m and energy mgh is sliding along a flat surface with a coefficient of kinetic friction μ and a length L. Which of the following correctly represents and expression for μ that would result in the box coming to rest exactly at the end of the surface?

   A) $\mu = h^2/L^2$
   B) $\mu = L/h$
   C) $\mu = L^2/h^2$
   D) $\mu = h/L$

1445. All of these scenarios include conservatives forces at work EXCEPT:

   A) a box of mass m being lifted upwards against gravity.
   B) two unlike charges being separated.
   C) a cart of mass m being slid across a rough surface.
   D) all of the above.

1446. According to Newton's first law, one can conclude that:

   A) a moving box will gradually slow to a stop if no net force is acting upon it.
   B) an object's acceleration can be given by the ratio of the force experienced to its mass.
   C) a moving object will continue at constant velocity indefinitely if no forces are acting upon it.
   D) any object resting on a surface must give rise to two equal and opposite forces.

1447. When a car locks its wheels, it will begin to slide instead of roll, as the wheels will no longer rotate properly. A car of mass m locks its wheels and slides all the way down a ramp of length d before stopping. If this ramp makes an angle of θ with the ground, what amount of energy is dissipated as heat during this process?

   A) $\mu_k mg\sin\theta$
   B) $\mu_k mgd\sin\theta$
   C) $\mu_k mg\cos\theta$
   D) $\mu_k mgd\cos\theta$

1448. Assume that the relevant coefficient of kinetic friction is 0.2, while that of static friction is 0.3. What force must be applied to a 1-gram sheet of paper to keep it stationary against a vertical wall?

   A) 0.03 N
   B) 0.05 N
   C) 0.3 N
   D) 0.5 N

1449. How far will a box of mass 16 kg, initially moving at 5 m/s, slide on a floor where the frictional force is 2 N?

   A) 25 m
   B) 50 m
   C) 100 m
   D) 200 m

1450. The plot below shows velocity as a function of time for a 6-kg dolly as it is rolled down a smooth marble hallway.

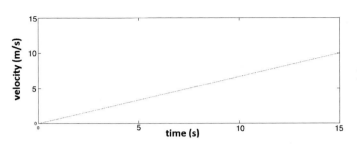

The force being applied to the dolly is:

A) 0.67 N
B) 4 N
C) 10 N
D) This answer depends on the time at which this force is measured.

1451. Four blocks of mass M are connected by a massless cord.

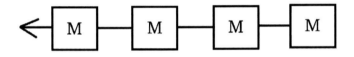

If the cord is pulled from the left with a force of 12 N, causing all of the blocks to accelerate, what net force will be experienced by the rightmost block?

A) 1/3 N
B) 1/4 N
C) 3 N
D) 4 N

1452. A crate of 3 kg rests on a ramp of 30° with a coefficient of static friction of 0.4. Upward force is applied to the crate, parallel to the slope of the ramp, in incremental values until it begins to accelerate.

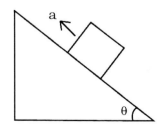

What is the approximate minimum force needed to accelerate the block?

A) 12 N
B) 20 N
C) 26 N
D) 34 N

1453. As shown in the following diagram, a weight is suspended by two ropes of negligible mass.

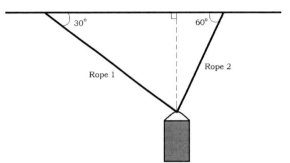

If the force felt on Rope 1 is 10 N, approximately what force is exerted on Rope 2?

A) 5 N
B) 6 N
C) 10 N
D) 17 N

1454. A 10-kg box is set on a cargo ramp with a 60° incline. In order for the box to remain in place, which of the following relationships must be true?

A) The coefficient of static friction for the ramp must be at least 1.7.
B) The coefficient of kinetic friction for the ramp must be at least 1.7.
C) The coefficient of static friction cannot exceed a value of 1, so the ramp must be lowered to a smaller angle in order for the box to be at equilibrium.
D) The coefficient of kinetic friction cannot exceed a value of 1, so the ramp must be lowered to a smaller angle in order for the box to be at equilibrium.

1455. Two objects are connected with a wire of negligible mass. Upon release, both begin to accelerate in a uniform manner.

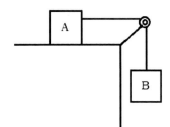

If the coefficient of kinetic friction between the box and the surface is μ:

A) the magnitude of energy lost to friction must be less than the change in kinetic energy of Object B.
B) the work done by Object B must be equal to the work done by the frictional force of the surface.
C) the work done by Object B must be greater than the work done by the frictional force of the surface.
D) Object B must be at least twice as heavy as Object A in order to overcome the forces of kinetic and static friction.

Questions 1456–1457 rely on the figure below

A 60-kg rider on a looping roller coaster, below, happens to bring a scale with him to sit on. Assume constant velocity throughout the loop.

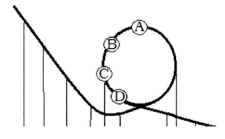

1456. At which labeled point will the scale give the lowest reading?

A) Point A
B) Point B
C) Point C
D) Point D

1457. At which point in the roller coaster's descent towards the loop is the force of kinetic friction the greatest?

A) The force of kinetic friction is largest at the top of the ramp.
B) The force of kinetic friction is largest at the bottom of the ramp.
C) The force of kinetic friction is uniform at all points on the ramp.
D) This answer is impossible to determine based on the information given.

1458. Three forces are acting on the object below.

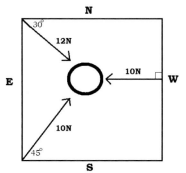

In which direction will the resultant force point? (Note: sin 30° = 0.5, cos 30° = 0.86, sin 45° = cos 45° = 0.7)

A) NE
B) NW
C) SE
D) SW

1459. What are the appropriate units for impulse?

A) kg*m
B) (kg*m)/s^2
C) (kg*m)/s
D) kg*m*s

1460. A television (m = 20 kg) is dropped from a height of 12 m onto a car in a collision which lasts 0.02 seconds and brings the falling TV to rest. The windshield absorbs 60 Ns of impulse (and shatters) with the remaining force being distributed over the car into the shocks. What is the impulse felt in the shocks of the car?

A) 250 Ns
B) 310 Ns
C) 2,400 Ns
D) 7 × 10^5 Ns

1461. A cart of mass m must travel along a looped circular track of radius R without falling off at the top of the loop. In order for this condition to be met, what must be the minimum centripetal and normal forces just as the cart passes by along the top of the loop?

A) $F_c = mg$, $F_N = 0$
B) $F_c = 0$, $F_N = mg$
C) $F_c = 0$, $F_N = 0$
D) $F_c = mg$, $F_N = mg$

1462. Suppose that a 5 kg mass is hung on the end of a massless string of length 200 cm. This string is capable of enduring a force of 200 N before breaking. If the mass is swung in a circle (with the plane of the circle perpendicular to the floor), what is the maximum velocity at which the mass can be swung without breaking the string?

A) 2.4 m/s
B) 7.7 m/s
C) 60 m/s
D) 80 m/s

1463. A molecular motor is capable of generating a torque of 40 pN-nm. If the amount of energy contained in 1 ATP molecule is 100 pN-nm, how many revolutions could the motor make using 4 ATP molecules?

A) 0 revolutions
B) 1.5 revolutions
C) 3 revolutions
D) 10 revolutions

1464. A ball of mass m = 2 kg and r = 10 cm rolls down a one-meter-tall incline without slipping. What will be the velocity of the ball at the bottom of the incline? Note that the moment of inertia of a solid sphere is $2/5mr^2$.

A) 1.5 m/s
B) 3.7 m/s
C) 4.5 m/s
D) 14.1 m/s

1465. The motor driving the rotation of a large metal hoop (R = 1 m) in a machine produces 100 Nm of torque. If the hoop accelerates at a rate of 2.5 rad/sec, how heavy must it be?

A) 25 kg
B) 40 kg
C) 100 kg
D) 250 kg

1466. A car enters a turn of radius r on an icy road at a velocity v. What angle (θ) is required to ensure that the car does not slide off the road?

A) $\sin \theta = v^2/rg$
B) $\sin \theta = v^2/g$
C) $\sin \theta = mv^2/r$
D) This question cannot be solved without the mass of the car.

1467. What is the apparent weight of an 80 kg fighter pilot at the bottom of a loop executed during training, if the radius of the loop is 300 m and his jet held a constant velocity of 150 m/s?

A) 85 N
B) 800 N
C) 6000 N
D) 6800 N

Questions 1468–1469 rely on the figure below

A ball attached to a string on a tabletop is swung in a circle with a constant velocity of v. The string is threaded through a small hole in the table such that it can be pulled on to be shortened.

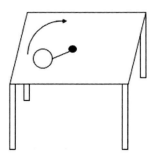

1468. If the string is pulled to reduce it to half of its original length, how will the velocity of the ball change?

A) The velocity of the ball will remain constant.
B) The velocity of the ball will decrease to one-half of its previous value.
C) The velocity of the ball will increase by a factor of 1.4.
D) The velocity of the ball will double.

1469. In the scenario described above, what torque is exerted on the ball by the string?

    A) 0 Nm
    B) 1.4 Nm
    C) 2 Nm
    D) Not enough information is available to solve.

1470. The graph below describes the velocity (v) as a function of time for a point on the outside of a rotating object.

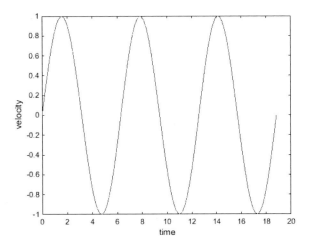

Given the moment of inertia (I) of the object, what force was applied?

    A) F = Isin(t)
    B) F = Icos(t)
    C) F = –Isin(t)
    D) F = –Icos(t)

1471. A gymnast leaps onto a trampoline and is propelled directly upward. If the trampoline acts as a perfectly elastic spring and air resistance can be assumed to be negligible, which is true?

    A) The gymnast's kinetic energy at the instant when she leaves the trampoline is less than her gravitational potential energy at the top of her projectile arc.
    B) The gymnast's elastic potential energy at the least stretched part of the trampoline is equal to her gravitational potential energy at the top of her projectile arc.
    C) The gymnast's elastic potential energy at the most stretched part of the trampoline is equal to her gravitational potential energy at the top of her projectile arc.
    D) The gymnast's elastic potential energy at the most stretched part of the trampoline is equal to her kinetic energy at the top of her projectile arc.

1472. Conservative forces include:

    A) gravity and air resistance.
    B) spring force and gravity.
    C) friction and air resistance.
    D) magnetic force and friction.

1473. A 1500-kg racecar accelerates from 0 m/s to 30 m/s in 4.2 seconds. How much more work is done by that car than by an identical one which accelerates from 10 m/s to 16 m/s in 8 seconds?

    A) 5.7 J
    B) 1.5×10^5 J
    C) 5.7×10^5 J
    D) 6.7×10^5 J

Questions 1474–1475 depend on the figure below

A physics student is designing an apparatus to project a 0.5 kg ball as far as possible across a football field. He proposes the following sketch to his teacher, in which a platform supporting a spring is tilted at a 30° angle. Friction and air resistance can be assumed to be negligible and the spring constant is 350 N/m.

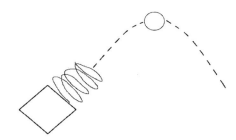

1474. If the spring is only partially pulled back, giving the ball an initial total velocity of 12 m/s, approximately how much kinetic energy does the ball have at its maximum height? Note that sin(30°) = 0.5 and cos(30°) = 0.866.

    A) 0 J
    B) 10.4 J
    C) 25 J
    D) 36 J

1475. If the projectile is instead assumed to experience air resistance, but friction is still ignored, which statement accurately describes conservation of energy during this process?

A) Total energy and mechanical energy are both conserved.

B) Total energy is conserved, but mechanical energy is not.

C) Mechanical energy is conserved, but total energy is not.

D) Neither total nor mechanical energy is conserved.

1476. The SI unit for energy can be written as:

A) $(kg*m^2)/s^2$.

B) N/m.

C) $(kg*m)/s^2$.

D) $kg/(m*s^2)$.

1477. A platform diver with a weight of 1090 N free-falls directly off a tall diving board. If she takes 1.4 s to hit the water, what was her gravitational potential energy at the top of the board?

A) 545 J

B) 10900 J

C) 21800 J

D) 11000 N

Questions 1478–1479 rely on the figure below

A football player kicks the ball at an unknown angle, Θ, according to the projectile arc shown below. The ball has a mass of 0.5 kg. Assume that air resistance is negligible for the duration of this process.

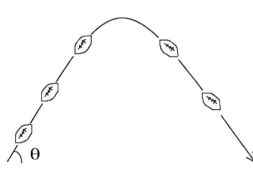

1478. The ball is kicked in such a way as to give it 36 J of initial kinetic energy.

Angle	Sin	Cos
15°	0.259	0.966
30°	0.5	0.866
45°	0.707	0.707
60°	0.866	0.5

If the vertical component of its initial velocity is 6 m/s, what is Θ? A table of sine and cosine values is given above.

A) 15°

B) 30°

C) 45°

D) 60°

1479. If the kinetic energy of the ball is 56 J when it hits the ground but was 25 J at its peak, with what initial horizontal velocity was it kicked?

A) 7 m/s

B) 10 m/s

C) 25 m/s

D) 100 m/s

1480. Mechanical energy consists of:

A) kinetic energy alone.

B) the sum of kinetic energy, friction, and air resistance.

C) the sum of kinetic and potential energy.

D) the sum of kinetic energy, potential energy, and friction.

1481. An engine is supplied with 100 g of a fuel with a heat of combustion of 50 MJ/kg. If this engine can sustain a force of 20 N over a distance of 5 km, the efficiency of the engine is:

A) 2%.

B) 10%.

C) 20%.

D) 100%.

1482. A motor in a model racecar operates at 50% efficiency and uses a fuel with a heat of combustion of 2 MJ/kg. This motor produces a constant force of 30 N, which is just enough to move the car across a rough carpet. Approximately how many grams of fuel would this motor need to propel the car 1000 m?

A) 0.03 g
B) 15 g
C) 30 g
D) 3000 g

1483. What minimum coefficient of friction must a rough, flat surface 10 m in length have if it is to stop a sliding cart with a mass of 100 kg and a velocity of 5 m/s?

A) 0.063
B) 0.13
C) 0.25
D) 1.25

1484. A mixture of gases is held in a flexible balloon. While absorbing 100 J of heat, the gases expand from 1 L to 3 L against atmospheric pressure. What is the change in internal energy of this mixture? (Note: 1 L atm = 101.3 J)

A) -2 L*atm
B) -1 L*atm
C) 1 L*atm
D) 3 L*atm

1485. A cylinder fitted with a piston exists in a high-pressure chamber (3 atm) with an initial volume of 1 L. If a quantity of a hydrocarbon material is combusted inside the cylinder to produce 1 kJ of energy, and if only 30% of this energy is lost to friction, what is the volume change of the gas inside the cylinder? (Note: 1 L atm = 101.3 J)

A) 0.99 L
B) 2.33 L
C) 3.32 L
D) 6.97 L

Questions 1486–1487 rely on the figure below

A driverless car is powered by a single motor. The graph below shows the relationship between the force generated by that motor and the velocity of the car.

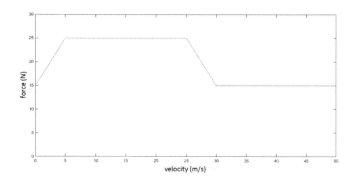

1486. How much power was generated by the motor during the interval from 0 to 20 seconds?

A) 25 W
B) 150 W
C) 175 W
D) 475 W

1487. Imagine instead that the force is constant while the total power output over the full 50-second interval is unchanged. The new force generated by the motor will be:

A) 15 N.
B) 18 N.
C) 20 N.
D) 25 N.

Questions 1488–1489 are related

1488. A pulley is connected via a rope to a crate of mass M. If the pulley is powered by a motor that can produce 145 J of work, approximately how high off the ground can the crate be lifted? Assume that the pulley and rope are massless, and that the crate is lifted slowly enough to make its kinetic energy very small.

A) 14.5 meters
B) (145*M) meters
C) (145/M) meters
D) (14.5/M) meters

1489. Consider a scenario similar to that described above, but now assume that the pulley has a mass of M' and a radius of 10 cm. Compared to when the pulley was massless, the final height of the crate will be:

A) less than the original height, since the kinetic energy of rotation must be considered.
B) more than the original height, since the kinetic energy of rotation must be considered.
C) the same as the original height.
D) Not enough information is given to determine which of the two heights will be higher.

1490. A man pulls on a rope connected to a massless pulley with a 50-kg steel beam secured at the other end. He exerts a constant power of 135 W for 10 seconds, but the beam is lifted only 50 cm. Approximately how efficient is this manual process? Assume that the beam rises at a constant, very small velocity.

A) 0.4%
B) 19%
C) 25%
D) 185%

1491. As the energy carried by a light wave increases, which of the following will NOT necessarily change as well?

A) Frequency
B) Wavelength
C) Velocity
D) Period

1492. Noise-canceling headphones contain a component that emits sounds of particular wavelengths to produce destructive interference with incoming sound waves. To accomplish this, what must be the phase difference between the incoming and outgoing waves?

A) 0°
B) 90°
C) 180°
D) 360°

1493. The functions sin(t) and cos(t) are how many degrees out of phase with each other?

A) 0° (in phase)
B) 45° ($\pi/4$ rad)
C) 90° ($\pi/2$ rad)
D) 180° (π rad)

1494. A photon with a momentum of 150 MeV/c has a frequency closest to which of the following? (h = 4.1×10^{-15} eV s and c = 3×10^8 m/s)

A) 10^{-13} Hz
B) 10^{16} Hz
C) 10^{22} Hz
D) 10^{44} Hz

1495. A sound wave of frequency 350 Hz is emitted from a speaker placed at x = 0. Another speaker, emitting the same frequency, is currently being placed at x = d, as shown in the figure.

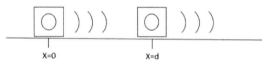

What should the value of d be, in meters, such that no sound is heard by an observer standing at x > d? Approximate that the speed of sound is 300 m/s.

A) 2 m
B) 3 m
C) 7 m
D) 175 m

1496. A photon with which of the following energies possesses a wavelength in the visible spectrum? (h = 4.1×10^{-15} eV s and c = 3×10^8 m/s)

A) 0.01 eV
B) 0.5 eV
C) 2.0 eV
D) 600 eV

1497. Which of the below plots correctly shows the relationship between the intensity of a sound source and the amplitude of the source?

A)

B)

C)

D)

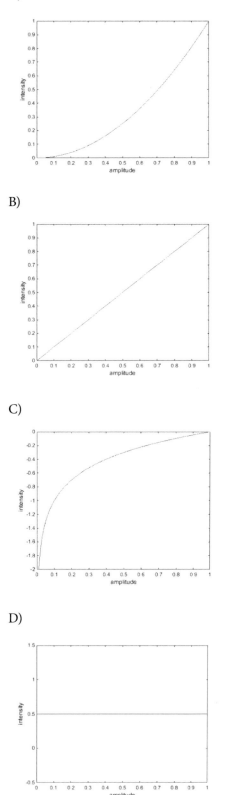

1498. Young's double slit experiment forms a classic example of which property of light?

A) Its diffraction when it encounters an obstacle
B) Its refraction when it enters a medium of a different refractive index
C) Its reflection away from a boundary at the same angle as the incident ray
D) Its speed of about 3×10^8 m/s in a vacuum

Questions 1499–1500 rely on the image below

Consider the following pipe, which is closed at x = 0 and open at x = L, and which contains a standing wave. The third harmonic occurs at 378 Hz.

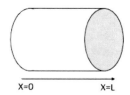

1499. Which of these listed frequencies could also be a harmonic of this pipe?

A) 63 Hz
B) 256 Hz
C) 630 Hz
D) 756 Hz

1500. Which of these statements is/are accurate?

I. The velocity of air molecules is zero at x = 0.
II. The velocity of air molecules is zero at x = L.
III. The velocity of air molecules is constant throughout the pipe.

A) I only
B) II only
C) III only
D) I and II

1501. A horizontal spring on a frictionless surface with a spring constant of k = 15 N/m holds 1000 J of energy when fully stretched. A 2-kg mass is attached to the spring. When released from the position described above, what acceleration does this mass experience?

A) 9 m/s^2
B) 45 m/s^2
C) 75 m/s^2
D) 133 m/s^2

1502. A student in need of a stopwatch decides to build one using a mass and string. She wants her pendulum to time a 1 min experiment in 15 full swings. Approximately what length of string does the student need to build this pendulum?

A) 1 m
B) 2 m
C) 4 m
D) 10 m

1503. A pendulum is released from rest from a small angle, Θ, for which a graph of velocity vs. time is shown below.

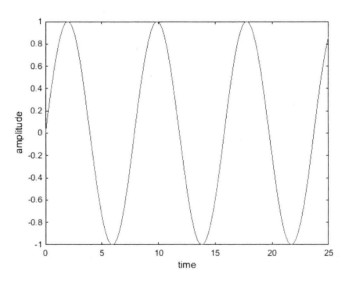

What is the approximate period of oscillation of this pendulum?

A) 3 seconds
B) 5 seconds
C) 8 seconds
D) 25 seconds

1504. Several astronauts want to use the swinging of a pendulum as a simple way to measure the gravitational force on another planet. If a 1 m pendulum with a 0.1-kg mass at the end oscillates with a period of 6.28 s, what is the acceleration due to gravity at the planet's surface?

A) 1 m/s^2
B) 5 m/s^2
C) 9.8 m/s^2
D) 50 m/s^2

1505. A certain spring has a spring constant of 100 N/m. How much must this spring be stretched in order to store the same amount of energy contained in a spring with k = 200 N/m stretched 20 cm?

A) 0.28 cm
B) 28 cm
C) 34 cm
D) 3.4 m

1506. The response of Spring A, a device used in many industrial applications, to an externally-applied load (force due to gravity) is shown below.

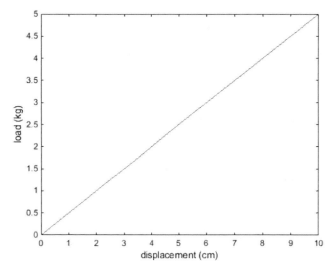

What is the spring constant of spring A?

A) 0.5 N/m
B) 5 N/m
C) 100 N/m
D) 500 N/m

1507. A spring system is shown below, with m representing the mass attached to the spring, k representing the spring constant, and x denoting the distance stretched or compressed from the spring's equilibrium position.

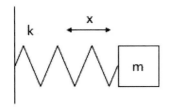

What is the highest velocity this mass can achieve upon its release?

A) k/m
B) $0.5kx^2$
C) $(x)(k/m)^{1/2}$
D) x^2k/m

1508. A student in an eleventh-grade physics class is designing a pendulum that must have a specific frequency. Which of the following variables will NOT affect this experiment?

A) The mass of the weight at the end of the pendulum
B) The length of the pendulum
C) The magnitude of gravity
D) All of the above will affect the frequency.

1509. A mass of 2 kg on a spring with k = 100 N/m will oscillate at the same frequency as a 2 kg mass on approximately what length of string?

A) 0.04 m
B) 0.2 m
C) 0.4 m
D) 1 m

1510. By what factor does the frequency of oscillation of a pendulum change when its length is quadrupled from 2 cm to 8 cm?

A) Its original frequency is multiplied by 0.5.
B) Its original frequency is multiplied by 2.
C) Its original frequency is multiplied by 4.
D) Its original frequency is multiplied by 6.

1511. A child's pool toy has a density of 570 kg/m³. When placed in a pool of pure water, what percentage of the toy will be above the surface of the liquid?

A) 5.7%
B) 43%
C) 57%
D) None; the toy will be fully submerged.

1512. Which of the following statements describes an accurate relation between P_{atm}, P_{gauge}, and $P_{absolute}$?

A) Gauge pressure is always less than absolute pressure.
B) Atmospheric pressure is always less than absolute pressure.
C) Gauge pressure always has a value of zero or greater.
D) When a container of water is placed in a vacuum, gauge pressure and absolute pressure are equivalent.

1513. A sample of distilled water is kept in a container with a width and length of 2 cm and a height of 8 cm. The density of the water is closest to:

A) 3.2×10^{-5} kg/m³.
B) 32 g/cm³.
C) 1 kg/L.
D) 1 kg/m³.

1514. A small metal disc is submerged in a tank of water at a depth of exactly 75 cm. However, the tank is located outside a mountain base at an elevation of close to 5000 m, causing the ambient pressure to be roughly 380 torr. What is the absolute pressure experienced by the submerged disc? (1 atm = 760 torr = 101 kPa)

A) 7500 Pa
B) 7880 Pa
C) 50,750 Pa
D) 58,250 Pa

1515. A variety of experiments are being conducted in a large tank of liquid. For a cylindrical object with a specific gravity of exactly 1.00, which is true?

A) The object will sink beneath the surface of the fluid.

B) At least part of the object will project above the surface of the fluid.

C) The object will sit exactly at the surface of the fluid, with its entire volume underwater but not sinking.

D) Not enough information is available to answer this question.

1516. A certain buoy used in nautical sports has a specific gravity of 0.40, allowing it to float remarkably well in most fluids. Which of the following objects has the same specific gravity as the buoy?

A) A fabric ball with a uniform density of 0.3 g/cm^3 and a volume of 58 cm^3

B) A cube-shaped stack of small cardboard boxes with a uniform density of 0.6 kg/L and a side length of 0.8 m

C) A wooden toy boat with a mass of 0.8 kg and a volume of 0.002 m^3

D) A metal marble that sinks to the bottom of a water tank when dropped in

Questions 1517–1518 rely on the figure below

An engineering student fashions a very large object with the intention of studying buoyancy. The object is cube-shaped with a side length of 5 m. The top half of the cube is composed of aluminum ($\rho = 2712$ kg/m^3), while the lower half is made of dogwood ($\rho = 750$ kg/m^3). The student places the object in a tank of hexanol ($\rho = 811$ kg/m^3).

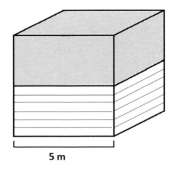

5 m

1517. The buoyant force experienced by the cube is:

A) 4.06×10^4 N.

B) 9.4×10^5 N.

C) 1.0×10^6 N.

D) 2.16×10^6 N.

1518. The student decides to try placing the cube on an underwater scale on the floor of the hexanol tank. Approximately what reading will the scale give for the cube's weight in hexanol?

A) 1.1×10^5 N

B) 1.1×10^6 N

C) 2.1×10^6 N

D) 2.1×10^9 N

1519. 5 mL of an unknown fluid is poured into a test tube, resulting in the situation pictured below.

For this fluid:

A) cohesive forces between fluid particles are greater than adhesive forces between fluid and glass.

B) cohesive forces between fluid and glass are greater than adhesive forces between fluid particles.

C) adhesive forces between fluid particles are greater than cohesive forces between fluid and glass.

D) adhesive forces between fluid and glass are greater than cohesive forces between fluid particles.

1520. In which of these cases would the surface tension of water produce the LEAST force upon the object described?

A) A remarkably light pencil with a length of 6 cm and a width of 0.5 cm floats in a bathtub.
B) A square piece of cardboard with a side length of 0.5 m floats on the surface of a still pond.
C) A rectangular sheet of mural paper with a length of 80 cm and a width of 25 cm lies atop a large puddle.
D) A circular foam packing peanut with a mass of 0.5 g and a radius of 2 cm floats in a sink.

1521. A 500-mL sample of mercury flows through a tube in the manner pictured below.

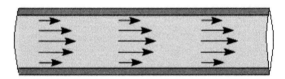

An observer notes that the mercury adjacent to the glass walls of the tube seems to travel significantly more slowly than the mercury in the hollow center. Additionally, the substance as a whole appears thick, like honey. This fluid can accurately be described as:

A) nonviscous, with turbulent flow.
B) nonviscous, with laminar flow.
C) viscous, with turbulent flow.
D) viscous, with laminar flow.

1522. A particular fluid is highly viscous and virtually incompressible. A student, tasked with making several hypothetical calculations, wrongly assumes that this substance is perfectly ideal. Which is likely to yield a result that deviates significantly from its actual value?

A) A calculation involving Bernoulli's equation
B) A calculation involving the continuity equation
C) Both of the above calculations will deviate significantly from their real values.
D) Neither of the above calculations will deviate significantly from its real value.

1523. Bernoulli's equation can be used to assess a moving fluid at various points throughout its travel. This relationship is often written as follows:

$$P_1 + \rho g h_1 + \tfrac{1}{2} \rho v_1^2 = P_2 + \rho g h_2 + \tfrac{1}{2} \rho v_2^2$$

In the equation above, potential units for P_2 include:

A) J.
B) N/m.
C) J/m³.
D) J/m.

1524. A biophysics student is studying the human circulatory system. To make his calculations easier, he assumes that blood perfectly mimics an ideal fluid and ignores any diffusion into or out of circulatory vessels. If no mistakes are made, this student will estimate that the highest volume flow rate is displayed in:

A) the aorta, as it is closest to the heart.
B) the capillaries, as they possess the smallest individual cross-sectional areas.
C) the capillaries, as they possess the largest combined cross-sectional area.
D) Blood should travel through all vessels with an equal volume flow rate.

Questions 1525–1526 rely on the figure below

Two cylindrical reservoirs are situated as shown below, held above the ground by metal pylons. The reservoirs are completely filled with water and connected by a thin pipe. An identical pipe of shorter length extends from the lower reservoir. Note that the upper reservoir is open to the air above.

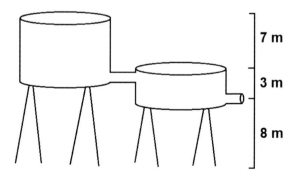

1525. Water is allowed to exit the system through the small pipe extending from the lower tank. About how far in the horizontal direction will this jet of water travel before reaching the ground?

A) 8 m
B) 9.6 m
C) 14.1 m
D) 17.6 m

1526. The small pipe extending from the lower tank is blocked to prevent the efflux of fluid. Assuming a specific gravity for water of 1.0, what is the gauge pressure at a point 6 m below the top of the first reservoir?

A) 1×10^4 Pa
B) 6×10^4 Pa
C) 1.2×10^5 Pa
D) 1.6×10^5 Pa

1527. A salt solution with a density of 1075 kg/m³ is moving through a closed series of vessels. All vessels are positioned at the same height, but one (tube 1) has a cross-sectional area twice that of the adjacent vessel (tube 2). The pressure exerted by the vessel should be higher in:

A) Tube 2.
B) Tube 1.
C) neither; the pressures should be equal.
D) This answer cannot be determined without more information.

1528. What is the kinetic energy of 50 cm³ of distilled water traveling at a velocity of 8 m/s?

A) 1.6 J
B) 1600 J
C) 32 kJ
D) 1600 kJ

1529. A sample of synthetic blood acts very similarly to an ideal fluid. If this sample moves at 4 m/s through a vessel with a cross-sectional area of 2 cm², through what area will it travel at 50 cm/s?

A) 0.16 cm²
B) 0.25 cm²
C) 16 cm²
D) 25 cm²

1530. The figure below relates to the Venturi effect, a phenomenon that relates the pressure exerted by a fluid to the cross-sectional area of the pipe through which it passes.

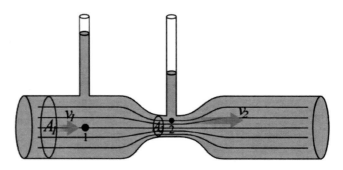

Which of these statements are FALSE?

I. The pressure exerted at point 1 is higher because the fluid moves more rapidly through that section of pipe.
II. The pressure exerted at point 2 is higher because the cross-sectional area is smaller at that position.
III. The pressure exerted at point 2 is lower because the fluid moves more rapidly through that section of pipe.

A) I only
B) II only
C) I and II
D) I and III

1531. Two charges in a particular medium with a dielectric constant ε experience an electrostatic attractive force, F. How would this force change if the dielectric constant were increased to 2ε?

A) The new force would be 0.25 times the original force.
B) The new force would be 0.5 times the original force.
C) The new force would be 2 times the original force.
D) The new force would be 4 times the original force.

1532. The energy required to move an electron through a 1.0 V potential is closest to which value?

A) 1 eV
B) 1.6 eV
C) 1 J
D) 1.6 J

1533. A charged particle is accelerated from rest to 100 m/s by an electric field. This particular particle has a mass-to-charge ratio of 2 kg/C. What strength of field is required to do this if the acceleration occurs in 20 μs?

A) 5×10^6 N/C

B) 1×10^7 N/C

C) 2.5×10^6 N/C

D) This answer cannot be determined from the given information.

1534. What velocity must an electron have in a magnetic field of 10 T (acting perpendicular to the velocity) in order to experience the same force as it would in a 250 N/C electric field?

A) 0.04 m/s

B) 10 m/s

C) 25 m/s

D) 250 m/s

Questions 1535–1536 are related

An electron in an electric field of $E = 1 \times 10^4$ N/C is accelerated from rest through a distance of 10 cm.

1535. What is the work done by the electric field on the electron? (1 eV = 1.6×10^{-19} J)

A) 10 eV

B) 100 eV

C) 1 keV

D) 1.6×10^{-19} J

1536. The electric field is shut off just as a magnetic field of 15 T is turned on. If the electron then makes a circle of radius R at a constant velocity, what amount of work is performed by the magnetic field?

A) 0 J

B) 14 J

C) 28πR J

D) This cannot be determined from the given information.

Questions 1537–1538 rely on the figure below

Numerous charged particles are present in an external electric field. The force (N) as a function of charge (C) for each is shown below.

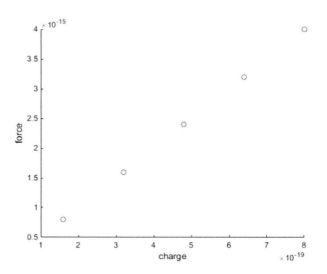

1537. What is the magnitude of this electric field?

A) 0.8×10^{-15} N/C

B) 4×10^{-15} N/C

C) 5×10^3 N/C

D) 5×10^4 N/C

1538. What force would be experienced by a 0.5 C charge?

A) 0.4×10^{-15} N

B) 2×10^{-15} N

C) 1×10^{-4} N

D) 2.5×10^3 N

1539. Below is a figure of a K^+ ion in an electric field.

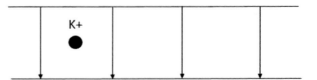

How strong must the field be to prevent the potassium ion from falling due to gravity?

A) 7×10^{-3} N/C

B) 7×10^{-6} N/C

C) 4×10^{-6} N/C

D) None of the above; in this situation, such an equilibrium is impossible.

1540. The Bohr model of the hydrogen atom assumes a circular electronic orbit around a single proton. Given that the distance between an electron and its associated proton is r, what is the velocity of the relevant orbit? Note: k = 1/(4πε) and Q = elementary charge.

A) $Q\sqrt{k/r}$
B) $Q\sqrt{k/(mr)}$
C) $\sqrt{kQ/(mr)}$
D) $Q/r\sqrt{k}$

1541. What is the resistance of a 100 W light bulb that is plugged into a standard 120-V power source?

A) 0.83 Ω
B) 1.2 Ω
C) 83 Ω
D) 144 Ω

1542. A moderately complex circuit contains a battery, four light bulbs (shown below as resistors), and two capacitors.

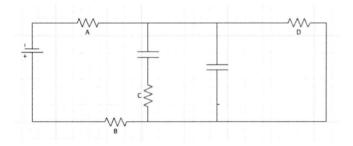

After the voltage source has been turned on for several minutes longer than is required to charge both capacitors, which light bulbs are lit?

A) A only
B) A and B
C) A, B, and D
D) A, B, C, and D

1543. Consider the circuit shown below.

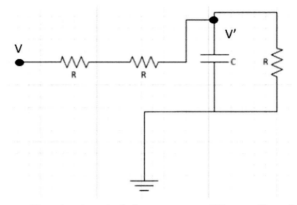

Keeping in mind the presence of V, as well as the knowledge that a current i flows through the first resistor, what is V' relative to the ground?

A) V
B) iR
C) V – 2iR
D) 0

1544. In the simple circuit depicted here, imagine that the component shown as a resistor is actually a bulb that serves as part of a large neon sign.

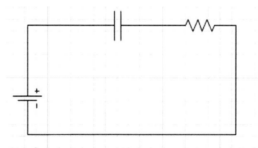

This bulb:

A) never turns on at all.
B) begins turned off, but gradually becomes brighter.
C) remains lit at constant brightness as long as current is exiting the battery.
D) starts off bright, but gradually dims.

1545. For the circuit below, assume that $R_1 = R_2$.

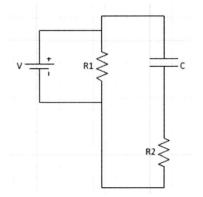

What is the ratio of the current through R_1 after a long stretch of time, to the current through R_1 a few seconds after the battery is turned on?

A) 1:0.5
B) 1:2
C) 1:1
D) 0:1

1546. For the circuit below, R = 100 kΩ and C = 50 μF.

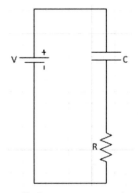

How long will this capacitor take to reach 63% of its full charge?

A) The capacitor will charge instantly.
B) 50 μs
C) 5 s
D) The capacitor will never reach this charge.

Questions 1547–1548 rely on the figure below

Consider the circuit system shown here.

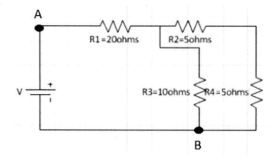

1547. If the current through R1 is equal to 2 A, what is the voltage at point A?

A) 5 V
B) 25 V
C) 50 V
D) 100 V

1548. The voltage at point B is:

A) 0 V.
B) 25 V.
C) 50 V.
D) 100 V.

1549. Below is a plot of time (in s) versus current (in mA) through a resistor.

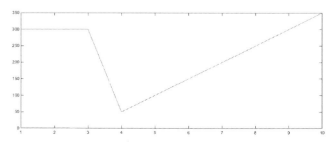

Approximately how much charge passed through this resistor during the interval pictured?

A) 0.3 C
B) 2 C
C) 3.35 C
D) 1000 C

1550. For this question, use the plot of time vs. current that is shown below.

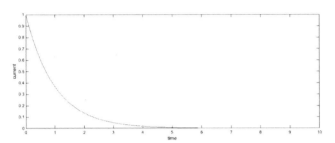

This graphical trend matches which type of circuit element?

A) A charging capacitor
B) A cooling resistor
C) A diode
D) An inductor

1551. Space heaters frequently generate heat by exploiting the fact that running a current through high resistance expels heat in proportion to the amount of resistance encountered. An engineer is designing a space heater using a coil of wire made of titanium, a metal with a rather high resistivity. However, tests of the prototype find that it does not generate enough heat. What change to the design could increase the resistance of the system?

A) Increasing the diameter of the wire in the coil
B) Increasing the length of the coiled wire
C) Replacing the coil with two coils in parallel, each half of the original length
D) Replacing the titanium coil with a copper coil of the same dimensions

1552. After determining how best to increase the resistance of his space heater design, an engineer must find the power consumed by the heater so his company can advertise its energy efficiency. The new heater has a total resistance of 360 Ω and is designed to function properly when plugged into standard American power sockets, which have a voltage of 120 V. How much energy will the space heater use per hour?

A) 40 J
B) 360 J
C) 2400 J
D) 144,000 J

1553. A 240 W heat lamp is designed to work with the standard voltage of the American power grid, 120 V. What must be the equivalent resistance of this lamp?

A) 30 Ω
B) 60 Ω
C) 120 Ω
D) 240 Ω

1554. A clock with a 12 V battery typically uses 3 watts of power. What current passes through this clock?

A) 0.25 A
B) 0.33 A
C) 3 A
D) 4 A

Questions 1555–1556 refer to the figure below

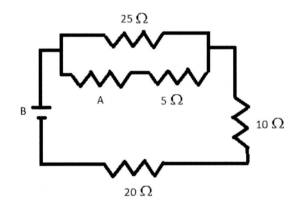

1555. If the resistor labeled A has a resistance of 95 Ω, the equivalent resistance of the entire circuit is:

A) 30.05 Ω.
B) 50 Ω.
C) 70 Ω.
D) 131.6 Ω.

1556. Suppose that resistor A has a resistance of 15 Ω, and that it exists in a circuit with a battery (B) that has an emf of 120 V. What is the approximate current in the circuit at the point just after the parallel branches rejoin?

A) 3 amperes
B) 4 amperes
C) 8 amperes
D) 40 amperes

1557. A capacitor with flat, circular plates of radius r is used as a component in a laptop computer. The designers find that they must double the circuit's capacitance to deal with certain power fluctuations. Which of the following setups would NOT double the capacitance?

    A) Replacing the capacitor with two parallel capacitors, each with radius r

    B) Halving the distance between the capacitor plates

    C) Replacing the capacitor with a new capacitor of radius $2r$

    D) Inserting a material with twice the dielectric permittivity of the previous material between the plates

Questions 1558–1559 rely on the figure below

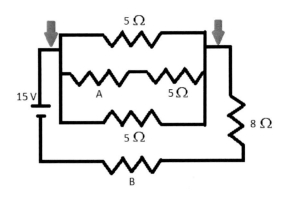

1558. Imagine that the resistor labeled A has a resistance of 5 W, while the resistances of B and the wire itself are negligible. By what amount does the voltage drop between the two arrows?

    A) 0.9 V

    B) 3 V

    C) 15 V

    D) It depends on the branch of the parallel element that is considered.

1559. If the circuit had a power consumption of 7.5 W, and the resistance of A was 5 Ω, the resistance of B would be:

    A) 5 W.

    B) 10 W.

    C) 15 W.

    D) 20 W.

1560. The American power grid supplies a 120 V alternating current to the end user, after it passes through a series of transformers that lower this voltage from the much higher levels (up to 7.5 × 10⁵ V) used for power transmission. What is the average value of the ε for a kitchen appliance plugged into the American power grid?

    A) 0 V

    B) 60 V

    C) 84 V

    D) 120 V

1561. In what unit is the strength of a magnetic field measured?

    A) Farad (F)

    B) Coulomb (C)

    C) Tesla (T)

    D) Ampere (A)

1562. Imagine a moving, charged particle traveling through an external magnetic field. How does the magnetic force exerted on the particle relate to its velocity and the direction of the field itself, respectively?

    A) The force is perpendicular to both the velocity vector and the field.

    B) The force is parallel to both the velocity vector and the field.

    C) The force is perpendicular to the velocity vector, but parallel to the field.

    D) The force is perpendicular to the field, but parallel to the velocity vector.

1563. A magnetic field generated by a prototype apparatus causes a charge to move through a quarter of a circle of radius 4 × 10⁻⁶ m. If this field exerts a magnetic force of 5 × 10⁻² N, how much work does it perform during this process?

    A) 6.3 × 10⁻⁶ J

    B) 2 × 10⁻⁷ J

    C) 2 × 10⁻⁸ J

    D) 0 J

1564. At a particular moment in time, a particle with a charge of -0.8 C that is moving toward the left is held in equilibrium while experiencing two forces: one due to gravity and pointing straight downward, and one due to an external magnetic field. For this scenario to make sense, this field must point:

A) directly upward.

B) directly downward.

C) out of the page.

D) into the page.

1565. Which of these particles will experience a force when subjected to a magnetic field with a strength of 4.37 T?

I.   A neutron traveling at 7×10^3 m/s

II. A proton moving at 0 m/s

III. A positive particle traveling at 800 km/s parallel to the field

IV. An electron moving at 800 m/s perpendicular to the field

    A)   III only

    B)   IV only

    C)   I and III

    D)   II and IV

1566. A negatively charged particle with a mass of 1.67×10^{-27} kg and a charge of -1.6×10^{-19} C is traveling at 5×10^4 m/s perpendicular to a 0.25 T magnetic field. What magnitude of magnetic force will this particle experience?

A) 2.09×10^{-24} N

B) 2.09×10^{-23} N

C) 2×10^{-15} N

D) The particle will not experience a force.

1567. If an object with a charge of +2.4 C is pulled upward by a magnetic field, an object with a charge of -1.2 C and the same velocity vector will be:

A) pulled upward with half of the force in the same field.

B) pulled upward with twice the force in the same field.

C) pushed downward with half of the force in the same field.

D) pushed downward with twice the force in the same field.

1568. A proton is subjected to a magnetic field in the absence of other forces. As a result, it moves in a perfect circle. The velocity of this proton can be written as which of the following?

A) $\dfrac{qBr}{m}$

B) qBr

C) $\dfrac{m}{qBr}$

D) $\dfrac{qB}{mr}$

1569. A square, closed segment of copper wire is placed in an external magnetic field of strength B that points into the page. If the strength of the field is decreased to 0.5 B, what will happen to the wire?

A) It will experience a counterclockwise current.

B) It will experience a clockwise current.

C) It will generate a magnetic field that points out of the page.

D) It will remain unchanged.

1570. In simple terms, electromagnetic induction is:

A) the promotion of a current by a changing magnetic field.

B) the promotion of a current by a static magnetic field.

C) the establishment of a magnetic field by a changing electric field.

D) the establishment of a magnetic field by a static electric field.

1571. Which of the following is a true statement?

A) Both sound and ultraviolet light waves are longitudinal.

B) Both sound and ultraviolet light waves are transverse.

C) Sound is a longitudinal wave, while ultraviolet light is a transverse wave.

D) Sound is a transverse wave, while ultraviolet light is a longitudinal wave.

1572. During a football game, you notice that the crowd is doing "the wave." In this activity, a section of people stand up and quickly sit down, causing a progression of standing people to move around the stadium. "The wave" is a:

A) longitudinal wave.

B) transverse wave.

C) standing wave.

D) None of the above are accurate.

1573. While visiting a beach with some friends, you see an explosion that appears to occur 10 miles down the coast. Assuming that you are located in the same vicinity, which person in your group will hear the explosion first?

    A) You, just standing on the sand.
    B) Your friend Alice, who is snorkeling about 15 m from the shoreline.
    C) Your friend Jim, who is leaning with his ear on a handrail that stretches all the way down to the explosion.
    D) All members of your group will hear the sound simultaneously.

1574. The table below provides the bulk modulus for several metals.

Material	Bulk modulus (GPa)
brass	70
copper	123
cast iron	100
stainless steel	163
cast steel	139

If their densities were roughly the same, through which of the following would you expect sound to travel the slowest?

    A) Copper
    B) Cast iron
    C) Cast steel
    D) Stainless steel

1575. A sound with which of the following wavelengths would have the highest pitch?

    A) 1.5 cm
    B) 1.4×10^3 mm
    C) 1.6×10^7 nm
    D) 1.7×10^{-6} km

1576. A jackhammer makes a loud tapping noise that is measured at approximately 130 dB. If $I_0 = 10^{-12}$ W/m^2, the intensity of this tapping sound is:

    A) 10^{-12} W/m^2.
    B) 10^{-5} W/m^2.
    C) 10 W/m^2.
    D) 130 W/m^2.

1577. After buying some speakers online, you note that their quietest setting is 3 dB, while their loudest is 33 dB. How many of these speakers playing at the lowest setting would you need to equal the intensity of one speaker playing as loudly as possible?

    A) 11
    B) 30
    C) 100
    D) 1000

1578. A criminal is mistakenly driving towards the police at 60 m/s while they drive towards him at 40 m/s. If the speed of sound is 340 m/s and the police car is emitting a siren at 2.4 kHz, what frequency will the criminal hear?

    A) 1.8 kHz
    B) 2.2 kHz
    C) 2.7 kHz
    D) 3.2 kHz

1579. A far-off star is moving away from the earth at a speed of 1.0×10^8 m/s. The star appears to be blue/green when viewed through a telescope. If blue/green light has a frequency of 6.0×10^{14} Hz, what is the frequency of the light the star is actually emitting?

    A) 4.5×10^{14} Hz
    B) 5.0×10^{14} Hz
    C) 7.0×10^{14} Hz
    D) 8.0×10^{14} Hz

1580. A crystal glass with a resonant frequency of 800 Hz is placed in a room full of helium gas. If the speed of sound in helium is 1.0 km/s, what is the wavelength of sound needed to break the glass?

    A) 1.25×10^{-3} m
    B) 0.8 m
    C) 1.25 m
    D) 800 m

1581. Photons are examples of:

    A) particles.
    B) waves.
    C) both waves and particles.
    D) neither waves nor particles.

1582. Of the colors given below, which has a frequency closest to 7.5×10^{14} Hz?

    A) Green
    B) Yellow
    C) Violet
    D) Red

1583. Orange light has a wavelength of 590-620 nm. Which of the following has a longer wavelength than orange light?

A) Blue light
B) X-rays
C) Gamma rays
D) Infrared light

1584. An X-ray with a frequency of 3×10^{16} Hz travels immediately atop an ultraviolet ray with a frequency of 3×10^{15} Hz. These light waves will exhibit:

A) constructive interference.
B) destructive interference.
C) both constructive and destructive interference.
D) neither constructive nor destructive interference.

Questions 1585–1586 rely on the figure below

Unpolarized light with an intensity of 100 kW/m² shines on a series of two vertical polarizers.

1585. The intensity of the light after passing through both polarizers will be:
A) 33 kW/m².
B) 50 kW/m².
C) 100 kW/m².
D) 200 kW/m².

1586. If the second polarizer is rotated 90°, what percentage of the original intensity will reach the eye?
A) 0%
B) 0.25%
C) 25%
D) 50%

1587. When white light moves from a vacuum to a glass prism, the component color that bends the most is:

A) blue light.
B) yellow light.
C) green light.
D) All colors of light bend the same when changing from one medium to another.

Questions 1588–1589 rely on the figure below

Monochromatic light with a wavelength of 580 nm is incident on a screen with two thin slits. Light leaves these slits and shines on an optical screen, creating the effect seen below.

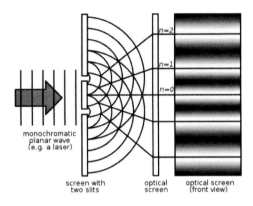

1588. What phenomenon gives rise to the bright band at n = 1?

A) Destructive interference
B) Constructive interference
C) The photoelectric effect
D) Dispersion

1589. A scientist measures the distance from one slit to a dark area, then measures the distance from the other slit to the same dark region. Which of the following could be the calculated difference between these two values?

A) 100 nm
B) 580 nm
C) 1160 nm
D) 1450 nm

1590. Superman gains his power from sunlight. If he begins at a standstill, what velocity can he attain if he directly converts the energy of a photon of yellow light (λ = 570 nm) into kinetic energy? Note that Planck's constant (h) = 6.62×10^{-34} (m^2kg) / s and that Superman's mass is 100 kg.

A) $\sqrt{\dfrac{2(6.62 \times 10^{-34})(3 \times 10^8)}{(570 \times 10^{-9})(100)}}$

B) $\sqrt{\dfrac{2(6.62 \times 10^{-34})}{(570 \times 10^{-9})(100)(3 \times 10^8)}}$

C) $\dfrac{2(6.62 \times 10^{-34})(3 \times 10^8)(570 \times 10^{-9})}{(100)}$

D) $\dfrac{2(570 \times 10^{-9})}{(6.62 \times 10^{-34})(3 \times 10^8)(100)}$

1591. The speed of light in table salt (NaCl) is approximately 1.95×10^8 m/s. What is the index of refraction of sodium chloride?

A) 0.65
B) 1.54
C) 6.5
D) The calculation of this value requires additional information.

1592. For the sake of this question, the index of refraction of ethanol can be approximated as 1.33. How can the velocity of light in ethanol be accurately compared to that in a vacuum?

A) Light travels 4/3 times faster in ethanol than in a vacuum.
B) Light travels 3/4 as fast in a vacuum as it does in ethanol.
C) Light travels 3/4 as fast in ethanol as it does in a vacuum.
D) Light travels equally rapidly in ethanol as it does in a vacuum.

1593. A ray of visible light travels through air to contact a glass surface, shown below.

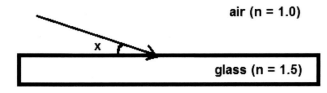

If x = 18°, what will be the angle of reflection with respect to the normal?

A) 11.2°
B) 18°
C) 39.3°
D) 72°

1594. An engineering student devises a multi-layered apparatus that can hold up to three different materials, stacked directly atop each other. He then places a small laser at point X, shown below. The laser sends a coherent beam of light through all three layers of the experimental setup.

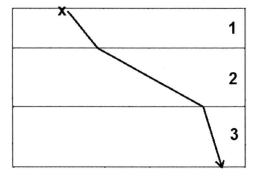

From these results alone, what are potential identities of media 1, 2, and 3? Note that n_{ice} = 1.31, $n_{diamond}$ = 2.42, and n_{glass} = 1.5.

A) 1 = vacuum; 2 = glass; 3 = ice
B) 1 = diamond; 2 = glass; 3 = vacuum
C) 1 = glass; 2 = vacuum; 3 = ice
D) 1 = ice; 2 = diamond; 3 = glass

1595. A beaker is filled with equal volumes of distilled water (n = 1.33) and olive oil (n = 1.48), which settle into two distinct layers. If light is then shone into this beaker from multiple directions, which of these statements is NOT true?

A) When light hits the oil-water boundary at a 33° angle to the interface, some of it will reflect back at a 57° angle to the normal.
B) When a ray moves from the oil into the water, it will bend away from the normal because light travels faster in water.
C) When a ray moves from the water into the oil, its angle of refraction with respect to the normal will be smaller than its angle of incidence.
D) When a ray initially moving through the oil hits the water at a 24° angle to the normal, its angle of refraction will be larger than 24° because light travels faster through oil.

1596. A vacuum has an index of refraction of 1.0, while that of liquid water is around 1.33. With this in mind, how much more rapidly will infrared light travel than ultraviolet light when both are moving through outer space?

A) IR rays will travel 1.33 times faster than UV rays.

B) UV rays will travel 1.33 times faster than IR rays.

C) Both forms of ray will move at the same speed.

D) This answer cannot be determined without knowing the relative frequencies of the two rays.

1597. As light travels from a medium with an index of refraction of 1.875 to one with a refractive index of 1.320:

A) wavelength increases while frequency remains constant.

B) wavelength increases while frequency decreases.

C) wavelength decreases while frequency increases.

D) wavelength remains constant while frequency increases.

1598. Of the scenarios below, which is most likely to lead to total internal reflection?

A) Light travels from air (n = 1.0) to diamond (n = 2.4) at an angle of incidence of 78°.

B) Light travels from diamond (n = 2.4) to air (n = 1.0) at an angle of incidence of 81°.

C) Light travels from water (n = 1.34) to glass (n = 1.5) at an angle of incidence of 13°.

D) Light travels from diamond (n = 2.4) to air (n = 1.0) at an angle of incidence of 9°.

1599. Assume that light is traveling from a material with a refractive index of n_1 to one with an index of n_2. With regard to total internal reflection, the critical angle ($<_{crit}$) can be expressed using the equation:

A) $\sin (<_{crit}) = n_2 / n_1$.

B) $\sin (<_{crit}) = n_1 / n_2$.

C) $<_{crit} = \sin^{-1}(n_1 / n_2)$.

D) $<_{crit} = \cos^{-1}(n_2 / n_1)$.

1600. An optometrist wishes to construct the most powerful converging lens that he can. In other words, he wants to create a lens that refracts, or bends, rays toward each other as efficiently as possible. To do so, he should:

A) make the lens from a very thin material.

B) submerge a regular glass lens (n = 1.5) in acetone (n = 1.33) instead of air.

C) replace a typical glass lens (n = 1.5) with a transparent material (n = 1.7) that is slightly thicker.

D) use a spherical lens with a focal length that is as high as possible.

1601. A lens with a focal length of -5 cm could be described as being:

A) concave and convergent.

B) concave and divergent.

C) convex and convergent.

D) convex and divergent.

1602. Which of the following is FALSE regarding optical aberration?

A) A mirror may exhibit spherical aberrations.

B) A mirror may exhibit chromatic aberrations.

C) A lens may exhibit spherical aberrations.

D) A lens may exhibit chromatic aberrations.

1603. An object is placed 30 cm to the left of a lens with a focal length of 20 cm. The image will appear:

A) 20 cm to the left side of the lens.

B) 20 cm to the right side of the lens.

C) 30 cm to the right side of the lens.

D) 60 cm to the right side of the lens.

1604. A small fir tree sits 10 m in front of a converging mirror that has a radius of curvature of 20 m. What will be true of the image that will form of this tree?

A) The image will appear larger than the tree itself.

B) The image will appear smaller than the tree itself.

C) The image will appear to be the same size as the tree.

D) No image will form.

1605. A boy stands exactly 40 m to the left of a large concave mirror (radius of curvature = 10 m). The image created will be:

A) real.
B) nonexistent.
C) inverted.
D) to the right of the mirror.

Questions 1606–1607 rely on the figure below

Light from a star passes through a diverging lens, as shown here. Both points A and B are located exactly one focal length from the lens.

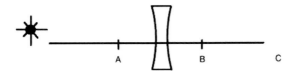

1606. At which point would you expect the image of the star to appear?

A) A
B) B
C) C
D) No image will form.

1607. In the situation above, what terms accurately describe the image?

A) Real and magnified
B) Virtual and magnified
C) Real and minimized
D) Virtual and minimized

1608. Myopia is a condition in which the lens of the eye focuses incoming parallel light between the lens and the retina, rather than converging on the retina itself. An individual with myopia would need a:

A) diverging lens to see objects that are far away.
B) converging lens to see objects that are far away.
C) diverging lens to see nearby objects.
D) converging lens to see nearby objects.

1609. An object is placed 10 m from a system of lenses.

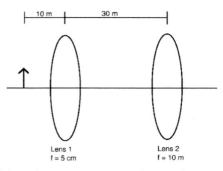

If these lenses are arranged according to the diagram above, where will the final image lie after light has left the object and passed through both lenses?

A) 10 cm to the right of Lens 1
B) 20 cm to the left of Lens 1
C) 10 cm to the left of Lens 2
D) 20 cm to the right of Lens 2

1610. Three microscope lenses are placed above an object, with individual magnifications of 2.0, -1.5, and -0.5. What is the total magnification of this optical system?

A) 0
B) 1.5
C) 2.25
D) 4.0

1611. C^{14} decays with a half-life of 5470 years. Throughout its lifetime, a certain plant constantly replenishes the C^{14} in its cells to compose 0.024% of its total carbon by fixing carbon from the atmosphere. How old must a plant fossil be if its carbon is 0.006% C^{14}?

A) 5470 years
B) 10940 years
C) 15410 years
D) 21880 years

1612. Cobalt-60 has a half-life of 5.2 years. How much cobalt-60 will remain after 26 years if you begin with 32 grams of the isotope?

A) 0 grams
B) 1 gram
C) 2 grams
D) 4 grams

1613. The figure below plots the decay of a newly discovered compound. The y-axis represents the mass of the compound remaining (in grams), while the x-axis gives time in weeks.

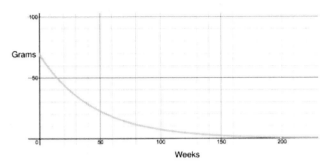

Approximately how many years will it take for a pure sample to degrade to 25% its original concentration?

A) 0.6
B) 1.2
C) 35
D) 63

1614. Of the elements given below, the species that is least likely to undergo alpha decay is:

A) He^3.
B) C^{12}.
C) Ne^{20}.
D) U^{238}.

1615. What element will remain if U^{238} undergoes one α, one $β^+$, one $β^-$, and two gamma decays?

A) Th^{234}
B) Np^{238}
C) Pa^{236}
D) U^{238}

1616. If Cl^{37} were to emit a gamma particle, the nucleus of which element would be left?

A) Potassium
B) Sulfur
C) Argon
D) Chlorine

1617. A certain element decays once, leaving behind a positron and Na^{24}. The initial element must have been:

A) Al^{28}
B) Ne^{24}
C) Mg^{24}
D) Na^{24}

1618. Which of the following will experience a force when moved through a perpendicular external magnetic field?

I.   An α particle
II. A $β^-$ particle
III. A $β^+$ particle
IV. A gamma particle

A) I and IV
B) II and III
C) I, II, and III
D) I, II, III, and IV

1619. A scientist is measuring the mass of a uranium nucleus. He finds a value that is less than the predicted mass, which he obtained by calculating the total masses of the protons and neutrons in the nucleus. This can most probably be explained by the fact that:

A) the negatively-charged electrons counteract the perceived mass of the atom.
B) the equipment used by the scientist is in error.
C) subatomic particles were lost through radiation.
D) the excess mass was converted into energy.

1620. The mass of a proton is 1.0072 amu, while the mass of a neutron is 1.0086 amu. Given that the measured mass of a helium nucleus is 4.0015 amu, how much energy is converted from mass during the formation of one such nucleus? (1 amu = 1.66×10^{-27} kg)

A) 3.0×10^{-2} J
B) 6.0×10^{-10} J
C) 1.5×10^{-20} J
D) 4.5×10^{-12} J

This page intentionally left blank.

Sociology

1621. What is a latent function of the Internal Revenue Service?

A) To provide a financial security blanket for lower-income and middle-income workers during retirement

B) To collect taxes

C) To provide employment

D) To audit individuals and corporations who do not follow the tax code

1622. According to a functionalist perspective, in the U.S., Social Security:

I. has a manifest function of providing employment.

II. is one part of a society that will never maintain equilibrium.

III. has a latent dysfunction of creating a means of identity theft.

IV. has a manifest function of providing a financial security blanket for lower-income workers.

A) I and II

B) I and IV

C) II and III

D) III and IV

1623. In certain countries, the American peace sign, which involves folding in all of the digits except the index and middle fingers, is interpreted as an insult. The study of this symbolism is part of:

A) micro sociology.

B) conflict sociology.

C) bilateral sociology.

D) meta sociology.

1624. A biologist is observing the interactions of monkeys through the lens of sociology. He studies two groups of baboons that inhabit a sparsely wooded island off the coast of Malaysia. The researcher notes that one group seems to have successfully staked a claim on the island's most plentiful freshwater spring, which also houses the largest grove of fruit trees and bushes. When the less fortunate group approaches, the healthier baboons growl menacingly. Which theoretical approach does this biologist most likely take when explaining the behavior of the more powerful baboons?

A) Causal determinism

B) Symbolic interactionism

C) Conflict theory

D) Social constructionism

Questions 1625–1626 rely on the figure below

In a study that spanned more than ten years, sociologists aimed to monitor the approaches used by primary-school students to call for their teachers' attention. The original cohort of experimental-group participants was told from a young age that they could alert a teacher in any of three ways: raising their hands, calling the teacher's name, or pressing a button that ignited a light on their desks. The control group consisted of a random assortment of public-school children who were treated like typical American students. Their preferences are depicted in table form below.

	Raise Hand	Call Teacher's Name	Press Button
Test Group	30%	30%	40%
Control Group	78%	12%	10%

1625. How would one evaluate the results of this study from a viewpoint of symbolic interactionism?

  A) Since the test group was not told how to notify the teacher, pressing the button became the majority choice since it was the most entertaining option.

  B) Since the test group was not told how to notify the teacher, pressing the button was randomly assigned as having the highest value for commanding attention.

  C) Since the test group was not told how to notify the teacher, there was no clear, shared understanding of the method of communication that is most appropriate.

  D) Since the test group was not told how to notify the teacher, the three choices became practically equal in favor.

1626. One might explain the results of the control group through the lens of social constructionism by saying that:

  A) obedience is a social construct, so the students knew to press the button.

  B) honor is a social construct, and calling the teacher's name honored the teacher the most.

  C) respect is a social construct, and the students knew that raising their hands was the most respectful choice.

  D) seniority is a social construct, and the students knew to ask the teacher before asking a question or giving an opinion.

1627. Anthropologists are studying a newly-discovered culture that was centered on a chain of islands in the South Pacific over a thousand years ago. It appears that, instead of bartering with various items, members of this island society traded types of rare stones in exchange for goods. What does this monetary agreement exemplify?

  A) Symbolic interactionism
  B) Exchange-rational choice
  C) Social constructionism
  D) Functionalism

1628. A proponent of feminist theory argues that male-dominated society has systematically oppressed women. He states that the motivations for this systematic oppression are multiple, but can be traced to a desire for social and political power. This individual's views in regard to feminist theory are most likely rooted in:

  A) conflict theory.
  B) social constructionism.
  C) functionalism.
  D) dysfunctionalism.

1629. Initially unsure of what to do, the owner of a professional sports team decides to fire the general manager and coaching staff, despite his affection for them. This decision is made when he realizes that his popularity is diminishing and that sponsors are backing out of their association with his perennially losing team. Exchange-rational choice theory explains that he does this because:

  A) he thinks that the rewards of this decision outweigh the punishments.

  B) he wishes to make the maximum amount of social and monetary profit.

  C) unable to make a rational choice, he instead is forced to weigh the benefits and punishments of his social exchange.

  D) he cannot make an objectively rational choice, but can attempt to do so anyway.

1630. All of the following are latent functions of a medical school, EXCEPT:

  A) to employ professors, researchers, and office workers.

  B) to educate future doctors.

  C) to provide medical services to local residents.

  D) All of the above are latent functions.

1631. During a physical education class, a primary school student is asked to name his favorite sport. After the student replies that he enjoys watching figure skating the most, the coach scolds him for enjoying a "girl's pastime." To what aspect of education does this coach's response best relate?

A) Social learning
B) Hidden curriculum
C) Bystander apathy
D) Social constructionism

1632. Which of the following scenarios is best accounted for by teacher expectancy theory?

A) A teacher raises his expectations for a student who is performing well on exams, causing him to grade the student more harshly.
B) A teacher lowers his expectations for a student that he views as unintelligent, and the student, after realizing this, begins to work harder to prove himself.
C) A teacher lowers her expectations for a student that she views as lazy, and the student, after realizing this, continues to slack off.
D) A teacher raises her expectations for a student who is performing well on exams, and the student, after realizing this, begins to underperform.

1633. A high school student (Max Johnson) has lived with his mother (Sara Lee) his entire life, but still visits his father (Jack Johnson) regularly. His father has a large family, whom the son loves and sees regularly. This type of kinship is best described as:

A) patrilineal descent.
B) matrilineal descent.
C) bilateral descent.
D) hybrid descent.

1634. Which description of a family best represents a patriarchy?

A) A family in which the father pays all financial expenses, while the mother makes most of the choices regarding the children's education
B) A family with a single father who pays for his children's education
C) A family in which the bedridden father gives commands to his wife and their children
D) A family in which one father is more assertive and commanding than the other father

1635. All of the following are social benefits that can be provided by family EXCEPT:

A) companionship.
B) socialization.
C) protection.
D) obedience.

1636. Which of these statements regarding cults is true?

A) They have practices that fall outside of what society considers to be normal.
B) They are led by an individual rather than by a multitude.
C) They can never become major religions.
D) They often survive and grow, but only to a certain point.

1637. A child is born to religious parents. She attends church regularly throughout her childhood, learns more about her religion at her public school each day during class, and eventually becomes a lawyer who relies upon her religious knowledge to interpret the law. This individual's religion is most likely a:

A) sect.
B) cult.
C) state religion.
D) component of a theocracy.

1638. Of the listed scenarios, which correctly describe types of abuse within a family?

    I.   A man suffers spousal abuse when his wife constantly belittles him in front of his children for not providing more money to the family.

    II.   A child suffers from neglect when her parents don't buy her a winter coat, yet make her walk miles to school in the snow.

    III.   A mentally disabled grandfather suffers elder abuse when his wealthy family refuses to pay for a nursing home and instead chooses to allow him to live alone in a dangerous neighborhood.

    IV.   A wife suffers from neglect when her husband leaves for long stretches of time for business meetings.

    A) I and III
    B) I, II, and III
    C) I, II, and IV
    D) II, III, and IV

Questions 1639–1640 rely on the figure below

A study researches the beliefs held by religious rural and urban populations in southern Louisiana. The results of the study are summarized here.

	Christian	Muslim	Jewish	Other
Rural	97%	1%	0.1%	1.9%
Urban	95%	3%	1%	1%

1639. Some of the religions that constitute the "other" category could be characterized as cults. What is most likely true of these religious groups?

    A) They result from a split from a major religion.
    B) They are unable to grow to become a major religion.
    C) They have practices that society deems unacceptable.
    D) They are intended as a means of social control.

1640. Which of the following is more likely true of the rural Christians in Louisiana when compared to urban Christians in Illinois?

    A) They are more superstitious.
    B) They are more likely to follow legal codes set forth in the Bible.
    C) They may to adhere to a sect that split from the Christianity practiced in urban centers.
    D) They are less likely to allow people to convert to their religion.

1641. A form of government in which decisions are dominated by the interests of a small class of wealthy stakeholders would best be characterized as:

    A) capitalistic.
    B) monopolistic.
    C) oligarchic.
    D) authoritarian.

1642. Which of these disorders is most reflective of the social phenomenon referred to as *medicalization*?

    A) Lung cancer
    B) Myocardial infarction
    C) Type II diabetes
    D) Alcoholism

1643. Of the following, which rights or obligations are part of Talcott Parsons' sociological conception of the *legitimate* sick role?

    I.   The patient is released from his or her normal roles or duties.

    II.   The patient is considered responsible for his or her condition.

    III.   The patient has the duty to cooperate with medical professionals and get well.

    A) I only
    B) III only
    C) I and III
    D) II and III

1644. Social epidemiology would be most relevant to specifically identifying the individuals who are most likely to develop and die from:

    A) Alzheimer's disease.
    B) prostate cancer.
    C) AIDS.
    D) leukemia.

1645. Since the 1960s, medical care has transitioned from a delivery model of direct pay to small, independent clinics, to an alternative system in which insurance companies handle payment to large, extended hospital systems. This shift in medical care is best described by the term:

A) socialization.
B) deindividuation.
C) collectivization.
D) bureaucratization.

1646. Which of these population demographics is the LEAST useful for determining an individual's risk of developing a disease?

A) Age
B) Per capita income
C) Household size
D) Ethnic background

1647. A sociological research study aims to analyze the meanings that patients and doctors ascribe to individual steps of the treatment process. In doing so, researchers hope to discover the ways that conflicting interpretations can result in misunderstandings and poor care outcomes. This study's approach seems most closely related to which set of social theories?

A) Conflict theory
B) Structural functionalism
C) Symbolic interactionism
D) Game theory

1648. A psychiatrist begins to meet with a patient who has severe schizophrenic delusions. This man is convinced that the CIA is using the mental health clinic to implant tracking devices in his brain. Handling this patient's issues ethically would be most challenging because of the need to respect which principle of medical ethics?

A) Beneficence
B) Nonmaleficence
C) Respect for autonomy
D) Equitable treatment

1649. A political scientist is interested in studying cultural differences between democratic and non-democratic societies. To do so, he asks if citizens of various countries agree with a number of statements. Democratic nations include the U.S. and France, while non-democratic countries include Russia and China. The table below gives the percentage of participants from each group who answered "yes, I agree" to each statement.

Question	USA	France	Russia	China
1. "The government should be able to restrict the publication of information that is harmful to national security."	7%	8%	73%	60%
2. "It is wrong to desecrate the flag of my country."	70%	71%	80%	70%
3. "It should be a crime to desecrate the flag of my country."	52%	23%	70%	62%

The marked difference in responses to statement #1 between democratic and non-democratic participants relates best to:

A) mores.
B) taboos.
C) folkways.
D) values.

1650. While the economy affects nearly all aspects of society, it tends to impact some more strongly than others. Which of the following statistics is LEAST likely to be significantly affected by a major economic downturn or recession?

A) Fertility rates
B) Health insurance coverage
C) College attendance rates
D) Church attendance rates

1651. A certain ancient language is known to have contained five times as many prepositions as modern American English. This difference can be explained as:

A) one culture having a different, less explanatory material culture that necessitated more detailed words.
B) a difference in the symbolic cultures of the ancient and contemporary societies.
C) the ancient culture's folkways' placing less importance on direction and prepositional placement.
D) an example of social learning affecting language.

1652. Which of these tasks could serve as part of the study of material culture?

I. Analyzing the number of unique objects that mothers buy to raise children in different parts of the world
II. Comparing the social value of a college education in different countries
III. Contrasting how often gifts were exchanged in ancient versus modern cultures
IV. Studying similarities in architectural aesthetics in different societies

A) I and III
B) II and IV
C) I, II, and III
D) I, III, and IV

1653. All of these collections of individuals are examples of societies EXCEPT:

A) a tribe of Plains Native Americans that once traversed the central and Midwestern United States.
B) a study group that meets three times a week after each chemistry lecture.
C) a pack of wolves in Alaska whose mothers exchange cubs after birth.
D) a group of trappers in the Russian taiga who share a communal home during the winter season.

1654. Cultural assimilation of a group is exemplified by:

A) a vegetarian Indian man who, after moving to the U.S. for medical school, begins to enjoy eating meat and watching football.
B) Indian residents of Milwaukee who choose to live close to each other and form a small neighborhood.
C) Russian immigrants in San Francisco who gradually start to integrate American cooking styles into their cuisine.
D) an English violinist studying in St. Petersburg, where she becomes more and more fascinated by Russian folk music.

1655. The descendants of German immigrants located in a small town in central Texas have held a yearly waltz competition since the mid-1850s. This scenario best relates to:

A) cultural transmission.
B) cultural diffusion.
C) cultural assimilation.
D) cultural retention.

1656. Of the situations below, which most accurately represents culture lag?

A) A donut chain in Philadelphia stops using certain unhealthy sweeteners after receiving bad press in a local newspaper.

B) Although less harmful energy sources are being developed, many regard this with suspicion for fear that it will change familiar rhythms of American culture.

C) Although processing speed in computer hard drives has increased immensely, it is difficult to extend battery life.

D) Despite the success of some electric car companies, these cars are still charged by fixed power sources which in turn depend on carbon-emitting municipal power companies.

Questions 1657–1658 rely on the figure below

Sociologists are examining the maintenance of cultural traditions among different generations of Russian immigrants living in the United States. To assess this complex topic, they first choose three Russian or American traditions, then survey a number of Russian-Americans to gain their opinions of each. The table below shows the percentage of participants in each group who celebrate or strongly identify with each concept.

	Novy God	Russian dance	American sports
1st generation	98%	85%	20%
2nd generation	94%	60%	50%
3rd generation	90%	20%	80%

1657. *Novy god*, which encompasses both New Year's Eve and New Year's Day, is a yearly holiday in Russian culture. Although it was briefly banned by the Soviet Union, it was reinstated in the mid-1940s. The celebration of *Novy god* in the United States can be seen as an example of:

A) cultural diffusion.
B) cultural assimilation.
C) cultural transmission.
D) cultural integration.

1658. As generations become more removed from the original immigrants, it appears that fewer Russian-Americans partake in Russian dance forms. In contrast, more and more of these individuals who grew up in American neighborhoods have begun to follow American sports. The partaking in Russian dance forms and the viewing of American sports can be characterized as, respectively:

A) cultural assimilation and cultural transmission.
B) cultural integration and cultural transmission.
C) cultural assimilation and cultural assimilation.
D) cultural transmission and cultural transmission.

1659. Katie, a sociology student, hears her friend say, "A subculture consists of a smaller region within a larger area. For example, if Dublin is a suburb of Columbus, and if everyone in the wider Columbus area shares similar values, then Dublin is a subculture." Which example of a subculture can Katie give to correct her friend's assumptions?

A) A group of product designers who attended the same art school and formed several design firms that share an aesthetic vision

B) Hackers living in different parts of the world that work for numerous governments and their own self-interests

C) A food industry conglomerate that starts an advertising campaign using celebrity endorsements

D) Politically opinionated individuals who endorse the limitation of government and believe that the capitalist model of society is broken

1660. It has long been noted that humans and certain apes share some cultural similarities. When one group of these apes was observed to cross to the other side of a large lake in order to flee poachers, they initially conflicted with their new neighbors. However, as time passed, the neighbors were seen adopting certain practices of the newly established group, including picking at their loved ones' teeth to promote dental hygiene. This teeth-picking behavior is an example of:

A) cultural diffusion.
B) cultural transmission.
C) cultural assimilation.
D) cultural integration.

1661. If a certain individual's master status is "professional piano player":

A) his master status is also an ascribed status.
B) his master status is also an achieved status.
C) at least one of his primary groups must consist of other musicians.
D) he most commonly uses other men his age with families as a reference group.

1662. A group or category of people to which an individual can compare himself is best known as a:

A) control group.
B) standard of comparison.
C) reference group.
D) primary group.

1663. Role strain is best exemplified by which of the following scenarios?

A) The leader of a volunteer group who is expected both to be nice to the volunteers she organizes and to be strict when they break rules or miss mandatory events
B) A twenty-one-year-old who is both a member of his college football team and a premed student
C) A mother whose time is needed in the capacities of caretaker to her children, PTA president, and employee at her job
D) An investment banker who grows increasingly insecure about his abilities, later quitting his job

1664. A student preparing for the MCAT meets with a study group twice per week for four months. All students take the exam on the same day and occasionally communicate afterwards. With respect to the student, other members of this group are LEAST likely to be part of a:

A) secondary group.
B) primary group.
C) peer group.
D) reference group.

1665. Gregory is extremely talented at baseball, but only rarely plays it because he prefers to sing in the local choir. However, Gregory is also a child actor on a television series and is most

commonly referred to by others in that respect. Which of the following statements is true?

A) Gregory's master status is "baseball player."
B) Gregory's master status is "singer."
C) For Gregory, "male" is an ascribed status.
D) For Gregory, "actor" is an ascribed status.

1666. A bureaucracy can best be categorized as:

A) a large but extremely personal organization that cares about each member.
B) a business or other group where everyone performs roughly the same task to get things done.
C) a startup company with a reorganized system in which "every employee is his own boss."
D) a company, governmental organization, or other group with a strict hierarchy of positions.

1667. An incoming college freshman wants to join a club to meet new friends. Her interests include sports, music, and, especially, volunteering. This student would most likely join what type of formal organization?

A) A normative organization
B) A coercive organization
C) A utilitarian organization
D) An oligarchy

1668. Which of these pairings properly match(es) the term with its definition?

I. Role strain – trouble satisfying the demands of multiple distinct roles that clash with each other
II. Role conflict – trouble satisfying multiple different aspects of the same role at once
III. Role exit – the act of giving up a certain role due to conflict with another role, life changes, or feelings of inadequacy

A) II only
B) III only
C) I and II
D) I, II, and III

Questions 1669–1670 rely on the table below

A theory known as the stereotype content model categorizes stereotypes into four groups according to two factors: warmth and competence. Each warmth-competence combination is associated with a certain stereotype, as shown below. As part of a high school psychology class, students were asked a number of questions about people in their lives. Results were then categorized separately for each student.

		Competence	
		Low	High
Warmth	Low	Contemptuous stereotype	Envious stereotype
	High	Paternalistic stereotype	Admiration

1669. Members of a participant's out-group would be LEAST prevalent in which category?

A) Low warmth, low competence
B) Low warmth, high competence
C) High warmth, high competence
D) High warmth, low competence

1670. James is a member of the high school soccer team. He most often identifies as "brother," since he primarily characterizes himself as a caretaker for his chronically ill sister, but his closest friends are his soccer teammates. Which individual would James most likely view with an envious stereotype?

A) A member of an opposing team, since that team would compete with James' in-group
B) His soccer coach, since he is both a well-liked and an extremely talented man
C) A member of his own team, since envious stereotypes involve high competence
D) His sister, since he secretly resents her illness holding him back

1671. In which of the below situations is group polarization most likely to occur?

A) A man who identifies as a fair-weather Michigan fan is made to listen to a recording of a Michigan football rally.
B) A man who identifies as a fair-weather Michigan fan is made to listen to a recording of a rival team's rally, then casually asked about his opinions afterward.
C) Two dozen men who are moderately excited about a new business idea spend three hours in discussion in a room together.
D) A woman who feels unbelievably excited about a new business idea spends an hour with two dozen men who feel neutral about it.

1672. Jamie and Rebecca, two college cheerleaders, must perform a gymnastics-heavy routine at their school's football game. Jamie performs better than she ever has when practicing alone, while Rebecca falls during an early part of the maneuver. With regard to social psychology, what may explain these events?

A) Jamie experienced social facilitation, while Rebecca experienced social loafing.
B) Rebecca experienced social facilitation, while Jamie experienced social loafing.
C) Jamie had practiced the feat often and found it fairly simple, while Rebecca was less familiar with it and perceived it as difficult.
D) Rebecca had practiced the feat often and found it fairly simple, while Jamie was less familiar with it and perceived it as difficult.

1673. When considering only a small group of adolescent girls, which of these statements is most accurate?

A) When peer pressure is present, conformity almost certainly is as well.
B) When one of the girls experiences conformity, peer pressure almost certainly is present.
C) Peer pressure and conformity are likely demonstrated within this group, but are unrelated to each other.
D) Neither peer pressure nor conformity are likely to be present at all.

1674. How can group polarization be defined?

   A) The tendency for group discussion to intensify members' original stances, toward either one extreme or the other
   B) The tendency for members of a group to make riskier decisions as a whole than they would have individually
   C) The tendency for group discussion to result in less extreme viewpoints than those of the individuals involved
   D) The tendency for members of a group to make more cautious decisions as a whole than they would have individually

1675. According to Irving Janis, some groups include members who voluntarily control information that enters the group, limiting the total range of possible decisions and reducing overall dissent. Janis called these individuals:

   A) mind soldiers.
   B) groupthinkers.
   C) mindguards.
   D) message constrictors.

1676. The story of Kitty Genovese exemplifies which concept within social psychology?

   A) Groupthink
   B) Social facilitation
   C) Bystander deindividuation
   D) Bystander apathy

1677. Imagine that an unidentified number of wealthy families are boating in separate yachts when they observe a small lifeboat on the verge of sinking in the distance. If a sociologist were to predict the appearance of a plot that graphed the number of separate families that observe this scenario versus the probability that one will stop and help, he would likely find:

   A) a positive correlation (between 0 and 1).
   B) no correlation at all (0).
   C) no correlation at all (-1)
   D) a negative correlation (between 0 and -1).

1678. All of the following would be expected to produce adverse results over half of the time EXCEPT:

   A) social facilitation.
   B) social loafing.
   C) the bystander effect.
   D) groupthink.

1679. Of the scenarios below, the bystander effect is most likely to be observed when:

   A) a single man walks past a child who has fallen off his bike and scraped his knee.
   B) several unrelated individuals in a crowded area walk past a child who has fallen off his bike and scraped his knee.
   C) a single man walks past a group of children, all of whom have fallen off their bikes and scraped their knees.
   D) a married couple walks past a child who has fallen off his bike and scraped his knee.

1680. If a jury experiences group polarization while deliberating on a murder case, they are likely to:

   A) forcefully state that the accused murderer is guilty.
   B) forcefully state that the accused murderer is innocent.
   C) have more trouble making a decision than if they had not experienced this phenomenon.
   D) either A or B is possible.

1681. Which of the following is an example of stereotype threat?

   A) Jon works extra hours at work for several months and receives a promotion.
   B) Jessie believes that all French people are arrogant and standoffish. She refuses to interact with her French neighbors, which further reinforces her belief.
   C) In her philosophy class, Amy is afraid to express her critique of an ethical system, as she believes that the class will think she's overly emotional because she's a woman. When she does speak up, she ends up crying and has difficulty speaking clearly.
   D) In the 1600s, many women were persecuted due to the belief that they were witches.

1682. Citizens of a particular city often blame skateboarders for crimes in which they were not remotely involved. What does this situation most clearly exemplify?

   A) False consensus
   B) Affirmative action
   C) Fundamental attribution error
   D) A scapegoat

1683. Before attending first grade, Jared is told by his mother that, like his brothers and sister, he will probably not succeed at math. If this situation illustrates a self-fulfilling prophecy, how will Jared react when he attends class?

    A) Jared will do poorly at math because he's naturally better at language and writing.

    B) Jared will do poorly at math because it matches the expectation held about him.

    C) Jared will do well at math because he knows that he must work harder than the other kids.

    D) Jared will do well at math because he wants to redeem the poor performance of his siblings.

1684. A study asked 2,500 adults whether they would trust the political opinions of people from various professions. Overwhelmingly, subjects responded that they would trust the opinion of a medical doctor or Ph. D more than a janitor or taxi driver. This demonstrates the power of:

    A) prestige.

    B) ethnocentrism.

    C) groupthink.

    D) stigma.

Questions 1685–1686 rely on the graph below

A group of developmental psychologists surveyed a large sample of young adults. In their questionnaire, they asked about the ethnic and racial identities of the participants as well as whether each individual had ever been diagnosed with attention deficit hyperactivity disorder (ADHD). The results are shown below.

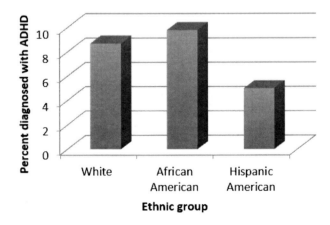

1685. If, when analyzing the data above, the researchers obtain a p-value > 0.5, how would the results of the study be affected?

    A) The role of ethnicity in the likelihood of ADHD diagnosis in young adults would be called into question.

    B) The researchers would conclude that only the difference in diagnosis rate between white Americans and Hispanic-Americans was statistically significant.

    C) Both the precision and accuracy of the results would be strengthened.

    D) The precision, but not the accuracy, of the results would be strengthened.

1686. Assuming that at least one of the discrepencies presented in the graph is statistically significant, the experimenters could conclude that:

    A) African-American young adults have the strongest genetic predisposition to ADHD.

    B) white American young adults are less likely to be diagnosed with ADHD than Hispanic-American young adults.

    C) ethnicity is the most important determining factor in whether a young adult will be diagnosed with ADHD.

    D) diagnosing clinicians may be influenced by racial bias.

1687. Prejudice differs from discrimination in that:

    A) prejudice involves racial and ethnic groups, while discrimination can include any biases possessed by an individual.

    B) prejudice is inherited, while discrimination is learned from experience.

    C) prejudice is a falsely held belief or attitude, while discrimination is an action or behavior toward an individual or social group.

    D) prejudice is an action or behavior toward an individual or social group, while discrimination is a falsely held belief or attitude.

1688. Which of the following is NOT a way in which unfair distribution of power can lead to discrimination?

A) Groups with large amounts of political sway can get candidates into office; thus, they can influence policy more readily than minority groups with less political power.

B) Certain unfair hiring policies influenced by bias lead to especially low-paying jobs for minority groups.

C) A specific law results in limitations on where members of a minority group live, go to school, and access healthcare, thus producing disparities.

D) People with low social power tend to have more access to resources because they band together and support each other.

1689. A member of a high socioeconomic class notices that a certain restaurant places its Hispanic-American workers in the kitchen at low wages. How might this person use the just-world hypothesis to explain his observation?

A) He would think the restaurant is being racist, and that it should instead pay its workers more fairly.

B) He would think that the hiring practices of the restaurant are fair, since the Hispanic workers could always try harder to obtain a better job.

C) He would think that, eventually, the restaurant manager would realize the error of his actions and improve his practices.

D) He would be blind to any injustice because the just-world phenomenon considers all moral positions to be equal.

1690. Affirmative action is best exemplified by:

A) a group that assembles outside a courthouse to protest against restrictions to abortion rights.

B) a woman who obtains an advanced degree and, through years of hard work, becomes a CEO in an industry that is typically run by men.

C) a young man who, after losing his job, chooses to focus on the positive results of his situation rather than the negatives.

D) a top medical school that creates several scholarships for individuals of underrepresented ethnic minority groups.

1691. Which of the following are examples of institutional, as opposed to individual, discrimination?

I. Mandatory literacy tests for voters in the Jim Crow South
II. Segregated schools for black children
III. Restaurant owners refusing to seat black customers

A) I only
B) I and II
C) II and III
D) I, II, and III

1692. While AIDS was first recognized as a disease in the early 1980s, it was not until several years later that efforts were made to raise public awareness of the disease and advocate resources towards finding a cure. AIDS (at first) primarily affected groups, namely heroin users and gay men, who were not seen as deserving of help due to their lifestyles. Which term most closely relates to this situation?

A) Social class
B) Prejudice
C) Social stigma
D) Groupthink

1693. A sociologist is researching racial disparities in hiring practices. She designs a study to assess discriminatory behavior by employers against job candidates, sight unseen. The researcher sends out several sets of resumes, all identical in terms of experience and qualifications, but with names listed with either stereotypically black (Trayvon, Omar, Jamal, etc.) or white (Walter, Chad, Trey, etc.) connotations. Within both groups, some resumes list a felony drug possession conviction, while the others do not. She obtains the following results, with the percentage given reflecting "candidates" who were asked to come in for an interview:

	Clean record	Felony record
"White" names	17%	8%
"Black" names	8%	2%

When confronted with the results, employers claim that they are not prejudiced, and that they always use racially neutral qualitative criteria to evaluate their candidates. Assuming that this statement is true, which statement best explains the results?

A) Qualitative criteria are inherently racist.
B) Different cultures have different ideas about what constitutes a quality applicant.
C) Qualitative criteria can be interpreted according to unconscious biases.
D) A history of discrimination leaves certain minorities with fewer resources to acquire the qualitative criteria desired by employers.

1694. Previous studies have determined that black patients with cardiac symptoms receive an inferior quality of care in comparison to white patients. An administrator at a neurology clinic wishes to determine whether a similar disparity exists at his facility. To do so, he recruits a group of elderly black men to feign stroke symptoms, observe their own treatment, and fill out a survey rating several aspects of their care on a scale of 1 to 5. Their average rating for most aspects was low, particularly on the scale for "The physician listens to my concerns," which averaged 1.5. Which of the following statements could be accurately made about this study?

A) Care quality was operationalized as a quantitative variable.
B) The results indicate that doctors are less sensitive to the concerns of the black volunteers.
C) The research design properly controlled for the subjective expectations of each volunteer.
D) The results demonstrate the preferential treatment of white patients.

1695. Despite efforts to achieve equality in healthcare, minority patients often receive subpar care compared to non-minorities, even at the same facility. Explorations of this phenomenon have determined that a variety of factors are involved. For example, minorities may have difficulty attending follow-up appointments due to inability to take time off from low-income service jobs, in which they tend to be overrepresented. Others find that as minorities tend to have fewer healthcare professionals in their social circle, they sometimes feel intimidated by physicians' expertise and accept misdiagnoses, even against their own

reservations. These findings can best be explained in terms of which social theory?

A) Structural functionalism
B) Behaviorism
C) Conflict theory
D) Status analysis

1696. Research has attempted to isolate the brain activation patterns that are linked to racial prejudice. Several studies have found that self-reported prejudice is related to increased activation in the amygdala when viewing photos of racial minorities. This link may be best explained by the amygdala's role in:

A) pattern recognition.
B) fear and aggression.
C) in-group bonding.
D) visual processing.

1697. Which of the following scenarios is LEAST likely to be caused by the phenomenon of stereotype threat?

A) After watching several videos of the career highlights of black basketball superstars like Michael Jordan and Kobe Bryant, white athletes perform worse at free throws than a control group that did not watch the videos.
B) Black and white students perform better on a mathematics test when they are not informed beforehand that Asians tend to have higher average scores.
C) Women in a certain male-dominated field receive higher performance marks, on average, than the men in the field.
D) Two middle-aged groups of immigrants take a test of English as a second language. One group is told that the test intends to analyze why younger people pick up languages faster, and its members perform worse than the other group (which is not given a reason for the test).

1698. Some job criteria can be implicitly discriminatory when, even if not formulated with discriminatory intent, their application results in disparate outcomes for different groups. Basing choices on which of the following criteria would most likely result in implicitly sexist hiring practices?

    A) Age
    B) Height
    C) Social skills
    D) Language fluency

1699. Which of these scenarios does NOT exemplify discrimination?

    A) A patient is more likely to follow treatment plans that come from a male doctor rather than a female one.
    B) An academic gives better projects to his Asian graduate students because he thinks they are smarter.
    C) A landlord will not rent to black tenants because he expects that they will not maintain the property.
    D) An older man is convinced that all gay men are pedophiles.

1700. Historically, much of the black population of the U.S. has lived in segregated neighborhoods that were frequently built in undesirable locations, such as downwind from factories. Additionally, due to underrepresentation in the political system, noxious industries and toxic waste disposal plants have often been sited near black neighborhoods. As a result, black neighborhoods often display significantly higher levels of environmental toxins such as lead and radon, and residents possess elevated risk of cancers and developmental abnormalities. These health problems can be best described as the legacy of which social phenomenon?

    A) Stigmatization
    B) Institutional discrimination
    C) Disenfranchisement
    D) Stereotyping

1701. When Johnny was younger, his mother would scold him every time he put his elbows on the table while eating. As a result, Johnny learned to keep his elbows off the table. Which norm is his mother instilling and how?

    A) Johnny's mother is instilling formal deviance via positive punishment.
    B) Johnny's mother is instilling formal deviance via positive reinforcement.
    C) Johnny's mother is instilling a folkway via positive punishment.
    D) Johnny's mother is instilling a folkway via positive reinforcement.

1702. Although social norms vary from community to community, many cultures administer similar consequences for disobeying their specific norms. Which of the statements below is / are true?

    I. Formal deviance generally results in legal sanctions.
    II. Informal deviance generally results in legal sanctions.
    III. Informal deviance generally results in social sanctions.
    IV. Both informal and formal deviance can result in stigma.

    A) I only
    B) II and IV
    C) II, III, and IV
    D) I, III, and IV

1703. Interestingly, a society's norms are often difficult to identify directly. In contrast, deviance (or violation of these norms) can be simpler to spot, making it a valuable tool to learn about socially accepted behavior. What cause-and-effect relationship below does NOT pair an example of deviance with the appropriate societal response?

    A) Violation of a more is generally punished by legal restitution.
    B) Violation of a formal norm can result in legal fines and incarceration.
    C) Violation of a folkway generally causes little more than hurt feelings.
    D) Violation of an informal norm can result in social sanctions.

Questions 1704–1706 rely on the figure below

A trendy fashion magazine, interested in America's odd obsession with fanny packs, is attempting to study the actual consumption of these items. The number of fanny packs sold over a 25-year span is shown here.

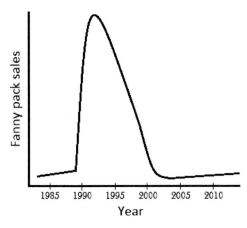

1704. Initially, the researchers are perplexed by the sudden peak in fanny pack sales between 1990 and 2000. They later realize that this brief popularity was due in part to the popularity of the TV series *Baywatch* (1989-2001), which glamorized the items. Which piece of evidence supports the idea that the fanny pack was a fad to which *Baywatch* contributed?

A) The quick emergence of the fanny pack as a popular item, as well as its subsequent rapid loss in popularity, correspond with the viewership of the *Baywatch* seasons.

B) The slow climb in fanny pack sales from 1989 to 1995 marks the item's permanent presence in society as a tribute to the *Baywatch* fandom.

C) The rapid decline in fanny pack sales from 1995 to 2000 may result from a fanny pack deficit due to extreme consumption of the items during *Baywatch*'s most popular years.

D) The viewership statistics for *Baywatch* in the average American household are the direct inverse of fanny pack sales.

1705. In 1992, mass hysteria erupted due to an undersupply of fanny packs. During this event, individuals rioted at the doors of a department store. Which crowd behavior theory is correctly paired with an analysis of the rioting consumers?

A) Crowds as gatherings; the riot was not an emergent behavior of the crowd, but simply the result of many violent fanny pack consumers coming together.

B) Emergent-norm theory; the reason for gathering was distinct from the temporary reason(s) the fanny pack consumers had for rioting.

C) Convergence theory; significant variation exists in the fanny pack crowd, and the individuals did not have impaired judgement when they were rioting.

D) Contagion theory; the hypnotic influence of the crowd, combined with the anonymity of the fanny pack purchasers, contributed to the crowd's irrational rioting behavior.

1706. In 2010, a teenager wears a fanny pack to a social gathering with her peers. When she arrives, she realizes that some other individuals are criticizing and mocking her. Her peers' behavior can be explained by the idea that:

A) informal norms in 2010 dictate that fanny packs are socially acceptable, and the teenager is experiencing legal sanctions.

B) informal norms in 2010 dictate that fanny packs are socially unacceptable, and the teenager has been deemed as deviant and stigmatized.

C) formal norms in 2010 dictate that fanny packs are socially unacceptable, and the teenager is experiencing legal sanctions.

D) formal norms in 2010 dictate that fanny packs are socially unacceptable, and the teenager has been deemed as deviant and stigmatized.

1707. The word *taboo* was introduced to English by Captain Cook after his visit to the South Pacific in 1771. Due to these origins, it is associated with Polynesian cultures; however, taboos are present in all societies. Which of the following are characteristics of a taboo?

   I.   Taboos are generally irrational in nature.
   II.   A taboo is a social norm that violently prohibits certain actions.
   III.   Individuals often believe that a supernatural authority governs the taboo.
   IV.   Defiance of a taboo will result in difficulty for the offender.

   A) I only
   B) II and IV
   C) I, II, and IV
   D) II, III, and IV

1708. A student experiencing anomie may:

   A) dream of becoming a physician, but cannot due to his extreme phobia of blood.
   B) dream of becoming a physician, but despite the support of his peers and family, cannot afford to continue school.
   C) dream of becoming a physician, but decide not to pursue his dream in order to care for his ill grandmother.
   D) dream of becoming a physician, but is not able to do so due to a lack of guidance and inability to integrate into society.

1709. Which factor does NOT play a potential direct role in the initiation of a riot?

   A) Bystander apathy
   B) Moral panic
   C) Mass hysteria
   D) Emergent properties of the crowd

1710. Mores are social norms that are given greater moral significance than other rules of social behavior. Which choice gives an example of a more found in a physician's profession?

   A) The physician's team is a group of medical professionals that assist the doctor in his or her duties.
   B) Malpractice insurance is required to protect the physician's personal and professional interests.
   C) The Hippocratic Oath is a vow taken by the physician to "first do no harm" and to treat patients with respect.
   D) Board certification is a process that ensures that the physician is qualified to treat and prescribe.

1711. While an individual's personality appears to develop in part due to genetics, it is also subject to social pressures. All of the following correctly match a type of socialization to its definition EXCEPT:

   A) primary socialization; an individual learns a behavior to be displayed in a small group that is part of a larger society.
   B) anticipatory socialization; an individual expecting certain social relationships will rehearse related behaviors.
   C) developmental socialization; an individual focuses on learning and developing social skills.
   D) resocialization; an individual replaces old behavioral patterns with new ones in order to enter a new phase of his or her life.

1712. Throughout history, there have been several well-documented incidences of "wild children," or children who are raised in isolation from human contact. One example is Sidi Mohamed, who was "adopted" by ostriches in the Sahara Desert from ages two to twelve. He was then rescued and successfully integrated into society. During his socialization process, it was important for Sidi Mohamed to accept or reject which societal traits?

   I.   Values
   II.   Behaviors
   III.   Attitudes
   IV.   Norms

   A) I and II
   B) II and IV
   C) I, II, and III
   D) I, II, III, and IV

Questions 1713–1714 rely on the figure below

In a longitudinal study, a group of 100 males in fraternities were surveyed every five years during the interval from ages 20 to 40. One of the survey questions asks the individuals how many alcoholic beverages they consume, on average, per week. The results are presented below.

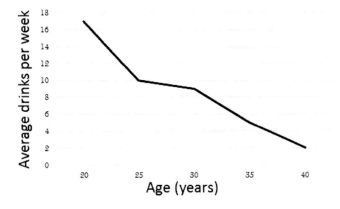

1713. The researchers hypothesize that the decrease in weekly alcohol consumption correlated with an increase in age due to changes in behavior patterns. Which type of socialization would account for this trend?

A) Resocialization
B) Primary socialization
C) Secondary socialization
D) Anticipatory socialization

1714. In follow-up interviews, the forty-year-old participants are asked what may have contributed to the displayed decrease in alcohol consumption. The men list their families, peers, and coworkers as influences. From this information, the researchers are most likely to hypothesize that:

A) the participants' reported decrease in consumption is false; they are still drinking the same as they were at age 20, but are afraid to report it due to their families.
B) the participants' decrease in consumption is due to the new social context created by various agents of socialization.
C) the participants' decrease in consumption is due to the unavailability of alcohol at home and at the workplace.
D) the participants' reported decrease in consumption is due mainly to social desirability bias.

1715. While the U.S. currently possesses the technology to differentiate human embryonic stem cells (hESCs) into neurons, no consensus has been met on the ethical guidelines of such research. Which of the following statements characterize this dilemma as a cultural lag?

I. American culture is taking time to catch up with the technological innovations related to hESCs.
II. The hESC studies are creating at least a small degree of social conflict.
III. The American government can make no attempt to consolidate guidelines until complete agreement is established by the public.
IV. The ethical disagreement on hESC research may lead to a breakdown of social solidarity.

A) I and II
B) II and IV
C) I, II, and III
D) I, II, and IV

Questions 1716–1717 rely on the figure below

The following graph, constructed by a sociology student, is intended to correspond to the stages of culture shock. While cultural assimilation involves many changes, he opts to graph only its effect on the individual's perceived happiness or overall contentment, measured from 1 (miserable) to 10 (overjoyed). He also labels four specific points on the curve.

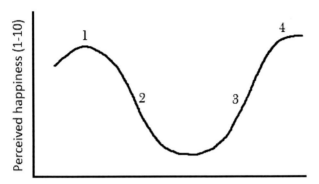

1716. Which of these pairings correctly matches the position on the graph above with its corresponding stage of culture shock?

A) 1: honeymoon
B) 2: acceptance
C) 3: negotiation
D) 4: adjustment

1717. Following the final stage shown in the graph (phase 4), several outcomes are possible. Which of these outcomes would NOT be likely at this time?

A) Rejection: the individual does not fully integrate and instead withdraws to isolation. She may also experience problems re-integrating after returning back home.
B) Cultural assimilation: the individual completely integrates into his host culture without losing his original identity.
C) Non-assimilation: the individual does not adjust to the new culture, and instead cycles between the honeymoon and negotiation phases.
D) Cosmopolitan: the individual adopts certain aspects he views as positive from the new culture, while integrate it with his previous beliefs to create a unique blend.

1718. Tasha, who has spent her entire life in Texas, recently decided to take a new job in Japan. When she first arrived, she was excited and loved the local food and culture, as well as her living space. However, she is now experiencing bouts of frustration, loneliness, and disconnect from her surroundings. She is also noticing physical symptoms such as insomnia and disruptions in her gut flora. What stage of culture shock is Tasha experiencing, and what will likely happen after a period of time?

A) Negotiation – Tasha is growing accustomed to the culture and developing a routine; she will soon be able to participate fully in her new society.
B) Negotiation – Tasha is feeling anxious about her new surroundings; she will soon grow accustomed to the culture and develop a routine.
C) Adjustment – Tasha is growing accustomed to the culture and developing a routine; she will soon be able to fully participate in her new society.
D) Adjustment – Tasha is feeling anxious about her new surroundings; she will soon grow accustomed to the culture and develop a routine.

1719. Jason recently moved to Turkey from Australia. He is having a difficult time adjusting, and he often compares the culture in Turkey to what he was previously accustomed to, believing that his Australian culture is superior. Which of these terms best explains Jason's attitudes?

A) Ethnocentrism
B) Cultural relativism
C) Xenophobia
D) Religiocentrism

1720. Multiculturalism is:

A) an ideology that promotes the growth of multicultural communities.
B) applied to demographic populations at the organizational level.
C) a concept that involves advocacy for equal rights for all individuals and respect for all cultures.
D) all of the above.

1721. Sociologists define self-concept as the way an individual evaluates and perceives him- or herself. Children begin to develop their self-concepts at a very young age. How can one accurately chronologize the development of the existential and categorical selves?

   A) The existential self comes first, followed by the categorical self; the child realizes her existence as a separate entity before understanding that she is an "object" in the world and can be categorized.

   B) The categorical self comes first, followed by the existential self; the child realizes her existence as a separate entity before understanding that she is an "object" in the world and can be categorized.

   C) The existential self comes first, followed by the categorical self; the child initially realizes that she is an "object" that is part of the experiences of others, then understands that she possesses her own separate experience.

   D) The categorical self comes first, followed by the existential self; the child initially realizes that she is an "object" that is part of the experiences of others, then understands that she possesses her own separate experience.

1722. In 1960, sociologist Thomas Kuhn studied self-image by asking participants of a study to answer the question "Who am I?" in twenty different ways. His list of answers to this query may include all of the following EXCEPT:

   A) physical description: I am tall.
   B) social roles: I am a teacher.
   C) personal traits: I am a mother.
   D) existential statements: I am a spiritual entity.

1723. Alfonso, a 15-year-old, has always been a good student and son. Lately, however, he has been exploring his identity and engaging in dangerous activities such as dirt biking. He even dyed his hair green! Which psychosocial crisis is Alfonso experiencing, and how can the resolution of this crisis contribute to the formation of his identity?

   A) Identity versus role confusion; resolution of this crisis indicates that Alfonso has come closer to finding his unique identity.

   B) Identity versus role confusion; resolution of this crisis does not contribute to Alfonso's identity formation.

   C) Intimacy versus isolation; resolution of this crisis indicates that Alfonso has come closer to finding his unique identity.

   D) Intimacy versus isolation; resolution of this crisis does not contribute to Alfonso's identity formation.

Questions 1724–1726 refer to the figure below

Exactly 200 boys, ages 6-9, are randomly selected for a study on the influence of television on the socialization of gender roles. A survey then determines their television viewership habits. Approximately 100 of the boys watch less than 30 hours of television per week, while the other group watches more than 30 hours each week. Finally, boys of both groups are asked which of a list of professions they would most likely choose.

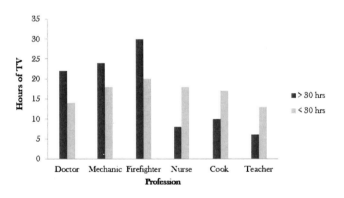

1724. Recent research has found that, in children's TV programs, men are usually more dominant and work in stereotypically male professions. For example, male characters are often shown as doctors, mechanics, and firefighters. In conjunction with the data presented above, which of these statements is most likely to be true of the ">30-hour" group?

   A) The children have not adopted the gender-stereotyped attitudes and behaviors seen on television.
   B) The children have adopted the gender-stereotyped attitudes and behaviors seen on television, but they have not yet internalized them in their own identity formation.
   C) The children have adopted the gender-stereotyped attitudes and behaviors seen on television, and they have internalized them in their own identity formation.
   D) No conclusion can be drawn from this data set.

1725. When one of the boys who watched more than 30 hours of television was asked why he wanted to be a nurse, he replied that his father is a nurse as well. Which of the following is NOT accurate?

   A) Family is an influential socialization force.
   B) The environment inside of his family home influenced this child's response.
   C) Television is one of many factors that may impact a person's attitudes and behavior.
   D) Since this child's father is definitely a stronger influence than the TV shows, this influence will continue as the child ages.

1726. A newly-released children's television show stars a boy who loves to cook. In an identical study, when surveyed immediately after the conclusion of this show's first season, 25 of the boys who watched more than 30 hours of weekly television respond that they aspire to be cooks. The most logical explanation for this trend is that:

   A) due to the small sample size of the original experiment, this variation could easily result from human error.
   B) the twenty-five boys may have watched the new show and have internalized the gender role depicted.
   C) the twenty-five boys may have watched the new show but have not yet internalized the gender role depicted.
   D) the twenty-five boys may or may not have watched the new show, but they likely watched fewer hours of shows depicting men in more "traditional" careers.

1727. Xixi is a thirty-year-old woman who was recently laid off and does not feel that she can find another job soon. Although her family is concerned about her well-being, Xixi tries her best to be optimistic. She often uses phrases such as "I am sure the right job will come along" or "this is a good opportunity for me to work on myself." The contrast between Xixi's internal emotions and her external emotional display exemplifies:

   A) impression management; Xixi is afraid of being perceived negatively by her family if she does not respond in an optimistic way.
   B) impression management; Xixi is attempting to influence her family's perception of her and to align this perception with her goals of finding another job.
   C) presentation of merchandise; Xixi is afraid of being perceived negatively by her family if she does not respond in an optimistic way.
   D) presentation of merchandise; Xixi is attempting to influence her family's perception of her and to align this perception with her goals of finding another job.

1728. How might the recent advent of social networking sites (SNSs), including Facebook, Myspace, and LinkedIn, affect an individual's self-presentation?

   I. SNSs optimize self-presentation because an individual is able to decide what is displayed.
   II. Activity from other users on an individual's profile, such as comments or picture tags, may reduce some control of self-presentation.
   III. SNSs do not contribute to self-presentation.

A) I only
B) II only
C) I and II
D) I, II, and III

1729. The dramaturgical approach of self-presentation is a theatrical metaphor that describes individuals "performing on stage" with the goal of gaining acceptance from their "audience." Of the definitions below, all correctly identify a component of this approach EXCEPT:

A) front stage: the actor knows that he or she is being watched by the audience and behaves accordingly.
B) back stage: the performer rehearses for his or her role by staying in character and gauging what others wish to perceive.
C) outside: the individual meets audience members independently and gives specific performances.
D) borders: the performer manages the people allowed to observe him or her to restrict access to the "performance."

1730. The image below is an American advertisement that shows Uncle Sam, a common symbol of American patriotism, recruiting personnel for World War I.

Sociological studies have shown that propaganda, a category that many would consider to include this ad, is an important component of the gradual indoctrination of ideas to the public. Which of these comments relating to this advertisement are true?

I. It serves as propaganda with a goal of changing the attitudes of the population towards joining the army.

II. The indoctrinated population is not expected to criticize the doctrine displayed.
III. The attempts at indoctrination by this ad serve as a form of public education.
IV. The attempts at indoctrination by this ad are not the same as socialization.

A) I and II
B) II and III
C) I, II, and IV
D) I, III, and IV

1731. Gender refers to one's characteristics that range from masculine to feminine. All of the following are considered gender characteristics EXCEPT:

A) biological sex.
B) gender identity.
C) education during development.
D) sex-based social structures.

1732. The human sex ratio is defined as:

A) the ratio of males to females in a population, which is approximately 1:1.5.
B) the ratio of males to females in a population, which is approximately 1:1.
C) the ratio of males to the total human population, which is approximately 1:2.5.
D) the ratio of males to the total human population, which is approximately 1:2.

1733. Gender imbalances occur when the ratio of males to females is disturbed. Which of these may cause such disturbances?

I. Natural or environmental factors
II. Gender-based abortions
III. Differential effects of aging

A) I only
B) I and II
C) II and III
D) I, II, and III

1734. According to the United States Census, the American population is divided into six ethnic and racial categories. All of these are recognized by the U.S. as distinct ethnic or racial groups EXCEPT:

A) White.
B) Native American and Alaskan Native.
C) Native Hawaiian and Other Pacific Islanders.
D) Hispanic and Latino Americans.

1735. It is estimated that 3% of the world's population consists of international immigrants. Which of these factors are reasons for the emigration of individuals from one country to another?

   I. Economic factors
   II. Personal factors
   III. Educational factors

    A) I only
    B) II only
    C) I and II
    D) I, II, and III

Questions 1736–1738 rely on the figure below

The demographic transition model, below, was proposed by Warren Thompson. It delineates the typical population changes that mark a transition from a pre-industrial to an industrial economic system.

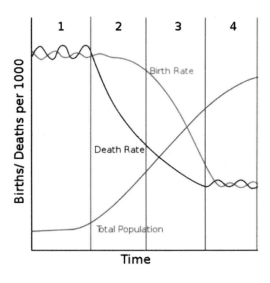

1736. Name the phases shown in this figure, from stage 1 to stage 4.

    A) Pre-industrial; urbanization; mature industrial; post-industrial
    B) Urbanization; pre-industrial; mature industrial; post-industrial
    C) Pre-industrial; mature industrial; urbanization; post-industrial
    D) Pre-industrial; mature industrial; post-industrial; urbanization

1737. In countries such as Germany, Italy, and Japan, the fertility rate has actually dropped below the mortality rate. In which stage do these nations currently exist, and what are the implications?

    A) The mature industrial age; these populations are now equilibrating and stable.
    B) The mature industrial age; these populations are shrinking.
    C) The post-industrial age; these populations are now equilibrating and stable.
    D) The post-industrial age; these populations are shrinking.

1738. Which of these are NOT reasons for the declining mortality rate that marks stage 2?

    A) Improvements in food supply
    B) Progress in agricultural technology
    C) Increased access to contraceptives
    D) Significant improvements in public health

1739. How can globalization influence a country?

    A) It can increase the nation's wealth.
    B) It can threaten cultural values.
    C) Both A and B are correct.
    D) Neither A nor B is correct.

1740. Which of these trends accurately describes urban and rural populations during the process of urbanization?

    A) Both urban and rural populations increase.
    B) Both urban and rural populations decrease.
    C) The urban population decreases, while the rural population increases.
    D) The urban population increases, while the rural population decreases.

Questions 1741–1742 rely on the figure below

A historical sociologist analyzes the changes to a certain country's population over the course of several centuries. Note that the results (shown below) give fertility rate as a measure of the number of births during one year per 1000 members of the population. Similarly, mortality rate is the number of deaths, per year, per 1000 individuals.

Year	1300	1400	1500	1600
Fertility rate (births per 1000 individuals)	25	24	12	10
Mortality rate (deaths per 1000 individuals)	27	17	10	11
Population (millions)	2	3.5	6	7

1741. According to this data, which type of societal change occurred at least in part between the years 1300 and 1400?

A) A demographic shift
B) A demographic transition
C) A demographic stagnation
D) A migration

1742. Assume that the four time periods listed in the table perfectly represent the four stages of demographic transition. During which interval might we expect children to require extensive schooling in order to be productive in society?

A) 1300-1350
B) 1400-1450
C) 1500-1550
D) 1550-1600

1743. During a certain period in societal development, children generally begin to require a higher level and longer duration of support from their parents. This, in turn, encourages adults to have fewer children. Of the four main stages of demographic transition, this interval constitutes:

A) Stage 1.
B) Stage 2.
C) Stage 3.
D) Stage 4.

1744. All of the following correctly describe globalization EXCEPT:

A) it tends to increase pollution.
B) it reduces the geographic constraints on ideas.
C) it involves the exchange of cultural ideas, aiding international business.
D) it increases job security due to increased global demand.

1745. Which of these locations is most likely a poor, densely populated urban area with dangerously inefficient sanitation systems?

A) An urban sprawl in a country with a low GDP
B) A slum in an undeveloped nation
C) A ghetto in a wealthy nation's capital
D) A society in stage 4 of a demographic transition

1746. A moderately impoverished country has recently seen its population grow at an alarming rate. The most likely cause of this population expansion is:

A) a high fertility rate.
B) a low mortality rate.
C) low unemployment due to globalization.
D) immigration.

1747. Of these statements about demographic shifts, which are most likely true of a wealthy, economically developed, and racially and ethnically diverse nation?

I. It will have a higher rate of immigration than emigration.
II. It will have a higher rate of emigration than immigration.
III. It will exhibit a high fertility rate.
IV. The approximate magnitude of its fertility rate cannot be determined without more information.

A) I and III
B) I and IV
C) II and III
D) II and IV

1748. A decline in the agricultural sector of a coastal African country will most probably result in:

A) decreased globalization due to a decrease in the export of crops.

B) increased globalization due to an increase in the export of crops.

C) urbanization and the formation of slums as citizens migrate to cities.

D) a nationwide shift towards stage 4 of a demographic transition.

1749. In "Country X," the public has held a generally negative opinion of immigrants for several decades. Recently, a number of citizens formed an organization meant not only to change this perception, but also to educate arriving immigrants about their legal rights as residents of the country. This group could best be categorized as a:

A) proactive social movement.

B) reactive social movement.

C) symbolic movement.

D) demographic movement.

1750. Most sociologists divide demographic transitions into either four or five distinct stages. In which of these intervals does a society's fertility rate remain stable while its mortality rate drops?

A) Stage 1

B) Stage 2

C) Stage 3

D) Stage 4

1751. A person who is thought to possess considerable power will:

A) have a highly lauded reputation.

B) have a lowly reputation.

C) have assets, but not necessarily income.

D) be more likely than average to have a high socioeconomic status.

1752. Property may include all of the following EXCEPT:

A) government-issued bonds.

B) an estate co-owned by three siblings.

C) a yearly salary.

D) a tax-deductible donation.

1753. Although white and minority populations are slowly trending towards equal pay, sociologists argue that the vast disparity in asset wealth in America will continue to define the wealth gap between white and most other populations. This pervasive lack of access to asset wealth is one example of:

A) cultural transmission.

B) cultural diffusion.

C) social stratification.

D) social reproduction.

1754. Mr. Jones achieves a good position as a municipal service worker. However, no matter how hard his children try, they are only allowed to reach the same level of seniority that he has attained. In fact, if they try to climb further up the social ladder, society will disallow them from seeking further education. Mr. Jones and his family probably live in a:

A) meritocracy.

B) class system.

C) caste system.

D) state of social poverty.

1755. A large city is hit especially hard by a recession, and its impoverished citizens begin to feel less socially tied to their fellow inhabitants. In one very poor neighborhood that was once lower-middle class but safe, crime rates have spiked and children are almost never seen playing outside. This situation is termed:

A) social poverty.

B) social degeneration.

C) anomie.

D) social exclusion.

1756. An individual who is a member of a higher socioeconomic class is more likely to:

I. have weak ties and a smaller network of connections.

II. have strong ties and a smaller network of connections.

III. have less social capital, since much has been spent on attaining his or her current high status.

IV. have more social capital, since more connected, wealthier people tend to wield more influence.

A) I only

B) II only

C) I and III

D) II and IV

Questions 1757–1758 rely on the figure below

In a 2011 study conducted by the U.S. Census, the national household wealth distribution was sampled and organized by racial or ethnic group. Some of the results of this census are summarized here.

Characteristic	Net Worth	Net Worth (Excluding Equity in Own Home)	Interest Earning Assets at Financial Institutions	Other Interest-Earning Assets	Regular Checking Accounts	Stocks and Mutual Fund Shares
AVERAGE HOUSEHOLD	68,828	16,942	2,450	18,181	600	20,000
White Alone	89,537	24,044	3,000	20,000	700	24,000
White Alone (Not of Hispanic Origin)	110,500	33,408	3,250	20,000	800	24,000
Black Alone	6,314	2,124	500	(B)	242	4,750
Asian Alone	89,339	29,339	4,500	(B)	900	19,000
Other (residual)	19,023	7,113	750	(B)	285	8,000
Hispanic Origin	7,683	4,010	700	(B)	300	8,000
Not of Hispanic Origin	84,680	22,280	3,000	20,000	652	20,000

1757. A sociologist notes that the disparity in net worth between racial groups can be partially attributed to inheritance. For example, the children of wealthy parents are likely to inherit money from family members. These children are then able to collect a down payment on a home, increasing their likelihood of eventually owning that home and considerably increasing their net worth. This process is cyclical, so wealth continues to be kept mainly within families and passed down to the next generation. According to this logic, in comparison to white families, Hispanic families are more likely to have:

A) strong ties.
B) less power.
C) more social capital.
D) less social capital.

1758. An economist who argues that liquid funds are the sole indicator of prosperity would consider which two racial groups to be approximately equally prosperous?

A) White and Asian
B) Asian and Black
C) White, Asian, and Black
D) All groups would be roughly equal in terms of financial success.

1759. A person's class consciousness can best be explained as:

A) her ability to discern where she lies within her familial hierarchy.
B) her cognizance of the social stratum in which she exists.
C) her willingness to strive for upward mobility.
D) her contentment with her current socioeconomic stratum.

1760. Johnny B. is a member of the lower middle class. What might be Johnny B.'s profession or employment status?

A) A craftsman who took college classes
B) A steelworker who didn't attend college
C) An unemployed member of his socioeconomic stratum, which comprises 20% of the total population
D) A newly hired clerk at an office supply store with no college education

Questions 1761–1763 rely on the figure below

Sociologists at the University of Townsville collected data regarding six different neighborhoods within Townsville from the U.S. Census Bureau and the local police department.

Neighborhood	Population	Annual homicide rate (per 1000)	Monthly gunshot reports	Employment rate (%)	Median household income	% White	% Black	% Latino	% Asian
Downtown	15,345	1.2	3.1	72.1%	$65,500	60	12	23	15
Upton Downs	15,678	0.2	0.4	73.4%	$54,300	80	4	5	11
Granville	11,231	7.4	25.4	49.7%	$21,300	4	70	25	1
University Park	7,567	0.5	2.1	59.9%	$41,200	50	15	15	20
Mira Vista	13,234	5.1	10.3	53.1%	$26,600	15	15	65	5
Chinatown	10,643	1.4	5.5	61.8%	$35,500	30	10	10	50

1761. Based on the table above, which of these neighborhoods is likely to have the lowest average birthweight?

   A) Chinatown
   B) Mira Vista
   C) Granville
   D) Upton Downs

1762. Using a completely randomized method, five individuals are chosen from each region. These people are then polled on a number of issues, including access to basic healthcare. Individuals from which neighborhood are most likely to lack health insurance?

   A) Mira Vista
   B) Downtown
   C) University Park
   D) Upton Downs

1763. Considering the information given, which of Massey and Denton's indices of segregation could be best estimated for Townsville?

   A) Exposure
   B) Concentration
   C) Clustering
   D) Centralization

1764. In some high-poverty, segregated neighborhoods, people struggle to find work and be socially mobile because they know few others near them who can connect them with job openings. This situation best relates to:

   A) a lack of cultural capital.
   B) social alienation.
   C) a lack of social capital.
   D) dependency.

Questions 1765–1766 rely on the table below

Some of the University of Townsville's statisticians aimed to explain the variance in lifespan among Townsville residents. To do so, they used regression models that incorporated various demographic variables. After determining that their results were significant, they constructed the following table.

Factor	Explained variance
Education	.22
Ethnicity	.10
Gender	.15

1765. Based on this table and on knowledge of the underlying phenomena, which of these individuals is likely to have the longest lifespan?

A) A white woman who dropped out of high school
B) A black man with a law degree
C) A black woman who is a college graduate
D) A Latino man with no high-school education

1766. Which demographic variable, when added to the model, has the potential to explain the most variance in lifespan?

A) Household size
B) Income
C) Genetic factors, such as oncogenes
D) Diet

Questions 1767–1768 rely on the figure below

A public health researcher in Townsville uses GIS mapping software to correlate soil lead level readings with the locations and demographics of several neighborhoods. A "safe" soil lead level is defined by the U.S. government as fewer than 300 parts per million (ppm). The GIS researcher also maps average atmospheric particulate concentrations in each region. His results are illustrated here.

Neighborhood	Population	% White	% Black	% Latino	% Asian	Average soil lead level (ppm)	Particulate level
Downtown	15,345	60	12	23	15	150.3	high
Upton Downs	15,678	80	4	5	11	100.7	low
Granville	11,231	4	70	25	1	385.8	medium
University Park	7,567	50	15	15	20	123.5	low
Mira Vista	13,234	15	15	65	5	293.5	high
Chinatown	10,643	30	10	10	50	189.3	medium

1767. Based on the above data, Townsville residents of which ethnicity are most at risk for developmental issues with language, working memory, and impulse control?

A) Black
B) Latino
C) Asian
D) It cannot be determined without more information.

1768. An epidemiologist is attempting to explain why Latinos have the highest risk of asthma in Townsville. Which of these facts is the LEAST relevant to this situation?

A) Granville and Mira Vista are historically industrial neighborhoods and retain a few factories to this day.
B) A major interstate highway was built through Mira Vista, Granville, and downtown Townsville in the 1960s.
C) Townsville International Airport is located in Mira Vista.
D) Granville is downwind of the Townsville Municipal Coal Plant.

1769. It has been hypothesized that the higher obesity rates in poor communities are due in part to a lack of fully-stocked grocery stores in these areas, leaving residents to rely on fast food and the cheap, high-calorie processed meals sold at convenience stores. This phenomenon is commonly referred to as:

A) economic segregation.
B) ghettoization.
C) the presence of food deserts.
D) social exclusion.

1770. Over the past few decades, industry has spread worldwide. While this transition has somewhat "flattened" the disparities in standards of living between regions of the world, it has also increased the inequality within countries. What term relates best to this major change?

A) Urbanization
B) Demographic transition
C) Globalization
D) Redistribution

1771. William, a fast-food worker, owes approximately $4500 on several credit cards. He attributes this financial situation to his mother and father, who tell him that credit cards are healthy and who lack any retirement savings. Which sociological concept does this situation illustrate?

A) Intergenerational mobility
B) Intragenerational mobility
C) Social reproduction
D) Social facilitation

Questions 1772–1773 rely on the figure below

Joseph Hickey and William Thompson, two sociologists, outlined the following breakdown of a particular nation's socioeconomic structure into five classes.

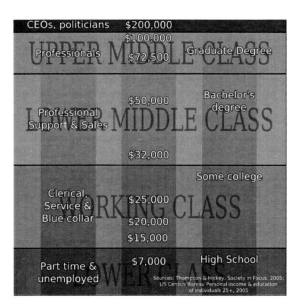

1772. What term can be used to describe the social structure of this nation?

A) A complete meritocracy with a class system
B) A partial meritocracy with a class system
C) A partial meritocracy with a caste system
D) An oligarchy with a class system

1773. Members of the uppermost strata according to this diagram likely possess:

A) low social capital and small networks with strong ties.
B) high social capital and small networks with weak ties.
C) high social capital and large networks with weak ties.
D) high social capital and small networks with strong ties.

1774. After reckless behavior and several arrests, a once-famous teen movie star is forced to declare bankruptcy. Five years later, she is working as a cashier and taking small, low-paying roles whenever she can get them. This situation exemplifies:

A) intergenerational mobility.
B) intragenerational mobility.
C) absolute poverty.
D) a caste system.

1775. James D., a bank executive, has a salary of two million dollars per year, plus bonuses when his division performs well. However, he lives in a neighborhood that contains even wealthier individuals from "old money" families. To which sociological term is this scenario most related?

A) Relative poverty
B) Absolute poverty
C) Both relative and absolute poverty
D) Neither relative nor absolute poverty

1776. The Wilson family lives in inner-city Detroit, where Mrs. Wilson (a single mother) makes $1800 per month. However, they spend a great deal of time with their neighbors, many of whom own houses and make approximately $40,000 annually. Mrs. Wilson and her four young children likely live in:

A) relative poverty.
B) absolute poverty.
C) both relative and absolute poverty.
D) neither relative nor absolute poverty.

1777. A family has lived in a Middle Eastern country for many years. While members of this family are very intelligent, they have been unable to rise above the rank of factory worker, and female members are banned from attending school. If these individuals were able, which of these actions would they likely take?

A) Emigrate from this nation to escape its caste system
B) Immigrate from this nation to escape its caste system
C) Emigrate from this nation to escape its meritocratic system
D) Immigrate from this nation to escape its meritocratic system

1778. A governmental or social system controlled by its wealthy members is specifically known as an:

A) oligarchy.
B) plutocracy.
C) bureaucracy.
D) partial meritocracy.

1779. A caste system and a meritocracy, respectively, are classified as:

A) two types of closed systems of stratification.
B) two types of open systems of stratification.
C) an open and a closed system of stratification.
D) a closed and an open system of stratification.

1780. How do the standards of living in a caste system differ from those in an open stratification system?

A) They do not; a caste system is a form of open system.
B) The standard of living for all citizens in a caste system is lower than the standard for individuals in an open system.
C) The standard of living for all citizens in a caste system is higher than the standard for individuals in an open system.
D) The standard of living for some citizens in a caste system is lower than the standard for those in an open system, but is higher for others.

1781. In a particular relationship, doubling thing A is shown to halve thing B, while reducing thing A notably increases thing B. How can this interaction be described?

A) The two factors are positively correlated, and thing A is the dependent variable.
B) The two factors are negatively correlated, and thing A is the dependent variable.
C) The two factors are positively correlated, and thing A is the independent variable.
D) The two factors are negatively correlated, and thing A is the independent variable.

1782. A researcher studying aging is examining the effect of grapefruit consumption on the breakdown of atorvastatin, a cholesterol medication. After deliberation, he opts to simultaneously test the relationship between grapefruit consumption and blood pressure in general. This researcher has:

A) added a new independent variable.
B) enhanced the power of his study.
C) added a new dependent variable.
D) added a potential confounding variable.

1783. When an experimental relationship is depicted in graph form, which axis usually corresponds to the independent variable(s)?

    A) The x-axis, and the dependent variable(s) are graphed on the y-axis
    B) The y-axis, and the dependent variable(s) are graphed on the x-axis
    C) Neither axis, but the dependent variable(s) are graphed on the y-axis
    D) Neither axis, but the dependent variable(s) are graphed on the x-axis

1784. Ideally, an experimental protocol should be designed to:

    A) remove confounding variables.
    B) remove moderating variables.
    C) remove both confounding and mediating variables.
    D) remove confounding, mediating, and moderating variables.

1785. Double-blind studies attempt to reduce the potential confounding effect of:

    A) the availability heuristic.
    B) confirmation bias.
    C) the social desirability bias.
    D) stereotype threat.

1786. Which of the studies listed below is most at risk of being confounded by the social desirability bias?

    A) A protocol that relies on self-submitted questionnaires from a carefully randomized group of participants
    B) A procedure in which heart rate is tested in a lab, but all participants are volunteers from the same university
    C) A setup that is entirely based on mathematical analysis of lab data, but only applies to a particular species of bacterium
    D) A clinical trial in which doctors, but not patients, know which participants receive a placebo

1787. Ecological validity is a form of:

    A) content validity.
    B) criterion validity.
    C) external validity.
    D) internal validity.

1788. A business psychologist is analyzing the relationship between the time of day and the security line at a typical airport. Across the United States, he notes that lines are significantly longer in the early afternoon than in the morning. However, in southwestern states, this relationship is hardly noticeable, while northeastern airports experience a drastic change from morning to afternoon. In this scenario, which type of variable is the state in which an airport is located?

    A) Confounding
    B) Dependent
    C) Moderating
    D) Mediating

1789. Which of these experimental protocols appears to have the highest external validity?

    A) A study that established a causal relationship between consumption of a rare fruit and development of a particular disease, with a p-value of <0.05
    B) A questionnaire about bipolar disorder in which every question was particularly relevant, but that was seen by very few participants
    C) A ten-year procedure that obtained a novel result, but that only applied to a tiny population in Africa
    D) A simplistic protocol that tested only one relationship, but that applied to students of a range of ages across the world

1790. In an attempt to determine whether Latino heritage makes one more likely to develop a certain spinal condition, researchers find a p-value of 0.07. If typical assumptions about statistical significance are made, which is true?

    A) The results are already statistically significant, as $p < 0.5$.
    B) The results are already statistically significant, as $p > 0.05$.
    C) The results are not statistically significant, and an increase in sample size has no chance of affecting the statistical significance of the results.
    D) The results are not statistically significant, but may become statistically significant if the sample size is increased.

1791. One cell line commonly used in biological research is the HeLa strain, which is derived from samples of a cancerous tumor from a woman named Henrietta Lacks. These cells are functionally immortal, in that they can divide indefinitely without dying, and were key to developing advances such as the polio vaccine. However, Mrs. Lacks was not informed that her cancer cells had been preserved before her death, and her family was surprised to find her medical records published without their knowledge years later. The case of Henrietta Lacks infringed on which principles of research ethics?

I.   Minimizing the risk of harm to subjects
II. Protecting the privacy and confidentiality of subjects
III. Obtaining informed consent

    A) I and II
    B) I and III
    C) II and III
    D) I, II, and III

1792. The "Tuskegee syphilis study" was an infamous experiment conducted by the U.S. government between 1936 and 1972. In this case, a large number of black male syphilitics were told that they would be receiving free treatment at clinics set up by the researchers. In reality, no members of the group were treated for syphilis, even after the discovery of penicillin as an effective cure, in an attempt to deliberately observe the progression of the disease in untreated patients. This study LEAST violated which tenet of research ethics?

A) Obtaining informed consent
B) Minimizing the risk of harm to subjects
C) Avoiding deceptive practices
D) Protecting the privacy and confidentiality of subjects

Questions 1793–1795 rely on the figure below

A sociology student is interested in preventative health. For a project, he surveys the residents of a local neighborhood about their healthcare habits and obtains the following results, broken down by income group as shown.

	Income over $50,000/year	Income $25,000-50,000/year	Income under $25,000/year
% with insurance	99%	94%	78%
% had physical exam in the past 12 months	62%	50%	29%
% had flu vaccine in the past 12 months	59%	43%	26%

1793. In regards to its participants, this is considered a:

A) longitudinal study.
B) cohort study.
C) cross-sectional study.
D) double-blind study.

1794. Suppose that the creator of this study decided to give the same survey to the same 1000 of the individuals from his original sample at yearly intervals to monitor changes in their healthcare use over time. Which term could properly be used to describe this new study design?

A) A retrospective study
B) A case study
C) A longitudinal study
D) An ecological study

1795. The student makes a final variation to the method for his procedure. Now, each year, he surveys individuals that live in this particular neighborhood to observe the ways that local healthcare trends change over time. This new design could most accurately be called a:

A) cohort study.
B) cross-sectional study.
C) retrospective study.
D) ecological study.

Questions 1796–1798 rely on the figure below

A Ph.D. wishes to establish a causal link between smoking and high blood pressure. To attempt this, he selects a random sample of 1241 individuals from the surrounding population, determines their overall rate of smoking (both regular and infrequent), and measures their blood pressures. The researcher then contacts the individuals from this initial sample every twelve months to determine how their blood pressure and smoking status change from year to year. After a total of 72 months, he obtains the results shown below. Note that all percentages represent the fraction of participants with high blood pressure, defined by the researcher as a reading of 140/90 or above.

Group	Year 1	Year 2	Year 3	Year 4	Year 5	Year 6
Daily smokers	16%	18%	20%	22%	24%	27%
Occasional smokers	12%	14%	15%	17%	18%	19%
Nonsmokers	11%	13%	14%	15%	16%	17%

1796. This study most closely exemplifies a:

A) longitudinal study.
B) cross-sectional study.
C) retrospective study.
D) case study.

1797. Imagine that the Ph.D. involved in this research instead wished to extend his data set backwards in time. For this reason, he collects medical records for the participants that include their smoking habits and blood pressure readings for many years prior to his initial testing. This change to the procedural design would cause this study to become a:

A) longitudinal study.
B) case study.
C) ecological study.
D) retrospective study.

1798. When aiming to establish a causal link between smoking and high blood pressure, it would be LEAST helpful to control for which of these listed variables?

A) Age
B) BMI
C) Gender
D) State of residence

1799. A certain genetic neurological syndrome is currently being studied to determine its effects on and interactions with other aspects of health. However, this syndrome is so rare that only approximately 1 in 500,000 neonates are born with it. Which type of study would a researcher of this condition benefit most from planning and executing?

A) An ecological study, as the living environments of those with the syndrome would yield a substantial amount of information

B) A case study, as the best approach here is to make a detailed study of a small number of individuals

C) A cohort study, as the researcher could thus examine the conditions of sufferers at a specific moment in time

D) A double-blind study, as that would minimize both conscious and unconscious bias on the part of the researcher

1800. The FDA is running a safety-and-efficacy trial for a new anti-cancer drug. To prevent either conscious or unconscious bias from influencing the treatment of the subjects, neither the researchers nor the patients involved are told who is given the experimental medication and who receives a known treatment with established safety and effectiveness. This type of information-handling procedure is best known as a:

A) single-blind study.
B) double-blind study.
C) case study.
D) clinical trial.

This page intentionally left blank.

Organic Chemistry

CHAPTER 7

1801. Which of the following are naturally occurring R-amino acids?

I. Glycine
II. Cysteine
III. Aspartic acid
IV. Proline

A) I only
B) II only
C) III and IV
D) II, III, and IV

1802. Which of the molecules below, if present in a 4 M aqueous solution, would not rotate plane-polarized light?

A)
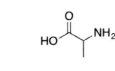

B)

C)

D)

1803. Of these statements, choose the one that is NOT true of chiral compounds.

A) Chiral centers are often carbon atoms, but can also exist around phosphorus or nitrogen.
B) All amino acids that are L in configuration are also S.
C) The direction of optical rotation cannot be determined by a molecule's R or S configuration alone.
D) A molecule with two or more chiral centers does not have to be optically active.

1804. A polycyclic species is shown below.

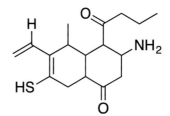

How many stereocenters are present in this molecule?

A) 5
B) 7
C) 9
D) 10

1805. An optically active molecule that rotates plane-polarized light clockwise reacts with methanol in solution via an S_N1 mechanism. In which direction will the product solution rotate plane-polarized light?

   A) Clockwise
   B) Counterclockwise
   C) No rotation will be observed.
   D) Optical rotation can only be determined experimentally.

Questions 1806–1807 rely on the table below

Sugar	Specific rotation
D-fructose	-92°
D-lactose	+52.3°

All measurements were obtained with a path length of 1 dm.

1806. In a mixed solution of D-fructose and L-fructose, if the observed optical rotation is -75.2°, what is the enantiomeric excess of D-fructose?

   A) 0.815%
   B) 39.1%
   C) 75.2%
   D) 81.5%

1807. The concentration of a dilute solution of D-lactose was determined to be 0.3 g/mL. What must be the observed optical rotation when this mixture is exposed to plane-polarized light?

   A) -27.6°
   B) -17.4°
   C) +15.69°
   D) +174.3°

1808. Which of the below molecules are designated as Z?

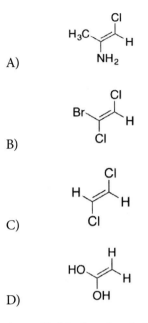

   A)

   B)

   C)

   D)

1809. A small chiral molecule is shown below.

Which of these structures represents the enantiomer of the above compound?

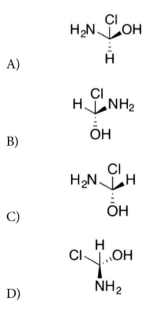

   A)

   B)

   C)

   D)

1810. Consider the species depicted below, with stereochemistry denoted in wedge-and-dash form.

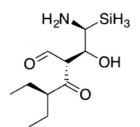

How many diastereomers of this molecule exist?

A) 3
B) 6
C) 8
D) 9

1811. The total number of possible structural isomers of pentane is:

A) two.
B) three.
C) four.
D) five.

1812. Isopentane and *n*-pentane are best described as:

A) configurational isomers.
B) conformational isomers.
C) geometric isomers.
D) enantiomers.

1813. All of the following are possible constitutional isomers of hexane EXCEPT:

A) *n*-hexane.
B) isohexane.
C) cyclohexane.
D) none of the above.

Questions 1814–1815 rely on the figure below

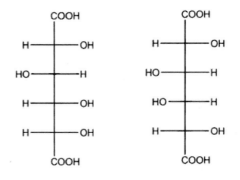

1814. In what way are these organic molecules related?

A) They are enantiomers.
B) They are diastereomers.
C) They are identical compounds.
D) They are structural isomers.

1815. What is true of the above compounds?

I.   They are impossible to separate via fractional distillation or extraction.
II. They most likely have at least somewhat different solubilities in aqueous solution.
III. Their physical properties are identical.

A) I only
B) II only
C) III only
D) I, II, and III

Questions 1816–1817 rely on the figure below

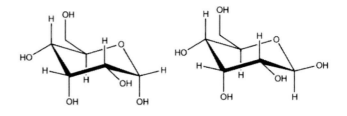

1816. The sugars shown above are most specifically described as:

A) anomers.
B) epimers.
C) configurational isomers.
D) all of the above.

1817. In order for the above sugars to be considered epimers, what would need to be true?

    A) They would need to display different configurations at a carbon other than the anomeric carbon.
    B) They would need to display different configurations at multiple carbons.
    C) One sugar would need to alter its configuration on at least two carbons.
    D) These structures are already epimers.

1818. The diagram below shows two straight-chain sugars in the form of Fischer projections.

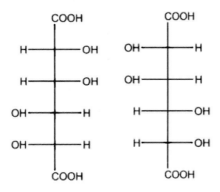

    These structures can be described as:

    A) enantiomers.
    B) meso compounds.
    C) diastereomers.
    D) identical molecules.

1819. Consider the structures shown below, with stereochemistry highlighted in dash-and-wedge form.

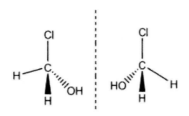

    Are these molecules identical, and would they rotate plane-polarized light in solution?

    A) No, they are not identical, and they do rotate plane-polarized light.
    B) Yes, they are identical, but they still rotate plane-polarized light.
    C) No, they are not identical, and they do not rotate plane-polarized light.
    D) Yes, they are identical, and they do not rotate plane-polarized light.

1820. Which of these methods constitutes a possible means of separating enantiomers?

    A) Distillation
    B) Recrystallization
    C) Reaction with a molecule like 1,5-pentanedial (glutaraldehyde)
    D) None of the above

1821. A high-school chemistry student is given a flask containing *n*-octane (boiling point = 125 °C). If she must react this compound in such a way as to raise its boiling point above 145 °C, what should she do?

    A) Use free-radical halogenation to add a chlorine atom to one of the compound's terminal carbons
    B) Utilize a Grignard reaction to further alkylate the compound, thus increasing its molecular weight
    C) Hydrolyze the compound into two smaller alkanes
    D) Isomerize the compound to make it more highly branched without changing its molecular formula

1822. One particular conformation of 1-bromopropane is shown below.

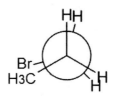

    This conformer can be described as:

    A) eclipsed and anti.
    B) staggered and gauche.
    C) fully eclipsed.
    D) staggered and anti.

1823. Which of these alkyl halides, under S$_N$1 conditions, would form the most stable carbocation?

A) 3-bromo-3-methylhexane
B) 4-chloro-2,2-di-*tert*-butylheptane
C) 1-bromodecane
D) 7-chloro-2,4,5-trimethyloctane

1824. In organic chemistry, radicals are extremely reactive species that possess at least one unpaired valence electron. In what order do the three steps of a radical reaction occur?

A) Propagation, initiation, termination
B) Initiation, termination, propagation
C) Termination, propagation, initiation
D) Initiation, propagation, termination

1825. Which of the following statements is true?

A) *Trans*-2-fluoro-3-iodohexane and *cis*-2-fluoro-3-iodohexane are geometrical isomers, with the former the more stable of the two.
B) *Trans*-2-fluoro-3-iodohexane and *cis*-2-fluoro-3-iodohexane are geometrical isomers, with the latter the more stable of the two.
C) *Trans*-2-fluoro-3-iodohexane and *cis*-2-fluoro-3-iodohexane are configurational isomers, with the former the more stable of the two.
D) *Trans*-2-fluoro-3-iodohexane and *cis*-2-fluoro-3-iodohexane do not exist.

1826. Consider the structures of *trans*-3-pentene and *cis*-3-pentene, two geometrically isomeric alkenes.

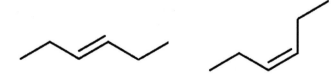

Which of these compounds is predicted to have the lower melting point?

A) *Trans*-2-pentene, because its molecules cannot stack as efficiently
B) *Trans*-2-pentene, because its molecules can stack more efficiently
C) *Cis*-2-pentene, because its molecules cannot stack as efficiently
D) *Cis*-2-pentene, because its molecules can stack more efficiently

1827. If you wish to promote an E2 reaction, you should use:

A) a substrate with an anti-periplanar hydrogen atom, a strong base, heat, and a polar aprotic solvent.
B) a substrate with an anti-periplanar hydrogen atom, a mild base, heat, and a polar aprotic solvent.
C) a tertiary substrate, a strong base, heat, and a polar aprotic solvent.
D) a tertiary substrate, a mild base, heat, and a polar protic solvent.

1828. A simple alkene is shown below.

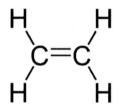

What is a non-IUPAC name for this structure?

A) Ethene
B) Ethylene
C) Acetylene
D) Ethyne

1829. Propyne is exposed to H$_2$ in a solution containing a chunk of solid platinum. If it reacts successfully, the original alkyne will:

A) be partially oxidized to form propene.
B) be partially reduced to form propene.
C) be fully oxidized to form propane.
D) be fully reduced to form propane.

1830. Dodeca-2,4,6,8-tetraene contains how many fewer pi bonds than sigma carbon-carbon bonds?

A) 4
B) 7
C) 11
D) 12

1831. A hydrocarbon with one pi bond is shown below.

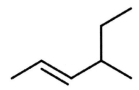

What is the IUPAC name for this molecule?

A) *Trans*-3-methyl-4-hexene
B) *Trans*-4-ethyl-2-pentene
C) *Trans*-4-methyl-2-hexene
D) *Trans*-4-methyl-3-hexene

1832. A fatty acid that contains three carbon-carbon double bonds, as well as one carbon-oxygen double bond, is termed a:

A) polyunsaturated fatty acid.
B) saturated fatty acid.
C) monounsaturated fatty acid.
D) tetraunsaturated fatty acid.

1833. When an alkene is exposed to HBr, the anti-Markovnikov product:

A) involves the bromine atom adding to the more substituted end of the alkene, and occurs during radical reactions.
B) involves the bromine atom adding to the more substituted end of the alkene, and occurs during the simple addition of HBr.
C) involves the bromine atom adding to the less substituted end of the alkene, and occurs during radical reactions.
D) involves the bromine atom adding to the more substituted end of the alkene, and occurs during the simple addition of HBr.

1834. Consider a reaction of the below molecule with hydrobromic acid.

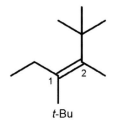

If a halogen atom were to add to this bond in Markovnikov fashion via reaction with HBr, to which labeled carbon would bromine attach?

A) Carbon 1, because it is more substituted
B) Carbon 2, because it is more substituted
C) Carbon 2, because it is less substituted
D) None of the above answers are accurate.

1835. The structure of anthracene, a cyclic compound, is shown here.

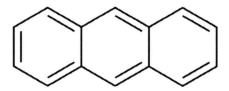

A chemist has a solution that is thought to contain this molecule, but also likely includes cyclohexane, 5-hydroxydecanoic acid, and propene. To detect the presence of any naphthalene, the chemist should use:

A) simple distillation.
B) acid-base extraction.
C) UV-Vis spectroscopy.
D) thin-layer chromatography.

1836. A number of organic chemistry students are conducting an experiment with the molecule below.

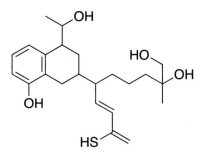

If they successfully react this species with $KMnO_4$ in aqueous conditions, which functional groups will the product contain?

I.   Alcohol
II. Ketone
III. Carboxylic acid
IV. Aldehyde

A) I only
B) II and III
C) I, II, and III
D) I, II, III, and IV

1837. Which of the combinations of reagents below will yield an aldehyde?

A)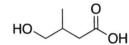

OH + PCC

B) O + Cr_2O_7 (acetic acid structure, OH)

C) OH + Cr_2O_7

D) OH + PCC

1838. A researcher hypothesizes that the carboxylic acid below may have potential applications in the fuel cells of electric cars.

According to IUPAC rules, the name of this molecule is:

A) 3-methyl-4-hydroxybutanoic acid.
B) 1-hydroxy-2-methylbutanoic acid.
C) 4-hydroxy-3-methylbutanoic acid.
D) 3,4-hydroxymethylbutanoic acid.

1839. In solution, water molecules can form a network of hydrogen bonds, a phenomenon that contributes to many unique properties. Molecules that have the ability to hydrogen bond with water include:

I. H_2N—...—O, OH

II. OH

III. HO—...

IV.

A) II only
B) II and III
C) I, II, and III
D) I, II, III, and IV

1840. The product of an oxidation reaction is shown below.

What is a possible identity of the original reactant?

A) 3-hydroxypentanoic acid
B) 1,4-pentadiol
C) 4-hydroxypentene
D) 4-oxopentanoic acid

1841. A pharmaceutical research team reacts a solution containing an unknown alcohol with $K_2Cr_2O_7$. When this reaction proceeds as desired, Cr^{6+} is reduced to Cr^{3+}, which is indicated by a color change from orange to green. However, the team noted that their solution exhibited no color change, which implies that:

A) the unknown alcohol must be primary.
B) the unknown alcohol must be tertiary.
C) the unknown alcohol is either primary or tertiary.
D) the unknown alcohol is either secondary or tertiary.

1842. A student is searching for the most acidic alcohol to facilitate a certain synthetic procedure. Of the molecules below, which is best suited for his purposes?

A)

B)

C)

D)

1843. Chromium trioxide (CrO_3) can be used to oxidize alcohols. Which of these species will be oxidized to the highest degree by CrO_3?

A) A primary alcohol
B) A secondary alcohol
C) A tertiary alcohol
D) All alcohols will be oxidized to the same degree.

1844. Equimolar amounts of the following alcohols are combined in aqueous solution. If the mixture is then heated, which compound would distill last?

A)

B)

C)

D)

1845. In general, alcohols are NOT known for:

A) acting as nucleophiles in the presence of an acidic catalyst.
B) serving as good leaving groups in substitution reactions.
C) their ability to exert strong intermolecular attractive forces.
D) remaining protonated at physiological pH.

Questions 1846–1847 rely on the figure below

Consider the following reaction scheme. The reaction proceeds in three experimentally-observable steps. Note that stereochemistry is deliberately omitted from the figure and need not be considered.

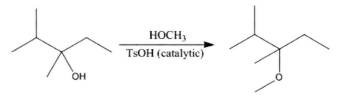

1846. The second step of this process results in the formation of a high-energy intermediate. The hybridization and molecular geometry of this species can best be described as:

A) sp^3 and tetrahedral.
B) sp^3 and trigonal planar.
C) sp^2 and trigonal planar.
D) sp^2 and bent.

1847. The first step of the reaction proceeds:

A) faster than the second, because it is a decomposition reaction.
B) faster than the second, because is a proton-transfer reaction.
C) slower than the second, because it is a decomposition reaction.
D) slower than the second, because it is a proton-transfer reaction.

1848. Though relatively slow, nucleophilic substitution reactions feature in a number of reaction schemes commonly employed in a laboratory setting. One such process, the Finkelstein reaction, involves the treatment of a primary alcohol with tosyl chloride, followed by addition of a halide salt. This series of steps permits the synthesis of a primary alkyl halide. Which of the following conditions would best optimize the speed and yield of the Finkelstein reaction?

A) Low pH with acetone as the solvent
B) Low pH with water as the solvent
C) Neutral pH with ethanol as the solvent
D) Neutral pH with dimethylformamide as the solvent

1849. A chemistry student is working with the organic molecule shown below.

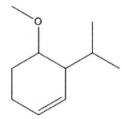

If she treats this species with 1-propyne in the presence of sodium hydride, the resulting reaction will proceed:

A) via an S_N2 pathway and yield 2-butyne, an organic salt, and hydrogen gas.
B) via an S_N2 pathway and yield a neutral organic derivative of the molecule shown, as well as methane and hydrogen gas.
C) via an S_N1 pathway and yield 2-butyne, an organic salt, and hydrogen gas.
D) via an S_N1 pathway and yield a neutral organic derivative of the molecule shown, as well as methane and hydrogen gas.

1850. The following image depicts an alcohol thought by researchers to have potential pharmaceutical applications.

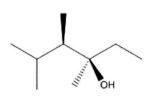

Treatment of this molecule with methanol under acidic conditions would most likely yield:

A) an enantiopure product.
B) a racemic mixture of products.
C) a meso product.
D) a mixture of diastereomers.

1851. How could one best increase the rate of reaction of 1-bromopropane with sodium cyanide?

A) By doubling the concentration of 1-bromopropane
B) By doubling the concentration of sodium cyanide
C) By acidifying the reaction medium
D) Both choices A and B would increase the reaction rate.

1852. Unlike S_N1 reactions, which require at least two steps, S_N2 reactions can proceed through a single transition state. This high-energy species is best described as:

A) pentavalent, because the nucleophile approaches from the side opposite the leaving group.
B) pentavalent, because the nucleophile approaches from the same side as the leaving group.
C) tetrahedral, because the nucleophile approaches the vacant orbital from the same side as the leaving group.
D) tetrahedral, because the nucleophile can approach the vacant orbital from either side of the species being attacked.

309

Questions 1853–1854 rely on the figure below

A chemist treats a sample of benzyl alcohol with one equivalent of sodium methoxide in an effort to produce the ether shown below. He is dismayed to find that this reaction yields almost none of the desired product.

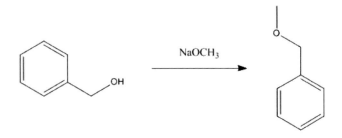

1853. The best explanation for the poor yield is that:

A) the electrophilic carbon is sterically hindered, preventing an effective nucleophilic approach.

B) the nucleophile is much too large to effectively coordinate at the electrophilic site.

C) the relative basicity of the nucleophile favors a proton transfer over a substitution.

D) the relative basicity of the nucleophile favors an elimination reaction over a substitution.

1854. Which of the following measures could potentially rescue the reaction and most effectively increase the yield of the desired product?

A) Treatment of the reactant with tosyl chloride and pyridine prior to the addition of sodium methoxide

B) Treatment of the reactant with tosyl chloride and pyridine following the addition of the sodium methoxide

C) Concurrent addition of tosyl chloride, pyridine, and sodium methoxide

D) Addition of acetic acid to the reaction mixture prior to addition of sodium methoxide

1855. A simple organic alcohol is treated with tosyl chloride. The resulting tosylate can best be described as:

A) a transition state, with a subsequent stable intermediate.

B) a stable intermediate, which can exist for some time in solution.

C) an unstable intermediate, which immediately undergoes rapid substitution.

D) an unstable intermediate, which typically undergoes spontaneous degradation.

1856. Which is more acidic, the proton on an –OH group or that present on an –SH group?

A) The proton on the –OH group, because oxygen is more electronegative than sulfur

B) The proton on the –OH group, because oxygen is smaller than sulfur

C) The proton on the –SH group, because sulfur is less electronegative than oxygen

D) The proton on the –SH group, because sulfur is larger than oxygen

1857. Isopropanol can be classified as:

A) a primary alcohol.

B) a secondary alcohol.

C) a tertiary alcohol.

D) a quaternary alcohol.

1858. Is *tert*-butoxide or ethoxide a stronger base?

A) Ethoxide, due to its electron-donating substituents

B) *Tert*-butoxide, due to its electron-donating substituents

C) *Tert*-butoxide, due to its electron-withdrawing substituents

D) Neither of these two compounds is basic.

1859. A student must demonstrate a substitution reaction for his laboratory partner. Specifically, he needs to conduct this reaction in such a way as to include the nucleophile in the rate-determining step. Which starting material and nucleophile should the student use, respectively?

A) A tertiary alkyl halide and a strong nucleophile

B) A tertiary alkyl halide and a moderate nucleophile

C) A primary alkyl halide and a strong nucleophile

D) A primary alkyl halide and a weak nucleophile

1860. Which of these solvents would be LEAST useful for a nucleophilic substitution reaction involving 3-bromo-3-methylheptane?

A) Acetone, due to its lack of an –OH or –NH bond
B) Ammonia, due to its basic tendencies
C) Ethanol, due to its ability to hydrogen bond
D) Water, due to its polar protic nature

1861. Which of the following statements is/are true?

I. The carbonyl carbon in an aldehyde is less sterically hindered than that of a ketone.
II. The carbonyl carbon in a ketone is more positively charged than in that of an aldehyde.
III. Aldehydes are more reactive than ketones.
IV. A C=O bond is shorter than a C=C bond.

A) I only
B) I and III
C) I, II, and IV
D) I, III, and IV

1862. Students in a chemistry lab are researching a certain ketone, shown in the figure below.

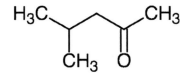

The correct IUPAC name for this structure is:

A) 4-methyl-2-pentanone.
B) 2-oxo-4-methylpentane.
C) 4,4-dimethyl-2-butanone.
D) 2-oxo-4,4-dimethylbutane.

1863. Of these structures, which does NOT contain an alpha hydrogen?

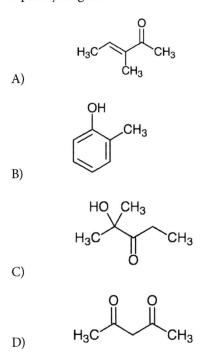

A)

B)

C)

D)

1864. A researcher is studying the effects of molecular structure on a variety of properties, including boiling point and acidity. Of the following compounds, which has the most acidic alpha proton?

A) Methyl propyl ketone
B) 2-hexanone
C) Acetylacetone
D) 2-butanone

1865. Place the following compounds in order of increasing boiling point: water, ethanol, methanol, and acetone.

A) Water, ethanol, acetone, methanol
B) Acetone, methanol, ethanol, water
C) Ethanol, methanol, acetone, water
D) Water, ethanol, methanol, acetone

Questions 1866–1867 rely on the figure below

A multi-step reaction is shown, in part, below.

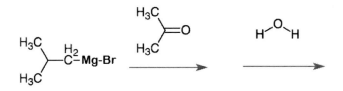

1866. The first step of this reaction can best be described as:

A) electrophilic substitution.
B) nucleophilic substitution.
C) nucleophilic addition.
D) electrophilic addition.

1867. How can the product formed by the overall reaction be most accurately characterized?

A) As a tertiary alcohol
B) As a secondary alcohol
C) As an acetal
D) As a ketone

Questions 1868 –1870 rely on the figure below

The following diagram shows several reactants and intermediates involved in a multi-step reaction.

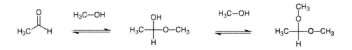

1868. Using the diagram above, correctly label the types of compound from left to right.

A) Aldehyde, alcohol, hemiacetal, alcohol, acetal
B) Ketone, alcohol, hemiketal, alcohol, ketal
C) Ketone, alcohol, hemiacetal, alcohol, acetal
D) Aldehyde, alcohol, hemiketal, alcohol, ketal

1869. If a laboratory researcher is attempting to conduct this reaction, which conditions should he use to facilitate the first step?

A) Acidic conditions only
B) Basic conditions only
C) Either acidic or basic conditions
D) Neutral conditions only

1870. After successfully completing the reaction, the researcher decides to regenerate the original reactants from the product molecules. What method will give him the best results?

A) Acid-catalyzed hydrolysis
B) Base-catalyzed hydrolysis
C) Addition of $NaIO_4$
D) In this case, no reverse reaction is possible.

1871. The figure below shows the simplest possible aldehyde.

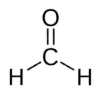

While this structure can be called by its IUPAC name of methanal, it is more commonly known as:

A) acetone.
B) acetylene.
C) acetaldehyde.
D) formaldehyde.

1872. What product is produced when 2-hexanol successfully reacts with chromium(III) oxide?

A) Hexanoic acid
B) 2-hexanone
C) Hexane
D) 1,2-hexanediol

1873. A pharmaceutical chemist is attempting to convert the molecule below into a primary alcohol for use in a nucleophilic substitution reaction.

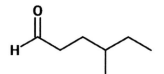

This could best be accomplished by:

A) adding the molecule to a dilute solution of $K_2Cr_2O_7$.
B) adding the molecule to a dilute solution of LAH.
C) reacting the molecule with one equivalent of propanal in water.
D) none of the above.

1874. Describe the basic procedure for synthesizing a Grignard reagent.

    A) Combine solid magnesium with an alkyl halide in diethyl ether and reflux.

    B) Combine solid magnesium with an alkyl halide in water and heat.

    C) Combine an alkyl magnesium compound with a halogen in diethyl ether and reflux.

    D) Combine an alkane with a diatomic halogen in water and heat.

1875. Which of the enol structures shown below is more stable than its ketone tautomer?

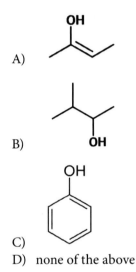

    A)

    B)

    C)

    D) none of the above

1876. A pharmaceutical chemist is studying the properties of the ion below.

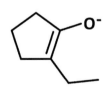

This structure represents:

    A) the kinetic enolate.

    B) the thermodynamic enolate.

    C) neither the kinetic nor the thermodynamic enolate.

    D) it is impossible to decide from the information given.

1877. Tautomerization can include conversion between:

    I. a ketone and an enol.

    II. an aldehyde and an enol.

    III. an enamine and an imine.

    IV. an enamine and an imide.

    A) I only

    B) I and II only

    C) I, II, and III

    D) I, II, and IV

1878. During the synthesis of a biologically relevant macromolecule, a chemist realizes that he has produced the thermodynamic enolate. In comparison to the kinetic enolate, this molecule has:

    A) a higher activation energy, but is more stable overall.

    B) a higher activation energy and is less stable overall.

    C) a lower activation energy, but is less stable overall.

    D) a lower activation energy and is more stable overall.

Questions 1879–1880 rely on the figure below

The following diagram depicts the general mechanism of an aldol condensation.

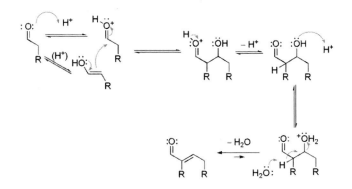

1879. The final product of the multi-step reaction above can best be described as:

A) an unsaturated dicarbonyl.
B) a saturated aldehyde.
C) a β,γ -unsaturated aldehyde.
D) an α,β-unsaturated aldehyde.

1880. The acid catalyst shown in this mechanism increases the rate of reaction by accomplishing which of the following?

A) increasing the electrophilicity of the carbonyl carbon
B) converting an oxygen atom into –OH to facilitate its immediate loss as a leaving group
C) converting the initial ketone to its enol tautomer
D) none of these; aldol condensations should not be acid-catalyzed.

1881. The hypothetical reaction shown below forms a coordination complex.

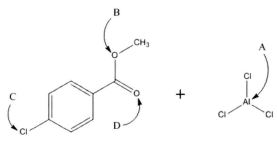

In the context of this process, which labeled atom represents the best nucleophile?

A) Atom A
B) Atom B
C) Atom C
D) Atom D

1882. Alpha helices display a measurable molecular dipole along their long axes. This property results from:

A) hydrogen bonding between spatially adjacent R groups on the exterior surface of the helix.
B) hydrogen bonding between backbone carbonyl oxygen atoms and protonated nitrogen atoms separated in sequence by several amino acid residues.
C) hydrogen bonding between backbone carbonyl oxygen atoms and protonated nitrogen atoms from amino acids that are directly adjacent in sequence.
D) hydrogen bonding between spatially adjacent R groups on the interior face of the helix.

1883. Consider the reaction scheme depicted below. The starting material is first treated with ethyl Grignard, after which the contents of the reaction vessel are quenched with a weak acid. Assume all reagents are present in molar equivalents.

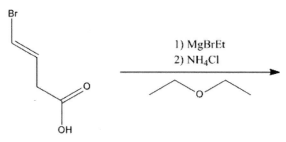

Considering the most likely product(s) of the given scheme, the reaction would best be described as a(n):

A) acyl transfer.
B) esterification.
C) addition reaction.
D) acid-base reaction.

1884. Which of these laboratory reagents would be most appropriate for the reduction of a carboxylic acid?

A) Lithium aluminum hydride
B) Sodium hydride
C) Sodium borohydride
D) Sodium cyanoborohydride

Questions 1885–1886 rely on the figure below

An organic chemist is especially interested in a certain carboxylic acid, depicted below. For the following questions, assume that the starting material is completely enantiopure.

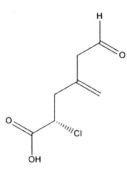

1885. Compared to the R group of aspartate, the conjugate base of this carboxylic acid would most likely be:

A) a weaker base, due to the inductive effect of the proximal chlorine atom.
B) a stronger base, due to the inductive effect of the proximal chlorine atom.
C) a stronger base, due to the potential for alternative resonance structures upon delocalization of chlorine lone pairs.
D) a weaker base, due to the potential for alternative resonance structures upon delocalization of chlorine lone pairs.

1886. The given carboxylic acid is reduced via reaction with excess lithium aluminum deuteride. Assume that the appropriate acidic workup is performed following this reduction. The final product(s) would best be described as:

A) a racemic mixture.
B) a mixture of two diastereomers.
C) a mixture of more than two diastereomers.
D) a single, unique product.

1887. The Krapcho decarboxylation provides a useful alternative to a traditional ester decarboxylation, which usually requires harsh acidic conditions

that could damage other valuable parts of the molecule. The Krapcho reaction is depicted below. Its first step involves an S_N2 attack by a halide ion, while the remainder of the reaction proceeds in a manner analogous to a traditional decarboxylation.

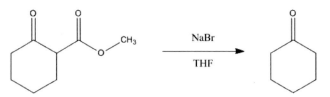

In addition to the major organic product, which side products would be formed in high concentrations during the reaction depicted above?

A) Carbon dioxide and methane
B) Carbon dioxide and water
C) Carbon dioxide and bromomethane
D) Carbon dioxide and methanol

1888. Generally, a free carboxylic acid is considered more electrophilic than its corresponding:

A) aldehyde.
B) acyl chloride.
C) amide.
D) ketone.

1889. A scientist contemplates the reaction of benzoic acid with ammonia, with the intention of synthesizing the corresponding amide via a nucleophilic substitution reaction. As one might expect, this reaction is rather slow. However, the formation of the amide product is thermodynamically favorable. Which of the following reagents, if added to the reaction vessel, is likely to increase the speed of this reaction?

I. Titanium tetrachloride, a Lewis acid
II. Acetic acid, a weak Brønsted acid
III. Palladium on carbon, a metallic catalyst

A) I only
B) II only
C) I and II
D) II and III

1890. Fischer esterification is easily achievable in acidic solution. An organic chemistry student plans to conduct such a reaction with the species shown below.

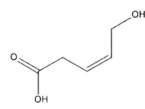

Which conditions should be used to obtain the highest possible yield of the desired cyclic ester product?

A) Hydrochloric acid in water
B) Anhydrous sulfuric acid
C) Hydrochloric acid in ethanol
D) Sulfuric acid in water

1891. Carboxylic acid derivatives include:

A) aldehydes and ketones.
B) amides and ethers.
C) esters and nitro groups.
D) thioesters and acyl halides.

1892. An organic chemist must choose a compound with the best possible leaving group for a tricky synthesis reaction. Of the following, he should use:

A) butanoyl chloride.
B) propanamide.
C) acetyl iodide.
D) acetic anhydride.

Questions 1893–1894 rely on the figure below

Propionic anhydride, shown below, is a molecule with a variety of synthetic applications. A team of scientists is focusing on the compound due to its role in the production of fentanyl, a powerful opioid used as an analgesic.

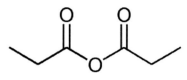

1893. Which of these reactions or multistep syntheses could produce the compound above?

A) Heat two equivalents of ethanoic acid in water.
B) Combine methyl propionate with propanol, then expose to heat and H_2SO_4.
C) Mix propionic acid with PCl_5, then extract the product; finally, combine it with additional propionic acid and heat.
D) Expose a dilute solution of propionic acid to heat, then add water, acid, and reflux for 25 minutes.

1894. Of the choices below, the only one that is LESS reactive than propionic anhydride is:

A) hexanamide.
B) NH_2^-.
C) propionyl bromide.
D) ethoxide.

1895. What is a possible explanation for the high stability of amides in comparison to acid anhydrides?

A) The leaving group on an amide is resonance-stabilized, while that of an anhydride is destabilized by a negative charge.
B) The leaving group on an amide is NR_2^-, which is highly reactive in comparison to the anhydride's carboxylate ion.
C) The nature of the nitrogen atom allows it to be equally electron-withdrawing as the surrounding alkyl substituents.
D) None of the above; amides are actually less stable than anhydrides.

1896. If you were to rank the carboxylic acid derivatives from least to most reactive, your list would include:

A) acyl halides before acid anhydrides, and acid anhydrides before amides.
B) amides before acid anhydrides, and acid anhydrides before acyl halides.
C) anhydrides before esters, and esters before acyl halides.
D) amides before esters, and acyl halides before carboxylic acids.

1897. The figure below shows a lactone, or cyclic ester.

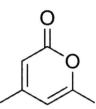

Which combination(s) of reagents could yield this compound?

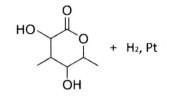

I.

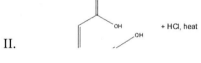

II.

+ HCl, heat

III.

OH ... + ... O ... + heat

A) I only
B) II only
C) I and III
D) II and III

1898. Cephalexin (a β-lactam antibiotic) and β-propiolactone most likely share which of the following features?

A) Both contain at least one ester group.
B) Both contain at least one amide group.
C) Both contain at least one cyclic ring.
D) Both contain at least three oxygen atoms.

1899. After conducting a synthesis of ethyl ethanoate, your chemistry professor decided that he is unhappy with the identity of this product.
If he knows that he can fix the issue using transesterification, which reagent might he add to his existing solution?

A) Methyl propionate
B) Ethanol
C) Hexanol
D) Water

1900. A theoretical reaction between acetic anhydride and one equivalent of ammonia is shown below.

In this process, what are the leaving group and nucleophile, respectively?

A) The leaving group is $C_2H_3O_2^-$, while the nucleophile is NH_3.
B) The leaving group is C_2H_3O, while the nucleophile is NH_3.
C) The leaving group is NH_3, while the nucleophile is C_2H_3O.
D) This reaction does not involve a nucleophilic attack.

1901. Urea, a metabolic waste product, contains which of the following functional groups?

I. Amide
II. Imide
III. Imine

A) I only
B) II only
C) I and III
D) II and III

1902. Methyl acetate is:

A) a three-carbon ether.
B) a three-carbon ester.
C) a four-carbon ester.
D) a four-carbon ether.

1903. With regard to leaving group alone, which of these species is the LEAST unstable?

A) Propionyl bromide
B) Propionyl iodide
C) Propionyl fluoride
D) Propionyl chloride

1904. If you wish to conduct a series of reactions beginning with 2-methylheptanoic acid, but fear that it is insufficiently reactive, you should:

A) expose it to PCl_5.
B) expose it to SOCl.
C) add it to aqueous solution.
D) react it with ethanol.

1905. Imipenem is a β-lactam antibiotic with a number of uses, including the treatment of *Pseudomonas* infections. The structure of imipenem must contain:

A) at least one oxygen atom, but no heterocyclic rings.
B) more than two heterocyclic rings.
C) at least one heterocyclic ring.
D) at least one nitrogen atom, but no heterocyclic rings.

1906. For an organic chemistry assignment, a student must carry out a reductive amination. If his starting reagent is an aldehyde, his product should be an:

A) enamine.
B) amine.
C) imide.
D) imine.

Questions 1907–1908 rely on the figure below

A chemist performs a standard reaction, the first step of which is depicted below.

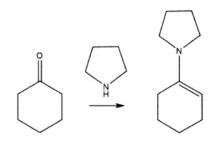

1907. The product of the above step is an:

A) imide.
B) amide.
C) enamine.
D) enamide.

1908. If the chemist reacts the depicted product with the smallest possible beta-unsaturated ketone, what species should form?

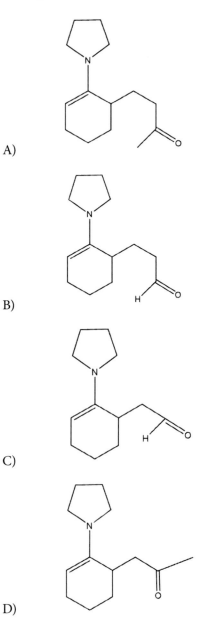

A)

B)

C)

D)

1909. The compound $(HC_2O)_2N(C_2H_5)$ can best be described as an:

A) imine.
B) imide.
C) enamine.
D) amide.

1910. Which of these listed compounds has the lowest pK$_b$?

A) Ammonia
B) *M*-chloroaniline
C) Aniline
D) Ethylamine

1911. The mixture of ethylamine and propionyl chloride should create:

A) N-ethylpropionamide.
B) N-propylethionamide.
C) aryl propionamide.
D) a primary amine.

Questions 1912–1913 rely on the figure below

The structure of penicillin has a characteristic β-lactam structure at its center, as shown here.

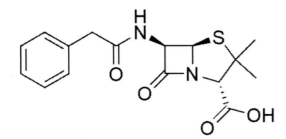

1912. Which of the following statements regarding the β-lactam structure is true?

A) It is composed of a thionyl enamine.
B) The bond between the nitrogen and the carbonyl carbon is able to rotate freely.
C) Significant ring strain exists.
D) The presence of an amide stabilizes the otherwise strained cyclic structure.

1913. All of these are true of the β-lactam functionality in particular, EXCEPT that:

A) it contains an amide.
B) the sigma bonds in the ring can rotate.
C) only one π bond is found in the structure.
D) its nitrogen-containing functional group can be hydrolyzed.

1914. The reaction of formaldehyde and cyanide should form a:

A) cyanate.
B) secondary amine.
C) tertiary amine.
D) cyanohydrin.

1915. Which of these molecules is a possible product of acid-catalyzed amide hydrolysis?

A) Diethylamine
B) Pentanal
C) 2-hexanone
D) Benzenamine

1916. In order to synthesize a quinone compound, a phenol must be:

A) oxidized.
B) reduced.
C) decarboxylated.
D) hydrolyzed.

1917. All of the following are true of a typical quinone EXCEPT that:

A) it contains two carbonyl groups.
B) it is aromatic.
C) it is conjugated.
D) it can be formed via reduction using CrO$_3$.

Questions 1918–1919 rely on the figure below

Phenol can undergo a series of redox reactions to eventually form hydroquinone. The first step of this process is shown below.

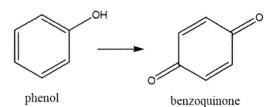

phenol   benzoquinone

1918. After a chemist finishes synthesizing benzoquinone, she wants to reduce her product to form hydroquinone. What is the structure of this product?

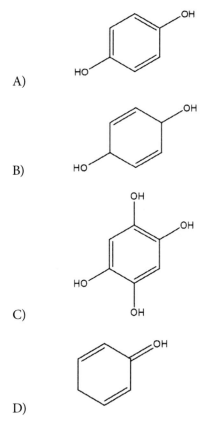

A)

B)

C)

D)

1919. Ubiquinone, commonly referred to as coenzyme Q, is classified as a type of benzoquinone. Which of these statements regarding ubiquinone are true?

I.   It is polycyclic.
II. It is conjugated.
III. It can be reduced.
IV. It can be oxidized.

   A) I and IV
   B) II and III
   C) I, II, and III
   D) I, II, III, and IV

1920. A student attempts to isolate a product from a reaction flask by taking advantage of differing acidities. If she knows that the flask contains an alcohol, a carboxylic acid, a phenol, and an amine, and if she plans to separate the compounds in order of decreasing acidity, how many other species will remain in the flask after she isolates the phenol?

   A) None
   B) One
   C) Two
   D) Three

1921. Polysubstitution of a phenol is best facilitated by using:

   A) a polar solvent.
   B) a nonpolar solvent.
   C) a molecule with electron-withdrawing substituents.
   D) a molecule with electron-donating substituents.

1922. Furan, a small organic compound used in many synthesis reactions, is:

   A) a molecule with an oxygen that is sp hybridized.
   B) a molecule with an oxygen that is sp^3 hybridized.
   C) a heterocyclic, nitrogen-containing species.
   D) a heteroaromatic species.

1923. Which of the following compounds has a conjugate base with the highest pK_b?

A)

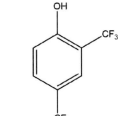

B)

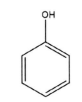

C)

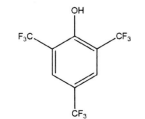

D)

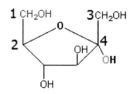

1924. Trichlorophenol can be synthesized by reacting phenol with:

A) chlorine and carbon disulfide.
B) chlorine and chromium trioxide.
C) acyl chloride and water.
D) chlorine and water.

1925. Consider the conjugate bases of these four compounds: an alcohol, a phenol, a carboxylic acid, and an amine. Which of these rankings correctly orders these species in terms of most to least basic?

A) Amine > alcohol > phenol > carboxylic acid
B) Amine > phenol > alcohol > carboxylic acid
C) Amine > alcohol > carboxylic acid > phenol
D) Amine > phenol > carboxylic acid > phenol

Questions 1926–1927 refer to the figure below

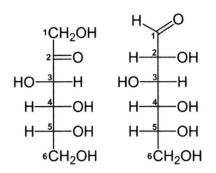

1926. How can the two molecules above be described in relation to each other?

A) Anomers
B) Epimers
C) Diastereomers
D) Structural isomers

1927. Which of the following carbohydrates is NOT an epimer of the molecule on the right?

A) Fructose
B) Galactose
C) Mannose
D) Allose

Questions 1928–1929 rely on the figure below

1928. This molecule can be described as a(n):

A) aldohexose.
B) ketopentose.
C) aldopentose.
D) ketohexose.

1929. Which carbon is the anomeric carbon?

A) C1
B) C2
C) C3
D) C4

1930. Cellulose differs from starch in that cellulose includes a(n):

A) α-1,4 acetal linkage.
B) β-1,4 acetal linkage.
C) α-1,6 acetal linkage.
D) β-1,6 acetal linkage.

1931. Lactose intolerance is common in some ethnicities. In fact, lactose tolerance is thought to be an adaptive trait that spread through the human population as cow milk became an increasingly large part of the human diet. Lactose intolerance is caused by adult deactivation of lactase synthesis. The lactase enzyme cleaves bonds between:

A) galactose and fructose.
B) galactose and mannose.
C) galactose and glucose.
D) glucose and fructose.

Questions 1932–1933 rely on the figure below

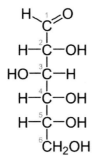

1932. If this carbohydrate were to isomerize into a furanose, the –OH group on which carbon would form a hemiacetal with Carbon 1?

A) C4
B) C5
C) C6
D) An acetal, not a hemiacetal, would form.

1933. To form maltose, the above sugar would form an α-1,4 linkage with:

A) glucose.
B) fructose.
C) galactose.
D) mannose.

1934. A scientist adds acid to an aqueous solution of 100% α-D-glucopyranose. What is he most likely to find in solution when he examines it again in a few hours?

A) 100% α-D-glucopyranose
B) 64% α-D-glucopyranose and 36% β-D-glucopyranose
C) 36% α-D-glucopyranose and 64% β-D-glucopyranose
D) 100% β-D-glucopyranose

1935. A glycoprotein might have an oligosaccharide chain composed of all of the following EXCEPT:

A) mannose.
B) glucose.
C) deoxyribose.
D) galactose.

1936. A simple disaccharide, maltose, is shown below.

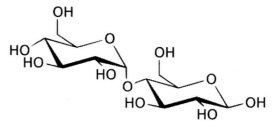

Which of these enzymes is most likely capable of hydrolyzing maltose?

A) Glucoinvertase, a brush-border enzyme with specificity for α-1,4 linkages
B) Sucrase-isomaltase, an enzyme expressed in erythrocytes with specificity for α-1,6 linkages
C) Cellulase, an enzyme produced by some fungi with specificity for β-1,4 linkages
D) β-1,6 glucanase, which is specific for β-1,6 linkages

1937. Scientists at a clinical research lab are particularly interested in the following carbohydrate.

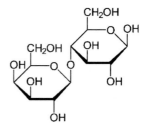

Immediately following an initial proton transfer, acid-catalyzed hydrolysis of this disaccharide will proceed through:

A) an sp³-hybridized oxonium intermediate.
B) an sp²-hybridized oxonium intermediate.
C) a secondary carbocation intermediate.
D) a secondary carbanion intermediate.

Questions 1938–1939 rely on the figure below

A complex multi-ring compound is generated during the course of a synthetic pathway.

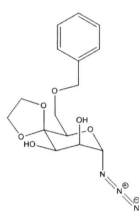

1938. Suppose the chemist responsible for synthesizing this species is concerned about possible side reactions involving the naked alcohol moieties. While leaving the rest of the molecule untouched and causing limited complications, protection of these groups would be most effectively achieved with:

A) acetic acid and catalytic sulfuric acid.
B) acetyl chloride and pyridine.
C) sodium hydride and methyl iodide.
D) tosyl chloride and sodium hydroxide.

1939. Conversion of the ketal group to a ketone could be accomplished by adding:

A) potassium *tert*-butoxide.
B) lithium aluminum hydride.
C) sodium hydroxide.
D) aqueous sulfuric acid.

1940. For the organic molecule shown below, stereochemistry has been deliberately omitted.

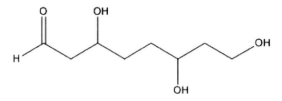

Treatment of this species with aqueous sulfuric acid would yield a major product best described as:

A) a bicycle containing one 7-membered ring and one 6-membered ring.
B) a bicycle containing one 6-membered ring and one 5-membered ring.
C) a bicycle containing two 6-membered rings.
D) a bicycle containing one 7-membered ring and one 5-membered ring.

1941. This is the structure of a simple ketal, a compound containing two oxygen atoms bound to the same carbon.

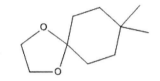

This molecule is treated with sulfuric acid in a solution of water labeled with ^{15}O. The products of the complete hydrolysis reaction will be:

A) a diol containing one ^{15}O and one ^{16}O and a ketone containing one ^{16}O.
B) a diol containing two ^{16}O atoms and a ketone containing one ^{15}O.
C) a diol containing one ^{15}O and one ^{16}O and a ketone containing one ^{15}O.
D) a diol containing two ^{15}O atoms and a ketone containing one ^{15}O.

Questions 1942–1943 rely on the figure below

The structure of sucrose, a dimer of glucose and fructose, is shown in the following figure.

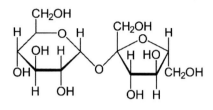

1942. The unique nature of the glycosidic linkage present in sucrose renders it resistant to hydrolysis, unlike that of other common disaccharides. Sucrase, a brush-border enzyme, rapidly increases the ordinarily sluggish degradation of sucrose into its component monosaccharides. Alternatively, sucrose may be hydrolyzed using:

A) Tollens' reagent.
B) hydrochloric acid.
C) sodium borohydride.
D) potassium hydroxide.

1943. The two monomeric subunits of sucrose are best described as:

A) structural isomers.
B) diastereomers.
C) enantiomers.
D) epimers.

1944. A number of common sugars can undergo a series of reactions that ultimately result in the formation of acrylamide, a neurotoxin. These processes, which occur during cooking and baking, are known as the Maillard reactions. One of the many steps of the Maillard reactions is depicted below.

Considering that this step occurs fairly early in the overall reaction pathway, which of these sugars is LEAST likely to participate in the Maillard reactions?

A) Fructose
B) Glucose
C) Galactose
D) Sucrose

1945. Glycogen is a highly branched carbohydrate composed of glucose monomers. While the majority of its synthetic workload is managed by glycogen synthase, the first step involves the addition of UDP-glucose to glycogenin, a process catalyzed by glycogenin itself. As glycogen synthase continues to add glucose monomers, glycogenin remains bound to the initial glucose unit, serving as a sort of scaffold for the growing glycogen polymer. The first step in glycogen synthesis is shown below; note that the liberation of UDP is not shown here.

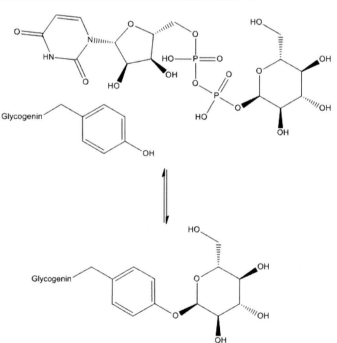

A biochemist obtains a pure sample of human glycogen. When he adds Tollens' reagent to his sample, he observes:

A) the generation of a silver mirror, as glycogen possesses exposed reducing ends.
B) the absence of a silver mirror, as glycogen possesses exposed reducing ends.
C) the generation of a silver mirror, as glycogen lacks exposed reducing ends.
D) the absence of a silver mirror, as glycogen lacks exposed reducing ends.

1946. An unsaturated free fatty acid must contain:

I.   an alkene or alkyne.
II. an ester.
III. a carboxylic acid.

    A) I only
    B) III only
    C) I and II
    D) I and III

1947. The species below undergoes a reaction analogous to the saponification of a triglyceride.

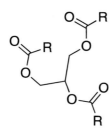

How many equivalents of NaOH / H_2O are required to drive this process to completion?

    A) 1
    B) 2
    C) 3
    D) None; this molecule will not react.

1948. Lipids are an important component of cell membranes. Which pair of terms lists a class of lipids that is necessary to maintain membrane fluidity and one that is used as markers for cell signaling, respectively?

    A) Triacylglycerols, cholesterols
    B) Phospholipids, waxes
    C) Cholesterols, glycosphingolipids
    D) Sphingolipids, cholesterols

1949. The glycerol backbone of a triacylglycerol is attached to three fatty acids via:

    A) ester bonds.
    B) disulfide linkages.
    C) carbon-carbon double bonds.
    D) ether linkages.

1950. Reactions are favorable when they increase the overall entropy of a system. Which class of lipids will have the most positive entropy when dissolved in water? Assume that the water itself does not react with any of these choices to form new molecules.

    A) Triacyglycerols
    B) Cholesterols
    C) Phospholipids
    D) Waxes

1951. The beginning of fatty acid synthesis, shown below, proceeds via nucleophilic addition.

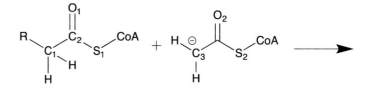

In this process, which numbered atom acts as the nucleophile and which acts as the electrophile, respectively?

    A) O2 and C2
    B) S2 and C2
    C) C3 and S1
    D) C3 and C2

1952. All of the following statements regarding the saponification of triacylglycerols are true EXCEPT:

    A) it yields two fatty acid salts and a glycerol molecule.
    B) it is the reverse of the esterification reaction between fatty acids and glycerol.
    C) it is a hydrolysis reaction.
    D) it utilizes OH⁻ ions for nucleophilic attack on carbonyl carbons.

1953. A biochemistry researcher is studying the potential laboratory applications of the molecule below.

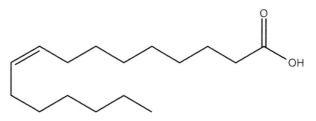

The correct name for this fatty acid is:

    A) *cis*-9-hexadecenoic acid.
    B) *cis*-10-hexadecenoic acid.
    C) *trans*-7-hexadecenoic acid.
    D) *trans*-9-hexadecenoic acid.

1954. A researcher has discovered a genetic disorder in plants that causes them to lose water through excess evaporation. The scientist noted that this condition is characterized by a deficiency in a certain class of lipids. Affected plants are most likely lacking:

A) cholesterols.
B) waxes.
C) free fatty acids.
D) glycosphingolipids.

1955. The diagram below depicts a macromolecule called a ganglioside.

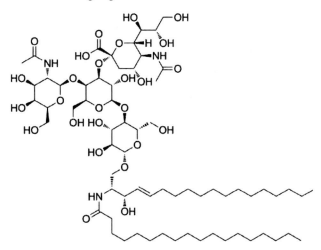

Tay-Sachs disease is caused by an accumulation of gangliosides in the brain. Based on the structure of this molecule, it is potentially a derivative of:

A) a cholesterol.
B) a phospholipid.
C) a free fatty acid.
D) a wax.

1956. What is the advantage of vacuum distillation over simple distillation?

A) Vacuum distillation is able to separate compounds with extremely similar boiling points.
B) Vacuum distillation provides suction to physically move the compound with the lower boiling point up the distillation column.
C) Vacuum distillation separates compounds that typically are not found in the liquid phase.
D) Vacuum distillation facilitates the separation of compounds with extremely high boiling points.

1957. A lab director emphatically tells his organic chemistry students to conduct a certain separation procedure using fractional distillation. Which two compounds might these students be separating?

A) Caprylic acid ($C_7H_{15}COOH$) and capric acid ($C_9H_{19}COOH$)
B) Heptanol and 2-methylbutanol
C) Hexanol and 2-methylpentanol
D) Octanoic acid and hexane

1958. Todd is attempting to finish an extraction begun by his lab partner. At this time, his separatory flask contains water and toluene, with benzylamine, 1,3-diphenylacetone, and phenol dissolved in the toluene layer. To separate out the benzylamine, he should add:

A) sodium hydroxide.
B) hydrobromic acid.
C) additional water.
D) potassium bicarbonate.

1959. One popular analytical procedure is thin-layer chromatography (TLC) involving a hexane mobile phase and a plate coated in silica gel. Which of the molecules below will adhere best to the plate?

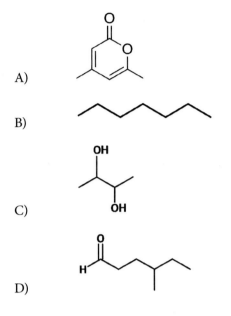

A)

B)

C)

D)

1960. Vacuum distillation aids in the separation of compounds because:

A) a compound will boil when its vapor pressure is greater than its partial pressure in the liquid mixture.
B) a compound will boil when its vapor pressure is equal to ambient pressure.
C) the addition of a nonvolatile solute to a liquid typically lowers boiling point.
D) the addition of a nonvolatile solute to a liquid typically increases boiling point.

Questions 1961–1963 rely on the figure below

A Ph. D. student conducts a TLC procedure to comparatively analyze three different compounds, labeled below as X, Y, and Z. He uses a silica stationary phase and a toluene solvent.

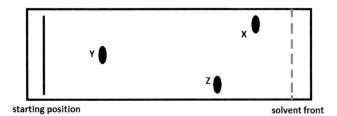

1961. According to the diagram above, the compound with the lowest R_f is:

    A) Compound X, because it is the smallest distance from the solvent front.

    B) Compound X, because it interacts the most favorably with the stationary phase.

    C) Compound Y, because it is the least polar.

    D) Compound Y, because it interacts least favorably with the solvent.

1962. The identities of Compounds X, Y, and Z, respectively, could be which of the following?

    A) Compound X = diphenyl; compound Y = oxalic acid; compound Z = propanol

    B) Compound X = glutaric acid; compound Y = ethane; compound Z = aniline

    C) Compound X = 1,2-propanediol; compound Y = pentanoic acid; compound Z = hexane

    D) Compound X = diethyl ether; compound Y = chloroform; compound Z = pentane

1963. The Ph. D. student discovers that compound Y is actually propanoic acid. An undergrad intern attempts to repeat the procedure, but his sample of Y is contaminated by substantial amounts of acetic acid and butanoic acid. Assuming that his other samples are pure, how will his results likely appear?

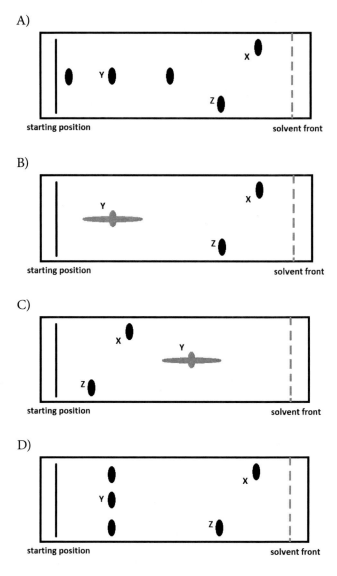

1964. In most forms of gas chromatography:

    A) the stationary phase is a gas, such as helium, while the mobile phase is a liquid on a solid, inert support structure.

    B) the stationary phase is a gas, such as hydrogen or oxygen, while the mobile phase is a liquid on a solid, inert support structure.

    C) the mobile phase is a gas, such as helium, while the stationary phase is a liquid on a solid, inert support structure.

    D) the mobile phase is a gas, such as hydrogen or oxygen, while the stationary phase is a liquid on a solid, inert support structure.

1965. Which solvent would be most suitable for the recrystallization of molecule 1, a solid collected after a synthesis procedure? Note that the known melting point for molecule 1 is 168 °C and the sample collected is displaying a melting point of 164-167°C.

   A) Solvent A, in which molecule 1 is very soluble at 80°C but far less soluble at 19.5°C
   B) Solvent B, in which molecule 1 is highly (and equally) soluble at all temperatures
   C) Solvent C, in which both molecule 1 and its common impurities are fairly soluble at 80°C but insoluble at 19.5°C
   D) None of the above; recrystallization either would not work or is not necessary for the purification of this sample.

1966. Which of these molecules would display little to no observable activity on an IR spectrum?

   A) Carbon dioxide
   B) Methane
   C) Nitrogen
   D) Nitric oxide

1967. While carbon dioxide exhibits four vibrational modes in space, its experimentally-obtained IR spectrum shows no more than two distinct peaks. This is partly because:

   A) the two oxygen nuclei exhibit nuclear spins that are equal in magnitude but opposite in direction.
   B) three of the vibrational modes are considered energetically degenerate.
   C) one of the vibrational modes is not observable by IR spectroscopy.
   D) two of the vibrational modes are not excitable by IR spectrometers of conventional power.

1968. In contrast to conventional X-ray crystallography, which provides information about inert systems, variations of NMR spectroscopy are frequently used to follow molecular processes in real time. For example, heteronuclear single quantum coherence (HSQC) may be employed to examine the binding of a small organic molecule to its protein target. HSQC probes the nuclear spin of a heteronucleus, typically nitrogen, after magnetic excitation of a nearby hydrogen nucleus. This interaction between these two nuclei, known as the nuclear Overhauser effect, is most likely:

   A) propagated through sigma bonds.
   B) propagated through pi bonds.
   C) propagated through space.
   D) propagated through solvent molecules.

1969. An organic molecule of particular significance is shown below.

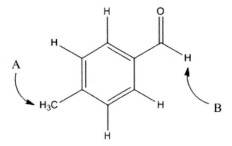

Compared to the hydrogen nucleus labeled A, the nucleus labeled B is considered:

   A) more shielded, and would thus display a peak shifted farther left on an NMR spectrum.
   B) less shielded, and would thus display a peak shifted farther left on an NMR spectrum.
   C) more shielded, and would thus display a peak shifted farther right on an NMR spectrum.
   D) less shielded, and would thus display a peak shifted farther right on an NMR spectrum.

1970. Phenytoin is a medication used to treat seizure disorders and a number of cardiac arrhythmias. The structure of this drug is shown below.

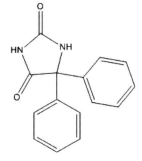

On the H¹ NMR spectrum for phenytoin, how many distinct peaks would be visible? Keep in mind that labile protons (such as those on the amide functional group) exchange rapidly with those of the solvent and that NMR samples are usually dissolved in $DCCl_3$.

A) One peak
B) Two peaks
C) Three peaks
D) Four peaks

1971. Compared to IR spectroscopy, ultraviolet-visible spectroscopy:

A) involves the induction of electronic excitations, and consequently exposes the sample to higher-energy light.
B) involves the induction of electronic relaxations, and consequently exposes the sample to lower-energy light.
C) relies on the unique vibrational energies of specific chemical bonds, requiring a higher incident energy.
D) relies on the unique vibrational energies of specific chemical bonds, requiring a lower incident energy.

1972. The structure of ethidium bromide (EtBr) is shown below. This molecule is a useful laboratory reagent because it can be induced to fluoresce under certain coordination conditions. It is also a known teratogen.

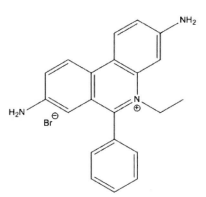

Considering the structure of EtBr, it would be most useful for staining an electrophoresis sample consisting of:

A) DNA that has been treated with sodium dodecyl sulfate.
B) DNA that has been run on a gel in its native state.
C) mRNA that has been treated with sodium dodecyl sulfate.
D) protein that has been run on a gel in its native state.

1973. Historically, mass spectrometry was used to characterize small organic compounds and simple salts. Recently, however, this technique has been applied to a much broader array of interesting molecules, including large proteins. Debate exists regarding the accuracy of the resulting data. Those who object to the use of mass spectrometry for the characterization of large proteins would most likely posit that:

I. the sample is likely to be damaged by the ionization process necessary to propel it through the device.
II. proteins in the gas phase exhibit marked structural differences compared to their native state in solution.
III. exposure to massive amounts of X-ray radiation destroys the sample too rapidly for any usable data to be obtained.
IV. the inherently static nature of solid-phase protein samples provides little insight into their biological behavior.

A) I only
B) I and II
C) I and III
D) II, III, and IV

1974. Collision-induced dissociation (CID) is a technique based on the principles of mass spectrometry that involves the bombardment of ionized molecules in the gas phase with neutral gas atoms. This method is often used to generate small peptide fragments of 20-30 residues from larger protein samples, but can also result in the creation of unpredictable free radicals. The resulting fragments can be readily sequenced and the data can be combined to elucidate the sequence of the original protein. This process is most analogous to:

A) SDS-polyacrylamide gel electrophoresis.
B) high-performance liquid chromatography.
C) Edman degradation.
D) native polyacrylamide gel electrophoresis.

1975. Traditional mass spectrometry most directly measures which of the following values?

A) The atomic mass of the sample
B) The mass-to-charge ratio of the sample
C) The charge density of the sample
D) The mass of the most abundant isotope in the sample

1976. A sample of nonanoic acid is analyzed using nuclear magnetic resonance (NMR) spectroscopy. Which of this molecule's protons will exhibit a peak that is farthest upfield?

A) The proton(s) on carbon 9, which will display a shift of around 1.0 ppm
B) The proton(s) on carbon 9, which will display a shift of around 11.5 ppm
C) The proton on the –COOH group, which will display a shift of around 1.0 ppm
D) The proton on the –COOH group, which will display a shift of around 11.5 ppm

1977. Of the following molecules, which is most likely to be analyzed using ultraviolet-visible spectroscopy?

A) Acetylene
B) Bicyclopropane
C) Cyclodecapentaene
D) Isopropanol

1978. Unlike IR spectroscopy, UV-Vis spectroscopy is:

A) reliant on the use of longer-wavelength light.
B) reliant on the use of higher-energy radiation.
C) less likely to be used to detect molecules like dodeca-2,4,6,8-tetradiene.
D) more likely to separate compounds on the sole basis of net charge.

1979. The organic molecule shown below is currently under study by a team of research chemists.

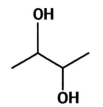

On the H^1 NMR spectrum for this species, how many distinct peaks should be visible?

A) 2 peaks
B) 3 peaks
C) 6 peaks
D) 10 peaks

1980. A chemist uses mass spectrometry to analyze an unknown sample. Along with an M^+ peak at approximately 102, he notes several peaks, one of which corresponds to an m/z value of 17. Of the listed choices, this sample is likely:

A) 2-pentanone, and the peak at m/z = 17 corresponds to a methyl group.
B) 2-pentanone, and the peak at m/z = 17 corresponds to a propyl group.
C) 3-hexanol, and the peak at m/z = 17 corresponds to a methyl group.
D) 3-hexanol, and the peak at m/z = 17 corresponds to a hydroxyl group.

This page intentionally left blank.

CHAPTER 8

Graph Practice

Questions 1981–1983 rely on the figure below

Wild-type *E. coli* is able to synthesize the amino acids needed for its own survival, a condition known as prototrophy. In contrast, some mutated *E. coli* strains are classified as auxotrophs, meaning that they have been rendered incapable of synthesis of one or more biomolecules. The table below depicts the growth patterns of four of these strains on various media. Note that (+) indicates growth, while (-) indicates a failure to grow or survive.

Medium	Strain A1	Strain A2	Strain A3	Strain A4
Phe⁺ Tyr⁺ Lys⁻	(+)	(-)	(+)	(+)
Phe⁻ Tyr⁺ Lys⁻	(-)	(-)	(-)	(+)
Phe⁻ Tyr⁻ Lys⁻	(-)	(-)	(-)	(+)

1981. Strain A1:

  A) can properly synthesize its own phenylalanine.
  B) cannot properly synthesize its own phenylalanine.
  C) cannot properly synthesize its own lysine.
  D) None of the above can be determined without more information.

1982. Given the data in the table alone, which of these amino acids can we NOT assess the ability of Strain A2 to synthesize?

  A) Lys only
  B) Phe only
  C) Phe and Tyr
  D) Lys, Phe, and Tyr

1983. Due to a mix-up with the cultures, it is discovered that one of the four strains is actually wild-type *E. coli*. This strain is most likely:

  A) A1.
  B) A2.
  C) A3.
  D) A4.

Questions 1984–1985 rely on the figure below

The Meyer-Overton correlation represents a breakthrough finding in the study of general anesthetics. Its two namesakes independently discovered a relationship between the minimum alveolar concentration required to achieve anesthesia and the solubility of the relevant compound in olive oil, a value that is denoted below as the olive oil: gas partition coefficient.

The Meyer-Overton correlation for anesthetics

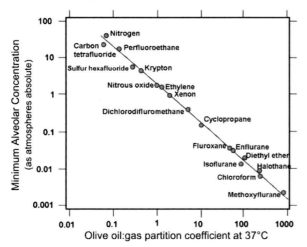

1984. If a modern researcher were to map a similar correlation between minimum alveolar concentration and solubility in distilled water, he would likely observe:

A) a correlation coefficient of between 0.5 and 1.

B) a correlation coefficient of 0.

C) a correlation coefficient of between -0.5 and -1.

D) a correlation coefficient of -1.

1985. In Meyer and Overton's experiments, what was the independent variable?

A) Minimum alveolar concentration

B) Anesthetic potency

C) Olive oil: gas partition coefficient

D) None of the above

Questions 1986–1987 rely on the figure below

Consider the general appearance of the following correlation matrix.

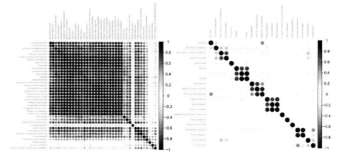

1986. Why does each matrix feature a dark-colored diagonal line ranging from the top left to the lower right?

A) Because the correlation between one variable and itself is always 1

B) Because the correlation between one variable and itself is always 0

C) Because these figures are set up to centrally feature the main independent/dependent relationship

D) Because these results were statistically significant

1987. The upper left quadrant of the left-hand matrix:

A) features more values that are positively correlated than the lower right quadrant.

B) features more values that are negatively correlated than the lower right quadrant.

C) features more values that are either positively or negatively correlated than the lower right quadrant.

D) features more values with near-zero correlation coefficients than the lower right quadrant.

1988. Consider the Michaelis-Menten graph shown below. Assume that the x-axis is measured in units/L, while the y-axis is given in s⁻¹units/L.

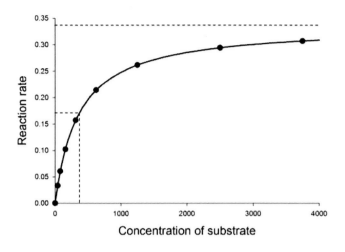

With regard to this plot, which of these statements is true?

A) When [S] <<< 1000 units/L, the reaction is zeroth order with regard to its substrate.

B) When [S] >>> 4000 units/L, the reaction is zeroth order with regard to its substrate.

C) When [S] >>> 4000 units/L, the reaction is first order with regard to its substrate.

D) This enzyme-catalyzed reaction is always first order with regard to its substrate.

1989. Reagent A combines with protons in a 1:1 ratio in an extremely favorable reaction. If this mechanism is first order in both Reagent A and H⁺, what is the relationship between solution pH and reaction rate?

A) Direct and linear
B) Direct and exponential
C) Inverse and exponential
D) Inverse and linear

1990. The typical progression of an enzyme-catalyzed reaction is shown below. Enzyme and substrate are placed in a glass vessel and left undisturbed for several minutes.

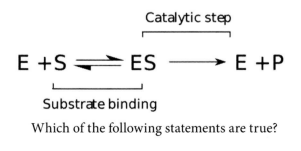

Which of the following statements are true?

I. When [E] increases, [ES] must simultaneously decrease.
II. When [P] increases, [S] must simultaneously decrease.
III. Both [S] and [ES] can increase at the same time.

A) I only
B) II only
C) I and II
D) I and III

1991. A nonviscous fluid is traveling through a network of tubes at equal height, but differing in their radii. Which graph best depicts the relationship between the hydrostatic pressure in a vessel and the square of the velocity through which fluid moves at that specific point?

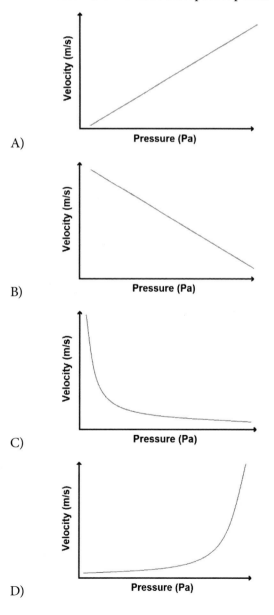

1992. A microwave is dropped off a hotel balcony by an unruly rock star in the midst of one of his "episodes." Assume that air resistance has a negligible effect.

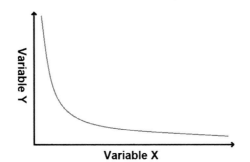

If the above graph relates to characteristics of the microwave's fall before it hits the ground, to what might Variables X and Y refer?

A) Variable Y is acceleration, while Variable X is the height of the microwave with respect to the ground.

B) Variable Y is velocity, while Variable X is the distance that the microwave has fallen at the relevant instant in time.

C) Variable Y is velocity, while Variable X is the height of the microwave with respect to the ground.

D) Variable Y is time, while Variable X is acceleration.

1993. How does the radius of curvature of a convex lens relate to its power?

A) The two quantities are directly proportional, and can be related using the equation r = 2/P.

B) The two quantities are directly proportional, and can be related using the equation r = P/2.

C) The two quantities are inversely proportional, and can be related using the equation r = P/2.

D) The two quantities are inversely proportional, and can be related using the equation r = 2/P.

1994. A petroleum engineer is conducting a series of calculations regarding a proposed drilling pipeline. First, he needs to find the velocity of oil through the pipe, which requires knowledge of its cross-sectional area.

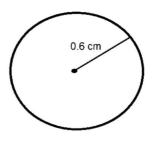

In SI units, what is the approximate area of this circular region?

A) 1.1×10^{-8} m^2

B) 1.1×10^{-4} m^2

C) 3.6×10^{-1} m^2

D) 3.6×10^{-1} cm^2

Questions 1995–1997 rely on the figure below

An exercise physiologist surveys a cohort of individuals regarding the frequency at which they engage in at least 45 minutes of heavy exercise. She then measures the resting heart rate of each participant and plots it on the following set of axes.

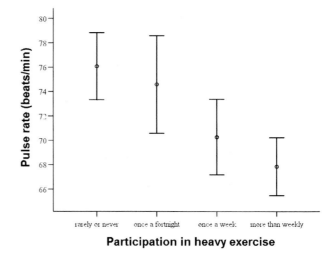

1995. Considering solely the participants who exercised at least once per week, what can be concluded?

A) Exercising more than once per week lowered resting pulse rate in comparison to exercising only once per week.

B) Exercising more than once per week raised resting pulse rate in comparison to exercising only once per week.

C) Exercising more than once per week increased cardiovascular health in comparison to exercising only once per week.

D) None of the above can be concluded.

1996. What change might the physiologist implement to her procedure to increase the odds that her data will be statistically significant?

A) Use a smaller p-value as a cut-off for statistical significance

B) Increase the sample sizes of all four of her experimental groups

C) Add a component to the study that measures the effect of body weight on pulse rate

D) Decrease the sample sizes of at least two of her experimental groups

1997. A second scientist mimics this experiment with only the "rarely or never" and the "once per fortnight" exercise groups. Interestingly, she arrives at nearly identical results. Based on the results in the figure, for the hypothesis that exercising once each fortnight is enough to at least somewhat decrease pulse rate, which of the following is the most likely p-value?

A) p = 0.01
B) p = 0.049
C) p = 0.4
D) p = 1.5

1998. A psychology student has marked the below graph as "important," but seems to have forgotten to label its axes while dozing off in the lecture hall.

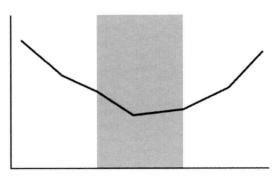

What might the x- and y-axis of this plot represent?

A) X-axis – quality of performance; y-axis – arousal

B) X-axis – arousal; y-axis – quality of performance

C) X-axis – likelihood that a particular word would be recalled; y-axis – position in a list of words

D) X-axis – position in a list of words; y-axis – likelihood that a particular word would be recalled

Questions 1999–2000 rely on the figure below

Consider the population pyramid of Angola (below), taken from census data corresponding to the year 2005.

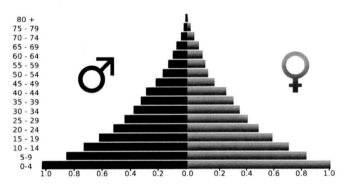

1999. In 1995, in which stage of demographic transition was Angola likely to be?

A) Stage 1
B) Stage 2
C) Stage 3
D) Stage 4

2000. From this figure, what conclusion can be drawn about the Angolan population in 2005?

A) A larger number of individuals are 40 years of age or older, rather than 39 or younger.

B) The likelihood that any one member of the population is a 45-year-old female is 0.4%.

C) It is technically possible for more 43-year-olds to be present in the population than 31-year-olds.

D) Since this diagram does not include non-native Angolans, it lacks a good deal of useful information regarding actual demographics.

2001. The graph below gives the risk of post-traumatic seizure (PTS) as a function of the severity of a traumatic brain injury (TBI).

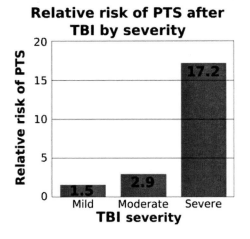

Relative risk of PTS after TBI by severity

What is the identity of the dependent variable, and which is the control group?

A) The dependent variable is PTS risk, and the control group is mild severity.
B) The dependent variable is PTS risk, and the control group is not shown.
C) The dependent variable is TBI severity, and the control group is mild severity.
D) The dependent variable is TBI severity, and the control group is moderate severity.

1. B is correct. DNA is structured with the nitrogenous bases on the inside of the helix, connected by H-bonds; this makes choice I true. Choice III correctly identifies the radius of a typical DNA helix as 20 angstroms.

   II: The sugar in DNA is deoxyribose, not ribose.
   IV: Purines bind to pyrimidines in double-stranded DNA.

2. B is correct. A nucleoside contains both a sugar and a nitrogenous base, but unlike a nucleotide, it does not include phosphate groups. Additionally, the sugar involved is either ribose or deoxyribose, both of which have five carbons.

3. A is correct. The sequence given represents part of the sense strand, which is not directly transcribed into mRNA. Instead, it is its complementary partner, the antisense strand, that is transcribed, meaning that the sense strand has the same sequence and directionality as the mRNA (but with uracil instead of thymine).

   B, D: These sequences include thymine, which is not present in RNA.
   C: This sequence is complementary to the fragment given. However, the resulting RNA should be complementary to the antisense strand, not the sense strand.

4. D is correct. Both adenine and guanine are purine bases, which have structures composed of two fused rings. In contrast, pyrimidine structures contain only one ring. A purine-purine base pairing would thus be wider than the typical purine-pyrimidine pairing.

   A, C: These statements incorrectly identify adenine and guanine as pyrimidines.
   B: This incorrectly states that the purine-purine base pairing would be narrower.

5. B is correct. We are told that each sample being tested should have a single mutated base pair. All of the choices are very close to the complement of the noncoding sequence given, but B has two base pairs that are mutated instead of one.

6. A is correct. The T_m is the point at which the dsDNA strand is 50% denatured. Choice A correctly estimates the T_m for each of the three samples based on the data seen in the graph.

   B: The T_m is incorrectly identified here as the point at which the strands are 90% denatured.
   C: While the numbers are correct here, Sample 1 and Sample 2 are mixed up.
   D: Here, the T_m is wrongly identified as the temperature at which 10% of the sample is denatured.

7. C is correct. From the experimental results, we can tell that Sample 3 has the highest T_m, followed by Samples 2 and 1, respectively. The question states that Sample 1 has the lowest cytosine content, while Sample 3 has the highest. Remember that G-C base pairs have three hydrogen bonds and A-T pairs have two. This makes DNA with a higher G-C content more difficult to denature.

8. C is correct. Though we are only given the percentage of adenine, we know that it should be identical to the percentage of thymine (35%), since the two always pair together. Similarly, the cytosine and guanine content must be equal. Finally, all the percentages should add up to 100%. $100 - 2(35) = 30$, leaving us with 15% for C and the same for G.

9. A is correct. For an organism to live at such high temperatures, its DNA must be very stable and resistant to denaturation. A higher G-C content leads to stronger DNA due to the increased number of hydrogen bonds between the strands. Sample A contains the DNA with the highest G-C content.

10. D is correct. We are looking for characteristics that resemble those of DNA. DNA is able to form a long, stable polymer of nucleotides. It can also be replicated with a high rate of accuracy, and it codes for mRNA, which is later translated into protein.

11. B is correct. Telomerase is required for DNA replication, as it contributes to maintaining the integrity of the genome. Because DNA polymerase reads the template from 3' to 5' and can only begin replication where a primer has been established, the 3' ends of chromosomes generally are not replicated. Telomerase adds a repeating sequence to prevent these ends from shortening during every

replication cycle. Ligase is also necessary, and has the role of joining the Okazaki fragments on the lagging strand.

I: *Taq* polymerase has a bacterial origin and is used in PCR, not natural human cells.
IV: Transcriptase enzymes are involved in transcription, not replication.

12. C is correct. In semiconservative replication, the parent dsDNA is denatured so that each strand can be used as a template to form a new piece of DNA. As a result, the two dsDNA products of the first replication will each contain one strand of original DNA and one new strand. After the fourth replication, a total of 16 dsDNA molecules will exist, or 32 single strands. Of those molecules, only two of them come from the original parent DNA. Thus, our fraction is 2/32, or 1/16.

13. D is correct. A dideoxynucleoside triphosphate lacks an -OH group at both its 2' and 3' positions. Since DNA polymerase requires a free 3' –OH to continue replication, ddNTPs serve as inhibitors of the chain elongation. In other words, incorporation of a ddNTP results in the termination of replication.

    A: Primers bind to the gene of interest and signal where DNA polymerase should attach. Primers are required for both strands of the dsDNA molecule.
    B: Heat-resistant *Taq* polymerase is the most common "lab polymerase" enzyme used in PCR reactions.
    C: Magnesium-containing buffer serves as a cofactor for *Taq* polymerase. Specifically, it stabilizes the negative charges on the two strands, which would otherwise repel each other.

14. B is correct. DNA polymerase catalyzes the elongation of new DNA strands. However, this enzyme cannot initiate DNA synthesis on its own, as it can only bind to a free –OH group that is already present on the developing strand. RNA primers provide these free 3' hydroxyl groups.

    A: While the replication fork does initially form at the site where replication begins, it then moves along the strands as they are unwound by helicase. The fork does not relate to the direct function of primers.
    C: Both parent strands are used as templates during DNA replication.

D: This more closely relates to the function of helicase.

15. A is correct. Telomerase adds the sequence "TTAGGG" to the 3' end of each telomere to compensate for DNA polymerase's inability to replicate the ends of chromosomes. Without telomerase, the chromosomes would gradually shorten.

    B, C: Neither reannealing nor supercoiling relates to telomerase.
    D: Since this condition is X-linked, males only need one copy to express the disease phenotype.

16. C is correct. The initiation process requires that the double helix be unwound and the hydrogen bonding between base pairs be broken. Initiation proteins target AT pairs because only two hydrogen bonds form between the bases, requiring less energy to break than the three H-bonds that connect guanine and cytosine.

    A: Both AT and GC pairs include one purine and one pyrimidine.
    D: Since DNA replication requires denaturation of the double helix, an inert structure would be an undesirable site to initiate the process. Inert compounds are unreactive and would be difficult to denature.

17. B is correct. This situation is possible, and in fact describes how retroviruses generally synthesize DNA. Eukaryotic DNA polymerase requires a free 3' -OH group, which is provided by a short RNA strand synthesized by primase enzymes. Retroviruses, on the other hand, use reverse transcriptase to form DNA from an RNA template. The retrovirus in the question lacks a primase and instead uses reverse transcriptase to elongate the 3' OH provided by the tRNA.

    A: tRNA does not mimic any enzymatic function.
    C: While this is true, it does not answer the question. Reverse transcriptase has a DNA polymerase activity and initiates synthesis by binding to a specific tRNA.
    D: Viruses do not contain ribosomes or other organelles.

18. B is correct. DNA polymerase is only able to read DNA from 3' to 5' and synthesize it from 5' to 3'. Point B represents the 5' end of the parent

DNA, which corresponds to the 3' end of the new strand. Thus, Point B is the location at which DNA polymerase will be forced to move away from the replication fork (from left to right).

A: This is the 3' end of the parent DNA, which corresponds to the 5' end of the new strand. The leading strand will form at this position.
C, D: At these locations, the parent double helix is still intact. No replication will occur there until the DNA is unwound.

19. D is correct. While the leading strand of DNA can be replicated continuously, the lagging strand must be synthesized in segments known as Okazaki fragments. This occurs because DNA polymerase can only read template DNA from 3' → 5', meaning that it can only elongate new strands from 5' → 3'. If this mutated polymerase could work in either direction, the lagging strand would be synthesized in an identical manner to the leading strand.

B: Normally, DNA polymerase reads template DNA from 3' to 5' and can only begin replication where a primer already exists. Because of this, the 3' ends of chromosomes generally are not replicated, and must be acted upon by telomerase to prevent shortening. If the polymerase could act in either direction, if anything, the telomeres should shorten less.
C: In normal replication, ligase activity is greater on the lagging strand because it must connect the Okazaki fragments. The absence of these fragments would reduce ligase involvement.

20. C is correct. This statement accurately describes a difference between the initiation of transcription and that of replication.

A: Transcription uses a DNA-dependent RNA polymerase; we can remember this because it requires a DNA transcript but catalyzes the lengthening of an RNA strand. Additionally, this choice does not specifically relate to the first step of these processes.
B: While this statement is true, it describes the elongation step of replication and the final product of transcription. The question specifically referenced initiation.

21. B is correct. A truncated protein product will form as the result of a nonsense mutation, or the replacement of a normal codon with a premature stop codon. In humans, the three stop codons are

UAA, UAG, and UGA. First, divide each given sequence into three-nucleotide segments. In choice I, one of these codons is UAA, while option III contains UGA.

II: While this sequence does include a UAA segment, it is split between codons, with the uracil nucleotide part of one codon and the two adenines present in another.
IV: Similarly, this choice contains UAG, but not as a single codon.

22. C is correct. While multiple proteins can stem from a single mRNA transcript, this is due to alternative splicing, not the triplet genetic code.

A, B, D: All of these statements identify strengths of the triplet code. The fact that each codon correlates to no more than one amino acid gives the code specificity. Degeneracy makes it possible for some point mutations to occur without changing the final protein product. Finally, the use of three bases allows for efficient recognition of a sequence and production of its corresponding protein.

23. B is correct. DNA resides in the nucleus, the organelle in which it is transcribed into mRNA. The finished mRNA transcript then enters the cytosol, where it is translated into protein at a ribosome.

A: This choice switches the names for the processes of transcription and translation.
C: Translation does not occur in the nucleus.
D: Transcription does not occur in the cytosol. D is incorrect because it states that the DNA starts outside of the nucleus.

24. A is correct. An anticodon is part of a tRNA molecule. It is able to bind to a corresponding codon because it possesses a complementary RNA sequence.

B: The lock-and-key model better describes enzyme-substrate interactions.
C: Since a codon is a three-nucleotide segment of RNA, its binding to an anticodon occurs via complementary RNA base pairing.
D: This statement is simply untrue.

25. B is correct. While there is no need to memorize the entire genetic code, remember that the most likely place for a silent mutation to be found is in the third base of a codon. The sequence in choice

B has two mutations, but both are found in this third, or "wobble," base. In fact, the two point mutations are identical, meaning that if one is silent, the other must be too.

A, D: Both of these choices contain only a single mutation, but neither is found in the third base of a codon. Mutations to the first or second base typically result in a change to the protein product. C: This is a nonsense mutation, which will truncate the protein.

26. D is correct. The table matches amino acids to their mRNA codons. However, we are given part of the sense DNA strand, which has the same sequence as the mRNA except with thymine instead of uracil. Converting this sequence to mRNA thus yields 5' UUUUUCGUG 3'. Starting from the 5' end and consulting the table gives our polypeptide in the N-to-C direction.

    A: The proper second codon is UUC (phenylalanine), not UUG (leucine). B: The sequence here represents the proper region of the polypeptide, but in the C-to-N direction. C: This answer would be correct if the given sequence had represented part of the antisense DNA.

27. A is correct. This mRNA sequence gives rise to part of a polypeptide consisting of histidine, serine, and glutamic acid. Histidine is basic, while glutamic acid is acidic; serine, while neutral, is highly polar. Remember, regions rich in polar residues are likely exposed to the solvent on the exterior or interior face of the plasma membrane. Only positioning within the cytosolic domain of the protein would make this possible.

    B, C, D: These choices identify hydrophobic areas of a transmembrane protein. It is highly unlikely for many basic, acidic, or neutral polar residues to appear in this region.

28. D is correct. Each codon consists of three consecutive nucleotides. At each position, one of four nitrogenous bases may be present. For this reason, the total number of distinct codons is 4^3 or 64.

    B: Due to the degeneracy of the genetic code, many more than 20 codons are able to exist. Some codons simply correspond to the same amino acid as others.

29. C is correct. "Wobble" base pairings, in which the third nucleotide of an anticodon is not complementary to the third base of its associated codon, are less stable than those that bind according to Watson and Crick rules. It therefore makes sense for the less stable codon-anticodon pairs to use a wobble form of pairing.

    A: These are the codons that experience more stable, not less stable, interactions.

30. D is correct. Retroviruses are positive-sense ssRNA viruses. These pathogens have a single-stranded RNA genome that must be reverse transcribed to form DNA. The DNA is then transcribed into RNA and used to synthesize viral proteins.

    A: Archaebacteria, like other prokaryotes, have DNA in their genomes. As such, they do not serve as an exception to the process described by the question stem. B: Fungi are eukaryotes, which follow the central dogma mentioned in the question. C: The term "DNA" should give away the fact that these pathogens are more likely to follow typical rules for the interpretation of genetic material than those in choice D.

31. C is correct. Since the mutant protein runs father on the gel, it must be shorter than its wild-type counterpart. Nonsense mutations replace an amino acid-coding mRNA codon with a stop codon, causing the translated protein to be truncated, or shortened.

32. D is correct. Since a single base was inserted, this certainly is an insertion mutation. Insertions (or deletions) of nucleotides in multiples of numbers other than 3 always produce a frameshift; in other words, the reading frame used during translation will move. Finally, this insertion caused the fourth codon to become UAG (a stop codon) instead of AGA, making this a nonsense mutation as well.

33. C is correct. The enzymes insert a random number of bases to connect the relevant genes; this number might or might not be a multiple of three. Only when that number is a multiple of three will the translational machinery read the genes "in frame." Thus, two-thirds of the antibodies will be out of

frame because statistically, only one-third of any set of random numbers is a multiple of three.

34. A is correct. "Wobble" deals with the idea that the last base of a codon does not determine the associated tRNA to the same extent as the first two bases. In other words, the last base can often be mutated without changing the amino acid that is introduced into the translated polypeptide. Since the final protein is unchanged, this exemplifies a silent mutation.

    B, C, D: These mutations all result in a change to the final protein product, unlike silent mutations in the "wobble" base of a codon.

35. B is correct. The question stem implies that a large portion of the genetic material from one chromosome has been shifted to a different chromosome. This is the definition of a translocation.

36. D is correct. A nonsense mutation requires a premature stop codon, and the only stop codon listed is UAG. Note that the other two such codons are UGA and UAA.

    A: This is a start codon, not a stop codon.

37. D is correct. The most reliable way to confirm the presence of a silent mutation is by analyzing the sequence of the associated gene. Thus, Sanger sequencing is the only DNA-analysis technique listed that can confirm such a mutation.

    A, B: While these techniques would show differences in protein size, for example, they would not be useful in assessing silent mutations because such mutations do not noticeably change the protein.
    C: Again, since silent mutations have no effect on protein structure or function, they would not be revealed by a Western blot.

38. D is correct. Classification of a nonsense mutation requires that a premature stop codon has been created. In this case, the insertion of a "G" after the fifth nucleotide causes the second codon to change from UAU to UAG, a stop codon.

    A: Nonsense mutations are often the result of frameshifts. However, in this case, the protein will be truncated before translation can continue with the altered frame that results from the insertion.

C: Nonsense mutations are among the most damaging of potential mutations, as they produce a shortened and often nonfunctional protein. Thus, they are very different from silent mutations, which have no noticeable effect on the protein produced.

39. B is correct. The graph shows a dramatic decrease in protein activity, or in other words, a near-complete loss of function. A frameshift mutation is the most potentially damaging of the choices listed. It could also introduce a stop codon where none previously existed, a common explanation for loss of protein function.

    A: This describes a missense mutation, which tends to be less harmful to overall protein function than frameshifts. Additionally, changing a residue not involved in the active site would likely not impair protein activity this dramatically.
    C: Silent mutations do not impact the function of the translated protein.
    D: This choice does not make sense for a number of reasons. For one, the graph shows lowered protein activity. While slowed translation would cause the protein to be produced less rapidly, it would not impact the function of that protein once made.

40. A is correct. Serine is a polar amino acid, while alanine is nonpolar. This will disrupt the hydrophobic effects related to protein folding.

    B: Serine and alanine are approximately the same size.
    C, D: These choices are likely too dramatic to result from a single missense mutation. It is more probable that protein function will be slightly impaired, but not entirely lost.

41. B is correct. DNA polymerase has inherent proofreading mechanisms that allow it to repair mismatches in the base-pairing sequence. Viruses are examples of organisms that can have genomes comprised entirely of either DNA or RNA.

    II: RNA is less stable than DNA, as it contains the sugar ribose compared to DNA's deoxyribose. This additional 2' hydroxyl group reduces the stability of the RNA molecule. As a result, mRNA degrades rapidly in the cytoplasm.
    III: A DNA strand can certainly hybridize with an RNA polymer. In fact, this process must be able to occur for transcription to take place.

42. A is correct. The single-stranded nature of RNA allows it to fold on itself and pair with its own nucleobases. This allows the macromolecule to adopt multiple three-dimensional shapes, which can fulfill a wide variety of roles; one of the most common is the hairpin loop. This flexibility contributes to RNA's many functions as mRNA, tRNA, rRNA, etc.

    B: RNA is often targeted for destruction. This explains why pre-mRNA undergoes post-transcriptional processing, including the addition of the poly(A) tail and the 5'-cap, both of which protect the molecule from degradation.
    C: mRNA, tRNA, and rRNA serve very distinct functions and cannot be interchanged. mRNA serves as the template for protein translation, tRNA is involved in codon-amino acid recognition, and rRNA is a main component of ribosomes.
    D: While RNA is less stable than DNA, this does not relate to the question's focus on RNA's structural variety.

43. B is correct. A major role of snRNAs involves the formation of the spliceosome. This cellular machinery is responsible for removing introns from pre-mRNA transcripts during post-transcriptional processing. If an organism stopped producing snRNA, this modification process would be most significantly impaired.

44. D is correct. Quaternary structure is a method of classification used for proteins, not RNA. It is proteins that form disulfide bonds between cysteine residues.

    A: While most biological catalysts are protein-based, ribozymes are composed of RNA and are capable of catalyzing biochemical reactions.
    B: Many types of viruses contain genomes that are composed entirely of RNA.
    C: Ribosomes are cellular organelles present in both prokaryotes and eukaryotes and are largely made up of rRNA.

45. C is correct. RNA contains ribose, a different five-carbon sugar than deoxyribose. The presence of a 2' hydroxyl group on this sugar molecule renders RNA more reactive and unstable than its DNA counterparts.

    A: RNA is indeed single-stranded. However, this feature does not have a direct impact on its stability. Instead, it allows the molecule to perform a variety of functions.
    B: While polymerase enzymes do make errors, this tends to lead to base pair mismatches, not a lack of stability of the entire molecule.
    D: This does not directly alter the stability of RNA.

46. B is correct. tRNAs are "charged," or bound to an amino acid, by enzymes known as aminoacyl tRNA synthetases. The amino acid corresponding to the tRNA molecule is attached to the 3' end of the RNA. Attachment takes place via covalent bonding to the CCA tail, which is indicated by the label B.

    A: This structure is the D arm, which is important in tRNA recognition.
    D: The structure with this label is the anticodon loop, which binds with the corresponding mRNA codon.

47. D is correct. The anticodon sequence of a tRNA molecule serves to pair with a specific codon within the mRNA transcript. If this sequence were to change, the codon recognized by the anticodon loop would also change.

    A: The wobble theory relates to the degeneracy of the genetic code; in other words, it refers to the fact that more than one distinct codon can correspond to the same amino acid. However, the last base of a codon is typically the "wobble" base. If a mutation changed the tRNA anticodon's recognition of either the first or second base, or even the third in some cases, the tRNA would pair with a different amino acid.
    B: Aminoacyl-tRNA synthetases should not lose their ability to recognize this tRNA. Instead, the change in the anticodon loop means that the synthetase enzyme will attach a different amino acid to the 3' end of the tRNA.

48. B is correct. Post-transcriptional modification allows for a single gene to produce a variety of mRNA transcripts, and thus, to form multiple distinct protein products. This is accomplished through the process of splicing, which is described in choice B.

    A, C: These are post-transcriptional modifications, but they do not add to the diversity of protein products. Instead, they increase the stability and longevity of the mRNA transcript.
    D: This is not a post-transcriptional modification.

49. D is correct. The poly (A) tail and the 5' cap are added as protection for the mRNA transcript. These post-transcriptional modifications do not affect the sequence of the transcript itself.

    A: RNA polymerase does lack the innate proofreading ability of DNA polymerase.
    C: DNA contains the template for every organelle, cell, and organ. Errors in DNA replication, if left unfixed, will be passed down to daughter DNA molecules. Errors in transcription, on the other hand, either result in a nonfunctional polypeptide, the intended polypeptide, or a dysfunctional protein that will likely be targeted for destruction.

50. A is correct. The acronym "snRNP" stands for "small nuclear ribonucleic protein." These structures combine with other proteins to form the spliceosome complex, which facilitates splicing of the pre-mRNA transcript.

51. D is correct. Choice I is a fundamental function of both the 5' cap and the poly(A) tail. Choice II is also correct, as eukaryotic translation often relies on cap-dependent initiation. The 5' cap contains a special tag that is required to interact with certain key ribosomal proteins. Finally, choice III is correct, since nuclear export of RNA is regulated by the cap binding complex (CBC). This complex binds specifically to capped RNA.

52. D is correct. Spliceosomes are primarily involved in alternative splicing, a process in which the spliceosome removes the introns and ligates the exons of the pre-mRNA transcript. This enables multiple distinct transcripts to be produced from a single gene and is responsible for much genetic diversity.

    A: Transcription would still occur. Only alternative splicing, which is part of post-transcriptional processing, would not.
    B: Spliceosomes are not involved in DNA replication.
    C: Since other steps of post-transcriptional processing would proceed normally, mature mRNA would still be different from pre-mRNA.

53. D is correct. siRNA is a class of dsRNA that is crucial in RNA interference. siRNA molecules are produced from small hairpin RNAs and dsRNAs in a process catalyzed by the Dicer enzyme.

    A: tRNA is involved in translation and amino acid recognition.
    B: rRNA is a primary component of ribosomes and functions in protein synthesis.
    C: While miRNA molecules are involved in RNA silencing, they are produced by RNA polymerase II.

54. B is correct. This question requires understanding of the complementary DNA strands involved in transcription. One strand is the sense (non-template) strand, while the other is the antisense (template) strand. mRNA is transcribed directly from the antisense strand, giving it the same base sequence as the sense strand. Thus, if a virus produces antisense RNA complementary to a gene's promoter sequence, the viral RNA will hybridize that sequence, blocking transcription from occurring.

    D: This is a tempting answer, as it correctly describes a function of miRNA. However, the question asks about the scenario's effect on transcription, not what occurs afterward.

55. A is the correct answer. Sigma factors are initiation factors that enable RNA polymerase to bind to promoter sequences. This is necessary for the initiation of RNA synthesis. Sigma factors are highly specific, and any given RNA polymerase holoenzyme is associated with a single sigma factor.

    B: The transcription bubble is unrelated to sigma factors.
    C: Since RNA polymerase has an innate ability to unwind DNA, it does not require a helicase enzyme.
    D: Sigma factors do not enable differentiation between nucleotides.

56. B is correct. During alternative splicing, a complex known as the spliceosome binds to the pre-mRNA and forms a loop, similar to that shown in the figure. Segments in the loop will be spliced from the mRNA sequence. Here, the fragments labeled B (an exon) and C (an intron) will be removed. Contrary to popular misconception, the removal of exons can occur during splicing. In fact, such

removal is a primary reason why numerous mRNA transcripts can be generated from a single gene.

57. B is the correct answer. The process described in the question stem is the definition of RNA interference.

    A: While base pairing is utilized in RNA interference, it does not adequately describe the entire process.

58. D is the correct answer. In the figure, label D indicates the poly(A) tail, a structure added to the end of each mRNA transcript during post-transcriptional processing. In eukaryotic cells, enzymatic degradation often occurs when the poly(A) tail is shortened beyond a particular threshold.

    C: This answer is partly true, as the poly(A) tail is part of the untranslated region. However, it is not involved in signaling the termination of translation.
    A: The genetic information that will be translated into the future protein is found within exons, indicated here by labels B and C.
    B: This function is fulfilled by the 5' cap, indicated by label A in the figure.

59. D is correct. Both DNA and RNA polymerase read DNA from 3'-5' and synthesize new strands of genetic material from 5'-3'.

60. C is correct. Ribozymes are RNA molecules that are capable of catalyzing biochemical reactions, including RNA and DNA ligation and the formation of peptide bonds.

    A: Viruses can have either DNA or RNA genomes.
    B: While RNA is more unstable than DNA, this does not make it unable to store genetic information.
    D: RNA contains many of the same bases as DNA, meaning that it certainly can hydrogen bond in a similar manner.

61. B is correct. Enzymes are not consumed during the reactions that they catalyze. Additionally, enzymes tend to have optimal temperature and pH ranges at which they function most efficiently. Outside of its optimal conditions, an enzyme can become denatured, or lose its shape and catalyzing ability.

    I: Ribozymes are capable of catalyzing biochemical reactions, but are composed of RNA, not protein.

II: An enzyme functions to lower the activation energy of a reaction. However, it does not do so only for the forward reaction; it necessarily reduces the reverse activation energy as well.

62. D is correct. This statement accurately describes the "lock and key" model, which postulates that an enzyme and its substrate have complementary geometric shapes.

    A, B, C: These describe characteristics of the "induced fit" model that make it advantageous in comparison to the older hypothesis.

63. A is correct. The primary structure of a protein is simply its amino acid sequence. While the other levels of structure certainly could be affected by such a change, they are not guaranteed to be (for example, if an amino acid was replaced by a similar residue, as in an alanine-to-valine mutation).

    B: Secondary structure refers to specific local interactions, such as those that form alpha helices and beta-pleated sheets.
    C: Tertiary structure forms the larger-scale three-dimensional conformation of the protein. This additional folding of the secondary structure is driven by hydrophobic interactions between the side chains.

64. B is correct. The heat used in the frying process denatures the tertiary structure of the protein. The protein unfolds, exposing its hydrophobic interior to the environment and facilitating bond formation with other protein molecules. This results in a more solid, hard egg white.

65. C is correct. Disulfide bonds, posttranslational modifications, prenylation, and the binding of metal ions are all made possible by cysteine's nucleophilic thiol group.

    A: Cysteine is traditionally considered a hydrophilic amino acid, and it is also capable of stabilizing hydrophobic interactions in micelles. However, this does not adequately explain cysteine's versatile role.
    D: This is correct, however, its thiol group must be unbound for many of the listed reactions.

66. D is correct. Notice that proline's side chain is actually bound to its amino group instead of projecting outward from the alpha carbon. This cyclic side chain results in a strict 60° angle

between proline and neighboring amino acids. Proline also plays a large role in beta turns.

A: This is untrue. Of the twenty main amino acids, glycine is the only one that is achiral.
B: Proline is indeed found both at the ends of beta sheets and as the first residue of alpha helices. However, this is not due to its amino group.
C: The carboxyl group can only form a peptide bond with one amino acid, not two.

67. A is correct. *Taq* polymerase, like any other enzyme, is sensitive to both pH and temperature. During PCR, the temperature is cycled to facilitate the denaturing and rewinding of the DNA double helix. The enzyme used must withstand these fluctuations in temperature without denaturing.

B: Polymerase enzymes catalyze the elongation of DNA strands; they do not play a role in the maintenance of established DNA structure.
C: The heat involved comes from the PCR apparatus, not the replication process.
D: Heat resistance has no direct relation to pH.

68. B is correct. The figure depicts a molecule labeled "D" that binds to the enzyme. When the molecule attaches, the enzyme changes conformation and the original substrate is prevented from binding. Since the molecule marked "D" does not bind in the active site, this is consistent with allosteric regulation.

C: Competitive inhibition occurs when an inhibitor competes with the substrate to bind to the active site.

69. D is correct. Many oral drugs are metabolized significantly, often with only a small percentage of the drug actually reaching the bloodstream. Cytochrome P-450 is the enzyme responsible for metabolizing most types of statin. Irreversible inhibition by bergamottin, a compound found in grapefruit juice, results in less statin being metabolized than usual. This can lead to potential overdose due to increased bioavailability.

A: Compounds in grapefruit juice do bind irreversibly to the cytochrome. However, nothing in the question stem indicated that a toxic product forms.
B: Halting digestion would not cause a specific negative reaction in relation to statin drugs.

C: Cytochromes do not play a direct role in the maintenance of stomach acidity.

70. B is correct. Increasing the enzyme's affinity for other molecules would reduce the rate at which it can act on its intended substrate. However, this should not completely shut down the pathway.

71. C is correct. Translation is the process by which mRNA is decoded by ribosomes to create proteins. Disrupted translation would alter protein production without compromising DNA or RNA levels.

A: DNA replication is the process by which DNA is copied. Disruption of DNA replication would result in an inability to progress in the cell cycle, but would not disrupt protein levels without affecting other nucleic acids.
B: Transcription occurs when mRNA is produced from a DNA template. Since RNA levels are not affected here, this choice does not make sense.
D: Bacteria do utilize translation to synthesize protein. Additionally, interruption of binary fission (a form of prokaryotic asexual reproduction) would simply prevent the bacterial cells from dividing.

72. D is correct. Translation begins with initiation, when the ribosome and initial tRNA assemble on the mRNA. This is followed by elongation, a phase during which the amino acid carried by the initial tRNA is transferred to the amino acid on the incoming tRNA. Next, the ribosome continues to read the mRNA and translocates to the next codon. Finally, after multiple elongation-translocation phases, the ribosome reaches the stop codon and the polypeptide is released. This constitutes the final termination step.

73. A is correct. "S" denotes Svedberg units, a form of measurement used for ribosomes. Prokaryotic ribosomes are 70S in total and are composed of two subunits: a smaller 30S structure and a larger 50S one. Consequently, we know that choice A is the only answer that both accurately names a prokaryotic subunit and pairs it with its correct description.

B, D: These options refer to the smaller (40S) and larger (60S) subunits that comprise the 80S eukaryotic ribosome. As tetracycline targets prokaryotic cells, these two choices are incorrect.

C: 70S correlates to the entire prokaryotic ribosome, not a single subunit.

74. D is correct. During translation, a tRNA anticodon matches with an mRNA codon and adds its charged amino acid to the growing polypeptide chain. The concept of "wobble" refers to unorthodox base pairings that can occur during this process. For example, one canonical Watson-Crick pair is guanine-cytosine. In contrast, translation can yield a pairing between guanine and uracil. Thus, a single tRNA may correspond to multiple mRNA codons, resulting in the often-mentioned "degeneracy" of the genetic code. The flexible, noncanonical base pairing described above tends to occur in the third nucleotide of a codon, making D the best choice.

A, B: These "codon mutations" would be harmful to the cell, as the translational integrity between mRNA and amino acid would be compromised.

75. A is correct. From the codon table supplied, we see that the original codon (UAU) codes for tyrosine, while the mutant version (UAA) is a stop codon. Introduction of a premature stop codon terminates translation and results in a shorter polypeptide.

B, C: UAA codes for neither cytosine nor tyrosine. D: The question stem never indicates that any of the translational machinery has been disrupted. In this case, translation will occur but will be halted prematurely.

76. B is correct. The mRNA sequence provided in the question is that of the wild-type transcript. Notice that the first codon is AUG, which (as the start codon) denotes methionine, the initial amino acid. The question describes the relevant mutation as C5W, meaning that the wild-type polypeptide's fifth amino acid, cysteine (C), has been changed to tryptophan (W). From the table, we see that tryptophan correlates to the codon UGG. Choice B accurately includes a UGG as its fifth codon while lacking any other mutations.

A: This is not a mutant transcript; in fact, it is identical to the wild-type sequence. C: The question describes a point mutation, in which only a single nucleotide is changed. In contrast, this option includes two altered bases. Additionally, GGC codes for glycine (G), not tryptophan (W).

D: Option D shows a two-nucleotide change from serine to tryptophan (S6W) in the sixth codon. This is not the mutation described in the question stem.

77. C is correct. The start codon corresponds to methionine in eukaryotes and to a modified "fMet," or N-formylmethionine, in prokaryotes. Additionally, statement III is correct; translation is facilitated by ribosomes in both cell types. Although these organelles differ in overall size (80S in eukaryotes compared to 70S in prokaryotes), both contain only two subunits.

II: Prokaryotic mRNA is polycistronic, not monocistronic. This means that a single prokaryotic mRNA transcript can code for multiple proteins.

78. C is correct. The question stem describes eRF1 as an omnipotent release factor that recognizes stop codons. More specifically, it mentions that this factor is eukaryotic. Humans and other eukaryotes possess 3 stop codons: UAA, UAG, and UGA. In contrast, prokaryotic stop codons are recognized by multiple release factors in two classes.

79. B is correct. We are looking for a situation in which information does not flow in the direction shown in the figure. Choice B discusses the M-MULV reverse transcriptase that synthesizes DNA (technically cDNA, or complementary DNA) from RNA. In contrast, the central dogma makes RNA from a DNA template.

A: This demethylation is consistent with the central dogma, as is the mention of transcription itself. Transcription converts information held by DNA into a more portable form, RNA. C: Here, modification of pre-mRNAs assists in their later translation into the target protein strands. This post-transcriptional step is critical for the integrity of the central dogma. D: The eubacterium described in this choice contains a unique DNA polymerase, but this still aligns with the steps shown in the figure. In fact, the ability of this organism to replicate DNA even in extreme conditions points to the tenacity of the central dogma.

80. C is correct. The P site is the region of the ribosome in which peptidyl tRNAs are formed. In other words, the tRNA molecule actually forms a

complex with the growing polypeptide at this site. Additional residues are added via the formation of peptide bonds.

A, B, D: The A site receives incoming tRNAs, while the E site serves as the location where the newly-formed polypeptide chain exit. Choices A and B reverse these roles.

81. D is correct. Prokaryotic genomes are made up of a single circular chromosome composed of double-stranded DNA. In contrast, human somatic cells contain 46 chromosomes (23 from each parent). These structures are also made of dsDNA, but are linear.

    A: These numbers are the reverse of those in reality.
    B: Again, this choice reverses eukaryotic and prokaryotic characteristics. The human genome contains a plethora of extraneous DNA that is ultimately spliced out before expression.

82. B is correct. In eukaryotes, dsDNA is wrapped around proteins known as histones. A DNA-histone subunit is termed a nucleosome. Finally, chromatin represents fully packaged DNA.

83. B is correct. The production of telomeres is essential for any dividing cell, but particularly for tumor cells, which replicate rapidly. If the action of telomerase is blocked, the cell will quickly lose genetic material from the ends of each chromosome with every subsequent division. Eventually, this will result in cell death. Although most tumors do produce telomerase for this reason, some cancer cells have found alternate methods to prevent the loss of DNA, such as copying a telomere from another chromosome.

84. A is correct. When the centromere falls in the middle of the chromosome, giving the arms a symmetrical appearance, the structure is metacentric. In contrast, a chromosome that has its centromere at the end is termed telocentric.

    C: Submetacentric refers to a chromosome with arms that are slightly different lengths, while acrocentric is used to describe a chromosome with arms of very different lengths.
    D: Antimetacentric chromosomes do not exist.

85. D is correct. Heterochromatin, the compact form of chromatin, is associated with decreased transcriptional activity. One feature that marks this structure is the methylation of guanine and cytosine nucleotides, a modification that inhibits transcription.

    A, C: Acetylated histone tails are associated with euchromatin, in which transcription rate is increased.
    B: Heterochromatin does not contain extra histone clusters.

86. C is correct. Euchromatin, the loose or less dense form of chromatin structure, contains acetylated histone tails. These modifications decrease the affinity of the nucleosome for the DNA, relaxing the overall structure. As this allows transcriptional enzymes more access to the DNA, it is associated with increased gene expression.

    A: Euchromatin does not contain extra histone clusters.
    B: Methylated guanine and cytosine nucleotides would decrease the rate of transcription of that segment of the chromosome. Euchromatin is associated with increased transcription.

87. C is correct. H1 is the component of the nucleosome that is positioned outside of the main histone "bead" structure. This protein holds DNA in place as it enters and exits the wound region of the nucleosome. H1 also provides stability to the structure.

    A, B, D: While all of these proteins are components of the nucleosome, they do not perform the same unique function as H1.

88. D is correct. Heterochromatin is very compact and thus appears dark when viewed under a light microscope. Euchromatin, in contrast, is loosely dispersed within the nucleus. This structure makes it less dense, so light that it is hardly visible through a microscope, and transcriptionally active.

    A: Although small details cannot be elucidated under a light microscope, both heterochromatin and euchromatin are large enough to see.
    B: Both forms of chromatin are found in the nucleus.

89. D is correct. Splicing out introns to remove them from a mature transcript is one of the major post-transcriptional modifications. Other modifications

include the addition of a 5' cap and a 3' poly(A) tail.

A, B: Neither of these statements are true.
C: While this choice is close, transcription of mRNA from DNA occurs before introns are spliced out. This action occurs immediately before export of a mature transcript from the nucleus for translation.

90. B is correct. DNA gyrase is present in prokaryotes and some eukaryotes. This enzyme serves to create supercoils in the DNA structure to facilitate replication with minimum strain.

    A: This function is performed by DNA helicase.
    C: This is the role of DNA polymerase, not DNA gyrase.
    D: This action is performed by primase.

91. D is correct. According to the definition of an operon, Gene A, Gene B, and Gene C fall under the control of a single promoter. Consequently, the rates of transcription for all three genes should be equal, and the same number of mRNA transcripts will be produced for all of them.

    A: Although Gene A is immediately downstream of the promoter, this does not alter the rate of transcription.
    B: While Gene B would have the longest mRNA transcript, that does not mean that it would have the most copies of that transcriptional product.

92. B is correct. Coding regions are the DNA segments that are directly transcribed into mRNA and then translated to protein products. Although such regions are certainly found within the operon, they do not regulate the rate of transcription.

    A: During transcription, the transcription factors that regulate gene expression bind to the operator sequence.
    C: The enhancer is the region where activators can bind to increase the rate of transcription.
    D: The promoter is a regulatory sequence that initiates transcription.

93. B is correct. Lactose is an inducer, a molecule that regulates gene expression by increasing transcription rate. This graph shows that the

addition of lactose increases the amount of *lac* mRNA.

A: If lactose was a repressor, it would inhibit gene expression. In that case, the addition of lactose would result in a decrease in *lac* mRNA levels.
C: Operators are DNA domains to which transcription factors bind and modify transcription rate. Since operators are DNA sequences within the operon, adding one to this culture and observing an effect does not make sense.
D. Operons are functional domains of DNA in which multiple genes are under the control of a single promoter. Since *lac* itself is the operon, lactose is not.

94. C is correct. In a positive repressible operon, an inhibitor can attach to the activator, blocking the activator from binding to the DNA. This results in the downregulation of transcription.

    A: Inducers activate gene expression either by inactivating repressors or by activating inducers. This question asks for the opposite effect.
    B: The enzyme RNA polymerase synthesizes new RNA strands. Adding more RNA polymerase would increase the rate of transcription, not stop it.
    D: Activators upregulate gene expression by increasing transcription.

95. A is correct. Negative control involves the binding of a repressor to block transcription, while positive control includes an activator protein that binds and stimulates transcription. The operon discussed in this question is controlled by a repressor, making this negative control. Secondly, this operon is "switched on" by an inducer, indicating an induction system.

    B: Negative repression is a "switch off" system in which a normally active gene can be inactivated by a repressor.
    C, D: Positive operon control involves an activator protein that binds and stimulates transcription. The question mentions a repressor, not an activator.

96. C is correct. Nucleases, which cleave DNA molecules, are not involved in transcription.

    A: Transcription factors bind to specific DNA sequences to regulate the rate of transcription.

B: RNA polymerases are the enzymes that synthesize mRNA molecules, making them very involved in transcription.

C: Histones are proteins that play a role in the packing of nucleic acids into chromosomes. Although this choice is tempting, histones are actually critical in transcriptional regulation; specifically, chromatin states formed by the histones dictate transcriptional activity. Heterochromatin is tightly packed chromatin that is transcriptionally inactive, while the loosely packed euchromatin is able to be transcribed.

97. A is correct. The Shine-Dalgarno sequence is the ribosomal binding site found exclusively in prokaryotic mRNA. Blocking this sequence would inhibit essential mRNA modifications in prokaryotes without disturbing eukaryotic cells.

    B: RNA polymerase II is the enzyme responsible for RNA synthesis in eukaryotes. Targeting this enzyme would likely harm host cells.
    C: The TATA box is a short sequence (TATAAAA) that functions as a basal promoter in eukaryotes. It, too, would be a poor target due to the potential to harm the host.

98. B is correct. During gene amplification, a section of the genome is replicated multiple times, resulting in an increase in the number of copies. Note that this occurs during a single cell cycle.

99. D is correct. Transcription factors can bind to the enhancer, a short region of DNA, to activate transcription. If the enhancer of the *yellow* gene set is deleted, the transcription of these genes cannot be activated and no black melanin will be produced. In other words, the wings will not contain any pigmentation.

    A: In this species, dark spots on the wings is the wild-type phenotype. Deletion of the enhancer will knock out this trait and cause the phenotype to deviate from its normal pattern.
    B, C: The question never indicates that the *yellow* gene set is involved in wing development.

100. B is correct. The promoter is the region of DNA to which RNA polymerase binds to initiate transcription. Consequently, it is essential for transcriptional regulation in both prokaryotes and eukaryotes. Repressors are proteins that inhibit gene expression by blocking specific regions of DNA or by preventing RNA polymerase from binding to the promoter. Repressors are found in both eukaryotes and prokaryotes

    II: Operons are functional groups of genes controlled by a single promoter. Operons are found only in prokaryotes.
    III: Enhancers are regions of DNA to which proteins can bind and activate transcription. Enhancers are present only in eukaryotes.

101. D is correct. A 7-methylguanylate cap is always added to the 5' end of pre-mRNA to protect it from degradation. Additionally, introns (noncoding regions) are excised through the use of an apparatus known as the spliceosome.

    I: It is a poly(A) tail, not a cap, that is added to the 3' end.
    III: Exons consist of DNA that is able to be expressed, so they remain part of the mature mRNA.

102. D is correct. All post-transcriptional modifications take place in the nucleus. As such, it is not pre-mRNA that exits to the cytosol, but a fully mature mRNA transcript.

    A: The methyl and phosphate groups mentioned here form a 5' cap that is added to pre-mRNA. This cap then plays a role in the regulation of translation.
    B: The poly(A) tail that is added to the 3' end does consist of a hundred or more adenine nucleotides.
    C: Introns, or noncoding segments, are spliced out of the pre-mRNA, leaving exons behind.

103. C is correct. Tumor suppressor genes, when functioning normally, are responsible for keeping rampant cell proliferation in check. Mutations in these genes can cause cancer cells to proliferate.

    A: An oncogene is an activated proto-oncogene. These genes promote rapid cell proliferation. Since it is diminished, not enhanced, *TP53* expression that promotes cancer growth, this answer is incorrect.
    B: The proto-oncogene is a healthy gene that, when activated, becomes a cancer-causing oncogene.

104. C is correct. The table shows that *JN87* has a similar trend in both lung cancer and leukemia patients. Specifically, it displays decreased

transcriptional activity. Tumor suppressor genes lead to cancer only when mutations occur to prevent them from functioning normally. In other words, the gene with the most drastically lowered mRNA levels in cancer patients is most likely to be a tumor suppressor.

A: RC18 is likely an oncogene. Since these genes promote cell proliferation, a cancer patient would be expected to display increased mRNA activity with regard to them.
B: Transcriptional activity of *AR12* appears to be relatively similar to that in healthy patients.

105. C is correct. Transcription of *RC18* appears to be drastically increased in both sets of cancer patients. Oncogenes are activated proto-oncogenes that tend to result in increased cell proliferation. In this particular study, it makes sense that the gene(s) with higher mRNA activity would be oncogenes.

A, B, D: *JN87* is far more likely to be a tumor suppressor gene than an oncogene.

106. B is correct. Acetylation promotes gene expression, while methylation discourages it. Thus, the genes that exhibit increased transcription in stressed mice are the ones that are most likely to be acetylated. Genes 1 and 3 both display significantly higher mRNA activity (and thus increased transcription) in the stressed groups than the healthy group.

A, C: Gene 2, which shows decreased levels of transcription in response to stress, is more likely to be methylated than acetylated.

107. B is correct. Methylation of a gene lowers its proclivity to undergo transcription. Since the stressed and partially stressed mice exhibit decreased transcription of Gene 2, it is this gene that is most likely to be methylated. If this epigenetic modification is heritable, Gene 2 will also be methylated in the newborn mice.

A, C, D: Genes 1 and 3, which display increased transcriptional activity, are more likely to be acetylated than methylated.

108. A is correct. DNA methylation inhibits transcription.

B: Acetylation, not methylation, stimulates transcription.

109. C is correct. MicroRNAs are responsible for post-transcriptional silencing. These short ncRNA molecules bind to mRNA, signaling its destruction or promoting degradation of its protective post-transcriptional modifications.

A, B: Both methylation and acetylation are both forms of pre-transcriptional silencing. In other words, they represent alterations to DNA, not mRNA.
D: tRNA mainly plays a role in the proper translation of processed mRNA.

110. A is correct. Small nuclear RNA (snRNA) molecules are involved in the splicing of pre-mRNA. Since this form of ncRNA was found near pre-mRNA, it is the most logical answer.

B: rRNA, or ribosomal RNA, is produced in the nucleolus and is located within or close to ribosomes.
C: tRNAs are likely to be found in the cytoplasm.
D: snoRNAs, or small nucleolar RNAs, exist in the nucleolus. The question stem referenced the nucleus.

111. C is correct. An organism's genotype is the total collection of genes it carries, while its phenotype is the observable characteristics that result from how those genes are expressed. The question tells us that the two strains have nearly identical genes (same genotype) but very different virulence (behavior / phenotype).

A: As explained in the question, the bacteria have nearly identical genes.
B: The question tells us that it is a "certain bacteria" with different strains – meaning different versions of the same species.
D: Nothing in the question addresses antibiotic resistance by the bacteria.

112. D is correct. Fraternal twins are the result of the fertilization of two different ova by two different sperm. Thus fraternal twins share only 50% of their genes, making them no more closely genetically related than any two siblings. Since 50% of their genes are different, the two boys have different genotypes. One of the boys exhibits a different result in a blood test, meaning they also have different phenotypes.

B, C: Remember that "phenotype" refers not just to characteristics that are observable with the naked eye, but also behaviors, products of behavior, and physiological and biochemical characteristics.

113. B is correct. Since an organism with the dominant gene will always display it, a researcher cannot tell simply through observation whether the fruit fly is WWEE, WwEE, WWEe, or WwEe. The typical way to make this determination is to carry out a test cross: a mating between the unknown individual and an individual known to be homozygous recessive (wwee) for the traits in question. Then, if any of the offspring demonstrate the recessive phenotype (ww or ee), we can conclude that the unknown organism was heterozygous for that trait.

   C: Northern blots assess RNA.
   D: Western blots assess for protein.

114. A is correct. Alleles are alternative forms of the same gene. In human blood types, there is one locus (location) that codes for blood group, and there are three possible alleles: I^A, I^B, and i, which give rise to blood types A, B, and O, respectively.

115. B is correct. In classical genetics, a hybrid is an organism that is heterozygous for the traits in question. More generally, a hybrid is simply the result of any cross between two genetically distinct individuals. Crossing a homozygous dominant individual with a homozygous recessive one will produce entirely heterozygous offspring.

   A, C: These would result in offspring genetically identical to the parents.
   D: This is a dihybrid cross in which both parents are hybrids for the traits, but the question asked us for a cross that would give only hybrid offspring.

116. D is correct. To display the recessive phenotype, an organism must have a genotype that contains two copies of the recessive gene. Thus the short stem flower must have genotype ll and we can eliminate choices B and C. To be recessive, the offspring must have inherited one copy of the l allele from each parent. The long-stemmed parent must then have a copy of the l allele, making its genotype Ll.

117. A is correct. While sickle cell disease is a dangerous affliction that can be deadly, sickle cell trait (being heterozygous for the trait) confers some survival advantages by increasing resistance to malaria. With malaria present as a selection pressure, those with resistance will be more likely to survive and pass on their trait. Thus, a recessive gene that is dangerous (or even fatal) in homozygotes can persist due to the advantage of being heterozygous. This is called hybrid vigor or heterosis.

   B: Negative selection pressure would tend to decrease a gene's frequency in the population.
   C: Inbreeding usually reduces fitness, although it does tend to increase the frequency of rare alleles.
   D: The question tells us that those who get sickle cell disease are less likely to survive in these regions, suggesting worse medical care, not better.

118. C is correct. The term "wild type" refers to the traits an animal typically possesses when found in nature. This usually refers to a dominant trait, but not always. If 98% of the grasshoppers have yellow eyes, then yellow is the wild type.

   A: "Dominant" refers to the interaction between the genes, not which trait is simply the most common. We have no reason to suspect that Bb individuals would stop showing black eyes.
   B: Selection pressures can decrease the frequency of a trait even if that trait is not negative and the pressure is not acting directly on that trait. For example, grasshoppers with black eyes may have had another trait (e.g. shorter legs) that was being selected against.
   D: The question tells us nothing about the fitness levels associated with the two eye colors.

119. D is correct. The impact a trait has on an individual's fitness is determined only by its impact on the individual's reproductive success. If a trait has no effect until after the reproductive life is over, it won't change the fitness of an individual and can continue to exist in the population. Even in the case of Huntington's disease, which is both dominant and fatal, it can persist simply because the disease doesn't typically strike until the person is in late middle or old age.

   A: Even moderate negative effects would reduce fitness and gene frequency over a long timeline.
   B: Spontaneous mutations are rare events in humans, given the exceptionally high accuracy of DNA polymerase and error-fixing machinery present in every cell.

C: Selective pressures can outweigh chance, and do so constantly – this is the basis of natural selection.

120. A is correct. A locus (plural: loci) is simply a location where a gene is found. Moving the genes from one chromosome to another will change their loci. An allele is simply a given variant of a given gene (e.g. H versus h). Nothing in the question suggests the genes themselves were changed.

    C, D: Since the individual is exhibiting no changes in traits, this suggests the genes themselves are operating normally. This means they can be transcribed just fine, and the break in the chromosome did not occur in a coding segment of DNA.

121. C is correct. Since the mother's father expresses the autosomal recessive trait, he must have two copies of the mutation and will pass one on to his daughter, making her an obligate carrier. The husband has a 1/24 chance of also being a heterozygote. Even if both parents are carriers, there is only a 50% chance that the child will be one as well (along with as a 25% chance that he will have cystic fibrosis, and a 25% probability that he will be homozygous dominant). To get our answer, multiply (1/24)(1/2) = 1/48, which is closest to choice C.

    B: This is closest to the chance that the child will actually have cystic fibrosis.

122. A is correct. The first cross yields only short flowers with petite blooms, indicating that these are the dominant traits. If you were to cross two of these progeny, you could expect a result that follows normal Mendelian ratios for a dihybrid cross: 9:3:3:1. Here, the "1" represents the 1/16, or 6.25%, that will display both recessive traits.

123. A is correct. Individuals with autosomal dominant diseases are almost always heterozygotes, as the possession of two mutated alleles is nearly always lethal. Therefore, this woman has a 50% chance of passing the Von Willebrand allele to each of her children. Due to the mentioned penetrance value, such a child then

has a 50% chance of expressing the trait. (0.5)(0.5) = 0.25, or 25%.

124. D is correct. All of the kittens have long hair, indicating that it is entirely dominant over the short allele. Since both orange and black, and not a blended mixture of the two, appear in these kittens' coats, color must follow a codominant inheritance pattern instead of displaying incomplete dominance.

125. D is correct. If you look only at the branch that is found within the box, you will note that neither parent expresses the trait, but one son does. This can be explained either by autosomal recessivity (in which both parents are carriers) or X-linked recessivity (in which the mother is a carrier).

    A: Autosomal dominant traits do not appear in children whose parents do not suffer from the disorder.

126. D is correct. The pedigree implies that the disorder is actually X-linked recessive, something that can be immediately suspected (but not proven) based on the fact that more males than females suffer from this disorder. (Further pedigree analysis shows that this must be the case.) Since "A's" father has the condition and must have given her his X chromosome, she is guaranteed to carry the disease allele.

127. B is correct. Since this trait appears to some extent in everyone who has the gene, it is 100% penetrant. However, variations in symptom severity always imply that a condition displays variable expressivity, meaning that some people express it more than others.

128. C is correct. A large gene pool yields increased genetic diversity, which leads to more opportunities for excellent biological fitness by way of adaptation to the environment. This reduces, rather than increases, the species' likelihood of extinction.

129. D is correct. We can see that the expression of this gene varies based on the season, but the percentage of members with the trait in the population remains constant over time. This means that, at times, at least some plants who have the gene are not expressing its associated trait. This indicates that there is penetrance of less

than 100%. We can make no conclusions about expressivity because we do not know how waxy the leaves are.

130. B is correct. We are given no information regarding dominance or recessivity, so we must take all potential allelic combinations into account. Three genes are present, with two possibilities each; thus, we can use 2^n to find that there are eight different combinations.

131. C is correct. The probability of nondisjunction is 1/130, or about 0.008. Assuming that this happens, the mother may have a baby with Turner syndrome (X0), triple X (XXX), or Klinefelter syndrome (XXY). If the child is Y0, it will not be viable and the pregnancy will be terminated far before term. We are asked for trisomies, which include only triple X and Klinefelter syndrome. So, if she has a viable baby after nondisjunction, it has a 2/3 chance of having a trisomy. Multiplying the probabilities as follows yields our answer: (1/130)(2/3) = 0.005 or a 0.5% chance.

132. B is correct. Only one X chromosome is required for expression of this dominant trait. However, in females, one chromosome is always randomly inactivated. Therefore, incomplete penetrance exists for X-linked dominant traits. Fathers always pass their X allele to their daughters, making I correct; however, mothers can pass either the mutated or normal X allele, giving them only a 50% chance of passing it along.

133. A is correct. For the woman to have symptoms of an X-linked disorder she must express the recessive allele. This can happen in one of many ways. She could possess only one copy of the X chromosome, which carries the mutation; in this case, her mother would not experience symptoms due to her normal X chromosome. The woman also could have an issue with inactivation in which the normal X is not expressed at all. Finally, the disease can be the result of random mutation. It is not possible for her to have inherited a faulty copy from both parents, because if her father had the mutation, he would express it due to the lack of an additional X chromosome.

134. A is correct. This child has a Y chromosome, so he will be genetically male. However, he is missing the gene responsible for male activation and differentiation and will therefore develop similarly to a female.

135. C is correct. This trait appears to be passed almost entirely to sons through their carrier mothers.

136. D is correct. The disease shows an X-linked recessive inheritance pattern, and the father of Individual "i" has the disease. He must then pass this gene to his daughter, making her an obligate carrier. She therefore has a 50% chance of passing this gene to her sons, which does not happen. However, she also has three daughters and has likely passed this trait to at least one of them. The father expresses this trait, so he must pass his mutant X chromosome to all of his daughters. Therefore, we would expect at least one of them to be deaf as well, which is not the case. Thus, D is the most sensible answer.

   A, B: These statements are false.

137. B is correct. The Y chromosome is only passed through men, and therefore can only be passed from fathers to their sons.

138. A is correct. When the mitochondria and chloroplasts were hypothetically engulfed by the larger cells, they became surrounded with an additional plasma membrane.

   B: This statement describes eukaryotes.

139. B is correct. Mitochondrial diseases are inherited maternally. Therefore, only mothers can pass them on to their children, so only the boy in option B is at risk.

140. B is correct. Coiling direction, as stated, is maternally inherited in the first generation. Therefore, all offspring in the F_1 generation should have a sinistral coil with a heterozygous genotype (S, S+). When two individuals from the F_1 generation later mate, note that both must be heterozygous for the dominant allele. Therefore, F_2 offspring are more likely to have a dextral coil.

141. C is correct. During meiosis, four haploid cells are created through meiosis I and meiosis II. Meiosis I includes prophase, metaphase, anaphase, and telophase in two subsequent incarnations.

   D: This is the correct sequence for mitosis.

142. D is correct. Mitosis creates two identical diploid cells and thus does not involve the process of crossing over.

    A: This is the effect of crossing over on meiosis, not mitosis.

143. A is correct. The centromeres are the attachment sites for the spindle fibers to pull apart the chromosomes during anaphase. This occurs during anaphase II in meiosis, as anaphase I only involved the segregation of homologous chromosomes (and not sister chromatids) into daughter cells.

144. B is correct. Mitosis and meiosis are correctly labeled, but 23 chromosomes should exist in each haploid cell, not 24.

145. D is correct. During synapsis, homologous chromosomes pair up together and undergo crossing over. Failure to correctly complete synapsis could be caused by an inversion, translocation, or nondisjunction. The gamete might undergo apoptosis due to being genetically inviable; it could also, however, continue on to complete meiosis. Several genetic diseases in humans are caused by failed synapsis.

146. B is correct. Genes that are on the same chromosome and near each other are most closely linked, due to the low probability that they will be separated during crossing over.

147. C is correct. The synaptonemal complex is a protein structure that forms between homologous chromosomes during meiosis. It plays an integral part in chromosome pairing, synapsis, and recombination.

148. D is correct. Independent assortment refers to the phenomenon by which genes for separate traits are passed independently of one another from parents to offspring. During meiosis, chromosomes undergo recombination and are pulled apart randomly, thus distributing traits in a manner independent from each other.

    C: Independent assortment does not happen during mitosis.

149. A is correct. In meiosis, the nuclear membrane breaks down in both prophase I and II. In mitosis, the nuclear membrane breaks down in prophase.

150. D is correct. The likelihood of independent assortment for genes on different chromosomes is 50%. If, however, genes on the same chromosome are situated sufficiently far apart, they could also approach a recombination frequency of 50%.

151. D is correct. The people who express the trait for red hair must possess two copies of the allele. We can therefore solve for q, knowing that 0.09 represents q^2. Once we have found that q = 0.3, we can use p + q = 1 to determine that p = 0.7. Finally, with these values in mind, the carrier rate must be expressed by 2pq = 2(0.7)(0.3) = 0.42.

    A) This would be found by incorrectly assuming that 9% was q, not q^2.
    B) This answer results from finding pq instead of 2pq.
    C) While this correctly describes the frequency of the allele for red hair, we are asked for the percent of heterozygous individuals.

152. C is correct. The 845 individuals described are those who express the dominant allele, meaning that they can be either homozygous or heterozygous for the trait. If we round 845 to 840, we can estimate that 84% of the population has the sulfur receptor; in other words, $p^2 + 2pq$ = 0.84. While this may be difficult to solve for p, we can easily use it to find q^2 using the equation $p^2 + 2pq + q^2 = 1$. Finally, we can calculate the percentage of homozygous dominant individuals by solving for p^2.

    A: This comes from using 84% as q^2 instead of $p^2 + 2pq$.
    B: This is q^2, not p^2.
    D: This results from the mistaken assumption that all of the individuals described in the question are homozygous dominant. In reality, most are heterozygotes.

153. B is correct. The table gives the percentages of the alleles in the gene pool, while the question mentions that the albino trait is recessive. Therefore, we can use the table to find q (the frequency of the albino allele) during both 1993 and 1997, then find q^2 (the percentage of fish actually expressing the trait). In 1993, q = 4.03% (or about 0.04), so q^2 = 0.0016. In 1997, q = 7.98% (or about 0.08), so q^2 = 0.0064. The difference

between these is 0.0064 – 0.0016 = 0.0048 or about 0.5%.

C: This is the difference in recessive allele frequency (q) between 1993 and 1997. The question asks for the difference in q^2.

154. C is correct. In 1995, light-colored rocks were added to the riverbank, making the albino fish better camouflaged and less likely to be preyed upon. This leads to natural selection of the albino allele over the pigmented one.

A: The population size was never discussed.
B, D: No information is given to support these choices.

155. A is correct. Genetic drift occurs when chance events cause changes in allele frequencies over time. Note that unlike natural selection, genetic drift does not favor specific traits that confer biological fitness.

156. C is correct. In this sequence, UAU has been changed to UAA, a stop codon. This will cause a truncated protein and is known as a nonsense mutation.

A: Silent mutations are those that do not affect the final protein product. Nonsense mutations, in contrast, often render the protein nonfunctional.
B: Missense mutations involve the mutation of one amino acid into another instead of into a stop codon.
D: Frameshifts are insertions or deletions that cause the translational reading frame to move.

157. A is correct. A mutation in the promoter sequence would prevent initiation of transcription entirely, resulting in a total lack of the relevant protein.

B: Since intron sequences are spliced out during post-transcriptional modifications, a mutation there would likely not affect the protein.
C: A mutation downstream of a gene would likely have no effect. Promoters and binding sites are all upstream of the gene of interest.
D: An error in RNA polymerase would affect transcription of every gene and would be lethal to the patient.

158. D is correct. Wild-type *Salmonella* cannot grow without histidine. Plate 1 serves as a control to prove this, explaining why there is no growth on that plate. However, if a carcinogen causes mutations to *Salmonella*'s genetic code, the bacterium may regain its ability to grow in a histidine-free environment. Therefore, Plate 2 is set up to test whether the PAH is a carcinogen. If growth had occurred on this plate, it could be concluded that the PAH did in fact mutate the *Salmonella* genome. However, no growth was seen.

A, C: Plate 3 is another control plate, intended to determine that *Salmonella* will grow on a histidine-rich medium. Growth on this plate is expected and does not imply anything about the PAH.
B: Plate 4 is, again, a control plate. It shows us that a known carcinogen does mutate the genetic code of *Salmonella*, resulting in a large amount of growth. Since Plate 2 does not look like this plate, PAH likely is not mutagenic.

159. D is correct. The five conditions for Hardy-Weinberg equilibrium are as follows: a large breeding population, random mating, no mutations that change overall allele frequencies, no immigration or emigration, and no natural selection. The scenario in choice I would lead to selection against the white foxes, while Choice II violates the criterion of "no migration." Choice III, though a tempting one to exclude, does describe some mutations taking place, which is enough to violate equilibrium. Finally, choice IV describes a small population size, not a large one.

160. B is correct. Since recombination is more likely with genes that are farther apart, H and J must be found at opposite ends of the chromosome. Similarly, I and K have the smallest recombination rate, so they must be the closest together. Now, we just need to determine whether the order is HKIJ or HIKJ. Let's first try HIKJ. We know that H and I are 0.23 units apart and that I and K are 0.09 units apart. This adds up to 0.34 as the total distance between H and K. However, we also know that H and J (the opposite ends of the fragment) differ by 0.34 units, meaning that if HIKJ were the correct order, K and J would be positioned 0.00 units apart. Since this is not possible, the accurate order must be HKIJ.

161. D is correct. When a selective force acts against both extremes of a population trait, those who fall

in the middle will predominate over time. This is a perfect example of stabilizing selection.

A: Speciation, or the formation of two different species from a common ancestor, is unrelated to the question stem.
B: Directional selection would be correct if the plants were pushed to grow either taller or shorter.
C: Disruptive selection only occurs when the moderate version of a trait is evolutionarily disfavored, forcing the species to diverge between two extremes.

162. A is correct. Directional selection is a phenomenon by which one phenotypic extreme is favored over others. Over time, this causes the allele frequency to shift in the direction corresponding to that phenotype. Here, when precipitation is high, the long-beaked birds are favored while the others suffer an evolutionary disadvantage.

D: Genetic drift is not a type of selection.

163. C is correct. Co-evolution, as its name implies, occurs when two species evolve in response to each other.

A: Parallel evolution involves the simultaneous, but separate, evolution of similar traits by two related species. The flowers and hummingbirds are not closely related at all.
B: This would require the flowers and birds to actually become more similar, which is not occurring; each is simply evolving in response to the other.
D: Divergent evolution occurs when two groups from one lineage become increasingly more disparate, which is not happening here.

164. B is correct. After the fire, moths able to hide in the black and white ash are not preyed upon; therefore, they are able to survive and pass their genes along. Since the population's alleles are seen to favor more extreme phenotypes over time, this is disruptive selection.

D: The bottleneck effect is not a type of natural selection.

165. C is correct. The bottleneck effect occurs when a disaster or other event results in a loss of a large portion of a population. All future members of the population then descend from a small number

of individuals, which drastically reduces genetic variability.

A: In a large population, random mating tends to increase genetic diversity.
B: Stabilizing selection generally results from forces that favor moderate phenotypes over more extreme ones. No such selective forces are present here.
D: Gene flow, or the transfer of genes from one population to another, increases genetic variation as well.

166. B is correct. When many distinct species arise from a single ancestor, particularly when these species are very different and fill separate ecological roles, adaptive radiation has occurred.

A: Commensalism is a form of symbiosis and does not relate to the question.
C: Evolutionary bottlenecks reduce genetic variation, not increase it.
D: Stabilizing selection, which is not described here, happens when an "average" trait is selected for against more extreme ones.

167. B is correct. Allopatric speciation occurs when populations, or parts of the same population, are separated by a physical barrier.

A: Sympatric speciation is that which occurs without a physical barrier. Since these beetles were separated by an ocean, this choice is incorrect.
C: Parapatric speciation occurs when segments of two distinct populations overlap. Due to environmental differences, these segments may develop into two species, but individuals in the overlapping areas can typically still interbreed.

168. C is correct. The molecular clock hypothesis posits that we can use the number of genetic differences between two species to calculate the amount of time that has passed since their divergence. If mutations do not occur fairly steadily, this would not make mathematical sense.

A, B: The mentioned hypothesis does not consider the harmful or beneficial effects of mutations.
D: The molecular clock hypothesis is concerned with microscopic changes in DNA, not the large-scale evolution of species.

169. D is correct. Darwin's theory of natural selection states that the individuals who successfully

produce the most offspring will pass on their genes more than other organisms. This is the definition of biological fitness.

A, B: These qualities do not matter if the organism in question never passes on its traits.
C: While this tends to correlate with fitness, reproduction can occur without generation of fertile young.

170. A is correct. Commensalism is a form of symbiotic relationship in which one of the organisms (the hermit crab) benefits and the other (the individual that has discarded its shell) is neither harmed nor helped.

B: Parasitism is seen when one organism benefits, while the other suffers. Here, neither species seems to be harmed.
C: Mutualism is a relationship in which both parties benefit.
D: Ectosymbiosis happens when one species lives on the surface of another. While the hermit crabs are living within another species' shells, they are not actually residing on members of that species.

171. B is correct. In general, eukaryotes are more complex than prokaryotes. Along these lines, prokaryotic cell membranes do not contain membrane-linked carbohydrates or sterol-type molecules.

172. C is correct. The fluid mosaic model describes a membrane as (effectively) a two-dimensional liquid that allows for the free diffusion of both phospholipids and proteins within its structure. Therefore, we would expect the rate of protein diffusion within a membrane to be based on its viscosity.

A, B: These would indicate that proteins are unable to freely diffuse throughout the membrane.
D: The fluid mosaic model does not address transport rates across the lipid bilayer.

173 D is correct. All three of the listed options are common functions of membrane-bound proteins. Metabolite transport is almost exclusively mediated by transmembrane proteins, while membrane-linked proteins connect the actin cytoskeleton to the cell membrane.

Finally, as seen with hormone receptors, transduction pathways are initiated by activation of certain transmembrane receptors.

174. C is correct. We are told two things about the receptor molecule in question: first, that it initiates a signal transduction pathway, and second, that it is a G protein-coupled receptor. Both of these tell us that it will be embedded in the cell membrane.

175. A is correct. Epithelial cells separate the lumen of the small intestine from the rest of the body and mediate the absorption of nutrients. Thus, these cells must form a barrier that does not allow fluid to pass. This is accomplished through tight junctions. A secondary effect of tight junctions is that they allow for the creation of polarity, since transmembrane proteins are unable to cross to the opposite side of the cell.

176. A is correct. Since the metabolites on the two sides of the cell have different values, some form of gradient must exist at the barrier between the two cells. The cell on the left has more total positive charge than that on the right, matching choice A.

C: Cells do not possess such a potassium sequestration system.

177. B is correct. Gap junctions connect cells and allow them to share cytoplasm and metabolites. It can be assumed that ions would flow to minimize the concentration gradient. This means that K^+ would travel to the right, opposite the direction of Cl^- flow.

178. D is correct. The faster the recovery, the more fluidity in the plasma membrane.

179. C is correct. Saturated fatty acids allow for efficient packing of the lipid structures in the membrane, lowering its fluidity. Therefore, the sample with the slowest recovery time would be the sample with the highest level of saturated fatty acids.

180. B is correct. In order for this species to thrive at high temperatures, its cell membranes must be very stable to avoid become overly fluid. Since unsaturated fatty acids increase the fluidity of plasma membranes, a low level of these would be expected in this organism. In contrast, cholesterol

and other sterol-like molecules function as a type of buffer. These compounds prevent high or low temperatures from adversely affecting the fluidity of cell membranes; therefore, high levels of these would be expected.

181. B is correct. $Ca(OH)_2$ will dissociate into one Ca^{+2} and two OH^- ions, giving its side of the beaker a total concentration of 9 M. Since glucose is a covalent compound, it will not dissociate in water. Therefore, the left side has a higher concentration of particles and water will flow from right to left.

182. C is correct. The higher the concentration of the compound, the higher the rate of diffusion, making I correct. Since the molecule is large and polar, it requires a protein channel for transport into the cell.

    II: The substance travels through a channel instead of diffusing through the membrane itself. Plasma membrane fluidity is irrelevant.
    III: Cellular volume itself is not important; it is the concentration gradient of the substance that impacts diffusion.

183. D is correct. Though sodium is not at equilibrium with regard to concentration alone, its influx has caused the cell to become more positive than the extracellular fluid. Electrostatic forces repel cations and prevent more sodium from entering the cell.

    A: Total solute concentration does determine water movement, or osmosis. However, the movement of individual molecules is impacted by other factors.
    B: There is no evidence to support this statement.
    C: Sodium chloride is soluble and will not form an inert salt.

184. B is correct. The theoretical pump sends two Na^+ ions out of the cell and brings one K^+ inward, effectively establishing a net negative charge. In other words, the pump is working to polarize the cell. If the cell is hyperpolarized, it will need to become more positive to return to its resting potential. Therefore, the pump will likely slow.

185. D is correct. Small, nonpolar molecules are membrane-permeable, while polar, charged, or very large particles require channels to pass through the lipid bilayer. Na^+, ATP, and glucose are all polar molecules. Only estrogen,

a steroid hormone, is nonpolar. Remember that steroids can passively diffuse across the plasma membrane.

186. D is correct. Both glucose and sucrose are large and very polar, making them unable to diffuse across hydrophobic membranes.

    A, B: These solutes cannot cross the plasma membrane without the aid of channels or transport proteins.
    C: Since concentration gradients are still present for both glucose and sucrose, equilibrium has not been reached for these individual compounds.

187. B is correct. Facilitated diffusion is a type of passive transport that involves transmembrane protein channels. These channels are highly specific for a certain molecule or ion. For example, a sodium channel does not allow transport of potassium.

    A: Facilitated diffusion is a passive, not active, process.
    C: Protein channels can assist molecules in entering and exiting the mitochondria, nucleus and endoplasmic reticulum, not just the cell itself.
    D: Passive processes always move molecules down their concentration gradients.

188. D is correct. We see that zinc is brought in even against its concentration gradient, so the process must be active transport. We see that the extracellular fluid is getting more concentrated even though it is losing zinc, therefore it must be gaining another ion. Zinc is being traded for another ion down its concentration gradient in order to shuttle zinc inside of the cell.

189. C is correct. Molecule A is absorbed at a rate directly correlated with its concentration outside the cell, suggesting that it can easily diffuse through the membrane under any conditions. In contrast, molecule B seems to display Michaelis-Menten kinetics, with the concentration of the compound impacting rate at low, but not high, concentrations. This implies that a protein is required to transport the molecule inside the cell. Therefore, molecule A is likely small and nonpolar, while molecule B must be large, polar, or both.

    A, D: CO_2, O_2, and testosterone are all nonpolar and freely diffuse through membranes. All would show similar rates of transport when graphed against concentration.

B: This is backwards. Glycine is polar, while testosterone (a steroid hormone) is nonpolar.

190. C is correct. The Na⁺/K⁺ ATPase pumps three sodium ions out of the cell for every two potassium ions it carries inward.

191. A is correct. From the question stem, we can assume that the cells of a bristlenose pleco are less highly concentrated in solute than a similar volume of ocean water. This is likely true because these organisms live in fresh water, and a cell must have a tonicity that is relatively similar to that of its environment to avoid losing or gaining fluid. In other words, *Ancistrus* cells are hypotonic to salt water. When placed in an ocean, these cells will shrink as water flows down its concentration gradient from low to high solute.

B, C: These choices are factually impossible regardless of the given information.
D: This would be true if *Ancistrus* cells contained more, not less, solute than an equivalent volume of ocean water.

192. B is correct. The term "isotonic" denotes that the solution in question has the same solute osmolarity as the compartment to which it is being compared.

A: We have no reason to consider only charged solutes when dealing with tonicity. In fact, fairly large or uncharged proteins (like serum albumin) contribute greatly to osmotic effects in the body.
C: A solution can be isotonic with regard to any other solution, not just the cytosol of a muscle cell.
D: This describes a hypertonic solution.

193. C is correct. For a water-permeable (but not solute-permeable) cell to gain water via osmosis, its contents must be hypertonic relative to its environment. In other words, it must include relatively more solute. Here, the extracellular fluid has a sodium ion concentration of 140 mEq/L, meaning that any cell with a larger ion concentration should absorb water. However, NaBr is virtually completely soluble in water, so 70 mEq/L of NaBr will dissociate into 140 mEq/L of Na⁺ and Br⁻ ions.

B, D: Since these cells are hypotonic in comparison to the fluid in the beaker, they will lose water instead of swell.

194. B is correct. The sodium-potassium pump is a type of primary active transport, in which two ions are pumped against their concentration gradients. In contrast, secondary transport involves the use of a previously-established concentration gradient to allow one particle to travel in a spontaneous direction. This action powers the motion of a single species against its own gradient.

A: Both primary and secondary active transport involve the use of ATP, whether directly or indirectly.

195. C is correct. Cotransporters move two different ions or molecules in the same direction across a membrane. Here, we know that sodium's concentration gradient is used to power the movement of glucose. Since sodium tends to be far more highly concentrated outside the cell (due to the action of the sodium-potassium pump), it will flow inward when allowed to move down its gradient. Since Na⁺ and glucose travel in the same direction, glucose molecules must enter the cell.

196. A is correct. Integral proteins are those that are tightly attached or embedded within the plasma membrane. All transmembrane proteins, which span the entire bilayer, are members of this larger class.

II: Many bacterial transmembrane proteins exist.
III: Some integral proteins are not transmembrane in nature.

197. D is correct. Pinocytosis, sometimes called "cell drinking," involves the engulfment of extracellular fluid and any associated solutes by one or more vesicles.

A: This is a broad term that includes both pino- and phagocytosis, as well as endocytosis that is mediated by specific receptors.
B: This is not an actual biological term.
C: Phagocytosis, a separate form of endocytosis, refers to the surrounding of potential pathogens by immune cells.

198. A is correct. During endocytosis, external molecules or pathogens are first engulfed in an

invagination of the cell membrane known as a vesicle. These vesicles initially deliver their contents to early endosomes, which are also membrane-bound. These contents then progress to late endosomes, which fuse with lysosomes for degradation.

B: This is not a scientific term.
C, D: While the protein probably was located in these structures earlier, the question asks where it was found immediately before entering the lysosome.

199. C is correct. Phagocytosis is a specific form of endocytosis. As such, it requires large amounts of ATP and is certainly classified as active transport.

    I: Passive transport is that which does not require energy, typically involving materials moving down a gradient of some kind.
    III: While pinocytosis is also a specialized type of endocytosis, phagocytosis is not a form of pinocytosis.

200. D is correct. This figure shows plasma membrane receptors binding to small molecules (or ligands) present in the extracellular region. The cell then engulfs these molecules in a membrane-bound vesicle. This perfectly exemplifies receptor-mediated endocytosis, which often incorporates the protein clathrin.

    A, C: All forms of endocytosis are active, as they require large amounts of ATP.
    B: Phagocytosis is not receptor-mediated in this manner.

201. C is correct. The mitochondrion is unique because it carries its own set of genetic material and is able to self-replicate.

    III, IV: These features are not unique to the mitochondria.

202. D is correct. It is eukaryotes, not prokaryotes, that use alternative splicing.

    A, B, C: All of these options accurately state differences between eukaryotic and prokaryotic cells.

203. A is correct. The nucleolus is the area of the nucleus where the genes that code for ribosomal RNA (rRNA) are translated.

B: DNA that is not being transcribed is typically compacted around the outside edge of the nucleus.
C: Translation always occurs in the cytoplasm, not the nucleus.
D: The genes for histones are transcribed in the same manner as the genes for non-histone proteins.

204. C is correct. While the electron transport chain does occur in the mitochondria, it takes place along the inner mitochondrial membrane.

205. D is correct. All nuclear import and export takes place through the nuclear pore complex. Proteins can use NES's to leave the membrane-bound structure, and NIS's to enter it. They may also use the RAN cycle for these processes.

206. C is correct. True organelles are present only in eukaryotes and not in either bacteria or Archaea. Therefore, it can be assumed that the development of organelles took place after both bacteria and Archaea had diverged from the cell line that would eventually become eukaryotes.

207. C is correct. The endosymbiotic hypothesis posits that mitochondria (and chloroplasts) began as small prokaryotes that were engulfed by, and eventually incorporated into, larger eukaryotic cells.

208. B is correct. First, transcription factors must enter the nucleus, since this is where transcription takes place. Second, to be certain that it is EGF that is activating the molecule in question, we must observe a change from before its addition to afterward. Only option B changes locations upon activation by the EGF molecule.

209. C is correct. Since it does not enter the nucleus, S6-K must affect the aspects of protein synthesis that are extranuclear, such as mature mRNA and the mitochondria.

    A: Splicing occurs in the nucleus.
    B: While this is possible, S6-K would not be directly affecting protein synthesis itself.

210. A is correct. Prokaryotes do not conduct splicing or other post-transcriptional modifications.

    B: While prokaryotes lack linear chromosomes, they do have proteins that bind to and condense DNA.
    C: Cell walls are common among prokaryotic species.
    D: Actin is a cytoskeletal protein; a prokaryote could certainly possess a cytoskeleton.

211. D is correct. The lysosome contains various enzymes and acid used to degrade many cellular macromolecules and sometimes the cell itself. The Golgi apparatus packages proteins and lipids and targets them to specific parts of the cell. Finally, the mitochondria are the site of both the Krebs cycle and the ETC.

    II: The smooth ER does not produce proteins.

212. C is correct. The endoplasmic reticulum is an extension of the outer layer of the nuclear envelope. This connects the ER directly to the nucleus.

213. B is correct. The lysosome is a specialized vesicle that buds off from the Golgi apparatus, then acts as the digestion center for the cell.

    A: Endocytotic vesicles are formed by invaginations of the cellular membrane. While they can bind to lysosomes if targeted for digestion, they do not represent the origin of the lysosome.

214. C is correct. Think of this mistake as similar to lysosomal rupture. The enzymes in the lysosome will dissolve the macromolecules found in the cell. This would likely result in cell death.

215. D is correct. The Golgi functions as a sort of cellular post office. It packages proteins into vesicles, then targets them to certain locations. This includes targeting proteins for excretion and forming vesicles that will later become lysosomes. Without the Golgi, none of the listed functions would be possible.

216. B is correct. For each structure, simply divide the number of organelles by the number of cells.

217. B is correct. An increase in the number of ribosomes in a cell sample indicates that the cells have increased their level of protein production.

This may be observed when cells are preparing to go through cell division and must synthesize enough proteins to support two cells.

218. C is correct. The smooth endoplasmic reticulum plays a critical role in the production of lipids and fatty acids in the cell.

    A: This is carried out by the rough, not the smooth, ER.
    B: Enzymes are produced at ribosomes like any other type of protein.
    D: Proteins are packaged into vesicles by the Golgi apparatus.

219. A is correct. An increase in smooth ER indicates an increase in the production of lipids and fatty acids. The liver is the main human organ that functions in fatty acid metabolism

    B: Muscle cells would have an increased need for ATP, not a heightened production of lipids.
    C: Red blood cells effectively have no organelles.

220. B is correct. Transmembrane proteins are translated in the rough ER. They are then packaged in a vesicle that heads to the Golgi apparatus. The Golgi then repackages the protein in another vesicle that is directed to the cell membrane.

    D: No ribosomes are directly attached to the cellular membrane.

221. B is correct. Macrophages must undergo rapid actin reorganization during the process of phagocytosis. If macrophages cannot use this behavior to engulf bacteria, it reflects a significant impairment in their function.

    A, C, D: These cells function more in the secretion of molecules and the activation of intercellular signaling. For this reason, they will be less heavily compromised by a slower pace of cytoskeletal reorganization.

222. A is correct. Gamma-tubulin is a component of the centriole, which acts as a center of microtubule reorganization. This protein forms a stable "base" for alpha and beta tubulin dimers to bind; this is a necessary process in the formation of microtubules, including the mitotic spindle. Disrupting the conformation of gamma-tubulin will prevent the binding of these dimers, so

mitosis will fail as soon as the spindle apparatus begins to form during prophase.

D: Yeast cells do utilize mitosis.

223. A is correct. Kinesins attach to vesicles and travel toward the + end of microtubules, which extend toward the cell membrane from microtubule organizing centers (like the centriole) that are more central to the cell. Note that the + end tends to be the location at which dimers rapidly add to the existing structure.

    B: Kinesins tend to move toward the +, not the -, end of microtubules.
    C, D: Dyneins usually move toward the center of a cell. The question describes vesicular transport away from the cell body.

224. C is correct. Ion transport relies on channels in the cell membrane. It does not directly require cytoskeletal proteins to occur.

    A: Cell movement relies on the polymerization of actin.
    B: Mitosis requires microtubules to form the mitotic spindle.
    D: Actin polymerization creates the invagination of the cell membrane involved in endocytosis.

225. B is correct. Epithelial tissue is linked by intermediate filaments (specifically keratin) that pass through the cells from side-to-side. The filaments of one cell are indirectly linked to those of another in structures known as desmosomes. This network of fibers helps to distribute mechanical stress among the cells. Other tissues do not rely on keratin to alleviate stress in this manner, and would not have their structural integrity disrupted so heavily.

226. D is correct. Eukaryotic and prokaryotic flagella have entirely different structures. In eukaryotes, a flagellum is primarily composed of a bundle of linked microtubules. The actual protein flagellin is only a component of prokaryotic flagella.

227. B is correct. Progeria is caused by a mutation that causes the synthesis of defective nuclear lamins. In healthy cells, lamins are comprised of intermediate filaments that form the structural support for the nuclear membrane.

A, C: Actin filaments and microtubules are not structurally involved in this part of the cytoskeleton.
D: Collagen is an extracellular fiber that is secreted by cells. Unlike the other choices, it is not even a component of the cytoskeleton.

228. B is correct. Microtubules tend to spontaneously collapse into free-floating dimers and re-form – unless they are stabilized by other proteins. This characteristic is known as dynamic instability. Thus, colchicine will inhibit any process that requires the reformation of collapsed microtubules. For choice I, mitosis requires microtubules to form the spindle apparatus, which separates chromosomes into distinct daughter cells. For choice II, motor proteins attached to vesicles use microtubules as "roads" to transport their cargo. Additionally, without microtubules, organelle placement and function is disrupted. (For example, the Golgi apparatus would tend to fragment, disrupting proper vesicular transport.)

    III: Cytokinesis relies on actin filaments to separate dividing cells. Since colchicine only directly affects microtubules, this process should proceed normally.
    IV: Filipodium extension also involves actin filaments and will not be directly impacted by colchicine.

229. C is correct. Cell movement relies on the continuous reorganization of actin filaments, the extension of which on the leading edge and retraction on the trailing edge helps drive the cell forward.

    A, B: Vesicular transport and organelle relocation depend on microtubules, not actin filaments.
    D: Intercellular signaling does not directly involve cytoskeletal proteins at all.

230. A is correct. Based on the table, type A can be identified as actin microfilaments, type B as intermediate filaments, and type C as microtubules. Muscle cells, like those within the myocardial layer of the heart, should have the highest concentrations of actin, since it, along with myosin, is a key component of myofibrils.

    B, C, D: Neurons, epithelial cells, and fat cells would not be expected to have such a high actin concentration.

231. B is correct. Hooke's cell theory describes three fundamental principles: that all living organisms are composed of one or more cells, that the cell is the basic unit of life, and that all cells come from pre-existing cells through some form of biogenesis.

    A: Living organisms can be unicellular.
    C: The cell, not protein, is the fundamental unit of life.
    D: This answer choice is both false and out of scope.

232. B is correct. Peptidoglycan is a key component of bacterial cell walls and is only produced by prokaryotes.

    A: Fungal infections are characterized by spores or chitin.
    C, D: Viruses and eukaryotic parasites do not synthesize peptidoglycan.

233. C is correct. The image depicts rod-shaped bacteria arranged in a line. The root word "strep-" indicates a string or chain, while "bacillus" denotes a rod-like shape.

    A: Spirochetes have a corkscrew-like appearance.
    B: Staphylococci would resemble circular bacteria ("coccus") in a cluster ("staphylo-").
    D: Diplobacilli consist of bacilli in groupings of two.

234. C is correct. The image depicts spherical bacteria arranged in grapelike clusters. "Staphylo-" indicates a clustered organization, while "-coccus" means "circular shape."

    A: Streptococcus are cocci, but they are connected in chains, not arranged in clusters.
    B: Any form of bacillus is rod-shaped, not spherical.
    D: *Borrelia burgdorferi* is a type of spirochete, meaning that it must possess a corkscrew-like appearance.

235. A is correct. Protozoans are uni- or multicellular eukaryotic organisms, all of which possess membrane-bound organelles.

    B, C: Bacteria and Archaea lack a nucleus or other membrane-bound internal structures. These organisms are classified as prokaryotes.
    D: Bacteriophage(s) are a type of virus that are only semi-living and have no organelles.

236. C is correct. The image depicts darkly-stained circular bacteria (cocci) and light-colored rod-shaped cells (bacilli). Gram's iodine allows crystal violet to form large complexes that may be retained in Gram-positive bacteria; this stains these cells dark purple. In contrast, Gram-negative bacteria (which lack thick peptidoglycan walls) appear light pink due to the counterstain.

237. A is correct. Gram positive bacteria have a thick peptidoglycan wall but entirely lack an outer membrane. This allows them to stain purple, as the complexes formed between crystal violet and Gram's iodine are unable to exit through the thick cell wall.

    B: Cells with a thin cell wall will give a negative result in Gram's iodine.
    C, D: These choices describe neither Gram negative nor Gram positive prokaryotes.

238. D is correct. Eukaryotic cilia and flagella are composed of bundles of microtubules. Note that this differs from prokaryotic flagella, which are formed from the protein flagellin.

    A: Intermediate filaments are less dynamic than actin or microtubular filaments. They are not involved in ciliary or flagellar structure.
    B: Myosin is present in muscle and aids in the process of contraction.
    C: Microfilaments are composed of actin and are found in the cytoplasm of eukaryotic cells, as well as in muscle.

239. D is correct. Unlike those of eukaryotes, bacterial flagella are made up of flagellin. This protein does not serve as the main component of any of the listed structures.

    A: Kinetochores are composed of microtubules, the structural building block of eukaryotic flagella.
    B: Desmosomes are loose cell-to-cell junction proteins composed of intermediate filaments.
    C: Microvilli are built from microfilaments, not flagellin.

240. C is correct. The basal body acts as a motor that solidly attaches the flagellar structure into the plasma membrane.

    A: The hook is an extracellular portion of the flagellum that allows for a curved, whip-like motion.

B: The wheel, sometimes called the sleeve, provides a pore through the outer membrane of the cell wall.

D: The filament is a helix-shaped structure used directly for propulsion.

241. B is correct. Binary fission is the direct duplication of the prokaryotic genome. This process therefore makes a clone with no genetic difference, assuming that random mutation can be ignored.

242. D is correct. Binary fission is an example of asexual reproduction in which the prokaryote simply duplicates its DNA and divides. Conjugation is the process of plasmid sharing between different bacterial cells, which allows for genetic exchange and increases total genetic diversity.

243. A is correct. Prokaryotes reproduce at a much higher rate than eukaryotes. In addition, they possess fewer checkpoints to correct errors, making mutations more likely to be passed on. These mutations are predominantly deleterious, but some can confer an advantage to their hosts.

244. B is correct. The size of the colony doubles every 12 minutes. Note that, in order for this colony to double in size to fill the petri dish, they simply require one additional round of replication.

245. C is correct. Tube 3 shows diffuse growth throughout the test tube, but with a slightly greater concentration of cells at the top. This displays preferential growth near an oxygenated environment.

246. D is correct. The first bacterium is exposed to the environment; therefore, it may be either an obligate aerobe, a facultative aerobe, or an aerotolerant anaerobe. However, the second bacterium must be an obligate anaerobe because it only grows in the bottom of the tube, away from the air. Tube 1 indicates an obligate aerobe, Tube 2 an obligate anaerobe, Tube 3 a facultative anaerobe, and Tube 4 an aerotolerant anaerobe.

247. C is correct. Facultative anaerobes are organisms that can create ATP through either aerobic or anaerobic respiration, in either the presence or absence of oxygen. Aerobic respiration creates more energy and is therefore preferred.

248. C is correct. The table shows growth of bacteria on different media and in differing sunlight exposure levels. *Streptomyces* shows similar growth in the presence and absence of sunlight, so it must be chemotrophic; additionally, it is unable to grow on minimal media alone, making it a heterotroph. *Pseudomonas* also shows growth in the absence of sunlight. As a consequence, this bacterium must also be chemotrophic. While this strain can grow on minimal media, it can only do so when exposed to the atmosphere. Therefore, it must be an autotroph.

249. A is correct. If the bacteria are phototrophs, they need exposure to sunlight to grow. Their placement in an incubator caused them to be devoid of sunlight.

B: Heterotrophs need an organic or inorganic source to from which to derive energy. The enriched media contained plenty of sugars intended for this purpose.
C: The loose seal on the dishes would allow some gas exchange, sufficient for autotrophs.
D: At an appropriate temperature and on appropriate media, bacterial colonies are able to divide exponentially, meaning that visible colonies should be evident after an overnight incubation.

250. C is correct. Negative chemotaxis describes movement away from a concentration of substances. Positive chemotaxis describes the opposite phenomenon, while neutral chemotaxis is not an observed event.

251. A is correct. Eukaryotic transcription occurs in the nucleus, while prokaryotes (who lack nuclei entirely) conduct it in the cytoplasm.

252. C is correct. Prokaryotic ribosomes have 70S ribosomes, which can be further divided into 30S and 50S subunits. In contrast, eukaryotes have 80S ribosomes composed of 40S and 60S subunits. Both prokaryotes and eukaryotes utilize tRNA during translation.

A: The 40S subunit is found in eukaryotic ribosomes, so targeting here would therefore be lethal to humans.

253. D is correct. Prokaryotes do not have membrane-bound organelles. Therefore, none of the structures in the figure, which depicts a eukaryotic cell, would be involved in post-translational processing.

254. A is correct. Plasmids are circular double-stranded pieces of DNA that can serve a number of roles, such as providing antibiotic resistance, coding for a sex pilus, or holding other genes that provide benefit to the host.

255. B is correct. Plasmids are used in laboratory settings to incorporate genes of interest into certain cells. This allows for the creation of specific genetically-altered organisms or for certain protein products.

    A: Most organisms are not naturally competent, meaning that they are incapable of taking up extraneous genetic information from the environment.
    C: Plasmids are capable of autonomous replication.
    D: A plasmid can be incorporated anywhere in the host genome, including within actual genes and promoter regions.

256. A is correct. Transformation occurs when bacteria take up plasmids from the environment.

257. C is correct. Conjugation occurs when a bacterium directly transfers genetic information to another. Most commonly, this information is the F factor, which is copied and transmitted through a pilus.

258. D is correct. The F factor is a plasmid that encodes for a sex pilus and allows for genetic exchange. Those positive for the factor can create such a pilus and transfer genetic information to individuals lacking the gene. When the F factor plasmid becomes spliced within the bacterium's chromosome, this results in an Hfr bacterium. When Hfr cells attempt to transfer the F factor via conjugation, genomic material can be transferred as well.

259. C is correct. Class 1 transposons are known as "copy-and-paste" transposons. These genetic elements first undergo transcription through the use of RNA polymerase. The mRNA transcript is then reverse transcribed back to DNA and finally inserted into another location in the genome.

260. B is correct. Transduction utilizes a bacteriophage as a vector for genetic exchange. Viruses (of which a bacteriophage is an example) have two stages in their life cycle, lytic and lysogenic. The lytic cycle is seen when the bacteriophage is actively copying its genetic material to create more viral bodies. This phase results in the lysis of the host cell. On the other hand, the lysogenic cycle is a dormant state during which viral DNA is incorporated into the host genome to be activated later.

261. C is correct. The indicated protein resides on the external surface of the viral envelope, meaning that it was derived from the external surface of the host cell membrane and was carried away with the viral capsid during budding. External membrane proteins are made in the host endoplasmic reticulum and travel to the membrane via intracellular vesicles.

    A: The protein may or may not be a recognizable antigen for immunoglobulin binding. Host proteins are often incorporated into the viral envelope, and since we are not told whether the indicated protein is of host or viral origin, there is no way of knowing if it will be recognized as foreign by the immune system. It may simply be a host protein, which would not bind the variable domain of an antibody.
    B: This is an extreme choice and unlikely, since the protein is associated with the membrane. The internal region of the lipid bilayer is hydrophobic. Protein association with the bilayer necessitates interaction between hydrophobic amino acid residues and the hydrophobic phospholipid tails.
    D: The protein could be viral in origin. Many viruses, including HIV, use host synthetic machinery to produce proteins that are then incorporated into the cell membrane. When the viral particle buds off, it carries these proteins with it in the viral envelope.

262. B is correct. The viral capsid is composed of identical protein subunits. This explains why viral capsids frequently exhibit a high degree of symmetry. By eliminating the need for many structurally different capsid proteins, it also allows the viral genome to remain relatively small.

A: The viral envelope, not the capsid, is composed of lipids.

D: The viral capsid proteins are encoded by viral genes.

263. C is correct. Viruses do not contain any membranous organelles. A viral protein capsid houses only genetic material and, occasionally, some enzymes and regulatory proteins.

A: This statement is true. The basic viral structure consists of a protein capsid surrounding the genetic material, which is either RNA or DNA.
B: This statement is true. Viruses mutate rapidly, due in part to the low fidelity of their replication mechanisms.
D: This statement is true. Viruses are parasites, since they cannot complete a replication cycle without a host.

264. B is correct. Viral penetration of a host cell typically requires interaction between proteins on the surface of the viral particle and receptors on the host cell membrane. We are told that HPV is non-enveloped, so the most external aspect of the viral particle is the capsid itself. Production of an antibody that prevents binding of a viral capsid protein with a host cell receptor is likely to inhibit the docking process and reduce infectivity.

A: Reverse transcriptase is an enzyme responsible for the synthesis of dsDNA from a coding strand of ssRNA. This is an essential step in the replication cycle of RNA retroviruses, but the question states that HPV is a DNA virus. Such viruses would have no reason to express reverse transcriptase.
C: Tumor suppressors are a large family of regulatory proteins that are generally involved in intracellular signaling pathways. They are not produced by viruses; in fact, viruses often inhibit tumor suppressor proteins in order to push the cell cycle forward and permit their own replication.

265. C is correct. Lambda phage is a bacteriophage, a type of virus that exclusively infects bacteria. Since all bacteria are prokaryotes, choice II is correct. Additionally, all viruses are parasites because they cannot complete a full reproductive cycle without a host.

I: Bacteriophages can infect cells through the transfer of either viral DNA or RNA.

III: As viruses, bacteriophages do not possess their own machinery for the production of proteins. All viral proteins are ultimately produced by host ribosomes.

266. B is correct. There is noticeable overlap between the locations of some of the viral genes. For example, the *vif* gene begins at base pair 5280, but the *pol* gene does not end until base pair 5300. It would be impossible for all of these genes to be produced using a single reading frame.

A: The figure offers nothing to suggest this is true, and if multiple reading frames are used, it is not unreasonable to assume that RNA splicing may take place.
C: This could be true, but nothing in the figure suggests it. Viral RNA often has a poly(A) tail and a 5' cap.
D: Again, the figure does not offer any evidence in support of this answer choice. In fact, HIV carries two copies of its genome in each capsid.

267. A is correct. Contact between viral and host DNA can result in recombination events. In eukaryotic cells, direct contact with viral DNA can only occur if the viral DNA enters the nucleus.

B: Viruses do not have cell membranes or complex internal signaling pathways.
C: Since we are told that KSHV causes cancer, it probably does not infect bacteria and would not be classified as a bacteriophage. Furthermore, a bacteriophage would not be sensitive to antibiotics.
D: Although we are told that KSHV uses DNA as its genetic material, it is a virus, meaning that it does not transcribe or translate its own DNA polymerase. Instead, it utilizes the host polymerase for replication.

268. A is correct. The genetic material must be positive-sense RNA. Upon entering the yeast cell, the viral RNA would be treated like host mRNA and quickly processed by yeast ribosomes. This would result in the production of all necessary viral proteins, including those required for RNA replication. In this way, new viral particles could be synthesized and released into the growth medium despite the initial absence of viral accessory proteins.

B: Negative-sense RNA is unlikely to be infectious without an accompanying viral protein to convert it to positive-sense RNA. Even if the negative-sense RNA were translated by host ribosomes, the resulting peptides would be nonfunctional and would not facilitate viral propagation.

C: We are told that the virologist injected the DNA into the cytoplasm of the yeast cells. Isolated DNA in the cytoplasm of eukaryotic cells cannot be processed by ribosomes; instead, it will be rapidly degraded by cytoplasmic exonucleases. RNA polymerase, which resides only in the nucleus, is necessary for the production of functional viral proteins. There is no reason to believe that viral DNA could have entered the nucleus in this case.

D: This is incorrect for the same reasons as option C. Furthermore, ssDNA is more unstable than dsDNA and cannot be processed by cellular ribosomes, regardless of sense.

269. C is correct. The primary structure of RNA is conserved across all organisms and viruses. It is always composed of A, U, G, and C.

   A: This statement is true. RNA contains a free hydroxyl group that can act as a nucleophile and permit hydrolysis.
   B: This statement is true. Since it lacks a complementary strand, reverse transcription frequently produces errors that can lead to the production of non-functional proteins or advantageous mutations.
   D: This statement is true, and is often the cause of pandemics such as Spanish flu or avian flu. Viruses often carry multiple distinct segments of genetic material, analogous to chromosomes in eukaryotes. If two viral particles infect the same cell, these segments can be exchanged and result in new combinations of viral traits.

270. D is correct. Ionizing radiation damages nucleic acids and leads to mutations. Since viruses depend on intact nucleic acids to transfer genetic information, it is unlikely that CDJ has a viral cause. Peptide bonds are less affected by ionizing radiation, and a hallmark of prion proteins is their thermodynamic stability.

   A: This statement does not support or refute either hypothesis. Antibiotics are only effective against bacterial infections, not prion diseases or viral infections.
   B: This supports the viral hypothesis. If the presence of prions is simply a result of a host

reaction to viral infection, the prions themselves are not the infectious agent. The prion hypothesis claims that consumption of prions causes CDJ, but the scenario outlined in this answer choice suggests that a viral infection could be the initial trigger.

C: This does not support either hypothesis more than the other. The crude lysates could contain virus particles or prions, either of which could infect the healthy animals and cause them to develop CDJ.

271. C is correct. The name "trisomy 21" indicates that three copies of chromosome 21 are present, in contrast to the wild-type genotype, which has only two. This error occurs during mitosis in the form of a nondisjunction; as a result, a gamete will possess an extra copy of the chromosome. In general, nondisjunction simply means that chromosomes do not separate during anaphase, resulting in a daughter cell with two copies of the chromosome and a daughter cell without any copies.

   A, B: Chromosomal crossover occurs during prophase I of meiosis. In this normal event, homologous chromosomes recombine to yield added genetic diversity. Crossing over does not result in trisomy 21.

272. B is correct. The phases of mitosis can be remembered using the acronym "PMAT," with prometaphase falling between prophase and metaphase. The first phase, prophase, is marked by condensing of the chromosomes. Shortly afterward, during prometaphase, the nuclear membrane disintegrates, and spindle fibers begin to contact the kinetochores. In metaphase, the chromosomes align along the central metaphase plate. Anaphase is the stage in which the pairs begin to separate and move to opposite poles of the spindle apparatus. Finally, during telophase, the nuclear membranes re-form around the two separate sets of genetic material.

273. C is correct. To answer this question, we must understand the role and mechanism of microtubules in cellular division. These fibers originate from the centrosomes and attach to the kinetochore, or central region of each chromosome. Microtubules position homologous pairs at the center of the cell during metaphase.

To do so, the apparatus must assemble and disassemble to adjust the chromosomes precisely at the center. Paclitaxel would prevent the tubulin from disassembling, thus freezing the spindle configuration, and the cell cycle would stop at metaphase.

274. D is correct. Homologous recombination, which occurs during meiosis, is another term for "crossing over." In this event, nucleotide sequences are exchanged between similar, but non-identical, chromosomes; this contributes to genetic diversity. Homologous recombination also serves as a method by which cells repair breaks in the DNA. However, it should not directly result in an inappropriate distribution of DNA, or aneuploidy.

    A: Nondisjunction occurs when homologous chromosomes improperly separate during cell division. This does result in an incorrect number of chromosomes in the resulting gametes.
    B: Merotelic attachment happens when both mitotic spindle poles attach to one kinetochore. Consequently, sister chromatids are distributed unevenly.
    C: Multipolar spindles, as their name implies, exist when more than two poles form on the spindle apparatus. This results in more than two daughter cells, with an unequal distribution of chromosomes among them.

275. D is correct. Since the chromosomes must be well-stained, the cells should be arrested during metaphase. At this time, the chromosomes are much more compact than they are during early prophase. The chromosome count of a eukaryotic cell is simply the total number of chromosomes; note that this count includes the two sex chromosomes. This man's karyogram shows that he has 46 chromosomes, which is the same as any wild-type human.

    A, B: Although chromosomes are condensed during prophase, they exhibit a denser conformation during metaphase. If staining of these chromosomes occurred in prophase, it would appear weaker due to the comparatively loose packing.
    C: This man has 44 autosomal chromosomes and 2 sex chromosomes. The question is asking for a chromosome count, which includes all 46.

276. B is correct. For both mitosis and meiosis to proceed as expected, DNA must be accurately replicated. This occurs during the S phase of interphase. Any mutations introduced during DNA replication can be dangerous or even lethal for the daughter cells.

    I: Meiosis is associated with sexual reproduction. In contrast, mitosis occurs in somatic cells and is used by organisms as a form of growth. It can also be categorized as a form of asexual reproduction.
    II, III: These statements are accurate for mitosis, which produces two genetically identical, diploid daughter cells. However, meiosis I results in two genetically different haploid cells. During meiosis II, these cells divide further to form the four haploid gametes with which we are typically familiar.

277. B is correct. The question stem is describing a tetrad, in which two homologous chromosomes (along with their identical sister chromatids) are joined at the chiasmata. Because the tetrads are lined up at the center of the cell, the metaphase plate, this indicates that the cell is experiencing metaphase I of meiosis. This is the phase when the homologous chromosomes (each containing two sister chromatids) are aligned.

    A: This is not indicated by the question stem.
    C, D: By the beginning of meiosis II, homologous chromosomes have already segregated into separate daughter cells. The scientist would not observe a total of four chromatids in either of these phases.

278. D is correct. At the onset of anaphase, multiple events take place in order to accurately and precisely separate the sister chromatids. However, the chromatin structure does not relax between metaphase and anaphase. The centromere structure must remain intact, as it continues to associate with the kinetochore and other factors related to the spindle apparatus.

    A: The kinetochore must have attachments to both poles for the chromatids to have the ability to migrate. This is referred to as "biorientation."
    B: Cohesin, a protein complex that holds the sister chromatids together, must be severed to allow sister chromatids to separate.
    C: Lastly, when the sister chromatids are about to segregate, the microtubules of the spindle

apparatus depolymerize, creating the tension to pull the chromatids apart.

279. A is correct. When analyzing the man's karyogram, we see that he is missing chromosome 15 entirely, but has two copies of chromosome 14 that are much larger than normal. We can speculate that chromosomes 14 and 15 have somehow become fused. This can result from a Robertsonian translocation, in which the long q arms of chromosomes are transposed to form one large derivative structure.

280. C is correct. This man's gametes will contain only 22 chromosomes, not the usual 23. As a result, when his sperm is joined with an egg, the resulting zygote will be aneuploid, or missing one chromosome. This instability can promote spontaneous abortions or miscarriages.

    B: The karyogram shows that this man's sex chromosomes are not affected by his condition. D: Although the man's gamete production may be unstable, there is no reason to believe that his condition would completely disrupt meiosis, especially considering that he is still diploid and has an even number of chromosomes.

281. C is correct. The cell spends close to 90% of its time in interphase, which includes the processes of DNA replication, protein synthesis, and cell growth.

    IV: Not all of the components of interphase are of equal length. The G_1 phase is longer than the S phase, while the G_0 phase varies highly based on cell type.

282. A is correct. The G_1 phase is the primary period of cellular growth. Based on environmental conditions, nutrients, and the presence of signaling molecules, the cell will either fully commit to the cell cycle and initiate the S phase, or it will enter G_0.

    B: This checkpoint is necessary for ensuring that all DNA has been replicated correctly. However, at this point, the cell has already committed to the cycle.

283. D is correct. Cell cycle checkpoints are incredibly important in the regulation of cell growth. Typically, if its environment lacks nutrients, a cell may enter the G_0 phase, while if DNA replication was inaccurate, it will remain in the G_2 phase. Cancer cells, on the contrary, often lack such checkpoints, making them prone to unrestricted proliferation.

    A: This is another quality of cancer cells. However, it relates more to tumor growth than to division.

284. D is correct. The G_0 phase is entered directly from the G_1 phase. However, if a cell notes the presence of poorly copied DNA, it must have already finished the S phase.

    A, B: Growth factors and cyclin-dependent kinases are necessary to drive a cell further into the cell cycle.
    C: Terminally differentiated cells are those that have reached full maturity but retain their functionality, such as nerve and cardiac muscle cells. These cell types remain in the G_0 phase.

285. B is correct. Neurons are terminally differentiated cells, which stop dividing but retain their function. Mature erythrocytes, which have no nuclei, do not divide at all.

    A: Liver cells are generally suspended in the G_0 phase. However, under certain conditions, these cells can return to the G_1 phase.
    C: Epithelial cells divide throughout an organism's life.

286. C is correct. The G_2 checkpoint is also known as the G_2-M DNA damage checkpoint. It functions primarily to identify incorrectly replicated DNA.

    A: The G_1 phase occurs before DNA replication.
    B: The S phase is the phase in which DNA is copied, not proofread.

287. B is correct. A cell will transition from the G_1 to the S phase when it is in a favorable environment and has acquired enough nutrients, in addition to containing the proper growth factors. If a cell enters the S phase prematurely, the G_2 checkpoint will still ensure that the DNA has been replicated correctly. However, due to the reduced time spent in the G_1 phase, the cell will be smaller in size and will thus yield smaller daughter cells.

288. B is correct. Cdk stands for cyclin-dependent kinase. As their name implies, these are enzymes that are activated by cyclin and signal cells to progress through a given phase of the cell cycle.

C: Tumor growth is often characterized by uncontrollable growth. As cip and kip are cell cycle inhibitors, their presence would inhibit cancerous growth.

D: Cdk1 is active during the G_1 phase and does trigger certain processes to prepare the cell for the S phase. However, the absence of Cdk1, while reducing the viability of the cell, would not completely prevent it from beginning DNA synthesis.

289. D is correct. The amount of cyclins and their corresponding Cdks vary drastically based on the phase in which the cell is found. Cyclin and Cdks serve to promote the cell cycle, and a perpetually high level of both of these species would push the cell forward in the cycle, even if other factors (such as nutrient availability and environmental conditions) were not favorable.

290. B is correct. During the G_2 phase, the cell has already passed through both the S and the G_1 stages, which indicates that it possesses sufficient nutrients and exists in favorable conditions. Completing the S phase means that the DNA has doubled its genetic information. Additionally, the G_2 phase immediately precedes mitosis, making it the last phase during which the cell can produce protein and organelles.

    D: At this point, the cell has split into two much smaller daughter cells.

291. C is correct. The cells of the webbing undergo apoptosis; they shrink in size, their nuclear DNA is degraded, and they separate into small membrane-wrapped fragments. Finally, nearby phagocytic cells engulf these pieces.

292. B is correct. The terms "autocrine" and "endocrine" are labeled appropriately, while "paracrine" and "juxtacrine" are reversed.

293. D is correct. These are the proper definitions of these terms.

    A, B: These choices attempt to incorporate apoptosis and regenerative capacity.

294. B is correct. As pluripotent cells develop into multipotent cells, they express a greater percentage of lineage-specific genes due to specialization. DNA methylation provides one of the mechanisms used to "turn off" genes not related to the newly specialized cells.

    A: Lineage potential, or the ability to differentiate into many cell types, decreases according to the arrow, as does the expression of pluripotent genes.
    C, D: Chromatin becomes more "closed" or specialized in the direction of the arrow.

295. A is correct. The ectoderm produces the epidermis, nervous system, eye lens, and hair.

    B: These cells are derived from the mesoderm.
    C: These cells are derived from the endoderm.
    D: This choice combines organs and tissue types that are derived from different lineages.

296. D is correct. Senescence is a term that relates to aging.

    A: This choice refers to a cell's potency.
    B: This option exemplifies regenerative capacity.
    C: This is apoptosis, not senescence.

297. B is correct. The embryo first undergoes division into a blastula, or hollow ball of cells. Next, some of these cells migrate inwards in a process called gastrulation. This produces the structure in the figure, the gastrula.

    A: A blastula is a hollow ball of cells that has not yet undergone gastrulation.
    C: A zygote is simply a one-cell fertilized egg.
    D: An egg would appear as a single cell, unlike this diagram.

298. C is correct. This layer of cells is the endoderm, which gives rise to the linings of internal organs.

    A: These types of cell would differentiate from the ectoderm, the outer layer of the gastrula.
    B: These arise from the mesoderm.

299. C is correct. Regenerative capacity refers to an organ's ability to rebuild itself. Humans exhibit partial regeneration in response to injury, with the liver representing an organ with high regenerative capacity. Thus, this structure can undergo extensive, but not complete, regrowth. In fact, a person can donate up to 50% of his liver and it will regrow the missing portion.

300. D is correct. Research has shown that telomeres, the repetitive sequences at the ends of chromosomes, shorten with each successive division. Eventually, this shortening can

become so severe that the cell may lose genetic information or be unable to undergo division.

301. C is correct. All three of these statements accurately characterize meiosis.

    III: Interphase II does not exist.

302. B is correct. This statement perfectly sums up the very general concepts of mitosis and meiosis.

303. C is correct. Spermatogenesis is the production of sperm, where one somatic cell gives rise to four germ cells. Oogenesis, in contrast, produces only one germ cell in addition to polar bodies.

304. B is correct. This cell has an odd number of chromosomes, meaning that it must be a haploid cell. Of the choices listed, only germ cells are haploid.

305. A is correct. During oogenesis, only one ovum is produced at a time. In addition, polar bodies are formed and quickly degraded. This, combined with the timing of oogenesis, is advantageous because it only produces one offspring at a time. In an animal like a human, who is not capable of carrying a large litter, this serves as a built-in mechanism to prevent unhealthy pregnancies.

306. D is correct. Of the four hormones listed, FH peaks at 7 days, while LH and estrogen peak at 14. The peak for progesterone is not shown, but this hormone exists at low levels throughout the cycle, except for at day 21. Therefore, it can be assumed that the peak is either right before or right after this date. This is the latest peak of the four hormones.

307. D is correct. Following implantation of the fertilized egg, hCG is released. This hormone mimics LH to stimulate high levels of estrogen and progesterone. Similarly, it is the drop in estrogen and progesterone which triggers a new cycle to begin.

308. B is correct. The percentages of DNA are based on a comparison to a cell in the G_1 phase, which would not yet have undergone replication. In comparison, a cell that has recently experienced replication will have twice the amount of DNA.

309. C is correct. Immediately following fertilization, the DNA of the ovum has combined with that of the sperm cell. Both of these cells would have 50% of the DNA of a somatic G_1 cell; therefore, the fertilized egg should contain 100%.

310. A is correct. The digestive enzymes in the acrosome are used to dissolve the protective coating on the ovum, allowing the sperm cell to enter and fertilize. Of the options given, this is the only reasonable choice.

    B, C, D: None of these describe sperm functions correctly.

311. B is correct. A zygote is formed by the fusion of gametes (one sperm and one ovum). As both gametes are haploid, fusion results in a single, diploid cell.

    A: An embryo is a multicellular organism with developing organ systems. The question specifies that the answer should be single-celled.
    C: Following the formation of the zygote, four cell divisions occur with no significant growth. The resulting ball of cells is known as the morula, which is not unicellular.
    D: A gastrula is a collection of cells containing three germ layers; these will develop and differentiate into organs during organogenesis. The question refers to a much earlier stage of development.

312. D is correct. The diploid cell produced by fertilization is known as a zygote. Following multiple divisions with no cell growth, the ball of cells becomes known as the morula. Further division results in the blastula, a compact, hollow collection of cells. Finally, an invagination into this structure results in three tissue layers, and the developing organism is now called the gastrula.

313. A is correct. The question states that spina bifida is a result of improper neurulation. Nervous tissue is derived from the ectoderm.

    B: The endoderm is the most internal layer; it forms the linings of many organs but does not relate to neurulation.
    C: The mesoderm is the middle germ layer. Blood, muscle, and kidney cells, among others, are derived from the mesoderm.
    D: This is not a germ layer.

314. C is correct. This question indicates that the ectoderm has been labeled, so all tissue derived from this layer should be labeled as well. The nervous system, skin, hair, and nails are all derived from the ectoderm.

A: These tissues are derived from the mesoderm.
B: These internal organs and linings are derived from the endoderm.
D: Although the skin, brain, and portions of the eye are derived from the ectoderm, erythrocytes arise from mesodermal tissue.

315. B is correct. In healthy developing organisms, maternal growth factors do not pass through the placenta. Thus, they play no role in pattern formation.

A, D: Signaling pathways allow a cell to communicate with itself and neighboring cells to coordinate cellular fate. This is critical for pattern formation.
C: A morphogen gradient does form across a developing embryo. This gradient signals cells regarding their relative positions, which is essential for position-based differentiation.

316. A is correct. The scientist has exploited pattern formation to specify which limb arises from a particular bud. While cells in the limb buds receive the same signals, they are interpreted differently to specify the limb that actually forms. This requires limb-specific transcription factors, which activate the transcription of specific genes to initiate differentiation.

B, C, D: Although changing the poles or zone of polarizing activity may seem sufficient at first, there is no indication that it will directly affect the cell's interpretation of the signals. Similarly, dissecting and reattaching the limb buds may not change the preexisting signaling pathways occurring in the developing embryo.

317. D is correct. Inhibiting differentiation would completely prevent organogenesis. Differentiation is the process by which stem cells mature into cells with specific functions. These clusters of differentiated cells give rise to organs and organ systems in organogenesis.

A, B, C: Intercalation is the process by which cells move to create thin layers. Pattern formation is the organization of cells based on their position, and requires cell movement or migration. All

of these options are related to cell position, not cell function. Consequently, they would not be directly affected if differentiation were stalled.

318. D is correct. The neural tube gives rise to the spinal cord, brain, and neural crest cells. The crest cells can then become pigment cells, neurons, and a variety of other cell types.

IV: The vertebral column is derived from the endoderm, not the neural tube.

319. D is correct. Maternal exposure to teratogens, maternal genotype, and maternal disease all are environmental and genetic factors that could predispose an embryo to developmental abnormalities. Teratogens are chemical agents that may disturb the development of an embryo, such as medications, drugs, or chemicals. More vulnerable maternal genotypes or existing maternal conditions, such as heart disease, may also increase the risk of pathological development.

320. A is correct. The marked structure is the neural tube. The neural tube develops into the central nervous system, including the brain and the spinal cord.

B: The peripheral nervous system is derived from other ectodermal tissue, not from the neural tube directly.
C, D: The notochord is the round tube-like structure immediately ventral to (and in this figure, below) the neural tube. In the developing embryo, the notochord defines the primitive axis.

321. C is correct. Epithelial cells do not directly connect to collagen and other fibers of the basement membrane. Instead, they possess transmembrane proteins called integrins that can connect to collagen, or, more typically, to a bridging protein like fibronectin, which itself attaches to collagen.

A: Interleukins are immune proteins that are not involved in cell-ECM junctions.
B: Cadherins form cell-cell junctions, not junctions between the cell and the extracellular matrix.
D: Connexins are gap junction proteins and are not involved in this type of connection.

322. D is correct. Tight junctions are necessary in all epithelial cell layers that have functions that

depend on preventing free diffusion between the sides of the layer. Such cells use transmembrane transport proteins to move molecules through the cell. In contrast, the free exchange of gas molecules is the entire purpose of lung tissue; lung capillaries are therefore extremely leaky and contain no tight junctions.

A, B, C: The blood-brain barrier, the selective transport of nutrients, and the exclusion of filtrate from the kidney ECM all rely on the presence of tight junctions to form a seal against diffusion.

323. D is correct. As a gland, the pancreas is composed primarily of epithelial tissue, making choice III correct. It secretes hormones like insulin and glucagon into the bloodstream, making statement I correct as well. However, it also secretes enzymes such as proteases into the GI tract, making it an exocrine gland in addition to its endocrine function. Interestingly, the GI tract is considered "exterior" to the organism as it is continuous with the surface of the skin, and indeed develops from an indentation of the outermost layer of the embryo. In this way, the action of the pancreas resembles that of other exocrine structures like sweat and sebaceous glands.

324. B is correct. Vitamin C is vital for the synthesis of collagen. A deficiency in collagen will severely weaken connective tissues, resulting in bleeding.

A: Proteoglycans are found in most connective tissues and play numerous roles, such as forming gels and regulating cell growth. However, they do not have a structural function like collagen does. C: While keratin is also vital to the strength of tissues like gums, it is an intracellular component of epithelial, not connective, tissues. D: Connexins help form cellular gap junctions; they do not play a role in the stability of connective tissue.

325. B is correct. The endothelium is the name given to the epithelial lining of the vasculature surrounding the inner space or lumen. Underneath this lining lies vascular smooth muscle, which is encompassed by the outer lining or adventitia. To prevent rupturing of the plaque,

it is best to strengthen the endothelium beneath which it is located.

326. C is correct. Chondrocytes are the cells involved in maintaining cartilaginous connective tissue throughout the body. Muscles, like that of the calf, are made of muscle cells, not cartilage. They would thus not be directly impacted by an issue with chondrocyte activity.

A, B, D: Tissues such as joint capsules, intervertebral discs, and ligaments would be negatively affected by impaired maintenance of cartilage.

327. B is correct. The uterus relies on motile cilia in its epithelium to move the embryo from the ovary and Fallopian tubes. Dysfunction of these cilia can result in an ectopic pregnancy. Cilia are present on most cells of the body, but motile cilia that move under their own power are found only in the uterine lining and the trachea.

328. B is correct. Layer 2 is the basement membrane, which connects the epithelial layer to the underlying connective tissue. The basal lamina is one layer of this membrane; the reticular lamina, composed of reticular fibers, is the other.

329. D is correct. The swollen, blobby appearance of these cells should alert you to their identity as carriers of lipid droplets. No structures characteristic of the other tissue types are visible, such as neurons (A), muscle cells with gap junctions (C), or villi (B).

330. B is correct. The fluid consists of proteoglycans and glycoproteins, which, along with water, are the major components of mucus. Of the mentioned tissues, which is known to secrete mucus? The name of choice B gives this answer away. Goblet cells in the mucosa (or epithelial lining) of the small intestine produce mucus, and cancers of these cells (known as adenocarcinomas) are not uncommon.

331. B is correct. Activation of the parasympathetic nervous system stimulates digestion while decreasing heart rate. The sympathetic nervous system has opposite effects. Deactivation of the parasympathetic system will cause sympathetic activity to dominate, producing the symptoms

mentioned in the question (inhibited digestion and increased heart rate).

C: The limbic system is associated with the activation of emotions in the brain.

D: The somatic nervous system controls voluntary muscle movements; it is not involved in regulating digestion or heart rate.

332. A is correct. In sympathetic pathways, almost all postsynaptic nerves secrete norepinephrine on their target effectors.

B: The enteric nervous system is another name for the "gut brain," the cluster of parasympathetic ganglia that are heavily involved in controlling digestion. As part of the parasympathetic system, it does not directly involve norepinephrine.

C, D: These systems secrete acetylcholine, not norepinephrine, on their final targets.

333. B is correct. Sensory (afferent) tracts are located toward the rear, or dorsal, side of the spinal cord. In contrast, motor (efferent) tracts lie toward the front, or ventral, and lateral sides. If only the dorsal nerves are severed, then motor neurons are still intact, and the soldier should retain motility of both voluntary and involuntary muscles.

D: The digestive tract, controlled by visceral motor neurons, should also remain motile, though its regulation will likely be disrupted by the lack of visceral sensory input due to the injury.

334 D is correct. Schwann cells produce the myelin sheath of peripheral neurons. The description of symptoms in areas such as the skin and skeletal muscles should indicate that such neurons are Guillain-Barré's target. Therefore, it must be Schwann cells that are dying, causing these peripheral nerves to become demyelinated.

A: Microglial cells perform maintenance in the brain; they do not relate to the symptoms described.

B: Astrocytes help support the blood-brain barrier.

C: Oligodendrocytes form the myelin sheath in the central nervous system. Since the CNS includes only the brain and spinal cord, demyelination there would not explain the symptoms.

335. C is correct. Many reflexes are involved in maintaining homeostasis, which can cause hormone levels to be adjusted in response to (for example) increased blood pressure.

A: Some reflex arcs, like the familiar "knee-jerk" reflex, pass directly from sensory to motor neurons without being integrated by an interneuron.

B: Reflex arcs certainly do not need to be located in the brain. In fact, one hallmark of a reflexive response is that it does not depend on the brain for control.

D: "Special senses" like vision and hearing can also trigger reflexes. For example, you might flinch at a noise or at an object hurling towards your face.

336. D is correct. The sympathetic nervous system is recognizable by its distinctive chained ganglia parallel to the spinal cord.

A: The dorsal root (or sensory) ganglia are also parallel to the spinal cord, but are not chained. While knowledge of these structures is not high-yield on the MCAT, you certainly should be familiar with both the sympathetic and parasympathetic nervous systems.

B, C: Parasympathetic (and enteric) ganglia are located near the organs they control, not near the spinal cord.

337. D is correct. In locked-in syndrome, it is the motor pathways that are inoperative. These pathways are efferent, as they travel away from the spinal cord. Since the sufferer maintains function in his internal organs, autonomic (or visceral) efferent pathways must be intact, but somatic (or voluntary) motor pathways are not.

338. B is correct. The dorsal root, or sensory, ganglia are distinctive in that they contain pseudobipolar neurons like type 4. In fact, the offset cell bodies of these neurons make up most of the mass of these structures. Such neurons allow unimpeded transmission of sensory impulses, as they do not have to travel through the cell body.

A, C: Neurons in the brain are more likely to be heavily branched, like type 3.

D: Special sensory neurons are likely to be bipolar, like type 2. In fact, you've likely heard of the bipolar neurons in the retina. Note that unipolar neurons (type 1) are rare in humans but present in some insects.

339. C is correct. The parasympathetic nervous system is responsible for delivering impulses to the genitals. These signals relax certain smooth muscles, allowing blood to flow into the penis during an erection. The parasympathetic system also delivers acetylcholine to all its effectors. Therefore, increasing the body's acetylcholine levels could help this patient with erectile dysfunction.

A, D: Dopamine and serotonin are not directly involved in physiological sexual responses.
B: The sympathetic nervous system, which secretes norepinephrine on most of its effectors, controls the orgasm. You can remember this using the mnemonic "P is for point, S is for shoot." Since this patient has erectile dysfunction, he is having difficulty becoming aroused in the first place, making the parasympathetic system a better target.

340. B is correct. The sympathetic nervous system promotes both vasoconstriction and dilation, depending on the organ. In other words, it activates areas necessary for "fight-or-flight" activity and deactivates areas unimportant to such a response. Digestive organs, like the large intestine and stomach, display reduced blood flow when the sympathetic system is active. This makes sense with what we already know about this system, as a threatened organism has more pressing issues to worry about than digesting its last meal.

II: Vessels within skeletal muscle are dilated under sympathetic stimulation to provide oxygen for vigorous activity.
IV: When the sympathetic system is activated, the bronchioles within the lungs are dilated. This increases the oxygen content in the lungs and triggers the lung vasculature to dilate automatically.

341. B is correct. Point B indicates the axon hillock, a special region of the soma from which impulses originate. First, the release and binding of neurotransmitters from neighboring cells triggers graded potentials in the dendrites. Should these potentials summate in a manner that exceeds the threshold, a large number of voltage-gated ion channels at the axon hillock will open. The hillock's position directly adjacent to the axon allows proper initiation of an action potential.

A: Action potentials are not generated in the dendrites. Graded potentials may very well occur at these sites, but the initiation of a full action potential requires depolarization at the axon hillock.
C: This label most directly points to a Schwann cell, which helps myelinate the axon. These cells do not depolarize and cannot initiate action potentials or graded potentials.
D: This point indicates the axon terminal, from which synaptic vesicles will be released. Generally, action potentials only conduct in a single direction.

342. C is correct. The image shows a neuron with an axon coated in Schwann cells, which produce myelin. Schwann cells can be distinguished from oligodendrocytes (the other myelin-producing cells) by their tendency to wrap closely around the axon instead of protruding outward. Schwann cells are present only in the peripheral nervous system.

A: Myelinated CNS neurons, which make up the white matter of the brain, are myelinated by oligodendrocytes.

343. D is correct. Conducting velocity is influenced by the radius of the axon, with thicker axons able to propagate action potentials more rapidly. Myelination also increases conducting velocity.

344. C is correct. Synaptic vesicles have tightly-controlled size constraints. Therefore, all vesicles contain a roughly similar amount of neurotransmitter. The release of even a single synaptic vesicle causes enough neurotransmitter to enter the synaptic cleft to provoke a measurable postsynaptic depolarization. That being said, the release of one vesicle may not necessarily be sufficient to elicit an action potential.

A: The target neuron does not necessarily produce or release the same neurotransmitter as its presynaptic partner.
B: Again, we cannot know if the amount of glutamate released is enough to trigger an action potential.
D: Synaptic glutamate diffuses out of the synapse and is typically recycled or metabolized

by neighboring astrocytes, rather than by the postsynaptic neuron.

345. C is correct. AMPA receptors open in response to the binding of ligand (specifically, glutamate). While they do permit the passage of sodium and potassium, they should not be confused with the voltage-gated ion channels responsible for the propagation of an action potential.

    B: Leaky channels allow ion passage with or without an input signal. An AMPAR requires the binding of glutamate before any ions are able to pass through.
    D: The figure shows the movement of both sodium and potassium ions through the channel. Since two different types of cations are able to pass, this receptor would be better described as a "nonspecific cation channel."

346. C is correct. The arrival of an action potential at the axon terminal triggers a rapid influx of calcium ions, which then initiates a number of critical neurotransmission events. This increase in intracellular calcium is the "change in cytoplasmic conditions" to which the question is referring. If synaptotagmin must directly respond to the presence of intracellular calcium, it must contain some sort of calcium-binding domain. The only protein listed in the answer choices that also binds calcium is calmodulin. It is most reasonable to assume that these two proteins may share structural similarities.

347. C is correct. Increased conduction through AMPA receptors would permit the more efficient passage of extracellular cations into the neuron, facilitating a more rapid postsynaptic response. With regard to statement II, the activation of scaffolding proteins would permit tight co-localization of AMPA receptors on the postsynaptic membrane, effectively increasing the likelihood of glutamate binding. Scaffolding proteins prevent diffusion of transmembrane AMPA receptors out of the postsynaptic density, which allows the postsynaptic neuron to remain sensitive to presynaptic inputs.

    III: AMPAR proteolysis is irrelevant. If the AMPA receptors were sequestered into the cell, they would be unavailable to bind neurotransmitters. Therefore, AMPAR endocytosis would desensitize the postsynaptic neuron to further input. Notably,

this is one mechanism by which long-term depression (LTD) is mediated.

348. A is correct. The question states that acetylcholinesterase is membrane-bound, and that it is responsible for the extremely rapid degradation of acetylcholine. Since physostigmine is an acetylcholinesterase inhibitor, the concentration of acetylcholine in the synaptic cleft will likely increase when the drug is present.

    C, D: These choices can be immediately eliminated because no part of the hydrolysis catalyzed by acetylcholinesterase is intracellular. In fact, acetylcholine, a charged molecule, never enters the postsynaptic cell.

349. D is correct. Although the definition of a neurotransmitter is fairly broad, these molecules must be small enough to rapidly diffuse across the synaptic cleft and exert physiological effects. Peptides are the largest molecules that can still be classified as neurotransmitters. A relatively large protein like neuroglobin would diffuse slowly in comparison to small organic molecules and soluble peptides. Neurotransmitters must also have a mechanism by which the signal can be shut off, either by degradation or synaptic clearance. The only mechanism by which a large protein could be removed from the synapse is endocytosis, which is relatively slow and energetically unfavorable.

    A: In addition to its peripheral immune functions, histamine is a neurotransmitter in the CNS and is involved in mediating wakefulness and attention. Many classical neurotransmitters are monoamines, including dopamine and serotonin.
    B: Although toxic in large amounts, small amounts of carbon monoxide are produced transiently in the brain, which facilitates communication between neurons. Nitric oxide, which is better studied, acts similarly.
    C: Substance P is involved in the propagation of signals associated with pain. It is both a neurotransmitter and a neuromodulator.

350. B is correct. We are told both that succinylcholine is an ester and that it resembles acetylcholine. This information suggests that, like acetylcholine, it is subject to enzymatic hydrolysis. The question also mentions that succinylcholine binds

without antagonistic activity to the same site as acetylcholine, but that it is nevertheless a potent paralytic agent. In reality, succinylcholine binds the receptor and briefly triggers an excitatory response, followed by a prolonged period of muscular inactivity resulting from sustained depolarization of the postsynaptic cell. In other words, the postsynaptic neuron is unable to repolarize, and instead remains in a refractory period with no ability to generate further impulses. In fact, patients exhibit involuntary muscle twitching, known as fasciculation, shortly after receiving IV succinylcholine.

A: If succinylcholine did not cause a depolarization while also not serving as an antagonist, it would not have a paralytic effect on patients.

351. A is correct. Due to their respective concentration gradients, sodium cations will enter the cell during the depolarization phase of an action potential, while potassium will exit the cell to repolarize it. Additionally, choice A accurately shows that ions are only able to enter and exit the cell at the nodes of Ranvier, or gaps in the myelin sheath. At other positions on the axon, multiple layers of myelin prevent significant ion movement.

B: This choice reverses the directions of Na^+ and K^+ movement.
C, D: These diagrams inaccurately show ions entering and exiting the cell at all locations along the axon. In reality, this only occurs at the nodes of Ranvier.

352. C is correct. The resting potential of a typical neuron is -70 mV. The terms "depolarization," "repolarization," and "hyperpolarization" are all given in reference to this value. Therefore, when a neuron depolarizes, its membrane potential becomes less negative than -70 mV. Between points 2 and 3, the opposite happens; the neuron's potential is dropping to a more negative value. It even briefly dips below -70, which is termed a hyperpolarization.

A, B: On the diagram above, depolarization is marked by point 1. It does not occur between points 2 and 3.
D: Hyperpolarization (marked by point 3) occurs after depolarization in the action potential shown.

353. B is correct. The label 1 marks the depolarization phase of the action potential. During the early parts of this phase, sodium channels either are already open or are rapidly opening as a result of a superthreshold stimulus. In contrast, K^+ voltage-gated channels, which are slower to open, will mainly remain closed until near the end of the depolarization period. Opening of these channels spurs the cell to repolarize and return to its resting state.

A: This is the reverse of the correct choice, and would be more apt near the beginning of the repolarization phase.
C: Inactivation is a complicated concept generally discussed in relation to sodium channels. For this question, note only that "inactive" is not synonymous with "closed." Many voltage-gated channels have two gates, an activation gate and an inactivation gate. When either is closed, transmission through the channel is blocked; however, inactivation gates are generally closed immediately after a channel has been open. These gates are not likely to be shut for potassium channels at the moment under discussion.
D: Most sodium channels will be open at this time.

354. B is correct. Remember, for a typical neuron, the concentration of sodium is much greater outside the cell than inside; the reverse is true for potassium. For this reason, addition of Na^+ leak channels will allow more sodium cations to enter the intracellular space. In contrast, a reduction in the number of K^+ leak channels will decrease the permeability of the membrane to potassium, trapping more of these cations inside the neuron. In total, both changes act to make the cell more positive in comparison to its environment.

D: Since the neuron becomes more positive, it will actually be easier to hit a threshold value and trigger an action potential.

355. D is correct. Hyperpolarization refers to any phase in which the cell becomes more negative (or polarized) than its resting value. Unless told otherwise, we can generally estimate that the resting membrane potential for a typical neuron is -70 mV. Thus, -85 mV, which is more negative, is a value that could certainly be attained during

the hyperpolarization "overshoot" of the action potential.

A, B: These values constitute depolarization, not hyperpolarization.
C: This is equal to the typical resting potential of a neuron. Note, of course, that different neurons have different resting potentials.

356. D is correct. Leak channels are named based on their tendency to remain open; in other words, they allow ions to "leak" in or out. In contrast, voltage-gated channels only open when the membrane potential exceeds or drops below a certain approximate value.

    B: In a typical neuron, the concentration of potassium is much greater inside the cell than outside. For this reason, the opening of leak channels would allow potassium to travel outward, down its concentration gradient. This would constitute a hyperpolarization.
    C: This choice mistakenly interprets the meaning of the word "hyperpolarize." Since the resting potential is relatively negative, a cell that "hyper" -polarizes becomes even more negative with respect to its environment.

357. D is correct. The opening of sodium voltage-gated ion channels promotes an initial depolarization, which triggers the opening of more of the same channels. If the resulting depolarization surpasses the threshold value, the neuron will fire. Inhibition of sodium transmission blocks all of these processes and makes an action potential virtually impossible.

    A, C: These choices would make slightly more sense if sodium did travel out of the cell. However, when its channels are opened, sodium moves down its concentration gradient to enter the neuron and cause depolarization.

358. B is correct. This description perfectly distinguishes absolute and relative refractory periods. Specifically, a neuron experiences an absolute period during the depolarization and early repolarization phases of an action potential, while the relative period encompasses the time when the neuron is hyperpolarized.

    A: The same neuron certainly can experience both relative and absolute refractory periods.
    C, D: These descriptions are untrue.

359. A is correct. Since the post-synaptic neuron became hyperpolarized (and thus less likely to reach the threshold required to execute an action potential), this term aptly describes the situation. GABA is the classic inhibitory neurotransmitter and often promotes such responses.

    B, D: Glutamate is an excitatory neurotransmitter. As such, it would likely depolarize, not hyperpolarize, a post-synaptic cell.
    C: Hyperpolarization constitutes inhibition, not excitation.

360. D is correct. The "all-or-none" principle states that a neuron will fire when it experiences a depolarization that surpasses its threshold, and will not fire when it does not. In other words, there is no "in-between" region in which the neuron fires more strongly or weakly. Since both stimuli surpass the threshold of -55 mV, this neuron should fire in an identical manner during both trials.

    A: The strength of the stimulus does not determine the strength of a single neuron's response. The neuron should fire equally in Trials 1 and 2.
    B: This choice tries to confuse us with negative numbers. -54 mV is more positive, or depolarized, than -55 mV. Thus, the neuron in Trial 2 does reach and surpass its threshold value.
    C: This is wrong. A neuron is less likely to fire when its potential is especially negative. However, as long as it passes its threshold potential, it will experience an action potential.

361. C is correct. The endocrine system is responsible for secreting hormones, not enzymes, to maintain homeostasis within the body. These hormones can be close- or far-acting, depending on the type and mode of transport. Some glands, most notably the pancreas, do serve both endocrine and exocrine functions.

362. A is correct. Pilocaratine is metabolized in the same way as iodine, which plays its primary role in the thyroid gland. From this limited information, we must also expect pilocaratine to be found there.

    B, C, D: The stomach, liver, and small intestine do not metabolize or store iodine, nor do they utilize iodine-based compounds.

363. D is correct. The adrenal gland is composed of two parts, the cortex and the medulla. The adrenal cortex produces aldosterone and cortisol, among others. The adrenal medulla secretes epinephrine and norepinephrine.

    A: Growth hormone is produced and secreted by the anterior lobe of the pituitary gland.
    B: Epinephrine is secreted from the adrenal medulla.
    C: Glucagon is released by the pancreas.

364. D is correct. Corticosteroids are released upon stimulation of the adrenal cortex by ACTH (adrenocorticotropic hormone), a tropic hormone secreted by the anterior pituitary. ACTH release is mediated by the release of CRH (corticotropin-releasing hormone) from the hypothalamus. Thus, release of CRH will stimulate the release of ACTH, triggering the student's high corticosteroid levels.

    A, C: Decreased ACTH or CRH would most directly result in decreased secretion of corticosteroids.
    B: Increased cortisone in the blood would promote negative feedback of the CRH/ACTH system, resulting in the inhibition of corticosteroid release.

365. B is correct. The anterior pituitary produces FSH, LH, ACTH, TSH, prolactin, endorphin, and GH.

    II: GHRH, or growth hormone releasing hormone, is secreted by the hypothalamus.
    IV: Oxytocin is synthesized by the hypothalamus and stored and released by the posterior pituitary.

366. C is correct. Melatonin is produced and secreted by the pineal gland; it is associated with sleep and the regulation of circadian rhythms.

    A: FSH is produced and secreted by the anterior pituitary.
    B: While ADH is secreted and stored by the posterior pituitary, it is actually produced in the hypothalamus. The posterior pituitary does not synthesize the hormones that it releases.
    D: Insulin is produced and released by the pancreas.

367. A is correct. The lab results show that this patient has high cortisone levels. This can be the result of a hormone-secreting tumor that releases either CRH, ACTH, or cortisone itself. We see that the values for CRH are normal, but that ACTH levels are significantly lowered. Therefore, the tumor must be secreting cortisone, a steroid hormone produced in the adrenal cortex. The decreased ACTH levels can be explained by negative feedback from the high amounts of cortisone.

    B: The hypothalamus does secrete CRH, but if that were the hormone released by the tumor, we would expect high (not low) ACTH levels.
    C: The anterior pituitary secretes ACTH, but again, ACTH is not elevated.
    D: While the symptoms may suggest a thyroid condition, T_3 and T_4 (hormones produced by the thyroid gland) are present at normal levels.

368. B is correct. Vasopressin, otherwise known as ADH, is a fast-acting hormone that increases water reabsorption in the collecting ducts of nephrons in the kidneys. Through this mechanism, it concentrates urine and results in less frequent urination.

    A: Over long periods of time, aldosterone does cause increased reabsorption of sodium and therefore water. However, this steroid hormone is not fast-acting.
    C, D: TSH and GH do not affect the kidneys' ability to concentrate urine.

369. A is correct. The parathyroid gland produces and secretes parathyroid hormone (PTH), which regulates calcium levels along with its antagonist hormone, calcitonin. PTH increases plasma calcium by increasing absorption in the small intestine and extracting calcium from bone, therefore decreasing bone density.

    B: PTH increases plasma calcium levels.
    C, D: PTH does not play a role in the regulation of metabolic rate. This relates more to the thyroid than the parathyroid gland.

370. D is correct. Aldosterone's main role is to increase blood pressure by stimulating extra water retention. To do this, it increases both sodium reabsorption and potassium secretion in the nephrons of the kidney.

    A: Calcium levels relate to calcitonin and PTH, not aldosterone.
    B: Aldosterone increases sodium reabsorption, so levels of that ion should be high, not low.

C: Aldosterone stimulates water reabsorption, leading to high blood pressure.

371. B is correct. Cholesterol plays a role in maintaining membrane fluidity and is a steroid precursor. Steroids then can be converted into bile salts. Cholesterol does not play a role in nucleic acid synthesis.

372. A is correct. Autocrine hormones bind to autocrine receptors on the same cell that released them

    B: Endocrine hormones travel longer distances using the circulatory system.
    C: Paracrine hormones secrete into the extracellular environment to effect nearby cells.
    D: Exocrine products are released through ducts rather than the bloodstream.

373. A is correct. Peptide hormones are large and usually polar, making them unable to enter the cell through the plasma membrane. They therefore must bind to extracellular receptors.

    B, D: Tyrosine-based and steroid hormones are small and nonpolar, allowing them to cross the plasma membrane and bind to intracellular targets.
    C: Gaseous hormones (such as NO) can freely diffuse through the plasma membrane.

374. D is correct. From the given structure, this is a steroid hormone, as it is relatively small and nonpolar. It will thus be able to traverse the plasma membrane and bind to intracellular receptors. Steroid hormones are long-acting, so we would expect this molecule to influence long-term gene expression rather that transient cAMP cascades or calcium influx.

375. C is correct. The question states that cells producing steroid hormones need a large smooth ER and Golgi. Therefore, we must find an organ that produces and secretes steroid hormones. The ovary synthesizes and releases estrogen and progesterone.

A: The anterior pituitary produces FSH, LH, ACTH, TSH, GH, and prolactin, none of which are steroid hormones.
B: The pancreas produces the peptides insulin and glucagon.
D: The adrenal medulla secretes epinephrine and norepinephrine, which are not steroids.

376. A is correct. SHH is released during development when the notochord is still present. The described concentration gradient implies that it is released to neighboring cells.

377. B is correct. cAMP is a secondary signaling molecule that works in the cell to activate or inactivate separate proteins and enzymes. This acts as a cascade to amplify the associated signal.

    A: "Attenuate" means "diminish." As part of a signaling cascade, cAMP amplifies the signal.
    C, D: GH, growth hormone, is a primary signaling molecule.

378. B is correct. Peptide hormones are unable to cross the plasma membrane and must instead bind to transmembrane receptors. These receptors must include a hydrophobic region to span the membrane, as well as hydrophilic regions on either terminal to bind with the peptide hormone and intracellular machinery.

379. B is correct. This accurately represents the steps in a GPCR cascade.

380. D is correct. If an inhibitor of the receptor is present, it will block glucagon from exerting its physiological effect. Glucagon raises blood glucose, so, if glucagon cannot act, plasma glucose will decrease.

381. C is correct. Asthmatic patients suffer from uncontrollable constriction of the bronchioles, a condition that results in the characteristic wheezing associated with an asthma attack. Although the sympathetic nervous system normally triggers contraction of smooth muscle, the beta-adrenergic receptors expressed by muscle in the bronchioles promote relaxation and subsequent bronchial dilation.

    A: The alveoli are not surrounded by muscle. Instead, they are pulled open during inspiration by a decrease in pressure in the pleural space; during passive expiration, they shrink elastically.

B: The trachea is a rigid tube held open by cartilaginous rings and is not surrounded by muscle. An anatomical upper airway obstruction is usually the result of laryngospasm (as opposed to muscular contraction), which occludes the tracheal opening but does not actually collapse the trachea.

D: The glottis is not closed by smooth muscle. Instead, it is occluded when the epiglottis falls to rest on top of it.

382. B is correct. The question stem states that increasing PEEP keeps alveoli inflated and allows gas exchange to occur. Premature infants are often unable to produce surfactant, putting them in danger of respiratory failure secondary to alveolar collapse. Grunting increases the pressure against which the infant must exhale, which forces some of the collapsed alveoli to inflate.

A: PEEP refers purely to pressure at the end of expiration. Asthmatic patients suffer from bronchoconstriction that prevents air from entering their lungs. Although they certainly may be in severe respiratory distress, their condition stems from difficulty with inspiration, not expiration.

C: Alveolar elasticity contributes to the spontaneous decrease in lung volume that occurs during expiration. In other words, the alveoli are elastic enough to shrink when air is exhaled. A patient with lowered elasticity would have trouble deflating his or her alveoli; however, increasing PEEP acts to keep the alveoli inflated. Thus, attempting to raise PEEP would not benefit this patient.

D: This individual has air trapped between his or her lung and chest wall, which slowly crushes the lung and prevents expansion. Although this does signify a problem with keeping the lung inflated, it is not alveolar in origin. From the question, we know only that an increase in PEEP serves to keep the alveoli from collapsing.

383. D is correct. According to the question stem, high blood pH leads to the laying of soft-shelled eggs. Alkaline, or high, pH is caused by the elimination of excess carbon dioxide, which promotes a shift in the equilibrium and reduces the amount of carbonic acid in the blood. An animal that is overheated tends to increase respiratory rate, or "pant," to raise the amount of cooler air passing through its body. This increase in breathing rate will be accompanied by increased elimination of carbon dioxide. As mentioned above, excessive exhalation of CO_2 leads to alkalosis, and thus to soft shells.

384. D is correct. Nose breathing is preferable to mouth breathing because the nasal passages are labyrinthine and richly vascularized. This increases the time that incoming air takes to reach the lungs, allowing it to be warmed, humidified, and filtered on the way. Intubation bypasses these protective functions. The necrosis mentioned in the question stem results from dry, cold air coming into direct contact with delicate tracheobronchial tissue. In contrast, pneumonia occurs when unfiltered air moves directly through the ET tube into the immunologically vulnerable lung space.

IV: Gas exchange occurs exclusively in the lower respiratory zone.

385. C is correct. Oxygen and carbon dioxide are small and nonpolar, and thus can use simple diffusion to pass directly through cell membranes.

A: Active transport involves energy expenditure, which is not required to achieve gas exchange. During inhalation, the partial pressure of oxygen in the atmosphere (and consequently, in the alveoli) is higher than the P_{O_2} in the blood coming from the pulmonary artery. For this reason, oxygen can simply move down its concentration gradient from the lungs into circulation.

B: While gases are bound to carrier proteins in the bloodstream, no protein is used to transport them between the circulatory system and the alveoli.

D: Small, hydrophobic molecules like O_2 and CO_2 do not require protein channels to cross lipid bilayers.

386. D is correct. We are explicitly told that asthma results from constriction of the bronchioles. As far as we know, the alveoli are unaffected, as is the gross anatomy of the lung. Asthmatics experience respiratory distress because, due to the extra bronchiolar resistance, they cannot fill or empty their lungs quickly enough; however, this does not change the volume that they could potentially inhale or exhale. In fact, asthma patients do not display significant changes in tidal volume, vital

capacity, or reserve volumes. The extremely small change in overall lung volume resulting from the decrease in bronchiolar diameter is negligible.

387. A is correct. A pregnant female in her third trimester experiences substantial pressure on her diaphragm from the growing fetus. Hence, it is impossible for her to maintain normal lung volumes. Compressed lungs result in a decrease in tidal volume (V_T or TV), the amount of air that enters and exits the lungs during one regular breathing cycle. Given this reduction, the woman must increase her respiratory rate in order to sustain both her own metabolic needs and those of the fetus.

388. B is correct. Increased tidal volume is one of several adaptations that occur in response to a high-altitude environment. (Production of 2,3-BPG also increases, as does hematocrit.) The ultimate result of these changes is that more oxygen can be extracted from the air and delivered to the tissues. During a normal breath, a substantial percentage of available alveoli are not utilized. Increased tidal volume (the volume breathed in and out during each breathing cycle) leads to increased recruitment and inflation of alveoli, which add to the surface available for gas exchange. This is important at high altitudes, where a lower total pressure results in a smaller amount of total oxygen present per liter of air.

A: Air is not "forced" out of the alveoli. This option describes some sort of positive-pressure breathing, which is the opposite of the way human breathing works.
C: Diffusion rate depends primarily on temperature. A change in lung volume alone will not alter this parameter.
D: We have no reason to assume this. In fact, alveolar collapse (atelectasis) usually affects only preterm infants or patients with chronic respiratory conditions.

389. A is correct. The respiratory center in the brain is bathed in cerebrospinal fluid (CSF) and responds with extreme sensitivity to changes in pH. Decreased pH of the CSF is a result of decreased plasma pH, which is a consequence of increased retention of carbon dioxide. Stimulation of respiration results in the excretion of CO_2 and, eventually, a return to a healthy pH.

B, D: Alkaline blood or CSF is a sign that breathing rate should be decreased, not increased. C: Plasma pH is not directly monitored by central chemoreceptors; it would be a better answer if the question referred to the peripheral receptors, the carotid and aortic bodies.

390. C is correct. At rest, ventilation is a subconscious process that is controlled by the pons and medulla oblongata, both of which are located in the brain stem (region B). However, we can easily alter the rate and depth of respiration using conscious thought. As a result, the cerebral cortex (region A) must also play a role, at least at times.

D: The region labeled C is the cerebellum, which is primarily responsible for coordination and motor control. It does not stimulate, monitor, or modify breathing.

391. B is correct. Vertebrates have a closed circulatory system, meaning that vessels feed into other vessels to form a closed loop. In contrast, an open system involves open-ended vasculature; invertebrates possess such systems, in which blood bathes organs and tissues in open sinuses or cavities. The human lymphatic system, which does not constitute a full loop, is also an open system.

I. The circulatory system contains two circuits: pulmonary and systemic.
II. Large lymphatic vessels do contain valves, making this choice incorrect. However, note that it is right about the circulatory system; veins contain valves, but arteries do not.
III: Leukocytes, or white blood cells, are present in both lymphatic and circulatory vessels.

392. B is correct. Veins (as well as arteries, arterioles, and venules) contain a layer of smooth muscle in their walls. This allows for processes such as vasoconstriction and vasodilation. Choice B describes common characteristics of smooth muscle: one nucleus per cell ("uninucleate"), rounded cells with tapered ends, and a lack of the striation found in other muscle types.

A: These characteristics describe skeletal muscle.
C: This choice includes qualities of cardiac muscle. The big giveaway is striation, which is not observed in smooth muscle.

393. B is correct. This vessel is the pulmonary artery, which is evidenced by the diagram's depiction of it as being attached to the right ventricle. The pulmonary artery is a rare exception among arteries, most of which contain oxygenated blood. However, the defining characteristic of such a vessel is that it carries blood away from the heart. The pulmonary artery brings deoxygenated, CO_2-rich blood from the heart to the lungs for oxygenation.

A: This large, curved vessel is the aorta. As all blood traveling to the systemic circuit must first pass through this artery, it must contain high-O_2, low-CO_2 blood.
C: These are the pulmonary veins, which bring recently oxygenated, low-CO_2 blood back from the lungs to the left side of the heart.
D: This statement is untrue; both CO_2 and O_2 concentrations vary between different vessels.

394. D is correct. Remember, the heart is generally drawn as if it belongs to a person who is standing facing you. In other words, the left side of the page represents the right side of the heart, and vice versa. For this reason, the label "5" represents the tricuspid valve, which separates the two right-hand chambers. Blood is carried from the systemic circuit in veins that merge to form the superior and inferior vena cavae, which deposit this deoxygenated blood into the right atrium.

C: The left, not right, side of the heart receives blood directly from the vasculature of the lungs.

395. C is correct. The continuity equation is often written as $A_1v_1 = A_2v_2$. This shows us that fluids travel slower through vessels with larger areas. Initially, one might assume that the small area of a single capillary is relevant here; however, remember that one artery branches off into many arterioles, which then each branch to form countless capillaries. Thus, it is the combined area of all capillaries – a huge value – that helps us answer this question. Alternatively, we could simply remember that blood must travel slowly through capillaries to maximize gas and nutrient exchange.

396. A is correct. In adults and healthy infants, the pulmonary artery carries deoxygenated blood from the heart to the lungs to undergo gas exchange. If this low-O_2, high-CO_2 blood is allowed to mix with aortic blood, the main adverse consequence will be a lowering of oxygen concentration in the aorta. Additionally, the high levels of CO_2 from the pulmonary artery will likely spread to the aorta, which normally contains minimal amounts of carbon dioxide.

B: The pulmonary artery usually holds deoxygenated blood. Allowing it to make direct contact with the aorta will, if anything, raise the oxygen concentration in this vessel.
C: A main symptom of babies with this condition is hypoxia, or low oxygen concentration in the tissues. Choice C is the reverse of this phenomenon.
D: This statement is untrue.

397. C is correct. The main role of albumin is related to the maintenance of oncotic pressure. This value, which represents the osmotic pressure that exists due to proteins, is necessary to promote the influx of water near the venous ends of capillary beds. Basically, albumin (like other proteins) is too large to diffuse in or out of a capillary. Instead, this protein stays in the capillary bed and draws water, with its associated toxins and waste products, from the tissues to the bloodstream.

A, B: Both oxygen and CO_2 are carried by hemoglobin, not albumin.
D: Diffusion only occurs at a significant level in the capillaries. All other vessels (arteries, etc.) have walls that are too thick to facilitate gas and fluid exchange.

398. A is correct. Arterial blood pressure is typically measured as systolic / diastolic, and these values are represented by labels 1 and 2, respectively. Systolic pressure is measured when the heart is contracting, and is always the higher of the two numbers. Here, it appears to be close to 120 mmHg, which is the standard value for a human. In contrast, diastolic pressure is the lower of the two and is taken when the heart is relaxed. The label "2" shows a value just under 80 mmHg, perfect for diastolic pressure. Finally, the much lower value marked by label 3 is a sensible pressure measurement for a systemic vein.

B: This choice reverses the systolic and diastolic pressures.

C: Asystole refers to a complete cessation of cardiac activity. It signifies a fatal or potentially fatal trauma and does not make sense here.

D: These pressures are given in the exact reverse order of the correct list.

399. D is correct. All blood vessels – arteries, arterioles, veins, venules, and capillaries – contain a thin inner lining composed of endothelial cells. This lining forms the interface, or immediate barrier, between blood and the remainder of the vessel, except in capillaries, which are made of endothelium alone. Lymphatic vessels also share this form of epithelium.

A: While this is partly true, other vessel types contain endothelium.

B: Smooth muscle is not required for endothelium to be present. Additionally, venules are also lined with a small amount of smooth muscle.

C: Gas diffusion takes place in capillaries alone; the other vessel types are too thick to properly allow for this diffusive process.

400. B is correct. Arteries, arterioles, veins, and venules contain walls with a layer of smooth muscle. However, capillary walls are composed solely of a one-cell-thick layer of endothelium to facilitate gas exchange. For this reason, while NO would certainly promote vasodilation somewhere, it would not be in the capillaries.

A: Only the heart itself contains cardiac muscle; the lining of arteries and other vessels includes smooth muscle.

C: This statement is untrue. Dilation of vessels near the skin causes more blood to be carried close to the body's surface. As a result, heat can dissipate and body temperature can remain at a safe level.

401 C is correct. Carbonic anhydrase is the enzyme responsible for interconverting carbon dioxide and carbonic acid. It is found within erythrocytes, which will settle to the bottom of the tube during centrifugation due to their high relative density.

A, D: Layer 1 represents the plasma, which is not the location of carbonic anhydrase, though it does contain many enzymes.

B: Layer 2 is the "buffy coat," which is composed of leukocytes. Leukocytes do not participate

in gas transport and do not carry carbonic anhydrase.

402. B is correct. DNA will only be found in nucleated cells. Layer 1, the plasma layer, contains no cells at all. Layer 3 contains erythrocytes, which do not have a nucleus or any DNA. Leukocytes, or white blood cells, do have intact nuclei in which DNA is present; these cells exist in the second layer.

403. A is correct. Erythrocytes do not contain any membranous organelles, including mitochondria. Despite their ability to use glycolysis for energy, these cells are somewhat metabolically insufficient. Cellular maintenance and repair are energetically demanding processes that erythrocytes are unable to maintain for more than a few months.

B: Erythrocytes are unable to make new proteins owing to a lack of genetic material, but they do contain functioning enzymes. Carbonic anhydrase is one example.

C: Hemoglobin serves to bind free oxygen in a stable form, which prevents its conversion to free radical species. Therefore, erythrocytes are not in any particular peril due to their role in oxygen transport. Furthermore, they do not have nuclei and cannot undergo genetic mutations to become cancerous.

D: Erythrocytes cannot become virally infected; they do not contain the DNA or necessary replication machinery to perpetuate viral proliferation.

404. A is correct. This phenomenon is known as peripheral edema, and is a result of reduced oncotic pressure in peripheral circulation. Proteins and other solutes in the blood are responsible for maintaining a concentration gradient that draws fluid out of the interstitial space and back into the plasma. Since we are told that albumin is a major solute in the blood, it is reasonable to conclude that its absence would disrupt this gradient and lead to fluid retention in the tissues.

B: Albumin does not play a role in clearing viral infections from the body. Primary viral infections are suppressed by the cell-mediated immune response, while secondary infections are cleared with the help of memory B lymphocytes and cell-mediated activity.

C: Hemoglobin is the sole oxygen-carrying protein in the blood. Albumin does not bind oxygen or interact with hemoglobin, which is found inside erythrocytes.

D: A reduction in protein content in the plasma would not increase blood viscosity. In fact, the ratio of solvent to solute would increase, so viscosity would actually be slightly lowered.

405. D is correct. Erythropoietin (EPO) is a hormone produced by the kidneys that stimulates production of erythrocytes. Increasing the red blood cell count results in an increased ability to carry oxygen due to an increase in available O_2 binding sites.

A: Removal of the stomach will eliminate the only endogenous source of intrinsic factor, which is produced by parietal cells. Intrinsic factor is essential for the absorption of Vitamin B_{12} from dietary sources. Vitamin B_{12} is necessary for erythrocyte formation; in fact, a low RBC count due to B_{12} deficiency is known as pernicious anemia.

B: Red blood cells are synthesized in the red marrow. Ablation, or destruction, will eliminate any capacity to form new erythrocytes from bone marrow progenitor cells.

C: Iron is an essential cofactor for hemoglobin. Functional hemoglobin cannot be made without iron, which must be obtained from dietary sources.

406. D is correct. We are told that ephedrine is a sympathomimetic drug and that it is similar to epinephrine. This information tells us that like other sympathomimetic molecules, ephedrine activates the sympathetic nervous system, which exerts many downstream effects. Among them is vasoconstriction, which is a critical step in effective hemostasis. Vasoconstriction could reasonably decrease clotting time and assist in stopping the bleed.

A: Histamine is an endogenous molecule with diverse effects. In the central nervous system, it is involved in regulation of arousal, which is why some older allergy medications (antihistamines) can cause drowsiness. Peripherally, histamine is released by mast cells during the allergic reaction to cause vasodilation. This would be an undesirable effect since our objective is to reduce blood flow through the ruptured nasal vessel.

B: Lidocaine is simply an analgesic. There is no reason to assume it has any effect on coagulation.

C: Tissue plasminogen activator (tPA) is a protein that converts plasminogen to plasmin. Plasmin is responsible for the breakdown of blood clots. Even if you did not know this, the choice states that tPA is a treatment for ischemic stroke, which suggests that it may have some antagonistic effect on clotting. Administration of tPA would likely disrupt any nascent coagulation and worsen the condition.

407. D is correct. The mother will only mount an immune response to an antigen that her immune system recognizes as foreign. For this reason, she must be negative for the Rh antigen. Furthermore, the formation of antibodies and the generation of a memory humoral response take between 48 and 96 hours. This means that the first pregnancy is at minimal risk for hemolytic disease of the newborn. After the first delivery, however, the maternal immune system has been exposed to fetal Rh. Thus subsequent exposure to Rh will elicit a much stronger response.

408. C is correct. From the question stem, we know that sickle-cell anemia is exacerbated by increased concentrations of deoxyhemoglobin. This form of hemoglobin predominates under conditions of hypoxia, low pH, and high carbon dioxide. Vigorous exercise and metabolic acidosis will promote the conversion of oxyhemoglobin to deoxyhemoglobin.

III: This will cause more molecules to assume the oxyhemoglobin form, which has a lower affinity for other hemoglobin molecules.

409. C is correct. The protein described seems to resemble myoglobin, as it is monomeric and plays an analogous role in maintaining an oxygen reserve in the tissues. Therefore, it must have a greater affinity for oxygen than does hemoglobin, which translates to a leftward shift on the graph. Due to its monomeric nature, this protein cannot possibly display binding cooperativity, so the curve for neuroglobin cannot be sigmoidal. The most logical answer choice is C.

410. D is correct. 2,3-BPG is a molecule that binds to hemoglobin and reduces its affinity for oxygen. We are given the entire chemical name for the compound, from which we can discern that

it contains two negatively-charged phosphate groups. Substitution of a histidine residue for serine will change the character of the binding pocket. Histidine has the ability to gain a proton and become positively charged, while serine is neutral. A replacement of His with Ser could thus reduce the affinity of the binding pocket for any negatively charged molecules, such as 2,3-BPG.

A: If true, this would give HbF a reduced affinity for oxygen, since diatomic gases such as CO compete with oxygen for the iron center in the heme group.
B: Carbaminohemoglobin has a lower oxygen affinity than hemoglobin that has not been carbamoylated. A modification that promotes carbamoylation would reduce oxygen binding.
C: The Fe(III) state of hemoglobin is unable to bind oxygen. Coordination with oxygen is made possible because iron is preserved in its Fe(II) state. Excessive generation of Fe(III) hemoglobin is one of the effects of cyanide poisoning, which can be fatal.

411. C is correct. The Bohr effect describes hemoglobin-oxygen affinity as being directly related to pH and inversely correlated with [CO_2]. Thus, in order to decrease this affinity, the pH must be low and the concentration of carbon dioxide must be high.

412. A is correct. As small, nonpolar gaseous molecules, oxygen and carbon dioxide can cross membranes via simple diffusion.

C: This specifically describes the simple diffusion of water.

413. D is correct. Hemoglobin is an iron-containing metalloprotein. This iron cofactor is especially important because it is located in the middle of the porphyrin ring and is directly involved in the binding of oxygen.

C: Zinc is bound as a cofactor to carbonic anhydrase, which is another important enzyme involved in gas homeostasis and regulation.

414. D is correct. The binding of a single oxygen atom to the iron complex causes the iron atom to move towards the center of the porphyrin ring. This induces a strain in the hemoglobin molecule and, through a conformational change, facilitates the binding of additional O_2 molecules to the same

hemoglobin. This process is known as cooperative binding.

415. D is correct. Iron is not a substrate of hemoglobin, it is part of hemoglobin. Remember, hemoglobin is an iron-containing metalloprotein.

C: Nitric oxide is an allosteric ligand that is bound to the thiol groups of hemoglobin. These ligands dissociate when hemoglobin releases oxygen from its heme site and are hypothesized to help oxygen transport in tissues.

416. C is correct. The shape of this curve is sigmoidal, or S-shaped. This is due to the cooperative binding exhibited by the hemoglobin molecule. As one oxygen binds to hemoglobin, conformational changes occur that enable the binding of additional substrate.

D: Hyperbolic curves are characteristic of noncooperative binding.

417. D is correct. Fetal hemoglobin is comprised of two alpha subunits and two gamma subunits, whereas adult hemoglobin contains two alpha and two beta subunits. This structural difference explains how fetal hemoglobin is able to extract oxygen from maternal hemoglobin. For this to occur, it must have a higher affinity, thereby shifting the curve to the left.

C: Maternal blood does not mix with fetal blood.

418. A is correct. Simple diffusion is the mechanism by which both oxygen and carbon dioxide move from the bloodstream into the alveoli and back. The movement of these gases is based on their concentrations in one location relative to the other.

419. A is correct. Alkalosis is a condition in which physiological pH is higher than normal. This would occur because carbonic anhydrase is a crucial enzyme that converts CO_2 and water to carbonic acid, which then dissociates into bicarbonate and protons. The forward reaction of carbonic anhydrase is extremely fast; thus, it is reasonable to expect that a lack of this enzyme will promote a buildup of carbon dioxide and water. Additionally, this will prevent the formation of protons, thus increasing the pH.

D: Increasing the breathing rate can increase pH, but this does not answer the question posed.

420. C is correct. An increase in breathing rate means that more carbon dioxide is exhaled. The bicarbonate buffer will act to restore the loss of carbon dioxide by forming carbonic acid from bicarbonate and protons. Reducing the amount of protons increases the pH.

421. A is correct. The lymphatic system exists under very low pressure, similar to the venous system. One-way valves are present to prevent backflow.

     C: The arterial circuit does not run parallel to the lymphatic vessels.

422. D is correct. Immune cells routinely sample antigens in the peripheral tissues and return to the lymph nodes through the lymphatic vessels to present them. Presentation will occur at the node that is most proximal to the site from which the migrating immune cell has come. The closest node to the foot is the popliteal lymph node, which will swell due to lymphocyte proliferation in response to infection.

423. B is correct. The question states that blood from the intestine travels to the liver, where it is subject to enzymatic modification. Amino acids, carbohydrates, and most other small molecules enter portal circulation after absorption in the small intestine. Triglycerides, in contrast, are absorbed via intestinal lacteals. Free fatty acids enter the lymphatic system directly, and are therefore exempt from first pass metabolism. A drug attached to a fatty acid is more likely to maintain its molecular integrity long enough to have a therapeutic effect.

424. D is correct. Neutrophils are instrumental in the rapid response to infection. While a potent T or B cell response takes several days to gain momentum, neutrophils are able to recognize and combat many types of pathogens within seconds of exposure.

     A, B: During a secondary exposure, the pathogen is usually eliminated before the onset of noticeable symptoms. This is due to a rapid and robust memory response and high levels of serum immunoglobulin remaining from previous exposure. Neutrophils may contribute to this response, but are not essential. We are also told that neutrophils live for only a few hours,

suggesting they have no role in the retention of immunological memory.
C: Neutrophils use reactive oxygen species to kill pathogens. If anything, neutropenia would reduce collateral damage from ROS during the immune response.

425. A is correct. Dendritic cells present antigens, in the context of MHC, to immature CD4+ T cells. The T cell will become activated if it has affinity for the antigen/MHC presented by the dendritic cell. An activated CD4+ T cell will produce a unique cytokine profile to regulate other immune cells and facilitate an effective response to the pathogen.

     B: Under some circumstances, macrophages can present antigens in the context of MHC. However, only T cells display the receptor capable of recognizing MHC. Macrophages are unable to interact with dendritic cells.
     C: B cells recognize intact antigenic domains. They do not recognize antigen fragments in the context of MHC. Furthermore, a memory B cell would be unlikely to recognize an antigen derived from an unfamiliar pathogen.
     D: Although cytotoxic T cells are capable of recognizing MHC loaded with antigen, they respond by perforating (or destroying) the presenting cell. While this is an effective way to kill an infected somatic cell, it would be counterproductive to the objective of the dendritic cell, which is to inform the immune system of a foreign invader.

426. B is correct. Patient #2 has an effective, but somewhat delayed, response to this pathogen. This suggests that he has no memory cells corresponding to the particular antigenic profile of his current infection.

     A, C: Prior antigenic challenge with this antigen would provide a more robust and rapid response. This would more closely resemble the steep increase in serum antibody levels exhibited by Patient #1.
     D: There is no reason to assume that Patient #2 is immunocompromised. Sluggish antibody synthesis is to be expected in the case of novel antigen exposure. A completely flat curve would suggest that he is mounting an inadequate immune response.

427. C is correct. Neonates gain maternal antibodies through breast milk. However, a baby who has never been exposed to any antigen will be slow to synthesize antibodies of her own. Maternal antibodies tend to bind any novel antigen with high affinity, masking exposure of the antigen to the neonatal immune system. Therefore, even though the infant may be immunocompetent, her immune system cannot actually "see" the pathogen. As long as breast-feeding continues, antibody levels should remain fairly constant.

    A: Antibiotics do not eliminate the need for an immune response. Even a patient on antibiotics will show an upward trend in antibody synthesis.
    B: An advanced AIDS patient will show virtually no response to an infection. Patient #3 does have a significant number of antibodies; they simply remain at a constant level.
    D: A vaccinated infant would show a steep upward trend in antibody synthesis, much like Patient #1.

428. A is correct. Patient A shows a red blood cell count that is below normal limits, as well as a dramatically lowered CD4+ T cell count. A deficiency in red blood cells is known as anemia, making I correct. HIV is a virus that infects and kills CD4+ T cells, resulting in the complete loss of immunocompetence associated with AIDS.

    III: Patient A has normal white blood cell and neutrophil counts, which would be unusual in a patient suffering from an infection such as pneumonia.

429. B is correct. Patient B has an extremely low platelet count, which would compromise his or her ability to effectively achieve hemostasis. This would prolong the damage caused by a hemorrhage in the brain, increasing the risk of death.

    A: Platelets do not play a significant role in directly fighting infection.
    C: Anaphylaxis is a severe allergic reaction with a number of diverse causes. It involves the activation of mast cells and the systemic release of histamine. No data regarding these cells is provided, making B the better answer.
    D: Myocardial infarction is the result of a clot in a coronary artery. Patient B, who will struggle to form clots, is not at high risk for this condition.

430. D is correct. Neutrophils are the only cell type listed that utilize free radicals to kill pathogens. Thus, they are the only cells likely to contain myeloperoxidase.

431. C is correct. VDJ recombination is the process by which genes for immunoglobulins are rearranged in developing lymphocytes to create novel gene products.

    A: Although the general concept might seem similar, VDJ recombination affects nuclear DNA and results in a permanent alteration of the gene product. RNA splicing does not change the DNA from which it was transcribed.
    B: Post-translational modification refers to chemical alterations made to completed proteins. Novel antibody sequences are determined well before translation occurs.
    D: Clonal selection is an important part of immunological development, but it is not directly responsible for the generation of antibody diversity. In fact, clonal selection eliminates many of the cell lines that express the novel antibodies developed during VDJ recombination.

432. B is correct. An IgG antibody is composed of two light chains and two heavy chains, all joined by disulfide linkages. Since DTT reduces disulfide bonds, it separates these subunits. However, because the two light chains are identical, they will not be distinguishable as separate bands on the gel. The same is true for the heavy chains.

    D: This is the number of subunits, not the number of distinct bands that will appear in the gel.

433. C is correct. Hemagglutination refers to erythrocyte aggregation that results from cross-linking by antibodies. In a laboratory setting, a blood sample that reacts positively with a given antibody will visibly thicken, informing the researcher of the presence of a relevant antigen. Since IgM offers the greatest number of available binding sites, it will be the most effective in causing aggregation of erythrocytes.

434. C is correct. The MHC subtype is completely irrelevant. All answer choices describe MHC that has been loaded with "self" peptides. Strong binding to such peptides on MHC results in autoimmunity, so the cells that behave in this way are selected against. However, T cells that do not

bind MHC loaded with peptides are also selected against because their inability to recognize MHC renders them unable to respond to antigen presentation. Only weak binding to MHC and a "self" antigen is an acceptable T cell behavior. Ultimately, this should lead to strong binding of the surviving T cell lines to foreign antigens bound to MHC.

435. C is correct. This suggests that the patient's own immune cells are not displaying a reaction to the cells of the thyroid. Since the question asks for a fact that provides evidence *against* the auto-immunity hypothesis, this fits the bill.

A: The release of thyroid cellular debris into systemic circulation does suggest thyroid damage, but provides little insight into its underlying cause.
B: Autoimmune diseases are often genetic, but so are many other conditions that could cause thyroid damage. This is a less compelling option than choice D.
D: The fact that the B cells in question cannot produce more than one type of antibody does not suggest that they will be unreactive to thyroid cells. In fact, a single B cell is always able only to produce identical antibodies that bind a common antigenic domain. These are known as "monoclonal antibodies." B lymphocytes that react to cells expressing TSH receptors are likely to cause an immune reaction to those cells, even if they are only stimulated by that single antigen.

436 D is correct. Using a whole viral particle increases the chance of presenting a viable antigenic domain to which antibodies may effectively bind. Intense heat is frequently used to denature viral enzymes and melt viral genetic material, eliminating its pathogenic potential.

A: Successful vaccines, according to the question, should provide lifelong immunity. A highly variable domain is unlikely to remain unchanged across all strains of the bacteria during the span of a human life. While a vaccine developed from this molecule may provide immunity for a few years, a new strain of *M. tuberculosis* is likely to display a new and unrecognizable form of the glycoprotein.
B: Since DNA is concealed within the viral capsid, it does not represent an ideal target for recognition by immune cells.

C: Although antibodies may be able to recognize this toxin and react accordingly (assuming the toxin is bound to the surface of the bacterium), such a toxic vaccine is likely to have noticeable negative effects on the patient.

437. C is correct. Erythrocytes are anucleate and incapable of synthesizing new proteins. Therefore, they are unable to produce MHC and do not express it under any circumstances.

438. C is correct. The information about organ transplants tells us that the MHC amino acid sequence varies among individuals and that immune cells can recognize this variation. This means the T cells must bind, at least partially, to amino acid residues from the MHC. Normal T cells only kill cells that they recognize as foreign. This could be because they detect "self" MHC loaded with foreign protein, or because they detect foreign MHC.

D: Though this choice is very close, it does not specify that a foreign protein is bound to the MHC.

439. B is correct. The question stem describes classic CD8+ T cell behavior. These cells are cytotoxic and play an essential role in the combating of intracellular infection.

A: T cells cannot produce antibodies; this is the role of B cells.
C: Complement activation does not mark cells for destruction by macrophages. Also, T cells do not activate the complement system.
D: This would be completely counterproductive to the intended purpose of cell recognition. Lysis of the T cell would prevent it from releasing its toxins into the infected target cell.

440. B is correct. We are told that the response to superantigen stimulation involves widespread cytokine release, which suggests that CD4+ T cells are involved. These cells promote generation of cytokines to direct other immune cells. The question also mentions that the inflammatory response is followed by widespread deactivation of immune cells, which implies that suppressor cells were probably activated by the nonspecific cytokine storm.

II. According to the question, the bacterium is extracellular and response to it is mediated by MHC II. CD8+ T cells do not bind MHC II and are not recruited during the response to extracellular pathogens.

441. D is correct. I, II, and IV all occur in the large intestine.

III: This happens in the small intestine.

442. A is correct. Bile is produced by the liver, then travels to the gall bladder, where it is stored until needed. Once the gall bladder receives the signal to release bile, the substance travels down the cystic duct and the common bile duct (which is shared by the liver), then into the duodenum.

443. B is correct. Two types of amylase exist: salivary and pancreatic. Both of these work to break down starches.

A: Lysozyme hydrolyzes β-1,4 linkages in bacterial cell walls.
C: Pepsin is a protease released into the stomach that digests protein.
D: Trypsin is a pancreatic protease.

444. C is correct. Between meals, glucagon stimulates enzymes in the liver to break down glycogen stores so that glucose can be released into the bloodstream.

A: Glucagon stimulates fatty acid breakdown in adipocytes to increase the fuel sources available in the blood.
B: Glucagon increases blood glucose levels, while insulin decreases them.
D: Glucagon increases gluconeogenesis in the liver and kidneys only.

445. C is correct. Low pH decreases secretion of gastrin by G cells because gastrin promotes HCl secretion. If not for this negative feedback mechanism, the pH would be lowered beyond optimal levels.

446. B is correct. The patient is in a prolonged state of starvation, so his body is producing a large amount of ketones to provide fuel. If this state continues for too long, the patient may develop ketoacidosis.

447. C is correct. The patient has normal blood sugar levels and a normal pH, meaning that his energy stores have returned to normal. After the ingested sugars are used, blood sugar levels will

start to drop, and the body must begin to utilize gluconeogenesis and glycogenolysis to keep blood glucose at a healthy level.

448. D is correct. This reaction involves the breakdown of triacylglycerides into glycerol and fatty acids. While it may take place in a number of places, of those listed, only D is correct. Lipase released by the pancreas into the small intestine catalyzes this reaction.

A, B: Within any cell, the interconversion of triacylglycerides and fatty acids take place in the smooth endoplasmic reticulum.
C: No reactions occur in the lacteals of the lymph system, though fatty acids do travel in chylomicrons through these structures.

449. B is correct. Structure B is a fatty acid, which is hydrophobic. As a result, it requires carriers for transport through the blood.

C: Triacylglycerides don't travel through the blood due to their large size.

450. B is correct. In the small intestine, the digestive system acts to decrease the acidity of the environment. To facilitate this, the pancreas releases bicarbonate along with enzymes that raise the pH to 6.

A: Trypsin cleaves proteins, while amylase cleaves sugars.
C: Goblet cells secrete mucus to protect the stomach lining from abrasion due to low pH.
D: Chief cells release the zymogen pepsinogen, which is then cleaved in the acidic environment of the stomach for activation.

451. B is correct. Label A points to the deeper, more interior layer of the kidney, which is termed the medulla. In contrast, the outer covering (B) is called the cortex. Note that this naming system extends to other organs as well; for example, the adrenal gland contains a cortex and a medulla. Finally, Label C points to the tube that carries filtrate out of the kidney. This structure is known as a ureter (humans have two) and brings fluid to the urinary bladder.

C, D: The urethra brings urine from the bladder to the outside of the body. It does not directly attach to the kidney.

452. C is correct. The question references the adrenal cortex, the outer region of the adrenal gland. This structure releases the corticosteroids, which include aldosterone and cortisol.

A: Norepinephrine, a catecholamine, is secreted by the adrenal medulla.
B: Renin actually is an enzyme, not a hormone. Additionally, it is released by the kidney, not the adrenal gland.
D: ADH is synthesized in the hypothalamus and secreted by the posterior pituitary.

453. A is correct. Overall, the teacher did a somewhat decent job explaining this vital physiological process. However, she incorrectly stated that glucose is reabsorbed in the loop of Henle, a structure that mainly absorbs water and sodium. Most reabsorption of biologically important solutes, including glucose, occurs in the PCT.

B: This statement is false. In fact, glucose in one's urine is a classic sign of untreated diabetes.
C: Secretion, or the transport of solute from the bloodstream into the nephron, is the opposite of the process that the teacher is describing.

454. A is correct. Filtration, secretion, and reabsorption are extremely easy terms to confuse. Remember, filtration refers to the general movement of plasma from the glomerulus (a tight network of capillaries) into the entrance of the nephron at the Bowman's capsule. This process is extremely general, with virtually any molecule smaller than protein allowed passage into the filtrate.

B: This is very close! However, filtration involves movement from the glomerulus into Bowman's capsule, not the other way around.
C: This is the reverse of the proper distinction.
D: This choice, too, is the virtual opposite of the correct answer. Filtration is accomplished mainly by physically forcing fluid to enter the nephron. As such, it is a passive process that relies on diffusion.

455. D is correct. Simple cuboidal epithelia are well-suited for solute transport and absorption. The two regions of the nephrons that are most likely to possess such a lining are the proximal and distal convoluted tubules. However, the PCT (which is especially specialized for reabsorption of glucose, amino acids, and other vital solutes) is lined with a brush border of microvilli. This is a unique characteristic in comparison to other parts of the nephron.

A: The collecting duct, a tough structure that is typically impermeable to water, does not play a major role in solute reabsorption.
B: The glomerulus is a tangled ball of capillaries clustered near the Bowman's capsule. The question stem gives no indication that Sample 1 came from a blood vessel.

456. C is correct. The loop of Henle is likely one of the most confusing aspects of MCAT-level physiology. While many students think that the loop actually concentrates urine itself, it simply prepares the medulla of the kidney for the later absorption of water. Specifically, the antiparallel nature of the loop establishes a countercurrent multiplier system that makes the inner medulla very solute-rich. Interestingly, the collecting duct also runs parallel to this long structure. When ADH is present, as in periods of dehydration, the collecting duct is made water-permeable through the introduction of aquaporin channels. Since the medulla is now so salty, water can passively exit the nephron and remain in the body.

B: While this represents the actual region from which water exits the nephron due to ADH, it does not answer the question.

457. C is correct. ADH is synthesized in the hypothalamus, stored in the posterior pituitary gland, and released when blood pressure is low. An end goal of this hormone is the retention of water through insertion of aquaporins in the collecting duct. Vasopressin is another term for ADH.

I: Aldosterone has the same general function as antidiuretic hormone, though its mechanism of action differs significantly. However, it is secreted from the adrenal cortex.

458. B is correct. The more important a molecule is, the more likely it is to be reabsorbed to prevent its loss from the body. For example, glucose tends to be entirely reabsorbed in the nephron in healthy individuals.

A: While this species does appear to be important, as a protein, it is too large to enter the filtrate in the first place.

C: Toxins are much more likely to be secreted than reabsorbed.

459. D is correct. Once angiotensinogen has been cleaved into its active form (angiotensin I), ACE acts upon that product to form angiotensin II. This species then facilitates the release of aldosterone in an attempt to raise blood pressure and retain water.

A: This is the role of renin.
B: This function is performed by angiotensin II.
C: While this choice does accurately mention characteristics of renin, this is not the function of angiotensin-converting enzyme.

460. B is correct. The urinary system includes the kidneys as well as organs used specifically for excretion (the urinary bladder, ureters, and urethra). This system is heavily dependent on hormonal input from the endocrine system, especially with regard to water balance.

A, C, D: The integumentary system (skin), digestive system, and skeletal system are all dependent on the kidneys for proper functioning. However, none of them display the same close relationship with the excretory system as choice B.

461. D is correct. The body excretes nitrogenous waste in the form of urea by way of the urea cycle. Furthermore, urea is a vital component of the countercurrent exchange system that enables the reabsorption of ions and water. Potassium can also be found in the urine, albeit in small amounts; most of it is reabsorbed in the loop of Henle. Finally, a healthy person would not expect to find glucose in his urine. However, diabetics can have such high levels of plasma glucose that the nephron is unable to reabsorb 100% of it, leading to the sugary urine that is a classic sign of the disease.

B: Platelets are too large to enter the filtrate from the glomerulus.

462. A is correct. These three processes best describe the general function of the kidneys and the activity that leads to the excretion of urine. Blood reaching the nephron is first filtered by the glomerulus. Next, ions and water are reabsorbed into the bloodstream, while toxins and protons are secreted into the nephron.

463. D is correct. Alcohol inhibits the production of ADH (antidiuretic hormone). This hormone is normally released to stimulate the translocation of aquaporins into the cells of the collecting duct, a process that increases the reabsorption of water. Without ADH, large quantities of ingested fluid will be excreted regardless of the individual's hydration level.

A: Consumption of large amounts of alcohol temporarily increases, not decreases, blood pressure.
B: Alcohol affects ADH, which acts on the collecting duct, not the DCT.
C: The proximal convoluted tubule does not play a major role in water reabsorption. Instead, it is the location of the reabsorption of anions and glucose. It also plays a role in the pH regulation of the filtrate.

464. A is correct. The Bowman's capsule is located at the beginning of the nephron. Here, blood is filtered, meaning that plasma (along with the ions, glucose, and other small molecules present) enters the nephron from glomerular capillaries. The glomerular blood pressure is high, which assists in forcing water and solutes into the Bowman's capsule.

B: Reabsorption of water occurs primarily in the loop of Henle, with the descending limb permeable to water and the ascending limb permeable to salts. Reabsorption of glucose and other solutes also occurs to a large degree in the proximal convoluted tubule.
C: Secretion does not occur in the Bowman's capsule.
D: Excretion refers to the eventual loss of urine from the body; this does not occur in the Bowman's capsule.

465. B is correct. The urea cycle produces urea from ammonia; it is necessary to prevent the buildup of ammonia, a toxic nitrogenous product. The process is cyclic, and the first set of reactants include ATP, ammonia, and carbonate, which is equivalent to water and carbon dioxide. The end products of the cycle are urea and ornithine, the

latter of which is reused during the next series of reactions.

C: While uric acid is present in the body, it is not the end product of the urea cycle. Buildup of uric acid can lead to gout and is associated with diabetes and kidney stones.

466. B is correct. While the descending limb of the loop of Henle is permeable to water, it is generally impermeable to Na⁺ and other ions. As filtrate progresses through the descending loop of Henle, its osmolarity increases as water flows out of the descending limb and into the interstitium.

C: This region is the ascending limb of the loop of Henle. Here, the nephron is fairly impermeable to water and impermeable to salts.
D: This region is the collecting duct. This structure is generally impermeable to water, except in the presence of antidiuretic hormone.

467. D is correct. The label D indicates the collecting duct, which is the tube where filtrate eventually appears after various secretions and reabsorptions. When blood pressure is low and the body needs to conserve water, antidiuretic hormone increases the permeability of the collecting duct to water, and water will flow out of the nephron and back into the interstitium.

A: This is the proximal convoluted tubule, not the collecting duct.
B: This refers to the descending limb of the loop of Henle, which is not the region that ADH acts upon.
C: This area is the ascending limb of the loop of Henle, which also does not directly relate to ADH.

468. D is correct. Drinking large amounts of water will decrease the concentration of ions in the plasma. However, the kidneys function to maintain homeostasis, and over time, more water will be excreted and the concentration of ions will be restored. This will happen mainly due to the inhibition of the hormones ADH and aldosterone, reducing the overall reabsorption of H_2O.

A: Remember, osmolarity here refers to the concentration of solutes, not that of water. Drinking large quantities of water will dilute the blood and decrease osmolarity.

B, C: These answers are correct in that the concentration of ions will initially decrease. However, the functioning of nephrons is not dependent on urination or on consumption of additional food.

469. A is correct. The renin-angiotensin system regulates blood pressure by stimulating the release of aldosterone, which increases sodium reabsorption. Water naturally follows the ion movement, thus increasing blood pressure and decreasing urine output. If this system were disabled, blood pressure could still be regulated by antidiuretic hormone, which operates through a mechanism independent of the renin-angiotensin system. Instead of directly involving sodium reabsorption, ADH functions by increasing the permeability of the collecting duct to water.

C: The renin-angiotensin system results in vasoconstriction. Vasodilation would have the opposite of the intended effect and decrease blood pressure further.
D: This system directly responds to decreased blood pressure, specifically a drop in blood flow to the kidneys. It is not immediately activated by high salt osmolarity.

470. B is correct. Aldosterone is a steroid hormone that plays an important role in the regulation of blood pressure. It acts on the distal tubule to increase the reabsorption of sodium and the secretion of potassium. This leads to increased water retention and a corresponding increase in blood pressure.

A: Aldosterone increases the secretion of potassium, which is not identical to reducing reabsorption.
C: Aldosterone does not play a direct role in the regulation of pH.
D: Aldosterone and ADH are generally released under the same conditions and do not directly inhibit the functioning of each other.

471. B is correct. Erection is triggered by parasympathetic nervous stimulation. Since the parasympathetic and sympathetic systems are in constant opposition, damage to the sympathetic branch leads to unchecked activation of parasympathetic pathways.

C: Damage to the spinal cord would constitute damage to the central nervous system.

D: The somatic nervous system is responsible for voluntary skeletal muscle control. The parasympathetic and sympathetic branches are subsets of the autonomic nervous system, which is involuntary.

472. A is correct. Sperm require relatively alkaline conditions to survive, but the vaginal tract is generally acidic. The seminal vesicles produce a basic solution to neutralize the vaginal pH and permit the survival of sperm. Dysfunctional seminal vesicles will reduce the chances of fertilization.

    B: Seminal fluid is released only during ejaculation, and does not play any part in establishing the baseline genitourinary environment. Males are less susceptible to urinary tract infections simply because the male urethra is longer.
    C, D: Sperm production and maturation occur in the testes and epididymis, respectively. These structures are anatomically and functionally separate from the seminal vesicles.

473. B is correct. Like most hormone axes in the body, the hypothalamic-pituitary axis is subject to negative feedback. A pituitary lesion will reduce or eliminate the secretion of FSH and LH. GnRH-secreting neurons in the hypothalamus will respond to this drop in serum hormone levels by increasing GnRH secretion.

    A: Testosterone production is stimulated by LH action on Leydig cells in the testes. Without LH production, synthesis of testosterone is likely to drop dramatically.
    C: Spermatogenesis is promoted by the action of FSH on the testes' Sertoli cells. When FSH production is limited, spermatogenesis is likely to decrease.

474. A is correct. Activin essentially magnifies the effects of FSH on its target cells. In males, FSH acts on Sertoli cells to stimulate spermatogenesis. An activin receptor agonist is a molecule that stimulates the activin receptor, exactly like endogenous activin.

C, D: According to the question, activin has a sensitizing effect. In other words, the normal effects of FSH are increased in the presence of activin.

475. D is correct. Progesterone is the dominant hormone during the luteal phase and is represented by the darkest line on the graph. The sudden drop in progesterone at the end of the luteal phase triggers uterine contractions, resulting in menses. In fact, progesterone also drops sharply just before parturition (birth), relieving the inhibition of uterine contractions that permitted the maintenance of pregnancy.

    A: Oxytocin actually stimulates uterine contractions, making it a poor choice for preventing labor.
    B: Prolactin levels do not increase until after birth. This implies that this hormone is unnecessary for maintaining pregnancy, and it likely has no effect on the uterine myometrium.
    C: Estrogen is also elevated during the luteal phase, but not nearly as much as progesterone. On the graph, it is represented by the second-highest line during the final week or so of the cycle. This suggests that progesterone is more instrumental in preventing contractions.

476. D is correct. Although FSH and LH both increase dramatically during the onset of puberty, they are both peptide hormones and do not at all resemble the structure of BPA. BPA is a small molecule with multiple six-membered rings, so it is reasonable to assume that it could mimic estrogen *in vivo*.

    C: hCG does have effects similar to LH, but it is also a peptide hormone.

477. C is correct. DNA damage can result from free radical activity generated by normal cellular reactions. This is why rapidly dividing cells often become cancerous. Any options that mitigate the metabolic load on the oocyte will help to preserve the integrity of its DNA. The oocyte is, in fact, surrounded by maternal follicular cells, which synthesize most of its required proteins and other molecules. These cells are expendable and gradually disintegrate as the oocyte travels down the tube. Supercoiling reduces base pair exposure

to the nuclear environment, lowering the chances of damage.

II: Available nutrients do not reduce the risk involved in the extremely active process of zygotic division.

478. C is correct. The sperm and oocyte meet in the Fallopian tube. The zygote continues to travel down the tube until it reaches the uterus. Implantation occurs in the uterine endometrium.

479. A is correct. The question informs us that hCG has a suppressive effect on T cells, which are responsible for controlling the presence of foreign cells. A substantial portion of the placenta develops from embryonic tissue, which is immunologically foreign to the maternal immune system. Although a complex mechanism exists to facilitate immunological tolerance of the fetus during pregnancy, it requires proper CD8+ T cell activity. Inactivation of the maternal immune system could result in unchecked placental infiltration through the myometrium. Normally, the placenta does not contact the myometrium at all and is restricted to the endometrial layer.

B: Inadequate trophoblast implantation has a number of causes. However, excessive hCG is more likely to facilitate implantation.
C: Inappropriate reactions to harmless antigens occur due to an overactive immune system. If anything, hCG-mediated suppression of T cell activity would decrease the likelihood of eclampsia developing.
D: This choice mentions that the overgrown tissue is "normal," implying that T cells are not responsible for controlling its activity. T cells only recognize foreign cells, and normally would never respond to cells displaying a "self" antigenic profile.

480. C is correct. Parturition is one of the rare examples of a positive feedback loop. Stimulation of oxytocin receptors located in the uterine wall increase uterine elasticity, which causes increased uterine stretch during subsequent contractions. This stimulates stretch receptors that feed back to the posterior pituitary gland to trigger more oxytocin production.

A: Progesterone secretion drops markedly just prior to the onset of parturition. It does not play

a stimulatory role in uterine contractions or oxytocin secretion.
B: hCG only remains high during the first trimester of pregnancy. It would provide no stimulatory effects during the third trimester.
D: In a healthy pregnancy, the placenta detaches from the endometrium soon after fetal delivery.

481. A is correct. One of the hallmarks of cardiac muscle tissue is an action potential with a "plateau" in its depolarization. Specifically, repolarization is delayed due to the action of slow-to-open voltage gated Ca^{2+} channels. This maintains the regular beat of the heart. Skeletal muscle, on the other hand, lacks such a plateau, and the opening of potassium channels is able to rapidly repolarize the cell.

B, D: These are conserved across both types of striated muscle.
C: ATP ultimately contributes energy for the contraction of all three types of muscle.

482. D is correct. The diaphragm is comprised of skeletal muscle, which explains why one is able to consciously take a deep breath. In contrast, one cannot consciously control the smooth muscle lining the aorta, ventricular muscle, or arrector pili (the muscles that make hairs on the arm or neck stand on end in the cold, producing "goosebumps").

483. C is correct. From the diagram, one should be able to tell that schematic B indicates single-unit muscle, which is composed of cells that are connected via gap junctions. This allows the action potential to propagate between cells, leading to simultaneous contraction. On the other hand, schematic A indicates multiunit muscle, in which each cell is innervated individually and contracts on its own. This is useful for precise contraction. Single-unit smooth muscle is found in the lining of blood vessels, the GI tract, and the uterus.

484. D is correct. Smooth muscle cells contain both thick myosin and thin actin filaments. However, the lack of sarcomeric organization results in the characteristic lack of striation and a "smooth" appearance. Unlike skeletal and cardiac muscle, smooth muscle also contains intermediate

filaments that are anchored to dense bodies distributed along the cytoplasm of the cell.

485. A is correct. In a simple reflex arc, a sensory neuron conducts the signal to the spinal cord where it synapses directly with a motor neuron. The motor neuron then sends the signal to the muscle that causes the knee jerk response. So in response to the sudden stretching of the patellar tendon, the quadriceps will flex causing a kick.

B: The patellar tendon reflex is an example of a simple reflex that does not require an interneuron to flex the quadriceps. While there are interneurons involved in relaxing the hamstring and sending signals to the brain, the question only asks about the jerking response.
C, D: Nothing in the question suggests that proteins are reshaping or that the child experienced pain.

486. A is correct. The sarcomere describes the arrangement of filaments in the smallest functional unit of muscle. Essentially, myofibrils are collections of parallel sarcomeres forming a filament. A muscle fiber is a multinucleate muscle cell containing numerous myofibrils, while a fasciculus is a unit of muscle that contains multiple fibers wrapped in connective tissue.

487. B is correct. Slow-twitch muscles are slow to fatigue, and therefore are featured in postural muscles that must remain contracted for extended periods of time. Therefore, they are likely to contain large amounts of myoglobin, a red protein that stores oxygen within muscle.

488. D is correct. Both A and C are true. Shivering results in the generation of heat through metabolism; moreover, blood is passed through the valves of veins in part due to contraction of skeletal muscle. Still, most of the driving force for fluid flow in the veins is generated from the pumping of the heart. Skeletal muscle also contributes to the flow of fluid through the lymphatic system.

B: Smooth muscle within the walls of blood vessels is responsible for the regulation of diameter, and therefore for the resistance to fluid flow.

489. A is correct. The question stem mentions that actin and myosin are not attached, but that they are positioned perpendicularly, implying that they are preparing for future binding. Hydrolysis of ATP into ADP and inorganic phosphate restores the myosin head to a 90° angle, "cocking" it for new attachment and the ensuing power stroke.

B: This occurs immediately after myosin binds actin and before the power stroke.
C: ATP binding of myosin does detach it from actin, but the myosin head remains "bent" until ATP is hydrolyzed.

490. A is the correct answer. Titin contains folded immunoglobulin domains that unfold with force, much like a slinky expands as one pulls on its ends. Logically, it makes sense that a protein that serves a protective function as a sarcomeric shock absorber would be found at the junctions of the sarcomere, in the I band.

491. A is correct. Thick filaments within the sarcomere of striated muscle are composed of the protein myosin. These filaments have protuberances known as "myosin heads" along both ends, which engage in the myosin ATPase activity that drives the cross-bridge formation cycle. Thick filaments are located in the A band of the sarcomere and interact with the adjacent thin filaments, which are made up of actin.

B: Titin is located along the junctions of the sarcomere in the I band, but it does not make up thick filaments.

492. D is correct. Acetylcholinesterase is an enzyme that degrades ACh, so its inhibition would magnify the effects of the neurotransmitter.

493. C is correct. Cardiac muscle cells have gap junctions at the intercalated disks; these allow the action potential to spread between cells, leading to the simultaneous contraction of cardiac tissue. Smooth muscle cells may also contain gap junctions if they are part of single-unit smooth muscle tissue, which is found within the GI tract and uterus.

494. D is correct. Both statements A and C are true. For skeletal muscle to relax, the conformation of myosin must change as ATP binds the myosin head, decreasing its affinity for actin and breaking the cross-bridge between thick and thin filaments. Additionally, the free Ca^{2+} concentration in the sarcomere itself must go down, returning

tropomyosin and troponin to their resting positions. This requires use of the Ca²⁺ ATPase in the sarcoplasmic reticulum.

B: ATP hydrolysis occurs earlier in the contraction cycle.

495. D is correct. A and B are both true. Increased frequency (not size, since action potentials are all-or-nothing) of action potentials results in greater recruitment of motor units. This results in a "stepping up" of force until maximal contraction, or tetanus, is reached.

496. B is correct. At death, metabolic processes cease and the supply of ATP is depleted. Myosin possesses an ATPase enzymatic activity at its heads. The detachment of myosin heads from the thin actin filaments involves entry of ATP into the cycle. Therefore, if no ATP is present, the cross-bridge will not be broken, and the sarcomere will be frozen.

497. A is correct. This is the definition of a tetanic contraction.

498. A is correct. Excitation-contraction coupling occurs when calcium channels in the sarcoplasmic reticulum change conformation in response to a depolarization propagated across the sarcolemma and into T-tubules. The calcium leaks out of the SR, down its concentration gradient, and results in the movement of troponin and tropomyosin from the myosin binding sites on the thin filaments. This starts the cross-bridge cycle.

B, C: These would appear to enhance muscle contraction, not impair it.

499. D is correct. Both A and B represent accurate statements. Skeletal muscle has no inhibitory signal, since it is innervated only by motor neurons. Therefore, cessation of a contraction signal is enough to cause the skeletal muscle to relax. ATP is needed to effect detachment of myosin thick filaments from the actin thin filaments. Calcium is brought back down to resting levels by a calcium ATPase pump in the sarcoplasmic reticulum, and troponin and tropomyosin return to covering myosin binding sites on actin.

500. B is correct. During contraction, the I band and H zone shorten, while the A band is unchanged.

501. B is correct. Flat bones are strong, flattened bones that provide protection to vital organs. Examples include the sternum, scapula, and ribs.

A: The femur is a long bone.
C: The vertebrae exemplify irregular bone.
D: The metatarsal serves as an example of a short bone.

502. C is correct. A long bone is characterized as a bone with an elongated body that is lengthier than its width, with growth plates at either end. The mandible is a type of irregular bone.

503. B is correct. The joint between the humerus and ulna is filled with synovial fluid and is thus considered a synovial joint. Most joints that move or allow for rotation can be characterized as this particular type.

A: Fibrous joints contain fibrous connective tissue and do not move. One example is the joint between plates of the skull.
C: Cartilaginous joints, which contain cartilage, allow very little movement. The connection between vertebral discs is one of these joints.

504. C is correct. Osteoblasts serve to promote the creation of new bone, while osteoclasts are responsible for bone reabsorption and recycling. Osteocytes are mature osteoblast cells that eventually become surrounded by the matrix that they secrete.

505. B is correct. Increased levels of plasma calcium will stimulate the secretion of calcitonin. This peptide hormone is responsible for activating osteoblasts, which take calcium from the blood to create new bone.

A: Osteoclasts are inhibited in the presence of high calcium.
C, D: These cells are not directly affected by blood calcium levels.

506. A is correct. Calcitonin "tones down" blood calcium levels by activating osteoblasts. Osteoblasts synthesize hydroxyapatite, a calcium-containing mineral. In other words, these cells absorb excess calcium in the blood with the goals

of both synthesizing new bone and lowering serum calcium levels.

B: Osteoblasts decrease serum [Ca^{2+}].

C, D: Calcitonin stimulates osteoblasts.

507. A is correct. Parathyroid hormone (PTH) is responsible for raising blood calcium levels. Without this hormone, plasma [Ca^{2+}] will be perpetually low, a condition that is known as hypocalcemia. Changes in blood calcium affect the ability of muscles to contract and relax.

B: It is excess calcium that needs to be excreted by the kidney, making this condition more likely to promote excessive urination.
C: Calcitonin, not PTH, stimulates osteoblast activity to create new bone.
D: Excessive calcium can result in constipation due to disruption of ion gradients in the colonic epithelium.

508. D is correct. Dihydroxycholecalciferol is the active form of vitamin D, which works in the kidney to increase calcium reabsorption. Calcitonin decreases serum calcium levels; this action is opposed by parathyroid hormone (PTH).

509. B is correct. Cartilage is composed of chondrin, a flexible matrix secreted by chondrocytes. All other choices accurately list differences between bone and cartilage.

510. D is correct. Ligaments are responsible for bone-to-bone connections, while tendons (like this one) serve to attach bone to muscle.

511. B is correct. Stratified, or multi-layered, epithelium is best suited for protective purposes, especially in tissues like the skin where the most external layers are constantly being lost. In addition, epidermal cells are "squamous," or flattened and thin.

A: The epidermis is not composed of columnar, or tall, rectangular cells; that would more closely reflect the shape of the simple epidermal cells lining the small intestine. Additionally, the term "endothelium" generally describes the specialized epithelium that lines blood vessels, not that of the skin.
C: The skin, with its vital protective role, could not be composed of a simple (single-layered) epithelium. Such a lining would be too permeable,

both to substances on the exterior and interior of the body.
D: Epidermal cells are squamous, not cuboidal (or boxlike in shape).

512. D is correct. As their name implies, sweat glands secrete sweat, a water-based solution that is derived from plasma and contains many salts. When this fluid evaporates from the skin (an endothermic process), it cools the exterior of the body. In contrast, sebaceous glands produce sebum, a waxy or oily substance that prevents the skin from becoming overly dry.

A: Sebaceous glands certainly secrete a fluid (albeit an oily one) onto the exterior of the skin.
B: Again, both sweat and sebaceous glands secrete fluids onto the skin, specifically the epidermis.
C: This one is somewhat more specific. However, remember that the epidermis is the outermost layer of the skin. The base of a sweat gland is buried somewhat deeper, in the dermis or hypodermis; sebaceous glands mainly originate from the dermis.

513. D is correct. The dermis is the tissue layer located immediately below the epidermis. It is composed mainly of connective tissue, such as collagen, and contains the bases of sebaceous glands and many sweat glands.

A: As the most exterior layer of the skin, the epidermis is shown marked with the label "1."
B: The hypodermis is located immediately below the dermis. In the diagram shown, it is not given a label, but consists of the fatty tissue underneath the layer marked "2."
C: While the dermis is found underneath the epidermis, this is not an actual anatomical term.

514. D is correct. It is the hypodermis, or most interior layer of human skin, that contains fat (or adipose) tissue. The hypodermis is not marked with a label, but is depicted by the light-colored fatty deposits at the very bottom of the image.

A: This is the epidermis, which consists of stratified squamous epithelium, not fat.
B: This label marks the dermis, or "middle" layer of the skin. The dermis is composed mainly of elastic fibers and collagen; again, it does not contain a notable amount of adipose tissue.
C: This label marks the base of a hair cell, and does not point to a layer at all.

515. B is correct. While vasodilation is certainly a mechanism by which the body aims to remain cool, the actual dilation is performed by arteries and arterioles, not capillaries. Remember, capillary walls consist only of a single endothelial layer. Since they lack smooth muscle entirely, they cannot possibly constrict or expand.

A: The subcutaneous layer (also known as the hypodermis) is mainly composed of fatty tissue. As such, it does assist in keeping the body warm.
C: This answer is similar to choice B, but is a true statement because it mentions arterioles, not capillaries. Blood vessels supplying the skin do constrict in cold weather to keep blood flow nearer to the warmer core.
D: Sweat glands, and the fluid that they secrete, play a major thermoregulatory role in warm temperatures.

516. C is correct. Melanin, a pigment derived from tyrosine, provides color to the eyes and skin. This pigmentation helps protect the skin from harmful and potentially cancer-causing UV rays. The patient described likely suffers from a form of albinism, a complete melanin deficiency marked by whitish skin and pink eyes.

A: These symptoms more likely denote a keratin deficiency. Keratin is a structural protein that gives the skin its flexibility and toughness.
B: Watch out for this choice! A melanin deficiency would certainly lead to a susceptibility to UV damage. However, UV light has a wavelength of 200-400 nm. The wavelength mentioned here is characteristic of infrared (IR) radiation.
D: These physical hallmarks would result from high production of melanin, the opposite of what is mentioned in the question stem.

517. B is correct. The diagram depicts a section of simple columnar epithelium. As a "simple," or one-layered, tissue, this epithelium is best suited for absorption or secretion. However, these functions are performed by a variety of organs, so we must look at the shapes of the individual cells. The column-shaped nature, as well as the cilia lining the top of each cell, are clear hallmarks of the intestinal lining.

A: The epidermis is categorized as a stratified squamous epithelium. Since the skin mainly plays a role in the protection of the body, it would not be likely to be found in a single layer. Instead, epidermal cells are arranged in many layers of thin, flattened epithelial cells.
C: Like the skin, the mouth is subject to constant contact with the outside environment. To provide the best protection against this external contact, it is also composed of a simple squamous epithelium.
D: This is very close! But nephrons are lined with cuboidal, not columnar, cells. While this is a specific detail, you should recognize the diagram shown as best resembling the lining of the intestine.

518. A is correct. Innate immunity is that which is nonspecific, meaning that it protects against most or all pathogens in a similar way. The skin, simply by protecting the interior of the body, certainly serves as part of the innate immune system.

B: Adaptive immunity only against specific pathogens, and only after prior exposure. This subdivision of the immune system is more closely associated with B cells, antibodies, and T cells.
C: Cell-mediated immunity is provided by immune cells (macrophages, T cells, etc.), not the skin.

519. C is correct. The skin (along with hair and nails) comprises the integumentary system. Remember that the skin is an organ; in fact, it is the largest organ in the human body.

520. A is correct. The question stem mentions that psoriasis involves overly rapid growth of keratinocytes, or young epidermal cells. In fact, it is this rapid growth that produces thick plaques on the exterior of a sufferer's skin. Choice A involves a medication that lengthens interphase, thus increasing the amount of time between cell divisions and slowing growth. In addition, this medication is topical, or intended for application directly to the skin.

B: This is the exact opposite of our desired effect. Tumors are characterized by rapid growth, so a growth factor implicated in tumor pathology would (if anything) make an individual's psoriasis worse.
C: The epidermis of the skin is a type of epithelium. In contrast, endothelium generally refers to the epithelial layer that lines blood

vessels. A treatment that targets this layer would have no effect on a skin condition.

D: Remember, just because a treatment is popular certainly does not mean that it is effective. In fact, cellulose is not digestible by humans, so this "remedy" likely passes straight through the digestive system without exerting a physiological effect.

521. A is correct. Anfinsen's experiment supported the idea that a protein's primary structure, or amino acid sequence, contains the information that directs secondary, tertiary, and quaternary structure. The disulfides within the enzyme were reformed via oxidation, allowing the enzyme to fully regain its conformation and, consequently, its function.

522. A is correct. Denaturation via SDS and mercaptoethanol effectively removes all forces that hold together secondary, tertiary, and quaternary structure. Therefore, the various subunits of Protein A would separate individually as they migrate along the gel. In a native gel, the protein is not denatured, and Protein A would migrate as a single, heavier molecule. This would result in slower travel.

C: This is possible if Protein A is comprised of identical, very massive subunits. However, it is less likely than A.

D: A smear occurs when fragments of protein are present across a range of sizes. The denatured sample would be expected to result in discrete bands, as only specific protein subunits should be present.

523. A is correct. In size-exclusion chromatography, proteins that are larger elute faster, as they are less likely to become trapped in the spaces within the stationary phase. In contrast, larger proteins migrate more slowly through a gel in electrophoresis. Size-exclusion chromatography yields no information on the presence of subunits or the nature of the protein's amino acid composition.

524. B is correct. The rigidity of the proline ring disrupts the formation of alpha helices and beta sheets. This is why proline is found at the "turns" in antiparallel beta sheets.

A, C: It is impossible for a protein to lack primary structure.

D: Tertiary structure is still possible, as residues in the protein may interact in a way that leads to some sort of protein folding.

525. A is correct. Leucine is a hydrophobic residue. Therefore, the presence of leucine side chains on the alpha helices can result in hydrophobic interactions that create so-called leucine zipper or scissor dimerization.

B: London dispersion forces are always present, but hydrophobic interactions are more significant.

526. C is correct. Sedimentation coefficient basically measures the efficiency of a particle's migration down a tube during centrifugation. Therefore, both the shape and mass of a particle are significant. This explains why sedimentation coefficients are not additive. A protein that is comprised of two subunits does not necessarily have a sedimentation coefficient that is the sum of the subunits' coefficients.

527. D is correct. Even though the band for Protein 3 is higher on the gel than either of the bands for Protein 2, the overall masses of the individual proteins are unknown. To actually assess this choice, we would need to know the sum of the masses of the subunits of Protein 2, which could easily add up to a value greater than that of Protein 3.

A, B: Remember, the smaller a protein subunit, the farther it should travel on an SDS-PAGE gel. For this reason, Protein 2 does appear to have the smallest subunit, while Protein 1 contains the largest.

C: This can be deduced from the presence of multiple bands in the lanes for Proteins 1 and 2.

528. B is correct. Both proteins contain heme, which allows them to carry oxygen.

A: Cooperativity requires the presence of multiple binding sites, but myoglobin only has one.

C: Myoglobin stores oxygen and supports aerobic respiration in muscle, specifically. In contrast, hemoglobin is the main oxygen carrier in the bloodstream and distributes oxygen in general to the tissues of the body.

529. D is correct. The Beer-Lambert law states that absorbance = εCl, where ε denotes the extinction coefficient, C represents concentration, and l is the path length in cm. Solving for C gives 10 M.

530. D is correct. Since we know neither the expected size of ABNF nor the position of the band in the gel, any protein could be responsible for this result. Additionally, the band may be due to multiple subunits or even distinct proteins if all are of similar size.

531. C is correct. IgA is an antibody found in the mucous membranes that helps prevent initial colonization by pathogens. IgE is primarily involved in the response to allergens, while IgM is responsible for the initial humoral response.

IV: IgD is the antigen receptor for B cells that have not yet been exposed to antigens.

532. C is correct. The wide variety of antibodies produced by the human body is possible due to the random recombination and alternative splicing of the gene segments that code for the variable regions. This allows for an immense number of unique immunoglobulins to be created in response to pathogens.

A: The modifications are done prior to translation.
B: This would be highly impractical.

533. A is correct. Kinesins have two conformations, one when bound to ATP and a second when bound to ADP. By hydrolyzing ATP into ADP, the kinesin can move down the microtubule. Then, replacing ADP with ATP causes the kinesin to reach out further out on the microtubule and the cycle continues.

534. D is correct. Actin strands polymerize at the (+) end and depolymerize at the (-) end. In polymeric form, ATP-bound actin (found at the (+) end) has a much higher affinity than the ADP-bound form present at the (-) end. Therefore, both A and B are true.

535. B is correct. Microtubules originate from the MTOC, which is located close to the center of the cell. Because microtubules grow from the (+) end, that end is located towards the periphery of the cell while the (-) ends are found close to the center. Kinesins travel toward the (+) ends

of microtubules, and therefore must carry cargo towards the outside of the cell.

C: Dyneins carry cargo towards the center of the cell.

536. B is correct. The antigen-binding domain of an antibody is also known as the variable domain. It is located at the end of the two arms of the structure. The variability of the structure allows antibodies to recognize very specific antigens.

A, C: Both of these are a part of the constant region, which does not bind to antigens.
D: This represents one of the hinge domains that connect the light chains to the heavy chains.

537. C is correct. Antibodies are recognized based upon their heavy chains (regions 1, 3, and 4). Heavy chains are part of the constant region and are the same among all antibodies within an organism. However, they vary between species.

538. C is correct. Treadmilling can occur when the polymer is able to grow at the (+) end but shrinks at the (-) end. We can see that this occurs in the region labeled 3.

539. B is correct. From the graph, we can see that the rate of polymerization at the (+) end is approximately equal to the rate of depolymerization at the (-) end. As a result, there will be no net growth of the polymer. This can be thought of as a type of steady-state reaction.

A, C: As stated above, the actin polymers would not be changing in size.

540. D is correct. Desmosomes are cellular junctions that are composed of cadherins. Since the cadherin gene is intact here, something else must be wrong with the cell. Desmosomes are anchored to the cytoskeleton via the intermediate filaments. Therefore, dysfunctional intermediate filaments would result in the inability to form desmosomes and is likely involved here.

541. D is correct. Both A and B are true. A reaction may be spontaneous yet also proceed extremely slowly. In addition, catalysts change the activation energy necessary to accomplish the reaction by altering the mechanism; this increases reaction rate while leaving free energy change unaffected. Because many physiological reactions are spontaneous but extremely slow, enzymes can

be used as "switches," where their presence or absence determines whether a reaction occurs on a practical timescale.

542. C is correct. The enzyme's active site best stabilizes the transition state. This should be intuitively consistent with the fact that enzymes reduce activation energy. If the enzyme stabilized the substrate, this would reduce the driving force of the reaction and raise the ΔG. Moreover, enzymes do not have high affinity for products as, quite simply, they need to release them for the reaction to proceed in the desired direction.

543. D is correct. B and C are true. By reducing the activation energy, the rates of the forward and reverse reaction increase. However, the spontaneity of the forward reaction and the nonspontaneity of the reverse reaction, or vice versa, are not affected.

544. A is correct. Because glucose and glucose 6-phosphate differ by one phosphate group, the correct answer will be a class of enzymes that accomplishes phosphorylation, which are kinases by definition. In most cells, the kinase that mediates this step is hexokinase. In special cells, including those of the liver, the kinase responsible is a specific hexokinase isoform called glucokinase.

545. B is correct. Glucose 6-phosphate and fructose 6-phosphate are isomers; thus, the second step of glycolysis is likely mediated by an isomerase (phosphoglucoisomerase).

A, C: Phosphorylation is accomplished by kinases, such as glucokinase, hexokinase, or phosphofructokinase.

546. B is correct. A typical rate vs. pH curve is parabolic in shape. After reaching an optimal pH, the activity of a particular enzyme will decline. This explains why enzymes from the stomach, such as pepsin, do not work efficiently in the small intestine, where the pH is higher due to bicarbonate secretion.

A: Rate and pH are not related in a linear fashion. Additionally, this plot shows no "peak" in optimal enzymatic activity.
C, D: This curve could only relate to an enzyme that has two distinct, very different optimal pH values. Enzymes typically do not exhibit

optimum activity in two entirely separate sets of conditions.

547. A is correct. Salivary amylase is first released in the oral cavity, while pepsin is released in the stomach, where it works in an extremely acidic environment. Of the given choices, only carboxypeptidase, made in the pancreas and delivered to the small intestine via ducts, operates efficiently at the pH of the small intestine.

548. C is correct. An enzyme reduces the activation energy for both the forward and reverse reactions. The direction of reaction in this case is governed by the relative amounts of reactants and products, i.e. the difference between the reaction quotient and equilibrium. In tissue, high amounts of carbon dioxide exist outside of the red blood cell, driving diffusion into the cell and consumption of the carbon dioxide by carbonic anhydrase. In the lungs, there is low carbon dioxide tension outside of the cell, driving production of the gas by carbonic anhydrase and subsequent diffusion out of the cell into the blood.

549. D is correct. The K_m value refers to the substrate concentration necessary to achieve half of the V_{max}, or maximal reaction rate. If competitive inhibitor is added, the apparent K_m value increases. The only possible choice that indicates an increase in K_m is D.

550. D is correct. A, B, and C may all affect the V_{max}. Changing the amount of enzyme affects how fast the reaction can occur, given availability of substrate. A noncompetitive inhibitor decreases the maximal rate of reaction while leaving the K_m unaffected. Finally, a mixed inhibitor in one that has effects that are a mix of both competitive and noncompetitive effects. Thus a mixed inhibitor changes both K_m and V_{max}.

551. D is correct. Vitamin C and the B complex vitamins are the two groups of vitamin that are water-soluble. Vitamin C, also known as ascorbic acid, can function as an antioxidant; it also serves as a cofactor in many enzymatic reactions, including collagen synthesis. The many different vitamin B members can function either as prosthetic groups, such as biotin, or as coenzymes, such as folic acid.

C: Vitamin A is made from a precursor, beta-carotene, which is a carotenoid. However, vitamin A is fat-soluble.

552. C is correct. The stabilization of the transition state is explained by the induced-fit model, but not the lock and key model. The induced-fit theory posits that the active site of the enzyme is shaped by interactions between itself and the substrate. The gradual molding of the active site to the substrate is what eventually stabilizes the transition state.

553. A is correct. Allosteric regulation is achieved through the binding of a molecule at a site on the enzyme other than the active site. In contrast, catalysis of a reaction is the main function of an enzyme and occurs at the active site. Thus, an allosteric molecule, by definition, cannot catalyze a reaction due to its binding location.

    B, C: These represent functions that an allosteric molecule can perform.
    D: This is the most common way by which an allosteric molecule can inhibit an enzyme.

554. B is correct. Coenzymes and prosthetic groups both fall under the category of cofactors. However, one difference between them relates to their binding to their associated enzymes. Prosthetic groups are tightly bound to the enzyme (such as zinc in carbonic anhydrase), while coenzymes are generally released from the active site after the reaction (such as NADH or riboflavin).

    A: This describes certain organic prosthetic groups, including biotin in pyruvate carboxylase.
    C: Prosthetic groups can be metal ions that are located at the enzyme core, but many other such groups are located elsewhere.
    D: This is a function of coenzymes, not prosthetic groups.

555. A is correct. This is a key characteristic of the induced-fit hypothesis and part of the explanation for the stabilization of the transition state.

556. B is correct. Iron is a part of the heme group, which is a cofactor of hemoglobin.

    A: This answer is tempting. However, remember that prosthetic groups are tightly bound to their parent compounds. Fe is able to shift while

binding oxygen; this describes the phenomenon known as cooperative binding.
    C: Coenzymes often dissociate from the parent compound following the reaction. However, iron atom must remain in the heme group in order for hemoglobin to function properly.

557. A is correct. Many coenzymes dissociate from the enzyme after catalyzing a reaction. Coenzymes can also transfer functional groups between molecules. If the iron atom were to separate from hemoglobin after binding to a single oxygen, the hemoglobin-oxygen binding affinity and the ability of hemoglobin to transfer oxygen would be drastically reduced. This is true because hemoglobin is capable of transferring four oxygen molecules; the binding of each of these molecules is enabled by the iron atom.

558. D is correct. This diagram shows a classic feedback inhibition mechanism, in which the final product of a metabolic pathway downregulates the activity of an earlier enzyme to limit its own production.

    C: Feed-forward mechanisms do not function like this and are quite rare.

559. B is correct. In this situation, enzymes A through E may serve many other functions in addition to the catalysis of P production. Thus, inhibiting only the final enzyme responsible for the production of P will minimize the potential detrimental effects on the organism while achieving the original intention.

560. C is correct. Phosphorylation can denature some proteins, while others require phosphorylation to function at all. Most enzymes are sensitive to charge, and the addition of phosphate groups can denature or renature them through alteration of the charge distribution on the enzyme.

561. D is correct. Enzymes lower the activation energy of the associated reaction, thereby allowing it to proceed faster. Enzymes do not change the energy state of either products or reactants and do not affect the total change in energy.

    B: Carbonic anhydrase mediates both steps of this reaction and will therefore lower the activation energies of both.

562. B is correct. When protons bind to hemoglobin, it decreases the affinity of the enzyme for its substrate, making oxygen less likely to bind. This decrease in affinity is the definition of negative cooperativity.

563. C is correct. To solve this equation, we must use the Michaelis-Menten equation, $V_o = \frac{V_{max}[S]}{K_m + [S]}$. Notice that increasing any value in the numerator will increase initial velocity, while increasing any value in the denominator will do the opposite. To break this equation down further, note that $K_m = \frac{k_{-1} + k_2}{k_1}$. Since increasing K_m will decrease reaction rate, decreasing k_{-1} (which makes K_m smaller) must increase the initial velocity.

564. C is correct. The rate of the reaction is dependent on the concentration of the reactants and the rate constant, which in this case is k_1. As the pyruvate dehydrogenase complex is created and bound with substrate, the amount of unbound enzyme and substrate decreases. Therefore, [PD]$_t$ - [PD-Y] is equal to the concentration of unbound enzyme [PD]. The rate at which [PD-Y] forms, then, is equal to k_1([PD]$_t$ - [PD-Y])[Y].

565. A is correct. K_m represents the substrate concentration needed for the reaction to reached ½ V_{max}. Here, V_{max} is approximately 3, so half of that value is near 1.5. Imagine drawing a line across from 1.5 to the curve, then down to the x-axis to determine concentration. Of the values listed, 2 is closest to the value of K_m.

566. D is correct. The Michaelis-Menten equation states that $V_o = \frac{V_{max}[S]}{K_m + [S]}$. Because the initial reaction rate is equal to one-fourth of its maximum value, we can substitute $(1/4)V_{max}$ for V_0. $(1/4)V_{max} = (V_{max}[S]) / (K_m + [S])$, which simplifies to $1/4 = [S] / (K_m + [S])$. Solving for K_m shows that it is equal to 3[S], or 150 mM.

567. C is correct. The y-intercept of a Lineweaver-Burk plot gives us the reciprocal of V_{max}. To find V_{max}, we must simply take the reciprocal of this value.

568. B is correct. We can solve for K_m either by finding the slope and multiplying by V_{max}, or by solving for the x-intercept and negating the reciprocal of that value. For the first method, slope is calculated as change in y divided by change in x. Here, that

yields 3/2. From the Lineweaver-Burk equation, we know that slope = K_m / V_{max} and that V_{max} is the reciprocal of the y-intercept. 3/2 = K_m / (1/3), so K_m = 1/2.

569. A is correct. Addition of enzyme increases [E], which will increase the rate and the V_{max} of the reaction. An increase in V_{max} will lower the y-intercept and decrease the value of the slope. K_m, or enzyme affinity, will remain unaffected.

570. C is correct. Enzymes only affect the kinetics of their associated reactions. They do not alter ΔG or ΔH.

571. A is correct. In competitive inhibition, the inhibitor and substrate are structurally similar, causing them to compete for binding with the active site. The enzyme's activity can be restored to its V_{max} via addition of extra substrate, which "drowns out" the effects of the inhibitor.

B: This describes allosteric or noncompetitive inhibition. In this type of inhibition, additional substrate cannot restore enzyme activity to its maximum value.
C: The two compounds are each interacting with the enzyme, not with each other.
D: As in choice C, nothing in the question indicates that Compounds A and B would chemically interact in any way.

572. C is correct. ATP is formed both via substrate-level phosphorylation during glycolysis and the Krebs cycle and, in more significant quantities, during oxidative phosphorylation. Likewise, NADH is formed during glycolysis and the Krebs cycle, while citric acid is formed only in the latter. All of these products, therefore, are formed downstream of phosphofructokinase. Allosteric inhibition of upstream enzymes by downstream products is the definition of negative feedback and maintains balance within the system.

A: Competitive inhibition is not allosteric.
B: Positive feedback does not restore balance; it accomplishes the opposite. Specifically, it occurs when downstream products amplify the activity of upstream enzymes.
D: There is no such thing as aerobic takeover. At any rate, phosphofructokinase is necessary for both aerobic and anaerobic respiration, and

inhibition of this enzyme would affect both pathways.

573. C is correct. K_m is defined as the concentration of substrate when the enzyme's activity is at half of the V_{max}, or maximal rate. V_{max} can be estimated as the value where the curves plateau. At the indicated substrate concentration in conditions A and C, the rate (V) appears to be half of that estimated maximum. We could also observe that compound C seems to be a noncompetitive inhibitor, which would have the same K_m as the uninhibited enzyme.

II: In condition B, the rate is much lower than half of its maximum value.

574. B is correct. The curve for Compound C shows that it decreases the enzyme's V_{max} while leaving its K_m unaffected. These signs indicate noncompetitive inhibition, which targets areas distinct from the active site. The potential binding positions mentioned in the question may be some such allosteric sites.

A, C: Compound B appears to promote an increased K_m, with a rate that approaches the original V_{max} as substrate concentration is raised. These signs indicate competitive inhibition, which does not involve allosteric sites.

575. D is correct. According to the induced fit model, substrates have structures that loosely complement the enzyme's active site contours. Upon preliminary interactions, the shape of the enzyme changes to even better accommodate the substrate and form the enzyme-substrate complex. Thus, competitive inhibitors, which bind the active site, would be expected to have structures that at least somewhat fit into that site as well. Moreover, the presence of negatively charged amino acids in the active site means that competitive inhibitors likely possess positively charged residues, such as lysine and arginine, to allow for strong non-covalent interactions.

C: Neither competitive inhibitors nor substrates mimic the structure of the enzyme itself. Instead, they complement all or part of the active site structure.

576. D is correct. Upon addition of substrate, the rate of reaction increases. This result could be observed at low substrate concentrations when

no inhibitor is present. It could also be seen along with noncompetitive inhibition (before the V_{max} plateau is reached) or competitive inhibition (at higher substrate concentrations). Therefore, Luke does not have sufficient information to distinguish between these choices.

577. A is correct. The slope of a line in a Lineweaver-Burk plot gives K_m/V_{max} for the reaction. The y-intercept denotes $1/V_{max}$, while the x-intercept corresponds to $-1/K_m$. In noncompetitive inhibition, the V_{max} is decreased, so the slope of the line should increase. Moreover, K_m remains the same, so the x-intercept should not change.

B: This line would result from competitive inhibition. The slope increases because the apparent K_m, the numerator, becomes larger. This also explains why the x-intercept moves towards the origin. However, since V_{max} is constant, the y-intercept does not change.

578: C is correct. The x-intercept of a Lineweaver-Burk plot is equal to $-1/K_m$. The graph indicates a value of $-a$ for the x-intercept of the dashed line. Solving the expression $-a = (-1/K_m)$ results in a value of $1/a$ for K_m.

579. A is correct. Zymogens are inactive precursors that can be covalently cleaved into functional enzymes. A classic example is the autocatalysis of pepsinogen by hydrochloric acid, which forms the digestive enzyme pepsin.

B: The question states that A is converted to B. Catalysts do not participate in reactions.
C: Molecule A is described as inactive, meaning that it would not bind to a substrate.

580. D is correct. 2,3-BPG is a metabolite, an isomer of a glycolytic intermediate. Its presence therefore indicates metabolic activity and implies a "need" for oxygen. It notably interacts with allosteric sites on hemoglobin (not the active sites, since those are occupied by O_2) to promote the release of oxygen. This is observed as a rightwards shift in the saturation curve.

A: 2,3-BPG does not interact with the active site of the hemoglobin molecule. Additionally, it is not an inhibitor; if it were, it would make gas exchange more difficult.
B, C: No covalent modification is occurring.

581. A is correct. The first step in this problem is to identify the site of potential autocatalytic (self-) cleavage. The ester is the site where this would take place; a nucleophile would attack the carbonyl carbon, causing the ester oxygen to leave. Choices II, III, and IV each contain an ester, which acts as the site for nucleophilic attack. The next step is to identify which zymogen would have a free nucleophile at pH 3. Molecule IV has a carboxylic acid, which would be deprotonated at pH 3, providing a negatively-charged terminal carboxylic acid that can act as a strong nucleophile for autocatalytic cleavage.

582. B is correct. You must recall that many digestive enzymes are synthesized as zymogens.

583. C is correct. The reaction depicts a hydrolysis mechanism, in which a molecule of water is used to split the substrate. Hydrolysis is a very common method of activating zymogens. By examining the reaction, you can see where the water molecule donates an H$^+$ and an OH$^-$.

584. A is correct. Allosteric activators will increase the initial rate of the reaction, but will not increase the V_{max}.

B: Curve B shows the effect of an allosteric inhibitor, which will slow the initial rate but will not decrease V_{max}.
C: Curve C is characteristic of an allosteric enzyme due to its sigmoidal shape.
D: Curve D is incorrect because the V_{max} of this reaction actually increases, which is not a result of allosteric activation.

585. C is correct. As seen on the graph, the enzyme becomes saturated at approximately 9 mM. Once an enzyme is saturated, increasing the substrate concentration will have no effect on the reaction rate or on V_{max}.

B: If the enzyme were not saturated, choice B would be correct.

586. A is correct. Recall that kinases are enzymes that are used to add and remove phosphate groups in biological systems.

587. B is correct. Allosteric inhibition slows the initial reaction rate, but the reaction will eventually reach the same V_{max}.

A: Enzyme A exhibits Michaelis-Menten kinetics, which can be characterized by the hyperbolic shape of Curve A.
C: Competitive inhibition slows the initial rate of the reaction, but as substrate concentration increases, the substrate will be able to overcome the inhibitor and the reaction will reach its original V_{max}.
D: Allosteric activation will increase the initial reaction rate so that the reaction can reach the same maximum at a faster pace.

588. B is correct. The question stem describes hemoglobin with the characteristics of an allosteric enzyme. These enzymes do not exhibit classical Michaelis-Menten kinetics. Here, the interactions between neighboring subunits affect the affinity of other subunits.

C: An amphiphilic molecule is one that is both polar and nonpolar. This is not relevant to the question.

589. B is correct. Hemoglobin is an allosteric enzyme, which will exhibit a sigmoidal kinetic curve.

A: This hyperbolic curve is characteristic of classical Michaelis-Menten kinetics.

590. D is correct. From the question stem, it is known that the negatively-charged molecule cannot bind at the active site. The description of this interaction is characteristic of allosteric regulation.

591. B is correct. cDNA is made from mRNA that has undergone post-transcriptional modification. These changes eliminate promoter and other regulatory sequences as well as introns, all of which are still present in the DNA from the genomic library.

A: Telomere sequences are added to the end of chromosomes, meaning that few genes will have them.
C: Post-transcriptionally modified DNA is used as template to make cDNA, not the other way around.
D: Intron, not exons, are not present in the cDNA clones.

592. C is correct. Most proteins that interact with the intact double helix bind to the major groove. This allows unambiguous interactions between the

amino acids of the protein and the DNA bases via H-bonding.

A: Restriction enzymes do not require DNA strands to have already been unwound.
B: The minor groove does not allow for base-specific unambiguous interactions.
D: Proteins may bind to the phosphates in the DNA backbone. But the phosphate groups are identical regardless of whether the associated base is A, C, T, or G. In other words, this would not allow for sequence-specific interaction.

593. B is correct. The *Drosophila* DNA inserts into the *Eco*RI recognition site within the ampicillin resistance gene. This means that ampicillin resistance will be knocked out while the tetracycline resistance gene remains intact. Therefore, tetracycline should be added to the medium to eliminate the bacteria that are neither tetracycline-resistant nor ampicillin-resistant.

A, C: Since these choices contain ampicillin, they would fail to select bacteria that have successfully incorporated plasmids with the knocked-out ampicillin resistance gene.
D: All bacteria, whether transformed or not, would grow on this medium.

594. D is correct. The *Drosophila* DNA insert knocks out only the gene for ampicillin resistance.

A: This would select for bacteria carrying the original plasmid without the *Drosophila* DNA insert.
B: This would select for cells in which the tetracycline gene has been knocked out. This situation would not be a logical result of the experiment described.
C: This would isolate bacteria that did not incorporate the plasmid at all.

595. C is correct. Choices A, B, and D would leave the ampicillin resistance gene intact. Since the situation in choice C does not involve the bacteria picking up the plasmid at all, the resulting colonies would not be resistant to ampicillin or tetracycline.

596. B is correct. Only AAGCTT, found in choice B, would result in a palindromic complement. Restriction enzyme recognition sites are palindromic double-stranded sequences.

597. C is correct. Under non-optimal conditions, both complete and partial digestion will occur. We will have a total of three different DNA segments as a result of full digestion (let's call them A, B, and C). In addition, three segments can also result from partial digestion (A+B, B+C, and A+B+C). These six segments have different sizes, so they would produce six different elution peaks in SEC.

D: SEC can be used with DNA as well as protein.

598: D is correct. The negatively charged phosphate groups present in nucleic acids prevent passage through the cell membrane. Therefore, the cells must be treated (by lysing, for example) to become permeable to the oligonucleotides.

A: Human cells do not have cell walls.
B: Since one function of the poly-A tail is to protect the mRNA from degradation, this choice is unlikely.
C: Eukaryotic mRNA does gain a 3' poly-A tail during post-transcriptional modifications.

599. D is correct. I, II, and III are true statements. A genomic library contains all of the sequences in the entire genome. In contrast, a cDNA library is constructed from nuclear mRNA, meaning that it would only contain sequences that had been recently transcribed.

600. A is correct. In Sanger dideoxynucleotide sequencing, all four ddNTPs are added to a single tube in which DNA replication is taking place. Remember, dNTPs are used to elongate the chain, while ddNTPs terminate replication. During primer extension, a large number of chains of various lengths are produced, all complementary to the template DNA. Since new strands are synthesized from 3' → 5', the 3' end of the complementary DNA chain will be nearest to the well, while the 5' end will be farthest. This makes A the accurate answer choice.

B: This is the complementary DNA sequence in reverse order.
C: This is the template DNA sequence in reverse order.
D: This is the complementary DNA sequence in the correct order, but we're looking for the sequence of the parent DNA.

601. C is correct. The majority of PCR protocols involve cyclical heating of the sample to promote

DNA denaturation. The polymerase used in this process must be resistant to temperatures that exceed the normal physiological range for most organisms. In fact, *Taq* polymerase is taken from thermophilic bacteria. It would therefore be difficult to denature this heat-stable enzyme using high temperatures alone.

A: Strong acid is sufficient to denature most proteins, and we have no reason to assume that *T. aquaticus* polymerase is exempt.
B: Guanidinium chloride, like urea, disrupts networks of hydrogen bonds. Since H-bonding is critical for maintaining specificity in protein structure, its disruption would likely result in denaturation.
D: Mechanical agitation of proteins in solution may sometimes cause the proteins to invert, exposing their hydrophobic interiors. This often results in protein aggregation. *T. aquaticus* certainly may be subject to such behavior under stress.

602. A is correct. Magnesium is a cofactor for *Taq* DNA polymerase. This ion aids in the coordination of the pyrophosphate leaving group, facilitating phosphodiester hydrolysis and the subsequent addition of incoming nucleotide triphosphates.

B: PCR requires free deoxynucleotide triphosphates (dNTPs). Free rNTPs are unnecessary in such a procedure.
C: Hydroxide ions would serve no conceivable purpose during PCR. In fact, they would probably hamper protein function and cause DNA denaturation due to the resulting basicity of the solution.
D: Pyrophosphate is a side product of DNA polymerization. Not only is this molecule unnecessary for conducting a PCR procedure, its presence in solution may actually reduce the rate of the forward reaction.

603. C is correct. During the cooler phases of PCR, the two DNA strands are able to remain coordinated with each other via hydrogen bonding. As heat enters the system, the complementary strands dissociate and lose their characteristic helical secondary structure. This change would most likely be observable when using CD spectroscopy.

A: We are told that CD spectroscopy focuses on secondary structure. Although the nucleotides involved do retain constant chirality, this property does not relate to this level of structure.
B: Since the DNA strands dissociate when subject to high temperature, the CD spectra are not likely to be identical regardless of reaction progress.
D: *Taq* polymerase is frequently used for PCR specifically because it does not denature during heating.

604. C is correct. During the melting phase, energy is absorbed by the intermolecular hydrogen bonds between the two DNA strands. Eventually, the energy input will exceed that which can be stored within these bonds, and the two strands will dissociate. Until this point is reached, however, the added heat energy will steadily be transferred to the bonds instead of contributing to an increase in molecular kinetic energy. Since temperature is a measure of the average kinetic energy of a sample, this value will remain fairly constant until the heat capacity of the DNA duplex has been exceeded.

605. B is correct. The principal stabilizing force that maintains the structure of the DNA double helix is the hydrophobic attraction between stacked base pairs. Hydrogen bonding is a secondary contributor to overall duplex stability, but it still must be disrupted before dissociation can happen.

III: Phosphate groups on opposing DNA strands do not interact noticeably. Furthermore, all such groups carry a negative charge at physiological pH, so they would not participate in any attractive interactions.
IV: Although this effect is likely to be somewhat disrupted by the increased temperature of the reaction vessel, this disruption is not required to permit DNA dissociation. In fact, under normal conditions, water molecules compete for H-bonding interactions with complementary base pairs; this actually opposes duplex stability. Again, this is why hydrophobic effects are the predominant forces that maintain the double helix.

606. D is correct. This is a way of saying that catalytic activity will be hampered by temperatures that are insufficiently high. Catalysis requires a number of conformational changes. A protein that is too cold will lack enough thermal energy to cycle through its conformational changes at an

optimal rate. As a result, this necessary catalysis will be somewhat sluggish.

A: This choice may initially seem plausible; however, we were told that all polymerization phases (of which there are many) run at 72°C. If the *Taq* enzyme required thermal activation, the very first of these phases might very well need to be preceded by a period of relatively high temperature. However, subsequent polymerization phases would not need to take place under these conditions.

B: Fully non-complementary strands do not anneal. Hydrogen bonding places strict geometric restrictions on the double helix that necessitate complementarity. This property is exploited during the process of DNA repair, since even a single mismatch induces a substantial distortion in the double helix that may be recognized by repair enzymes.

C: While this statement is true, the primers do not dissociate during the polymerization phase. They must remain bound to permit the initiation of replication.

607. A is correct. If primers are complementary to each other (or if a primer is complementary to itself), primer nucleotides may anneal with one another to form a small, useless dimer. Selection of primer sequences that do not exhibit this characteristic will decrease the chances of promoting this side reaction, ultimately optimizing the desired PCR.

B: Since magnesium is an essential component of a PCR solution, a metal chelating agent would likely reduce the reaction rate.

C: Although hydrogen bonding favors the addition of complementary nucleotides, errors may occasionally occur. Relatively high pyrimidine concentration in solution increases the probability that a pyrimidine will be wrongly incorporated into the growing strand, simply due to the law of mass action. Since *Taq* polymerase has limited proofreading ability, this error is unlikely to be resolved. Optimally, PCR involves the use of equal concentrations of all four dNTPs.

D: PCR is error-prone and works best when used to amplify DNA strands that are not particularly large.

608. A is correct. A rightward shift implies that a higher temperature must be reached to "melt," or denature, 50% of the DNA. GC units feature three hydrogen bonds, one more than the number of bonds between AT nucleobases. In other words, the separation of GC pairs requires a larger amount of energy input in the form of heat.

C, D: The slope of the researcher's graph is impossible to predict. DNA denaturation is a dynamic process that depends greatly on the sequences involved. During the course of heating, hydrogen bonds are constantly being broken and reformed, which ultimately determines the shape of the curve. To conclude, while either C or D might be true, neither is predictable, and neither constitutes the most likely change that would result from the difference between telomere and exon DNA.

609. B is correct. The original sample is composed of messenger RNA, which features a 3' poly(A) tail. The presence of this tail could be detected by a complementary probe, most likely a single-stranded thymidine repeat oligonucleotide. Note that the question stem describes the primers as random nucleotides that do not repeat, so they would not bind the poly(A) tail. Since reverse transcriptase starts at the 3' end, the transcribed cDNA cannot possibly contain any segment transcribed from this tail region. Thus, neither the poly(A) nor a complementary poly(T) sequence will appear in the final amplified cDNA, and we do not need to consider the risk of false positive labeling by a poly(T) probe.

610. A is correct. Since the target proteins are denatured, any interaction that depends on secondary or higher levels of structure is unlikely to occur. This eliminates all answer choices except for A. Since denaturation does not involve the destruction of individual amino acid residues, it is perfectly reasonable to assume that such cross-linking could still occur and lead to identification of the prey protein.

611. C is correct. Western blots typically use antibodies to bind to a protein of interest within a tissue homogenate or extract. They can be used to determine the identity and size of a protein produced by a cell.

A: This would require a polymerase chain reaction (PCR).

B: The choice here resembles some sort of sequencing technique, perhaps Sanger sequencing.

D: This would require a northern blot.

612. C is correct. Eugenics, whose principles can be traced back as far as ancient Greece, has become increasingly associated with negative consequences, particularly after the Nazis integrated this "science" into their philosophy and practice. While positive in theory, the critique of eugenics lies in the fact that the selection procedure for adjusting the human population resides within the hands of those in power and is thus subject to abuse.

613. B is correct. Embryonic stem cells are found in the inner mass of the blastocyst. As far as is now known, they represent the only pluripotent human stem cells.

A, B, D: While stem cells can be found in various adult tissues, we have no evidence that they are pluripotent.

614. B is correct. In a knockout experiment, the researcher genetically modifies the organism to inactivate a particular gene. Here, the strain in which Gene B was knocked out could not metabolize lactose. This indicates that Gene B is essential for this process.

615. D is correct. If the new strain, in which Gene C is knocked out, also could not metabolize lactose, both B and C must be necessary for lactose metabolism.

616. D is correct. This is a classic practical use of biotechnology. The newly-formed virus can be used as a vaccine so that the body can produce antibodies for the surface protein. The presence of these immunoglobulins will speed the activation of the immune system in case of infection.

617. B is correct. During a western blot, proteins are first run on an electrophoretic gel. The gel is then transferred to a nitrocellulose membrane, after which a fluorescently labeled marker is introduced, allowing visualization. In this experiment, Colony C clearly produces the protein of interest, which is about 15 kDa in size.

618. A is correct. If the wrong antibody was used, it would bind to an entirely different protein and would give us no information about the protein of interest.

619. C is correct. One of the drawbacks of gene therapy is the vector randomly integrates the new DNA sequences. This could possibly lead to integration into a region that would activate an oncogene. As leukemia is a cancer of the white blood cells, this choice makes the most sense.

620. A is correct. Immunohistochemistry uses labeled antibodies to distinguish particular proteins in tissue samples. Either radioactive elements or linked, color-producing enzymes can be used as labels.

621. D is correct. The low pI of protein A indicates that it contains many charged residues, making it more likely to be soluble and less likely to be buried within the lipid bilayer. Protein B has a more neutral character, meaning that it more likely contains predominantly hydrophobic residues. Proteins containing large numbers of hydrophobic or nonpolar amino acids tend to reside within the membrane.

622. D is correct. SDS, or sodium dodecyl sulfate, is a detergent commonly administered before protein separation. SDS denatures the protein, making it linear. As an anionic substance, it also coats the protein with a negative charge. This allows proteins to be separated on the basis of charge alone, without deviations in charge skewing the results.

A: Larger proteins will travel slowly through a polyacrylamide gel; it is the smallest proteins that should reach the end first.
B: This would be true of a reducing agent, not SDS.
C: SDS denatures secondary, tertiary, and quaternary structure. However, the primary structure is simply the amino acid sequence of the protein. Denaturing this level of structure is both unattainable for SDS and undesirable for the overall procedure.

623. A is correct. Since both children suffer from the disease even though only one parent was affected, this condition must be dominant. It also must be autosomal, since the father was able to pass the trait down to children of both genders.

C, D: Since the father has this disease but the mother does not, this disorder cannot be sex-linked (which usually means X-linked). A father can only give his Y chromosome to his sons and his X chromosome to his daughters. However, both children inherited the disease from him, so it must be encoded on an autosome.

624. C is correct. The mutant protein must be smaller, or closer to the bottom of the gel, than the wild-type version. Since the mutant has more lysine residues, which are basic, the overall peptide will also have a higher pI than the wild-type variant.

    A: These two proteins are the same weight. Instead, they need to differ by 25 kDa.
    B: While this choice accurately relates the proteins in terms of weight, the mutant should not have a lower pI than the wild-type protein.
    D: This wrongly gives a mutant protein that weighs more than the wild-type. Remember, in a gel separation procedure, heavier proteins do not move as far down the gel as lighter variants.

625. A is correct. The question stem describes the general procedure of a western blot.

    B: A northern blot detects RNA, not protein.
    C: While ELISA does detect protein, it does not need a nitrocellulose membrane. It generally tests for specific antibody-antigen interactions and is less time-consuming and expensive than western blotting.
    D: While a 2D SDS-PAGE protocol does involve a gel, it does not include antibody detection.

626. C is correct. FISH, or fluorescence *in situ* hybridization, is used for the detection of DNA sequences, not in protein identification. Specifically, it involves probes that bind to complementary regions of the chromosome.

    A, B, D: While these three techniques differ significantly from each other, all at least relate to protein.

627. B is correct. According to the question, the first protein to elute from the column should be the smallest protein in the sample. The largest absorbance peak occurs very early on the x-axis, which represents time; this makes choice B correct.

    A: We cannot say that there were few "large" proteins – for all we know, all of the proteins in the sample could be quite large. We know only their relative sizes.
    C: Though the graph does appear to have only four major peaks, there could be multiple similarly-sized proteins within each peak.
    D: The data gives no indication of this contamination.

628. A is correct. ELISA is a fairly simple procedure that tests for antibody-antigen interactions. Unlike SDS-PAGE, it does not involve sodium dodecyl sulfate as a reagent, and unlike regular gel electrophoresis, it does not involve an agarose gel.

629. C is correct. Reducing agents are most often used in such procedures to reduce disulfide bridges into free thiol groups. As these bridges are part of the tertiary structure, C is a correct statement.

    A: Denaturing primary structure would be undesirable in an SDS-PAGE procedure.
    B: This is accomplished by SDS, not a reducing agent.
    D: This is the reverse of the correct response.

630. C is correct. SDS denatures higher-level protein structure, including quaternary structure. If this protein was composed of two distinct subunits, and if these subunits were separated by the addition of SDS, they would appear on the gel as two proteins of different weights.

    A: Degraded proteins appear as a smear on a gel. Additionally, we have no reason to believe that this occurred.
    B: SDS does not break peptide bonds, which connect amino acid residues in a protein's primary structure.
    D: We are told that this protein has been purified.

631. D is correct. HPLC is a powerful form of liquid chromatography. Unlike other forms of liquid chromatography, which rely on gravity, HPLC utilizes high pressures to force a sample through a smaller, more tightly packed stationary phase. This process is a more effective purification and analytical method than many traditional forms of chromatography.

    IV: The mobile phase (solvent) in HPLC is no different from the mobile phases used in other forms of chromatography. Hexane, toluene, and water are common solvents.

632. C is correct. As stated in the question stem, cellulose is a polar substance. This means that polar compounds will interact with the cellulose, or stationary phase, and spend a greater proportion of time bound to it. In contrast, methane is a nonpolar substance, meaning that it will spend more time in the mobile phase and thus travel farther on the plate. R_f values are calculated by dividing the distance traveled by the substance by the distance traveled by the solvent front. Thus, the substance that travels farther on the paper will have a larger R_f value.

633. A is correct. In reversed-phase chromatography, the stationary phase is hydrophobic, while the mobile phase is hydrophilic. Arginine, as a charged amino acid, will elute out first, as it will not interact with the hydrophobic stationary phase at all. Serine has a polar side chain and will interact minimally with the hydrophobic environment, while phenylalanine has a hydrophobic side chain and will interact most strongly to the stationary phase.

    B: This describes the proper order for traditional chromatography, which has a polar stationary phase and a nonpolar mobile phase.

634. D is correct. A His6 tag is a label consisting of six histidine residues. It is often used in laboratory settings and has a high affinity for transition metals, such as nickel and cobalt. Affinity chromatography is most often used to purify proteins bound to tags and generally involves selective binding of the protein to one of these metals.

635. A is correct. Size-exclusion chromatography separates compounds based on size. In this technique, the stationary phase is composed of beads with tiny pores. Smaller molecules can get trapped in these beads, while larger molecules move past them and remain in the mobile phase.

    C, D: Size-exclusion chromatography does not separate based on polarity.

636. C is correct. Size-exclusion chromatography separates compounds based on size. Since methane is a small molecule relative to benzene, it will be trapped within the pores of the column's stationary phase. Benzene will largely avoid this, allowing it to elute out in the earlier fractions.

    D: This is backwards. As a larger molecule, benzene should be able to travel through the column more quickly.

637. B is correct. In a typical ion-exchange column, the resin that makes up the stationary phase contains charged functional groups that interact with charged compounds in the mixture. Specifically, an anion-exchange column has positive groups that retain the anionic components that enter the column. Since glutamic acid is negatively charged, it will interact with the resin, causing it to elute later than alanine.

    A: Ion-exchange columns do not separate molecules based on size.

638. C is correct. The stationary phase of this paper is alumina, which is a polar substance. Thus, polar compounds will bind to the alumina with greater affinity, causing them to travel a shorter distance along the paper.

    B: This answer results from the incorrect assumption that the solvent is polar and the stationary phase is nonpolar.

639. B is correct. R_f values are calculated by dividing the distance traveled by a sample by the distance traveled by the solvent front. In this scenario the equation looks like: R_f = 4 cm / 10 cm, which gives 0.4.

640. D is correct. Thin-layer chromatography is used for analysis, not purification. Specifically, it characterizes samples by their R_f value. It can also be used to identify compounds in a mixture and determine overall purity.

641. A is correct. From the figure depicting the two forms of alanine, we can see that these stereoisomers are non-superimposable mirror images. For this reason, the L- and D-isomers must be examples of enantiomers. Furthermore, in nature, only L amino acids are produced in cells and used to form protein. Although D amino acids are occasionally incorporated into bacterial cell walls, they are not used in protein production.

642. D is correct. If none of the fractions rotate plane-polarized light, they must either be achiral, contain a racemic mixture, or contain a meso compound. Since the scientist previously attempted to isolate separate enantiomers, we

can assume that the solution is not racemic (as, by definition, that would contain more than one isomer). The simplest solution is that he simply has an achiral amino acid, the only standard example of which is glycine.

B, C: Both leucine and isoleucine are chiral. However, since we do not know the direction or amount that either rotates plane-polarized light, we cannot assume that the rotation of one would cancel the other.

643. A is correct. At a pH of 1.0, alanine's carboxyl and amino groups are both protonated. The carboxyl group is neutral, while the amino group has a positive charge; the overall molecule thus has a net charge of +1. Based on this fact, cation-exchange chromatography would be most effective. In this method, the solid phase contains negatively charged ions. As it flows through the column, alanine will be attracted to this phase while negative and neutral molecules will pass through. The alanine can then be eluted by changing the pH or by washing the column with stronger cations.

B: While this is close, alanine will be a cation, not an anion, under these conditions. Anion-exchange chromatography results in negatively charged molecules binding to the column while all other components elute out of it.

644. A is correct. A zwitterion is a molecule that contains both negative and positive charges. For this question, it is useful to have knowledge of a few pK_a values that relate to amino acids. The carboxyl group pK_a is about 2, while the amino group has a pK_a of around 9-10. For this reason, we can infer that on average, alanine will have a deprotonated carboxylic acid at any pH above 2 (giving it a negative charge) and a protonated amino group at any pH below 9 (giving it a positive charge). Overall, the molecule will be neutral at pH 5.

B: At a pH of 12, tyrosine's amino group, carboxylic acid group, and side chain phenol will all be deprotonated. This results in an amino acid with a net charge of -2. While we do not need to know pK_a values for every side chain, we at least know that tyrosine will not be neutral.
C: At a pH of 4, lysine's amine is protonated, while its carboxylic acid is deprotonated.

However, lysine's R group contains a primary amine with a pKa of about 10. At pH 4, this amine will be protonated, giving lysine a net charge of +1.
D. At a pH of 1, both glycine's amino group (pK_a = 9.6) and carboxylic acid group (pK_a = 2.3) are protonated, resulting in a net charge of +1.

645. C is correct. Disulfide bonds are formed between the terminal thiol groups of cysteine residues. These bonds are important in the maintenance of the protein's tertiary structure, and in keratin, the larger the number of disulfide bonds, the curlier the hair. Reducing these bonds breaks them into free thiol groups and relaxes the hair.

D: While methionine does contain sulfur, it cannot form disulfide bonds with either cysteine or other methionine residues.

646. A is correct. The formation of a polypeptide takes place via a dehydration reaction. Here, the labeled amino acid will form a covalent peptide bond with another residue. The incoming amino group acts as a nucleophile and attacks the carbonyl carbon, and the labeled oxygen molecule is released as water.

B: Dehydration reactions release water molecules, not O_2 molecules.
C: Immediately after its incorporation into a polypeptide, the amino acid should be found at the C-terminus, not the N-terminus. Additionally, the labeled oxygen atom will already have been lost.

647. B is correct. The isoelectric point is the pH at which glycine is most likely to exist as a neutral salt. For amino acids with neutral side chains, this point exists exactly halfway between the first and second pK_a values, which are represented by the half-equivalence points on the curve above. Here, (2.3 + 9.6) / 2 = 5.95.

648. D is correct. The solution begins at a pH of 6, which is very close to point B in the figure. This represents the first equivalence point of the titration. At such positions, the curve is very steep, meaning that the addition of a significant amount of strong base certainly should increase the pH of the solution. At a pH more basic than the pI of glycine, the molecule as a whole should

be negatively charged, as both the carboxy and the amino termini will be deprotonated.

649. D is correct. Anion-exchange chromatography separates substances using a positively-charged stationary phase. Consequently, the beads in the column bind anions, or negatively-charged molecules. Glycine will have a net negative charge at any pH more basic than its pI, but the more basic the solution, the larger the percentage of glycine molecules with a full -1 charge. The choice with the most basic pH is choice D.

A: At such a low pH, both the carboxyl and amino groups will be protonated, resulting in a net charge of +1. While this would work perfectly in a cation-exchange column, it will be repelled by an anion-exchange one. The glycine would be lost in the eluent and washes instead of adhering to the column.

650. C is correct. As covalent bonds, peptide bonds do not easily break – this requires either an enzyme or slow hydrolysis.

A, B, D: These are all characteristics of peptide bonds.

651. B is correct. Numeral II states that K (lysine) is not a zwitterion at physiological pH (~7.4). At this pH, every amino acid has a negatively-charged carboxyl group and a positively-charged amino group. However, lysine also has an amino functionality on its side chain with a pK_a of 10.5. As a result, this R group has a positive charge under the described conditions, and lysine has a net positive charge of +1. In contrast, zwitterions are neutrally charged.

I: Lysine has a net positive charge (+1).
III: Lysine is a basic amino acid.

652. D is correct. Ion-exchange chromatography separates compounds based on their net charge. In this case, the stationary phase is positive, meaning that negatively-charged compounds will take longer to elute because they will interact more with the stationary phase. Therefore, we would expect the polypeptide that elutes first to contain fewer negative amino acids than the one that elutes second. D (aspartic acid) is negatively charged at physiological pH, so we would not expect it to be common in the first eluent.

A, B, C: Alanine, histidine, and proline are not negatively-charged amino acids.

653. C is correct. Entropic penalties are incurred when amino acids are exposed to an environment in which they are poorly soluble. In this case, the surface of a protein is likely to face an aqueous environment, so hydrophilic residues are favored and hydrophobic residues incur a penalty. Leucine, valine and phenylalanine are all hydrophobic amino acids.

A, B, D: Histidine, serine, glutamic acid, and threonine are not hydrophobic.

654. C is correct. At pH 1, the amino group (pK_a ~ 9.2) on tyrosine is protonated and positively charged. In addition, the carboxylic acid group (pK_a ~ 2.2) is also protonated, making it neutral. Therefore, the overall charge on the molecule is +1.

655. A is correct. Chiral column chromatography separates compounds based on their optical rotation (D or L). If the correct stationary phase is used, it can be used to resolve racemic mixtures of chiral amino acids. Therefore, we must choose the option that is achiral. Glycine, which lacks a chiral center, is a perfect answer.

656. B is correct. The tertiary structure of a protein is driven by the tendency of hydrophobic residues to bury themselves inside the molecule, away from water, as well as interactions between side chains. Specifically, a substitution involving two amino acids that vary in polarity, charge, or sulfur content could alter tertiary structure. Of all the options listed, replacing lysine (a basic, positively-charged AA) with leucine (a nonpolar, neutral AA) is most likely to promote such a change.

A: Val and Met both have nonpolar, neutral R groups.
C: Ser and Thr are polar uncharged AAs.
D: Both Asp and Glu are polar, negatively-charged residues.

657. D is correct. The most entropically favored conformation of a globular protein involves the burial of hydrophobic residues inside the molecule, away from the aqueous environment that surrounds the protein. Thus, we must choose the amino acid that is most hydrophobic. F (phenylalanine) is the only nonpolar amino acid listed.

658. B is correct. The table lists three pK$_a$ values. From outside knowledge, we should know that all amino acids have a carboxyl and an amino group, corresponding to pK$_a$ values of about 2 and 9 – 10.5, respectively. Therefore, Group 1 must represent the carboxylic acid, while Group 3 must be the amine. This means that Group 2 is the R group.

A: Since we do not know the pH in which it is currently found, we cannot guarantee that this is true.
C: The unknown amino acid could not be lysine, as it lacks a basic side chain.
D: At physiological pH, X will likely carry a -1 net charge.

659. C is correct. From the table, we can infer that X has an acidic R group due to its low pK$_a$. In fact, this side chain likely includes a carboxylic acid, which tend to have pK$_a$ values near 4. COOH groups become deprotonated at physiological pH, giving them a negative charge and an overall polarity. Altogether, this information implies that X will be found on the surface of a protein, adjacent to the aqueous external environment.

A: Hydrophobic, not hydrophilic, residues are found in the interior of proteins.
B: Nucleic acids, not amino acids, abound in DNA.
D: Because the transmembrane domain of a protein is located within the lipid bilayer, the amino acids found in this region tend to be hydrophobic.

660. D is correct. In titrations of weak acids and weak bases, one equivalence point is found for each acidic or basic functional group. Because the amino acid shown in the picture has two amino groups and one carboxylic acid group, three equivalence points will be observed during its titration with NaOH.

661. A is correct. The question stem references proline, a structurally unique amino acid. Proline can be spotted by the fact that its amino terminal is directly attached to its side chain in the form of a heterocyclic ring. This feature causes proline to promote "kinks," or bends, in the secondary structures of proteins in which it is incorporated.

B: This double-ringed compound is tryptophan, a larger molecule than proline.

C: This structure is that of histidine. While this basic amino acid also contains a heterocyclic ring, its side chain is not covalently bound to its amino group.
D: The residue shown here is phenylalanine, not proline. Phenylalanine is given the one-letter abbreviation "F."

662. B is correct. Disulfide linkages are those that form between two free –SH groups, yielding S-S bonds. To break these linkages, one must simply add hydrogen back to the two sulfur atoms involved. In organic chemistry, one may conceptualize reduction as either the loss of bonds to oxygen or the gain of bonds to hydrogen. As such, a reducing agent would break these bonds. Note that disulfide linkages form between two cysteine residues.

A: An oxidizing agent, not a reducing agent, would better facilitate the formation of disulfide bonds.
C: This answer is close! But the term "cystine" already describes two linked cysteine residues.
D: As it represents individual residues that are linked by peptide covalent bonds, primary structure is much more difficult to denature than the other levels of protein arrangement.

663. C is correct. Be sure to memorize both the three-letter and the one-letter abbreviations for all twenty standard amino acids! W denotes tryptophan, an aromatic residue with two fused rings. Y stands for tyrosine, while F refers to phenylalanine; both of these molecules also contain aromatic rings.

A, B, D: T refers to threonine, not tyrosine. Threonine lacks a ring and instead features a two-carbon alcohol as its R group. Additionally, P denotes proline, which is not aromatic.

664. D is correct. The amino acid known simply as "N" is asparagine. Like glutamine, this residue contains an extra nitrogen atom in the form of an amide functionality. Remember, amides are neutral overall, not basic.

A: This describes lysine (K).
B: The feature depicted here better matches methionine (M).
C: You should know that this is alanine, a residue that is given the shorthand symbol "A."

665. B is correct. Aromatic compounds are those that contain planar, conjugated rings and follow Hückel's rule, which stipulates that the system must possess 4n + 2 pi electrons. (To simplify this rule, remember that "n" denotes any integer, meaning that aromatic systems may contain 6, 10, or 14 pi electrons, and so on.) Phenylalanine, a classic example of an aromatic amino acid, fits all of these qualifications.

I: The side chain of threonine is not conjugated. III: While tyrosine is aromatic, this choice incorrectly states Hückel's rule.

666. D is correct. The given formula is that of methionine, a residue that contains a thioether functionality as part of its side chain. Since it does not possess a free –SH group, it cannot establish disulfide linkages with the R groups of other amino acids.

A: The given structure is too large to correspond to cysteine. Even if you do not know the exact molecular composition of either of these residues, remember that cysteine is a three-carbon molecule, since its side chain contains only one C atom.
B: Cystine is a term used to describe two bound cysteine residues, which cannot possibly be the case here as only one sulfur atom is present.

667. A is correct. This is the structure of glutamine. While you do not need to be able to discern this molecule from asparagine (a residue that is extremely similar in structure), the answer choices should give away that this residue begins with G. The three-letter abbreviation for glutamine is Gln, while its one-letter code is Q.

B, D: Glu and E reference glutamic acid. That structure contains a carboxylic acid, not the amide that is characteristic of glutamine.
C: This is incorrect for the same reason as choice B. Additionally, G stands for glycine.

668. C is correct. Since all standard amino acids share the same backbone, we simply need to compare the side chains of these four choices. Glutamate, the conjugate base of glutamic acid, has a –COO⁻ functionality as part of its side chain. As such, it possesses an added resonance structure in comparison to the other three species.

A, B, D: None of the side chains of these molecules exhibit resonance.

669. D is correct. The start codon, AUG, codes for methionine. Met (M) is one of the two main sulfur-containing amino acids, along with cysteine (Cys, C).

670. C is correct. Lysine (Lys) is denoted by the single letter K.

A, B, D: L is leucine, Y denotes tyrosine, and N correlates to asparagine.

671. C is correct. This question asks you to recall which amino acids are basic. Arginine and histidine are the only basic residues listed. Note that lysine is basic as well.

II: Aspartic acid is an acidic amino acid and can thus act as a proton donor.
IV: Proline is a nonpolar amino acid and lacks any acid or base side chain functionality.

672. B is correct. A peptide bond is resonance-stabilized, which gives the bond a partial double bond character. This strengthens and stabilizes the interaction.

A: Peptide bonds are cleaved by hydrolysis and formed via dehydration reactions.
C: The breakdown of peptides into individual amino acids actually increases the entropy of the system, and is thus favorable.
D: This is not true.

673. D is correct. Disulfide bonds are cleaved via a reduction reaction.

674. C is correct. First, identify which oxygen will be replaced with an amino group. Here, it must be the center carbonyl, since that represents a ketone while the other two are carboxylic acids. When the central carbonyl oxygen is replaced with an amino group, aspartic acid or aspartate will be formed.

675. B is correct. The one-letter codes for serine, threonine, tyrosine, histidine, and arginine are S, T, Y, H, and R, respectively. These amino acids occupy 7 residues in this peptide, 2 of which are threonines. Thus, there are five potential phosphorylation sites.

676. B is correct. Methionine is not capable of forming disulfide bonds.

677. C is correct. The four amino acids listed are polar and would thus be soluble in water and other polar solvents. However, we wish to form a precipitate, which would occur in a nonpolar solvent such as hexane.

678. A is correct. The cleavage of a Cys-Cys disulfide bond involves a reduction reaction, so it must be coupled with an oxidation. The transition from NADH to NAD⁺ fits in this category.

    B: This reaction depicts a carboxylic acid being reduced to an aldehyde.
    C: This reaction depicts the reduction of FAD to $FADH_2$.
    D: This is the dissociation of water, and would not be coupled to a redox reaction.

679. C is correct. C-terminal amino acids will have a free carboxyl group, as will any aspartate or glutamate residues. Choice C has one aspartate, on glutamate, and the C-terminal serine contributes the third potential methylation site.

    A: This sequence could be methylated at the glutamate (E) and the C-terminus residues L, yielding 2 methylation sites.
    B: This sequence could be methylated at three glutamate residues, as well as at the terminal proline, yielding 4 methylation sites.
    D: This sequence could be methylated at aspartate (D) and the C-terminus L, yielding 2 methylation sites.

680. A is correct. Isoleucine and alanine are both hydrophobic amino acids that are typically buried in the protein core.

    B: The protein's exterior is typically made of hydrophilic amino acids to enhance solubility and favorable interactions with the environment.

681. B is correct. This sequence is mostly composed of lysine (K) and arginine (R), along with one alanine and one histidine residue. Basic amino acids like lysine and arginine are charged at physiological pH; this charge makes the side chain hydrophilic. Since the environment immediately surrounding a protein is water-based, hydrophilic entities will be found on the surface.

    A, C: Most of this protein's residues are not hydrophobic. Note that hydrophobic regions are usually found deep within the structure of the protein to protect the residues from water.

682. C is correct. During electrophoresis, charged polypeptides will migrate towards the pole with the opposite charge. Therefore, to migrate towards the positive terminal, a molecule must be negative overall. All polypeptides have a carboxy and an amino terminus, which are negatively and positively charged, respectively, at a pH of 7. The overall charge of the molecule will thus depend on the R groups. At a relatively neutral pH, an acidic amino acid will have a negatively charged side chain, while a basic amino acid will have a side chain that is positive. Since the segment in choice C contains two acidic residues (Asp and Glu) and only one basic one (Arg), it has a charge of -1.

    A: This segment has one acidic residue (Glu) and one basic one (Arg), yielding a charge of 0.
    B: This segment has one acidic residue (Glu) and two basic ones (Lys and Arg), yielding a charge of +1.
    D: This segment has one acidic residue (Asp) and one basic one (Arg), yielding a charge of 0.

683. D is correct. As a basic amino acid, lysine has a carboxylic acid group (pK_{a1}) and two amino groups (pK_{a2} and pK_{a3}). At a pH of 7, the carboxylic acid will be deprotonated (contributing a -1 charge), while both amines will be protonated (contributing a total charge of +2). Lysine will thus have a charge of +1. By the time it reaches a pH of 10, the amine that has a pK_a of 8.95 will have lost its proton, resulting in a net charge of 0.

    A: This change would be observed when going from a pH of 10 to 12, for example.
    B: This would occur when going from a pH of 12 to 10.
    C: This change could be seen when going from a pH of 10 to 7.

684. D is correct. The isoelectric point, or pI, represents the pH at which the molecule has a net neutral charge. For lysine, this will occur at a pH between the molecule's pK_{a2} and pK_{a3}, due to the fact that the carboxylic acid will be negative, one of the amino groups will be positive, and the remaining amine will be neutral. The pI is thus the average of 8.95 and 10.53.

    A: This is the average of pK_{a1} and pK_{a2}. This calculation would work for acidic amino acids (such as glutamic acid), but lysine is basic.

B: 7.2 is the average of all three pK_a values. Never average three values when solving for the pI.
C: This is very close to the pK_{a2} of the molecule; however, the pI must also take pK_{a3} into account.

685. A is correct. The titration curve displays three pK_a values (the points halfway along the flat parts of the curve), representing three groups that can potentially be deprotonated. This indicates that the amino acid in question must be either acidic or basic. Note that pK_{a1} and pK_{a2} are both in the acidic range. As an amine-based group could not lose its proton at such a low pH, the amino acid's side chain must be a carboxylic acid. Our answer, then, can only be aspartic or glutamic acid.

B: Lysine is a basic amino acid. Its titration curve would have two pK_a values in the basic range.
C, D: Both serine and glycine have uncharged side chains, so their titration curves will show only show two pK_a values.

686. B is correct. This amino acid has an acidic side chain, meaning that the relevant pK_a must be either pK_{a1} or pK_{a2}. The only question is whether the side chain COOH is more or less acidic than the α-carboxy group. The positively charged amino group is an electron-withdrawing substituent that most drastically affects the backbone (α) COOH. Since it withdraws electron density from that group, it makes it easier for the group to lose a proton, therefore increasing its acidity. In other words, the side chain carboxylic acid must be less acidic and thus is represented by pK_{a2}.

C: pK_{a3} corresponds to the pK_a of the amino group.
D: pI is an attribute of the whole amino acid, not a specific functional group.

687. B is correct. Here, an effective buffering agent must decrease the concentration of free protons in the plasma. Physiological pH is mentioned as being between 7.3 and 7.4; at this pH, acidic amino acids like glutamic acid have deprotonated side chains. These COO⁻ groups can pick up some of the H⁺ ions and reduce the acidity of the plasma.

I: At a pH of around 7, the side chain of arginine (a basic amino acid) will already be protonated, so it cannot play a role in buffering the overly acidic solution.

III: Since acidosis is a decrease in blood pH, hydrogen ion concentrations are increased, not decreased.

688. B is correct. The three basic amino acids to know are lysine, histidine, and arginine. Lysine contains an amino group in its side chain, while histidine has an imidazole ring and arginine contains a guanidine group. Azide groups are composed of three consecutive nitrogen atoms, a structure not found in any of the major amino acids.

689. A is correct. Amino acids are also termed α-amino acids, since the amino group is attached to the alpha carbon. A gamma-carboxylic acid, then, must describe a molecule with a carboxylic acid located at the gamma-carbon (the third position away from the original carbonyl carbon). Aspartic acid does not contain such a group, and glutamine and asparagine do not have side chains with COOH groups at all.

B, C, D: Glutamic acid contains a carboxylic acid at the gamma position. Even if you cannot distinguish glutamic and aspartic acid, note that these three choices all contained both molecules. Glutamate is shown in the figure below.

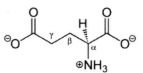

690. C is correct. Enzymes work best at physiological pH, which differs significantly from the pKa values of the side chains of basic enzymes. The presence of such residues in the active site therefore does not affect the pH of the environment surrounding the site itself.

A: The side chain amino group can be deprotonated by the substrate, then covalently attach to the substrate using its new lone pair of electrons.
B: The basic side chain is usually positively charged, allowing it to act as an electrophilic center. It can thus attract and interact with nucleophilic substrates.
D: In many cases, the amino acid itself does participate in the enzymatic reaction, reacting with the substrate in an acid-base or a nucleophile-electrophile fashion.

691. D is correct. Le Châtelier's principle states that any change to the conditions of a chemical equilibrium must result in readjustments to establish a new equilibrium. Specific changes to reactant or product concentration, temperature, volume, or pressure would force a system to readjust.

    III: Catalysts affect the kinetics, not the thermodynamic equilibrium, of the reaction.

692. B is correct. Homeostasis is the regulation of specific variables within the body to maintain a stable and constant internal condition. Examples of such variables include body temperature, plasma pH, and blood sugar. Body height, however, is neither internal nor something that fluctuates in the short term, nor do processes fluctuate to maintain it.

693. B is correct. The spontaneity of a reaction can be determined by the reaction $\Delta G° = \Delta H - T\Delta S$. Values of $\Delta H < 0$ and $\Delta S > 0$ will always result in $\Delta G° < 0$, which is spontaneous. Secondly, the rate of this reaction exists independently of the state functions (entropy, enthalpy, Gibbs free energy), and depends on kinetics: temperature and the amount of reactants versus products (A is incorrect). Because pH represents the concentration of protons (an eventual product of this reaction), it will have an effect on the reaction rate.

694. D is correct. The reaction quotient (Q) is measured as the relative concentrations of the products divided by that of the reactants. Due to the large amount of carbon dioxide produced by respiration during exercise, there is a larger than usual concentration of CO_2, a reactant, present. This makes Q an unusually small number. When Q is less than the equilibrium value (K), the reaction favors the products. This means that the system shifts to the right to make more products (HCO_3^- and H^+) in order to reestablish equilibrium.

695. D is correct. Enzymes change the kinetics, but not the thermodynamics, of a reaction. In other words, K_{eq} cannot be altered by changes to enzyme activity.

696. D is correct. ΔG is defined as $G_{products} - G_{reactants}$. This reaction is exergonic because the free energy of the reactants is higher than that of the products ($\Delta G < 0$). Consequently, it can be considered spontaneous. Removing the enzyme catalyst would change the activation energy, but not any of the free energy values.

    A, C: Endergonic reactions occur when $\Delta G > 0$, or when $G_{products} > G_{reactants}$.

697. B is correct. Le Châtelier's principle states that, with a decrease in product concentration, the system will shift right to reestablish equilibrium. (Note that this process does not change K_{eq}.) ΔG represents the change in Gibbs free energy of the system at a specific point in time, and is given by $\Delta G = -RT \ln Q$ for a system that is not at equilibrium. Here, Q is the reaction quotient, and is calculated as [products] / [reactants]. Due to the decrease in products, Q is smaller than at equilibrium ($Q < K_{eq}$). This corresponds to a decrease in ΔG.

698. C is correct. The rate of a reaction is the number of particulate collisions in a given amount of time. The rate is affected both by temperature and by the presence of a catalyst.

    III, IV: Enthalpy and entropy are thermodynamic quantities, not kinetic ones. As such, they predict spontaneity, but do not affect the rate directly.

699. D is correct. The first law of thermodynamics states that energy is always conserved. In terms of biological systems, this means that energy cannot be spontaneously produced (C) or destroyed (B), and that the energy transfer between molecules cannot result in the spontaneous creation or elimination of energy (A).

700. C is correct. It is extremely difficult for organisms to alter the temperature of a specific subcellular compartment. All of the other choices occur often.

701. B is correct. NADH is constantly being recycled in cells by converting it back and forth between its oxidized and reduced forms through coupled redox reactions. If cells could not recycle NADH, you would run out of it in a matter of seconds.

702. B is correct. Fatty acids are the most energy-dense fuel taken in by the body. The longer the fatty

acid chain, the more ATP can be produced in metabolism.

A: Sugars are the least efficient fuel as compared to fats and proteins.

C: Proteins can be used in metabolism when there is a lack of other fuel sources available (fats and sugars). Catabolism of proteins yields more ATP than sugars but less than fats.

D: Vitamins are not regularly metabolized for fuel. They are typically involved in metabolism as cofactors for other reactions.

703. A is correct. When ATP is converted to ADP, the terminal phosphate group (labeled P_1 in the figure) will be donated onto another molecule. To begin this reaction, the molecule initiates nucleophilic attack on P_1.

    B: Nucleophilic attack on P_3 would result in the cleaving of a pyrophosphate (PP_i) as a leaving group and the generation of a molecule of AMP.

704. B is correct. If it is known that ATP goes to AMP, two phosphate groups must be lost; thus a pyrophosphate (or double phosphate group) is the side product of this reaction.

705. B is correct. Both NADH and $FADH_2$ are formed when NAD^+ and FAD, respectively, are reduced in redox reactions during processes such as glycolysis and the TCA cycle. Once in their reduced form, NADH and $FADH_2$ carry electrons to the electron transport chain to generate ATP.

    A, C: $FADH_2$ is a flavoprotein and is embedded in the mitochondrial membrane as part of the electron transport chain. NADH is not a flavoprotein and, while it indirectly participates in the electron transport chain by donating electrons, it is not embedded in the mitochondrial membrane.

    D: NADH and $FADH_2$ cannot be used interchangeably.

706. D is correct. The transition from NAD^+ to NADH is a reduction reaction, and thus must be coupled with an oxidation reaction. Choice D shows a reaction in which the hydroxyl group in the reactant is oxidized to a carbonyl group in the product.

    A, C: These are both reduction reactions.
    B: This is not redox chemistry.

707. B is correct. Two ATP molecules are typically spent in the beginning of glycolysis to attach two phosphate groups; this number would increase to four. Then four units of ATP are generated in the second half of glycolysis (two for each three-carbon unit). The net production of ATP under these conditions would thus be zero.

708. A is correct. The hydrolysis of ATP is an exergonic reaction that generates energy to power unfavorable processes. By coupling the hydrolysis of ATP to another reaction, the net sum of the energies of the two reactions will be exergonic overall.

    I: The hydrolysis of ATP is exergonic and favorable, so it couples to other reactions that are endergonic and unfavorable.
    III: The hydrolysis of ATP is not reversible without added energy.
    IV: Other oxidation reactions would couple with reductions. There would be no benefit to coupling with the hydrolysis of ATP, as that is not a redox reaction.

709. D is correct. Based on the behavior of the coenzyme NAD^+, it can be deduced that the reagent, ethanol, will be oxidized in this reaction (since it is coupled to a reduction reaction). The oxidized form of ethanol is acetaldehyde.

    A: This is the reduced form of ethanol. The reduction of ethanol would not couple with the reduction of NADH.
    B: The molecule depicted, acetic acid, is two oxidation states above ethanol. Since NAD^+ is only reduced one step to NADH, we are looked for the oxidation state of ethanol that is only one step up.
    C: This molecule has three carbons, while ethanol only has two. Therefore, this molecule could never be formed merely from a redox reaction with ethanol.

710. B is correct. Recall that inorganic phosphate is incorporated onto the 3-carbon moieties in the second half of glycolysis through coupling of this reaction with the reduction of NAD^+.

    A, C, D: These are not true statements.

711. D is correct. ATP synthase reduces oxygen in the final step of the electron transport chain in order to utilize the proton gradient and generate ATP.

A: While this is considered aerobic respiration, no oxygen is utilized during the citric acid cycle.
B, D: Both of these processes are anaerobic in nature.

712. C is correct. During glycolysis, NADH is produced in the cytosol, while during the citric acid cycle, it is produced inside of the mitochondrial matrix.

713. C is correct. Erythrocytes, or red blood cells, do not contain a nucleus or mitochondria and therefore cannot use the citric acid cycle or electron transport chain to create ATP. Neurons, epithelial tissues, and T-cells do have mitochondria and can therefore utilize aerobic respiration.

714. B is correct. Glycolysis and gluconeogenesis can proceed in the presence and absence of oxygen. Fermentation requires anaerobic conditions to become active. The citric acid cycle, on the other hand, requires aerobic conditions.

715. D is correct. During glycolysis, one glucose, two NAD⁺, two H⁺, and two ATP molecules are consumed to yield two pyruvate, four ATP, and four NADH. Acetyl-CoA is formed from the pyruvate dehydrogenase complex before the citric acid cycle.

716. A is correct. Hexokinase is the first enzyme to catalyze a step of glycolysis, which occurs in the cytoplasm.

B: Pyruvate dehydrogenase converts pyruvate into acetyl-CoA. This process occurs in the mitochondria.
C, D: Both of these enzymes are found in the citric acid cycle which takes place in the mitochondria.

717. A is correct. Glycolysis requires two ATP molecules in order to advance and produces a total of four ATP per molecule of glucose. This results in a net of 2 ATP for the reaction.

B: This answer accurately reflects the total, but not the net, production of ATP during glycolysis.
C: This is the total for one molecule of pyruvate during aerobic respiration.
D: This is the total for one molecule of glucose during aerobic respiration.

718. D is correct. The net reaction below is written with correct stoichiometric ratios.

Acetyl-CoA + 3 NAD⁺ + FAD⁺ + GDP + Pᵢ + 2 H₂O → 2 CO₂ + 3 NADH + FADH₂ + GTP + 2H⁺ + CoA

719. C is correct. The electron transport chain is present on the inner mitochondrial membrane and pumps protons from the matrix into the intermembrane space. DNP is an uncoupling agent which allows protons to leak back across this membrane, therefore destroying the gradient.

A, B, D: The electron transport chain is present along the inner mitochondrial matrix.

720. D is correct. Oxidative phosphorylation utilizes a proton gradient to drive ATP production, creating 36 ATP per molecule of glucose.

721. D is correct. This reaction is part of the glycolysis/gluconeogenesis pathway and involves condensation into an aldol. In fact, it is mediated by aldolase.

722. A is correct. This reaction includes the isomerization of dihydroxyacetone phosphate into glyceraldehyde-3-phosphate. This reaction is catalyzed by triosephosphate isomerase. An isomerization reaction takes place when one molecule is transformed into another species that has exactly the same atoms, but with a different arrangement.

723. B is correct. This reaction is part of the glycolysis/gluconeogenesis pathway and is catalyzed by phosphofructokinase. Kinases are enzymes that add phosphate groups to molecules.

724. A is correct. A reduction in either glucose, NAD⁺, or ADP will result in a slowing or halt to glycolysis.

725. C is correct. Glycolysis produces a total of four ATP molecules. However, two such molecules as an "initial investment." This results in a net production of only two ATP.

726. D is correct. Hexokinase mediates the first step in glycolysis by adding a phosphate group to the sixth carbon in order to trap glucose within the cell. Glucokinase is an isozyme of this molecule that is used in the liver. Glucokinase has a much

lower affinity for glucose and is used to maintain blood sugar levels.

727. A is correct. Hexokinase has a much higher affinity for glucose than its isozyme, glucokinase. Therefore this enzyme will be saturated with glucose at much lower concentrations. Eight hours after a meal is long enough to imply fairly low blood sugar, making glucokinase inactive due to its low K_m.

728. C is correct. Glycolysis has three irreversible steps. These are catalyzed by hexokinase, phosphofructokinase and pyruvate kinase.

    A: Pyruvate carboxylase is an enzyme utilized in gluconeogenesis.
    B: Aldolase catalyzes a reversible reaction.
    D: Citrate synthase catalyzes an irreversible reaction in the Krebs cycle.

729. B is correct. In an oxygen-poor environment, the citric acid cycle will slow while glycolysis is activated further. Glycolysis utilizes ADP, NAD^+, and glucose to form ATP and NADH. Note that aerobic organisms depend on the citric acid cycle and oxidative phosphorylation to produce the majority of their ATP; without these processes, ATP will not be abundant.

730. C is correct. Aerobic organisms utilize the Krebs cycle and oxidative phosphorylation to create ATP. Each pyruvate molecule can be converted into three NADH and one $FADH_2$ molecule. One unit of NADH can produce three ATP from the ETC, while each $FADH_2$ promotes the production of two such nucleotides.

731. C is correct. A phosphate group is both polar and negatively charged, so it would not be able to pass through the hydrophobic cellular membrane. One of the benefits of phosphorylation is that it restrains the molecule and keeps it from exiting the cell.

732. B is correct. Phosphofructokinase-1 phosphorylates fructose 6-phosphate in one of the three regulated steps of glycolysis. ATP, the product of glycolysis, will allosterically inhibit this reaction.

    A: Fructose-1,6-bisphosphatase is a gluconeogenic enzyme that catalyzes the dephosphorylation of fructose 1,6-biphosphate to fructose 6-phosphate.

C, D: An excess of ATP would downregulate glycolytic reactions and upregulate gluconeogenic reactions.

733. B is correct. ATP and acetyl-CoA are regulators of this final step of glycolysis.

734. B is correct. Since the glucose molecule entering glycolysis has already been phosphorylated, 1 ATP can be saved, boosted the net total to 3 ATP produced.

735. D is correct. CO_2 is a product of both anaerobic and aerobic respiration through glycolysis. Aerobically, 2 pyruvates and 2 molecules of CO_2 will be generated, whereas aerobically, 2 molecules of methanol and two molecules of CO_2 will be generated.

    A: H_2O is not generated in glycolysis.
    B: Lactate is a product that is exclusive to anaerobic fermentation.
    C: Acetyl-CoA is a product that is exclusive to aerobic respiration.

736. A is correct. A sucrose disaccharide is made up of one D-glucose and one D-fructose unit. Once these monosaccharaides are phosphorylated, they will each be able to enter into the glycolytic cycle after steps 1 and 2, respectively.

737. D is correct. 1 glucose molecule yields 2 ethanol and 2 CO_2 molecules, so following these stoichiometric coefficients shows that 5 moles of glucose would yield 10 moles of each product.

738. C is correct. Lactate itself cannot be metabolized further into producing anymore ATP. However, it can be reincorporated into a glucose molecule through gluconeogenesis. While glycolysis only produces 2 ATP per glucose molecule, the reaction rate is very rapid and thus is sufficient to power oxygen-deprived muscles.

739. B is correct. Recall that "kinases" are enzymes that can phosphorylate and dephosphorylate molecules, and recall that pyruvate kinase is responsible for converting PEP into pyruvate.

740. C is correct. The question stem specifically states that the toxin is released within the mitochondrial matrix. Thus, it will not affect glycolysis, which takes place in the cell's cytosol.

741. D is correct. When alpha-ketoglutarate is formed, isocitrate loses electrons. The loss of electrons characterizes an oxidation reaction. During this reaction, NAD^+ is simultaneously reduced to form NADH and H^+.

    A: Dehydration reactions result in the loss of water, typically to a leaving group or in the creation of a double bond.
    B: Hydration reactions involve the addition of water.
    C: A decarboxylation reaction results in the loss of carbon dioxide.

742. C is correct. A patient who has taken this drug will see an increase in CO_2 in his or her blood. This yields a decreased plasma pH through the action of the blood buffer system.

743. C is correct. During the Krebs, cycle for every molecule of acetyl-CoA, three units of NADH and one of $FADH_2$ are produced. Therefore, if nine molecules of $FADH_2$ are formed, 27 NADH molecules must be created as well.

744. A is correct. The only step that creates GTP during the citric acid cycle is the conversion of succinyl-coA to succinate.

    B: This reaction produces $FADH_2$.
    C, D: Both of these reactions produce NADH.

745. B is correct. Carnitine is used to transport fatty acids into the mitochondria. Fatty acids are utilized to create acetyl-CoA for the citric acid cycle; without acetyl-CoA, the cycle cannot progress.

    A, C: Both of these processes occur in the cytoplasm and are therefore unaffected by carnitine.

746. C is correct. Fumarate is hydrogenated by addition of water across its double bond to form malate.

    A: This is the structure of isocitrate, an earlier intermediate in the citric acid cycle.
    B: This is alpha-ketoglutarate, another early Krebs cycle molecule.
    D: This structure denotes oxaloacetate, not malate.

747. D is correct. Succinate dehydrogenase utilizes FAD as its oxidizing agent. All of the other enzymes use NAD^+.

748. B is correct. Citrate synthase is the first enzyme in the citric acid cycle and converts acetyl-CoA to citrate. Additionally, excess acetyl CoA will force some of these molecules back in the direction of pyruvate, their precursor.

749. B is correct. Pyruvate is first converted to acetyl-CoA, which produces one NADH. Acetyl-CoA then enters the Krebs cycle to produce three NADH, one $FADH_2$, and one GTP molecule, which is immediately converted to ATP. Finally, each NADH yield three ATP molecules, while and each $FADH_2$ is converted to two; this happens during oxidative phosphorylation. In total, this results in the creation of 15 molecules of ATP.

750. C is correct. Products of the TCA cycle will act to inhibit it. These include ATP, citrate, and NADH. In contrast, high levels of low-energy molecules such as AMP, ADP, and NAD^+ stimulate the TCA cycle. therefore stimulated in times of high acetyl-CoA. Pyruvate carboxylase is an enzyme used in gluconeogenesis that converts pyruvate to oxaloacetate, during high levels of acetyl-CoA gluconeogenesis is stimulated. Pyruvate dehydrogenase is responsible for conversion of pyruvate to acetyl-CoA and is therefore inhibited in times of high acetyl-CoA.

751. C is correct. NADH dehydrogenase, also known as complex I, is the first protein in the ETC and is responsible for oxidizing NADH. Ubiquinone, another electron acceptor, is alternatively known as Q, a molecule that can be reduced to QH_2. Finally, cytochrome C is complex III, the third of the large protein complexes in the mitochondrial ETC. The role of Complex III (a one-electron carrier) is to oxidize one molecule of ubiquinol.

    D: Plastocyanin is involved in photosynthesis; specifically, it functions as an electron shuttle between photosystems I and II. However, it plays no role in mitochondrial oxidative phosphorylation.

752. B is correct. Complex II does not contribute to the proton gradient and instead oxidizes $FADH_2$ and reduces ubiquinone. Complex II is hypothesized

to reduce the production of reactive oxygen species.

A: Complex I is known as NADH dehydrogenase, and is responsible for oxidizing NADH. It pumps four protons from the matrix into the intermembrane space.

C: Complex III is known as cytochrome c. It contains a heme group and is responsible for the oxidation of ubiquinol. It pumps a total of four protons into the intermembrane space.

D: Complex IV is also known as cytochrome c oxidase, and is the final protein complex in the electron transfer chain. It reduces oxygen to water and pumps a total of four protons into the intermembrane space.

753. D is correct. As electron carriers, NADH and $FADH_2$ must be oxidized to generate the proton gradient used for ATP synthesis. NADH is oxidized by Complex I, while $FADH_2$ is oxidized a step later by Complex II. If a mutation rendered the NAD^+ coenzyme nonfunctional, $FADH_2$ would still provide the electrons needed to facilitate oxidative phosphorylation; the process would simply slow down.

754. C is correct. Oxidative phosphorylation is a metabolic pathway in which cells regenerate ATP through a series of redox reactions. The statement given here most accurately highlights the "coupled" relationship shared by the two main components of oxidative phosphorylation. As an endergonic process, ATP production must be paired with a more favorable reaction to proceed.

A: This statement does not include the actual production of ATP, a major part of the coupling described in the question stem.

D: This describes the role of oxygen in the electron transfer chain, but does not characterize the coupled relationship.

755. A is correct. Complexes I, III, and IV pump protons (H^+ ions) from the mitochondrial matrix into the intermembrane space. This generates the electrochemical gradient that can then be used for ATP synthesis. Since protons are moved out of the matrix and into the intermembrane space, the intermembrane space will be comparatively positive.

B: Protons are indeed pumped out of the matrix. However, this makes the matrix more negative, not more positive.

756. D is correct. Oligomycin, as stated in the question stem, inhibits proton flow through the enzyme ATP synthase. This would wholly prevent the regeneration of ATP in the mitochondria. Note that ATP synthesis in the cell as a whole would still persist (albeit at a lower level), as glycolysis does not require the proper functioning of ATP synthase.

757. B is correct. The prompt mentions that oligomycin prevents protons from flowing through ATP synthase. This would not have a direct impact on the existing proton gradient, which would have built up previously but would not be able to be relieved.

A: The electron transport chain will cease almost entirely after the addition of oligomycin. Additionally, the electrochemical gradient already established by the presence of protons in the intermembrane space would tend to repel more protons from entering the space.

C: Most likely, the gradient would dissipate over time, due to proton leak back into the matrix. However, it would be unlikely to drop to 50% after a fairly short interval.

C: This would be more likely to occur if an uncoupling agent, like 2,4-dinitrophenol, had been administered.

758. C is correct. The F_1 portion, one of the two main "fractions" of ATP synthase, is located inside the mitochondrial matrix.

A: It is the F_0 fragment of ATP synthase that is embedded in the membrane.

759. A is correct. In the figure, the F_0 portion of ATP synthase is embedded in the mitochondrial membrane, while the F_1 fraction is located at the bottom of the figure, within the matrix. Based on this layout, protons would flow from the top of the figure towards the bottom.

B: This reverses the direction of proton movement. During oxidative phosphorylation, protons travel down their gradient from the intermembrane space back into the mitochondrial matrix. In this process, the ions move directly through ATP synthase.

760. D is correct. Ultimately, the products of oxidative phosphorylation are ATP, water, NAD$^+$, and FAD. These products are not retained in the same way that oxaloacetate is during the citric acid cycle.

A, B, C: These statements accurately describe oxidative phosphorylation.

761. B is correct. Gluconeogenesis must overcome the three irreversible glycolytic steps. The enzymes used to achieve this are glucose 6-phosphatase, fructose 1,6-bisphosphatase, PEP carboxykinase and pyruvate carboxylase.

A, C: These enzymes are shared between glycolysis and gluconeogenesis.
D: Pyruvate kinase is used in the last step of glycolysis.

762. C is correct. Gluconeogenesis is the process of creating glucose from sources including lactate, which is converted to pyruvate in the Cori cycle in the liver. Pyruvate formation is the last step in glycolysis and therefore the first step in gluconeogenesis. Furthermore, glycerol can be converted to fructose 1,6-bisphosphate. In contrast, succinate is a part of the citric acid cycle and cannot be incorporated directly into gluconeogenesis.

763. B is correct. The figure shows changes in ΔG, with each drop representing a step of glycolysis. We can see that Steps 1, 3, and 10 exhibit significantly larger negative ΔG values than the other steps and are therefore irreversible glycolytic steps.

764. D is correct. Gluconeogenesis must overcome the three irreversible steps in glycolysis. Step 1 indicates glucose's conversion to glucose 6-phosphate; in glycolysis, this reaction is mediated by hexokinase. During gluconeogenesis, this step is bypassed by glucose 6-phosphatase.

A: Hexokinase is the enzyme responsible for this step in glycolysis.
B: Fructose 1,6-bisphosphatase bypasses Step 3 in glycolysis.
C: Aldolase is a shared enzyme between glycolysis and gluconeogenesis. This catalyst serves to mediate Step 4 in the figure.

765. A is correct. Gluconeogenesis takes place predominantly in the liver and, to a lesser extent, in the kidney. The liver helps maintain blood glucose levels.

B, C, D: Gluconeogenesis does not occur in these organs.

766. A is correct. Glycolysis occurs in all cells, while gluconeogenesis only occurs in the liver and cortex of the kidney.

767. D is correct. The predominant role of gluconeogenesis is to maintain blood glucose levels in times of fasting. This is controlled almost exclusively by the liver.

A: This process describes glycolysis.
B: Gluconeogenesis requires ATP in order to progress.
C: The process described is fermentation, which is used by cells to restore NAD$^+$ in order to continue anaerobic respiration.

768. B is correct. In times of high ATP, pyruvate kinase is inactivated, which stops glycolysis. Pyruvate is then shuttled into the gluconeogenic pathway. Low levels of ADP activate enzymes that function in gluconeogenesis, further promoting this process. Finally, ADP is required to activate many enzymes in the citric acid cycle; therefore low levels of ADP will inactivate this cycle.

769. C is correct. High levels of acetyl-CoA indicate high energy production in the cell. Typically, all acetyl-CoA is shuttled into the citric acid cycle. When levels rise in the cell, however, glycolysis is inactivated and gluconeogenesis is stimulated.

770. B is correct. Pyruvate carboxylase is the first enzyme used in gluconeogenesis to bypass pyruvate kinase. If this enzyme is inhibited, the liver will be unable to convert pyruvate to glucose and will therefore be unable to increase blood sugar. Thus, this patient will be expected to have lower-than-normal blood glucose levels, as seen in patient B.

A: Patient A has high blood glucose, but otherwise normal lab results.
C, D: Blood pH is regulated by levels of carbon dioxide and lactic acid. Neither process is affected by pyruvate carboxylase.

771. D is correct. Gluconeogenesis and the pentose phosphate pathway both share the molecule glucose 6-phosphate, a glycolytic intermediate.

The pentose phosphate pathway begins with the production of glyceraldehyde 3-phosphate, which can be fed into the citric acid cycle and the electron transport chain. Lastly, the product ribose 5-phosphate is important in the production of nucleic acids.

772. D is correct. Xylulose 5-phosphate is an intermediate in the pentose phosphate pathway and is produced during the second step of the non-oxidative portion of the pathway. It is also a reactant during the last step of this portion, in which is reacts with erythrose 4-phosphate to form G3P and F6P.

B: The primary function of the pentose phosphate pathway is to produce NADPH, a vital molecule responsible for enabling anabolic reactions in the body.
C: Glyceraldehyde 3-phosphate (G3P) is produced in the third step of the non-oxidative portion of the pathway.

773. A is correct. The primary function of the pentose phosphate pathway is to produce NADPH. Thus, low levels of NADPH will most likely stimulate the pathway. Additionally, glucose-6-phosphate (G6P) is the first molecule involved in this process; therefore, high levels of G6P must promote these reactions much more than low levels.

774. B is correct. NADPH is most often used for anabolic reactions and is a key part of fatty acid synthesis. Acetyl-CoA is combined with malonyl-CoA to form fatty acids. If the concentration of acetyl-CoA is high, the first step of the pentose phosphate pathway will be inhibited, as there will be no need for reactants of fatty acid synthesis.

775. D is correct. The oxidation phase begins with glucose 6-phosphate. This molecule is oxidized to eventually form ribulose 5-phosphate and NADPH. NADPH is the molecule that is necessary for the synthesis of acetyl-CoA, which, in turn, is responsible for fatty acid synthesis.

A: The isomerization phase yields xylulose-5-phosphate, which can be rearranged to form carbon chains of different lengths. The identity of these products is dependent on the metabolic needs of the cell. However, fatty acid synthesis does not use these carbon chains.

B: Here, the two most notable products are glyceraldehyde 3-phosphate and fructose 6-phosphate. These products are not important in fatty acid synthesis.
C: This is not a phase of the pentose phosphate pathway.

776. A is correct. Removing the phosphate group on the ribose-containing adenine would turn NADPH into NADH. These are two different molecules with very different functions. While NADPH is primarily used in anabolic pathways (including nucleic acid and lipid synthesis), NADH is an electron carrier in cellular respiration. Thus, removing the phosphate group would change both the name of NADPH and its function.

777. D is correct. Polypeptide elongation relies on the function of aminoacyl-tRNA synthetases and their corresponding amino acids and tRNA. NADPH does not play a role in this process.

778. B is correct. NADPH serves an important function in anabolic pathways, such as lipid and nucleic acid synthesis. Thus, it is sensible to maintain greater amounts of NADPH in the body for use. This is contrary to the relationship between NAD^+ and NADH and closely relates to these molecules' respective functions.

779. C is correct. Transketolase is active during the non-oxidative portion of the pentose phosphate pathway. It is responsible for catalyzing the production of glyceraldehyde 3-phosphate and fructose 6-phosphate.

B, D: These are steps in protein synthesis, not the pentose phosphate pathway.

780. B is correct. Transketolase is responsible for catalyzing the reaction to form glyceraldehyde 3-phosphate and fructose 6-phosphate. Both of these products are part of glycolysis.

781. A is correct. Since we know that high use of ATP causes the forward reaction to predominate, we can expect more of its products to be present when the cell is in an energetically demanding state. However, ATP will be used rapidly, leaving high concentrations of intracellular AMP. Simultaneously, the cell will be performing glycolysis at a high rate in an effort to feed the

citric acid cycle and the electron transport chain. Thus, high [AMP] coincides with rapid glycolytic behavior, and we can infer that AMP upregulates one or more glycolytic enzymes. In reality, AMP is a main effector of phosphofructokinase.

II: Based on the equation, concentrations of ADP will decrease when energy demand is high. Thus, we have no evidence to indicate that it would stimulate glycolysis, which produces more energy. III: Though ATP is a product of the reaction above, it does not promote glycolysis. In fact, high concentrations of ATP signal that sufficient energy is present. In a classic negative feedback mechanism, this causes the cell to slow down, not speed up, ATP production.

782. D is correct. Glycolysis is a catabolic process with a negative net change in free energy. In this process, irreversible (or committed) steps refer to reactions that are very difficult to reverse due to their highly negative ΔG values. Thus, the correct answer choice is the one that represents the most negative ΔG°, as it will have the smallest tendency to proceed in the reverse direction.

A, B, C: All of these ΔG° values are less negative, and therefore less irreversible, then -20.9 kJ/mol.

783. B is correct. Insulin, a peptide hormone, helps cells take up glucose from the bloodstream. Type 1 diabetics lack the ability to properly produce this hormone. Thus, giving a dose of insulin to this patient would promote an influx of glucose into cells that were previously unable to gain it from the blood. Because these cells were improperly acquiring and utilizing glucose before, we can infer that they were not producing ATP at a maximal rate. The insulin treatment allows them to take in glucose and produce ATP through glycolysis, while also stimulating the citric acid cycle and the electron transport chain. Since pyruvate is a glycolytic product, its levels should increase after insulin administration.

A: Plasma glucose levels should certainly decrease, as that is a main function of insulin. C: As outlined above, an insulin injection would stimulate glycolysis in a diabetic individual. Thus, intermediates in gluconeogenesis should decrease. D: As a result of increased glycolytic flux, overall ATP levels will increase. This change typically correlates with a drop in AMP concentration.

784. C is correct. Glycogenolysis denotes the breakdown of glycogen, a polymer of glucose that is stored by the body for future energy needs. The body utilizes glycogen when food consumption does not provide sufficient energy; in other words, glycogenolysis occurs when one has not eaten recently or exists in a state of increased ATP demand. Eating a carbohydrate-rich meal would significantly reduce the need for such a process.

A: The sympathetic system is stimulated when the body activates the "fight-or-flight" response. When this occurs, epinephrine prepares the muscles for energy-intensive work by increasing heart rate and releasing glucose from storage. This latter function is performed via glycogenolysis. B: Glucagon promotes the breakdown of glycogen to increase blood glucose levels. D: Similarly to choice A, heavy exercise implies that muscles need an unusually large amount of energy. This energy is provided in the form of ATP produced from glucose that is removed from storage.

785. C is correct. If blood flow stops, so does the transport of oxygen. In such conditions, cells cannot generate ATP through mitochondrial respiration, though they can still use anaerobic processes such as glycolysis and fermentation. Therefore, extended cardiac arrest leads to a decrease in ATP concentration in the cells of vital organs, inhibiting their function.

A: As outlined above, glycolysis and fermentation can continue even when oxygen is completely lacking. For this reason, "complete absence" is too strong. B: Though blood pH would decrease after cardiac arrest (due to both lactic acid production and CO_2 buildup), we have no reason to believe that it would cause cell lysis. D: Increased levels of plasma CO_2 lead to acidification, which is a drop in pH, not an increase.

786. B is correct. The enzyme evidently binds its substrate more effectively when ATP levels are low. This means that it is probably involved in a process that generates ATP, of which glycolysis is a perfect example. This question is a prime demonstration of the cellular regulation of

carbohydrate metabolism to meet energetic demands.

A: Glycogenesis is stimulated during times of energetic abundance, allowing excess glucose to be stored as glycogen for later use. Here, Enzyme X is most effective when cellular [ATP] is high.
C, D: From outside knowledge, we should know that the digestive system is not directly affected by ATP levels. Instead, this regulation occurs once nutrients have been taken up into the bloodstream and cells.

787. A is correct. K_m refers to the substrate concentration at which an enzyme has reached ½ of its V_{max}. As the figure shows, when ATP concentrations are low, a smaller substrate concentration is required to reach the same velocity. This leads us to the conclusion that [ATP] positively correlates with the K_m of Enzyme X. Additionally, because the low-[ATP] and high-[ATP] curves have very similar V_{max} values, the inhibition of Enzyme X by ATP must be competitive.

C, D: If the relevant inhibition were allosteric, differing concentrations of ATP would yield significant changes in V_{max}.

788. D is correct. After several hours of fasting, the body begins to generate glucose from alternative sources such as pyruvate, fatty acids and amino acids. We can therefore expect food deprivation to promote gluconeogenesis, as the cells attempt to maintain glucose levels in this manner. This response is due in part to an increase in the transcription of gluconeogenic genes, leading to increased mRNA levels.

B: Glucagon is released when blood glucose levels are low, as they would be during the initial hours of starvation.
C: This choice is backwards. Increasing glycogen synthesis during fasting would be counterproductive. Specifically, it would further reduce plasma glucose levels and put more energetically vital molecules away in storage.

789. D is correct. As the final electron acceptor in the electron transport chain (ETC), oxygen is reduced to form H_2O. Thus, the radioactively-labeled O atoms would be found in water.

A: Glucose is broken down during glycolysis, but it does not directly interact with O_2.

B: CO_2 is produced during the citric acid cycle, well before O_2 enters into carbohydrate metabolism.
C: NADH donates electrons, or is oxidized, during the ETC; however, it does not react with oxygen directly.

790. B is correct. Glucagon induces the liver to release glucose into the bloodstream by breaking down its stored glycogen via glycogenolysis. Thus, this hormone increases blood sugar levels and must be released when these levels are too low. Low plasma glucose is known as hypoglycemia. Administration of IMG to a hypoglycemic patient would help normalize his or her glucose levels.

A: Since glucagon would exacerbate hyperglycemia by increasing plasma glucose concentrations, it would not be used to treat this condition.
C, D: Though diabetes does involve dysregulation of blood glucose levels, diabetics can have large fluctuations in these readings due to insulin administration or nutrient consumption. Without information regarding the specific clinical situation, we cannot know whether glucagon would help a particular diabetic individual.

791. C is correct. Cholesterol does not determine the saturation of membrane lipids. It is diet, along with other biochemical processes, that does this.

A: This could certainly happen in a cholesterol-deficient individual. Cholesterol is composed of multiple hydrophobic aromatic rings, which are attracted to the nonpolar tails of lipid molecules. This attraction helps "plug" holes between the tails, making the membrane less permeable.
B: An increase in rigidity is likely to occur as well. The presence of cholesterol increases membranes fluidity, as its location between lipid tails prevents the tails from contacting and crystallizing with each other.
D: The lipid rafts that surround membrane proteins also tend to contain cholesterol, helping to secure these proteins in the membrane. A lack of cholesterol would destabilize these rafts.

792. D is correct. When a G protein-coupled receptor (GPCR) binds a ligand, the associated protein's α subunit exchanges a bound GDP molecule for GTP, thus transitioning to an active conformation. Typically, the α subunit

later hydrolyzes this GTP back to GDP, causing the system to return to an inactive state. If the α subunit lost its enzymatic activity, it would remain in its active conformation and would continually stimulate its target protein. In cases of cholera, this promotes the oversecretion of ions into the lumen of the digestive tract and causes the diarrhea for which cholera is infamous.

A, B: Inhibiting the GTPase functionality of the G-protein system does not alter its ability to become activated by ligand molecules or its subunits' potential to separate.
C: This is the reverse of the correct result.

793. B is correct. The plasma membrane is a lipid bilayer composed of phospholipids with polar "heads" and nonpolar "tails." These self-organize so that the polar heads face water, either inside or outside the cell, while the nonpolar tails face each other. In a hydrophobic solvent like ethane or methane, the tails would instead be prone to facing outward, while the polar heads would be repelled from the nonpolar fluid and point toward each other. Cell membranes could not possibly work on Titan like they do on Earth.

A: This statement is factually incorrect. Even the cells of our own bodies can undergo anaerobic respiration.
C: Molecules tend to get more, not less, stable at low temperatures. Of course, due to the mentioned temperature difference, cells would require distinct proteins with conformations that work in such a cold environment.
D: Nitrogen gas is extremely unreactive; in fact, Earth's atmosphere is mostly nitrogen as well.

794. B is correct. The cell membrane potential relates to the ion concentrations by way of the Nernst equation, which can be written as $V_m = 2.3026$ $[(RT / zF) * (\log (P_c[C_o^+] + P_A[A_i^-]) / (P_c[C_i^+] + P_A[A_o^-]))]$, where R is the gas constant, T is temperature, z is the effective charge of the ions involved (usually 1), F is Faraday's constant, and P is the permeability of the relevant type of ion. Note also that $[C_o^+]$ represents the concentration of various cation species outside the cell, while $[A_i^-]$ denotes the concentration of anions inside. Assuming that the membrane potential is determined by a single species of cation (K^+), the anion terms cancel, as does the permeability factor for K^+. Finally, squaring the concentrations

inside and outside the cell allows us to resolve the problem using log identities. $\log ([K_o^+]^2 / [K_i^+]^2) = \log [([K_o^+] / [K_i^+])^2] = 2*\log ([K_o^+] / [K_i^+])$. The value of the potential must therefore be doubled compared to its prior value.

795. C is correct. Of the listed molecules, only dopamine is not a nonpolar sterol or a small gas molecule (both types of molecules that can traverse the membrane unassisted). Dopamine, a catecholamine, relies on vesicular transport, the breakdown of which causes conditions like Parkinson's disease.

796. A is correct. If ion concentrations equalized on both sides of the plasma membrane, cell potentials would depolarize (become less negative), not hyperpolarize. In fact, it is the variation in ion concentration that establishes membrane potentials in the first place.

B: Transport of sodium, which requires proper gradient formation, enables the secondary active transport of glucose.
C: Ca^{2+} levels in muscle cells would rise in the situation described, as it is a Na^+-Ca^{2+} antiport that establishes the balance of Ca^{2+} ions in muscles at rest. In other words, increasing the intracellular Na^+ concentration would cause more movement of Ca^{2+} inside the cell. Certain heart medications correct for weak contractions by raising $[Ca^{2+}]$ in this manner.
D: Sodium transport is vital for the formation of the osmotic gradient that helps the kidneys reabsorb water.

797. B is correct. Lipids are typically inserted in the cytosolic leaflet of the ER after synthesis. Proteins positioned between the two leaflets, known as flippases, move lipids into the inner leaflet; the activity of these transporters would not be affected by a halt in vesicular transport. Choice III also makes sense; remember, the nuclear membrane is continuous with the ER. Thus, as lipids move freely according to the fluid mosaic model, they should be able to migrate from the ER to the surface of the nuclear membrane.

III: The movement of lipids and embedded membrane proteins between the ER and the Golgi apparatus requires vesicular transport. For this reason, the lipid in question would not be found here.

798. B is correct. Lipid rafts surround proteins and serve signaling purposes, as implied by this question. The hydrophobic molecules that form these rafts tend to have long, saturated tails to aid in their adherence to each other and to their associated protein(s). As molecule B has the longest tail of the saturated fatty acids shown, it would be most likely to exist near a transmembrane protein.

799. D is correct. Because the double bonds present in unsaturated fatty acids create "kinks" in the molecules' tails, lipids containing these acids have trouble adhering to each other as strongly as lipids with mainly saturated tails. The higher the unsaturated lipid concentration, the more fluid and permeable a membrane will be. Of the fatty acids in the diagram, D is the most unsaturated; thus, it is most likely to exist in a more permeable membrane.

800. C is correct. As seen in the diagram, the receptor is composed of two subunits that join tightly when activated by insulin. This is a dead giveaway that the receptor must be a receptor tyrosine kinase (RTK), a common example of a dimeric transmembrane receptor. We can also obtain clues from the biochemistry of the listed amino acids.

    A, B: Phenylalanine and tryptophan are highly aromatic residues that lack an -OH group to easily attach a phosphate.
    D: Cysteine does have an available –SH (thiol) group, but these functionalities are not typically known for binding to phosphate molecules.

801. B is correct. Beta-oxidation involves several steps. Dehydrogenation of the fatty acid yields a molecule each of $FADH_2$ and NADH, while cleavage of the structure produces acetyl-CoA. These products are then utilized in other metabolic pathways. $FADH_2$ and NADH are used in the electron transport chain, while acetyl-CoA is fed into the Krebs cycle.

    IV: ATP does not directly result from the oxidation of fatty acids.

802. B is correct. The Atkins diet induces a state of physiological ketosis, which forces the body to utilize stores of fat for energy due to extremely low glucose intake. The sweet-smelling breath and perspiration come from the metabolism of ketone bodies, the primary metabolic molecule present during ketosis. The specific molecule responsible for the smell is acetone, which is both excreted in urine and exhaled.

803. D is correct. Fatty acid metabolism involves the process of beta-oxidation, which ultimately splits fatty acid chains into acetyl-CoA. This molecule enters the Krebs cycle in the same way as acetyl-CoA that is produced via aerobic cellular respiration.

    C: While glycolysis is the first step in the oxidation of glucose, it refers only to the processes that occur in the cytosol and that lead to the production of pyruvate. D is a more specific choice.

804. B is correct. The final step of beta-oxidation involves the cleavage of the molecule by thiolase, which ultimately yields one unit of acetyl-CoA, as well a new fatty acid that differs from the original by two carbons. Thus, to find the number of acetyl-CoA molecules that will be formed from a fatty acid, we can simply divide its total number of carbons by two. In this case, linoleic acid has 18 carbons, which will yield 9 molecules of acetyl-CoA.

805. B is correct. Protein kinase A is an important enzyme for the regulation and control of fatty acid metabolism. Signaling molecules such as glucagon, epinephrine, and norepinephrine activate this kinase through binding to G protein-coupled receptors, an action that produces cyclic AMP. Activated protein kinase A phosphorylates hormone-sensitive lipase, which is the enzyme responsible for hydrolyzing stores of fat.

806. A is correct. Oleic acid has eighteen carbons and a single double bond. It also has a double bond on its ninth carbon from the non-COOH end, which is *trans* here.

    B: *Cis* conformation indicates that the two hydrogens on the doubly bound carbons are on the same side, which is not accurate.
    C, D: Linoleic acid has the same number of carbons as oleic acid. However, its structure includes two double bonds.

807. D is correct. Unsaturated fats give cellular membranes greater fluidity and functionality,

which lowers the freezing temperature of the membrane. This can be seen in everyday examples, such as bacon fat, which is made up of mostly saturated lipids. Bacon fat hardens rapidly in comparison to olive oil, which is composed mainly of unsaturated fats and is liquid at room temperature.

C: The lipid bilayer is not metabolized for energy.

808. A is correct. Fats are typically ingested as triglycerides. However, these structures cannot be immediately absorbed, and must be emulsified by bile salts and digested by pancreatic lipase to free fatty acids and monoglycerides. Free fatty acids are generally absorbed and packaged into both chylomicrons and lipoproteins. Through binding to the membranes of adipocytes or muscle cells, these molecules can be released and stored as triacylglycerols.

809. D is correct. The table shows the percentage of each molecule type that is generally carried by these lipoproteins. Chylomicrons and VLDLs are the most common transporters of triacylglycerols, as shown by their values of 84 and 50 percent, respectively. HDLs, however, are responsible for collecting a wide variety of fat molecules, as shown in the table.

A, C: These are the two most prevalent carriers of triacylglycerols.

810. B is correct. Chylomicrons are commonly used to transport triacylglycerols from the intestines to the tissues. However, they are not the only transport molecules. If some sort of trauma were to stop the production of these lipoproteins, transport of triacylglycerols would decrease significantly.

C: Lipids like VLDLs would still transport triacylglycerols to some extent in the absence of chylomicrons.

811. B is correct. First, recognize that the intermediate being alluded to is acetyl-CoA. An eight-carbon fatty acid chain would require four acetyl-CoA molecules, and each glucose molecule yields two acetyl-CoA units. Thus, it would take two glucose monomers to generate enough acetyl-CoA to make an 8-C fatty acid.

812. A is correct. Glycogen synthase is used to elongate glycogen chains by adding new α-1,4 linkages. In this glycogen molecule, both hydroxyl groups 5 and 6 are capable of joining with a new sugar unit via an α-1,4 linkage.

B, D: α-1,6 linkages are used to create branches in a glycogen molecule. Branching enzyme, not glycogen synthase, is responsible for creating these bonds.

813. B is correct. Transferase will take a segment of the branched chain that is one unit away from the branch site and relocate it to the parent chain, creating a new α-1,4 linkage.

A: The bond between these subunits can only be cleaved by α-1,6 glucosidase, and this enzyme only functions on the final sugar of a branched chain.

814. C is correct. The acyl group is transferred from acetyl-CoA to the enzyme carnitine acyltransferase, which then carries that group across the membrane via a transmembrane protein. Once on the other side, the acyl group is rejoined to a fresh CoA molecule by another carnitine acyltransferase enzyme.

A: CoA is a large, polar molecule.

815. D is correct. Recall that ammonia is the byproduct of amino acid metabolism. Ammonia is converted into the body's most prevalent nitrogen-containing compound, urea.

816. C is correct. These three statements are true. The branching of glycogen increases its solubility because it arranges its many hydroxyl groups in such a way that surrounding water molecules can easily hydrate them. Additionally, the enzymes used in glycogen degradation can only work on the non-reducing end of glucose, so by creating a branched structure, more of these active ends are exposed for reaction.

I: By keeping many glucose subunits as a single entity, intracellular osmotic pressure is minimized.

817. D is correct. This is why some amino acids are termed "essential" – because the body cannot make them, so they must be ingested.

818. B is correct. If an individual were using proteins as her primary fuel, she would quickly run down her muscular protein stores and would be forced to degrade proteins from organs. This would cause organ failure. Under starvation conditions, muscular atrophy can be observed when both sugar and fat supplies have been depleted.

    A: Ketoacidosis is caused by an excess of ketone bodies, which are generated from the oxidation of fatty acids, not proteins.
    C: If the body is burning proteins instead of sugar, if anything, hyperglycemia would result.
    D: Fat stores should not become smaller because this individual is not drawing her energy from fat.

819. C is correct. During starvation, as glucose (dashed line) supplies decline, fatty acid oxidation and ketone body (solid line) synthesis will take over to supply metabolic fuel.

820. C is correct. First, realize that the solid line corresponds to the increase of ketone bodies during starvation. In the event that these molecules run out, the body will need to rely on its next energy source, protein. Remember, proteins are the body's last resort during starvation.

821. B is correct. In response to low blood glucose levels, the body will act to produce more glucose and to use less of this macromolecule whenever possible. This results is a decrease in the rate of glycolysis (I). Next, low blood glucose levels will increase the rate of the two pathways that produce glucose in the body, glycogenolysis (II) and gluconeogenesis (III).

    IV: Ketone bodies are produced in response to low blood sugar, specifically when the body has expended its stored glycogen and glucose. Therefore, this pathway should increase in response to prolonged low blood glucose levels.

822. A is correct. Glucagon is produced by the pancreas in response to low blood sugar. This peptide acts antagonistically to insulin. It increases plasma glucose levels by stimulating gluconeogenesis, glycogenolysis, and other glucose-producing processes.

823. B is correct. To a much lower extent than in the liver, gluconeogenesis does occur in the kidneys.

Note that this process does not occur in cells of any other organs.

824. D is correct. Only the liver and (to a lesser extent) the kidneys are able to carry out gluconeogenesis. Other organs, such as the muscles, are relatively unaffected by glucagon. Muscle cells must have a constant supply of ATP and are constantly undergoing glycolysis. If this were to happen at the same time as gluconeogenesis, it would create a futile cycle.

    A: All cells are attached to blood vessels, at least indirectly.
    B: Glycolysis occurs in all cells.
    C: Muscle cells are affected by many hormones, such as epinephrine.

825. C is correct. Type II diabetes is marked by an acquired resistance to insulin. Despite high blood sugar levels and unimpeded insulin production, cells do not respond properly to the hormone. This results in the systematic appearance of hyperglycemia.

    B: Glucagon and insulin are antagonistic.
    D: If they were unable to metabolize glucose at all, these mice would die very quickly.

826. D is correct. Hyperglycemia is synonymous with high blood sugar. Additionally, insulin resistance implies that the patient will continue to suffer from high plasma glucose, regardless of insulin secretion. By reading the graph carefully, we see that Patient 2 has increased blood glucose levels in spite of his higher levels of insulin.

    A: This better relates to hypoglycemia.

827. D is correct. Glucagon levels increase in response to low blood sugar. In both Patients 1 and 2, blood glucose increases throughout the duration of the test, returning to baseline right as the test concludes. For this reason, glucagon levels would be expected to be low.

828. B is correct. Between 75 and 100 minutes, there is a clear spike in the concentration of glucagon and a later spike in gluconeogenic rate. An increase in glucagon concentration generally results from low blood sugar levels. Therefore, we can infer that the mouse's blood glucose levels were falling at some point between 75 and 100 min.

829. C is correct. In addition to glucagon, epinephrine can also trigger increased rates of gluconeogenesis. This neurotransmitter is released in vast quantities during the fight-or-flight response.

830. B is correct. In a similar fashion to diabetes, obese patients tend to develop a resistance to leptin due to its perpetually high levels. This reduces its physiological effect on the individual.

    A: A consistent mutation across a large group of obese patients is unlikely.

831. C is correct. Nucleotides participate in a number of distinct cellular processes. Their most well-known function is the storage and reproduction of genetic information in the form of DNA, making option I accurate. Additionally, nucleotides (like ATP) participate in the storage and transfer of metabolic energy. Finally, they also participate in intracellular signaling in the form of cAMP or cGMP.

    III: While it is possible that a nucleotide could be used to facilitate protein degradation, this is not a main function.

832. A is correct. cAMP is formed from ATP when two phosphates are cleaved. The remaining phosphate forms a cyclic bond with the 3' carbon of the structure.

833. C is correct. A nucleoside consists of a five-carbon pentose sugar and a nitrogenous base, either a purine or a pyrimidine. Purine bases consist of a pyrimidine ring attached to an imidazole group; as a result, both B and D are correct statements. Finally, an N-glycosidic linkage attaches the pentose sugar to the nitrogenous base. This makes A accurate as well.

    C: A phosphodiester bond connects two nucleotides in a poly-nucleotide strand. Nucleosides do not contain phosphate.

834. A is correct. The spliceosome, which cuts and reattaches premature mRNA transcripts, is an RNA-based enzyme. This serves as an example of RNA's function in post-transcriptional modification.

835. D is correct. Nucleotides contain three main components: a nitrogenous base, a five-carbon sugar, and at least one phosphate group. Here, the student has drawn pyrimidine (a nitrogenous base), arabinose (a five-carbon sugar), and an attached triphosphate. This makes the structure a nucleotide.

836. C is correct. G-C base pairs are connected by three hydrogen bonds, while A-T pairings are linked by only two. Therefore, the higher the guanine content, the higher the melting temperature. Sample 3 has the highest T_m and is therefore the correct answer.

837. D is correct. Melting temperature is, in essence, a measure of DNA stability. Due to mutation of 1% of the bases, significantly fewer hydrogen bonds will connect the two strands, even after reannealing. This lowers the melting temperature of the DNA.

    A: While 1% is significant enough to change the melting temperature, it would likely not be significant enough to prevent reannealing entirely.

838. A is correct. One of the key differences between RNA and DNA is that RNA contains uracil, while DNA includes thymine. Sample 1 is the only sample that does not contain thymine at all; thus, its corresponding organism must have an RNA genome.

839. A is correct. G-C base pairs are more stable than A-T or A-U pairings. At perpetually low temperatures, an organism's genome would need a high adenine content to ensure that the dsDNA strands can be unwound and separated during transcription or replication. (Typically, heat facilitates this process.) Therefore, A is the best choice.

840. B is correct. The largest difference between DNA and RNA is that RNA has a ribose sugar, while DNA includes 2'-deoxyribose. In a hypothetical double-helical mRNA structure, the 2' OH group exists in close proximity to the backbone of the helix. This can result in reactions that cleave the backbone of the structure, lowering its stability.

    A: Uracil is simply a thymine molecule with one extra methyl group. This minor alteration does not affect its hydrogen binding properties.
    C: While accessory proteins do attach to the DNA, they are not primarily responsible for the stability of the double-helical structure.

841. C is correct. If contraction does not occur in the absence of acetylcholine, other molecules at the junction must be unable to serve as alternative ligands. This suggests that the nicotinic receptor is highly specific for ACh. Additionally, we are told that muscle contraction is reversed by the breakdown of acetylcholine, meaning that the ligand must rapidly dissociate from the binding pocket to become subject to hydrolytic cleavage by this enzyme. If affinity were higher, the ligand would remain bound and would be invulnerable to the actions of acetylcholinesterase.

D: While this is likely too specific for the MCAT, this answer can be tempting due to the fact that the ACh receptor also binds nicotine. However, regardless of this information, the receptor should not be considered to have low specificity. No receptor demonstrates binding to a single molecule 100% of the time, and nicotine is a structural analog of acetylcholine.

842. B is correct. The hydration cage that typically forms around soluble ions is held in place by hydrogen bonding between the cooperating water molecules. Hydrogen bonding, like other attractive forces, weakens with increased distance. Thus, the larger potassium ions are more weakly coordinated by their solvating water molecules. This allows them to be stripped of their hydration shells at a smaller energetic penalty than sodium ions.

A: Na^+ ions are smaller than K^+ ions.
C: As both of these ions can effectively be considered point charges, their differences in charge / electron distribution are negligible. Additionally, as ions from the same group of the periodic table, they would interact similarly with the channel residues.
D: This is untrue; both sodium and potassium cations have +1 charges.

843. A is correct. The figure shows that the S-loop enters the channel from the extracellular side, which necessitates movement back in the extracellular direction in order to prevent occlusion of the pore. In other words, depolarization must cause the loop to shift outward and expose the open channel. Since depolarization involves a positive shift in transmembrane voltage, positive residues will be repelled away from the cytoplasm. For this

reason, the S-loop must be primarily positively charged.

C, D: If the majority of residues were negatively charged, they would either remain still or be pulled slightly further into the cytoplasm during depolarization.

844. C is correct. In an alpha helix, the amino acid residues are directed outward, away from the long axis of the helix. A single helix spanning a lipid bilayer would be composed almost entirely of hydrophobic residues, making choice A extremely tempting. However, since the transmembrane domain of this channel is composed of multiple (six, specifically) helices that must also make contact with each other, they cannot be wholly hydrophobic. Instead, the face of each helix that associates with an adjacent helix is likely to be primarily hydrophilic, which permits the formation of salt bridges between neighboring residues. In contrast, the face of the helix that is exposed to the interior of the lipid bilayer will be primarily hydrophobic. The result is a helix that is roughly half hydrophobic and half hydrophilic.

845. A is correct. Receptor tyrosine kinases, when activated, phosphorylate their own tyrosine residues, creating a docking site for any protein that expresses an SH2 domain. The identity of the activating ligand (here, IGF-1) is irrelevant. If PI3K is involved in a receptor tyrosine kinase signaling cascade, it is reasonable to assume that it would have an SH2 domain; in fact, it does.

B: G protein-coupled receptor activity does not involve receptor tyrosine kinases. For this reason, an SH2 domain is unlikely to serve a purpose here.
C: Nothing in choice suggests the presence of phosphorylated tyrosine residues.
D: SH2 has no catalytic function (although we are not told this in the question stem). However, we do know that PLC recognizes phosphate groups that are bound to lipids. SH2 domains only bind phosphates that are attached to tyrosine residues.

846. C is correct. According to the signaling cascade shown in the figure, PTEN acts to inhibit Akt. Akt activates mTOR, which eventually leads to angiogenesis and protein synthesis, two processes that are instrumental in the development of malignancies. Since PTEN appears to keep these

processes in check, it is likely a classic tumor suppressor protein.

A: As stated above, mTOR ultimately activates angiogenesis and protein synthesis. One would thus expect mTOR activity to increase in malignant cells.
B: VEGF, a downstream target of mTOR, clearly contributes to angiogenesis.
D: PDK1 activates, instead of inhibiting, Akt. This ultimately leads to the activation of other signaling pathways that lead to oncogenic processes.

847. A is correct. We are told that downregulation of FOXO contributes to cancer progression. Thus, under normal conditions, FOXO must arrest uncontrolled growth, possibly by triggering apoptosis. The text preceding the figure tells us that Akt is a kinase, and the figure indicates that it inhibits FOXO activity. If Akt activity (phosphorylation) prevents the action of FOXO (the triggering of apoptosis via activation of nuclear genes), then FOXO must be unable to enter the nucleus and exert its effects when in its phosphorylated state.

848. C is correct. Upon dissociation from the beta-gamma complex, the alpha subunit is able to move across the internal face of the cell membrane and interact with a number of targets. This can continue until the hydrolytic activity of the alpha subunit, which is relatively slow, cleaves GTP and subsequently inactivates the G protein.

A: This is false; at rest, a single GPCR can attach to only one G-protein.
B: Even if this statement were true, it would not lead to signal amplification because it would still activate, at most, a single receptor molecule.
D: This is completely untrue; it is the enzymatic activity of a G protein that allows it to hydrolyze GTP.

849. A is correct. Since we are told that Ras resembles a typical G protein alpha subunit, it is reasonable to assume that it binds and hydrolyzes GTP in a similar manner. In short, Ras is active when GTP is bound and inactive when attached to GDP. Since NF-1 is a GTPase activator, it must trigger the hydrolysis of GTP and the subsequent inactivation of Ras. Therefore, if NF-1 is

inactivated, Ras will remain active longer than it normally should.

850. B is correct. Since Ras is located downstream of Bcr-Abl, TKIs that previously facilitated the inactivation of Bcr-Abl will now be ineffective in halting the progression of this signaling pathway. From this question alone, we do not know the exact role of Ras in the pathway, but this is the only option that describes a downstream mutation that could feasibly cause increased activation.

A: We are told that Bcr-Abl is constitutively active. Therefore, its ability to receive input signals is irrelevant.
C: The question stem states that TKIs work by binding the RTK, not its partner.
D: While we aren't told specifics about the relationship between the RTK and Grb2, we do know that TKIs work to prevent this interaction. For this reason, this relationship must be essential for the progression of cancer. Thus, a mutation that mimics the desired effects of the TKI would not confer resistance to TKI therapy. If anything, it would improve responsiveness of the cancer to this medication.

851. C is correct. We are told that TNFα is produced by macrophages; these cells become activated during robust immune activity, which enhances their phagocytic functions. This information suggests that TNFα participates in such a heightened immune response to fight cancerous cells. However, the malignant cells are likely to adapt to circumvent this attack. Reduction in the number of available TNFα binding sites by elimination of receptors would reduce the cytokine's effect and minimize the damage the immune response has on the cancer. If TNFα normally induces apoptosis, production of an apoptotic inhibitor would also decrease its effects and permit cancer survival. Finally, malignancies require increased blood supply to support their uncontrolled growth, and the question asks specifically about metastatic cancer, which grows rapidly.

II: Although the stem suggests that TNFα is elevated in cancer patients, this certainly does not imply that it is produced by the malignant cells themselves. In contrast, chronic elevation is the result of a persistent, albeit marginally effective, immune response with detrimental side effects.

852. C is correct. Carboplatin bears some resemblance to a nucleotide, suggesting that its target is DNA. Irreparable intercalation of DNA results in activation of the apoptotic pathway. As a sequential and tightly-controlled process, apoptosis minimizes damage to surrounding cells that would normally result from exposure to toxic cellular contents, particularly mitochondrial complexes. To do this, cellular contents are packaged into small vesicles as the cell blebs apart; these vesicles are then picked up by macrophages.

A: This vesicular release does not occur in cells that undergo necrosis.
B: The question mentions that the parent compound was successful, suggesting that it did not cause widespread necrosis (a generally harmful form of externally-caused cell death). Specifically, necrosis usually results from acute toxic, traumatic, or ischemic insult to the cell.
D: This does not accurately describe apoptosis.

853. C is correct. In non-apoptotic cells, ICAD exists in a bound state with CAD, which is a DNase. It may help to know that CAD actually stands for "caspase-activated DNase," while ICAD stands for "inhibitor of caspase-activated DNase." When ICAD is cleaved by an effector caspase, it loses its structural integrity and can no longer remain associated with its partner. This relieves the inhibition of CAD and permits subsequent DNA degradation, a hallmark of apoptosis. Note that this answer can also be achieved by elimination, as much of the above information is too specific to be high-yield on the MCAT.

A, D: The question states that caspase activation requires the action of cytochrome c. This protein is typically buried in the mitochondria, while caspases are said to be found in the cytosol. Since proteins would ordinarily be unable to pass through a lipid bilayer, the mitochondria (or at least, its outer membrane) must lose its structural integrity prior to caspase activation. This breakdown implies that the electron transport chain has already halted, since a proton gradient would be impossible to maintain. Similarly, while Bax does bind to the outer membrane during apoptosis and cause it to leak cytochrome c, this occurs long before caspase activation.
B: According to the question stem, caspases are proteases, not nucleases. As such, they cannot cleave DNA.

854. C is correct. The question stem tells us that Fas ligand serves a cytotoxic role; in other words, it induces the death of cells that it contacts and binds. Unlike CD8+ cells, CD4+ T cells do not have substantial cytotoxic activity. Although they do express Fas, they have no reason to express Fas ligand.

A: Cells of the blood-testes barrier express Fas ligand in order to promote apoptosis in lymphocytes that threaten to infiltrate the immunologically privileged testes. Exposure of the testes to immune cells would result in significant inflammation upon recognition of sperm, which are immunologically foreign.
B: The placenta separates the maternal from the fetal circulation. It would make perfect sense for cells lining this barrier to express Fas ligand to prevent maternal immune cells from reaching the fetus, which is immunologically foreign.
D: Metastatic cancer cells frequently express Fas ligand. They use it to induce apoptosis in immune cells that would otherwise clear them from the body and prevent further cancerous growth.

855. D is correct. DAG (diacylglycerol) is a lipid comprised of two fatty acid tails bound to a glycerol unit. This structure is very similar to that of prostaglandin. In fact, DAG is actually one of several prostaglandin precursors.

A: Testosterone is a lipid derivative; as such, it resembles DAG in that both are very hydrophobic. However, as a steroid, its structure contains several carbon rings instead of long alkyl tails.
B: ATP is a nucleotide, not a lipid.
C: Histamine is a small amino acid derivative. Like choice B, it is not a lipid at all.

856. A is correct. The figure shows PLC bound to GTP, or guanosine triphosphate. Judging from its name, phosphatidylcholine contains a phosphate moiety, which would likely be recognized by PLC. Arachidonic acid is a lipid without a phosphate moiety. Overall, choice A best resembles the figure; in fact, PLC does perform this reaction in the course of mediating the immune response.

B: Both arachidonic acid and thromboxane are signaling lipids that do not contain phosphate groups. As such, this answer choice bears no special resemblance to the role of PLC depicted in the figure.
C: Structurally, inositol does not resemble a phospholipid. More specifically, this would imply that PLC cleaves its own active second messenger product, which would immediately eliminate the signal and prevent the desired opening of calcium channels.
D: Cholesterol is very large and contains a number of carbon rings; it does not resemble the phospholipid substrates normally bound by PLC. Although many enzymes are promiscuous, it is unlikely that the active site of PLC could accommodate a molecule so markedly different in structure.

857. A is correct. From the term "ceramidase," we can assume that this is the enzyme responsible for the breakdown of ceramide. Thus, cells treated with an inhibitor of this enzyme should display elevated ceramide levels. Concurrently, they have been induced to produce excess Bax, a known proapoptotic protein that apparently interacts with ceramide. If an increase in both ceramide and an apoptosis-inducing protein does not promote apoptosis, this strongly suggests against the hypothesis mentioned in the question stem. In fact, it seems more likely that ceramide inhibits apoptosis, possibly by binding to Bax through its aforementioned ceramide-binding domain.

B: The question stem mentions that most lipids remain in a specific membrane, so it would be perfectly reasonable if elevated mitochondrial ceramide did not elevate ceramide levels in the plasma membrane. Also, note that mitochondrial membrane properties change significantly during the course of apoptosis. If known apoptotic inducers (namely chemotherapeutic agents) cause an increase in ceramide in the mitochondria, this suggests that ceramide at least might be involved in committing the cell to apoptosis.
C: Since lipids do not tend to move through and between membranes, the experiment described here does not support or refute the hypothesis. It is unlikely that the ceramide ever reached its cellular targets.
D: Bcl-2 could act downstream of ceramide, meaning that its overexpression would arrest the proapoptotic pathway without canceling any upstream signaling. If this were true, ceramide would remain elevated, but the cell would survive due to overexpression of this downstream anti-apoptotic factor.

858. B is correct. The question stem implies that SREBP enters the nucleus when the cell is cholesterol-deficient. Since we are told that cholesterol biosynthesis is tightly controlled, SREBP presumably acts to activate genes that increase the concentration of intracellular cholesterol. Synthesis of LDL receptors will enable the cell to import cholesterol by binding circulating LDL and taking it in via endocytosis.

A: Increased expression of these enzymes would further increase SREBP levels in the cell. This would constitute a positive feedback loop, which is inconsistent with the description of cholesterol biosynthesis as "tightly regulated."
C: The wording of this answer choice indirectly tells us that HMG-CoA synthase does not perform the rate-limiting step of cholesterol biosynthesis; it performs the step that immediately precedes it. Biochemical regulation typically targets enzymes involved in the rate-limiting step of the pathway, since altering other steps produces sluggish and generally insignificant chances in metabolic output.
D: If SREBP acts to protect the cell from a drop in cholesterol levels, it would not make sense for it to increase synthesis of a protein involved in cholesterol export.

859. A is correct. As nonpolar molecules, steroids generally pass directly through the plasma membrane and bind soluble cytoplasmic receptors.

B: The blood-brain barrier is penetrable by hydrophobic molecules, which include steroids and many drugs. Estrogen and testosterone, for example, are critical for proper neuronal development, even into early adulthood.
C: The question tells us that ganaxolone does elicit a rapid response, but this would make it atypical. Most steroids work by altering gene expression, which is a slow process.
D: Most steroids do alter gene expression; it is their primary method of effecting cellular function.

860. B is correct. If aspirin is prescribed to reduce the risk of myocardial infarction (heart attack), it likely plays some role in inhibiting thrombosis. This implies that thromboxane A2 is involved in the progression of the clotting cascade. Stimulation of vascular smooth muscle will result in vasoconstriction, an early step in the coagulation process. This choice also makes sense, as we would expect aspirin to inhibit the constriction of blood vessels.

    A: According to the question stem, thromboxane A2 is a derivative of prostaglandin. Since prostaglandins typically do not alter gene transcription, it is not reasonable to assume that a derivative would be able to do so.
    C: Since prostaglandins are small lipids, it would be unusual for them to form cross-links with large fibrous proteins, particularly one subject to such physical strain.
    D: It is cholesterol that alters membrane fluidity. Prostaglandins and their derivatives are small signaling molecules that bind protein receptors.

861. C is correct. From Weber's law, we know that the waiter notices 1-dB, or 2%, differences in sound intensity. This is evident because the question states that he notes the difference between 50 and 49 dB. This applies for increases in sound as well, so if the café is initially at 55 dB and gradually increases to 60, the waiter will notice when the sound intensity reaches (1.02)(55) or about 56 dB.

862. B is correct. The absolute threshold is the point at which the sensory system is activated, but not necessarily when the sound is perceived.

    C: This confuses the threshold of conscious perception with the absolute threshold.
    D: 130 dB is not a threshold level relevant to perception, although it could represent a pain threshold.

863. D is correct. Even though a signal is sent to the animal's central nervous system at 2 dB, we cannot be certain if it noticed the sound. The threshold must fall somewhere between 2 and 3 dB.

864. C is correct. The table shows the stressed subjects able to perceive a sound at a lower intensity than the other group. Additionally, this choice is consistent with signal detection theory.

A: This represents adaptation, as (according to this statement), the stressed subjects have become more accustomed to the sounds. However, it does not match the data.
B: The relevant threshold of conscious perception was higher for sound and lower for odor, so this statement is untrue.

865. C is correct. Because the stressed subjects had been previously exposed to the same types of sound as were played during the study, they were likely able to ignore them more and focus on the task at hand when compared with the distracted healthy subjects.

    I: This represents signal detection theory more than it does adaptation.
    II: This mentions the fact that the healthy subjects were less perceptive of the sounds, but does not relate to adaptation because they were not already used to this form of stimulus.
    III: The healthy subjects do not have a response bias, as they hear the sounds for the first time during the study procedure.

866. B is correct. This choice correctly orders the pathway traversed by incoming visual information. The optic tracts precede the brain itself, while the lateral geniculate nucleus represents the entry point for visual information into the brain.

867. C is correct. Magnocellular cells detect motion, which accounts for the child's perception of the bee flying by. Cones detect color (in a bee, yellow), which it is assumed that the boy can see. Finally, Meissner's corpuscles are responsible for the feeling of light touch, which pertains to the bee lightly brushing his face. However, parvocellular cells detect stationary objects in fine detail, but do not work well with fast-moving objects like the bee.

868. D is correct. The auditory cortex is responsible for processing sound information in the temporal lobe after it has passed through the medial geniculate nucleus. It is not mentioned that these patients have trouble perceiving sound. Note that some information is also sent to the inferior colliculus, which helps keep the eyes focused on singular points even when the head is rotating.

This key part of the vestibulo-ocular reflex could easily be damaged in these people.

B: In the auditory pathway, the medial geniculate nucleus precedes the inferior colliculus.
C: The lateral geniculate nucleus is the point at which visual information enters the brain. The patients' troubles could stem from a deficiency of the visual system.

869. C is correct. The arrangement of hair in different parts of the cochlea allows us to hear sounds of different frequencies. This is why cochlear implants cause patients to hear sounds of higher frequencies, as the part of the cochlea in which they are implanted is receptive to these pitches.

870. C is correct. While the bakery smells might be distracting at first, the man's brain adapts, allowing him to focus on more relevant stimuli.

A: This is not related to adaptation as much as it is to response bias.
B: This is a physical habit formed from experience. It does not pertain to the resident's altered perception of light.
D: Like B, this is a habit learned from experience and does not describe adaptation.

871. C is correct. The choroid is a layered region of the eye that contains connective tissue and blood vessels; it is located beneath the retina but above the sclera. Since the choroid is responsible for absorbing excess light, it is likely that this patient has an issue with the choroids of her eyes.

A: The cornea is the transparent region of the eye immediately in front of the pupil and iris. While it does serve a number of functions, it does not absorb bright light.
B, D: These structures are mislabeled. In the diagram, the label 3 denotes the retina, while the sclera is structure 4.

872. A is correct. The sympathetic nervous system triggers "fight-or-flight" responses, among which is pupil dilation.

B, C, D: The parasympathetic nervous system promotes pupil constriction. For this reason, the desired effect actually could be produced using a parasympathetic inhibitor. However, note that the question specifically asks for a system that the doctor should stimulate.

873. B is correct. Both rods and cones are photoreceptors located in the retina. Specifically, rods contain rhodopsin and are responsible for perceiving light and dark. Since they can operate in much more poorly lit environments than cones, they facilitate night vision.

A: Cones are responsible for perceiving color and are located primarily in the central region of the retina. Cones require a significant amount of light to function, which is why humans do not see color well at night. The individuals mentioned in the question do not seem to have issues with their cones.
C, D: It is much more likely that insufficient, not excessive, rhodopsin expression would cause the problem described. Similarly, having large numbers of photoreceptors in general would not cause a night vision deficiency.

874. C is correct. The lateral geniculate nucleus is the first "stopping point" for visual information once it reaches the brain. If both James' occipital lobe and visual pathway leading to the brain are healthy, it is his lateral geniculate nucleus that is most likely damaged.

A, D: Both the optic chiasm and the optic tracts are parts of the visual pathway that precede the brain. These structures are described in the question stem as healthy.
B: The visual cortex is located in the occipital lobe, which is again undamaged in James' case.

875. B is correct. Group 1 displays extremely poor results when observing moving objects. Both magnocellular and parvocellular cells are located within the lateral geniculate nucleus, or LGN. In particular, magnocellular cells are responsible for perceiving motion, though they do not discern the fine details of moving objects.

A: Parvocellular cells do not detect movement. Instead, they perceive color and can discern the specific visual details and shapes of stationary objects.
C: Horizontal cells help ganglion cells organize the large amounts of visual information transmitted by retinal cells; they do not perceive motion.

876. C is correct. Group 2 appears to be some sort of visually healthy control group, while Group 1 has serious difficulty detecting motion. In contrast,

members of Group 3 can identify moving, but not stationary, objects. For this reason, participants in Group 3 most likely have healthy magnocellular cells, the structures in the LGN that detect movement. Since Groups 1 and 2 are capable of discerning the shapes and details of fixed objects, they most likely have healthy parvocellular cells.

I: Magnocellular cells perceive moving objects. Since members of Group 1 are deficient in this area, this statement is false.
II: Individuals from Group 3 certainly may have damaged parvocellular cells, since they have so much trouble identifying stationary objects.

877. C is correct. Bipolar cells receive information from the eye's photoreceptors (rods and cones) and transmit it to the ganglion cells.

A: Horizontal cells also receive information from photoreceptors and convey it to ganglion cells. However, they relate better to the organization and regulation of that information than simply the passing of it onward to the next layer of the retina.

878. D is correct. Rods are rhodopsin-containing photoreceptors responsible for perceiving light and dark, while magnocellular cells are neurons in the lateral geniculate nucleus (LGN) that detect motion. Of course, photoreceptors are found in the retina while the LGN is part of the thalamus, so few patients would suffer damage to both; even so, D is the best answer.

A, C: Parvocellular cells are responsible for perceiving the shape and detail of stationary objects.
B: Cones detect color, which is normal in the case of A.K.

879. C is correct. The human blind spot is present because the optic disc, which leads to the optic nerve, contains no photoreceptors. In humans, it makes sense that this region does not include rods or cones, especially since the blind spot is small and not enormously evolutionarily disadvantageous. However, we can assume that the scientists have the capacity to add photoreceptors without impairing the normal functions of their synthetic visual system.

A: It is true that the fovea contains no rods, which prevents light and dark from being perceived at that position. However, the fovea itself does not constitute the eye's blind spot.
B: The macula contains the fovea and already has a high concentration of cones.
D: Changing the shape of the eye to an oval would not allow the current "blind spot" to receive visual information, since photoreceptors would still not be present.

880. C is correct. The optic chiasm is the point at which optic fibers on the nasal side begin to travel to the opposite hemisphere of the brain, causing them to cross paths. It is in the retina where signals are transmitted from bipolar to ganglion cells.

A, B, D: All three of these statements are true.

881. B is correct. The stapes, one of the three bones of the middle ear, precedes the organ of Corti. Its role is to transmit vibrations from the middle to the inner ear through the oval window of the cochlea. Damage to the patient's stapes would result in the symptoms described.

A: The pinna is part of the outer ear and precedes the auditory canal. The question stem describes the patient's external auditory canal as normal.
C: The basilar membrane does surround the organ of Corti, but is responsible for protecting it, not for conducting sound.
D: The vestibule does not transmit sound. Instead, it is responsible for perceiving linear acceleration.

882. C is correct. The vestibule is part of the bony labyrinth of the inner ear; it helps us perceive linear acceleration as well as maintain balance. Impairment of the other listed structures would not cause the balance issues mentioned in the question stem.

883. D is correct. The semicircular canals mainly function to sense rotational head and body acceleration. Since these particular desert iguanas do not move in a rotating pattern, semicircular canals would not be especially beneficial to their survival.

A: The scalae are chambers within the cochlea. As these lizards (as far as we know) are able to hear in a similar fashion to humans, they would require fairly similar cochleas.
B: The Eustachian tube helps the ear maintain equal pressure with the environment. The

iguanas' ears would still need to perform this task.

C: The vestibulocochlear nerve is another term for the auditory nerve, which is necessary if these iguanas are to hear at all.

884. A is correct. The organ of Corti is housed within the ear, while the other listed terms are part of the brain. For this reason, the organ of Corti must be listed first. Fibers then travel to the inferior colliculus, then to the medial geniculate nucleus (a region of the thalamus). From here, they move to the auditory cortex for final processing.

C: While some fibers carrying auditory information do synapse in the superior olive, they do so before, not after, reaching the MGN.
D: The auditory cortex should be the last structure in the pathway.

885. C is correct. Group 3 has by far the highest "minimum" values for perceived frequency and loudness. In other words, sounds must be both high-pitched and very loud to be noticed by these individuals. For this reason, they stand to benefit most. (Note that normal benchmarks are 25 Hz and 0 dB; some people can even hear sounds with negative decibel values.)

A: Group 1 begins hearing sounds at around 25 Hz and 0 dB. Since these are normal values, this is either the control group or a collection of individuals with hearing losses that cannot be determined from the given data.
B: On average, these people hear sound at a normal minimum frequency. While they do display a deficiency in hearing sounds that are quieter than 5 dB, this represents very mild hearing loss. Cochlear implants are meant for individuals with more extreme impairments.

886. D is correct. An inability to perceive one's spatial positioning could indicate damage to the vestibule in the inner ear. However, the given data relates only to hearing – specifically, to perceived frequency and loudness. This is not enough information to support a conclusion as to which group may consist of individuals with vestibular damage.

887. C is correct. The superior olive, located in the brain stem, is responsible for sound localization.

A: The ampullae are parts of the semicircular canals that are covered in hair cells. They help sense rotational acceleration, not the location from which a sound has traveled.
B: The medial geniculate nucleus is a part of the thalamus that receives and passes on auditory input. It, too, is uninvolved in sound localization.

888. A is correct. The vestibule is part of the inner ear. The label "4" represents the tympanic membrane, not the vestibule.

B, C, D: All three of these structures are properly labeled and comprise the ossicles, three small bones found within the middle ear.

889. D is correct. The superior olive, a region in the brain stem, is responsible for localizing sound. In contrast, the inferior colliculus helps us coordinate head rotation with a visual focus on a specific point. All four of the Roman numerals incorrectly convey this information.

I: The auditory cortex is essential for processing auditory information, but not specifically for sound localization or fixation on a point in the visual field.
II: The inferior colliculus, not the superior olive, is responsible for the function described here.
IV: The semicircular canals do not assist in sound localization; instead, they perceive rotation of the body or head.

890. D is correct. The ampullae are part of the semicircular canals, which help us perceive rotational acceleration. Note that these canals function both to detect head movement relative to the body and body motion in general (as when a person spins while keeping her head still).

A, B: The utricle and saccule are components of the vestibule. This inner ear structure assists in the perception of linear, not rotational, acceleration.

891. C is correct. Options I, II, and III are all correct definitions.

IV: Taste buds are not grouped based on the taste sensation that they are able to detect. All taste buds respond to all five of the currently known tastes.

892. C is correct. The vestibular sense, effectively, is the sense of balance. This is controlled by the cochlea

and the inner ear. Additionally, it does not relate to any of the other three choices.

893. D is correct. Hearing is processed by the auditory cortex, which is located in the temporal lobe. This form of sensation does not relate to the medulla at all.

A: All somatosensory information is sent to the somatosensory cortex.
B: Taste signals are processed by the taste center, which is located in the thalamus.
C: Smell-related information is passed along the olfactory tract to higher-order parts of the brain, including the limbic system.

894. D is correct. The student has lost the ability to feel pain and temperature, both of which are the responsibility of free nerve endings. Therefore, the free nerve endings are likely affected by the nerve disorder.

A: Olfactory chemoreceptors are responsible for smell and are in no way related to touch.
B: Merkel's disks are somatosensory nerves that typically respond to deep pressure and texture.
C: Meissner's corpuscles, also somatosensory nerves, respond to deep pressure and vibrations, two of the sensations that the student is able to feel.

895. A is correct. First, balance-related tasks test the vestibular sense. Next, the doctor asks the patient to touch body parts without being able to see them, which assesses the patient's proprioception; this sense refers to locate and perceive where our body is in space. Finally, the patient must identify objects by touch, which relates to somatosensation.

896. B is correct. The two senses shown in the table that are at a healthy baseline for all patients are the responses to smell and taste. Both of these are controlled by chemoreceptors.

897. D is correct. The bacterium appears to be affecting different types of mechanoreceptors. Therefore, it is reasonable to assume that the response(s) of other mechanoreceptors could be altered. The body's sensation of vibration is controlled by mechanoreceptors; although we do not always conceptualize it in this manner, sound itself is simply a vibrational stimulus. Therefore, the response to sound might be impacted.

C: Proprioception is the ability to orient and locate one's body in space. This is not directly under the control of mechanoreceptors.

898. C is correct. The table shows a patient's response as a percentage of what would be considered normal. It is certainly possible for a nerve condition to cause increased, instead of decreased, sensation; this is the obvious case with Patient 3.

A: Patient 1 has a decreased response to sound, but the other two type of stimuli seem to generate remarkably normal responses.
B: Patient 2 displays an increased response to smell, which is controlled by chemoreceptors.

899. B is correct. All types of sensory information, with the exception of smell, pass through the thalamus at some point. Therefore, degeneration of this part of the brain would cause a near-universal decrease in sensation, with the exception of the sense of smell. The olfactory sense could even be increased to compensate for the loss of the other senses.

900: A is correct. The vestibular sense controls our ability to balance and orient ourselves. Often, a defect in this system results in nausea and vertigo. One common cause of such a problem is the puncture of the semicircular canal(s).

B: While many infections of the inner ear can promote vestibular problems, this option clearly states that the infection acts only on the auditory nerve, not the surrounding tissue.

901. C is correct. Bottom-up processing refers to perception that is not influenced by preconceived notions or ideas. In other words, it's entirely data-driven and is generally used for unfamiliar objects. Here, the newborn has never seen a banana before, so perception of it will be determined solely by sensory input.

A: Here, we see an example of the Gestalt principle of closure. This is the idea that a space enclosed by an incomplete contour will be perceived as a closed figure.
B: This is an example of top-down processing, in which an individual uses background knowledge to influence perception.

D: This young woman is exemplifying signal detection by discerning a specific stimulus within a field of many other stimuli.

902. A is correct. When a person uses the Gestalt principle of proximity, he or she perceives objects that appear close together in space as being grouped together.

B: The principle of closure refers to our tendency to perceive objects as complete regardless of any gaps. In other words, our brains "fill in" images to form a coherent perception.
C: Feature detection is the biological process of interpreting a stimulus. While this is certainly part of perception in general, feature detection itself is not a Gestalt principle.
D: Parallel processing, or the ability to simultaneously interpret different types of stimuli, also is not a Gestalt principle.

903. A is correct. This is the definition of the law of Prägnanz.

B, D: While probably somewhat true, these do not relate to the law of Prägnanz.
C: Our brain uses both bottom-up and top-down processing, depending on the circumstance. It would be foolish to assume that one is better than the other. They also have nothing to do with the law of Prägnanz.

904. B is correct. This is a classic example of top-down processing, which occurs when the brain uses known information to interpret a stimulus. In this case, the man can recognize familiar words, even with missing letters, because he has seen them or similar words before.

A: Bottom-up processing occurs without any previously-learned information.
C: The Gestalt principle of similarity states that similar objects will be grouped together perceptually. Reading the sign does not demonstrate this.
D: The Gestalt principle of proximity describes our tendency to assume that objects that appear close together in space are members of the same group. It does not apply to this scenario.

905. D is correct. If you weren't familiar with these terms before, you can use the word structure to deduce their meaning. "Mono" means "one," "bi"

generally means "two," and "-ocular" refers to eyes.

906. C is correct. The law of closure states that the brain will interpret objects (such as shapes, letters, or figures) as complete even when they are not, as long as they are partially outlined. In the NBA symbol, we perceive a basketball player in the outline of two very unrelated shapes.

A, D: These examples relate to top-down processing and inductive reasoning.
B: Thomas' actions represent a switch from binocular to monocular vision.

907. D is correct. The ability to perceive the relative sizes of multiple objects can be performed using only one eye. Thus, this counts as a monocular cue.

A, B: These cues are binocular, as they require two eyes.
C: Somatosensation is the sense of touch, or the faculty relating to perception of bodily sensations. It is neither a monocular nor a binocular cue.

908. A is correct. Motion parallax is exactly what John experiences in the car: objects that are closer to him move faster across his field of view than objects positioned farther away.

B: Jeff's experience is simply a form of acclimation to sensory input.
C: This phenomenon occurs because the perilymph in Anna's inner ear is still moving when she stops spinning. This creates the sensation that the world is rotating; it is not motion parallax.
D: While a minimum speed is certainly required to perceive motion, this example does not answer the question.

909. D is correct. The only known difference between these groups is that participants in one could determine depth, while those in the other could not. The determination of relative size and depth are monocular and binocular cues, respectively. For this reason, we can assume that both groups had at least one eye open, but the first likely had the other closed while the second was allowed to use both eyes.

A, B, C: These distinctions do not explain the observed difference between the two groups.

910. C is correct. Perceptual constancy is the idea that, despite observed changes, our brain tends to interpret familiar objects as having the same size, shape, and brightness over time. It is this idea, not the law of similarity, that relates to the roller coaster.

    A: While Gestalt therapy does deal with emotions, the Gestalt principles of perception relate to visual stimuli.
    B: This statement is untrue.
    D: The Gestalt principle of good continuation suggests that, when one observes objects that appear to intersect, one will interpret them as two distinct objects. This does not relate to the question stem.

911. A is correct. A person who is fully awake will display beta waves when analyzed with electroencephalography. These waves are characterized as having high frequencies and low amplitudes.

    III, IV: Alpha waves are emitted when an individual is not fully awake or is less alert. Alpha waves are synchronous, but beta waves are not.

912. D is correct. Cortisol levels are elevated when awake and alert.

913. D is correct. An electromyogram measures muscular activity during the sleep cycle. Moderate muscle function is characteristic of all of the cycles, except REM sleep.

914. D is correct. Beta waves are emitted both when someone is fully awake and when one is in REM sleep. The only difference between these two conditions is that the beta waves present during REM sleep display a less consistent frequency.

    A: Stage 2 sleep exhibits theta waves, K-complexes, and sleep spindles.
    B: Stage 3 sleep exhibits delta waves, which have high amplitudes and high frequencies.
    C: Stage 4 sleep also exhibits delta waves with generally smaller frequencies than in Stage 3.

915. C is correct. In REM sleep, an EMG will display less muscular activity than when one is physiologically awake.

    A: EEG readings under both conditions will include prominent beta waves.

B, D: Both heart rate and respiration are similar between individuals in REM sleep and those who are alert.

916. B is correct. The anterior pituitary is likely be overstimulated, as it is responsible for releasing adrenocorticotropic hormone. ACTH effects the release of cortisol from the adrenal cortex.

    A: The posterior pituitary gland is unrelated to this scenario.
    D: The pineal gland releases melatonin, which does have an important role in regulating sleep cycle. However, the sleep-deprived individuals appear to have elevated cortisol levels, not melatonin levels.

917. A is correct. Light plays an essential role in regulating sleep cycle. The results of the study could be affected, depending on whether the sleep-deprived individuals were studied in a room with plenty of sun versus one with dim lighting.

918. C is correct. The cognitive dream theory posits that dreams are just stream-of-consciousness scenarios that are randomly ordered by the dreamer's brain.

    A: Activation-synthesis theory holds that there is a causal connection between neural activation and dream content.
    B: Problem-solving dream theory includes the hypothesis that we attempt to solve problems while dreaming without being limited by the rules of reality.

919. D is correct. Somnambulism (sleepwalking) occurs in individuals during Stages 3 and 4 of the sleep cycle.

    A, B: Both of these precede slow-wave sleep (Stages 3 and 4), which is when sleepwalking is observed.

920. B is correct. The pons typically prevents us from physically responding to our dreams. However, sufferers of night terrors experience the symptoms of anxiety, raised heart rate, and increased respiration that are described in the question stem. When these symptoms manifest, it appears the pons is acting abnormally by allowing dreams to affect the physical reality of these people.

921. C is correct. Because the pianist notices the ringing phone but is still able to focus on the task

at hand, this situation best relates to Treisman's attenuation model. This theory proposes that we "turn down," or attenuate, the intensity of less important stimuli to focus on other tasks. Perhaps if the phone were to ring for the entire performance, the perceived intensity of that stimulus would increase and the pianist's playing might be affected.

A, B: The Broadbent model of selective attention would apply only if the stimulus had not registered in the pianist's mind at all. Broadbent posited that some stimuli are filtered out of our attention entirely, forming a bottleneck where only relevant stimuli remain eligible for higher processing and storage in memory.

922. D is correct. Treisman's model requires that stimuli at least be perceived by the subject, albeit at low levels if they are not relevant to the task at hand. This teacher does not notice the students talking at all. Therefore, she has not simply "attenuated," or weakened, this distracting stimulus; she has filtered it out entirely, which would fit Broadbent's model more than Treisman's.

923. C is correct. The resource model of attention proposes that we are capable of dividing our attention (or "multitasking") as long as our total attentional resources exceed those required by the combined tasks at hand.

924. D is correct. Groups 2 and 3 were tasked with cooking while answering math questions. They differ only in that Group 3 must also listen to distracting noises. However, since both sets of participants completed their respective tasks in the same amount of time, we can conclude that Group 3 was able to limit the intensity of the stimuli provided by the sounds, to the point that it did not affect completion time. This would fit Treisman's model, which posits that we can "weaken" unhelpful or distracting stimuli so that we notice, but are not drastically affected by, them. However, it is also possible that the subjects did not notice the distracting sounds at all, which would relate more closely to the Broadbent model of selective attention.

C: The resource model of attention is better suited to explain our capacity to finish multiple tasks at the same time. It does not go as far as to

hypothesize why Group 3, which was exposed to additional distracting stimuli, could still finish its tasks in the same amount of time as Group 2.

925. A is correct. Automatic processing, a form of unconscious functioning that is sometimes known as "muscle memory," explains why familiar tasks are easier than less familiar ones. Additionally, multitasking is usually simpler and more efficient when we are performing actions that we are used to. Since the chefs cook so often, they can use automatic processing to finish making the omelettes much faster than can a group of random individuals.

B: Members of Group 3 could only have utilized automatic processing if they were performing a particularly familiar task. For example, if every individual in this group was a mathematics professor, perhaps they could have utilized automatic processing to complete the math problems. However, we are given no indication of their skills or professions.

926. B is correct. Opioids can cause euphoria (a strong feeling of happiness) while reducing pain. In fact, most opioids are prescribed as painkillers.

A: Barbiturates do cause feelings of relaxation, but that is not identical to euphoria.
C: Stimulants certainly do promote euphoria. However, these drugs, which promote alertness and generally speed up a person's system, do not necessarily dull pain.
D: Hallucinogens may cause euphoria, but are not known to diminish pain in the same way as opioids.

927. C is correct. Stimulants possess multiple mechanisms of action, including the stimulation of neurotransmitter release, downregulation of the effects of inhibitory neutransmitters, and inhibition of neurotransmitter reabsorption. Often, the same stimulant works through multiple pathways to alter both the release and the reuptake of chemicals including dopamine and norepinephrine.

IV: It is alcohol that most commonly suppresses functioning of the cerebellum, causing clumsiness.

928. C is correct. The mesolimbic pathway is the reward pathway most commonly tied to

addiction. It appears to be involved in the response to other rewarding behaviors, such as gambling and human affection, in addition to drug dependency.

929. B is correct. Heroin, like other opiates, acts as a pharmacological endorphin. Interestingly, the term "endorphin" is even derived from the phrase "endogenous morphine." The constant stimulation of specific receptors by the drug causes a downregulation of endorphin production by the body. When an individual ceases to use opiates, painful withdrawal symptoms occur due to this underproduction or even complete stoppage of endorphin release.

C: GABA is an inhibitory neurotransmitter; a deficiency in this chemical would not cause the symptoms referenced.
D: Interestingly, heroin does not act on a dopaminergic pathway nearly as directly as some other drugs. Instead, it (and other opiates) bind to mu-opioid receptors in the brain.

930. C is correct. Treisman's attenuation model explains that certain stimuli, although perceived, can be "attenuated" or weakened in intensity until further notice. This allows the subject to focus a majority of attention on relevant tasks while virtually ignoring distractions. Here, the dog initially attenuates the intensity associated with the sound of his name; this way, he can focus on something currently more important to him (digging a hole). However, as he hears his name again, the intensity of the stimulus increases, causing him to stop the task at hand and return home.

A, B: If this scenario followed the Broadbent model, the dog would not even perceive the sound of the human yelling because it would be eliminated entirely at a "bottleneck" of stimuli.

931. D is correct. The preoperational stage is Piaget's second stage of development. A grasp of the concept of object permanence signifies the end of the sensorimotor stage (ages 0-2) and the beginning of the preoperational stage (ages 2-7, approximately).

A: This quality will appear during the concrete operational stage.

B: This trait is a hallmark of the formal operational stage, which occurs long after the preoperational phase.
C: Crystallized intelligence refers to the use of learned skills and knowledge. This is a quality of adult development and tends to peak in middle age.

932. A is correct. Fluid intelligence refers to the capacity to arrive at novel solutions through logical thought and without the use of outside knowledge. This young person certainly demonstrates such intelligence by solving a Rubik's cube when he has never seen one.

B) This action is a quality of Piaget's sensorimotor stage of development. It does not demonstrate fluid intelligence.
C) Tempting answer! But this is a demonstration of crystallized intelligence, or the application of previously learned knowledge and skills.
D) This scenario describes a quality of Piaget's preoperational stage. Like choices B and C, it does not demonstrate fluid intelligence.

933. B is correct. Kohlberg famously outlined three stages of moral development: preconventional, conventional, and postconventional. In the preconventional stage, exemplified by young children, the individual is primarily concerned with the consequences of actions. Thus, subject A's response that the thief might get caught and go to jail relates to this perspective. In contrast, the conventional stage is marked by concern with the respect of societal rules and the maintenance of social order. In stating that stealing is wrong and that society wouldn't function if everyone stole, subject C demonstrates this perspective. Finally, the postconventional stage is characterized by abstract ideas of morality and the observance of universal human ethics. Subject B's response that personal property is a universal right best fits this stage of development.

934. D is correct. Symbolic thinking is the ability to use symbols or other indirect representations to describe objects or ideas. This mode of thinking is closely related to imaginative play (for example, consider a child who uses pieces of paper to represent food while playing "house"). The preoperational stage, which lasts from around ages two to seven, is marked by the development

of symbolic thinking. It is also qualified by egocentrism and centration, or the tendency to focus on one aspect of a concept and neglect all others.

A: A child in the sensorimotor phase would be an infant; he or she would not engage in symbolic thinking.
C, D: These phases occur after the preoperational stage.

935. A is correct. Erikson divided a typical lifetime into eight phases, each exemplified by a certain conflict. "Integrity vs. despair" represents the final phase and is marked by the individual's reflections on his or her life. If the person successfully resolves this conflict, he or she will emerge with wisdom, understanding, and peace with their own death. If not, the result often includes feelings of bitterness, resentment, and a feeling that life has been meaningless.

B, C, D: All of these stages precede the final phase of life and would not form the representative conflict of an 80-year-old individual.

936. C is correct. According to the data in the table, the more closely related one is genetically to an individual with bipolar disorder, the higher one's own risk of developing it. However, the information also indicates that having a twin with bipolar disorder does not guarantee that one will suffer from it (otherwise, the risk would be 100%). Given the extreme difference between 85% and 15-25% (which is seen when one has a regular sibling with the condition), genetics seem to play a larger role than environment. Note, however, that we would need more information as well as statistical analyses to determine this, which is why the correct answer says "likely."

A: This is far too extreme. Also, again, if genetics were the only determining factor, we'd expect to see a 100% risk of diagnosis for individuals with a bipolar identical twin.
B: While the study does measure diagnoses, it appears to use the same criteria for each group. Since we still observe a drastically heightened risk for those with an identical twin suffering from the disorder, we can assume that genetics play some role.

D: This answer is partially correct, but nothing in the data suggests that environment is a more important deterministic factor than genetics.

937. C is correct. The "zone of proximal development" refers to skills that an individual is very close to learning, but that require help from a "more knowledgeable other," or individual with experience in that skill, to be fully mastered. According to Vygotsky, without the "other," a person cannot easily progress in learning the relevant task.

A: 10,000 hours is commonly cited as the amount of time required to become an expert at a certain activity. It does not apply to the zone of proximal development.
D: Peers who are also at the beginner level do not qualify as "more knowledgeable others."

938. C is correct. A person does not need to successfully master or resolve each conflict to enter the next stage of personality development. While resolution may be healthier in general, it is not required, either at that point or later in life.

D: The idea of a "more knowledgeable other" is one of Vygotsky's concepts, not Erikson's.

939. B is correct. The "physiological revolution" occurs during adolescence, which coincides with Erikson's conflict between identity and role confusion. During this developmental stage, an individual's body is undergoing the sometimes-uncomfortable changes associated with puberty. At this point, he or she is pressured to answer the question: "Who am I?"

A: This stage falls prior to identity vs. role confusion. It is marked by an attempt to use one's abilities and intelligence to succeed in the world.
C: This stage comes after identity vs. role confusion. In it, individuals learn how to have intimate relationships with others.
D: This is the first stage of development, characterized by the act of learning to trust oneself and the environment.

940. B is correct. This girl already has a genetic susceptibility to an anxiety disorder, as her father has the condition. Her tumultuous childhood could then have secured the probability that she would then develop the disorder herself. This occurs often with psychiatric disorders, where

environmental factors seem to "bring out" the expression of certain genes.

A: This scenario is entirely genetic.
C: Such a cultural influence on personality does not involve genetics at all.
D: The act of taking an SSRI does not influence genetic expression in the way the question is asking.

941. C is correct. Roman numerals I, II, and III all correctly identify one of Gardner's multiple intelligences.

IV: Fluid intelligence is a component of the general intelligence factor theory, not the theory of multiple intelligences.

942. B is correct. As described, the confirmation bias causes people to overvalue information that confirms their previously-held opinions, while neglecting facts that challenge these viewpoints. Thus, even the massive amount of information provided by the Internet cannot alter many beliefs.

A: The affect heuristic relates to emotion, which is not implicated here.

943. D is correct. Algorithms follow a step-by-step method of problem-solving that is nearly foolproof with regard to finding a definitive solution. This is the method most commonly used by computers. However, it is disadvantageous because it can be an extremely time-consuming process, especially for complex problems.

B: This more closely resembles a schema or script than an algorithm.
C: The description here gives the benefits and pitfalls of using intuition, which is very different from an algorithm.

944. C is correct. Deductive reasoning begins with a set of rules, then uses them to draw a conclusion. To be both sound and valid, the rules must be accurate, and the drawn conclusion must fit within the parameters set by these rules. Choice C has rules that are scientifically accurate ("all atoms have mass" and "calcium is an atom"), and a correct conclusion is drawn from these stipulations.

A: This is a sound argument but is not valid. Many athletes are unable to run quickly, making the initial rule a false statement.

B: Here, our conclusion is not sound. Many other animals also have four paws.
D: This is an example of inductive reasoning, where a larger conclusion is drawn from a series of smaller observations.

945. C is correct. This theory states that there are multiple different forms of intelligence, including emotional, musical, logical-mathematical, and many more. While this musical savant may be considered well below average in many of these categories, he would still be considered a genius when it comes to his musical intelligence.

946. A is correct. This is a classic example of the availability heuristic, a bias that is seen when people make decisions based on available information. It often results in the overestimate of certain rates or outcomes that we hear about often. For example, every plane crash is a national news story, while nobody notices when a plane lands safely on the ground. Thus, we tend to assume that there is a much higher rate of plane crashes than there actually is.

947. B is correct. Heuristics are very closely tied to cognitive biases. Often, the repeated use of a heuristic leads to the development of cognitive biases. Therefore, the individuals who are told the real-life answers would likely undervalue these results and overvalue the next example of an incident in the news or other source, causing their wrong opinions to persevere.

948. B is correct. The data in the table clearly shows that identical twins who grew up in either the same or different households have closer IQ scores than the corresponding fraternal twins.

A: The term "always" is too strong here, especially since this statement can be false when the identical and fraternal twins grew up under different circumstances.
D: Fraternal twins are actually no more genetically related than any non-identical brothers or sisters.

949. A is correct. The evidence in the figure implies that there are both genetic and environmental components to intelligence. With this in mind, there should be no reason why identical twins

(who are genetically identical) would vary more than entirely unrelated people.

B, C, D: All of these agree with the figure that there is both a genetic and an environmental component to intelligence.

950. A is correct. The frontal lobe develops slowly in children and allows for the ability to plan, organize, and make judgment calls. Childhood damage to this region could result in the described deficits later in life.

B, C: The amygdala and limbic system are involved in emotional arousal, not planning.
D: The hypothalamus is a part of the limbic system.

951. D is correct. The first stage of memory is encoding, or the initial adaptation of a piece of information into a memory. The second stage, storage, involves the preservation of that encoded fragment in a memory system (short-term, long-term, etc.). The final stage is retrieval, in which these stored memories are accessed again by the person who formed them.

952. B is correct. In general, pieces of information will proceed from sensory to short-term to long-term memory, though most do not make it through this entire sequence. Both echoic (auditory) and iconic (visual) memory are subsets of sensory memory, making I correct. Though II does not include long-term memory, it accurately describes the progression of the information that enters short-term memory but never proceeds further.

III: Iconic memory is a type of sensory memory, not a subsequent step in the process.
IV: Working memory never precedes sensory memory, since the latter is the first and shortest-lived element in this progression.

953. C is correct. The self-reference effect explains that people best recall information when it relates to themselves. If Bill associates Tom's name with his own during encoding, he will more easily retrieve that name later.

A: This technique is the method of loci.
B: While combining the names with their phonetic pronunciations might increase depth of processing, it is not related to the self-reference effect.
D: This technique is maintenance rehearsal.

954. A is correct. Recognition involves the simple identification of information that has previously been memorized. The subject needs only to decide whether presented information matches his or her memory of the topic. Multiple-choice tests are a classic example of recognition, since answers are presented to the subject and do not need to be freshly retrieved.

C: While related to recognition, recall is much more difficult, as it requires retrieval of a memory with few or no cues. For example, a student taking a free-response exam must rely on recall.

955. D is correct. Maintenance rehearsal involves shallower processing than elaborative rehearsal, making it less effective as an encoding technique. Here, maintenance might consist of constant repetition of the same structural characteristics, while elaboration would involve forming a variety of connections between the amino acids and other information that has already been learned.

A: Increasing depth of processing generally does lead to more effective encoding.
B: Mnemonics are often used when encoding new information, and thy certainly could help in this case.
C: This method resembles chunking, another useful encoding technique.

956. C is correct. Automatic processing relates to encoding, not retrieval. Specifically, it involves encoding that is accomplished without conscious effort.

A, B, D: All three of these choices can serve as cues to aid memory retrieval.

957. B is correct. When presented with items in list format, people tend to remember the first and last entries better than any of those in the middle. This phenomenon is called the serial position effect. Specifically, the primacy effect relates to the first term while the recency effect relates to the last (or most recently heard).

958. A is correct. Long-term memories are thought to be organized within interconnected webs called semantic networks. In these networks, each distinct concept or term exists as a node. When information needs to be retrieved, certain nodes are activated first, and this "memory cascade"

spreads to adjacent nodes in a process known as spreading activation.

959. A is correct. LTP is the strengthening of synaptic connections due to high-frequency stimulation. In other words, when a healthy individual performs the same task repeatedly, the synapses associated with that task become more closely connected. LTP is thought to play an integral role in both learning and the storage of memories, and since the wild-type mice have the only functioning memory of the three groups shown, they likely experience the most LTP.

B: The word "only" is strong here. The other groups may have been able to encode information into short-term memory, for example; they just couldn't store it until the next trial.
C: LTP is thought to enhance memory, not impair it.
D: This is false. Additionally, the HP4 mice had little improvement throughout the trials, implying that their memory is impaired and not likely to be undergoing a large amount of LTP.

960. D is correct. Glutamate is generally excitatory, while GABA is inhibitory. While they act on different receptors, a broadly active glutamate inhibitor like APV will cause large-scale inhibition. Similarly, a GABA receptor agonist would increase activity at inhibitory GABA synapses.

A, C: These are backwards, since they will increase the activity of glutamate receptors.
B: This is inhibitory, but only acts on hippocampal neurons "selectively." The question stem states that APV acts in multiple regions of the brain.

961. C is correct. The storage of facts or general knowledge is accomplished by semantic memory, a type of explicit memory. Declarative memory is simply a synonym for explicit memory, making that choice correct as well.

III: Episodic memory is the memory of events that occurred in our lives. For example, a recollection of the first day of school would be an episodic memory. The question stem gives a scientific fact, which is semantic, not episodic.

962. B is correct. Spaced repetition is a technique intended to improve encoding. Only declarative

(or explicit) memory is consciously encoded, but that category includes both semantic and episodic memory. Semantic memory does relate to facts and concepts, making B the correct answer.

A: Working memory is short-term, while spaced repetition is intended to facilitate long-term encoding.
C: Explicit memory is consciously, not unconsciously, retrieved.
D: Nondeclarative and implicit memory are interchangeable terms. Since implicit memory is unconscious, it does not make sense to try to use techniques to encode it more efficiently.

963. C is correct. What Jack used is similar to priming, a technique in which stimuli are used as "hints" to facilitate the retrieval process. Priming is a type of implicit memory, a category that includes memories that are not consciously recalled. Even when the subject does not notice the priming (like Jack's mom), he or she becomes more likely to recall a related piece of information later. Here, Jack's mother implicitly remembered to get pizza after being primed with relevant stimuli.

964. D is correct. If Philip memorizes the names of the fifty states, that information will be present in long-term, not working, memory. Specifically, it will be encoded within semantic memory, which deals with the recollection of facts and ideas.

A, B: Working memory is most often defined as the part of short-term memory that is able to "hold" fragments of information for use in cognitive processes. Both the memory game and the math challenge are examples of such cognitive tasks.
C: One proposed facet of working memory is the visuospatial sketchpad, in which visual information is held for short-term use. Remembering the location of objects in a room would require this system to function properly.

965. B is correct. Facts and concepts are stored in semantic memory, which is a type of declarative or explicit memory. Completing an action that has become second nature, like riding a motorcycle, requires procedural memory. Finally, playing a video game in which certain actions are rewarded is not directly related to memory at all, but certainly involves operant conditioning.

A: Riding a motorcycle relates to procedural memory, which is implicit, not explicit.

C: Episodic memory stores recollections of events from our past. Remembering the tax codes is semantic, not episodic.

D: Working memory is a subset of short-term memory. Riding a motorcycle is a complex, learned action and would be encoded in long-term memory instead.

966. D is correct. Nondeclarative memory includes procedural memory, which relates to physical movements and actions. The motor cortex, along with the cerebellum and basal ganglia, is thought to play an integral role in the functioning of this system. In addition, actions that are second nature (such as riding a bike) are encoded within procedural memory and require the motor cortex to execute.

A: Nondeclarative memory includes conditioned responses.

B: While similar, these two terms are not identical. Nondeclarative memory does encompass procedural memory, but also includes priming as well as responses that have been learned through conditioning.

C: Context effects certainly can improve recall of a semantic memory. For example, if you learned a list of facts in a very cold room, you'll likely remember those facts better in a room of similar temperature. In other words, you recall that information most efficiently when the context matches that which was present during encoding.

967. A is correct. Baddeley's model of working memory proposes that this type of memory is controlled by a system termed the "central executive." This organizing system coordinates two other structures, the visuospatial sketchpad and the phonological loop. The sketchpad holds visual information to be used and manipulated by the central executive, while the loop is the site of auditory information for the same purpose.

968. D is correct. While elaborative rehearsal is an effective method to aid encoding, this information is not being committed to prospective memory. Prospective memory involves remembering that you need to do something in the future, and has nothing to do with memorizing details or facts.

A, B, C: These are all effective memorization strategies. Note that this information is being encoded into semantic memory, which is a type of declarative memory.

969. A is correct. The two additional cards serve as new information that interferes with the recall of old knowledge. This is the definition of retroactive interference.

B: Proactive interference occurs when old knowledge hinders the ability to encode new memories.

C: The students are making false alarm errors. They are mistakenly thinking that the two cards were present in the original set when they actually were not.

D: Priming is a process that makes proper recall more likely. The new cards do the opposite – they impair correct recall of the original five cards.

970. C is correct. This child is having problems with her procedural memory, which relates to the learning of physical movements. The cerebellum is thought to play a primary role in the encoding of procedural memories.

A: The hippocampus relates to explicit memory. Holding and moving a pencil is a procedural, or implicit, action.

B: Declarative memory is explicit and involves the recollection of facts and occasions.

D: Hearing has nothing to do with this girl's impairment.

971. C is correct. Ataxia refers to impaired coordination of muscle movements, such as those required to walk. It does not relate to short-term memory.

A, B, D: All of these pairings correctly match a disease with an associated symptom.

972. B is correct. Interference can be retroactive, in which the learning of new information makes recalling old memories more difficult. Alternatively, it can be proactive, in which old information impairs the encoding of new memories.

A, D: The terms "retrograde" and "anterograde" describe amnesia, not interference.

C: "Reactive" is not a type of interference.

973. A is correct. Source monitoring is the process we use to isolate the source of a particular memory. Specifically, it helps us decide whether memories reflect real experiences or are simply distorted from dreams, our imagination, or unrelated events.

B: While priming could be relevant here, the movie causes this woman to mistakenly describe the wrong individual. Hence, nothing in this scenario aided proper retrieval of the thief's appearance.
C: Serial positioning relates to the retrieval of items from a list. Specifically, it generally involves the primacy and recency effects, neither of which is relevant here.
D: In signal detection theory, a correct rejection involves accurately stating that a certain stimulus was never presented. This situation results in a false alarm, not a correct rejection.

974. B is correct. Alzheimer's disease is most commonly associated with dementia, a serious decline in cognitive skills. This usually includes retrograde memory loss. Korsakoff's syndrome, a disorder that results from severe thiamine deficiency, also causes the loss of older memories. In fact, Korsakoff's is generally connected with confabulation, or the presentation of false or distorted memories.

III: BPD is a personality disorder associated with unpredictable behavior, irritability, and drastic mood changes. It is not generally associated with memory loss.
IV: Ebbinghaus' disease is not a real condition.

975. C is correct. This question actually relates to classical conditioning, not to memory (which the other choices focus upon). William has a conditioned response to his phone's ringtone that later becomes more specific; this is the definition of stimulus discrimination.

A, B: While the descriptions for these terms (the forgetting curve and retroactive interference) are basically correct, the question stem does not involve a memory struggle or impairment.
D: Anterograde amnesia is the inability to form new memories, not a difficulty retrieving past ones.

976. D is correct. In both situations, Jenny learns new information, which impairs her retrieval of older, previously encoded memories. These are classic cases of retroactive interference.

A, B, C: Proactive interference occurs when information from the past interferes with the encoding and retrieval of new memories.

977. C is correct. Ebbinghaus' curve of forgetting shows how retention of memorized material decreases over time, especially if it is not rehearsed or otherwise emphasized. Information is forgotten most rapidly in the days right after memorization.

B: This is close, but it states that memories are stored before they are encoded. In reality, encoding occurs first, followed by storage and later retrieval.
D: Spaced practice is an effective learning technique and should not decrease retention.

978. B is correct. The recency effect is our natural ability to recall the last word of a list more easily than terms in the middle. It is a specific type of serial position effect. Since the last term on this list is "literature," most participants would remember it more easily (as seen in the table), but the individual described in the question would lack this advantage.

A: This answer would be correct if the individual had an impaired ability to experience the primacy effect.
D: This might make sense if the question referenced serial position effects in general, but it only mentions the recency effect.

979. D is correct. Retroactive interference happens when the learning of new information impairs the proper retrieval of older memories. Here, more recent terms (tulip, flowerpot, etc.) cause participants to struggle at recalling the related word "gardening."

A: Context effects relate to our ability to best recall material when our environment or mental state resembles that which we experienced during encoding. They are not relevant here.
B: While free recall usually is harder than recognition, this does not relate to the researcher's introduction of the new terms.

980. A is correct. Anterograde amnesia is a defect in the ability to form new memories, often as a result of hippocampal damage. Since this man cannot encode and store the new information regarding his nurse's name, he certainly could suffer from this condition. The other answers do not make sense given the information in the question.

B: Dissociative fugue is an often-temporary loss of identity and personal memories. It often ends in the victim wandering to unfamiliar locations.
C: Since the man can remember how to perform physical tasks, his procedural memory is probably fine.
D: This is backwards; retrograde amnesia refers to the inability to recall old memories.

981. D is correct. The two main regions of the brain involved in the production and comprehension of language are Broca's and Wernicke's areas. Aphasia of either of these regions would result in a deficiency in some aspect of verbal communication. Note also that Broca's area is found in the frontal lobe, while Wernicke's is part of the temporal lobe. So, progressive damage to either of these lobes could also affect the ability to process and produce coherent language.

982. B is correct. The learning theory posits that language acquisition results from operant conditioning – in other words, from rewards and punishments. Essentially, parents and other adults react to their child's first words with excitement and praise, and this motivates the child to speak more often and with increasing complexity.

A. This statement embodies the nativist theory of language development.
C. The explanation here is actually the direct opposite of the theory referenced in the question stem.
D. This relates more to social interactionist theory than to learning theory.

983. C is correct. The idea of sensitive developmental years is a part of the nativist theory of language acquisition. Specifically, the years in question span from an age of two until puberty. During this time, children are able to develop a mastery of language and the basic rules of syntax via exposure to human interaction. If a child was deprived of this social contact, he or she would never be able to gain a full grasp of language. In

fact, this does occur in cases of extreme abuse or neglect.

A: Students learning a second language are likely far older than the "sensitive years" in question.
B: According to nativist theory, the sensitive period begins around age two. As a result, this baby is too young to provide proper support for the question stem.
D: A six-year-old would still fall within the sensitive period of development and (in most cases) would not speak in the same manner as an adult. Even if this were true, it would not provide as strong of evidence as choice C.

984. D is correct. While the social interactionist theory does focus on factors like interaction with adults and interpretation of one's environment, it is also biological in nature. This theory posits that a strong relationship exists between the development of the brain and a child's ability to speak and command his or her language. If brain scans actually revealed this connection, it would provide strong evidence for this theory.

A, C: Neither of these theories directly connect language acquisition to the development of the brain.
B: Tempting as it may sound, this is not a theory that relates to language acquisition.

985. A is correct. Wernicke's area is located in the back of the temporal lobe. It controls the comprehension of speech and written language the ability to produce coherent sentences. This patient has clearly lost the ability to produce coherent sentences but continue to be able to speak and produce words indicative of damage to Wernicke's area.

B. The limbic system is involved with emotions and language production.
C. Broca's area controls the production of language. Damage to the Broca's area results in the inability to produce any words.
D. The auditory cortex controls our ability to hear sounds.

986. B is correct. From the table, we see that the children who developed the best grasp of language were those with families that were deemed supportive. Even foster children with multiple homes developed language more adeptly than individuals in a single unsupportive

home with absentee or neglectful parents. This aligns with the learning theory of language development, which states that language is learned via operant conditioning. In an unsupportive home, the children would not receive enough positive reinforcement to properly incentivize mastery of language and syntax.

A: This is not a theory of language development.

987. D is correct. As its name implies, the learning theory proposes that language is acquired through associative learning – specifically, through operant conditioning and positive / negative reinforcement. It does not limit language development to a certain age range. (Remember, operant conditioning in general can be effective at any age.) Although the children from the unsupportive homes did appear to "catch up" to the other two groups, that can certainly be explained by changes in reinforcement or punishment during their teenage or young adult years.

988. A is correct. Of all the languages listed in the table, Language 1 clearly has the most words to describe the color red. While we do not know whether this trend extends to other colors, it is safe to at least assume that speakers of this language pay far more attention to the exact shade of red when remembering and describing objects that they see.

D: While members of all cultures would likely perceive similar shades when looking at the same object, those who speak Language 2 or Language 4 (for example) would be more constrained by words when trying to describe its nuances.

989. C is correct. The most striking aspect of Language 5 is that it does not include even a single word to describe the concept of snow. Therefore, this language likely developed and is spoken in a part of the world that never sees snow – in other words, a warmer region. Of the answers listed, only the Amazon rainforest fits this description.

A, B, C: Even if we do not know much geography, we certainly can conclude that parts of North America see a great deal of snow, as does eastern Europe. The mountainous region of Nepal contains Mount Everest, where snow is also commonplace.

990. B is correct. The Sapir-Whorf hypothesis holds that the language a person speaks influences a person's thoughts and decisions. For example, if a person's language has no word for something, then the person will not be able to easily entertain thoughts about that thing. Here, the language has no words for numbers. Thus adult speakers of the language would have difficulty understanding numbers and developing basic numeracy.

991. D is correct. The concept of "universal emotions," which had previously been posited by Darwin, was fleshed out most fully by psychologist Paul Ekman. The emotions that he listed as universal to all cultures include happiness, sadness, surprise, fear, disgust, and anger; a seventh emotion, contempt, has been debated as well. Jealousy is not a universal emotion.

A, B, C: All three of these emotions are considered to be universal.

992. C is correct. This answer describes the facial expressions associated with fear. Widened eyes and raised eyebrows characterize this response, as does an open mouth in most cases.

A: These facial expressions are associated with disgust. They can best be identified by the wrinkled nose commonly seen when an individual smells something rotten.
B: These expressions are those linked to anger, especially the deep stare.
D: The expressions listed in this choice are associated with surprise. They can be distinguished from those seen in a fearful individual by the open, dropped jaw.

993. A is correct. In general, an adaptive role is one that relates to an evolutionary advantage. Darwin postulated that emotions evolved because they gave the individuals who experienced them such a benefit in survival and reproduction. For example, early humans who felt fear may have been better at avoiding dangerous predators.

B, C: Evolution works on the level of changes to the gene pool over time. Both of these choices describe learned changes occurring on the individual level.
D: While this may be true, the question asked about the adaptive role of emotion in general. This choice seems to explain the prevalence of humans

who feel love over those who feel more unpleasant emotions, which we do not know even exists.

994. B is correct. The James-Lange theory of emotion posits that physiological changes, like increased heart rate or breathing, cause a subsequent experience of emotion. For example, imagine that someone jumps in front of you in a haunted house. This theory predicts that your heart rate will speed up first, and you will feel fear as a result.

A: This statement describes the Cannon-Bard theory of emotion.
C: The inclusion of conscious appraisal of the stimulus makes this the Schachter-Singer, not the James-Lange, theory.
D: This is the reverse of the order hypothesized in the James Lange theory.

995. B is correct. According to the Cannon-Bard theory, physiological arousal and the experience of emotion happen simultaneously. Since skin temperature appears to start increasing at the 5-second mark, the correct answer is the value that is closest to this point in time.

A: This is prior to the steep increase in skin temperature shown on the graph. The friend could not possibly experience emotion before the stimulus itself.
C: Since 8 seconds is well after the increase in skin temperature begins, this choice reflects the James-Lange, not the Cannon-Bard, hypothesis.
D: The mention of thinking best relates to the Schachter-Singer theory, which suggests that physiological arousal happens first, then cognitive appraisal of the stimulus, and finally emotion.

996. B is correct. According to the Schachter-Singer theory, a physiological response to a stimulus happens first, followed by cognitive appraisal of the situation. This appraisal then results in the experience of a related emotion. In this scenario, both the stimulus and the change to skin temperature occurred at the 5-second mark, but the friend did not push the button until 7 seconds in. This indicates that the physiological sensation happened before the experience of emotion.

A: The Cannon-Bard theory of emotion suggests that physiological response and emotion happen simultaneously. If the friend had pushed the button at or immediately after the 5-second mark, this would be a logical answer.
C: This is not a real theory of emotion.
D: Similarly, this theory does not exist. Note that it is similar to the James-Lange hypothesis, which also places physiological response before the experience of emotion. However, that theory is not an answer choice.

997. D is correct. The amygdala is an almond-shaped component of the limbic system. This structure is thought to play an integral role in both memory and fear.

A: The cerebellum coordinates and regulates muscle activity. On the MCAT, it is most commonly referenced in connection to fine motor and balance-related movements.
B, C: The occipital lobe is associated with vision, while the thalamus acts to relay information and integrate sensory inputs. Neither has a notable connection to the emotion of fear.

998. C is correct. The Yerkes-Dodson law, which is based on experimental evidence, states that people tend to perform best when they are moderately aroused. In other words, a "sweet spot" of arousal exists where performance seems to peak. This is thought to be true because high levels reflect heightened nervousness and lessened concentration, while low levels often correlate with decreased motivation or even sleepiness.

D: Different people certainly may have different optimal levels of arousal, and this varies even more with the task that is being performed. However, the Yerkes-Dodson law is better described by choice C.

999. A is correct. The prefrontal cortex is linked to executive functions, including planning, decision-making, and inhibition of behavior. It also is associated with the reduction of emotional feelings, particularly fear and anxiety. In other words, proper functioning of this region is required for the inhibition of overwhelming or negative feelings, so damage to it might produce the symptoms described.

B: The amygdala is strongly associated with the perception of fear. However, damage to this region would likely result in lowered fear and anxiety, which is the opposite of this patient's problem.

C: The hippocampus plays a role in forming memories, but is not directly involved in emotion.

D: The olfactory bulb is involved in the sense of smell.

1000. B is correct. Emotions differ from moods primarily in their duration. Specifically, an emotion is generally perceived on the order of seconds, while a mood (happy, melancholy, excited) can last for days or more.

A: We can only speculate as to what animals feel, and evidence certainly does not support this choice. Perhaps animals experience both emotions and moods, perhaps not; this likely also depends on the species.

C: Both "healthy" and "unhealthy" people can experience both emotions and moods. While depressed mood is a hallmark of major depressive disorder, this choice does not accurately describe the differences between these two broad terms.

D: Both emotions and moods can be caused by outside stimuli and still represent internal states.

1001. B is correct. Cognitive appraisal of stress consists of two stages: primary and secondary. During primary appraisal, the person analyzes the potential stressor along with the surrounding environment to determine whether it represents a threat. If a threat (and thus a source of stress) is detected, secondary appraisal ensues, in which the individual decides whether and how he can reasonably cope with the situation. Here, John already knows that his grandmother's death is stressful; he is now considering how he can best cope with this situation during finals.

C, D: These are not components of the cognitive appraisal of stress.

1002. D is correct. When an individual performs constant reappraisal of stress, he or she monitors the stressor to determine whether it still represents a significant threat. Elaine does this by periodically looking behind her. In doing so, she continually allows herself to evaluate the situation and plan potential next steps.

A: Isaac uses cognitive appraisal to turn a situation into eustress (positive stress). This does not constitute constant reappraisal.

B: In this situation, Robert briefly appraises the potential stressor and makes a quick decision. The question stem is asking for something entirely different.

C: This type of mass stress can be caused by a significant catastrophe or disaster; however, it is unrelated to constant stress reappraisal.

1003. B is correct. Reframing is a common psychological technique by which a patient attempts to see something from a different perspective. Eustress refers to positive or healthy stress. By asking George to attempt to perceive his obstacles as eustress, the psychologist is encouraging him to think about them in a more positive way and to contemplate them as motivating, not upsetting.

A, C: These choices, despite their differences in wording, basically revolve around avoiding stress entirely. This is not what the psychologist is asking George to do.

D: This choice focuses on distress (negative or unhealthy stress), not eustress.

1004. D is correct. Individuals with PTSD often feel near-constant hyperarousal stemming from heightened sympathetic (fight-or-flight) responses. Symptoms include tension, irritability, insomnia, angry outbursts, and a tendency to be easily startled.

A: These symptoms relate more to the re-experiencing cluster, as they involve the individual "reliving" stressful aspects of his or her trauma.

B: These are symptoms of the avoidance cluster.

C: While these experiences do sound like they relate to extreme arousal, they are associated with mania, not PTSD. In other words, someone with bipolar disorder is more likely to experience them.

1005. C is correct. Our bodies respond to stress through activation of the sympathetic nervous system. Part of this system involves the release of cortisol, a hormone with a number of effects, including a shift in metabolism from using sugar as an energy source to using fat. The cortisol release mechanism begins when the hypothalamus secretes corticotropin-releasing hormone (CRH), which stimulates the anterior pituitary to release adrenocorticotropic hormone (ACTH). Finally, in response, the adrenal cortex secretes cortisol into the bloodstream.

A: The hypothalamus (a part of the brain) and the adrenal gland (an endocrine organ) do not communicate via direct nerve stimulation.
B: It is the hypothalamus that releases CRH, while the anterior pituitary secretes ACTH. In other words, this choice is backwards.
D: The thyroid is not directly involved with the mechanism mentioned in the question stem.

1006. B is correct. Make sure to note the positions of the error bars! According to the graph, no statistical significance exists between the results for cognitive behavioral therapy and those for meditation, which display overlapping bars. However, the lower end of the error bar for the combination of two therapies is still above the higher end of that for CBT. For this reason, we see that the stress-reducing effects of the combined therapy are statistically significant.

A: Although the meditation column does appear higher than that for cognitive behavioral therapy, we cannot draw a conclusion due to the overlap in the error bars.
C: This choice results from inaccurately reading the graph. A larger reduction in stress, by percentage, is indicated by a highest bar in the figure.

1007. D is correct. Ultimately, this question is simply asking us to explain the premise of CBT. This type of therapy seeks to identify harmful, or maladaptive, thought patterns and behaviors. The goal is then to use systematic techniques to adjust these behaviors to be healthier and more functional. Thus, CBT can be used to reduce stress by identifying triggers and adjusting the individual's perception of his or her stressors.

A: As Freudian concepts, these components of the personality would likely be a greater part of the psychoanalytic approach.
B: This choice represents a more humanistic approach to therapy and personal development.
C: This is a technique called "age regression therapy" in which the subject gains access to childhood memories as a method to address

past trauma and emotional hang-ups. It does not relate to CBT.

1008. C is correct. Long-term stress has been demonstrated to correlate with a number of adverse medical outcomes. Specifically, it seems to have a hand in causing heightened blood pressure, a weakened immune system, and skin problems. Chronic stress has also been shown to exacerbate the courses of diseases such as AIDS, cancer, and diabetes.

A: These symptoms are actually the reverse of those that occur in an individual suffering from long-term stress.
B: Actions like substance abuse and unusual food consumption represent behavioral, not physiological, effects.
D: These effects are emotional, not physiological.

1009. A is correct. Acute stress arises from daily situations that are unpredictable, represent a threat to the individual's ego, or are difficult to control. Andrew's trouble finding his car keys before work represents this kind of short-term stress. Note that "acute" refers to duration rather than intensity of symptoms, although acute symptoms are very often intense.

B: Here, Gerald is experiencing chronic stress, seemingly in the form of PTSD.
C, D: These are also examples of chronic stress, as they are long-term in nature.

1010. C is correct. When exposed to a stressor, an individual's body responds in a number of ways to assist in handling the situation. Most of these responses stem from sympathetic nervous activity, and many (such as increased alertness and a minimized perception of pain) are essential to keeping us safe in dangerous scenarios.

A, B: These are some of the negative consequences of chronic stress.
D: No evidence suggests that stress increases IQ or cardiovascular fitness. Additionally, stress (whether eustress or distress) is not likely to directly promote a sense of tranquility.

1011. C is correct. It is thought that hypersensitivity of dopaminergic receptors in multiple areas of the brain is responsible for the symptoms of schizophrenia. Conversely, in Parkinson's disease, neurons in the substantia nigra release insufficient amounts of dopamine, causing issues with movement. The administration of dopaminergic antagonists to treat schizophrenia can result in Parkinson's-like symptoms.

1012. B is correct. SSRIs, or selective serotonin reuptake inhibitors, decrease the amount of recycling (reuptake) of serotonin by presynaptic neurons. As a monoamine, serotonin clearance will also be inhibited by MAOIs, which, in combination, can result in a dangerous condition called serotonin syndrome.

A: Benzodiazepines are often prescribed for anxiety. These medications cause an increase in GABA, which is not a monoamine.
C: Similarly, melatonin is not a monoamine. It is involved in regulating the sleep cycle and does not have a significant risk of interacting with MAOIs.
D: Nitrous oxide, a gas, is itself used as a neurotransmitter and also should not interact with MAOIs.

1013. D is correct. The description of the symptoms of Huntington's disease includes impairment in the smoothness of movement, a process in which the basal ganglia are heavily involved.

A: Although the cerebellum also controls coordinated movement, it is nowhere near the striatum, which is located near the center of the diagram.
B, C: The hippocampus and thalamus both lie near the area indicated, but are involved primarily with memory and sensory integration, respectively.

1014. D is correct. Dilation of lung blood vessels in response to O_2 content is triggered by direct stimulation of the vasculature by O_2; nerve cells are not involved.

A: This process involves reflex arcs that include baroreceptors.
B, C: These responses stem from reflex arcs that include thermoreceptors.

1015. C is correct. Endorphins are known as the "natural painkillers" of the brain, and are released en masse after activities like vigorous exercise and sex. However, they are also continuously secreted at low levels during normal activity. As opiates like heroin and morphine act on the same receptors as endorphins, these receptors are downregulated when an addict becomes habituated to such substances. This renders him (or her) less sensitive to his own natural endorphins, so he will experience understimulation of these pathways when drug use is ceased, resulting in generalized pain.

1016. D is correct. The key word here is "downregulation," a decrease in a cell component in response to an external variable. Childhood lead exposure results in fewer NMDA receptors becoming localized on the cell membrane.

A, B: Action on glutamate instead of NMDA receptors does not constitute the downregulation described in the question stem.
C: This process would be characteristic of an NMDA receptor antagonist, not a downregulator.

1017. C is correct. A dopaminergic receptor antagonist would have the opposite of the desired effect; it would make these receptors less sensitive to the already-limited quantities of dopamine.

A, B: The contradictory nature of these statements make choosing one tempting. However, pay close attention to the prompt's mention of the paradoxical symptoms of Parkinson's disease: the resting tremors are caused by dysfunctional inhibition of involuntary impulses, while the simultaneous rigidity of voluntary movements is caused by dysfunctional excitation of voluntary signals.
D: This is straightforwardly correct; a problem with dopamine synthesis could be alleviated by an increase in dopaminergic precursors like l-DOPA.

1018. A is correct. The frontal lobes are involved in executive functions like decision-making.

1019. C is correct. In addition to playing many roles in the peripheral nervous system (such as muscle activation and synaptic transmission of autonomic nervous signals), acetylcholine is also used in the CNS in areas related to arousal, attention, and motivation.

A, B, D: While these neurotransmitters serve as intercellular messengers in various parts of the body, they not used by the PNS.

1020. D is correct. The typical neuron's resting potential is -70 mV. If the cell were depolarized, it could easily rise to the threshold level (approximately -55 mV), and an action potential would be triggered. Therefore, an inhibitory neuron must instead hyperpolarize its target neuron to prevent this response. GABA accomplishes this by opening Cl⁻ channels, which lowers the resting potential (say, to -80 mV) and makes it more difficult for the excitatory entrance of Na⁺ ions to raise the cell potential to threshold level.

1021. C is correct. Cortisol is released by the adrenal glands in response to stress. This secretion comprises one of the functions of the sympathetic nervous system, or "fight or flight" mechanism.

A: A tumor in the thyroid gland would not cause elevation of cortisol.
D: We have no reason to conclude something this specific.

1022. B is correct. The parasympathetic nervous system is responsible for "rest and digest" functions. It is activated during relaxation or immediately after meals.

A, C, D: All of these behaviors would activate the sympathetic nervous system.

1023. B is correct. The hypothalamus is involved with the "four F's": fighting, fleeing, feeding, and fornication. Receptors in the hypothalamus also regulate metabolism, water balance, and temperature in the body.

A: The thalamus functions mainly as a relay station for incoming sensory signals.

C: The thyroid gland is principally involved with metabolism.
D: The major function of the parathyroid is the regulation of calcium and phosphate levels.

1024. D is correct. The genetic constitution of an individual may be expressed in a variety of ways, depending on environmental triggers or suppressors of the transcription of particular genes.

B: In general, environment does not promote heritable modifications, though exceptions have been found.

1025. A is correct. Neurulation occurs three to four weeks after fertilization and marks the formation of the developing nervous system. It is characterized by the furrowing of the notochord out of the ectoderm to produce the neural groove.

B: The neural tube differentiates into the spinal cord well after neurulation takes place.
C: Forming of the rhombencephalon, mesencephalon, and prosencephalon happens after neurulation.
D: The prefrontal cortex isn't actually fully formed until an individual reaches his or her mid-twenties.

1026. D is correct. The three major subdivisions of the embryonic brain are the prosencephalon (forebrain), mesencephalon (midbrain), and rhombencephalon (hindbrain). They give rise to the structures that are listed in the Roman numerals above.

1027. C is correct. DNA methylation represents one of the most well-studied epigenetic modifications. The term "epigenetics" refers to non-heritable changes in expression that do not change the sequence of DNA itself.

1028. A is correct. "Monozygotic" is another term for "identical." Remember, identical twins share all of their DNA, while fraternal twins are no more related than any two non-twin siblings. For this reason, the high concordance rate between monozygotic twins implies a genetic influence on schizophrenia.

1029. B is correct. Because the limbic system (which corresponds to emotion) develops more rapidly than the prefrontal cortex (which corresponds to rationality), adolescent behavior tends to be more emotional in origin than that of adults.

1030. B is correct. While in the womb, the fetus produces many more neurons than are necessary. This total amount of cells is pruned over the course of one's lifetime. An important point, however, is that the newborn possesses few neural networks. These form from learning and environmental shaping.

1031. C is correct. All of these disorders do contain the prefix "schizo-," which means "split" or "apart" in Greek. However, this term can have multiple implications. Schizophrenia ("split mind") is a disorder characterized by perceptual abnormalities like hallucinations, as well as delusions and disjointed thought patterns. Note that its name does not denote multiple personalities, but a separation of mental functions. Schizotypal personality disorder (from "schizophrenic phenotype") is similarly characterized by odd and disturbed thought patterns (particularly those relating to paranormal activity), along with perceptual distortions that lead the individual to attribute excessive personal significance to normal events. However, these abnormalities are much less severe than in schizophrenia, and typically do not include hallucinations or extreme delusions, which signify a complete break from reality in many schizophrenics. Schizotypal individuals also display a difficulty with social relationships, which may stem from their odd beliefs and perceptions.

II: Schizoid personality disorder is characterized by a feeling of separation (hence "apart"), coldness, and apathy toward others, and is not associated with the listed symptoms.

1032. B is correct. Borderline personality disorder is characterized by an unusual intensity of emotions. Individuals with BPD often have trouble seeing people in anything other than black-or-white terms (as wholly good or completely evil). In addition, these views and associated emotions are prone to sudden flips to the opposite extreme based on minor provocations.

A, C, D: BPD is not marked by emotional unavailability, miscomprehension, or devaluation.

1033. C is correct. People with NPD lack empathy toward others. As a result, they have trouble seeing the impact of their attempts to prop up or affirm their own self-esteem on the people around them. Their social and romantic relationships tend to be superficial, as they do not have interest in (and indeed have trouble comprehending) the needs and wants of others as opposed to their own.

A: Narcissists do have emotions, though they tend to be self-centered.
B, D: These choices are close! Narcissists often lack self-esteem or self-regard, and their behavior is an attempt to secure it through external validation. However, this question specifically asks about the way in which those with NPD deal with others, rather than the "why."

1034. B is correct. Antisocial personality disorder, also known as sociopathy, is characterized by a distinct lack of emotional affect toward things that would provoke a strong emotional response in other people, particularly those involving sympathy or remorse. Sociopaths do not feel regret for harmful actions in the same way that "normal" individuals do, and they tend to see people as means to an end; in other words, they lack a "conscience." As a result, they tend to lack internal compunctions against engaging in harmful (and often criminal) behavior, and when combined with the impulsivity that also frequently marks this disorder, they are far more likely to land in the prison system than people with the other personality disorders listed.

1035. B is correct. Many personality disorders are especially interesting because they are categorized as ego-syntonic. This term means that symptoms are not painful or frustrating; rather, individuals with the disorder see their condition as rational or normal.

A, C, D: These terms are not commonly recognized.

1036. C is correct. Freud's theory of the personality includes three components. The id represents a person's base, animalistic, and often unconscious wants and urges, while the ego represents rational self-interest. Last of all, the superego contains the internalized moral codes of the individual's society. These three components mutually oppose each other and fight to control behavior. In this case, the superego won.

D: The libido, a part of the id, sums up wants and urges related to love and sexual desire. According to Freud's ideas of childhood and development, it is this component that often relates to various fixations.

1037. D is correct. Other than this example, all of the listed experiments are cases in which external influences were able to determine behavior, overriding what individuals would describe their "normal" personalities to be. In contrast, Piaget's experiments, which assessed the abilities of children at various ages to perceive things like object permanence or the viewpoints of others, did not involve an external influence that provoked behavior deviating from the norm.

A: Here, the external influence on the "guards," who were suddenly placed in a position of power, caused them to manifest such cruel and uncaring behavior that Zimbardo called an early halt to the experiment.
B: In the case of Milgram's experiment, test subjects who described themselves as independent-minded were convinced to give another subject increasingly painful electric shocks, even to the point where the confederate acting as the other subject pretended to die. Here, the actual participants dramatically changed their behavior based solely on repeated commands from the perceived authority running the experiment.
C: In Bandura's "Bobo doll" experiment, children who witnessed adults act aggressively toward a doll were much more likely to themselves attack and beat the doll than those who did not.

1038. D is correct. In Kohlberg's view, the pre-conventional stage (which is characteristic of small children) involves moral motivations in which decisions are made based on their direct consequences, such as punishment, and particularly in relation to the self.

A: In the conventional stage, moral judgments are made through comparison to society's rules and expectations.
B: Kohlberg did not outline an "unconventional" stage.
D: In the post-conventional stage, moral decisions are based on abstract principles like fairness and universal human rights.

1039. D is correct. Goldberg's five dimensions are agreeableness (the degree to which one values getting along with others), extraversion (the degree to which one engages with people and the external world) conscientiousness (a person's level of self-discipline and focus on achievement) neuroticism (the degree to which one experiences negative emotions like anxiety, depression, or anger) and openness to experience (the amount of value placed on novelty, creativity, and variety of experiences). Rigidity is not a factor on this list!

1040. C is correct. Biological theories of personality emphasize the genetic and evolutionary roots of personality over environmental influences or life choices. From the correlation given for social liberalism, we see that identical twins hold views that are highly correlated, while fraternal twins (who are only as genetically related as regular siblings) correlate significantly less.

A: Psychoanalytic theories emphasize Freud's idea of the unconscious and his three divisions of personality. Nothing in the data has Freudian implications.
B: Humanistic theories emphasize man's drive for self-actualization.
D: Situationist theories focus on the effects of external environmental factors. The data shown actually imply that the opposite – genetic influences – strongly influence social views.

1041. C is correct. Intrinsically motivated activities are those that we desire to engage in due to internal factors. In other words, we are intrinsically motivated when we do something because it is enjoyable or rewarding. In contrast, actions are extrinsically motivated when they are rewarded or otherwise motivated by outside forces.

A, D: If Dave mows the lawn to earn money, he is not doing so out of internal, personal motivation.

Whether he loves money or not is irrelevant; he is mowing the lawn to gain a tangible reward.

B: Since Pauline is motivated by her final class grade, she is extrinsically motivated.

1042. A is correct. This child is already intrinsically motivated to play with the science kit, as evidenced by the fact that she does so for hours on her own with no outside rewards. Research has shown that offering rewards (extrinsic motivation) to people who are already intrinsically motivated actually makes them less willing to engage in the task. For this reason, leaving the child alone is preferable to rewarding her in any predictable way.

1043. C is correct. A drive is a feeling of tension that results from some need, whether physiological or more complex. According to the drive reduction theory, we are motivated to act to reduce drives, as they are generally unpleasant.

A: This describes reflexes, not drives.
B: Drives usually are not pleasant. Additionally, drive reduction theory posits that we act to reduce, not increase, drives.
D: This more closely describes instincts, which differ subtly from drives. Instincts are biologically innate from birth and do not need to be taught to individuals of the species in question. Drives, in contrast, are (usually) short-term urges to fulfill a need.

1044. A is correct. The Yerkes-Dodson law posits that a person will perform best on a task when he is moderately aroused, or physically and mentally alert. At very low arousal levels, the person will not be involved enough to do well at the task, while at high levels, he may be too nervous or agitated to perform at his best.

B: This shows the opposite of the Yerkes-Dodson relationship.
C, D: The correlation between quality of performance and arousal is not linear.

1045. B is correct. The expectancy-value theory states that motivation is the product of both "expectancy," or how well we predict a certain activity will go, and "value," or our predicted benefit from completing the activity. Choice B describes a course in which the student predicts moderate success and a high amount of value.

A: Here, we see a course with high expected success but little to no value. Since this theory gives motivation as the product of expectancy and value, a value of zero should result in a motivation of zero regardless of the success expected at the endeavor.
C: Again, motivation = expectancy × value. An expected chance of success of zero thus yields zero motivation as well.
D: This choice reflects the same expectancy as choice B, but less value to the student.

1046. C is correct. A primary drive is one that springs from a basic physiological need, while a secondary drive is one that might relate to, but does not directly come from, such a need. The most common examples of primary drives are hunger and thirst. However, the drive to earn money is a secondary motivation, regardless of what that money will be used for. Additionally, a desire to eat food when one is not hungry stems from a social rather than a physiological requirement, and the aggression tied to sports, similarly, is not based in a primary biological need.

III: This choice is the only primary drive of the four descriptions given. Finding shelter in very cold weather directly results from the human body's need to remain warm.

1047. B is correct. Drives are unpleasant urges or tensions, like thirst, resulting from unmet needs, like the lack of hydration. According to drive reduction theory, we base our actions on our motivation to reduce these drives.

A: Drive augmentation theory does not exist. Since drives are generally unpleasant, we would not want to "augment," or enhance, them.
C, D: While these are theories of motivation, they relate to excitement and external rewards, specifically.

1048. C is correct. The opponent-process theory, which is often used as a model to explain drug addiction, states that many human behaviors have two opposing components. This can be used with regard to emotional responses. For example, a drug addict feels pleasure (the euphoria associated with certain neurotransmitter) when he takes the drug, but withdrawal (the lack of these neurotransmitters, causing unhappiness) when he stops. Even more interestingly, the opponent-process theory also relates to physical symptoms. Since heroin is a depressant, the drug addict's body compensated by "speeding itself up" after many instances of taking the drug, with an increased heart rate, shaky muscles, etc. While the addict did not notice this while he was still on the substance, once he stopped, this "opponent process" became the only thing he experienced and caused withdrawal symptoms.

A, D: These are both incorrectly defined theories of motivation.
B: While arousal theory is properly defined here, the desire to maintain a certain arousal level does not specifically relate to drug withdrawal.

1049. C is correct. According to Maslow, individuals must fulfill the needs at the bottom of the pyramid first before moving upward to higher-level goals. This occurs because more basic needs, like hunger and thirst, are distracting and prevent attention from being given to aims like earning love and gaining the esteem of others. If this individual is on the "love / belonging" rung of the pyramid, he must have met his physiological and safety-related goals.

1050. D is correct. Maslow hypothesized that individuals must fulfill the needs at the bottom of the pyramid first before moving upward to higher-level goals. Since self-actualization appears immediately above the "esteem" section of the diagram, it will be this individual's next focus.

A: Love and belonging are below esteem, not above it. On Maslow's pyramid, more basic needs are lower and must be satisfied first.
B: This improperly defines self-actualization, which is the human desire to fulfill our full potential in some way.
C: As the most basic of the needs shown, physiological requirements will be met before turning attention to more abstract goals.

1051. B is correct. The cognitive component of this man's attitude includes factors such as memories and impressions, which are represented by his recollection of his childhood trauma on a freeway.

A: The affective component, which consists of emotions and feelings, is best represented by this man's general feeling of dislike toward freeways.
C: Here, the behavioral component is simply this man's avoidance of freeways. In other words, it includes behaviors or actions that stem from his attitude.

1052. C is correct. Attitudes tend to have the most predictable effects on behavior when they are highly specific. Since this person specifically wishes to build muscle and not just to become more athletic, it is very likely that he or she will start lifting weights.

A: Although alcohol is present at some parties, this correlation is not nearly as strong as that described in choice C. Perhaps this individual will attend parties that do not involve drinking, or perhaps he or she will simply refrain from alcohol consumption while out.
B: While avoiding fast-food restaurants might be associated with being more fit, this is not a causal relationship.
D: Joining an online dating site is only one potential way to combat loneliness. For all we know, this individual will instead choose one of the many other alternatives, like attending club meetings or joining a sports team.

1053. B is correct. Public declarations can strongly impact personal behavior. In other words, an individual who openly speaks out in favor of recycling might be more likely to actually recycle, lest someone see him or her act hypocritically.

1054. B is correct. Role-playing is simply the adaptation of one's behavior to fit a role, often for an educational or training purpose. Research has shown that role-playing can absolutely impact attitude. Here, a young German previously had Jewish friends and was presumably fairly unbiased against Jewish culture. When he joins the army and must take on the entirely new role of a soldier, he starts to feel and act in anti-Semitic ways.

A, C, D: These scenarios do not directly involve role-playing; choices A and D simply depict individuals doing their jobs. Choice C does not even seem to include a change in attitude, as we do not know the wealthy child's previous feelings toward less affluent individuals.

1055. C is correct. The elaboration likelihood model draws a distinction between the central and peripheral methods of persuasion. When a listener is persuaded via the peripheral route, he or she does not truly analyze the points made by the speaker. Instead, the listener clings to superficial qualities like the speaker's sense of humor, attractiveness, or the general impression made on others. Thus, a peripherally-engaged listener has the ability to form general impressions of the speaker's presentation, but does not attempt to gain specific ideas that relate to the qualities of his points.

A: The anti-control peripheral listeners lack the motivation to deeply analyze the speaker's argument. In part, they likely do not wish to be convinced that they are mistaken.
B: Since the anti-control listeners are only engaged in the peripheral, or relatively unimportant, components of the speaker's presentation, they currently do not possess the ability to delve deep into the arguments and points made.

1056. C is correct. If the anti-control listeners who changed their attitudes were engaged by peripheral components of the speaker's argument, then their attitude changes will likely be only temporary. According to this model, central components are ones that relate intrinsically to the speaker's point of view, while peripheral aspects include shallower qualities like his or her appearance or perceived impact on others. The more central the components that convince the listener, the more likely any attitude shift provoked by the argument will be long-term and meaningful.

1057. A is correct. Social cognitive theory claims that individuals learn attitudes and behaviors by observing those of others. Of these choices, only the child who seems to let violent movies shape his behavior demonstrates actions that were impacted by observation.

B: Here, the actions and behaviors of this boy are not influenced by observation. He simply seems to prefer others who resemble his own family.

C, D: These scenarios do not depict individuals whose behavior or attitudes stem from the emulation of others. Instead, they seem to involve the contradiction of or purposeful rebellion against mimicking other people.

1058. C is correct. Cognitive dissonance theory explains how the ideas that we use to justify difficult decisions tend to take root as perceptions of our personal values. In other words, we "talk ourselves into" valuing things that reinforce the belief that we made the correct choice. Here, if the unhappy couple decides to remain married because marriage is an important bond that is worth some short-term discontent, they will likely internalize that idea as being inherently truthful and moral in order to justify their decision. If they choose to divorce, they might gain a strong belief in the notion that personal happiness is more powerful than adherence to a social construct, such as marriage.

1059. C is correct. Since so much time and effort has already been devoted to their marriage, this couple might justify continuing the relationship simply due to their high assessment of the work invested in it. This factor relates to cognitive dissonance and explains the disproportionate value that can be placed on such relationships, even when they are unhappy.

1060. C is correct. Role-playing can cause an individual to adopt new attitudes that were not previously present. Here, however, we know only that this soldier has a criminal history and that he displays violent behavior. For all we know, this man may have always been like this; we cannot conclude that his attitude has changed because of his role as a soldier.

A, B: These scenarios are great examples of the potential effect of public declarations on behavior. The motivational speaker, who makes a living portraying himself as confident and successful, is likely to continue maintaining such a self-image. Similarly, the chef is more likely to change his glove habits after yelling at another person for a similar offense. Both of these individuals are partially influenced by the fear of being perceived as hypocrites if they contradict their own declarations.

D: Here, this person would not have previously felt qualified to make medical decisions. However, his role as a caretaker influences him to feel more confident about these choices.

1061. D is correct. Nonassociative learning involves a change in response to one stimulus, in contrast with associative learning, which forms a connection between multiple stimuli or between a stimulus and a response. Habituation, in which the response to a stimulus decreases after it is administered multiple times, is an example of nonassociative learning. The same is true for sensitization, in which multiple administrations of the same stimulus amplify the response.

A: Both of these behaviors are most commonly defined as modifications of the stimulus required to produce a response during classical conditioning. Classical conditioning is a form of associative learning. Note that while habituated stimuli can also be subject to discrimination or generalization, these phenomena are not actual types of habituation.
B: Again, habituation properly answers this question, but classical conditioning does not.
C: Both of these types of learning are associative.

1062. B is correct. The process occurring here is habituation, or the decrease in response during repeated exposures to the same stimulus. Both habituation and its opposite, sensitization, are types of nonassociative learning.

A: Learning can be either associative or, as in this example, nonassociative.
D: Associative learning includes phenomena like classical and operant conditioning. It involves establishing a more complex connection between multiple stimuli or between a stimulus and a response.

1063. A is correct. Stimulus discrimination occurs whenever the conditioned stimulus required to generate a response is made more specific. Its opposite, stimulus generalization, occurs when a specific stimulus was previously needed to provoke a response, but similar stimuli are now able to do so as well.

II: While very closely related, these two terms are not identical. Dishabituation refers to the recovery of an old response to a previously habituated stimulus. Sensitization, in contrast, is actually defined as an intensification of a response after multiple administrations of the same stimulus. In other words, dishabituation involves the strength of a response returning to its previous value, while in sensitization, the response becomes even stronger over time.
III: Escape and avoidance learning are types of negative reinforcement, as an unfavorable stimulus is removed to facilitate an increase in the desired behavior.

1064. D is correct. Habituation involves a decrease in the magnitude of the response after repeated exposures to the same stimulus. A classic example of habituation involves hearing loud or initially bothersome noises. After being subject to the noise for a period of time, a normal person learns to ignore it and eventually does not even notice the stimulus. Donnie, who cannot experience habituation, would be unable to do this.

A: This relates more to muscle fatigue, which is independent of habituation.
B: This choice discusses the adaptation of sensory neurons. In this phenomenon, a neuron responds less to a certain stimulus over time, and in the future may not fire at all. Sensory adaptation is distinct from habituation, a form of nonassociative learning.
C: This relates to observational learning and even to the cerebellum, but not to habituation.

1065. A is correct. Mirror neurons are most related to observational learning and are also thought to play a role in empathy. The "Bobo doll" experiment tested the tendency of children to mimic behavior exhibited by adults; this is a clear example of observational learning.

B: Inattentional blindness relates to selective and divided attention, not observational learning.
C: Harlow's study dealt with attachment, which does not directly relate to mirror neurons.
D: This study relates to the two-factor theory of emotion, an alternative to the James-Lange and Cannon-Bard theories. This concept does not directly involve mirror neurons.

1066. C is correct. Ataxia is actually defined as an inability to perform proper muscle movements.

As such, it does not directly relate to learning or memory.

A, B, D: All three of these choices relate to either learning, memory, or both, and all three terms are properly defined.

1067. D is correct. Since the children are using observational learning to mimic the adults' behavior, they will display heightened activity in their mirror neurons. Mirror neurons are thought to be located in the premotor cortex (part of the frontal lobe), as well as in parts of the parietal lobe.

1068. B is correct. Vicarious emotions, which closely relate to empathy, are emotions that are felt "on the part of" someone who is being observed. In other words, when a person watches another individual do something embarrassing, he may vicariously feel embarrassment even though he (the observer) did not do anything to be ashamed of. Note that vicarious emotions can be felt even if the person being watched is not experiencing them himself.

A: Since the child is not actually doing what the adult is doing (as far as we know), this choice is incorrect.
C: Mirror neurons are hypothesized to play a role in empathy in addition to the mimicking of physical behaviors.
D: Piaget's preoperational stage includes children of approximate ages 2-6. The teenagers in this experiment are much too old to be part of this stage.

1069. D is correct. *Aplysia californica* is a species of sea hare studied by Eric Kandel and his team in their famous experiments on non-associative learning. Habituation refers to a decrease in response after the same stimulus is administered multiple times. Since we wish to restore the original withdrawal response, we want dishabituation to occur. Shocking the animal, or presenting another new stimulus, can bring the previously-habituated response back to a stronger level.

A, C: While both of these choices are partially correct, we want to promote dishabituation, not habituation.
B: This research deals with nonassociative learning. Since *Aplysia californica* is a very simple animal (similar to a sea slug), it likely would not respond well to associative learning. As aspects of operant conditioning, reinforcers and punishments are associative.

1070. B is correct. Problem solving is a complex psychological process with the goal of finding a solution to an issue, usually one requiring multi-step logic or reasoning. The trial-and-error approach is often used to reach this goal. In this method, various attempts are made to solve the problem in different ways, until one attempt proves successful (or until the organism gives up).

A, D: Observational learning occurs when an organism watches another individual in order to learn a behavior. Classical conditioning involves the pairing of an originally neutral stimulus with one that produces a known, instinctual response. Both of these methods of learning are generally simpler than problem solving.
C: Shaping involves the reinforcement of actions that are simple at first, then progressively build up to form more complex behaviors. It often relates to operant conditioning, but is not directly connected to problem solving.

1071. C is correct. An unconditioned stimulus is one that naturally produces a particular response (for example, food causing Pavlov's dogs to salivate). In contrast, a conditioned stimulus does not evoke an innate reaction, but was associated with the unconditioned stimulus until that reaction was "learned." A neutral stimulus, not an unconditioned stimulus, becomes conditioned.

1072. A is correct. Acquisition is defined as the conversion of a neutral stimulus into a conditioned one through a pairing with an unconditioned stimulus.

B: An unconditioned stimulus naturally evokes a particular response before any learning takes place. It is thus impossible (and unnecessary) to change an unconditioned stimulus into a conditioned one.
C: A conditioned stimulus is one that produces a reaction due to its association with an unconditioned stimulus. One of these types of stimuli cannot transition into the other.

D: This is stimulus generalization, not acquisition.

1073. D is correct. The bell, originally a neutral stimulus, has become conditioned, causing Johnny to perform the conditioned response of standing up. Here, Johnny also begins to respond to similar, but not identical, stimuli. This "broadening" of an originally specific stimulus is the definition of generalization.

1074. B is correct. Originally, the sight of the teacher turning toward the closet does not evoke any particular response in the toddlers. However, associating it with the unconditioned stimulus of fun (from the toys and blocks) gradually causes the children to respond with increased activity. Thus, the teacher's turning has become a conditioned stimulus.

A: The toys and blocks always produce a positive response in the children, at least during the course of this situation. They therefore play the role of unconditioned, not neutral stimuli.
C: The children, not the teacher, are performing the conditioned response here.
D: The children do not initially respond to the teacher's movement toward the closet. Unconditioned responses are those that occur naturally, before learning has taken place.

1075. B is correct. A primary reinforcer is one that is naturally positive or negative, even before any associative learning takes place. Food and water are classic primary reinforcers, making I correct. A secondary reinforcer is not reinforcing on its own, but has become associated with a primary reinforcer. Choice III is correct because the clicking sound has no natural benefit or risk, but has turned into a usable reward through its pairing with the primary reinforcer of food.

II: The tokens described here are secondary, not primary, reinforcers.
IV: Water is a primary reinforcer.

1076. C is correct. Stimulus discrimination occurs whenever the conditioned stimulus required to generate a response is made more specific. In other words, any stimulus within a broad category (all flashing lights) originally was able to elicit a conditioned response. Through selective reinforcement of some stimuli over others, this category was narrowed to certain light flashes only.

A: This is stimulus generalization, not discrimination.
B: This is an example of extinction.
D: This situation exemplifies shaping, or the teaching of a complex behavior by rewarding simple, then successively more difficult, steps.

1077. B is correct. The sound of the drawer is not initially reinforcing on its own. During days 1-3, it provokes no response in the cat, making it a neutral stimulus. While it later becomes conditioned through its pairing with the unconditioned stimulus (food), that occurs much later in the experiment (days 14-20).

1078. C is correct. Spontaneous recovery is the reappearance of a conditioned response even after the associated conditioned stimulus has become extinct. Here, the student stops pairing the drawer-opening noise with food during days 14-20. Extinction has clearly taken place by day 21, when the cat begins to ignore the drawer. However, the cat's conditioned behavior of running toward the drawer briefly reappears in days 25-26.

1079. D is correct. This is an example of second-order conditioning, in which a neutral event is paired with a previously conditioned stimulus instead of an unconditioned one. While this process can be effective, the question mentions that the rabbits have only recently formed an association between the coins and food. If so, the coins cannot possibly be a more effective reinforcer than food itself, and the scientist has no reason to use them.

A: If the tone is only occasionally paired with the coin, it will take longer for the rabbits to associate the two stimuli.
B: This doesn't make sense. Spontaneous recovery occurs after the response to a conditioned stimulus has already been extinguished. The question does not mention the extinction of the association between the coin and food. Even if the change in choice B were implemented, it would reduce the efficacy of the procedure, since pairing the tone with a reinforcer in the process of extinction would be less likely to motivate the rabbits to respond.
C: Increasing the time that the tone (the neutral stimulus) is paired with the coins sounds like a

good idea. However, remember that the coins are not innately reinforcing, and that they have only recently become conditioned. If the coins are presented without food (whether with or without the tone) for a long enough interval, the rabbits' response to them will extinguish. Thus, this is a worse answer than choice D, which involves the unconditioned reinforcer of food.

1080. A is correct. Associative learning is that which establishes a connection between multiple stimuli or between a stimulus and a response. In general, associative learning includes both operant and classical conditioning. Habituation, or the decrease in response during repeated exposures to the same stimulus, is a type of non-associative learning.

C: Instrumental conditioning is another name for operant conditioning.

1081. D is correct. A continuous reinforcement schedule rewards every instance of a desired behavior, making it more effective than any other schedule at increasing the frequency of that behavior. The downside is that the behavior will extinguish rapidly once reinforcement is stopped, but this doesn't matter because the coach doesn't need it to persist for very long.

A, B: Both of these schedules are slower at producing learning than continuous reinforcement.
C: Intermittent reinforcement includes both variable-interval and fixed-interval schedules, making this a clear wrong answer. Also, intermittent schedules are slower at producing learning than continuous ones.

1082. B is correct. Shaping involves the reinforcement of actions that are simple at first, then progressively build up to form more complex behaviors. Choice B is a classic example of shaping, since the boy is rewarded for small movements (picking up his toothbrush), then for more complicated but related actions, and finally is able to complete an entire task.

A: Shaping is not spontaneous; it requires each step to be reinforced. This choice only mentions reinforcement of the child's initial use of "da-da."
C, D: These situations involve changes from one complex behavior to another, not a

progressive increase from simple actions to more complicated ones.

1083. B is correct. The instructor contacts his students after certain amounts of time, not a certain number of responses, making this either a fixed-interval or a variable-interval schedule. Since he checks in after inconsistent time periods ("every one to three days"), it must be variable-interval.

1084. A is correct. Fixed-ratio schedules are highly susceptible to extinction because the subject immediately notices when reinforcement stops. Variable-interval schedules, in contrast, result in slower extinction, since the subject continues to hope that a reward is coming.

B: Escape and avoidance learning are types of negative reinforcement.
C: All forms of punishment are intended to decrease the frequency of specific behaviors.
D: This is an extreme statement, and depends on both the frequency of reward and the definition of "effective." Variable schedules, for example, are much more effective at resisting extinction after reinforcement has ceased.

1085. A is correct. The researcher wants to increase the frequency of lever-pulling, meaning that he must use reinforcement, not punishment. This scenario involves negative reinforcement because something aversive is being removed. Finally, while both avoidance and escape learning are types of negative reinforcement, avoidance is relevant in this case because the rats have the potential to avoid the cold temperature entirely. Escape learning, in contrast, would not involve a warning sound, requiring the aversive condition to be present at least briefly before the rats act to end it.

1086. C is correct. The library is aiming to decrease the number of instances of overdue books, meaning that they must be using some form of punishment. Specifically, this situation exemplifies negative punishment because something desirable (library privileges) is being taken away.

1087. B is correct. Variable-ratio schedules are the most effective at quickly producing large numbers of responses.

A: Neither of the two schedules will be better able to make the child truly enjoy reading - that's entirely up to him.

C: The total amount of the reward has nothing to do with the reinforcement schedule. This manager could simply use a variable-interval schedule with small, infrequent cash bonuses.

D: The yoga teacher requires a reinforcement method that is resistant to extinction, which is true for both variable-ratio and variable-interval schedules.

1088. A is correct. Classical conditioning involves involuntary actions, while operant conditioning involves conscious, voluntary ones. Specifically, classical conditioning pairs a neutral stimulus with an unconditioned one, like pairing the ringing of a bell with the presentation of food. Over time, the neutral stimulus becomes "conditioned" and elicits the same response as the unconditioned stimulus (e.g., dogs begin salivating when the bell is rung).

B: Operant, not classical, conditioning focuses on rewards and punishments. In addition, unconditioned responses occur naturally and would not need to be rewarded.

C: Both operant and classical conditioning are types of associative learning.

D: Operant, not classical, conditioning was introduced by B. F. Skinner, who performed experiments in his famed "Skinner boxes."

1089. D is correct. From the graph, we can see that the frequency of hand-raising remains fairly constant until around day 25, when it increases sharply. At that point, the professor must have changed his reward procedure to one that is more effective. Continuous reinforcement, in which every instance of a desired behavior is rewarded, results in faster learning than any other reinforcement schedule, as well as fast extinction. It would thus explain the results shown in the scatter plot.

A: This is a fixed-ratio schedule.

B: This accurately describes a fixed-ratio schedule, but it involves students being rewarded more rarely than in the original procedure, which would not produce the sharp increase in hand-raising shown in the graph.

C: This is a form of negative punishment, since something desirable (movie privileges) is being removed.

1090. C is correct. From the graph, it is evident that instances of the desired behavior drop sharply after day 50. This decrease in behavior after reinforcement has ceased is called extinction.

B: While the original professor was using positive reinforcement, the new teacher did not establish any method at all, and certainly did not punish the students.

1091. B is correct. Self-concept refers to our full set of conscious ideas about ourselves, while identity is generally used in relation to the categories we belong to. In other words, our identity might be racial ("I am an Asian-American"), gender-based ("I am a woman"), etc. In contrast, our self-concept includes less group-based qualities like personality traits and our perceptions of our own bodies.

A: This is the reverse of the correct answer.

C, D: Both of these choices describe the actual self and the ideal self, two facets of the self-discrepancy theory, instead of self-concept and identity.

1092. D is correct. Self-efficacy refers to a person's perspective of his or her ability to complete tasks. In other words, it is our belief in our own "effectiveness" or competence in a certain field. In contrast, self-esteem is a person's measure of his or her own value or worth as a person. An individual may have high self-efficacy without having high self-esteem, and vice versa.

A: A person might have full confidence in his ability to complete a task well while still having low self-esteem. This is especially true if he perceives factors other than his own competence (like attractiveness or height) as impactful on his value as a person.

1093. B is correct. Identity can be defined as our relationship within categories or groups of people. For example, one person can have a racial or ethnic identity ("I am an African-American"), a gender identity ("I am male"), and a class identity ("I am a member of the middle class"), plus more, all at once.

A, C: Since self-concept refers to a person's entire collection of conscious ideas about himself, he can only have one self-concept.

1094. C is correct. The self-discrepancy theory includes the actual self (how we perceive ourselves to be in reality), the ideal self (how we wish we could perceive ourselves), and the ought self (how we think others wish they could perceive us).

A: These are the three parts of the psyche according to Sigmund Freud.

1095. D is correct. Since this statement involves Jeffrey blaming his loss on one of his personal traits (strength), it best exemplifies an internal locus of control. Individuals with internal loci believe that they have the power to influence the outcomes of events in their lives.

C: A statement that would better exemplify an external locus might be something like, "I lost because it was rainy outside." In that case, Jeffrey would be showing that not he, but an outside force (the weather), controlled the competition.

1096. A is correct. Both gender identity and class identity are properly defined here.

III: This choice is switched with the definition in IV. Ethnic identity involves the non-physical aspects of a person's culture.
IV: Racial identity refers to a person's genetic physical features, such as dark skin or curly hair, that are used to place him or her in a particular category.

1097. D is correct. An individual's locus of control is based on his perception of his own level of involvement in, or control over, the events that occur in his life. A person with an external locus of control might answer with "I failed a test because the professor didn't like me," while someone with an internal locus might say "I didn't do well because I didn't study enough, but if I had studied, I could've changed the outcome."

A: This question would be a good gauge of self-esteem, not locus of control.
B: This question relates more to self-efficacy (our perception of our ability to "get things done") or even optimism, but not locus of control.
C: This question simply asks when a challenge was most recently faced, so it will not directly tell

the psychiatrist anything about locus of control, self-esteem, or self-efficacy

1098. D is correct. Self-esteem refers to a person's perception of her own value or worth as a person. Since we do not know whether any of these students base their perceived self-worth on math ability, the table cannot possibly give us enough information.

A: High predicted scores correlate more with self-efficacy (our perception of our own competence in completing tasks) than self-esteem.
B: This would only tell us how accurately the student was able to gauge his own math ability, and nothing else.
C: While this would certainly show us the student who is best at math, it would not tell us anything about self-esteem.

1099. D is correct. Learned helplessness occurs when an individual gives up and stops trying to avoid an aversive consequence. It generally happens over time, after long periods during which the individual's actions do not have the desired result. An external locus of control is closely correlated with learned helplessness, since people with such loci feel like they do not have a large amount of power to control their own lives. Denise performed much worse than expected on the first and second exams, so her poor score on the third could have resulted from this phenomenon.

A, B: Simply performing poorly is not a marker of learned helplessness. Additionally, the question asked which student developed learned helplessness during the year; Max performed consistently on all three exams and did not do noticeably worse than his initial prediction.
C: This is backwards; an internal locus of control is unlikely to lead to learned helplessness.

1100. C is correct. The ought self is one of the three parts of the self-discrepancy theory. It refers to our perceptions about what others want to see in us. Since this woman is thinking about how others would like to perceive her, the ought self is the most relevant choice.

A: The actual self includes perceptions of how we actually are.

B: The ideal self includes our thoughts about how we should be or how we wish we were.

1101. D is correct. This statement sums up the defining principles of social interactionism, a perspective that is also closely tied to language.

A: Social interactionism does not revolve around self-improvement.
B: The concept of universal meaning would be rejected by a true social interactionist. This perspective holds that we discover and define our own systems of meaning throughout our lives.
C: This is Freud's concept of psychosexual development.

1102. A is correct. The concept of the looking-glass self states that we shape our identities based on our perception of the way others view us. In other words, regardless of Anthony's actual personality or of his friends' actual thoughts about him, since he believes that his friends view him as successful, he will feel like a successful person.

B: Others' *actual* perceptions of us are not the focus of the looking-glass self model.
C: Anthony's optimism is irrelevant to this question.
D: Similar to choice B, Anthony's actual behavior is not the focus of the looking-glass self idea. Instead, this model is centered on our ideas of what others think of us.

1103. B is correct. Vygotsky proposed the idea that some tasks are easily accomplished by a child, while others are well outside the child's abilities. However, some skills fall in between those two categories and can be completed with help from a more knowledgeable other. In this way, the young person is able to learn to perform the action on his own.

A: Kohlberg dealt with moral decisions, not actions like writing one's name.
C: Erikson focused on a number of conflicts that, according to him, help define our identity. For example, a newborn infant must face the conflict of trust vs. mistrust. The question stem does not indicate that one of Erikson's conflicts is being experienced.
D: Freud proposed that two components of identity are the id (the unconscious, instinctive part) and the ego (the conscious, realistic part). This has little to do with the question stem.

1104. B is correct. The ought self is part of self-discrepancy theory, which was originally put forth by Edward Higgins. While that specific name is unlikely to appear on the MCAT, you should understand the other components of this theory, which are the actual self and the ideal self. You should also know that this idea is not Freudian.

I: This is one of Freud's five stages of psychosexual development, seen from approximately age 5 to puberty.
II: The death instinct is uniquely Freudian, and is often mentioned along with the sex / survival instinct. Now, these concepts are often called the Thanatos and Eros drives, respectively, though Freud did not use those exact terms.
III: Freud often referenced a fixation as an excessive focus on a certain aspect of the libido. For example, a child could suffer from an oral or an anal fixation.

1105. C is correct. The question stem focuses on moral decision-making, the development of which was studied by Lawrence Kohlberg. Kohlberg's three main stages of moral reasoning are preconventional, conventional, and postconventional. Since James is an adult who usually makes ethical decisions based on the desire to conform, he exhibits conventional moral reasoning.

A, B: Erikson's stages do not relate specifically to moral choices. In addition, his initiative vs. guilt conflict happens around ages 3-6, while integrity vs. despair, his last stage, occurs after age 65.
D: James does not appear to have reached this stage, in which individuals base decisions around complex ideas such as the overall good of humanity.

1106. B is correct. Groupthink is marked by excessive stereotyping, which is the opposite of this choice. While B might be true in some cases, Janis' symptoms of groupthink mentioned a high level of stereotyping of outsiders, not a low level of stereotyping of those present within the group.

A, C, D: All three of these choices are among Janis' eight hallmarks of groupthink.

1107. C is correct. According to the table, only in the game stage can a child consider the roles of multiple other individuals at once. Since this is exactly what this child is doing (not to mention the fact that he is performing in a Shakespeare play!), he must currently fall within this developmental stage.

1108. B is correct. Mead identified the generalized other as a hallmark of late-stage development of the self. When a person assumes the perspective of this other, he is able to imagine the expectations of others and of society as a whole, and can plan his behavior accordingly.

A, D: These are not actual psychological terms.
C: The "more knowledgeable other" relates to Vygotsky's zone of proximal development. It is not connected to Mead's work with the self.

1109. D is correct. Mead proposed the concepts of the I and the me, which make up two parts of his theory of the social self. Here, the me represents our internalized set of societal values and attitudes – in other words, it includes the attitudes and behaviors that we have learned are socially acceptable, and that result in the socialized self. Choice D best sums up this concept.

A: This is most closely related to the id, which is Freud's concept, not Mead's.
B: Again, this describes a Freudian concept: the superego.
C: With the mention of free will and individuality, this choice more closely resembles Mead's I, not the me.

1110. C is correct. Deindividuation involves the loss of aspects of one's own identity when one joins a group. A person experiencing deindividuation will instead acquire aspects of the group identity, and will be prone to actions that he or she otherwise would never consider. Much of this stems from the relative anonymity provided by the group, which can lead to a mob mentality. Young individuals who join gangs are classic examples of those likely to undergo deindividuation.

A: Social loafing, or the tendency to expend less effort than usual during group projects or tasks, is not related to the question stem.
B: Social facilitation is a phenomenon in which those who typically perform well on a task tend to do even better in front of a group. Again, it is unrelated here.

D: Individuation refers to the general process of identity formation that begins when we are very young. While this answer is close, Erika has been experiencing individuation long before joining the clique, so it is not a process that she would be at risk of participating in.

1111. D is correct. Situational attributions are those that blame the external environment or chance, while dispositional attributions place blame on the person's own personality. Here, Dave initially attributed his failure to his professor, not himself; as such, he made a situational attribution. He next vacillated toward blaming his own lack of hard work (a dispositional factor), before finally settling on luck as the cause (another situational attribution).

1112. A is correct. Attribution theory is a field of study that deals with our perceptions of the causes of events and behaviors. As such, it includes misattributions and biases (like the fundamental attribution error and the self-serving bias), but also applies to situations where we properly attribute causes or motivations.

B: This is the reverse of the correct answer; attribution theory deals with motivations or explanations, not consequences.
C, D: These choices describe the self-serving bias and the fundamental attribution error, respectively. Again, these biases certainly relate to attribution theory, but are not sufficient definitions of the concept as a whole.

1113. D is correct. The fundamental attribution error refers to the common tendency to blame others' actions on dispositional, rather than situational, factors. For example, you easily could have concluded that your cousin was also stuck in traffic (a situational factor), but instead decided to attribute his lateness to his personality. In contrast, self-serving bias describes our tendency to attribute bad things that happen to ourselves as being due to situational factors (bad luck, etc.) instead of dispositional factors.

1114. A is correct. Kelley's cues include distinctiveness (how likely the person is to behave this way in different situations), consensus (how many other individuals typically exhibit the behavior, or how accepted it is in society), and consistency (how similar the person's behavior is over time). Familiarity is not one of these types of cue.

1115. B is correct. A consensus cue focuses on the closeness of the behavior to that which is typically expected by society. In other words, when people act just like everyone around them, we tend to attribute their behavior to situational factors. However, when individuals deviate from common social behavior, we use that deviation to assess their personality. Here, most individuals on the train clearly were either unwilling or incapable of stopping the mugging. Since Mike did so, the motivation behind his actions will be cited as dispositional and the public will gain a favorable impression of his personality.

   A: Distinctiveness cues relate to a single person's actions during a variety of scenarios. If the person tends to act similarly in all situations, we see those actions as inherent to his or her personality; if not, we tend to consider situational factors. Since we have no idea how Mike typically acts in other scenarios, this choice is not accurate.
   C: This is the reverse of the proper interpretation of a consensus cue. When individuals align with the consensus (in other words, when they act similarly to most other people), we generally perceive their behavior as situational, not dispositional.
   D: Familiarity cues are not one of the three types of cues used to make attributions.

1116. A is correct. Kelley's covariation model outlined three factors that we use to make attributions: distinctiveness cues, consensus cues, and consistency cues. Distinctiveness cues monitor a single individual's actions across a variety of scenarios. If the person tends to act similarly in all situations, we see these actions as inherent to his personality; if not, we tend to attribute the unusual actions to situational factors. Here, Kyle is cruel in one situation, but kind in virtually all others. As a result, Amanda rates his behavior

within his fraternity as high in distinctiveness and does not let it sway her good opinion of him.

   B: Consensus cues focuses on the closeness of the behavior to that which is typically expected by society. The question stem does not mention Amanda's comparison of Kyle's behavior to societal expectations.
   C: Consistency cues relate the person's behavior over time, not across a variety of circumstances at roughly the same time.

1117. B is correct. The correspondent inference theory focuses on the perception of a person's behavior as corresponding to his or her personality. In other words, it attempts to dictate when we will make dispositional attributions. According to this theory, we tend to make such attributions when the action is seen as intentional, when it directly harms or benefits us, and when it differs from what is typically expected by society. In choice B, the woman does something unusual to purposely and directly benefit you. As a result, you will likely perceive her to be a good or generous person.

   A: The correspondent inference theory states that we tend to attribute accidental behaviors to situational factors.
   C: Similarly, actions that comply with others or with societal expectations are typically seen as situational, not as particularly relevant to an individual's personality.
   D: Like choice A, this action is portrayed as non-intentional, since the director had no choice but to fire the employees.

1118. A is correct. In short, the fundamental attribution error (FAE) is a human tendency to blame the behavior of others on dispositional, rather than situational, causes. Studies have shown that the FAE is more prevalent in individualist than collectivist cultures, likely because cultures that pride themselves on individualism are more focused on the personalities of certain members and less on outside factors that could affect the group. As a collectivist culture, Country A is the best answer to this "least" question.

1119. C is correct. The defensive attribution hypothesis stems from the human fear that terrible consequences might happen to us simply due to chance. To avoid being scared by this idea, we tend to blame the victims of an accident or to draw distinctions between ourselves and them (as in, "He's nothing like me, so this could never happen to me"). Here, Alice feels comforted by the idea (true or otherwise) that the young man was drinking and driving, as that is a behavior that she can avoid.

A: This statement is the opposite of what the mentioned hypothesis would predict. Alice will not want to consider the idea that she, too, could die in a car accident.
B: This is a misinterpretation of the word "defensive." Hopefully, Alice won't need to worry that the boy's death was actually her fault.
D: Feeling sad due to empathy does not relate to the defensive attribution hypothesis.

1120. B is correct. The fundamental attribution error refers to a common tendency to blame others' actions on dispositional, rather than situational, factors. Specifically, it most often relates to actions that are personally harmful to us, such as the classic example of being cut off by another driver. Here, Margaret blames another player's actions on bad intentions, as though the player maliciously wanted to undermine Margaret's abilities. For all Margaret knows, the player could have been distracted or caught the ball for a completely unrelated reason.

A, D: The fundamental attribution error relates to our interpretation of the cause of someone else's behavior, not our own.
C: While this answer may initially appear tempting, Alex seems to understand that the referee is having some health issues in his family. This represents a situational, not a dispositional, factor.

1121. B is correct. Heuristics are cognitive shortcuts and include the representativeness heuristic, the availability heuristic, and several more. While we tend to focus on the mistakes these heuristics can lead to, they are generally helpful. Many complex decisions would take much longer to evaluate without such shortcuts.

C: This describes a script, not a heuristic.
D: This is a description of the halo effect.

1122. A is correct. Situational attributions are those that relate to the environment or outside factors.

In this case, you could have blamed the other driver's personal traits, but instead attributed his behavior to an external circumstance (being late and in a hurry).

B: Dispositional attributions are those that relate to the person's character or personality. Here, assuming that the other driver cut you off because he was just a rude person is a dispositional attribution.

1123. D is correct. The self-serving bias is our natural tendency to cite dispositional factors when we succeed, while attributing our failures to situational, or external, causes. Here, the student uses a dispositional attribution when he does well in tennis, but blames his failures on outside factors unrelated to himself.

A: In this example, the student uses situational attributions both when he succeeds and when he fails.
B: This more closely reflects confirmation bias.
C: Here, the student uses dispositional attributions in cases of success and failure.

1124. C is correct. A schema is a conceptual framework that we use to organize information on a certain topic. Similarly, a script is a specific schema that is used for activities involving steps in a certain order. Finally, heuristics are mental shortcuts that assist in decision-making processes.

III: Iconic memory is a subtype of sensory memory; specifically, it relates to visual information regarding our surroundings. Sensory memory is extremely short-lived and does not play a notable role in decision-making.

1125. B is correct. At first, the mother has not formed a belief regarding the new variant of flu, but happens to see stories about its deadliness. When she subsequently starts to believe that the flu is very dangerous, this exemplifies the availability heuristic, since the mother relied on information that was readily available (the news stories) as the sole basis for her assessment. Later, she falls victim to belief perseverence when she ignores the a statement about the flu's recovery rate and perseveres in her belief about flu's deadliness.

A, D: Since the mother had not initially formed an opinion about the flu, confirmation bias and belief perseverance should not come first.

C: Object permanence is related to infant and child development, not bias.

1126. A is correct. The just-world hypothesis is a bias toward believing that the world is fair – that good actions are rewarded and bad actions are punished. This is very similar to a belief in karma, or that people eventually get what they deserve.

B: This is the halo effect, or tendency to use limited information to categorize people as either good or bad.
C: This is not technically a bias at all, and could simply be a normal preference. At the very least, it does not relate to the just-world hypothesis.

1127. C is correct. The representativeness heuristic involves predicting the outcome of events based on similar events that have occurred in the past. While this can involve assumptions of similarity (for example, assuming that two patients with similar symptoms suffer from the same disease), it also includes this fallacy. Previous events (the births of four female children) are used to assume that future children will be male, based on a desire to group these events together into a representative sample.

1128. D is correct. This choice is the only one that does not predict the outcome of an event based on previous results. The probability of having a child of either gender is 50% regardless of the genders of the older children.

1129. B is correct. According to the actor-observer bias, we tend to attribute the behavior of others to dispositional factors, while making situational attributions about our own actions. In other words, we are either the "observer" (as we watch others) or the "actor" (as we ourselves behave). Here, George is the observer when he blames Robert's offensive joke-telling on his personality, and the actor when he tells the same kind of joke himself.

1130. D is correct. The availability heuristic involves the use of information that is readily available to make decisions. In this scenario, the most readily accessible pieces of knowledge (comments from others, etc.) actually contradict the theorist's views, but he ignores them in favor of his radical belief.

1131. B is correct. Low levels of either serotonin or norepinephrine can lead to major depressive disorder.

II: It is high, not low, levels of glucocorticoids that contribute to depression.
IV: Dopamine is typically released during pleasurable experiences and would not trigger depression at high levels.

1132. C is correct. Bipolar II disorder is marked by manic episodes that alternate with intervals of major depression. These states of mania are slightly lower in intensity than those experienced by patients with bipolar I disorder.

A: Major depressive disorder is characterized by depressive episodes only.
B: SAD is a type of major depressive disorder with a seasonal onset.

1133. B is correct. The biopsychosocial approach looks at the intersection between the sociocultural, psychological, and biomedical influences on mental health to create a holistic outlook.

1134. D is correct. Reactive attachment disorder is observed when an infant fails to healthily attach to its caregivers or parents. Additional symptoms can include withdrawal, sadness, a lack of interest in games, and a tendency to avoid social interaction. These hallmarks are similar to those of autism spectrum disorder, so a patient cannot be diagnosed with both RAD and autism.

C: Although the listed symptoms are similar to depression, a RAD patient does not need to have MDD.

1135. C is correct. This situation describes the exact symptoms for conversion disorder. Often times the development of conversion disorder comes after the patient experiences a traumatic event. The patient develops a neurological disorder with no clear neurological cause for the symptoms. After a thorough exam rules out any underlying neurological diagnosis a final diagnosis of conversion disorder can be reached.

A: Acute stress disorder is a less intense version of PTSD
B: Generalized anxiety is defined by undue worrying about many different things and does not involve any neurological symptoms.

1136. D is correct. While twins do appear to share the same psychological disorder at a higher rate than regular siblings, we do not have nearly enough information to draw a conclusion. In addition to the issues mentioned in the question stem, we also have no data regarding the overall prevalence of mental disorders in twins versus non-twin individuals.

1137. B is correct. If two random people are more likely to share the same disorder than members of a set of twins, this implies that genetics actually reduce the observed similarity between mental illnesses suffered.

1138. B is correct. Seasonal affective disorder is defined as a seasonal onset of major depressive disorder, typically during the winter. It is correlated with the abnormal metabolism of melatonin. This fits the trend of these patients, who reported decreased levels of happiness in the winter for multiple years.

1139. A is correct. This is not a valid treatment for seasonal affective disorder. SAD stems from a lack of sunlight, which promotes abnormalities in the metabolism of melatonin and results in diminished serotonin levels. If anything, choice A would worsen this condition.

    B: Although antidepressants would probably not be the best option, SAD is technically a form of major depressive disorder.
    C: Bright light therapy is intended to counteract the direct cause of SAD: a lack of sunlight.
    D: Therapy, while not specific to this scenario, can always serve as effective treatment for mental disorders that may have an underlying psychological root.

1140. B is correct. Somatic disorders typically arise secondarily to bodily symptoms. One example is illness anxiety disorder, a form of anxiety and fear of developing a severe medical condition. Another is conversion disorder, in which patients may even be blind but have no physical reason for this phenomenon.

1141. B is correct. Schizophrenia is a psychotic disorder with a variety of subtypes and a wide array of symptoms. However, to be diagnosed with schizophrenia, an individual must have either disorganized speech, delusions, or hallucinations. He or she also must have had at least two classic schizophrenia symptoms for at least six months. Patient B has had delusions, specifically delusions of persecution, for a full year. She also displays negative symptoms, which are those that represent a lack of some healthy behavior. "Flat affect," or emotionless speaking, and reduced motivation are negative symptoms.

    A: Though hallucinations are a symptom of schizophrenia, this man needs to have at least one other symptom (delusions, negative symptoms, catatonia, etc.) to obtain a diagnosis.
    C: This description sounds like Alzheimer's disease, not schizophrenia.
    D: Patient D likely has a somatic disorder, possibly conversion disorder, which is marked by sudden physical symptoms that appear to have no physiological basis.

1142. C is correct. Negative symptoms are those that represent missing or lacking behavior. For example, avolition (lack of motivation) and flat affect (lack of emotion in speech or facial expression) are negative symptoms.

    A: The word "negative" here refers to the lack of normal behavior, not an adverse symptom. Paranoid delusions are positive, not negative, symptoms.
    B: Though the lack of motivation is a negative symptom, the definition here describes positive ones.
    D: We have no reason to believe that hallucinations do not decrease with medication. Additionally, this does not relate to negative symptoms.

1143. D is correct. According to the stress-diathesis model, individuals develop schizophrenia due to a combination of two factors: genetic predisposition (the "diathesis") and trauma, abuse, or other stressors during their lifetimes (the "stress"). Oscar is thought to be experiencing the prodromal phase, or pre-schizophrenic onset phase, of the disorder. Additionally, he has undergone recent stress, making him a good candidate for this researcher to study.

    A, B: We have no reason to believe that these individuals possess the diathesis or have experienced any extreme stress. Thus, while they may be useful subjects in some sort of control

group, they are not especially relevant here. Additionally, Amelie is far younger than the average age of schizophrenic onset, which is 18 for men and around 25 for women.
C: While this man is at least schizophrenic, he has not experienced recent stress and is thus not a great fit for experiments evaluating this model.

1144. D is correct. Positive symptoms are symptoms that are felt in addition to healthy human experience. In contrast, negative symptoms represent missing or lacking behavior. Anhedonia, or the lack of enjoyment of activities that were previously fun, is a negative symptom; it also applies more to depression than to schizophrenia. Anterograde amnesia, or the inability to form new memories, is not seen in schizophrenic patients.

I, IV: Disorganized speech and delusions are classic examples of positive symptoms, along with hallucinations.

1145. C is correct. The data in the table clearly shows that BPD diagnoses are much more common in white, healthy females than in white, healthy males. While this data isn't nearly enough to draw a conclusion to other races or health statuses, the answer choice says that BPD "may" have a higher rate in females, which cannot be disputed. In fact, research has shown that BPD is around twice as common in females as in males.

A, D: This table measures prevalence (the percentage of people currently diagnosed with a disease), not incidence (the percentage of people newly diagnosed each year). Even if we assume that this sample is representative, if 2.8% of all individuals polled currently have BPD, it would be unreasonable to expect that same number to be newly diagnosed in a single year.
B: We cannot ascertain that this is true. It's equally possible that individuals who already have BPD happen to be drawn to alcohol and drugs.

1146. A is correct. The DSM-V groups personality disorders into three clusters, labeled A, B, and C. While intimate knowledge of this categorization method is not high-yield on the MCAT, it is helpful to know which disorders are most similar. Both narcissistic personality disorder and BPD fall under Cluster B in the current

DSM, along with two others: histrionic and antisocial personality disorder.

B, C: While these are personality disorders, they are part of different "clusters" than BPD.
D: SAD is not a personality disorder, nor is it even categorized as a disorder of its own in the DSM-V. Instead, it is listed as a subtype of major depressive disorder (MDD).

1147. A is correct. Ego-syntonic disorders are those that align with the patient's self-concept. In other words, instead of feeling sick or abnormal, the patient feels good and may even enjoy her disease, considering it to be part of her usual behavior. A number of personality disorders, as well as anorexia nervosa, are classic examples of ego-syntonic conditions.

B: Anxiety disorders generally give their sufferers a large amount of trouble and would not be described as ego-syntonic.
C, D: Ego-dystonic diseases are perceived by the patient as "wrong" or in conflict with the patient's true self. This does not match the description in the question stem.

1148. D is correct. Catalepsy refers to the decreased, stiffened muscle movement that is often seen as a symptom of catatonic-type schizophrenia. Alternatively, this type of psychotic disorder can result in the exact opposite: dramatically increased motor activity or rates of speech.

A: This description matches echolalia, not echopraxia.
B: Long periods of depression that are not sufficiently severe to receive a diagnosis for MDD are known as dysthymia, not anhedonia.
C: The description given here is the exact opposite of mania, which involves elevated mood, lessened sleep, and temporarily increased self-esteem.

1149. C is correct. Schizophrenia is the most well-known of the psychotic disorders, while schizotypal personality is a disorder with some similar features, including odd behavior, avoidance of social situations, and belief in magic or other supernatural phenomena.

A: Both of these conditions are personality disorders. The question states that Roxanne has a psychotic disorder.

B: This is the reverse of the information given in the question stem. Roxanne should have a psychotic disorder, but has a personality disorder in this choice, while the opposite is true for Marisol.

D: Bipolar I disorder is a mood disorder, not a psychotic one.

1150. C is correct. Multiple personality disorder is the old name for dissociative identity disorder (DID).

A, B: While these are also dissociative disorders (or, in the case of dissociative fugue, common experiences of those with dissociative disorders), they do not match the information given in the question.

D: Hypochondriasis is the previous name for somatic symptom disorder, which is not dissociative.

1151. D is correct. An individual's in-group is anyone with whom he or she feels a sense of belonging. Here, this player's teammates, the fans who support him and cheer him on, and his parents could all be considered to be part of his in-group.

II: The crowd in the opposing team's stadium is likely not going to be supportive of the player or his team. These would be counted as part of his out-group.

1152. D is correct. Although the mentioned politicians do not support the pilot's mission, it is never stated that they oppose the military itself or its soldiers. It is also not explicitly stated that the pilot supports his own mission. Of the choices, it is most likely that the pilot will feel most akin to a fellow citizen.

A, B, C: All of these form part of the pilot's out-group. However, it is possible that the enemy pilots could be considered part of the American's reference group, since they play similar roles but target each other's allies.

1153. A is correct. A reference group may consist of anyone against whom one compares and evaluates oneself. Here, the American soldiers might have compared their professionalism, success, or even the attractiveness of their uniforms to the French and, from these references, evaluated their own worth.

C: Since the French and American soldiers were allies, it is unlikely that the French soldiers would have been part of the Americans' out-group.

D: A primary group must have consistent, direct interaction with the individual. In this scenario, the Americans and French were still housed in separate trenches despite their allegiance.

1154. A is correct. A primary group is made up of people with whom an individual has close relationships that last a long time. A secondary group is defined by more temporary, less intimate relationships.

1155. D is correct. The concept of social facilitation deals with the performance of tasks in front of other individuals. According to this idea, simple or familiar actions can often be executed better in a social environment, but advanced or unfamiliar tasks are performed better in private. Thus, golfers who are not yet familiar with the game's intricacies would likely perform more poorly in public than when alone.

A, B: Both of these choices contradict the Yerkes-Dodson law, a theory related to social facilitation. This law posits that individuals perform best when moderately aroused, as opposed to at either end of the arousal spectrum.

1156. B is correct. The stereotype content model sorts relationships along two scales: competence and warmth. When two individuals are part of different in-groups, they tend to perceive each other with either low or high competence, meaning that they either consider them incapable and worthy of pity or capable and competitive. As Patricia is actively vying against Ellen on the dance floor, she certainly would view her as highly competent. Additionally, since the two girls are no longer close friends, we can assume that Patricia sees Ellen with low, not high, warmth. These factors combine to produce an envious stereotype.

A: Patricia probably used to see Ellen this way! But, since the two are now competing to the detriment of their friendship, choice B is a better answer.

C: If this were true, Patricia would see Ellen as having low competence. This stereotype is generally reserved for groups that are liked but pitied, such as very old people and those with some disabilities.

D: A contemptuous stereotype stems from a position of low perceived warmth and low competence. As Ellen is highly competitive at dance, this viewpoint is unlikely.

1157. A is correct. A reference group consists of those against whom the first violinist can compare and evaluate herself. This is most true of her fellow violinists.

C: The conductor might be considered to be part of the violinist's in-group.
D: The violinist's parents and siblings would be considered her family or primary group.

1158. B is correct. Social loafing references the idea that individuals tend to expend less effort when performing a task as part of a larger group. Here, the government auditor does a worse job because his mistakes are less likely to be noticed. Since the job is shared by everyone in his team, he feels that some of his responsibility is diffused to others.

1159. D is correct. None of these psychological terms capture this scenario.

A: Social facilitation describes how individuals who are executing familiar, simple tasks perform better in public, while those who are less familiar with the activity tend to perform worse. However, this contestant is described as experienced.

1160. A is correct. This statement describes the bystander effect. If many members of the crowd indifferently walk by, it becomes less likely that others will act to relieve the biker's plight.

B: This describes social loafing.
C: Although the bystander effect is sometimes described as bystander apathy, this is because empathy is diffused through the crowd to a point where individuals in the crowd feel less empathy for the victim.

1161. B is correct. The likelihood that a subject would help the elderly woman decreased as the number of people on the street increased. This is a classic example of the bystander effect, the phenomenon in which people tend not to help individuals in distress when other people are present. It

has been shown (and is demonstrated in this experiment) that the frequency and timeliness of help decreases as more and more people are near the distressed individual.

A: Deindividuation is a phenomenon in which a person in a group loses his or her sense of self, becomes part of an anonymous crowd, and may be in a group exhibiting mob mentality. This does not apply to this situation described.
C: Social facilitation refers to the changes in an individual's performance level when he knows he is being observed. It applies to the performance and execution of tasks, not to the act of helping a person in distress.
D: Groupthink refers to a tendency of groups to make incorrect or poor decisions when members wish to maintain harmony and form a group consensus. It does not apply here.

1162. C is correct. In social situations, the behavior of an individual often changes significantly, as large groups provide a level of anonymity and thus remove a sense of personal identity. This is known as deindividuation. In this scenario, the people wearing masks deviate from their typical behavior because they experience deindividuation.

A: This situation exemplifies peer pressure.
B: The leaders in this case are experiencing group polarization.
D: This is an example of social loafing.

1163. C is correct. This answer gives the basic definition of "identity shift." This concept was introduced by Wendy Treynor, who focused on conflicts (both internal and external) and the way that we change our personal behavior and standards to minimize them.

1164. D is correct. Groupthink is a phenomenon in which members of a group arrive at incorrect or suboptimal conclusions due to a desire to maintain harmony among themselves. In this situation, the town leaders make a decision that they know is not the best due to their desire for the group to get along.

A: Peer pressure relates more to the intention to avoid rejection and maintain approval from others. Since the question references decision-making in particular, groupthink is a better answer.

B: While deindividuation is another group phenomenon, it refers specifically to an individual's deviation from usual behavior due to the relative anonymity provided by the group. It does not particularly relate to decision-making.
C: Social loafing relates to the effort expended by participants in a group task, which has nothing to do with the question.

1165. B is correct. This answer describes the basic principles of group polarization and groupthink.

C: This is the exact reverse of the correct answer.

1166. B is correct. Two major components of group polarization are informational influence and normative influence. Informational influence relates to group members' desire to be accurate or "right" about an idea. When a member holds a minority opinion, she may assume that she is wrong and change her mindset to reflect that of the majority. This explains why the dominant viewpoints end up being reflected in the ideas that emerge.

A: Normative influence refers to the pull a group member feels to be socially desired, accepted, admired, or simply liked. It does not particularly relate to decision-making or the perceived "correctness" of an idea.
C, D: These answers are not actual influences that contribute to group polarization.

1167. C is correct. Informal social control includes the less overt methods of social control (shame, criticism, ridicule, etc.). This form of control causes people to abide by societal norms even without any explicit law or regulation.

A, B: These are examples of formal social control.
D: Although not an actual law (and certainly easier to break), the actions of the volunteers still represent an overt or formal form of social control.

1168. B is correct. Peer pressure is seen when social equals, or peers, exert an influence that causes someone to change his or her attitudes, behavior, or values. In this situation, Eric's fellow employees exert a subtle influence on him that makes him more inclined to go out for lunch. This pressure is not direct coercion – in other words, he will not be fired if he does not comply

– but he is still pressured because he wishes to remain part of the group.

A: While deindividuation is another group phenomenon, it refers specifically to an individual's deviation from usual behavior due to the relative anonymity provided by the group. Eric has not become anonymous or begun to lose touch with his own identity; he simply feels pressure to conform.
C: Groupthink is the social phenomenon in which groups make poor decisions based on a desire for harmony. The question stem never mentioned group decision-making.
D: Social facilitation refers to the changes in an individual's performance level when he knows he is being observed. It applies to the performance and execution of tasks, not to pressures exerted to conform.

1169. C is correct. Group polarization is the tendency for opinions, beliefs, and decisions to become more extreme in a group setting than the actual, privately held beliefs of group members. In the above example, attending the meeting caused members to shift from predominantly "weakly agree" to "strongly agree."

1170. D is correct. Peer pressure certainly can be a good thing. For example, consider a young man who feels influenced to do his homework and perform well on his math exams because all of his friends are good students. On the other hand, peer pressure can be negative as well. Imagine a second young man who chooses to use drugs at a very young age because all of his friends are doing the same.

A: Peer pressure doesn't always cause an individual to exhibit deviant behavior.
B: This statement relates more to deindividuation, not peer pressure.

1171. C is correct. Impression management theorists define the authentic self as who the person "actually is," including both positive and negative aspects. In contrast, the ideal self is who the person would like to be, while the tactical self is that which is used to manipulate or when trying to conform to expectations.

A: These are the three Freudian components of identity.
B: Middle stage is not a psychological term.

1172. D is correct. In order to confer a biological advantage, a behavior must increase reproductive success or assist in survival. Protecting against threats while enhancing access to resources and mates would accomplish this.

B: This is a potential disadvantage of aggression.
C: This statement is not true.

1173. C is correct. The proximity effect posits that we experience greater attraction to people who are physically closer to us.

A: Reciprocal liking refers to our tendency to like people better when they like us.
B, D: These refer to memory and do not represent principles of attraction.

1174. C is correct. This is the definition of the term in question.

D: This represents a secure attachment style.

1175. A is correct. Studies of human attraction have found that we gravitate toward people who possess the golden ratio, or the body and facial proportions that relate in a particular numerical way.

1176. B is correct. Studies have shown that we tend to be attracted to people if we think that they are attracted to us. This phenomenon is called reciprocal liking. This clearly matches the experimental results.

A: This is not a principle of attraction.
C, D: These are two terms for the same concept, which refers to the idea that humans prefer stimuli to which they have been previously exposed.

1177. D is correct. Network support is that which provides another individual with a sense of belonging. By establishing a group meeting and inviting the troubled students, she could help them feel less isolated and more connected.

A: This represents esteem support, not network support.
B: This choice epitomizes material support.
C: This represents emotional support.

1178. C is correct. Empathy refers to the ability to identify with another person's emotions or "walk a mile in their shoes." Research suggests that both men and women feel empathy relatively

equally, but women are more likely to express it outright (by crying, verbally expressing genuine concern, etc.)

A, B: These statements are not true at all.
D: This statement relates more to the tendency of males and females to express emotion (anger, etc.), rather than their feelings of empathy.

1179. B is correct. Self-handicapping refers to a cognitive defense strategy in which people create excuses and "put themselves down" in an attempt to reduce the disappointment of themselves and others when (or if) they fail.

1180. D is correct. The dramaturgical approach uses the metaphor of a theatrical performance to describe impression management tendencies. When an individual is being observed and is trying to present a certain image, he is acting according to his front-stage self. In contrast, back stage references the person's actions when he is "off stage," not attempting to conform to an audience, and free to act without the restraint of his front-stage persona.

1181. C is correct. Foraging behavior relates to the act of searching for food and resources. Since eagles consume fish as part of their diet, this choice is a perfect example.

A, B: These represent mating behaviors. Choice B directly describes the act of mating, which choice A refers to preparation for potential young. Neither of these activities relate to the hunt for food.
D: This is aggression, not foraging.

1182. D is correct. Foraging refers to exploratory or searching behavior with the intent of finding food. Many species demonstrate the ability to learn such behaviors, both from their own experimental trial and error and by observing other members of their population.

A, C: Animals certainly can learn foraging behavior. Additionally, these choices can be eliminated for other reasons: foraging is not a result of gene expression alone, and countless species outside of humans and primates exhibit such actions.
B: Humans do not have to teach animals to forage. If this were true, many animal species would have a much harder time surviving.

1183. C is correct. The dove's strategy involves first displaying aggression, but running in the face of an escalated conflict. Thus, when two doves encounter each other, both will display aggression initially. However, neither will escalate the fight. For this reason, neither will have a reason to run and they will share the resource. This can also be inferred from the table, where the result of a dove vs. dove meeting is given as W/2.

A: If this were true, the payoff of such a meeting would be given as 0.
B: The question stem never indicates that doves actually fight, only that they attempt to display aggression at first.
D: Similar to choice A, if this statement were accurate, the result would be given in the table as W (100% of the relevant resource).

1184. B is correct. When two hawks meet, both will display aggression and escalate to a fight. In this situation, one hawk must inevitably win because neither of the two birds will flee. Thus, Bird A will win about half of the time and lose the other half. As such, he will gain (on average) half of the resource in question. However, as he will also risk the cost of injury, that value must be subtracted from his overall reward.

A: The winner would take the entire resource, not half.
C: We cannot assume that Bird A will always win. In fact, this choice contradicts the payoff given by the matrix.
D: The question gives no mention of a hawk fleeing under any circumstance.

1185. D is correct. From the matrix, we see that a hawk has two possible payoffs: $V/2 - C/2$ (when fighting another hawk) and V (when meeting a dove). If the dove population, the hawk will win fewer clear victories, causing V to drop. In contrast, since the hawk will now fight more often, C (the risk of an injury) will rise. As a result, the V/C ratio will decline, causing the hawk population to dwindle. With fewer predators, the population of doves can then climb until a new V/C ratio is achieved.

A: While a hawk will always beat a dove in a direct meeting, if fewer doves exist, the hawks will be forced to fight more often and take the corresponding cost (C). As such, the hawk

population can still drop and re-establish an equilibrium.
B: According to the question stem, doves never actually fight.
C: This is the reverse of what will actually occur.

1186. C is correct. The selfish gene, proposed by Richard Dawkins, expresses the idea that organisms display altruistic behavior to ensure the survival of genes that they have in common with the organism receiving the benefit of the behavior. In other words, while this selflessness does not directly appear to benefit the animal displaying it, it actually helps carry on that animal's genes through related organisms. The closer the relationship between the two individuals, the more likely altruism is to manifest.

A: This is simply an untrue statement.
B: In theory, this may be true, though the idea of selfless versus selfish animals does seem somewhat oversimplified. But all else aside, this does not explain the concept mentioned in the question stem.
D: This statement is extreme; the concept of the selfish gene simply explains why altruism can be beneficial, not that it always is.

1187. A is correct. Fisherian selection suggests that, if a strong enough mating preference for elaborate ornamentation exists, this preference could undermine natural selection even if the feature is otherwise non-adaptive. Fisher hypothesized that, since males of a certain appearance propagate with females who strongly prefer such features, this cycle can continue over many generations. In other words, males progressively become more extreme in appearance, while females continue to desire this type of display. This positive feedback mechanism is called the Fisherian runway.

B, C: These concepts help explain altruistic behavior, not ornamentation.
D: This is the basis of game theory, which here relates to a hypothetical comparison of organisms competing for resources. It does not explain ornamentation in male animals.

1188. B is correct. According to the concept of sensory bias, an organism can gain mating opportunities by exploiting a preference that is already desirable in a non-mating context. A classic example involves guppy fish in Trinidad and Tobago. Guppies have a natural preference for shiny orange objects because they resemble orange fruit, an especially desirable type of food. In this system, orange fish are mated with more frequently due to this seemingly evolutionarily neutral preference.

A: This statement does not relate to sensory bias.
C: This sentence is far too extreme. Biological fitness, or the tendency to propagate and pass down genes to viable offspring, depends on a variety of factors.
D: The example given here relates more to Fisherian selection than to sensory bias.

1189. D is correct. The question stem asks for two things: a facial expression and a behavior conserved across species. The baring of teeth fits both of these requirements, as it is an expression that many species use as a sign of aggression.

A: This behavior is not a facial expression and seems to happen only with bees.
B: This is a strictly human phenomenon. While several facial expressions seem to be universal across all or most cultures, the question asks for a behavior displayed "between," not "within," species.
C: Rising up on back legs represents body language, not a facial expression.

1190. C is correct. According to foraging theory, foraging behavior will be selected for when it results in the greatest gain in resources with the least cost. This group of monkeys experiences a large gain (a new, easy-to-obtain food source) with minimal cost, at least as far as we know.

A: The cost of traveling multiple miles would outweigh the benefit of a small number of berries.
B: This statement describes a large cost (losing fights), meaning that the behavior of this bird is unlikely to be highly evolutionarily beneficial.
D: If these tigers eat their offspring before they reach reproductive age, they will be strongly selected against. Either tigers who do not exhibit this behavior will become more prevalent, or this species will die out.

1191. A is correct. ^{238}U, like all isotopes of uranium, has an atomic number of 92. Remember, it is this value that determines an element's identity, so all isotopes of the same element must have the same atomic number. This number is equal to the number of protons in one uranium atom.

B: This stems from the assumption that the mass number is always equal to twice the number of protons. Remember, an isotope does not need to have the same number of protons as neutrons. Here, for instance, uranium has 92 protons and 146 neutrons.
C: This is the mass number of this element, not the number of protons.

1192. C is correct. Radon-222, like all isotopes of radon, has 86 protons. It therefore must have (222 – 86) or 136 neutrons, yielding a ratio of 86:136. This relationship can be simplified to 43:68.

A: This results from the mistaken idea that elements tend to have equal numbers of protons and neutrons. Instead, we must actually calculate these numbers from the mass number and the periodic table.
D: While the number of protons is correct here, the number of neutrons is far too large.

1193. C is correct. For our purposes, we can treat protons and neutrons as though they have the same mass. However, this question references "uncharged nucleons," meaning neutrons. One ^{35}Cl atom contains 18 neutrons, so half of that number gives us 9. Since the mass of one neutron is 1.67×10^{-27} kg, we can multiply by 9 to get 1.5×10^{-26} kg.

A: This is the mass of all 18 neutrons rather than half of them.

1194. B is correct. When denoting the mass and atomic numbers of an element, the mass number is written above the atomic number. The mass number is simply the total number of nucleons, or (120 + 125) = 245. The atomic number is the quantity of protons, not neutrons.

A: This flips the relative positioning of the two values.
C: Remember, atomic number denotes the number of protons.
D: This choice makes both of the mistakes mentioned above.

1195. C is correct. Atoms are the tiny units that compose matter; they consist of electron(s) and a central nucleus. The term "ion" refers specifically to charged atoms. Luckily, the number of moles of a substance directly relates to the number of particles by way of Avogadro's number, so a direct comparison of moles is all we need to find our answer. However, two moles of a molecule is not equivalent to two moles of atoms. For example, since methanol has a formula of CH_3OH, it contains a total of six atoms per molecule. In contrast, NaCl will dissociate into two ions: Na^+ and Cl^-. In this solution, we have 0.25 moles of NaCl, which can be thought of as (0.25 moles * 2) or 0.5 ions. For atoms, we have (2 moles * 6) + (0.25 * 2) or 12.5; remember that ions are technically atoms as well! This gives us a ratio of 0.5:12.5 or 1:25.

A: This is simply the ratio of moles of ions to moles of methanol.
B: This is the ratio of molecules of NaCl to atoms in methanol, but neglects to involve moles or account for the two ions that NaCl produces.
C: This answer is incorrect in several ways. It likely was derived from a 6:2 ratio, or the ratio of atoms in methanol to ions in NaCl. However, this question asks for the ion-to-atom ratio. Additionally, this answer does not account for the moles present.

1196. C is correct. The number of molecules or atoms in one mole is reflected by Avogadro's number. Thus, we can divide the number of molecules by this number to find moles. $(1.2 \times 10^{92}) / (6.0 \times 10^{23}) = 2.0 \times 10^{68}$.

B: This result likely stems from a mistake with scientific notation. When dividing one exponential term by another, the exponents are subtracted, not divided.
D: This is the product of the number of molecules and Avogadro's number. Instead of multiplying the two, we need to divide.

1197. A is correct. To find the molar mass, we must first calculate the number of moles of Molecule 2, then divide the given mass by this value. $(6 \times 10^{26}$ molecule) / $(6 \times 10^{23}$ molecules per mole) = 1000 moles. 200 g / 1000 moles yields a molar mass of 0.2 g/mol.

C: This is equivalent to the number of moles divided by the mass. Remember to pay attention

to units! Molar mass is measured in g/mol, not mol/g.
D: This choice probably results from an order-of-magnitude error.

1198. B is correct. Calcium chloride will dissociate into three ions in water. This reaction occurs as follows: $CaCl_2 \rightarrow Ca^{2+} + 2Cl^-$. In other words, for every 1.5 moles of overall compound, 4.5 moles of ions will be present.

A: This choice assumes that calcium chloride does not ionize in water.
C: This value would be the approximate number of ions if $CaCl_2$ did not dissociate. However, the question asks for the number of moles of ions.

1199. C is correct. The molar ratio of phosphorus (P) to P_4 is 4:1. Thus, given 0.5 moles of P_4, there are 4*0.5 or 2 moles of phosphorus.

A: This is 0.5 / 4, not 0.5*4.
B: While this accurately describes the number of moles of P_4, it does not account for the 4:1 ratio of P to P_4.
D: This choice neglects to account for the data in the table, which states that 0.5 moles of P_4 are present.

1200. C is correct. A molecule is a general term for any distinct chemical structure that contains two or more atoms. A compound is a type of molecules that contains more than one element. For example, while O_2 is a molecule, it is not a compound because it contains oxygen alone. Methane is both a molecule and a compound, and because it contains four moles of hydrogen in each mole of itself, two moles of methane include eight moles of hydrogen.

IV: CH_4 does not ionize in water.

1201. A is correct. Electron affinity relates to an element's desire to gain an electron. For the majority of elements, this quality increases as you move upwards and to the right on the periodic table. However, the nitrogen-containing group is an exception to this rule. Carbon has an electron configuration of $[He]2s^22p^2$, so the addition of another electron would give carbon a half-filled p orbital and is thus highly favorable. Nitrogen, on the other hand, has an electron configuration of $[He]2s^22p^3$. Addition of another electron would alter nitrogen's half-filled valence state and produce a partially-filled orbital. Therefore, nitrogen will have a lower electron affinity than expected, making this choice more likely than the others.

B, C, D: These statements correctly reflect the periodic trends relevant to the relationship between carbon and nitrogen.

1202. B is correct. The table shows successive ionization energies for an unknown element. The first IE value is very small, indicating that it is very easy for this element to lose a single electron. However, the second ionization energy is higher than any other, implying that removing a second electron is energetically unfavorable. We can conclude that this electron is being removed either from a full or half-filled orbital. Alkali metals fit this trend; after the first ionization they have reached noble gas configuration, so removal of a second electron would disturb a complete octet and is highly energetically costly.

B: Alkaline earth metals would be expected to have low first and second ionization energies, since they must lose two electrons to reach a noble gas configuration.
C: Noble gases have very high first ionization energies, since an electron must be taken from a complete octet.
D: Halogens would not have second ionization energies that are so markedly higher than their first IE values.

1203. D is correct. First, we must determine what type of element is being ionized. Due to the very low first ionization energy value followed by the very high second IE, we can conclude that the element belongs in either the alkali metal or the oxygen-containing group. Next, we simply must add three electrons to each answer choice to find a configuration that matches either of these groups. Adding three electrons to choice D results in $1s^2 2s^2 2p^3 3s^2 3p^6 4s^1$, which is the ground state of potassium. As an alkali metal, potassium fits the data shown in the graph.

A: After adding three electrons, this configuration becomes $1s^2 2s^2 2p^3$, which is the ground state for nitrogen. The element shown in the figure does not match this group of the periodic table.

B: Adding three electrons makes this configuration $1s^2 2s^2 2p^5$, or the ground state for fluorine. The results shown in the table do not match those that would be seen with a halogen.
C: This configuration plus three electrons yields $1s^2 2s^2 2p^6 3s^2 3p^6$, which is the ground state of neon, a noble gas.

1204. A is correct. Atomic radius increases as you move down and to the left along the periodic table. Rubidium is the lowest and farthest to the left of these four elements, followed by strontium, oxygen, and fluorine.

C: While this choice is actually scientifically correct, the question asks for the elements to be placed in decreasing, not increasing, order.
D: This is the reverse of the correct trend.

1205. D is correct. To establish a complete octet, bromine needs only one additional electron. Therefore, when bromine adds an electron, it will become more stable and release energy. Potassium, in contrast, prefers to lose an electron to have a full octet. For this element, adding another electron is unfavorable and will require energy in an endothermic process.

1206. A is correct. Atomic radius increases as you move down and to the left along the periodic table. Therefore, potassium will generally have a larger radius than magnesium. However, be careful when dealing with charged species. Potassium that has been ionized has lost an electron, gaining the electron configuration of argon. This causes its effective nuclear charge to be distributed over fewer electrons, pulling them closer and reducing the radius of the ion. The uncharged species is thus larger than K^+.

1207. C is correct. Ionic character is determined by the electronegativity difference between bonded elements. Therefore, the pair with the largest difference will exhibit the most ionic character. The easiest way to examine this is to look for the atoms' distance apart on the periodic table. Hydrogen and fluorine are on opposite sides, meaning that hydrogen is relatively electropositive, while fluorine is actually the most electronegative of the elements. These two atoms are farther away than any other pair, resulting in the bond with the most ionic character.

1208. A is correct. Electron affinity can be defined as an elements' desire to gain an electron. Argon is a noble gas, meaning that it already has a complete octet. It therefore would have no desire to gain or lose electrons.

    B, C: Beryllium and sodium both have low electron affinities. Be desires to lose two electrons to reach a noble gas configuration, while sodium prefers to lose one.
    D: The formation of bonds indicates that carbon does desire to gain electrons, making this statement incorrect in relation to the question.

1209. C is correct. The electronegativity difference results in the oxygen group, which is more electronegative, withdrawing electron density from the carbon group. This leaves carbon with a partial positive charge, a characteristic of a good electrophile.

    A: Electron affinity has no direct effect on the polarization of bonds.
    B: While this is true, it is not the cause for the carbonyl carbon's electrophilic nature.
    D: Oxygen is electron-withdrawing, making this statement false.

1210. D is correct. Members of the alkali metals have one valence electron. When this electron is lost, these elements gain a noble gas configuration, making them very stable. For this reason, alkali metals have very low ionization energies and lose an electron extremely easily. In this reaction, hydrogen gas is produced and the metal forms its corresponding oxide.

    A: While alkali metals do have low electronegativities, this relates more to their ability to form ionic bonds, not their reactivity in water.
    B: Alkali metals have very low electron affinities. In fact, they are actively trying to lose one of their electrons to reach a stable noble gas configuration.
    C: Alkali metals are not catalysts for combustion reactions, nor would this explain their reactivity.

1211. C is correct. Alkali metals are located in the first column of the periodic table; they include sodium and potassium. These metals are highly reactive with water. Due to their extreme tendency to lose a single electron and reach a noble gas configuration, they serve as good reducing agents.

    III: Alkali metals form hydrides, such as NaH, when they bind to hydrogen. These compounds are actually basic, not acidic.

1212. B is correct. Noble gases are inert because they already possess a full, eight-electron valence shell. This configuration displays maximum stability.

    A: Noble gases do not form diatomic molecules.
    C: A half-full valence shell would only have four electrons, like carbon, not eight, like a noble gas.
    D: This choice describes a solid, not a noble gas.

1213. A is correct. Halogens have seven valence electrons. To obtain a stable noble gas configuration, they must pick up an additional electron. When an element gains an electron, it is reduced.

1214. D is correct. Two of the most well-known chemical hallmarks of transition metals are their ability to possess multiple oxidation numbers and their tendency to form brightly-colored compounds. This second characteristic stems from the arrangement of their d electrons.

    B: Some halogens are brightly colored in their atomic states. They do not, however, have multiple stable oxidation states.

1215. C is correct. All of the listed molecules are alkali metals, with the exception of beryllium, an alkaline earth metal. Alkali metals react especially well with water due to their low ionization energies, and they become more reactive as you move down the group. Therefore, Be is the least reactive with H_2O, while Li, Na, and K (in that order) are more so.

1216. A is correct. The oxidation state of atom 2 is +2, meaning that it tends to lose two electrons to form a stable valence shell. This is characteristic of an alkaline earth metal.

1217. C is correct. Let's begin with atom 1. The table states that it has an oxidation state of +1, making it a group 1 element. Next, we see that it forms a diatomic and an amphipathic oxide. Since Na, K, and Li (for example) never form diatomic species, the only element that fits this description is hydrogen. Next, atom 3 does not exist in a diatomic state, eliminating oxygen as a potential identity and leaving us with choice C.

1218. A is correct. Atom 1 has an oxidation state of -1, a clear characteristic of a halogen. For atom 2, the table lists multiple distinct stable oxidation states. This is typical of a transition metal, as these species possess a d subshell that can be filled, half-filled, or empty without losing large amounts of stability.

1219. C is correct. Calcium, as an alkaline earth metal, has a typical oxidation state of +2. It is not as reactive with water as are alkali metals, but it certainly will still react fairly rapidly. As a species that readily loses electrons, it possesses reducing potential. Finally, as a lone atom in space, this metal is diamagnetic, meaning that it includes only paired electrons. (While calcium acts slightly differently in metal form, this is outside the scope of the MCAT.)

1220. C is correct. All nitrate salts are soluble, so this test would not provide any new information.

A: Ion-exchange chromatography with subsequent titration could be used to determine the charge of the ion. While it is already known that its charge is positive, this method could distinguish between a +1, +2, +3, or +4 charge.
B: The most reactive elements with water are the alkali metals, followed by the alkaline earth metals. By comparing the reactivity of the unknown species with one of these known elements, the student could reveal the group of the atom.

1221. D is correct. Protium is the most common, well-known form of hydrogen. Deuterium and tritium are hydrogen isotopes, containing one proton and two neutrons and one proton and three neutrons, respectively. While isotopes may vary in their physical properties, the chemical identity of an isotope is the same as its parent atom – here, hydrogen.

IV: While a helium ion has the same number of electrons as a hydrogen ion, He always possesses two protons, making it a different chemical species from H.

1222. C is correct. The Bohr model is built on the Rutherford model, which previously postulated that the nucleus was positive in charge. The Bohr model improved on this idea by integrating a quantum physical understanding of the Rutherford model.

A: This is the Dalton model of the atom.
B: This statement describes the Thompson model of the atom, also known as the "Plum Pudding" model.
D: This better relates to Heisenberg's uncertainty principle.

1223. A is correct. Bohr proposed "stationary orbits," or orbits at the specific distances at which an electron is stable. These orbits are associated with energy levels. Jumping between orbits must then require either the absorption or the emittance of a photon with a frequency that is related to the difference in energy levels between the orbits and to Planck's constant.

B: This is very close. However, the Bohr model only gives accurate results for one-electron systems and when the charged points move at speeds significantly lower than the speed of light.
C: This is not explained by the Bohr model; rather, it represents the function of filters used in X-ray imaging.
D: Electromagnetic radiation was discovered in the 1800s, while the Bohr model came into existence in 1913.

1224. D is correct. A set of quantum numbers describes a specific electron and how its nature is unique from that of other electrons. This cannot be used to infer the charge density of an entire atom, especially since each electron has a different set of quantum numbers.

1225. B is correct. The 4s orbital has a higher energy than the 3d block. Thus, the two 4s electrons will be removed before any of the 3d electrons.

A: This represents the configuration for ground state nickel.
D: This would be the logical answer if the differences in energy level between the orbitals were not taken into consideration.

1226. B is correct. Hund's rule states that orbitals will be occupied in order of increasing energy and that every orbital of a subshell must contain a single electron before any are paired. In this diagram, the 3d subshell shows a pairing of electrons while one orbital is still empty, which violates Hund's rule.

A: The Pauli exclusion principle posits that no two electrons can have identical quantum numbers.

C: The Heisenberg uncertainty principle, which states that it is impossible to simultaneously measure the position and momentum of a particle, is irrelevant here.

D: The Schrödinger equation describes how a quantum state and system changes over time.

1227. C is correct. Electron excitation is responsible for countless reactions and mechanisms. Photons are the most common form of energy used to excite electrons, but collision with other particles can promote similar stimulation. Excited electrons will, over time, fall back to their ground states. At this time, they will emit electromagnetic radiation at a specific wavelength that corresponds to the difference between energy levels.

1228. D is correct. Heisenberg's uncertainty principle posits a limit to the precision with which certain physical properties of a particle can be known. Position and momentum form a pair of properties that exemplifies this principle.

1229. D is correct. Nitrogen is located in the second principal energy shell, meaning that its "n" value must be 2. The azimuthal quantum number refers to the subshell (s, p, d, etc.). Since the question is asking for a p electron, this quantum number must be 1. The range of magnetic quantum numbers can all apply here, since the question is not specifying the particular axis of the electron.

A: Here, the magnetic quantum number is larger than the azimuthal number, which is impossible.

1230. C is correct. Cobalt is located in the 3d block, where it possesses more than 5 "d" electrons. Thus, all five of its "d" orbitals will be at least partially filled. Specifically, these are d_{xy}, d_{xz}, d_{yz}, $d_{x^2-y^2}$, and d_{z^2}.

D: This is the total number of "d" electrons held by cobalt, not the number of relevant orbitals.

1231. A is correct. Due to conservation of energy, a photoelectron's energy cannot be greater than that of the incident photon.

II: This is false; the energy of a photoelectron may only be less than that of the incident photon. This concept is due to the existence of the work function, a quantity of energy required for an electron to be released at all. Since some of the incident photon's energy is devoted to overcoming this threshold, not all of it can be converted to kinetic energy for the ejected electron.

III: The threshold frequency is simply the frequency that must be surpassed for a photoelectron to be emitted. It is the energy of the incident photon (and whether it surpasses this threshold) that determines whether ejection occurs.

IV: The intensity of the incident ray determines the number, not the individual energies, of the ejected photoelectrons.

1232. D is correct. Diamagnetic materials are those that contain no unpaired electrons. Cadmium, which possesses five fully-filled d orbitals, is the only diamagnetic element of the choices given.

A, B, C: All of these elements are paramagnetic. In other words, if you were to write out their electron configurations, you would notice that they each contain at least one unpaired electron.

1233. B is correct. The effective nuclear charge can be found by subtracting the number of electrons in all shells preceding the one in question from the nuclear charge (the number of protons). Shells 1-3 contain 28 electrons, while an iodine nucleus possesses 53 protons. Thus, the effective nuclear charge on the n = 4 subshell is (53 – 28) or 25.

C: This is simply the number of protons in an iodine nucleus. Number of protons is not the same as effective nuclear charge, which also takes into account shielding from more interior electron shells.

1234. C is correct. A higher-energy state is one that is more excited than the ground state. Transition to such a state requires the input of energy, and would not release energy in the form of light. All other choices are true statements.

1235. C is correct. Note that the final energy is less than the initial energy, which must be true if the electron emitted a photon. Specifically, the difference between these two energy values will give us the energy of the emitted photon. Thus, to calculate frequency, use the equation $hf + E_{final} = E_{initial}$. This yields a frequency of 0.4 Hz.

A: This follows from a mistake with scientific notation.
B, D: The value given in choice D comes from mistakenly adding the final and initial energies instead of subtracting. The answer in choice B reflects the same mistake, plus an order-of-magnitude error.

1236. B is correct. To most easily determine the final principal quantum number, we must be familiar with the different series of spectra. The Lyman series (ultraviolet rays) involves any emission in which the ground state of the electron is n = 1. The Balmer series (visible rays) includes emissions in which the final state is n = 2. Finally, the Paschen series (infrared) contains any emission with a final state of n = 3. Here, the initial principal quantum number, or excited state, does not matter when answering this question.

A, D: These would fall under the Balmer series, as n_{final} = 2. In general, the Balmer series relates to emissions of visible light.
C: This emission would be in the Lyman series, as n_{final} = 1. The Lyman series entirely relates to UV rays.

1237. D is correct. From the information given, we cannot discern the principal quantum numbers of the excited electrons. We can only identify which shells they returned to when re-entering a lower state. Therefore, the samples could have emitted different series of light (resulting in infrared, UV, or visible rays), all while initially existing in an excited state of n = 6.

1238. B is correct. Effective nuclear charge can be found by subtracting the total number of electrons in all shells preceding the one in question from the nuclear charge (the number of protons). Selenium has an atomic number of

34. The atom pictured appears to be oxidized (Se^{2+}), as we would expect the outermost shell to have 6 electrons if the atom were neutral. In other words, the diagram includes 32 electrons. Starting from the first ring, the number of electrons in each shell is, respectively, 2, 8, 18, and 4. (Note that this information corresponds to the atom's electronic configuration.) To calculate the effective nuclear charge when n = 4, then, we only need to find (34 – 28), or 6.

A: Effective nuclear charge is not equal to the number of valence electrons.

1239. B is correct. Even if this atom is oxidized twice, the shells interior to n = 4 will still contain same number of electrons. Similarly, selenium will still include 34 protons. Thus, the effective nuclear charge (as calculated for #1238) will not change.

1240. C is correct. To calculate the frequency, we must use the following equation: $hf = R(1/n^2_{final} – 1/n^2_{initial})$, in which n_{final} = 3 and $n_{initial}$ = 6. (We know that the final principal quantum number must be 3 because infrared light is emitted, placing this emission as part of the Paschen series.) Plugging in values yields an approximate frequency of $f = 2.75 \times 10^{14}$ Hz.

A, B, D: These values result from using different values for n_{final}. For this question, it is critical to know which final principal quantum numbers correspond to which types of light (infrared, UV, etc.).

1241. C is correct. All combustion reactions should have oxygen, which is bimolecular, as a reactant. Since calcium has a +2 charge, it will combine with oxygen to form CaO, and one molecule of O_2 will be required for every two molecules of Ca.

A: Like other metals, calcium forms a unimolecular solid. This choice treats it as bimolecular.
B: Oxygen gas is bimolecular, not unimolecular.

1242. A is correct. When carbonate-containing compounds decompose, they form carbon dioxide and an oxide. Here, that oxide is MgO.

B, C: These choices both have carbonate as a product; keep in mind that carbonate will typically decompose into carbon dioxide. Even if we did not know this, the question references the production of an oxide, which is not seen in these choices.

D: Like choice C, this misbalances the charges on the reactant molecule. Magnesium has a +2 charge, while carbonate has a charge of -2.

1243. D is correct. Since each cation and anion switches the ion to which it is bound, this is a double displacement. Precipitation reactions involve the formation of a solid (an insoluble compound) from aqueous ions. Since solid lead bromide forms during the process shown above, this is a precipitation reaction as well.

1244. D is correct. This reaction must be balanced before any assessments can be made, giving us $2KBr\,(aq) + Pb(NO_3)_2\,(aq) \rightarrow PbBr_2\,(s) + 2KNO_3$ (aq). Since the molar ratio of lead nitrate to potassium nitrate is 1:2, statement II is accurate. There also is a 2:1 molar ratio of potassium bromide to lead bromide, making III true as well. Finally, statement IV is true because the reactants contain two bromine atoms for every six oxygen atoms.

I: The balanced ratio of KBr to KNO_3 is 1:1, not 1:2.

1245. C is correct. When zinc is oxidized, it loses two electrons to become Zn^{2+}. Correspondingly, hydrogen is reduced from H^+ to H in a process requiring two moles of H^+ for each mole of Zn.

A: Zinc, like other metals, is unimolecular.
B: For oxidation is to occur, H^+ must be reduced. Here, hydrogen has the same oxidation state on the reactant and product sides of the equation.
D: As an ion, zinc is Zn^{2+}, not Zn^+. Additionally, H_2 is gaseous, not aqueous.

1246. C is correct. Like other redox reactions, this can be written as two separate half-reactions. For the oxidation half-reaction, $Na \rightarrow Na^+ + e^-$. For the reduction component, $O_2 + 4e^- \rightarrow 2O^{2-}$. However, the sodium half-reaction must be multiplied by four to give the same number of electrons on both sides. When we combine the two, we find that $4Na + O_2 + 4e^- \rightarrow 2Na_2O + 4e^-$.

1247. D is correct. Since nitrate has a charge of -1, iron(II) nitrate must include two nitrate ions for each iron atom. On the product side, aluminum has a +3 charge, meaning that aluminum nitrate must include three nitrate anions. The pure metals (aluminum and iron) should both be neutral and unimolecular.

A: Aluminum is not bimolecular. Additionally, the charge of aluminum ion is +3, not +2.
B: Nitrate has a +1 charge, while Fe(II) has a +2 charge. For this reason, $FeNO_3$ is not the proper reactant.
C: Like A, this choice mistakenly assumes that the charge of aluminum ion is +2.

1248. A is correct. On the reactant side, magnesium and sulfide ions have +2 and -2 charges, respectively. Magnesium maintains this +2 charge on the product side, while sulfur changes its oxidation state to +6. Oxygen, however, initially has an oxidation state of -1, but becomes -2 as a component of water. For this reason, oxygen, not magnesium, is reduced.

B: While this equation is balanced, it gives hydrogen peroxide as H_4O_4 instead of H_2O_2.
C, D: As stated above, magnesium is neither oxidized nor reduced in this reaction.

1249. B is correct. This is not a redox reaction, as no atoms change oxidation states at all. Barium has a +2 state throughout the reaction, nitrogen is +5, hydrogen is +1, oxygen is -2, and sulfur is +6.

A: Since solid barium sulfate is forming from two aqueous reactants, this is a precipitation reaction.
C: Since each cation and anion switches the ion to which it is bound, this is a double displacement reaction.

1250. C is correct. This equation is not given in its balanced form. When we do balance it, we find that $Ba(NO_3)_2 + H_2SO_4 \rightarrow BaSO_4 + 2\,HNO_3$. In other words, for every mole of barium nitrate, three total moles of product will form (two moles of HNO_3 and one mole of $BaSO_4$). Thus, for every 5 moles of barium nitrate, 15 moles of product will be created.

A: This results from misreading the question, which calls for the total number of product molecules produced. Even the unbalanced equation gives a 1:2 ratio of $BaNO_3$ to products, not 1:1.
B: This incorrect answer likely comes from neglecting to balance the equation given.

1251. C is correct. First, we need to find the molar ratio of each element compared to the others. Let's start with carbon. 36.1 g C × (1 mol C / 12 g C) = 3 mol C. For hydrogen, 5.3 g H × (1 mol H / 1 g H) = 5.3 mol H. Finally, 48.1 g O × (1 mol O / 16 g O) = 3 mol O, and 10.5 g N × (1 mol N / 14 g N) = 0.75 mol N. Since nitrogen has the smallest molar value, we can use it to find the simplified overall ratio. Start with carbon: 3 mol C / 0.75 = 4 mol C. For hydrogen, 5.3 mol H / 0.75 = 7 mol H, and for oxygen, 3 mol O / 0.75 = 4 mol O. The empirical formula is $C_4H_7NO_4$. Finally, since this compound has the same molar mass that was mentioned in the question stem, this also represents the molecular formula.

1252. B is correct. First, remember that all of the carbon in the original compound ends up in the form of carbon dioxide, while all of the hydrogen will be present as part of the water. Thus, we need to determine how many moles of the measured CO_2 are carbon and how many moles of the measured H_2O are hydrogen. 900 mg of CO_2 contains 0.245 grams of carbon, which is 0.02 moles. 360 mg of H_2O contains 0.04 grams of hydrogen, which is 0.04 moles. Finally, the remaining mass left unaccounted for in the original compound must represent oxygen. So, 1980 mg – 245 mg – 40 mg = 1695 mg oxygen, or about .10 moles. Since carbon is present in the smallest molar value, our ratio (and empirical formula) must be CH_2O_5.

    A: This is the molecular, not empirical, formula.

1253. B is correct. Let's use dimensional analysis to find this answer. Grams × 1 mol / grams × (6.02×10^{23} particles / mol) = particles, which is exactly what we want to solve for.

    A, C: Multiplying the mass by the molar mass yields g^2 / mol instead of canceling g.

1254. B is correct. We first must use Avogadro's number to find moles, then find the molar mass of resveratrol and convert to grams. With some simple math, we can find that one mole of resveratrol has a mass of 228 g. Finally, 3.0×10^{24} molecules × (1mol / 6×10^{23} molecules) × (228 g / mol) = 1140 g, or approximately 1.1 kg.

    A: This is the answer you would get if you mistakenly divide Avogadro's number by the total number of molecules instead of performing the reciprocal of that operation.
    C: This is the number of moles of resveratrol, not kilograms.
    D: This is the number of grams of resveratrol, not kilograms.

1255. C is correct. Density = mass / volume. We are given both mass and volume, but neither is written in the same units as the answer choices. First, then, let's convert volume to cubic meters. Remember, even though 100 centimeters equals one meter, 100 cubic centimeters does not equal one cubic meter! Instead, one cubic meter equals $(100 \text{ cm})^3$, or 10^6 cubic centimeters. In other words, one cubic centimeter equals 10^{-6} cubic meters. $0.1 \text{ cm}^3 = 0.1 \times 10^{-6} \text{ m}^3 = \times 10^{-7} \text{ m}^3$. Next, 160 mg = 0.16 g = 0.00016 kg = 1.6×10^{-4} kg. Finally, 1.6×10^{-4} kg / 10^{-7} m^3 gives our answer.

    A: This results from a mistake in the conversion of cubic centimeters to cubic meters.
    C: You would get this answer if you found g / m^3 instead of kg / m^3.

1256. B is correct. The molar ratio can be determined by finding the coefficient for each molecule in the balanced equation. As always, first ensure that the equation is balanced; conveniently, this one already is. Because oxygen has a coefficient of 12 and water has a coefficient of 11, the molar ratio is simply 12:11, meaning that for every 12 moles of oxygen reacted with sucrose, 11 moles of hydrogen are produced.

1257. A is correct. When calculating the number of mole of a product, find the initial amount of reactant(s) and use the appropriate molar ratio. 684 g sucrose × (1 mol sucrose / 342 g) × (23 mol total products / 1 mol sucrose) gives 46 moles of product.

    C: This is the number of moles of water produced, but the question asks for the amount of gas. Since both CO_2 and H_2O are in the gaseous state, both must be included.
    D: This is the number of moles of CO_2 produced.

1258. D is correct. The formal charge is calculated by adding the number of nonbonding electrons and half of the number of bonding electrons, then subtracting that value from the total number of valence electrons for each atom. For oxygen, 6 − (4 + 2) = 0. For sulfur, 6 − (0 + 6) = 0.

C: These are the atoms' oxidation states.

1259.   D is correct. In the original state of sulfur trioxide, both sulfur and oxygen have formal charges of zero. If sulfur gains an extra bond from the benzene ring while losing one to oxygen, it retains the same formal charge. However, because the oxygen gains two nonbonding electrons while losing two bonding electrons, its formal charge changes. We can calculate it as 6 − (6 + 1) = -1.

C: This choice can result from subtracting half the number of bonding electrons and the full number of nonbonding electrons, which is backwards.

1260.   C is correct. First, we need to convert the volume to cubic meters. 2.5×10^4 cm^3 × (1 m^3 / 10^6 cm^3) = 2.5×10^{-2} m^3. Then, 50 mg / 2.5×10^{-2} m^3 yields 20×10^2 mg / m^3, or 2000 mg / m^3.

A: This answer might be found if the correct value, 2×10^3 mg / m^3, was mistaken for 2×10^{-3} mg / m^3. It is also the same as the correct answer in units of g / m^3.

B: The value shown here comes from a mistaken use of volume / mass.

1261.   C is correct. To calculate the limiting reagent, we must use stoichiometry to determine how much sulfate is required to react with 50 mg of methane (or vice versa). However, we cannot do this before converting grams to moles. 0.05 g CH$_4$ × $\frac{1\,mol}{16\,g}$ = 0.003 mol methane, which requires 0.003 mol SO$_4^{2-}$, or 0.3 g, to fully react. Since we have only 0.06 g of SO$_4^{2-}$, sulfate must be the limiting reagent. 0.06 g SO$_4^{2-}$ × $\frac{1\,mol}{96\,g}$ = approximately 0.0006 mol, which reacts with 0.0006 mol, or 0.01 g, of CH$_4$. We will thus have 0.04 g of methane in excess once the sulfate has been exhausted.

A, B: Sulfate, not methane, is limiting in this reaction.
D: 10 mg is the amount of methane that reacts, not the amount remaining after sulfate is completely exhausted.

1262.   C is correct. According to the reasoning used for #1261, sulfate is the limiting reagent here. We can thus use the given amount of 0.06 g sulfate

to find how much hydrogen sulfide should form. As always, though, we must first convert grams of sulfate to moles. 0.06 g SO$_4^{2-}$ × $\frac{1\,mol}{96\,g}$ = approximately 0.0006 mol. Since sulfate reacts to form hydrogen sulfide in a 1:1 molar ratio, 0.0006 mol of HS$^-$ will be formed. Finally, we must convert to grams of hydrogen sulfide. 0.0006 mol HS$^-$ × $\frac{1\,mol}{33.065\,g}$ = about 0.02 grams of HS$^-$.

A: This is the number of grams, not mg, of HS$^-$.
B: This is the mass of methane reacted, not the mass of HS$^-$ formed.
D: This is the number of milligrams of sulfate, the limiting reagent. Though sulfate reacts to form hydrosulfide ion with a 1:1 ratio, note that this ratio works only for moles, not grams.

1263.   A is correct. To find the percent composition of carbon in the balloon, the total mass of all other elements present must be calculated. For convenience, we can assume that there are 100 mol of gas in the balloon. Let's begin with argon, which has a mole fraction of 0.10. This is equivalent to 10 mol (0.10 × 100 mol), and since Ar has a molecular weight of approximately 40 g/mol, we can conclude that 400 g of Ar are present. For carbon dioxide, which has a molecular weight of 44 g/mol, 26 mol is equivalent to 1144 g; note, however, that only 312 g of this amount is carbon. Finally, though we do not know the mole fractions of nitrogen and oxygen, we know that the remaining mole fraction of 0.64 is divided evenly between them, giving us 32 mol (or 1024 g) of O$_2$ and 32 mol (or 896 g) of N$_2$. The percent composition of carbon is (312 g C / 3464 g total mass) x 100, or about 9%.

B: This results from using 16 g/mol as the molecular weight for oxygen gas and 14 g/mol as that of nitrogen gas. Remember, both of these elements are found in their bimolecular forms (O$_2$ and N$_2$) in nature.
C: A calculated answer of 26% results from equating the mole fraction of carbon dioxide to the percent composition of carbon.
D: This choice is far too large, and may result from finding the percent composition of CO$_2$ instead of carbon alone.

1264.   B is correct. Glutamine has a molar mass of 146 g/mol. The molar mass of nitrogen is 14 g/mol, so the two equivalents of nitrogen present in one mole of glutamine have a mass of 28 g. (28 / 146) × 100 = 19%. This can also be obtained by discerning that 28 is slightly less than one-fifth of 146, so our answer should be slightly less than 20%.

A: This choice can be found by mistakenly taking the mass of one equivalent of nitrogen (14 g) and dividing by the molar mass of glutamine. In reality, each mole of glutamine contains two equivalents of N.
C: If you divided 28 g by the mass of glutamine that is not due to nitrogen (146 g – 28 g = 118 g), you'd get this answer. In reality, composition by mass must be found by taking the mass of our component of interest and dividing by total mass.

1265. C is correct. First, the equation must be balanced, showing that the accurate mole ratio is 1:1:4:1 (with water having the coefficient of 4). Ammonium dichromate has a molar mass of approximately 250 g, so 750 g represents 3 moles. Since the molar ratio of ammonium dichromate to nitrogen gas is 1:1, 3 mol $(NH_4)_2Cr_2O_7$ will yield 3 mol, or 84 g, of N_2.

B: Remember, the molar mass of N_2 is 28 g / mol, not 14 g / mol.
D: 168 g is the mass of N, not the mass of N_2, which is the quantity asked for in the question stem.

1266. D is correct. Since the molar mass of ammonium dichromate is about 250 g, 500 g represents 2 moles of the compound. Complete decomposition of this amount should produce 2 mol, or 56 g. The student's actual yield of 12 g thus represents a significant percent error: (|12 g – 56 g| / 56 g) × 100% = 79%.

A: This is the percent yield rather than the percent error. Percent yield = (actual / theoretical) × 100.
C: To find percent yield, take (actual – theoretical yield) and divide by the theoretical value. This choice results from dividing by the sum of the theoretical and actual yields, or 68 g.

1267. C is correct. First, the balanced equation described by the question must be written: 3 $CuS + 8 HNO_3 \rightarrow 3 Cu(NO_3)_2 + 3 S + 4 H_2O + 2$ NO. Since the 6:16 molar ratio of copper sulfide

to nitric acid is equivalent to the 3:8 ratio in the balanced equation, the two reagents are present in stoichiometric quantities. Neither is limiting; both will be exhausted if the reaction runs to completion.

A, B: These choices most likely result from improper balancing of the reaction described.

1268. B is correct. Since the question states that equimolar amounts of all four substances are present, we can simply take the mass of copper in one mole of copper nitrate and divide by the sum of the molar masses of these species, including copper nitrate itself. The total of the four molar masses is 187.6 + 32.06 + 18 + 30, or about 267.7. Thus, the percent composition of Cu is equal to (63.5 / 267.7) × 100% = 23.7%. Note that rounding to 60 / 270 makes the math significantly easier and simplifies to 2 / 9, or 22%.

C: This error can be attributed to dividing 63.5 by 204, which is the mass of the products excluding copper. Since the copper in copper nitrate is part of the total mass of the species in the beaker, it must be included in the denominator.

1269. A is correct. The chemical equation must first be balanced before we attempt to find an answer. This yields 2 $H_3PO_4 + 3 Mg(OH)_2 \rightarrow 6$ $H_2O + Mg_3(PO_4)_2$, or a 2:3:6:1 ratio. Next, we need to determine the limiting reagent. Since 6 mol of magnesium hydroxide requires 4 mol of phosphoric acid to fully react, and since we have only 2 mol of H_3PO_4, phosphoric acid is the limiting reagent. 2 mol of H_3PO_4 yields 1 mol of $Mg_3(PO_4)_2$.

B: The given equation must be balanced before any calculations can be made. While the unbalanced equation makes it appear that 2 moles of H_3PO_4 will produce 2 mol of $Mg_3(PO_4)_2$, this is incorrect.
D: This answer results from two separate mistakes: leaving the reaction unbalanced and assuming that magnesium hydroxide is the limiting reagent.

1270. A is correct. Using the reasoning for #1269, we know that the balanced reaction is 2 H_3PO_4 + 3 $Mg(OH)_2 \rightarrow 6 H_2O + Mg_3(PO_4)_2$ and that phosphoric acid is limiting. Theoretically, a complete reaction should yield 1 mol, or 263 g, magnesium phosphate. Percent yield can be calculated by taking (actual yield / theoretical yield) × 100% = (13.15 g / 263 g) × 100% = 5.0%.

D: This results from confusing percent error with percent yield.

1271. B is correct. Here, we should use $M_1V_1 = M_2V_2$, keeping in mind that V_2 must include both the 1.85 L of water and the original 0.15 L of solute. $M_2 = M_1V_1 / V_2 = (0.15 \text{ L} \times 0.75 \text{ M}) / 2 \text{ L} = {\sim}0.06$ M.

A, C: These answers likely result from mistakes with scientific notation.
D: To obtain an answer this large, you may have left the volume of ethylene glycol in milliliters instead of converting to liters.

1272. D is correct. Since molarity reflects the number of moles of solute per liter of solution, we first must discern how many moles of acetone are present. Acetone has a molar mass of 58 g, so 174 g C_3H_6O × (1 mol C_3H_6O / 58 g) = 3 mol acetone. We can ignore the density of the solvent, as it is unnecessary when calculating the volume of the solution. The molarity is thus 3 mol acetone / 0.350 L solution, or 8.6 M.

B: This can be attributed to using mL instead of L when making the final calculation.
C: Confusing molarity with molality would lead to this choice. Since molality represents the number of moles of solute per kilogram of solvent, it could be calculated as (3 mol acetone) / (0.700 kg solvent) = 4.2 m.

1273. B is correct. Molality is measured in moles of solute per kilogram of solvent. To find moles of solute, we must take 49 g H_3PO_4 × (1 mol H_3PO_4 / 98 g) = 0.5 mol H_3PO_4. Next, use density to calculate the mass of the solvent: 2000 mL carbonated water × (1.5 g/mL) = 3000 g, or 3 kg. Finally, 0.5 mol / 3 kg = 0.17 m.

C: 0.25 is the molarity, not molality, of the solution. Remember, we cannot take (0.5 mol H_3PO_4) / (2 L carbonated water) here, as that gives us units of mol/L, not mol/kg.

1274. A is correct. Molarity is measured as moles of solute per unit volume of solution, while molality represents moles of solute per kilogram of solvent. As the volume of solvent increases, the denominators of both of these measurements

will increase as well, causing both to become lowered overall.

D: Under the conditions described, this could only be true if the mass of solute were increased as well.

1275. B is correct. Since succinic acid is a dicarboxylic acid, and since carboxylic acids readily become deprotonated, succinic acid is diprotic. Normality is a measurement that is very similar to molarity, except that it measures moles of equivalents per liter of solution. Here, 472 g $C_4H_6O_4$ × (1 mol / 118 g $C_4H_6O_4$) = 4 moles of $C_4H_6O_4$, which possess 8 equivalents of protons. The normality is thus (8 equivalents of H^+) / 2 L = 4 N.

B: This is the molarity, not the normality, of the acidic solution.
D: This is the number of equivalent protons, and would be the correct answer if this solution had a volume of 1 L. However, we must divide by 2 L in this case.

1276. B is correct. Here, mole fraction can be calculated as the number of moles of carbon dioxide present divided by the total moles of gas. 250 mL HCl × (2 mol HCl / 1000 mL) × (1 mol CO_2 / 1 mol HCl) = 0.5 mol CO_2. To find our answer, take 0.5 mol CO_2 / 1.5 total moles in the vessel = 0.33.

C: An answer of 0.50 likely results from dividing by the moles of gaseous H_2O and NH_3 alone. Remember, when calculating mole fraction, the denominator must include all of the species present, including CO_2 itself.

1277. D is correct. Mass percent can be calculated by dividing the mass of NaCl by the mass of the entire solution. Because the reaction was run in an open container, CO_2 should not be included; as a gas, it easily leaves the solution. To find the number of grams of NaCl, take 250 mL HCl × (2 mol HCl / 1000 mL) × (1 mol NaCl / 1 mol HCl) = 0.5 mol NaCl × 58 g/mol = 29 g NaCl. For H_2O, 0.5 mol H_2O × 18 g/mol = 9 g H_2O. The total mass of the solution is thus 38 g, and 29 g / 38 g × 100% = 75%.

B: This is the mass percent of water, not NaCl.
C: 0.5 is the mole fraction of NaCl (and the mole fraction of water as well). The question asked for percent by mass.

1278. A is correct. Since phosphoric acid is triprotic, the complete deprotonation of 0.5 moles of H_3PO_4 will require 1.5 moles of hydroxide, or the full amount present. Each of these OH- molecules will gain a proton, leaving us with 19.5 moles of water and 0.5 moles of PO_4^{3-}. The total number of moles in solution is 19.5 + 0.5, or 20 moles. Thus, the mole fraction of PO_4^{3-} is 0.5 / 20, or 0.025.

1279. C is correct. To find the percent by mass of phosphate anions, we must find the mass of phosphate present. 2 mol PO_4^{3-} × (95 g / 1 mol) = 190 g PO_4^{3-}. The percent by mass is thus 190 g PO_4^{3-} / 330 g total, or about 58%.

    B: This choice comes from taking 95 g / (95 + 140 g). In other words, it would be the proper percentage if only one mole of phosphate anion were present.
    D: This is 95 g / 140 g, which incorporates only one mole of phosphate and does not include the mass of phosphate in the total value.

1280. D is correct. As the flask is well-sealed, we can assume that the molarity on the label is correct (and if it weren't, the question would be impossible to answer). (3 mol compound / 1000 mL) × (1 ml / 2 g) = 0.0015 mol / g, or 667 g/mol.

1281. A is correct. Collision theory states that reaction rate is dependent on the number of molecules that collide in a favorable way. As concentration increases, so will the total number of favorable collisions.

    II: Virtually all reactions do increase in rate as temperature is increased. However, this is separate from the changes that occur to their equilibria. Exothermic reactions, which release heat, will experience a shift toward the reactants when temperature is raised. For this reason, the relative amount of products compared to reactants will drop.
    III: Activation energy is the difference in energy between the starting species and the high-energy transition state. Since reactants and products typically have different potential energies, the energetic distance between them and the transition state will differ. This will yield different activation energies for the forward and reverse reactions.

    IV: Catalysts do lower the activation energy, which corresponds to the energy of the transition state. However, they do not impact ΔG, which is the free energy difference between reactants and products.

1282. D is correct. Unless a reaction is specified as an elementary or single-step process, its rate law can only be determined experimentally.

    A: This resembles the equation for this reaction's equilibrium constant. Unlike K_{eq}, the rate law should not include a term corresponding to the products.
    C: This would be correct if the reaction was known to be an elementary, or one-step, reaction. Since the nature of this process was not specified, we cannot use stoichiometric coefficients as exponents when writing the rate law.

1283. D is correct. Between the first and fourth trials, [C] is doubled while [A] and [B] are held constant. Despite the change to [C], the rate remains the same, indicating that the reaction is zeroth-order for C and making that reactant absent from the rate law. Between trials 1 and 2, [A] is quadrupled while [B] and [C] are held constant, and the rate also quadruples; this implies that A is first order in the law. Finally, a tripling of [B] (while [A] and [C] are constant) causes the rate to increase by a factor of 9. For this reason, the reaction must be second order for B: $3^n = 9$, so n = 2.

1284. B is correct. The rate law was determined in #1283 to be rate = $k[A][B]^2$, so we can ignore the initial concentration of reagent C. However, we do not yet know the rate constant. Although we can use any of the trials in the table to find it, let's use trial 1, as the numbers are fairly easy to deal with. 0.004 mM/s = k(0.5 mM)(1 mM)^2, so k = 0.008 $s^{-1}mM^{-2}$. Finally, we can plug in our known values to answer the question. Rate = (0.008 $s^{-1}mM^{-2}$)(2 mM)(4 mM)^2, or 0.256 mM/s.

    A: If you calculated this value, you likely forgot to square the concentration of B. Note that according to the table, this reaction is second order for that reagent.
    D: This choice neglects to include the rate constant. Remember, we must first calculate that

value, then use it in the rate law to find initial rate.

1285. B is correct. C represents the reaction intermediate that is formed in this two-step reaction. Note that its total potential energy is less than that of either transition state, but greater than that of the product (E) that will later form.

A: Points B and D represent the high-energy transition states that are briefly produced during this reaction. These extremely unstable states are transient; for this reason, they are not considered intermediates, which are generally stable enough to be isolated.
C: Point E represents the final product of the forward reaction.

1286. D is correct. ΔG refers to the free energy difference reactant or intermediate and a product; in other words, it is the linear distance between the energies of the relevant species. For the second step of the forward reaction, the starting material is the intermediate (C), while the product is the final compound formed, E. The distance between the two is marked by line 4.

A: This is the activation energy for the first step of the forward reaction.
B: Line 2 represents the ΔG of the entire two-step reaction, not the second step alone.
C: This denotes the activation energy, not the ΔG, of the second step.

1287. D is correct. The question stem states that this is a one-step reaction, so we can use the equation to determine the rate law. This gives us rate = $k[\text{1,3-dibutene}]^2$ – in other words, a bimolecular, or second-order, reaction. Since rate must be given in units of M/s while concentrations are given in M, the rate constant, k, must have units of $M^{-1}s^{-1}$.

1288. C is correct. The rate of a zeroth-order reaction is independent of reagent concentration.

A: This would be accurate if the reaction were first order with respect to H_2.
B: Similarly, this choice would make sense if the reaction were second order with respect to H_2.
C: As we do not know whether this is a single- or multi-step reaction, we cannot determine the

reaction order from the equation alone. As such, it certainly could be zeroth order overall.

1289. C is correct. The question stem mentions that this reaction is bimolecular, which means that it must have an overall reaction order of 2. The rate law given in choice C is trimolecular, which would make it third order overall. Note that to find overall reaction order, simply add the exponents of all reactants involved in the rate law.

A, B: These are second-order, or bimolecular, reactions. (For A, 1 + 1 = 2, while for B, 2 is the only exponent involved.)
D: While this rate law initially appears to be missing its rate constant (k), note that it is absolutely possible for k to equal 1. In that case, this would also be a sensible second-order rate law.

1290. B is correct. First, it must be determined which of the three steps is rate-limiting. Since the question stem states that both unimolecular steps (2 and 3) are "extremely fast," the bimolecular step (Step 1) must be the slowest, and therefore the rate-limiting, step. The rate law can thus be written directly from that step.

A: This law uses the reactants and coefficients present in the overall reaction. Since that process is a multi-step reaction, we cannot use it alone to deduce the rate law.
C, D: These laws include B, an intermediate. Additionally, they are not written using Step 1 alone.

1291. C is correct. Equilibrium is reached when the concentrations of products and reactants plateau at the right side of the graph. Here, since the value of $[H_2]$ - $[HI]$ is negative, $[HI]$ must be greater than either $[H_2]$ or $[I_2]$.

D: Reactant and product concentrations certainly do not have to become constant at equilibrium.

1292. B is correct. The reaction will shift to counteract the stress that is placed on it. In this case, it will shift to the right, consuming reactants and making products, in response to the increase in reactant concentrations. This returns the value of the reaction quotient (Q) to that of the equilibrium constant (K).

1293. D is correct. At equilibrium, the forward and reverse reactions are occurring at the same rate. Thus, we can expect that ^{14}C would be found incorporated into all carbon-carrying species.

1294. D is correct. When pressure is increased, the reaction will shift in a way that minimizes the total number of gas molecules in the system. In the given reaction, this shift will be toward the reactant side to counteract the increase in pressure.

   I: This wrongly implies that the reaction shifts toward the side with more gaseous molecules. IV: As the new equilibrium will involve relatively more reactant molecules, this is impossible.

1295. C is correct. $K_{eq} = \frac{[A]a[B]b}{[C]c[D]d}$, where A and B represent products and C and D represent reactants. Here, a, b, c, and d represent the related coefficients in the balanced equation.

   A: This is the reciprocal of the correct answer.
   B: This choice neglects to include NOCl, which (as neither a solid nor a pure liquid) must be involved in the expression.
   D: Since the "2" in Cl_2 is not a coefficient, chlorine should not be squared.

1296. C is correct. If the relative amount of products is too small, the reaction is not at equilibrium; specifically, it must travel to the right to reach its equilibrium value. The ratio in question is Q, the reaction quotient, which here is less than K.

1297. D is correct. The overall reaction is equal to (Reaction 2 + Reaction 3 – Reaction 1). K_{eq} of this process as a whole, then, is $(K_2K_3) / K_1$.

   A, C: K values should not be added or subtracted when combining individual steps of a reaction.
   B: K_1 should be present in the denominator, as its reverse reaction is a component of the process given in the question stem.

1298. D is correct. Spontaneity is determined by the overall change in Gibbs free energy. $\Delta G_{rxn}°$ is -29.5 kJ/mol, so this process is spontaneous.

   A: K_{eq} is 8. In fact, K_{eq} cannot have a negative value.
   B: $\Delta G_{rxn}°$ is not positive.
   C: This reaction is spontaneous due to its negative ΔG.

1299. D is correct. K_{eq} is not affected by pressure changes, although it does vary with temperature.

1300. B is correct. Setting up the equation $10 = [A_6]/[A_3]^2$ tells us that $A_3 = 0.1$. From this value, we know that the mole fraction of the compound in question is 0.5.

1301. C is correct. While most chloride salts are soluble, silver chloride (AgCl) is a notable exception and forms a white, opaque precipitate in water.

   A: Both ammonium and nitrate always form soluble salts.
   B: Similarly, salts of alkali metals (including both sodium and potassium) are soluble. In other words, both the KCl contaminant and the HCl would dissociate completely in water. While an enormous amount of KCl could lead to a solution saturated with chloride ion, this choice specifically mentions that the amount was small.
   D: This contaminant would simply neutralize the HCl, yielding water and a soluble NaCl salt.

1302. D is correct. K_{sp}, or the solubility product, is an equilibrium constant similar to K_a or K_{eq}. It is equal to the concentrations of product ions, each raised to the power of their respective coefficients and multiplied together. Here, $CaOH_2 \rightarrow Ca^{2+} + OH^-$. For this reason, calcium ion is given an exponent of one while hydroxide ion is squared.

   A, C: These choices wrongly characterize the coefficients given to calcium and hydroxide ions.
   B: Remember, solids and pure liquids are never included in equilibrium constants! As a solid, calcium hydroxide should not be present in this expression.

1303. B is correct. Zinc phosphate has a formula of $Zn_3(PO_4)_2$. As such, its K_{sp} expression can be written as $K_{sp} = [Zn^{2+}]^3[PO_4^{3-}]^2$. Our phosphate and zinc concentrations are 0.005 M and 0.0001 M, respectively; these can be converted to 5×10^{-3} M and 1×10^{-4} M for easier calculations. Now, we simply need to evaluate whether the ion product (a quantity analogous to Q) exceeds the K_{sp}. $(1 \times 10^{-4})^3 = 1 \times 10^{-12}$, while $(5 \times 10^{-3})^2 = 25 \times 10^{-6}$. The product of these terms is 25×10^{-18}, or 2.5×10^{-17}. As this quantity is far greater than the K_{sp}, this substance will precipitate.

D: As its very small K_{sp} shows, zinc phosphate is insoluble in water.

1304. D is correct. We see from the table that $Mn(OH)_2$ has a smaller K_{sp} (in other words, one with a more negative exponent) than $Mg(OH)_2$. For this reason, statement II is correct. For statement III, remember that molar solubility is defined as the moles of a substance that can dissolve in one liter of solution. This value correlates to K_{sp}, and since $Mg(OH)_2$ and $Mn(OH)_2$ dissociate into the same number of ions, we can compare their K_{sp} values directly. As a result, we know that statement III is true as well.

I: Don't let negative exponents throw you off! Since the K_{sp} value for CuS has the most negative exponent, it is the smallest of the three numbers. Therefore, CuS is the least soluble of the salts under discussion.

1305. C is correct. As an equilibrium constant, K_{sp} only responds to changes in temperature. Specifically, if the researcher increased the ambient temperature (and thus the temperature of her solution), K_{sp} would rise.

A, B, D: Neither changes in ion concentration nor the common ion effect can actually alter the K_{sp} of a compound.

1306. D is correct. Since chromium(II) hydroxide has a formula of $Cr(OH)_2$, its K_{sp} expression is $[Cr^{2+}][OH^-]^2$. To translate between molar solubility and K_{sp}, let's give molar solubility a variable, "x." In other words, "x" moles of $Cr(OH)_2$ dissolve in a single liter of water. Since a 1:1 ratio exists between dissolved $Cr(OH)_2$ and the amount of aqueous Cr^{2+} present, we can say that our $[Cr^{2+}]$ value is also "x." However, two OH^- ions enter solution for every molecule of $Cr(OH)_2$ that dissociates, meaning that our value for $[OH^-]$ must be "2x." When we plug in these variables, we see that $K_{sp} = (x)(2x)^2$, or $K_{sp} = 4x^3$. $4[(7 \times 10^{-9})^3]$ is equal to $4(343 \times 10^{-27})$, or approximately 1400×10^{-27}. Manipulating scientific notation yields our answer, 1.4×10^{-24}.

A: This is a mistaken use of scientific notation.
B: This value was likely obtained by assuming that $K_{sp} = x^2$. That equation would only hold true if our original compound dissociated into two ions instead of three.

C: This calculation results from using the equation $K_{sp} = 2x^2$; in other words, forgetting to square the "2" coefficient in relation to $[OH^-]$.

1307. B is correct. The common ion effect stems from Le Châtelier's principle, a set of rules that govern chemical equilibria. If a solution contains a particular salt, and the same cation or anion that is present in that salt is then added to solution, its solubility will decrease. For example, here, the student begins with an unsaturated BaF_2 solution. If he were to add either Ba^{2+} or (as in this case) F^-, the BaF_2 salt will become less soluble. This occurs because the concentration of product ions has increased, shifting the equilibrium back toward the solid BaF_2.

A: There is no "common ion" here; the only salt involved is $CaCO_3$. If calcium chloride (or a similar salt of calcium) had been added instead, this would be a better answer.
C: The common ion effect decreases, not increases, solubility. Hence, the observations described here are impossible.
D: These two salts do not contain any common ions.

1308. B is correct. To find this answer, we simply need to calculate the molar solubility, or the amount of calcium oxalate that dissolves in one liter of water. When one molecule of $CaC_2O_{4(s)}$ dissolves, it forms one Ca^{2+} ion and one $C_2O_4^{2-}$ ion. Thus, we can write its K_{sp} expression as $K_{sp} = [Ca^{2+}][C_2O_4^{2-}]$, or $2.7 \times 10^{-9} = x^2$. As all components are present in a 1:1 ratio, our molar solubility (and the amount of oxalate ion in one liter of solution) is equal to "x." To find the square root of 2.7×10^{-9}, it is easiest to first convert to 27×10^{-10}. *27* is slightly greater than 5, so our answer is closest to 5.2×10^{-5}.

A: This is simply the K_{sp} of this compound, which is not what the question asks for.
C: The value shown here is the correct answer multiplied by 5. The fact that we begin with 5 moles of calcium oxalate is irrelevant; only a small amount can dissolve in water whether we have 1 mole or 100.
D: This choice most likely results from an error in calculating the square root of 2.7×10^{-9}. Remember, do not take the root of the exponent along with the coefficient! Instead, find

the square root of the coefficient, then cut the exponent in half.

1309. C is correct. Remember, molar solubility is distinct (both numerically and in definition) from K_{sp}, the solubility product. Molar solubility is defined perfectly in choice C.

A: This is the definition of K_{sp}, not molar solubility.
B: This is the reverse of the correct description. If molar solubility actually did represent the volume of solvent required to dissolve one mole of solid, it would be an enormous quantity for many insoluble substances.
D: Notice that this choice uses the term "unsaturated." Since unsaturated solutions can contain any molar amount of solid (up to the saturation point of the compound), this does not make sense.

1310. A is correct. For this question, consider Le Châtelier's principle. The dissociation expression for copper carbonate can be written as follows: $CuCO_3 \ß\rightarrow Cu^{2+} + CO_3^{2-}$. Just as the addition of a common ion would decrease this solubility by forcing the equilibrium toward the solid salt, the formation of a complex ion will remove some copper cation from solution, pushing the equilibrium in the opposite direction (toward the dissociated ions). For this reason, side reactions that form a complex tend to increase solubility.

C, D: These choices are too extreme. Like most carbonates, $CuCO_3$ certainly is not completely soluble. On the other hand, all compounds dissolve somewhat (even if to only a tiny degree) in solution.

1311. C is correct. Perchloric acid ($HClO_4$) is one of the strong acids you should know for the MCAT.

A: Nitrous acid (HNO_2) is weak. Make sure you do not confuse it with nitric acid (HNO_3)!
B: Hypochlorous acid ($HClO$) is weak.
D: Sulfurous acid (H_2SO_3) is weak. Do not confuse it with sulfuric acid (H_2SO_4)!

1312. D is correct. The product of the K_a of an acid and the K_b of its conjugate base is always equal to K_w. HSO_4^- and SO_4^{2-} are conjugates, so this statement is true.

A, C: $K_a * K_b$ is always equal to K_w, but the value of K_w is only 10^{-14} at 25 °C.

B: This is a common mistake. $K_a * K_b = K_w$, but only for the K_a of an acid and the K_b of its conjugate base. The K_a and K_b of the same species will (almost certainly) not multiply to equal K_w.

1313. B is correct. Acetic acid ($HC_2H_3O_2$) acts as a Brønsted-Lowry acid in this reaction because it donates a proton to form H_2O. Its conjugate, the acetate anion ($C_2H_3O_2^-$), is thus the conjugate base of a Brønsted-Lowry acid.

D: While acetate has the ability to accept a proton and therefore is a Brønsted-Lowry base, it is not strong. In contrast, it is stabilized by resonance, making it less likely to react and a weaker base.

1314. A is correct. The conjugate base of any Brønsted-Lowry acid is the species that exists after that acid has lost a proton. Here, that is ClO_2^-. Next, we must decide whether ClO_2^- is strong or weak. Remember, the weaker the original acid, the stronger its conjugate base (and vice versa). $HClO_2$ is a moderately weak acid, so it will have a moderately basic conjugate. However, ClO_2^- is not a hydroxide compound that dissociates completely, nor is it an ion like NH_2^- that is able to deprotonate even extremely weak acids. For that reason, ClO_2^- is categorized as a weak base.

1315. C is correct. For choice I, use the K_w expression, $K_w = [H^+][OH^-]$. According to the log rules, this can easily be changed into $\log(K_w) = \log[H^+] + \log[OH^-]$. Multiplying the entire equation by -1 yields $-\log(K_w) = -\log[H^+] - \log[OH^-]$, or $pK_w = pH + pOH$. Next, simply remember that $K_a * K_b = K_w$. Rearranging this equation yields choice III, which is thus correct.

II: K_a and K_b must be multiplied to yield K_w, not added. Only logarithmic terms like pH and pOH should be added directly.

1316. C is correct. The student cannot predict that simply because KOH is a strong base, the final solution will be basic. Instead, he must calculate the relative amounts of H^+ and OH^- in solution. He begins with (0.80 M)(0.050 L) = 0.040 mol HF and (0.75 M)(0.040 L) = 0.030 mol KOH. In this case, then, KOH is the limiting reagent and will fully react with HF, leaving excess HF (and thus excess H^+) in the final solution.

A: HF is a weak acid, unlike HCl, HBr, and HI.

B: A pOH that is greater than 7 signifies that the pH is less than 7, making the solution acidic overall. While this is true in this particular case, it has nothing to do with the strength of KOH.
D: Blue litmus will turn red in acidic, not basic, solution.

1317. B is correct. The higher the pK_a value, the weaker the acid, so Acid B must be weaker than Acid A. Comparatively weak acids have comparatively strong conjugate bases, and the stronger the base, the larger its K_b value.

A: As stated above, Acid B is weaker than Acid A. Weaker acids dissociate less in aqueous solution.
C: This is backwards. Since $pK_b = -log(K_b)$, the smaller the pK_b, the stronger the base. Acid B has a stronger conjugate base than Acid A, so it should have a smaller pK_b value.
D: $K_a = 10^{-pK_a}$, so the K_a for Acid B will be equal to $10^{-5.8}$. Be careful with negative exponents! This value falls between 10^{-5} and 10^{-6}, not 10^{-4} and 10^{-5}.

1318. D is correct. The compound with the lower pK_a will be the stronger acid. An acid is relatively strong when it has a more stable conjugate base (anion), which makes it better able to readily lose a proton. The two factors that contribute most to the stability of an anion are resonance and the presence of electron-withdrawing groups (also known as inductive effect) on the molecule. Fluorine atoms and nitro groups are classic examples of electron-withdrawing substituents.

A, B: The acid on the left has fewer electron-withdrawing groups than the structure on the right and an equal amount of resonance. For these reasons, it is a weaker acid.
C: Fluorine and NO_2 are electron-withdrawing.

1319. D is correct. The most basic ion is that which has the largest K_b. Since this table gives only K_a values, we must use the equation $K_a*K_b = K_w$. Remember that this relates the K_a of an acid with the K_b of its conjugate base, not the K_a and K_b of the same species! For this reason, since K_w is a constant at any particular temperature, the correct answer will be the ion whose conjugate acid has the smallest K_a. The conjugate of CO_3^{2-} is HCO_3^-, which has a K_a of 4.8×10^{-11}.

A, B, C: The K_a values of H_2SO_3, $H_2PO_4^-$, and $HC_2O_4^-$ are 1.5×10^{-2}, 6.2×10^{-8}, and 6.4×10^{-5},

respectively. All of these values are larger than 4.8×10^{-11}.

1320. C is correct. Since $K_a*K_b = K_w$, $pK_a + pK_b = pK_w$. At 25 °C, pK_w is equal to 14. Remember, though, that this equation relates the pK_a of an acid with the pK_b of its conjugate base, not the pK_a and pK_b of the same species! In other words, $pK_a(H_3PO_4) + pK_b(H_2PO_4^-) = 14$. Since the K_a for H_3PO_4 is 7.5×10^{-3}, its pK_a must fall somewhere between 2 and 3, but closer to 2 (let's call it 2.2). $pK_b = 14 - 2.2$, making C the only logical answer.

A: This mistakenly gives the approximate pK_a of H_3PO_4.
B: This is close to the answer that would be calculated from using the K_a of $H_2PO_4^-$ instead of that of H_3PO_4.

1321. C is correct. This flask contains 1 M HCl that is diluted by a factor of 10, yielding a total concentration of 0.1 M hydrochloric acid. Since HCl is a strong acid, we can assume that [HCl] = [H^+]. Finally, since $pH = -log[H^+]$, $pH = -log(0.1) = 1$.

A: This is the pH of undiluted 1 M HCl.

1322. C is correct. HF is a weak acid, while NaOH is a strong base. After neutralization, the two species that will remain in solution are F^-, Na^+, and H_2O. As a weak acid, HF has a fairly decent conjugate base, while the other two species are neutral.

A: HF is not a strong acid.
D: Due to their 1:1 molar ratio, NaOH and HF will fully neutralize each other, regardless of their differing strengths.

1323. D is correct. The pK_a and pK_w for both reactions are large, positive values. This means that the reactants will dissociate to a very small extent. For this reason, HCN and H_2O will dominate in solution.

A, B, C: Very small amounts of H_3O^+ and OH^- will be produced by the auto-ionization of the water, and very little H_3O^+ and CN^- will be made from the dissociation of HCN.

1324. B is correct. HCN is a very weak acid, with a pK_a of 9.2. To find our answer, we must discern how much H^+ is formed from the dissociation of this species in water. Remember, for every H^+ ion that forms, one CN^- ion will form as well; for this reason, we can set x^2 equal to the K_a, $10^{-9.2}$. Rounding this to 10^{-9} and taking its square root is roughly equal to $10^{-4.5}$, which correlates to a pH between 4 and 5.

A: This would be true if HCN were a strong acid.
C, D: Since HCN is not a base, these choices are impossible in aqueous solution.

1325. B is correct. pH can have a value that is either below 0 or above 14. For example, consider a solution of 10 M HCl. Its pH is $-\log(10)$, or -1.

A: This is accurate; any acid on its own in aqueous solution will yield a pH at least slightly less than 7.
C: This statement is true, as is the reverse.
D: Through stoichiometry, one can see that this is correct.

1326. D is correct. Pure water always has an equal number of hydroxide and hydrogen ions. While pH does decrease with increasing temperature, pOH decreases as well.

1327. A is correct. K_w is only equal to approximately 10^{-14} at 25 °C.

I: Since pH decreases with increasing temperature, more dissociation must take place when more heat energy is available. Thus, this reaction must be endothermic.

III: pH = pOH for pure water at all temperatures.

IV: While pH does drop when the temperature is high, pOH changes in the same manner. A solution is only acidic when more protons are present than hydroxide ions.

1328: C is correct. H_2O (l) $\longleftrightarrow$ H^+ (aq) + OH^- (aq). When writing an equilibrium constant expression, remember to disregard pure liquids and solids. Thus, $K_w = [H^+][OH^-]$.

1329. C is correct. Due to Le Châtelier's principle, basic compounds dissolve best in acidic solution. Specifically, the presence of protons neutralizes some of the free hydroxide ions, pushing the equilibrium toward dissociation. 2 M of a strong acid would certainly accomplish the student's goal of raising the number of Ca^{2+} ions in solution.

A: Bases dissolve especially poorly in basic solution due to the common ion effect.

B: While this would likely help a very small amount, 0.05 M of a weak acid is hardly a change at all.
D: It is true that none of these alterations will change K_{sp}, but they can still force the reaction toward the ion products in order to re-establish equilibrium.

1330. B is correct. The initial number of moles of acid present is (8 M)(0.250 L) or 2 moles. Regardless of the strengths of the species involved, this quantity requires 2 moles of OH^- ions to fully neutralize and 1 mole to "half neutralize."

A, C: Acid and base strength does not affect the quantity required for a neutralization reaction. This can be proven through use of simple stoichiometry.
D: The question stem references the half-equivalence point, not the equivalence point.

1331. D is correct. Choice I is a classic buffer, with equal amounts of a weak acid and its conjugate base. Choice III contains the same conjugate pair, but with more moles of acid. Remember, the concentrations of acid and conjugate base do not have to be equal to produce a buffer, just to produce one where pH = pK_a. Finally, Choice IV appears to contain a strong base, which should not appear in a buffer solution. However, note that the number of moles of NaOH is exactly half that of $HC_2H_3O_2$, meaning that the base will deprotonate one-half of the acetic acid molecules. This will leave a solution with equal amounts of $HC_2H_3O_2$ and $NaC_2H_3O_2$, a perfect buffer.

II: While this involves a weak acid and a weak base, they are not a conjugate pair.

1332. C is correct. To manufacture a buffer, an acid should be selected with a pK_a as close to the desired pH as possible. However, the numbers given are K_a values, not pK_as. To convert, remember that pK_a is simply the negative log of K_a. We can estimate negative log values by gauging what values each of these K_as falls between. For acetic acid, 1.8×10^{-5} is very close to 1×10^{-5}, but falls slightly on the side of 1×10^{-4}. Its pK_a, then, must be slightly less than 5.

A: Acids dissociate less in acidic solutions due to the common ion effect. If the solution already has a high concentration of H^+ ions, the reaction shifts toward the reactants to regenerate the undissociated HF.

B, C: Changing the concentration of a product or reactant will never change K_a. Like other K values, K_a is an equilibrium constant and only changes in response to changing temperature.
B: This one is very close! However, 6.3×10^{-5} is closer to 1×10^{-4} than 1×10^{-5}, so the pK_a must be closer to 4 than 5, and not as close to 4.8 as choice C.

1333. D is correct. The Henderson-Hasselbalch equation can be written as either $pH = pK_a + \log\frac{[\text{conjugate base}]}{[\text{acid}]}$ or $pOH = pK_b + \log\frac{[\text{conjugate acid}]}{[\text{base}]}$.
A: The log term should not be subtracted here. This would wrongly imply that more conjugate base produces a lower pH.
B: K_a should not appear in this equation, since the other terms are logs. Note that $-\log[H^+]$ is the same as pH.
C: This incorrectly places the base concentration in the numerator of the fraction.

1334. C is correct. If this solution contains equal concentrations of HCO_3^- and CO_3^{2-}, we must be at one of the titration's half-equivalence points. Here, pH must equal pK_a – but which one? Since the first proton on H_2CO_3 has already been removed, we are at the second half-equivalence point, and the relevant pK_a is pK_{a2}. $pK_{a2} = -\log(K_{a2})$, which should fall between 10 and 11.

B: We would get an answer similar to this one if we used the first K_a value instead of the second.

1335. C is correct. $[HF] = [F^-]$ at the half-equivalence point, since this is where exactly half of the original hydrofluoric acid has been neutralized to form NaF. At the equivalence point, no HF would remain.

A: 0.5 L of 1 M NaOH contains 0.5 moles of OH^- ions, which will neutralize the 0.5 moles of H^+ present in our original solution. This position represents the equivalence point. Since a weak acid is being titrated with a strong base, the solution will be basic at this point due to the presence of the weakly basic salt NaF.
B: The products of this neutralization are NaF and H_2O. As the conjugate base of a weak acid, F^- is basic, making NaF a basic salt.
D: As stated above, 0.5 L of 1 M NaOH is needed to reach the equivalence point, so half of that

volume would bring the titration to the half-equivalence point.

1336. C is correct. Point B is the first equivalence point. Here, the first proton on H_2CO_3 has been fully neutralized, leaving a solution that contains only HCO_3^-. Point C is the second half-equivalence point, at which the second proton has been removed from half of the molecules as well. In both of these cases, HCO_3^- is present while H_2CO_3 is not.

A, D: Point A is the first half-equivalence point, where the first proton has been removed from exactly half of the H_2CO_3 molecules. Here, $[H_2CO_3] = [HCO_3^-]$.

1337. A is correct. Point A is the first half-equivalence point, meaning that we need to add exactly half of the volume required to neutralize the first proton, or one-quarter of the amount needed to fully neutralize H_2CO_3. We can use $N_1V_1 = N_2V_2$: (1.5 N H_2CO_3)(500 mL) = (2.25 M NaOH)(x mL). Solving for x, we get a volume of 333 mL. However, remember that this equation gives us the volume of base needed to fully neutralize the acid! To answer this question, we need to divide by four, giving us 83.3 mL.

1338. C is correct. As temperature increases, pK_w becomes smaller. Since $pH + pOH = pK_w$, and since pH = pOH for a neutral solution, both pH and pOH must decrease with increasing temperature.

A: The pH of a neutral solution is only 7 at 25 °C, when $pK_w = 14$.
B: A solution of pure water is neutral, and in neutral solutions, $[H^+] = [OH^-]$. pH, then, must equal pOH.
D: This is backwards. The increasing pK_w shows that as water temperature rises, the dissociation reaction favors the product ions.

1339. A is correct. $pH + pOH = pK_w$, and pH = pOH for a neutral solution. Substituting pH in for pOH, we get 2(pH) = 12.70, or pH = 6.35.

1340. B is correct. Any titration of a weak acid or base will be most effective as a buffer at the half-equivalence point. At the half-equivalence point, $[HA] = [A^-]$, so $pH = pK_a$. You can also remember that the half-equivalence point falls in the middle of the flattest point on a titration curve, where pH is changing the least.

1341. C is correct. The oxidation state of carbon in H_2CO_3 can be found by starting with the elements with known oxidation states. Oxygen generally has an oxidation number of -2 (with some exceptions, such as in H_2O_2). Hydrogen tends to have an oxidation number of +1. Since the overall compound is neutral, we are left with $(2)(+1) + C + (3)(-2) = 0$, or C = +4. For H_2CO_3 to be converted into HCO_3^- and CO_3^{2-}, it simply loses one or two protons; this does not change its oxidation state.

D: This gives the charges on the overall compounds, not the oxidation states of carbon alone.

1342. A is correct. Here, let's begin with oxygen, since it exists in its elemental form on the reactant side of the reaction. Oxygen thus begins with an oxidation state of zero. It ends with a number of -2, meaning that it was reduced, or gained electrons. In contrast, carbon begins with an oxidation state of -2 and ends with one of +4; this is a loss of electrons, or oxidation.

B, D: The oxidation state of hydrogen does not change in this reaction.

1343. C is correct. The better reducing agent is the metal that is more likely to oxidize itself (in other words, it reduces a different species). Here, Na^+ has a more negative reduction potential; in other words, it is less likely to reduce than Mg^{2+}. However, we need to switch the signs of the reactions to find their oxidation potentials. Na (s) thus has an oxidation potential of +2.71, while Mg (s) has an oxidation potential of +2.38. Mg (s) is the better choice for a reducing agent.

A, B: A good reducing agent does not gain electrons (reduce); it loses electrons, or oxidizes. D: Mg (s) is less likely to give up electrons than Na (s).

1344. B is correct. Good oxidizing agents are species that are especially prone to reduction, while good reducing agents are those that are likely to oxidize. Here, Cl_2 has the highest reduction potential, so it is the best oxidizing agent. If we reverse the reaction involving sodium, we see that Na (s) has the most positive oxidation potential and is thus the best reducing agent.

A: This is the reverse of the correct answer. C, D: Na^+ is the product of the reaction with the highest oxidation potential, while Cl^- is formed by the reaction with the most positive reduction potential. Oxidizing and reducing agents must be reactants, not products.

1345. C is correct. Reactions in galvanic cells occur spontaneously. Since Cu^{2+} has a more positive reduction potential than Zn^{2+}, it is Cu^{2+} that will reduce and Zn(s) that will oxidize. Oxidation and reduction always occur according to the mnemonic "RED CAT": reduction happens at the cathode and oxidation takes place at the anode.

B, D: Regardless of the type of cell, oxidation never occurs at the cathode and reduction never occurs at the anode.

1346. C is correct. A more positive E_{cell} indicates a reaction that is more spontaneous in the forward direction. While $E°_{cell}$ is a set value, it refers to the reaction at standard conditions (25 °C, 1 atm, and 1 M concentrations of all reactants). If reactant concentrations are increased, the reaction will be pushed forward and more products will be formed.

A, B: Decreasing the E_{cell} makes the reaction less spontaneous and would produce fewer moles of product.
D: While the standard state cell potential cannot be changed, the cell potential in general can be altered by modifying the experimental conditions.

1347. C is correct. Oxidation always occurs at the anode regardless of the type of cell.

1348. B is correct. In a galvanic cell, nickel would oxidize and lead would reduce, resulting in a potential of $0.23 + (-0.13) = 0.10$ V. In an electrolytic cell, lead would oxidize and nickel would reduce, yielding a potential of $0.13 + (-0.23) = -0.10$ V.

I: This results from adding the reduction potentials of both reactions together. In reality, one of these reactions would need to be an oxidization.

IV: This value comes from adding the oxidation potentials of the two reactions, but neglects the fact that one reaction must be a reduction.

1349. A is correct. Reactions occurring in galvanic cells are always spontaneous, meaning that they have positive E_{cell} values. Positive cell potentials correlate to negative ΔG values, since both refer to spontaneous reactions. Similarly, these reactions must have K values that are greater than one, because they favor the products, not the reactants.

1350. A is correct. Perchloric acid is $HClO_4$, meaning that Species A must be $NaClO_4$. In this compound, as in most cases other than peroxides, oxygen has an oxidation state of -2. Sodium has an oxidation number of +1, while chlorine has one of +7 and the overall compound is neutral.

1351. B is correct. Since the cathode is composed of solid nickel metal, the relevant half-reaction must be $Ni^{2+} + 2 e^- \rightarrow Ni (s)$. For this reason, raising $[Ni^{2+}]$ would increase the favorability of this reaction. According to Le Châtelier's principle, such a change would increase the reactant concentration and drive the associated redox reaction toward the products.

A: While sodium does seem to have a very positive oxidation potential, and while this does appear to make the metal a good choice for an anode, Na (s) is actually highly explosive in water. For this reason, it would be an unwise choice to include in aqueous solution.
C: This is the reverse of the correct answer; Cd^{2+} is a product, not a reactant.
D: Under standard conditions, this galvanic cell would have an $E°_{cell}$ of 0.12 V. A positive value like this one certainly denotes a spontaneous reaction.

1352. D is correct. Note that this question asks for E_{cell} (the cell potential), not $E°_{cell}$ (the standard-state cell potential). As a result, we cannot assume that this student constructs his apparatus under standard conditions. For this reason, factors like temperature, pressure, and the relative concentrations of reactants are unknown, and we cannot rule out any of these choices as potential answers.

A: This negative value represents the $E°_{cell}$ of an electrolytic cell composed of these two metals. Such cells are nonspontaneous, meaning that the lead cation would reduce (E° = -0.13 V) while the copper metal would oxidize (E° = -0.34 V). (-0.13) + (-0.34) = -0.47.
B: While this value could not be obtained under standard conditions, that fact is irrelevant for this question.
C: Similar to choice A, this is the $E°_{cell}$ of a lead/copper galvanic cell. Lead metal would oxidize, yielding an E° value of 0.13 V, while copper cation would reduce and give an E° of 0.34 V. (0.13) + (0.34) = 0.47.

1353. B is correct. Concentration cells are a form of galvanic (spontaneous) cell. Specifically, they include the same species in both half-cells, and thus function only if the two sides contain different concentrations. Here, for example, one half-cell is highly concentrated in Sn^{2+}, making that side very positive. The other side is significantly more dilute. Thus, electrons will move from the dilute to the concentrated side until an equilibrium is established.

A: This choice properly identifies the cell as galvanic; however, its half-cells contain entirely separate species.
C, D: Concentration cells are not electrolytic. In fact, they function only because different concentrations of the same ion can produce a very small positive potential.

1354. C is correct. Regardless of the type of cell, the anode is always the site of oxidation. Here, we are told that the apparatus constitutes a galvanic cell and that silver ion is more prone to reduction than zinc ion. Thus, the silver electrode must serve as the cathode, leaving the zinc electrode to function as the anode. Remember, while electrons travel from anode to cathode, current moves in the opposite direction (from cathode to anode).

A: While Ag can be oxidized, the question stem implies that this is unlikely.
B: Here, the silver electrode is the site of reduction. For this reason, electrons would flow towards it, not away.
D: It is silver, not zinc, that is reduced in this case.

1355. C is correct. Structure A is the salt bridge, an important component of a galvanic cell like this one. Let's first imagine what would occur without such a structure. Here, electrons flow from right to left in an effort to reduce Ag^+ to solid silver metal. After only a short time, however, the left-hand half-cell would become highly negative in comparison to the half-cell on the right. As electrons would now be traveling against their charge gradient, the process would grind to a premature halt. On the other hand, when a salt bridge is present to connect the two solutions, otherwise uninvolved ions can move to neutralize this charge difference. In this case, one sulfate ion will travel to the right for every two electrons that move to the left.

A, B: Electrons move through the wire, not the salt bridge.
D: This is the reverse of the correct answer. As negative species, sulfate ions would not travel in the same direction as electrons.

1356. B is correct. Anions and cations travel through a salt bridge in opposite directions. Here, since electrons move from right to left, we might previously have assumed that SO_4^{2-} ions would travel the other way to neutralize the resulting charge gradient. Now, however, we realize that Na^+ ions are present instead. These cations will move from right to left in a 1:1 ratio with electrons, preventing charge buildup and allowing the reaction to continue as long as possible.

A: Sulfate certainly did not participate in the redox reaction described, but it still could have functioned as an important species due to its relationship with the salt bridge.
D: Na^+ has a highly negative reduction potential and is thus incredibly unlikely to reduce.

1357. A is correct. While the anode is the site of oxidation in all cells, its sign is not always the same. Specifically, remember that electrolytic cells are nonspontaneous. Since electrons always flow from anode to cathode, the anode of such a cell must be positive. The resulting positive-to-negative electron flow exemplifies a nonspontaneous process.

B: Galvanic cells have negative (-) anodes. This way, electrons can flow from a negative to a positive region, a process that is spontaneous in nature.

1358. D is correct. If Q > 3, ln(Q) must be larger than 1. For this reason, the quantity $\frac{RT}{nF}$ ln(Q) gives rise to a positive value that must be added to E°. Thus, E (the cell potential) will be greater than E° (the standard-state cell potential).

A: Q cannot possibly be equal to 0, as ln(0) represents a quantity that does not exist.
B: When Q = 1, ln(Q) = 0. In this case, the value of T does not matter; the product of zero and any other number is always zero.
C: This is the reverse of the accurate relationship.

1359. A is correct. In essence, rechargeable batteries work via reversible redox processes. When such a cell is discharging, it is releasing stored energy; this is similar to the spontaneous process seen in galvanic cells. However, this question asks about recharging. Here, we must use an external power source to move electrons in a way that would be naturally nonspontaneous, just as an electrolytic cell does.

C: A concentration cell is a type of galvanic cell. It thus is more closely related to discharge than to recharge.
D: A half-cell includes only one "half" of a redox reaction – either reduction or oxidation. As no redox process can occur without two half-reactions, this choice does not make sense.

1360. C is correct. If the external concentration of ion "X" is ten times smaller than its internal concentration, then the log term in the equation will yield a value of -1. Plugging in a valence of +1 gives (61)(-1), or -61 mV.

A, B, D: All three of these sets of conditions will produce an equilibrium potential of +61 mV, not the desired -61 mV.

1361. D is correct. Based on the name and chemical formula, we can determine that this is an anionic structure that is associated with Na^+. This could only occur by way of an ionic bond. Additionally, the structure includes 12 carbons and 25 hydrogens, indicating that the carbons are attached by single bonds (which are also covalent). Finally, multiple pi bonds exist as part of the sulfate group.

1362. B is correct. NaH contains a bond between a positively-charged sodium and a negatively-charged hydrogen atom. This is a clear example of an ionic bond.

    A, C: These involve atoms with less significant electronegativity differences.
    D: Hydrogen bonds are intermolecular and require the presence of –OH, –FH, or –NH.

1363. C is correct. Methane (CH_4) contains four hydrogen atoms bound to a central carbon. In each bond, one electron is donated by C and one by H. Both carbon and hydrogen have relatively similar electronegativities, making this a nonpolar covalent bond.

1364. A is correct. The potential energy of the two hydrogen atoms begins at a baseline level. Due to the stability conferred by a bond, it then drops, reaching a minimum at the ideal bond length for H_2. However, if they continue to move closer together, they will begin to repel each other and bring the potential energy back above the baseline.

1365. A is correct. The stronger a bond, the shorter it will be. Ethyne has a triple bond between the two carbons, making it the strongest; ethene has a double bond, and ethane has a single bond.

1366. B is correct. Each double bond contains one sigma and one pi bond. Since three double bonds are present in the central ring of the structure, there are also three pi bonds.

    D: This is the number of visible sigma bonds in the diagram.

1367. A is correct. An sp³-hybridized carbon is one that is bound to four substituents. In such a structure, all three p orbitals are hybridized with the single s orbital. To put this simply, the central carbon must have four single, and no double, bonds attached to it. This applies to three of the carbon atoms in epinephrine. Remember to fill in the extra hydrogens as needed.

1368. B is correct. Bond order denotes whether a bond is single, double, or triple in nature. The higher the bond order, the shorter the associated length. Unknown #1 is notably shorter than either the N-N single or double bond; we can thus assume that it is a triple bond, with an order of 3.

Unknown #2's bond length is almost identical to that of the known N=N bond, making it likely to be a double bond.

1369. D is correct. The bond length mentioned in the question stem is longer than any of those listed in the table. The best way to increase bond length without changing bond order is to replace one of the atoms in the bond with a larger one. Here, either sulfur or phosphorus is worth trying.

1370. A is correct. Carbon dioxide is a linear molecule. Even though each C-O bond is polar, the overall symmetry causes the individual dipoles to cancel. Since no molecular dipole is present, CO_2 would not align with the magnetic field.

1371. A is correct. We are looking for a structure that is both as stable as possible and correctly labeled in terms of formal charges. To find the formal charge on an atom, take its group number (or ground-state number of valence electrons), then subtract the number of bonds in which it participates and the number of electrons in its lone pairs. For example, take one of the negatively-charged oxygen atoms in choice A. Oxygen typically has 6 valence electrons, so $6 - (1 + 6)$ yields -1. Since phosphate has an overall charge of -3, three oxygens must be single-bonded and one must be double-bonded. Phosphorus, the central atom, can form five bonds (here, three single and one double) due to its d orbitals.

    B, D: These structures unnecessarily scatter the formal charges on the atoms. In general, make as many atoms neutral as possible (eliminating D, in which every atom has a non-neutral formal charge). When possible, allow the peripheral atoms to hold a charge and make the central atom neutral.
    C: These negatively-charged oxygen atoms are incorrectly labeled. They should be neutral [6 $- (2 + 4) = 0$], while the singly-bonded oxygen should hold a negative charge. Additionally, phosphorus has an incorrect charge as well as seven bonds.

1372. B is correct. Remember that carbon atoms always prefer to form four bonds, so one oxygen atom must be doubly bound to the central carbon while the remaining two must have single bonds.

The three resonance structures of carbonate are shown below.

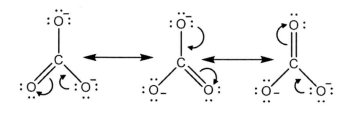

1373. C is correct. First, draw the Lewis structure of the sulfate anion. You will see that the central sulfur atom is doubly bound to two oxygen atoms, while the other two oxygens are connected by single bonds. As a result, the sulfur atom has four bonding groups and no lone pairs, yielding a tetrahedral geometry.

A: Octahedral molecular geometry exists when there are six (not four) bonding groups connected to the central atom.
B: A square pyramidal shape, as its name implies, occurs when four bonding groups are arranged in a "square" around the central atom, with an additional substituent above to form the shape of a pyramid. This geometry exists only when a central atom is bound to five substituents and contains a single lone pair.
D: A square planar geometry is formed when a central atom is connected to four substituents (forming a square shape), as well as two lone pairs. As stated above, the sulfur atom in sulfate does not contain lone pairs at all.

1374. B is correct. The tertiary carbon has three bonding groups and no lone pairs. This is the hallmark of a trigonal planar geometry.

A: If this carbon were tetrahedral, it would need to be bound to four substituents. As each carbon in the benzene ring has a double bond, this is impossible.
C: A square planar geometry requires four substituents and two lone pairs, a condition that is not present in the molecule shown.
D: This is similar to a tetrahedral geometry, but includes three substituents and one lone pair instead of four substituents. In any case, the carbon referenced in the question is only bound to three groups.

1375. C is correct. The structure shown in the question stem, as well as three additional resonance forms, is shown below.

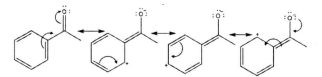

All three of these structures contain a positively charged carbon atom somewhere on the benzene ring. Note that the original form, in which all atoms have neutral formal charges, is more stable than any of those three.

1376. A is correct. As an element in group 5A with available d orbitals, phosphorus can form five single bonds. Bromine, like the other halogens, tends to form one bond. Remember, the most stable Lewis structures are those that minimize formal charges; for this reason, structure A is our clear answer.

B: Here, the bromine atoms are given two lone pairs instead of three, but are still depicted as neutral. If this situation were somehow possible, these atoms would be significantly electron-deficient and thus positively charged.
D: These structures vastly overcomplicate the distribution of charge.

1377. D is correct. A trigonal pyramidal geometry is found in molecules where the central atom has three substituents and one lone pair of electrons. Though it is not drawn in the figure above, nitrogen (as an atom that prefers to have five valence electrons) has a single lone pair. This pair repels the groups away from itself, creating a pyramid shape when considering the atoms alone.

B: While a tetrahedral shape is similar to that displayed above, it requires the central atom to have four substituents and no lone pairs.

1378. C is correct. A bent geometry appears when a central atom is bound to two substituents while also containing two lone pairs. Water, or H_2O, is a classic example. If nitrogen triiodide were to lose an iodine atom (unstable as the resulting structure would be), it would now be bound to two atoms instead of three. To maintain a full octet, nitrogen would gain an additional lone pair, yielding the bent shape described above.

B: This answer is tempting! But a linear geometry requires perfect 180° angles between atoms. As such, it would only occur if the central nitrogen contained two bound substituents and no lone pairs.

1379. C is correct. The molecular geometry of a compound certainly can be determined from its molecular formula. The easiest way to do so is to first draw the Lewis structure of the species. In addition, as regions of relative electron density, lone pairs do repel other bonding groups. This is what creates a bent structure in molecules like water.

II: The molecular geometry is directly affected by valence electrons on the central atom alone. Electrons on peripheral atoms are not used when deducing the overall shape of the species.

1380. D is correct. All three of the statements are true. Sulfur trioxide has three equivalent resonance structures, each of which possesses one S=O bond and two S-O bonds. Since this species contains three bonding groups and no lone pairs, it has a trigonal planar molecular geometry. Finally, the molecule as a whole is uncharged, and each individual atom has a neutral formal charge as well.

1381. B is correct. A hydrogen bond forms when a hydrogen atom is bound to nitrogen, oxygen, or fluorine and can interact with lone pairs on adjacent molecules. Here, the carboxylate group will gain an H atom, giving it the required –OH group for this form of interaction.

A, B: Dipole-dipole interactions and London forces are weaker than hydrogen bonds.
D: Covalent bonding is intramolecular, not intermolecular.

1382. C is correct. If these choices were closer, you would need to consider factors like branching of the carbon chain. However, molecular weight directly correlates with boiling point. Since 1-octene is much heavier than the other molecules, it will boil at the highest temperature.

1383. B is correct. Low vapor pressure always corresponds to high boiling point, a property

that directly relates to the strength of intermolecular attractions. Choice B depicts a molecule that can hydrogen bond, making it able to exert the strongest attractive forces of the molecules listed.

A: This nonpolar structure can only generate London forces, which are the weakest type of intermolecular attraction.
C, D: These molecules exert dipole-dipole forces.

1384. C is correct. This ketone can interact with other like molecules via dipole-dipole forces. These attractions are a direct result of its carbonyl (C=O) bond. Since carbon and oxygen differ in their electronegativities, this bond represents a moderately strong dipole.

A: The pictured species does not possess an –OH group.
B, D: Neither of these characteristics contribute to the ability to exert dipole-dipole forces.

1385. A is correct. This question is tricky, as it mixes intra- and intermolecular forces! Remember, intramolecular bonds (which attach atoms of the same molecule) are always stronger than intermolecular attractions. Nonpolar covalent bonds are intramolecular.

B: This is the strongest of the listed intermolecular forces.

1386. D is correct. Gaseous hydrogen is composed of two atoms of identical electronegativities. Therefore, it lacks a dipole entirely and can only participate in the weakest attractions, London forces.

1387. D is correct. This statement perfectly describes hydrogen bonding in DNA. Guanine and cytosine are attached by three H-bonds, while adenine and thymine are only connected by two.

1388. D is correct. All of the molecules listed are ketones, which can exert dipole-dipole interactions. We therefore can only compare these species by size. The smaller the molecule, the less energy required to remove it from solution. 2-propanone is the smallest of these choices.

1389. C is correct. This question is basically asking for the species with the lowest boiling point, or that which exerts the weakest intermolecular forces. As an entirely nonpolar molecule, this must be neon. We are also given a hint by the fact that neon is a noble gas, which implies that it has already surpassed its boiling point at room temperature.

1390. A is correct. The more G-C bonds present, the higher the denaturation temperature of the helix. Choice A contains only 10% thymine, giving it a total of 20% A-T and 80% G-C bonds. As a result, it is the most stable of those listed.

1391. D is correct. Boyle's law relates the volume and pressure of a gas as follows: $P_1V_1 = P_2V_2$. In other words, doubling the volume of a gas should cut pressure in half, and quadrupling the volume of a gas should reduce pressure to one-fourth of what it was before.

    A, B: While these statements are true, they relate temperature and volume, not pressure and volume. As such, they relate to Charles' law.
    C: Boyle's law gives volume and pressure as indirectly proportional. This choice incorrectly describes them as directly related.

1392. A is correct. Remember, temperatures must be changed to Kelvin when dealing with the ideal gas law. This gas begins with a temperature of 288 K and must increase about 1.25-fold to reach 356 K. According to the equation PV = nRT, if all other factors remain constant, pressure must change by this amount as well. A 125% change in pressure results in a new value of 1.25 atm. Note that it is also perfectly fine to plug in all values to the ideal gas law to find this answer.

    D: This answer is far too large, it results from keeping temperature values in Celsius. Remember, an increase from 15°C to 83°C is not a fivefold increase when converted to Kelvin values.

1393. A is correct. To make gas-related calculations easier, we assume that the particles comprising ideal gases have no volume of their own. For that reason, all of the volume is assumed to be occupied by the gas itself, not the particles (in other words, gases expand or contract perfectly to fill their containers). Another main assumption of the ideal gas law is that particles

themselves do not experience intermolecular forces from other particles in the gas.

    B, D: Ideal gases themselves certainly occupy a volume; for example, consider a gas in a 2 L container. It is the particles that are assumed to have negligible volume.
    C: Even for an ideal gas, the force exerted by collisions on the walls of the container cannot be ignored. In fact, it is this force that allows pressure within the vessel to be measured.

1394. B is correct. Gases behave least ideally at high pressure and low temperature. In other words, they deviate most from ideal behavior under conditions that favor formation of a liquid. While choice B clearly involves the lowest temperature, it is not immediately easy to compare pressures, as they are given in different units. However, one gigapascal (or GPa) is equivalent to 1×10^9 Pa. Thus, choice B involves an extremely high pressure of 1×10^{11} Pa.

    A: This pressure and temperature are actually very close to standard conditions (101,500 Pa and 298 K). Hence, the container would not be under an unusually high pressure or low temperature.
    C: These conditions involve low pressure (2.5 $\times 10^4$ Pa) and high temperature, which is when gases behave most ideally, not least.

1395. D is correct. Since the sample contains 1 mole of gas, we can rearrange the ideal gas law to find our expected PV/RT ratio: 1. The given value is higher, implying that either pressure or volume is larger than expected. For the ideal gas law to work properly, two main assumptions are necessary: that the volume of particles themselves is negligible and that no intermolecular forces are present between particles. However, these assumptions become especially untrue at low temperature and high pressure. Given this information, D is the only sensible answer.

    A: Low, not high, temperature causes deviations from the ideal gas law.
    B: While low temperature could cause an unexpected calculation, the value found by the scientist is higher than expected (1.05 instead of 1).
    C: High, not low, pressure causes deviations from expected ideal behavior.

1396. C is correct. The kinetic molecular theory of gases states that the average KE of one mole of any gas is proportional to 32 RT, meaning that the only factor involved is temperature. Thus, our answer will be the particle with the smallest temperature in Kelvin. Choice C has a Kelvin temperature far lower than that of any other choice. Note, of course, that it is impossible to exactly determine the KE held by any one particle; however, the question asks for the most likely answer.

D: While this choice has the smallest molecular weight, that attribute is irrelevant. With a temperature of 135 + 273 = 408 K, this particle should have substantially more KE than choice C.

1397. C is correct. The molar masses or molecular weights of the gases are irrelevant. The same number of moles of any gas will always occupy the same volume, as long as surrounding conditions are identical; instead of differing in volume, the gases will simply have different densities. In other words, one mole of any gas at STP occupies exactly 22.4 L, and three moles of any gas (which we have here) occupies 3*22.4 or 67.2 L.

A: This is the volume taken up by one mole of any gas at STP. However, the given information allows us to deduce that we have three moles.
B, D: These choices incorrectly take into account the fact that krypton's molar mass is twice that of argon.

1398. C is correct. Dalton's law states that the total pressure in a vessel is the sum of the partial pressures of the components. Moreover, the partial pressure of a gas is proportional to its mole fraction in the container. We already know that the total number of moles in the flask is 0.5 + 0.25 + 0.75 = 1.5 moles. Since exactly one-third of this is ammonia, the total pressure is 3*415 torr, or 1245 torr.

B: This value would be calculated if we assumed the mole fraction of ammonia was one-half – in other words, if we confused ammonia with helium.
D: This choice could result from confusing ammonia with oxygen, which has a mole fraction of one-sixth.

1399. C is correct. Graham's law can be used to compare the rates of diffusion of two gases. This equation can be written as $\frac{\text{rate 1}}{\text{rate 2}} = \frac{\sqrt{\text{molar mass 2}}}{\sqrt{\text{molar mass 1}}}$; in other words, the rate of diffusion of a gas varies with the reciprocal of the square root of its molar mass. Here, let's give helium "Rate 1" and our unknown gas "Rate 2." This equation becomes $\frac{0.8 \text{ m/s}}{0.1 \text{ m/s}} = \frac{\sqrt{\text{molar mass 2}}}{\sqrt{4\text{g/mol}}}$, and the molar mass of Gas A can be calculated at 256 g/mol.

A: This is the square root of Gas A's molar mass.
B: This choice could be found by misremembering Graham's law as $\frac{\text{rate 1}}{\text{rate 2}} = \frac{\text{molar mass 2}}{\text{molar mass 1}}$.

1400. C is correct. Both diffusion and effusion involve the net movement of gas particles from high-concentration to lower-concentration regions. Diffusion can be thought of as the "spreading out" of particles in a container in which they can move relatively freely, while effusion involves the movement of particles through a small gap. Graham's law, which describes both forms of motion, can be written as $\frac{\text{rate 1}}{\text{rate 2}} = \frac{\sqrt{\text{molar mass 2}}}{\sqrt{\text{molar mass 1}}}$ when two gases are being directly compared. In other words, I is certainly true. While statement III mentions density instead of molar mass, remember that one mole of any gas will occupy the same volume under the same conditions. For that reason, density and molar mass are directly proportional.

II: According to Graham's law, diffusion rate is proportional to the square root of the molar mass of the gas, not to the molar mass itself.

1401. C is correct. The reaction shows carbon dioxide undergoing a phase change from gas directly to solid. Such a transition is termed deposition.

A: Don't fall for this trap answer! While dry ice is often mentioned in regard to sublimation, that reaction involves a direct transition from solid to gas. The reaction shown describes the opposite process.
B: Condensation involves a change from gas to liquid, not gas to solid.
D: Decomposition is not a type of phase change. Instead, it refers to a reaction during which a single, larger compound is broken into at least two smaller compounds.

1402. D is correct. In choice I, the temperature of the water increases while pressure stays the same; additionally, the ice melts into liquid water. This process requires a significant heat input, both to raise the temperatures of the solid and liquid states and for the phase change itself. Choice II does not involve a temperature increase, but does describe vaporization; this process requires a specific amount of energy known as latent heat or the heat of vaporization. Finally, choice III describes sublimation, or the direct transition from solid to gas. This process can be facilitated by either a pressure drop or a temperature increase, but since pressure actually rose, III must be a correct choice here.

IV: This choice is the reverse of the correct answer. Condensation, or the transition from vapor into liquid, generally releases heat energy.

1403. D is correct. This process must be broken down into steps. First, ice at -5 °C becomes ice at 0 °C. Plugging known values in to $Q = mc\Delta T$ yields $Q = (100 \text{ g})(2.03 \text{ J} / (\text{g°C}))(5 \text{ °C}) = 1015$ J. Next, ice at 0 °C is melted to form water at the same temperature. Since this is a phase change, we must use the latent heat of fusion, giving us (100 g)(334 J/g), or 33400 J. Finally, the temperature of water is increased from 0 to 15°C. This step requires (100 g)(4.18 J / (g°C))(15 °C), or 6279 J. In total, 1015 J + 33400 J + 6279 J = 40685 J.

A: This fails to take the heat of fusion into account. Remember, even though temperature remains constant during the transition, a phase change from solid to liquid still requires heat input.
B: While this value does not completely neglect the heat of fusion, it fails to multiply it by the mass. In other words, make sure to use (334 J/g) (100 g) instead of simply 334 J.
C: This answer likely results from confusing the specific heats of ice and liquid water.

1404. D is correct. Since water has a density of 1 g/mL, an 80-mL sample of pure water must weigh 80 g, or 0.08 kg. Here, the relevant value of the two that are given is the heat of vaporization. (0.08 kg)(2256 kJ) can be approximated as (8×10^{-2}) (2.25×10^3), or 180 kJ. However, since the answers are written in joules, the correct answer is 180×10^3 or 1.8×10^5 J.

A: The phase change from liquid to gas certainly does require energy. Remember, the equation $Q = mc\Delta T$ can only be used when temperature is changing. For phase transitions themselves, use $Q = mL$, where L is the latent heat (H_{vap} or H_{fusion}) of the substance.
B: This answer results from neglecting to convert kJ to J.
C: This value is equal to (0.08 kg)(334 kJ/kg). However, 334 kJ/kg is the heat of fusion, which is the amount required to melt a substance from solid to liquid. This is not the correct phase change.

1405. C is correct. The compound is a liquid during the middle portion of the graph, from approximately the 400-J to the 575-J mark (halfway between 550 and 600 J). Prior to that segment, the compound is melting, while immediately afterwards, it is undergoing vaporization. Since we only need to find the specific heat, we can rearrange the equation $Q = mc\Delta T$ into $c = \frac{Q}{m\Delta T}$. When we plug in 175 J for Q, 50 g for m, and 2° for T (since temperature increased from 15 °C to 17 °C during that segment), we find that c = 1.75 J / (g°C).

A: This closely resembles the specific heat of the solid phase, so it could have been found by mistakenly using the first segment of the graph. Here, temperature increases from 10 °C to 15 °C while about 175 J are added.
B: This choice is the approximate specific heat of the gas phase. During this last section of the graph, temperature increases from 17 °C to 21 °C from the addition of 200 J.

1406. B is correct. The phase with the largest specific heat will display the most gradual upward rise in the figure. In other words, the greater the specific heat, the more joules that must be added to increase temperature by one degree, and the smaller the slope of a graph like this one. It is the middle segment, from 400 to about 575 J, that rises the least rapidly. This section corresponds to the liquid phase.

A, C: The solid and vapor phases are denoted by the first and last segments of the graph, respectively. Both of these regions have a much larger slope than that corresponding to liquid. D: Different phases of the same compound can certainly have different specific heat values. For example, consider H_2O; its liquid phase has a significantly higher c value than either its solid or vapor phases.

1407. D is correct. Since such minor changes are able to interconvert the sample between all three phases, we might assume that we are near this substance's triple point. However, for carbon dioxide as well as the vast majority of substances, the vapor is less dense than the liquid phase. For this reason, a decrease in pressure could never cause gaseous CO_2 to condense to liquid. On the contrary, such a change promotes solid-to-liquid, liquid-to-gas, and solid-to-gas transitions.

    A: This statement defines the triple point, not the critical point.
    B: While this definition of the critical point is accurate, it does not answer the question. At the critical point, a small pressure increase could never solidify the compound.
    C: This choice is tempting! But, as stated above, the student's observations are factually impossible.

1408. D is correct. Fusion is just a fancy word for melting.
    A: This is condensation.
    B: This is freezing.
    C: This is either deposition or freezing. It's unclear since the answer choice doesn't specify whether the CO_2 starts as gas or liquid.

1409. B is correct. The most notable feature of water's phase diagram is the slightly negative slope of the line separating the solid and liquid phases. While most compounds have a solid phase that is denser than liquid, the opposite is true for H_2O; picture ice cubes floating atop a glass of water. For this reason, an increase in pressure can actually cause ice to melt. For most other substances, this would not be possible, and the line between solid and liquid would have a positive slope. In this diagram, the relevant line is labeled as line B.

    A: This line separates the solid and gas phases.

C: This line separates the liquid and gas phases.

1410. C is correct. Point 1 falls along the line separating the gas and solid phases. At or immediately below this point, a pressure increase would cause deposition, not freezing, to occur.

    A: This is true. Since point 3 is located on the line separating solid from liquid, a temperature increase would certainly facilitate melting.
    B: This is also true. Lines A, B, and C all represent equilibria of some sort. Specifically, line C falls between the liquid and gas phases. Any point on this line thus represents the boiling point at its respective pressure, and here, equilibrium exists between the two phases.
    D: This statement is also correct. As we travel up line C, the liquid and vapor phases become more and more difficult to distinguish. Eventually, we reach point 4, which is known as the critical point; here, these phases are no longer distinct at all, and the substance is called a supercritical fluid.

1411. B is correct. Freezing point depression can be calculated using $\Delta T_f = K_f mi$, where k_f is a constant, m is molality, and i is the Van't Hoff factor, or number of dissolved particles per molecule. In other words, the choice with the highest value of mi is our answer. NaCl dissociates into two ions (Na^+ and Cl^-), so 1.5 moles of that salt in 1 L of solution has a molality of 1.5 m, an i value of 2, and a total value of mi of 3. This is higher than any other choice listed.

    A: Calcium phosphate is insoluble, so it will produce a negligible number of particles and will only slightly affect the T_f.
    C: Since KOH dissociates into two particles, this choice has an i value of 2. But don't be fooled by the molality; we've added an additional liter of solution, so the molality value is (2.5 moles KOH) / (~2 kg solvent) = 1.25 m. This yields an mi value of 2.5, lower than choice B.
    D: Similarly, the concentration looks large here, but the actual molality of the solution is (4 moles glucose) / (~2 kg solvent), or 2 m. Since glucose does not dissociate, this is also our mi value and is lower than the "mi" for B.

1412. C is correct. For boiling point elevation, use the formula $\Delta T_b = K_b mi$. Since we're solving for the unaltered boiling point of diethyl ether, we can rewrite this as $T_{final} - T_{initial} = K_b mi$, where T_{final} is 49.7 °C and $T_{initial}$ is the quantity that must be found. Glucose is organic and does not dissociate, making i = 1, and the molality can be found by calculating (0,35 mol glucose) / (0.05 kg solvent) = 7 m. Plugging in these values yields 49.7 °C – $T_{initial}$ = (2.16 °C*kg / mol)(7 m)(1) or 49.7 °C – $T_{initial}$ = 15.1. $T_{initial}$, then, is closest to 34.6 °C.

A: This is the ΔT_f value, not the original boiling temperature.
B: This value resembles the answer obtained if you assume that glucose dissociates into two particles. Remember that as an organic compound, glucose remains intact in solution.
D: This is 49.7 °C – K_b, which is not what the question asks for.

1413. B is correct. Boiling point can be defined as the temperature at which a substance's vapor pressure is equal to the ambient pressure.

D: Boiling point and vapor pressure relate similarly for all solvents.

1414. D is correct. To calculate freezing point depression, the formula $\Delta T_f = K_f mi$ is typically used. While molecular weight is not directly involved in this equation, it can be found from molality. Water typically freezes at 0 °C, so ΔT_f = -9.3 °C. As sucrose is organic, it does not dissociate and i = 1. We can plug in values to get -9.3 °C = (1.86 °C/m)(m)(1), showing that molality = 5 mol sucrose / kg solvent. Since only 10 mL, or 0.01 kg, of water was used, 17.1 grams of sucrose must correspond to 0.05 moles. 17.1 g / 0.05 mol = 342 g / mol.

A: This results from a mistaken calculation, likely an error with the decimal places associated with water. 10 mL of water is 0.01 L, which equals roughly 0.01 kg.

1415. A is correct. When a nonvolatile solute is added to a solvent, it reduces the mole fraction of that solvent in the solution. Since nonvolatile solutes do not readily evaporate, this also decreases the solution's vapor pressure. A lowered vapor pressure makes the solution more difficult to boil, resulting in an elevated boiling point.

B, C: Freezing point elevation and vapor pressure elevation are not colligative properties.
D: Vapor pressure elevation is not a colligative property, but even more importantly, this pairing does not make sense. A higher VP marks a solution that is more readily available to boil (and would have a lower BP).

1416. A is correct. Note that this is an "except" question! We thus need to find the choices that would not increase the osmotic pressure, which is calculated using π = iMRT. Increasing the amount of water without changing solute concentration results in a decreased molarity, which lowers π.

I: Increasing NaCl concentration increases the molarity of solute, increasing π.
II: Increasing albumin concentration increases the molarity of solute, increasing π. Note that this occurs despite the fact that albumin is much too large to diffuse through the membrane! In fact, in physiological systems, albumin's size makes it one of the molecules that most affects osmotic pressure by "pulling" water back into the capillaries.
IV: Increasing T increases π according to the equation for osmotic pressure.

1417. C is correct. Using such a membrane allows all solutes to move down their concentration gradients, which would explain the results described here.

A: This describes a normal semipermeable membrane (though, in the body, capillary walls are permeable to small solutes). Protein would be incapable of crossing such a membrane.
B: 100 daltons is 1000 times smaller than 100 kilodaltons, the number described in choice C. The albumin-like protein used in this experiment is much larger than 100 Da and would not cross this membrane.
D: This does not explain why all solutes were able to cross the membrane.

1418. D is correct. As a dicarboxylic acid, Molecule Z will dissociate in water; specifically, both of its carboxylic acid groups will be deprotonated. This results in more total particles than the solution containing Molecule X, a neutral amide. Since all other factors are identical, the solution with fewer particles will show a smaller degree of boiling point elevation.

A, B: Since the two molecules are added in equimolar amounts, molecular weight does not matter.

C: This choice would be correct if the question asked for the solution with the higher boiling point.

1419. C is correct. Sodium chloride is a nonvolatile solute because it does not have a significant vapor pressure of its own. Note, however, that NaCl and other nonvolatile compounds typically lower the vapor pressure of a solution.

A: This statement is correct. Even at temperatures well below their boiling points, liquids virtually always evaporate to some extent. In other words, ethanol can enter the gas phase when its vapor pressure is lower than P_{atm}; it just won't be boiling.
B: This is also true. Water can hydrogen bond, meaning that its intermolecular forces are stronger than those present in acetone. Larger intermolecular forces produce lowered vapor pressure and increased boiling points.
D: 380 torr is equivalent to 0.5 atm, so this water is at its boiling point. Technically, boiling point can be defined as an equilibrium between the liquid and vapor phases.

1420. B is correct. R is the gas constant, which is used in a variety of equations and can be given in multiple different ways. When calculating osmotic pressure, one of the more common versions of R is used: 0.0821 (L*atm) / (mol*K). Here, this can be found using the units of the other terms in the equation. π is measured in atm, i is unitless, M is measured in mol/L, and T is typically given in Kelvin. We can plug in to get atm = (mol/L) (R) (K) and obtain the correct answer.

A: This answer would be obtained if molality were used instead of molarity.
C: This is the reciprocal of the correct answer.

1421. C is correct. Let's immediately convert one of the given units to make them match. Since one millimeter is equal to 1×10^{-3} m, 56 mm/min is equal to 5.6×10^{-2} m/min. However, it is easier to convert meters into millimeters. 1 m is equal to 1000 mm, so this answer can be found by taking

1000 mm ÷ 56 mm/min = about 18 minutes. Finally, 18 min × 60 s/min = 1080 s. Note that rounding is generally fine on the MCAT, so it would be acceptable to estimate this value at 20 min × 60 s/min = 1200 s

A: 18 is the number of minutes taken, not seconds.
D: This incorrectly uses 100 s/min as the minute-to-second conversion rate.

1422. C is correct. Displacement and velocity are vectors, meaning that they have both direction and magnitude. In contrast, distance and speed are scalars and only convey magnitude.

III: Work is a scalar, as it does not give any indication of the direction in which the work was performed.

1423. C is correct. Displacement is the direct distance that separates the initial and final positions. Each time the guard makes a full circle, he winds up where he originally began. At those times, the distance between start and finish is zero meters.

A: Displacement is a vector, while distance is a scalar quantity. In circular motion, the two certainly are not always equal.
B: This is a tempting choice. However, the guard is moving in a circle. Even near the beginning of his patrol, his total distance traveled is greater than his displacement, since the distance includes his entire circular path while displacement is the "shortest distance between two points."
D: As a vector, displacement is negative any time the guard finds himself behind his original position.

1424. D is correct. Speed is a scalar, not a vector. Unlike velocity, which conveys both magnitude and direction, speed can only ever be a positive value.

C: This answer would be correct if the question had asked about velocity instead of speed.

1425. A is correct. Velocity is the change in position (or displacement) over time; it is measured in meters per second. Acceleration, then, is the change in velocity over time and is given in m/s^2.

1426. B is correct. First, it is necessary to convert all of these values to have the same units. Let's convert them to m/s, simply for the sake of using SI units. Starting with choice A, 800 μm/ms × 1000 ms/s × 1 m/10⁶ μm = 0.8 m/s. For choice C, 0.100 km/min × 1 min/60 s × 1000 m/km = 1.7 m/s. Finally, 320 cm/hr × 1 hr/60 min × 1 m/100 cm = 0.05 m/s. 34 m/s is by far the largest value of the four.

1427. C is correct. The graph shows us that at a time of 6 seconds, the projectile has a negative velocity. Since velocity is a vector, its sign gives the direction of motion. A negative sign denotes backwards movement, and the flat slope of the graph at that point means that the projectile is not accelerating.

A, B: A flat slope on a position vs. time graph would indicate that no motion is occurring, but this is a velocity vs. time graph.
D: No acceleration, either positive or negative, is taking place at this time.

1428. D is correct. Since the question asks about the magnitude of acceleration, we can ignore its direction or sign. Acceleration can simply be found by determining the slope at the relevant position of the velocity vs. time graph. At a time of 1 s, the slope is 1 unit/s, while at t = 3, the slope is -1 unit/s. Since we can ignore the sign, these have equal magnitudes. At t = 6 s, the slope is zero (horizontal), as it is at t = 9.5 s.

1429. B is correct. If the orbit's radius is 160 km, its diameter is 320 km and its circumference is 320π, or around 1000, km. Since the planet's velocity is given in m/s, we'll need to convert either km or m. To avoid large numbers, let's convert 200 m/s to 0.2 km/s. We can thus see that traveling 1000 km will take 1000 km ÷ 0.2 km/s = 5000 s, or about 83 minutes.

A: This results from mistaking circumference as the product of radius and pi, instead of diameter and pi. As a result, the answer is only half as large as it should be.
D: This is the correct answer, but in seconds, not minutes.

1430. C is correct. The SI units for the quantities described are "MKS units," or meters, kilograms, and seconds.

1431. B is correct. First, use $F = ma$ to find acceleration. 150 N = 7.5 kg (a), giving an acceleration of 20

m/s². Now, we can plug values in to the formula $v_f^2 = v_i^2 + 2a\Delta x$ to calculate distance. (40 m/s)² = (0 m/s)² + 2(20 m/s²)(x) shows that x = 40 m.

A: This comes from forgetting to square v_f in the formula $v_f^2 = v_i^2 + 2a\Delta x$.
C: This answer results from mistakenly using $v_f^2 = v_i^2 + a\Delta x$.

1432. C is correct. Let's start by listing our known values. The height of the cliff, or vertical distance, is 20 m. The initial velocity is 10 m/s, but remember that this is entirely horizontal! The initial vertical velocity is 0 m/s and the acceleration can be estimated at 10 m/s². First, use vertical components and the equation $\Delta x = v_i t + \frac{1}{2}at^2$ to find time. 20 m = ½(10 m/s²)(t²) means that t² = 4, so t = 2. Next, use horizontal components to find range, which is equal to the product of initial horizontal velocity and time. Range = (10 m/s)(2 s) = 20 m.

A: This results from using 10 m/s as the initial vertical velocity, when in reality there is no initial velocity in the vertical direction.
D: This answer can be obtained if you accidentally assume that t = 4 (instead of t² = 4).

1433. D is correct. Time in flight does not depend on mass; in other words, if two objects of different masses are simultaneously dropped from the same height, they will hit the ground at the same time. Additionally, though the briefcase is thrown horizontally while the ball is dropped, both objects begin with a vertical velocity of zero.

1434. C is correct. Time in flight is determined by vertical, not horizontal, components. Increasing the total velocity while leaving the angle unchanged must also increase the vertical velocity (and thus the time). For III and IV, let's do some math. Originally, Timothy was kicking at a 30° angle, meaning that the vertical component of that velocity was (8 m/s)(sin 30), or 4 m/s. With this information, we can use $v_f = v_i + at$ to find the time of flight from the initial kick to the peak of the projectile arc. 0 m/s = 4 m/s + (10 m/s²)(t) yields a time of 0.4 s. Remember, though, that the total time of flight is twice this value, or 0.8 s. When Timothy changes his angle to 45°, the vertical component of that value becomes (8 m/s)(sin 45), or about 5.6 m/s; this corresponds to a total flight time of 1.1 s. When he makes the angle 90°, the new velocity of 6 m/s is entirely vertical. 0 m/s = 6 m/s + (10 m/s²)(t) yields an initial-to-peak time of 0.6 s, or a total time in flight of 1.2 s.

II: Simply increasing horizontal velocity will increase range, but not flight time.

1435. C is correct. This question gives a lot of information, so let's take it one step at a time. The easiest quantity to examine first is the kinetic energy, since all KE at the top of an arc must be due to horizontal velocity. We can set ½mv² equal to 1000 J and find that the horizontal velocity at that position – and all positions, if we ignore air resistance – is 5 m/s. Range = v_xt, so the kangaroo travels (5 m/s)(1.7 s) or 8.5 m.

A: This would be the calculated height of the kangaroo if we mistakenly assume 1000 J of potential energy instead of kinetic.
B: This value is near that which would be found if mv2, instead of ½mv2, was used.
D: Projectiles have no kinetic energy due to vertical motion at the peaks of their travel, but certainly can have KE from horizontal movement.

1436. C is correct. The horizontal component of velocity does not affect the rate at which an object falls, so Jake's and Phil's baseballs will fall at the same rate. When Jake's ball hits the ground, it has fallen 30 m, so Phil's ball must also have fallen 30 m.

A: This answer comes from incorrectly using the horizontal velocity of Jake's ball to solve for time.

1437. D is correct. Since we're asked to solve for a horizontal component (range), we need to use other horizontal components in our calculation. The horizontal velocity is given by 20 cos(65°) m/s.

A, B: These choices use an acceleration of 9.8 m/s². Since this is a vertical component, it should not be used in the same equation as horizontal velocity. Additionally, choice B uses the vertical component of velocity, which cannot directly give us the range.
C: This uses the total velocity of 20 m/s instead of the horizontal fraction of that amount.

1438. B is correct. The slope of the graph at point B gives us the car's acceleration at that position. At point B, the slope is 4/6, or 2/3. In other words, the car is accelerating at a rate of roughly 0.67 m/s². Since its "initial" velocity (at point B) is 1 m/s, its velocity 15 seconds later is given by $v_f = v_i + at$ or vf = 1 m/s + (0.67 m/s²)(15) = 11 m/s.

A: This value results from forgetting to add the 1 m/s that the car already has at point B.
C: If we mistake the velocity at point B (1 m/s) for the acceleration, this answer would result.
D: This is the velocity the car would be traveling if it continued at its velocity at point A for 15 s.

1439. A is correct. A negative sign for velocity indicates that the object is traveling backwards, not that it is slowing down. For part of the interval mentioned here, the car is speeding up in the reverse direction.

B: This is correct, since velocity is negative.
C: This statement is also true. The car's velocity at point A is 3 m/s. In the 4 s it spends in the air, it would move a horizontal distance of (3 m/s)(4 s) or 12 m.
D: This is true. The word "magnitude" tells us to ignore the sign given to the acceleration. If we do this, we see that the slope of the line at t = 3.9 s is greater than that at t = 6 s.

1440. C is correct. We have to work backwards here, since mass is not directly involved in any kinematics equation. Let's start by finding the height from which the beam fell. Since it had no vertical velocity at the time when it began to fall, we can easily use $\Delta x = v_i t + \frac{1}{2}at^2$ and drop the $v_0 t$ term. $\Delta x = \frac{1}{2}$ (10 m/s²)(0.9 s)² yields around 4 m for Δx. Now, we simply need to find the mass that 1800 J would lift 4 m. The most logical way to do this is to use W = Fd = mgh, giving us 1800 J = 40(m). The beam must have a mass of 45 kg.

B: This answer results from neglecting the ½ in $\Delta x = \frac{1}{2}at^2$.
D: This is the weight of the beam (450 N), not its mass.

1441. B is correct. The total energy of a system should be conserved so long as no non-conservative forces are at work. While rare exceptions do exist, they relate to cases like nuclear fusion reactions, in which a relatively small amount of mass can be converted to energy. For the MCAT, assume that total energy is conserved unless something like friction is explicitly mentioned.

I: Kinetic energy is not conserved as an object accelerates in a gravitational field. Consider a baseball that is thrown directly upward. At the bottom of the arc, it has a maximum amount of KE; at the top, it has a minimum.
III: By definition, momentum is not conserved when external forces are acting. To simplify this, consider momentum as mass*velocity. While the object's mass will not change during this process, its velocity certainly will.
IV: Like kinetic energy, potential energy is not conserved here. The object will gain or lose PE depending on its position relative to the ground.

1442. A is correct. According to the question, air resistance and velocity are related, allowing us to write out the following equation: $F_{air} = -kv^2$. Next, we can set up a free-body diagram in which gravity is acting downward while air resistance pulls the ball upward. This gives us $F_{net} = ma = g - kv^2$. Finally, we can solve for acceleration by dividing both sides by mass, yielding $a = (g - kv^2) / m$.

B: This equation has the gravitational force and the drag force acting in the same direction. While this would be true if the object were rising, the question mentions that it is in free fall.
C: This choice neglects to include any term for air resistance.

1443. A is correct. If Urbanium has a circumference that is two times larger than that of Earth, it must also have a radius that is twice as large. While we do not need to plug in actual values to solve this problem, we should be familiar with the equation $F_{grav} = \frac{Gm_1 m_2}{r^2}$. Using this relationship, we see that a doubling of the planet's mass should double the gravitational force, but a doubling of its radius should decrease it by a factor of 4. As a result, an object on Urbanium must experience a gravitational force (and thus acceleration) that is half what it would be on Earth.

B: 10 m/s^2 is the approximate g value on Earth, not Urbanium. Remember, the gravitational force is inversely proportional to the square of the radius, not the radius alone.
D: This answer might result from reversing the effects of the mass and the radius. In other words, if mass (in the numerator) were squared while radius (in the denominator) was not, this value would make sense.

1444. D is correct. The box begins with energy equal to mgh and to bring the box to rest, the work done by friction would also have to be equal to mgh. The work due to friction is force time distance and the force of friction is μ times the normal force. So we have the equations $F_f = \mu F_N$ which we can rewrite $F_f = \mu mg$. The work due to friction is then $W = \mu mgL$. We can write the equation $mgh = \mu mgL$ to solve for an expression for μ that would bring the car to a stop at the end of the surface. Eliminating m and g gives $\mu = h/L$.

1445. C is correct. Friction, like air resistance, is a nonconservative force. Since this cart is being dragged across a "rough surface," we can assume that friction is present and able to dissipate some of the cart's kinetic energy.

A, B, D: Gravity and electrostatic forces are conservative.

1446. C is correct. Remember, Newton's first law states that objects in motion remain in motion unless acted upon by an outside force, while objects at rest remain at rest unless acted upon in a similar manner. In other words, an object moving with a constant velocity will continue moving, at that velocity and in the same direction, until some force acts to stop or change its motion.

A: This is actually untrue. If no net force is acting upon a moving object, it would have no reason to slow or stop.
B: It is Newton's second law that puts forth the equation $F_{net} = ma$, not his first law.
D: This is Newton's third law, which involves the existence of equal and opposite forces. The question asks about Newton's first law.

1447. D is correct. This car does not come to a stop out of nowhere – it is consistently acted upon and slowed by kinetic friction. Thus, the amount of energy dissipated as heat is same as the car's change in potential energy; this is also the work done by friction during the slide. When an object slides down an incline, frictional force is given by $\mu_k mg\cos\theta$. Since work is equivalent to force*distance, the work done by friction is $\mu_k mgd\cos\theta$.

A, B: For inclined planes, sine is generally used when finding the gravitational force on an object. Since we are dealing with the frictional force, we should use cosine instead. Additionally, choice A forgets to multiply by d, meaning that it gives a value for force and not energy.

C: Similarly, this choice neglects to include the variable d. Remember, we are dealing with friction! For nonconservative forces such as this one, the amount of work done is proportional to the distance over which it acts.

1448. A is correct. All that is necessary here is to set the weight of the paper equal to the frictional force. Since the paper is not sliding, we must use the coefficient of static friction. This yields $(0.001 \text{ kg})(10 \text{ m/s}^2) = 0.3F_N$, which can be simplified to $0.01 \text{ N} = 0.3F_N$. From this equation, we know that F_N (the normal force, which we exert directly against the wall) must be about 0.03 N.

B, D: To calculate these values, it is likely that the coefficient of kinetic friction was used instead of that of static friction. Additionally, choice D is still an order of magnitude too large.
C: Here, again, this choice likely results from an order-of-magnitude error when solving for normal force.

1449. C is correct. Given the force and mass that are mentioned, the deceleration due to friction must be a = F / m = (2 N) / (16 kg), or $1/8 \text{ m/s}^2$. To keep our signs consistent, let's call it an acceleration of $-1/8$ m/s, since friction opposes the box's original direction of motion. This value can be plugged in to the kinematics equation $v_f^2 = v_0^2 + 2ax$, which we can then solve for x. Luckily, $v_f = 0$ m/s, making this easy to simplify into $25 \text{ m}^2/\text{s}^2 = (0.25 \text{ m/s}^2)(x \text{ m})$. From this equation, we know that x = 100 m.

D: This value may come from forgetting the 2 in the "2ax" portion of the equation.

1450. B is correct. From the graph, it can be directly observed that acceleration is constant at 10/15 m/s^2, which is equal to $2/3 \text{ m/s}^2$. (Note that

this value is simply the slope of the line; the slope of a velocity vs. time graph will always yield acceleration, though it may not always be constant). After plugging both this value and given mass into F = ma, we find that F = (6 kg)(2/3 m/s²) = 4 N.

A: This is the acceleration (0.67 m/s²), not the applied force.
D: While this would be true if acceleration were not uniform, it actually is constant throughout the full 15-second interval.

1451. D is correct. A 12-N force is being exerted on a system with a mass of 4M. We can therefore plug in to Newton's equation for net force to yield $F_{app} = 4Ma$. Next, solving for acceleration gives us a $= F_{app}/4M$. Since all of the blocks are connected, they will accelerate at the same rate. Substituting into Newton's equation gives $F = M(F_{app}/4M) = F_{app}/4$. Now, all that remains is to plug in our applied force value, 12 N. Force = 12 N / 4 = 3 N.

1452. C is correct. The crate will begin to accelerate once all opposing forces have been overcome. These opposing forces include static friction and the relevant component of gravity. For the sake of simplicity, set our net force equation up as $F_{net} = F_{applied} - (F_g + F_s) = 0$ N, or $F_{applied} = F_g + F_s$. Now, note that the force of gravity that actually acts is equal to mgsin30, or (3 kg)(10 m/s²)(0.5), which is 15 N. At its maximum value, static frictional force is equal to $F_N\mu_s$, which can be calculated as $F_s = mg\cos30(\mu_s) = (3 \text{ kg})(10 \text{ m/s}^2)(0.866)(0.4) = 10.4$ N. Finally, $F_{applied} = 15$ N + 10.4 N = 25.4 N.

1453. D is correct. Since the object is not moving, the horizontal components of tension must be in equilibrium. Rope 1 displays a tension of 10 N, the horizontal component of which is (10 N)(cos 30) or 8.6 N. Now, we know that the force felt by the second rope follows the equation 8.6 N = $F_2\cos60$. Rearranging to solve for force gives us $F_2 = (8.6) / (\cos 60)$, or about 17.2 N.

1454. A is correct. Since the box is not moving, we need to determine a sufficient coefficient of static friction, which can be accomplished using $F_s = \mu_s F_N$. $F_N = mg\cos60 = (10 \text{ kg})(10 \text{m/s}^2)(\cos 60) = 50$ N. Now, the gravitational force that can actually act on the box is $F_g = mg\sin60 = (10 \text{ kg})(10 \text{ m/s}^2)(\sin 60)$ or 86.6 N. Next, place these values into our equation for static friction to determine the coefficient of static friction. 86.6 N= μ_s(50 N), so μ_s = (86.6) / (50) = 1.7.

B, D: Kinetic friction can only be applied when the object is sliding against the surface in question.

1455. C is correct. In order for the system to accelerate, a net force must be present. Work is equal to force applied over a distance (W = Fd). Therefore, since a net force is causing the boxes to accelerate, the forces in the direction of acceleration must be greater than those opposing this acceleration.

1456. A is correct. A scale measures a person's weight by finding the normal force, which is equal and opposite to the perpendicular force on a particular surface. Here, two other forces are involved: gravity and the centripetal force. Since centripetal force always points to the center of an object's circular path, it will always point inward and away from the track, just like the normal force. We can therefore ignore this value and focus on gravity. At point A, the smallest possible gravitational component is pointing into the surface of the track; in fact, no gravity is pointing toward the surface at all. This explains why people feel weightless at the top of similar loops.

B, C, D: At all of these positions, some component of gravity is still pointing down and against the surface of the loop.

1457. C is correct. Kinetic friction is dependent only on the coefficient of friction and the normal force and does not take velocity into account. The normal force is constant throughout the descent, as the path of the coaster is linear. Therefore, the force of friction will remain constant throughout the coaster's descent.

1458. B is correct. To solve this problem, we must break each force into its components, then determine the resultant force. Let's begin by finding the horizontal components. For the 12 N force, this value is equal to (12)(cos 30), while it is (10)(cos 45) for the 10 N force that comes from the east. As both of these forces point west, they can be added. The 10 N force from the west will oppose this total value and therefore must be subtracted in our net force equation. We can

now calculate the net horizontal force: F_{net} = (12)(cos 30) + (10)(cos 45) – 10 N = 7.4 N westward. Doing the same for the vertical components tells us that 1 N of force points in the northern direction. Thus, the resultant force must point NW.

1459. C is correct. Impulse is the product of force and time, giving it units of (kg*m*s)/s². This simplifies to (kg*m)/s.

1460. A is correct. Impulse is the change in momentum. Falling from h = 12 m means the TV is going 15.5 m/s when it hits. It has a mass of 20 kg and p of 310 kg m/s. The windshield absorbs 60 of this, leaving 250 for the shocks.

1461. A is correct. When the cart reaches the top of the loop, it must have a centripetal force pushing radially outward with a magnitude equal to the force of gravity to keep it from falling. At this point, the cart will not be pushing against the track. Therefore, the centripetal force will equal the gravitational force (mg), while the normal force will be 0.

1462. A is correct. A is correct. The point in the circle where the force will be greatest (and therefore, where the string is most likely to snap) is at the top of the circle. Here, both the gravitational force and the centripetal force point radially inward. Therefore, we must solve for the velocity that gives F_c + mg = 200. With F_c = mv/r², v = sqrt (6), which is about 2.4.

1463. B is correct. Since energy = (torque)(angle), we can set the amount of energy in the ATP molecules (400 pN-nm) equal to the torque (40pN-nm) multiplied by the angle (which we are solving for). The resulting angle is 10 radians, which is close to 3π radians. As a single revolution consists of 2π rad, this constitutes approximately 1.5 revolutions.

1464. B is correct. The kinetic energy at the bottom of the ramp is equal to the difference between the potential energy at the top and the energy lost to rotation. Since the energy of rotation is 0.5Iω^2 (where ω is equal to v/r), all factors related to mass and radius will cancel, leaving only v = sqrt(100/7). As this value must fall between 3 and 4, only B can be correct.

1465. B is correct. Using the formula torque = $I\alpha$, and knowing that the moment of inertia for a ring is represented by the simplest possible formula (MR^2), we can solve for mass. 100 / 2.5 = M = 40 kg.

1466. A is correct. Set the centripetal force equal to the component of the weight that acts parallel to the slanted road. This yields $mv^2/r = mg\sin\theta$. Note that this question can be solved without the mass, since that factor cancels.

1467. D is correct. To find the pilot's weight at the bottom of the loop, add gravitational force and centripetal force. Plugging the given values into $mg + mv^2/R$ gives us 6800 N.

1468. D is correct. This problem can be solved by setting the initial and final values for angular momentum equal. Angular momentum is given as $L = mvR$. For this reason, the velocity must double to compensate for R being halved.

1469. A is correct. No torque is applied to the system, as the angle between the displacement and force vectors is zero. Sin(0) = 0.

1470. B is correct. From the graph, we can see $v(t) = \sin(t)$, so the acceleration is given by $a(t) = \cos(t)$. Since $F = I\alpha$ (and in this case, $\alpha = a$), $F = I\cos(t)$.

1471. C is correct. If the spring is perfectly elastic, it will not lose any energy to friction, and the gymnast's maximum elastic potential energy will be equal to her maximum kinetic energy. In turn, if she is projected directly upward, her maximum KE will be equal to her maximum gravitational potential energy, which she possesses at the peak of her arc.

    A: If this were true, the gymnast would be gaining energy throughout the projectile arc. This is not possible unless an outside force is doing work on her body.
    B: The least stretched part of the trampoline is where the gymnast possesses her minimum, not maximum, elastic potential PE. Elastic PE = $\frac{1}{2}kx^2$, so where x is smallest, elastic PE is also at a minimum value.
    D: If the gymnast was propelled straight upward, her total velocity at the top of the arc will be zero, and she should have no kinetic energy.

1472. B is correct. Conservative forces are those that do work that does not depend on the path taken. In other words, the work done by a conservative force only depends on the starting and ending positions, and is zero if those positions are the same. Conservative forces can also be thought of as those that act in situations where mechanical energy is conserved. Gravity is a classic example of a conservative force, and the force exerted by a spring is a member of this category as well.

    A, D: Air resistance and friction are path-dependent forces. If they are present during a scenario, mechanical energy will not be conserved.
    C: Again, this choice pairs two nonconservative forces, and may be obtained from misreading the question

1473. C is correct. According to the work-energy theorem, work is equal to the change in kinetic energy throughout a process. The first racecar does not possess initial kinetic energy, so its ΔKE is equal to $\frac{1}{2}$ (1500 kg)(30 m/s)^2 = $\frac{1}{2}$ (1.5×10^3)(9×10^2) = 6.75×10^5 J (note that rounding would absolutely be acceptable in a test-day scenario). The change in kinetic energy of the second car is equal to $\frac{1}{2}$ (1500 kg)(16 m/s)^2 – $\frac{1}{2}$ (1500 kg)(10 m/s)^2, or $\frac{1}{2}$ (1500) (256 – 100). Since these numbers are even trickier to work with, convert $\frac{1}{2}$ (1500) into 750 and use scientific notation. We get (7.5×10^2)(1.56×10^2), or approximately 11 × 10^4, or 1.1×10^5, J. Finally, the question asks for the difference in work exerted by the two cars. 6.75×10^5 J – 1.1×10^5 J = about 5.7×10^5 J.

    A: This comes from mistaken subtraction. 6.75×10^5 J – 1.1×10^5 J is not simply 5.7; these values are the same as saying 675000 – 110000. The exponent, 10^5, must remain in the answer.
    D: This choice results from using $\frac{1}{2}$ (1500 kg)(6 m/s)^2 for the second car's change in kinetic energy. Remember that you must actually calculate the initial and final kinetic energies and find the difference between their values. $\frac{1}{2}$ (1500 kg)(6 m/s)^2 yields a different number from $\frac{1}{2}$ (1500 kg)(16 m/s)^2 – $\frac{1}{2}$ (1500 kg)(10 m/s)^2.

1474. C is correct. At its maximum height, all of the ball's velocity will be horizontal, meaning that horizontal motion is the only contributor to the kinetic energy at that position. Since no air resistance is experienced, we simply need to find the initial horizontal velocity of the ball. We can use $\cos(30°) = v_{horizontal} / v_{total}$, or $0.866 = v_{horizontal} / (12 \text{ m/s})$. Estimating $v_{horizontal}$ as around 10 m/s (though in reality, it is slightly greater) yields a kinetic energy of ½ (0.5 kg)(10 m/s)² or 25 J.

A: This choice is easy to pick if you mistakenly think that all of the ball's energy at its peak will be potential. This would be true if the ball had no horizontal velocity, but it does.
B: This is the ball's horizontal velocity (10.4 m/s), not an energy value.
D: This is the total kinetic energy possessed by the ball at the time of its launch.

1475. B is correct. Mechanical energy is defined as the sum of kinetic and potential energy. This value is only conserved when the sole forces present are conservative ones. Since air resistance is nonconservative, some mechanical energy will be lost as heat.

C, D: Total energy is always conserved, according to the law of conservation of energy. While this does have rare exceptions, as in the mass-to-energy conversion involved in nuclear reactions, it certainly does apply in this case.

1476. A is correct. Energy is measured in joules, which are equivalent to N * m (just think of the fact that work is also measured in joules, and W = FdcosΘ). One newton is the same as one (kg*m) / s², so multiplying that set of units by meters yields our answer.

B: This is N / m, while joules are N * m. The units given in this choice are those used for the spring constant in Hooke's law.
C: These are the units for newtons, not joules.
D: This actually gives the units for pressure, which has SI units of pascals. One pascal is equivalent to one J / m³, which can also be written as it is in choice D.

1477. B is correct. First, we must find the height from which the diver dropped. To do this, we can use the kinematics equation $\Delta x = v_i t + ½ at^2$. At the instant she began to fall, the diver had a vertical velocity of 0 m/s, so this simplifies to $\Delta x = ½ at^2$. When we plug in 1.4 seconds as "t" and 10 m/s² as "a," we see that the diver's initial height was 10 m. Since she has a weight of 1090 N (or 109 kg),

her initial gravitational potential energy is mgh, or (109 kg)(10 m/s²)(10 m) or 10900 J.

C: This answer could come from misremembering the kinematics equation above as $\Delta x = v_i at^2$.
D: A choice of this value likely results from using the either the wrong variable or the wrong equation when solving. It is the only choice in Newtons, but the problem asks for energy..

1478. B is correct. We are given a value for total initial kinetic energy, as well as part of the initial velocity (the vertical component). To make this easier, let's first use 36 J to find the value of the total initial velocity. 36 J = ½ (0.5 kg)(v)² gives us 144 = v², or v = 12 m/s. Now, draw a triangle using Θ, with the total velocity value as the hypotenuse. We can see that $\sin \Theta = v_{vertical} / v_{total}$, or (6 m/s) / (12 m/s). The sin value for Θ is 0.5, so it must be a 30° angle.

1479. B is correct. At its peak, all of the ball's kinetic energy is due to horizontal movement, since its vertical velocity is zero. In other words, 25 J = ½ (0.5 kg)(v_x)². 100 J = (v_x)², and v_x at the peak is equal to 10 m/s. Since the problem tells us to treat air resistance as negligible, this must also be the ball's initial horizontal velocity, since without air resistance, no acceleration takes place in the horizontal direction.

A: This choice may result from using KE = mv² instead of KE = ½ mv².
C: This is the total initial velocity, not just the horizontal component. It results from using 56 J instead of 25 J. If 56 J = ½ (0.5 kg)(v)², 225 J = (v)² and v = 25 m/s.
D: This is v_x^2, not v_x.

1480. C is correct. Mechanical energy is that which comes from the position and movement of an object. It can be found by taking the sum of kinetic energy and potential energy.

A: Potential energy, or the energy due to position, is also included as a component of mechanical energy.
B, D: Nonconservative forces like air resistance and friction are not part of mechanical energy.

1481. A is correct. The basic formula to use here is efficiency = (energy out) / (energy in). First, then, we must find the energy output, or the amount of work that was actually done by the engine. To do so, multiply the force by the given distance: 20 N * 5000 m, or 1×10^5 J. Now, find the energy input: 50 MJ/kg * 0.1 kg = 5 MJ, or 5×10^6 J. 1×10^5 J divided by this value yields 0.02, or 2%.

1482. C is correct. This problem requires multiple steps, the first of which is to find the amount of energy required by the motor. Energy, like work, is measured in joules. For this reason, we can use W = Fd, or 30 N * 1000 m. This yields 3×10^4 J, which must be doubled to 6×10^4 J, as only half of the energy provided by the fuel is able to perform useful work. Finally, we must divide by the heat of combustion (2×10^6 J/kg), giving us 0.03 kg or 30 g.

A: This is the correct answer in kilograms, not grams.
B: 15 g would be a logical choice if this motor were perfectly efficient. However, as it has an efficiency of only 50%, it requires twice the expected amount of fuel.

1483. A is correct. First, set the initial kinetic energy of the cart equal to the product of the frictional force and the distance. (This should be done because it is the work provided by friction that must stop the cart, or dissipate all of its kinetic energy.) We can now solve for the coefficient of friction: $(10 \text{ m})(mg\mu) = 0.5mv^2$, or $(10 \text{ m})(10 \text{ m/s}^2)(\mu) = (0.5)(5 \text{ m/s})^2$. This equation shows us that μ must be 0.125, or about 0.13. Note that larger coefficients would work as well; 0.125 is simply the coefficient required to stop the cart after traveling the full 10-m length of the surface.

C: To obtain the choice shown here, you may have forgotten to account for kinetic energy as $\frac{1}{2}mv^2$ instead of simply mv^2.
D: This value is far too large. It likely results from setting the frictional force equal to kinetic energy while neglecting to include the 10-m length of the flat surface. Remember, force and energy have different units and cannot be directly equated.

1484. B is correct. Since the gas is doing work, it loses internal energy. However, it also gains energy from the heat influx. First, let's find the amount of energy lost during the expansion alone. W = PΔV, or (1 atm)(2 L), meaning that the energy change during this process is -2 L*atm.

We now must convert J (the units given for heat) into L*atm, for which we can remember the conversion factor 1 L*atm = 101.325 J. It is now evident that the gaseous mixture gained approximately (100 J) / (101.325 J/L*atm) or 1 L*atm of heat energy. Summing these values yields (-2 L*atm) + (1 L*atm) = -1 L*atm.

A: -2 L*atm is the energy change resulting from the expansion alone, but neglects the mentioned influx of 100 J.
C: This results from using the reverse of the correct signs. The 2 L*atm lost during the expansion should be negative, while the energy gained from the addition of heat should be positive.
D: This answer treats both the energy changes as positive instead of giving the proper signs.

1485. B is correct. The energy used for expansion must come from the energy of combustion, minus the amount lost to friction. Since the burning of the hydrocarbon produced 1 kJ but lost 300 J, 700 J of energy contribute to the expansion mentioned in the question. Using the conversion factor 101.325 J = 1 L*atm, we see that this value is approximately 7 L*atm. Since this is the work done during the combustion, we can equate it to PΔV, then divide by P (which is 3 atm, not 1). This yields 2.33 L as the change in volume.

C: This is the approximate final volume of the container (1 L + 2.33 L). The question stem asks for the change in volume alone.
D: This value would be logical if the pressure outside the chamber had been 1 atm, not 3.

1486. D is correct. This is a force vs. velocity graph; thus, to find the power, we simply need to find the area under the curve during the relevant interval. Initially, this might not be obvious! However, think of the region outlined by the curve as a rectangle. In this case, we would find the area under the curve by multiplying the two sides: (N) × (m/s) = (Nm/s), or J/s. These are the same units as those used for power (W)! To find the entire area from 0 to 20 s, it is easiest to divide the curve into three regions: a rectangle from 0 to 15 N that spans from 0 to 20 s, a small triangle from 15 to 25 N that ranges from 0 to 5 s, and another rectangle from 15 to 25 N that spans from 5 to 20 s. The combined area of these regions is 475 W.

A: This is the area of the small triangular region alone.

B: Like choice A, this value only includes part of the total area. Specifically, it accounts for the rectangular part of the trapezoid from 15 to 25 N and from 5 to 20 s.

C: This choice neglects to include the rectangle from 0 to 15 N (in other words, the bottom region of the curve).

1487. C is correct. The question stem mentions that the total power output is unchanged. To find this value, simply determine the area under the curve between 0 and 50 seconds (in total, 1000 W). If this were instead to be bounded by a flat horizontal line, it would form a rectangle of length 50 and height 20 (since 50*20 = 1000). In other words, a constant force of 20 N over 50 s would produce the same total power output. This also makes logical sense, as a quick glance at the graph shows the motor spending the same approximate amount of time at 15 N and 25 N.

1488. D is correct. The problem implies that the kinetic energy can be ignored; in other words, all work is devoted simply to lifting the crate against gravity. We can thus equate the work done by the motor to the crate's change in potential energy. 145 J = Mgh, or 145 J = (M)(10 m/s^2)(h). Solving for h yields 14.5/M.

A: This choice assumes a mass of 1 kg, which certainly might not be true.

B, C: These values neglect to include gravity (10 m/s^2). Additionally, choice B likely results from an algebra mistake.

1489. A is correct. In the previous problem, we could find height by equating 145 J (the energy generated by the motor) to Mgh (the final potential energy of the crate). Here, however, we must also consider the energy consumed by the rotation of the pulley. In other words, 145 J = Mgh + rotational KE. No matter what numerical value is actually given to the rotational KE term, it must still result in a decrease in the final "h."

1490. B is correct. First, calculate the power output exerted by the man: (135 J/s)(10 s) = 1350 J. We can now equate this value to the change in potential energy of the crate, since little of the man's energy input goes to accelerating the crate above a very low velocity. For this PE value, we

have (50 kg)(10 m/s^2)(0.5 m) = 250 J. Efficiency = (energy out) / (energy in), or 250 J / 1350 J. This gives us a measured efficiency of just under 20%.

A: This tiny value results from using 1 kg, instead of 50 kg, as the crate's mass.

D: Efficiency can never be greater than 100%. This value likely comes from dividing 250 J by 135 J – in other words, from neglecting to account for the 10-second time interval.

1491. C is correct. Energy depends on the frequency of a light wave. Furthermore, the velocity of light is constant within a given medium, so if the frequency changes, so must the wavelength. Period and frequency are inverses, so period would change as well. Therefore, the velocity is the only feature that would not change.

1492. C is correct. The waves must be out of phase in order to completely destructively interfere. This requires a 180° phase difference.

1493. C is correct. If you look at a sine and a cosine curve together, you can see that the sine function reaches the starting point of the cosine curve, cos(0), after one-quarter of a period. This is equal to 90°.

1494. C is correct. Since E = pc and E = hf, we can set pc equal to hf. Solving for f yields f = pc/h. By plugging in the given momentum and using the constants given, we get [{150 × 10^6 / 3 x 10^8}(3 × 10^8)] / (4.1 × 10^{-15}). The only answer with the correct order of magnitude is C.

1495. B is correct. First, note that the waves must be 180° out of phase in order to destructively interfere. We know from the problem that the period is 1/350 s; from the phase information, we also know that the waves must be spaced a half-period apart. To find this distance in space, multiply the time separation by the velocity of the wave to get (1/2)(1/350)(300), or 3/7. Now, the wave can actually be any odd number of half-periods apart (1/2, 3/2, 5/2, etc.) since a full period would lead to unwanted constructive interference. From here, we can generalize our formula to identify 3n/7 as the required separation, where n must be odd. Only B fits this criterion (n = 7).

1496. C is correct. Using the equation E = hc/λ and solving for λ shows that only B gives a wavelength between 400 and 700 nm.

1497. A is correct. In reality, intensity is proportional to the square of the amplitude. Since amplitude is shown on the x-axis here, we need only to look for an exponential shape. B implies a linear relationship, C wrongly denotes a logarithmic relationship, and D indicates that these two values are unrelated.

1498. A is correct. In the referenced experiment, Young observed interference patterns between light from two sources passed through small slits (here, the slits represent the obstacles). Because light diffracts, or bends, when passing through the slit, the interference pattern appeared.

1499. C is correct. Since 378 Hz is the third harmonic, 126 Hz must be the fundamental frequency. This makes A incorrect, as it is a non-integer multiple. B and D may also be eliminated, as even-numbered harmonics do not exist in pipes with one closed and one open end.

1500. A is correct. Since the pipe is closed at x = 0, a node exists there, meaning that the air is still.

II: L represents an antinode or point of maximum amplitude, making this a false statement.
III: The velocity cannot possibly be constant throughout a region that contains both nodes and antinodes.

1501. C is correct. First, use the equation $U = \frac{1}{2} kx^2$ to solve for x, which is the distance stretched. 750 J = $\frac{1}{2} kx^2$, meaning that 1500 J = (15 N/m)(x^2). This can be solved to find that $x^2 = 100$ m^2 and x = 10 m. Then, we can equate the spring force to mass*acceleration using kx = ma. Plugging in values yields (15 N/m)(10 m) = (2 kg)(a), or a = 75 m/s^2.

A: This is the value for x, or the displacement of the mass (10 m), not acceleration.
B: This answer could have been obtained by using $U = kx^2$ instead of $U = \frac{1}{2} kx^2$.
D: This is the value for x^2 (100 m^2), not acceleration.

1502. C is correct. To measure 60 seconds with 15 full swings, the period of the pendulum must be 4 seconds. Period and length are related by the equation $T = 2\pi \sqrt{l/g}$, which can be rearranged to l = $(T/2\pi)^2(g)$. Replacing T with 4 s and g with 10 m/s^2 yields about 4 m.

D: A length of 16 m could be mistakenly calculated using the equation $T = 2\pi (l/g)$.

1503. C is correct. Period is defined as the time it takes for an object to complete one full cycle of its periodic motion. On the graph, this is the amount of time for the sinusoid to return to its original position.

B: This is half of the period, or the time from a "peak" to a "trough" on the graph. The full period is the distance from peak-to-peak or trough-to-trough.
D: 16 seconds represents two periods.

1504. A is correct. For a pendulum, period, length, and gravitational acceleration are related by the equation $T = 2\pi\sqrt{l/g}$. Note that mass is not included in this formula. Plugging in 6.28 s for T and 1 m for length gives us 6.28 = $2\pi \sqrt{1m/g}$, or $1^2 = 1m/g$. On this planet, then, g = 1 m/s^2.

1505. B is correct. The elastic potential energy of a spring can be found using the equation $U = \frac{1}{2} kx^2$. Since we have two springs here, we can equate their potential energy values in $k_1 x_1^2 = k_2 x_2^2$. Inserting given values makes this equation (100 N/m)(x_1^2) = (200 N/m)(0.04 m), or $x_1^2 = 0.08$ m. If this seems difficult to evaluate without a calculator, another method is to simplify to $100x^2 = 8$ and find the square root of both sides, yielding 10x = $\sqrt{8}$ = 2.8 or x = 0.28 m.

A: Since these values are all given in centimeters, we need to convert 0.28 m into centimeters to get 28 cm. 0.28 cm is thus two orders of magnitude too small.
D: This likely results from a mistaken unit conversion.

1506. D is correct. Spring constants are given in units of N/m, meaning that we simply need to convert the mass of the load to newtons and the displacement to meters. While any point on this graph will give the same answer, let's choose the upper right-hand corner, where mass = 5 kg and displacement = 10 cm. Newtons, or force, can be found by multiplying the mass of the load by gravity. This yields F = (5 kg)(10 m/s^2) = 50 N, while a displacement of 10 cm is equivalent to 0.1 m. Last of all, the spring constant can be found using k = F/x, where F = 50 N and x = 0.1 m.

A: This choice results from a mistake with units. It was likely obtained by taking 5 kg / 10 cm instead of 50 N / 0.1 m.
B: This is another unit mistake; it comes from dividing 50 N by 10 cm.

1507. C is correct. The maximum kinetic energy possessed by the spring, if assumed to be ideal, is equal to its maximum elastic potential energy. If we set the elastic PE of a spring system (U = ½ kx²) to the kinetic energy of the block, we get kx² = mv². Solving for v yields choice C.

A: An expression like this one has units of N/(m*kg), not m/s, as velocity should.
B: While this represents the elastic potential energy, and thus the kinetic energy that can be converted, in a spring system, it does not give us velocity.
D: This answer is on the right track, but gives us v², not v.

1508. A is correct. The period of a pendulum is given by T = $2\pi\sqrt{l/g}$. Since frequency is simply the inverse of period, these are the only variables that will affect the experiment described in the question. Note that mass is not included in this equation.

B, C: Length (l) and acceleration due to gravity (g) do affect the period and frequency of a pendulum.

1509. B is correct. For the spring and the pendulum to have identical frequencies, they must have the same period as well. The period of a pendulum is given by T = $2\pi\sqrt{l/g}$, while that of a spring is T = $2\pi\sqrt{m/k}$. When we set these equations equal to each other, we get l/g = m/k, or l / (10 m/s²) = 2 kg / (100 N/m). The length of the string is thus 20 / 100 or 0.2 m.

1510. A is correct. According to the equation f = $\frac{1}{2\pi}\sqrt{\frac{g}{l}}$, frequency will decrease when a pendulum is lengthened. While this is enough information to obtain the correct answer, we can also solve for the exact magnitude of decrease. Since length is quadrupled and the variable for length is raised to the ½ power in the equation, we will see a

decrease by a factor of 2 (or, as otherwise stated, the original frequency will be cut in half).

1511. B is correct. To find the fraction of the toy that is submerged, we can use its specific gravity, or the ratio of its density to that of water. Since water has a density of 1000 kg/m³, this toy's specific gravity is 0.57. From this, we already know that 57% of the toy is beneath the surface, but this question asks for the amount that sticks out above the water. 100% - 57% = 43%.

A: An answer like this one likely results from an order-of-magnitude error made when calculating specific gravity.
C: This is the percentage submerged, not above the surface.
D: Any object with a specific gravity less than one will float at least somewhat in water.

1512. D is correct. Absolute pressure is the sum of the relevant gauge and atmospheric pressures. In a vacuum, no atmospheric pressure is present, making $P_{absolute} = P_{gauge}$.

A: Gauge pressure can be equal to absolute pressure, as in the correct choice.
B: Atmospheric pressure can equal absolute pressure in cases where no gauge pressure is present. The surface of a liquid is one example.
C: This choice is tempting, but negative gauge pressure exists! For example, consider the thoracic cavity during "negative pressure" breathing. We know that inhalation is promoted by a low absolute pressure (lower than P_{atm}) in this cavity. Since $P_{absolute} = P_{atm} + P_{gauge}$, this could only be true if P_{gauge} is negative.

1513. C is correct. The dimensions of the container are irrelevant; this question is simply asking for the density of water, which you should know in a variety of different units. For example, water has a density of about 1 g/cm³, 1 g/mL, or (like this choice) 1 kg/L.

A, B: Both of these answers mistakenly attempt to incorporate the volume of the container, which is 32 cm³.
D: The density of water in these units is 1000 kg/m³, not 1 kg/m³.

1514. D is correct. The question asks for absolute pressure, which includes both gauge and atmospheric pressure. First, let's find the gauge pressure using the equation P = ρgy, where ρ denotes the density of the fluid and y refers to the depth of the object. Since all answer choices are in Pascals, we need to use SI units to find our answer, meaning that we should use 0.75 m, not 75 cm, for y. The density of water is 1000 kg/m³ and gravity, as always, is 10 m/s², yielding a gauge pressure of (1000 kg/m³)(10 m/s²)(0.75 m) or 7500 Pa. Finally, we must add atmospheric pressure, which is 380 torr. Since 760 torr is equal to 101,500 Pa, 380 torr is equivalent to 50,750 Pa and our final answer is 58,250 Pa.

A: This represents the gauge pressure. Absolute pressure must also include the contribution from ambient pressure.
B: The value here could only be obtained by adding the gauge pressure (7500 Pa) and the atmospheric pressure in torr. However, P_{atm} must be converted to Pascals as well.
C: This is the atmospheric pressure. Absolute pressure must also include the contribution from gauge pressure.

1515. D is correct. This question is trying to trick us into assuming that the liquid in the tank is water. Since we do not know the actual identity of the fluid, we have no idea whether this object will sink or float.

C: This would occur if the liquid were water.

1516. C is correct. The buoy's specific gravity tells us that the ratio of its density to that of water is 0.4. In other words, since water has a density of 1000 kg/m³, the buoy must have a density equal to 400 kg/m³. We can then find the density of the boat using ρ = mass / volume, or ρ = 0.8 kg / 0.002 m³. From this math, we find that the boat also has a density of 400 kg/m³.

A: Since we are given density here, we do not even need to consider volume. A density of 0.3 g/cm³ is equivalent to 300 kg/m³, a value smaller than that of the buoy.
B: Similar to choice A, the side length is irrelevant here. A density of 0.6 kg/L can be converted to 600 kg/m³, significantly larger than the density of the buoy.
D: If this marble sinks in water, its specific gravity must be larger than 1.

1517. C is correct. Buoyant force can be calculated using the equation $F_b = ρVg$. The entire object

will be submerged, meaning that V is simply the object's volume. For a cube, finding volume is simple: just cube the length of a single side, which in this case yields 125 m³. Note, however, that ρ represents the density of the fluid, not the object. For this reason, we only need to calculate (811 kg/m³)(125 m³)(10 m/s²), or approximately 1 × 10⁶ N.

A: This answer is a miscalculation of the volume. It was most likely found by forgetting that volume is the length of one side cubed, not simply the length of one side (5 m).
B: Though this answer is very close to the correct one, it is slightly too small. It results from using the density of the dogwood (750 kg/m³) as ρ.
D: This choice mistakenly uses the density of the object as ρ, resulting in an answer that is far too large.

1518. B is correct. Using $F_b = ρVg$, we know that the buoyant force on the cube is 1 × 10⁶ N. However, we also need to know the weight of the cube in air, for which we need to calculate its mass. Since the volume of the cube is 125 m³, 62.5 m³ is composed of aluminum and 62.5 m³ is made of dogwood. For the aluminum, (62.5 m³)(2712 kg/m³) is approximately (6.0 × 10¹)(2.7 × 10³), or 16.2 × 10⁴ kg. For the dogwood, (62.5 m³)(750 kg/m³) is about (6.0 × 10¹)(7.5 × 10²), or 4.5 × 10⁴ kg. Finally, we can add these values to obtain a total mass of around 20.7 × 10⁴, or 2.1 × 10⁵, kg. This yields a weight of 2.1 × 10⁶ N. Last of all, the apparent weight of the cube in hexanol is the difference between the actual weight and the buoyant force, or 1.1 × 10⁶ N.

A: This is not the apparent weight and fails to account for gravity.
C: This is the weight of the cube in air, which is not what the question asks for.

1519. A is correct. The image shows a convex meniscus, similar to that seen with mercury. In this case, the fluid "bulges upward" because fluid particles are more attracted to each other than to the glass sides of the tube. Attractive forces between like particles are known as cohesive forces, while those between particles of different substances are termed adhesive forces.

C: This choice confuses the definitions of cohesive and adhesive forces.

D: The scenario described here resembles that between water and glass in a capillary tube. Those interactions would produce a concave, not convex, meniscus.

1520. D is correct. The maximum force on a floating object due to surface tension is proportional to the length of its edges that touch the fluid. In other words, force is dependent on the circumference or perimeter of the object. Since all of these objects float in water, our answer will be the choice with the smallest circumference. The packing peanut has a radius of 2 cm, making its circumference 4π cm – a value much smaller than that of any other choice.

C: The mural paper has a circumference of 210 cm, or 2.1 m. This answer is tempting if the question is misread as asking about the largest force instead of the smallest.

1521. D is correct. Viscosity can be conceptualized as the internal friction of a fluid. In other words, a viscous fluid is one that resists flow. The question stem describes mercury as "thick" and mentions its slow travel, implying that it (like all real fluids) has at least some degree of viscosity. In contrast, laminar flow is a quality of an ideal fluid; substances that move in this manner travel in parallel layers, with a lack of up-and-down motion. The figure is a perfect depiction of laminar flow.

A, C: Turbulence is the opposite of laminar fluid motion. If this sample had turbulence, the diagram would depict more "bumpy" or up-and-down movement instead of perfectly parallel straight arrows.

1522. A is correct. Both Bernoulli's and the continuity equation assume that the relevant fluid is ideal. However, the concept of an ideal fluid involves multiple assumptions. Ideal fluids are nonviscous (unlike the one described here) and incompressible (like the one described here). Bernoulli's equation, often referred to as "conservation of energy for fluids," relates much more closely to viscosity than compressibility. Viscosity can be thought of as the internal friction of a fluid – a quality that causes it to dissipate energy as it travels. Hence, a very viscous fluid is subject to a nonconservative

force and would not be properly assessed by Bernoulli's equation alone.

B, C: The continuity equation, often written as $A_1v_1 = A_2v_2$, relates much more to compressibility than to viscosity. An incompressible fluid will adhere fairly well to the principles underlying this relationship, regardless of the energy that it dissipates due to friction.

1523. C is correct. Bernoulli's equation is sometimes known as "conservation of energy for fluids." As such, we may wrongly deduce that all terms in this relationship have units of joules (J). However, consider ρgh_1. Since ρ denotes density, ρgh_1 can be written as $[(mgh_1) / volume]$. In fact, every term in Bernoulli's equation has units of (energy) / (volume), or J/m^3. Another way to discern this trend is to remember that P_1 and P_2 refer to pressure, a value often measured in Pa or N/m^2. Multiplying both the numerator and the denominator by meters yields $(N*m)/m^3$. Once we realize that one $N*m$ is equivalent to one joule, we have our answer.

B: Pressure, with its SI unit of the pascal, can be measured as the quotient of force and area (N/m^2). However, N/m is not a proper set of units.
D: Joules per meter is another way of denoting energy per unit length. When dealing with the energy held by a fluid, we care about volume, not length.

1524. D is correct. While blood (like any real fluid) is not actually ideal, we are told that we can assume otherwise for this particular question. Ideal fluids follow the law of continuity, which states that volume flow rate (VFR) is equal at every point in a system at a particular instant in time. This principle can best be conceptualized through simple logic. If a fluid is incompressible, only a certain volume can possibly fit in a vessel at one time. Larger vessels will thus experience slower blood flow, while ones with smaller total areas will be moved through more quickly. In the end, VFR (measured in m^3/s) is constant everywhere.

C: This choice is attempting to confuse VFR and velocity. Altogether, capillaries do cover a very large cross-sectional area, causing fluid to travel especially slowly through them. However, in an ideal situation, the VFR does not differ between capillaries and other vessels. Additionally, the question asks for the highest rate, not the slowest.

1525. D is correct. This question becomes much easier when broken into steps. First, we must find the horizontal velocity of water exiting the tank; next, we simply need to use kinematics formulas to calculate the time that this jet spends in the air. The initial part of this question requires the use of Bernoulli's equation: $P_1 + \rho gh_1 + \frac{1}{2} \rho v^2_1 = P_2 + \rho gh_2 + \frac{1}{2} \rho v^2_2$. Let's call the very top of the upper reservoir "Point 1," while "Point 2" refers to the pipe through which water exits. Since both ends of the system are open to atmospheric pressure, we can drop P_1 and P_2. Now, think of the remaining terms in relation to energy conservation. At the top of the system, water can be estimated to possess only potential energy; at the bottom, all of that energy has been converted to kinetic. When we finally simplify our original equation, we get $v = \sqrt{2gh}$, or $v = \sqrt{2(10)(10 \text{ m})}$. This gives us a final velocity of $v = \sqrt{200}$, or around 14.1 m/s. Since all of this velocity is horizontal, we can multiply by the time of flight to find the range. Using $\Delta x = v_i t + \frac{1}{2} at^2$, and remembering that flight time is determined only by vertical components, we get $8 \text{ m} = \frac{1}{2} (10)t^2$. The time that the spraying water is in the air is close to 1.25 s, and the horizontal distance traveled is about (14.1 m/s)(1.25 s) or 17.6 m.

A: This is the vertical, not horizontal, distance traveled after leaving the pipe system.
B: This answer comes from using 3 m as the change in height of the water. Here, since water in the upper tank possesses all of the potential energy that comes with that height, we must use 3 m + 7 m or 10 m.
C: 14.1 m/s is the velocity of the exiting water, not the distance that it travels horizontally.

1526. B is correct. The specific gravity is unhelpful unless we know the density of pure water, which is generally given as 1000 kg/m³. (While many other units can be used for this quantity, it is best to use kilograms and meters when dealing with SI units such as pascals.) From here, we just need to use the equation $P = \rho gy$, where y denotes depth. This yields [(1000 kg/m³)(10 m/s²)(6 m)], or 6×10^4 Pa.

A: The calculations likely used to obtain this answer use 1 m (the height above the bottom of the upper reservoir) instead of 6 m. Remember, this equation always necessitates the use of depth, not height above a reference point.
C: This answer may result from using 12 m (the height above the ground) instead of 6 m.
D: The value here is the absolute pressure, or the sum of the gauge and atmospheric pressures. This is not what the question asks for.

1527. B is correct. According to Bernoulli's equation, when the height of a fluid is constant, it will exert a greater pressure when it is traveling more slowly. (In other words, hydrostatic pressure and kinetic energy are inversely correlated.) Here, the salt solution will move more slowly through Tube 1, which has a larger area. This can best be understood through the continuity equation, often written as $A_1v_1 = A_2v_2$.

1528. A is correct. To solve this problem, simply remember that the kinetic energy per unit volume for a fluid is given by $\frac{1}{2} \rho v^2$. For this reason, its total kinetic energy is simply $\frac{1}{2} \rho v^2$ * volume. Make sure to memorize the density of pure water, which is 1000 kg/m³ (or 1 g/cm³, or 1 kg/L; you should know this value in multiple different units). Finally, ensure that your units align by converting volume to cubic meters. 1 cm³ = 1×10^{-6} m³, so 50 cm³ = 50×10^{-6}, or 5×10^{-5}, m³. [$\frac{1}{2}$ (1000 kg/m³)(8 m/s)²](5×10^{-5} m³) = $(3.2 \times 10^4)(5 \times 10^{-5})$, or 1.6 J.

B: This is $\frac{1}{2}$ (50)(8 m/s)². As 50 cm³ is a volume, not a mass, we cannot find the answer via this route.
C: 32 kJ is equivalent to 3.2×10^4 J, the amount of kinetic energy per cubic meter of this fluid. In other words, if you obtained this answer, you likely forgot to account for the given volume by multiplying by 5×10^{-5} m³.
D: This is $(3.2 \times 10^4 \text{ J})(50)$. Remember to avoid mixing different units for the same measurement! Here, we cannot leave the volume in cubic centimeters, as we already used meters as part of our given density.

1529. C is correct. This question relates to the continuity equation, $A_1v_1 = A_2v_2$. Watch your units! The new velocity (50 cm/s) is one-eighth of the previous value (4 m/s), so the new cross-sectional area must be eight times larger.

A: This is one-eighth of the given area. If velocity decreases when passing by a certain point, cross-sectional area must increase.

B, D: These choices mistakenly relate 4 m/s to 50 m/s (or 4 cm/s to 50 cm/s). If this were the case, the new velocity would be 12.5 times larger than the old one. However, the question stem gives one value in meters and the other in centimeters, so we must convert one of the two.

1530. C is correct. According to Bernoulli's equation, when gravitational potential energy (or height) is relatively constant, a slower-moving fluid will exert a greater pressure than a more rapidly-moving one. Additionally, the continuity equation states that fluids travel more quickly through regions of smaller cross-sectional area. When we combine these facts, we see that this fluid travels more quickly past Point 2 than Point 1, making statement I incorrect. Additionally, the figure depicts the hydrostatic pressure at Point 2 as lower, not higher, than that at Point 1.

III: This statement is perfectly accurate. Fluid moves rapidly through Point 2 due to the constriction in the pipe; this results in a lower hydrostatic pressure, and thus a lower column of fluid, at that location.

1531. B is correct. Coulomb's law is typically given as $F = k \frac{Qq}{r^2}$. Technically, Coulomb's constant k is equal to $\frac{1}{4\pi\varepsilon}$, so doubling ε halves the force generated.

1532. A is correct. This is the definition of an electron-volt. It can also be found by using the formula V = U/q and solving for U in units of eV.

1533. B is correct. We can solve this by setting F = ma equal to Eq, then solving for E. This gives us E = ma/q. We can calculate acceleration by dividing the change in velocity (100 m/s) by the time (20 μs) to get $a = 5 \times 10^6$ m/s². We then can plug in 2 for m/q because this is the mass-to-charge ratio given in the problem. This yields 10×10^6, or 1×10^7, N/C.

1534. C is correct. Here, set the magnetic force equal to the electric force, giving qvB = Eq or vB = E. Solving for v rearranges this into v = E/B, so we may just divide 250 by 10 to get 25 m/s. Tesla are

the SI unit for magnetic fields, so we do not need to convert any units.

1535. B is correct. First, the equation for work is W = Fd, where (here) F = Eq. Using W = Eqd with E = 1×10^4, q = 1.6×10^{-19}, and d = 0.01 m, we get 1.6×10^{-17} J, or 100 eV.

1536. A is correct. Magnetic fields act perpendicularly to the velocity of a charged particle. Therefore, according to W = Fdcosθ, they perform no work.

1537. C is correct. The slope of the line that can be drawn through the points represents the value of the E-field.

D: This results from an error in the use of scientific notation.

1538. D is correct. Since E = F/q, to find the force on the charge, simply multiply its value by that of the electric field in N/C. Thus, the answer is (0.5 C)(5000 N/C) = 2500 N.

1539. D is correct. Remember, electric field lines point in the direction that a positive particle will be pushed. Since both gravitational force and the force generated by the field will drag the potassium ion downward, no equilibrium can exist here.

1540. B is correct. For this problem, set the centripetal force equal to the electrostatic force, yielding $(kQQ)/r^2 = mv^2/r$. Solving for v gives v = sqrt(kQ²/(mr)). Here, Q can be pulled out of the square root expression.

1541. D is correct. Using the relevant equation for power (P = V²/R) and solving for R yields [(120)(120)] / 100, or 144 Ω.

1542. C is correct. For a bulb to be lit, current must flow through it. When fully charged, capacitors resemble open circuits, so current will flow only through resistors A, B, and D. The presence of a capacitor is preventing the active flow of charge through the branch that contains resistor C.

1543. C is correct. The total voltage drop throughout the entire circuit must be V. Therefore, the voltage at V' relative to the ground is equal to V minus the drop across the two resistors between V and V'. In other words, the voltage at V' is V – 2iR.

1544. D is correct. When the current first begins to flow, it is unimpeded by the capacitor, which allows the bulb to shine brightly. As the capacitor charges, acting progressively more and more like an open circuit, the lightbulb receives less current and dims.

1545. C is correct. When the battery is first connected, current will flow through both parallel resistors, causing the total I value to be twice as high as when the R_2 branch is "disconnected" by the charged capacitor later. However, since this high current is split evenly between the branches, R_1 actually receives the same amount of current at both times.

1546. C is correct. The amount of time that it takes a capacitor to reach 63% of its final charge is known as the time constant, which is equal to RC. Plugging in the given values yields 5 s.

1547. C is correct. First, simplify this circuit by combining R2 and R4, which are in series. This 10 Ω combination is in parallel with R3, which gives an equivalent resistance of 5 Ω. Finally, this entire structure exists in series with the 20 Ω resistor, giving a total resistance of 25 Ω. Using V = IR, we can see that the voltage generated by the battery (and that at point A) is 50 V.

1548. A is correct. The voltage at the negative terminal of the battery must be zero. Since the voltage drop across a wire can be assumed to be zero as well, and since no resistors separate point B from the negative terminal, 0 V is our answer.

1549. B is correct. Here, our answer (the total current that flows through the resistor) is simply equal to the area under the curve. This comes to approximately 2000 mC, or 2 C.

1550. A is correct. When the current across a capacitor is decreasing in the manner shown, the voltage across its plates must be increasing. In other words, it is charging.

1551. B is correct. The resistance of a circuit element is defined by the equation R = ρL/A, where ρ is the resistivity of the metal, L is the length of the element, and A is the cross-sectional area. Using this equation, we see that increasing L should increase R proportionally.

A: This increases the cross-sectional area of the wire, represented by A in the equation. Such a change would lower resistance.
C: This change effectively doubles the cross-sectional area (A), as charges now have an alternate path through which to move. Note that this effective increase in area is one reason why the equivalent resistance of a parallel set of resistors is always lower than that of individual resistors in that element.
D: A change in the wire material to copper would lower the value of ρ, lowering R. While the resistivities of these metals are not given, an astute student should remember that the question stem noted titanium as having a high resistivity. Switching from this metal to copper, a material commonly used in wires due to its low resistance, would not give the desired effect.

1552. D is correct. Power is given in units of watts, or joules per second. Voltage has units of joules per coulomb, while current has units of coulombs per second. In other words, multiplying voltage and current yields power in an equation most commonly given as P = IV. But how can we find the value of the current? Since resistance is given, we can simply use V = IR and rearrange to I = V/R. Now, we know that I = 0.333 A, a value that we can use to find the power, 40 W. Finally, we must convert this value, currently in joules per second, to joules per hour by multiplying by (3600 s / 1 hour).

1553. B is correct. Power = voltage × current, an equation generally given as P = IV. When we plug in our known values for P and V, we obtain (240 W) = (I)(120 V), meaning that current must be equal to 2 A. This value can then be inserted into Ohm's law, V = IR, to find overall resistance.

1554. A is correct. Starting with P = IV, we can rearrange to obtain I = P / V. The current (I) is therefore equal to 3 W / 12 V, or 0.25 A.

1555. B is correct. For n resistors in series, $R_{eq} = R_1 + R_2 + … + R_n$. For n resistors in parallel, $(1/R_{eq}) = (1/R_1) + (1/R_2) + … + (1/R_n)$. However, here we have resistors in series with a parallel element. First, then, we need to treat the parallel element as a single resistor and find its own equivalent resistance. Notice that resistor A and the 5-Ω resistor are in series within a single parallel branch. We can thus say that, combined, they provide the same resistance as one 100-Ω resistor positioned on that branch. To calculate the equivalent resistance of the parallel element in the diagram, we plug the numbers in as follows: $(1/R_{total}) = (1/25) + (1/100) = (4/100) + (1/100) = (5/100)$, or $(1/20)$. The parallel set of resistors thus has an equivalent resistance of 20 Ω. Then, to find the resistance of the entire circuit, $R_{total} = 20$ Ω + 10 Ω + 20 Ω = 50 Ω, choice A.

A: This choice is found by incorrectly assuming that, for n resistors in parallel, $R_{eq} = (1/R_1) + (1/R_2) + … + (1/R_n)$. In other words, if you perceived the equivalent resistance of the parallel set of resistors to be 1/20 Ω instead of 20 Ω, you would calculate a final answer of 30.05 Ω.
D: This value results from confusing the formulas for series and parallel resistors.

1556. A is correct. The current (I) is constant throughout series elements of a circuit. When it reaches a junction where branches align in parallel, the current splits in inverse proportion to the respective resistances, but still adds up to the same total value. Here, voltage is given, so we simply need to calculate the equivalent resistance for the entire circuit. The two resistors on the bottom branch, so we can add them to obtain 20 Ω. Next, we need to find the effective resistance of the parallel branches together: $(1/R_{total}) = (1/25) + (1/20) = (4/100) + (6/100) = (10/100)$, or 1/10. Thus, the parallel element has an equivalent resistance of 10 Ω. Finally, we can simply add 10 Ω + 10 Ω + 20 Ω to get 40 ohms. Current then must be found using V = IR, which can be rearranged to yield I = V/R. 120 V / 40 W = 3.0 A.

B: This choice is found by incorrectly assuming that, for n resistors in parallel, $R_{eq} = (1/R_1) + (1/R_2) + … + (1/R_n)$. As a result, you would mistakenly think the equivalent resistance of the parallel set of resistors to be 1/10 Ω instead of 10 Ω, so you would calculate a total R_{eq} of 30.1 Ω.
C: If you used V = IR with values of 15 Ω and 120 V, you would find this answer. Remember, when using the total voltage of the battery to find current, you must use R_{eq}, which represents the effective resistance of the circuit as a whole! You cannot use the resistance of a single circuit element.

D: This is the equivalent resistance, not the current.

1557. C is correct. Capacitance (in farads) can be calculated using the equation C = εA/d, where ε is the dielectric permittivity of the material between the plates (a measure of how readily electric charge is "felt" through the material), A is the plates' area, and d is the distance between the plates. In other words, capacitance does increase in proportion to area; however, doubling the radius of a circle quadruples – not doubles – the area. (Remember that the area of a circle is given by πr^2).

A: Capacitors in parallel display an effective capacitance equal to the sum of their individual values, as the area of the plate is effectively increased. Thus, this change would double the capacitance.
B, D: Halving the distance would also double the capacitance, as would inserting a material with twice the dielectric permittivity as before. Both of these changes can be assessed using the equation given above.

1558. A is correct. First, we must find the equivalent resistance of the circuit as a whole, beginning with the parallel element. When we plug in our known values, we obtain $(1/R_{total}) = (1/5) + (1/5) + [1/(5 + 5)] = (2/5) + (1/10) = (4/10) + (1/10)$, or 1/2. The parallel set of resistors thus has an equivalent resistance of 2 Ω. The total resistance in the circuit, then, must be 2 + 8 or 10 Ω. Voltage will drop across a circuit element in proportion to its fraction of total resistance. Thus, as the parallel element between the red arrows has 2/10 or 20% of the total resistance, the voltage will drop by (15 V * 0.20) = 3 V, or choice A.

A: This choice assumes that the parallel equivalent resistance is 0.5 Ω instead of 2 Ω. If that were true, then it would contain 0.5 / 8.5 or approximately 5% of the total resistance.
C: This is the total voltage of the battery, not the voltage drop across the parallel element.
D: This statement is untrue; voltage drops are always identical across parallel branches. Here, the drop across each branch is 3 V.

1559. D is correct. The voltage and power are given, allowing us to find I using P = IV. I = 7.5 W /

15 V, or 0.5 A. Next, the resistance of resistor B can be found using the equation V = IR. As explained above for #1558, the equivalent resistance for the parallel element containing resistor A is 2 W. Finally, we can find the resistance of B as follows: V = IR$_{total}$, so R$_{total}$ = V/I. (2 Ω + 8 Ω + B) = V/ I = 15 V / 0.5 A = 30 Ω. (10 Ω + B) = 30 W, so B = 20 Ω, choice D.

1560. A is correct. An AC current reverses its polarity at a constant rate; in other words, it goes from 120 V to -120 V in a sine-wave pattern. Since it spends identical amounts of time with a negative and a positive voltage, the average EMF of an AC current is zero. For this reason, this type of current is generally measured as an RMS (root mean square) value instead.

1561. C is correct. Magnetic field strength is measured in Teslas.

A: This is the unit for capacitance.
B, D: These units denote charge and current, respectively.

1562. A is correct. The magnetic force, magnetic field, and relevant velocity are all perpendicular. (In other words, magnetic force acts to pull a moving particle in a circular arc.) This relationship is memorable through use of the right-hand rule, one version of which has a person's thumb correspond to the particle's velocity, fingers denote the magnetic field lines, and palm face in the direction of the charge on a positive particle.

1563. D is correct. Magnetic fields always exert a force on a moving particle that is perpendicular to both the particle's velocity and the field itself. Remember, the equation for work is W = FdcosΘ. This relationship tells us that only the force exerted parallel to the object's motion contributes to the work, of which there is none here.

A: This value comes from using W = Fd. Remember, only a particular component of the force can be incorporated to this equation.
B: This is simply the product of the force and the radius. Even if we could use W = Fd here, the radius does not represent the distance traveled or the displacement of the particle.

C: The choice here results from an error when dealing with scientific notation, as well as the mistake described for option B.

1564. D is correct. For this question, use the right-hand rule. Since this particle is traveling with a leftward velocity vector, first point your thumb toward the left. Next, because the magnetic force exists in equilibrium with the downward-pointing gravitational force, the magnetic force must be exerted in the upward direction. To account for this, ensure that your palm is facing upward. At this point, your fingers should point out of the page; however, this rule is typically used for positive charges, so you must switch this final direction. The magnetic field must point into the page instead.

A: This is the direction of the magnetic force, not the field.
B, C: These answers may have been obtained by assuming that the particle was positively, not negatively, charged.

1565. B is correct. The magnetic force experienced by a particle in a magnetic field is given by F = qvBsinΘ, where q denotes charge, v stands for velocity, and B gives the strength of the field. From this relationship, it is evident that a particle must possess both velocity and a charge (whether positive or negative) to be affected by a magnetic field. Additionally, it must be moving in a manner that is at least partially perpendicular to the field lines.

1566. C is correct. To solve this problem, simply consider F = qvBsinΘ, where q denotes charge, v stands for velocity, and B gives the strength of the field. Plugging in our known values yields F = (-1.6 × 10^{-19} C)(5 × 10^4 m/s)(0.25 T), or 2 × 10^{-15} N.

A, B: Both of these values stem from a use of mass instead of charge. Remember, mass is not present in the equation for the magnetic force on a moving particle.
D: This would be true if the particle were moving parallel to the field lines.

1567. C is correct. Magnetic force on a moving particle is equal to qvBsinΘ. Here, compared to the first object, the new object has a charge with half the magnitude and the opposite sign. As a result, it will experience half of the magnetic force and in the opposite direction.

1568. A is correct. Since the magnetic force is directing this proton in a circular path, it can be set equal to the equation for centripetal force, F = $\frac{mv^2}{r}$. Specifically, this yields qvB = $\frac{mv^2}{r}$, which simplifies to v = $\frac{qBr}{m}$.

B: This results from setting magnetic force equal to centripetal acceleration, not centripetal force.
C: This is the reciprocal of the correct answer.

1569. B is correct. This scenario relates to electromagnetic induction and to Lenz's law. This law, which brings to mind conservation of energy and even Le Châtelier's principle, states that a change to a magnetic field will always generate a current that counteracts that change. Here, the external field is becoming weaker, or less heavily positioned into the page. To resist this change, it will induce a current that promotes a field pointing the same direction, into the page. The right-hand rule tells us that this current must travel clockwise.

A, C: These would be true if the magnetic field were increasing.
D: This could only occur if the field were unaltered as well.

1570. A is correct. Electromagnetic induction closely relates to Lenz's law. This law states that a change to a magnetic field will tend to generate a current that counteracts that change. In other words, magnetic flux "prefers" to remain constant whenever possible.

B: Static magnetic fields do not generate an electromotive force.
C, D: While electric activity can induce the presence of a magnetic field, the term "electromagnetic induction" refers to a different concept.

1571. C is correct. Sound is a longitudinal wave in which the medium is compressed in the same direction that the wave propagates. Light is a transverse wave involving electric and magnetic fields. Note that the fact that the question deals with UV light is irrelevant; all light on the

electromagnetic spectrum consists of waves that are transverse in nature.

1572. B is correct. "The wave" causes an up-and-down oscillation of people, while the wave itself moves forward through the stadium. Since this oscillation is perpendicular to the direction of the wave's travel, it is transverse in nature.

A: Longitudinal waves occur when the direction of oscillation is the same as the direction of the wave's propagation.
C: While this is a wave of people standing, it is not a standing wave. A standing wave, also called a stationary wave, refers to a situation involving nodes and antinodes. Often, standing waves are tested in reference to closed/open pipes or stringed instruments.

1573. C is correct. Generally speaking, sound travels fastest through solids, slower in liquids, and slowest through gases. This occurs because solids have higher bulk moduli, meaning that they are comparatively difficult to compress but easily regain their original shapes once pressure has been released (up to a point). Since sound waves propagate by compressing and "rarefacting" the medium they travel in, the material with the highest bulk modulus will generally be traveled through most rapidly.

A: Sound travels slowest through gases (in general).
B: While sound does travel faster through water than air, it moves even more rapidly through most metals and other solids.
D: Sound certainly travels at different speeds through different phases of matter.

1574. B is correct. The velocity of a sound wave in a certain material is given by v = $\sqrt{\frac{B}{\rho}}$, where B is the bulk modulus of the material and ρ is its density. Because cast iron has the smallest bulk modulus of the metals given, sound will travel more slowly through it than the others.

D: This is the metal with the highest bulk modulus, so sound should travel through it the most quickly (assuming that densities are roughly equal). The question asks for the material that would give the lowest velocity.

1575. D is correct. Pitch is the perceived frequency of a sound, and frequency and wavelength are inversely proportional. Consequently, the sound with the lowest wavelength should have the highest pitch. However, since our choices are in different units, it is not immediately obvious which is smallest. If we convert to centimeters, it becomes clear that this choice (0.17 cm) is our answer.

B: 1.4×10^3 mm is equal to 140 cm.
C: 1.6×10^7 nm is equal to 1.6 cm.

1576. C is correct. We can use the equation dB = 10 log $\frac{I}{I_0}$ and plug in the given variables. This yields $130 = 10 \log\left(\frac{I}{10^{-12}W/m2}\right)$, which can be simplified to $13 = \log\left(\frac{I}{10^{-12}W/m2}\right)$. When we remove the logarithm, we get $10^{13} = \frac{I}{10^{-12}}$. Intensity is thus equal to $(10^{13})(10^{-12})$, or 10.

B: This choice likely results from a miscalculation of $(10^{13})(10^{-12})$. The product of these terms should be 10^1, not 10^{-1}.
D: Intensity and the decibel measurement are not identical.

1577. D is correct. Each 10-dB increase reflects a tenfold increase in intensity. In other words, to produce a sound of 13 dB, you would need 10 3-dB speakers. To make a sound measured at 23 dB, you would need 100, and to make a 33-dB sound, you would need 1000.

1578. D is correct. For this question, you must use the equation for the Doppler effect, $f' = f\left(\frac{V \pm V_0}{V \pm V_s}\right)$. If both cars are moving closer to each other, they both act to increase the perceived frequency of sound. We can thus plug in our known values to obtain $f' = 2.4$ kHz $\left(\frac{340+60}{340-40}\right) = 2.4$ kHz $\frac{400}{300}$ = 3.2 kHz.

A, B: Since the two cars are headed towards each other, the frequency perceived by the criminal should be higher, not lower, than the emitted frequency.

1579. D is correct. The Doppler effect applies to light as well as sound waves, with an associated equation of $f' = f\left(\frac{V \pm V_0}{V \pm V_s}\right)$. If the star is moving away from Earth, the perceived frequency of light will be lower than the actual frequency ("red shift"), ruling out answers A and B. To decide between the remaining choices, remember that you are given the perceived frequency, not the original

frequency. Plugging values into the equation gives us 6.0×10^{14} Hz = f $\left(\frac{3.0 \times 10^8}{3.0 \times 10^8 + 1.0 \times 10^8}\right)$. This simplifies to $6.0 \times 10^{14} = 0.75f$. Solving for the original frequency yields 8.0×10^{14} Hz.

A: This value could be calculated if you incorrectly assumed that the star was moving towards the earth.

1580. C is correct. Breaking the glass requires a sound wave with a frequency that matches the resonant frequency of the glass (800 Hz). Using the equation v = λf, we can solve for wavelength. In this case, $\lambda = \frac{1000 \text{ m/s}}{800 \text{ hz}}$, or 1.25 m.

A: This answer results from forgetting to convert the speed of sound into m/s.
B: This is f / v, not v / f.

1581. C is correct. Photons exhibit wave-particle duality. With qualities like wavelength, frequency, and interference, they implicate their wavelike nature. However, they also are measured in discrete quantities and are involved in the photoelectric effect, indicating their particle nature.

1582. C is correct. We know that the speed of light is 3×10^8 m/s and that the given frequency is 7.5×10^{14} Hz. These values can be plugged into the equation c = λf to yield a wavelength of 4×10^{-7} m, or 400 nm. While it is not necessary to know the specific frequencies and wavelengths of colors like yellow and green, you should know that 400 nm is the smallest wavelength still categorized as visible light. The color with the shortest wavelength within the visible spectrum is violet.

D: The wavelength of red light, which is the longest-wavelength, lowest-frequency color, is 700 nm.

1583. D is correct. You can rephrase this question as "which of the following has the highest wavelength," making the information about orange light irrelevant. Of the options, infrared light has the longest wavelength. Remember, infrared means "below red," or "having a lower frequency than red light." For that reason, we know that infrared rays possess a longer wavelength than any member of the visible spectrum.

A: Blue light has a wavelength of 450-490 nm. Because blue light is closer to violet (and ultraviolet) light, it must have a higher frequency, higher energy, and shorter wavelength than orange light.

1584. C is correct. Because the frequencies of these two waves are not the same, their wavelengths must also differ. These mismatched wavelengths will sometimes exhibit constructive interference and sometimes display destructive interference depending on how they are matched in a particular moment.

1585. B is correct. The intensity of unpolarized light will be cut in half as it passes through a single polarizing filter. Because the second polarizer is oriented in the same direction as the first, it will not change the intensity of the light that reaches it. In other words, the intensity of vertically-polarized light is not changed when it moves through a vertical polarizing filter.

C: The polarizers will block some of the light from passing through.
D: Simple polarizing filters cannot increase the intensity of light that reaches them. For that to happen, another light source would need to be contributing as well.

1586. A is correct. When two polarizing lenses are oriented at a 90° angle, no light will be able to pass through. In this scenario, the first polarizer remains vertical, while the second has been turned horizontally. This means that only vertical components of light will make it through the first filter, but only horizontal components (of which none remain) will pass through the second.

1587. A is correct. When light travels from air into glass, it will bend toward the normal at an angle determined by the index of refraction. However, different colors of light have different refractive indices in glass, with red (the color with the longest wavelength) having the smallest index of refraction and thus bending the least. In contrast, violet light has the shortest wavelength and thus bends most dramatically. Blue is closest to violet on the visible part of the electromagnetic spectrum.

D: Different colors of light do bend by different amounts when entering and exiting a medium. This phenomenon helps to explain why rainbows are able to form.

1588. B is correct. In the double-slit experiment described above, bright bands of light are created by constructive interference. In other words, at points where the two waves interact "in phase," an especially bright beam is produced.

A: Destructive interference gives rise to the dark bands, not the bright ones. Destructive interference occurs when two or more waves interact "out of phase" and cancel out some of each other's intensity.
C, D: These terms are unrelated to the dark and light bands seen on the screen.

1589. D is correct. Since the area described is a dark region on the optical screen, it must result from destructive interference. This tells you that the two waves involved must be completely out of phase, or differ by a half-wavelength. Given that the wavelength is 580 nm, the difference between the distances traveled must be $d = 290 + 580n$ where $n = 1, 2, 3$, etc.

A: The waves involved here must be completely out of phase. Since their wavelengths are 580 nm, a difference of 100 nm is not sufficiently large.
B, C: These distances would lead to completely constructive interference, as they are perfect multiples of 580 nm. This type of interference would create bright bands of light.

1590. A is correct. Combining the equations $E = hc$ and $c = \lambda f$ leads to $E = hc/\lambda$, which represents the energy of a photon. If this is perfectly converted into kinetic energy, we can set the two equal to get $hc/\lambda = \frac{1}{2}mv^2$. After rearranging this equation for velocity, we get $v = \sqrt{\frac{2hc}{\lambda m}}$.

1591. B is correct. Index of refraction, or "n," is a medium-specific value that relates the velocity of light through a material with the velocity at which light moves through a vacuum. More specifically, these quantities relate according to the equation $v = c / n$, where v and c are the velocities of light in the relevant medium and in a vacuum, respectively. Light travels through a vacuum at 3×10^8 m/s, which is a constant that you should have memorized. In contrast, it is said to move through NaCl at 1.95×10^8 m/s. Rearranging our earlier equation gives us n = c / v; thus, the index of refraction of NaCl is $(3 \times 10^8$ m/s) / $(1.95 \times 10^8$ m/s) or around 1.5.

A: As light can never travel more rapidly than it does in a vacuum, indices of refraction are never less than one.

1592. C is correct. The index of refraction (n) of a medium relates the speed of light through that material with 3×10^8 m/s, the speed at which light moves through a vacuum. These terms can be compared through use of the equation v = c / n, where v and c are the velocities of light in the relevant medium and in a vacuum, respectively. When we plug in our known values, we see that v = c / 1.33, or v = c / (4/3). Remember, dividing a term by a fraction is the same as multiplying the same term by its reciprocal! Thus, v = (3/4)c, and the velocity of light in ethanol is three-fourths (or 75%) of that in a vacuum.

A, B: These choices both say the same thing. Additionally, light can never travel faster through any medium than it does through a vacuum.
D: The material through which electromagnetic radiation travels certainly affects its velocity.

1593. D is correct. For a ray that contacts a flat surface, the angle of incidence is equal to the angle of reflection. However, note that this question asks for the angle with respect to the normal! The diagram shows the angle x with respect to the surface itself. In contrast, the normal is the line that runs perpendicular, or at a 90° angle, to the glass surface. For this reason, both the angle of incidence and that of reflection can be measured as (90 – 18) or 72° when compared to the normal.

A: This value resembles that which would be found using Snell's law and an angle of incidence of 18°. This is wrong for multiple reasons: Snell's law is used only for refraction, and even if this question did not deal with reflection, 72° (not 18°) would need to be plugged in.
B: Again, be sure to notice what the question is asking for. In general, in optics, angles are measured with respect to the normal; avoid assuming that the angles shown in diagrams should be used exactly as written.

C: The angle given here was likely found by using Snell's law to calculate the ray's angle of refraction upon entering the glass. While the angle used was at least correct (72°), this question asks about reflection.

1594. C is correct. Several possibilities exist for the identities of these three substances; however, only one is given as an answer choice. We see that, when moving from medium 1 to medium 2, the ray bends away from the normal; this indicates that it has traveled from a higher-n to a lower-n material. However, when later entering medium 3, the ray moves back towards the normal, implying that it has re-entered a substance with a comparatively high refractive index. This trend – high to low and back to high – is only displayed by the materials in choice C.

A, D: Both of these choices are the reverse of the correct trend. Here, we see a transition from low n (either 1 or 1.31) to high n (either 1.5 or 2.42), then back to a low-index medium. Such answers could result either from misreading the figure or from mistakenly considering angles with respect to the surface instead of to the normal line.

1595. D is correct. Most of this statement is true; when light travels from a medium with a high index (oil) to one with a low index (water), the ray will bend away from the normal. For this reason, its angle of refraction will certainly exceed 24°. However, a higher n implies that light travels more slowly, not more quickly, through a particular medium. Thus, light moves faster through water than through oil.

A: Make sure to note when angles are given in relation to the normal, and when they are not! When dealing with a flat surface, the angle of incidence always equals the angle of refraction. Here, a 33° angle to the oil-water interface is the same as a 57° angle to the normal, which is the line that runs perpendicular to that boundary.
B, C: These statements are also perfectly accurate.

1596. C is correct. Both IR and UV – along with visible light, microwaves, and a number of other forms – are types of electromagnetic radiation, commonly known as "light." All types of light move equally quickly in a vacuum, like that present in space. Specifically, they travel at 3×10^8 m/s.

D: Frequency does not matter here. According to the equation $c = \lambda f$, both types of radiation will move with the same velocity in a vacuum. UV light does have a higher frequency, but that simply means that IR rays possess longer wavelengths.

1597. A is correct. Here, light rays are moving from a region of high n to one of relatively low n. According to the equation $c = v / n$, the light will speed up during this transition. From here, it is helpful to remember this relationship: velocity $= \lambda f$. Since light is increasing in velocity, the product of wavelength and frequency must increase in a corresponding manner. Furthermore, the frequency of light does not change when that light transitions between media. Thus, it must be wavelength that rises to yield the predicted increase in speed.

1598. B is correct. For total internal reflection to occur, two main criteria must be met. First, light must be traveling from a medium with a high index of refraction to one with a lower index, preferably with a large difference between the two. Second, the angle of incidence must be relatively large. Choice B meets both of these conditions. In fact, the behavior of light at a diamond-air interface is one of the most commonly cited examples of total internal reflection.

A: The direction of light's movement is reversed here. Total internal reflection (or a refraction so significant that light "bends back" into the medium) requires the incident ray to be moving from a high-n material to one with a low n.
C: This choice is actually that which is least likely to produce the effect mentioned by the question, as it involves a small angle and two media with very close refractive indices.
D: This situation is close! However, remember that total internal reflection is favored by high, not low, angles of incidence with respect to the normal.

1599. A is correct. The critical angle is the angle of incidence above which total internal reflection will occur. In other words, this is the angle that yields an angle of refraction of 90°. (Thus, larger angles will yield larger $<_{refraction}$ values, meaning

that the light must bend back into the original medium.) We can find our answer using Snell's law: $n_1\sin\Theta_1 = n_2\sin\Theta_2$, or $n_1\sin\Theta_1 = n_2\sin(90°)$. Since the sine of 90° is 1, this simplifies to $n_1\sin\Theta_1 = n_2$, which can be rearranged into $\sin\Theta_1 = n_2 / n_1$. As Θ_1 represents the critical angle, we have our answer.

D: Snell's law involves sine, not cosine.

1600. C is correct. Though lenses can be intimidating, the basic principle is simple: they operate by refracting light. The greater the difference between the index of refraction of the lens material and that of the surrounding environment, the more the rays will bend. Here, originally, the optometrist used a glass lens in what we can assume is air, meaning that the respective refractive indices of the two media were 1.5 and 1.0. Raising the n of the lens to 1.7 will improve the strength of the apparatus, as will increasing its thickness, which will simply give light more medium through which it must travel at its bent angle.

A: This will reduce the amount of medium through which the bent rays must travel. In fact, it can be helpful to remember that thinner lenses are generally weaker ones.
B: This change will reduce, instead of increase, the difference in the indices of refraction of the two materials.
D: Remember, the power of a lens is the reciprocal of its focal length! In other words, a high focal length correlates to a weak lens.

1601. B is correct. A mirror or lens with a negative focal length must be diverging. For a lens, that is concave; for a mirror, it is convex.

1602. B is correct. Spherical aberrations are caused by imperfect surfaces, such as dings, bends, or ridges. This occurs in both lenses and mirrors. In contrast, chromatic aberrations occur as a result of diffraction, which requires light to travel through different media rather than reflect, as it does when incident on a mirror.

1603. D is correct. Use the formula $\frac{1}{f} = \frac{1}{d_o} + \frac{1}{d_i}$ and plug in 20 for f and 30 for d_o. Solving yields $d_i = 60$.

1604. D is correct. The focal length of any mirror is equal to half of its radius of curvature, which, in this case, is 10 m. In any converging system, when an object is placed at the focal point, no image will be created. You can prove this mathematically through the use of $\frac{1}{f} = \frac{1}{d_o} + \frac{1}{d_i}$. If $f = d_o$, then d_i does not exist.

1605. C is correct. If the radius of curvature is 10 m, then the focal length is half of that, or 5 m. Plugging into $\frac{1}{f} = \frac{1}{d_o} + \frac{1}{d_i}$ allows us to solve for all three variables. However, even this is unnecessary, as converging systems in which the object is more than one focal length from the lens always yield real, inverted images.

1606. A is correct. Since this is a diverging system, the image must form in front of the lens. Additionally, because the star is so far away, you can assume that the incoming light hits the lens in parallel. Either mathematically or through the use of a ray diagram, you can see that the image will appear at the focal point.

1607. D is correct. Because the image produced is on the same side as the object, it is termed virtual. (This is true for lenses only; if the image were on the same side as the object in a mirror, it would be real.) This narrows the choices to B and D. To decide, one must determine the magnification using $m = -\frac{d_i}{d_o}$. As we can assume that the star is much farther away than the image, the magnification approaches zero. In other words, the image will be smaller than the object.

1608. A is correct. Because the lens of the eye cannot focus light that is approaching in parallel, it must have more trouble dealing with distant objects. A diverging lens will cause the rays of light to bend outward, correcting the extra converging power possessed by the lens of a myopic individual.

1609. D is correct. First, solve for the image created by the first lens. Using $\frac{1}{f} = \frac{1}{d_o} + \frac{1}{d_i}$, we see that the first image distance is 10 cm. This image may then be viewed as the object for the second lens. Since "Image 1" is 10 cm behind the first lens, it falls 20 cm in front of the second ($d_o = 20$ cm).

Solving in a similar manner as above yields a distance of 20 cm to the right of Lens 2.

1610. B is correct. In order to determine the total magnification of a system of lenses, simply multiply the individual magnifications. (2)(-1.5)(-0.5) = 1.5.

1611. B is correct. If the plant originally had 0.024% C^{14}, then after one half-life (5470 years), it should have 0.012%. Another half-life would bring its concentration to 0.006%; two half-lives is equivalent to 10940 years.

A: This is only a single half-life, at which point C^{14} would comprise 0.012% of total carbon.
C: 15410 years is three half-lives, which would bring the C^{14} concentration to 0.003%.
D: This value represents four half-lives, which would bring the C^{14} concentration to 0.0015%.

1612. B is correct. 26 years represents five half-lives. Since half of 32 g is 16 g, that is the amount which remains after a single half-life, or 5.2 years. A second half-life brings this value to 8 g, then 4 g, then 2 g. Finally, after the fifth half-life, the remaining concentration is half of 2 g, or 1 g.

A: This value is too small. It may have been obtained if you assume that half of the compound (16 g) is gone after one half-life, and that the remaining 16 grams decays during the second half-life. However, this represents linear, not exponential, decay.
C: This represents the amount remaining after four half-lives.
D: This represents the amount left after only three half-lives, not five.

1613. B is correct. The graph shows that it takes about 30 weeks for the compound to decay from 70 grams to 35 grams. In other words, its half-life is about 30 weeks. For a sample to go from 100% to 25%, two half-lives, or about 60 weeks, must pass. 60 weeks is closest to 1.2 years.

A, C: These values are very close to a single half-life in years and weeks, respectively.
D: This answer would be correct if the question had asked for the time period in weeks, not years.

1614. A is correct. In alpha decay, an atom loses two protons and two neutrons. Since He³ has only a single neutron, it is not capable of alpha decay.

B, C, D: Whether it is likely or not, these elements at least have more than two protons and two neutrons. They are thus able to undergo alpha decay.

1615. A is correct. Alpha decay occurs when an unstable element loses two protons and two neutrons, otherwise known as a helium nucleus or α particle. β⁺ decay converts a proton into a neutron, while β⁻ decay turns a neutron into a proton. In other words, the two types of beta decay cancel each other out. Finally, gamma decay does not change the parent element. Our final answer must have two fewer protons and four fewer mass units than our starting compound, making Th²³⁴ the correct answer.

B: This choice would result from a single β⁻ decay.
C: This results from one β⁺ decay.
D: This is an example of gamma decay, which doesn't change the nucleus involved.

1616. D is correct. In gamma decay, the nucleus of the decaying element does not change. In a process that can be referred to as a "settling" of the nucleus, the element emits a high-energy photon, otherwise known as a gamma ray or gamma particle.

A: A potassium nucleus possesses two more protons than Cl³⁷. None of the major forms of radioactive decay results in the gain of two protons at once.
B: A nucleus of this element could be produced from β⁻ decay.
C: An argon nucleus could result from β⁻ decay.

1617. C is correct. β⁺ decay occurs when a proton is converted into a neutron and a positron, or β⁺ particle. The parent element in β⁺ decay has one more proton and one fewer neutron than the daughter nucleus.

A: For this element to be converted directly into Na²⁴, it would need to undergo alpha decay.
B: This element can produce Na²⁴ after one β⁻ decay, but that form of radioactive decay gives off an electron, not a positron.

D: This choice would only be correct if the question had described gamma decay.

1618. C is correct. Any charged particle will be subjected to a force when moved perpendicularly to a magnetic field. An alpha particle is two neutrons and two protons, which has a +2 charge. A β⁻ particle is just an electron, which has a -1 charge; in contrast, a β⁺ particle is a positron, which has a +1 charge.

IV: A gamma particle is a photon, meaning that it carries no charge. As such, it is not influenced by the magnetic field.

1619. D is correct. All nuclei weigh less than the sum of their component protons and neutrons, a phenomenon known as mass defect. When subatomic particles come together to form a nucleus, some of their mass is converted into energy. You can calculate this relationship using the famous equation $E = mc^2$.

1620. D is correct. First, calculate the mass defect. A helium nucleus has two protons and two neutrons, meaning that the total mass of the protons is 2.0144 amu while that of the neutrons is 2.0172 amu. Combining these values gives a predicted mass of 4.0316 amu. Because the actual mass is 4.0015 amu, the mass defect is roughly .030 amu. The next step is to convert the mass to kilograms, the units required for the equation $E = mc^2$. 0.03 amu × (1.66 × 10⁻²⁷ kg / amu) = 4.98 × 10⁻²⁹, or about 5 × 10⁻²⁹, kg. Finally, plug in to $E = mc^2$. E = (5 × 10⁻²⁹) (3 × 10⁸)² = (5 × 10⁻²⁹) (9 × 10¹⁶) = 4.5 × 10⁻¹² J.

A: This value is far too large, and comes from keeping the units for mass in amu. For the equation $E = mc^2$, mass must be converted into the SI base unit of kilograms.
C: This value results from neglecting to square the speed of light in the equation $E = mc^2$.

1621. C is correct. A latent function is an unintended benefit of a social structure. In this case, one latent function of the IRS is to provide employment to the many accountants, management staff, and service workers that work for this organization.

A: This describes Social Security.
B, D: These are manifest, not latent, functions of the IRS.

1622. D is correct. A latent dysfunction is an unintentional negative consequence of a societal structure. Here, one adverse effect of Social Security is that it creates a means of identity theft, since Americans rely so heavily on social security numbers as proof of identity. Additionally, choice IV describes Social Security's manifest function.

I: This is a latent function.
II: According to a functionalist philosophy, successful societies can reach and maintain a dynamic equilibrium.

1623. A is correct. Micro sociology is the study of expressions, symbolic gestures, and other small, individual components of society.

B: Conflict sociology is the study of the way that distinct groups compete for resources. It deals with the idea that those who hold control of limited resources possess an advantage over those who do not.

1624. C is correct. Conflict theory accounts for the fact that some baboons monopolized resources in order to give themselves an advantage over others. As in conflict theory, the main focus of the question stem is to depict favored and marginalized groups who clash over resources.

B: Though it does relate to language (similar to the growling mentioned here), symbolic interactionism does not account for competition over resources.
D: It is unclear what, if any, role socially constructed values play in this narrative.

1625. C is correct. Symbolic interactionism accounts for the fact that we agree upon certain gestures, words, and other symbols, to which we assign meaning. Since the test group was never told which symbols were socially appropriate, they lack a cohesive understanding of the method preferred by outside society.

A: While the button might provide some entertainment, this does not relate to symbolic interactionism.
B: Words like "value" are typically associated with social constructionism, which explains how we assign importance to certain social constructs. Symbolic interactionism is more concerned with meaning than with value.

1626. C is correct. Social constructionism accounts for respect as a notion upon which society places a certain amount of value. By choosing to raise their hands respectfully, students are acknowledging respect as a social construct that is important to them.

A, B, D: Although these are plausible, none relate as directly to the question stem as choice C.

1627. C is correct. Social constructionism accounts for our assignment of meaning to certain constructs, including money, obedience, and trustworthiness. Here, the ancient culture chose to assign meaning to the rare stones as a form of currency.

1628. A is correct. Conflict theory explains how groups compete for resources to attain power or superiority. Here, the two groups are categorized as men and women. According to this individual, men have consolidated political and social power for their own prosperity.

B: Social constructionism is more relevant to the assignment of value to certain social constructs. This man is more concerned with the fact that men have attempted to dominate these arenas than the notion that they are social constructs in the first place.

1629. A is correct. Exchange-rational choice theory relates to the logical deliberation between options by way of measuring the social exchanges that could occur in consequence. Some choices yield more benefits than punishments, others are the opposite, and still others seem to have a neutral exchange value. Here, the owner decided that his firing of the coaching staff would result in more rewards then punishments.

1630. B is correct. A latent function is an unintended consequence, while a manifest function is an intentional or main result. Medical schools exist primarily to educate future doctors.

A, C: These are latent functions. Although medical schools do employ many people and provide medical services, these are secondary to their primary goal of education.

1631. B is correct. Hidden curriculum refers to implicit or unspoken values that are taught in school.

Often, parts of the hidden curriculum are not even intentional, but are conveyed unconsciously by teachers or administrators. This coach seems to believe that boys should act like boys and girls should act like girls. However, this idea clearly is not part of a written syllabus for the class. By scolding his student, he is enforcing a hidden curriculum.

1632. C is correct. Expectancy theory describes how the expectations that a teacher transmits to a student can cause the student to act in accordance to these expectations.

A: This choice only describes the teacher's actions, not the student's response.
B: Neither of these options describe a student acting in a way that matches his teacher's expectations.

1633. A is correct. Kinship systems relate to family. We know that Max has formed many strong bonds with individuals on his father's side. We also know that he shares his father's, not his mother's, last name. For this reason, patrilineal descent is the best answer.

C: This might be the case if the student felt and expressed equal kinship with those on both sides of his family.

1634. C is correct. A patriarchy describes a family in which the male "head of the house" keeps most or all of the authority. Although this father is bedridden, he still is described as having enough authority to order his wife and children around.

A: This cannot be a patriarchy, as the wife still possesses the power to make some important choices.
B: While this father does seem to have most of the power, we cannot know if this is due to a patriarchal system or to the fact that he is a single parent.
D: In the case of a family with two fathers, patriarchy is a more difficult term to apply.

1635. D is correct. While one might learn obedience from familial influences (just as one might learn virtually anything), obedience itself is not as clear of a benefit as the other choices.

1636. A is correct. By definition, cults revolve around practices that are considered either abnormal or outright unacceptable.

B: The definition of a cult does not constrain the number of individuals that can lead it.
C: Cults can evolve into major religions. By some definitions, even Christianity exemplifies a cult that became one of the world's largest religions.
D: Cults can survive and grow without any defined limits.

1637. D is correct. While a state religion is officially recognized by the government, it does not form a component of the laws by which the nation operates. For this reason, if not for the description of this individual as a lawyer who uses religion in her work, a state religion would be a sensible answer. However, since laws do function in accordance with her religion, this woman most likely lives in a theocracy.

1638. B is correct. Abuse is an umbrella term that covers spousal abuse, negligence, and elder abuse.

IV: No clear instance of abuse is mentioned by this example. Negligence applies more specifically to instances where the party being abandoned or ignored is suffering physical or long-term mental harm.

1639. C is correct. In general, cults have at least some practices that are frowned upon by mainstream society.

A: This describes a sect, which is the result of a deviation from another religion.
B: This is untrue.
D: This is not necessarily the intention of all cults.

1640. C is correct. A sect is defined as a religious group that arose from a split from a larger religion. It is more likely to find these types of religious organizations in rural areas than in urban ones..

A: While this might be true, it is not implied by the study.
B: This would be true of a state religion or one found in a theocracy, but there is no specific mention of it here.
D: There is no evidence to suggest this is true.

1641. C is correct. An oligarchy (from the Greek "*oligos-*," or "few," and "*-cracy*," or "rule by") is a political situation where a small group of people effectively run society.

A: An oligarchy is not necessarily capitalistic; for example, many former communist countries were effectively oligarchies. Nor are all capitalistic countries themselves oligarchies.
B: Oligarchies are distinct from monopolies, or markets dominated by a single seller.
D: While some oligarchies are authoritarian, not all need to be. Some such governments permit a degree of individual freedom while restricting political decision-making to the favored class.

1642. D is correct. Medicalization is the process by which a condition is viewed as a disease (and thus deserving of help from the medical profession), rather than as something else, such as a habit, personality trait, character flaw, or lifestyle choice. Here, alcoholism is the only disease listed that was not always perceived as having clear biological roots that can be treated by doctors. As science and the public have learned more about the neurological changes associated with addiction, alcoholism has started to be seen as a treatable disease; in other words, it has been medicalized.

A, B, C: These illnesses have virtually always been seen as diseases and have needed no such change in status.

1643. C is correct. The sick role is a socially constructed role that individuals enter when they become ill. One can acquire the sick role legitimately (by actually being sick) or illegitimately (by faking illness or deliberately / negligently failing to take care of one's health). As part of Parson's conception of this role, patients are released from normal duties like work or family care due to the infirmities brought on by the illness, making statement I accurate. However, the patient now has the obligation to do his best to relieve others of these burdens as quickly as possible, by trying to become well and taking the advice of doctors and other medical staff.

II: In Parson's conception of the *legitimate* sick role, a sufferer is not considered responsible for his own illness; it is something that has been inflicted on him. This choice might instead be correct if the question asked about the illegitimate sick role.

1644. C is correct. Social epidemiology studies the ways that social factors (such as lifestyle choices, demographic characteristics, and cultural practices) influence the development of specific diseases. As the probability of acquiring HIV is strongly linked to certain behavioral practices (IV drug use and promiscuous sex), social epidemiology will be able to most narrowly pinpoint the groups at risk for this disease.

B: The question asks for a disease whose risk factors can be isolated using social epidemiology. As of now, Alzheimer's has exceedingly broad risk factors (basically age, although other characteristics are considered to play a role). Similarly, the main risk factors for prostate cancer are a male gender and an older age, also broad categories.
D: No narrow criteria currently exist for predicting which individuals will develop leukemia.

1645. D is correct. Bureaucratization is the tendency for a segment of society to become increasingly controlled by bureaucracies, or organizations governed by rigid administrative rules and formal hierarchies. In this case, informal client relationships and small practices have been replaced by formalized insurance systems like HMOs and PPOs along with large, hierarchically-organized hospital systems.

A: Socialization more properly refers to the idea of deeply involving government in a specific social function. While this has happened to some degree, it does not capture changes that have occurred to the private sector as well.
B: Deindividuation, a concept in group psychology, occurs when an individual subsumes his identity and self-awareness into a group (like a gang or mob).
C: This term would be accurate if the question stem mentioned the government nationalizing and running hospitals itself, which has not happened in the US.

1646. C is correct. Household size, by itself, tells us relatively little about an individual's health. Its main relevance is its correlation to other factors (for example, more impoverished families generally tend to have larger households overall).

A: An individual's age directly relates to his or her ability to fight off and recuperate from disease; thus, it is highly relevant to the social epidemiology of a population.
B: Per capita income, or "income per person," directly correlates to the resources available to an individual or family. The higher the income, the greater the ability to purchase health insurance and obtain preventive care.
D: Ethnic background is relevant because many genetic diseases, like sickle-cell anemia and Tay-Sachs disease, are highly prevalent within certain ethnic groups.

1647. C is correct. Symbolic interactionism deals with how the perceived meanings of objects (or symbols) interact with each other and with larger institutions. In this case, the study focuses on systems of meaning constructed around steps in the journey through the healthcare system.

A: Conflict theory is interested in determining the resources held by societal groups (like races or classes) and ascertaining the material and social effects on their lives.
B: Structural functionalism would more likely study *how* the healthcare system organizes resources to address social problems.
D: Game theory is a mathematically-based discipline that focuses on the rational maximization of outcomes when making decisions. It is not a school of sociological thought.

1648. C is correct. While this patient is capable of making decisions, he likely has difficulty recognizing his own best interests in any rational manner. For this reason, such a severely delusional man would present issues relating to the ethical need to respect patient autonomy. Mental illness, as well as other disorders that hinder patients from making effective decisions (like comas), presents an ethical dilemma that is currently is the subject of ongoing legislative and judicial debates.

1649. D is correct. The responses to the survey reveal that the citizens possess different values regarding free speech. In other words, they have very dissimilar opinions in relation to the

importance that society as a whole should attach to this freedom.

A, C: Mores and folkways relate more to informal standards of behavior than to opinion. Mores more closely resemble rules, while folkways are closer to cultural guidelines; even so, neither carries a formal legal sanction like a government prohibition.
B: A taboo is an action that is strongly disapproved of by society; these behaviors may or may not have associated legal sanctions as well. However, this revulsion or disapproval typically comes from the idea that violating the taboo breaks some sacred standard, such as incest or polygamy. Free speech does not relate to such a standard.

1650. D is correct. Church attendance, as a factor that stems from deep and often permanent religious conviction, is much less affected by economic factors than the other choices.

A: When unemployment rates rise, people tend to get married later and postpone having children until they are better suited for them. While this is not true for every family, fertility rates do fall during recessions.
B: At least in our current system, high unemployment does mean that fewer people can afford health insurance coverage.
C: Recessions impact college attendance rates in a number of ways. Some students may postpone entry to the job market by entering graduate school, while others may be discouraged by the high cost of attendance and forgo a higher education entirely.

1651. B is correct. Symbolic culture includes all aspects of a society's culture that are not material. In other words, it is comprised of language, traditions, collective behaviors, and so on. As language is a major component of symbolic culture, we can conclude that the large difference in preposition number between the two societies represents a symbolic distinction. While we cannot be certain of any more details, we can guess that the ancient society gained value from having numerous and more descriptive prepositional phrases.

A: Language is not a part of material culture.

C: This choice would make more sense if the older society's folkways placed an increased emphasis on direction, which could in turn necessitate more descriptive prepositions. However, this answer choice mentions a decreased, not increased, emphasis.

D: The scenario described does not involve social learning.

1652. D is correct. To put it simply, material culture includes tangible objects or "things." Buildings, gifts, toys, furniture, and food all fall within this subdivision of culture. Roman numeral I describes objects directly, while III discusses gifts and IV mentions physical buildings.

II: This is part of symbolic, not material, culture. The social value of a college education is not an object; it is more of a perception, and can vary both between and within societies.

1653. B is correct. Admittedly, "society" is not a strictly-defined term; nevertheless, a study group that only meets three times per week likely has not established the same shared identity that the other choices involve. In addition, unlike any of the other three answers, this group absolutely might stop meeting once their classes no longer coincide. In general, a society is simply a group of individuals located in the same region who share at least some elements of culture or collective identity.

C: Animals, even simple ones like ants, often live in societies. Whether animals have culture is more hotly debated.

1654. C is correct. Cultural assimilation requires that one party begin to blend aspects of other cultures into their own. By using American cooking techniques in the preparation of Russian food, the immigrants in this question are assimilating into American culture.

A: This choice does describe the assimilation of a lone individual, but the question asks for an example of a group.

B: By living in a predominantly Indian area of the city, these residents are less likely to integrate American traditions into their familiar culture. While some assimilation may occur anyway, this is not the best answer.

D: Again, this example relates to an individual rather than a group. Additionally, the fact that this woman is becoming interested in Russian music does not necessarily imply assimilation, or cultural blending.

1655. A is correct. Cultural transmission is the continuation of a cultural tradition through successive generations. In other words, it involves the "passing down" of cultural behaviors and knowledge from adults, usually parents, to children. Here, we see that the dancing competition has existed in this town for over one hundred and fifty years. It is a part of the original immigrants' culture that has been maintained throughout the years, rather than diluted or replaced with other traditions.

B: Diffusion would require that the waltzing tradition be spread to other townspeople. Here, only the descendants of the German immigrants seem to be participating.

C: While it is likely that even second- or third-generation Germans experienced significant assimilation, the yearly waltz competition does not directly relate to this concept.

1656. B is correct. Culture lag is a phenomenon where material culture advances faster than symbolic culture. This progress, and the resulting disconnect between the public and technology, often leads to conflict. In this case, although the material culture associated with advanced energy technologies has progressed, the symbolic importance of this advancement is lost to many voters. Still attached to the notion that fossil fuels should be our main source of energy, they regard these new eco-friendly technologies with suspicion.

1657. C is correct. Cultural transmission is the continuation of a cultural tradition through successive generations. In other words, it involves the "passing down" of cultural behaviors and knowledge from adults, usually parents, to children. This term is the best choice here, as *Novy god* exemplifies a cultural tradition that has been maintained over the course of several generations.

A: Cultural diffusion would be appropriate only if it were found that more and more non-Russian Americans began celebrating *Novy god* – in other words, that a Russian tradition was spreading.

1658. C is correct. Both the diminished participation in a Russian tradition and the increased identification with an American one represent cultural assimilation. These younger generations of Russian-Americans are becoming increasingly assimilated into American culture.

B: Cultural integration is not a proper sociological term. Even if it were, it would not apply to the trend displayed here with Russian dance. Note that a lack of participation in a Russian tradition does not necessitate increased participation in American pastimes; for this reason, we cannot say that these individuals are undergoing "integration" from the information regarding dance alone.

1659. A is correct. A subculture is a smaller group within a society whose members share values, often an environment, and common goals. These product designers have not only shared a space, but also hold a common vision for their products and how they should conduct business. This perfectly exemplifies a subculture.

B: These hackers do not seem to share values or goals with each other. They simply operate according to their varying interests.
C: This is simply an example of marketing and does not relate to subcultures.
D: The people described here make for a tempting choice! It is true that members of a subculture often hold views that are different from, and even in opposition to, those possessed by most of society. However, nothing in this choice mentions that these individuals are located near each other or even in the same country. In general, subcultures fall within larger cultures, so people who hail from entirely different regions of the world would be less likely to comprise one.

1660. A is correct. Cultural diffusion represents the spread of a cultural practice or tradition from one group to another (or between individuals in a single group). Here, one group's penchant for teeth-picking gradually diffuses to the other group, causing members of that group to begin picking at other apes' teeth as well.

1661. B is correct. Achieved statuses are positions that we earn through our own accomplishment. A professional piano player has most likely chosen

that career voluntarily and certainly has earned his status through hard work.

A: An ascribed status is one that we are born with or assigned. Examples include height and gender.
C: A primary group is one that includes long-lasting, close relationships. This individual is not necessarily close with other musicians.
D: A reference group is one that is used to compare oneself to. While we don't know exactly which groups this individual uses for reference, the question stem only tells us that he is a professional musician. We have no idea whether he has a family, and must conclude that he likely compares himself to other musicians.

1662. C is correct. A reference group is one that is used to compare oneself to. For example, an athlete might evaluate his own training schedule and overall performance against those of other athletes.

A: A control group is a group within an experimental design that does not receive the experimental condition. The question stem has nothing to do with any experiment or study.
B: While this is not incorrect, it is not the term used in sociology.
D: A primary group is one that includes long-lasting, close relationships, such as a family or tight-knit group of friends.

1663. A is correct. Role strain occurs when a person has trouble meeting multiple demands of the same role. Only choice A describes a single role or position (volunteer leader) with multiple conflicting requirements to fulfill.

B, C: These choices relate more closely to role conflict. Do not get these terms confused! Role conflict occurs when multiple distinct roles are in competition with each other for an individual's resources.
D: This choice describes role exit, not role strain.

1664. B is correct. A primary group includes members with close, long-lasting relationships. Members of an MCAT study group might spend a lot of time together for a brief period, but are unlikely to stay close long after their exam. Additionally, the question emphasizes that they only speak "occasionally" after the test.

A: A secondary group is more temporary and less closely connected than a primary group. Members choose to join a secondary group for a specific purpose, such as studying for the MCAT.

C: A peer group is one made up of individuals of similar ages; its members also share interests and are generally of the same status. Most students preparing for the MCAT fall into the same peer group.

D: A reference group is one that is used to compare oneself to. A student preparing for an exam would likely gauge his study habits and test performance against members of his study group.

1665. C is correct. An ascribed status is one that we are born with or assigned. Examples include gender, race, and height.

A, B: Gregory's master status is unlikely to be baseball, since others do not think of him as a baseball player. The same is true of singing, regardless of how much he enjoys the activity. Gregory's master status is far more likely to be "child actor."

D: Since becoming an actor is an accomplishment, it is categorized as an achieved, not an ascribed, status.

1666. D is correct. A bureaucracy is an organizational system used in governments, companies, and other large groups. One of several characteristics of a bureaucracy is a strictly hierarchical structure, with bosses and employees fulfilling distinct functions.

A: Bureaucracies are large, but they are impersonal, not personal.

B: In a bureaucracy, each member performs a specialized function. Having each worker in a company (for example) do the exact same job does not make sense in a bureaucratic setting.

C: This is the opposite of the correct answer.

1667. A is correct. A normative organization is voluntarily joined and exists to perform some moral activity. Volunteer groups are classic examples of normative organizations.

B: A coercive organization is not voluntary, so this freshman would not be able to choose to join one.

C: A utilitarian organization is one where members are paid or otherwise compensated, such as a job.

D: An oligarchy is a governmental system in which most power is held by only a few people. This has nothing to do with the question stem.

1668. B is correct. Role exit occurs when an individual leaves a role. It can happen for a variety of reasons, but the most common ones include conflict with another role or a large personal change.

I, II: These definitions are confused. Role strain involves a single role with multiple aspects that are sometimes at odds, while role conflict relates to multiple distinct, conflicting roles.

1669. C is correct. An in-group is one that an individual feels membership in, while an out-group is one to which the individual does not belong. Generally, members of one's in-group are favored while those in an out-group are disliked or discriminated against. If a participant views someone with an admiration stereotype (high warmth, high competence), that participant is seeing the person in a very positive way, meaning they are likely a member of the in-group.

1670. A is correct. If James views someone with an envious stereotype, he perceives them with low warmth but admits that their competence is high. This is most common when the person in question is a member of a competing out-group, such as an enemy team.

B: James would likely view his own coach with an admiration stereotype.

C: While the envious stereotype does involve high perceived competence, a member of James' own team would fall into his in-group and would likely be viewed with high warmth.

D: James' sister probably is characterized under the paternalistic stereotype: high warmth, low competence.

1671. C is correct. Group polarization is a phenomenon in which members of a group tend to take stronger viewpoints after discussion than they would have on their own. Note that original opinions do not drastically change, but simply become more extreme. Here, since these people originally feel positive about the idea, they are likely to view it even more positively after talking in a group for several hours.

A, B: Neither of these scenarios involves a group at all.

D: Since the vast majority of this group already feels neutral, it is not as good of an answer as choice C. If anything, the woman's opinions are likely to become less (not more) extreme.

1672. C is correct. The experiences of both of these individuals can be explained by social facilitation. According to this idea, individuals tend to perform better in front of groups when the task in question is fairly simple or familiar, but perform worse when they are less comfortable with what they are doing.

A, B: Neither of these individuals is experiencing social loafing. This phenomenon is more relevant to group activities like team sports and group projects.

1673. B is correct. Conformity represents adherence to the standards of a group; it closely relates to the obedience of group rules and norms. Typically, conformity does not occur without some form of outside pressure. If we are only considering this closed group of young people, we can assume that such pressure comes from peers within the group.

A: One can experience peer pressure without conforming. For example, consider a male who has just turned twenty-one. Though all of his friends may pressure him to drink alcohol, he can certainly choose whether to conform (and drink) or not (and abstain).

C, D: These concepts are both related and present in most peer groups.

1674. A is correct. Group polarization is a phenomenon in which members of a group tend to take stronger viewpoints after discussion than they would have on their own. Note that original opinions do not drastically change, but simply become more extreme. In other words, if group members are individually somewhat risk-averse, their group decision will be even more so. On the other hand, if each of the people involved likes to take risks, their final decision is likely to be extremely risky.

C: This is the opposite of group polarization.

1675. C is correct. The presence of mindguards is one of Janis' eight proposed features of groupthink.

A, B, D: None of these terms were ever defined or even mentioned by Janis.

1676. D is correct. Kitty Genovese, a young woman from New York City, was stabbed in front of a number of witnesses, none of whom called the authorities. While this event has been largely studied and its accounts questioned, it still serves as a classic example of the bystander effect, also known as bystander apathy. This relates to the tendency of people to avoid helping those in distress when other individuals are present. This concept is thought to stem from the idea that "someone else will do it," a viewpoint that (when held by everyone present) causes nobody to actually step in.

A, B: While both of these terms are concepts in group psychology, neither is especially relevant to the described situation.

C: This choice is a combination of two psychological terms that, in combination, make no sense.

1677. D is correct. This question relates to the bystander effect, or the tendency of people to avoid helping those in distress when other individuals are present. Thus, we can infer that the more wealthy families that see the distressed lifeboat, the more they will conclude that "someone else will help" and go on their way. As a result, the two values are negatively correlated.

C: No correlation gives a coefficient of 0, not -1.

1678. A is correct. Social facilitation can result in improved performance in front of a crowd, especially when the task being performed is familiar and fairly easy.

B: This tends to yield negative consequences, as it involves the decreased effort of individuals in a group.

C: This interesting phenomenon is almost always negative (and sometimes deadly), as it explains why people sometimes do not stop to help others in need.

D: The psychological phenomenon listed here generally results in more reckless or illogical decisions.

1679. B is correct. The bystander effect is the tendency of people to avoid helping those in distress when other individuals are present. This concept is thought to stem from the idea that "someone else will do it," a viewpoint that (when held by everyone present) causes nobody to actually step in. Here, the question stem describes the region as crowded, implying that many potential bystanders are present. Such a situation forms a classic environment for the bystander effect to take place.

A: Since only one bystander is mentioned here, he is unlikely to think that someone else will help the unfortunate boy. As such, he is far more likely to help the boy himself.
C: This unlikely situation involves multiple victims, not multiple bystanders.
D: This choice is close! However, since the only individuals who seem to witness the child's distress are together, they are more likely to help him than are a number of unrelated people.

1680. D is correct. Group polarization is a phenomenon in which members of a group tend to take stronger viewpoints after discussion than they would have on their own. Note that original opinions do not drastically change, but simply become more extreme. In other words, if jury members individually thought the murderer to be guilty, their final decision will even more strongly convey this opinion. On the other hand, if each of the jurors previously felt that he may be innocent, their final decision is likely to sway in the opposite direction.

1681. C is correct. Stereotype threat occurs when a person worries about confirming adverse stereotypes about his or her social group. In this example, Amy fears that speaking up in class will confirm the negative belief that women are overly emotional.

A: This is a great example of meritocracy, but certainly does not relate to stereotype threat.
B: The situation here is a self-fulfilling prophecy, not stereotype threat. While the two are not completely unrelated, stereotype threat must involve one's own social group, not that of others.
D: This fact is unrelated to the concept in the question.

1682. D is correct. In this situation, the citizens are displaying prejudice against the skateboarders by assigning blame for crimes they did not commit. In other words, they are expressing their anger about certain events against a social group that they dislike. This is a classic example of a scapegoat. Another common example is the Nazis' blame of the Jewish people for Germany's problems before and during the Holocaust.

A: False consensus involves an individual's biased belief that other people agree with them. In other words, it is our tendency to assume that our opinions are normal or typical. Although this may be true of the citizens, it doesn't relate to their false assignment of blame.
B: Affirmative action refers to policies that attempt to adjust for past discrimination. It certainly is not relevant here.
C: Fundamental attribution error is the undue emphasis that people tend to place on dispositional factors when judging the behavior of others. This psychological bias does not relate to the question.

1683. B is correct. A self-fulfilling prophecy refers to a prediction or judgment that, simply by being made, makes itself likely to actually happen. In other words, the prediction creates a situation that confirms its own accuracy. In this case, Jared is told that he will fail at math because his siblings did not do well. If this is a self-fulfilling prophecy, he actually will do poorly because of this expectation.

A: While Jared may be better at English, this situation does not involve his poor performance as a result of others' expectations.

1684. A is correct. Prestige refers to the level of respect given to a person, often in the context of occupation. In this situation, the experimental group indicated that they would trust the opinions of certain individuals on the basis of their jobs alone. This shows that the status and respect obtained through those professions hold a degree of power.

B: Ethnocentrism, or the act of judging another culture by the standards of one's own, does not apply here.
C: Groupthink is a phenomenon in group psychology when the desire to conform or

maintain harmony results in a quick consensus. Once again, this is not relevant.

D: Stigma is an extreme form of disapproval shown to a certain person or group based on their perceived deviations from social norms. This too does not apply here.

1685. A is correct. When conducting a study, the possibility always exists that differences in the data were not actually caused by the variable being tested. In statistics, this is called the null hypothesis, and a p-value is used to assign statistical significance to results. Traditionally, a p-value smaller than 0.05 indicates that the results are statistically significant. Specifically, this means that there is a less than 5% chance that the observed data was caused by random error. If the p-value were actually greater than 0.5, there is over a 50% chance that the results were not caused by the independent variable (ethnicity), meaning that any conclusion drawn from this data must be seen as very unreliable.

B: As far as we know, none of the correlations seen in the study will be statistically significant.
C, D: These results mistakenly portray a large p-value indicating a highly significant relationship. In reality, such a substantial p-value would call into question both the precision and the accuracy of the experiment.

1686. D is correct. The differences in diagnosis rate could be caused by a number of factors, one of which could be previously-held ethnic bias influencing the diagnosing clinician. Note also that choice D says "may," making it less extreme than the other options.

A: The data do show African-Americans as having the highest ADHD diagnosis rate, but this could be due to a number of non-genetic factors.
B: This statement is the reverse of the correlation seen in the graph.
C: While a correlation between ethnicity and young adult ADHD diagnosis clearly appears to exist, we certainly cannot say that ethnicity is the most important factor. This is particularly true given that we have such limited information.

1687. C is correct. Prejudice is an unjustified attitude or mindset regarding an individual or group. In

contrast, discrimination is the actual behavior resulting from such an attitude.

A: Both prejudice and discrimination can involve bias against virtually any group or person.
B: As far as we know, neither prejudice nor discrimination is inherited; in any case, this is not the difference between the terms.
D: This is opposite of the correct answer.

1688. D is correct. Social power is the capacity to make changes or produce effects by influencing the actions of other people. Thus, a group with low social power is one that has less influence on others and on society in general. Such a group would have a diminished ability to acquire resources, not an enhanced one.

A, B, C: Political disparities, hiring practices based on prejudice, and unfair laws can all perpetuate discrimination. Additionally, all relate to one or more groups having more power than others.

1689. B is correct. The "just-world phenomenon" refers to a perception that the world is fundamentally fair and that individuals "get what they deserve." In the context of prejudice and discrimination, people of high status can use this fallacy to explain away an otherwise unfair situation. Thus, the person in this question would likely believe that the workers deserve the jobs they have and possess the ability to move up in the world. By holding this belief, he can maintain the perception that the world is just.

A: Such a perception would involve admitting unfairness, which is contradictory to the just-world phenomenon.
C: The just-world hypothesis posits that individuals who act cruelly or unjustly will be punished, while those who are good will earn rewards. It does not state that unfair individuals later change their ways.
D: This statement is untrue.

1690. D is correct. Affirmative action refers to policy, laws, or (in this case) scholarships that are intended to favor disadvantaged groups. Specifically, these policies benefit groups that have suffered from discrimination in the past, with the intention of establishing overall fairness.

A: Peaceful assembly has little to do with affirmative action.

B: The success of this woman seems to be due to her own efforts, not to affirmative action.

C: This choice describes positive thinking or optimism, which is very different from what the question mentions.

1691. B is correct. Institutional discrimination occurs at a society-wide level, as opposed to discriminatory acts performed by lone individuals. Some overlap does exist – after all, decisions about society are made by individuals. But institutional discrimination, as a rule, tends to affect an entire group of people at once, not just a person or small number of people from that minority group. As it often relates to laws or policies, it can be more difficult to eradicate. Here, situations I and II are examples of institutional discrimination against African-American people prior to the civil rights era.

III: This form of discrimination certainly occurred as well, but each instance was perpetuated by an individual restaurant owner and specifically affected certain black customer(s). For this reason, it is individual discrimination.

1692. C is correct. Certain lifestyles are frequently viewed with disapproval across wide sectors of society, in a phenomenon known as social stigma. AIDS acquired some of this stigma through association with its sufferers and was seen as "the gay disease" or "the junkie's disease" for quite some time. Because these groups were, in some ways, seen as having brought the disease on themselves through their stigmatized behavior, it was a slow process to mobilize the wider health community to improve prevention awareness and develop countermeasures.

1693. C is correct. In theory, there is nothing inherently racist about using qualitative criteria. However, because they rely on subjective determinations of quality, they can fall victim to subjective, even unconscious, biases.

B, D: These statements are actually true, but do not properly relate to the question stem. The prompt makes clear that the resumes were the same, except for the names and felon status.

1694. A is correct. A latent variable like the quality of physician care would be impossible to study directly, as it is multifaceted and subject to so much personal opinion. In this study, the quality of care was expressed on a numeric scale. For this reason, we can say that it was operationalized as a quantitative variable.

B, D: These conclusions cannot be validly drawn, as the study did not include a control group to compare to the black volunteers. Maybe the doctors at this clinic are just terrible to everyone!

C: We see no sign that subjective expectations were controlled for. Specifically, we have no indication what level of care each volunteer would consider worthy of a 1 or a 5. Perhaps they are just very picky, or perhaps they actually gave the clinic more credit than it deserved. This is a wide-ranging problem with self-reported assessments.

1695. C is correct. The mention of low-wage jobs is a clear reference to social class, as is the description of social circles, from which arise differences in the perceived status attributed to healthcare professionals. Class and status disparities are classic hallmarks of conflict theory.

A: Structural functionalism relates more to the activities of institutions.

B: Behaviorism is a psychological theory that de-emphasizes internal mental states.

D: This is not a recognized term.

1696. B is correct. The amygdala is a component of the limbic system. Activation of this region is linked to "fight-or-flight" emotions such as fear and aggression.

1697. C is correct. Stereotype threat occurs when an individual is anxious to avoid fulfilling a negative stereotype. As a result, his or her performance declines; in other words, he or she does exemplify the stereotype anyway. In choice C, no stereotype is explicitly mentioned, but we can assume that females would be negatively viewed in a male-dominated profession. If the female professionals are actually higher-performing, they did not fulfill the stereotype.

A, B, D: All three of these choices are examples of such stereotypes. In A, the idea that white people are bad at basketball "comes true" when the athletes are reminded of it. Similar results are seen with regard to the idea that non-Asians are inferior at math (B) or that older people are mentally slow (D).

1698. B is correct. Men, on average, are taller than women. Therefore, looking for either short or tall employees would definitely favor either males or females.

A, C, D: These characteristics are not nearly as heavily determined by gender as height.

1699. D is correct. Discrimination must involve an action that affects the target of a prejudice. For example, refusing to take a group of people seriously constitutes discrimination, as does withholding rights or resources from a minority group. However, simply having a bigoted opinion is only a sign of prejudice, not an outright act of discrimination.

1700. B is correct. The conditions described result from institutional discrimination, which affects an entire group in society and often relates to policies or actual laws.

A: This term refers to the social disapproval given to certain behaviors or lifestyle choices. The question stem does not go as far as to say that black individuals were stigmatized. Additionally, institutional discrimination relates more broadly to the entire situation described.
C: This is close, but disenfranchisement is a subtype of institutional discrimination, and not the best answer.
D: Stereotyping does not refer to society-wide effects as strongly as choice B does.

1701. C is correct. Here, the idea of elbows on the dinner table as inappropriate is an informal norm that causes individuals to behave in a certain way. More importantly, the violation of this norm carries no heavy consequence; Johnny would not be sentenced to jail time for placing his elbows on the table, nor would he be stigmatized by society. Due to its minimal moral significance, this is a folkway. Furthermore, Johnny's mother administers something negative (a scolding) if he commits this undesired behavior. As such, she is using positive punishment.

A, B: Formal deviance is a violation of social norms that results in legal sanctions. Johnny's mother certainly is not encouraging such behavior.
D: Positive reinforcement involves a reward given for proper behavior, which is not the case here.

1702. D is correct. Deviance is a word used for the violation of social norms. Specifically, formal deviance is the disobedience of formal norms, including laws; this behavior results in legal sanctions such as fines and imprisonment. Predictably, informal deviance involves the breaking of less explicit norms, such as societal standards and expected roles. This form of deviance results in social sanctions that include shame, criticism, and disapproval. Finally, either type of deviance may result in social stigma, making statement IV correct.

II: Informal deviances is generally not enforced by law.

1703. A is correct. Mores, which specifically relate to moral norms, play a major role in dictating the accepted practices in society. Mores also relate to taboos; for example, a feeling of disgust at the idea of incest is considered a more. Violation of a more usually does not result in legal restitution.

B: Formal norms are rules applied to society by governing parties, such as the federal or state laws or other codes of conduct. Violation of these norms (or laws, by-laws, or codes) results in legal punishment such as jail time and mandatory fines.
C: A folkway is a social convention that is not considered to bear moral weight. Consequently, deviation from a folkway is often a matter of personal preference, and (at most) results in others perceiving the violator as impolite.
D: Informal norms are unwritten rules that govern behavior and are reinforced by society. When one breaks an informal norm, one could certainly be sanctioned by society.

1704. A is correct. A fad is a specific type of collective behavior in which a particular fashion, activity, or other thing becomes extremely popular within a culture. Fads are generally characterized by a quick emergence and subsequent dramatic loss in popularity after only a brief period of time. In addition, fads often arise regardless of the inherent quality of the object or idea. Choice A supports the characterization of fanny packs as a fad; additionally, it isolates a correlation between this trend and the *Baywatch* viewership, indicating a potential relationship for future investigation.

B: Due to the decrease in fanny pack sales post-2000, it is safe to say that the fanny pack does not have a permanent presence in society. Additionally, such a lasting effect is not even a hallmark of a fad.
C: No evidence points to the idea that the observed drop in sales was due to product unavailability, nor is this choice relevant to the concept of a fad.
D: This statement actually contradicts the hypothesis that *Baywatch* contributed to the fanny pack fad.

1705. D is correct. Answering this question requires a solid understanding of the four listed theories of crowd behavior. Contagion theory posits that crowds exert a hypnotic influence, and the subsequent irrational frenzy can include behaviors that people would never consider when alone. All of the other choices incorrectly define their theories.

A: Crowd as "gatherings" is a theory that contrasts individuals and large groups; it states that a crowd is composed of a varied number of individuals, friends, and cliques. Unlike contagion theory, crowd as "gatherings" proposes that crowds do not, in themselves, alter judgment. Choice C actually includes this definition, but wrongly pairs it with convergence theory.
B: Emergent-norm theory is a combination of ideas that propose that crowd behavior results from a combination of participant anonymity, shared emotions, and the gathering of like-minded individuals in a society.
C: Convergence theory hypothesizes that it is not the crowd itself that provokes violent behavior. Instead, the event draws like-minded individuals, who encourage each other to participate in rioting activities. This definition is given in choice A, but is incorrectly matched with the theory of crowds as "gatherings."

1706. B is correct. From the graph, we see that fanny packs have recently been contextualized in society as unpopular or even abnormal. This is considered an informal norm, or an unwritten rule that governs behavior. Since the teenager is violating this social norm, her behavior is deviant, and she is unfortunately stigmatized by her peers.

A: The consequences of informal deviation do not include legal sanctions. The teenager cannot be fined or incarcerated for wearing a fanny pack.
C, D: A formal norm is a rule or law made by a governing body. Fanny packs are not illegal, and thus their wearing is not controlled by formal norms.

1707. D is correct. Taboos are strong prohibitions of certain actions that are deemed either accursed or too sacred to engage in. Examples include incest and patricide, which are considered two universal taboos. Believers often fear that some form of godly or supernatural authority enforces the taboo. Although breaking a taboo is generally not punishable by law, it is considered an informal deviance and is thus stigmatized by society.

I: Although it was once believed that taboos arose from irrational fears, they are now thought to have served historical functions in society. For example, Sigmund Freud postulated that taboos arose from social attitudes forbidding actions that could disturb the social order. These actions (according to him) may exist as strong unconscious desires, but must be suppressed by societal expectations and norms.

1708. D is correct. Anomie refers to a state of social disorder characterized by a breakdown of social norms and a loss of bonds between individuals and their community. It can also be explained as a "mismatch" of norms that otherwise serve to guide the society's citizens. Choice D discusses the student's inability to integrate into society, as well as a general lack of guidance; this relates to anomie better than any other answer.

A: Phobias do not relate to anomie.
B, C: These choices attribute the student's behavior to factors independent of a connection to society. Here, the student clearly still experiences relationships and ties to his

surrounding community, such as his supportive interactions with peers and family (choice B) or his caregiver relationship with his grandmother (choice C).

1709. A is correct. Bystander apathy, also known as the bystander effect, is a social phenomenon in which observers are less likely to help a victim when other people are present. Although riots certainly do include bystanders, their lack of action does not directly initiate such violence or rebellion.

B: Moral panic is a fear held by a group of people that their lives are threatened by an evil. This panic can certainly incite a riot; in fact, it often frames violence as a way to reassert society's moral values.
C: Mass hysteria is a group phenomenon that can cause odd behavior and even physical symptoms. Although it is a short-term event, it may result in mass chaos and violence in a crowd.
D: Collective behavioral theories do propose that emergent properties in a crowd may contribute to riots. In other words, while the individuals themselves may be generally peaceful, the hypnotic environment of a crowd (coupled with individual anonymity) can cause such violence to emerge.

1710. C is correct. Like the question states, a more is a norm with moral significance. Although breaking a more is not necessarily condemned by law, its deviance results in social sanctions. Although the other choices are important aspects of a physician's practice, only the Hippocratic Oath involves higher moral principles of little to no legal consequence. The oath holds doctors accountable for higher moral duties outside the basic roles of treating patients and providing medication.

1711. A is correct. Primary socialization describes the initial act of learning the values, behaviors, and norms of a culture. The definition given here relates better to secondary socialization, where an individual learns a subset of behaviors and norms that apply to a specific group within society as a whole.

B, C, D: These choices correctly pair the type of socialization with its description.

1712. D is correct. When experiencing socialization, an individual must accept or reject society's values, behaviors, attitudes, and norms. In other words, all of the choices are important for Sidi Mohamed to familiarize himself with after being reintroduced to society.

1713. A is correct. Resocialization is a process in which an individual replaces previous behavior patterns with new ones as he or she shifts into a new phase of life. While resocialization is often drastic (as when a young person joins the military), it would certainly apply to males adjusting to their exit from the college fraternity lifestyle. It is likely that in this shift in lifestyle at least partially accounts for the participants' altered drinking habits over time.

B, C: Primary socialization occurs in young children as they first learn the expectations and values of their societies. In contrast, secondary socialization is marked by the act of learning norms and values that apply to a subgroup within society. Since this study highlights a change in an already-established social behavior (rather than the introduction of new behaviors), these choices are incorrect.
D: Anticipatory socialization is the process by which a person practices for future social relationships. This form of socialization is not relevant to the study described.

1714. B is correct. Agents of socialization are individuals, groups, or institutions that are critical in the socialization of individuals. Family members, friends, and coworkers can all serve as such agents. From the results, the researchers are likely to hypothesize that these agents may have influenced the behavior of the study's participants.

A, D: Social desirability bias refers to the tendency of individuals to answer survey questions in a way that makes them look good to others. In other words, choices A and D are basically the same; both imply that participants would lie about their excessive drinking. Nothing in the data or question stem allows us to assume that all, or even most, of the 100 participants have been dishonest about their alcohol consumption.
C: Since no information is given to imply that alcohol is unavailable to the older participants,

and since the decline in consumption is very gradual and steady, we can infer that the trend shown is more likely due to a change in participant behavior.

1715. D is correct. Cultural lag is a theory that explains certain social problems. It posits that a culture often takes time to catch up with new technological advances, and that this "lag" creates social conflict due to public disagreement regarding the application of the technology. In the case of hESCs, not every member of the population has yet been educated on the benefits and risks of this technology, making I correct. Due to this lag, distinct populations may have different opinions on the ethics of hESC research, leading to social problems and conflict (statement II is correct as well). Finally, this disagreement can lead to at least minor breakdown of social solidarity (III is correct).

III: The question stem gives no indication that this statement is true. Additionally, the concept of cultural lag never requires the public to reach a full agreement before moving forward with an ethical issue.

1716. A is correct. The first phase of culture shock is the honeymoon, in which the individual views the new culture in a romanticized or overly positive light. Next comes negotiation, where the individual may feel anxious, lonely, homesick, or frustrated. Following this phase is the adjustment period, marked by a feeling of growing accustomed with the culture along with a return to a positive attitude. The final of the four stages is acceptance, where the individual can now participate fully in his or her new culture.

1717. C is correct. "Non-assimilation" is not an outcome of culture shock; even if it were possible, it would be unlikely to involve the cycling described by this choice. Generally, there is some sort of conclusion to an individual's experience in a new culture.

A: This is certainly a potential outcome. In the case of rejection, the individual does not adjust well to the new culture and will often perceive it as hostile.
B: In this outcome, a group of people known as "adopters" are able to completely assimilate into the new culture. Note that this result is possible, but rare; in fact, it only occurs in 10% of cases.
C: This is believed to result in 30% of cases. Individuals known as "cosmopolitans" end up with a unique blend of their new and old cultures.

1718. B is correct. Following the initial honeymoon phase, Tasha is showing signs of anxiety, loneliness, and homesickness. All of these are symptoms of the negotiation phase, the second phase of culture shock. We can anticipate that, following this period of time, she will enter the third phase (adjustment). During this time, Tasha will get used to her new culture and begin new routines.

A: This choice incorrectly describes acceptance (the fourth and final stage of culture shock) as immediately following negotiation.

1719. A is correct. Jason is displaying an ethnocentric ideology; in other words, he is judging another culture by the standards of his own, and generally believes that his own Australian culture is superior to others.

B: Cultural relativism (the belief that all cultures must be understood in their own contexts) is the virtual opposite of the viewpoint described in the question stem.
C: Xenophobia is an unreasonable fear of outside cultures. While often confused with ethnocentrism, this term is not the best answer because no indication is given that Jason fears the Turkish culture.
D: Religiocentric constructs claim cultural superiority due to a divine association. The question never mentions religious beliefs.

1720. D is correct. Multiculturalism is an ideology that promotes interaction between cultural groups. It involves advocacy for equality and respect so that these cultures may live in peace, making C correct. Additionally, multiculturalism is reflected by the demographic populations of organizations that include businesses, neighborhoods, and schools. Finally, a main aim of this perspective is to promote the growth and spreading of multicultural communities.

1721. A is correct. The categorical self can only develop after the formation of the existential self. Together, these two aspects contribute to the existence of the self-concept. During the maturation of the existential self, the child discovers that she is distinct from others and that she can interact with the world throughout time and space. Following this revelation, she can develop the categorical self, in which she realizes that other entities may interact with her – in other words, that she also exists as an "object" in the world.

1722. C is correct. A personal trait is given by an individual as a self-description; in other words, it relates to the person's perception of his or her intrinsic traits. Examples include "I am optimistic" and "I am friendly." The statement "I am a mother" actually describes a social role, or a position shaped by our relationships and interactions with others. The descriptor of "mother" denotes a role fulfilled through a connection with another individual, her child.

A: Physical traits are external appearances that an individual would describe him- or herself as possessing. "I am tall" is certainly a physical description.
B: Like "mother," "teacher" is a social role, as it is earned via certain interactions with others.
D: Existential statements are abstract answers to Kuhn's question. This descriptor is a great example of such an answer.

1723. A is correct. Alfonso's behavior fits neatly into Erik Erikson's theory of adolescent development, which highlights "identity vs. role confusion" as a major conflict. Erikson believed that, during this stage, the adolescent will try different behaviors to either solidify or resolve uncertainty about his identity. The variation in Alfonso's behavior, such as his rebellious act of hair-dying, is his way of experimenting with himself. He is accepting or rejecting certain goals and values to become a unique individual.

B: While this crisis does not need to be resolved for Alfonso to move on in his development,

it will certainly result either in a positive solidification of his identity or in confusion.
C, D: "Intimacy vs. isolation" is the stage of psychosocial conflict that follows "identity vs. role confusion." Here, the individual explores his relationship with others.

1724. C is correct. In this study, the boys were asked which profession they would most like to have. The question stem specifically mentioned "doctor," "mechanic," and "firefighter" as stereotypically male-dominated careers. The qualitative trend shown in the graph is that the more television the children watch, the more likely they are to choose one of these three professions (and the less likely they are to choose any of the others). From this, we can infer that these boys have at least partially adopted the gender-stereotyped attitudes and behaviors that they see regularly on TV. Additionally, remember that this study used male participants. It is thus likely that these boys have internalized the gender roles depicted on television as ones that are expected of them personally.

A: Whether unconsciously or consciously, the boys who watched more TV have certainly responded to media influences on their perceptions of gender.

1725. D is correct. From this information alone, we cannot determine whether the father or the media has a greater influence on this child, nor can we predict what he will feel in the future. Perhaps the boy has only been watching a large amount of television for a short time, while he has been exposed to his father for much longer.

A: Studies have shown that family is likely the most influential of the socialization factors.
B: This is a very moderate choice (and thus difficult to contradict). Attitudes, behavior, and values learned from his family will certainly play a role in guiding this child.
C: As this boy grows, he or she will interact with other socializing forces, such as alternate forms of media, community, and peers.

1726. B is correct. The premise of this program – a boy who enjoys cooking – has introduced the idea that a new role may be acceptable for males in this society. The boys in the ">30-hour" group have likely internalized this gender-related information; this is evident because they have not only accepted this new gender role in other males, but can even picture themselves as cooks.

A: The original sample size of 200 individuals is not especially small for such a procedure.
D: We have no reason to believe this. As the majority of shows are described as depicting men in traditional roles, and as these boys still watched more than 30 hours of TV per week, it is more likely that they began watching the cooking show than that they stopped watching other programming.

1727. B is correct. Impression management is the effort (whether intentional or unconscious) to control the way that other people view oneself. More specifically, individuals usually wish to project an image that is generally consistent with their long-term goals. In the case of Xixi, she hopes to display a positive and confident attitude to her family.

A: This choice is close, but portrays impression management as occurring solely for the purpose of pleasing others. In reality, this process is also an important way that we match our behavior to our own self-perceptions.
C, D: "Presentation of merchandise" is a business term used to denote the process of altering the public perception of a product to make it more desirable. As humans are not objects up for sale, sociologists instead use the term "impression management."

1728. C is correct. Self-presentation is the act of displaying a certain image of oneself to others. In a way, SNSs have optimized this process, as the individual gets to choose his or her custom profile pages along with specific pieces of information to divulge. However, some forms of social media allow people to comment or share pictures of other individuals, reducing that person's control of his or her self-presentation.

III: This statement is both too extreme and factually untrue.

1729. B is correct. The dramaturgical approach consists of four main parts: the front stage self, the back stage self, outside, and borders. When on the front stage, the actor is behaving in front of audience members with the goal of winning their approval. However, the back stage exists when the audience is not present, allowing the actor to step out of character. The back stage is not a venue for the rehearsal of audience-pleasing behaviors.

C, D: Both of these descriptions are accurate.

1730. C is correct. Indoctrination is the process by which individuals come to unquestioningly accept a set of beliefs or attitudes. Due to its negative connotation, this concept is considered more extreme than regular socialization, which is generally perceived as positive. Thus, choice IV is correct. This propaganda aimed to indoctrinate the idea of patriotism and duty toward military service, thus attempting to change public perceptions and making statement I accurate as well. Finally, members of the population are not expected to question or criticize this new patriotic attitude.

III: Indoctrination is not the same as education. Although the citizens are "learning" to be patriotic, this ad conveys an element of suppression and lack of intellectual exercise. In contrast, education is more open and less directed toward a single point of view.

1731. C is correct. Many factors influence a person's gender, including biological sex (or that assigned at birth), gender identity, and societal influences. Education, however, does not directly relate to an individual's gender formation.

1732. B is correct. For humans, the sex ratio denotes the number of males to that of females in the total population. This ratio is approximately 1:1, though it can vary based on events like war or selective illness. In general, however, biological sex is determined by the 50/50 chance of obtaining either a second X or a Y chromosome during fertilization.

1733. D is correct. Gender imbalances occur when selecting factors favor the survival of one gender over the other. These include natural factors (such as sex-linked diseases), abortion of fetuses of a particular gender, and the fact that females tend to have a longer life expectancy than males.

1734. D is correct. Hispanic and Latino Americans are not considered as a distinct ethnic or racial category. Instead, each of the other categories may include these individuals. The six racial or ethnic groups recognized by the U.S. Census are White, Native American and Alaskan Native, Asian American, African American, Native Hawaiian and Other Pacific Islanders, and those with two or more racial backgrounds.

1735. D is correct. Economic factors, especially job opportunities, are leading reasons for emigration and immigration. In addition, personal factors may be involved, including the presence of friends or family in a different country. Finally, many people leave their home nations for chances at a better education, especially for marginalized groups.

1736. A is correct. In stage 1, which marks pre-industrial society, both birth and death rates are high and the population exists in an equilibrium. In the next stage, urbanization, the developing country improves its food supply and sanitation (thus decreasing its mortality rate) while the birth rate remains unaltered. In stage 3, the mature industrial age, birth rates decrease due to contraceptives, women's rights, and an increase in wages. Finally, the last stage is the post-industrial phase. Here, both low birth rates and low death rates are present, and the population is at equilibrium again.

1737. D is correct. These countries are considered to fall into the post-industrial age of demographic transition. At this time, since the birth rate is now lower than the death rate, the general population must decrease over time unless offset by immigration or other outside factors.

1738. C is correct. Stage 2, also known as the urbanization phase, is characterized by a lower mortality rate. However, increased access to contraceptive methods would impact the birth rate, not the death rate.

A, B: Both of these could lead to an increase in food supply for the population as a whole, preventing deaths from hunger.
D: Public health advances, such as sanitation improvements, vaccinations, and access to affordable care, would decrease the number of preventable deaths.

1739. C is correct. Globalization, or the growing interdependence that exists between nations, has a variety of effects, both positive and negative.

For example, an increase in international trade and migration might contribute to a particular country's wealth. However, the spread of ideas may threaten cultural values, as previously isolated citizens gain access to unfamiliar cultures.

1740. D is correct. Urbanization is the large-scale movement of people from rural, agricultural areas to urban regions. As a result, city populations increase while rural ones drop. Urbanization generally occurs at the same time as modernization and industrialization.

1741. B is correct. A demographic transition is a shift in a population from a less highly developed or preindustrial society to an industrial, more technologically advanced one. Note that only part of this shift – Stage 1, specifically – takes place between 1300 and 1400. Stage 1 is marked by high fertility and mortality rates, as one might expect in a society with poor medicine and less advanced economics.

A: The demographics of this population likely do shift substantially during the period referenced. However, a demographic transition is more relevant to the given information, as it accounts for changing fertility and mortality rates.
C: Demographic stagnation is not a term that will appear on the MCAT.

1742. B is correct. It is Stage 3 of a demographic transition that is marked by mandatory education and a shift away from encouraging children to work. We can find this interval by isolating the range in the data where the birth rate is falling, while still remaining higher than the mortality rate. After the year 1500, the birth and death rates are nearly identical; before 1400, they are also similar, albeit much higher. Thus, the only window in which Stage 3 could exist is between 1400 and 1500, yielding choice B as the best answer.

1743. C is correct. During Stage 3 of a demographic transition, the mortality rate continues to drop due to advances in medicine. Additionally, this is when the fertility rate starts to fall as well. Stage 3 is also marked by a shift toward requiring more schooling to teach children to fill productive roles in society; these changes prevent children from working, causing them to require more parental support. In turn, parents begin to have fewer babies.

A: Stage 1 is marked by high mortality and high fertility rates. At this time, society is far from reaching the industrial era, and the education of children is not a prime focus.

B: Stage 2 exhibits a decrease in mortality rate but little change in birth rate. The question implies that the correct answer is the stage during which fertility rate begins to drop.

D: Stage 4 occurs well after the transition to an industrialized society; it thus occurs later than the events described here.

1744. D is correct. This choice is too broad; globalization does not increase job security everywhere. Specifically, it reduces job security in countries where manufacturing and other forms of labor-intensive employment can now be outsourced to nations with cheaper labor.

A, B, C: These are three classic features of a shift to a more global perspective.

1745. B is correct. "Slum" is the term used for an impoverished section of an urban area that is heavily populated. While a poorly maintained or inefficient sanitation system is not a prerequisite to classify a region as a slum, it certainly would not be unusual in such areas.

A: An urban sprawl is not necessarily inhabited by poorer individuals. The term simply qualifies a seemingly unplanned, expansive suburban area.

C: A ghetto is a subtype of a slum; specifically, it is a slum that is racially or ethnically segregated. Since ghettos can also be characterized as slums, and since we are given no information about racial demographics, B is the better answer.

D: A Stage 4 society is post-industrial and marked by relatively low birth and mortality rates. We have absolutely no reason to believe that such a society would be impoverished or shoddily constructed.

1746. A is correct. A high fertility rate denotes an increase in births, which would certainly promote population growth. Additionally, such a change is more likely than a simple reduction in mortality rate to cause a population spike. After all, a lowered mortality rate only allows people who are already part of the population to remain

alive longer; in contrast, a peak in birth rate can add a very large number of new individuals to the society fairly rapidly.

C: Low unemployment – in other words, more easily attainable jobs – would not cause the alarming spike described. Perhaps more parents would have children due to their increasingly favorable economic position, but the direct cause of the increase would still be increased fertility.

D: Immigration to an impoverished country is unlikely to occur to a large degree.

1747. B is correct. Wealthy countries like the one described often serve as sought-after destinations for immigrants seeking employment and a safe place to live. This makes statement I correct. Additionally, Roman numeral IV is also accurate. Fertility rate cannot be discerned simply from the economic success of a country; we need at least some population data.

II: Don't confuse emigration with immigration! The emigration rate is the pace at which citizens leave a country. Since the nation described is economically prosperous and diverse, individuals and families are more likely to attempt to enter it than to desire to leave.

1748. C is correct. As the country's agricultural industry suffers, more unemployed citizens will be forced to leave rural areas and move to cities in search of work. This is the very definition of urbanization. Unfortunately, as larger and larger numbers of relatively impoverished people move in from the farmland, limited resources will necessitate the formation of slums. These are simply the poorer, more run-down and generally crowded regions of large cities.

1749. A is correct. A proactive social movement is one that aims to initiate change, generally in a progressive or positive way. Here, citizens intend to change the negative attitude that permeates their nation with regard to immigrants.

B: A reactive movement is one formed in response to something else. Most commonly, these movements act in response to some progressive trend, aiming to maintain the status quo and prevent change. For example, if a second group later formed with the intent of perpetuating the negative perception of immigrants, that would be a reactive social movement.

1750. B is correct. A society is in stage 2 immediately prior to full-scale industrialization. During this phase, the mortality rate drops due to advances in medical care. However, the fertility rate remains relatively stable, provoking a net population increase.

A: This very early stage is characterized by similarly high fertility and mortality rates.
C: This phase occurs immediately after the transitions mentioned in the question stem. During Stage 3, the mortality rate does fall, just as it does during stage 2. However, stage 3 marks the beginning of a downward trend in fertility rate as well.
D: At this time, the fertility and mortality rates are again similar, but both are now relatively low. However, note that the overall population is still climbing somewhat.

1751. D is correct. When someone is said to have power, it means that he or she has a significant capacity to influence the actions of others. While being powerful and having a high socioeconomic status do not always go together, individuals in higher business or social positions tend to have both money and power. For this reason, an individual known to be powerful has a greater chance of being somewhat wealthy than one with unknown or low levels of power.

A, B: Reputation and power do not correlate perfectly. Many individuals have power, or control over others, but are generally disliked or even hated.
C: No guaranteed relationship exists to connect total assets with power.

1752. D is correct. A donation, tax-deductible or otherwise, does not fit the broad definition of property. This category includes virtually all material objects or quantities that are seen as belonging to the individual in question. Alternatively, property can be conceptualized as including income (C) or assets (A and B). Giving a donation, in contrast, means that a person is losing or relinquishing money or objects, and thus reducing his or her total amount of property.

1753. D is correct. Social reproduction is the tendency for demographic facts to repeat themselves throughout successive generations. For example, if Jane's parents are poor and have unhealthy spending habits, she will more than likely learn the same behaviors and perpetuate a loop of poverty. The idea that certain minority groups will continue to possess less overall wealth than the white population relates perfectly to this intergenerational trend.

A, B: These terms relate more closely to assimilation or interaction between cultures. They do not have any special relevance to money or wealth.
C: Social stratification is the broad notion that different classes (upper, middle, lower middle, etc.) manifest themselves in society and carry associated stereotypes and expectations.

1754. C is correct. A caste system is marked by strict constraints on the movement between social classes. In the vast majority of cases, then, one is born into the same class that one will die in. If it is true that, no matter how hard Mr. Jones' children work, they can only ever reach a certain social standing, this society is almost certainly a caste system.

A: A meritocracy would display significantly more potential for socioeconomic movement. In this type of system, the merits of one's efforts "pay off" and upward mobility is very possible.
B: In a class system, unlike in a caste system, movement from one social level to another is possible. If this family lived in a class system, they would not reach a "ceiling" of achievement above which further promotion is impossible.

1755. C is correct. Anomie is a state of social discord or breakdown that results from a splitting of social ties. Often, this occurs to some extent in areas that were once peaceful but have recently suffered due to economic failure and other factors. This leads to a general confusion and lack of moral guidance provided by society, which citizens had previously trusted and relied upon.

1756. D is correct. People of higher socioeconomic status are more likely to form stronger ties with a smaller total number of individuals. The stronger the bonds and the smaller the group, the more personal influence they can exert over other people's opinions and behavior; consequently, this makes them better able to use that influence to benefit others as well as themselves. In addition, they will be likely to have more social capital, or networking capacity that can be used to obtain benefits.

I: Weaker ties with a large network are more characteristic of individuals from a lower socioeconomic class.
III: Those with higher socioeconomic status nearly always possess more social capital, a concept that wealthy individuals often use to their own advantage.

1757. D is correct. Social capital can be thought of as "networking power" or the ability to gain advantages through personal connections. This value loosely correlates with one's socioeconomic status. From the table, we see that Hispanic families have significantly less average equity in their homes than white families. Since they then possess less of an opportunity to buy property and pass this asset wealth to future generations, the Hispanic population is likely to be more impoverished and have a lower average socioeconomic status. These positions generally carry very little social capital.

A: The strength of personal ties cannot be inferred through data alone. However, this is likely backwards anyway; it is the individuals with high socioeconomic statuses that tend to form strong ties within a smaller, more influential network.
B: Power is an individual's ability to control or provoke others to behave in a certain fashion. This does not always relate to wealth or net worth.

1758. A is correct. The data shows that white and Asian families have high, and relatively similar, amounts of money in savings. Note that this sum should include funds from both interest-earning savings accounts and regular checking accounts.

1759. B is correct. Class consciousness, a concept originally proposed by Karl Marx, is the capacity to acknowledge one's current place in the socioeconomic class system. Marx believed that many individuals, especially those who were more impoverished, did not accept or accurately consider their own social class. He posited that they thus lacked feelings of solidarity that would otherwise be both possible and beneficial, for the working classes in particular.

A: This choice incorrectly uses the word "familial." Class consciousness does not relate to any sort of family hierarchy.
C, D: The concept in question is more of an awareness than a feeling of either ambition or happiness with one's own position.

1760. A is correct. As an individual who falls into the lower middle class, Johnny B may certainly have attempted some form of brief, incomplete college education and to have ended up specializing in a trade.

B: A steelworker with no college education will most likely exist in the lower or working class.
C: Although we cannot know for certain whether Johnny B. is employed (perhaps he was recently laid off from a lower middle class job), we can be sure that it is the lower, not the lower middle, class that forms about 20% of the American population.
D: A new, likely young clerk who never attended college will almost certainly be categorized in the lower (working) class.

1761. C is correct. Factors that tend to correlate with low birthweight include maternal stress and a lack of access to prenatal care. From the table, we see that Granville has the highest crime rate (a cause of prenatal stress) and the lowest income and employment rate (factors that tend to limit access to healthcare). None of the other neighborhoods rank quite as poorly in these statistical measures.

1762. A is correct. Of the listed choices, Mira Vista has both the lowest employment rate and the lowest income. In the U.S., most health insurance is obtained either through one's employer or by paying large premiums. Unemployment and low income make it more difficult for individuals and families to become insured. We can thus expect a random Mira Vista resident to be statistically more likely to be uninsured than a resident of the other neighborhoods mentioned.

1763. A is correct. Exposure is the only index (of those given) that does not require land area or geographic information, which are not provided in the table. Exposure is a measure of the frequency at which ethnic groups will contact each other. This could be estimated using the ethnic breakdowns and population numbers of each region.

B: Concentration defines the proportion of the total city area that is occupied by a minority. Since the table gives no physical measurements of land area, this cannot be approximated.
C: Of Massey and Denton's indices, clustering describes the extent to which minority-occupied areas tend to adjoin one another. Again, we cannot estimate this without knowing more about the geography of Townsville.
D: Centralization rates the closeness of minority groups to the city center. Like choices B and C, this requires too much geographical information to be assessed.

1764. C is correct. Social capital is the collective value of social networks and the connections that may arise from those networks. The benefits of social capital include access to job openings, which promote social mobility. The question stem describes a neighborhood that appears to be low in social capital.

A: Cultural capital includes non-financial assets such as style of dress, manner of speech, and appearance. This concept is not as relevant to the question stem as choice C.
B: Social alienation, or the process of becoming disaffected and isolated from mainstream society, is also an incorrect choice. While lacking connections is a form of isolation, social capital relates better to the prompt's emphasis on social mobility.
D: One is dependent when one requires sustenance from others or from the state. While this is a common situation for unemployed individuals, it does not relate to networking or personal connections.

1765. C is correct. This question tests the concept of intersectionality; remember, one person can simultaneously belong to multiple advantaged or disadvantaged groups. According to outside knowledge, several factors are closely linked to lifespan. Specifically, a higher level of education tends to be linked to a longer life, white and Asian individuals tend to live longer than Latinos and African-Americans, and women tend to live longer than men. To answer this question, then, let's determine which individual has the fewest health "strikes" against him or her (male, low education level, etc.). The given variance will then tell us which "strikes" are more severe than others. For choice C, while the described individual is African-American, that is the only "strike" against her; females and college graduates tend to be relatively healthy. Choice A also describes one "strike" (minimal education), but the table implies that education explains more of the variance in lifespan than does ethnicity. We can therefore expect the status of a college degree to confer a greater advantage than a white ethnicity, and choice C is the best answer.

B: This individual possesses two adverse demographic qualities; he is both male and African-American.
D: As this man has three "strikes" (Latino ethnicity, male, and low education), he would have the shortest, not longest, expected lifespan.

1766. B is correct. Income is heavily associated with lifespan, as money allows one access to insurance, preventative care, and healthier food.

A: Household size does not tend to correlate, at least directly, with lifespan.
C, D: These both strongly affect the length and quality of a person's life, but they are not demographic variables!

1767. A is correct. The developmental problems mentioned are associated with childhood lead exposure. We then simply must ascertain which ethnic group is concentrated in the area(s) with the highest lead levels. In Townsville, African-Americans disproportionately tend to live in Granville, which has far and away the highest lead levels in the soil.

B: Latinos make up a large proportion of the population in Mira Vista, the neighborhood with the second-highest measured levels of lead. However, Latinos are not as heavily concentrated in this neighborhood as blacks are in Granville.

1768. D is correct. Asthma is exacerbated by high atmospheric particulate levels, which coal emissions would tend to promote. However, we are looking for connections between Latino-heavy areas and potential risk factors for asthma. Granville is only 25% Latino; thus, compared to factors that affect the mainly-Latino area of Mira Vista, choice D does not relate to the question stem.

A: Industrial emissions are a major source of particulates. Emissions in Mira Vista, where Latinos are most densely concentrated, is definitely a factor that could raise the risk of asthma.
B: Auto emissions also promote particulates and increase asthma risk. A highway in Mira Vista would absolutely affect a predominantly Latino population; downtown and Granville are also more than 20% Latino.
C: Aircraft emissions are similar to auto exhaust in their tendency to emit particulates, and again, Mira Vista is mainly Latino.

1769. C is correct. Food deserts, or impoverished regions that lack access to fresh or healthy food, relate perfectly to the question stem.

A: Economic segregation, or the separation by income and social class, does relate to the existence of food deserts. However, this concept is too broad to be the correct choice.
B: Ghettoization is the confinement of a minority to a limited territory that often possesses subpar services. Similarly, social exclusion is the tendency for minorities to be excluded from institutions and relegated to the fringe of society. Again, these terms are too broad to be the most relevant answers.

1770. C is correct. Globalization is the process by which the world becomes more interconnected. This worldwide change is especially relevant to economic interactions.

A: When a region experiences urbanization, its population moves from rural to predominately urban areas. This transition is often caused by industrialization, but is not synonymous with the global implications of industry.
B: Classically, a demographic transition first involves a fall in mortality rate, which is soon followed by a drop in fertility rate. This change accompanies industrialization and development, but is not a term for the large-scale change itself.

D: Redistribution is the re-allocation of resources from one social group to another and can occur under a variety of circumstances.

1771. C is correct. Social reproduction explains the idea that socioeconomic class can be passed from one generation to the next through intangible characteristics, like education. Here, William's parents taught him unhealthy financial habits, increasing the chance that he will also lack wealth and will perpetuate an unfortunate cycle.

A, B: No mobility, or movement between socioeconomic classes, is described here.
D: Social facilitation refers to performance in front of a group, not inheritance of class-related qualities.

1772. B is correct. Hickey and Thompson conducted their research in the United States, which is organized as a partial meritocracy. A meritocracy is a system of social or governmental organization in which hard work and talent are rewarded with success. The U.S. and Canada are largely meritocratic societies, which explains why you often hear of "rags-to-riches" stories. However, virtually no true meritocracies exist, as those who are born to wealthy or politically powerful clans typically possess an advantage. Additionally, the diagram shows the existence of five distinct classes.

C: No meritocracy can also qualify as a caste system.
D: An oligarchy is a society that is ruled by a very small handful of individuals. While the diagram does depict a small "upper class," it never implies that only certain individuals can reach this status.

1773. D is correct. The highest stratum shown in the diagram is the upper class, a group that includes about 1% of Americans. These individuals have high social capital, meaning that they possess valuable social networks and personal connections. Additionally, these networks tend to be relatively small and closely knit.

C: Large, weakly-associated networks are characteristic of lower socioeconomic strata.

1774. B is correct. Intragenerational mobility includes changes to an individual's socioeconomic status (whether good or bad) that occur during the course of his or her lifetime. Here, a woman begins as a movie actress, a highly-regarded position that tends to be well-paid. When she transitions to her new job as a cashier, it serves as a perfect example of downward intragenerational mobility.

A: This form of social mobility involves changes that occur over one or more generations. We do not know the socioeconomic status of either the woman's parents or her potential children.
C: While the woman is certainly less wealthy than she used to be, we have no way of knowing whether she falls near the poverty line. She may have more than enough money to survive.
D: Caste systems are rigid and resist mobility in general.

1775. A is correct. Relative poverty exists when an individual or family is less wealthy than those around them. Interestingly, this phenomenon is seen among people of virtually any socioeconomic class; if you are a millionaire and your neighbors and relatives are billionaires, you technically live in relative poverty.

B: Absolute poverty is marked by an income that falls below the poverty line and by a financial struggle to obtain essential goods and services.

1776. C is correct. Mrs. Wilson is making approximately $21,000 per year for her family of five, while (in the U.S.) the poverty line for a family of four currently falls at $27,890. Individuals and families who live below the poverty line generally exist in absolute poverty. Additionally, many of the Wilsons' neighbors have a higher socioeconomic status, putting this unfortunate family in relative poverty as well.

1777. A is correct. The nation in question appears to be a caste system, or one that values ascribed qualities over achieved ones. In such systems, it is extremely difficult for those in the lower castes to experience upward social mobility, even if they are very smart or talented. This family would thus be likely to move to a nation with a meritocratic system, in which people are rewarded for their hard work and achievement. Only choice D identifies this concept along with the proper use of the term "emigrate."

B, D: One does not "immigrate" away from a particular country. Remember, the term "immigrate" refers to the act of entering a new nation, while "emigrate" is the proper word to use for the act of leaving a familiar one.

1778. B is correct. A plutocracy is a nation that is controlled by the rich or upper-class members.

A: An oligarchy is a society that is ruled by a very small handful of individuals. While these ruling individuals are likely wealthy, choice B is a more specific term.
C: A bureaucracy is a hierarchical system of organization that may or may not be controlled by wealthy individuals.
D: A meritocracy is a system of social or governmental organization in which hard work and talent are rewarded with success. Virtually no complete meritocracies exist, as those who are born to wealthy or politically powerful clans typically possess an advantage. The question stem describes the opposite of any form of meritocracy.

1779. D is correct. A closed system is one that resists social mobility. One perfect example of such a system is a caste system, in which individuals are almost always born to the same socioeconomic class in which they will live for their entire lives. In contrast, an open system is one whose members can travel between social classes. Such is the case in a meritocracy, in which achieved status and talent dictate the level to which an individual can rise.

1780. D is correct. While caste systems tend to be negatively portrayed due to their near-complete lack of social mobility, it cannot be denied that individuals in upper castes likely live better than those in the lower strata of an open system.

A: A caste system is a classic example of a closed system.

1781. D is correct. A negative correlation implies that as one variable increases, the other decreases. This inverse relationship is displayed here. Additionally, a dependent variable is one that varies due to intentional changes to an independent variable. From this definition, we know that thing B is dependent, while thing A is independent.

1782. C is correct. A dependent variable is one that varies outside of the direct control of the researcher. The goal of an experiment is to identify which, if any, independent variables have a decisive impact on dependent variables. Here, two dependent variables exist: blood pressure and the rate of atorvastatin breakdown.

A: An independent variable is one that is manipulated by the researcher to examine its effect on one or more dependent variables. Here, the only independent variable is the amount of grapefruit in one's diet.
B: We cannot possibly know how statistically significant this study's results can be, as we know nothing about sample sizes or variation in the data.
D: A confounding variable is one that is not being directly studied, but that has the potential to skew a study's results. While such variables certainly may exist here, none are mentioned outright.

1783. A is correct. Since the values of an independent variable are controlled by the experimental procedure, it is typically plotted along the x-axis. In contrast, the quantity or extent of a dependent variable relies upon its relationship with the independent variable. As a result, it is most sensible to graph it along the y-axis, where a quick glance can compare the difference between higher and lower values.

1784. A is correct. Confounding variables are factors that stem from the failure to properly control an experiment. For example, imagine that researchers are examining the effect of thing A on thing B. If they completely neglect to consider thing C, which also has an effect on thing B, it may lead them to an incorrect conclusion regarding thing A. Therefore, a protocol should always strive to remove or lessen the effect of these variables.

B, C, D: Mediating variables are simply those that explain the relationship between the independent and dependent variable. Using our above scenario, imagine that thing A affects thing B due to a connection they share, known as thing D. We cannot – and would not desire to – remove the effect of thing D, as it is an integral part of the relationship under analysis. The same goes for moderating variables, which are factors that alter the strength of the correlation being studied.

1785. B is correct. In a double-blind study, typically a clinical trial, neither the patients nor the doctors (or other administrators of medication) know which patients receive the experimental treatment. This reduces the impact of confirmation bias. Here, this form of bias tends to make doctors falsely see more improvement in patients who are being treated than in those receiving a placebo.

1786. A is correct. Social desirability bias refers to the human tendency to portray oneself as better or more socially acceptable than one really is. This is a major problem with studies that rely on questionnaires, as those surveyed tend to say that they have higher salaries, drink and participate in risky behavior less, and have more friends than they actually do.

B: This experiment is more vulnerable to sampling bias than to the mentioned phenomenon.
C: This study lacks external validity, but is at virtually no risk of the social desirability bias.
D: While less effective than a double-blind study, this protocol does not relate to the question.

1787. C is correct. External validity refers to the generalizability of a particular experimental finding. A study with ecological validity is set up in a manner in which the testing situation does not alter potential results, making the obtained data more likely to be relevant to the outside world.

1788. C is correct. This question is tricky! A moderating variable is one that affects the strength of a relationship between separate independent and dependent variables. Here, time of day (the independent variable) always seems to affect the length of the security line (the dependent variable). However, this relationship may be strong or weak, depending on location. Thus, geographical region (Southwest, Northeast, etc.) moderates the relationship between the main variables in this study.

A: Confounding variables can be thought of as factors stemming from the failure to properly control an experiment. Here, the researchers are intentionally examining distinctions between cases in various states; location did not simply skew their results.

D: A mediating variable is one that explains the relationship between independent and dependent variables. In other words, location would need to explain how time of day relates to the length of an airport line.

1789. D is correct. External validity refers to how well the experimental results may be generalized to other situations. If the experimental method described in choice D is relevant to a wide range of individuals, this procedure is externally valid.

A, C: Both of these protocols are testing something that is too specific ("rare fruit," "tiny population"). A study that finds a specific correlation under certain conditions, but likely does not apply to other environments or to "real life," lacks external validity.
B: This procedure appears to possess content validity, but (as far as we know) only applies to individuals with bipolar disorder.

1790. D is correct. Typically, a statistically significant result is one for which the p-value is less than 0.05. (This means that the observed interaction has more than a 95% chance of being due to the concluded relationship, and less than a 5% chance of resulting from luck.) Here, the p-value is originally larger than 0.05, but statistical power can be increased by raising the sample size. Since 0.07 is only slightly larger than 0.05, D is a logical answer.

1791. C is correct. Statement II is very relevant; this principle was certainly violated, as Mrs. Lacks' medical records were published without her or her family's knowledge. In addition, the question stem states that neither Mrs. Lacks nor her family were informed of the doctors' plans.

I: The harvesting and later proliferation of Mrs. Lacks' tumor cells posed no significant health threat to her. Furthermore, it had the potential to benefit either her or others with a similar form of cancer (if, say, an effective HeLa-specific toxin was found). For this reason, the case of Henrietta Lacks did not violate the principle of harm minimization.

1792. D is correct. The only ethical violation not mentioned is a violation of privacy and confidentiality; whatever the researchers' other faults, they did not divulge private information about the research subjects. In fact, they tried to keep the existence of this experiment a secret.

A, B, C: The researchers did not inform the participants of the purpose of the study and certainly were not interested in minimizing the risk of harm, as they led them to think they were being treated when they were not. This practice is also extremely deceptive.

1793. C is correct. This procedure examines certain subsets of a population (in this case, income groups) at a specific moment in time, making it a cross-sectional study.

A: A longitudinal study observes the same subjects over a period of time. As described in the question stem, this survey was given only once.
B: A cohort study is a type of longitudinal study, making this choice wrong as well. Specifically, cohort studies examine a specific group over a certain time interval to determine their risk of contracting a disease.
D: In a double-blind study, neither the researchers nor the participants are informed which treatment is experimental and which is a control. While this is a classic way to minimize unconscious bias, it has nothing to do with the observational study described here.

1794. C is correct. As this new method follows the same subjects over an extended period of time, it is a longitudinal study.

A: Retrospective studies examine records from dates prior to the beginning of the research. This is not relevant to the information given.
B: Even with its new parameters, this study is not nearly in-depth and detailed enough to qualify as a case study. Such studies typically have a narrow, detailed focus, digging into contextual factors that affect the (usually few) research subjects rather than emphasizing broad trends for a large sample.
D: An ecological study would focus on risk factors present in a geographical area. While the individuals here do originate from the same region, they are free to move; additionally, it is

the individuals themselves who are the object of the study, not the features of their location.

1795. D is correct. This final survey procedure represents an ecological study, which is a type of observational study. We can discern this because its objective is to determine the health risk factors and data specific to a defined geographic area. This differs from the previous procedure in that the same individuals are not questioned repeatedly; it is the location, not the people in it, which serves as the student's main focus.

A: A cohort study would examine a set group of individuals over a period of time, with an emphasis on the determination of their risk of contracting a disease. In contrast, the participants referenced in the question stem are in flux, as people are free to move in and out of the neighborhood.
B: A cross-sectional study gives a picture of a situation at a defined moment in time; it does not look at trends over long intervals.
C: This is not a retrospective study, as it does not examine records from prior to the date on which the research began.

1796. A is correct. Longitudinal studies observe the same subjects over a period of time. These protocols have several advantages, one of which is the idea that individuals are compared to themselves instead of others, allowing for more accurate monitoring of trends. Since this smoking study follows subjects through several years of observation, A is the best choice.

B: A cross-sectional study is the near opposite of a longitudinal procedure. Instead of studying the same participants over a time interval, it takes a sample of a population at a single point in time.
C: This is not a retrospective study, as it does not examine records from prior to the date on which the research began.
B: The goals and protocol of this study are not nearly in-depth and detailed enough to qualify as a case study. Such studies typically have a narrow focus and delve into contextual factors that affect the (usually few) subjects involved. They do not aim to emphasize broad trends for a large sample.

1797. D is correct. By extending the timeframe backward, and by looking at records that were compiled prior to the research itself, the Ph.D. would have changed this study to be retrospective in nature.

A: Tempting answer! But this study was already longitudinal, even before the change outlined in the question stem. The question asks what the study would become, not what it already was.
B: The goals and protocol of this study are still not sufficiently in-depth and detailed to qualify as a case study. Such studies typically have a narrow focus and delve into contextual factors that affect the (usually few) subjects involved. They do not aim to emphasize broad trends for a large sample.
C: This would not be an ecological study. That type of protocol would zero in on risk factors related to a specific location, not certain individuals, as we are told here.

1798. D is correct. Of the options given, location alone has the least significant effect on blood pressure. The other variables should certainly be controlled for, as a failure to do so could yield skewed results where blood pressure was high for a reason unrelated to smoking.

A: With age, arteries harden and blood pressure regulation systems break down. As a result, age is a potential confounding variable in this study. We thus need to show that smoking is associated with a BP difference in both young and old individuals, ruling out the possibility that the results are an artifact of older people's poor health.
B: BMI, as a measure of obesity, is highly associated with elevated blood pressure. We must control for this variable (or for another obesity-related index) to ensure that smokers with higher blood pressure readings than nonsmokers are not simply more overweight.
C: Gender has differing effects on blood pressure. For people below 55, men tend to display higher pressure readings than women, but this trend reverses in older groups. We certainly want to control for gender to make sure that any trend that seems to relate to smoking does not stem from a gender imbalance among the participants (if more smokers were men, for instance). Controlling for gender would also help reveal whether smoking is associated with higher BP for both men and women, which adds to the value of the study.

1799. B is correct. Case studies tend to have a very narrow, detailed focus; they aim to thoroughly elucidate the contextual factors that affect a small number of subjects, as opposed to establishing broad trends for a large sample. Here, the most remarkable information given is the incredibly small number of individuals with this disease. This rules out the use of other methods that rely on larger samples. Additionally, the emphasis on contextual interactions between this syndrome and the health of the subjects would also benefit from a case study methodology.

A: While an ecological study does focus on the surrounding environment, nothing in the question stem indicates that this is the researcher's goal. In fact, so few sufferers of this disease exist that they would likely be spread across entirely disparate places and living situations, making even the establishment of experimental groups difficult.
C: A cohort study begins with a group of healthy individuals and tracks changes in their health (or other variables) over time. Most often, the goal of such an approach is to determine the participants' risk of developing a disease. Since the described condition is genetic and observable at birth, establishment of a healthy cohort would be impossible. Additionally, the rarity of this syndrome is so extreme that assembly of even a moderately-sized cohort would be very hard.
D: While double-blind studies do minimize bias in clinical trials, no drug or medication is mentioned in the given information. Those researching this condition would more likely choose an observational procedure.

1800. B is correct. In a double-blind protocol, neither researchers nor participants are informed which treatment is experimental and which serves as a control. This helps avoid unconscious bias on the part of the clinicians, who might otherwise see what they want to see and perceive the experimental group as healthier.

A: A single-blind study would prevent the patients, but not the researchers, from knowing the identities of the individuals in each experimental condition.
C: Case studies are observational procedures that tend to have a detailed focus on factors affecting a few individuals with a particular disease. The

question asks about the handling of information, not the construction of the study as a whole.
D: This is in fact a clinical trial, but the question asks about the information-handling method described. For this reason, B is a better choice.

1801. B is correct. Glycine is the only amino acid that is achiral. All other common residues have S configurations, with the exception of cysteine, the only common amino acid designated as R.

1802. D is correct. Imagine that you rotate the substituents on the right chiral carbon upwards. It can then be seen that this molecule has a line of symmetry. Symmetrical molecules with multiple chiral centers are known as meso compounds and do not rotate polarized light.

A: This is the amino acid alanine, which is a chiral compound and is not meso.
B: This structure might appear to possess a line of symmetry, but since the spatial arrangement of the hydrogen and chlorine atoms are opposite, this molecule is not meso.
C: This is a chiral compound and is clearly not meso.

1803. B is correct. While all common chiral amino acids exist in their L forms in humans, not all are designated as S. Specifically, cysteine is the lone R residue. The D/L naming convention is determined by the placement of the amino group and is thus independent of the R-group, while the R/S convention assigns priority to the atoms surrounding the chiral center and is affected by the side chain.

C: This is true; the direction of optical rotation must be determined experimentally.
D: Meso compounds have multiple chiral centers but are not optically active.

1804. A is correct. Since a stereocenter must have four different substituents, only five such centers exist in this molecule. A double bond counts only as a single substituent, making all carbon atoms with two single and one double bond achiral.

1805. C is correct. During an S_N1 reaction, the stereochemistry of the original substrate is lost when the leaving group detaches and the carbocation intermediate forms. The nucleophile will attack this ion without a stereochemical preference; thus, a racemic mixture will form, containing 50% of each enantiomer. Racemic mixtures do not rotate light overall.

1806. D is correct. To solve this problem, use the following equation: enantiomeric excess = (observed optical rotation*100) / specific rotation. The specific rotation of D-fructose is given by the table, and that of its enantiomer, L-fructose, must have the same magnitude but an opposite sign (+92°).

1807. C is correct. Use the following equation: specific rotation = (observed optical rotation) / (path length * concentration). The specific rotation and path length are provided in the table, and the question stem mentions the concentration.

1808. B is correct. E-Z designation utilizes Cahn-Ingold-Prelog priority rules, in which a higher priority is assigned to atoms with larger atomic numbers. Z indicates that the two highest-priority groups are on the same side of the double bond, while E denotes that they fall on opposite sides. In choice B, Br is given the highest priority, followed by Cl; both fall on the same side in a configuration that resembles the *cis* designation.

A, C: These resemble *trans* structures, meaning that they are classified as E.
D: This molecule has neither an E nor Z configuration.

1809. C is correct. The easiest way to identify inverted stereochemistry is to find a structure that switches the solid wedge and dash. In choice C, all atoms are arranged in the same position as in the original molecule, but OH now points into the page and H is now protruding outward. Thus, these molecules are enantiomers.

A, B, D: These represent the exact same molecule as the original, drawn from different perspectives.

1810. B is correct. A diastereomer is a stereoisomer with stereochemistry that varies from the original molecule at at least one, but not every, chiral center. The number of stereoisomers of a molecule is equal to 2^n, where n denotes its number of stereocenters. Since this compound has three chiral centers, eight stereoisomers exist. However, two are enantiomers, leaving six diastereomers remaining.

1811. B is correct. The best way to find this answer is to actually draw out all of the possible configurations for C_5H_{12}. This yields three molecules with this formula and different connectivities.

1812. A is correct. Configurational and structural isomers are synonymous. Both isopentane and *n*-pentane contain five carbons and twelve hydrogens, but these atoms are bonded differently.

B: A conformational isomer is a species formed by rotation around one single bond. Conformers are much more similar to each other than configurational isomers.
C: Geometric isomerism generally requires the presence of a double bond.

1813. C is correct. Cyclohexane has a different molecular formula (fewer hydrogen atoms) than *n*-hexane and isohexane.

A, B: Both of these are constitutional isomers, as they share the same molecular formula.

1814. B is correct. In this case, only one stereogenic center varies between the two structures. Thus, these could be described as either epimers or diastereomers.

C: Because one stereogenic center is different, these are not two drawings of the same compound.
D: Structural isomers have the same molecular formula, but different construction of bonds between atoms. Here, it is the stereochemistry that distinguishes the two Fischer projections.

1815. B is correct. Diastereomers, unlike enantiomers, exhibit different physical properties. This quality allows them to be separated fairly easily. In other words, while their solubilities, boiling points, and melting points are likely similar, they are not identical.

I: Diastereomers are easier to separate than enantiomers.
III: Enantiomers, not diastereomers, have indistinguishable chemical and physical properties.

1816. A is correct. Anomers are a subtype of epimer that differ only at the anomeric carbon. This is true of the two sugars shown, as their anomeric hydroxyl groups point upward and downward, respectively.

B: While this is also an accurate term, the question asks for the most specific form of classification.

C, D: These are not configurational isomers, as they differ only in their stereochemistry.

1817. D is correct. Although these isomers are most specifically described as anomers, they are also classified as epimers. Epimers are molecules that differ at a single stereogenic center, which is true of the two sugars relevant to the question.

1818. A is correct. The two structures are enantiomers, as they represent non-superimposable mirror images. Enantiomers are fairly simple to spot because they differ in configuration at every chiral center.

B: These structures cannot be folded onto themselves across a plane of symmetry.

C: Diastereomers must be identical at one or more chiral centers, which these are not.

D: These molecules differ at more stereogenic centers than just the anomeric carbon.

1819. D is correct. These compounds are optically inactive, meaning that they do not rotate plane-polarized light. This is true because they contain two identical substituents (hydrogen atoms) bound to the only chiral center, which is also what makes them identical.

1820. D is correct. Enantiomers, which share physical and chemical properties, cannot be resolved using typical laboratory techniques. These include methods like distillation, recrystallization, and extraction, which are useless until the original species are reacted to form diastereomers. Enantiomers can be separated by reaction with a chiral compound, but glutaraldehyde (as its IUPAC name shows) is achiral.

1821. A is correct. Boiling point is mainly determined by intermolecular forces and molecular weight. Since unsubstituted alkanes are able to exert only London dispersion forces, they typically display low boiling points. However, if this student were able to halogenate *n*-octane, she would be giving it a polar bond between the chlorine atom and one carbon. This would allow the product

to experience dipole-dipole forces, raising its boiling temperature.

B: As a straight-chain hydrocarbon, *n*-octane will not react with a Grignard reagent. Grignard processes are typically used to alkylate compounds that contain carbonyl functionalities.

C: Higher, not lower, molecular weights make compounds more difficult to boil.

D: Branching, which decreases the surface area available for intermolecular attractions, tends to lower the boiling point.

1822. C is correct. The diagram shows the compound in the form of a Newman projection. This method of depiction makes it easy to see which substituents are subject to steric strain from other groups. Here, the substituents on the front carbon are arranged as close as possible to those on the back carbon (which is not directly visible). This represents an eclipsed conformation. Furthermore, the two largest groups (CH_3 and Br) are directly adjacent to one another. This energetically unfavorable arrangement is known as fully eclipsed.

A: Anti implies that the largest substituents are 180° from each other, which is not possible here.

B: A staggered conformation exists when substituents on the front and back carbons are 60° from each other.

D: This is the most stable potential conformer. Again, the given compound is not staggered.

1823. A is correct. The more alkyl substituents bound to a particular position, the more stable the potential carbocation. Remember, however, that S_N1 reactions require the loss of a leaving group before such a charged species can form. Here, our leaving groups are halogen atoms. For this reason, we are looking for an answer in which the halogen is located on a highly substituted carbon. (If you can't tell from the IUPAC names, try drawing out the structures.) Choice A represents a tertiary alkyl halide.

B, D: Despite the clear presence of many substituents on these carbon chains, the molecules as a whole are only secondary alkyl halides. The methyl and *tert*-butyl groups are located on different carbons from the halogen atoms.

C: This primary structure represents the least stable potential carbocation of the listed choices.

1824. D is correct. An initiation step represents the original formation of a radical, while propagation references a step in which a pre-existing radical reacts to form a new one. Finally, termination involves interaction between two radical species to re-form a typical, less reactive molecule.

C: This is the reverse of the correct answer.

1825. D is correct. The compound named in the question stem contains only single bonds. Substituents are able to freely rotate around such bonds, an action that is prevented in alkenes. In other words, bound atoms or groups are never "locked" in place when positioned around a single bond. For this reason, cis and trans isomers do not exist in alkanes.

1826. C is correct. The *cis* isomer of this alkene should melt at a lower temperature than the *trans* isomer. In general, this trend is true of alkenes, as the *trans* form (pictured on the left in this case) is better able to stack on top of like molecules. Better stacking equates to more surface area over which intermolecular forces may be exerted, making the substance more difficult to melt.

B: This question asks for the alkene with the lower, not higher, melting point.

1827. A is correct. E2 reactions are bimolecular eliminations. These reactions are analogous to S_N2 mechanisms, as both are second-order and involve a one-step mechanism. Unlike S_N2 reactions, however, E2 processes must involve a hydrogen that is "anti" to the leaving group. Additionally, use of a strong base tends to push a reaction toward E2, while E1 reactions can proceed with weaker basic species. Finally, like S_N2 processes, E2 reactions prefer aprotic solvents.

D: These conditions would favor an E1, not an E2, mechanism.

1828. B is correct. The diagram depicts the simplest possible alkene. While this molecule is termed "ethene" according to IUPAC nomenclature, its common name is ethylene.

C, D: Both of these terms denote the same structure, a simple two-carbon alkyne.

1829. D is correct. Catalytic hydrogenation is a form of reduction. (Remember, in organic chemistry, reduction tends to involve the net gain of bonds to hydrogen!) Here, an alkyne is reduced to form the corresponding alkane, or singly-bound carbon structure.

A, C: Oxidation typically involves reaction with an oxygen-rich compound. Exposure to hydrogen gas is the exact reverse of this idea.
B: While this partial reduction can occur, it requires the presence of Lindlar's catalyst. Simple reaction with H_2 and a platinum or palladium catalyst will fully reduce an alkyne to an alkane.

1830. B is correct. This twelve-carbon structure includes eleven sigma bonds between carbons, as well as four pi bonds. Remember, double and triple bonds must contain one sigma bond before they "add" bonds made from pi orbitals! Since the question asks for the difference between pi and sigma quantities, the answer is 11 – 4 or 7.

A: This value simply represents the number of pi bonds in this alkene.
C: Similarly, this is the number of sigma carbon-carbon bonds, not the difference that the question seems to want.
D: This is the number of carbon atoms in dodeca-2,4,6,8-triene.

1831. C is correct. Here, the highest number of carbons that can be found in a single chain is six, making this a form of hexene. Additionally, remember to start numbering at the end that contains the high-priority double bond. Since that bond connects the second and third carbons, it should be labeled "2." Finally, the methyl group is found on the fourth carbon.

A: This name neglects to start numbering from the end closest to the double bond.
B: Remember to use the longest chain possible that still contains important functional groups, even if it is not initially obvious! This chain is six, not five, carbons long.
D: The double bond begins with the second carbon from the left, not the third.

1832. A is correct. An unsaturated fatty acid is one that contains one or more multiple bonds, meaning that it is "unsaturated" with hydrogen atoms. Since this molecule includes three double bonds, it is polyunsaturated.

B: This refers to a fatty acid that entirely lacks double bonds.

C: This choice would be correct if the molecule contained only one double bond.

D: This is not a term in common usage. Additionally, the molecule in question appears to contain three, not four, C=C bonds.

1833. C is correct. When an alkene is reacted with hydrobromic acid, the Markovnikov product typically forms. Since this product includes the halogen bound to the more substituted end of the bond, it tends to be especially stable. Radical reactions, particularly those initiated by peroxides, form an exception to this rule. In these processes, hydrogen adds to the less substituted end, while the bromine ion adds to the other position.

B: This statement represents Markovnikov addition.

1834. D is correct. While the diagram attempts to hide this, both ends of the double bond are equally substituted. In fact, both have the same substituents: one *tert*-butyl group and one alkyl group each. For this reason, neither end would be specifically prone to Markovnikov addition, in which the halogen atom adds to the more substituted of the two atoms.

1835. C is correct. To answer this question, first ask yourself how anthracene differs from the other three molecules. Most notably, it is both cyclic and aromatic. Next, we need to find an analytic method that would give a unique reading for this compound. The best answer is UV-visible spectroscopy, which is mainly used to analyze conjugated systems. The larger the system, the more shifted the UV absorption peak, implying that anthracene's peak would likely appear distinct enough to notice its presence.

A: This technique separates compounds on the basis of boiling point. As a twelve-carbon structure with both an alcohol and a carboxylic acid group, 5-hydroxydodecanoic acid is probably similar enough to anthracene to boil at a close temperature (in reality, these substances boil about twenty degrees apart). Additionally,

distillation is a separation method and cannot be directly used for detection.

B: Extraction, another separation technique, utilizes differences in solubility, particularly acid-base properties. Alkanes and alkenes are too similar to be isolated in this manner.

C: Finally, though TLC could theoretically be used as an inexact detection method, it separates compounds on the basis of polarity. Two of the potential contaminants are nonpolar, just like anthracene.

1836. C is correct. $KMnO_4$, like a number of other oxygen-containing reagents, is an oxidizing agent. The original molecule contains a primary and a secondary alcohol, which will be oxidized into a carboxylic acid and a ketone, respectively. It also contains a tertiary alcohol (as well as a phenol ring), neither of which can be oxidized without breaking a carbon-carbon bond. These substituents will thus remain in the form of alcohols. Note that $KMnO_4$ is a strong oxidant, which is why it can oxidize the primary alcohol directly to a carboxylic acid without first forming an aldehyde.

IV: An aldehyde would form only if the students were reacting the primary alcohol with a weak oxidant, such as PCC.

1837. D is correct. Only primary alcohols, which are positioned at the ends of carbon chains, can be oxidized to form aldehydes. Additionally, this can only be accomplished using weak oxidants, such as PCC. A stronger oxidizing agent would cause a primary alcohol to gain two bonds to oxygen and form a carboxylic acid.

A: Isopropanol is a secondary alcohol and thus would be oxidized to a ketone.

B: Acetic acid is already fully oxidized to a carboxylic acid; it would actually need to be reduced to yield an aldehyde.

C: Ethanol is a primary alcohol and could theoretically be converted into an aldehyde. However, Cr_2O_7 is a strong oxidant and would oxidize ethanol directly into acetic acid.

1838. C is correct. If we follow IUPAC naming conventions, the highest-priority group on this molecule is the carboxylic acid. We thus know that the rightmost carbon should be given the number "1" and that the suffix should be "-oic acid." The other functional groups ("hydroxy" and "methyl") are then listed in alphabetical order with the numbered carbon to which they are attached.

A: This choice numbers the substituents correctly, but does not list them in alphabetical order.

D: The numbers for two different substituents should not be listed together, as they are here.

1839. D is correct. Molecules I, II, and III contain either O-H or N-H bonds, allowing them to donate hydrogen bonds (remember, this process requires bonds between hydrogen and either fluorine, oxygen, or nitrogen). Choice IV is slightly trickier, as this cyclic ether cannot H-bond with itself. However, the question asked which could form hydrogen bonds with water, which already has the requisite O-H bonds present. The hydrogen in water could thus interact with the oxygen in this ether, making all four Roman numerals correct.

1840. B is correct. 1,4-pentadiol is a five-carbon chain with two hydroxyl groups. The terminal –OH, located at carbon 1, is a primary alcohol and can thus be oxidized directly to a carboxylic acid. (Note that this requires a strong oxidant, like $KMnO_4$ or Cr_2O_3.) The hydroxyl group at carbon 4 is secondary and will be oxidized to a ketone.

D: This is the product (the molecule shown in the question stem), not the potential precursor for which we are asked.

1841. B is correct. Tertiary alcohols cannot be oxidized further, as that would require the breaking of a carbon-carbon bond. Such an alcohol, when reacted with $K_2Cr_2O_7$, would remain unchanged. This is indicated by the question stem.

A: Potassium dichromate would oxidize a primary alcohol to a carboxylic acid. Since this would reduce the chromium cation, this transition would be coupled with a color change.
D: Similarly, a secondary alcohol can be oxidized to a ketone. If potassium dichromate were used for this process, this reaction would produce the color change described.

1842. D is correct. A good way to determine relative acidity is to consider the stability of the conjugate base. The more stable the base, the easier it is for the associated acid to lose a proton; in other words, the more stable the conjugate, the stronger the acid. One factor that contributes to this stability is inductive effect, or the presence of electron-withdrawing groups; these pull electron density toward themselves, making an anionic atom less negative. Here, Cl is such an electron-withdrawing group. These atoms "spread out" the density that would otherwise be held entirely by the single oxygen atom.

A: Here, both tert-butyl and NH_2 are electron-donating, meaning they add even more electron density to the anionic oxygen. This added density makes the hydroxyl group more unlikely to lose its proton, increasing the pK_a.
B: Ethanol lacks the electron-withdrawing effects exhibited by the dichloro groups in choice D.
C: As in choice A, this tert-butyl group is electron-donating, making this alcohol less acidic.

1843. A is correct. Oxidation of an alcohol involves the formation of additional bonds to oxygen to replace existing carbon-hydrogen bonds. In the presence of a strong oxidizing agent, like CrO_3, a primary alcohol will be oxidized to a carboxylic acid. As the resulting species has three carbon-oxygen bonds, it is more oxidized than any other potential product.

B: Secondary alcohols can only be oxidized to ketones, which is one degree of oxidation below carboxylic acids.
C: A tertiary alcohol cannot be oxidized, as that would require breaking a bond to carbon.

1844. D is correct. As distillation separates compounds based on their boiling points, this question is basically asking which alcohol has the highest BP. Boiling point depends mainly on the strength of intermolecular forces that a molecule experiences. In alcohols, this can generally be reworded to state that the more hydrogen bonding an alcohol can exhibit, the higher its boiling point will be. Molecular weight also plays a role in this trend, as heavier compounds are more difficult to vaporize. Choice D, as both the molecule with the most –OH groups (and thus the highest degree of hydrogen bonding) and the heaviest compound, will boil at the highest temperature.

1845. B is correct. Hydroxyl (-OH) substituents make poor leaving groups, as they are unstable on their own in solution. These groups typically need to be either protonated (to form water) or modified with a mesylate or tosylate to activate them as leaving groups.

A: Alcohols are weak nucleophiles, but they are certainly nucleophilic enough to react with an acid-activated electrophile.
C: Due to their –OH groups, alcohols are classic examples of species that hydrogen bond in solution. H-bonds are strong intermolecular forces.
D: Most alcohols have pK$_a$s that range between 10 and 18 (around 15 on average), so they will be protonated at a physiological pH of 7.4.

1846. C is correct. This reaction utilizes an S$_N$1 mechanism, which involves the formation of a high-energy carbocation intermediate. Since the carbocation formed during this particular process is substituted by three alkyl groups, it is tertiary; since it lacks lone pairs, we must only consider these three substituents when determining both its hybridization and its geometry. Therefore, this carbocation is sp^2-hybridized with trigonal planar geometry.

1847. B is correct. The first step in the process shown in the figure involves the transfer of a proton from the acidic reaction medium to the tertiary alcohol. In general, acid-base chemistry is faster than carbocation formation, which is an extremely slow process due to the inherent instability of the positively-charged carbon atom. In fact, we know that carbocation formation is invariably the rate-limiting step in any E1 or S$_N$1 reaction.

1848. D is correct. Since the initial substrate is primary, it cannot form a carbocation; as a result, we know that the reaction described must proceed according to an S$_N$2 mechanism. S$_N$2 reactions progress most rapidly in polar aprotic solvents, of which the only ones listed are acetone and dimethylformamide. However, an acidic environment would protonate and reduce the available concentration of the halide anion in solution, slowing down the substitution. Optimally, the reaction should instead be conducted at neutral pH, as choice D mentions.

B, C: Both ethanol and water are polar protic; in other words, they can hydrogen bond and would stabilize the nucleophile in solution. Such solvents are better suited for S$_N$1 reactions.

1849. A is correct. Theoretically, if a carbocation were to form, it could only be on the methoxy carbon shown above (making the oxygen atom and its large organic substituent the leaving group). This carbocation would not be sufficiently substituted, which forbids an S$_N$1 mechanism. Note also that, while protonation of the oxygen atom could facilitate substitution at the adjacent ring carbon, this is impossible due to the strongly basic environment promoted by sodium hydride. Instead, the methoxy carbon will undergo nucleophilic attack by the conjugate base of 1-propyne, resulting in the formation of a four-carbon molecule, 2-butyne.

1850. D is correct. The molecule shown has two chiral centers, but only one (the carbon bound to the –OH group) represents a viable site for nucleophilic substitution. Therefore, the other center will remain unchanged under the described reaction conditions. Since the question stem mentions a weak nucleophile (methanol) while the diagram shows a potential tertiary carbocation, we can conclude that this reaction will occur via an S$_N$1 mechanism, yielding products that are racemic with respect to that chiral center. However, since the other stereocenter remains unaltered by the reaction, the two resulting products will be diastereomers rather than enantiomers.

1851. D is correct. Since 1-bromopropane is primary, this reaction must proceed according to an S$_N$2 pathway; in other words, its rate-limiting step is bimolecular. The rate of this reaction depends entirely on the probability that the substrate (1-bromopropane) will collide favorably with the nucleophile (cyanide anion) in solution. Doubling the concentration of either reactant will increase the likelihood of these favorable interactions.

C: Acidification will cause the cyanide ions (weak bases) to become protonated. The resulting HCN molecules will serve as poor nucleophiles compared to CN$^-$, and the reaction will slow down significantly.

1852. A is correct. As a result of steric constraints imposed upon the geometry of the transition state, the nucleophile always approaches the electrophile from the side opposite the leaving group. (This is why you may have heard an S_N2 reaction described as a "backside attack.") Since none of the orbitals are empty (all are occupied by atoms or lone pairs), the transition state reaction center is transiently coordinated by five different substituents.

1853. C is correct. As a strong base, methoxide will readily deprotonate the benzyl alcohol shown above. The resulting negatively-charged oxygen atom is a terrible leaving group. The reaction effectively stops at this point, and the benzylate salt will undergo no further relevant chemistry.

    A: The electrophilic carbon is primary in nature, which is perfectly suitable for an S_N2 attack.
    B: Here, the nucleophile is methoxide, which is quite small. Only large nucleophiles, such as *tert*-butoxide, are unfavorable for S_N2 reactions.
    D: This would be an acceptable answer if the substrate were able to undergo elimination. However, benzyl alcohol does not contain any beta hydrogen atoms, making elimination impossible.

1854. A is correct. Tosylation of benzyl alcohol will prevent it from transferring a proton to the alkoxide. During the course of the tosylation reaction, the proton will instead be transferred to pyridine, creating an insoluble pyridinium chloride salt that will crash out of solution and is easily removable.

    B: This will not increase the desired yield at all. By this point, the proton will have already been abstracted by the nucleophile, and the relatively high pK_a of methanol precludes it from returning the proton to the reactant.
    C: This measure may somewhat increase the yield of the desired product. However, note that methoxide (as the conjugate base of methanol, a very weak acid) is a stronger base than pyridine, and that proton transfer has the potential to happen much faster than tosylation. For this reason, there is a significant chance that benzyl alcohol will still be deprotonated by methoxide before protection can occur.
    D: This will have little effect overall. While the weak acid will convert a negligible amount of

benzyl alcohol to its protonated form, the alcohol will be unable to leave in the form of water as this would produce a primary carbocation.

1855. B is correct. Tosylates are perfectly stable in solution. Although they are frequently used as precursors to later substitution products, they can exist without degrading for as long as any other laboratory-grade organic molecule. Tosyl groups are commonly added to protect particularly reactive substituents from side reactions during synthetic procedures.

    A: A tosylate is certainly not classified as a transition state. As highly unstable species, transition states exist for an immeasurable amount of time and cannot be observed using ordinary techniques.

1856. D is correct. Since sulfur is much larger than oxygen, the conjugate base of a thiol-containing molecule is better able to delocalize negative charge, increasing its stability. Remember, the more stable the conjugate base, the stronger the acid.

    A: While electronegativity does promote acidity, this trend exists across a period, not down a group. Here, atomic radius has a more substantial effect.

1857. B is correct. Unlike *n*-propanol, its straight-chain isomer, isopropanol possesses an –OH group on its second carbon. The hydroxyl oxygen is thus bound to a carbon that is attached to only two alkyl substituents. This is the definition of a secondary alcohol.

1858. B is correct. *Tert*-butoxide, the highly substituted conjugate of *tert*-butanol, is a very strong base. This idea stems from the fact that the negative charge is fully concentrated on *tert*-butoxide's lone oxygen atom. Additionally, its alkyl substituents donate added electron density to that position, localizing the charge further and resulting in high reactivity.

    A: Ethoxide has fewer electron-donating substituents than *tert*-butoxide.
    C: Electron-withdrawing groups strengthen acids, not bases.

1859. C is correct. The question stem describes an S_N2 procedure. These processes, formally known as bimolecular nucleophilic substitution reactions, happen in one step and involve a "backside attack" by a strong nucleophile. Since the attacking atom must bind at the same time as the leaving group is removed, these reactions require an unhindered substrate and a powerful nucleophile.

A, B: Tertiary substrates are used for S_N1 reactions, not S_N2 procedures. In an S_N1 reaction, the nucleophile is not part of the rate-determining first step.

1860. A is correct. Acetone is a polar aprotic solvent, meaning that it cannot donate hydrogen bonds. S_N2 reactions proceed best when in the presence of these solvents, but the reaction referenced in the question stem is S_N1. (We know this because the original alkyl halide is tertiary.) S_N1 reactions are facilitated by the presence of polar protic solvents.

B, C, D: These solvents are polar protic. Due to their large dipoles, they are easily able to stabilize charged species, including the unstable cation formed during the rate-determining step of an S_N1 procedure.

1861. D is correct. For statement I, remember that a ketone's carbonyl carbon is hindered by two methyl groups, while the same carbon in an aldehyde has only one. As a result, ketones can be more easily approached by nucleophiles, making these compounds more reactive as well. Finally, in comparison to C=C bonds, C=O bonds are shortened slightly due to the electronegativity of the oxygen atom.

II: In a ketone, each methyl group donates a small amount of electron density, and thus negative charge, to the carbonyl carbon. This reduces the net positive charge on that carbon atom.

1862. A is correct. When asked questions about nomenclature, remember to first identify the highest-priority functional group. In this case, only one group is present, so it must be identified in the suffix of the name (-one). Next, identify the longest carbon chain, being sure to start from the end that will give the ketone the lowest possible number. Starting from the right side of

the compound gives 2-pentanone, and we also have a methyl group on the 4-carbon.

B, D: The highest-priority functional group should be named in the suffix, not the prefix, of the compound's name.
C: This is technically a five-carbon chain, not a four-carbon chain with a methyl group.

1863. B is correct. An alpha hydrogen is one bound to the carbon immediately adjacent to a carbonyl carbon. Of the four structures given, A, C, and D contain such hydrogen atoms. Choice B does not include a carbonyl at all.

1864. C is correct. Each of these compounds contains at least one alpha proton, which are especially acidic due to the potential resonance stabilization of the conjugate base. However, acetylacetone is a dicarbonyl compound. Specifically, it has two carbonyl groups that flank a single, middle carbon, which is alpha to both of them. If you draw the resonance states for this compound after the central carbon has been deprotonated, you'll see that both carbonyls contribute a stabilizing effect, making these hydrogens highly acidic.

1865. B is correct. Multiple factors are involved in this question. First, when all else is equal, a higher molecular weight leads to a higher boiling point; for this reason, ethanol must have a higher BP than methanol. This eliminates choices A and D. Next, note that acetone is the only compound in the list that is unable to hydrogen bond with other like molecules. As a result, it exerts the weakest intermolecular forces and should have the lowest boiling point.

1866. C is correct. The figure depicts a Grignard reaction, a highly useful organometallic process used to form carbon-carbon bonds. The carbon-magnesium bond is polarized, giving the carbon a moderately negative charge. As such, this carbon atom can act as a nucleophile and attack the partially positive carbonyl carbon on acetone.

B: While this reaction does contain a nucleophile, substitutions involve one molecule or atom that replaces another. In other words, they generally require a leaving group, which acetone does not have.

1867. A is correct. The full reaction occurs as follows:

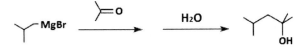

As shown above, the hydroxy group in the product molecule is attached to a carbon that is itself bound to three other carbon atoms. This is a classic tertiary alcohol.

C: Acetals are derived from reactions between alcohols and aldehydes, not ketones. Additionally, they require two oxygen atoms to be bound to the same carbon, which is not the case here.
D: While one of the reactants is a ketone (acetone), the product is not.

1868. A is correct. The first reactant is an aldehyde, or a carbonyl bound to both an R group and a hydrogen. Reaction with one equivalent of alcohol produces a hemiacetal, or "half acetal," while reaction with a second equivalent forms a full acetal. These compounds are interesting in that they include two oxygen atoms bound to the same carbon. For a hemiacetal, one of those is part of an –OH group, while the other is part of an ether (-OR). For an acetal, both oxygen atoms exist within –OR groups.

B, C: A ketone is a carbonyl that is bound on both sides to alkyl groups. The initial reactant in this series is an aldehyde, not a ketone.
D: Hemiketals and ketals are derived from ketones, as their names imply. This reaction begins with an aldehyde.

1869. C is correct. The first step in this reaction is the formation of the hemiacetal. Since the oxygen atom in methanol is a fairly good nucleophile, and since nucleophiles readily attack the carbons of carbonyl groups, this step can occur under either acidic or basic conditions. Note that the formation of the acetal, the second step, is only possible under acidic conditions.

1870. A is correct. Under acidic conditions, one of the electronegative oxygen atoms in the acetal can be protonated, creating a more favorable leaving group. Such a group is necessary if we wish to lose the methanol groups and regenerate the carbon-oxygen double bond.

B: Basic conditions are most effective when some target molecule must be deprotonated. Here, deprotonation serves no purpose; in fact, even a strong base cannot deprotonate the ether groups present on the product acetal.
C: $NaIO_4$ is used to cleave geminal diols, not geminal ethers.
D: Acetal formation is reversible; in fact, its reversibility is what makes it so chemically useful. In many multi-step reactions, aldehydes or ketones are temporarily converted to acetals or ketals to protect from reaction with nucleophiles. Later, acid-catalyzed hydrolysis can be used to recover the "hidden" aldehyde or ketone.

1871. D is correct. This one-carbon aldehyde is commonly referred to as formaldehyde. For the MCAT, it is best to know this structure, as well as those listed in the other three answer choices.

A: Acetone is a ketone, not an aldehyde.
B: Acetylene is a two-carbon alkyne; it is not an aldehyde, like the diagram shown.
C: While acetaldehyde is an aldehyde, it contains two carbons, not one.

1872. B is correct. Like many chromium-containing reagents, chromium(III) oxide, or Cr_2O_3, is a strong oxidizing agent. In general, such reagents increase the number of bonds formed between carbon and oxygen and decrease those between carbon and hydrogen. Here, we begin with 2-hexanol, a secondary alcohol. Oxidizing this molecule as thoroughly as possible results in production of the corresponding ketone, shown below.

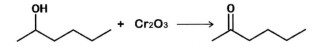

A: While oxidation of alcohols can produce carboxylic acids, those alcohols need to be primary, not secondary. 2-hexanol does not have the ability to form an additional bond to oxygen.
C: This choice lists a compound that is reduced in comparison to 2-hexanol, not oxidized.
D: Cr_2O_3 does not add novel –OH groups where none existed before.

1873. B is correct. The easiest way to change this molecule into a decent nucleophile is to reduce it to a primary alcohol. The oxygen in a relatively unhindered –OH group has two lone pairs, attracting it to electropositive atoms. LAH (or LiAlH$_4$) is a strong reducing agent that can easily convert aldehydes to their corresponding alcohols.

A: Like many of the chromium-containing reagents, potassium dichromate is an oxidizing agent. This would have the opposite of the intended effect.
C: Reacting two aldehydes under neutral conditions will likely do nothing. At the very least, it will not accomplish this scientist's goal.

1874. A is correct. A Grignard reagent is an organometallic compound (for example, CH$_3$MgBr) that can be used to add alkyl groups to aldehydes or ketones. Such reagents are generally produced by adding the associated alkyl halide (here, CH$_3$Br) to a vessel containing diethyl ether and small pieces of solid Mg.

B: Water cannot be used in the reaction flask, even in tiny amounts, when synthesizing such a reagent. If it is present, the Grignard reagent will react to form an alkane and be useless for future reactions.
C: This choice is the reverse of the correct procedure. We must begin with an alkyl halide (like CH$_3$Br), not CH$_3$Mg.
D: This choice does not mention magnesium, an important component of a Grignard reagent.

1875. C is correct. In general, keto forms are more stable than their enol counterparts. However, an exception to this rule exists when the enol tautomer establishes a conjugated system. In choice C, the enol forms a benzene ring, which is highly stable and unlikely to be disrupted by the formation of a ketone.

A: Like most such structures, this enol is more stable in its keto form. Note that the structure shown is not conjugated.
B: This molecule is not an enol.

1876. B is correct. The thermodynamic product is the one that is more "thermodynamically" stable, but is more difficult to synthesize due to a higher activation energy. In general, thermodynamic enolates are those that are more substituted than their kinetic counterparts. Here, the double

bond has formed in the position of greater steric hindrance (between carbons 1 and 2).

A: If this were our enolate, it would have the double bond between carbons 1 and 5 (the less substituted position adjacent to what formerly was the carbonyl carbon).

1877. C is correct. Tautomerization is the conversion between specific, easily interchangeable isomers. The most common form of this reaction, known as keto-enol tautomerism, involves conversion between a ketone or aldehyde and its corresponding "enol," a structure with an –OH group immediately adjacent to a C-C double bond. However, a similar reaction can occur with imines and enamines, nitrogen-containing functional groups analogous to the keto and enol forms, respectively.

IV: Imides are functional groups composed of a nitrogen atom between two carbonyl groups. These structures are analogous to acid anhydrides and do not participate in tautomerization with enamines.

1878. A is correct. This question deals with kinetic vs. thermodynamic control, two competing pathways by which certain reactants can produce multiple distinct products. The thermodynamic product is the one that is more "thermodynamically" stable, but is more difficult to synthesize due to a higher activation energy. This product is favored by energy-rich conditions, such as high temperature. In general, the thermodynamic enolate is that which is more substituted – it is more stable once produced, but steric hindrance gives its synthesis reaction a high E$_a$.

B: If these were the characteristics of our product, it would be unlikely to be formed at all.
C: This describes the kinetic enolate, which is easier to form (lower E$_a$) but less stable.
D: These qualities describe neither the kinetic nor the thermodynamic enolate. In fact, if such a product could form, it would likely be the only one due to its high favorability.

1879. D is correct. The term unsaturated refers to molecules that do not possess the maximum possible number of hydrogen atoms (in other words, those that contain double or triple bonds). As this aldehyde possesses a double bond between the alpha and beta carbons, choice D gives its most accurate nomenclature.

A: Dicarbonyl compounds contain two carbon-oxygen double bonds, which this aldehyde does not.
B: No molecule with one or more double bonds can ever be accurately referred to as saturated.
C: On a carbonyl compound, the beta position is the atom two positions away from the carbonyl carbon, while the gamma position is one atom away from that (on the side more distant from the carbonyl). This double bond does not fall between these two positions. Instead, it is an α,β bond.

1880. A is correct. As evident from an early step in the reaction mechanism, an H⁺ ion protonates the carbonyl oxygen. This protonation makes the carbon-oxygen double bond significantly weaker, allowing the carbonyl carbon to become even more electrophilic (or partially positive) than before. This facilitates the reaction by increasing the chance that the nucleophilic enol will attack.

B: While this is close, protonation converts –OH into $-OH_2$ (water) immediately before its loss as a leaving group. This choice wrongly describes this conversion as –O to –OH.
C: The mechanism depicts an aldehyde, not a ketone.
D: Acid catalysis is one of the most well-known ways to efficiently carry out an aldol condensation.

1881. D is correct. Remember, nucleophiles are atoms that are comparatively electron-rich and thus tend to react with partially positive species. Atom D, the carbonyl oxygen, has two pairs of localized electrons. Localized electron pairs are confined to a single atom and are thus more available to react.

A: The aluminum atom, which has no unpaired electrons, could be considered electron-deficient. Nucleophiles should generally have an excess of electron density.
B, C: Although these atoms do have free electron density, their lone pairs are delocalized due to the presence of alternative resonance structures. Since this density is distributed over a larger portion of the molecule, it is less available to participate in a reaction.

1882. B is correct. In an alpha helix, all carbonyl groups are oriented in the same direction; this results in a slight dipole moment. While these groups are not consecutive in terms of the amino acid sequence, they are spatially adjacent. This allows them to hydrogen bond.

A: R groups vary greatly in character, and many do not have the ability to form hydrogen bonds at all. Since all alpha helices display the property described, it most likely does not result from such a wildly variable factor.
D: Amino acid side chains are directed outward, away from the long axis of the helix.

1883. D is correct. Due to the relative acidities of the participating compounds, a proton transfer is much more likely to occur before any other reaction type. All Grignard reagents function as strong bases and must be present in excess in order to successfully esterify carboxylic acids. Note that proton transfer reactions occur more rapidly than almost any other reaction class. If such an exchange is possible, it will usually be the first step of the reaction.

1884. A is correct. Carboxylic acids, like esters, are relatively less prone to reduction than ketones and aldehydes. Reduction of a carboxylic acid requires a strong reducing agent, such as lithium aluminum hydride (LAH).

B: Sodium hydride is completely insoluble in most solvents; its solubility is similar to that of sand. This makes it an excellent choice when a strong base is required but nucleophilic behavior is undesirable. However, since reduction requires a nucleophilic attack on the carbonyl group, sodium hydride is inappropriate in this case.
C: While sodium borohydride is more than adequate for the gentle reduction of ketones and aldehydes, it is too weak to serve as an adequate reductant here.
D: Due to the presence of the electron-withdrawing cyano group, sodium cyanoborohydride is an even weaker reductant than sodium borohydride. It is typically used in reductive amination reactions, but would not suffice to reduce a carboxylic acid.

1885. A is correct. The presence of an electronegative chlorine atom on the alpha carbon will reduce the amount of available electron density at the oxygen atoms. This lowers the ability of these oxygens to form new bonds with protons, decreasing their basicity. Alternatively, one might consider that the presence of an electron-withdrawing substituent makes the protonated form of the molecule more acidic, which necessarily makes its deprotonated form a worse base.

C, D: No resonance structures are made possible by delocalization of the chlorine atom's lone pairs. These electrons are localized.

1886. B is correct. Lithium aluminum deuteride is sufficiently reactive to reduce both carbonyl groups. Although complete reduction of the carboxylic acid moiety forms a secondary alcohol that lacks chirality, reduction of the aldehyde creates a new chiral center. Since the aldehyde is geometrically planar, deuteride atoms may add from either face, producing an equal mixture of stereoisomers with respect to that particular site. The other chiral center, with the chlorine atom, will remain untouched by the reaction. Therefore, the reduction results in an equal mixture of two diastereomers.

1887. C is correct. Bromomethane is formed by the first step of the reaction, in which the ester is demethylated. Carbon dioxide is a product of all decarboxylations.

A: This reaction never forms free methane. The methyl group is attacked by the bromide ion and remains bound to it for the remainder of the reaction.
B: Since the starting material is an ester, rather than a free carboxylic acid, no reasonable source of water is present.
D: We are told that the reaction begins with an S_N2 attack. Methanol could only be produced if the bromide ion attacked the carbonyl directly; this would require acidic conditions.

1888. C is correct. Carboxylic acids are less reactive than most of their derivatives because the potential resonance effect renders the carbon center relatively electron-rich. Amides can also display this resonance behavior, but since nitrogen is less electronegative than oxygen, the amide bond exhibits a greater degree of resonance character in which the nitrogen is sp^2-hybridized. As a result, an even greater amount of electron density is concentrated around the carbonyl carbon, which reduces the electrophilicity of the amide group.

A: The hydrogen substituent of an aldehyde donates almost no electron density to the carbon center, leaving it more electron-deficient than a carboxylic acid.
B: Acyl halides are generally very reactive. Although the chlorine atom can donate electrons to the carbon via resonance, this resonance contributor is very minor. The electron-withdrawing effect of the Cl atom, which makes the carbonyl carbon more partially positive, far outweighs any resonance donation.
D: In a ketone, the carbon atoms adjacent to the carbonyl are weakly electron-donating, but do not offer as much supplemental electron density as an adjacent oxygen atom would provide through resonance.

1889. C is correct. A Lewis acid is likely to complex with the carbonyl group, further polarizing the C=O bond and increasing the electrophilicity of the carbon atom. A similar effect can occur upon addition of a weak acid, where the proton coordinates with the carbonyl oxygen atom to further polarize the bond. (Critically, it should be noted that ammonia would probably also form a coordination complex with $TiCl_4$. In addition, NH_3 has the potential to accept a proton from a weak acid. However, we are told that the amide formation is thermodynamically favorable. Since neither of these two side reactions is productive in any way, they will simply reverse in solution, allowing the favorable overall reaction to proceed instead.)

III: Pd/C is used to catalyze hydrogenation reactions, which have mechanisms that differ significantly from those of nucleophilic substitutions.

1890. B is correct. Ideally, acidic conditions serve to effectively protonate the carbonyl of the carboxylic acid and further polarize the bond. However, some species react in alternative ways. Since sulfuric acid is a poor nucleophile, it is unlikely to cause any undesirable side reactions. In reality, note that side reactions between two different organic acid molecules are unavoidable. That is, a second molecule of the organic acid could be induced to add across the double bond.

With this in mind, we are asked only to identify the catalyst that offers the highest possible degree of success.

A: This would likely result in a side reaction, specifically an electrophilic addition across the alkene.
C: Here, ethanol would promote the esterification of the carboxylic acid to form an ethyl ester. This is an unnecessary side reaction that could be avoided with a different selection of solvent.
D: Although water will not react with the carboxylic acid to form any undesirable products, it could add across the alkene to yield a diol instead of the intended cyclic molecule.

1891. D is correct. A carboxylic acid derivative is a molecule that can be synthesized from a carboxylic acid via nucleophilic acyl substitution. Alternately, such a compound is one that contains a carbonyl group immediately adjacent to a heteroatom, generally one that is electronegative. A thioester includes a carbonyl next to a sulfur atom, while an acyl halide contains a carbonyl next to a halogen.

A: Both of these molecules contain only carbon or hydrogen next to their carbonyl carbons. These atoms are neither heteroatoms nor especially electronegative.
B: While an amide is a carboxylic acid derivative, an ether is not. Don't confuse ethers with esters!
C: A nitro group is simply an $-NO_2$ substituent. This structure cannot be directly synthesized from a carboxylic acid.

1892. C is correct. Of the carboxylic acid derivatives, acyl halides are the most reactive because they contain the best leaving groups (halogen atoms). However, both butanoyl chloride and acetyl iodide are acyl halides. To distinguish between the two, remember that iodide is the most stable halogen in solution due to its large size. For this reason, I^- is a much better leaving group than Br^-, Cl^-, and especially F^-.

B: The leaving group on this molecule is NH_2^-, which is extremely unstable in solution. For this reason, amides are notably unreactive.
D: While acid anhydrides do possess good leaving groups, they are not quite as good as the halogen atoms present on acyl halides.

1893. C is correct. The process described here involves two steps. First, PCl_5 is used to synthesize an acyl halide, a common first step in such reactions due to the high reactivity of these compounds. Next, the newly generated propionyl chloride is reacted with propionic acid, forming propionic anhydride and losing Cl^- as a leaving group.

A: While this will form an anhydride, it will not have enough carbons. Ethanoic acid is a two-carbon molecule, but both sides of propionic anhydride are shown to have three-carbon chains.
B: Reaction of an ester (such as methyl propionate) with an alcohol simply yields another ester, not an anhydride.
D: The added water and reflux at the end of this procedure are counterproductive. Such conditions facilitate hydrolysis, which is often acid-catalyzed. This reaction will break the desired anhydride into two carboxylic acids.

1894. A is correct. Propionic anhydride is an acid anhydride, one of the more reactive of the carboxylic acid derivatives. Amides, in contrast, are the least reactive, since their leaving groups are extremely unstable in solution. Hexanamide is an amide, as evident from its nomenclature.

B, D: Neither of these ions are carboxylic acid derivatives. In fact, both are fairly strong bases, as they are the conjugates of extremely weak acids. Bases like these are highly reactive, as they need to gain a proton to restore stability.
C: From the name of this compound, we can see that it is an acyl halide; these molecules are highly reactive due to the presence of a good leaving group.

1895. B is correct. Remember, stability is the opposite of reactivity. Thus, this question is asking why anhydrides are more reactive than amides, which relates to the differences between their leaving groups. Consider a primary amide, for which the leaving group is NH_2^-. As a strong base, this group is extremely reactive, making it unlikely to leave in the first place. In comparison, the leaving group of an anhydride is a carboxylate ion, which displays resonance between the two oxygen atoms. Since this makes the group stable in solution, it can easily leave and the anhydride can participate in a variety of reactions.

A: Amides do not have resonance-stabilized leaving groups. In fact, their LGs are incredibly unstable on their own, making the compound as a whole unlikely to react.
C: Alkyl groups are electron-donating, not electron-withdrawing.
D: Amides certainly are more stable – or less reactive – than anhydrides.

1896. B is correct. The hardest part of this question is not becoming confused. We are told to order the derivatives beginning with the least reactive; of those listed, amides are by far the most inert. In fact, our full list would go as follows: amides < esters and carboxylic acids < acid anhydrides < acyl halides. Only choice B ranks three members of this list correctly.

A: This choice ranks from most to least reactive, which is the opposite of what the question asks.
C: Anhydrides are significantly more reactive than esters.
D: While amides would rank before esters on this list, acyl halides are far more reactive than carboxylic acids, placing them last in the order specified.

1897. B is correct. Lactones are generally produced via intramolecular nucleophilic attack; this creates the cyclic structure. Choice II contains a good nucleophile (-OH) in a position where it can easily access the carbonyl carbon on the same chain. Such a ring closure will form the compound given in the question stem. Additionally, this type of reaction is a dehydration, which are facilitated by heat and acidic conditions.

I: This is close to the given structure; in fact, it is only missing the two double bonds in the ring. However, these bonds could only form from the molecule in choice I via an elimination reaction, which requires a base. H_2 and Pt are used in catalytic hydrogenation, which actually reduces (removes) double bonds.
III: Combination of these reagents could, at best, result in the –OH attacking the carbonyl carbon of acetone. However, there is no possibility for ring closure.

1898. C is correct. Since we certainly do not need to be familiar with these specific structures, we must use the information given in the question.

Cephalexin is a lactam, or cyclic amide, while β-propiolactone is a lactone, or cyclic ester. Since both structures are at least partially cyclic, C is the best answer.

A: While β-propiolactone certainly contains an ester, we have no way of knowing whether cephalexin does. Lactams are cyclic amides, which have a nitrogen atom in the alpha position instead of an oxygen.
B: Similarly, while we know that cephalexin must contain an amide, we cannot be sure about β-propiolactone.
D: Again, we have no way of knowing this. Esters may contain as few as two oxygen atoms, while amides may contain only one. In fact, β-propiolactone has only two O atoms.

1899. C is correct. Transesterification involves the conversion of one ester to another via reaction with an alcohol. The –OH acts as a nucleophile and attacks the ester's carbonyl carbon, replacing the previous R group on the ester with its own. Here, only choices B and C are alcohols. However, the R group on choice B is an ethyl group, which will simply react with ethyl ethanoate to produce the same product as before. As we know that the professor was unhappy with his previous results, hexanol is the best choice.

A: Methyl propionate is an ester, which will not react noticeably with another ester molecule.
D: If anything, water will hydrolyze the ethyl ethanoate, which is not desirable here.

1900. A is correct. The leaving group on an acid anhydride includes both the carbonyl functionality and the oxygen atom immediately adjacent to it. In fact, this is why anhydrides are so reactive – their leaving groups have resonance, making them especially stable in solution. For that reason, the LG here is the entire acetate ion, not just C_2H_3O. Finally, as an attacking molecule with a lone pair, NH_3 is a classic nucleophile and will be drawn to electropositive regions.

1901. A is correct. The structure of urea is shown below.

As is evident from this image, urea is an amide-containing molecule.

II: An imide is similar to an acid anhydride, but with a central nitrogen atom instead of oxygen. As urea does not include two carbonyl functionalities, this choice is false.
III. Imines involve carbon-nitrogen double bonds.

1902. B is correct. Typically, esters end in the suffix "-oate," but since this molecule is a derivative of acetic acid, it simply ends in "-ate." In any case, this species cannot possibly be an ether, which are designated by the full word "ether" in their nomenclature. Acetate substituents contain two carbons, while methyl contains one, yielding three in total.

1903. C is correct. In essence, this question is asking for the most stable (or least reactive) choice. Of the four halogens present in these molecules, fluorine serves as the worst leaving group. To understand this concept, consider the periodic table. As a member of a higher period than chlorine, bromine, or iodine, fluorine is a very small atom. As such, it poorly delocalizes the negative charge gained when it exits as a leaving group. The worse the leaving group, the less reactive the compound, and an unreactive molecule is by definition more stable.

B: This represents the most reactive, and thus least stable, acyl halide listed.

1904. A is correct. Phosphorus pentachloride (PCl_5) is a reagent commonly used to convert carboxylic acids into acyl halides. This particular reaction would produce 1-methylheptanoyl chloride, which (like other acyl halides) is highly reactive due to its halogen leaving group.

B: It is thionyl chloride ($SOCl_2$), not SOCl, that would accomplish the described goal.
C: If anything, water would simply attack the carbonyl carbon of this carboxylic acid, producing the exact same molecule as the original species.
D: Reaction of a carboxylic acid with an alcohol forms an ester. Esters are nearly identical to carboxylic acids in terms of reactivity.

1905. C is correct. Since this compound is likely unfamiliar, we must use its name to discern its chemical structure. The described antibiotic is said to be a lactam, or cyclic amide. Thus, its structure contains at least a single ring with an incorporated nitrogen atom.

A: Lactams are nitrogen-containing. While imipenem may also include oxygen, we have no way of knowing this.
B: This choice is impossible to ascertain from the given information alone.

1906. B is correct. Reductive animation reactions always result in the production of an amine, specifically from some sort of carbonyl. The fact that his starting material is an aldehyde is a distractor.

A, C, D: While enamines, imides, and imines can be formed from both aldehydes and ketones, these species do not form during reductive animation.

1907. C is correct. This is the first step of a Stork enamine alkylation reaction. For this process to occur, an enamine must first be produced. This structure can be identified by the presence of an amine on one carbon that is connected to another carbon atom via a double bond.

A: An imide is characterized by a nitrogen neighbored on both sides by acyl groups.
B: An amide includes a nitrogen adjacent to a carbonyl group. Other types of amides include nitrogen next to sulfonyl and phosphoryl groups.
D: An enamide is an amide with an adjacent double bond.

1908. A is correct. A beta-unsaturated ketone has a double bond between its beta and alpha carbons. If we add the smallest possible beta-unsaturated ketone to the enamine shown, the final product should be four carbons larger than the intermediate enamine.

B, C: These represent the addition of an aldehyde.
D: Because this carbonyl group occurs in the middle of a three-carbon chain, a beta carbon does not exist at all. Instead, there are two alpha carbons (both once removed from the carbonyl carbon).

1909. B is correct. This is an example of an imide, which is characterized by one acyl group on either side of a nitrogen that may also be attached to an additional R group.

1910. D is correct. This question is asking for the most basic species. Alkyl groups stabilize positive molecules, making alkyl amines the most basic, followed by ammonia and aryl amines.

A: Ammonia is less basic than an alkyl amine, such as ethylamine.
B, C: Both of these are examples of aryl amines.

1911. A is correct. N-ethylpropionamide is an amide. This type of molecule results from the combination of an alkyl amine and an acyl chloride, such as propionyl chloride.

B: This represents an incorrect naming of the same structure.
C: An aryl amine will be cyclic, which the proper product will not be.
D: This neglects the presence of the carbonyl functionality.

1912. C is correct. Because the C-N bond on the acyl group has sp^2 character, the ring cannot rotate around its sigma bonds to find a conformation that presents the least strain.

A: No enamine is present here, as no C-C double bonds exist outside of the benzene ring.
B: The opposite is true; the bonds do not rotate freely.
D: Regardless of the presence of an amide, ring strain is not stabilized.

1913. B is correct. Because the ring contains an amide, giving the C-N bond sp^2 character, the sigma bonds in this cyclic structure cannot rotate.

C: One π bond is present, between the oxygen and the carbon. Note that the question asked about part of the molecule, not penicillin as a whole.
D: All amides, one of which is seen here, can be hydrolyzed.

1914. D is correct. Cyanohydrins result from the reaction of an aldehyde with cyanide.

B, C: A cyanohydrin contains a primary amine, as the carbon that serves as part of cyanide nucleophilically attacks the carbonyl group. This leaves the cyanide nitrogen attached only to its original carbon.

1915. A is correct. When an amide is hydrolyzed, the two products are a carboxylic acid and an amine.

B, C: One of the products is a carboxylic acid, which does contain an acyl group. However, neither a ketone nor an aldehyde could be directly produced via the described mechanism.

1916. A is correct. To form a quinone – a conjugated dicarbonyl compound – more carbon-oxygen bonds must be added to a phenol. This is the definition of oxidization.

B: Reducing a phenol would eliminate bonds between carbon and oxygen. This does not make sense, as a quinone must have two oxygen atoms while a simple phenol contains only one.
C: This would unnecessarily involve removal of a carbon atom.

1917. D is correct. Chromium trioxide is used in oxidation reactions. Reduction is unlikely to form a quinone, which is a highly oxidized compound.

A: Quinones include two carbonyl groups.
B: Quinone compounds are aromatic. Even benzoquinone, which initially might not appear to be aromatic in nature, possesses delocalized C-O double bonds. This allows the molecule to display aromaticity.
C: All quinones are conjugated.

1918. A is correct. Because benzoquinone is reduced, we should predict a product with fewer carbon-oxygen bonds. Here, C=O bonds are reduced to C-O ones.

B: We cannot assume that reduction would result in a loss of aromatic character.
C: This structure is equally oxygenated in comparison to benzoquinone.
D: From the question stem, we have no reason to assume that a hydroxyl group would be lost.

1919. B is correct. By definition, all quinones are conjugated. In addition, because the C-O bonds in benzoquinone display sp^2 hybridization, we can assume that they may be reduced to sp^3 structures. In other words, a hydrogen atom can be added to each carbon atom that originally participates in a C=O bond.

1920. C is correct. Here, the carboxylic acid is the most acidic, followed by the phenol, which has a lower pK$_a$ than a simple alcohol due to its potential to exhibit resonance. Finally, the amine is the least acidic of these four molecules. In other words, only the alcohol and the amine will remain after the phenol is isolated.

1921. A is correct. Polar solvents are most commonly used during polysubstitution.

B: Nonpolar solvents are best used for monosubstitution.

1922. D is correct. Furan is a five-membered aromatic ring that contains an oxygen. Because it is aromatic in nature, and because its ring structure contains oxygen as well as carbon, it can be considered heteroaromatic.

A, B: The oxygen in furan is sp^2 hybridized, as it possesses double bond character.
C: This statement would better describe pyrrole, a similar compound that contains nitrogen instead of oxygen.

1923. C is correct. Since stronger acids tend to have weaker conjugate bases, this question, in essence, is asking for the strongest acid. The phenol that contains the most electron-withdrawing substituents will be the most acidic. Here, the trifluoride groups are electron-withdrawing, meaning that they pull negative charge away from the potentially deprotonated oxygen atom. This stabilizes the compound and strengthens its acidity.

D: Alkyl groups are electron-donating.

1924. D is correct. In order to chlorinate the phenol, Cl_2 and water (a polar solvent) should be used.

A: Nonpolar solvents are better used for monosubstitution.
B: Chromium trioxide is typically used in oxidation reactions, not halogenations.

1925. A is correct. As common bases themselves, amines should clearly be listed first, while carboxylic acids should be last. To compare a phenol with a regular alcohol, remember that a stronger acid must have a weaker conjugate base. As resonance-stabilized species, phenols are more acidic than alcohols, meaning that alcohols have the more basic conjugates of the two.

1926. D is correct. These molecules (fructose on the left, glucose on the right) possess the same atomic components, but lack identical bonding between these atoms. For this reason, they are structural isomers.

A: Anomers differ only in the orientation of the –OH group on the anomeric carbon of the cyclized molecule.
B: Epimers have different stereochemistry at a single chiral center, but display identical bonding. The pictured molecules differ in their bonded arrangement of atoms.
C: Diastereomers do not display different bonding between atoms.

1927. A is correct. As a ketose, fructose cannot possibly be an epimer of glucose, an aldose. Epimers differ only in the stereoconfiguration at a single chiral center.

B, C, D: Galactose differs from glucose in its configuration at C4, mannose differs at C2, and allose differs at C3.

1928. D is correct. The image shows a furanose form of fructose. As this molecule contains six carbons, it is a hexose, as opposed to a pentose (which contains five). Note also that the deacetalized form of this carbohydrate must include a ketone group. For this reason, it is a ketose, rather than an aldose, and a ketohexose overall.

1929. D is correct. The anomeric carbon is that which is bound to two separate oxygen atoms in the cyclic structure. This is the carbon that would be a ketone group on the deacetalized, long-chain fructose molecule.

1930. B is correct. Cellulose contains β-1,4 acetal linkages between glucose molecules. Humans lack an enzyme to cleave these bonds, which explains why we cannot digest cellulose. Starch contains α-1,4 acetal linkages, which we can break down.

1931. C is correct. Glucose and galactose are the monosaccharide components of the disaccharide lactose. They are connected by a β (1→4) acetal linkage that is cleaved by lactase.

A: This combination forms lactulose, not lactose.
B: No common disaccharide consists of these two components.
D: These are the monomeric components of fructose.

1932. A is correct. Furanoses are cyclized forms of carbohydrates that contain five-membered rings, including an oxygen atom bonded to the anomeric carbon. To form a five-membered ring with C1 (the anomeric carbon), the hydroxyl group on C4 must attack the aldehyde on C1.

B, C: These would form rings that are too large to be classified as furanoses.
D: An acetal requires two –OR groups. In reality, one –OR and one –OH group would be present.

1933. A is correct. The depicted molecule is glucose. Maltose is composed of two glucose molecules that are connected by an α (1 → 4) linkage.

B: This combination would produce sucrose, which also contains a different linkage.
C: These two monomers would produce lactose (if the linkage were β).
D: Glucose and mannose do not combine to form a common disaccharide.

1934. C is correct. The β anomer of glucose is slightly more stable than the α anomer. When provided with a catalyst, such as an acid, the α anomer will tend to mutarotate (or change its configuration) into the β anomer until an approximate 1:2 anomer ratio is achieved.

1935. C is correct. Deoxyribose is a component of DNA. It is not found in the oligosaccharide chains of glycoproteins. The other listed monosaccharides are common components of these chains.

1936. A is correct. Essentially, this question is simply asking us to identify the type of linkage that joins the two subunits of maltose. Notice how the anomeric carbon projects its oxygen atom in the direction opposite that of carbon 6. Since these two atoms are opposed, this must be an α linkage. The anomeric carbon (carbon 1) is joined via a glycosidic linkage to carbon 4 of the adjoining sugar. Therefore, this is an α (1-4) glycosidic linkage and would be suitable for hydrolysis by glucoinvertase.

1937. B is correct. After protonation of the bridging oxygen atom, electrons from the left-hand ring oxygen will move down to displace this protonated atom. This creates an intermediate featuring a positively-charged oxygen with a bond order of three. By definition, this is an oxonium ion.

A: Although the first step of the reaction does proceed through an sp^3-hybridized oxonium intermediate, the subsequent step features a planar, sp^2-hybridized oxonium ion.
C: The resonance structure that would involve a carbocation is vastly outweighed by the more favorable oxonium structure. It should therefore be considered insignificant in the context of this mechanism.
D: It would be extremely difficult to form a carbanion under acidic reaction conditions. This does not occur during the course of this reaction.

1938. B is correct. Acetyl chloride, though still not perfect, is the most viable option for a protecting group presented. Importantly, acetylation of the free alcohol groups can be achieved without the need for acid catalysis that could damage the ketal. Generation of acidic conditions *in situ* should be effectively prevented by the presence of pyridine, which forms an insoluble precipitate with chloride.

A: Here, the use of catalytic acid threatens to break open the cyclic ketal.
C: While sodium hydride is not nucleophilic and should not displace the azide group, it is an extremely strong base. Global deprotonation will yield a free alkoxide ion adjacent to the azide. This presents the possibility of a ring-closing reaction, making this set of reagents undesirable given the alternatives.
D: Tosyl chloride would be an excellent choice for this protection reaction if it were not presented for use with sodium hydroxide. Free hydroxide ions would likely displace the tosyl groups and regenerate the naked alcohol functionalities.

1939. D is correct. Ketals may be effectively hydrolyzed by treatment with strong acid and water.

B: While lithium aluminum hydride is a powerful reducing agent, it is unlikely to have an effect on a ketal.
A, C: Ketals are resistant to basic conditions.

1940. A is correct. Here, the primary product (given below) is an acetal formed by the reaction between the terminal aldehyde and two of the hydroxyl groups.

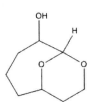

In consideration of ring strain, it is the two hydroxyl groups most distal to the aldehyde that are likely to participate. Involvement of the proximal hydroxyl would form an extremely tight ring, which is unfavorable given the transition state required for the initial nucleophilic attack on the aldehyde. In reality, the resulting acetal features two rings – one 7-membered and one 6-membered – that share a bridging oxygen atom. The proximal hydroxyl group resides untouched on the larger ring.

1941. B is correct. Here, a cyclic ketal is hydrolyzed into the ketone from which it is derived. During this hydrolysis reaction, the attacking nucleophile is simply a solvent water molecule. The oxygen nucleus from the labeled water is the same atom present in the ketone carbonyl of the final product. The diol retains both of the oxygen nuclei originally present in the ketal, which are unlabeled.

D: This implies that none of the three product oxygen atoms are labeled, which is impossible given that the starting material contains only two O atoms.

1942. B is correct. The glycosidic linkage shown above is an acetal. All acetals are acid-sensitive.

A: Tollens' reagent is useful for identifying reducing sugars, as it reacts with free aldehydes to produce a silver mirror. However, sucrose is not a reducing sugar. Tollens' reagent does not accomplish the hydrolysis described.
C: Sucrose contains no carbonyl groups that could be reduced by sodium borohydride. Reducing sugars do contain an aldehyde moiety that could potentially react with $NaBH_4$, but sucrose is not a reducing sugar. Additionally, we are asked about a hydrolysis, not a reduction.
D: A strong base would be unlikely to facilitate the hydrolysis of an acetal. Acetals and ketals are resistant to basic conditions.

1943. A is correct. Glucose and fructose are structural, or configurational, isomers. Remember that glucose is a hexose, meaning that it contains a six-membered ring. In contrast, fructose (a pentose) includes a five-membered ring. Both monosaccharides contain the same number of carbon, oxygen, and hydrogen atoms.

B, C, D: Since they differ in their connectivity, these two molecules cannot possibly be any form of stereoisomers.

1944. D is correct. From the diagram alone, we should recognize a component of imine synthesis. Such a synthesis reaction occurs between a carbonyl and a free amine. Since non-reducing sugars, such as sucrose, do not contain free carbonyl groups (either aldehydes or ketones), they are unable to undergo the nucleophilic attack by the lysine residue that is displayed above.

A, B, C: All three of these monomers are reducing sugars.

1945. D is correct. A positive Tollens' test is indicated by the formation of a silver mirror, or shiny Ag precipitate. This requires the presence of a reducing sugar. According to the reaction scheme provided, glucose monomers are joined to glycogenin through their reducing ends; each subsequent monomer also binds in a similar fashion. Glycogen, therefore, has no free reducing ends.

B, C: These choices incorrectly describe Tollens' test. A silver mirror forms only if a reducing sugar is present, as such a molecule can reduce silver cation to solid Ag.

1946. D is correct. The term "unsaturated" indicates that there is at least one multiple bond, generally an alkene, in the molecule. Additionally, any fatty acid, as its name implies, must have a carboxylic acid at one terminal.

II: Don't get your lipid-based molecules confused! An ester forms when a free fatty acid binds with glycerol to comprise part of a triacylglyceride.

1947. C is correct. In a saponification reaction, OH^- acts as a nucleophile and attacks one of the carbonyl carbons to cleave the associated ester bond. Since one equivalent of NaOH / H_2O is required to hydrolyze each ester, and since this molecule (like a stereotypical triglyceride) contains three esters, three equivalents are required.

D: Saponification (a word that means "soap-making") is simply a specific term for the cleavage of ester bonds in fats. This molecule can certainly undergo a similar reaction, which will form a triol (or three-hydroxyl alcohol) and three carboxylic acids.

1948. C is correct. Cholesterols are cyclic molecules that exist in the phospholipid bilayer to maintain fluidity and shape; without them, the bilayer would be too rigid. In contrast, glycosphingolipids are sphingolipids with a sugar attached to the head group. These molecules protrude from the membrane to act as tags for cell signaling.

A: Triacylglycerols are not membrane lipids, a category that includes cholesterol, glycolipids, and phospholipids.
B: While phospholipids are the predominant component of cell membranes, they contribute to rigidity, not fluidity. Waxes are not membrane lipids.
D: Sphingolipids are used to protect cells from the external environment. Note that special classes, such as glycosphingolipids, are used for cell signaling; however, this choice is still backwards.

1949. A is correct. To form a triacylglycerol molecule from its component parts, three free fatty acids must be joined with glycerol via an esterification reaction. Technically, a triacylglycerol is a triester.

1950. C is correct. This question is asking for the molecule that interacts most favorably with water. In general, lipids are hydrophobic, meaning that they would form a low-entropy mixture in water; however, phospholipids are amphipathic due to their charged phosphate head and hydrocarbon tails. In other words, they are partially polar. As a result, compared to the three other molecules, phospholipids would have the most favorable (or "least unfavorable") interactions in aqueous solution.

1951. D is correct. At the time depicted in the diagram, C_3 has been deprotonated by a base, leaving it

negatively charged and thus nucleophilic. In contrast, C_2 is partially positively charged due to its proximity to the carbonyl oxygen. For this reason, C_3 will attack C_2 in this early step of fatty acid synthesis.

1952. A is correct. A triacylglycerol consists of a glycerol backbone bound via ester linkages to three fatty chains. Thus, the saponification of such a molecule will yield three (not two) fatty acid salts and one glycerol molecule.

B, C, D: All of these statements accurately characterize saponification.

1953. A is correct. When naming a fatty acid, number the carbon atoms starting at the carbonyl. We can find the prefix from the total number of carbons in the chain (16 carbons = "hexadec-"), while "-oic acid" is always used as the suffix. For unsaturated fatty acids, we must specify both the nature (cis vs. trans) and the location of the double bond; since the bond spans two carbons, we use the lower number. Finally, "-en-" is inserted in between the prefix and suffix to designate the alkene.

B: When marking the location of a C=C bond, be sure to use the lower of the two numbers.
C, D: The main substituents on the double bond are cis, not trans.

1954. B is correct. Waxes are highly hydrophobic lipids that are used, among other applications, to create seals that lock in moisture. Plants typically have a waxy layer on their leaves to prevent water loss.

1955. C is correct. Sphingolipids are characterized by at least one long hydrocarbon chain, as well as a nitrogenous headgroup. Sphingolipids are additionally characterized by the presence of nitrogen.

A: Cholesterol is a nonpolar structure with four fused rings. It does not resemble the macromolecule shown.
B: The image given in the question stem does not even contain phosphorus.
D: Waxes are generally simpler than this molecule. Additionally, they contain neither rings nor nitrogen atoms.

1956. D is correct. A compound will boil when its vapor pressure is equal to the ambient pressure to which it is exposed. Adding a vacuum to the distillation apparatus dramatically lowers ambient pressure, making compounds that typically have high boiling points more prone to vaporization. For example, consider a compound that boils at 300 °C at 1 atm of pressure – this substance would be nearly impossible to vaporize without using a vacuum.

A: This is fractional, not vacuum, distillation.
B: This statement is incorrect; the purpose of the vacuum is not to "suck up" the compound.
C: All forms of distillation separate liquids.

1957. C is correct. Fractional distillation is used to separate compounds with very close boiling points (generally less than 25 °C apart). The apparatus is very similar to that used for simple distillation, except a long fractionating column is placed directly above the distillation flask. As compounds must travel up the entire column in the vapor phase to move into the flask used to collect the products, enhanced separation is achieved. Of the pairs mentioned, hexanol and 2-methylpentanol are likely to have the most similar boiling points. Both are six-carbon alcohols; 2-methylpentanol just demonstrates slightly more branching, lowering its BP a few degrees.

A: While these two carboxylic acids are similar, one is an eight-carbon structure while the other contains ten carbons. This difference in molecular weight is drastic enough to make A a worse answer than C.
B: Similarly, this choice contains one eight-carbon alcohol and one five-carbon one, which will differ significantly in BP.
D: Due to its ability to form hydrogen bonds, pentanoic acid will have a much higher boiling point than hexane.

1958. B is correct. Benzylamine is a basic compound. To separate a base from other molecules dissolved in the organic layer, we must use an acid to protonate it. As a charged (and thus very polar) compound, our protonated amine will then move into the water layer where it can be isolated.

A, D: Bases such as these might be added to separate out acidic compounds, but benzylamine is a base.

1959. C is correct. The key to this question is understanding that silica (SiO_2) is a highly polar molecule. Therefore, this TLC procedure involves a polar stationary phase and a nonpolar mobile phase (hexane, or C_6H_{14}). Compounds prefer to associate with other molecules of similar polarities, so the most polar molecule listed will interact best with the silica plate. Here, that molecule is 2,3-butanediol, as its hydroxyl groups allow it to form multiple hydrogen bonds.

A, D: Due to the dipole moment provided by the carbonyl group, both of these molecules are somewhat polar. However, neither can donate hydrogen bonds. Note that choice D is an aldehyde, not a carboxylic acid.
B: This is heptane, a very nonpolar molecule that will interact least with the polar plate.

1960. B is correct. Boiling point is defined as the temperature at which a compound's vapor pressure is equal to the atmospheric (or ambient) pressure. We typically think of heating as the only way to cause a substance to boil, but according to this relationship, an alternate method involves lowering the ambient pressure. This can be achieved through vacuum distillation, and is typically used to separate compounds that would otherwise be very difficult to boil.

A: This relationship can be true at temperatures other than the boiling point; additionally, it does not explain the role of vacuum distillation.
C: This statement is backwards.
D: While adding a nonvolatile solute (for example, NaCl) to a liquid will raise its boiling point, this does not relate to vacuum distillation. Instead, this is the colligative property of boiling point elevation.

1961. D is correct. R_f is a measure of the distance traveled by a compound in comparison to the distance covered by the solvent front. In other words, the lowest R_f will be attained by the molecule that traveled the shortest distance along the plate. Here, that is Compound Y, which did so because it interacted more readily with the plate than with the solvent.

A, B: Compound X has the highest R_f of the three compounds shown.

C: Since silica is a polar material, and since Compound Y attached so readily to the silica plate, we can assume that Compound Y is the most, not the least, polar.

1962. A is correct. Remember, silica is highly polar, while toluene is nonpolar. Note also that Compound Y adhered most closely to the stationary phase (the plate), while Compound X interacted best with the mobile phase (the solvent). For this reason, we must choose an answer in which Y is most polar, X is most nonpolar, and Z falls somewhere in between. Choice A fulfills this condition, as oxalic acid (a dicarboxylic acid) is extremely polar while the cyclic hydrocarbon diphenyl is very nonpolar.

B: This is the reverse of the expected trend. Here, Compound X (glutaric acid) is the most polar of the three.
C: Here, Compound Z is the most nonpolar molecule mentioned. Since Z falls between the other two on the diagram, this is impossible.
D: All three of these compounds are nonpolar.

1963. B is correct. This student's sample of Compound Y is contaminated by two compounds that are very similar in terms of polarity (note that all three molecules are three-to-five-carbon carboxylic acids). Since his sample is impure, the student will see a smear on the plate, not a distinct spot. However, due to their similarities, these contaminants will only produce a small smear and will not change the relative positioning of the spot by a large amount.

A: The two extra spots on this TLC plate are too distinct and far apart. Three compounds that are so similar in terms of polarity should be much closer together on the silica.
C: Here, compound Y suddenly travels much farther on the plate than both X and Z. Contaminants like those described should not change the relative positioning so drastically.
D: On a diagram like that above, the added spots or smears from impurities should run horizontally next to spot Y, not vertically.

1964. C is correct. Most gas chromatography conducted in organic chemistry lab (and the only type likely to be referenced on the MCAT) is gas-liquid chromatography. The liquid comprises the stationary phase, while an inert gas (like helium or nitrogen) passes through the apparatus as the mobile phase.

A, B: In general, it doesn't make sense to use a gas as a stationary phase, as it will move through the column instead of remaining still. Thus, these choices reverse the identities of the stationary and mobile phases.
D: Hydrogen and oxygen are not inert gases. While they might be fine to use with certain compounds, gas chromatography generally requires an inert mobile phase to avoid further reactions with the components of the mixture.

1965. A is correct. Recrystallization is a method used to remove impurities from solid samples. For these procedures, we must choose a solvent in which our compound is relatively insoluble at cold temperatures but relatively soluble at warm ones. This way, we can heat our compound / solvent mixture to dissolve the sample, then cool the vessel to recrystallize it and exclude impurities from its new structure.

B: If molecule 1 is always soluble in this solvent, we would have difficulty re-forming the desired solid even when we cooled the solvent mixture.
C: We do not want the contaminants to share the properties of molecule 1. If we used this solvent, both molecule 1 and its impurities would dissolve when the solution was heated, but would re-form a contaminated solid when the apparatus was later cooled.
D: Recrystallization should certainly work for a contaminated solid. Additionally, the melting point data given confirms that this solid is likely impure.

1966. C is correct. To be IR-active, a molecule must have an inducible dipole moment. (While a permanent dipole is not necessary, it also confers IR activity.) N_2, a nonpolar diatomic molecule, has no dipole moment; electron density is shared equally between the two nitrogen atoms. When excited by infrared light, the molecule is only induced to stretch along its axis, which does not change its overall dipole moment. It exhibits no bending or asymmetric stretching vibrational modes.

A: Carbon dioxide has no permanent dipole moment, but a temporary one can be induced upon excitation.

B: Although methane does not have a permanent dipole due to its tetrahedral geometry, it has many vibrational modes that create a degree of asymmetry sufficient to induce a dipole.
D: Nitric oxide has a permanent dipole because oxygen is more electronegative than nitrogen.

1967. C is correct. The symmetric stretching mode of this molecule does not induce a dipole. It is thus effectively invisible to IR spectroscopy.

A: IR spec does not observe or invoke a nuclear spin; that role is played by NMR.
B: Technically, only two of the vibrational modes are considered degenerate. The scissoring mode, in which the linear structure bends about the central carbon, can occur in two spatial dimensions. However, both modes require the same input of energy and are indistinguishable when using IR spectroscopy.
D: This is not true. A normal IR spectrometer is more than capable of providing structural information about nearly any small organic molecule.

1968. C is correct. We are told that HSQC is useful for exploring ligand-binding interactions, which typically do not involve the formation of new covalent bonds. In other words, the ligand and protein remain chemically separate. Nevertheless, HSQC is able to return usable data concerning the process being measured; this is only possible if the interaction occurs through space.

D: The question defines HSQC as a variation of NMR spectroscopy, which provides accurate data regarding interactions over short molecular distances. It would be unlikely for nuclear coupling to occur across distances on the order of several bonds.

1969. B is correct. The proximity of hydrogen B to the electron-withdrawing carbonyl of the aldehyde suggests that it resides in a zone of relative electron deficiency. This exposes the nucleus to the magnetic pulse from the NMR device, causing it to resonate at a frequency distinct from that of hydrogen A.

A, D: These choices do not make sense. A decrease in shielding allows the nucleus to be more exposed to the external electromagnetic pulse from the NMR device, shifting it to the left

of the spectrum. Note that traditionally, all peaks are considered in reference to tetramethylsilane (TMS), a molecule containing chemically indistinct hydrogen atoms that are more heavily shielded than those of almost any other organic molecule. This establishes a reference point on the extreme right of the spectrum.

1970. C is correct. The question strongly hints that the amide protons will not appear in the spectrum. This leaves only the protons bound to carbon atoms, which appear on the phenyl substituents. Since the two rings reside in a chemically identical environment with respect to one another, their corresponding hydrogen nuclei are indistinguishable. Furthermore, the H nuclei positioned across from one another on each ring are also chemically identical for NMR purposes.

1971. A is correct. UV-Vis spectroscopy involves the exposure of a sample to incident light sufficient to promote electrons of the highest occupied molecular orbital (HOMO) to the lowest unoccupied molecular orbital, or LUMO. As its name implies, the incident light lies in the UV-visible region, which includes waves of higher energy (and shorter wavelength) than the infrared region.

C, D: These choices better represent IR, not UV-Vis. IR spectroscopy works by exposing a sample to relatively low-energy (long-wavelength) light, which is sufficient only to induce bond vibrations.

1972. B is correct. Considering its polycyclic structure and abundant conjugation, EtBr seems to resemble a nucleotide base. Furthermore, its relatively large size in comparison to endogenous bases suggests that it may interact most favorably with a pair of nucleotides. SDS will denature DNA just as readily as it will protein, which compromises the helical structure. Although EtBr can be used to stain single-stranded nucleic acids, the staining is much more effective when applied to native nucleic acid molecules instead.

A, C: Denatured nucleic acids do not retain their helical structure, so EtBr (which appears able to bind base pairs) is likely to intercalate poorly. Since we are told that the mentioned fluorescence depends on favorable coordination, it is reasonable to assume that the stain is less useful for these molecules.

D: Given the alternative options, there is no reason to assume that EtBr would bind with any specificity to protein.

1973. B is correct. Mass spectrometry requires mobilization of the sample in the gas phase, which is typically accomplished via bombardment with ions. While the actual degree of damage sustained by a protein sample during this process is up for debate, it constitutes a reasonable concern. Additionally, statement II is correct; molecules pass through a mass spectrometer in a vacuum and are stripped of their surrounding water molecules (or lipid molecules, in the case of membrane-associated proteins). Although no consensus has yet been reached, it is reasonable to suggest that such a dramatic deviation from cellular conditions could alter the structure of the protein under observation.

III: This would be a valid objection against the use of X-ray crystallography, but mass spec does not involve the use of X-ray radiation to visualize molecular structure.
IV: Mass spectrometry is used to observe molecules in the gas phase, not the solid phase. Again, this choice applies more to X-ray crystallography, which does deal principally with solid-phase samples.

1974. C is correct. The question stem describes a process in which a larger biological polymer is degraded to facilitate analysis of its simple components. Edman degradation involves the sequential cleavage of terminal amino acid residues from a polypeptide, the identities of which may then be determined by other methods. This is the technique that most closely resembles CID.

A: Although SDS-PAGE does involve the dissociation of protein subunits prior to analysis, SDS does not break covalent bonds. The question stem informs us that CID sometimes generates free radicals, which can only happen if covalent bonds are broken. Furthermore, CID generates peptides that are 20-30 residues in length, which is much too small for most intact subunits. Again, this suggests that peptide bonds must be broken during the CID process.

B, D: Neither of these techniques involves the systematic decomposition of the sample of interest.

1975. B is correct. In mass spec, the movement of the sample through the device is proportional to both its mass and its charge, neither of which can be measured directly. However, by clocking the time of flight of the particle, the mass-to-charge ratio can be obtained.

A: While this can be easily obtained from the mass-to-charge ratio, it is not the most directly measured value.
C: Ideally, every particle would be given an equal charge density during the ionization process. Even if differences do exist, this is not the parameter being measured.
D: Mass spectrometry produces data for all isotopes present in the sample.

1976. A is correct. With regard to NMR, upfield refers to the right-hand side of a spectrum. Here, signals appear if they correspond to nuclei that are shielded, or physically distant from electronegative atoms. The most shielded nuclei belong to those of the hydrogen atoms that are far from the –COOH terminal. As such, they will possess very low ppm values.

B, C: The ppm values for these two hydrogen nuclei are switched here.
D: While this carboxylic acid proton likely will exhibit such a shift, high numbers like this one are located downfield, not upfield.

1977. C is correct. While you do not need to understand the details of UV-Vis for the MCAT, you should know that it is typically used to assess the presence of highly conjugated systems. Conjugation refers to the presence of alternating double bonds within the structure of an organic molecule. From its name alone, we can infer that choice C (a ten-carbon cyclic compound with five double bonds) has such a structure.

A: Acetylene is another name for ethyne, an unconjugated alkyne.
B: This highly strained molecule contains two rings, but neither of them are conjugated.
D: This alcohol does not possess any double bonds at all.

1978. B is correct. Read this question carefully to note that it is asking for a trait of UV-Vis, not IR spec. As their names imply, IR spectroscopy utilizes infrared radiation, while UV-Vis uses ultraviolet light. UV radiation has a higher frequency, shorter wavelength, and higher energy than infrared rays.

C: UV-Vis spectroscopy is often used to analyze conjugated species like this one.
D: Neither of these analytic techniques deals directly with the charge of the species involved.

1979. B is correct. To answer this question, we must determine the number of sets of chemically equivalent hydrogen nuclei on this molecule. The three protons on the leftmost carbon are chemically identical to each other and to those on the rightmost carbon, so they constitute one set of H nuclei. The tertiary carbons each possess a single proton, both of which are identical; finally, the protons on the –OH groups are indistinguishable as well. In total, three different "types" of distinct protons exist here.

C: The answer here may result from neglecting to notice that this molecule is perfectly symmetrical.
D: This is the number of total protons in the molecule, not the number of visible peaks.

1980. D is correct. In mass spectrometry, the M^+ peak correlates to the molecule as a whole after it has lost a single electron. For this reason, we can deduce that the molecular weight of the sample is 102 amu, identical to that of 3-hexanol. Additionally, the m/z ratio is equivalent to the mass of a particle divided by its charge, which is typically +1. As –OH has a mass of 17 amu, D is the best answer.

A, B: 2-pentanone has a molecular weight of about 86 amu.
C: Methyl would likely have an m/z ratio of 15, not 17.

1981. B is correct. Strain A1 grows in an environment where it is given external phenylalanine, but fails to grow when this biomolecule is removed. Since the only change between the first and second rows is this removal of Phe, Strain A1 must have a mutation that prevents the synthesis of this aromatic residue.

C: Strain A1 grows when lysine is the only amino acid that is missing from the plate.

1982. C is correct. From the first row of the table, it is evident that Strain A2 cannot make its own lysine. Since all subsequent trials are conducted on media where lysine is still missing, we cannot tell which (-) results are due to the absence of Phe and Tyr, and which are simply the result of the lack of Lys.

A, D: As lysine is the only amino acid missing from the first plate, we know that Strain A2 cannot synthesize it.

1983. D is correct. We are told that wild-type *E. coli* can produce all of the amino acids required for its own propagation. In other words, it should grow regardless of the presence of external AAs in the medium. Since Strain A4 grows in all three trials, it is the most likely identity of this wild-type sample.

1984. A is correct. The given plot shows that minimum alveolar concentration and solubility in olive oil are directly related. However, olive oil is a lipid-based, hydrophobic compound, while water clearly possesses a hydrophilic nature. For this reason, the relationship asked about in the question stem would be the inverse of what is pictured. In other words, as aqueous solubility rises, the minimum alveolar concentration would rise as well (and the potency would fall). Strong direct correlations are given positive coefficients, with maximal values of 1.

B: A value of 0 implies that no correlation exists at all.
C, D: These resemble the relationship that is pictured in the diagram, not the one that is referenced by the question.

1985. D is correct. The given information never says that Meyer or Overton conducted an experiment at all. Instead, they simply noted a correlation between two already-known qualities of common anesthetic compounds. By definition, an independent variable is one that is manipulated by the researcher to assess resulting changes in a separate, dependent variable. Since these scientists could not possibly have manipulated minimum concentration (a known value for each anesthetic) or solubility, D is the best answer.

1986. A is correct. A correlation matrix allows the correlation values between many (here, dozens) of variables to be plotted in the same system. However, since each variable is correlated with each other factor, this necessarily involves the correlation of every variable with itself. As (for example) glycolysis is 100% directly correlated with glycolysis, this must yield a diagonal line in which every correlation coefficient is 1.

B: A correlation coefficient of 0 implies that no relationship exists between the two variables at all.
C: This does not accurately reflect the setup of a correlation matrix.
D: We have no way of knowing if this is true.

1987. C is correct. Since this diagram is in black and white, it is impossible to discern between a strong positive (1) and a strong negative (-1) correlation. However, we can observe that no correlation (0) is represented by white or light-colored dots. For this reason, we can certainly tell that more correlations of some kind exist in the top left than in the bottom right.

1988. B is correct. A typical enzyme-catalyzed reaction at low substrate concentration is first order with regard to substrate. This is evident from the graph, as the addition of more substrate directly influences the reaction rate. However, as [S] increases and the reaction velocity nears V_{max}, it undergoes a shift to become zeroth order. At this time, even the addition of a substantial amount of extra substrate does not influence the reaction rate due to enzyme saturation.

1989. C is correct. From the question stem, we can infer that the described reaction will proceed most rapidly when the largest number of H^+ ions are present in solution. In other words, a pH increase must promote a decrease in reaction rate, making this relationship inverse. Additionally, due to the logarithmic nature of pH, this relationship will not be linear. Remember, an increase of a single pH unit signifies a tenfold decrease in proton concentration.

1990. A is correct. For every ES molecule that forms, one free E molecule must have been used up. This makes statement I accurate; in addition, it explains why III cannot be true unless more substrate were being added.

II: The key word here is "simultaneously." Imagine that a single ES complex catalyzes its reaction and releases its components: a free enzyme molecule and one particle of product. During this instant in time, [P] increases, as does [E], but [S] is unaffected.

1991. B is correct. Consider Bernoulli's equation, which states that $P + \rho gh + \frac{1}{2}\rho v^2 = $ constant. Additionally, the question stem mentions that height is equal throughout this system of tubes, meaning that we can simplify to $P + \frac{1}{2}\rho v^2 = $ constant. From this relation, it is clear that hydrostatic pressure and v^2 are inversely related. However, note that it is the sum, not the product, of these terms that is a constant value. For this reason, the correct graph should be linear, not curved.

C: This would be a better choice if $(P)(\frac{1}{2}\rho v^2) = $ constant.

1992. C is correct. Here, we see an inverse relationship and a non-linear curve. This implies that, as one variable increases, the other decreases, and that one changes substantially in response to a small change of the other. Velocity and height off the ground are perfect choices, as the microwave will increase its velocity by the same amount over progressively smaller distances as it falls.

A, D: When air resistance is not considered, acceleration of a falling object is a constant 9.8 m/s^2. For this reason, both of these graphs would display straight horizontal or vertical lines.
B: This implies that the microwave is somehow slowing down during its fall.

1993. D is correct. The larger the radius of curvature, the thinner – and weaker – a lens will be. This relationship can be described mathematically using two known equations, $r = 2f$ and $P = 1/f$. Rearrangement yields $f = 1/P$, and substitution into the first equation gives $r = 2/P$.

A, B: These choices wrongly imply that, as radius of curvature increases, power increases as well.

C: The given equation in this choice is the reciprocal of the correct answer.

1994. B is correct. 0.6 cm is the same as 6×10^{-1} cm, which in turn is equivalent to 6×10^{-3} m. Area = πr^2, so our answer is approximately $(3.14)(6 \times 10^{-3}$ m$)^2$ or 113×10^{-6} m^2. Manipulating the scientific notation of this value yields 1.13×10^{-4} m^2.

A: This results from an improper use of scientific notation.
C, D: This is the area in square centimeters, which is not the SI unit for length.

1995. D is correct. The question stem asks us to consider only the two measurements on the right side of the plot. Here, note that the error bars overlap significantly. This means that, while the mean or average pulse rate may be lower for the more-than-weekly exercise group, there is a significant possibility that these results are due to chance alone. For this reason, we can draw no statistically significant conclusion.

B: This is actually the opposite of what the graph depicts.
C: This statement is reaching too far. Even if the measured differences in pulse rate were significant, we cannot equate a low resting heart rate to cardiovascular health in general.

1996. B is correct. This question is basically asking for a way to increase the statistical power, or the likelihood that the results will be significant and able to support the experimental hypothesis. One classic way to increase power is to raise the sample size; another is to minimize any potential error.

A: This would actually lower the power, as it would set an even more difficult-to-attain threshold for statistical significance.
C: Adding a new independent variable would not affect the power.

1997. C is correct. In the scientific community, a typical p-value is $p < 0.05$. If this is attained, it means that less than a 5% chance exists that the experimental results were due to chance. From the graph, however, we note that a huge overlap is present between the error bars of the two groups in question. For this reason, we can assume that they do not differ by a statistically

significant amount, and that p must be greater than 0.05.

A, B: Both of these values represent significant results.
D: A p-value cannot exceed 1.

1998. D is correct. This graph depicts the serial position effect, a phenomenon in which humans tend to remember the first and last words of a list better than those in the middle. Only the organization of the axes in choice D makes sense.

A, B: The Yerkes-Dodson law posits that individuals perform best when they are moderately aroused or alert. Here, choice B implies the opposite. Option A makes even less sense, as it conveys the idea that high arousal simultaneously correlates with two very different performance extremes.

1999. A is correct. The population pyramid shows that individuals of ages 0-4 form a comparatively large segment of the population. In contrast, even the five bars that correspond to ages over 60 are much smaller in total than that single group. Since fertility rate is clearly still high, we can narrow down the answers to stages 1 or 2, especially since the question references a time ten years prior to that depicted in the pyramid. Since very few Angolans seem to be elderly, we can assume that mortality rates were fairly high in recent years, making A the best choice.

2000. C is correct. The population pyramid only gives age ranges. Even though substantially more individuals of ages 30-34 are present than those of ages 40-44, we have no way of knowing the breakdowns within these categories.

A: This directly contradicts the figure.
B: Since the prevalence of female Angolans between 45 and 49 is only about 0.2%, this is impossible.
D: We have no reason to believe that this population pyramid includes only individuals who were born in Angola.

2001. B is correct. The dependent variable is the factor that is under study; specifically, it is that which is not directly manipulated by the researcher. Here, TBI severity is the independent variable, while

PTS risk is dependent. Additionally, note that all three of the bars shown ("mild," "moderate," and "severe"), technically consist of individuals who have had traumatic brain injuries. Note also that all three are assigned values greater than 1. From this information, we can see that the control group must be that which actually has a risk of "1": uninjured or healthy patients, who are not shown here directly.

Image Attributions

The following images are used with permission, compliant with relevant Creative Commons standards.

146:By Lordjuppiter (Own work) [CC BY-SA 3.0 (http://creativecommons.org/licenses/by-sa/3.0)], via Wikimedia Commons

200: By Grant, B. D. and Sato, M [CC BY 2.5 (http://creativecommons.org/licenses/by/2.5)], via Wikimedia Commons

320:By OpenStax College [CC BY 3.0 (http://creativecommons.org/licenses/by/3.0)], via Wikimedia Commons

329: Department of Histology, Jagiellonian University Medical College [CC BY-SA 3.0 (http://creativecommons.org/licenses/by/3.0)], via Wikimedia Commons

336:By OpenStax College [CC BY 3.0 (http://creativecommons.org/licenses/by/3.0)], via Wikimedia Commons

338:By Pseudounipolar_bipolar_neurons.svg: Juoj8 derivative work: Jonathan Haas [CC BY-SA 3.0 (http://creativecommons.org/licenses/by-sa/3.0)], via Wikimedia Commons

341 – 342; 351:By Selket [GFDL (http://www.gnu.org/copyleft/fdl.html) or CC-BY-SA-3.0 (http://creativecommons.org/licenses/by-sa/3.0/)], via Wikimedia Commons

344 – 345:By Diberri [CC BY-SA 3.0 (http://creativecommons.org/licenses/by/3.0)], via Wikimedia Commons

352 – 353:By OpenStax College [CC BY 3.0 (http://creativecommons.org/licenses/by/3.0)], via Wikimedia Commons

390:By Cancer Research UK (Original email from CRUK) [CC BY-SA 4.0 (http://creativecommons.org/licenses/by-sa/4.0)], via Wikimedia Commons

398:By OpenStax College [CC BY 3.0 (http://creativecommons.org/licenses/by/3.0)], via Wikimedia Commons

401 – 402:KnuteKnudsen at English Wikipedia [CC BY 3.0 (http://creativecommons.org/licenses/by/3.0)], via Wikimedia Commons

466 – 467:By Artwork by Holly Fischer [CC BY 3.0 (http://creativecommons.org/licenses/by/3.0)], via Wikimedia Commons

609:By Jpark623 [CC BY-SA 3.0 (http://creativecommons.org/licenses/by-sa/3.0)], via Wikimedia Commons

641 – 643:By Alejandro Porto [CC BY-SA 3.0 (http://creativecommons.org/licenses/by-sa/3.0)], via Wikimedia Commons

758 – 759:By Mitochondriale_Elektronentransportkette.svg: Klaus Hoffmeier derivative work: Matt [Public domain], via Wikimedia Commons

800:By Yikrazuul (Own work; ISBN 978-3540418139 S. 802+579) [CC BY-SA 3.0 (http://creativecommons.org/licenses/by-sa/3.0)], via Wikimedia Commons

843 – 844:By Cthuljew (Own work) [CC BY-SA 3.0 (http://creativecommons.org/licenses/by-sa/3.0) or GFDL (http://www.gnu.org/copyleft/fdl.html)], via Wikimedia Commons

846 – 847:By Tbatan [CC BY 3.0 (http://creativecommons.org/licenses/by/3.0)], via Wikimedia Commons

855 – 856:By Yikrazuul [CC BY-SA 3.0 (http://creativecommons.org/licenses/by-sa/3.0)], via Wikimedia Commons

871:By BruceBlaus. When using this image in external sources it can be cited as: Blausen.com staff. "Blausen gallery 2014". Wikiversity Journal of Medicine. DOI:10.15347/wjm/2014.010. ISSN 20018762. (Own work) [CC BY 3.0 (http://creativecommons.org/licenses/by/3.0)], via Wikimedia Commons

888:By 10.1371_journal.pbio.0030137.g001-L.jpg: Chittka L, Brockmann (10.1371_journal.pbio.0030137.g001-L.jpg) [CC BY 2.5 (http://creativecommons.org/licenses/by/2.5)], via Wikimedia Commons

1049 – 1050:By User:Factoryjoe (Mazlow's Hierarchy of Needs.svg) [CC BY-SA 3.0 (http://creativecommons.org/licenses/by-sa/3.0)], via Wikimedia Commons

1354 – 1356:By Hazmat2 (Own work) [CC BY 3.0 (http://creativecommons.org/licenses/by/3.0)], via Wikimedia Commons

1409 – 1410:By Matthieumarechal [GFDL (http://www.gnu.org/copyleft/fdl.html) or CC-BY-SA-3.0 (http://creativecommons.org/licenses/by-sa/3.0/)], via Wikimedia Commons

1521:By Lucho w2ed (Own work) [CC BY-SA 3.0 (http://creativecommons.org/licenses/by-sa/3.0)], via Wikimedia Commons

1986 – 1987:By abhi asus 1987 (Own work)) [CC BY-SA 3.0 (http://creativecommons.org/licenses/by-sa/3.0)], via Wikimedia Commons

1998:By Obli [CC BY-SA 3.0 (http://creativecommons.org/licenses/by-sa/3.0)], via Wikimedia Commons

2001:By User:Delldot (Own work) [GFDL (http://www.gnu.org/copyleft/fdl.html) or CC BY-SA 3.0 (http://creativecommons.org/licenses/by-sa/3.0)], via Wikimedia Commons